Lecture Notes in Computer Science 10645

Commenced Publication in 1973
Founding and Former Series Editors:
Gerhard Goos, Juris Hartmanis, and Jan van Leeuwen

More information about this series at http://www.springer.com/series/7412

Halimah Badioze Zaman · Peter Robinson
Alan F. Smeaton · Timothy K. Shih
Sergio Velastin · Tada Terutoshi
Azizah Jaafar · Nazlena Mohamad Ali (Eds.)

Advances in Visual Informatics

5th International Visual Informatics Conference, IVIC 2017
Bangi, Malaysia, November 28–30, 2017
Proceedings

 Springer

Editors
Halimah Badioze Zaman
Universiti Kebangsaan Malaysia
Bangi, Selangor
Malaysia

Peter Robinson
University of Cambridge
Cambridge
UK

Alan F. Smeaton
Dublin City University
Dublin
Ireland

Timothy K. Shih
National Central University
Jhongli
Taiwan

Sergio Velastin
Carlos III University of Madrid
Madrid
Spain

Tada Terutoshi
Toyo University
Kawagoe
Japan

Azizah Jaafar
Universiti Kebangsaan Malaysia
Bangi, Selangor
Malaysia

Nazlena Mohamad Ali
Universiti Kebangsaan Malaysia
Bangi, Selangor
Malaysia

ISSN 0302-9743   ISSN 1611-3349   (electronic)
Lecture Notes in Computer Science
ISBN 978-3-319-70009-0   ISBN 978-3-319-70010-6   (eBook)
https://doi.org/10.1007/978-3-319-70010-6

Library of Congress Control Number: 2017957842

LNCS Sublibrary: SL6 – Image Processing, Computer Vision, Pattern Recognition, and Graphics

Preface

The twenty-first century is a visual century. With the advent of Industry 4.0 or Fourth Industrial Revolution (4IR), visual informatics has become a crucial aspect of computer science. Specifically, it is a multidisciplinary field of computer science, information technology, and engineering, which integrates areas such as computer vision, image processing, pattern recognition, computer graphics, simulation, virtual reality, data visualization and analytics, cyber security as well as social computing, applied in various knowledge domains such as education, medical and health, finance, agriculture, and security. The Institute of Visual Informatics (IVI), Universiti Kebangsaan Malaysia (UKM) – or The National University of Malaysia – is a centre of excellence (CoE) established as an outcome of the First Visual Informatics Conference (IVIC) held in 2009. The institute, which conducts research in the aforementioned basic areas, conducts master's and doctoral (PhD) degree programs by research, as well as short professional practical certifications currently in the areas of data science and visual analytics. The institute has successfully graduated five master's and 28 PhD students since its inception in 2010 through 2017. We are indeed indebted to the international fraternity from the last four IVIC conferences (2009, 2011, 2013, and 2015), who have given us support that has resulted in the establishment of the institute. Our smart partnerships, through this conference, will not only help the institute to grow but will enhance research in this area internationally that can be applied by private organizations and governments in the respective countries.

The Visual Informatics Research Group and the Institute of Visual Informatics (IVI) at UKM once again hosted this 5th International Visual Informatics Conference (IVIC 2017), with the objective of bringing together experts to discuss and share new knowledge and ideas in this research area so that more concerted efforts can be undertaken nationally and globally. Like the previous IVIC conferences, this conference was conducted collaboratively by the visual informatics fraternity from various public and private universities and industry from different parts of the world. This fifth conference was co-sponsored by MyVIC Sdn. Bhd. (a local private company), the ICT Cluster of the National Council of Professors (MPN), the Malaysian Information Technology Society (MITS), the Malaysian Research Education Network (MyREN), the Malaysian Digital Economy Corporation (MDeC), the Malaysian Communications and Multimedia Commission (MCMC), and the Malaysian Administrative Modernization Planning Unit (MAMPU). The conference was co-chaired by six professors from UK, Ireland, Spain, Japan, Taiwan, and Malaysia.

The theme of the conference, "Visual Informatics: Changing Landscapes in 4IR Through Data-Driven Decisions" reflects the importance of big data in this fourth industrial revolution digital economy. It also portrayed the belief of the organizers (both locally and globally) of the importance of open data and sharing of big data and analytics, which would lead to the creation and innovation of new products through data-driven decisions. The changing landscapes of industry 4.0 (4IR) require data-driven decisions be made, based on big data analytics that would allow for more comprehensive and accurate visual insights, for more précise predictions of data that would result in an efficient data-driven decision-making for economic and social good. Thus, the theme of the conference was relevant, apt, and timely.

The conference focused on four tracks — Visualization and Data-Driven Technology, Engineering and Data-Driven Innovation, Data-Driven Societal Well-Being and Applications, and Data-Driven Cyber Security — which lasted for two days (November 28 and 29, 2017) and ended with a one-day workshop (November 30, 2017). There were five keynote speakers and 68 paper presentations based on topics covered by the four main tracks. The reviewing of the papers was conducted by experts who represented the Program Committee from Asia, Europe, Oceania, and USA. Each paper was reviewed by three reviewers and the acceptance rate was 51%. The reviewing process was managed using EasyChair.

The conference also included the first meeting of a national task force on big data represented by stakeholders from the private sector, academia, and government agencies in Malaysia. The objective of the task force is to consolidate big data and big data analytics initiatives, and help the government in formulation of policies relating to BD, BDA, as well as open data. The conclusion and recommendations made by the task force will be submitted to the appropriate governing body.

On behalf of the Organizing and Program Committee of IVIC 2017, we thank all authors for their submissions and camera-ready copies of papers, and all participants for their thought-provoking ideas and active participation in the conference. We also thank the vice-chancellor of UKM (host university), and the vice-chancellors and deans of all IT faculties of the IHLs for their support in organizing this conference. We also acknowledge the sponsors, members of the Organizing Committees, Program Committee members, support committees, and individuals who gave their continuous help and support in making the conference a success. IVIC has grown from strength to strength and it is our fervent hope that it can one day be held in different host countries in Asia, Europe, Oceania, the UK or the USA.

November 2017

Halimah Badioze Zaman
Peter Robinson
Alan Smeaton
Timothy Shih
Sergio Velastin
Tada Terutoshi
Azizah Jaafar
Nazlena Mohamad Ali

Organization

The 5th International Visual Informatics Conference (IVIC 2017) was organized by the Visual Informatics Research Group and Institute of Visual Informatics, Universiti Kebangsaan Malaysia (UKM), in collaboration with 18 local public and private universities in Malaysia, the Malaysian Information Technology Society (MITS), the Multimedia Development Corporation (MDeC), the Malaysian Research Educational Network (MyREN), and the ICT Cluster of the National Professors' Council (MPN).

Local Executive Committee

Chair

Halimah Badioze Zaman (UKM)

Deputy Chair

Zaharin Yusoff (SunwayUni)

Secretary

Azizah Jaafar (UKM)

Assistant Secretary

Nazlena Mohamad Ali (UKM)

Treasurer

Rabiah Abd. Kadir (UKM)

Assistant Treasurer

Zuraini Zainol (UPNM)

Program Committee

Program Co-chairs

Halimah Badioze Zaman	Universiti Kebangsaan Malaysia, Malaysia
Peter Robinson	University of Cambridge, UK
Alan F. Smeaton	Dublin City University, Ireland
Timothy K. Shih	National Central University, Taiwan
Sergio Velastin	Universidad Carlos III de Madrid, Madrid, Spain
Tada Terutoshi	Toyo University, Japan

Technical Program Committee

Abdul Hadi Abd Rahman
Abdullah Gani
Ahmad Sobri Hashim
Alan Smeaton
Aliimran Nordin
Ang Mei Choo
Aslina Baharum
Azizah Jaafar
Azlina Ahmad
Bavani Ramayah
Elankovan A. Sundararajan
Ely Salwana Mat Nayan
Faaizah Shahbodin
Fatimah Dato' Ahmad
Hanif Baharin
Hoo Meei Hao
Ibrahim Ahmad
Ibrahim Mohamed
Lilly Suriani Affendey
Maizatul H.M. Yatim
Masnizah Mohd
Mohamad Nazri Ahmad
Mohamad Taha Ijab
Mohammad Nazir Ahmad
Mohd Nazri Ismail
Mohd Rizal Mohd Isa

Mohd. Murtadha Mohamad
Muslihah Wook
Nazlena Mohamad Ali
Nor Azliana Akmal Jamaludin
Norasiken Bakar
Norshahriah Abd Wahab
Norshita Mat Nayan
Nur Intan Raihana Ruhaiyem
Nursuriati Jamil
Prasanna Ramakrisnan
Puteri Nor Ellyza Nohuddin
Rabiah Abd Kadir
Rosmayati Mohemad
Suraya Hamid
Suraya Yaacob
Suzaimah Ramli
Syahaneim Marzukhi
Syed Nasir Syed Zakaria Alsagoff
Ummul Hanan Mohamad
Wan Mohd Nazmee Wan Zainon
Wan Nural Jawahir Hj Wan Yussof
Zainab Abu Bakar
Zuraini Zainol
Zuriana Abu Bakar
Zurida Ishak

Local Arrangements Committee

Technical Committee

Fatimah Ahmad (UKM) – Head
Azizah Jaafar (UKM)
Nazlena Mohamad Ali (UKM)
Puteri Nor Ellyza Nohuddin (UKM)

Rabiatul Adawiyah Ab. Rashid (UKM)
Irna Hamil Hamzah (UKM)
S.P. Vanisri S.P. Batemanazan (UKM)

Publicity (Web Portal)

Aliimran Nordin (UKM) – Head
Norshita Mohd Nayan (UKM)
Ang Mei Choo (UKM)
Dayang Rohaya Awang Rambli (UTP)
Norasiken Bakar (UTeM)

Suzilawati Kamarudin (UTM)
Maizaitulaidawati Md Husin (UTM)
Rossilah Jamil (UTM)
Bahari Belaton (USM)
Suraya Hamid (UM)

Aslina Baharum (UMS)
Norshahriah Abd Wahab (UPNM)
Prasanna Ramakrisnan (UITM)
Bavani Ramayah (Nottingham)

Rabiah Ahmad (UTeM)
Hoo Mei Hao (UTAR)
Faaizah Shabodin (UTeM)

Logistics

Riza Sulaiman (UKM) – Head
Mohd Taha Ijab (UKM)
Syed Nasir Syed Zakaria Alsagoff (UPNM)

Muslihah Wook (UPNM)
Ahmad Hanif Ahmad Baharin (UKM)
Ummul Hanan Mohamad (UKM)

Sponsorship

Azlina Ahmad (UKM) – Head
Halimah Badioze Zaman (UKM)
Wan Fatimah Wan Ahmad (UTP)
M. Iqbal Saripan (UPM)
Bahari Belaton (USM)
Ahmad Sufril Azlan Mohamed (USM)

Adriana Md Rizal (IBS/UTM)
Suziah Sulaiman (UTP)
Noor Afiza Mat Razali (UPNM)
Zaharin Yusoff (SunwayUni)
Ahmad Rafi Mohamed Eshaq (MMU)

Workshop

Mohamad Taha Ijab (UKM) – Head
Bahari Belaton (USM)
Wan Fatimah Wan Ahmad (UTP)

Amelia Ritahani Ismail (UIA)
Syed Nasir Asagoff (UPNM)
Ho Chiung Ching (MMU)

Tour

Azreen Azman (UPM) – Head
Aliimran Nordin (UKM)

Conference Management System

EasyChair

Sponsoring Institutions

Universiti Kebangsaan Malaysia (UKM)
Sunway University
Universiti Pertahanan Nasional Malaysia (UPNM)
Universiti Teknologi PETRONAS (UTP)
Universiti Sains Malaysia (USM)
Universiti Teknologi MARA (UiTM)
Universiti Teknikal Malaysia (UTeM)
Universiti Putra Malaysia (UPM)
Universiti of Nottingham

KDU University College - Penang (KDU)
Al-Madinah International University (MEDIU)
Universiti Teknologi Malaysia (UTM)
Universiti Malaysia Sarawak (UNIMAS)
Universiti Malaya (UM)
Multimedia University (MMU)
Universiti Tenaga Nasional (UNITEN)
Universiti Malaysia Sabah (UMS)
Universiti Islam Antarabangsa Malaysia (UIAM)
International University of Malaya-Wales (IUMW)
Universiti Utara Malaysia (UUM)
National Professors' Council (MPN)
MyVIC
Malaysian Research Educational Network (MYREN)
Unit Pemodenan Tadbiran Dan Perancangan Pengurusan Malaysia (MAMPU)
Malaysian Information Technology Society (MITS)
CyberSecurity Malaysia

Contents

Engineering and Data Driven Innovation

Data Driven Societal Well-being and Applications

Keynote

Vehicle Detection Using Alex Net and Faster R-CNN Deep Learning Models: A Comparative Study

Jorge E. Espinosa[1], Sergio A. Velastin[2,3]([⊠]), and John W. Branch[4]

[1] Facultad de Ingenierías,
Politécnico Colombiano Jaime Isaza Cadavid – Medellín, Medellín, Colombia
jeespinosa@elpoli.edu.co
[2] University Carlos III - Madrid, Madrid, Spain
sergio.velastin@ieee.org
[3] Queen Mary University of London, London, UK
[4] Facultad de Minas, Universidad Nacional de Colombia – Sede Medellín,
Medellín, Colombia
jwbranch@unal.edu.co

Abstract. This paper presents a comparative study of two deep learning models used here for vehicle detection. Alex Net and Faster R-CNN are compared with the analysis of an urban video sequence. Several tests were carried to evaluate the quality of detections, failure rates and times employed to complete the detection task. The results allow to obtain important conclusions regarding the architectures and strategies used for implementing such network for the task of video detection, encouraging future research in this topic.

Keywords: Convolutional Neural Network · Feature extraction · Vehicle classification

1 Introduction

Currently traffic management is supported by urban traffic analysis. Traditionally, vehicle counting and road density evaluations are done with inductive loop sensors and increasingly with video information. Nevertheless, video detection faces different challenges due to changes in illumination conditions and high vehicle densities with frequent occlusions. Most video detection systems are based on appearance features or motion features. Appearance features [1–4] such as shape, color, edge maps and texture, are used to detect vehicles even in stationary positions. Other works are based on HOG (Histogram of Oriented Gradients) and some variations of it [5, 6]. Motion features are obtained based on the dynamics of the traffic movement. Such methods are generally based on background subtraction [7], use of frame difference [8], Kalman filter [9], optical flow [10, 11], etc. For a detailed survey of traditional vehicle detection methods please see [12].

On the other hand, *deep learning theory* (DL) applied to image processing is the current dominant computer vision theory especially in tasks such as image recognition.

© Springer International Publishing AG 2017
H. Badioze Zaman et al. (Eds.): IVIC 2017, LNCS 10645, pp. 3–15, 2017.
https://doi.org/10.1007/978-3-319-70010-6_1

Since 2010 the annual image recognition challenge known as the ImageNet Large-Scale Visual Recognition Competition (ILSVRC) [13] is being dominated by this approach.

For vehicle detection, several works using Deep Learning in vehicle detection are reported in the literature. Earlier approaches relied on 2D Deep Belief Networks (2D-DBN) [14], learning features by means of this architecture and using a pre-training sparse filtering process [15] or Hybrid architectures (HDNN) which overcome the issue of the single scale extraction features of traditional DNNs [16]. Color as a discriminative feature is used in [17] and [18]. There are also pre-training schemes [19] that obtain competitive results even with low resolution images and implementable in real time as in [20]. More recently, detection and classification of multiples classes is performed using integrated models as Fast R-CNN and Faster R-CNN [21–26]. Reports exist of methods able to recognize vehicle make and models (MMR) [27, 28], re-identification architectures for security urban surveillance [29–31], strategies using DBN [14, 32–34] that work with relatively few labelled data and models that are able to classify even the pose or orientation of the vehicle [23, 35, 36]. Generally most of the detection and classifications models are implemented using different CNN architectures such as CaffeNet [37, 38], GoogLeNet [39], and VGGNet [26] used in [27]. AlexNet [40] is used by Su et al. [18] in conjunction with GoogleNet [39] and NIN (Network in Network) [41].

Nevertheless, as far as we know, there are no comparative studies of DL strategies used for vehicle classification, nor on the use of CNNs already trained for feature extraction to perform vehicle discrimination in video sequences.

This work compares the results of a CNN used for feature extraction and a CNN integrated model network, both used for the task of classifying vehicles in video sequences. The paper is organized as follows: Sect. 2 gives a brief explanation of the architecture of the convolutional neural networks, explaining the advantage of the use of an already-trained network for feature extraction and the benefits of the integrated CNN model. Section 3 shows the classification approaches, describing the characteristics of the models built for the video detection task. Section 4 shows the results of the two models, comparing and explaining the results. Section 5 presents the conclusions and proposes some future work.

2   CNN Architectures Used

In this section, we describe the principal characteristics of the CNN AlexNet and the Faster R-CNN networks used in this comparative study.

2.1   AlexNet

AlexNet is considered the pioneer work of CNN networks, even after the work of Yann LeCun [42]. The AlexNet model was introduced in the paper "ImageNet Classification with Deep Convolutional Networks", were the authors created a "large, deep convolutional neural network", used to win the 2012 ILSVRC (ImageNet Large-Scale Visual Recognition Challenge) [43]. The network was trained on ImageNet data, with over 15 million annotated images from a total of over 22,000 categories.

The architecture of "AlexNet" has 23 layers, integrating 5 convolution layers, 5 ReLu layers (Rectified units), 2 layers for normalization, 3 pooling layers, 3 fully connected layers, one probabilistic layer with softmax units and finally a classification layer ending in 1000 neurons for 1000 categories (Fig. 1).

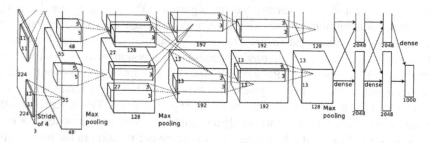

Fig. 1. Alex Net architecture. [40]

The main characteristics of the network includes the use of ReLU for the nonlinearity functions that decrease the training time as ReLUs are faster than the conventional *tanh* function used in MLP. For training proposes, the authors used techniques as data augmentation consisting in horizontal reflections, image translations or even patch extractions. Dropout layers were also included to overcome the problems of vanishing gradient and overfitting. The model was trained using batch stochastic gradient descent, using specific values for momentum and weight decay. It took nearly six days for training using two GTX 580 GPUs.

2.2 Faster R-CNN

The problem of object detection involves the detection of different classes of objects in each image. Traditionally, the strategy used was to deploy a two-class classifier (object vs non-object) in conjunction with a sliding window search. The amount of all windows scales and ratios returned could be huge, and then it was necessary to implement methods like non-maximal suppression for reducing the redundant candidates. This was the origin of object proposal algorithms, with strategies to limit search using calibration information [44], Branch & Bound [45] or grouping adjacent pixels merging them to find a blob region as in Selective Search [46]. These methods also included pre defining windows based on objects candidates as in Spatial Pyramid Pooling [47], or Edge boxes [48]. A valuable comparison of such methods was done by Hosang et al. [49]. The pre- filtering strategy has been used with positive results combining it with CNN networks for classification as in R-CNN [50] but employing too much time in the training process. To improve the training process time, Fast R-CNN [21] has been proposed that swaps the extracting strategy of detecting regions and running CNN. A high-resolution image is fed to the CNN network, the network produces a high resolution convolutional feature map. The region proposal produces regions over the feature map (conv5). The convolutional features of these regions are then fed into fully connected layers, with a linear classifier and a bounding box linear regression module to define regions. This model continues slowly at test time. Faster R-CNN addressed this issue by combining features of a fully convolutional network to perform both region proposals and object detection. Since region proposals depended on features of the image that were already calculated with the forward pass of the CNN (first step of classification), the model reuses the same CNN results for region proposals instead of running a separate selective search algorithm. The region proposal network (RPN) shares convolutional layers with the object detection network, then only one CNN needs to be trained and region proposals is calculated almost for free. Then, additional convolutional layers are used to regress region bounds with scores for object proposal at each location. The RPN works by moving a sliding window over the CNN feature map and at each window, generating k potential bounding boxes and scores associated for how good each of those boxes is expected to be. This k represents the common aspect ratios that candidates to objects could fit, caller anchor boxes. For each anchor box, the RPN output a bounding box and score per position in the image. This model improves significantly the speed and the object detection results.

Besides achieving the highest accuracy on both PASCAL VOC 2007 and 2012, Faster R-CNN was the basis of more than 125 proposed entries in ImageNet detection and localization at ILSVRC 2016 [51] and in the COCO challenge 2015 was the foundation of the winners in several categories [25]. Figure 2 shows the network structure of the Faster R-CNN framework. Both the region proposal network and the object classifier share fully convolutional layers. These layers are trained jointly. The region proposal network behaves as an attention director, determining the optimal bounding boxes across a wide range of scales and using nine candidate aspect ratios to be evaluated for object classification. In other words, the RPN tells the unified network where to look.

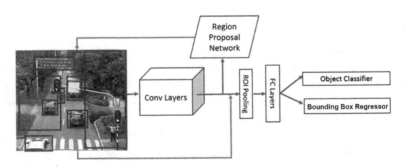

Fig. 2. Faster R-CNN network structure. Modified from [24]

3   Detection and Classification Approaches

An initial ROI (region of interest) step is implemented, allowing the user to select the precise area of analysis. This step optimizes performance and speeds up the processes of detection and classification, by reducing the area of analysis in the video sequences. Two models, AlexNet and Faster R-CNN were used for vehicle detection and classification in this research.

3.1   AlexNet Model

In the AlexNet model, object detection is performed based on background subtraction, using a Gaussian Mixture Model according to Zivkovic [52, 53]. Once the objects are detected, these are classified as vehicles on three categories: motorcycles, cars or buses. Other possible objects detected are classified as part of the urban environment ("urb-Tree"), any possible remaining detection is assigned to the "unknown" class. The classifier is constructed using a multiclass linear SVM trained with features obtained from a pre-trained CNN. Those features have been extracted for a set of 80 images per category, including the "urbTree" category created from the urban traffic environment. This approach to image category classification is based on the work published by Matlab in "Image category classification using deep learning" [54] and extended in [55] for Motorcycles classification. Here, we extend the categories to include the bus set. The classifier trained using CNN features provides close to 100% accuracy, which is higher than the accuracy achieved using methods such as Bag of Features and SURF. As in [55] the set of images categories has been created corresponding to images related to motorcycles, cars, buses and urban environment related objects ("urbTree"). Those images were obtained from different angles and perspectives in urban traffic in Medellin City (Colombia). Examples of each category are shown in Fig. 3.

Fig. 3.   Examples of cars, motorbikes and buses.

Following the strategy described in [55] by using the selected images, the pre-trained CNN "AlexNet" network is used for feature extraction, this technique is detailed described by Razavian et al. in [56]. For this work, the AlexNet network is only used to classify four categories. This pre-trained network was used to learn motorcycles, cars and buses features obtained from the extended dataset, with 80 images per category and 80 examples of the class "urbTree" created from the urban environment. In the end, the total number of examples is only 320.

Features are extracted from the training set, propagating images through the network up to a specific fully connected layer (fc7), extracting activations responses to create a training set of features, which is used later for classification.

For classification, as in [55], a multiclass SVM classifier is trained using the image features obtained from the CNN. Since the length of the feature vector is 4096, a fast stochastic gradient descent solver is used as training algorithm. In this case the classifier is trained with only 96 examples (24 per category). The validation set, which corresponds to the remaining 224 examples (56 by category) is then classified. The classifier accuracy is evaluated now with the features obtained on this set. Figure 4 shows the results in a confusion matrix. The classifier mismatches three bus images classifying those as cars; one car image is classified as bus and another as a motorcycle. The mean accuracy obtained is 0.978.

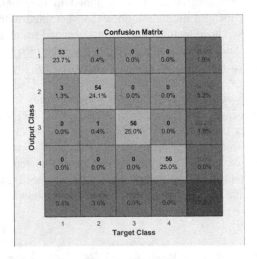

Fig. 4. Confusion matrix of the experiments (Class 1: Buses 2: Cars 3: Motorcycles 4: urbTree)

3.2 Faster R-CNN Model

The Faster R-CNN [25] model used in this research, is the one available for download at https://github.com/ShaoqingRen/faster_rcnn. The model is an object detection framework based on deep convolutional neural networks, which includes two networks: A Region Proposal Network (RPN) and an Object Detection Network. Both networks are trained for sharing convolutional layers to obtain real time results.

The model can be run based on two referenced CNN networks: ZF Net [57] or VGG16 [26]. In this research, we chose VGG16, which corresponds to the best performance results given the network layer configuration that the literature reports on the use of this architecture.

The VGG16 based model is pretrained with the ImageNet dataset. After downloading, both networks (RPN and ODN) are retrained in the PASCAL VOC 2007 dataset (Fig. 5) [58]. Based on the dataset used for retraining, the ODN is able to classify detections on 20 categories as follows:

- Person: person
- Animal: bird, cat, cow, dog, horse, sheep
- Vehicle: aeroplane, bicycle, boat, bus, car, motorbike, train
- Indoor: bottle, chair, dining table, potted plant, sofa, tv/monitor

20 classes

Fig. 5. Examples of each category in PASCAL VOC 2007 dataset [58].

For this experiments all classes different to bus, car or motorbike, are renamed as "unknown" to obtain comparative metrics for the results evaluation. As a preliminary step for video detection and classification, the user defines a ROI within which the detection and classification takes place.

4 Experiments and Results

We selected a video sequence of a real urban environment took in Medellín Colombia, over a secondary street of two lanes. The sequence consists of 1812 RGB frames (640 × 480), during daylight and good weather conditions. The sequence includes 36 different cars to detect (including sedan, VAN or taxis), 7 motorbikes and 1 Bus, which is the class assigned to a detected truck.

An XML-coded ground truth was obtained by means of ViPER [59] tool for annotation, and is used to compare the results of the two models. We use the performance metrics reported in [60]. These metrics have been extended to take into account the multiclass nature of the experiment.

The evaluations for Faster R-CNN are performed based on the NMS parameter threshold, used to reduce the redundancy on proposed regions. This threshold corresponds to the IoU overlap of the proposed regions. Results described in Table 1 and Fig. 6, show that decreasing the IoU threshold criteria increases the correct detection rate in total and for each class analyzed, but at the same time increases the False Alarm Rate. Best results correspond to a NMS threshold of 0.6 with a F1-Score of 0.76.

Table 1. Rates of Faster R-CNN results. NMS (non maximal suppression) – CDR: correct detection rate, Bikes: CDR for motorcycles, Cars: CDR for cars, Bus: CDR for buses or trucks. DFR: Detection Failure Rate. FAR: False Alarm Rate. PR: Precision. RC: Recall. F1:F1-score.

NMS threshold	CDR	CDR bikes	CDR cars	CDR buses	DFR	FAR	PR	RC	F1
0.30	0.75	0.26	0.83	0.33	0.25	0.38	0.62	0.75	0.68
0.40	0.73	0.21	0.81	0.32	0.27	0.31	0.69	0.73	0.71
0.50	0.72	0.18	0.80	0.33	0.28	0.22	0.78	0.72	0.75
0.60	0.70	0.13	0.78	0.29	0.30	0.16	0.84	0.70	**0.76**
0.70	0.65	0.09	0.74	0.23	0.35	0.13	0.87	0.65	0.75
0.80	0.61	0.06	0.70	0.07	0.39	0.10	0.90	0.61	0.73

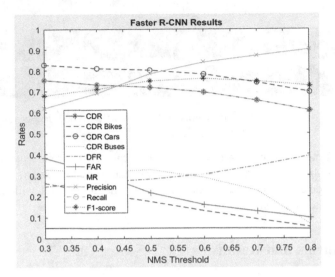

Fig. 6. Faster R-CNN rates results.

Meanwhile, working with the AlexNet classifier in conjunction with the GMM background subtraction, results are obtained in terms of the parameters of the background subtraction algorithm. First, the history parameter is evaluated against a fixed Mahalanobis distance of 128. History corresponds to the number of frames (LoH) that constitutes the training set for the background model. The best results obtained are for a history of 500 frames (F1 = 0.57). Fixing this number, we then proceed to change the Mahalanobis distance parameter (Tg). This parameter is a threshold for the squared Mahalanobis distance that helps decide when a sample is close to the existing components. A smaller Tg value generates more components. A higher Tg value may result in a small number of components but they can grow too large. The best result is obtained with LoH of 500, and Tg of 20, achieving a CDR of 0.66 with a FAR of 0.32 (Fig. 7 and Tables 2, 3).

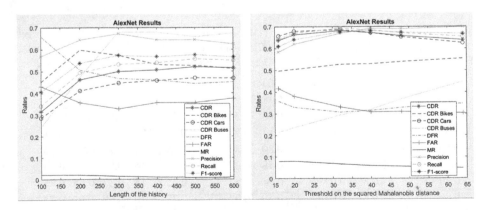

Fig. 7. Alex Net rates results

Table 2. Rates of Faster R-CNN results. NMS (non maximal suppression) – CDR: correct detection rate, Bikes: CDR for motorcycles, Cars: CDR for cars, Bus: CDR for buses or trucks. DFR: Detection Failure Rate. FAR: False Alarm Rate. MR: Merge Rate. PR: Precision. RC: Recall. F1:F1-score.

LoH	CDR	CDR bikes	CDR cars	CDR buses	DFR	FAR	MR	PR	RC	F1
100	0.32	0.45	0.29	0.24	0.66	0.43	0.02	0.57	0.34	0.41
200	0.46	0.60	0.41	0.47	0.51	0.36	0.02	0.64	0.49	0.54
300	0.50	0.57	0.45	0.68	0.47	0.33	0.01	0.67	0.53	0.57
400	0.51	0.53	0.46	0.68	0.46	0.36	0.01	0.64	0.54	0.57
500	0.52	0.53	0.47	0.66	0.44	0.36	0.01	0.64	0.56	**0.58**
600	0.51	0.51	0.47	0.67	0.45	0.38	0.01	0.62	0.55	0.56

Table 3. Rates of Faster R-CNN results. NMS (non maximal suppression) – CDR: correct detection rate, Bikes: CDR for motorcycles, Cars: CDR for cars, Bus: CDR for buses or trucks. DFR: Detection Failure Rate. FAR: False Alarm Rate. MR: Merge Rate. PR: Precision. RC: Recall. F1:F1-score.

Tg	CDR	CDR bikes	CDR cars	CDR buses	DFR	FAR	MR	PR	RC	F1
16	0.64	0.50	0.66	0.22	0.36	0.42	0.08	0.58	0.64	0.61
20	0.66	0.50	0.68	0.24	0.33	0.38	0.08	0.62	0.67	0.64
32	0.68	0.53	0.69	0.29	0.31	0.33	0.07	0.67	0.69	0.67
40	0.67	0.53	0.67	0.32	0.32	0.31	0.06	0.69	0.68	**0.68**
48	0.66	0.54	0.65	0.37	0.33	0.31	0.06	0.69	0.67	0.67
64	0.64	0.55	0.62	0.45	0.35	0.30	0.05	0.70	0.65	0.66

The results obtained show that Faster R-CNN outperforms Alex Net+GMM model, not only in the correct detection rate obtained while producing less false detections, but also in time spending in the analysis. Both model were analyzed on a Windows 10 Machine with a core i7 7th generation, 4.7 GHz, and 32 GB of RAM, using an NVidia Titan X (Pascal) 1531 MHz GPU, achieving close to real time in Faster R-CNN model (40 ms per frame) while AlexNet+GMM took almost 100 ms per frame.

5 Conclusions and Future Work

This paper has compared the performance of two deep learning models for vehicle detection and classification in urban video sequences. Although the AlexNet model is used for feature extraction in an ad-hoc set of examples oriented to urban scenarios, the pre-trained Faster R-CNN model achieves better results in correct detections according to F1-score measure. It is important to remark that the Faster R-CNN model does not use any dynamic attributes for vehicle detection whereas GMM background subtraction used in AlexNet model. In fact, as the merge rates (MR) result shows, GMM background subtraction still has issues with stationary vehicles and occluded scenarios. In Faster R-CNN, the RPN component results could be improved providing some urban context information as restriction size of the regions.

For future work, we intend to improve the results of the RPN component of the Faster R-CNN model enriching it with traffic context information, and improve the classification component with feature extraction using a Deep Architecture as AlexNet, ZF or VGG, with a wider set of urban road user classes (e.g. trucks, vans, cyclists, pedestrians).

Acknowledgments. S.A. Velastin is grateful to funding received from the Universidad Carlos III de Madrid, the European Union's Seventh Framework Programme for research, technological development and demonstration under grant agreement no. 600371, el Ministerio de Economía y Competitividad (COFUND2013-51509) and Banco Santander. The authors wish to thank Dr. Fei Yin for the code for metrics employed for evaluations. Finally, we gratefully acknowledge the support of NVIDIA Corporation with the donation of the GPUs used for this research. The data and code used for this work is available upon request from the authors.

References

1. Tsai, L.W., Hsieh, J.W., Fan, K.C.: Vehicle detection using normalized color and edge map. IEEE Trans. Image Process. **16**(3), 850–864 (2007)
2. Ma, X., Grimson, W.E.L.: Edge-based rich representation for vehicle classification. In: 10th IEEE International Conference on Computer Vision (ICCV 2005), vol. 1–2, pp. 1185–1192 (2005)
3. Buch, N., Orwell, J., Velastin, S.A.: 3D extended histogram of oriented gradients (3DHOG) for classification of road users in urban scenes (2009)
4. Feris, R.S., et al.: Large-scale vehicle detection, indexing, and search in urban surveillance videos. IEEE Trans. Multimed. **14**(1), 28–42 (2012)
5. Chen, Z., Ellis, T.: Multi-shape descriptor vehicle classification for urban traffic. In: 2011 International Conference on Digital Image Computing Techniques and Applications (DICTA), pp. 456–461 (2011)
6. Chen, Z., Ellis, T., Velastin, S.A.: Vehicle detection, tracking and classification in urban traffic. In: 2012 15th International IEEE Conference on Intelligent Transportation Systems, pp. 951–956 (2012)
7. Gupte, S., Masoud, O., Martin, R.F., Papanikolopoulos, N.P.: Detection and classification of vehicles. IEEE Trans. Intell. Transp. Syst. **3**(1), 37–47 (2002)
8. Cucchiara, R., Piccardi, M., Mello, P.: Image analysis and rule-based reasoning for a traffic monitoring system. IEEE Trans. Intell. Transp. Syst. **1**(2), 119–130 (2000)
9. Messelodi, S., Modena, C.M., Zanin, M.: A computer vision system for the detection and classification of vehicles at urban road intersections. Pattern Anal. Appl. **8**(1–2), 17–31 (2005)
10. Huang, C.-L., Liao, W.-C.: A vision-based vehicle identification system. In: Proceedings of 17th International Conference on Pattern Recognition, ICPR 2004, vol. 4, pp. 364–367 (2004)
11. Ottlik, A., Nagel, H.-H.: Initialization of model-based vehicle tracking in video sequences of inner-city intersections. Int. J. Comput. Vis. **80**(2), 211–225 (2008)

12. Tian, B., et al.: Hierarchical and networked vehicle surveillance in its: a survey. IEEE Trans. Intell. Transp. Syst. **16**(2), 557–580 (2015)
13. ImageNet Large Scale Visual Recognition Competition (ILSVRC). http://www.image-net. org/challenges/LSVRC/. Accessed 24 Oct 2016
14. Wang, H., Cai, Y., Chen, L.: A vehicle detection algorithm based on deep belief network. Sci. World J. **2014**, e647380 (2014)
15. Dong, Z., Pei, M., He, Y., Liu, T., Dong, Y., Jia, Y.: Vehicle type classification using unsupervised convolutional neural network. In: 2014 22nd International Conference on Pattern Recognition (ICPR), pp. 172–177 (2014)
16. Chen, X., Xiang, S., Liu, C.L., Pan, C.H.: Vehicle detection in satellite images by hybrid deep convolutional neural networks. IEEE Geosci. Remote Sens. Lett. **11**(10), 1797–1801 (2014)
17. Hu, C., Bai, X., Qi, L., Chen, P., Xue, G., Mei, L.: Vehicle color recognition with spatial pyramid deep learning. IEEE Trans. Intell. Transp. Syst. **16**(5), 2925–2934 (2015)
18. Su, B., Shao, J., Zhou, J., Zhang, X., Mei, L.: Vehicle color recognition in the surveillance with deep convolutional neural networks (2015)
19. Zhang, F., Xu, X., Qiao, Y.: Deep classification of vehicle makers and models: the effectiveness of pre-training and data enhancement. In: 2015 IEEE International Conference on Robotics and Biomimetics (ROBIO), pp. 231–236 (2015)
20. Bautista, C.M., Dy, C.A., Mañalac, M.I., Orbe, R.A., Cordel, M.: Convolutional neural network for vehicle detection in low resolution traffic videos. In: 2016 IEEE Region 10 Symposium (TENSYMP), pp. 277–281 (2016)
21. Girshick, R.: Fast R-CNN. In: Proceedings of IEEE International Conference on Computer Vision, pp. 1440–1448 (2015)
22. Wang, S., Liu, F., Gan, Z., Cui, Z.: Vehicle type classification via adaptive feature clustering for traffic surveillance video. In: 2016 8th International Conference on Wireless Communications Signal Processing (WCSP), pp. 1–5 (2016)
23. Chabot, F., Chaouch, M., Rabarisoa, J., Teulière, C., Chateau, T.: Deep MANTA: a coarse-to-fine many-task network for joint 2D and 3D vehicle analysis from monocular image. arXiv preprint arXiv:170307570 (2017)
24. Fan, Q., Brown, L., Smith, J.: A closer look at faster R-CNN for vehicle detection. In: 2016 IEEE Intelligent Vehicles Symposium (IV), pp. 124–129 (2016)
25. Ren, S., He, K., Girshick, R., Sun, J.: Faster R-CNN: towards real-time object detection with region proposal networks. In: Advances in Neural Information Processing Systems, pp. 91–99 (2015)
26. Simonyan, K., Zisserman, A.: Very deep convolutional networks for large-scale image recognition. arXiv preprint arXiv:14091556 (2014)
27. Liu, D., Wang, Y.: Monza: image classification of vehicle make and model using convolutional neural networks and transfer learning. http://cs231n.stanford.edu/reports/2015/ pdfs/lediurfinal.pdf. Accessed 16 Oct 2017
28. Gao, Y., Lee, H.J.: Local tiled deep networks for recognition of vehicle make and model. Sensors **16**(2), 226 (2016)
29. Liu, X., Liu, W., Mei, T., Ma, H.: A deep learning-based approach to progressive vehicle re-identification for urban surveillance. In: European Conference on Computer Vision, pp. 869–884 (2016)
30. Bromley, J., et al.: Signature verification using a "siamese" time delay neural network. IJPRAI **7**(4), 669–688 (1993)
31. Su, B., Shao, J., Zhou, J., Zhang, X., Mei, L., Hu, C.: The precise vehicle retrieval in traffic surveillance with deep convolutional neural networks. Int. J. Inf. Electron. Eng. **6**(3), 192 (2016)

32. Cai, Y., Sun, X., Wang, H., Chen, L., Jiang, H.: Night-time vehicle detection algorithm based on visual saliency and deep learning. J. Sens. **2016** (2016)
33. Wu, Y.Y., Tsai, C.M.: Pedestrian, bike, motorcycle, and vehicle classification via deep learning: deep belief network and small training set. In: 2016 International Conference on Applied System Innovation (ICASI), pp. 1–4 (2016)
34. Huang, B.-J., Hsieh, J.-W., Tsai, C.-M.: Vehicle detection in Hsuehshan Tunnel using background subtraction and deep belief network. In: Asian Conference on Intelligent Information and Database Systems, pp. 217–226 (2017)
35. Zhou, Y., Liu, L., Shao, L., Mellor, M.: DAVE: a unified framework for fast vehicle detection and annotation. In: Leibe, B., Matas, J., Sebe, N., Welling, M. (eds.) ECCV 2016. LNCS, vol. 9906, pp. 278–293. Springer, Cham (2016). doi:10.1007/978-3-319-46475-6_18
36. You, R., Kwon, J.-W.: VoNet: vehicle orientation classification using convolutional neural network. In: Proceedings of 2nd International Conference on Communication and Information Processing, pp. 195–199 (2016)
37. Caffe — Deep Learning Framework. http://caffe.berkeleyvision.org/. Accessed 05 Sept 2016
38. Luo, X., Shen, R., Hu, J., Deng, J., Hu, L., Guan, Q.: A deep convolution neural network model for vehicle recognition and face recognition. Procedia Comput. Sci. **107**, 715–720 (2017)
39. Szegedy, C., et al.: Going deeper with convolutions. In: Proceedings of IEEE Conference on Computer Vision and Pattern Recognition, pp. 1–9 (2015)
40. Krizhevsky, A., Sutskever, I., Hinton, G.E.: ImageNet classification with deep convolutional neural networks. In: Advances in Neural Information Processing Systems, pp. 1097–1105 (2012)
41. Lin, M., Chen, Q., Yan, S.: Network in network. arXiv preprint arXiv:13124400 (2013)
42. Lecun, Y., Bottou, L., Bengio, Y., Haffner, P.: Gradient-based learning applied to document recognition. Proc. IEEE **86**(11), 2278–2324 (1998)
43. ImageNet Large Scale Visual Recognition Competition 2012 (ILSVRC 2012). http://www. image-net.org/challenges/LSVRC/2012/. Accessed 30 Aug 2017
44. Brown, L.M., Fan, Q., Zhai, Y.: Self-calibration from vehicle information. In: 2015 12th IEEE International Conference on Advanced Video and Signal Based Surveillance (AVSS), pp. 1–6 (2015)
45. Lampert, C.H., Blaschko, M.B., Hofmann, T.: Efficient subwindow search: a branch and bound framework for object localization. IEEE Trans. Pattern Anal. Mach. Intell. **31**(12), 2129–2142 (2009)
46. Uijlings, J.R., Van De Sande, K.E., Gevers, T., Smeulders, A.W.: Selective search for object recognition. Int. J. Comput. Vis. **104**(2), 154–171 (2013)
47. He, K., Zhang, X., Ren, S., Sun, J.: Spatial pyramid pooling in deep convolutional networks for visual recognition. IEEE Trans. Pattern Anal. Mach. Intell. **37**(9), 1904–1916 (2015)
48. Zitnick, C.L., Dollár, P.: Edge boxes: locating object proposals from edges. In: Fleet, D., Pajdla, T., Schiele, B., Tuytelaars, T. (eds.) ECCV 2014. LNCS, vol. 8693, pp. 391–405. Springer, Cham (2014). doi:10.1007/978-3-319-10602-1_26
49. Hosang, J., Benenson, R., Dollár, P., Schiele, B.: What makes for effective detection proposals? IEEE Trans. Pattern Anal. Mach. Intell. **38**(4), 814–830 (2016)
50. Girshick, R., Donahue, J., Darrell, T., Malik, J.: Rich feature hierarchies for accurate object detection and semantic segmentation. In: 2014 IEEE Conference on Computer Vision and Pattern Recognition, pp. 580–587 (2014)
51. ILSVRC2016. http://image-net.org/challenges/LSVRC/2016/results. Accessed 30 Aug 2017
52. Zivkovic, Z.: Improved adaptive Gaussian mixture model for background subtraction. In: Proceedings of 17th International Conference on Pattern Recognition, ICPR 2004, vol. 2, pp. 28–31 (2004)

53. Zivkovic, Z., Van Der Heijden, F.: Efficient adaptive density estimation per image pixel for the task of background subtraction. Pattern Recognit. Lett. **27**(7), 773–780 (2006)
54. Image Category Classification Using Deep Learning - MATLAB & Simulink Example. https://www.mathworks.com/help/vision/examples/image-category-classification-using-deep-learning.html. Accessed 28 Feb 2017
55. 8th International Conference on Pattern Recognition Systems |Universidad Carlos III de Madrid — Madrid, Spain. http://velastin.dynu.com/icprs17/programme.php. Accessed 30 Aug 2017
56. Razavian, A.S., Azizpour, H., Sullivan, J., Carlsson, S.: CNN features off-the-shelf: an astounding baseline for recognition. In: 2014 IEEE Conference on Computer Vision and Pattern Recognition Workshops, pp. 512–519 (2014)
57. Zeiler, M.D., Fergus, R.: Visualizing and understanding convolutional networks. In: Fleet, D., Pajdla, T., Schiele, B., Tuytelaars, T. (eds.) ECCV 2014. LNCS, vol. 8689, pp. 818–833. Springer, Cham (2014). doi:10.1007/978-3-319-10590-1_53
58. The PASCAL Visual Object Classes Challenge 2007 (VOC 2007). http://host.robots.ox.ac.uk/pascal/VOC/voc2007/index.html. Accessed 31 Aug 2017
59. ViPER: The Video Performance Evaluation Resource. http://viper-toolkit.sourceforge.net/. Accessed 31 Aug 2017
60. Yin, F., Makris, D., Velastin, S.A.: Performance evaluation of object tracking algorithms. In: IEEE International Workshop on Performance Evaluation of Tracking and Surveillance, Rio De Janeiro, Brazil, p. 25 (2007)

Visualisation and Data Driven Technology

Improvement on the Efficiency of Technology Companies in Malaysia with Data Envelopment Analysis Model

Lam Weng Hoe[1,2,3(✉)], Lam Weng Siew[1,2,3], and Liew Kah Fai[1,2]

[1] Department of Physical and Mathematical Science, Faculty of Science,
Universiti Tunku Abdul Rahman, Kampar Campus, Jalan Universiti,
Bandar Barat, 31900 Kampar, Perak, Malaysia
whlam@utar.edu.my
[2] Centre for Mathematical Sciences, Universiti Tunku Abdul Rahman,
Kampar Campus, Jalan Universiti, Bandar Barat,
31900 Kampar, Perak, Malaysia
[3] Centre for Business and Management, Universiti Tunku Abdul Rahman,
Kampar Campus, Jalan Universiti, Bandar Barat,
31900 Kampar, Perak, Malaysia

Abstract. Efficiency evaluation is vital as it is able to determine the financial performance of the companies. Efficiency describes how well the companies in utilizing their inputs to generate outputs. The objective of this study is to propose a financial ratio based Data Envelopment Analysis (DEA) model to evaluate and compare the efficiency of listed technology companies in Malaysia for the period of 2011–2015. In DEA model, the efficiency is defined as the ratio of sum-weighted outputs to sum-weighted inputs. In this study, LINGO software is used to solve the DEA model. The results of this study indicate that ELSOFT, GTRONIC, KESM, MPI and VITROX are ranked as efficient technology companies in Malaysia. Besides that, the potential improvement for each inefficient company can be identified based on the benchmark efficient companies. This study is significant because it helps to identify the efficient technology companies which can serve as benchmarks to other inefficient companies for further improvement. Moreover, it is a pioneer study of proposing DEA model with financial ratio to evaluate and compare the efficiency of technology companies in Malaysia.

Keywords: Data Envelopment Analysis · Technology company · Linear programming model · LINGO software

1 Introduction

Technology sector is one of the dominating sectors in Malaysia as this sector has made a significant contribution in the economic growth of Malaysia. Technology company is a type of business entity that focuses primarily on the development and manufacturing of technology. Nowadays, technology has become an important dimension of national growth and development [1]. Furthermore, continuous improvement in technology is

© Springer International Publishing AG 2017
H. Badioze Zaman et al. (Eds.): IVIC 2017, LNCS 10645, pp. 19–30, 2017.
https://doi.org/10.1007/978-3-319-70010-6_2

essential for the economic growth in this competitive world. Therefore, efficiency evaluation is used to measure and assess the financial performance of the technology companies [2].

Data Envelopment Analysis (DEA) is a mathematical linear programming model which measures the relative efficiency of a set of companies [2]. In DEA model, the efficiency of the company is measured as the ratio of as sum-weighted outputs to sum-weighted inputs [3]. Charnes et al. [4] introduced the DEA model to measure the efficiency of the companies with multiple inputs and outputs. Mohamad and Said [5] mentioned that continuous improvement in performance is the first priority in today's world of business. Based on the past studies, DEA model has been applied to evaluate the financial performance of the companies by using financial ratio such as bank [3, 6, 7] and healthcare company [8] in different countries. However, the influence of financial performance on the survival of the technology companies is usually ignored. In fact, the financial performance of the technology companies is important because it gives impact on the economic growth of the country. Therefore, this paper aims to fill the research gap by studying the financial performance of the technology companies in Malaysia. The objective of this paper is to propose a financial ratio based DEA model to evaluate and compare the financial performance of listed technology companies in Malaysia stock market. The rest of the paper is organized as follows. The next section discusses about the data and methodology of the study. Section 3 presents the empirical results of this study. Section 4 concludes the paper.

2   Data and Methodology

2.1   Data

The data of this study consists of all listed companies from technology sector in Malaysia Main Market. These listed companies represent the overall performance of technology sector in Malaysia stock market. The data of this study are collected from the companies' financial annual reports from the year 2011 until 2015 [9].

Based on the past studies [10–15], the financial ratio such as current ratio, debt to assets ratio, debt to equity ratio, return on asset, return on equity and earnings per share are considered in this study. Current ratio is defined as the capability of the company to satisfy its current liabilities with current assets [16, 17]. Debt to asset ratio indicates the proportion of all assets that are financed with debt [18, 19]. Debt to equity ratio is defined as the measurement of the riskiness of the company's capital structure in terms of the relationship between the funds supplied by investors and creditors [18, 19]. Earnings per share (EPS) is the amount of earning gained during a period per share of common stock [18]. Return on assets (ROA) is the amount of net profit earned relative to the level of investment in total assets [19, 20]. Return on equity (ROE) measures the overall efficiency of the company in yielding the return in comparison to the total amount of shareholders' equity [17, 19, 21]. In this study, current ratio, debt to assets ratio and debt to equity ratio are treated as inputs that needed to be minimized. On the other hand, return on asset, return on equity and earnings per share are adopted as outputs that needed to be maximized.

2.2 Data Envelopment Analysis

DEA is a linear programming model which evaluates the relative efficiency of a set of companies by considering multiple inputs and outputs [7, 22, 23]. In DEA model, the efficiency is defined as the ratio of sum-weighted outputs to sum-weighted inputs. The formulation of the DEA model is presented as follows:

$$\text{Maximize } h_k = \frac{\sum_{r=1}^{s} t_r y_{rk}}{\sum_{i=1}^{m} w_i x_{ik}} \tag{1}$$

Subject to

$$\frac{\sum_{r=1}^{s} t_r y_{rj}}{\sum_{i=1}^{m} w_i x_{ij}} \leq 1, \; j = 1, 2, 3, \ldots, n \tag{2}$$

$$t_r \geq \varepsilon, \; r = 1, 2, 3, \ldots, s \tag{3}$$

$$w_i \geq \varepsilon, \; i = 1, 2, 3, \ldots, m \tag{4}$$

where
h_k is the relative efficiency of decision making unit-k (DMU$_k$)
s is the number of outputs
t_r is the weights to be determined for output r
y_{rj} is the observed value of r-type output for entity j
m is the number of inputs
w_i is the weights to be determined for input i
x_{ij} is the observed value of i-type input for entity j
ε is the positive value
n is the number of entities

The objective function (1) aims to maximize the efficiency of k-decision-making unit (DMU). Constraint (2) ensures that the efficiency of each company is within the range, $0 < h_k \leq 1$. The fractional objective function can be converted into a linear programming form by maximizing the sum-weighted outputs and setting the sum-weighted inputs equal to unity as shown in constraint (5) and (7) [7, 24]. The weights t_r and w_i represent the importance of each output and input variable to maximize the efficiency of each company.

$$\text{Maximize } h_k = \sum_{r=1}^{s} t_r y_{rk} \tag{5}$$

Subject to

$$\sum_{i=1}^{m} w_i x_{ij} - \sum_{r=1}^{s} t_r y_{rj} \geq 0, \ j = 1, 2, 3, \ldots, n \tag{6}$$

$$\sum_{r=1}^{m} w_i x_{ik} = 1 \tag{7}$$

$$t_r \geq \varepsilon, \ r = 1, 2, 3, \ldots, s \tag{8}$$

$$w_i \geq \varepsilon, \ i = 1, 2, 3, \ldots, m \tag{9}$$

In this study, LINGO software is used to solve the DEA model. LINGO is an optimization software for solving linear programming model, non-linear programming model, goal programming model and integer programming model [25–30].

3 Empirical Results

Table 1 presents the empirical results of the efficiency and ranking of technology companies in Malaysia.

Table 1. Efficiency and ranking of technology companies

Companies	Efficiency (%)	Rank
AMTEL	42.93	13
CENSOF	16.76	17
CUSCAPI	27.35	14
DIGISTA	4.77	18
ECS	43.16	12
EFORCE	66.13	10
ELSOFT	100.00	1
GRANFLO	78.74	7
GTRONIC	100.00	1
INARI	82.82	6
JCY	50.30	11
KESM	100.00	1
MPI	100.00	1
NOTION	24.29	15
PANPAGE	21.90	16
UNISEM	67.92	9
VITROX	100.00	1
WILLOW	73.32	8

As shown in Table 1, the major findings of this study show that five technology companies are ranked efficient since they manage to achieve 100.00% efficiency score. These efficient companies are ELSOFT, GTRONIC, KESM, MPI and VITROX. This implies that these efficient companies have fully utilized their inputs optimally in maximizing the outputs. Therefore, these efficient companies obtain the first ranking based on the DEA model. On the other hand, AMTEL, CENSOF, CUSCAPI, DIGISTA, ECS, EFORCE, GRANFLO, INARI, JCY, NOTION, PANPAGE, UNI-SEM and WILLOW are classified as inefficient companies since their efficiency score are less than 100.00%. The efficiency score for GRANFLO, INARI and WILLOW are in the range of 73.32% to 82.82%. In summary, ELSOFT, GTRONIC, KESM, MPI and VITROX are ranked as efficient companies among the technology companies in Malaysia over the study period.

Table 2 presents the contribution of input and output weights in maximizing the efficiency for each technology company.

Table 2. Contribution of input and output weights in maximizing efficiency.

Companies	Current ratio (Input 1)	Debt to assets ratio (Input 2)	Debt to equity ratio (Input 3)	EPS (Output 1)	ROA (Output 2)	ROE (Output 3)	Efficiency (%)
AMTEL	0.40	0.00	99.60	99.57	0.43	0.00	42.93
CENSOF	1.54	98.46	0.00	0.30	99.40	0.30	16.76
CUSCAPI	2.07	0.00	97.92	0.21	99.57	0.21	27.35
DIGISTA	0.23	99.77	0.00	0.87	98.26	0.87	4.77
ECS	0.16	0.00	99.84	100.00	0.00	0.00	43.16
EFORCE	2.94	0.00	97.06	99.12	0.88	0.00	66.13
ELSOFT	0.40	0.00	99.60	99.57	0.43	0.00	100.00
GRANFLO	2.07	0.00	97.93	0.14	99.73	0.14	78.74
GTRONIC	0.40	0.00	99.60	99.57	0.43	0.00	100.00
INARI	0.24	0.00	99.76	0.23	0.23	99.53	82.82
JCY	0.21	99.78	0.00	0.33	0.33	99.33	50.30
KESM	0.54	99.46	0.00	99.69	0.00	0.31	100.00
MPI	0.81	0.00	99.19	99.77	0.00	0.23	100.00
NOTION	0.81	0.00	99.19	99.77	0.00	0.23	24.29
PANPAGE	0.98	99.01	0.01	0.69	0.69	98.63	21.90
UNISEM	99.98	0.01	0.01	97.89	2.11	0.00	67.92
VITROX	1.36	0.00	98.64	0.27	0.27	99.47	100.00
WILLOW	0.24	0.00	99.76	0.24	0.24	99.52	73.32
Overall (average)	6.41	27.58	66.01	49.90	22.39	27.71	61.13

As shown in Table 2, DEA model provides the contribution of input and output weights in maximizing the efficiency for the technology companies in Malaysia. In this study, the overall output weights in the maximization of efficiency of the technology companies is mostly contributed by EPS (49.90%), followed by ROE (27.71%) and lastly ROA (22.39%). On the other hand, the overall input weights in the maximization of efficiency of the technology companies is mostly contributed by debt to equity ratio (66.01%), followed by debt to assets ratio (27.58%), and finally current ratio (6.41%).

Table 3 displays the reference set of efficient companies which serve as benchmark to inefficient companies for further improvement.

Table 3. Reference set for inefficient companies

Inefficient companies	Efficiency (%)	Efficient companies (optimal coefficients)				
		ELSOFT	GTRONIC	KESM	MPI	VITROX
AMTEL	42.93	0.126	0.084		0.029	
CENSOF	16.76	0.005				0.225
CUSCAPI	27.35	0.103				0.178
DIGISTA	4.77	0.082	0.099			
ECS	43.16		0.463		0.005	
EFORCE	66.13	0.121		0.007		0.542
GRANFLO	78.74	0.529				0.041
INARI	82.82	0.784	0.151			
JCY	50.30	0.504	0.257			
NOTION	24.29	0.179		0.039	0.017	
PANPAGE	21.90	0.738				0.025
UNISEM	67.92			0.093		0.041
WILLOW	73.32	0.084	0.593			

As shown in Table 3, the efficient companies such as ELSOFT, GTRONIC, KESM, MPI and VITROX serve as reference sets or benchmark to the inefficient companies for further improvement. AMTEL has an efficiency score of 42.93% and it is inefficient when compared with ELSOFT, GTRONIC and MPI according to the optimal coefficients. Based on the optimal solution of DEA model, AMTEL needs to benchmark the efficient companies such as ELSOFT, GTRONIC and MPI as reference sets with their optimal coefficients of 0.126, 0.084, and 0.029 respectively in order to achieve 100% efficiency score. The target improvement value for the inefficient company is determined as sum of the products of respective optimal coefficients for the reference sets multiplied by the matrix column ratios of reference sets. Based on Table 3, the target improvement values for inputs and outputs of AMTEL are determined as follows:

$$
\begin{bmatrix}
\text{Target Value} \\
\text{EPS} \\
\text{ROA} \\
\text{ROE} \\
\text{Current ratio} \\
\text{Debt to asset ratio} \\
\text{Debt to equity ratio}
\end{bmatrix}
= 0.126
\begin{bmatrix}
0.060730 \\
18.542089 \\
19.656255 \\
9.440078 \\
0.069970 \\
0.077571
\end{bmatrix}
+ 0.084
\begin{bmatrix}
0.163180 \\
26.940999 \\
27.064339 \\
55.651241 \\
0.004975 \\
0.005007
\end{bmatrix}
+ 0.029
\begin{bmatrix}
0.300132 \\
11.115824 \\
11.728142 \\
45.697625 \\
0.087334 \\
0.101352
\end{bmatrix}
$$

$$
=
\begin{bmatrix}
0.030221 \\
4.936188 \\
5.104988 \\
7.224925 \\
0.011800 \\
0.013172
\end{bmatrix}
$$

In summary, the target improvement values of inputs and outputs for other inefficient technology companies are determined and presented in Table 4.

Table 4. Potential improvement for inefficient technology companies

Companies			Current actual value	Target value	Potential improvement (%)
AMTEL	Outputs	EPS	0.030221	0.030221	0.00
		ROA	4.936188	4.936188	0.00
		ROE	5.031504	5.104988	1.46
	Inputs	Current ratio	16.827984	7.224925	−57.07
		Debt to asset ratio	0.029428	0.011800	−59.90
		Debt to equity ratio	0.030679	0.013172	−57.07
CENSOF	Outputs	EPS	0.005701	0.010433	83.01
		ROA	5.062774	5.062774	0.00
		ROE	5.151173	6.127274	18.95
	Inputs	Current ratio	8.879676	1.489521	−83.23
		Debt to asset ratio	0.215517	0.036152	−83.23
		Debt to equity ratio	0.356991	0.044227	−87.61
CUSCAPI	Outputs	EPS	0.012019	0.014238	18.47
		ROA	5.835332	5.835332	0.00
		ROE	6.599691	6.788561	2.86
	Inputs	Current ratio	7.709120	2.108511	−72.65
		Debt to asset ratio	0.130954	0.035531	−72.87
		Debt to equity ratio	0.156042	0.042679	−72.65

(*continued*)

Table 4. (*continued*)

Companies			Current actual value	Target value	Potential improvement (%)
DIGISTA	Outputs	EPS	0.007584	0.021090	178.07
		ROA	4.177063	4.177063	0.00
		ROE	4.088619	4.280195	4.69
	Inputs	Current ratio	131.529626	6.272770	−95.23
		Debt to asset ratio	0.130060	0.006203	−95.23
		Debt to equity ratio	0.203774	0.006826	−96.65
ECS	Outputs	EPS	0.076939	0.076939	0.00
		ROA	10.559108	12.518402	18.56
		ROE	10.628793	12.578403	18.34
	Inputs	Current ratio	60.109887	25.967853	−56.80
		Debt to asset ratio	0.006443	0.002720	−57.78
		Debt to equity ratio	0.006487	0.002802	−56.80
EFORCE	Outputs	EPS	0.033255	0.033255	0.00
		ROA	14.228041	14.228041	0.00
		ROE	16.744300	16.918789	1.04
	Inputs	Current ratio	7.006728	4.633442	−33.87
		Debt to asset ratio	0.148933	0.096169	−35.43
		Debt to equity ratio	0.177050	0.117080	−33.87
GRANFLO	Outputs	EPS	0.023372	0.033934	45.19
		ROA	10.701505	10.701505	0.00
		ROE	10.983147	11.482543	4.55
	Inputs	Current ratio	6.667781	5.250821	−21.25
		Debt to asset ratio	0.057235	0.043477	−24.04
		Debt to equity ratio	0.062164	0.048953	−21.25
INARI	Outputs	EPS	0.060246	0.072243	19.91
		ROA	18.177910	18.602827	2.34
		ROE	19.494864	19.494864	0.00
	Inputs	Current ratio	19.079734	15.801995	−17.18
		Debt to asset ratio	0.067297	0.055602	−17.38
		Debt to equity ratio	0.074336	0.061566	−17.18

(*continued*)

Table 4. (*continued*)

Companies			Current actual value	Target value	Potential improvement (%)
JCY	Outputs	EPS	0.050977	0.072472	42.17
		ROA	15.654375	16.255608	3.84
		ROE	16.848608	16.848608	0.00
	Inputs	Current ratio	37.846108	19.037314	−49.70
		Debt to asset ratio	0.072620	0.036529	−49.70
		Debt to equity ratio	0.080767	0.040368	−50.02
NOTION	Outputs	EPS	0.024927	0.024927	0.00
		ROA	3.358685	3.716970	10.67
		ROE	3.965568	3.965568	0.00
	Inputs	Current ratio	10.841365	2.633715	−75.71
		Debt to asset ratio	0.102424	0.022801	−77.74
		Debt to equity ratio	0.115372	0.028028	−75.71
PANPAGE	Outputs	EPS	0.020611	0.045947	122.93
		ROA	12.220372	14.233494	16.47
		ROE	15.171770	15.171770	0.00
	Inputs	Current ratio	32.521280	7.127714	−78.08
		Debt to asset ratio	0.253556	0.055572	−78.08
		Debt to equity ratio	0.374153	0.062062	−83.41
UNISEM	Outputs	EPS	0.023502	0.023502	0.00
		ROA	1.431203	1.431203	0.00
		ROE	1.584330	1.720194	8.58
	Inputs	Current ratio	0.983460	0.668051	−32.07
		Debt to asset ratio	0.217768	0.027873	−87.20
		Debt to equity ratio	0.284897	0.038122	−86.62
WILLOW	Outputs	EPS	0.032264	0.101918	215.89
		ROA	17.482116	17.543850	0.35
		ROE	17.710862	17.710862	0.00
	Inputs	Current ratio	46.111377	33.808849	−26.68
		Debt to asset ratio	0.012786	0.008844	−30.83
		Debt to equity ratio	0.012962	0.009504	−26.68

Based on the optimal solution of DEA model, each inefficient company is recommended for the target improvement values of inputs and outputs as shown in Table 4. For AMTEL, it is recommended to reduce the inputs and increase the output in order to become efficient company. Therefore, the input potential improvements of current ratio, debt to asset ratio and debt to equity ratio for AMTEL are −57.07%, −59.90% and −57.07% respectively. As for the output potential improvement, AMTEL is recommended to increase the ROE from 5.031504 to 5.104988 which contributes 1.46% improvement. As shown in Table 4, all inefficient technology companies are recommended to reduce further on the inputs such as current ratio, debt to asset ratio and debt to equity ratio in order to become efficient companies.

4 Conclusion

This paper aims to propose a financial ratio based DEA model to evaluate and compare the financial performance of the listed technology companies in Malaysia stock market. The results of this study show that ELSOFT, GTRONIC, KESM, MPI and VITROX are ranked as efficient technology companies since they manage to achieve 100% efficiency score. In this study, the overall output weights in the maximization of efficiency of the technology companies is mostly contributed by EPS, followed by ROE and ROA. On the other hand, the overall input weights in the maximization of efficiency of the technology companies is mostly contributed by debt to equity ratio, followed by debt to assets ratio and finally current ratio. Besides that, the potential improvement for each inefficient company can be determined based on the benchmark efficient companies identified by the DEA model. This study is significant because it helps to identify the efficient technology companies which can serve as benchmarks to other inefficient companies for further improvement.

Acknowledgements. The authors express gratitude to the research grant project number FRGS/1/2015/SG04/UTAR/02/3 for the support.

References

1. Sohn, S.Y., Moon, T.H.: Decision tree based on data envelopment analysis for effective technology commercialization. Expert Syst. Appl. **26**(2), 279–284 (2004)
2. Memon, M.A., Tahir, I.M.: Relative efficiency of manufacturing companies in Pakistan using data envelopment analysis. Int. J. Bus. Commer. **1**(3), 10–27 (2011)
3. Řepková, I.: Banking efficiency determinants in the Czech banking sector. Procedia Econ. Financ. **23**, 191–196 (2015)
4. Charnes, A., Cooper, W.W., Rhodes, E.: Measuring the efficiency of decision making units. Eur. J. Oper. Res. **2**(6), 429–444 (1978)
5. Mohamad, N.H., Said, F.: Measuring the performance of 100 largest listed companies in Malaysia. Afr. J. Bus. Manag. **4**(13), 3178–3190 (2010)
6. Sillah, B.M.S., Harrathi, N.: Bank efficiency analysis: Islamic banks versus conventional banks in the Gulf Cooperation Council countries 2006–2012. Int. J. Financ. Res. **6**(4), 143–150 (2015)

7. Mukta, M.: Efficiency of commercial banks in India: a DEA approach. Pertanika J. Soc. Sci. Humanit. **24**(1), 151–170 (2016)
8. Lam, W.S., Liew, K.F., Lam, W.H.: An empirical comparison on the efficiency of healthcare companies in Malaysia with data envelopment analysis model. Int. J. Serv. Sci. Manag. Eng. **4**(1), 1–5 (2017)
9. Bursa Malaysia, Company Announcements—Bursa Malaysia Market. http://www.bursam alaysia.com/market/listed-companies/company-announcements/#/?category=all. Accessed 15 May 2017
10. Ong, P.L., Kamil, A.A.: Data envelopment analysis for stocks selection on Bursa Malaysia. Arch. Appl. Sci. Res. **2**(5), 11–35 (2010)
11. Dalfard, V.M., Sohrabian, A., Najafabadi, A.M., Alvani, J.: Performance evaluation and prioritization of leasing companies using the super efficiency data envelopment analysis model. Acta Polytechnica Hungarica **9**(3), 183–194 (2012)
12. Mohamad, N.H., Said, F.: Using super-efficient DEA model to evaluate the business performance in Malaysia. World Appl. Sci. J. **17**(9), 1167–1177 (2012)
13. Arsad, R., Abdullah, M.N., Alias, S.: A ranking efficiency unit by restrictions using DEA models. In: AIP Conference Proceedings, vol. 1635, no. 1, pp. 266–273 (2014)
14. Rahmani, I., Barati, B., Dalfard, V.M., Shirkouhi, H.: Nonparametric frontier analysis models for efficiency evaluation in insurance industry: a case study of Iranian insurance market. Neural Comput. Appl. **24**(5), 1153–1161 (2014)
15. Zamani, L., Beegam, R., Borzoian, S.: Portfolio selection using data envelopment analysis (DEA): a case of select Indian investment companies. Int. J. Curr. Res. Acad. Rev. **2**(4), 50–55 (2014)
16. Price, J.E., Haddock, M.D., Brock, H.R.: College Accounting, 10th edn. Macmillan/McGraw-Hill, New York (1993)
17. Ablanedo-Rosas, J.H., Gao, H., Zheng, X., Alidaee, B., Wang, H.: A study of the relative efficiency of Chinese ports: a financial ratio-based data envelopment analysis approach. Expert Syst. **27**(5), 349–362 (2010)
18. Östring, P.: Profit-Focused Supplier Management. Am. Manag. Assoc. Int., United State (2003)
19. Fraser, L., Ormiston, A.: Understanding Financial Statements. Pearson Prentice Hall, Upper Saddle River (2004)
20. Ercan, M.K., Ban, U.: Financial Management. Fersa Publication, Gazi Copy Purchaser, Ankara (2005)
21. Akguc, O.: Financial Statement Analysis, 13th edn. Arayis Publication, Istanbul (2010)
22. Sofianopoulou, S.: Manufacturing cells efficiency evaluation using data envelopment analysis. J. Manuf. Technol. Manag. **17**(2), 224–238 (2006)
23. Parthiban, P., Zubar, H.A., Katakar, P.: Vendor selection problem: a multi-criteria approach based on strategic decisions. Int. J. Prod. Res. **51**(5), 1535–1548 (2013)
24. Martic, M.M., Novakovic, M.S., Baggia, A.: Data envelopment analysis - basic models and their utilization. Organizacija **42**(2), 37–43 (2009)
25. Lam, W.S., Lam, W.H.: Portfolio optimization for index tracking problem with mixed-integer programming model. J. Sci. Res. Dev. **2**(10), 5–8 (2015)
26. Lam, W.S., Lam, W.H.: Mathematical modeling of enhanced index tracking with optimization model. J. Numer. Anal. Appl. Math. **1**(1), 1–5 (2016)
27. Lam, W.H., Lam, W.S.: Mathematical modeling of risk in portfolio optimization with mean-extended Gini approach. SCIREA J. Math. **1**(2), 190–196 (2016)
28. Lam, W.S., Jaaman, S.H., Ismail, H.: Enhanced index tracking in portfolio optimization. In: 2013 International Conference on Mathematical Sciences and Statistics, vol. 1557, pp. 469–472. AIP Publishing, New York (2013)

29. Lam, W.S., Jaaman, S.H., Ismail, H.: Index tracking modeling in portfolio optimization mixed integer linear programming. J. Appl. Sci. Agricult. **9**(18), 47–50 (2014)
30. Lam, W.S., Jaaman, S.H., Lam, W.H.: A new enhanced index tracking model in portfolio optimization with sum weighted approach. In: 2016 4th International Conference on Mathematical Sciences, vol. 1830, pp. 1–7. AIP Publishing, New York (2017)

Visualization Principles for Facilitating Strategy Development Process in the Organization

Suraya Ya'acob[1(✉)], Nazlena Mohamad Ali[2], Hai-Ning Liang[3],
Norziha Megat Zainuddin[1], and Nor Shita Mat Nayan[2]

[1] Advanced Informatics School, Universiti Teknologi Malaysia,
Kuala Lumpur, Malaysia
{suraya.yaacob,norziha.kl}@utm.my
[2] Institut Visual Informatik, Universiti Kebangsaan Malaysia, Bangi, Malaysia
{nazlena,norshita}@ivi.ukm.my
[3] Department of Computer Science and Software Engineering,
Xi'an Jiaotong Liverpool University, Suzhou, China
HaiNing.Liang@xjtlu.edu.cn

Abstract. Visualization is essential to facilitate human cognitive activities especially to handle information complexities. There is a huge effort to develop various kind of visualization tools in order to facilitate human cognitive activities in the organization. One of the major activity in the organization is the strategy development process (SDP). This activity often involves complex cognitive activities (CCA) and always happen in the collaborative settings in the organization. Therefore, it is essential for visualization to facilitate SDP from Collaborative-CCA perspectives. In order to do that, this paper intend to highlight three visualization principles that able to facilitate SDP in the organization. Using the systemic view as a fundamental, the visualization principles are; (i) higher level visual structure, (ii) lower level visual structure, and (iii) the interconnection between higher and lower level visual structure. Consequently, by applying focus group observation, this paper demonstrates the usefulness of the visualization principles in facilitating SDP. Finally, this research will further evaluate and consult current visualization techniques, methods and tools in facilitating SDP.

Keywords: Visualization · Knowledge Visualization · Strategy · Strategy Development Process · Complex Cognitive Activities · Collaboration

1 Introduction

Knowledge Visualization (KV) has been widely used to facilitate the cognitive process in an organization. From basic presentations aids like Power Points, Prezi and Keynote to more sophisticated tools like Decision Support System, Knowledge Management, Business Intelligent and currently Big Data – visualization has been used to facilitate cognitive process. This is because, visualisation provides ways to ease the understanding of complex knowledge and improving managerial judgement by transforming

H. Badioze Zaman et al. (Eds.): IVIC 2017, LNCS 10645, pp. 31–42, 2017.
https://doi.org/10.1007/978-3-319-70010-6_3

complex text into visual representation form. According to [1], the importance of visual representation to support decision making has been emphasized and explored by many researchers [1–3]. Align with visualization advancement, we can see the trend of visualization use has been expanding rapidly to support specific and special application like strategy planning in the organization. So far, we can see the visualization paradigm shift towards creating an effective, rightful and valuable solution for the users is parallel to the increasing complexities and massiveness of information in the organization [4]. It is clearly that understanding the human perceivedness and organizational context of use are essential for current visualization needs. Because through these understanding, it can help generate a more useful, relevant and comprehensive visualization solution for strategy development process.

Therefore, this paper is focusing on visualization for strategy planning in the organization. In brief, As CCA, Strategy Development Process (SDP) has higher level of cognitive complexities and when doing strategy planning collaboratively, it increases the difficulties to communicate among the group members and pose numerous cognitive overload, emotional and social challenges. Therefore, in facilitating strategy planning, it is essential for visualization to tackle the CCA and collaborative challenge as well (Collaborative-CCA).

2 Working Background

Knowledge visualization (KV) was introduced in 2004 and has been well accepted since then. Burkhard and Eppler [5] define KV as *"the use of visual representations to improve the transfer and creation of knowledge between at least two persons"*. Through an understanding of users, knowledge transfer and perception should be better, more efficient, and generate further aggregate knowledge. With a focus on business and management, KV designates all graphic means that can be used to construct and convey complex insights, experiences, attitudes, values, expectations, perspectives, opinions and predictions to enable someone to re-construct, remember and apply these insights correctly. KV aims at understanding the functions, augmenting knowledge creation, and identifying the cognitive and organization needs of users from the perspective of cognitive, perception and social communication, and as such can supply some insights for us to determine how to design visualizations.

Meanwhile, strategy is a designation of method, action or plan to achieve a desired future such as long-term business goal or the solution for any problem. In pursuit of that, strategy development process is the course of action to plan and design the method, action or plan and making decision on allocating its resources to pursue the strategy. Usually, the outcomes is the strategy planning that use as a mechanism to control and guide the strategy development that widely used by military, companies, government sectors and communities. According to [2, 6], SDP can be overwhelming challenge because it compounds with time pressures, uncertainty, constant distraction and internal tensions. From visualization perspectives, SDP is mainly dealing with information complexities and uncertainties. Thus, SDP is a Complex Cognitive Activities (CCA) that requires interaction between various parts of tasks, actions and events for solving a higher level of cognitive activities [7]. In contrast with basic cognition, CCA is a higher cognitive process that involved more that storing and encoding memories as it must come with the ability to presuppose the availability of knowledge and put it to use. [8] recognized CCA as the processes that lead to understanding and the ability to transform and use knowledge in the appropriate context settings. Since CCA often involves a higher level of thinking and knowledge, the process of strategy planning tends to answer the questions of 'how' and 'why' (higher level knowledge). The questions of how and why require an understanding of the lower level of knowledge (remembering, understanding and knowing) before a user can make an analysis and a synthesis in response to higher levels of knowledge [9] in which the visualization need to support the reasoning in this kind of cognitive process. By focusing to SDP from CCA perspective, we concentrate to facilitate the uncertainties of information and higher level of cognitive complexities.

In the organization, [10] has observed that SDP always happen in the collaborative settings. Apparently, the meetings, discussions and brainstorming are among the familiar settings to plan the strategy in the organization. This is because, to develop the comprehensive strategy, it is not feasible to tackle by single people, the organization needs the view and opinion from experts and skilful managers from various domain. Based on [11], collaborative enhances the traditional interaction by bringing together many experts so that each can contribute toward the common goal of the understanding of the object, phenomenon, or data under investigation. In this condition, experts and decision makers are among the most potential collaborators to handle the increasingly large, complex and various domain and fields that are involved in the SDP [12]. Thus, by having multiple collaborators is what transforms the cognitive process and give rise to its challenges.

The crucial challenges of SDP learned from [13] highlighted the lack of facilitation for the convergence (synthesis) during Collaborative-CCA. To handle convergence challenge, [14] suggested the approach of summarization and abstraction. Summarization can be achieved by capturing the essence of information with fewer information elements and representing it with fewer information elements. Through summarization methods, we will select only unique information, then merge similar contributions to keep only the essential, and finally select an instance of similar pieces of information to represent multiple instances. Abstracting information can be performed by creating higher level concepts that encompass relevant information from the original set. The purpose of abstraction is to make the content more cognitively manageable by allowing people to pay attention to relevant information and to ignore other details. Abstraction can be done by generalizing a set of similar objects regarded to be a specific generic type/object. It can also be attained by aggregating the relationships between objects in a hierarchical manner. Both of abstraction and summarization approach can help to eliminate redundancy, similarity and overlap during the convergence of cognitive.

When dealing with visualizations, abstraction and summarization techniques can be automatic and carried out by users. As of yet, there is little research about summarization and abstraction techniques in complex visualizations, and as such, these techniques will need to be developed and tested. In order to support summarization and abstraction for visual structure synthesizing, the research considers three kernel theories as the foundation. Each of the theories will be described in the next paragraph: (i) General System Theory, (ii) Overview concept, (iii) Cycle of expectation formation.

2.1   Overview Concept

The concept of summarization and abstraction is closely related to understand the interconnection and provide the big picture in the sense of holism. Hence, from the visualization-computational based perspective (for instance – IV, KV, Visual Analytics, Data Visualization), an overview concept is the key element that should consider the systemic view for big data interfaces. Overview is the key element in the classical visual information-seeking mantra - *Overview first, zoom and filter then details on demand* by Schneiderman [15]. However, the context of meaning for overview is incomplete for the systemic point of view. According to [16], the meanings and uses of the notion of overview from an information visualization research mainly discuss a technical sense of systemic, in which an overview is a display that shrinks an information space and shows information about it at a coarse level of granularity. Although this mantra suggests the importance of a user's initial high-level view of the data in framing further analysis, it seems to capture only the modest parts of overview. In particular, the emphasis on getting an overview first and preferably pre-attentively is at odds with descriptions of overviewing as actively created throughout a task. By having the synthesis through summarization and abstraction means the users should be able to understand the reality and overall situation. They should be clear of the main driver, capable of identifying the key points and see the interconnections between various perspectives, understand the interconnection between various elements and finally, give them readiness to handle any emergence of ideas, information or tasks during Collaborative-CCA. Therefore, we attempt to extend the technical function of an overview to suffice the demonstration of the systemic view. Thus, we extend an overview concept towards the systemic view.

2.2   General System Theory

Since the inevitable of the systemic view in the current visualization-computational base is rooted from the theory of analytical reductionism. It states that the system is a 'sum of its parts' and the account system can be broken down into different individual accounts. That theory is applicable for a complicated system but clearly a mismatch for complex matters. Therefore, it is important to implement the theory that can provide the overview in the sense of systemic. The systemic concept has been mentioned by Aristotle 2000 years ago when he explained the significant holism is something over and above its parts and not just the sum of them all [17]. According to [18], the concept of system thinking is rooted from the General System Theory (GST). GST had been introduced by Von Bertalanffy in the 1930s and under system science, GST evolved to System Thinking around 1950 to the current date. Within that, Checkland, Ackoff and Senge are among the key persons that contributed to the significance of GST in handling complex challenges, especially for the organization and management perspectives.

GST approaches the problem like a supply chain. Rather that reacting to individual parts that arise, GST will understand the underlying interconnection between various elements within a system – looks for patterns over time and seek for the root case. One of the famous metaphors to describe GST is an Iceberg Model [19]. There are four levels of GST from the Iceberg Model, namely: (i). Events as the reaction on what just happened, (ii). Pattern and trends to anticipate what trends been there over time, (iii). Underlying structure is the design that influenced the pattern to understand the interconnection between parts and (iv). Mental model as the platform to transform the assumptions, beliefs and values that people hold about the system as illustrated in Fig. 1.

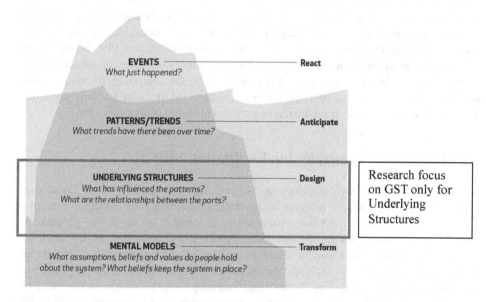

Fig. 1. Iceberg model as metaphor for general system thinking (Source: [19])

Because of the large extent of the GST level to be examined, we propose to concentrate the systemic view for visual representation on level three – underlying structures. Our study seeks an importance of the underlying structure of the Iceberg metaphor to clarify the interconnectedness between elements of information to represent system as a whole. Based on [18, 20], the research is aware that presenting visualization for the systemic view must at least contain the interconnection between elements and also between the higher levels of information (for instance: abstraction, key points and perspectives) and lower level information (details). So far, literature review in the visualization-computational field finds that the visual representation design focus is sufficient in presenting data part by part for lower level details. Therefore, to achieve a higher level of information, we argue to have higher level structure to complement a lower level of object data in forming the cycle of expectation.

2.3   Forming the Cycle of Expectation

For higher level thinking (analysis, synthesis and create), [19] describes the process as how people interpret the visualization as 'the cycle of forming expectation'. Basically, to interpret visualization, the process is between making hypotheses at a higher level structure and later confirming the hypotheses. The confirmation can be done through checking the relevant details at a lower level. Object data will recur iteratively until the users are satisfied and get the full understanding of the problem or the phenomena. From the cycle of formation, [20] emphasizes the importance of a higher level of visual structure to fill the gap in understanding how people communicate and reason with visual information, especially for complex cognitive processes. Meanwhile, IV from the overview concern basically operates at a lower level of abstraction and focuses mainly on raw data and information. A study from [15] mentioned that overview basically operated at a lower level of abstraction and focus mainly on the raw data/information. Therefore, to achieve a higher level of abstraction, [19, 20] suggest to have higher level structure of IV to complement the lower level of object data in forming the cycle of expectation. They argue that the encoding of visualization structure which is similar to how human structure information in their cognitive thinking would be useful in understanding the complex cognitive processes.

3   Visualization Principles for Facilitating SDP

Based on the convergence challenge and approaches described in Sect. 2 and suggestion by [10], the research propose the systemic concept as a visualization principles basis for SDP facilitation. Since visualization is capable to explicitly present the underlying structures between the information parts, it will help to show and draw the visual representation structure in order to synthesize the information complexities during SDP. This will help to clarify the interconnection and provide the big picture of the SDP context of use. Basically, this visualization principles have been theorized by extending the overview concept towards the systemic view. Then using GST, the research proposed the systemic view by embedding the underlying structure (layer 3 of the iceberg) to underpin the concept of the synthesis visual structure. Moreover, the cycle of formation will help to strengthen the needs for higher level and lower level of multi-view visual structure as to support synthesis for higher level thinking. The visual structure synthesizing claims three elements within this principle; (i) higher level visual structure, (ii) lower level visual structure, and (iii) the interconnection between higher and lower level visual structure.

3.1   Higher Level Visual Structure

In terms of the higher levels, [20, 21] have argued that the encoding of the visualization structure should be similar to how people structure information and this would be useful in helping them carry out complex activities. In addition, they highlight the use of metaphors to frame higher level visual structures and, by doing so, allow the abstract overviews. It is important that the overviews will allow users to make hypotheses about the information space at a higher level and enable them to confirm (or reject) these hypotheses at a lower level. Thus, it is clearly understood that the context of use for the macro level is essential as the rationales for this part (steps 1–3 from the context of use). As many cycles would need to be carried out, the structure need to be fluid, and fluidity of visualizations may not be easy to have when metaphors alone are used. There is a need to go beyond the metaphors. This is because, the importance of the metaphor has been highlighted as higher level visual structures to allow for the abstraction overviews for the visual representation. We argue that lack of metaphor alone as higher level visual structures to handle complexities and provide a systemic structure. Thus, we propose multiple-view properties as a synthesis visual structure to complement the concept of higher level information with the lower details to generate the systemic view of visual representation design. In order to create multiple-view properties of the visual structure, the context of use from the perspective details is also important to indicate the elements needed in the multiple-view properties. Thus, we suggest step 4 of the tasks-processes, step 5 of function and step 6 of knowledge needed is important to rationalize multiple-view properties for the higher level visual structure. The combination of these will help to form a more comprehensive visual structure as to guide the higher level of abstraction during the collaborative-CCA process.

3.2   Lower Level Visual Structure

Much of the literature has focused on the lower level representations. Thus, the research can easily choose, apply and combine the current visual structure as the lower level to present and guide the detailed information. The selection of these can be rationalized from the context of use on the detail parts in which are step 4, 5 and 6. According to [22], to reduce and manage the cognitive load, the overwhelming of the details can be clustered and categorized according to the key components. The selection of the key components can be according to the priority business and activity goal in the context of use – either based from function, tasks or knowledge in the context of use.

3.3   Interconnection Between Higher and Lower Level Visual Structure

According to [18, 20], contextual visual design must at least show the interconnection between higher levels of the information space (abstraction, key points, and perspectives) and lower levels (concrete details). It is important to handle the analytical and synthetical process and furthermore the divergence to the convergence phase. This is because the users develop abstractions of the higher levels by accessing and manipulating the lower level details. Therefore, the relationship between these lower and higher elements is important to facilitate the reasoning process. To support the process, the cycle of formation can strengthen the main relationship between the higher level and lower level of visual structures.

4   The Demonstration of Visualization Principles for SDP

The research has demonstrated and evaluated the visualization principles for SDP. Based on the needs to identify how visualization principles can effectively facilitate SDP, the unit of analysis for this research is the interactivity process between the user and visualization design. The demonstration and evaluation has been made through focus group observation by applying case study in the natural and collaborative settings. Initially, the visualization principles design has translated into paper-based visual representation. The paper based instrument has been used because it is open ended, free and easy to use and, due to the unfinished look has encouraged the users to amend it during SDP. Therefore, from the observation, the research can see the potential of this instrument to facilitate the users to develop the strategy planning. The paper-based instruments will be put in front of the group to facilitate them during the experiment and the users were reminded to use the instrument as the guidelines, reference and central point of view during SDP. Three collaborative groups have been selected to perform SDP in the meeting settings as shown in Fig. 2. Each of the group consists 4–6 people. During the focus group, the group members need to collaborate during the SDP to achieve the goal. Within 120 min (2 h), the group has been assigned to develop 3 strategy plan for inter-agencies collaboration in the public sector. Since the demonstration and evaluation is a case study basis, the focus group seems to be more flexible and opened to adapt the real case necessities. Due to the limited pages, this paper will focus only on the demonstration part and the evaluation findings will be presented in the future work.

Fig. 2. The settings for paper-based instruments in the strategy development process.

4.1   The Usefulness of Visualization Principles for SDP

Generally, the demonstration found the usefulness of visualization principles as visual representation instrument to facilitate SDP during the focus group observation, in other words, it justified the usefulness of visual structure synthesizing to facilitate SDP. The visual representation instrument is useful as a main reference during the discussion among the group members. The group used the instrument to guide them to handle each of the task in achieving the activities' goal. The elements provided in the higher level visual structure (the paper in blue color) serve as the points to guide the process and trigger an ideation in the lower level visual structure (List-shortlist, journey mappings and free style sketching). They also can write, draw, delete, connect and mark any information in the lower level visual structure based on the need during the SDP. Hence, interactivity between all these information (content and context) are explicitly shown, pointed and remarked. These can influence the interactivity between the users and the instruments and the communication among themselves. One of the examples is when one of the participant communicated among the group members to convince the abstraction of the think-tank group as the second strategy by using the details and elaboration from the lower level instrument (visual mappings). To convince this point of abstraction, the content inside the instrument will evolve when other group members give feedbacks during the communications. This process will iterate until the group is satisfied to decide the think-tank group as one of the public service collaborative professionalism strategies.

4.2   The Usefulness of Higher Level Visual Structure

From demonstration, the applicable design for the higher level visual structure has been transformed into a paper-based platform and highlighted using a blue color background paper. During the experiments, the research found 2 from 3 groups rarely put any content inside the higher level visual structure. Then after the experiments, the researcher had asked the group member about the function of the higher level visual structure (the diagram in the blue paper). The respondents from group 2 said that the higher level visual structure was useful because it eased their understanding about the process to be taken and the elements to consider during the experiment. Hence, they used it as the guidelines, while the content for details discussion about the understanding will be put in the lower level structure since it is a more proper place. The respondents from group 3 also agreed with the usefulness of the higher level visual structure as easy guidelines. Additionally, they mentioned the guidance on the basic elements let them have the similarity points of view to consider during the strategy development, especially for group 3 since each of the group members came from a different scheme of service in the public sector. They have different background, scope of works and interests that might lead them to have different points of consideration during the strategy development.

4.3   The Usefulness of Lower Level Visual Structure

There are three types of diagrams that have been used as lower level visual structures for the experiment namely List-shortlist, Journey Mappings and Freestyle sketching. Firstly, list-shortlist contributes as an intermediate between the higher and lower level visual structure. The list as shown in (a) plays a role to support the divergence phase in identifying the possible strategies. Then, from the lists, the group must converge to choose three best strategy plans using the shortlist visual structure as shown in (b). We can see that the users quite hesitated about the convergence process and took long time to come out with the three selections. For this reason, it is important to further clarify the convergence from the lists into the shortlist of 3 strategy plans. Secondly, Journey Mappings has been used to elaborate and discussed for each of the strategy that has been develop during SDP. Each of the visual mapping hold the details discussion for each of the strategy plan. The experiments showed the usefulness of the lower level visual structure to hold the content of discussion. It is explicit about the points of discussion in which the users can see the evolvement of the constructive content throughout the discussion. From here, the users have the reference to refine, amend and rationalize the convergence for each of the strategies as an abstraction point. Thirdly, the research also provided freestyle sketching (blank paper without any structure) because SDP is context dependent, thus any emergence condition can occur during the process. The free style sketching is useful to cater this need. As an example, group 3 needed an additional blank paper to explain the details about the value of the strategy to the stakeholders and power redundancies among the agencies for the third strategy plan – the central knowledge base. The freestyle sketching helped the users to understand situation clearly.

Additionally, we want to clarify the importance for the cycle of formation during the collaborative CCA process especially between the lower level visual structure (in this case is the visual mappings) and its intermediate-higher level visual structure (in this case is the lists-shortlist). As mentioned above (in paragraph i), the intermediate higher levels structure used the list to diverge all the possibilities and then used the shortlist to converge into 3 strategy plans. For the lower level visual structure, each plan will be discussed and elaborated in detailed using visual mappings. The elaboration from the lower level visual structure was useful to rationalize the convergence for each of the strategy plans. The feedback looping process from lower level to the higher level and vice versa helped to refine, amend and rationalize the abstraction for each of the strategy plan. Furthermore, the highest level visual structure (the Kaplan Model House on the blue paper) helped to elaborate and describe the lowest level of visual mappings in a more centered and relevant point of view, which indirectly helped to refine the abstraction to be more relevant. From here, the research found the convergence-divergence process from top-down or right-left (higher level to the lower level) help to identify the possible abstraction. Then the feedback loop from bottom-up or left-right (lower level to the higher level) helps to refine, rationalize and confirm the abstraction.

4.4 The Usefulness of Open Ended Organizing and Structuring

The visual representation instrument is useful as contextual guidelines. The combination of multiple visual structures helped to coordinate, manage and organize the incoming of information content during the experiment. Through an open-ended and multiple feedback loops, users are free to amend and put new input in the instruments for every emerging information and idea, in addition to the instrument morphing itself to include new information. As a result, the users were able to construct and develop their knowledge according to the content construction in the instrument. At the end of the experiment, the visual structure has been filled in and well utilized. The visual structure arranged the information according to the tasks given, thus it helped to reduce the cognitive load by chunking the big amount of information into smaller portion and then structuring and organizing the information that helped to enhance the information processing. Further than that, an explicit visual structure was useful to hold the centralized memory during SDP. The users have one point of reference center to clarify and check the collective memories.

5   Conclusions and Future Works

Strategy Development Process is a complex cognitive activity that involves information complexities and required higher level thinking. Since SDP always take place in the collaborative settings in the organization, it has increase the complexity challenge and the convergence issue has become more significant since it involves distinguished background of the multiple collaborators that increase the cognitive processes. Therefore, this paper has concentrate and elaborate three visualization principles for Strategy Development Process and the demonstration of it. From the demonstration, the research found the usefulness of: (i) higher level visual structure, (ii) lower level visual structure and (iii) the interconnection between higher level and lower level visual structure to facilitate SDP. Due to the limited pages in this paper, the evaluation results and findings from the demonstration will be presented in the future work. Through the observation during the demonstration, the results show the effectiveness of visualization principles to facilitate SDP. At the same time, the observation also gain deeper understanding about how these challenges has being taken in the real organization settings. Furthermore, using description and task settings from the real users' own job perspectives enrich and expand the description for each of the visualization principles.

References

1. Yee, J., Walker, A., Menzfield, L.: The use of design visualisation methods to support decision making. In DS 70: Proceedings of 12th International Design Conference on DESIGN 2012, Dubrovnik, Croatia (2012)
2. Platts, K., Eppler, M.: A framework for visualisation in the strategy process. In: Proceedings of 13th International Conference on Industry Engineering and Management Systems, Graz, Austria (2007) doi:10.1016/j.lrp.2008.11.005
3. Bresciani, S., Blackwell, A.F., Eppler, M.: A collaborative dimensions framework: understanding the mediating role of conceptual visualizations in collaborative knowledge work. In: Proceedings of 41st Annual Hawaii International Conference on System Sciences, p. 364. IEEE (2008)
4. Hundhausen, C.D.: Evaluating visualization environments: cognitive, social and cultural perspectives. In: Huang, W. (ed.) Handbook of Human Centric Visualization, pp. 115–145. Springer, Heidelberg (2014). doi:10.1007/978-1-4614-7485-2
5. Eppler, M.J., Burkhard, R.A.: Knowledge visualization. Università della Svizzera italiana (2004). doi:10.3929/ethz-a-005004486
6. Kernbach, S., Eppler, M.J., Bresciani, S.: The use of visualization in the communication of business strategies: an experimental evaluation. Int. J. Bus. Commun. 52(2), 164–187 (2015). doi:10.1109/IV.2010.55

7. Sedig, K., Parsons, P., Dittmer, M., Haworth, R.: Human-centered interactivity of visualization tools: micro- and macro-level considerations. In: Huang, W. (ed.) Handbook of Human Centric Visualization, pp. 717–743. Springer, New York (2014). doi:10.1007/ 978-1-4614-7485-2

8. Schleicher, D.J., McConnell, A.R.: The complexity of self–complexity: an associated systems theory approach. Soc. Cogn. **23**(5), 387–416 (2005). doi:10.1.1.669.6203

9. Krathwohl, D.R.: A revision of Bloom's taxonomy: an overview. Theory Pract. **41**(4), 212–218 (2002). doi:10.1207/s15430421tip4104_2

10. Ya'acob, S., Ali, N.M., Nayan, N.M.: Systemic visual structures: design solution for complexities of big data interfaces. In: Badioze Zaman, H., Robinson, P., Smeaton, A.F., Shih, T.K., Velastin, S., Jaafar, A., Mohamad Ali, N. (eds.) IVIC 2015. LNCS, vol. 9429, pp. 25–37. Springer, Cham (2015). doi:10.1007/978-3-319-25939-0_3

11. Isenberg, P., Elmqvist, N., Scholtz, J., Cernea, D., Ma, K.L., Hagen, H.: Collaborative visualization: definition, challenges, and research agenda. Inf. Visual. **10**(4), 310–326 (2011). doi:10.1177/1473871611412817

12. Mengis, J., Eppler, M.J.: Understanding and managing conversations from a knowledge perspective: an analysis of the roles and rules of face-to-face conversations in organizations. Org. Stud. **29**(10), 1287–1313 (2008)

13. Ya'acob, S., Ali, N.M., Nayan, N.M.: Handling emergence of dynamic visual representation design for complex activities in the collaboration. Jurnal Teknologi **78**(9–3), 1–11 (2016). doi:10.11113/jt.v78.9713

14. Kolfschoten, G.L., Brazier, F.M.: Cognitive load in collaboration: convergence. Group Decis. Negotiat. **22**(5), 975–996 (2013). Springer. doi:10.1109/HICSS.2012.156

15. Shneiderman, B.: The eyes have it: a task by data type taxonomy for information visualizations. In: Proceedings of IEEE Symposium on Visual Languages, pp. 336–343 (1996). doi:10.1109/VL.1996.545307

16. Hornbæk, K., Hertzum, M.: The notion of overview in information visualization. Int. J. Hum.-Comput. Stud. **69**(7), 509–525 (2011). doi:10.1016/j.ijhcs.2011.02.007

17. Corning, P.A.: The re-emergence of "emergence": a venerable concept in search of a theory. Complexity **7**(6), 18–30 (2002). doi:10.1002/cplx.10043

18. Mengis, J.: Integrating knowledge through communication-the case of experts and decision makers. In: Proceedings of OKLC, pp. 699–720 (2007). doi:10.1007/978-3-319-02958-0_29

19. A Systems Thinking Model: The Iceberg. https://www.nwei.org/iceberg/. Accessed June 2016

20. Ziemkiewicz, C., Kosara, R.: Implied dynamics in information visualization. In: Proceedings of International Conference on Advanced Visual Interfaces, pp. 215–222. ACM (2010). doi:10.1145/1842993.1843031

21. Ziemkiewicz, C., Kosara, R.: Embedding information visualization within visual representation. In: Ras, Z.W., Ribarsky, W. (eds.) Advances in Information and Intelligent Systems. SCI, vol. 251, pp. 307–326. Springer, Heidelberg (2009). doi:10.1007/978-3-642-04141-9_15

22. Paas, F., Renkl, A., Sweller, J.: Cognitive load theory and instructional design: recent developments. Educ. Psychol. **38**(1), 1–4 (2003). doi:10.1207/S15326985EP3801_1

Analysis of Visually Impaired Users' Navigation Techniques in Complex and Non-complex Layout by Using Spectrum

Bavani Ramayah[1(✉)] and Azizah Jaafar[2]

[1] Faculty of Science, University of Nottingham (Malaysia Campus), Semenyih, Selangor, Malaysia
bavani.r@nottingham.edu.my
[2] Institute of Visual Informatics (IVI), University Kebangsaan Malaysia (UKM), Bangi, Malaysia
azizahj@ukm.edu.my

Abstract. Visually Impaired (VI) users who assist by screen reader use various navigation techniques during their web navigation activities. This paper analyzed the usage of various navigation techniques in complex and non-complex layout. This study also examines the navigation behavior of VI users based on navigation techniques employed by VI users. This paper emphases on method called Spectrum which used to represent their navigation techniques in complex and non-complex layout. This effort provided a new frontier in analysing qualitative data in more efficiently. This study proven that VI users' navigation techniques in complex layout is differ from non-complex layout and it strongly influenced by information scent.

Keywords: Visually impaired users · Spectrum · Navigation · Modular layout · Complex layout

1 Introduction

Internet become the inseparable element in our daily life. The rapid growth of information technology (IT) pushed towards the needs of Internet as the main communication medium particularly among Visually Impaired (VI) Users. VI users rely on interpretation of screen reader to proceed with their navigation activities in web pages. However, VI users facing more challenges in the web sites consist of multi column layout which referred as complex or modular layout [1–4]. VI users employed various types of navigation techniques such as browsing, searching techniques in screen reader and general searching techniques [4] during their navigation activities. The adaption of various types of navigation techniques by VI users as hunter mode or tourist mode influences their navigation behaviour. Users with hunter mode have targeted information they are looking for when accessing a web site [4]. However, users with tourist mode prefer to navigate around the web site to have an overview of the web pages before looking for any information [4].The objective of this study is to examine the navigation techniques used by VI users and analyze their navigation behavior in

© Springer International Publishing AG 2017
H. Badioze Zaman et al. (Eds.): IVIC 2017, LNCS 10645, pp. 43–49, 2017.
https://doi.org/10.1007/978-3-319-70010-6_4

complex and non-complex layout. The major questions motivating this research are (a) What are the navigation techniques used by VI users in complex and non-complex layout (b) What is VI users' navigation behavior in complex and non-complex layout?

2 Web Navigation by VI Users

For a VI user, an audio mediated software called screen reader read the web content directly from the source code. As we know, source code only has one column with information one after another line and the screen reader will read the source code starts from the heading followed by navigation bar, body text and images. Therefore, the images that appear first for the sighted users may appear as last item for VI users. VI users only able to navigate the web pages without any barriers if the web pages are designed to be flexible [5, 6] for the various navigation techniques used by VI users such browsing, searching techniques in screen reader and general searching techniques.

Browsing is the technique employed by VI users to glance random through the web sites by using screen reader [2, 7]. VI users obtained the overview of the web page by using arrow and tab for general browsing. This technique consumes more time since it jumps from one link to another link displayed in the web page. Searching techniques through screen reader is the most common navigation method employed VI users. Screen reader such as JAWS could display link list tab, link list arrow and heading tags [8]. Keyboard shortcuts such as "insert+F6" for links and "insert+F6" for headings are very useful for VI users to continue their web navigation. For instance, when they press on "insert+F7", it will display a list of links within the web page. VI users will continue their navigation based on the links displayed in a pop-up box. Navigation by using headings and subheadings techniques in screen reader will allow VI users to jump from one section to another section or other subsections effortlessly. General searching techniques consists of searching by using keywords and search box [2]. They will track the destination point by correlate the keyword and search results by moving from one section to another section.

Since VI users adapting multiple techniques during their web navigation, it is vital to explore about the influences towards their navigation behavior in various types of layout. There are number of studies focused on accessibility issues in various types of web sites and user experiences [9–16]. However, in-depth investigation about VI users' navigation techniques that influences their navigation behavior is needed to unfold the hidden reason behind the issues occurs rather than focusing on finding drawbacks of existing web sites which is incompatible for VI users.

3 Spectrum

There are number of existing research explored about VI users' experiences and navigation behavior [17–21]. In these studies, the data obtained from finding were presented in column and charts. It is difficult to see underlying behavior by using table form even it is become norm in usability studies. Therefore, it is important to represent information to have more visually encapsulate form to show the relationship among the information in a way that makes it visually accessible. Slone [22] developed semi pie chart called Spectrum for this purpose. Spectrum could represents various forms of related data with multiple layers. This paper adapted a method called Spectrum [22] in representing VI users' navigation techniques in complex and non-complex layout. The exploration in this method is highly required in order convert the navigation techniques into navigation behavior to have in-depth understanding of VI users' interpretation process.

4 Methodology

4.1 Participants

There were total of twelve VI users participated in the study. They were selected based on experience in internet and screen reader. They were six males and six females. All of them are VI users who are active internet users. The range of age of the participants is between 21–64 years old. All participants use JAWS for their web activities.

4.2 Platform

Facebook was selected as an observation platform in this study. There are two versions of Facebook: a desktop version (https://www.facebook.com/) and mobile version (https://m.facebook.com/). Facebook desktop version designed for desktop users and its considered as complex layout since the information arranged in multi column to include large amount of information in single page [1]. The Facebook mobile version is designed for mobile users and it's considered as non-complex layout since the information arranged in single column layout. These two versions of Facebook pages are selected as platform for this study to observe VI users' web activities in windows environment and analyse their navigation techniques.

4.3 Data Collection

Participants were given five tasks within the desktop version Facebook pages and mobile version Facebook pages. The participants are been requested to make best guess about how to proceed with their tasks using the information that have been given in the webpage. Equipment such as computer, audio recorder and camcorder were used for the observation. The observation was conducted in naturalistic environment.

4.4 Qualitative Data Analysis

Data such as navigation techniques were recorded based on the observation of VI users' navigation activities. Spectrum was employed to represent the navigation techniques. Web navigation techniques particularly, browsing, searching techniques in screen reader, general searching using keywords were conceptualized based on specific codes in spectrum as shown in Table 1. Participants are grouped within regions A if combinations of three navigation techniques are employed by VI users during their navigation activities. However, participants are grouped within regions B if combinations of two navigation techniques and region C if combinations of one navigation technique is employed by VI users during their navigation process. For example, if a participant uses two navigation techniques such as browsing and searching techniques in screen reader, they would be grouped within region B.

Table 1. Details of data collection

Region	Details of data
A	Combination of Three navigation techniques only
B	Combination of Two navigation techniques only
C	Combination of One navigation technique only

5   Results and Discussions

The participants were grouped under three types of region based on the usage of navigation techniques. Figure 1 shows the summary of navigation techniques in Facebook Desktop version in form of spectrum. The plotted spectrum indicates that 58.3% (7 out of 12) of participants classified under region A where VI users applied combinations of three types of navigation techniques in completing their assigned tasks. However, there are 33.3% (4 out of 12) of the participants are classified under region C where they employed one combinations of navigation techniques in completing their tasks. There are only 8.3% (1 out of 12) of participants are classified under region B where they employed combination of two types of navigation techniques in completing their tasks. The majority of VI users employed combination of multiple techniques in completing their tasks in desktop version Facebook web layout.

Figure 2 shows the summary of navigation techniques in mobile version Facebook web layout. The plotted spectrum indicates that the total of twelve participants classified under region C. All of them employed single navigation technique in completing

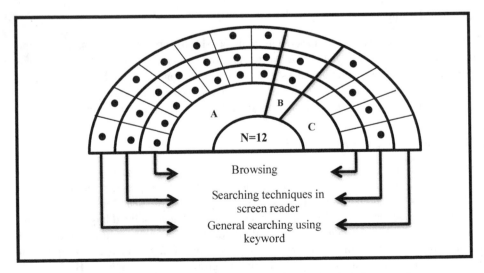

Fig. 1. Summary of navigation techniques in Facebook desktop version

their tasks. However, none of the participants are classified under region A and B in Facebook mobile version. In addition, majority of participants used searching techniques in screen reader in performing their tasks in mobile version Facebook layout. The plotted spectrum for desktop version Facebook web layout look more composite compare to spectrum for mobile version Facebook layout. As discussed earlier, Facebook desktop version is classified as complex layout however Facebook mobile version is classified as non-complex layout. The plotted spectrums in Figs. 1 and 2 clearly shows that navigation techniques used by VI users are strongly influenced by complexity of web layout. The selection of their navigation techniques created comfort zone among VI users to continue with their navigation activities. If the web layout is less complex, single navigation techniques employed by the VI users. However, they encountered multiple failures and not able to reach to their destination point if they used single navigation techniques in Desktop version Facebook layout. Therefore, VI users used multiple techniques in Desktop version and it directed them to their destination point more rapidly. This shows that the complication of web content strongly influences their navigation pattern.

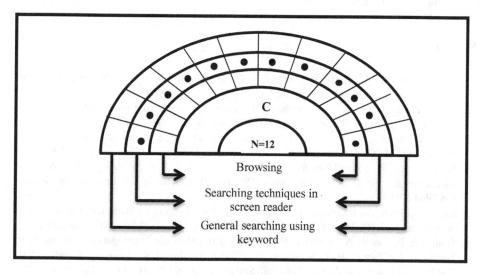

Fig. 2. Summary of navigation techniques in Facebook mobile version

This study also discovered that there is strong effect of information scent in VI users' navigation behavior and this become the hidden reason of adapting various types of navigation techniques in complex and non-complex layout. Information scent is part of information foraging which had been discussed by researchers [24–30]. However, there is only limited research had discussed the important and the influence of information scent during the navigation activities among VI users such as Takagi [23] and Vigo [27]. Contrary to the recent research by Vigo [30], this study proven that VI users' navigation techniques is depends on layout complexity where it strongly influenced by information scent. This unexpected finding provides useful evidence about information scent which previously applied among sighted users only.

6 Conclusion and Future Work

In this research, analysis of navigation techniques were carried out in complex and non-complex layout by using spectrum. Slone [22] employed this method to group the participants based on pattern similarity. This method had been modified to the form which is suitable to convert the qualitative data collected from VI users' navigation techniques in this study. This method able to show the relationship between navigation techniques and complexity of web page which it make visually accessible. This is very rare approach introduced by Slone [22]. This effort provided a new frontier in analyzing qualitative data in more efficiently. This study also has discovered the influence of information scent and this become the reason of adapting multiple techniques in complex layout. This research responded the needs to further investigate the influence of information scent in order to explain VI users' navigation behavior in more detail. To conclude, this research outcome will provide insights into VI users' navigation behavior especially for user interface designers who want to have better understanding on how VI users who solely depend on screen reader navigate in complex and non-complex web pages.

References

1. Francisco-Revilla, L., Crow, J.: Interpreting the layout of web pages. In: Proceedings of 20th ACM Conference Hypertext hypermedia - HT 2009, p. 157 (2009)
2. Ramayah, B., Jaafar, B.: Understanding the impact of web layout and emotional changes towards navigation. J. Theoret. Appl. Inf. Technol. **76**(3), 289–295 (2015)
3. Francisco-Revilla, L., Crow, J.: Interpretation of web page layouts by blind users. In: Proceedings of 10th Annul. Joint Conference Digital Libraries - JCDL 2010, p. 173 (2010)
4. Baumgartner, R., Fayzrakhmanov, R., Gattringer, R., Göbel, M., Holzinger, W.: Web 2.0 vision for the blind. In: Proceedings of WebSci10: Extending the Frontiers of Society On-Line (2010)
5. Lazar, J., Allen, A., Kleinman, J., Malarkey, C.: What frustrates screen reader users on the web: a study of 100 blind users. Int. J. Hum. Comput. Interact. **22**(3), 247–269 (2007)
6. Ramayah, B., Jaafar, A., Yatim, N.F.M.: Visually impaired user's navigation experiences in Facebook. In: Zaman, H.B., Robinson, P., Olivier, P., Shih, T.K., Velastin, S. (eds.) IVIC 2013. LNCS, vol. 8237, pp. 788–796. Springer, Cham (2013). doi:10.1007/978-3-319-02958-0_71
7. Weinreich, H., Obendorf, H., Herder, E., Mayer, M.: Not quite the average. ACM Trans. Web **2**(1), 1–31 (2008)
8. Center for Persons with Disabilities. http://webaim.org/resources/shortcuts/jaws
9. Aizpurua, A., Harper, S., Vigo, M.: Exploring the relationship between web accessibility and user experience. Int. J. Hum.-Comput. Stud. **91**, 13–23 (2016)
10. Power, C., Freire, A.P., Petrie, H., Swallow, D.: Guidelines are only half of the story: accessibility problems encountered by blind users on the web. In: Proceedings of SIGCHI Conference on Human Factors in Computing Systems, pp. 433–442 (2012)
11. Raufi, B., Ferati, M., Zenuni, X., Ajdari, J., Ismaili, F.: Methods and techniques of adaptive web accessibility for the blind and visually impaired. Procedia - Soc. Behav. Sci. **195**, 1999–2007 (2015)

12. Ramayah, B., Jaafar, A., Mohd Yatim, N.F.: Accessibility issues of social networking sites to blind users in Malaysia. In: Visual Informatics International Seminar 2012 (VIIS 2012) (2012)
13. Kuzma, J.M.: Accessibility design issues with UK e-government sites. Gov. Inf. Q. 27(2), 141–146 (2010)
14. Rorissa, A., Demissie, D.: An analysis of African e-Government service websites. Gov. Inf. Q. 27(2), 161–169 (2010)
15. Shi, Y.: The accessibility of Chinese local government web sites: an exploratory study. Gov. Inf. Q. 24(2), 377–403 (2007)
16. Chiang, M.F., Cole, R., Gupta, G.S., Kaiser, G.E., Starren, J.B.: Computer and world wide web accessibility by visually disabled patients: problems and solutions. Surv. Ophthalmol. 50(4), 394–405 (2005)
17. Yoon, K., Dols, R., Hulscher, L., Newberry, T.: An exploratory study of library website accessibility for visually impaired users. Libr. Inf. Sci. Res. 38(3), 250–258 (2016)
18. Brady, E., Sato, D., Ruan, C., Takagi, H., Asakawa, C.: Exploring interface design for independent navigation by people with visual impairments. pp. 387–388 (2015)
19. Pereira, L.S., Ferreira, S.B.L., Archambault, D.: Preliminary web accessibility evaluation method through the identification of critical items with the participation of visually impaired users. Procedia Comput. Sci. 67, 77–86 (2015)
20. Sahib, N.G., Tombros, A., Stockman, T.: Investigating the behavior of visually impaired users for multi-session search tasks. J. Am. Soc. Inf. Sci. Technol. 65(1), 69–83 (2014)
21. Loiacono, E.T., Djamasbi, S., Kiryazov, T.: Factors that affect visually impaired users' acceptance of audio and music websites. Int. J. Hum.-Comput. Stud. 71(3), 321–334 (2013)
22. Slone, D.J.: The influence of mental models and goals on search patterns during web interaction. J. Am. Soc. Inf. Sci. Technol. 53(September), 1152–1169 (2002)
23. Takagi, H., Saito, S., Fukuda, K., Asakawa, C.: Analysis of navigability of web applications for improving blind usability. ACM Trans. Comput. Interact. 14(3), 13–es (2007)
24. Blackmon, M.H., Polson, P.G., Kitajima, M., Lewis, C.: Cognitive walkthrough for the web. In: Proc. SIGCHI Conference on human Factors in Computing Systems. Chang. Our World, Chang. Ourselves - CHI 2002, no. 1, p. 463 (2002)
25. Pirolli, P., Card, S.: Information foraging. Psychol. Rev. 106(January), 643–675 (1999)
26. Pirolli, P.: Rational analyses of information foraging on the web. Cogn. Sci. 29, 343–373 (2005)
27. Vigo, M., Leporini, B., Paternò, F.: Enriching web information scent for blind users. In: Proceeding of 11th International ACM SIGACCESS Conference on Computer Accessibility - ASSETS 2009, p. 123 (2009)
28. Kitajima, M., Toyota, M.: Simulating navigation behaviour based on the architecture model Model Human Processor with Real-Time Constraints (MHP/RT). Behav. Inf. Technol. vol. 31, no. March 2016, pp. 41–58 (2012)
29. Patterson, R.E., Blaha, L.M., Grinstein, G.G., Liggett, K.K., Kaveney, D.E., Sheldon, K.C., Havig, P.R., Moore, J.: A human cognition framework for information visualization. Comput. Graph. 42, 42–58 (2014)
30. Vigo, M., Harper, S.: Challenging information foraging theory: Screen reader users are not always driven by information scent. In: HT 2013 – Proceedings of 24th ACM Conference on Hypertext and Social Media, pp. 60–68 (2013)

DengueViz: A Knowledge-Based Expert System Integrated with Parallel Coordinates Visualization in the Dengue Diagnosis

Jodene Yen Ling Ooi and J. Joshua Thomas(✉)

Department of Computing, School of Engineering, Computing and Built
Environment, KDU Penang University College, George Town, Penang, Malaysia
jodeneoyl@gmail.com, joshopever@yahoo.com

Abstract. The DengueViz is a knowledge-based expert system integrated with parallel coordinates as its visualization technique to diagnose dengue. The dengue diagnosis results includes the dengue classifications and their probability according to the interactions of users with the system. The knowledge base of this system consists of 140 rules for the classification of dengue. The integration of parallel coordinates visually presents the large amount of dengue information into a single visualization, where data interactions such as the selection of axes, filtering and highlighting reduces the clutter for it to be more comprehensible and enhances the correlation between the attributes of the information.

Keywords: Dengue · Knowledge-based expert system · Information visualization · Parallel coordinates · Visual data interactions · Dengue classification · Probability diagnosis

1 Introduction

Dengue is one of the most rapidly spreading mosquito-borne viral diseases in the world, with an estimation of 3.9 billion people across 128 countries at risk of dengue infections worldwide [1]. In Malaysia, there was an average of 110 dengue cases each day and 28 deaths per month in 2015; this was more than a 50% increase in the number of deaths compared with the previous year [2]. In 2016, the trend was expected to continue rising with the increasing number of dengue cases, where the Malaysian Ministry of Health had expected the number of dengue cases to spike between the months of June and August [3].

One of the root cause of the upward trend in the number of dengue cases and deaths despite the many efforts of the World Health Organization (WHO) [1], government and non-government organizations in prevention and control of dengue transmission is due to the characteristics in the classification of dengue infections which are similar to those of influenza and other diseases such as Chikungunya and Malaria [4]. Therefore, clinical diagnosis of dengue is often difficult; the dengue infection would have most probably evolved to a more severe form by the time a diagnosis is made, which significantly increases the mortality rates of dengue patients [1]. In addition, when dengue is not diagnosed accurately, proper dengue patient management could not be provided,

© Springer International Publishing AG 2017
H. Badioze Zaman et al. (Eds.): IVIC 2017, LNCS 10645, pp. 50–61, 2017.
https://doi.org/10.1007/978-3-319-70010-6_5

exposing the dengue patient to bites from female *Aedes aegypti* mosquitoes. When the infected mosquito bites another person, the dengue virus will be transmitted [1], leading to a higher risk of the widespread transmission of dengue virus in the neighborhood.

In order to overcome the problems mentioned above, the main aim of DengueViz is to assist in the diagnosis of dengue from the clinical and blood test characteristics of patients by integrating parallel coordinates as the information visualization technique into the knowledge-based expert system. The outline of the rest of the content is as follows: Sect. 2 Literature Review – describes expert systems, dengue diagnosis, parallel coordinates as an information visualization technique; Sect. 3 Methodology – describes the process flow of the system; Sect. 4 Implementation – describes the implementation techniques of the components of the knowledge-based expert system and the plotting of parallel coordinates; Sect. 5 Results – explains the end products of the system; and Sect. 6 Conclusion summarizes the system.

2   Literature Review

2.1   Expert Systems

Knowledge-Based Expert System. An expert system is one of the branches of artificial intelligence, where the system is capable of stimulating behaviors of (human) experts in reasoning and problem-solving using its domain-specific expert knowledge base [5]. Its high performance and responsiveness in distributing expertise in a reliable and consistent manner provides quality problem solving in its expert domain. Although its application is capable of solving real world problems, the expert system is limited to the extent of knowledge provided. This means, an inadequate knowledge base will still produce inaccurate or inefficient solutions.

The knowledge-based expert system provides the system with its ability for dengue diagnosis and classification from the clinical and blood test characteristics of patients. The two main components in knowledge-based expert system are described below:

- Knowledge Base. The knowledge base of an expert system contains the collection of facts acquired and represented in a specific manner to be integrated and processed by the inference engine of the expert system [6]. Typically, the knowledge base of an expert system is developed from a combination of several verified sources, including human experts, to provide sufficient knowledge of high integrity for the reasoning of the inference engine in order to solve real-world problems. To assist in the diagnosis of dengue, the knowledge base of DengueViz should contain clinical and blood test characteristics for the classification of dengue.
- Inference Engine. The inference engine holds the reasoning ability of the expert system based on the facts and rules from the knowledge base, through forward or backward chaining mode [7]. If the goal of the system is not known, the inference engine implements the forward chaining mode, where rules from the knowledge base are applied to produce possible outcomes as its goal; on the contrary, if the goal is known, the inference engine applies its rules to prove the desired outcome in a goal-driven backward chaining mode, to avoid any superfluous reasoning paths [7]. The goal of DengueViz is the classification of dengue, hence it implements the backward chaining mode.

Applications in Medicine. One of the earliest knowledge-based expert system in the field of medicine was developed in 1974 at the Stanford University, called MYCIN, which was developed to diagnose bacterial infections [8]. The efficiency of MYCIN was demonstrated with a series of successful experiments by the developers, proving the capabilities of medical expert systems in generating an accurate diagnosis, as well as providing drug prescriptions at the dosage adjusted for each patient according to the patient's health and conditions [8]. Since then, more expert systems have been developed in this field to improve the quality of healthcare all around the world. Main applications include the replication and transfer of knowledge from experts to the public, with roles in disease diagnosis, medical procedure interpretation, and prediction of medical complications and instructions of proper medical care [5].

2.2   Dengue Diagnosis

Dengue Clinical and Blood Test Characteristics. Clinical characteristics of dengue include: sudden high fever of 38.5°C and above; severe headache; pain behind eyes; muscle or joint pain; rash; abdominal pain; bleeding from gums nose, or mouth; skin bruising; anorexia; vomiting or nausea; fatigue or lethargy; black stools; lymph node enlargement; liver enlargement; shock; and positive tourniquet test [4]. Besides the age of patient and duration of fever, blood test characteristics include: platelet count (/mm3); white blood cell count (WBC) (/mm3); hemoglobin count (g/dL); hematocrit levels (%); aspartate aminotransferase count (AST) (units/L); and alanine transaminase (ALT) (units/L) [4].

While the WHO publication serves as useful guidelines for dengue classification, the characteristics are still considered not specific enough [9], causing dengue to often be misdiagnosed as other diseases. To get a better insight on the dengue characteristics, dengue-related research journals are studied and summarized, as in Table 1 below. Common characteristics are noted, where they appear in more than one research journal and affect the majority of the sample size of that particular research.

Table 1. Common characteristics in dengue classification for adults and children

Researchers	Location	Description	Common characteristics
Watt et al., 2003 [10]	Thailand	Dengue in adults	• Headache
Chang et al., 2009 [11]	Taiwan		• Muscle joint pain
Mitra et al., 2017 [12]	India		• Rash
			• Bleeding
			• Decreased platelet count
			• Increased AST and ALT
Xuan et al., 2004 [13]	Vietnam	Dengue in children	• Headache
Pongpan et al., 2013 [14]	Thailand		• Vomiting
Pone et al., 2016 [15]	Brazil		• Anorexia
			• Abdominal pain
			• Rash
			• Skin bruising
			• Bleeding
			• Decreased platelet count
			• Increased AST and ALT

Dengue Classifications and its Probabilities. According to WHO, classifications of dengue include: Dengue Fever, Dengue Hemorrhagic Fever (a more severe form of dengue fever with the presence of bleeding), and Dengue Shock Syndrome (the most severe form of dengue fever with the presence of shock or plasma leakage) [4].

For an increased specificity in the dengue diagnosis in DengueViz, each dengue classification will be generated along with its probabilities respectively. The probability of each classification is derived from the sum of the certainty points associated with each clinical characteristic. The default value for the certainty point of each characteristic is 1; the value is increased with the increase in severity and importance of the characteristic. The certainty points for each characteristic according to their respective dengue classification is summarized in Table 2 below.

Table 2. Clinical characteristics of dengue and their certainty points

Classification	Clinical characteristics	Certainty points	Remarks
Dengue fever	Sudden high fever	2	Common dengue characteristics
	Severe headache	2	
	Pain behind eyes	1	Default points
	Muscle or joint pain	2	Common dengue characteristics
	Rash	2	
	Abdominal pain	2	
	Vomiting or nausea	2	
	Anorexia	2	
	Fatigue or lethargy	1	Default points
	Positive tourniquet test	6	Preliminary dengue test
Dengue hemorrhagic Fever	Skin bruising	10	Blood below skin
	Bleeding from gums nose, or mouth	12	Hemorrhagic indicator
	Black stools	10	Blood in stools
Dengue shock syndrome	Lymph node enlargement	15	Internal organs affected
	Liver enlargement	15	
	Shock	25	Shock indicator

2.3   Integrating Parallel Coordinates Visualization

The main aim of information visualization is to visually present data in a way that is more intuitive and comprehensive, in a format that could be easily recognizable, navigated and managed, while preventing information overload [16]. One of the most suitable information visualization technique for presenting a large amount of data with multiple attributes is the parallel coordinates. The scalability of its framework allows as many axes to be plotted as required [17]. However, the visualization of large multi-dimensional data tend to look messy and too complicated to comprehend. Therefore, visual data interactions is an important part of the visualization to find correlation between the information.

There are many interactions that could reduce the clutter in parallel coordinates; common interactions include deletion and addition of axes, highlighting and filtering of data [18]. A brief overview of the interaction techniques in DengueViz are explained below:

- Deletion and addition of axes: allows unnecessary information to be temporarily taken off the parallel coordinates and added back whenever required with ease [18].
- Highlighting: helps bring to attention only important details in the parallel coordinates [18].
- Filtering: presents only a range of data values to be further analyzed in detailed as well as shows the differences between filtered and unfiltered data values [18].

3   Methodology

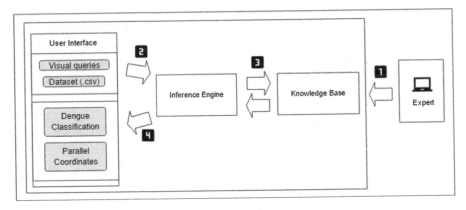

Fig. 1. System flow

The system flow will be explained in a chronological order of 4 parts as shown in the Fig. 1 above:

- The knowledge base of DengueViz is first filled with knowledge extracted from expert sources, i.e. research journal and WHO publications, in forms of IF-THEN rules.
- Users interact with the system either through visual queries, or import a CSV dataset of dengue information for the visualization in parallel coordinates. The user's inputs are passed to the inference engine of the system.
- The inference engine then processes the information and checks the knowledge base for rules that match the conditions of the user's inputs. For inputs that match more than one rule, the certainty points from each rule is combined to obtain the probability of the related dengue classifications.
- Finally, the inference engine returns the results to the user interface, displaying the dengue diagnosis in terms of its classification and probability. The parallel coordinates visualizes the information with parallel coordinates along with the newly generated dengue diagnosis.

4 Implementation and Experiments

4.1 Knowledge Base

The knowledge base contains the characteristics for the classification of dengue in the diagnosis process, as facts derived from the WHO publications and research journals. The facts are stored in the form of IF-THEN rules. There is a total of 140 rules in the knowledge base of the system, each containing a different combination of clinical and blood test characteristics for the respective dengue classifications.

There are certain conditions that must be adhered in the implementation of the knowledge base. For a disease to be classified as Dengue Fever in the system, the sudden high fever clinical characteristic must be present, accompanied by at least 2 other clinical characteristics [4], as referred from the dengue fever classification in Table 2 above. As Dengue Hemorrhagic Fever is a more severe form of Dengue Fever [4], the conditions in the Dengue Fever rules must first be fulfilled and similarly, the Dengue Shock Syndrome is a more severe form of the Dengue Hemorrhagic Fever and the same condition applies. The relationships between the 3 dengue classifications are illustrated in the Fig. 2 below.

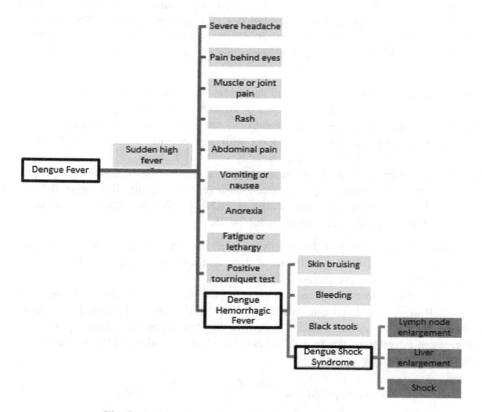

Fig. 2. Relationship between the dengue classifications

4.2 Inference Engine

In DengueViz, the C Language Integrated Production System (CLIPS) expert system shell [19] is integrated to play a role as its inference engine. CLIPS provides a ready-made framework for the development of the expert system inference engine, without its knowledge base [20]. As CLIPS runs from only a command line interface (CLI), an additional extension library, CLIPSJNI [19] is required to run it in a Java environment for the graphical user interface (GUI) of the system.

The main role of the inference engine is to check for rules with conditions matching the user's inputs. From the rule structure of the knowledge base as discussed above, it is common that there is more than one matching rule especially when more characteristics are selected by the user. As several rules are matched at the same time, probability for the respective dengue classification is calculated as mutually inclusive events, represented by the following mathematical expression:

$$Probability(DF) = \frac{100(cer1 + cer2) - (cer1 \times cer2)}{100} \qquad (1)$$

; where cer1 and cer2 are probabilities from rules 1 and 2 respectively.

Example. Some rules from the knowledge base of the system are described below for this example, where the clinical characteristics and certainty points of the characteristics are referred from Table 2 above. The sum of certainty points from each characteristic is used to provide a probability value in classifications for each rule respectively.

Rule 1: If sudden high fever, severe headache and rash is present, then dengue diagnosis is dengue fever with a probability value of 6.

Rule 2: If sudden high fever, severe headache, rash, and skin bruising is present, then dengue diagnosis is dengue fever with a probability value of 6 and dengue hemorrhagic fever with a probability value of 12.

Rule 3: If sudden high fever, severe headache, rash, skin bruising, and shock is present, then dengue diagnosis is dengue fever with a probability value of 6 and dengue hemorrhagic fever with a probability value of 12 and dengue shock syndrome with a probability value of 25.

From the rules above, if the patient experiences sudden high fever, severe headache, and rash, it fulfils the conditions of Rule 1. Therefore the dengue diagnosis is a 6% probability of Dengue Fever.

Later, if the patient starts experiencing skin bruising, it would match the conditions of both Rules 1 and 2. To calculate the new probability of the Dengue Fever classification, the Eq. (1) above is used. The dengue diagnosis is now an 11.64% probability of Dengue Fever from the probability calculated in (2), with a 12% probability of Dengue Hemorrhagic Fever.

$$Probability(DF) = \frac{100(6+6) - (6 \times 6)}{100} = 11.64\% \qquad (2)$$

If the condition of the patient worsens with the presence of shock, it would match the conditions of Rules 1, 2, and 3 as above. The new Dengue Fever probability would be 16.94% as calculated in (3), and 22.56% for the probability of Dengue Hemorrhagic Fever as in (4), with a 25% probability of Dengue Shock Syndrome.

$$Probability(DF) = \frac{100(11.64 + 6) - (11.64 \times 6)}{100} = 16.94\% \qquad (3)$$

$$Probability(DHF) = \frac{100(12 + 12) - (12 \times 12)}{100} = 22.56\% \qquad (4)$$

The certainty point of the rules are then doubled if the patient belongs to a more vulnerable age group, such as a child or elderly, or has blood test results that deviates from the healthy range. For example, if the patient above is a child with sudden high fever, severe headache, and rash, the probability of Dengue Fever would be calculated as in (5), resulting in a 21.93% probability.

$$Probability(DHF) = \frac{100(11.64 + 11.64) - (11.64 \times 11.64)}{100} = 21.93\% \qquad (5)$$

4.3 Plotting the Parallel Coordinates

The parallel coordinates is plotted using the Java Graphics 2D library, each element had to be plotted individually according to the following implementation flow as below:

- *Read dataset.* The dataset from the CSV file of patient information is first processed. Each attribute is plotted as the axes, and each data row is plotted as the data line of the parallel coordinates.
- *Axes plotting.* The number of axes in the parallel coordinates depends on the number of attributes in the CSV file. Each axis is labelled according to the attribute it represents, with data tics as labels to represent data values in the attributes.
- *Data line plotting.* Data lines are plotted to show the relationships between the dengue information attributes. As data lines are plotted from one axis to the other, their positions in each axis should always be noted to plot a continuous line in the parallel coordinates.

4.4 Visual Data Interactions

The system allows three basic parallel coordinates interactions. As the interactions are only mouse-related events, they are registered by the system using the Java MouseEvent library. The visual data interactions are implemented as below:

- *Filtering.* The main aim of the filter is to isolate a range of data value in the selected axes. The filter (upper and lower) boundaries are at the highest and lowest points of the axes by default. However, the boundaries can be changed by mouse dragging motion over the upper or lower boundaries. Filtering changes the color of data values outside the filter boundaries to a lighter color to allow a better visibility of the selected data value range.

- *Highlighting.* The highlighting brings attention to only one or more selected data value in the parallel coordinates. By mouse hovering over the data line, it temporarily changes it to a brighter color to provide a preview. By clicking on the data line, the data line is highlighted, and the mouse is free for other interactions. Clicking on the same data line again reverts the highlighted data line to its original state.
- *Axes selection.* The list of attributes in the dataset of the dengue information is displayed at the side of the system application window as checkboxes for each individual attribute. Selecting the checkbox enables the attribute to be plotted as an axis in the parallel coordinates and vice versa.

5 Results

Following the implementation, the final result is a system capable of producing a dengue diagnosis of the dengue classifications with its respective probabilities, integrated with the parallel coordinates as the information visualization technique.

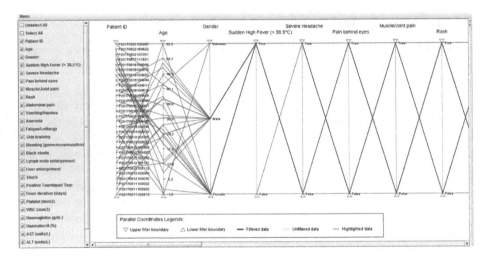

Fig. 3. Parallel coordinates prior to any data interactions

Figure 3 above shows a screenshot of the system at default state where no visual data interactions had been applied. The panel at the utmost left shows the list of attributes in the CSV file of dengue information in checkboxes. All the checkboxes are selected by default; this means all the attributes are plotted as the axes of the parallel coordinates. As for the parallel coordinates, the axes and its labels are in blue, whereas the data lines are in dark blue. The red triangles at the top and the bottom of the axes shows the upper and lower filter boundaries respectively. The legends of the parallel coordinates are displayed at the bottom of the window for reference purposes.

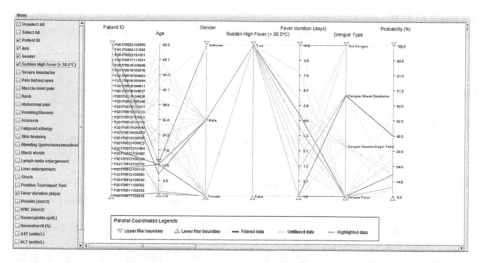

Fig. 4. Parallel coordinates after data interactions of filtering, highlighting and axis selection

The Fig. 4 above shows the parallel coordinates after applying visual data interactions. As only several attributes are selected from the left panel, only several axes plotted. The positions of the filter boundaries have been moved, the data lines outside the filter boundaries are in light blue to differentiate them from the filtered data lines. In this case, the filter boundaries only select dengue patients between the ages 0–12. After filtering, there are only 4 patients left. One of the data line is orange in color to demonstrate the highlighting of the selected data line. The parallel coordinates displays the Dengue Type and the Probability axis to show the classification of dengue and its probabilities in percentages accordingly, as diagnosis results generated from the inference engine of the system.

6 Conclusion

In conclusion, DengueViz demonstrates its capabilities in assisting dengue diagnosis by generating the dengue classification with its probability respectively; integrating the diagnosis results to the parallel coordinates for information visualization purposes. The terms probability is associated with the diagnosis result as an indication that the system is still in its prototyping stage, and it is not able to replace a medical care expert. More testing in the real world environments are required to improve the accuracy and the reliability of the system. However, it is able to assist medical care experts in making a more informed decision on dengue diagnosis so that the suitable treatment can administered to the patient.

Acknowledgements. KDU College (PG) Sdn Bhd has funded the work as an internal research grant scheme to the Department of Computing to conduct the computational medical research.

We thank KDU Penang University College, Intelligent Processing Applications (IPA) research cluster under the Department of Computing has provided the venue to conduct and complete the research work.

References

1. World Health Organization (WHO). http://www.who.int
2. The Star: 50% rise in dengue deaths (2016). http://www.thestar.com.my/news/nation/2016/01/06/50-rise-in-dengue-deaths-health-ministry-upward-trend-also-observed-in-other-countries
3. Arbee, A.: Dengue cases to spike between June and August: Health Ministry. (2016). https://www.nst.com.my/news/2016/04/137488/dengue-cases-spike-between-june-and-august-health-ministry
4. World Health Organization (WHO): Dengue Haemorrhagic Fever: Diagnosis, Treatment, Prevention and Control. Geneva (1997)
5. Desai, M.N., Kartikeyn, B., Dahiya, V.: Applications of expert system in medical field. J. Expert Syst. **2**, 150–152 (2015)
6. Darai, D.S., Singh, S., Biswas, S.: Knowledge Engineering-an overview. Int. J. Comput. Sci. Inf. Technol. **1**, 230–234 (2010)
7. Sharma, T., Tiwari, N., Kelkar, D.: Study of difference between forward and backward reasoning. Int. J. Emerg. Technol. Adv. Eng. **2**, 1–3 (2012)
8. Shortliffe, E.H.: Mycin: a knowledge-based computer program applied to infectious diseases. In: Proceedings of the Annual Symposium on Computer Application in Medical Care, pp. 66–69. PubMed Central, California (1977)
9. Srikiatkhachorn, A., Rothman, A.L., Gibbons, R.V., Sittisombut, N., Malasit, P., Ennis, F. A., Nimmannitya, S., Kalayanarooj, S.: Dengue- how best to classify it. Clin. Infect. Dis. **53**, 563–567 (2011)
10. Watt, G., Jongsakul, K., Chouriyagune, C., Paris, R.: Differentiating dengue virus infection from scrub typhus in thai adults with fever. Am. J. Trop. Med. Hyg. **68**, 536–538 (2003)
11. Chang, K., Lu, P.-L., Ko, W.-C., Tsai, J.-J., Tsai, W.-H., Chen, C.-D., Chen, Y.-H., Chen, T.-C., Hsieh, H.-C., Pan, C.-Y., Harn, M.-R.: Dengue fever scoring system: new strategy for the early detection of acute dengue virus infection in Taiwan. J. Formos. Med. Assoc. **108**, 879–885 (2009)
12. Mitra, S., Gautam, I., Jambugulam, M., Abhilash, K.P., Jayaseeelan, V.: Clinical score to differentiate scrub typhus and dengue: a tool to differentiate scrub typhus and dengue. J. Glob. Infect. Dis. **9**, 12 (2017)
13. Xuan, C., Phuong, T., Nhan, N.T., Kneen, R.: Clinical diagnosis and assessment of severity of confirmed dengue infections in vietnamese children: is the world health organization classification system helpful? Am. J. Trop. Med. Hyg. **70**, 172–179 (2004)
14. Pongpan, S., Wisitwong, A., Tawichasri, C., Patumanond, J., Namwongprom, S., Casimir, G.J., Tokiwa, K., Vasarhelyi, B.: Clinical Study Development of Dengue Infection Severity Score. ISRN Pediatr. **2013**, 1–6 (2013). doi:10.1155/2013/845876
15. Pone, S.M., Hökerberg, H.Y.M., De Oliveira, R. de C.V., Daumas, R.P., Pone, T.M., Pone, M.V.D.S., Brasil, P.: Clinical and laboratory signs associated to serious dengue disease in hospitalized children. J. Pediatr. (Rio J) **92**, 464–471 (2016). doi:10.1016/j.jped.2015.12.005
16. Chittaro, L.: Information visualization and its application to medicine. Artif. Intell. Med. **22**, 81–88 (2001). doi:10.1016/S0933-3657(00)00101-9

17. Thomas, J.J, Khader, A.T., Belaton, B.: A parallel coordinates visualization for the uncapaciated examination timetabling problem. In: Badioze Zaman, H., Robinson, P., Petrou, M., Olivier, P., Shih, T.K., Velastin, S., Nyström, J. (eds.) IVIC 2011. LNCS, vol. 7066, pp. 87–98. Springer, Heidelberg (2011). doi:10.1007/978-3-642-25191-7_10
18. Steinparz, S., Abmair, R., Bauer, A., Feiner, J.: InfoVis – parallel coordinates (2010). http://courses.iicm.tugraz.at/ivis/surveys/ss2010/g3-survey-parcoord.pdf
19. Riley, G.: CLIPS (2013). http://www.clipsrules.net
20. Kumar, S., Prasad, R.: Importance of Expert System Shell in Development of Expert System. Int. J. Innov. Res. Dev. **4**, 128–133 (2015)

Intake and Preparation of Malay Confinement Dietary Ontology Framework

Nur Liyana Lazim[1], Muhammad Hamiz Mohd Radzi[1(✉)],
Haryani Haron[2], and Mohammad Bakri Che Haron[1]

[1] Fakulti Sains Komputer & Matematik, UiTM Cawangan Melaka Kampus
Jasin, Merlimau, Malaysia
hamizradzi@tmsk.uitm.edu.my
[2] Fakulti Sains Komputer & Matematik, UiTM Cawangan Selangor Kampus
Shah Alam, Shah Alam, Malaysia

Abstract. In the rapid development of science and technology, indigenous knowledge needs to be preserved to avoid the extinction of knowledge. Indigenous knowledge can be defined as the knowledge that is being used by the local people in a certain community to live. The indigenous knowledge that is widely used in Malaysia is the Malay Confinement Dietary (MCD). Confinement is the restrictions that are placed on the diets and practices for the mothers during the month right after the delivery of their baby. Mothers in confinement needs to consume confinement dishes to restore back their health. However, mothers in confinement might not get the correct nutrients due to the intake and preparation of the confinement dish. The knowledge of the intake and preparation of the confinement dish are based on the knowledge and experiences of the midwives which will lead to data extinction if it is not being preserved. Therefore, ontology framework to preserve the knowledge of the intake and preparation of MCD is proposed in this paper. By preserving this kind of knowledge, it can be valuable and useful for the future generation to get to know previous generation's practice regarding MCD.

1 Introduction

In general, science and technology are two different disciplines, but they form a tight relationship among each other especially for research and development of society. The objective of science is to organize and grow knowledge by constructing and testing theory based on acknowledged and significant data. The objective of technology is to apply the findings to produce goods and services or to enhance the techniques used in industry or science. Indigenous knowledge (IK) cannot be left aside even in the rapid evolution of science and technology. The term 'indigenous knowledge' is defined as the knowledge systems developed by a society which adverse to the scientific knowledge that is commonly known as 'modern' knowledge [1]. In Malaysia, one of the IK that widely being practiced up until today is Malay Confinement Dietary (MCD). IK plays a big role in the MCD. Confinement is defined as the restrictions placed on diet and practices during the month right after delivery. During the confinement period, consumption of certain foods helps in improving or recovering health,

© Springer International Publishing AG 2017
H. Badioze Zaman et al. (Eds.): IVIC 2017, LNCS 10645, pp. 62–70, 2017.
https://doi.org/10.1007/978-3-319-70010-6_6

while other foods are restricted as they might cause illness either immediately or in the future [2]. Usually, mothers in confinement will need nutrients like carbohydrates, proteins, fats, minerals (mainly calcium and iron), vitamins, and water [3]. This nutrition can be found in the foods taken by the mothers in confinement [4].

However, the intake and preparation of the foods may affect the number of nutrients in food. When preparing the confinement dish, the number of nutrients in food is reduced. In other words, nutrient is altered from the food when it is exposed to oxygen, light or heat. Moreover, nutrients can also be completely conveyed out of food to the fluids that are introduced during a cooking process [5]. As an example, when boiling mud crabs in the plain water, the nutrients from the mud crab will be transferred to the broth. The broth is compact with nutrients and benefits of the mud crab like curing dengue fever [6] Besides that, the right way for the intake of confinement dish helps in nutrient absorption. Nutrient absorption takes place when digestive bacteria and enzymes work together to breakdown foods into molecules. Most of these molecules enter the blood stream that will eventually give benefits to the body [7].

Apparently, the information of the intake and preparation that need to be integrated with MCD is going to an extinction because the distributed, disorganized and unapproved information is not been preserved [8]. Hence, an ontology model is being used to preserve this knowledge. An ontology comprises of a illustrational terminology with express meanings by the implications of the terms in the terminology in addition to a group of definite proverbs which restrain the understanding and refined use of these terms [9]. An ontology can be helpful in depicting and characterizing the information of knowledge and making it simple for individuals to learn and convey the structure of information [10]. Furthermore, ontology is utilized for computational derivation as in breaking down the algorithms, inputs and outputs of implemented systems and internal structures to theoretical and conceptual terms. Besides that, ontology plays a big role in advancing correspondence between executed computational system, human and amongst people and actualized computational systems [11].

Currently, there is an existing ontology model that represents the nutrients required for mothers in postpartum period. The ontology model is then integrated with the phytochemicals from herbs, fruits and vegetables along with the colors of the phytochemicals in MCD ontology model. However, the current ontology model does not emphasize on the intake and preparation of MCD [12]. Therefore, if the intake and preparation ontology can be integrated with the current MCD ontology, mothers in confinement are able to know methods of preparing the dish and what is the appropriate intake needed according to the midwives' knowledge. Hence, this paper intends to construct ontology framework of intake and preparation for MCD that can be integrated with the existing MCD ontology model to preserve the knowledge held by the traditional midwives.

2 Knowledge

Knowledge is defined as facts, information and skills required through experience. As per stated by Miller and Bakrania [13], knowledge can be divided into tacit and explicit. Explicit knowledge comprises of rules, facts, policies and relationships which can be organized in electronic form or paper like manuals, documents, databases and procedures which is very easy to be disseminated to others [14–16]. In addition, journals, books and other information that can learned from the computer can be categorized as explicit knowledge. Meanwhile for tacit knowledge, it is defined as the knowledge that governs personal skills, and its transfer requires face-to-face contact or even coaching [16]. This type of knowledge is usually hard to be disseminated to another individual by writing it down or verbalizing it as it can be found in the minds of human like cultural beliefs and mental models [14, 17]. For example, tacit knowledge can be the knowledge that a child learned from their mother how to chew food based on his personal experience.

Tacit knowledge is the intuitive knowledge which is rooted in context, experience, practice and values. This type of knowledge is also hard to communicate as it is transferred through socialization and mentoring. One of the example of tacit knowledge is the indigenous knowledge. Based on [18, 19], IK is a form of knowledge that being utilized by the local people in certain group in order to live. IK can be disseminated via laws, songs, stories, legends, rituals and folklore. Furthermore, IK adopts a holistic approach as it exists in all aspects of life [20]. The existence of IK is crucial for the protection and the development of biodiversity [21, 22]. Barker [23] stated that, IK is more specialized to natural resources like the knowledge of plants, trees, animals, folk medicine, health and nutrition. However, this type of knowledge varies based on the geographical area [24]. Different area might have different cultural beliefs and knowledge because IK depends on the knowledge of the people for them to adapt with the area they are staying. These IK can be preserved through the knowledge management technique.

3 Knowledge Management and Ontology

When it comes to knowledge management, it is the process that integrates the tacit and explicit knowledge. Recapping about these two types of knowledge, tacit and explicit knowledge are very dependent with one another. Explicit knowledge implies the means of "collecting" the knowledge management methodologies, while on the other hand, tacit knowledge implies the means of "connecting" knowledge management methodology [25]. Knowledge management is the process of managing tacit and explicit knowledge and their activities that supports the entire process of discovering, illustrating, disseminating and use of knowledge [26]. According to Ruggles and Holtshouse [27], one of the vital characteristics of knowledge management is representing knowledge in documents, databases and software. For the sake of representing knowledge, conceptual models will be developed based on the decisions which is the modelling of knowledge. Knowledge modelling according to [28] is an interdisciplinary field that extents the approaches to obtain, clarify, evaluate, apprehend, model and express knowledge in a way to ease its preservation and to guarantee that it can be accumulated, replaced, makeshift, disseminated and reapplied.

Therefore, an example of knowledge model that is widely used is ontology [29]. According to [30], there are two different views on the term "ontology" which are the philosophical roots view and in its application to computer science. In the view of philosophical roots, philosophers are more interested in the philosophical ideas. In the context of its application to computer science, ontology engineers focus more on how ontologies can be used to illustrate, use and disseminate pieces of domain knowledge and how they can be applied in application. Hence, ontologies are the pieces of domain knowledge that will be developed in a machine interpretable language. [31–33] agreed with the proposed definitions that explains ontology in the computer science aspect: "*An ontology is a formal and explicit specification of a shared conceptualization*". Ontology is important as it explains the most commonly used terms in a specific domain which leads to constructing a skeleton and it allows the dissemination of knowledge. In Malaysia, the IK that is widely used among the Malays is the Malay Confinement Dietary (MCD) which can be preserved by using ontology.

4 Malay Confinement Dietary

MCD is the prohibition from consuming a numerous food items. Malays believe that foods are divided into 'hot' and 'cold'. After giving birth, it is believed that mothers lost a lot of 'hot' blood, thus, mothers need to balance the 'hot' and 'cold' states within the body through heat therapy [34, 35]. The heat therapy involves the consuming of 'hot' foods during confinement. Furthermore, mothers in confinement need to cover back the nutrients that they have lost due to giving birth. Mothers in confinement will need nutrients like carbohydrates, proteins, fats, minerals (mainly calcium and iron), vitamins, and water [3]. These nutrients can be found in the food intakes of confinement dietary. However, mothers in confinement might not get the correct nutrients due to the lack of knowledge of the volume of intake and the preparation method of the confinement dietary [36, 37]. The intake of confinement dietary is crucial for mothers to know during their confinement period. The intake in this research covers the time for a particular food needed to be taken for a mother to achieve the correct nutrients for their body. Most of the intake knowledge can only be fetched from midwife's experience [38]. Besides that, the preparation of confinement dish is as important as the intake because these preparation methods may lead to the loss of nutrition. Preparation of the confinement dish can be classified to five different processes which are, freeze, dry, cook, cook and drain, and reheat. The 2-D column representation in Figs. 1 and 2 below show the nutritional loss due to the preparation of the confinement dish [39].

Based on the data, most of the vitamin lost from the preparation of food is when it is dried up, but there are no minerals lost. However, a mineral lost the most is when the food is cooked and drained. Besides the method of preparation for the confinement dish which is stated before, this study also focuses on intake of the food. According to [35] mothers in confinement are just permitted to eat grilled meat or fish with rice. They are not allowed to eat oily or fried foods along with drinking cold water as they disrupt the blood circulation and cause muscle aches and back pain [40]. However, since this tacit knowledge of how the food should be prepared and taken, traditional Malay midwives' advices are needed according to the food data had been collected by the previous ontology knowledge model by [12].

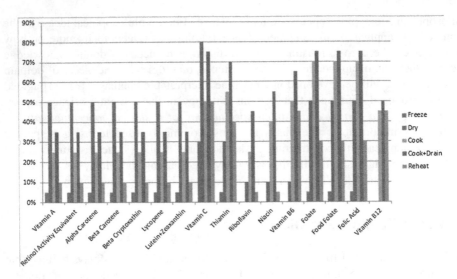

Fig. 1. 2-D column representation on the vitamins loss [39]

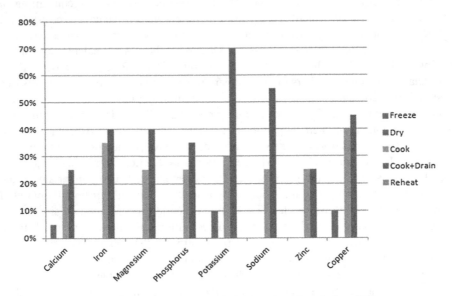

Fig. 2. 2-D column representation on the minerals loss [39]

5   Designing Ontology Framework

A research methodology is supposed to support the overall of research development. In this paper, the methodology that will be used for designing the ontology framework of the intake and preparation of MCD consists of seven steps as shown in Fig. 3.

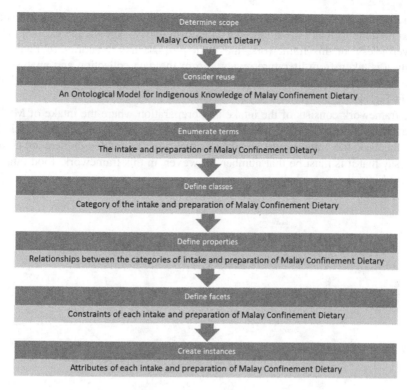

Fig. 3. Steps in developing ontology model.

According to Fig. 3, the step of creating an ontology framework starts by defining the domain or scope of the ontology model which is the MCD. Then the choice of reusing existing ontology model which is An Ontological Model for Indigenous Knowledge of Malay Confinement Dietary. Then the related terms of the intake and preparation of MCD is listed down. The terms are divided into types and subtypes where the type method of preparation has subtypes like steam, grill and boil. The type and subtypes are defined based on the top-down development process where the type is defined first then the subtypes which is then organized into a hierarchical taxonomy. Furthermore, more details on the classes are defined such as the properties of the class which is then became the slots of the class. The slots of each classes must be described with the value type, allowed values, cardinality and other features. For example, slot-value type for nutrient deficiency is number. Lastly, the individual instances of a class are defined.

6   Intake and Preparation of MCD Ontology Framework

At this moment, the collection of intake and preparation for MCD is unorganized and unstructured. There are few journals suggesting the food preparation for the mother in confinement period. However, there is less information about the intake as it only can be gathered through a tacit knowledge of Malay midwives. Hence, data collection needs to be done to make the traditional Malay midwives' knowledge explicit.

Nevertheless, in this framework, the main purpose the categories of intake and preparation is taken from literature review. From the data collection and analysis, the framework comprises of 2 main classes. The classes are the Intake and Preparation as shown in Fig. 4.

The framework consists of the intake and preparation where the intake of MCD is categorized to three subclasses which are the breakfast, lunch and dinner. Basically, most of the basic food intake must be taken 3 times a day even though there are no hard rules to say that it is must be that number. However, in this framework, food intake is categorized into those 3 subclasses.

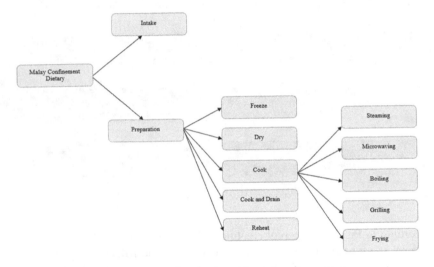

Fig. 4. Suggested main class of ontology framework.

Meanwhile for preparation of MCD, it is divided into five classes which are freeze, dry, cook, cook and drain, and reheat [31]. This preparation is important as the mother need to have right amount of nutrient and mineral to heal faster. The most important class of preparation is Cook. This Cook class can be divided into five subclasses which are the steaming, microwaving, boiling, grilling and frying. According to [27], most of the Malay traditional midwives would suggest that the method of preparation is Grilling. However, the details of intake and preparation can only be gathered through midwife's experience. Hence, this framework can only be completed into an ontology model once the interview with a traditional Malay midwife is done.

7 Discussion

If knowledge is not being preserved properly, it may lead to its extinction. In this paper, intake and preparation of MCD is considered as knowledge that needs to be preserved. This is because, mothers in confinement need to have right amount of nutrient and mineral to heal faster. One of the ways to boost the nutrients and mineral is through the foods taken during confinement. Hence, a proposal of the ontology framework is hoping to overcome the problem. Based on the framework, the food intake will have a relationship on how the food should be prepared. However, now, the classes in the framework is just some main classes that are taken from literature review. It can only be completed to a model after the data collection through interview with traditional Malay midwives is done. In the interview later, for each food in the existing MCD model, the intake and preparation method according to this framework will be gathered from the knowledge of the midwives. Nevertheless, with this framework, it gives a clearer idea on how to lead the interview with midwives to preserve the indigenous knowledge of intake and preparation of MCD.

Acknowledgments. The authors are grateful from the support to this work financially by UiTM Melaka.

References

1. Ajibade, L., Shokemi, O.: Indigenous approach to weather forecasting in Asa L.G.A. Kwara State, Nigeria. Indilinga: Afr. J. Indig. Knowl. Syst. **2**, 37–44 (2009)
2. Fok, D., Aris, I., Ho, J., Lim, S., Chua, M., Pang, W., Saw, S., Kwek, K., Godfrey, K., Kramer, M., Chong, Y.: A comparison of practices during the confinement period among Chinese, Malay, and Indian mothers in Singapore. Birth **43**, 247–254 (2016)
3. William, S., Sears, M., Holt, L.H.: The Pregnancy Book: A Month-By-Month Guide. Little, Brown (1997)
4. The Importance of Postpartum Nutrition. http://www.yummymummyclub.ca/family/pregnancy/20121127/the-importance-of-postpartum-nutrition
5. Bender, A.: Nutritional effects of food processing. Int. J. Food Sci. Technol. **1**, 261–289 (2007)
6. Wong, L., AbuBakar, S.: Health beliefs and practices related to dengue fever: a focus group study. PLoS Negl. Trop. Dis. **7**, e2310 (2013)
7. Improving Nutrient Absorption: What You Need to Know. https://www.hyperbiotics.com/blogs/recent-articles/76292739-improving-nutrient-absorption-what-you-need-to-know
8. Haron, H., Hamiz, M.: An ontological model for indigenous knowledge of Malay confinement dietary. J. Softw. **9**, 1302 (2014)
9. Campbell, A.E., Shapiro, S.C.: Ontological mediation: an overview. In: Proceedings of IJCAI Workshop on Basic Ontological Issues in Knowledge Sharing (1995)
10. Noy, N.F., McGuinness, D.L.: Ontology development 101: a guide to creating your first ontology (2001)
11. Michael, G.: Ontology: applications and design. Commun. ACM. **45** (2002)
12. Hamiz, M., Haron, H., Sanusi, A., Bakri, M.: Integration of Malay confinement dietary and phytochemicals ontology model. Adv. Sci. Lett. **4**, 400–407 (2016)
13. Miller, P., Bakrania, M.: Mobilising the power of what you know: a practical guide to successful knowledge management. Century Business (1998)
14. Botha, A., Kourie, D., Snyman, R.: Coping with Continuous Change in the Business Environment. Elsevier Science, Burlington (2014)
15. Wellman, J.: Organizational Learning: How Companies and Institutions Manage and Apply Knowledge. Palgrave Macmillan Ltd., London (2009)

16. Wyatt, J.: Management of explicit and tacit knowledge. J. Roy. Soc. Med. **94**, 6–9 (2001)
17. Nonaka, I.: A dynamic theory of organizational knowledge creation. Organ. Sci. **5**, 14–37 (1994)
18. Rajasekaran, B., Warren, D., Babu, S.: Indigenous natural-resource management systems for sustainable agricultural development—a global perspective. J. Int. Dev. **3**, 387–401 (1991)
19. Modern Science and Native Knowledge: Collaborative process that opens new perspective for PCST. http://www.raco.cat/index.php/quark/article/viewFile/55038/63353
20. Acharya, D., Shrivastava, A.: Indigenous herbal medicines. Aavishkar Publishers, Distributors, Jaipur (2008)
21. Gadgil, M., Berkes, F., Folke, C.: Indigenous knowledge for biodiversity conservation. Ambio. **22**(2/3), 151–156 (1993). Biodiversity: Ecology, Economics, Policy
22. Ajibade, L.: Knowing the unknown through the known: the case for indigenous knowledge in sustainable development. Afr. Res. Rev. **2**, 218–233 (2008)
23. Barker, D., Indigenous knowledge. International encyclopedia of geography: people, the earth, environment and technology (2006)
24. Langill, S.: Indigenous knowledge: a resource kit for sustainable development researchers in dryland Africa (1999)
25. Koenig, M.: What is KM? Knowledge Management Explained. http://www.kmworld.com/Articles/Editorial/What-Is-.../What-is-KM-Knowledge-Management-Explained-82405.aspx
26. Davenport, T.H.: Saving IT's soul: human-centered information management. Harv. Bus. Rev. **72**, 119–131 (1994)
27. Ruggles, R., Holtshouse, D.: The knowledge advantage. Capstone (1999)
28. Gómez-Pérez, A., Fernández-López, M., Corcho, O.: Ontological Engineering. Springer, London (2010)
29. Corcho, O., Fernández-López, M., Gómez-Pérez, A.: Ontological engineering. In: Semantic Web Services. 44–70 (2007)
30. Gruber, T.R.: A translation approach to portable ontology specifications. Knowl. Acquis. **5**, 199–220 (1993)
31. Studer, R., Benjamins, V., Fensel, D.: Knowledge engineering: principles and methods. Data Knowl. Eng. **25**, 161–197 (1998)
32. Borst, W.N.: Construction of Engineering Ontologies for Knowledge Sharing and Reuse. Centre for Telematics and Information Technology, Enschede (1997)
33. Introduction to the Semantic Web. http://www.cambridgesemantics.com/semanticuniversity/%0Aintroductionsemanticweb
34. Syed Jamaludin, S.: Beliefs and practices surrounding postpartum period among Malay women. In: Proceeding of Social Sciences Research ICSSR, pp. 409–417 (2014)
35. Zamani, A.: Traditional practices in postnatal care: the Malay community in Malaysia. Trinity Stud. Med. J. **2**, 30–31 (2001). http://tsmj.ie/wp-content/uploads/2015/07/Traditional-Practices-In-Postnatal-Care-The-Malay-Community-In-Malaysia.pdf
36. Spritzler, F.: How cooking affects the nutrient content of foods. https://authoritynutrition.com/cookingnutrientcontent/
37. Tyagi, S.B., Kharkwal, M., Saxena, T.: Impact of cooking on nutritional content of food. DU J. Undergrad. Res. Innov. **1**(3), 180–186 (2015)
38. Fadzil, F., Shamsuddin, K., Ezat, S., Puteh, W.: Traditional postpartum practices among Malaysian mothers. J. Altern. Complement. Med. **19**, 1–6 (2015). https://doi.org/10.1089/acm.2013.0469
39. Nutritional Effects of Food Processing. http://nutritiondata.self.com/topics/processing
40. Deraman, A.A., Wan Mohamad, W.R.: Adat dan pantang larang orang Melayu (Siri Penge). Penerbit Fajar Bakti, Selangor (1995)

Hybrid Improved Bacterial Swarm (HIBS) Optimization Algorithm

K. Shanmugasundaram, A.S.A. Mohamed$^{(\boxtimes)}$, and N.I.R. Ruhaiyem

School of Computer Sciences, Universiti Sains Malaysia (USM),
11800 Gelugor, Penang, Malaysia
ks14_com026@student.usm.my,
{sufril,intanraihana}@usm.my

Abstract. This paper proposed a hybrid improved bacterial swarm optimization (HIBS) algorithm by combining bacterial foraging optimization algorithm (BFO) with particle swarm optimization (PSO) to improve the performance of the classical BFO algorithm. Adaptive step size is introduced instead of fixed step size by random walk of the Fire Fly Algorithm (FFA) in the tumble move of the bacterium at the chemo-taxis stage of BFO. So that, the slow convergence of the BFO algorithm is mitigated. PSO algorithm is acted as mutation operator to attain the global best. So, the trapping out in the local optima by PSO is being avoided. BFO algorithm is used to attain the local best optimality. The new algorithm is tested on a set of benchmark functions. The proposed hybrid algorithm is compared with the original BFO and PSO algorithm. It has been proved that the proposed algorithm shows the significance than the classical BFO and PSO algorithms.

Keywords: Adaptive step size · Bacterial Foraging Optimization · Particle Swarm Optimization · Fire Fly Algorithm

1 Introduction

Bacterial Foraging Optimization (BFO) is a swarm intelligence algorithm used to solve real time applications and engineering optimization [3]. Similarly, Particle Swarm Optimization is also most successful swarm intelligence based algorithm in solving the optimization problems for more than a couple of decades [18]. Moreover, the BFO algorithm is being suffered by the slow convergence. This is due to the fixed step size in the tumble stage of bacterium in BFO, it faces two serious issues:

(i) If the step size is very small then it requires many generations to reach optimum solution. It may not achieve global optima with less number of iterations.
(ii) If the step size is very high then the bacterium reaches to optimum value quickly but accuracy of optimum value is very low [12].

The PSO algorithm has its own limitations like ending up in the local minimum. The underlying principle behind this problem is the fast rate of information flow

H. Badioze Zaman et al. (Eds.): IVIC 2017, LNCS 10645, pp. 71–78, 2017.
https://doi.org/10.1007/978-3-319-70010-6_7

between particles, resulting in the creation of similar particles with a loss in diversity that increases the possibility of being trapped out in the local optima resulting in premature convergence. The premature convergence of the PSO algorithm and the slow convergence of the BFO algorithm is mitigated by deploying the proposed hybrid improved bacterial swarm (HIBS) algorithm.

2 Related Works

The combination of more than one swarm based meta-heuristic algorithms is hybridized in order to yield the optimized solutions and better accuracy than the individual algorithm. The classical swarm intelligence algorithms namely bacterial foraging optimization (BFO), particle swarm optimization (PSO), ant colony optimization (ACO), artificial bee colony (ABC) and fire fly algorithm (FFA) are being hybridized among themselves by combining its continuous and discrete versions and they have their own hybrid variants [8, 16, 19]. Similarly, the algorithm is being combining with another algorithm to form the hybridized algorithms like BFO-PSO [4, 6, 7, 13, 15, 17], FFA-PSO [21]. In addition to that, they might be hybridized with the evolutionary based algorithms to form the hybridized versions like GA-PSO [11], DE-BFO-PSO [4].

The key motivation of the hybridized swarm intelligence algorithm is to mitigate the weaknesses of the individual algorithms. Biswas [4] proposed the hybrid BFO-PSO algorithm in order to increase the convergence speed and accuracy of the BFOA algorithm and at the same time, PSO algorithm is used as a mutation operator to attain the global best value. This algorithm showed its effectiveness in solving certain difficult real-world multimodal optimization problems. Bakwad [2] proposed BFO-pfPSO algorithm in which all the bacteria position and direction are updated after all fitness evaluations instead of each fitness evaluation in chemotaxis step. In order to accelerate the global performance of BFO, the bacteria update their current positions by pfPSO called as a mutation in which no velocity updates and also no inertia weights and acceleration constants.

An Improved Bacterial Foraging optimization (IBFO) algorithm is introduced by Yan et al [8]. Here, the social co-operation is introduced in order to guide the bacteria tumbling towards better directions and also step size is adjusted adaptively using decreasing step size. The BFO algorithm is hybridized with the PSO algorithm for velocity updates and crossover DE for the position and adaptation is done in the step size of chemotaxis is implemented as ACBSFO_DES in (Jarraya et al. 2013). In ABFO_PSO algorithm, the step size is used to calculate the magnitude of the velocity of the particle in PSO [1].

The hybrid BFO-PSO is used as the feature selection algorithm for detecting the bundle branch block in which the size of the database used might be reduced gradually and also classifier training time might be increased in [6]. In FABFO [9], the elimination –dispersal and reproduction steps are discarded in order to increase the speed of convergence and time complexity is reduced. The feature selection of muzzle point pattern of cattle is done by using the hybrid chaos BFO and PSO algorithm [17]. The hybrid BFO and PSO algorithm proved its state-of-the-art nature which is shown in the recent research of feature selection of face modality in the multimodal biometric recognition [7].

3 Proposed Methodology

The proposed Hybrid BF-PSO algorithm, a new algorithm that combines BFO with PSO algorithm, is endowed with high convergence speed and excellent accuracy. The combination of Bacterial Foraging Optimization and Particle swarm optimization algorithms are merged to form hybrid BF-PSO algorithm to mitigate the weakness of the individual.

This can be otherwise stated as the PSO performing a global search and providing a near optimal solution very quickly which is followed by a local search by BFO at the chemo taxis which fine-tunes the solution and gives an optimum solution of high accuracy. PSO has an inherent disability of trapping in the local optima, but it has high convergence speed whereas BFO has the drawback of having a very poor convergence speed but the ability not to trap in the local optima [13]. The proposed Hybrid BF-PSO method performs a local search through the chemotactic movement operation of bacterial foraging whereas the global search over the entire search space is accomplished by a particle swarm operator. There are three major changes have been deployed in the proposed Hybrid BF-PSO algorithm.

3.1 Adaptive Step Size in the Tumbling of Bacterium at Chemotaxis

The Step size C(i) is calculated in the tumble stage of the ith bacterium. It is used for the bacterium movement with fixed step size value in the random direction within the range of −1, 1. It delays in reaching the global solution. So, in the proposed BFO, the fixed step size is changed into varying step size ranging between [0, 1] using the random walk procedure of the firefly algorithm to reach the optimum at the earliest convergence which is given as following:

$$C(i) = \alpha(\text{rand} - 1/2) \tag{1}$$

where α is the randomization variable, rand is a random number generator within the range between [0, 1]. The step size C(i) is deployed into the given below, which is responsible for the Tumble move of the ith bacterium.

$$\theta i(j + 1, k, l) = \theta i(j, k, l) + C(i) * \emptyset j \tag{2}$$

where $\Theta i(j + 1, k, l)$ is the new position of the ith bacterium, $\Theta i(j, k, l)$-previous position of the ith bacterium, C(i)-step size, $\emptyset j$–previous direction of the ith bacterium.

3.2 Local Best by BFO Algorithm

In the proposed HBF-PSO algorithm, the BFO algorithm is used for local search whereas the PSO algorithm is influenced into the BFO algorithm as mutation operator in the reproduction stage of BFO, performing a global search and providing a near optimal solution very quickly. The PSO algorithm has an inherent disability of trapping in the local optima, but it has high convergence speed whereas BFO has the drawback of having a very poor convergence speed but it has the ability not to trap in the local optima [17]. The proposed Hybrid BF-PSO method performs a local search through the chemotactic movement operation of bacterial foraging whereas the global search over the entire search space is accomplished by a particle swarm operator. The BFO algorithm is used to find the local best (pbest) in the HBF-PSO algorithm:

$$\theta i(j+1,k,l) = \theta i(j,k,l) + C(i) * \emptyset j \qquad (3)$$

$$Pbest = f(\theta i(j+1,k,l)) \qquad (4)$$

where $\Theta i(j + 1, k, l)$ is the new position of the ith bacterium, $\Theta i(j, k, l)$ previous position of the ith bacterium, C(i)-step size, $\emptyset j$ –previous direction of the ith bacterium and *Pbest* is the local best of fitness value of $\Theta i(j + 1, k, l)$.

3.3 Global Best by PSO Algorithm

The PSO algorithm is used to find the global best (gbest) value in the HBF-PSO algorithm. PSO algorithm is acted as mutation operator in the BFO algorithm to update the direction and position of the ith bacterium which is given as followings:

$$\emptyset(j+1,k,l) = w * \emptyset(j) + c1 * rand * (pbest - \theta(i)) + c2 * rand * (gbest - \theta(i)) \qquad (5)$$

$$\theta(j+1,k,l) = \theta(j,k,l) + \emptyset(j+1,k,l) \qquad (6)$$

where $\emptyset(j + 1, k, l)$– new direction of the ith bacterium, $\Theta(j + 1, k, l)$-new position of the ith bacterium, w-inertia weight, c1, c2 – acceleration constants, rand-random number between the range[0,1], *pbest*- local optimum value, *gbest*-global optimum value, $\Theta(j, k, l)$ previous position of the ith bacterium, $\emptyset(j)$- previous direction of the ith bacterium. Positions and directions of the bacteria is updated by PSO algorithm only after the chemo taxis stage in which all the fitness evaluations is done in the chemo taxis.

The Database used for the proposed research is Bhosphorous hand image database. It consists of 642 persons left and right-hand images. The left and right-hand images belong to the same person in which each person has 3 poses of images from left as well as right hands. Total of 642 × 2 × 3= 3,852 samples l, 828 samples of the left hand and 816 samples of right-hand images are used for training. The sample images of the left-hand and right-hand images with 3 poses are shown in Fig. 1. The segmenting of the features of the hand can be optimised using segmentation strategy either by boundary based or region based approaches [21–25].

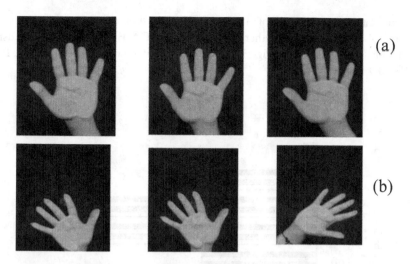

Fig. 1. Sample images from the hand database Bhosphorus (a) left-hand images of the same person with 3 poses (b) right-hand images of the same person with 3 poses.

4 Results and Discussions

In order to test the effectiveness of the proposed HIBS algorithm, the performance of the proposed HIBS algorithm will be evaluated by using the well-known four benchmark objective functions and being compared with the performance of the individual BFO, PSO algorithms which are also shown in detail in Table 1. It has been observed that the hybrid BFO-PSO algorithm is performed better than the original BFO and PSO algorithms on all the three benchmark functions except in the Ackley function.

Table 1. Results obtained by BFO, PSO and HIBS (HBF-PSO) algorithms using benchmark functions

Function	BFO	PSO	HIBS (HBF-PSO)
F1-Rosenbrock	0.31628	0.63834	**0.04371**
F2-Ackley	3.7583	**2.38452**	3.2183
F3-Griewank	3.0254	3.8596	**2.7563**
F4-Rastrigin	4.2356	6.29718	**3.38678**

The Equal Error Rate (EER) value of HBF-PSO is compared with other hybrid algorithms like Genetic Algorithm and Bacterial Foraging Algorithm (GA-BFO), GA-Genetic Algorithm and Bacterial Foraging Algorithm and Particle Swarm Optimization (PSO) using the Bhosphorous database along with the weighted sum score fusion. Among all the algorithms, the HIBS algorithm is reported with the minimal EER value 0.03827 and 0.04371 for left and right hand based samples respectively. The

Bhosphorus database comprises of 3852 samples. The Fig. 2 shows the EER value comparison of HBF-PSO with other algorithms like GA-BFO and GA-PSO using weighted sum score fusion. The Fig. 3 shows the EER value evaluation for BFO, PSO and HBF-PSO respectively.

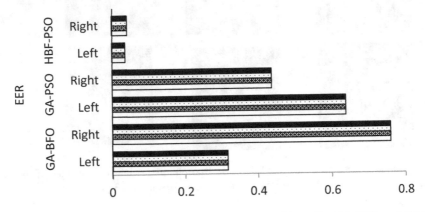

Fig. 2. EER value comparison of HBF-PSO with other algorithms like GA-BFO and GA-PSO using weighted sum score fusion

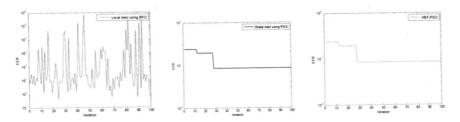

Fig. 3. EER value comparison of HBF-PSO with other algorithms like GA-BFO and GA-PSO using weighted sum score fusion

5 Conclusion

In this paper, the HIBS algorithm (Hybrid BFO-PSO) is proposed to mitigate the individual weaknesses of original BFO and PSO algorithm. In addition to that, the best fitness is achieved by adapting the step size in the tumble stage of bacteria at the chemotaxis stage in the BFO algorithm using random walk procedure of Fire Fly Algorithm (FFA). Moreover, the local best and global best is achieved by using BFO and PSO respectively in the Hybrid Improved Bacterial Swarm (HIBS) algorithm. The optimization performance of HIBS algorithm is tested with the set of benchmark functions and compared with the original BFO and PSO algorithms. The results proved that the proposed HIBS algorithm performed better on three benchmark functions out of four functions.

Acknowledgements. The author wish to thank Universiti Sains Malaysia for the support it has extended in the completion of the present research through Short Term University Grant No. 304/PKOMP/6313280.

References

1. Alostaz, A., Alhanjouri, M.: A new adaptive BFO based on PSO for learning neural network. i-Manager's J. Comput. Sci. **1**, 9 (2013)
2. Bakwad, K.M., Patnaik, S.S., et al.: Hybrid bacterial foraging with parameter free PSO. In: IEEE World Congress on Nature and Biologically Inspired Computing (2009)
3. Kevin, M.: Biomimicry of bacterial foraging for distributed optimization and control. IEEE Control Syst. Mag. (2002)
4. Biswas, A., Das, S., Abraham, A.: Synergy of PSO and bacterial foraging optimization: a comparative study on numerical benchmarks. In: Corchado, E., Corchado, J.M., Abraham, A. (eds.) Innovations in Hybrid Intelligent Systems. ASC, vol. 44, pp. 255–263. Springer, Heidelberg (2007). doi:10.1007/978-3-540-74972-1_34
5. Jarraya, Y., Bouaziz, S., Alimi, A.M., Abraham, A.: A hybrid computational chemotaxis in bacterial foraging optimization algorithm for global numerical optimization. In: IEEE International Conference on Cybernetics, pp. 213–218 (2003)
6. Kora, P., Kalva, S.R.: Hybrid bacterial foraging and particle swarm optimization for detecting Bundle Branch Block. SpringerPlus **4**(1), 481 (2015)
7. Kumar, S., Sing, S.K.: Hybrid BFO and PSO Swarm Intelligence Approach for Biometric Feature Optimization, Nature-Inspired Computing Concepts, Methodologies, Tools, and Applications. IGI Global, Hershey (2017)
8. Yan, X., Zhu, Y., Chen, H., Zhang, H.: Improved bacterial foraging optimization with social cooperation and adaptive step size. In: Huang, D.-S., Jiang, C., Bevilacqua, V., Figueroa, J. C. (eds.) ICIC 2012. LNCS, vol. 7389, pp. 634–640. Springer, Heidelberg (2012). doi:10. 1007/978-3-642-31588-6_81
9. Daas, M.S., Chikhi, S., Batouche, M.: Bacterial foraging optimization with double role of reproduction and step adaptation. In: Proceedings of International Conference on Intelligent Information Processing, Security and Advanced Communication, vol. 71. ACM (2015)
10. Hanmandlu, M., Kumar, A., Madasu, V.K., Yarlagadda, P.: Fusion of hand based biometrics using particle swarm optimization. In: 5th International Conference on Information Technology: New Generations, pp. 783–788. IEEE (2008)
11. Cherifi, et al.: Multimodal score-level fusion using hybrid GA-PSO for multibiometric system. Informatica **39**, 209–216 (2015)
12. Datta, T., et al.: Improved adaptive bacteria foraging algorithm in optimization of antenna array for faster convergence. Prog. Electromagn. Res. **1**, 143–157 (2008)
13. Chen, C.-H., et al.: Hybrid of bacterial foraging optimization and particle swarm optimization for evolutionary neural fuzzy classifier. Int. J. Fuzzy Syst. **16**, 422–433 (2014)
14. Yang, X.-S.: Firefly algorithms for multimodal optimization. In: Watanabe, O., Zeugmann, T. (eds.) SAGA 2009. LNCS, vol. 5792, pp. 169–178. Springer, Heidelberg (2009). doi:10. 1007/978-3-642-04944-6_14
15. Mao, L., et al.: Particle swarm and bacterial foraging inspired hybrid artificial bee colony algorithm for numerical function optimization. Math. Probl. Eng. (2016)
16. Kumar, A., et al.: A new framework for adaptive multimodal biometrics management. IEEE Trans. Inf. Forensics Secur. **5**, 92–102 (2010)

17. Kumar, A., et al.: Adaptive management of multimodal biometrics fusion using ant colony optimization. Inf. Fusion **32**, 49–63 (2016)
18. Kennedy, J., Kennedy, J.F., Eberhart, R.C., Shi, Y.: Swarm Intelligence. Morgan Kaufmann, Burlington (2001)
19. Hanmandlu, M., Kumar, A., Madasu, V.K., Yarlagadda, P.: Fusion of hand based biometrics using particle swarm optimization. In: Fifth International Conference on Information Technology: New Generations, pp. 783–788. IEEE (2008)
20. Kora, P., Krishna, K.S.R.: Hybrid firefly and particle swarm optimization algorithm for the detection of Bundle Branch Block. Int. J. Cardiovasc. Acad. **2**, 44–48 (2016)
21. Ruhaiyem, N.I.R., Mohamed, A.S.A., Belaton, B.: Optimized segmentation of cellular tomography through organelles' morphology and image features. J. Telecommun. Electron. Comput. Eng. (JTEC) **8**(3), 79–83 (2016)
22. Thevar, V.V., Ruhaiyem, N.I.R.: Concept, theory and application: hybrid watershed classic and active contour for enhanced image segmentation. In: Visual Informatics International Seminar (2016)
23. Ruhaiyem, N.I.R.: Semi-automated cellular tomogram segmentation workflow (CTSW): towards an automatic target-scoring system. In: Proceedings of International Conference on Computer Graphics, Multimedia and Image Processing (CGMIP 2014), Kuala Lumpur, Malaysia, pp. 38–48 (2014)
24. Ruhaiyem, N.I.R., Boundary-based versus region-based approaches for cellular tomography segmentation. In: Proceedings of 1st International Engineering Conference (IEC 2014), Erbil, Iraq, pp. 260–267 (2014)
25. Ruhaiyem, N.I.R.: Multiple, object-oriented segmentation methods of mammalian cell tomograms, Ph.D. Thesis, Institute for Molecular Bioscience, The University of Queensland (2014) doi:10.14264/uql.2014.554

Towards Big Data Quality Framework for Malaysia's Public Sector Open Data Initiative

Mohamad Taha Ijab[1(✉)], Azlina Ahmad[1], Rabiah Abdul Kadir[1],
and Suraya Hamid[2]

[1] Institute of Visual Informatics, Universiti Kebangsaan Malaysia (UKM),
43600 Bangi, Selangor, Malaysia
{taha,azlinaivi,rabiah}@ukm.edu.my
[2] Faculty of Computer Science and Information Technology, Universiti Malaya,
50603 Kuala Lumpur, Malaysia
suraya_hamid@um.edu.my

Abstract. This paper is about the conceptual development of the Big Data Quality Framework for Malaysia's Public Sector Open Data Initiative (My-PSODI). At the moment, there is a lack of Big Data Quality Framework in existence particularly that is focusing on the specific context and needs of Malaysia's Public Sector Open Data initiative. Most of existing data quality frameworks are catering the needs of traditional data types (i.e., structured data) and are very generic in nature. Due to the explosion of big data which consists mostly of unstructured data and structured data, and Malaysia's vision of leveraging data in modernizing its service delivery, a new framework addressing the needs of Big Data for Malaysia is needed. Based on an extensive literature review, we develop a conceptual framework and systematic methodologies of how to construct the said framework to its fruition.

Keywords: Big data · Open data · Data quality framework

1 Introduction

In 2015, Malaysia was ranked 51st in the Open Data Barometer against ninety two other countries in terms of our open data readiness, implementation, and impacts [1]. Malaysia's standing in the said Open Data Barometer is indeed worrying. Malaysia was ranked much lower than our neighbouring countries such as Singapore in 24th position, the Philippines in 36th position, and Indonesia in 40th position.

The reasons for this are, in many aspects, some data champions in the ministries and government agencies tasked with sharing their datasets for the Malaysia's Open Data portal (http://data.gov.my) still do not share their data, or if the data are shared, they are not in machine-readable format such as still in PDF format. Further, data are not timely available and updated, not free and not openly licensed, not accurate and in general is of not good quality. Thus, we feel that this research is timely and set the tone for Malaysia's long term strategy in enhancing its open and big data quality strategy, and also in improving its position in the Open Data Barometer ranking.

© Springer International Publishing AG 2017
H. Badioze Zaman et al. (Eds.): IVIC 2017, LNCS 10645, pp. 79–87, 2017.
https://doi.org/10.1007/978-3-319-70010-6_8

2 Malaysia's Public Sector Open Data Initiative (My-PSODI)

Malaysian Administrative Modernisation and Management Planning Unit (MAMPU) or Unit Pemodenan Tadbiran dan Perancangan Pengurusan Malaysia) has been given the mandate by the Government of Malaysia to spearhead the modernisation of government service delivery by leveraging on big data on the platform called Open Data portal.

MAMPU, in its "Analitis Data Raya Sektor Awam (DRSA) - Strategi, Cabaran dan Halatuju" document has stated that data readiness and data quality is one of the six critical success factors for Malaysia's Public Sector Open Data initiative [2, 3]. In addition to that, MAMPU's Data Engineering Process, in its Step 3 also placed high importance on Data Acquisition and Exploration (see Fig. 1) and specifically mentioned on Data Quality issue (see Fig. 2).

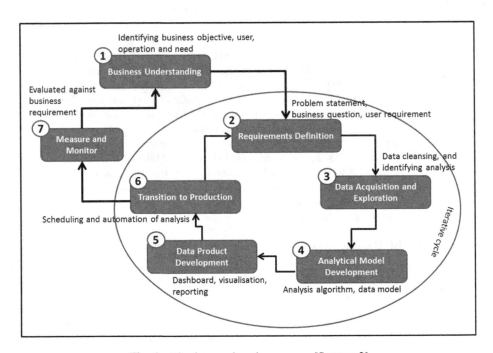

Fig. 1. Big data engineering process [Source: 2]

As can be seen in the figures above, each data needs to be explored and verified its quality before a "data exploration report" and "data quality report" can be produced. However, this methodological approach has not been properly implemented and the procedural way of exploring the data for ensuring and verifying its quality has not been performed by the data champions. Thus, this research is imperative to be performed to help data champions in the ministries and agencies specifically, and MAMPU generally to ensure the data and datasets that they share with the Malaysian publics in the My-PSODI are of high quality.

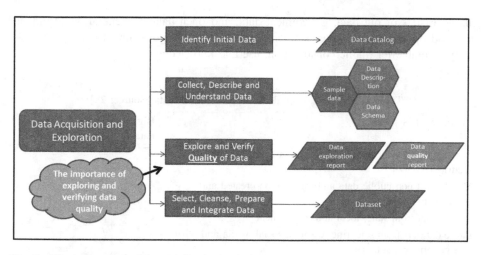

Fig. 2. The importance of data quality in the data acquisition and exploration stage [Source: 2]

3   Literature Review

Data is part of our everyday life and an essential asset in numerous businesses and organisations [4]. The quality of the data (i.e., the degree to which the data characteristics fulfill specific requirements) can have a tremendous impact on the businesses themselves, the companies, or even in human lives. In fact, research and industry reports show that huge amounts of capital are spent to improve the quality of the data being used in many systems, sometimes even only to understand the quality of the information in use. Considering the variety of dimensions, characteristics, business views, or simply the specificities of the systems being evaluated, understanding how to measure data quality can be an extremely difficult and challenging task.

3.1   Big Data, Open Data, and Government Data

Big data is defined as linkable information that has large data volumes and complex data structures [5]. Gartner defined big data as "high-volume, - velocity and - variety information assets that demand cost-effective, innovative forms of information processing for enhanced insight, decision making and process automation." [6]. Mining big data for beneficial use requires capability of extracting valuable and quality information from large datasets or streams of data that due to its volume, variety and velocity [7]. The characteristics of big data include the "5Vs": Volume, Velocity, Variety, Veracity and Value. Open data is defined by its use. [29] defines open data as "accessible public data that people, companies, and organisations can use to launch new ventures, analyse patterns and trends, make data-driven decisions, and solve complex problems". On the other hand, government data is usually data created and held by public authorities such as ministries and government agencies.

The different terms used to describe data (i.e., big data, government data, and open data) can sometimes create confusion. Table 1 below shows the different and common characteristics of big data, government data, and open data. In general, government data and open data are almost similar except that not all government data are necessarily available for public consumption, use and knowledge.

Table 1. Big data, open data and government data [Source: 29]

Characteristics	Big data	Gov. data	Open data
Non-public data for marketing, business analysis, national security	√	–	–
Mostly still non-public data and information created and gathered by government	–	√	√
Public data from state, local and government	√	√	√
Large datasets from scientific research, social media and other non-government sources	√	√	√
Large public government datasets	√	√	√

3.2 Consequences of Poor Quality Data

It is posited by [11] that the data quality rule remains "garbage-in, garbage-out," where one cannot expect accurate results based on inaccurate data, and therefore this rules applies in the context of large datasets or big data too. With the huge volume of generated data, the fast velocity of arriving data, and the large variety of heterogeneous data, the quality of data is far from perfect [9]. Studies have shown that poor quality big data is prevalent in large databases and on the Web which caused waste in resource, low service efficiency and high costs in repairing the data and even causing severe losses [10, 12, 16]. Since poor quality data can have serious consequences on the results of data analyses, the importance of veracity (the fourth characteristic of big data) and value of big data is increasingly being recognised.

It has been estimated that erroneous data costs US businesses 600 billion dollars annually [1]. In some enterprises, they find data error rate of approximately 1%–5%, and for some companies, it is above 30% [14]. The direct consequence of poor data quality is in terms of the data cleaning process (discovering rules, detecting/checking for inconsistencies, and data repairing) which will cost companies for about 30%–80% of the development time and budget for improving the data rather than quickly using the data for actual analysis, visualisation and decision making [9]. Therefore, it is very vital that data quality is ensured and verified right from the earliest stage of data preparation.

4 Conceptual Big Data Quality Framework

Currently, comprehensive analysis and research of data quality standards and quality assessment methods for big data are still lacking [8]. Quality is basically defined as "the degree to which a set of inherent characteristics fulfill the requirements" [15]. Other people define quality as "fitness for use" [16] and "conformance to requirements" [17]. [18] claims that data are of high quality if they are fit for their intended uses in operations, decision making and planning.

Data quality is said to be demonstrated through "data quality dimension", which is a set of data quality attributes that represent a single aspect of data quality and fifteen data quality dimensions were identified [16]. These 15 dimensions are: believability, accuracy, objectivity, reputation, value-added, relevancy, timeliness, completeness, appropriate amount of data, interpretability, ease of understanding, representational consistency, concise representation, accessibility, and access security.

Researchers such as [19] describe six evaluation criteria of data, namely authority, accuracy, objectivity, currency, coverage/intended audience, and interaction/transaction features of data. [20] study data quality and set up an emiotic-based framework for data quality with 4 levels and a total of 11 quality dimensions. These 4 levels are syntactic, semantic, pragmatic and social while the data dimensions are well-defined, comprehensive, unambiguous, meaningful, correct, timely, concise, easily accessed, reputable, understood, and awareness of bias.

[21] propose six quality metrics of high quality data including currency, availability, information-to-noise ratio, authority, popularity, and cohesiveness. [22] summarise the following data quality dimensions: accuracy, correctness, completeness, currency, volatility, timeliness, consistency, accessibility, believability, reputation, objectivity, value- added, relevancy, and ease of understanding. In more recent literature, [12] identifies the following data quality dimensions: accuracy, completeness, timeliness, consistency, and relevancy.

[23] investigates data quality from the aspects of physical, empirical, syntactic, semantic, pragmatic, social, and deontic quality. [13] propose the data quality attributes of accuracy, integrity, consistency, completeness, validity, timeliness, and accessibility. [24] claim that data quality have two dimensions: intrinsic and contextual dimensions. From the intrinsic dimension, the attributes are accuracy, timeliness, consistency, and completeness. Whereas, the contextual attributes are reputation, accessibility, believability, relevancy, value-added, and quantity. [25] highlights the data quality dimensions as accessibility, appropriate amount of data, believability, completeness, consistent representation, ease of manipulation, free-of-error, interpretability, objectivity, relevancy, reputation, security, timeliness, understandability, and value-added. [26] identify the data quality dimensions of accuracy, completeness, redundancy, readability, accessibility, consistency, and trust.

5 The Proposed Big Data Quality Framework for My-PSODI

As shown by the brief literature review on data quality above, and as agreed by a number of researchers such as [8, 12, 22, 24, 27] who argue that data quality is indeed being presented in the literature as a multidimensional, and multifaceted concept. There is no consensus among the various proposals, neither on the number of dimensions, nor on their definitions or metrics of data quality. Further, [10] claim that nearly 200 terms have been identified on data quality elements, and there is little agreement in their nature, their definitions or even measures. In probably to ratify this issue, [24] suggest that the definition of data quality should be seen as "domain aware" and should be defined by the data owners and users themselves.

According to [8, 9], data quality depends not only on its own features but also on the business environment using the data such as who produces the data, the processes surrounding the preparation of data, and also the data users themselves (i.e., what specific purpose the data is used for). Generally, the principle of 'the one whom providing the data is the one who responsible for quality' is commonly found [12]. However, the problem with this notion is that user's requirements which are considered to be important are not taken into account. This view is supported by [8] who argue that data quality standards are regularly developed from the perspective of data producers (data champions) instead of the data consumers (data users). Thus, in this research, we are developing the big data quality framework by combining the perspectives of the data producers (data champions), data drivers (the main government stakeholder), data experts and also the data users themselves. Thus, the definition, dimension, elements, and measures of data quality will be more comprehensive and holistic.

Furthermore, as to scope down our research, adapting from [8], the data quality elements that we are proposing in the Malaysia's Big Data Quality Framework for My-PSODI are: Accessibility, Timeliness, Authorisation, Credibility, Clarity, Accuracy, Authenticity, Integrity, Consistency, Completeness, Auditability, Fitness for Use, Readability, and Structure. These data elements are grouped into five data quality dimensions of Availability, Usability, Reliability, Relevance, and Presentation Quality [8].

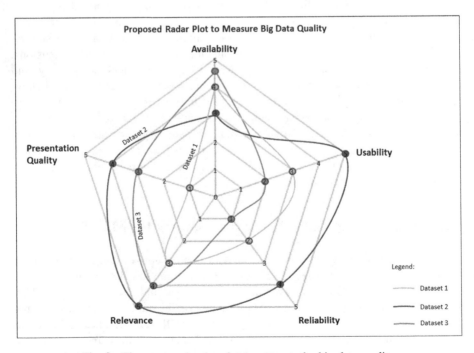

Fig. 3. The proposed radar plot to measure the big data quality.

The indicator of either the data is of highest quality or lowest quality will be measured, assessed, compared and given by the data champions and data owners themselves based on our to be developed metrics tool. Additionally, upon collating all the data, the data champions or data owners would be able to provide a certain ranking on their dataset according to a radar plot that we are also proposing (refer Fig. 3). For example, in Fig. 3, the data champion would state that the Availability of their Dataset 1 is at DQ 4 level, the Usability of their Dataset 1 is at DQ 3 level, the Reliability of their Dataset 1 is at DQ 2 level, Relevance of their Dataset 1 is at DQ 3 level, and the Presentation Quality of their Dataset 1 is at DQ 1 level. This will easily provide a snapshot of Dataset 1 is actually of poor quality overall. On the other hand, Dataset 2 will be relatively at a higher data quality rank as it scored 5 for Usability, 5 for Relevance, 4 for Presentation Quality, 4 for Reliability, and 3 Availability.

6 Conclusion

"Big Data and Open Data" are Malaysia's latest ICT initiatives as supported by the Prime Minister's Office of Malaysia. Thus, this research is directly relevant and linked to the Government Policy, namely the 11th Malaysian Plan for 2016 to 2020. The 11th Malaysia Plan in its Chap. 9 on "Transforming Public Service for Productivity" emphasises on leveraging data to enhance outcomes and to lower costs" [28].

The strategy to achieve this broad objective is by proliferating open data among government ministries and agencies, encouraging cross-agency data sharing, and leveraging big data analytics (BDA). For this task, MAMPU is appointed as the strategic advisor for My-PSODI and play its role in modernising of government service delivery.

The Public Sector Open Data initiative also allows the creation of new products from the government based on the big data and will enhance the service quality which takes into account the needs of the citizens. In broader sense, the Public Sector Open Data initiative will not only improve service delivery, but also to help support the Malaysia Goverment to achieve Vision 2020. The proposed Big Data Quality Framework in this paper includes the data elements of Accessibility, Timeliness, Authorisation, Credibility, Clarity, Accuracy, Authenticity, Integrity, Consistency, Completeness, Auditability, Fitness for Use, Readability, and Structure. These data elements are then grouped into five relevant data quality dimensions of Availability, Usability, Reliability, Relevance, and Presentation Quality, accordingly. Thus, this research is imperative and highly relevant as our proposed Big Data Quality Framework will certainly facilitate better data analytics and meaningful decision making, and subsequently help materialising the 11th Malaysia Plan, Vision 2020 and the longer term vision of Transformasi Nasional 2050 (TN50).

References

1. Open Data Barometer (2017). http://opendatabarometer.org/
2. MAMPU Analitis Data Raya Sektor Awam (DRSA): Strategi, Cabaran dan Halatuju (2013). http://www.mainpp.gov.my/index.php/nota-kursus-latihan/category/3-it?download=10:drsa-penang-anis-suhailis-mampu-latest
3. MAMPU. Garis Panduan Analitis Data Raya Sektor Awam – Program Kesedaran Dasar dan Garis Panduan ICT Sektor Awam (2016). http://www.mampu.gov.my/ms/penerbitan-mampu/send/89-program-kesedaran-dasar-dan-garis-panduan-ict-sektor-awam/215-7-taklimat-7-gp-drsa
4. Laranjeiro, N., Soydemir, S.N., Bernardino, J.: A survey on data quality: classifying poor data. In: IEEE 21st Pacific Rim International Symposium on Dependable Computing, 18–20 November, Zhangjiajie, China (2015)
5. Khoury, M.J., Ioannidis, J.P.A.: Big data meets public health. Science 346(6213), 1054–1055 (2014). doi:10.1126/science.aaa2709
6. Gartner, Big Data Definition (2012). http://www.gartner.com/it-glossary/big-data/
7. Abdel Hafez, H.A.: Mining big data in telecommunications industry: challenges, techniques, and revenue opportunity. Int. J. Comput. Electr. Autom. Control Inf. Eng. 10(1), 183–190 (2016)
8. Cai, L., Zhu, Y.: The challenges of data quality and data quality assessment in the big data era. Data Sci. J. 14(2), 1–10 (2015)
9. Saha, B., Srivastava, D.: Data quality: the other face of big data. In: IEEE 30th International Conference on Data Engineering (ICDE), 31 March–4 April, Chicago, IL (2014)
10. Chen, M., Song, M., Han, J., Haihong, E.: Survey on data quality. In: 2012 World Congress on Information and Communication Technologies (WICT), 30 October–2 November, Trivandrum, India (2012)
11. NIST: NIST Big Data Interoperability Framework, vol. 1, Definitions (2015). http://nvlpubs.nist.gov/nistpubs/SpecialPublications/NIST.SP.1500-1.pdf
12. Lucas, A.: Corporate data quality management: from theory to practice. In: 5th Iberian Conference on Information Systems and Technologies (CISTI), 16–19 June, Santiago, Spain (2010)
13. Abdullah, N., Ismail, S.A., Sophiayati, S., Mohd Sam, S.: Data quality in big data: a review. Int. J. Adv. Soft Comput. Appl. 7(3), 16–27 (2015)
14. Fan, W., Geerts, F.: Foundations of data management. Synth. Lect. Data Manag. 4(5), 1–217 (2012). Morgan & Claypool
15. General Administration of Quality Supervision, Inspection and Quarantine of the People's Republic of China. Quality management systems-fundamentals and vocabulary (GB/T19000—2008/ISO9000:2005), Beijing (2008)
16. Wang, R.Y., Strong, D.M.: Beyond accuracy: what data quality means to data consumers. J. Manag. Inf. Syst. 12(4), 5–33 (1996)
17. Crosby, P.B.: Quality is Free: The Art of Making Quality Certain. McGraw-Hill, New York (1988)
18. Juran, J.M.: Juran on Leadership for Quality: An Executive Handbook. The Free Press, New York (1989)
19. Alexander, J.E., Tate, M.A.: Web Wisdom: How to Evaluate and Create Information on the Web. Erlbaum, Mahwah (1999)
20. Shanks, G., Corbitt, B.: Understanding data quality: social and cultural aspects. In: Proceedings of the 10th Australasian Conference on Information Systems, pp. 785–797. MCB University Press Ltd., Wellington (1999)

21. Zhu, X., Gauch, S.: Incorporating quality metrics in centralised/distributed information retrieval on the world wide web. In: SIGIR 2000 Proceedings of the 23rd Annual International ACM SIGIR Conference on Research and Development in Information Retrieval, 24–28 July, Athens, Greece (2000)
22. Batini, C., Scannapeico, M.: Data Quality: Concepts, Methodologies and Techniques. Springer, Berlin (2006)
23. Krogstie, J.: Capturing enterprise data integration challenges using a semiotic data quality framework. Bus. Inf. Syst. Eng. **57**(1), 27–36 (2015)
24. Taleb, I., Dssouli, R., Serhani, M.A.: Big data pre-processing: a quality framework. In: 4th IEEE International Congress on Big Data, Santa Clara, CA 29 October–1 November (2015)
25. Juddoo, S.: Overview of data quality challenges in the context of big data. In: International Conference on Computing, Communication and Security (ICCCS), Mauritius, 4–5 December (2015)
26. Batini, C., Rula, A., Scannapieco, M., Viscusi, G.: From Data Quality to Big Data Quality, Big Data Concepts, Methodologies, Tools, and Applications, pp. 1934–1956. IGI Global, Hershey (2016)
27. Ijab, M.T., Ahmad, A., Abdul Kadir, R.: Challenge of data quality: towards a big data quality framework. In: IMPACT: Technologies for Society's Well-Being, Universiti Kebangsaan Malaysia (UKM), p. 44 (2016)
28. Economic Planning Unit - EPU Malaysia, 11th Malaysia Plan (2017). http://rmk11.epu.gov.my/index.php/en/muat-turun-dokumen
29. Gurin, J.: Big Data and Open Data: What's What and Why Does It Matter? The Guardian (2014). https://www.theguardian.com/public-leaders-network/2014/apr/15/big-data-open-data-transform-government

Bridging the Gap in Personalised Medicine Through Data Driven Genomics

Ummul Hanan Mohamad[(✉)], Mohamad Taha Ijab,
and Rabiah Abdul Kadir

Institute of Visual Informatics, Universiti Kebangsaan Malaysia (UKM),
43600 Bangi, Selangor, Malaysia
ummulhanan@ukm.edu.my

Abstract. Personalised medicine has been visualised as the ultimate healthcare practise, as the treatment will be customised to the patient's need. This will eliminate the "one-for-all" approach, thus reducing the potential drug's side effects, ineffective drug doses and severe complications due to unsuitable drugs prescribed. As the cost for genomics sequencing started to plummet, this condition has driven extensive studies on many disease genomics, generating genomics big data. However, without an in-depth analysis and management of the data, it will be difficult to reveal and relate the link between the genomics with the diseases in order to accomplish personalised medicine. The main reason behind this is that genomics data has never been straightforward and is poorly understood. Therefore, this paper purposely discusses how the advances in technology have aid the understanding of genomics big data, thus a proposed framework is highlighted to help change the landscape of personalised medicine.

Keywords: Big data · Personalised medicine · Data driven genomics

1 Introduction

Genome, the complete set of genes, contains DNA genetic makeup. Human has approximately three billions DNA base pairs, organised in 23 sets of chromosomes. On average, sequencing a whole human genome will yield approximately 100 gigabytes of raw data [1]. In support towards personalised medicine, genomics studies are vigorously carried out to help scientists understand the different pharmacological responses between patients when they are subjected to the same medical treatment. Several related genomics research areas [2–4] include pharmacogenomics (the study on how genes affect the drug responses), functional genomics (the study on genes' functions and interactions at the level of DNA, RNA and protein) and computational genomics (the use of computational analysis to interpret genomics data). With respect to personalised medicine, many disease research are concentrating on the study of genetic variations and gene expression profiling, utilising thousands of genome, thus generating petabytes of biological data [5].

Personalised medicine main objective is to improve the diagnostic and treatment of diseases at a molecular level in order to be able to tailor the medical treatment to one's personal need [6]. Thus, without the availability of reliable tools and systems to analyse

© Springer International Publishing AG 2017
H. Badioze Zaman et al. (Eds.): IVIC 2017, LNCS 10645, pp. 88–99, 2017.
https://doi.org/10.1007/978-3-319-70010-6_9

abundant datasets, this will definitely be challenging. Nevertheless, progress in these data-intensive genomics research, computational advances, and development towards better healthcare management has uplift the biomedical research from hypothesis-driven into a data-driven research paradigm.

Since the completion of Human Genome Project in 2003, the genomic research had exposed new avenues to allow better understanding of human diseases, yet we are also dealing with new problems due to the deluge of biological data within a short span of time. With patients getting more control of their health information, this has impacted the health decision and treatment. It is imminent that the future personalised medicine will be genotype-guided.

The reduction of genomics sequencing cost is one of the keys that led to the massive accumulation of diverse, digital data. These data or known as "Big Data" can no longer be handled by the traditional database software; thus the urgency for reliable analytic tools. Big data differs from the normal data based on these parameters (4V's); volume, variety, velocity and veracity. In terms of volume, the amount of biological data generated from genomics research may exceed beyond Exabytes (1 billion gigabytes). The second 'V' is variety in which the data comes from many forms (structured, semi-structured and unstructured) and sources (databases, digital health information, publications, reports etc.); leading to a challenge to standardise the data. In addition, velocity is also an important aspect since genomics data is increasing exponentially. Veracity or authenticity, ensures data reliability without compromising the data security.

The genomics big data are now changing the way data is generally handled; i.e. data storage, data integration, data management, data processing, data analysis and data security. We envisioned the overall perspectives of the challenges associated with the genomics big data in regard to personalised medicine, the solution from progressive information technology and at the end of this paper, we will proposed a framework that unifies the concepts and ideas to pave the way towards the genomics-dependent personalised medicine in this digital fourth industrial revolution (4IR) era.

2 Data Driven Genomics Challenges in Personalised Medicine

Genomics research has been extensively carried out in the last decade, which includes the Human Genome (HG) project, International HapMap project, Cancer Genome Atlas [7], genome wide association studies (GWAS) [8] and 1000 Genome to name a few. Human Genome project, for instance, aimed to complete the mapping of the entire human genes to enhance a better understanding of the genes function and its correlation to the human diseases [9]. Meanwhile, International HapMap project focused to identify the patterns of the genetic variation in human that can be associated with certain diseases, drug responses, health conditions and even variations that are influenced by environments [10]. In addition, Cancer Genome Atlas catalogued the cancer-linked genetic mutations while Genome Wide Association Studies (GWAS) searched for genes responsible for other diseases, i.e. diabetes, cardiac diseases and hypertension, by comparing genetic variants frequency in people with and without the disease. The study on human genetic variations is carried out in-depth by the 1000 Genome project.

All of the mentioned projects are carried out purposely to bridge the gap in personalised medicine in the context of genomics. By definition, personalised medicine is an individualised, genetic-guided approach that utilises predictive tools to determine the health risks and to design personalised health plans in order to precisely manage a patient's disease or predisposition to disease [11]. As mentioned, the important predictive tools include big data capture and storage tool (to keep genomics big data and medical records), collaboration tools (to allow data sharing among experts), predictive analysis tool (to improve data analysis) and decision support tools (to guide treatment decisions by the clinicians).

Despite having enormous collection of genomics data from the genomics research, there are many challenges that we need to overcome before personalised medicine can be implemented successfully. Among the challenges are (i) high cost to store data, (ii) complex genomics data, (iii) lack of depositories, (iv) difficult data integration, (v) limited analytical tools and (vi) concern on data protection.

2.1   High Cost to Store Data

One of the challenge is the cost to store data versus the cost to obtain data [5]. As claimed by [12], storing genomics data is very much pricier due to the need for vast computing power and advanced software tools. Handling massive amount of genomics data not only require data storage solutions, it also need feasible computational algorithms for genomics data assembly, data compression, parallel cloud computing as well as practical protocols to secure private data within a cloud-computing environment. In addition, getting more localised servers to handle the data is no longer a reasonable solution due to limitations in data integration and mobility. Due to this, many scientists opt to simply store the real sample and re-sequence the genes of interest (when needed) rather than storing the data itself. This practise is discouraging, as there is a high probability that when the data is not stored, it is also unlikely to be shared. As a result, we will continuously have gaps in understanding the relationships between genes and diseases. Nonetheless, for personalised medicine, we need to gather and analyse as much personalised genomics data for the data to be significant, before any precise decision on personalised medicine can be derived.

2.2   Complex Genomics Data

In addition, the genomics data is also complex and harder to define. At most time, there are too many different variables interacting in which we do not have a good understanding of. For example, to pave the way towards personalised medicine for breast cancer treatment, scientists need to analyse the data from many different aspects. Genomics data had revealed that (i) individual with BRCA1 or BRCA2 genes mutations have an increased risk of breast cancer [13] and (ii) individual expressing the HER2 protein [14] are at greater risk of breast cancer recurrence. As such, these genes have been used as one of the many predictive biomarkers in genetic screening test to obtain a personalised genomics data. However, adding in data such as the analysis of gene regulatory network to determine the expression of gene of interest, analysis of pharmacogenomics datasets to depict the suitability for the drug therapy, combined with detailed family histories will lead to a very complicated problem before a conclusive decision can be made.

2.3 Lack of Depositories

Next, lack of depositories that can house the petabytes of data also becomes a limitation towards realising personalised medicine. It is estimated that the completion of International Cancer Genome Consortium (ICGC) and The Cancer Genome Atlas (TCGA) project in 2018 will yield around 15 petabytes of data from 450 thousand individual genomes [15]. In other words, a personalised genomics data particularly the human oncology study had yielded more than 30 Gigabytes. This ultimately showed how massive a genomic data can be, elevating the need for advance computational infrastructure, beyond the common technical capacity of any single site or server. In addition, the depositories need to be able to sustain the data migration and allow access from many different locations with acceptable downloading capability. There is definitely no point of having genomics big data without having the appropriate technology to support the outcome in parallel.

2.4 Difficult Data Integration

Besides that, there is also difficulty in data integration due to the different data types [16]. For example, sequencing will reveal personalised genomics data while healthcare will have the patient's electronic medical records. Although both are digital data, there is yet to be any tools that can easily merge and integrate these different data types to expedite the understanding of disease and treatment. So far, a considerable amount of medical information has been collected, but majority remained inaccessible for research or public health purposes. In many countries, the available data not only is managed poorly, but insignificant amount of it was kept up-to-date into the databases [17]. This problem needs to be tackled well before we can make full use of the data to accomplish the objective of personalised medicine.

2.5 Limited Analytical Tools

Nonetheless, genomics data analysis is also limited by the available analytical tools and expertise. Many of the molecular biologist doing hands-on research has little experience using bioinformatics software. This is mostly due to the fact that wet lab research is usually time consuming, leaving less time to develop bioinformatics skills. Besides that, funding is mainly spent on research that generates data, when only a smaller amount goes to the data analysis. Even so, the existing computer infrastructure are also not optimised to solve biological problems [18]. To make it worst, software developer typically has less experience with the hands-on, thus resulting into the lack of biologist-friendly software. This situation does not only cripple the potential collaborations, it also undermines the innovations of reliable software. Moreover, this also deters the potential to fully explore and unlock the personalised genomics data and use them to our advantage.

2.6   Concern on Data Protection

Moreover, protection of data also becomes a major concern prior to the implementation of personalised medicine. As discussed by [19] on the HeLa genome, personalised genomic data differ from the traditional medical data as it carries not only the genetic information of the patient's, but also contain the genetic information of the family members for many generations. Since genomics data can reveal many things such as the health status, the drug responses and tendency towards certain diseases, it is very essential to implement a stronger and more sophisticated security measure to maintain the data confidentiality. Despite requiring the data to understand the biology of disease and the mechanism of treatment, we must not let any abuse to the data privacy poses any threat to the individual and their family.

3   Conquering the Challenges of Genomics Big Data Towards Personalised Medicine

As shown in Fig. 1, these are the steps to bridge the gap towards personalised medicine in the genomics context: (i) manage the genomics big data, (ii) identify the functions and impact of genomics variations, (iii) integrate the data to discover the relations between genetics and phenotypes, and (iv) transform the findings into medical practise [20].

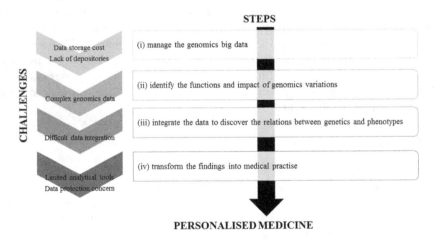

Fig. 1. Steps to bridge the gap towards personalised medicine in the genomics context

Without a proper integrative workflow system that prepare and compare the genomics and clinical data for cross-study, personalised medicine will just be another pipedream. Since the progress in the genomics studies has been highly encouraged by the advances in information technologies, it is very much anticipated that the challenges that arose from the data-intensive genomics science are addressed using a similar approach.

3.1   Manage the Genomics Big Data

The problem with genomics data deluge is that it requires proper storage facilities. A common practise such as using localised servers can no longer support this since they are limited in terms of capacity, accessibility, computing power and stability. For example, it is predicted that 2–40 Exabyte of data storage capacity is needed just to store the data of human genomes by 2025 [21]. In addition, many of the medical and health records now have been transformed into a digital data to improve documentation, reference and expedite the accessibility.

[22] claimed that cloud computing is the best storage solution for genomics big data. The advantages include low cost, high capacity, greater efficiency, easier access and integration of the data. Bionimbus [23] is one of the example of this cloud computing platform that address the data storage issue while exercising data control and security. So far, it has been efficiently used to process and align the acute myeloid leukaemia sequencing data that generally contained around 8 GB file size per sample and alignment of around 12 h to complete using 8 CPUs.

The explosion of sequencing data also requires compatible data compression method. General algorithms such as Lempel-Ziv may offer efficiency in terms of compatibility and speed, however customised algorithms will also be needed to further reduce the storage footprint and compression time [24]. GDC2 algorithm had shown promises to aid in the genomics data compression as it has four times the ability to perform almost 10 K compression of about 1K human genomes compared to the existing compressors. The data processing speed ranged around 200 MB/s, allowing the storage of entire human genome collection at a relatively lower cost.

As an example, we have a database that contained the genome of 1000 individuals. Improvement to this database will include better organization of the data and links to other related data such as the medical records. This will expedite the tracking of certain required traits when we want to develop future clinical trials to expedite the way towards personalised medicine. Current drug clinical trials are time consuming in terms of assessing the drugs effect and usage suitability. With the improved database, we can deploy the tool to carry out the virtual clinical trial to quickly identify drug risk based on the genomics data. It is often that with proper management of the genomics big data that we could clearly identify, draws the links and derive a conclusion on the best treatment for a particular disease.

3.2   Identify the Functions and Impact of Genomics Variations

A fundamental problem in the genomics data processing is the genome assembly. This is due to the large amount of fragmented genome reads produced during the next-generation sequencing (NGS) that require large memory capacity to assemble the genome. Without the availability of proper analytical tools, this could be the limitation to the progress of genomics research. The initiation of long-read sequencing technologies such as Pacific Biosciences (PacBio) and Oxford Nanopore have allowed for high quantity and quality assurance of the data at a moderate computational cost and allow up to 100-fold contigs assembly.

After a complete assembly of the data, the data need to be aligned with the reference genome for further annotation and comparison. Unlike prior technology which compare and align two sequences directly, the new tools adopt a two-step seed-and-extend strategy to increase the speed [25] such Basic Local Alignment Search Tool (BLAST, Spliced Transcripts Alignment to a Reference (STAR), Burrows-Wheeler Aligner (BWA) and Bowtie. The strategy was either to generate indexes based on the query sequences or organise the database into compact binary files for quicker alignment time. In the future, there will be even greater demand to develop new algorithms capable of delivering the task in a practical timeline.

Besides that, development of visualisation tools has allowed for simulation of many molecular processes in cells and predictions of drug effects in humans. This has speed up the clinical trial and reduces the unnecessary side effects. Despite the ever-growing improvement of many genomics analysis tools, there is also a need to have trained biologists in the data science. This effort has been recognised by the National Institutes of Health (NIH), thus leading to the launch of Big Data to Knowledge Initiative (BD2K).

To address this step effectively, we must strengthen the collaborating platform to engage more interaction and knowledge sharing among the genomics scientists, data scientists, bioinformaticians, clinicians and IT experts. Occasionally, the answer to unsolved issues in certain gene functions or impact of the genetic variations is exposed from the study of the particular disease in different perspectives.

3.3 Integrate the Data to Discover the Relations Between Genetics and Phenotypes

Another detrimental factor that deters the understanding of disease is the inconsistent terms used to describe the data. Scientists, clinicians and business acquaintances often classify diseases and describe symptoms differently. Due to this semantic irregularity, it is troublesome and difficult to populate the required data. As example, without proper standard ontologies, carcinoma or sarcoma will not be retrieved as the comparable data for cancer.

Consequently, the growth of many databases, has driven the development of specific ontologies. Gene ontology (GO), Kyoto Encyclopedia of Genes and Genomes (KEGG) and Medical Subject Headings thesaurus (MESH) are some of the useful collection of terms that can easily identify the relations among biological components. Ontologies do not only allow for better classification of data, it also depicts a better representation of the biological data, effectively organise the information, enable the statistical analysis and supports web searching [26].

Unfortunately, all the genomics data are often disconnected from medical records and individualised personal data. This condition dampens the progress in understanding the genetics and phenotypic relationships in the human disease. Therefore, it is best if depositories with the ability to manage different data types are developed. For example, it could store not only the genomics data from sequencing, the system will be able to merge the personalised genomics data from genetic screening, laboratory test result information, health records, lifestyle info and environmental exposures. These depositories will pave the way towards personalised medicine in such a way that it will expedite the tracking of the required information, from as miniscule as individual to larger pool as in a particular community.

3.4   Transform the Findings into Medical Practise

As mentioned earlier, genomics data contains very sensitive information not only of the patient's but includes the large member with familial ties. Thus, for the data to be made available publicly for research or medical purposes, the privacy of the data must be safely guarded through cyber security approach. [27] projected the development of a secure cloud computing, named GeneCloud, for conditions that crucially require data security. This platform differs from the public cloud computing in which the operations are executed in a secure sandbox that prevents any disclosure of sensitive data regardless of the intention. GeneCloud analytics program is also governed by the policies made by the data stakeholders.

Apart from a specialised method for data security, other common approaches can also be added to provide an extra precaution steps for data protection. Example are encryption, two-factor authentication and authorisation limits on number or duration and monitoring using a blockchain. Despite all the potential data security measures, policies on protecting genomics data especially on personalised genomics data must be carefully thought and implemented. The absence of these policies is perhaps one of the factors that contribute to insufficient data collection. Without sufficient data, the findings will not be significant enough to be translated into a medical practise.

In order to be able to implement the personalised medicine medical practise in healthcare facilities, a personalised medicine system that fulfills these criteria is recommended: automatically assess individual data to calculate the required drug dosage and to pre-screen any drug side effects and potential drug complications, based on the individual genomics data.

4   Discussion

Approaching this digital 4IR pace, technology breakthrough has driven the current medical processes into a more predictive and preventive approach of the disease management. Novel developments and waves of innovations are making data acquisition and analytics much easier, improving the medical collaboration platform, succumbing to more personalised treatment procedures with the aim to decrease the loss of human life.

Figure 2 highlighted the proposed framework to bridge the gaps towards personalised medicine in the genomics context; (i) improve current tools and pipelines, (ii) expand the cloud collaboration platform, (iii) create hybrid depositories and (iv) develop automated personalised medicine system.

In order to effectively manage the large-scale robust genomics data, it is proposed that we first improve the available current tools and pipelines to be compatibly efficient. It will be difficult to overcome the other challenges if we are struggling with the basic requirements to handle genomics big data.

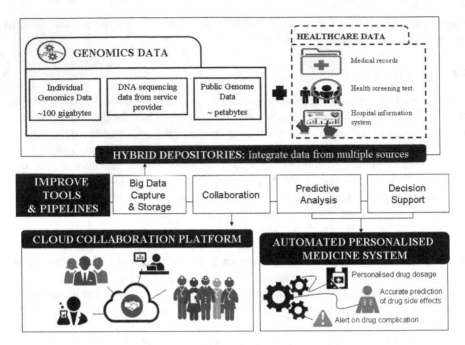

Fig. 2. Framework to bridge the gap towards personalised medicine in genomic context.

One of the important aspects to consider is to improve the available current tools and pipelines to be compatibly efficient. Why the available current tools? It is often quicker to improve a current tool rather than to build one from scratch. However, rather than having so many tools for a similar function or to obtain the same result, it is best to focus on the tools that are crucially needed. As example, the tools to identify pattern between the data in personalised genomics and medical records or develop the algorithm to determine the efficacy of drug dosage based on the genomics data. Besides that, we can also deploy a real-time health mobile application that can monitor and provide direct provision of care to patients. This can help improve clinical data gathering and improve the delivery of healthcare across the world.

[28] mentioned, "The considerable variation in clinical presentation and molecular etiology of genetic disorders, coupled with their relative individual rarity, makes it clear that no single provider, laboratory, medical center, state or even individual country will typically possess sufficient knowledge to deliver the best care for patients in need of care". This statement indirectly supports the essential need for a cloud collaboration platform to ensure that personalised medicine can achieve its objective. As we continue to gather massive information at an ever-increasing rate in this 4IR era, it is often that the importance of knowledge sharing is overlooked. The data and information are meaningless if the knowledge is not shared and informed to the medical community and vice versa. In addition, cloud collaboration platform also allows for real-time sharing among many expert groups from any places in the world, to which the traditional knowledge sharing methods have limitations. This will also serve as an

interactive medium to solve the current issues that hamper the progress of personalised medicine or any related genomics deadlock.

Next, despite our best intention to unlock the full potential of genomics data, we are frequently deterred by the intricacy of genomics data. It is possible that the missing information of the genetic mechanism or molecular interaction of the disease lies in the other semi-structured or unstructured data. This condition is alarming, as we are most likely to be relying on limited scope of data, resulting into less significant, inconclusive decisions. Without reliable data comparisons, it will be difficult to project a cohesive procedure in the application of personalised medicine through data-driven genomics. Thus, developing hybrid depositories with the ability to merge different data types may allow exploration of genomics data in different outlook to unveil the key components in understanding the human diseases.

As we are pacing towards the 4IR, we need to properly equip the healthcare facilities to support the personalised medicine system. Incorporation of artificial intelligence, augmented reality, simulations and visualisation techniques into the automated system will guide the personalised treatment decisions by assessing the information derived from the personalised genomics data. In addition, the systems need to be flexible to continuously integrate new findings, automated to provide accurate and unbiased individualised treatment, highly secured to prevent data corruption and data loss. This system may be implemented by stages, to prevent any unpredictable con-sequences to the healthcare system.

5   Conclusion

In conclusion, personalised medicine is not a laid-back quest, yet it is not impossible task to accomplish. The benefits are huge, comprising from individual perspective to community and global population. In terms of the personal advantage, personalised medicine will encourage everyone to be more attentive to their health as well as their families'. In the future, having a personalised genetic data will drive the decision to lead a healthier and better lifestyle.

Despite the numerous gaps to bridge before we can fully make use of the genomics data and putting personalised medicine into practice, it is necessary that we take a step forward from now. Simply start by strengthening the available current tools and pipelines that we need to handle the burst of genomics big data. Genomics data will be increasing exponentially, regardless of us being ready or not.

In addition, biological and data scientist also need to equip ourselves with the skills and expertise to decipher the genomics big data into translational medical application. In this 4IR era, conventional method of knowledge and expertise transfer is no longer feasible to accommodate the speed of data accumulation. Thus, this is where the cloud collaborating platform will be of used, to support transfer of technology, problem solving, knowledge sharing and research collaborations among many institutions.

Next, personalised medicine requires detailed analysis of not only the core geno-mics data, it also involved other forms of genomics related data. Examples are the clinical data, personalised genetic screening, laboratory DNA test, gene expression analysis and health reports to name a few. This is essential to direct us to genomics driven decision in customised medicinal treatment. Therefore, without the availability of hybrid depository that can capture, link, organise and perform analysis from different types of data, we will be incapable to plan the strategies to develop the personalised medicine structural systems.

Moreover, detailed policies to balance the need of data privacy, integrity and accessibility must be constructed to ensure maximum data protection. This ensures that the personal genomics info is not exposed to digital abuse or bio-crime such as in insurance fraud and genetics identity theft. It would also be helpful to initiate the preparations towards practising personalised medicine in parallel. The initiatives may also include deploying a rapid learning model for clinical practises to speed the knowledge management and healthcare integrative system that will give automated decisions of personalised medicine treatment to patient.

References

1. Grossglauser, M., Saner, H.: Data-driven healthcare: from patterns to actions. Eur. J. Prev. Cardiol. **21**, 14–17 (2014)
2. Jain, K.: Textbook of Personalized Medicine (2015)
3. Bielinski, S., Olson, J., Pathak, J.: Preemptive Genotyping for Personalized Medicine: Design of the Right Drug, Right Dose, Right Time—Using Genomic Data to Individualize Treatment Protocol. Mayo Clinic, Rochester (2014)
4. Alyass, A., Turcotte, M., Meyre, D.: From big data analysis to personalized medicine for all: challenges and opportunities. BMC Med. Genom. **8**, 33 (2015)
5. O'Driscoll, A., Daugelaite, J., Sleator, R.: "Big data", Hadoop and cloud computing in genomics. J. Biomed. Inform. **46**, 774–781 (2013)
6. Jameson, J., Longo, D.: Precision medicine—personalized, problematic, and promising. Obstet. Gynecol. Surv. **70**, 612–614 (2015)
7. The cancer genome atlas pan-cancer analysis project. Nature (2013)
8. Ng, M., Shriner, D., Chen, B., Li, J., Chen, W.: Meta-analysis of genome-wide association studies in African Americans provides insights into the genetic architecture of type 2 diabetes. PLoS Gen. **10**, e1004517 (2014)
9. Wilson, B., Nicholls, S.: The Human Genome Project, and recent advances in personalized genomics. Risk Manag. Healthc. Policy **8**, 9 (2015)
10. Zhang, W., Ng, H., Shu, M., Luo, H., Su, Z., Ge, W.: Comparing genetic variants detected in the 1000 genomes project with SNPs determined by the International HapMap Consortium. J. Genet. **94**, 731–740 (2015)
11. Offit, K.: Personalized medicine: new genomics, old lessons. Hum. Genet. **130**, 3–14 (2011)
12. Muir, P., Li, S., Lou, S., Wang, D.: The real cost of sequencing: scaling computation to keep pace with data generation. Genome **17**, 53 (2016)
13. Tung, N., Battelli, C., Allen, B., Kaldate, R., Bhatnagar, S.: Frequency of mutations in individuals with breast cancer referred for BRCA1 and BRCA2 testing using next-generation sequencing with a 25-gene panel. Cancer **121**, 25–33 (2015)
14. Cooke, T., Reeves, J., Lanigan, A., Stanton, P.: HER2 as a prognostic and predictive marker for breast cancer. Ann. Oncol. **12**, S23–S28 (2001)
15. Jennings, J.L., Hudson, T.J.: International Cancer Genome Consortium (ICGC). Cancer Res. **76**, 130 (2016)

16. Louie, B., Mork, P., Martin-Sanchez, F., Halevy, A.: Data integration and genomic medicine. J. Biomed. **28**, 5–16 (2007)
17. Khatri, P., Draghici, S.: Ontological analysis of gene expression data. current tools, limitations, and open problems. Bioinformatics **21**, 3587–3595 (2005)
18. Merelli, I., Pérez-Sánchez, H., Gesing, S.: Managing, analysing, and integrating big data in medical bioinformatics: open problems and future perspectives. BioMed Res. (2014)
19. Alzu'bi, A., Zhou, L., Watzlaf, V.: Personal genomic information management and personalized medicine: challenges, current solutions, and roles of HIM professionals. Perspect. Health Inf. Manag. **11**, 1c (2014)
20. Fernald, G.H., Capriotti, E., Daneshjou, R., Karczewski, K.J., Altman, R.B.: Bioinformatics challenges for personalized medicine. Bioinformatics **27**, 1741–1748 (2011)
21. Stephens, Z.D., Lee, S.Y., Faghri, F., Campbell, R.H., Zhai, C., Efron, M.J., Iyer, R., Schatz, M.C., Sinha, S., Robinson, G.E.: Big data: astronomical or genomical? PLoS Biol. **13**, e1002195 (2015)
22. Dove, E.S., Joly, Y., Tassé, A.-M.: Genomic cloud computing: legal and ethical points to consider. Eur. J. Hum. Genet. **23**, 1271–1278 (2015)
23. Heath, A.P., Greenway, M., Powell, R., Spring, J., Suarez, R., Hanley, D., Bandlamudi, C., McNerney, M.E., White, K.P., Grossman, R.L.: Bionimbus: a cloud for managing, analyzing and sharing large genomics datasets. J. Am. Med. Inform. Assoc. **21**, 969–975 (2014)
24. Deorowicz, S., Danek, A., Niemiec, M.: GDC 2: compression of large collections of genomes. Sci. Rep. **5**, 11565 (2015)
25. Madden, T.: The BLAST sequence analysis tool (2013)
26. Subhani, M., Anjum, A., Koop, A.: Clinical and genomics data integration using meta-dimensional approach. In: Proceedings of the 9th International Conference on Utility and Cloud Computing, pp. 416–421 (2016)
27. Beck, M., Haupt, V., Roy, J., Moennich, J., Jäkel, R.: Genecloud: secure cloud computing for biomedical research. In: Krcmar, H., Reussner, R., Rumpe, B. (eds.) Trusted Cloud Computing. Springer, Heidelberg (2014). doi:10.1007/978-3-319-12718-7_1
28. Directors, A.B.: Laboratory and clinical genomic data sharing is crucial to improving genetic health care: a position statement of the American College of Medical Genetics. Genet. Med. (2017)

Using Data Mining Strategy in Qualitative Research

Nadhirah Rasid[1], Puteri N.E. Nohuddin[1(✉)], Hamidah Alias[2],
Irna Hamzah[1], and A. Imran Nordin[1]

[1] Institute of Visual Informatics, Universiti Kebangsaan Malaysia, 43600 Bangi,
Selangor, Malaysia
sitinadhirah.abdrasid@gmail.com
[2] Department of Pediatrics, Faculty of Medicine, Universiti Kebangsaan
Malaysia, Cheras, 56000 Kuala Lumpur, Malaysia

Abstract. Analyzing qualitative data can be tedious if it is done manually. There are several techniques available to conduct qualitative research such as thematic analysis, grounded theory and content analysis amongst other techniques. The data collected from these techniques are usually huge in amount. Little has been done to apply data mining strategy to analyzes data gathered using qualitative methodology. In this paper, we present a work done to apply text mining technique to analyzes data gathered from interviews – unstructured data. The aim of this study is to develop patterns of pediatric cancer patient's activities in the ward. The result shows a pattern that suggests patients are mostly playing video games while receiving treatment and when they feel bored in the ward. This proposes that data mining techniques can be used to provide an initial insight of the information gathered qualitatively.

Keywords: Experience mining · Text mining · Pediatric · Cancer · Interview

1 Introduction

There are several studies conducts available to apply qualitative research in children with cancer such as grounded theory, ethnography, phenomenology and illness narrative amongst other techniques [1]. Through these conducts, the data collections include interviews, observations, memo records, diary study, field notes, written anecdotes of experiences and many more. Typically, the type of data gathered from these data collections consists of unstructured data. Unstructured data is varied and flexible data where it comes in many formats, including text, document, image, video and more. Unstructured data analytics can expose important interrelationships that were problematic or impossible to verify before [2]. Examples of unstructured data are "tweets" of Twitter [2] and biomedical text [3]. The challenging part when it comes to analyze unstructured data are the data volumes are so large and difficult to deal with, to find the most important data points, does all data need to be stored, does all data need to be analyzed, and how to make the data used to best advantage [4].

Analyzing qualitative data (unstructured data) can be challenging. It depends on the background knowledge and experiences of the researcher, theoretical framework built,

© Springer International Publishing AG 2017
H. Badioze Zaman et al. (Eds.): IVIC 2017, LNCS 10645, pp. 100–111, 2017.
https://doi.org/10.1007/978-3-319-70010-6_10

sampling and ability to interpret enormous amounts of information. The results produced from qualitative research is valuable as it gives bigger understanding of the realities which describe people behavior, routine, lives and their minds [1, 5] argues that applying qualitative research design in children with cancer allows us to capture their complex social process, cultural description and their experiences. Hence, it is crucial for researchers to be able to analyze correctly to produce better understanding of the meaning and the consequences of the results. The main problem arises when a junior researcher with limited background knowledge and experience attempts to conduct qualitative research. The massive amounts of information collected could be intimidating and this could make them to produce inaccurate interpretation. Hence, in this paper we are investigating the use of data mining technique to analyze qualitative data. We aim to apply one specific data mining technique called text mining technique to analyze data gathered from the interviews conducted with the parents/guardians of pediatric cancer patients. We argue that the patterns produced will help researchers to get an initial insight of the overall view.

2 Background and Related Work

2.1 Pediatric Cancer

Children and young adults are the highest-risk group of cancer diagnosis in Malaysia [6] and the most common cancer in childhood is B-precursor acute lymphoblastic leukemia (B-ALL) [7]. The treatments received by pediatric cancer patients were chemotherapy, radiotherapy, surgery, bone aspiration, or bedside procedure where it is required the patients to stay in the ward throughout the treatment session.

A research was conducted to see if correlation lies between specialist cancer care and quality of life for young people with cancer through systematically select and analyze published research on teenage and young adult experience of cancer [8]. The method used were systematic review and meta-synthesis where it is focused on terms such as population, intervention, outcome, and study type. This study came up with 315 identified studies which results the mediators and consequences of cancer care that impact on young people's quality of life after a cancer diagnosis such as psychosocial function, importance of peers, experience of healthcare, importance of support, impact of symptoms, striving for normality, impact of diagnosis, positive experiences, and financial consequences [8].

2.2 Interview Study

Interview study has been conducted in many study to understand one's experience, beliefs, satisfactions, or expectations [9] used interview study to consider patient and caregiver's beliefs and expectations about home hemodialysis. Other techniques used to analyze the interview study are purposive sampling and thematic analysis where it results seven (7) major themes which has positive themes: flexibility and freedom, comfort in familiar surroundings and altruistic motivation, and negative themes: disrupting sense of normality, family burden, housing constraints, and isolation from peer support.

Similarly, [10] also used interview as one of the method to scrutinize the nature and content of post-intensive care memories in traumatized intensive care patients where thematic and content analysis are used to further analyzed the interview study.

Another study [11] focusing on the interview method in education where the purpose was to delve into how students identify that they used social media to support their studies. 11 questions were proposed as a guide in the semi-structured interviews where the interviews focused on the student's perceptions and experiences. The data collected was summarized using key points and principal themes where the data is group according to the interview questions and categorized the feedback to three user categories which are frequent, medium and infrequent users who use social media to support their studies.

Furthermore, [12] used other way to capture one's experience in a study where official surveys, volunteered testimonials and in-class participation are approached to see if students were more attracted, motivated and engaged in the curriculum for higher education. In this study, one of the way to keep the students to participating in curriculum is using gamification and the student's feedback and experiences from this gamification approach is remarkable.

[13] focusing on quantitative study using Q methodology which allowed the investigation of subjective viewpoints and perceptions in implementing water-reuse policy. This method provides the researcher with a "systematic and rigorously quantitative means for examining human subjectivity".

2.3 Data Mining

Data mining is a data-driven, investigative process of knowledge finding where it is focused on discovery and mining valuable patterns of information from large and complex databases [14]. There are a few techniques in data mining such as classification [15], clustering [16], association rule [17], and text mining [18].

Classification is used as a tool to groups element in a set of data into one of predefined set of classes or categories [15]. This method makes use of mathematical techniques such as decision trees, linear programming, neural network and statistics. For example, used classification techniques such as J48, Naive Bayes and One-R classifier algorithm using WEKA work form to attain classification response for fraud detection dataset. Not only that, these classifiers were also compared over different parameters which it can helps the e-commerce companies to choose optimal classification algorithm [15].

Clustering aims to group items with similar characteristics within the same cluster [16]. For example, clustering techniques were used in detecting temporal pattern and cluster changes in social networks where it is used the Cattle Tracing System (CTS) database in operation in Great Britain (GB). The purposes were to identify frequent pattern trends and cluster similar trends using Self Organizing Map (SOM) technology [19].

Association rule often used to determine interesting correlation among items in large dataset [17]. For example, association rule is widely used in disease prediction such as breast cancer, heart disease and diabetes [20].

Data mining is widely used in healthcare research like in a research about the early detection lung cancer risk using data mining techniques. Data mining techniques used in this study are K-means clustering algorithm for finding relevant and irrelevant data, and AprioriTid algorithm and decision tree algorithm to spotted important frequent pattern. The finding results developing tools for lung cancer prediction system [21].

In qualitative study, data mining techniques such as self-organizing map and decision tree analysis were used as tools to analyzed health informatics data to find meaningful patterns in such large and complex database [14].

There are several studies which combining qualitative study and data mining technique such as understanding communication patterns in MOOCs [22]. The most frequent technique used in analyzing qualitative data is text mining techniques.

2.4   Text Mining for Qualitative Research

Focusing on one of the data mining techniques is text mining where it is commonly used in analyzing unstructured textual data. Text mining is widely used in healthcare [23], education [24], market prediction [25], social media [26], and others that involve massive, pattern and unstructured data. Several studies have been conducted using text mining technique in analyzing qualitative data such as mining questions [27] and understanding customer satisfaction through online hotel reviews [28].

In a research paper conducting competitive analysis using text mining on social media like Twitter and Facebook sites of three (3) largest pizza chains that is Pizza Hut, Domino's Pizza and Papa John's Pizza. The purpose of this study was to bring out business value. Furthermore, the comparison could help the company to discover weaknesses, find new opportunity and arrange their social media strategy [26].

There were also reviewed study about text mining technique for market prediction where the problem was to determine the relation lies between textual information and economy. This review study focused on two main review which are review of foundational integrative background concept and review of the major possible work. A review of foundational integrative background concept focusing on the efficient market hypothesis (EMH), behavioral-economics, adaptive market hypothesis (AMH), market's predictability, fundamental vs technical analysis, algorithmic trading, and sentiment and emotional analysis while review of the major possible work aiming for general survey, input dataset, textual data, pre-processing, machine learning, and findings of the reviewed work. This paper has suggested some aspects for market prediction based on online text mining which are semantics, syntax, sentiment, text-mining component, textual source or application-market specialization, machine learning algorithms, integration of technical signals, relation with behavioral-economics research, availability and quality of experimental datasets, and evaluation methods [29].

A study was conducted for low tech, low cost text mining, insights from the text mining literature, and an experiment with trend analysis in business intelligent by using design science as a simple methodological framework. This study came out with five (5) stages process for qualitative researchers who wish to conduct experiment using text mining which were problem awareness, process suggestion, development, evaluation of text mining process, and results [30].

Another study was comparing text mining with qualitative research in the perspectives of grounded theory, content analysis and reliability. It is shows that text mining has the same objective with certain qualitative methods and it could maintain consistency, verifiable and reliability results of qualitative research [31].

3 Methodology

3.1 Interviews with Parents/Guardians of Pediatric Cancer Patients

The aim of this study is to demonstrate that text mining is a tool for qualitative research. Thus, for the experiment set up, this study uses pediatric cancer patient's data in order to list out all the possible patient's experiences and activities in the ward while they received treatment.

This study was conducted qualitatively through interview session with their parents about their experiences and activities before, during and after cancer diagnosis and hospitalized. Interview method was commonly used in research about experience [32], satisfaction [9], opinion or belief [33] and more.

3.1.1 Participants

The interviews involved ten (10) patient's guardians who stayed with patients throughout the treatment session in the ward. All guardians who participated were patient's mother with age range between 35 and 52 years old.

3.1.2 Procedures

The interviews were conducted in the pediatric oncology ward, 4D at Pusat Perubatan Universiti Kebangsaan Malaysia (PPUKM), Cheras. All the interviews were performed at separate time where it took about 30 min to one (1) hour each.

Distinct set of questions were used for each interview where the outcomes from the first interview was used to create new set of questions for the second interview. Then the result form second interview was used to create new set of questions for the next interview and so on until the 10th interview.

Every interview was recorded using voice recorder to make sure that no information is missed during data transcription. Consent form was given to the guardian before the interview session began to acknowledge them that the interview will be recorded. The information recorded were then converted into text transcript in Microsoft Excel for data analyzing. For data analyzing, text mining technique was used to extract the valuable information from the interview session.

3.2 Qualitative Data Analytic Framework (QDAF)

The flow of this research follows proposed framework called Qualitative Data Analytics Framework (QDAF). This framework contains four (4) modules which were data set, pre-processing, text mining, visualization.

Data set of this research was the textual data from the interview session undergone pre-processing where the data was cleaned to removed unnecessary term. After pre-processing is formed, text mining process took place where Voyant Tools is used to analyzed the textual cleaned data and the result from this process will be presented using visualization. Figure 1 below shows QDAF used in this study.

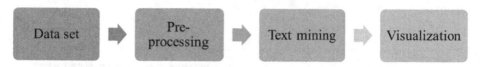

Fig. 1. Qualitative Data Analytics Framework (QDAF)

Figure 1 shows the Qualitative Data Analytics Framework (QDAF). It consists of four (4) stages namely data set, pre-processing, experience mining, and visualization.

3.2.1 Data Set

Data set is a collection of related set of information such as in this study, the data set was the information about experience and behavior of pediatric cancer patients in the ward which gathered from the interview session with patient's guardian.

The data collected was unstructured textual data which contain question and answer between interviewer and the participant (mother). All the interview data was stored in 10 separated files. Figure 2 below shows the original unstructured interview data set.

> Interviewer: What is the reaction when the patient is in the hospital?
>
> Mother: He said that he felt lonely here because they have no friends. The first thing that he complained was he wants to go home because he has no friends here. He has no friends to play with. He said that I cannot be his friend because I was his mother. As for his opinion, a mother cannot play with him. He can tell the difference between mother and friend. He needs friends to play together. My husband has passed away. Some of my friends told my son to let me marry again. But he does not allow me to marry. He just let me be friends only.
>
> Interviewer: How old is the patient?
>
> Mother: My son is 5 years old and 9 months. My son says that the situation is not encouraging him in the hospital because he cannot play with anyone, even though he has a lot of toys. Sometimes he invites nurses to play with him. The situation here limits my son to play with friends, to share his thoughts that can be expanded with toys.

Fig. 2. The original unstructured textual data of the interview

3.2.2 Pre-processing

Before the process of text mining, a pre-processing stage needs to be conducted to remove errors and inconsistencies from the dataset as it can improve the quality of data as well as the accuracy and effectiveness of text mining.

First step in text pre-processing was converted all words into lowercase to ensure that various forms of keywords such as 'mother', 'Mother' and 'MOTHERS' are identified similarly. Then punctuation marks, numbers, whitespace and symbols were removed from the text documents.

Next step was to stem and remove stop words. Stemming is the process of reducing inflected or derived words to their word stem while stop words are terms that considered as not important and do not value in the content of the files while. The example of word stemming is "playing" or "play" will become "plai". The cleaned data was stored in 10 separated files which represented each interview. Figure 3 below shows the cleaned textual data which stored in 10 separated Excel files according to participant.

1	befor patient diagnos or hospit what the activ perform by the patient	my son often plai bicycl and plai footbal he also plai alongsid with brother and sister
2	why patient like the activ	of passion for bike
3	when should patient do these activ	my son is plai on the bike sinc the ag of five he plai often in the even bike when return from school
4	how long it take in on session of the activ	quit a long time so i must call m to come home more than an hour other activ he did is go to catch grasshopp with cousin t activ is cri out school holidai and when cousin came to our hous after he catch it he took it back home and show it to me
5	the patient s stai in hospit patient is still do favorit activ	my son like to plai videogame and surf you tube to watch ctoon he love download videogame from the internet

Fig. 3. Cleaned textual data stored in 10 separated Excel files

Tables 1 and 2 below shows part of the stemming process and stop words performed in the study.

Table 1. Stemming process

Word	Stem	Word	Stem
Activities	Activ	Chemoterapy	Chemotherapi
Play	Plai	Online	Onlin
Hospital	Hospit	Tired	Tire
Cry	Cri	Bored	Bore
Outside	Outsid	Worry	Worri

Table 2. Stop words

	Stop	Words	
Long	Veri	Just	Wai
Hi	Thi	Sometime	Ani
Ar	Dure	Tell	Condit
Want	Doe	Thei	Ag
Because	Make	Allow	Tire
Ye	Onli	Wa	Differ

3.2.3   Text Mining

After data pre-processing is done, text analysis take place where the cleaned data is analyzed using Voyant Tools to extract the word frequencies and pattern of patient's experience and activities in the ward.

Voyant Tools is an open-source, online medium available for performing text analysis, statistical analysis and data mining which developed by Stéfan Sinclair and Geoffrey Rockwell. It is contained a lot of ways to represented the most counted words such as word cloud, trends, links, correlations, document terms, and other styles which can be adjusted according to the terms and stop words.

3.2.4   Visualization

Visualization is any techniques of creating images, graphs, or diagrams to represent the results of any analyzation or test for quick or better understanding. Not only that, visualization also helps user to figure out mistakes with their data or inputs [34].

The results from text mining were interpreted using visualization where it is presented in word frequencies table, word cloud, termsberry, trends, and link between patient's activities and experiences in the ward. All the visualization came from the Voyant Tools itself.

4   Result and Discussion

This section discussed the results from the text analysis using Voyant Tools.

Table 3. List of 16 important terms

Term	Frequencies	Term	Frequencies
Patient	305	Bore	48
Play	249	Friend	31
Videogame	192	Televise	25
Son	143	Happi	19
Active	124	Chemoterapi	18
Hospital	78	Phone	15
Treatment	76	Sleep	15
Home	73	Library	14

Table 3 above shows the list of 16 important terms occur from the 10 interview files. It is representing the frequencies of the important word like "videogame" word occur 192 times which indicates as the third highest frequency of word. Figure 4 illustrates the trends for the top five (5) most frequent words out of 998 terms in every file which represent each interview with the patient's mother such as "plai" which indicates the word "play" occur 34 times in Patient 6's file, "activ" which indicates "activity" occur 14 times in Patient 4's file, "patient" occur 35 times in Patient 5's file, "son" occur 21 times in Patient 10's file, and word "videogame" occur 0 times at Patient 7's file.

Instead of using term table and graph of trends, the most frequent used words also can be visualize in the form of word cloud which Fig. 5 represent the word cloud with the 25 most frequent words occur in the 10 interview files where "patient", "plai", "videogame", "son", and "active" appeared as the biggest word indicated the most frequent words followed by "time", "hospit", "feel", "treatment", "home", "game", "like", "cld" which indicate the word "child", "school", "bore", "wle" indicate the

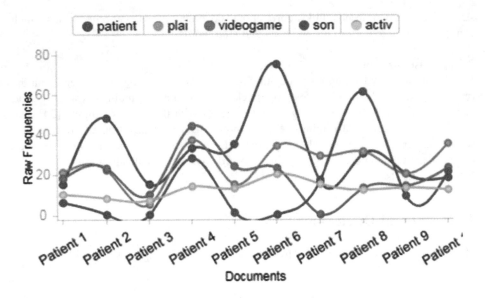

Fig. 4. Trends of five (5) most frequent word in the 10 files.

word "while", "make", "daughter", "watch", "thei" stands for "their", "help", "veri", "ask", "father", and "friend". The word "child" and "while" became "cld" and "wle" because the stop word "hi" has been removed from all files to improve the data accuracy.

Fig. 5. Word cloud with the most frequent words.

Figure 6 below point up the link between eight (8) most frequent words occur in the interview. For example, the largest bridge is between the word "videogame", "plai" and "patient" which represent that video game, play and patient are the strongest link among all. This illustrates that whenever patient play, they were playing video games. Another strong link is between word "plai" and "game" followed by link between "patient" and "feel".

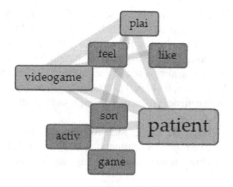

Fig. 6. Link between the most frequent words.

5   Conclusion and Future Work

The purpose of this study is to list out all the possible experiences and activities of pediatric cancer patients while receiving treatment in the ward through qualitative study. The text mining results represent strong relationship between patient and video game. It is shows positive integration where parents used video game to empower patients while staying in the ward for treatment session.

The advantage of using text mining for this study was it can extract frequent significant terms from the unstructured data which were collected for qualitative research and those frequent terms represent the pediatric cancer patient's experience during treatment session in the ward.

For future work, the experiment will be proceeding with diverse set of qualitative study which will represent the pediatric cancer patient's experiences and activities deeper using different technique of analyzing.

References

1. Woodgate, R.: Part I: an introduction to conducting qualitative research in children with cancer. J. Pediatr. Oncol. Nurs. **17**, 192–206 (2000)
2. Rama Prasath, A., Ramya, M.M.: Automated drusen grading system in fundus image using fuzzy c-means clustering. Int. J. Eng. Technol. **6**, 833–841 (2014)
3. Zhu, F., Patumcharoenpol, P., Zhang, C., Yang, Y., Chan, J., Meechai, A., Vongsangnak, W., Shen, B.: Biomedical text mining and its applications in cancer research. J. Biomed. Inform. **46**, 200–211 (2013)
4. Katal, A., Wazid, M., Goudar, R.H.: Big data: issues, challenges, tools and good practices. In: 2013 6th International Conference Contemporary Computing, IC3 2013, pp. 404–409 (2013)
5. Malterud, K.: Qualitative research: standards, challenges, and guidelines. Lancet **358**, 483–488 (2001)
6. Zainal, A.O., Nor Saleha, I.T.: National Cancer Registry Report (2011)

7. Lee, D.W., Kochenderfer, J.N., Stetler-Stevenson, M., Cui, Y.K., Delbrook, C., Feldman, S. A., Fry, T.J., Orentas, R., Sabatino, M., Shah, N.N., Steinberg, S.M., Stroncek, D., Tschernia, N., Yuan, C., Zhang, H., Zhang, L., Rosenberg, S.A., Wayne, A.S., Mackall, C.L.: T cells expressing CD19 chimeric antigen receptors for acute lymphoblastic leukaemia in children and young adults: a phase 1 dose-escalation trial. Lancet **385**, 517–528 (2015)
8. Taylor, R.M., Pearce, S., Gibson, F., Fern, L., Whelan, J.: Developing a conceptual model of teenage and young adult experiences of cancer through meta-synthesis. Int. J. Nurs. Stud. **50**, 832–846 (2013)
9. Tong, A., Palmer, S., Manns, B., Craig, J.C., Ruospo, M., Gargano, L., Johnson, D.W., Hegbrant, J., Olsson, M., Fishbane, S., Strippoli, G.F.M.: The beliefs and expectations of patients and caregivers about home haemodialysis: an interview study. BMJ Open **3**, e002148 (2013)
10. Wade, D.M., Brewin, C.R., Howell, D.C.J., White, E., Mythen, M.G., Weinman, J.A.: Intrusive memories of hallucinations and delusions in traumatized intensive care patients: an interview study. Br. J. Health. Psychol. **20**, 613–631 (2015)
11. Hrastinski, S., Aghaee, N.M.: How are campus students using social media to support their studies? An explorative interview study. Educ. Inf. Technol. **17**, 451–464 (2012)
12. Iosup, A., Epema, D.: An experience report on using gamification in technical higher education. In: Proceedings of 45th ACM Technical Symposium on Computer Science Education, SIGCSE 2014, pp. 27–32 (2014)
13. Ching, L.: A quantitative investigation of narratives: recycled drinking water. Water Policy **17**, 831–847 (2015)
14. Castellani, B., Castellani, J.: Data mining: qualitative analysis with health informatics data. Qual. Health Res. **13**, 1005–1018 (2003)
15. Alam, F., Pachauri, S.: Comparative study of J48, Naive Bayes and One-R classification technique for credit card fraud detection using WEKA. Adv. Comput. Sci. Technol. **10**, 1731–1743 (2017)
16. Fan, C., Xiao, F., Wang, S.: Development of prediction models for next-day building energy consumption and peak power demand using data mining techniques. Appl. Energy **127**, 1–10 (2014)
17. Slimani, T., Lazzez, A.: Efficient Analysis of Pattern and Association Rule Mining Approaches. arXiv preprint arXiv:1402.2892 (2014)
18. He, W.: Examining students' online interaction in a live video streaming environment using data mining and text mining. Comput. Hum. Behav. **29**, 90–102 (2013)
19. Nohuddin, P.N.E., Coenen, F., Christley, R., Setzkorn, C.: Detecting temporal pattern and cluster changes in social networks: a study focusing UK cattle movement database. In: Shi, Z., Vadera, S., Aamodt, A., Leake, D. (eds.) Intelligent Information Processing V, IIP 2010. IFIP Advances in Information and Communication Technology, vol. 340, pp. 163–172. Springer, Heidelberg (2010). doi:10.1007/978-3-642-16327-2_22
20. Vijiyarani, S., Sudha, S.: Disease prediction in data mining technique – a survey. Int. J. Comput. Appl. Inf. Technol. **2**, 17–21 (2013)
21. Ahmed, K., Emran, A.A., Jesmin, T., Mukti, R.F., Rahman, M.Z., Ahmed, F.: Early detection of lung cancer risk using data mining. Asian Pac. J. Cancer Prev. **14**, 595–598 (2013)
22. Eynon, R., Hjorth, I., Yasseri, T., Gillani, N.: Understanding Communication Patterns in MOOCs: Combining Data Mining and qualitative methods. arXiv preprint arXiv:1607.07495 (2016)
23. Dangare, C.S., Apte, S.S.: Improved study of heart disease prediction system using data mining classification techniques. Int. J. Comput. Appl. 0975–888 **47**, 44–48 (2012)

24. Yukselturk, E., Ozekes, S., Türel, Y.K.: Predicting dropout student : an application of data mining methods in an online education program. Eur. J. Open Distance e-Learning **17**, 118–133 (2014)
25. Khadjeh Nassirtoussi, A., Aghabozorgi, S., Ying Wah, T., Ngo, D.C.L.: Text mining of news-headlines for FOREX market prediction: a multi-layer dimension reduction algorithm with semantics and sentiment. Expert Syst. Appl. **42**, 306–324 (2015)
26. He, W., Zha, S., Li, L.: Social media competitive analysis and text mining: a case study in the pizza industry. Int. J. Inf. Manag. **33**, 464–472 (2013)
27. Bajaj, K., Pattabiraman, K., Mesbah, A.: Mining questions asked by web developers. In: Proceedings 11th Working Conference Mining Software Repositories - MSR 2014, pp. 112–121 (2014)
28. Berezina, K., Bilgihan, A., Cobanoglu, C., Okumus, F.: Understanding satisfied and dissatisfied hotel customers: text mining of online hotel reviews. J. Hosp. Mark. Manag. **25**, 1–24 (2015)
29. Khadjeh Nassirtoussi, A., Aghabozorgi, S., Ying Wah, T., Ngo, D.C.L.: Text mining for market prediction: a systematic review. Expert Syst. Appl. **41**, 7653–7670 (2014)
30. Rose, J., Lennerholt, C.: Low cost text mining as a strategy for qualitative researchers. Electron. J. Bus. Res. Method **15**, 2–16 (2017)
31. Yu, C.H., Jannasch-Pennell, A., Digangi, S., Yu, C.H.: Compatibility between text mining and qualitative research in the perspectives of grounded theory, content analysis, and reliability. Qual. Rep. **16**, 730–744 (2011)
32. Berglund, M., Westin, L., Svanstrom, R., Sundler, A.J.: Suffering caused by care patients' experiences from hospital settings. Int. J. Qual. Stud. Health Well-Being **7**, 1–9 (2012)
33. Turnbull, M.: A qualitative investigation into the experiences, perceptions, beliefs and self-care management of people with type 2 diabetes (2015)
34. Morton, K., Balazinska, M., Grossman, D., Mackinlay, J.: Support the data enthusiast. Proc. VLDB Endow. **7**, 453–456 (2014)

An Integrated Social Media Trading Platform for B40 Social Media Entrepreneurship

Johnlee Jumin[✉], Mohamad Taha Ijab, and Halimah Badioze Zaman

Institute of Visual Informatics, Universiti Kebangsaan Malaysia (UKM),
43600 Bangi, Selangor, Malaysia
p88950@siswa.ukm.edu.my, {taha,halimahivi}@ukm.edu.my

Abstract. Statistically, there are 2.7 million Malaysian households categorized under the Bottom 40 (B40) category with 56% of them are living in urban areas and the remaining 44% live in rural areas. Malaysia's Eleventh Malaysia Plan refers B40 as household with a mean monthly income of RM3,860. For the betterment of the B40 community in the country, the Government of Malaysia aims to double the B40 household incomes by Year 2020 and this is facilitated via various multisector initiatives, especially those championed by Malaysia Digital Economy Corporation [1]. It is observed by some studies that the younger generations in the B40 community are very exposed to the Internet and social technologies in general. They use social media application as a medium for many activities including interacting with family and friends, organizing events, for learning purposes, purchasing and selling products online, and thus becoming B40 social entrepreneurs themselves. Leveraging on this phenomenon, this paper proposes the development of an integrated social media trading platform which combines many popular social media such as Facebook and Instagram into a single platform that will be offered to the B40 social entrepreneur community in Malaysia to conduct their businesses on this platform. The integrated trading platform will cover a broad set of features such as storefront, payment, shipping, after sales service, customer management, and advisory from mentor. The integrated platform is also designed to enable the B40 social entrepreneurs to understand their customers better through sentiment analysis and social media analytics to boost their social entrepreneurship.

Keywords: Social computing application · B40 · Sentiment analysis · Social entrepreneurship

1 Introduction

Social media is the collective of online communications channels dedicated to community-based input, interaction, content-sharing and collaboration. Social media run on web-based technologies, desktop computers and mobile technologies (e.g., smartphones and tablet computers) to create highly interactive platforms through which individuals, communities and organizations share, co-create, discuss, and modify user-generated content or pre-made content posted online. They introduce substantial and

© Springer International Publishing AG 2017
H. Badioze Zaman et al. (Eds.): IVIC 2017, LNCS 10645, pp. 112–119, 2017.
https://doi.org/10.1007/978-3-319-70010-6_11

pervasive changes to communication between businesses, organizations, communities and individuals. Social media changes the way individuals and large organizations communicate [2].

Researchers observe that young social entrepreneurs use the social media platform for their online business [3]. Online business is generally any business on the Internet that sells products, services, or advertising online. The difference between a website and an online business is that the latter sells something using the global communications infrastructure of the Internet. It is posited that by fully leveraging on the social media platform, particularly an integrated one will improve the social entrepreneurship among the B40 community [4].

Social entrepreneurs among the B40 community are using many social media trading platforms and that cause issues such as difficulty in posting advertisements, managing products, managing customer transactions, managing payment, managing complaints, and after sales service. Presently, there are limited single, integrated social media trading platform that B40 community social entrepreneurs can use for free. There exist such integrated platforms such as SproutSocial, IFTTT, Everypost, Buffer, Agorapulse, and Tweetdeck but they are expensive to join.

This paper posits that social entrepreneurs are generally unable to understand the sentiment of their customers as complaints or compliments are not captured and analyzed properly on the existing social media. If they understand their customers' sentiments, it would be easier for them to make improvement in their trading to achieve customer satisfaction. Further, social entrepreneurs among B40 community lack support and mentoring from experts or other successful business people, or the government agency. Hence, there is a need to provide such advisory (mentoring) services by the industry mentors or government's agency experts to these B40 social entrepreneurs in guiding them to be successful entrepreneurs.

2   Literature Review

Towards researching this topic, this paper reviews the central concepts pertaining to the proposed development of the integrated trading platform for B40 social entrepreneur community by leveraging on social media analytics and sentiment analysis. These concepts are B40, social media, social entrepreneurship, social media analytics and sentiment analysis.

Based on [5], the B40 category refers to whose salary bracket is RM3,860 and below. Majority of these households have single income earners and more than half of the household's heads (52%) have no recognized education background. With poor education background, low skills level and in certain cases, living in remote locations, the B40 households are limited in their economic mobility and ability to secure higher paying jobs as well as income opportunities [6]. Studies have also shown that there is low ICT adoption among poor communities in Malaysia, which is part of the B40 group [2].

In terms of social media, according to [7], social media is many things. Social media according to [8] can be defined as (i) Web 2.0 Internet-based applications, (ii) social media is engine by user-generated content as its lifeblood, (iii) individuals and groups are able to create user-specific profiles for a site or app designed and maintained by a social media service, and (iv) social media services facilitate the development of social networks online by connecting a profile with those of other individuals and/or groups.

While the Internet and the World Wide Web have always been used to facilitate social interaction, the emergence and rapid diffusion of Web 2.0 functionalities during the first decade of the new millennium enabled an evolutionary leap forward in the social component of web use. This and falling costs for online data storage made it feasible for the first time to offer masses of Internet users access to an array of user-centric spaces they could populate with user-generated content, along with a correspondingly diverse set of opportunities for linking these spaces together to form virtual social networks [7]. Social media play increasingly important roles as a marketing platform. More and more retailers use social media to target teens and young adults, and social networking sites are a central venue in that trend. Online shopping nowadays become a trend and brings a lot of impact to customers and seller [9]. As for the social media uses, mostly 65% user is adults. Those within the ages of 18 to 29 is the group communities that have been using the most of social networking and women usually use social networking more than men. Other than that, studies also show that low income group actively use the social networking [7].

Pertaining to the concept of social entrepreneurship, in principle, social entrepreneur is a mission-driven individual who uses a set of entrepreneurial behaviors to deliver a social value to the less privileged, all through an entrepreneurially oriented entity that is financially independent, self-sufficient, or sustainable [10]. Entrepreneurs are conceptualized as individuals who see the world differently and envision the future better than others do. They seize opportunities that otherwise would go unnoticed. They perceive and accept risks differently than others. Although the use of the term social entrepreneur is growing rapidly, the field of social entrepreneurship lacks rigor and is in its infancy compared to the wider field of entrepreneurship. Success stories of individuals solving complex social problems are being used to legitimize the field of social entrepreneurship [11]. Further, a social entrepreneur is someone who takes reasonable risk on behalf of the people their organizations serve. The interest in social entrepreneurs stems from their role in addressing critical social problems and the dedication they show in improving the well-being of society [12].

According to [13], social entrepreneurship has several definitions and its definitions have been debated by researchers. One group of researchers refers to social entrepreneurship as not-for-profit initiatives in search of alternative funding strategies, or management schemes to create social value [14]. Another group views social entrepreneurship to alleviate social problems and catalyze social transformation, pointing to the importance of entrepreneurial environment and its process of becoming "social" [15]. In this research, we conceptualize social entrepreneurship encompasses the activities and processes undertaken to discover, define, and exploit opportunities to enhance social wealth by creating new ventures or managing existing organizations in an innovative via social media platform. This transformation is also made possible by the powerful forces entrepreneurship unleashes, where ordinary people conceive innovative ideas, organize production, assume risk, and engage customers to accumulate wealth or address pressing social causes, often across national borders [12].

All social media interactions can be analyzed for insights via a process called social media analytics. Therefore, for the social media trading by the B40 social entrepreneur community, there are high possibility that their volume of sales on social media is high and these transactions (i.e., selling, buying, paying, shipping, resolution/conflict handling) provide a lot of data that can be analyzed for insights to make their social entrepreneurship businesses better in the long run. This can also be achieved through the implementation of sentiment analysis. Sentiment analysis mainly deals with the evaluation type of opinions which imply positive or negative sentiments that include the emotions [16]. Emotions are closely related to sentiments. The strength of a sentiment or opinion is typically linked to the intensity of certain emotions, e.g., joy and anger. Opinions that we study in sentiment analysis are mostly evaluations. Emotions have been studied in multiple fields, e.g., psychology, philosophy, and sociology. The studies are very broad, from emotional responses of physiological reactions (e.g., heart rate changes, blood pressure, sweating and so on), facial expressions, gestures and postures to different types of subjective experiences of an individual's state of mind. Scientists have categorized people's emotions into some categories. However, there is still not a set of agreed basic emotions among researchers [17]. Sentiment analysis was also used to characterize social relations. Sentiment classification is usually formulated as a two-class classification problem, positive and negative. Training and testing data used are normally product reviews [6].

3 Existing Social Media Application Supporting Online Trading

There are many advantage of integration of social media nowadays. The user will not just be able to post in just one place, user also get all the messages and replies from across platform in one place, track competitor's activities of what they are up to, and the most important that user can use integration tool to generate analysis report to help user understand what is currently happening in their business and making smart decision. In this section, we briefly review the examples of existing system of integrated social media, namely IFTTT, SproutSocial, EveryPost, Buffer, Agora Pulse and TweetDeck.

IFTTT is an integrated social media application which have a feature that doing service for social media, with the functionality of save photo into Dropbox, backup photo, and post into social media. SproutSocial also an integrated social media, which having a feature such as listing the page of social media, an addition to handling user, message, task, feeds, publishing, and report, also post on the social media. On the other hand, EveryPost is a social media integrated system which having a functionality posting on social media and give an analytical report. Buffer is another integrated social media system having the functionality of handling the posting on social media, generate analytic report, and having a schedule part. Agora Pulse, one of the social media integrated systems that can list all the user page on social media, ease the task of monitoring and publishing on social media, and provide report. Lastly, TweeetDeck is a popular Twitter-based integrated system that have a functionality such as handling notification, message, activity log, user wall page, and posting into social media.

From the review of the existing systems, it is found that there is a need to have a single integrated social media trading platform particularly one that is addressing the needs of the B40 social entrepreneurs in Malaysia. The integrated platform will make it easier for the social entrepreneurs compared to the need of handling multiple social media platforms and numerous accounts to maintain and remember. Other than that, the integrated social media platform is proposed to handle not only trading posts, but also the one that is able in handling other business transactions such as store front, payment, shipping, conflict resolution, advisory or mentoring and sentiment analysis. These capabilities are conjectured to help the B40 social entrepreneurs to boost their online business when using the integrated social media system.

4   The Conceptual Framework of Integrated Social Media Trading Platform for B40 Community

Based on the review of the literature, a conceptual framework is derived as to provide a high-level understanding on how the concepts reviewed are combined and guide this entire research. The proposed conceptual framework is shown in Fig. 1.

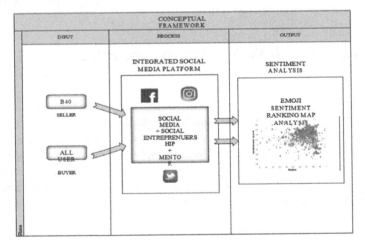

Fig. 1. Proposed conceptual framework.

This proposed conceptual framework consists of three components: input, process, and output. The input will consist of B40 community social entrepreneurs and all types of users (i.e. buyers on the social media trading platform). The second component is the trading process which is the core of this research (i.e., the integrated social media trading platform). Besides that, there is a mentoring part where the social media expert will become the user advisor to the B40 social entrepreneurs. The third component is the output where the inputs from the social media interactions are performed analyzed (i.e. sentiment analysis).

There are few features that will be included into this new proposed system. The features are shown below:

(a) **Single Interface with Single Sign On**

Single sign-on (SSO) is a session and user authentication service that permits a user to use one set of login credentials (e.g., name and password) to access multiple applications. The service authenticates the end user for all the applications the user has been given rights to and eliminates further prompts when the user switches applications during the same session. On the back end, SSO is helpful for logging user activities as well as monitoring user accounts. User can login into this application and then it's will automatically access all different type of user's social media account.

(b) **Trading Module**

Trading module is where the selling and buying activity. All the conversations with the customers will be displayed there. The store front is also part of the trading module.

(c) **Payment Module**

The payment module is a merchant service provided by an e-commerce application service provider that authorizes credit card or direct payments processing for e-businesses, online retailers, bricks and clicks, or traditional brick and mortar. Buyer will pay through this system and proceed with system confirmation.

(d) **Mentoring Module (Q & A)**

The mentoring module is about support from the expert and is aimed at encouraging the social entrepreneurs to manage their own business learning in order that they may maximize their potential, develop their skills, and improve their performance. Social entrepreneurs can ask advice from the expert on finding solution or improve their selling performance.

(e) **Reporting Module**

The reporting module is a collection of information organized in a narrative, graphic, or tabular form, prepared on ad hoc, periodic, recurring, regular, or as

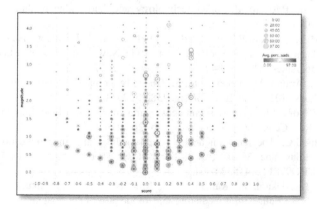

Fig. 2. Sentiment analysis module

required basis. All the user and buyer activity will be displayed there in most simple form that that user can understand easily.

(f) **Sentiment Analysis Module**

Sentiment analysis module, (refer Fig. 2) is about the use of natural language text processing, text analysis, computational linguistics, and biometrics to systematically identify, extract, quantify, and study affective states and subjective information. This analysis will determine which action is suitable to taken to improve the social entrepreneurship business activity.

5   Conclusion

Social media is a powerful medium for the community to interact among them. B40, is one of the groups in the community that using the social media as a platform for their business. Utilizing social media and forming of social entrepreneurship, the social entrepreneurs in the B40 community can maximize their income by social media integrated platform. With the addition of sentiment analysis, this community even can make a better decision for their business advancement and growth. Therefore, the proposed integrated social media trading platform in this paper is posited to provide an advantage to this community to enhance their use of social media as a trading platform as well as to improve their social entrepreneurship skills.

References

1. Report: Digital Malaysia: Increasing digital economic contribution for the nation (2012)
2. Arshad, N.H., Salleh, S.S., Aris, S.R.S., Janom, N., Mastuki, N.: Strategic analysis towards the formulation of micro sourcing strategic trusts. Int. J. Adv. Comput. Sci. Appl. 43–52 (2013)
3. Oprica, R.: Social networking for social entrepreneurship. Procedia - Soc. Behav. Sci. **92**, 664–667 (2013). doi:10.1016/j.sbspro.2013.08.735
4. Janom, N., Syazrah, W.N., Arshad, N.H., Salleh, S.S., Ruzaini, S., Aris, S., Mastuki, N.: Investigating the B40 crowd worker technology and knowledge readiness in Malaysia, pp. 12–15 (2014)
5. Bernama: SMEs, M40 and B40 expected to benefit from 2017 Budget—New Straits Times —Malaysia General Business Sports and Lifestyle News. https://www.nst.com.my/news/2016/10/181563/smes-m40-and-b40-expected-benefit-2017-budget
6. Gonçalves, P., Araújo, M., Benevenuto, F., Cha, M.: Comparing and combining sentiment analysis methods (2014). doi:10.1145/2512938.2512951
7. Perrin, A.: 65% of adults now use social networking sites – a nearly tenfold jump in the past decade. Pew Res. Cent. 2005–2015 (2015). doi:202.419.4372
8. Pan, B., Crotts, J.C.: Theoretical models of social media, marketing implications, and future research directions. Soc. Media Travel. Tour. Hosp. Theory, Pract. Cases 73–86 (2012). doi:10.1017/CBO9781107415324.004
9. Mohammed, J., Alekam, E., Kamariah, N., Mat, N., Nur, T., Tunku, A., Noraini, A., Kamaruddin, N.S.: Full, partial mediating and moderating play a significant role in online purchase items in Facebook among Facebook users (2014)

10. Zbuchea, A.: Social Entrepreneurship – a Perspective of the Young Romanians **4**, 409–426 (2016)
11. Abu-Saifan, S.: Social entrepreneurship: definition and boundaries. Technol. Innov. Manag. Rev. 22–27 (2012)
12. Choi, N., Majumdar, S.: Social entrepreneurship as an essentially contested concept: opening a new avenue for systematic future research. J. Bus. Ventur. **29**, 363–376 (2014). doi:10.1016/j.jbusvent.2013.05.001
13. Raudsaar, M., Kaseorg, M.: Social entrepreneurship as an alternative for disabled people **2**, 120–125 (2013). doi:10.5176/2010-4804
14. Braunerhjelm, P., Hamilton, U.S.: Social entrepreneurship – a survey of current research
15. Alvord, S.H., Brown, L.D., Letts, C.W.: J. Appl. Behav. Sci. (2004). doi:10.1177/0021886304266847
16. Cambria, E.: An introduction to concept-level sentiment analysis. In: Castro, F., Gelbukh, A., González, M. (eds.) MICAI 2013. LNCS, vol. 8266, pp. 478–483. Springer, Heidelberg (2013). doi:10.1007/978-3-642-45111-9_41
17. Liu, B.: Sentiment analysis and opinion mining. Direct **5**, 1–167 (2012). doi:10.2200/S00416ED1V01Y201204HLT016

Association Rule Mining Using Time Series Data for Malaysia Climate Variability Prediction

Rabiatul A.A. Rashid[1(✉)], Puteri N.E. Nohuddin[1],
and Zuraini Zainol[2]

[1] Institute of Visual Informatics, National University of Malaysia,
43600 Bangi, Selangor, Malaysia
rabiatul.rashid@gmail.com, puteri.ivi@ukm.edu.my
[2] Department of Computer Science,
Faculty of Science and Defence Technology,
National Defence University of Malaysia,
Sungai Besi Camp, 57000 Kuala Lumpur, Malaysia
zuraini@upnm.edu.my

Abstract. Many studies have been conducted to determine how data mining can be used in predicting climate change. Previous studies showed many data mining methods have been used in related to climate prediction, however classification and clustering methods are widely used to generate the climate prediction model. In this study, Association Rule Mining (ARM) is used to discover hidden rules in time series climate data from previous years and to analyze the relationship between the discovered rules. The dataset used in this study is a set of weather data from the Petaling Jaya observation station in Selangor for the year 2013 to 2015. This paper aims to utilize ARM for extracting behavioural patterns within the climate data that can be used to develop the prediction model for climate variability. The proposed framework is developed to provide a better approach in understanding how ARM can be used to find meaningful patterns in the climate data and generate rules that can be used to build a prediction model.

Keywords: Association rule mining · Climate variability · Climate prediction

1 Introduction

Climate change can be defined as trends in the average climate that happen over a long-term period, usually over decades or centuries. The earth's climate changes due to different factors such as natural changes in the earth's orbit, the amount of incoming sun radiation and also the effect of greenhouse gases. Global warming is one of the event of climate change that happen slowly and gradually.

However, climate variability is a phenomena in which the climate fluctuates from year to year variation, above or below a long-term average value [1]. It usually happens over a short period of time within months, seasons or even years. El Nino and El Nina are examples of events cause by climate variability. Current events of climate

© Springer International Publishing AG 2017
H. Badioze Zaman et al. (Eds.): IVIC 2017, LNCS 10645, pp. 120–130, 2017.
https://doi.org/10.1007/978-3-319-70010-6_12

variability can be addressed as risks associated with the future climate change [2]. Extreme changes in climate can affect human in many aspects such as in the production of agriculture, impact on food security and also in human health. Due to this factor, many researches have been done in predicting climate due to the need to reduce climate risk, whereby weather prediction models are one of the alternatives that can be used to determine future risk in changes of climate variability [3].

Observation station, which equipped with remote sensors like satellites and weather radars will generate a huge amount of time series climate data. The rapid growth of geographical information and availability of multi-source data has also contributed many climates qualitative analysis and one of the interesting technique that has been used is data mining technique [4].

Time series data is a collection of well-defined values that obtained from sequential measurement over time. Time series data mining is a process of discovering non trivial patterns of sequential data that contain measurable value over a time interval. Therefore, many studies have been conducted to see the suitability of time series analysis to be used in area such as predicting sales performance [5], disease epidemic detection for healthcare authorities [6], forecasting tourist demand [7], animal farming distribution [8] and also climate prediction [9].

Climate variability consists of time series data where knowledge can be extracted from the uncertain time series that can be used in climate prediction [10]. In this paper, ARM is used to generate rules and to build a prediction model using climate time series data. The study focuses on finding patterns and generate the suitability rules that can be used in predicting climate.

2   Previous Work

Data mining is a part of the process in Knowledge Discovery in Databases (KDD) [11], where data mining is used to extract knowledgeable information from the huge amount of data. Differ to standard statistical methods, data mining techniques are programmed to search for meaningful information without depending on the prior knowledge of the data, but the patterns discovered in the data are based on the data mining task that is used in the analysis [12]. The most commonly used techniques in data mining to predict climate are: clustering, classification, association rule mining, sequential pattern mining and also regression.

2.1   Data Mining in Climate Prediction

There are many studies that used data mining for climate prediction. The common techniques used in data mining are classification, clustering and also ARM. However, these methods are still popular research topics due to the need of searching for the most accurate technique in predicting climate. Climate prediction is known to be a complicated analysis because it involves many elements such as temperature, humidity, wind speed, rainfall and many more [13].

The target in climate variability prediction is to find significant changes that will affect human activities such as drought, heavy rainfall and also extreme temperature.

Many previous studies used several methods of data mining to build their prediction model, for example, in the study [12] both Artificial Neural Networks (ANN) and Decision Tree are used to develop classification rule for the prediction of future weather conditions using historical data. Meanwhile, [14] used k-Nearest Neighbor method in classification technique to build a weather prediction model. Another study by [15] used different methods in classification to build a rainfall prediction model based using the climate data. All studies show how data mining has proven to be significant to be used in climate prediction.

2.2 Association Rule Analysis in Climate Prediction

ARM is used to discover association and relations between the variables in databases. The two most popular algorithms in ARM are Apriori and FP-Growth, where Apriori aims to identify the frequent item sets that satisfied the minimum support and the generated rules that will satisfy the minimum confidence value [16]. Meanwhile FP-Growth uses a prefix-tree (FP-tree) data structure to store compressed and crucial information about the frequent item sets in the database. The FP-Growth algorithm will build conditional parameters based on the FP-tree structure to generate the full sets of frequent patterns [17]. Researchers have shown much interest to use ARM to build climate prediction model. In the study of [4, 18, 19], the researchers used an ARM approach to build their prediction models using climate data from the previous years. In classification and clustering algorithms, data needs to be categorized in a specific group. However, in ARM rules are discover from large data sets by discovering all relationships among data [18]. This method is considered relevant due to facts that climate prediction involves a variety of elements and factors.

2.3 Time Series Prediction

Time series data is a type of data that consist a real value that taken from a regular time interval. Time series data analysis is commonly used in weather and climate prediction, financial and marketing strategy [20]. Time series data mining is a combination of time series analysis and time series data mining. This method creates a process that can be used to discover temporal patterns that are reliable to do time series prediction [21]. The time series data are important in helping to build a prediction model. ARM using time series data can discover meaningful association relationships that occur with particular events of the time such as climate variability.

3 Methodology

3.1 Association Rule Mining

The method that we are using in this study is based on the process of discovering meaningful rules in the climate data. ARM is one of the techniques in data mining that can be used to extract meaningful associations, frequent patterns, and correlations between sets of items in the data repositories [22]. ARM is one of the technique in data mining that uses unsupervised data to discover rules from large data sets by discovering all knowledgeable relationships between the data [23]. The rules generated will then be analyzed and meaningful rules are used to show patterns and association in the climate data which then are extracted and used to develop the prediction model.

All rules in ARM are measured using the strength of threshold support and confidence. It is a form of $X \rightarrow Y$, where X and Y are item sets. The value of the support is calculated as follow:

$$\text{Support, } Supp(X) = X/T$$

$Supp(X)$ is where X shows how many times that the item occurs and T is the total number of the transaction.

The confidence of a rule is the percentage of transaction in T that contain X that also contain Y. It is calculated as:

$$\text{Confidence}(X \rightarrow Y) = Supp \ (X \cup Y)/Supp(X)$$

In a set of transactions T, the goal of ARM is to find all rules that is:

- Support $\geq$ *minsupp threshold*
- Confidence $\geq$ minconf threshold

where *minsup* and *minconf* are the corresponding support and confidence thresholds.

In this study, we will also look at the lift value if the rules generated. Lift value in ARM is the ratio of the confidence to expected confidence. Lift is one of the parameters to show interest in ARM analysis. It is calculated as:

$$\text{Lift} = \text{Confidence}/\text{Expected Confidence}$$

The lift value will give information about the increase in probability of generated rules.

3.2 Climate Variability Prediction Framework (CVPF)

In this study, we are using an approach that is suitable for analyzing the time series data on climate variability. In this CVPF approach, ARM is used to generate and discover meaningful pattern and rules within the climate data. Since the generated patterns and rules can be in a huge amount, clustering method is used to cluster the patterns and rules according to the attribute characteristics.

The CVPF consists of data analysis module that we develop to identify the rules that consists in the climate data variables and then to cluster the rules based on their similarities. In this framework (see Fig. 1), it consists 3 stages of (i) Data Processing, (ii) Rule Analysis and (iii) Prediction Model. In stage (i), it consists of two main activities that are data cleaning and data normalization. Data cleaning is a proses of identifying the inaccurate data from the datasets and replacing, or modifying, or deleting the data. Meanwhile, normalization is a proses of organizing the columns and tables of a relational database to reduce data redundancy and improve data integrity.

In the Data Processing stage, the data will be cleaned and data scheme will be produced and applied in the normalization process. The output from normalization will then be used in stage (ii) as input data.

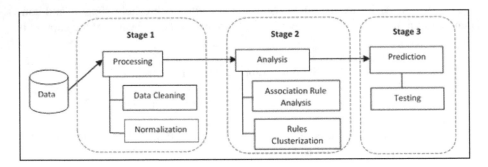

Fig. 1. Climate variability prediction framework (CVPF)

In stage (ii), ARM is used to analyze the data and to find the meaningful rules within the datasets. The FP-growth algorithm is one of the fastest and popular association rule algorithms for frequent item set mining. Based on the research [24], the major advantage of FP-Growth algorithm is, it uses compact data structure and eliminates repeated database scan. Therefore the information about the data set is greatly compressed. Due to these advantages, this study chose to use FP-Growth algorithm will be used to find patterns and to generate rules that will be used in the prediction model.

Generated patterns and rules will be analyzed and after all relevant rules identify, the next step is to cluster all the rules. In the rules *clusterization* process, all significant rules will be clustered based on their characteristics. This step will show the strength of the rules that will be used in the prediction. The prediction model will be built in stage (iii) and the model will be tested using the existing climate data to evaluate the proposed technique.

4 Experiment and Expected Outcome

The data used in this research is the climate data for Petaling Jaya, Selangor from the year 2013 to 2015 and the data was obtained from the Institute of Climate Change, The National University of Malaysia. It composed of monthly data for each year and the data details are as in Table 1.

Table 1. Details of attributes in dataset

Attribute name	Attribute type	Attribute measurement
Humidity	Double	Percentage of relative humidity, %
Temperature	Double	°C
Wind speed	Double	m/s
Rainfall	Double	mm
Number of rain days	Integer	days

In this experiment, a few support and confidence values were set to observe the number of rules generated by the algorithm. After conducting a few experiments, the value 15% support threshold and 70% confidence threshold had produced more significant and meaningful pattern that can be used in this analysis. Table 2 shows the details frequent sets, patterns that produce in each year analysis.

Table 2. Details of ARM analysis

Year	Support value	Confidence value	Number of lift rules	Number of confidence rules
2013	15	70	188	94
2014	15	70	288	160
2015	15	70	88	22

Figure 2 presents the total number of rules based on the confidence value generated for each year. For each year, the number of rules generated are different. However, for all three years the percentage of confidence for rules generated is 100% and 75%. The confidence value in ARM indicates how reliable this rule is. The higher the value of percentage, the more likely the variable occur in a group if it is known that all body variables are contained in that group.

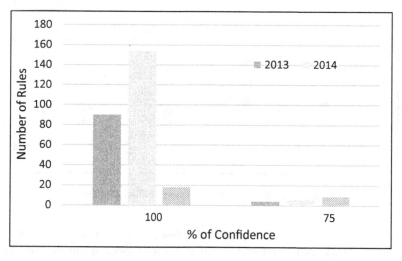

Fig. 2. Number of patterns based on percentage of confidence

From Fig. 2, the analysis of the rules generated are as below:

- For the year 2013, 94 rules were generated with the most frequent rules indicates meaningful relationship between variables for rainday ≥ 21.6 days. Rules for rainday ≤ 11.4 days and 14.8 < rainday < 18.2 days were also generated, however the number of rules describing for this month is less and is not significant to be used in climate prediction.

- Generated result for the year 2014 show that 161 rules were generated to show meaningful relationships between the attributes. The generated rules show a bigger range of months that can be used in climate prediction. The rules show detail relationship between variable for rainday $\geq$ 21.4 days, rainday < 7.6 days, 16.8 $\leq$ rainday < 21.4 days.
- In 2015, 98 rules were generated, and the most frequent rules generated are for 17.0 $\leq$ rainday < 20.0 days. Rules for other range of months were too few to be significant in predicting.

Data for year 2013 and 2014 generated more rules, showing the details of relationship among variables and more significant pattern that can be used in climate prediction compare with the result from year 2015.

Figure 3 shows the number of patterns generated based on the lift value. Lift value shows the significant strength of the rules to be used in the prediction model. Higher lift value means the pattern generated is more reliable to be in the prediction models. From Fig. 3, it indicates that patterns generated with a higher lift value in more reliable to be used in climate prediction model.

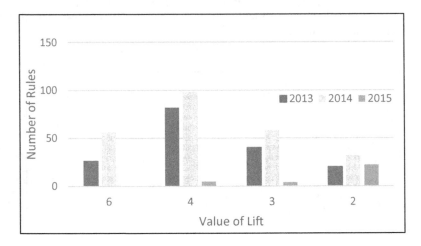

Fig. 3. Number of patterns based on the lift value

From the experiment, we can identify rules that can be used as rules in prediction, since the rules shows detailed information of all related factors in climate event such as to predict raining seasons. The selected patterns are based on the high confidence percentage. In Table 3 it shows the pattern that can be used to predict rain days. The patterns in this table show meaningful rules that can be used in climate prediction.

The rules in Table 3 show that in the year 2013, numbers of rules show a significant relationship for rainy days. From the rules, it shows that for rainday $\geq$ 21.6 days, the variables related are temperature < 27.62°C, windspeed < 1.06 m/s, humidity < 82.3%.

Table 3. Example of rules for rainy days

Year	Generated rules
2013	{rainday ≥ 21.6} → {humidity < 82.3, temperature < 27.62 windspeed < 1.06} 100.0
	{rainday ≥ 21.6} → {humidity < 82.3, temperature < 27.62} 100.0
	{rainday ≥ 21.6} → {humidity < 82.3, windspeed < 1.06} 100.0
2014	{humidity < 82.5 temperature < 27.46, windspeed < 0.9400000000000001 rainfall < 624.0} → {rainday ≥ 21.4} 100.0
	{humidity < 82.5 temperature < 27.46 windspeed < 0.9400000000000001} → {rainday ≥ 21.4} 100.0
	humidity < 82.5, windspeed < 0.9400000000000001, rainfall < 624.0} → {rainday ≥ 21.4} 100.0
2015	{humidity < 74.61999999999999, temperature < 28.64} → {17.0 ≤ rainday < 20.0} 100.0
	{humidity < 74.61999999999999, windspeed < 1.2 rainfall < 437.96} → {17.0 ≤ rainday < 20.0} 100.0
	{humidity < 74.61999999999999} → {17.0 ≤ rainday < 20.0} 75.0

For 2014, the significant rules generated shows pattern that for range rainday ≥ 21.4 days, the related variables are temperature < 27.46°C, windspeed < 0.94 m/s, humidity < 82.5% and rainfall < 624.00 mm.

Meanwhile, for the year 2015, the rules generated shows pattern for rainy days that happened in month < 3.2 that is between January until March. The patterns show for range 17.0 ≤ rainday < 20, the related variable value is temperature < 28.64°C humidity < 74.619%, windspeed < 1.2 m/s and rainfall < 437.96 mm.

From the generated rules, similar rules and pattern for each year are identified. The pattern will be used as a prediction model to predict the weather and climate in future years. In Fig. 4, it shows similarities of rules generated for number of raindays are between 19–21 days where most of the elements in that range are similar. This pattern shows that the Petaling Jaya area is expected to experience a significant rainfall of about 440 mm to 620 mm. The total amount of rainfall during this period is high and brings the risk of flash floods in the vicinity of Petaling Jaya. These expectations can be used by authorities such as the Department of Irrigation and Drainage to monitor the availability of drainage in Petaling Jaya to reduce the risk of flash floods.

Meanwhile, in Fig. 5, the resulting rule indicates that the amount of rain received would decrease between 350 mm to 160 mm only. This pattern shows that during this period the amount of rain received is greatly reduced compared when the raindays are between 7–15 days. This situation will affect water supply and this information can be used to control the water supply around Petaling Jaya to prevent the occurrence of water shortage problems to the surrounding residents.

From the analysis that we made, it shows that ARM can discover a huge number of meaningful patterns. In this study, we used time series based data to conduct experiments using FP-Growth algorithm and the results show plenty of meaningful rules that can be used in the prediction model.

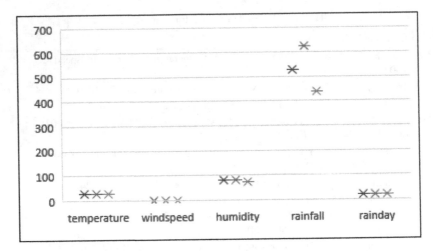

Fig. 4. Climate pattern in petaling jaya during rainning season for year 2013, 2014 and 2015

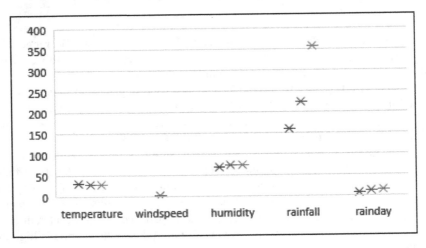

Fig. 5. Climate pattern in petaling jaya during dry season for year 2013, 2014 and 2015

5   Conclusion

From this study, it is proven that ARM can find the meaningful patterns in the climate data and generate rules that can be used to build a prediction model. The high confidence value and the lift value show the strength of the pattern and the rules are significant to the association. From the experiments, patterns of rain and dry seasons have been identified based on the rules generated. However, the data used in this study are based on monthly data. It is possible to have more detail analysis if daily climate data is used in future study.

Moving forward, this study will focus on how to cluster the generated rules and apply clustering method on the patterns. Each cluster will be grouped based on their rules characteristic and behavior. The result from this association rule clustering method will be used to build a prediction model. The model will the test with real data to valid the accuracy and suitability of the model in predicting climate.

Acknowledgements. Authors would like to thank Institute of Climate Change, The National University of Malaysia for providing the climate data to be used in this study.

References

1. Grant, M.S.: Climate variability and climate change (2010)
2. Siwar, C., Alam, M., Murad, A.W., Quasem, A.-A.: A review of the linkages between climate change, agricultural sustainability and poverty in Malaysia. Int. Rev. Bus. Res. Pap. **5**, 309–321 (2009)
3. Beer, T.: Climate variability and change: a perspective from the oceania region. Geosci. Lett. **1**, 5 (2014). doi:10.1186/2196-4092-1-5
4. Gouda, K.C., Chandrika, M.: Data mining for weather and climate studies. Int. J. Eng. Trends Technol. **32**, 29–32 (2016)
5. Yu, X., Liu, Y., Huang, X., An, A.: Mining online reviews for predicting sales performance: a case study in the movie domain. IEEE Trans. Knowl. Data Eng. **24**, 720–734 (2012). doi:10.1109/TKDE.2010.269
6. Rashid, R.A.A., Nohuddin, P.N.E., Zainol, Z., Kamarudin, S.: Dengue Epidemic Detection Using Data Mining Techniques for Healthcare Monitoring Initiative (2017, to appear)
7. Claveria, O., Torra, S.: Forecasting tourism demand to Catalonia: neural networks vs. time series models. Econ. Model. **36**, 220–228 (2014). doi:10.1016/j.econmod.2013.09.024
8. Nohuddin, P., Coenen, F., Christley, R.: The application of social network mining to cattle movement analysis: introducing the predictive trend mining framework. Soc. Netw. Anal. Min. **6**, (2016) doi:10.1007/s13278-016-0353-x
9. Esling, P., Agon, C.: Time-series data mining. ACM Comput. Surv. **45**, 1–34 (2012). doi:10.1145/2379776.2379788
10. Radzuan, N.F.M., Othman, Z., Bakar, A.A.: Uncertain time series in weather prediction. Procedia Technol. **11**, 557–564 (2013). doi:10.1016/j.protcy.2013.12.228
11. Ramamohan, Y., Vasantharao, K., Chakravarti, C.K., Ratnam, A.S.K.: A study of data mining tools in knowledge discovery process. Int. J. Soft Comput. Eng. **2**, 191–194 (2012)
12. Olaiya, F.: Application of data mining techniques in weather prediction and climate change studies. Int. J. Inf. Eng. Electron. Bus. **4**, 51–59 (2012). doi:10.5815/ijieeb.2012.01.07
13. Joshi, A., Kamble, B., Joshi, V., Kajale, K., Dhange, N.: Weather forecasting and climate changing using data mining application. Int. J. Adv. Res. Comput. Commun. Eng. **4**, 19–21 (2015). doi:10.17148/IJARCCE.2015.4305
14. Abrar, M., Tze, A., Sim, H., Shah, D., Khusro, S., Lecturer, S., Author, C.: Weather prediction using classification. Sci. Int. **26**, 2217–2223 (2014)
15. Zainudin, S., Jasim, D.S., Bakar, A.A.: Comparative analysis of data mining techniques for Malaysian rainfall prediction. Int. J. Adv. Sci. Eng. Inf. Technol. **6**, 1148–1153 (2016)
16. Suresh, H., Raimond, K.: Mining association rules from time series data using hybrid approaches. Int. J. Comput. Eng. Res. **3**, 181–189 (2013)

17. Kamsu-Foguem, B., Rigal, F., Mauget, F.: Mining association rules for the quality improvement of the production process. Expert Syst. Appl. **40**, 1034–1045 (2013). doi:10.1016/j.eswa.2012.08.039

18. Rana, D.P., Mistry, N.J., Raghuwanshi, M.M.: Novel usage of Gujarati calendar in temporal association rule mining for temperature analysis of Surat, India. In: Proceedings of 2014 International Conference Soft Computing Machine Intelligence ISCMI 2014, pp. 38–41 (2014). doi:10.1109/ISCMI.2014.20

19. Alshareef, A., Bakar, A.A., Hamdan, A.R., Abdullah, S.M.S., Jaafar, O.: Pattern discovery algorithm for weather prediction problem. In: Proceedings of 2015 Science and Information Conference SAI 2015. pp. 572–577 (2015). doi:10.1109/SAI.2015.7237200

20. Yoo, J.S.: Temporal data mining: similarity-profiled. In: Holmes, D.E., Jain, L.C. (eds.) Data Mining: Foundations and Intelligent Paradigms. Intelligent Systems Reference Library, vol. 23, pp. 29–47. Springer, Heidelberg (2012). doi:10.1007/978-3-642-23166-7_3

21. Mishra, S., Saravanan, C., Dwivedi, V.K., Pathak, K.K.: Discovering flood recession pattern in hydrological time series data mining during the post monsoon period - proquest. Comput. Appl. **90**, 35–44 (2014)

22. Qureshi, Z., Bansal, J., Bansal, S.: A survey on association rule mining in cloud computing. Int. J. Adv. Res. Comput. Commun. Eng. **3**, 318–321 (2013)

23. Liu, X., Zhai, K., Pedrycz, W.: An improved association rules mining method. Expert Syst. Appl. **39**, 1362–1374 (2012). doi:10.1016/j.eswa.2011.08.018

24. Kumar, B., Rukmani, K.: Implementation of web usage mining using APRIORI and FP growth algorithms. Int. J. Adv. Netw. Appl. **404**, 400–404 (2010)

An Ontology-Based Hybrid Recommender System for Internet Protocol Television

Mohammad Wahiduzzaman Khan, Gaik-Yee Chan[✉],
Fang-Fang Chua, and Su-Cheng Haw

Faculty of Computing and Informatics,
Multimedia University, Cyberjaya, Malaysia
gychan@mmu.edu.my

Abstract. Internet Protocol Television (IPTV) has gained popularity in providing TV channels and program choices to broad range of user. The service providers are attempting ways to attract more users' subscription and as from user point of view, they would like to have channel or program recommendations based on their preferences as well as public suggestions. This motivates us to propose an ontology-based hybrid recommender system. This system applies content-based and collaborative filtering in IPTV domain to increase users' satisfaction. The preliminary experimental results show that our proposed system works more effectively by eliminating the cold-start problem, over specialization, data sparsity and new item problems and efficiently by using the ontological user profile for computation of recommendations.

Keywords: Collaborative filtering · Content-based · Hybrid recommender system · Internet protocol television · Ontology

1 Introduction

One of the benefits of Internet Protocol Television (IPTV) is that it carries a broader catalog of videos for a wider range of demographics and tastes. Hence users have more options to choose from. However, human beings are pretty bad at choosing between many options. We may get overwhelmed, thus leading to making poor choices or perhaps choosing none of the many options. Consequently, we require intelligent system of predicting whether a user will be interested in a particular item or not and such an intelligent system is known as a recommender system. Significant amount of research in the field of recommender system have been carried out since the mid-1990s [1–7] till recent years [8–13]. Generally, there are two main approaches towards prediction and recommendation. One is the collaborative filtering approach and the other content-based. These two traditional approaches also tag along with many problems such as the cold-stat problem, the new user or item problem, over specialized problem and so on that needed to be resolved before quality recommendation could be produced.

Hence, hybrid approach, combining content-based, collaborative filtering, knowledge-based and/or ontological approach evolve for improving quality of recommendations. Ontology, a new trend in recommendation system, represents shared

© Springer International Publishing AG 2017
H. Badioze Zaman et al. (Eds.): IVIC 2017, LNCS 10645, pp. 131–142, 2017.
https://doi.org/10.1007/978-3-319-70010-6_13

conceptualization in certain domains [13]. Ontology is used to define sets of concepts relevant to a domain and the relationships between these concepts in a way inter-pretable by both human and machine. When designing a new recommender system, it is very important to select a suitable recommendation approach which will produce satisfactory recommendations to the users effectively and efficiently.

Therefore, in this paper, we propose using ontological user profile for a hybrid (content-based with collaborative filtering) recommendation system known as OHRS. The preliminary results from our experiments using dataset in the IPTV domain do indeed shows that OHRS performs more effectively and efficiently than purely content-based or collaborative filtering approach.

The organization of the paper is as follows, Sect. 2 discusses related works, Sect. 3 describes our proposed ontology-based hybrid recommender system, OHRS, Sect. 4 presents performance evaluation of OHRS and Sect. 5 concludes with discussion on future works.

2   Background and Related Works

The following sub-sections describe the recommender systems which can be broadly categorized into collaborative filtering, content-based, and hybrid [14].

2.1   Collaborative Filtering Approach

Collaborative filtering represents a process that filters items based on users' opinions. This approach is categorized into user-based and item-based approach [1–3].

User-based or memory-based filtering represents users as vectors in the space of size m, the number of items in the system. User-based collaborative filtering recom-mends items for users in two steps. First it finds similar user in terms of rating pattern on items with the target user. Next, it predicts items for target users by using the ratings of those users with similar rating patterns.

The disadvantage of this approach is its degraded efficiency because the process of finding similar users requires s^2 vector multiplications, where vector length is equal to m and s is the number of users in the system [11]. This approach thus has performance and scaling issues.

Under the item-based or model-based collaborative filtering approach, similarity of items is determined by ratings provided by other users on a particular item. For example, the movie "Game of thrones" with genre as Action, actor is Emilia Clarke. In this example, the movie is represented by features used by content-based approach. For another example, "Game of thrones" is represented based on users' rating, User 1 rated it 5, User 2 rated it 3, User 3 rated it 1, and User 4 rated it 5. Item-based collaborative filtering approach is thus more suitable to be used for this second type of representation.

Initially, a model is built to find similarities of all pairs of items. Next, it uses the most similar items to a target user's already-rated items for generation of recommen-dations for the target user. For example, if User 1, User 2 and User 3 all rated Item 1 with high values. Both User 1 and User 3 also rated high for Item 2 and User 2 has not try Item 2 yet so item-based collaborative approach may recommend Item 2 to User 2.

Nevertheless, traditional collaborative filtering approach has limitations, for example, the new user or new item problem and data sparsity problem. When there is a new user, not much information is known about this new user's preferences. For collaborative filtering approach, the system has to learn the new user's preferences through other users' ratings. One way to resolve this problem is by hybrid of content-based and collaborative filtering approach. Research in [15] has proposed various techniques in order to address this problem.

Collaborative filtering approach depends highly on users' ratings. Hence, only when a new item has gotten a substantial amount of ratings, then it will be recommended to a user. This new item problem could be resolved using hybrid-based approach.

If available data is very little as compared to predicted data in a recommender system, then data sparsity problem arises. For example, in a movie recommender system, some movies might have been rated by a small number of users. These movies will not be recommended to a user even though they have been rated highly by this small group of users. One way to resolve this issue is to use user information for computation of recommendations. Two users will not only be similar if they rate the same item similarly but also share some similar demographic information such as age, gender and so on [3].

2.2 Content-Based Approach

Content-based approach is also known as cognitive filtering. One such research in content-based recommender system is [5]. Content-based recommender system recommends items based on item profile as well as user profile. The content of every item consists of features or attributes that give meaningful descriptions to the item. For example, the item 'Movie' has features such as Genre, Actor and Director that describe that particular movie. The user profile is represented with user profile items such as ratings for items. If a user likes Action type of movie and watches "The dark knight", most likely, this user will also like "The dark knight rises". The reason being both of the movies share the same genre, actor and director.

However, before implementing a content-based recommender system, several issues need to be considered. First, an efficient method has to be used to extract related features from the items automatically. In addition, these features have to be represented in such a way that both the user profile and the items are linked in a meaningful way. Third, the machine learning algorithm should be able to learn the user's profile based on identified items. It can then make recommendations using the learned user's profile [4].

Content-based approach suffers from various shortcomings and one of these is limited content analysis. Content-based approach has to work within a limited range of features which are associated with the items the recommender system wants to recommend. In order to get a sufficient set of features, the content is automatically parsed. Otherwise, the features have to be manually assigned to the items. However, it will not be practical to manually assign attributes to items because resources are limited [1]. It is mentioned in [4] that automatic information retrieval technique could be used to extract features from text documents. But automatically extract features from multimedia data that are graphical and video in nature would be difficult. Additionally, if two items have the same features, they could not be distinguished. For example, a text-based documents represented by keywords cannot be distinguished by content-based systems whether one is well-written or the other badly written [4].

Over specialization seems to be a major problem of content-based approach. When a recommender system recommends items to a user using user profile, item profile and user's previous transactions, it will be confined within that user's choices, thus providing the same sort of recommendations all the time. For example, for a person who never watches a super-hero movie, he or she will never be recommended with any great super-hero movie of all time.

A content-based recommender system will only work well when the user has rated the items in a sufficient number of times before it can really understand the user's preferences to provide reliable recommendations. In such a case, the new user who has not rated enough number of items may not get recommendations in an accurate manner [4]. Nevertheless, this problem could be resolved by hybrid-based approach.

2.3   Hybrid Approach

Hybrid recommender systems, by combining different recommendation techniques, aim to perform better by eliminating shortcomings of the conventional approach. Conventional approaches are for example, collaborative filtering, content-based, and knowledge-based. Consequently, various hybrid recommendation techniques evolved with the aim to produce outputs which could outperform any single conventional approach. Some researches involved in this area are [4, 8, 9, 11]. Unlike the first two conventional approaches which applies learning algorithms, knowledge-based approach mainly exploit domain knowledge by making inferences on users' needs and preferences. Nevertheless, the most common hybridizing methodology is still combining content-based with collaborative filtering.

Research in [4] has also shown that hybrid recommender system using knowledge-based approach could address the cold-start problem. Cold-start problem occurs when learning-based techniques are used in collaborative filtering and content-based approaches. During machine learning phase, these approaches most often, require users to input their ratings or preferences manually which in a way is difficult to be obtained.

Traditional recommender systems that are predicting user rating uses very little information about the user [6]. It does not take advantages of user behavior. For example, classical collaborative filtering approaches rely explicitly on user ratings rather than user interest on particular concept or feature. Thus, traditional recommendation approaches including hybrid recommendation approach perform poorly on small amount of data [6].

Traditional recommender system, both content-based and collaborative filtering approach, suffers from scalability problem. This is due to the computation to obtain the nearest neighbors increases with the number of user in the system [6]. Singular value decomposition coupled with neural network seems to be an efficient technique for resolving the scalability problem [2].

Ontological recommender system sets a new trend in recommendation systems. Some research done in ontology-based recommender systems are [6, 7, 12, 13]. Ontology deals with the concepts and their interrelations of a specific domain [13]. By representing the user profile and recommendable items ontologically, preferences would be in more detailed and richer, thus better than the standard keywords-based representation. In ontology, terms are interpreted with other terms following their semantic relations. The hierarchical structure of ontology has made analysis of preferences at various levels of abstraction. With tremendous modeling and reasoning power, ontology could be used to store and exploit user preferences, thus allowing a greater margin of knowledge to be shared and reused. The ontology-based recommender system as proposed in [13] uses spreading activation technique to learn the user profile dynamically too.

3 Our Proposed Recommender System-OHRS

An over view architecture of our proposed ontological-based hybrid recommender system, OHRS, is as shown in Fig. 1 (read from left to right, top to bottom in the sequence of number 1, 2, and so on).

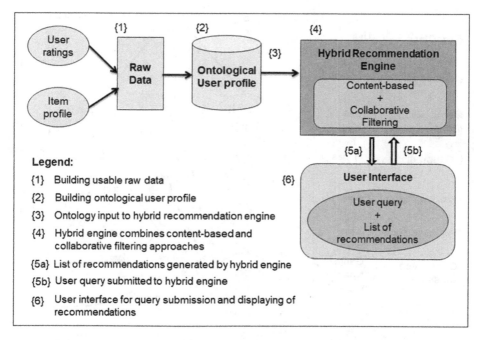

Fig. 1. An overview of OHRS

As seen from Fig. 1 (step 1), our OHRS makes use of MovieLens 100K dataset [16] in order to generate ontological user profile and item profile. The MovieLens dataset consists of two separate data sets, one dataset (Movie dataset) contains about 9K of records with movie id, movie titles and genre. Another data set (Rating dataset) contains 100K records with 671 users providing 6500 movies' ratings. Records in these two data sets are combined and formed into our raw data set (Rating-Genre dataset) consisting of about 800 records of 10 users (user id from 1 to 10) with average 80 different movies of genre per user rating, where user id 1 rated only the least number, i.e. 20.

As mentioned in [13] that ontology could be used to formally and semantically represent a shared concept of a specific domain. Ontology defines concepts and their relationships relevant to a specific domain and represent them in both human and machine readable form. Based on this ontology concept, thus, each element in the movie domain could be linked hierarchically and semantically [10]. Thus for our proposed system, the four columns of data such as User id, Movie id, Rating and Genre from the Rating-Genre dataset are transformed to a hierarchically and semantically linked data structure as shown in Fig. 2a. These hierarchically and semantically linked structures shall serve as the inputs to the ontological user profile (Fig. 1, step 2).

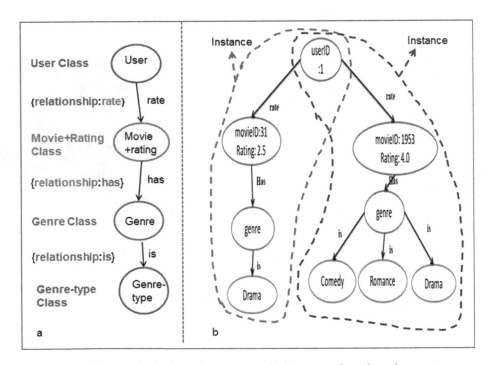

Fig. 2. (a) A generic ontology data structure (b) Instances of ontology data structure

Referring to Fig. 2a, classes (user, movie, genre, genre-type) are used to represent the different concepts of the movie domain in an abstract manner. The property belonging to two classes are semantically linked through a relationship, for example, the user class and movie-rating class has 'rate' relationship, i.e. user rates a movie. Each class also has a certain number of attributes, for example, the movie class has movie id as an attribute and rating attribute values ranging from 1–5 where value 1 is the lowest rating and the value 5 is the highest rating for that particular movie.

The ontology user profile database consists of instances of such hierarchically and semantically linked data structures (Fig. 2b showing two instances) where an instance represents a specific individual belonging to that class and has particular values for each of its attributes. For example, one instance of user id 1 rated movie id 31 with rating 2.5 where the movie genre is a Drama. At another instance, user id 1 rated movie id 1953 with rating 4.0 where the movie genre is a Comedy, Romance as well as Drama.

Due to ratings are subjectively provided by each user, there is a need to normalize the rating values. We normalize user rating by using Eq. 1 [6].

$$W_{a,n} = \frac{r_{a,n}}{5} \tag{1}$$

where $W_{a,n}$ is the weighted preferences value of a user a for an item n. Weighted preferences values range from 0 to 1 where 1 is the highest preference and $r_{a,n}$ is user a's ratings for item n in the scale of 0 to 5. We then formulate ontological user profile by using Eq. 2 [6],

$$W_{a,f} = \frac{1}{N} \sum_{f \in Features(dn)} W_{a,n} \tag{2}$$

where N is the number of movies watched by user a. $W_{a,f}$ is the ontological user preferences value of user a for a feature f, feature f is the genre of a movie, and d_n is the list of movies for feature f. Our ontological user profile containing normalized rating values (weighted preferences values) are tabulated as shown in Table 1.

Table 1. Ontological user profile with weighted preferences values

User id #	Genre						
	Action	Animation	Adventure	Children	Comedy	Crime	Documentary
User id 1	0.1	0.06	**0.165**	0.05	0.07	0.01	0
User id 2	0.142	0.029	0.103	0.034	0.192	0.053	0
User id 10	0.226	0	0.165	0	0.139	0.07	0

Table 1 shows partial ontological user profile with weighted preferences values as computed from Eq. 2 for three users, user id 1, 2, and 10. These preferences values range between 0 to 1 where 0 means lowest preference and 1 means highest preference. User id 1 rated a total of 20 movies, and out of these 20 rated movies, 8 are Adventure type of movies.

Table 2 displays the 8 Adventure movies rated by user id 1 with original ratings and normalized ratings where the normalized ratings are calculated using Eq. 1.

Table 2. Normalized ratings for user id 1

Movie id	1129	1287	1371	1405	2105	2193	2294	2968
Original rating	2.0	2.0	2.5	1.0	4.0	2.0	2.0	1.0
Normalized rating	0.4	0.4	0.5	0.2	0.8	0.4	0.4	0.2

After calculating normalized user rating, we then calculate ontological concept value for user id 1 for concept Adventure using Eq. 2. For example, N, the total number of movies rated by user id 1 is 20 and d_n is the list of movies with Adventure feature (refer to Table 2, Row 3). Applying these values to Eq. 2,

$$W_{1,adventure} = \frac{1}{20} * (0.4 + 0.4 + 0.5 + 0.2 + 0.8 + 0.4 + 0.4 + 0.2)$$

$$W_{1,adventure} = \frac{1}{20} * 3.3$$

so $W_{1,adventure} = 0.165$ as shown in Table 1 (Column 4, Row 3). This is interpreted as user id 1 has highest preference value of 0.165 for Adventure type of movie and preference value of 0 for Documentary type of movie. This means user id 1 mostly prefers watching Adventure type of movie over the other types of movies.

Refer to Fig. 1 (step 4), the hybrid recommendation engine consisting of combination of content-based and collaborative filtering approaches will make use of the ontological user profile data to generate similarity neighborhoods. To compute the similarity among users, the ontological distance of each user profile is calculated from Euclidean distance formula [12] Eq. 3,

$$distance_{a,b} = \sqrt{\sum_{f \in features} \left(W_{a,f} - W_{b,f}\right)^2} \tag{3}$$

where $distance_{a,b}$ represents ontological similarity between user a and user b. Once all the distances have been computed then by inversing this value, we get the user-user similarity value. For inversing the value, we use Eq. 4, [12].

$$Sim(a,b) = \frac{1}{distance_{a,b}} \tag{4}$$

These inversed user-user similarity values for 10 users are tabulated as shown in Table 3. We are inversing values in order to achieve some meaningful values for recommendation calculation using Eq. 5 [12].

As shown in Table 3, user-user similarity value for user id 1 and user id 2 is $Sim(1, 2)$ = 3.749 (Table 3: Column 2, Row 3 and Column 3, Row 2) and user-user similarity value for user id 1 and user id 6 is $Sim(1, 6)$ = 4.918 (Table 3: Column 2, Row 7, or Column 7, Row 2), which represents the highest values for user id 1. This means, based on ontological concept, user id 1 and user id 6 have similar rating patterns on similar movies.

Table 3. User-user similarity values for 10 users

User ID	1	2	3	4	5	6	7	8	9	10
1	0	3.749	3.049	3.336	2.614	4.918	4.342	3.517	2.517	4.433
2	3.749	0	8.074	3.704	4.454	6.473	3.716	6.515	6.085	5.116
3	3.049	8.074	0	3.555	3.61	5.868	3.585	6.996	4.793	4.443
4	3.336	3.704	3.555	0	3.498	5.387	6.768	3.623	2.628	3.698
5	2.614	4.454	3.61	3.498	0	3.401	2.867	3.275	4.127	2.872
6	4.918	6.473	5.868	5.387	3.401	0	5.959	7.342	3.46	6.236

After calculating user-user similarity values, we need to find the k most similar users or the nearest similar user neighborhood. For our experiment, we use $k = 5$, i.e. five most similar users. The k most similar users can be calculated by sorting the user-user similarity values in descending order for target user than pick the top k users from the list. Referring to Table 3, Row 2 for user id 1, the five most similar users are user id 6, 10, 7, 2, and 8.

In order to generate top-N movie as recommendation for a user, we need to calculate predicted user rating by using Eq. 5 [12],

$$P_{a,i} = \overline{r_a} + \frac{\sum_{b \in V} Sim(a,b) * (r_{b,i} - \overline{r_b})}{\sum_{b \in V} Sim(a,b)} \qquad (5)$$

where $P_{a,i}$ is the predicted rating of user a for movie i. $Sim(a,b)$ is the similarity value of user a and b. This evaluation even aims to generate recommendation that the user has not seen before. For example, user id 1 has not yet watched five movies (Table 4, Row 1) with movie ids 1204, 293, 1148, 1223 and 745. However, these movies have been watched by the peers (or neighbors: user id 6, 10, 7, 2 and 8), therefore, we compute the predicted scores on these items.

Table 4. Predicted user rating for user id 1

Movie id	1204	293	1148	1223	745
Predicted user rating (user id~1)	4.289	4289	4.123	4.123	4.123
User rating (Neighbors)	5	5	5	5	5
Genre/ concept	Adventure/ Drama/War	Action/Crime/ Drama/Thriller	Animation/ Children/ Comedy/ Crime	Adventure/Animation/ Children/Comedy/Sci-Fi	Animation/ Children/ Comedy

The recommendation list (refer to Table 4, Row 2) is then sorted according to the user's predicted rating for each item in descending order. Therefore, top-N items with high ranking in users predicted ratings are included in the recommendation list.

The top-N recommendations are displayed through the user interface (Fig. 1, steps 5–6). The recommendation list is tabulated as shown in Table 4 for user id 1. Here we are showing top-5 recommendations for user id 1 with the predicted rating and other neighbors' original ratings.

For our initial implementation, the user interface shows only the recommendation list pushed out from our OHRS. For future implementation, the OHRS user interface shall capture more context-aware attributes such as location, duration or time of watching the movie or user demographic such as age, education level, incomes and so on to facilitate recommendations to be pulled out from the system.

4 Performance Evaluation of OHRS

This section discusses the performance of our OHRS through a few scenarios. Each scenario represents a typical problem encountered by traditional content-based or collaborative filtering approach. Such problems could be the cold-start problem, over-specialization problem, new user or the new item problem, the data sparsity problem and degraded efficiency issue.

Now if we use the same raw dataset (Rating-Genre dataset) and calculate user-user similarity based on Pearson correlation formula, then run a query regarding top-N recommendation for user id 1 with traditional collaborative filtering approach, it will not be able to recommend a single item. This is due to the fact that user id 1 has not rated items that are rated by any of the other users from user id 2 to user id 10.

However, our OHRS has eliminated such problem because our approach is not just considering user rating on the same item but it also considers user likelihood for a particular ontological feature or concept. As shown in Table 4, OHRS is able to recommend the top-5 predicted item for user id 1 thus eliminated the cold-start problem which traditional recommendation system has failed to do.

For our experimental purpose, we added manually a new item, movie id 521356 and also put 5.0 as user id 6's rating for the newly inserted item. We then run our algorithm again to find the predicted user rating for user id 1. The predicted user rating for movie id 521356 as calculated for user id 1 is 4.015, close to the original rating of 5 from user id 6. Recommending a new item to a certain user is made possible using our OHRS, thus solving the new item problem.

The ontological data set for our experiment consists of only 10 users with their ratings, in which user id 1 has rated the least number of movies, i.e. 20. Even with this small number of users and ratings, our OHRS is able to recommend top-5 recommendations based on predicted ratings for user id 1 as shown in Table 4. Hence, data sparsity does not represent a problem for our system.

Our OHRS will not confine a user's taste only on the concept that he or she favors most. It also broadens the user's taste by providing recommendations for various concepts based on the ontological user profile. As shown in Table 4, Row 4, we are recommending top-5 items for user id 1 in which the genre belonging to other concepts such as Drama, Comedy, Sci-Fi and so on although user id 1 has highest preferences value for the Adventure type of movies.

Traditional content-based, collaborative filtering or hybrid approach requires extensive computation and memory storage thus creating efficiency issue. For example, if n is the number of item in the system, we would need $n * n$ matrix for computing item-item similarity values. Similarly, if m is the number of user in the system, it will take $m * m$ matrix to compute similarity among users. However, generating recommendation from our ontological user profile database will not requires $n * n$ or $m * m$ matrices for computation of item-item or user-user similarity values. This is due to the fact that data in our ontological user profile database are represented in classes and stored as instances for easy and fast access as compared to the traditional rows and columns representation.

5 Conclusion and Future Work

In this paper, we have demonstrated that our OHRS does indeed is more effective and efficient than some traditional content-based and collaborative filtering recommender systems. It can more effectively recommend items by eliminating problems such as cold-start, new item, sparsity and over specialization. Moreover, it is able to perform more efficiently due to the fact that it does not require extensive matrices computation and memory storage.

Nevertheless, further enhancements can be explored from ontology-based knowledge technologies such as group oriented recommendation and query driven recommendation. To improve further the quality of recommendation, it may be possible to add more context-aware attributes such as location, duration or time of watching the movie or user demographic such as age, education level, incomes and so on to the OHRS. Performance evaluation could then be based on large and real-time datasets for prediction of user ratings and recommendation on the basis of 10 to 100 nearest neighbors. Additionally, for performance bench marking, Root Mean Square Error (RMSE) and Mean Absolute Error (MAE) could be used. These measures compare the predicted with the actual ratings and provide an indication that the lower their values, the higher would be the accuracy.

Acknowledgement. This work is supported by the funding of TM R&D from the Telekom Malaysia, Malaysia.

References

1. Shardanand, U., Maes, P.: Social information filtering: algorithms for automating "word of mouth". In: Human Factors in Computing Systems Conference, pp. 210–217 (1995)
2. Billsus, D., Pazzani, M.J.: Learning collaborative information filters. In: 5th International Conference on Machine Learning, pp. 46–54 (1998)
3. Pazzani, M.J.: A framework for collaborative, content-based, and demographic filtering. Artif. Intell. Rev. **13**, 393–408 (1999)
4. Burke, R.: Hybrid recommender systems: survey and experiments. User Model. User-Adap. Inter. **12**(4), 331–370 (2002)

5. Pazzani, M.J., Billsus, D.: Content-based recommendation systems. In: Brusilovsky, P., Kobsa, A., Nejdl, W. (eds.) The Adaptive Web. LNCS, vol. 4321, pp. 325–341. Springer, Heidelberg (2007). doi:10.1007/978-3-540-72079-9_10
6. Cantador, I., Bellogín, A., Castells, P.: A multilayer ontology-based hybrid recommendation model. AI Commun. 21(2–3), 203–210 (2008)
7. Middleton, S.E., Roure, D.D., Shadbolt, N.R.: Ontology-based recommender systems. In: Staab, S., Studer, R. (eds.) Handbook on Ontologies. IHIS, pp. 779–796. Springer, Heidelberg (2009). doi:10.1007/978-3-540-92673-3_35
8. Bambini, R., Cremonesi, P., Turrin, R.: A recommender system for an IPTV service provider: a real large-scale production environment. In: Ricci, F., Rokach, L., Shapira, B., Kantor, P. (eds.) Recommender Systems Handbook, pp. 299–300. Springer, Boston (2011). doi:10.1007/978-0-387-85820-3_9
9. Park, D.H., Kim, H.K., Choi, I.Y., Kim, J.K.: A literature review and classification of recommender systems research. Expert Syst. Appl. 39, 10059–100072 (2012)
10. Carrer-Neto, W., Hernandez-Alcaraz, M.L., Valencia-Garcia, R., Garcia-Sanchez, F.: Social knowledge-based recommender system. Application to the movies domain. Expert Syst. Appl. 39, 10990–11000 (2012)
11. Pripuzic, K., Zarko, I.P., Podobnik, V. Lovrek, I.,Cavka, M., Petkovic, I., Stulic, P., Gojceta, M.: Building an IPTV VoD recommender system: an experience report. In: 12th International Conference on Telecommunications, pp. 155–162. IEEE (2013)
12. Zhang, Z., Gong, L., Xie, J.: Ontology-based collaborative filtering recommendation algorithm. In: Liu, D., Alippi, C., Zhao, D., Hussain, A. (eds.) BICS 2013. LNCS, vol. 7888, pp. 172–181. Springer, Heidelberg (2013). doi:10.1007/978-3-642-38786-9_20
13. Bahramian, Z., Abbaspour, R.A.: An Ontology-based tourism recommender system based on spreading activation model. In: International Conference on Sensors and Models in Remote Sensing and Photogrammetry, pp. 83–90 (2015)
14. Adomavicius, G., Tuzhilin, A.: Toward the next generation of recommender systems: a survey of the state-of-the-art and possible extensions. IEEE Trans. Knowl. Data Eng. 17(6), 734–749 (2005)
15. Rashid, A.M., Albert, I., Cosley, D., Lam, S.K., McNee, S.M., Konstan, J.A., Riedl, J.: Getting to know you: learning new user preferences in recommender systems. In: International Conference of Intelligent User Interfaces, pp. 127–134 (2002)
16. Grouplens, Movielens 100K Dataset. http://grouplens.org/datasets/movielens/100k/

Self-Regulated Learning and Online Learning: A Systematic Review

Noor Latiffah Adam[(⊠)], Fatin Balkis Alzahri, Shaharuddin Cik Soh,
Nordin Abu Bakar, and Nor Ashikin Mohamad Kamal

Faculty of Computer and Mathematical Sciences, Universiti Teknologi MARA,
40450 Shah Alam, Selangor, Malaysia
{latiffah, shahar, nordin,
nor_ashikin}@tmsk.uitm.edu.my, bieybalkis@gmail.com

Abstract. Self-regulated learning (SRL) is an academically effective form of learning, which learners must set their goals and make plans before starting to learn. As an ongoing process, learners need to monitor and regulate their cognition, motivation, and behavior as well as reflect on their learning process. These processes will be repeated as a cyclic process. The emerging technologies have changed the learning environments. Technology delivers teaching to learners via online. In online learning, information of education and learners do not share the same physical setting. Online learning should provide opportunities for learners to master necessary tasks. Online learners may use SRL strategies. In this research, we have collected, synthesized, and analyzed 130 articles on various topics related to SRL that published from 1986 to 2017, focusing on online learning and mathematics. We noted several models, phases, and few other topics discussed under SRL.

Keywords: Online learning · Self-regulated learning · Strategies · Mathematics

1 Introduction

As the technology emerged, online learning had become a popular form of education today. Within the past decade, it has contributed toward a major impact on education and the trend is increasing. Online learning is a way of studying for an internationally recognized qualification without needing to attend classes. It takes place over the Internet. Online learning is catalyzing a pedagogical shift in how we teach and learn. There is a shift away from top-down lecturing and passive learners to a more interactive, collaborative approach in which learners and instructor co-create the learning process. Learners should use an appropriate strategy to make sure they can learn from the online learning environment. One of the suitable strategies is self-regulated learning (SRL).

There were many educational researchers have conducted research on SRL. Zimmerman [56] stated that American educational leaders stressed on the importance of individuals assuming personal responsibility and control for their own acquisition of knowledge and skills. The implication are the learners must become active as they are self-regulated learners. SRL requires both will and skill from the learners. Therefore

© Springer International Publishing AG 2017
H. Badioze Zaman et al. (Eds.): IVIC 2017, LNCS 10645, pp. 143–154, 2017.
https://doi.org/10.1007/978-3-319-70010-6_14

education should help learners to be aware of their own thinking, to be strategic and to direct their motivation toward valuable goals. Learners learn to be their own teachers or masters as the final goals. This means that learners need to move from teaching to self-reflective practice [59]. For this research, we will focus on mathematics subject. Mathematical understanding is typically conceived to occupational success and personal management in daily life. Therefore mathematics is a core discipline in education across primary, secondary, and higher education curricula [17]. There are many research focus on mathematics subject in relation to self-efficacy beliefs, motivation, and mathematics achievement [6, 32, 36, 40–42, 44, 49]. Usually, learners will have some difficulty in order to understand mathematical problem texts and perceiving alternative ways of solving the problems, and also a lack of confidence when calculating the solutions. Learners' problem-solving difficulties do not always from lack of mathematical knowledge but from ineffective activation of their knowledge [47]. This could happen because learners are lack of metacognitive skills that need control, monitor, and reflect on solutions processes. With the existence of online learning, learners could master the mathematics subject as there are many resources available online. In online learning, when learners use strategies that are related to self-regulation, they can regulate their personal functioning and benefit from the online learning environments.

1.1 Online Learning

The growth of technology has changed the ways of learners to study. In daily life, the learner is surrounded with digital devices and they do not need to expand extra effort to get used to them as technology is assumed to be a natural part of the environment [14]. This has given the learners more learning opportunities and help them to master in their learning. There are many definitions of online learning and it is described as a way of instruction via computer or mobile devices with Internet connections. Delen and Liew [14] said that online learning is "the use of the Internet to access learning materials; to interact with the content, instructor, and other learners; and to obtain support during the learning process, to acquire knowledge, to construct personal meaning, and to grow from the learning experience". Online learning also has different terms used to describe it, one of the terms is e-learning.

With the introduction of computer and Internet, online learning or e-learning tools and delivery methods have been expanded. The first Mac in 1980's enabled learners to have computers in their homes hence making it easier for them to learn about particular subjects and develop certain skills sets. Then in the following decade, virtual learning environments began truly thriving with learners can gain access to online information and e-learning opportunities [60]. These opportunities give learners to learn by themselves and enhance their skills in the study. While studying in the classroom, the instructor may not be able to focus entirely on each of learners, this will likely to cause certain learners who do not understand what have been taught. Hence learners may need to learn and revise by themselves. Therefore, online learning can play a big role and help learners to learn. While learning via online learning, learners need to use specific strategies to make sure they can learn and benefit from it. The specific strategies that learners can use are self-regulated learning.

1.2 Self-Regulated Learning

Self-regulated is not a mental ability or academic performance skills. It is defined as a self-directive process by which learners transform their mental ability into academic skills. Those abilities will control over learner's own thoughts, feelings, motivations, and actions within the external environment that relate to acts of self-regulation [5]. Those abilities of skills are important for learning both and beyond the formal learning environment.

SRL is described as being a master of their own learning [56]. The learners take control of metacognitive, motivational, and behavioral aspects of their learning [26, 33, 36, 51, 53, 56]. Self-regulated learners who plan, organize, self-instruct, self-monitor, and self-evaluate at the various stage during learning process is called metacognitive. For motivationally is where the learners perceive themselves as competent, self-efficacious, and autonomous. Lastly for behaviorally, the learners select, structure, and create environments that optimize the learning. The learners' self-regulated thoughts and actions will be oriented toward achieving the learning goals. Hence the learners become active seekers and processors of information. They are aware when they know a fact or possess a skill and when they do not. The learners also will always seek out for information when need and take necessary steps to master it. They will investigate, monitor, and modify learning to achieve the goals. These characteristics are important for learners who are near to completion of formal learnings.

There is a self-oriented feedback loop in which learners monitor the effectiveness of their learning methods or strategies and respond to feedback in a variety of ways [43]. Other article suggested a cyclical model consists of three (3) phases [57]. The first phase is called Forethought phase which includes the key processes of goal setting and social modeling to set the stage for action. Then, the second phase is Performance Control phase which involves processes that occur during learning. Finally is Self-Reflection phase which occurs after performance phase. Learners will react to their effort by self-evaluating their progress and adjusting strategies as necessary through the cyclic of processes. According to this cyclic model, SRL strategies consists of cognitive and metacognitive activities or strategies [8, 10, 18, 23, 36, 46]. The cognitive strategies are related to dealing with subject domain while metacognitive strategies are related to thinking about and regulating the cognitive. Often the term of metacognitive is simply defined as "cognitive of cognitive" or "thinking about thinking" [14, 31]. Hence, the metacognitive can be understood as a competence of reflecting on mental task critically and efficiently and effectively organize the relevant learning and thinking processes. Zimmerman [53] explains that self-regulation is not a process that occurs at the individual level but is determined by interactions with environment and also personal and behavioral influences. Learners can learn through observing and interacting with parents, teachers, peers and who demonstrate these behaviors.

There is an important aspect of theories of self-regulated learning where learners' learning and motivation are treated as interdependent processes that cannot be apart from each other. The learners are rather to seek out their opportunities to learn, to compare and to reactive to their learning outcomes. They may do self-initiated activities to promote self-observation, self-evaluation, and self-improvement. This shown that SRL involves more than a capability to execute a learning response by the learners.

Besides, it also more than a capability to adjust learning responses to new or changing conditions from the feedback. At this level, learners are not only self-directed in a metacognitive sense but are self-motivated as well.

2 Research Method

We analyzed topics that being addressed in SRL research. During our analysis, we identified several topics that being addressed. The topics are model and phases of SRL, strategies used by learners in SRL, and self-regulation in online learning environments. To examine research on SRL, we conducted a systematic review and analysis in two phases. First, we accumulated and gather related articles, and finally discuss the topics addressed in SRL.

2.1 Accumulation of Related Articles

SRL research have been published in many journals, hence we searched through thirty year period (1986–2017) of random journals. We search any journals that related to SRL, online learning and mathematics in order to get 130 articles. The articles were searched through *Google Scholar* and UiTM's library, *EzAccess*. The research articles were searched by using phrases such as "Barry Zimmerman", "self-regulated learning", "self-regulated learning and mathematics", and "self-regulated learning and academic achievement". As we looking for research articles in the topic area of SRL, we eliminated any result that was a book review.

2.2 Related Topics

Related topics that will be discussed in the findings section begin with model and phases of SRL. Although there are several types of SRL model that was invented by some researchers, all of the models is said to be a cyclic process. Learners who follow the model in order to achieve a better performance in their learning will keep the process ongoing as a circle. Then, we discussed strategies that have been suggested by researchers for the learners to follow as self-regulated learners. The strategies are cognitive, metacognitive, self-efficacy or motivation, behavior, resource management, three model of Zimmerman and 15 SRL strategies. Then we will discuss self-regulated learning in online learning. Finally, we highlight the relationship between mathematics and self-regulated learning.

3 Findings

We have collected more than 150 articles related to SRL, online learning, and mathematics. As SRL becoming an issue among educators, we can see the increasing number of articles available per year from 1998 until 2017.

3.1   Model and Phases

All the model inventors (researchers) agreed that SRL is a cyclical process, composed of different phases. However, the models present different phases and sub-processes. In general terms, we can conclude that the models have three identifiable phases. The phases are (a) preparatory that includes task analysis, planning, having goals, and setting the goals; (b) performance which the actual task is done while monitoring and controlling the progress of performance; and (c) appraisal that learners reflects, regulates and adapts for future performances. Zimmerman's and Pintrich's models emphasize a clearer distinction among the phases and sub-processes that occur within them [1, 4, 7, 11, 13, 16, 20–22, 24, 25, 29, 34, 36, 37, 50, 52, 54, 55]. For Boekaerts's, Winne and Hadwin's, and Corno and Mandinach's models are more explicit, making SRL an open process that has recursive phases [27, 38, 39].

Winne and Hadwins's model does not make a clear distinction between the phases that belong to each that state SRL is presented as a loop that evolves over time. The Zimmerman's and Pintrich's models might allow for more specific interventions because the measurement of the effects might be more feasible. For example, if a teacher recognizes that one of the students has a motivation problem while performing a task, applying some of the subprocesses presented by Zimmerman might have a positive outcome. But for other three models, they might suggest more holistic interventions, as they perceive the SRL as a more continuous process composed of more inertial related sub-processes. Table 1 will illustrate the differences between the five different models and their phases [33].

Table 1.   Phases of SRL models

Models	Preparatory phase	Performance phase	Appraisal phase
Zimmerman	Forethought – task analysis, self-motivation beliefs	Performance – self-control, self-observation	Self-reflection – self-judgement, self-reaction
Pintrich	Forethought, planning, activation	Monitoring, control	Reaction, reflection
Boekaerts	Identification, interpretation, primary and secondary appraisal, goal setting	Goal striving	Performance feedback
Corno and Mandinach	Alertness, selectivity	Connecting, planning	Monitoring
Winne and Hadwin	Task definition, goal setting, planning	Applying tactics and strategies	Adapting metacognition

3.2   Strategies in SRL

Learners can use several strategies to adapt SRL in their learning routine. In general, the learners used the same strategies and did not really different from each other. The strategies that commonly used are cognitive, metacognitive and the three phases of

Zimmerman's model. There are also other strategy which are self-efficacy, motivation, behavior, resource management, and learning strategies (motivation, concentration, information processing, and self-testing).

Cognitive and metacognitive activities or strategies are part of SRL [58]. Cognitive strategies refer to rehearsal, elaboration, and organization strategies [19, 53]. The rehearsal strategies definition is a recitation of an item that learners want to learn and say the word aloud when to read it and highlighting the text. For elaboration, it is said as paraphrase and summarize the material that being learn. When learners select the main ideas and outline the text, learners already did the organizational strategies. By having cognitive strategies, learners will be more aware of their own knowledge, for example, mathematical knowledge. They may also know their strengths and weaknesses as well as their progress in the subject.

With cognitive strategies, metacognitive strategies become critical for SRL. Metacognitive strategies are planning, goal setting, monitoring and reflection to meet the goal [14, 19, 47, 51]. The activities under this strategies are goal setting, self-monitoring, and self-evaluation. The goal setting is referred to as deciding on specific learning outcomes, while self-monitoring involves comparing the goals with current accomplishments with the use of cognitive strategies. Self-monitoring can be varied as it depends on learning context. For self-evaluation, it is a learners' self-judgment on their performance. Self-evaluation and self-monitoring occur almost at the same time. Based on the results where learners compared their performance to the goals, they will decide whether they need to change cognitive strategies or just keep going with the strategies and increase the efforts [10].

Next, resource management strategies are time and effort management, seeking help from others, seeking information, and structuring environment for learning. It depends on knowledge of the subject that learners have and what resources they can use. Activities for resource management are not directly related to cognitive and metacognitive but it is important for academic success.

Self-efficacy is learners' confidence and belief in their ability to perform a task [2, 3, 15, 35, 40, 41]. Learners with high self-efficacy tend to be confident and motivate themselves to acquire learning while for low self-efficacy learners, they have less motivation and will think that achieving goals is difficult. Learners with high self-efficacy have more effort than low self-efficacy learners when they meet obstacles in learning. Volition also important in SRL [10]. Volition is learners' will power to accomplish their goals where volition is related to the use of cognitive and resource management activities.

SRL become a cyclical phases – forethought phase, performance phase and self-reflection phase [17, 38, 43, 59]. In forethought phase, there are two processes which are task analysis and self-motivation. Task analysis involves goal setting and strategic planning. Learners will set their specific goals can increase their performance and academic success. While for self-motivation, it is related to self-efficacy that learners' beliefs they are capable of learning. The second phase is a performance that consists of self-control and self-observation. Self-control related to forethought phase where it is about the method choosing by the learners. Learners will use of imagery, self-instruction, attention focusing, and task strategies in this processes. Self-observation refers to self-recording personal events to find out the cause of the events.

3.3 SRL in Online Learning

As learners always spend most of their time outside the classroom learning environment, they tend to study via online learning. Instructors and learners will consider the methods and strategies that are used in online learning as an important issue when comparing it with traditional instruction method which is face-to-face learning. By learning via online learning, it will provide the opportunities for learners to master necessary tasks by using appropriate strategies such as SRL [7, 13, 27].

SRL is one of the methods for learner performance in both traditional and online learning. When learners use strategies of SRL, they can regulate their personal functioning and benefit from the online learning by changing their behaviors accordingly. The perception of freedom of action as learners can act according to their own wishes, expectations and need in a supportive context, where they can get resources that needed, will help them to translate their own needs, expectations and wishes into clear intentions which are goal setting. Learners need to control their own learning practice in online learning in order to benefit from it, hence self-regulated strategies are really helping them in this process. For learners who may lack strong SRL skills, external supports provided by the Internet may support and enhance learner's self-regulated learning. As learners learn by themselves through the Internet, they can get any information and resources needed.

For instance, additional resources such as image, video, graphics, and animation can provide to learners to prompt their use of information seeking strategies. This may also help learners to improve their skills and learning over time. It is accepted by researchers that learners can improve their SRL by using activities that aim at training metacognitive strategies, executive attention and emotion regulation. When studies, learners usually used SRL strategies related to note-taking, seek information and monitoring. Thus it can be stated that the use of SRL strategies can give a positive relationship with academic performance [7].

3.4 Mathematics and Online Learning

As the alternative to face-to-face learning, learners can learn mathematics subject using online learning. Learners can learn mathematics via online learning because they can get many resources on the web on this subject. This will help them to improve their skills and understanding about all topics within the subject.

The online learning conditions in these studies were less likely to be instructor-directed than they were to be learner-directed, independent learning or interactive and collaborative in nature. Online learners typically have the opportunity to practice their skills or tests their knowledge. Thus, finding of the meta-analysis is that classes with online learning on average produce stronger learner learning outcomes than do classes with solely face-to-face instruction [28].

In learner's performance and achievement, mathematics via online learning are convenient, based on metacognitive strategies that enable the learners to plan and allocate learning resources, monitor their own knowledge levels at different points during learning acquisition, as well as motivation-emotions regulation refers to learners' thoughts, actions, and behaviours when learning that affect their efforts, persistence, and emotions when performing academic tasks [47]. These components are capable of increasing the learner's potential and performance level, moreover, learners are surrounded with digital devices in their daily life, and they do not need to expend extra effort to get used to them because "technology is assumed to be a natural part of the environment" [27].

3.5   Mathematics and SRL via Online Learning

Research on self-regulation of mathematics learning has been mainly undertaken within theoretical perspectives which are Zimmerman's model based on social-cognitive theory and theories of problem-solving. As been discuss before Zimmerman's model consists of three phases in the cyclical process. Then the theory of problem-solving is less elaborated than Zimmerman's model as the concerned of self-regulation components. It is focused on cognitive and metacognitive strategies that accompany an expert problem-solving process, namely orientation toward the task, planning a solution process or approach to the task, monitoring during task execution, evaluating the outcome, and reflecting on a solution or learning process [12].

In mathematics education, problem-solving has been a central focus. Mathematical problem solving been characterized as an activity that involves learners' engagement in cognitive strategies including accessing and using previous knowledge and experience. A successful problem solving involves coordinating previous knowledge, experiences, representations and patterns of inference, and intuition in an effort to generate new representatives of original problem-solving activity [21]. The mathematical problem solving should include experiences for learners to posing questions and formulate their own problems. Although mathematical problem solving is the most valuable aspects of mathematics, it becomes the most difficult topic for learners. Learners need to have different skills in order to have the ability to construct the solution in multi-step of processes. Hence, a coordinating framework was employed in the problem-solving process that consists of five categories. The categories are a knowledge base, problem-solving strategies, monitoring and controlling solution process, beliefs and affect, and practices. This shown that SRL and problem solving are linked to each other and help learners have better performance in their studies.

4   Discussions

From the researchers point of view, online regulated learning on mathematics strategies and methods are positive in enhancing learner's learning and knowledge [8, 9, 30, 48]. Nussbaumer et al. [31] have characterized learning strategies as purposeful, in the sense that they are consciously applied to attain the desired outcome. Learning strategies are different from study skills in that the latter can be automatized, whereas strategies require conscious effort [8]. Intrinsic motivation revealed to be the main factor predicting learners' regulation of their behavior and the learning environment. Intrinsic (belonging naturally) motivation also predicts the use of strategies indicating deep information processing, such as critical thinking and theoretical approach [48].

Some of the articles stated that online learning or blended learning can produce best features of classroom interaction and live instruction to personalize learning, allow thoughtful reflection, and differentiate instruction from learner to learner across a diverse group of learners. As we can see, the online learning represents a shift in instructional strategy and represents a fundamental shift in the way of delivery of the learning and instructional model of self-learning or distance learning. Some educators realize that the roles of schools, classrooms, and teachers are already changing. Online learning is beneficial to the learner who looks for options in learning mathematics based on their preferences. Moreover, technologies are growing fast; these advantages are the most precious ways to enhance the performance of the learner.

In developing learner's learning on mathematics via online, there is a large body of literature indicating both learning strategies and self-efficacy; both are critical to learner's success [49]. The method that always researchers examine is metacognitive, and this method is stated in many others researcher's paper [45]. Research has shown benefits from using metacognitive tools integrated to keep learners on track and remind them to use strategies such as note taking and reflection. We found that learner's study strategy and self-efficacy applied to a web-based setting or searching for information and learns using the Internet is not substantially different from learner learning in traditional developmental classes.

5   Conclusions

To achieve a better, optimal learning outcomes and performances, learners need to be self-regulated, motivated and engaged in the learning process. The emerging of technologies have changed the learning environments. Hence, we need to extend our investigation in the online learning environment and identify the effective interactions to enhance SRL of learners. More research to investigates the role of SRL in online courses will extend SRL theories to online environments and improve efforts to enhance learner's success in online courses, generally.

Acknowledgments. This work is supported by UiTM Internal Research Grants Scheme (600-IRMI/DANA 5/3/ARAS (0179/2016) from the research Management Center (RMC), Universiti Teknologi MARA, Shah Alam, Selangor. The appreciation also goes to Faculty of Computer and Mathematical Sciences, Universiti Teknologi MARA, Shah Alam, Selangor for giving a moral support in the production of this paper.

References

1. Abdullah, M.F.N.L., et al.: Students' discourse in learning mathematics with self-regulating strategies. Procedia - Soc. Behav. Sci. **191**, 2188–2194 (2015)
2. Agustiani, H., et al.: Self-efficacy and self-regulated learning as predictors of students academic performance. Open Psychol. J. **9**(1), 1–6 (2016)
3. Alegre, A.A.: Academic self-efficacy, self-regulated learning and academic performance in first-year university students. Propósitos y Represent. Rev. Psicol. Educ. la USIL **2**(1), 101–120 (2014)

4. Azevedo, R.: Theoretical, conceptual, methodological, and instructional issues in research on metacognition and self-regulated learning: a discussion. Metacogn. Learn. **4**(1), 87–95 (2009)
5. Bandura, A.: Social cognitive theory of self-regulation. Organ. Behav. Hum. Decis. Process. **50**(2), 248–287 (1991)
6. Bandura, A.: Social foundations of thought and action: A social cognitive theory. Prentice-Hall, Upper Saddle River (1986)
7. Barnard-brak, L., et al.: Profiles in self-regulated learning in the online learning environment. Int. Rev. Res. Open Distance Learn. **11**, 1 (2010)
8. de Boer, H., et al.: Effective strategies for self-regulated learning : a meta-analysis (2012)
9. Cetin, B.: Academic motivation and self-regulated learning in predicting academic achievement in college. J. Int. Educ. Res. **11**(2), 95–106 (2015)
10. Cho, M.-H.: The effects of design strategies for promoting students' self-regulated learning skills on students' self-regulation and achievements in online learning environments. Assoc. Educ. Commun. Technol. **27**(1999), 19–23 (2004)
11. Cifarelli, V., et al.: Associations of students' beliefs with self-regulated problem solving in college Algebra. J. Adv. Acad. **21**(2), 204–232 (2010)
12. De Corte, E., et al.: Self-regulation of mathematical knowledge and skills. In: Handbook of Self-Regulation Learning Performance, May 2016 (2011)
13. Delen, E., Liew, J.: The use of interactive environments to promote self-regulation in online learning: a literature review. Eur. J. Contemp. Educ. **15**(1), 24–33 (2016)
14. Fauzi, K.M.A.: The enhancement of student's mathematical connection ability and self-regulation learning with metacognitive learning approach in junior high school. In: 7th International Conference Research and Education in Mathematics, pp. 174–179 (2015)
15. Hodges, C.B., Kim, C.: Email, self-regulation, self-efficacy, and achievement in a college online mathematics course. J. Educ. Comput. Res. **43**(2), 207–223 (2010)
16. Huang, Y.-M., et al.: Supporting self-regulated learning in web 2.0 contexts. Turkish Online J. Educ. Technol. - TOJET **11**(2), 187–195 (2012)
17. Jain, S., Dowson, M.: Mathematics anxiety as a function of multidimensional self-regulation and self-efficacy. Contemp. Educ. Psychol. **34**(3), 240–249 (2009)
18. Jones, M.H., et al.: Homophily among peer groups members' perceived self-regulated learning. J. Exp. Educ. **78**, 378–394 (2010)
19. Junus, K., et al.: Social, cognitive, teaching, and metacognitive presence in general and focus group discussion: case study in blended e-learning Linear Algebra class. In: Proceedings of - Frontiers in Education Conference (FIE. 2015), February 2015
20. Kitsantas, A.: Fostering college students' selfregulated learning with learning technologies. Hell. J. Psychol. **10**(3), 235–252 (2013)
21. Kramarski, B., et al.: How can self-regulated learning support the problem solving of third-grade students with mathematics anxiety? Math. Educ. **42**(2), 179–193 (2010)
22. Lai, C.-L., Hwang, G.-J.: A self-regulated flipped classroom approach to improving students' learning performance in a mathematics course. Comput. Educ. **100**(May), 126–140 (2016)
23. Leidinger, M., Perels, F.: Training self-regulated learning in the classroom: development and evaluation of learning materials to train self-regulated learning during regular mathematics lessons at primary school. Educ. Res. Int. **2012**, 1–14 (2012)
24. Loch, B., Mcloughlin, C.: An instructional design model for screencasting: engaging students in self-regulated learning. In: ASCILITE 2011 Changing Demands, Changing Directions, pp. 816–821 (2011)
25. Magno, C.: Developing and assessing self-regulated learners. Assess. Handb. Contin. Educ. Progr. **1**, 26–41 (2015)

26. Marchis, I., Balogh, T.: Secondary school pupils' self-regulated learning skills. Acta Didact. Napocensia **3**(3), 147–152 (2010)
27. Mcmahon, M., Oliver, R.: Promoting self-regulated learning in an on-line environment. In: World Conference on Educational Multimedia, Hypermedia and Telecommunications, pp. 1299–1305 (2001)
28. Means, B. et al.: Evaluation of Evidence-Based Practices in Online Learning. Structure, p. 66 (2009)
29. Moos, D.C., Ringdal, A.: Self-regulated learning in the classroom: a literature review on the teacher's role. Educ. Res. Int. **2012**, 1–15 (2012)
30. Núñez, J.C., et al.: Implementation of training programs in self-regulated learning strategies in moodle format: results of a experience in higher education. Psicothema **23**(2), 274–281 (2011)
31. Nussbaumer, A., et al.: A competence-based service for supporting self-regulated learning in virtual environments. J. Learn. Anal. **2**(1), 101–133 (2015)
32. Pajares, F., Valiante, G.: Students'self-efficacy in their self-regulated learning strategies: a developmental perspective. Psychol. Int. J. Psychol. Orient. **45**(4), 211–221 (2002)
33. Panadero, E.: A review of self-regulated learning: six models and four directions for research. Front. Psychol. **8**, 1–28 (2017)
34. Perels, F., et al.: Is it possible to improve mathematical achievement by means of self-regulation strategies? Evaluation of an intervention in regular math classes. Eur. J. Psychol. Educ. **24**(1), 17–31 (2009)
35. Phan, H.P.: The Development of english and mathematics self-efficacy: a latent growth curve analysis. J. Educ. Res. **105**(3), 196–209 (2012)
36. Pintrich, P.R.: The role of goal orientation in self-regulated learning. In: Handbook of Self-Regulation (2000)
37. Rahimi, E., et al.: A learning model for enhancing the student's control in educational process using web 2.0 personal learning environments. Br. J. Educ. Technol. **46**(4), 780–792 (2015)
38. Rogers, D., Swam, K.: Self-regulated learning and internet searching. Teach. Coll. Rec. **106** (9), 1804–1824 (2004)
39. Roll, I., Winne, P.H.: Understanding, evaluating, and supporting self-regulated learning using learning analytics. J. Learn. Anal. **2**(1), 7–12 (2015)
40. Salmerón-Pérez, H., et al.: Self-regulated learning, self-efficacy beliefs and performance during the late childhood. Relieve - e-J. Educ. Res. Assess. Eval. **16**(2), 1–18 (2010)
41. Sartawi, A., et al.: Predicting mathematics achievement by motivation and self-efficacy across gender and achievement levels. Interdiscip. J. Teach. Learn. **2**(2), 59–77 (2012)
42. Schunk, D.: Self-evaluation and self-regulated learning. Graduate School and University Center, City University of New York (1996)
43. Schunk, D.H., Zimmerman, B.J. (eds.): Self-regulation of Learning and Performance: Issues and Educational Applications. Lawrence Erlbaum Associates Inc., New Jersey (1994)
44. Shih, S.: Children's self-efficacy beliefs, goal-setting behaviors, and self-regulated learning. J. Natl Taipei Teachers Coll. **15**, 265–282 (2002)
45. Shukor, N.A., et al.: A preliminary study on socially shared regulation during online collaborative mathematics learning. In: 2015 IEEE Conference on e-Learning, e-Management e-Services, IC3e 2015, pp. 1–7 (2016)
46. Sperling, R.A., et al.: Metacognition and self-regulated learning constructs. Educ. Res. Eval. **10**(2), 117–139 (2004)
47. Tzohar-Rozen, M., Kramarski, B.: Metacognition, motivation and emotions: contribution of self-regulated learning to solving mathematical problems. Glob. Educ. Rev. **1**(4), 76–95 (2014)

48. Virtanen, P., et al.: Self-regulation in higher education: students' motivational, regulational and learning strategies, and their relationships to study success. Stud. Learn. Soc. **3**, 1–2 (2015)
49. Wadsworth, L.M., et al.: Online mathematics achievement: effects of learning strategies and self-efficacy. J. Dev. Educ. **30**(3), 6–14 (2007)
50. Wigfield, A. et al.: Influences on the development of academic self-regulatory processes. In: Handbook of Self-regulation of Learning and Performance, pp. 33–48 (2011)
51. Williamson, G.: Self-regulated learning: an overview of metacognition, motivation and behaviour. J. Init. Teach. Inq. **1**, 25–27 (2015)
52. Yidizli, H., Saban, A.: The effect of self-regulated learning on sixth-grade Turkish students' mathematics achievements and motivational beliefs. Cogent Educ. **3**(1), 1–17 (2016)
53. Zimmerman, B.J.: A social cognitive view of self-regulated academic learning. J. Educ. Psychol. **81**(3), 329–339 (1989)
54. Zimmerman, B.J.: Becoming a self-regulated learner: an overview. Theory Pract. **41**(2), 64–70 (2002)
55. Zimmerman, B.J.: Investigating self-regulation and motivation: historical background, methodological developments, and future prospects. Am. Educ. Res. J. **45**(1), 166–183 (2008)
56. Zimmerman, B.J.: Self-regulated learning and academic achievement: an overview. Educ. Psychol. **25**, 3–17 (1990)
57. Zimmerman, B.J., Martinez-Pons, M.: Pursuing Academic Self Regulation: a 20-Year Methodological Quest. McGraw Hill, Singapore (2004)
58. Zimmerman, B.J., Martinez-Pons, M.: Development of a structured interview for assessing student use of self-regulated learning strategies. Am. Educ. Res. J. **23**(4), 614–628 (1986)
59. Zimmerman, B.J., Schunk, D.H. (eds.): Self-regulated learning: from teaching to self-reflective practice. Guilford Publications Inc., New York (1998)
60. e-learning Concepts, Trends, Applications. https://www.talentlms.com/elearning/elearning-101-jan2014-v1.1.pdf

A Hybrid Model of Differential Evolution with Neural Network on Lag Time Selection for Agricultural Price Time Series Forecasting

Chen ZhiYuan[(⊠)], Le Dinh Van Khoa, and Lee Soon Boon

The University of Nottingham Malaysia Campus,
43500 Semenyih, Selangor Darul Ehsan, Malaysia
{zhiyuan.chen, hcxd11}@nottingham.edu.my,
lsboon99@gmail.com

Abstract. The contribution of time series forecasting (TSF) on various aspects from economic to engineering has yielded its importance. Lot of recent studies concentrated on applying and modifying artificial neural network (ANN) to improve forecasting accuracy and achieved promising results. However, the selection of proper set from historical data for forecasting still has limited consideration. In addition, the selection of network structure as well as initial weights in ANN has been proved to have significant impact on the performance. This paper aims to propose a hybrid model that takes advantages of optimization algorithm: differential evolution (DE) in combine with ANN. The DE operates as features selection process that evaluates useful historical data known as lag to involve in learning process. Besides, DE will perform pre-calculation to determine the set of weight use for ANN. This proposed model is examined on agricultural commodity's price to evaluate its accuracy. The experimental results is compared and surpassed the popular TSF technique autoregressive integrated moving average (ARIMA) and traditional multilayer perceptron (MLP).

Keywords: Time series forecasting · Artificial neural network · Differential evolution · Lag time selection

1 Introduction

The selection of an appropriate number of historical values, known as lag, has been indicated as the most important factor that effect the efficient of TSF. TS defined as list of data represent the statistical value of a certain property in (ascendant) timing order. The list of data type can be adopted consist of continuous or discrete numeric data. Mathematically denote as a sequence of ordered observation $s_t \in R$ in equal interval of time t. As TS provides coherent description of data, this information is significantly useful for a wide range of fields such as engineering, financial, economics. Since TS consists of useful information such as data trending, seasonal of data behavior and impact of noise factor. The study of TS for accurate forecasting long term data yield important effect to various fields. Many studies on statistical modelling have results in common linear forecasting model such as ARIMA. In common, these approaches consider TS as linear problem and attempt to describe using a linear model. However,

© Springer International Publishing AG 2017
H. Badioze Zaman et al. (Eds.): IVIC 2017, LNCS 10645, pp. 155–167, 2017.
https://doi.org/10.1007/978-3-319-70010-6_15

according to G. Bontempi linear model have following disadvantages. Linear methods interpret all the structure in a time series through linear correlation deterministic linear dynamics can only lead to simple exponential or periodically oscillating behavior, so all irregular behavior is attributed to external noise while deterministic nonlinear equations could produce very irregular data [1].

As moving to more complicated data, the solution of linear model easily falls to underfitting issue. In these particular problems, nonlinear model such as support vector machine, neural network is highly refers. In a time series viewpoint, the inputs refer to list of past values and target denotes by the values of next data sequence. From a certain defined learning patterns, ANN and SVR are suitable to produce the generalization. Since these approaches assume that historical data has influence on next value, the selection of number of past data use for regression is one of the challenge of TSA. By selecting an appropriate set of lag that have critical influence and eliminate useless or redundancy lag values, the training performance can be enhanced in term of time and accuracy. Various lag time selection approaches have been studied for both linear and nonlinear model [2, 3, 4]. Earlier studies employed model assessment by evaluating likelihood properties to determine lag sequences. These trial and error approaches consists of Akaike Information Criterion (AIC) and Schwarz Bayesian Information Criterion (BIC). These techniques are strongly recommended for linear model such as vector auto regression. However, as the moving to nonlinear model, due to the differences in the nature of problem observation, implication of aforementioned methods cannot reserve the correctness. Studies on comparison of time series in view of linear pattern ARIMA and nonlinear pattern particle swarm optimization (PSO) indicated the advantages of nonlinear model [5].

Since the purpose of lag selection is to determine the best set of past values that minimize the error, the problem is referred to optimization solutions. Recent studies have tried to exploit search space using bio-inspired optimization algorithms such as genetic algorithm (GA), PSO. In this study, we would like to propose a hybrid algorithm that composes of differential evolution DE and NN. The DE determines the lags sequence that involves in operation and also initializes network's weights. On the other hand, ANN is adopted as the core learning engine to produce the ending prediction.

2 Related Work

As mentioned in previous chapter, understanding on dataset properties is important to deliver a proper forecasting model. Throughout this research, a dataset of agricultural commodities price in Malaysia from 2010 to 2014, was employed to verify forecasting performance. In the term of agricultural commodities price, various studies have indicated multiple impact factors that associate with the price that categorize into demand and supply. The level of supply of an agricultural commodity is a function of many factors such as seasonality, technology, trade etc. On the other hand, when the demand of a commodity falls, the price of that commodity also falls all else being equal. The demand of agricultural commodities is commonly influenced by seasonality, changes in taste, and prices of substitutes. Prices of agricultural commodities may also change with changes in government policies such as taxes and subsidies or inputs used in the production process. As the price was result from different endogenous, exogenous conditions, fuzzy logic usually applied as a solution [6]. However, in this particular problem, the affect from various features implies that the variables are infeasible to be linked by a linear relation. Moreover, the form of the relation is still vague and the only limited samples on these features are available and also inconsistent. Therefore, the implication of nonlinear model should be examined in full consideration. Experiments from studies of Cortez has compared the surpass performance between machine learning technique like SVM, ANN and classical approach Holt Winters in forecasting [7]. Earlier research of Zhang has proposed a merging solution of nonlinear ARIMA and linear model ANN to take the advantages from each of them [8]. The series was fitted by ARIMA model first before applying for the ANN training. As a result, this method can avoid the overfitting problem, reduce the model uncertainty. Later study also applied Zhang's model to examine various real world problems [9, 10]. Other combination between nonlinear and linear model was involved in using auto regression (AR) approach with ANN for hydrologic forecasting [11]. Recent study, adopted auto regressive moving reference (ARMR) with modified recurrent network (RNN) has yielded smaller prediction error and higher correlation between target returns and predicted returns [12].

Various studies have applied ANN as the core engine or partial components for prediction. In an experiment on calculating cumulative rainfall by Rivero, ANN was implemented as a filter for Bayesian method [13]. The trend of hybridizing neural network with other optimization algorithm to solve real problem has reached various remarkable results [14, 15]. However, each specific problem requires different network structure. The configuration consists of number of hidden layers, number of perceptron for in each layer, activation function as well as connection network. The initial weights were also considered as an important factor that limits the explored space for later training process. Recent studies have implied optimization algorithm at preprocessing step to enhance the accuracy. Some researchers used colony optimization algorithm for exploring initial space. Ribeiro, proposed a heuristics topology for lag selection using Particle Swarm Optimization (PSO) combine with Support Vector Regression and ANN as learning engine [16]. Instead of applying direct encoding strategy that determine the parameters of network; indirect encoding can be used to modify the network topology. For instances, a study on applied PSO for lag selection has implemented PSO to modified network and learning mechanism [17]. Meanwhile Brasileiro inspired Artificial Bee Colony for adjusting parameters and good set of lags [18]. Different searching approach was also examine in preprocessing step such as Ganji hybridize GA with learning technique [19]. Other researchers modify the network structure or introduced kernel for adaptive lag selection. Parras Gutierrez refined the neural network training with radial basis kernel literature for automatic lags determination [20]. Later works of Mohammadi has adopted the RBF network to examine the emergency supply demand [21].

Among different optimization algorithms, the evolutionary computations has been adopted widely and innovated into different branches. Due to the abundant selection among EC methods, several studies have been conducted to evaluate the performance of different EC methods. On the comparison done by Vesterstrom and Thomsen among DE, PSO with other extension of EA, the results has indicated the dominant of DE in compared with others EC for both noisy and noise free environment [22]. Due to its ease computation and high quality results, various studies were proposed to enhance DE performance [23, 24]. As a consequence, recent studies have high consideration on the combination between DE and ANN [25]. The adjustment on both IES and DES also enhance the prediction accuracy. Donate and Cortez has implied estimation distribution algorithm (EDA), which belongs to evolutionary engine, to selected list of useful lag to combine with ANN [26]. Although the performance of EDA has been proved to surpass the traditional genetic algorithm and DE, the study is still fresh and new that required further studies on comparison and hybridization. Therefore, the main motivation of this paper is to obtain ANN models through a fully automatic process, due to not all users who need to deal with forecasting are ANN experts.

3 Material and Method

The hybrid system will be designed based on biological inspired algorithms. Differential evolution is a branched of evolutionary computing, which imitate the natural selection process, first introduced by Storn and Price [27]. Meanwhile, ANN functions in a similar method as human neural sending signal.

3.1 Differential Evolution

Firstly, in preprocessing step, DE is performed as features selections components. As a population based computation strategy, this process contains 4 main operators: initialization, mutation, recombination and selection.

Initialization
At first, a population of possible sets of lags has been randomly generated. These individual has been represented as vector of lags weight with length equal to a predefined maximum lag allowed *lmax*. The initial value in each dimension of chromosome vectors was assigned randomly and uniformly distributed. In a population with size n, the ith individual will be formulated as

$$\vec{X}_i = \left[x_{i,1}, x_{i,2}, \ldots, x_{i,d} \right], (i = 1, 2, \ldots n) \tag{3.1}$$

$$subject\ to : x_{i,j} = x_j^{lb} + random_{i,j}[0, 1]\left(x_j^{ub} - x_j^{lb} \right), x_{i,j} \in \left[x_j^{lb}, x_j^{ub} \right]$$

whereas: d represents number of d previous lags, x_j^{ub} and x^{lb} indicate the upperbound and lowerbound at j^{th} lag. In lag selection process, the chromosomes have binary values 0, 1 in each element of individual. For instances, a chromosome can have its elements as following *(0, 1, 1, 1, 0,..., 0, 1)*, whereas 1 denoted for selected and 0 is eliminated from the model.

Mutation
The purpose of this operation is to calculate differentiation within population based on the distance and direction of lags values. According technique, the offspring can be

considered as the adjustment of searching vector through alternative differentiation's direction with calculated step length rather than inherit character from parent's value. For each individual, the mutation vector will be defined by rescale the target with a predefined weight factor and adding difference vector. The obtained vector will be known as donor vector while the weight will be notate as mutation factor.

DE/current to best/1 is defined as

$$\vec{V}_i = \vec{X}_i + F_1\left(\vec{X}_{r2} - \vec{X}_{r3}\right) + F_2\left(\vec{X}_{best} - \vec{X}_i\right) \tag{3.2}$$

DE/random to best/1 is defined as

$$\vec{V}_i = \vec{X}_{r1} + F_1\left(\vec{X}_{r2} - \vec{X}_{r3}\right) + F_2\left(\vec{X}_{best} - \vec{X}_{r1}\right) \tag{3.3}$$

whereas x_i is the current individual, x_{best} refers to the best individual in term of fitness; F_1, $F_2 \in (0,2]$.

r_1, r_2, $r_3 \in \{1, 2, ..., N\}$, r_1, r_2, r_3 are randomly selected and mutually exclusive. Real constants contribute to the decision of amplifying differential variation of $\left(\vec{X}_{r2} - \vec{X}_{r3}\right)$, and $\left(\vec{X}_{best} - \vec{X}_i\right)$, or $\left(\vec{X}_{best} - \vec{X}_{r1}\right)$. A higher value of F will create a larger diversity within population meanwhile a smaller value result in faster convergence rate.

Recombination

This process will produce new trial vectors by incorporating with fittest individuals in previous generation. These trial vectors will have their elements taken from either donor vector or target vector respectively. Depend on the purpose of evaluation, new trial vector in a generation can be determined by 2 different methods which are binomial and exponential crossover. The simpler and faster recombination technique, binomial or uniform crossover, formulate as

$$v_{i,j}, if\left(rand_{i,j}[0, 1) \le CR \, or \, j = j_{rand}\right) \tag{3.4}$$

$$u_{i,j} = \begin{cases} v_{i,j}, & if\left(rand_{i,j}[0, 1) \le CR \, or \, j = j_{rand}\right) \\ x_{i,j}, & otherwise \end{cases} \tag{3.5}$$

subjects to CR denotes the crossover rate, the higher rate, the more likely that trial vector will adopt donor components.

The other strategy, additional computation is required. Mathematically, the model for determining was specified by following formula

$$u_{i,j} = \begin{cases} v_{i,j}, & for \, j = \langle n \rangle_D, \langle n+L \rangle_D, ..., \langle n+L-1 \rangle_D \\ x_{i,j}, & for \, all \, other \, j \in [1, D] \end{cases} \tag{3.6}$$

subjects to the brackets indicates the modulo function which D is modulus; L's value will initialed at 0 and steady increment until a random number is larger than crossover rate or L surpassed D.

Reselection

Finally, the population will be recalculated through selection process. In term of fitness, trial vector will be compared with target vector to evaluate fitter solution. Replacement occurs if generated vector is better than its parents.

$$\vec{X}_{i,G+1} = \begin{cases} \vec{U}_{i,G}, & if\, f(\vec{U}_{i,G}) \le f(\vec{X}_{i,G}) \\ \vec{X}_{i,G}, & if\, f(\vec{U}_{i,G}) > f(\vec{X}_{i,G}) \end{cases} \tag{3.7}$$

The fitness function will be defined by the root mean squared error function. Therefore the objective of DE process is to minimize the prediction error as much as possible

3.2   Design of NN Architecture

The network constructs of 3 layers: input, hidden, output layer. The input layer will be designed as following. Assume the maximum lags defined in DE operation is t then the number of input nodes $node_{inp} = 2 * t + 1$. In particular, the values of input node would be decides as below:

The first t nodes represent the consequence of t past values. Meanwhile the next t values indicate the impact of each lag to the next step evaluation by scaling with a coefficient. This coefficient indicates by the time different between that lag and the oldest lag in the sequence. Consequently, closer later time tend to have more influence to the result. Mathematically, the input vector would be presented as

$$\vec{i}_i = \left[y_{i-1}, y_{i-2}, \ldots, y_{i-t}, \delta_{i-1,i-t} y_{i-1}, \delta_{i-2,i-t} y_{i-2}, \delta_{i-t} y_{i-t} \right],$$

subject to y_{i-k} indicates the commodity price of k previous lags; $\delta_{i-1,i-t}$ denotes the time different between lag $(i-1)^{th}$ and the oldest lag. The rest node described the current evaluation in term of time differences and bias.

The number of hidden nodes will automatically define as half of input nodes

$$node_{hidden} = \lceil node_{input}/2 \rceil$$

Finally, one node in the output produces the end price forecasting. To preserve the uniform characteristics, nodes in layers are fully connected; in addition, sigmoid formula which maintains the output in range [0, 1] was selected as the activation function from input layer to hidden layer. The NN use backpropagation learning method.

The hybrid model operates in following sequences:

Step 1: Initialize list of binary chromosome and execute DE process
Step 2: Return DE output will be used to determine lag features that become input node in network. Initialize network structure.
Step 3: Generate chromosome and replace with the weight in network structure.
Step 4: Execute the DE process to adjust the weights, the objective function is to minimize RSME function

Step 5: Final weight in DE process will be initialized for the network and start training process with back propagation retrain

Step 6: Validate the learning by cross validate with 20% of instances from training set

Step 7: Retrain step 5 if the learning has not validated or reach the maximum iteration

Step 8: Output the final model and be available for forecasting with test set.

4 Experimental Design

This study used dataset of Malaysian agricultural commodities price, obtained from Federal Agricultural Marketing Authority (FAMA). This dataset records the price of 53 different agricultural items spending from vegetables to fruits, and meat categories in all states of Malaysia. This 5 years dataset started from the beginning of 2010 to the end of 2014 and milestones were recorded in date. In general, the time interval between any 2 adjacent milestones is 3 days, which also implied that approximately 553 observations for each commodity. As the time interval is inconsistent and the main features are historical prices, which also nonlinear, this dataset is capable to determine the feasibility and effectiveness of provided model.

4.1 Data Preparation

At first, 53 commodities classified into 3 different categories fruits, vegetables, and meat before applied individual item to the model. Due to the fact that the prices are diverse among states, the experiment simplified as the mean price value at each milestone. It is worth to note that, at some specific date, only some states were available for price records. Therefore the mean price did not guarantee for entire states of Malaysia. Within 663 observations, 80% records (from Jan 2010 to Nov 2013) extracted for learning process and the rest 20% (from Dec 2013 to Dec 2014) preserved for testing. In order to adapt with the output of sigmoid function that range from [0, 1], target normalization has been executed. To prepare the case that forecasting prices exists the maximum and minimum prices, the boundary target will be widen as below formula:

$$t' = \frac{t_i - t_{lowerbound}}{t_{upperbound} - t_{lowerbound}},$$

whereas $t_{lowerbound} = t_{min}/2$; $t_{upperbound} = t_{max} \times 2$

Moreover, attributes normalization also performed to standardize the input influence which avoid the case wider range attribute dominate the narrower.

4.2 Model Assessment

In order to determine the accuracy of model forecasts, 3 evaluation methods that calculate the error metric have been applied. Assume $\hat{y}_i$ defines the forecasting value at ith milestones among N-step ahead prediction; y_i denotes the actual value, then the formulas of error evaluate as

$$Mean\ squared\ error\ MSE = \frac{1}{N}\sum_{i=1}^{N}(\hat{y}_i - y_i)^2$$

$$Mean\ absolute\ percentage\ error\ MAPE = \frac{1}{N}\sum_{i=1}^{N}\left|\frac{\hat{y}_i - y_i}{y_i}\right|$$

$$Mean\ absolute\ error\ MAE = \frac{1}{N}\sum_{i=1}^{N}|\hat{y}_i - y_i|$$

4.3 Parameter Configuration

The population of all DE processes consists of 50 individuals. Each individual in lag selection process represent as a vector with the length of maximum lag. On the other hand, the individuals describe weight value has the length of (2 + number input) x number hidden nodes. Since the searching space is still in acceptable range, that does not exists 500 dimensions, experiments from previous study indicate that, the result can be reach within small generations [23, 24]. Hence, the evolutionary generation has been limited to 100 cycles. Other parameters decided as following: the mutation strategy using 1 individual current to best with fitness F_1, F_2 to be 0.5, 1 respectively; crossover rate CR to be 0.7.

Since the searching space has been explored in advanced through DE, the learning rate of ANN was designed to be high at the beginning and getting decay for fast convergence. In detail, learning rate was 0.6 with momentum of 0.15; the decay rate was 0.005 for later epochs. The parameters also adjusted through trial and error process.

4.4 Result and Discussion

In order to preserve the objective, both ANN and the hybrid model were conducted with the same network structure as well as weight values at initial state. Consequently, all the learning rate, momentum, decay parameters were configured similarly. The difference between 2 network models only determined after DE processes which evaluated set of selected lag and refined the weight values. The graph describes total error through training epochs has reveal the supreme of hybrid model against MLP. In overall, the hybrid DE-ANN has managed to reduce the error to half. It is also worth to note that with conventional MLP, the learning process tend to converge after first 100–150 epochs, meanwhile the hybrid model continue to learn until reach 200 epochs. Within 53 items, the list of selected commodities to demonstrate in this paper (green spinach, red chili, watermelon, chicken egg) followed below conditions to guarantee the diversity of time series properties. Non seasonal item like green spinach will demonstrate a chaotic time series since price varied frequently. Seasonal item with watermelon and partly seasonal item with red chili are useful for verify the learning of seasonal in series behavior. Lastly, government price controlled item such as chicken egg is present for a stable series.

In green spinach series, the hybrid model only required approximately 10 epochs to reach the best state of MLP learning (0.000336) and set the record to 0.000214. As the case of red chili, the training speed of MLP has reduced after 3 iterations while hybrid model maintain the gradient for next 15 epochs. Similarly, the same learning trend also reflect in watermelon and chicken egg figure, with the error of (MLP, hybrid) are (0.000489, 0.000244) and (0.000164, 0.000125) respectively Table 1.

Table 1. Total error in training process in comparison with MLP

Total error	Red chili	Green spinach	Watermelon	Chicken egg
Hybrid	0.000463	0.000214	0.000244	0.000125
MLP	0.000587	0.000336	0.000489	0.000164

Model Comparison on Green Spinach's Price

According to the result from evaluation metric, using MSE, MAPE, MAE category, hybrid model has managed to predict closer than classical ARIMA or ANN model. Different from statistical model ARIMA which perform poorly on trend (Fig. 1), the applied of ANN on forecasting model has the ability to reveal this property concisely (Fig. 2). Obtained results indicated the output from various forecasting model in compare with real value started from Dec 5th, 2013 to Dec 9th, 2014. The hybrid model has managed to decrease the MSE measurement of ARIMA and ANN to 64.67% and 83.17% respectively. In case of MAE and MAPE index, the accuracy has improved 55.57%, 54.32% from ANN, and 63.9%, 62.93% from ARIMA.

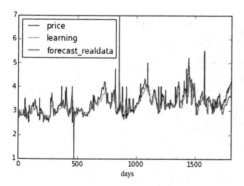

Fig. 1. Learning and forecasting of ANN on green spinach

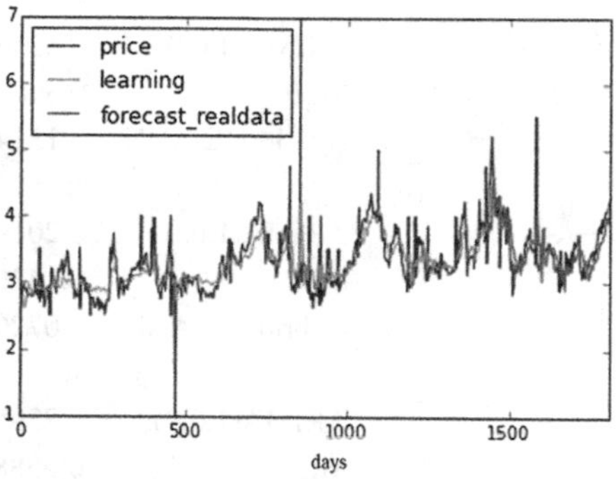

Fig. 2. Learning and forecasting of hybrid on green spinach

Model Comparison on Red Chili's Price

Similar as green spinach case, the performance of models involve in ANN clearly surpass ARIMA model. The y-axis represent for commodity's price, measures in Malaysian ringgit currency. The x-axis describes the time spend from Jan 2010 to Dec

2014 in daily unit. The training set start from Jan 5th, 2010 to Dec 19th, 2013 (441 instances) while the rest 110 instances (Dec 24th, 2013–Dec 11th, 2014) preserved for testing. Several experiments have been conducted to adjust the appropriate parameters. As a result, Figs. 3 and 4 demonstrate high quality of forecasting model as the results were much closed to the actual price. Although both ANN and hybrid model produce good predictions, the performance of hybrid model is slightly better according to the evaluation metric. Particularly, the improvement of hybrid in compare with ANN is 54.32% with MAPE, 55.57% with MAE and 66.97% with MSE Table 2.

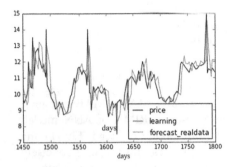

Fig. 3. Forecasting of ANN on red chili   **Fig. 4.** Forecasting of hybrid on red chili

Table 2. Forecasting performance in comparison with other models

Model assessment	MSE	MAE	MAPE
Green spinach			
ARIMA(1,0,0)	0.625645	0.641748	0.17022
MLP	0.398031	0.521386	0.13814
Hybrid DE-ANN	0.131443	0.231655	0.063094
Red chili			
ARIMA(1,0,0)	0.201945	2.155813	7.316197
MLP	0.142683	1.593539	3.4846
Hybrid DE-ANN	0.072609	0.803349	1.231218
Watermelon			
ARIMA(1,0,0)	0.229507	0.604138	0.466711
MLP	0.058865	0.153702	0.037487
Hybrid DE-ANN	0.036199	0.092206	0.020862
Chicken egg			
ARIMA(1,0,0)	0.119432	0.047971	0.006065
MLP	0.097394	0.038257	0.004839
Hybrid DE-ANN	0.073721	0.029845	0.004117

5 Conclusion and Further Study

A hybrid model of DE ANN that required DE in lag selection and initial weights process has been proposed to forecast agricultural commodity's price. The study of using a set of proper lags in TSF has not been put in full consideration. Most well-known methods BIC/AIC have been strongly implied by statistical theory and applicable in regression solution rather than machine learning method. The trend of studies on lag selection recently concentrates on evolutionary computing such as PSO or GA. Due to the remarkable performance that not only explore searching space but also exploit local region, DE has been adopted to examine the contribution of historical data. As assessing the impacts of each lag time for next prediction, DE simplified network architecture by eliminating insignificant lags.

Among feasible machine learning approaches, forecasting model constructed by ANN has been proved to be an efficient solution for various forecasting problems [9, 15, 21]. Since traditional ANN uses gradient descend approach for learning process, a weak weights initialization will lead the train model get trap in local optima. Therefore, DE in this research also enhances ANN accuracy by propose a promising set of weights at beginning. For both DE operations, the error measurement has been used as objective function for minimization. As the list of lag was optimized through searching process and weights were refined at initial step, the learning operation has been advanced further in compare with MLP.

In order to demonstrate hybrid model, dataset described Malaysia agricultural commodity's price of 53 items was used. When conducts with selective items, broaden from vegetables, fruits to meats, model managed to imitate the trend behavior in entire series as well as partial time interval. It also outperformed powerful linear model ARIMA as well as ANN in term of MAPE, MAE, MSE. Consequently, result from experiments indicates that performance of selected lag, obtained through DE operations, has overwhelmed the full set in initialization.

Although the model achieved high quality results, further studies should be implemented to compare with more advanced hybrid approaches. In addition, extra experiments should be conducted in common dataset such as Canadian lynx series to verify the efficiency. Furthermore, the replacement of backpropagation learning with DE approach is a promising solution to improve accuracy.

References

1. Bontempi, G., Ben Taieb, S., Le Borgne, Y.-A.: Machine learning strategies for time series forecasting. In: Aufaure, M.-A., Zimányi, E. (eds.) eBISS 2012. LNBIP, vol. 138, pp. 62–77. Springer, Heidelberg (2013). doi:10.1007/978-3-642-36318-4_3
2. Broersen, P.M.T.: The quality of lagged products and autoregressive Yule-Walker models as autocorrelation estimates. IEEE Trans. Instrum. Meas. **58**, 3867–3873 (2009). doi:10.1109/TIM.2009.2021206
3. Rahman, S.A., Huang, Y., Claassen, J., Kleinberg, S.: Imputation of missing values in time series with lagged correlations. In: IEEE International Conference on Data Mining Workshops, ICDMW, pp. 753–762 (2015)

4. Araujo, R.D.A, Junior, A.R.L., Ferreira, T.A.E.: Morphological-rank-linear time-lag added evolutionary forecasting method for financial time series forecasting. In: 2008 IEEE Congress on Evolutionary Computation, CEC 2008, pp. 1340–1347 (2008)
5. De Oliveira, J.F.L., Ludermir, T.B.: A hybrid evolutionary system for parameter optimization and lag selection in time series forecasting. In: Proceedings - 2014 Brazilian Conference on Intelligent Systems, BRACIS 2014, pp. 73–78 (2014)
6. Wong, W., Bai, E., Chu, A.W.: Adaptive time-variant models for fuzzy-time-series forecasting. IEEE Trans. Syst. Man Cybern. Part B Cybern. **40**, 1531–1542 (2010)
7. Cortez, P.: Sensitivity analysis for time lag selection to forecast seasonal time series using neural networks and support vector machines. In: The 2010 International Joint Conference on Neural Networks (IJCNN), pp. 1–8 (2010)
8. Zhang, G.P.: Time series forecasting using a hybrid ARIMA and neural network model. Neurocomputing. **50**, 159–175 (2003). doi:10.1016/S0925-2312(01)00702-0
9. Ömer Faruk, D.: A hybrid neural network and ARIMA model for water quality time series prediction. Eng. Appl. Artif. Intell. **23**, 586–594 (2010). doi:10.1016/j.engappai.2009.09.015
10. Khashei, M., Bijari, M.: A new class of hybrid models for time series forecasting. Expert Syst. Appl. **39**, 4344–4357 (2012). doi:10.1016/j.eswa.2011.09.157
11. Jain, A., Kumar, A.M.: Hybrid neural network models for hydrologic time series forecasting. Appl. Soft Comput. J. **7**, 585–592 (2007). doi:10.1016/j.asoc.2006.03.002
12. Rather, A.M., Agarwal, A., Sastry, V.N.: Recurrent neural network and a hybrid model for prediction of stock returns. Expert Syst. Appl. **42**, 3234–3241 (2015). doi:10.1016/j.eswa.2014.12.003
13. Rivero, C.R., Pucheta, J., Laboret, S., Herrera, M., Sauchelli, V.: Method: application to cumulative rainfall. IEEE Trans. Lat. Am. Trans. **11**, 359–364 (2013)
14. Araujo, R.DA., Vasconcelos, G.C., Ferreira, T.A.E.: Hybrid differential evolutionary system for financial time series forecasting. In: 2007 IEEE Congress on Evolutionary Computation, pp. 4329–4336 (2007)
15. Araújo, R.D.A., Oliveira, A.L.I., Meira, S.: A hybrid model for high-frequency stock market forecasting. Expert Syst. Appl. **42**, 4081–4096 (2015). doi:10.1016/j.eswa.2015.01.004
16. Ribeiro, G.H.T., de M. Neto, P.S.G., Cavalcanti, G.D.C., Tsang, I.R.: Lag selection for time series forecasting using particle swarm optimization. In: International Joint Conference on Neural Networks, pp. 2437–2444 (2011)
17. Cai, X., Zhang, N., Venayagamoorthy, G.K., Wunsch, D.C.: Time series prediction with recurrent neural networks trained by a hybrid PSO-EA algorithm. Neurocomputing. **70**, 2342–2353 (2007). doi:10.1016/j.neucom.2005.12.138
18. Brasileiro, R.C., Souza, V.L.F., Fernandes, B.J.T., Oliveira, A.L.I.: Automatic method for stock trading combining technical analysis and the Artificial Bee Colony Algorithm. In: 2013 IEEE Congress on Evolutionary Computation, CEC 2013, pp. 1810–1817 (2013)
19. Huang, G., Wang, L.: Hybrid neural network models for hydrologic time series forecasting based on genetic algorithm. In: 2011 Fourth International Joint. Conference Computational Science Optimization, pp. 1347–1350 (2011). doi:10.1109/CSO.2011.147
20. Parras-Gutierrez, E., Rivas Santos, V.: Time series forecasting: Automatic determination of lags and radial basis neural networks for a changing horizon environment. In: International Joint Conference on Neural Networks IJCNN, pp. 1–7 (2010)
21. Mohammadi, R., Fatemi Ghomi, S.M.T., Zeinali, F.: A new hybrid evolutionary based RBF networks method for forecasting time series: a case study of forecasting emergency supply demand time series. Eng. Appl. Artif. Intell. **36**, 204–214 (2014). doi:10.1016/j.engappai.2014.07.022

22. Vesterstrom, J., Thomsen, R.: A comparative study of differential evolution, particle swarm optimization, and evolutionary algorithms on numerical benchmark problems. In: 2004 Congress on Evolutionary Computation, CEC2004, pp. 1980–1987 (2004)
23. Neri, F., Tirronen, V.: Recent advances in differential evolution: a survey and experimental analysis. Artif. Intell. Rev. **33**, 61–106 (2010)
24. Segura, C., Coello Coello, C.A., Hernández-Díaz, A.G.: Improving the vector generation strategy of Differential Evolution for large-scale optimization. Inf. Sci. (Ny) **323**, 106–129 (2015). doi:10.1016/j.ins.2015.06.029
25. Wang, L., Zeng, Y., Chen, T.: Back propagation neural network with adaptive differential evolution algorithm for time series forecasting. Expert Syst. Appl. **42**, 855–863 (2015). doi:10.1016/j.eswa.2014.08.018
26. Peralta Donate, J., Cortez, P.: Evolutionary optimization of sparsely connected and time-lagged neural networks for time series forecasting. Appl. Soft Comput. **23**, 432–443 (2014). doi:10.1016/j.asoc.2014.06.041
27. Storn, R., Price, K.: Differential evolution – a simple and efficient heuristic for global optimization over continuous spaces. J. Glob. Optim. **11**, 341–359 (1997)

Identifying the Qur'anic Segment from Video Recording

Haslizatul Mohamed Hanum[1(✉)], Norizan Mat Diah[1],
and Zainab Abu Bakar[2]

[1] Universiti Tenologi MARA, 40450 Shah Alam, Selangor, Malaysia
haslizatul@salam.uitm.edu.my
[2] Al-Madinah International University, 40100 Shah Alam, Selangor, Malaysia

Abstract. This paper describes a system to identify Quran recitation (referred as Qur'anic) segment from speech video recording using the extracted acoustic signal. Identifying the Qur'anic sequence pattern from mixed-combination of speech and Qur'anic signal will contribute to more efficient segmentation of video segments. The random forest classifier algorithm is employed to classify the dynamic pattern of the extracted audio. Two feature sets which are pitch and intensity are extracted from the audio, and constructed into sequence of speech patterns which then classified as Qur'anic or non-Quranic segments. A collection of 40 segmented videos were trained and compared with the segmented videos which have been segmented manually. This project achieves classification accuracy of 57% using pitch and 85% using intensity. While using pitch feature only, 85% of the identified segments match the manually segmented collection while using intensity feature gives 95% match accordingly).

Keywords: Video segmentation · Acoustic feature pattern · Segment model

1 Introduction

The segmentation of the video can be done by differentiating between the speech, music, recitation or background signal extracted from the video recording. Segmentation of a video recording involves the identification of an argument for separating an input video stream into each segment. This step is necessary for advance one-dimensional and multi-dimensional signal data processing [1]. There are few techniques that can be used to identify the segments of video such as using video key-frame and/or acoustic features extracted from the video. However, it is di cult to determine the video key-frame, when the video is only displaying the speaker's face image. We are interested to identify the segment variability especially when most of the video frames show only the speaker's image throughout the video duration such as in religious (Sermon) speech. Therefore, this project proposes an enhancement of the identification of Quran recitation (refers from now on as Qur'anic) segment from speech video recording by evaluating the pitch and intensity features extracted from the recording's audio.

This paper presents the technique to identify the Qur'anic sequence pattern (QSP) utilizing the acoustic features extracted from religious speech video recording.

© Springer International Publishing AG 2017
H. Badioze Zaman et al. (Eds.): IVIC 2017, LNCS 10645, pp. 168–174, 2017.
https://doi.org/10.1007/978-3-319-70010-6_16

Random Forest technique is used to perform binary classification on the sequence patterns to enhance video segmentation into speech-recitation-speech structure. A method for speech pattern extraction using acoustic features is also described. We would like to draw your attention to the fact that it is not possible to modify a paper in any way, once it has been published. This applies to both the printed book and the online version of the publication. Every detail, including the order of the names of the authors, should be checked before the paper is sent to the Volume Editors.

2 Research Background

Recitation of the Quran refers to the reading with *tarteel*, *tajwid*, or *taghbir* aloud, reciting, or chanting of portions of the Quran verses. There are the rules to recite the verses which include the pronunciation, intonation and the caesuras that linked up the verses to deliver in a musical-like form.

Alghamdi [4] presented a set of labels which cover all the Arabic phonemes and their allophones to represent the Qur'anic corpus. Thus, they applied method for transcription to Qur'anic recitation to collect a sufficient Qur'anic speech database for training and testing. However, transcribing the Qur'anic recitation delivered by various Scholars may not be cost efficient. It is best to extract the audio features and build models special for Qur'anic segment.

Quran recitation segments have been defined in other research using various features, for example using MFCC and acoustic features. The viability of Mel-Frequency Cepstral Coefficient (MFCC) is found useful to identify Qur'anic recitation segment [7]. They said that MFCCs are based on the known variation of the human ears critical bandwidths with frequency which is the speech signal which was expressed in the Mel-frequency scale, to capture the important characteristic of phonetic in speech. A linear frequency spacing of this scale is below 1000 Hz and a logarithmic spacing above 1000 Hz. Normal speech waveform may vary from time to time depending on the physical condition of the vocal cord of the speakers. MFFCs are less susceptible to the said variations rather than the waveforms of the speech [8]. Hassan [5] proposed the technique of classification used to recognize the *Qalqalah Kubra* pronunciation (an Arabic grammar rule known as *tajweed*) using the Mel-Frequency Cepstral Coefficient (MFCC) extracted from the recitation audio. To classify the pronunciation of *Qalqalah Kubra* their described the use of Multilayer Perceptron using the MFCC features.

Recent research done on the recordings of Quran recitation such as in [3] include construction of an acoustical Arabic syllables database as a step towards a syllable-based Arabic speech verification/recognition system. Hafeez [6] proposed the development of speaker dependent live Quranic verse recitation recognition system using (CMU) Sphinx-4 based on HMM. The system aims to recognize and evaluates the accuracy of the recitation of Quranic verses. In order to generate the acoustic model, they used transliteration mechanism for the Arabic language. This system was trained using recitation from competent reciters and also the users themselves. After being trained various ways, the experiments showed that the accuracy in recognition word obtained was 67% for Arabic word with Arabic alphabet, 96% for transliteration words with syllables, 94% for transliteration compound words with syllables, and 81% for transliteration syllable with syllables.

From the related works that have been studied, acoustic features are the most suitable features that can be used in this project. Those features can be used to identify the features of Quran recitation types of an audio.

2.1 Speech Segment Model

Segment model applied on speech frames detects and groups similar neighboring frames into short segments, which was originated by segment model for speech recognition [9]. This idea of segment modeling is very similar to discovery of song's dynamic texture (DTM) for music summarization. Song structure is discovered by clustering similar patterns on sequence of cepstral features on series of frames represented as song features [10]. Segment modeling was applied to the task of song segmentation (i.e., automatically dividing a song into coherent segments that human listeners would label as verse, chorus, bridge, etc.) by modeling audio fragments from a song as samples from a DTM model.

This project performed a classification analysis of the training data using the Random Forest classifier algorithm because of its ability to build and predict faster and runs efficiently on large databases [11]. In general, random forest is a collection of decision tree classifiers. Each tree will be selected randomly at each node from a small group of features, in order to split the features in the training set. After that the best split will be calculated based on the features. The input vector will be taken by each tree, then classifying it and outputting the input vectors own vote on the feasible class label. Random forest collected together some trees that have been trained in a randomized way and commonly achieves higher-ranking stability and generalization compared to other simple classifier [12].

Thambi [11] analyzed if selecting a subset of the features can help improve the performance of the SND system. Towards this, they experimented with different feature selection algorithms, and observed that correlation based feature selection gave the best results. Then, they continue the experiment with different decision tree classification, and note that random forest algorithm outperformed other decision tree algorithms. They further improved the SND system performance by smoothing the decisions over 5 segments of 200 ms. each. Their baseline system achieved a classification accuracy of 94.45% and the final system with 8 features has a classification accuracy of 97.80%.

Lu [13] proposed a random forest based method for auditory context classification. The main difference of the proposed context-based method from other previous ones, which usually adopt a HMM-based model, is that the author employed a bag-of event model for auditory contexts, based on the observation that auditory contexts typically lack of obvious temporal evolution characteristics of the audio events, therefore they obviated explicit modeling of temporal correlation of events at the context level. The training and testing set contain around 100 and 150 mono channel audio samples, respectively, for each audio event and context category. The typical sample length is 1–3 s for audio events, and 15 s to 2 min duration for contexts. With 44.1 kHz sampling rate, they showed the effectiveness of the proposed random forest based framework, and combination of several heterogeneous features incrementally enhances the average performances.

Based on the previous studies that have been explored, this paper evaluates the similar features on Malay speech with random forest classifier because of its ability to perform higher prediction with higher accuracy.

3 Qur'anic Segment Identification

In this project, we identify the Qur'anic segment manually from the speech video recording by watching the video and listening to the speech content. Then, we extract and evaluate the pitch and intensity features from the identified Qur'anic segments and use Random Forest classifier to classify the features into Qur'anic versus non-Qur'anic classes as shown in Fig. 1. Finally, we test the correctness of the identified Qur'anic segment.

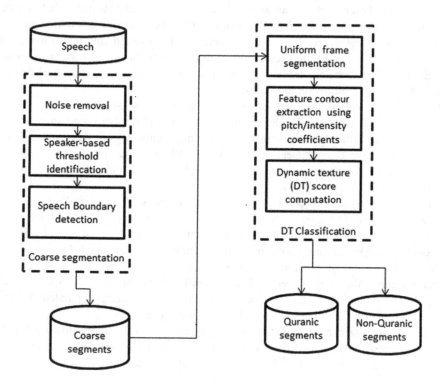

Fig. 1. The proposed Qur'anic segment identification methodology

3.1 Data Preparation

The data in this study consist of one speech video recording in mp4 format that have been downloaded from YouTube. The videos entitled 'sakaratul maut' (death) contain speech delivered by a male Islamic Scholar.

This process of segmentation can be done by segmenting video manually beginning with cutting the video from the long duration into short video segments depending on their content information. From the process, the types of segmented files which are speech segment, Quran recitation segment were identified.

First of all, the collected speech video recording was segmented manually by cutting the video using YTD Chrome Downloader after listening and identifying the two types of content from the whole video recording. A student from the University was trained to listen to and segment the video. From the segmentation process, 32 segmented videos in WMV format were identified. The segmented videos were saved into one folder. The files were labelled as either Qur'anic audio segments or speech audio segments.

3.2   Audio Pre-processing

There were 20 Qur'anic segments in WMV format from Audio Segmented audio files were extracted. To characterize an audio signal, there are many features that can be used. In this project, pitch and intensity features have been explored. First of all, the audio from each segmented video was extracted and converted into audio using an online audio converter at http://audio.online-convert.com/convert-to-wav. The audio from the identified Qur'anic segment were extracted to evaluate the characteristics of pitch and intensity features on those segments.

Coarse segmentation was performed after removal of noise and identifying the speaker's threshold value. Using pause duration, the boundaries between words can be identified to help refine the segments. Then, feature contours were constructed from each pitch and intensity coefficients extracted from 10 ms signal frames. The contours are constructed as Qur'anic sequence pattern (QSP's) and the ratio and weight of the contour was computed as in [14].

The pitch and intensity features were extracted using Praat tool. From the 20 manually identified Qur'anic segments, aggregate measures of pitch and intensity including min, max and mean attributes were combined with QSPs ratios and weights were computed. The measures were used to train and test a classifier for the Qur'anic segments. The value of pitch range for male speaker is set to 100–250 Hz. The extracted features then were saved as Praat's *TextGrid* and saved in a dedicated file. Then, the files containing the features were saved as Comma Separated Values (CSV) file format which then used for classification process.

Data is normalized to scale between the range 0 to 1 using the following Eq. 1, where x_{ij} represents the actual data, min_j and max_j are the minimum and maximum values of the data respectively and X_{ij} is the normalize data.

$$X_{ij} = \frac{x_{ij} - X_{min_j}}{X_{max_j} - X_{min_j}} \tag{1}$$

3.3   Identification of Qur'anic Segment

In this paper, results of classification analysis using the Random Forest classifier algorithm are presented. Random forest is chosen because of its ability to build and predict faster and runs efficiently on large databases. We examined the extracted pitch and intensity features within each segment and across segments along the Qur'anic and non-Qur'anic segments. Sequences of the QSPs are learned from the collection of these audio segments and aggregate measures were obtained. For each segment, it is classified as one of binary classes: a Qur'anic (1) or a non-Qur'anic (0) classes.

4   Result

The accuracy results of the pitch feature in order to identify the types of segments into either a Qur'anic or a speech type is 57%. Intensity feature offer a higher and more reliable measure for the identification of Quran recitation segment with the accuracy result of 85%. Thus, the intensity feature can be used for distinguishing between the Qur'anic audio segments from the speech segments.

From all the identified Qur'anic segments, the ones that were classified using pitch feature match 85% of the corresponding segments that have been identified manually. The intensity feature offer similar result with 95% match to the corresponding manually identified segments.

5   Conclusion

The dynamic texture model has been successfully applied to various computer vision problems, including video texture synthesis video recognition, and motion segmentation [15]. The treatment of a time-series as a sample from a linear dynamical system is also known as a texture pattern (TP) in the computer vision literature, where a video is modeled as sequences of vectorized image frames. For speech document, we consider representing the audio segments with the corresponding sequence of audio feature vectors. Similar approach is used for the Malay speech with Islamic content, as within the speech, they are fragments of Qur'anic verses recited in song-like intonation (*tarannum*). This paper concludes that the identification of the Qur'anic segment from the speech can be achieved by evaluating the pitch and intensity features.

It is important to identify the segments of Qur'anic Recitation especially when a database is required for a speech recognition system. It is also used to build other systems for example speaker verification and speech syntheses [4]. Automatic video segmentation is useful for video indexing and search applications by offering a visual guideline for the video content navigation [2].

Acknowledgment. This research is supported by Universiti Teknologi MARA (UiTM), Shah Alam, Selangor under the UiTM Internal Grant 600-IRMI/DANA 5/3/LESTARI (0111/2016). Special thanks to the members of the Faculty of Computer and Mathematical Sciences at UiTM for the encouragement to pursue research at the faculty. Thank you to Liliana Nulkasim for evaluating and manually segmenting the video contents and constructing the Malay speech collection closely supervised by the first author.

References

1. Prochazka, A., Kukal, J., Vysata, O.: Wavelet transform use for feature extraction and EEG signal segments classification. In: 3rd International Symposium on Communications, Control and Signal Processing (ISCCSP), pp. 719–722. IEEE (2008)
2. Yang, H., Meinel, C.: Content based lecture video retrieval using speech and video text information. IEEE Trans. Learn. Technol. **7**(2), 142–154 (2014)
3. Abdo, M.S., Kandil, A.H.: Semi-automatic segmentation system for syllables extraction from continuous arabic audio. Signal **7**(1), 535–540 (2016)
4. Alghamdi, M., El Hadj, Y.M., Alkanhal, M.: A manual system to segment and transcribe arabic speech. In: Signal Processing and Communications (ICSPC), pp. 233–236. IEEE (2007)
5. Hassan, H.A., Nasrudin, N.H., Khalid, M.N.M., Zabidi, A., Yassin, A.I.: Pattern classification in recognizing Qalqalah Kubra pronunciation using multilayer perceptrons. In: IEEE Symposium on Computer Applications and Industrial Electronics (ISCAIE), pp. 209–212 IEEE (2012)
6. Hafeez, H., Mohiuddin, K., Ahmed, S.: Speaker-dependent live quranic verses recitation recognition system using Sphinx-4 framework. In: IEEE 17th International Multi-Topic Conference (INMIC), pp. 333–337 (2014)
7. Razak, Z., Ibrahim, N.J., Tamil, E.M., Idris, M.Y.I., Yusoff, Z.M.: Quranic verse recitation feature extraction using Mel-frequency cepstral co-efficient (MFCC). In: 4th International Colloquium on Signal Processing and Its Applications, pp. 978–983 (2008)
8. Hasan, M.R., Jamil, M., Rabbani, M.G., Rahman, M.S.: Speaker identification using mel frequency cepstral coefficients variations. In: International Conference on Electrical and Computer Engineering (ICECE), vol. 1, no. 4, Dhaka, Bangladesh (2004)
9. Chin-Hui, L., Soong, F.K., Biing-Hwang, J.: A segment model based approach to speech recognition. In: International Conference on Acoustics, Speech, and Signal Processing (ICASSP), pp. 501–541 (1988)
10. Barrington, L., Chan, A.B., Gert, R.G.: Lanckriet: modeling music as a dynamic texture. IEEE Trans. Audio Speech Lang. Process. **18**(3), 602–612 (2010)
11. Thambi, S.V., Sreekumar, K.T., Kumar, C.S., Raj, P.R.: Random forest algorithm for improving the performance of speech/non-speech detection. In: 2014 First International Conference on Computational Systems and Communications (ICCSC), pp. 28–32. IEEE (2014)
12. Yang, L., Su, F.: Auditory context classification using random forests. In 2012 IEEE International Conference on Acoustics, Speech and Signal Processing (ICASSP), pp. 2349–2352. IEEE (2012)
13. Lu, L., Jiang, H., Zhang, H.: A robust audio classification and segmentation method. In Proceedings of the ninth ACM international conference on Multimedia, pp. 203–211. ACM (2001)
14. Hanum, H.M., Bakar, Z.A.: Sentence segmentation and phrase strength estimation in Malay continuous speech. In: Proceedings of the International Conference on Speech Prosody, vol. 2016, pp. 1163–1166 (2016)
15. Chan, A.B., Vasconcelos, N.: Modeling, clustering, and segmenting video with mixtures of dynamic textures. IEEE Trans. Speech Audio Process. **30**(5), 909–926 (2008)

Document Clustering in Military Explicit Knowledge: A Study on Peacekeeping Documents

Zuraini Zainol[1(✉)], Syahaneim Marzukhi[1], Puteri N.E. Nohuddin[2],
Wan M.U. Noormaanshah[1], and Omar Zakaria[1]

[1] Department of Computer Science, Universiti Pertahanan Nasional Malaysia,
Kem Sungai Besi, 57000 Kuala Lumpur, Malaysia
{zuraini, syahaneim, omar}@upnm.edu.my,
wanmuhamadumarullah@gmail.com
[2] Institute of Visual Informatics, Universiti Kebangsaan Malaysia,
43600 Bangi, Selangor, Malaysia
puteri.ivi@ukm.edu.my

Abstract. In Military domain, knowledge can also be categorized into explicit knowledge and tacit knowledge, where the explicit military knowledge can be any form of knowledge that can easily articulated, codified, accessed and stored into various media forms. Further, advanced computer technologies give a convenient platform for digitizing documents, producing web documents and electronic documents, including this explicit military knowledge (e.g. military peacekeeping documents). The main goal here is to discover useful knowledge from military peacekeeping documents. Yet, text mining is a powerful technique that is widely used for discovering useful patterns and knowledge specially in unstructured text documents. This paper describes Text Analytics of Unstructured Data (TAUD) framework for analyzing and discovering significant text patterns exist in the military text documents. The framework consists of three (3) components: (i) data collection (ii) document preprocessing and (iii) text analytics and visualization which are word cloud and document clustering using K-Means algorithm. The findings of this study allow the military commanders and training officers to understand and access the military knowledge which they had learnt and gathered during the training programs before they can be deployed into a peacekeeping mission.

Keywords: Military knowledge · Text mining · Visualization · Patterns

1 Introduction

Peacekeeping is one among a range of activities undertaken by the United Nations (UN) to maintain international peace and security throughout the world [1]. Peacekeeping has seen to be one of the tools to the UN to assist host countries that having difficulty from conflict to peace. Military personnel are the backbone and the most visible component of a peacekeeping operation. UN military personnel can be called upon to: protect civilians and UN personnel, monitor a disputed border, monitor and

© Springer International Publishing AG 2017
H. Badioze Zaman et al. (Eds.): IVIC 2017, LNCS 10645, pp. 175–184, 2017.
https://doi.org/10.1007/978-3-319-70010-6_17

observe peace processes in post-conflict areas, provide security across a conflict zone, assist in-country military personnel with training and support, assist ex-combatants in implementing the peace agreements; they may have signed and implement their mandated [1]. Therefore, in order to implement their mandated tasks, the military personnel need to prepare adequately before deployment. This preparation covers every aspect of UN Peacekeeping such as equipment and training in amongst others Protection of Civilians, the use of force and the rules of engagement. In addition, the military personnel also conduct and discipline in every important training item. Thus, the knowledge regarding training and equipment training, important information and in-depth understanding of the mission including previous and current conflicts, are vital to them.

One example of the military personnel explicit knowledge is UN Peacekeeping Training Manual that can be downloaded from the UN website [1]. These Guidelines describe the core roles and scope of operational employment activities for UN Military Experts on Mission in UN Department of Peacekeeping Operations (DPKO)-led peacekeeping missions. Next, these Guidelines link the roles of these military personnel to the skill sets that have been identified by DPKO as generally common to their operational employment across all UN peacekeeping missions). These training manual also covers important topics such as: weapon training, military training in UN operating techniques, safety measures and precautions, specialized training areas and exercises.

The advancement of technology nowadays resulted a convenient platform to digitize documents, produce web documents and electronic documents in order to assist the military personnel during UN peacekeeping missions. Whereas, these documents can be managed efficiently and effectively for keeping, copying and reproducing documents and knowledge. Further, many document management techniques are developed to improvise methods for handling and analyzing content of documents. Since the task of the military personnel is varied and crucial, therefore, the military personnel explicit knowledge; important information and in-depth understanding of the mission are vital to them. In order to extract the knowledge and identify hidden information pattern of the mission from various sources (e.g. data from reports, briefings, books, guidelines, notes and information) efficient technique is needed (e.g. data mining technique). Using data mining technique, knowledge can be extracted through the process of sorting and selecting meaningful and useful information from a large pool of data. Here, the data warehouse will store data from various sources and transactions, whereas the knowledge is extracted using the data mining technique such as text mining for discovering useful patterns and knowledge in unstructured text documents. Thus, the aim of this paper is to determine a technique of analyzing the unstructured text data in discovering the useful knowledge from military peacekeeping documents.

The rest of this paper is organized as follows. Section 2 explores Knowledge discovery, text analytics and military explicit knowledge and some related work on related topics. Section 3 discusses the framework for the proposed technique. Section 4 discusses the experiment and results. Finally, we conclude this paper with future work in Sect. 5.

2   Background and Related Work

In this section, some background information on Military Explicit Knowledge, knowledge discovery using text analytics and document clustering are discussed.

2.1   Military Explicit Knowledge – UN Peacekeeping Training Manual

Knowledge plays a key role in the information revolution and is widely associated to process information or skills acquired during a learning process. Major challenges are to select the "right" information from numerous sources and transform it into useful knowledge. Knowledge that has been documented is called as explicit and knowledge based on undocumented lesson learned and experiences are known as tacit knowledge. Tacit knowledge is based on common sense and often stored in human's mind [2] whereas explicit knowledge is based on academic accomplishment are both underutilized [3]. In Military domain, knowledge can also be categorized into: (i) explicit knowledge and (ii) tacit knowledge. In the military context, the explicit military knowledge is referred as knowledge that can easily articulated, codified, accessed and stored into various media forms such as (i) Doctrine, (ii) Tactics, Techniques and Procedures (TTPs), [4] etc. Throughout the experiments, UN Peacekeeping Training Manual is also known as 'Training Guidelines for National or Regional Training Programmes" from the UN website will be used as datasets [1]. Here, the training manual is used as the military explicit knowledge. This training manual comprises several basic topics on weapon training, general military, training in UN operating techniques, safety measures and precautions, specialized training areas and exercises.

2.2   Knowledge Discovery Using Text Analytics

Text Mining (TM) or Text Analytics (TA) is one type of data mining technique. TA is used for extracting or mining knowledge from the text document. According to [5], Knowledge Discovery in Text (KDT) is a process of identifying valid, novel, potentially useful and ultimately understandable patterns in unstructured text data. Text mining is similar to data mining but the data mining dealing with structure data and text mining dealing with unstructured or semi structure data [6]. TA is often used for analyzing the unstructured text documents in search of useful information and knowledge hidden from text resources. TA is an extension of data mining, which involves multiple disciplines areas such as Information Retrieval (IR), Statistics, Web Mining, Computational Linguistics and Natural Language Processing (NLP). TA can also be described as intelligent text analysis, text data mining and knowledge discovery in text. For example, TA is used in healthcare for investigating patient health outcomes and providing clinical decision making for health practitioners [7].

Figure 1 depicts four (4) main stages of TA: (i) the collection of document from different sources (e.g. emails, online news, reports, manuals and many more), (ii) retrieve documents, perform pre-processing and transformed them into suitable format for text analysis, (iii) apply the text mining techniques to the document where interesting patterns and knowledge are extracted and (iv) analyze the output text data where these patterns and knowledge are presented to users, which can be used for assisting decision makers in any application domains.

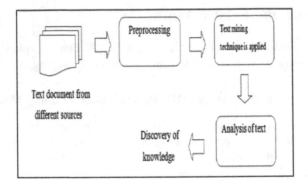

Fig. 1. Overview of four (4) main steps in TA process [6].

2.3 Document Clustering

Clustering is the process of finding meaningful groups in data. In clustering, the objective is not to predict a target class variable, but to simply capture the possible natural groupings in the data [6]. Therefore, clustering analysis is a method for grouping homogenous objects into respective categories [8, 9]. The most common application of clustering is to explore the data and find all possible meaningful groups in the data. Clustering analysis is broadly used in many applications such as market research, data analysis [10], image processing [11], biology [12], machine learning [13], information retrieval [14], spatial data analysis [15], customer or user profiling [10], web-log record analysis for websites [16], document clustering [17–20], etc. In other words, clustering is finding groups of objects such that the objects in a group will be similar (or related) to one another and different from (or unrelated to) the objects in other groups. In this paper, the method used is based on the concept of dividing similar text into same cluster. Each cluster contains a number of similar documents. There are several algorithms that are applied in this technique such as follows:

- K-means clustering
  K-means clustering is a type of unsupervised learning, that is applied to unlabeled data (i.e., data without defined categories or groups). The goal of this algorithm is to find groups in the data, with the number of groups represented by the variable k [21]. The algorithm works iteratively to assign each data point to one of k groups based on the features that are provided. Data points are clustered based on feature similarity.

- Hierarchical clustering
  Hierarchical clustering is a method of cluster analysis that look for building a hierarchical cluster [22]. In hierarchical clustering, a nested set of clusters is created. As the name is hierarchical, each level of hierarchy separates a set of clusters. Each of the items in the lower hierarchy has their own unique cluster, but as it goes up to the topmost hierarchies, all items belong to the same cluster. Figure 2 shows the example of hierarchical clustering that organizes objects into a dendrogram whose branches are the desired clusters

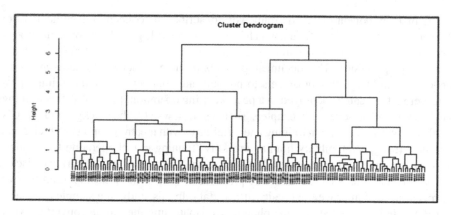

Fig. 2. The example of hierarchical clustering (dendrogram) adapted from [23]

3 Overview of Text Analytics in Military Explicit Knowledge Framework

In our previous paper [24], we have proposed a framework for Text Analytics of Unstructured Data (TAUD) for analyzing and discovering significant text patterns exist in the military text documents. Basically, TAUD consists of three (3) main components: (i) Document Collection; (ii) Data Preprocessing in Military Peacekeeping Document and (iii) Analyzing and Visualizing Selection of Terms (see Fig. 3).

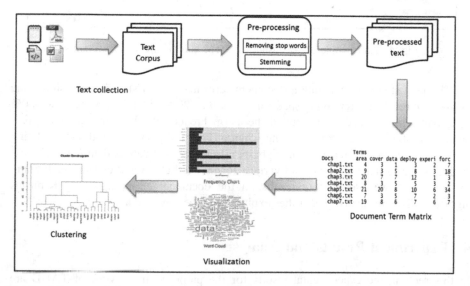

Fig. 3. A framework for text analytics in military peacekeeping document adopted from [24]

The first component of TAUD framework describes the collection documents from UN Peacekeeping Training Manual which is aimed to provide guidelines for actual troops contributing governments in the preparation and training before they can be deployed into a peacekeeping mission. This document presents training guidelines for assisting commanders and military training officers to prepare and conduct in country training programs before they can be deployed in a peacekeeping operation. Generally, this training manual consists of seven (7) chapters such as follows: (i) the background of UN peacekeeping, (ii) the weapon training and familiarity with theatre weapons, vehicles and equipment (iii) general military training areas (iv) training in UN operating techniques, (v) safety measures and precautions, (vi) specialized training areas and (vii) exercises.

The second component explains the preprocessing task. It is an important task as preprocessing will improve the quality of text data. In this study, the sample of dataset from PDF file is converted into the plain text format using the online converter. After that, the chapters are distributed into seven (7) documents of plain text. In this phase, five (5) common data preprocessing tasks are carried out. For example, (i) exploring the text data, (ii) converting text to lowercase, (iii) removing numbers, symbols, punctuations, english stop words, and stemming (iv) striping white space, and (v) removing sparse terms. Removal of unnecessary words will assist in document clustering. The cleaned data is then stored into seven (7) plain text files (see Fig. 4).

Docs	Terms area	deploy	forc	militari	oper	peacekeep	personnel	pko	train	troop
chap1.txt	4	3	7	9	9	13	5	13	26	5
chap2.txt	9	8	18	16	31	24	6	18	11	6
chap3.txt	20	12	3	2	13	4	7	10	44	16
chap4.txt	8	5	2	3	16	3	14	14	30	3
chap5.txt	21	10	34	6	21	11	5	19	50	5
chap6.txt	7	7	3	3	9	3	11	5	16	11
chap7.txt	19	7	7	11	9	4	12	18	48	4

Fig. 4. An example of screenshot for DTM after removing sparse terms

The next step is to generate a document term matrix (DTM). Figure 4 shows the example of results for removing sparse in DTM with 20 terms in 7 documents with 0% of sparsity. In this study, we applied the Term Frequency - Inverse Document Frequency (TF-IDF) as the term weighting scheme. The third phase focused on visualizing the selection keywords/terms. In this phase, all cleaned text data is then ready for text analytics and visualizing them into various forms word cloud and cluster dendogram. In this paper, we added more results on the document clustering using K-means algorithm. This result will be further explained in the next section.

4   Experiment Results and Analysis

In this section, the experimental results for the proposed framework of TAUD are presented and discussed. The preprocessed dataset consists of a DTM of seven (7) documents and 20 terms were used as an input dataset for analyzing the military

Fig. 5. Word cloud with 100 most frequently occurring words

peacekeeping documents. Figure 5 shows a word cloud which highlights the most frequently used words in text documents. As shown in Fig. 5, the keywords "train", "oper", "peac" and "area" are the top four (4) frequently used words in text documents which validates that seven (7) documents present information that related to peace-keeping operation and training. In this experiment, we customize the word cloud by setting the maximum number of keywords to be plotted is 100. It indicates that the size of keywords is corresponding to the frequency of the keyword.

Figure 6 presents the cluster dendogram for the 20 terms in the seven (7) documents. From the dendrogram, we can see that the cluster analysis has placed "train" in the first group. The second cluster consists of "data", "report", "home", "experi", "import", "organ", "personnel", "troop", "deploy" and "unit". This is because there are couple of chapters explained the importance of organization and unit, experience personnel and troops before they can be deployed. The third cluster consists of the keywords "area", "oper", and "pko". They are clustered together into one group of chapters on the operation's area for PKO (Peacekeeping Operation). The fourth cluster comprises of keywords "peacekeep", "military", "force", "observ", "cover" and "level". This relates to the chapters on military peacekeeping observers and force covers all levels.

K-means clustering is one of unsupervised learning algorithm that can be applied to understand the underlying structure of a dataset. For example, by using text data, K-means clustering can provide a great way to form the thousands of words being used in the military peacekeeping training manual. Figure 7 presents the K-means clustering for the 20 terms in the seven (7) documents. From the diagram, we can clearly see that the first cluster consists of keywords "oper", "pko", "forc", "area" and "peacekeep". The keyword "train" is placed in the second cluster. The third cluster consists of the keywords "troop", "personnel", "deploy", "cover", "observ", "level", "unit" and "militari". The fourth cluster comprises of keywords "data", "report", "experi", "import", "home" and "organ". This relates to the chapters on military peacekeeping observers and force covers all levels.

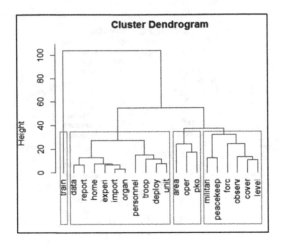

Fig. 6. Cluster dendrogram (hierarchical) with four (4) main clusters

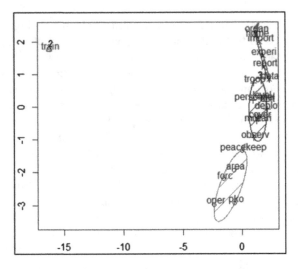

Fig. 7. K-means clustering with 4 clusters

5 Conclusion

This paper describes Text Analytics of Unstructured Data (TAUD) framework for analyzing and discovering significant text patterns exist in the military text documents. The framework consists of three (3) main components: (i) data collection (ii) document preprocessing and (iii) text analytics and visualization which are word cloud and document clustering using K-Means algorithm. In the first component, the document is collected from United Nations (UN) Peacekeeping Training Manual which is aimed to provide guidelines for actual troops contributing governments in the preparation and training before they can be deployed into a peacekeeping mission. Generally, this training manual consists of seven (7) main chapters. In the second component, the preprocessing task is performed. It is an important task as preprocessing will improve the quality of text data. Here, the dataset (i.e. United Nations (UN) Peacekeeping Training Manual from PDF file) is converted into the plain text format and the five (5) basic steps of data preprocessing are carried out. In the third component, all cleaned text data is then ready for text analytics and visualizing them into various forms word cloud and cluster dendogram. Based on the document term matrix (DTM) that was applied in the second component (i.e. document preprocessing), 20 terms in 7 documents were used as an input dataset for analyzing the military peacekeeping documents. The results highlight the most frequently used words and important terms in the seven (7) documents related to peacekeeping operation and training. The findings of this study (i.e. visualization from word cloud, dendogram clustering, K-means clustering) allow the military commanders and training officers to understand and access the military knowledge which they had learnt and gathered during the training programs before they can be deployed into a peacekeeping mission. For future work, this research will extend the dataset to include all tacit knowledge and explicit military knowledge peacekeeping documents that can give more understandings for discovering useful knowledge and patterns.

Acknowledgements. The authors would like to thank Universiti Pertahanan Nasional Malaysia (UPNM) and Kementerian Pendidikan Malaysia (KPM) under NRGS/2013/UPNM/PK/P3 for sponsoring this publication.

References

1. United Nation peacekeeping (2017) http://www.un.org/en/peacekeeping/. Accessed 20 June 2017
2. Yusof, W.S.E.Y.W., Zakaria, O., Zainol, Z.: Establishing of knowledge based framework for situational awareness using Nonaka's and Endsley's models. In: International Conference on Information and Communication Technology, pp. 47–50. IEEE Xplore (2016). 10.1109/ICICTM.2016.7890775
3. Smith, E.A.: The role of tacit and explicit knowledge in the workplace. J. Knowl. Manage. **5**(4), 311–321. MCG University Press (2010). ISSN 1367–3270
4. Nohuddin, P.N., et al.: Knowledge management in military: a review for Malaysian armed forces' communities of practices. J. Converg. Inf. Technol. **7**(6), 178–184. Advanced Institute of Convergence Information Technology Research Center, Malaysia (2010). doi:10.4156/jcit.vol7.issue6.22
5. Feldman, R., Dagan, I.: Knowledge discovery in textual databases (KDT). In: KDD. vol. 95, pp. 112–117 (1995)
6. Shrihari, R.C., Desai, A.: A review on knowledge discovery using text classification techniques in text mining. Int. J. Comput. Appl. **111**(6), 12–15 (2015)
7. Massey, G.: Extracting relevance from unstructured medical data. http://www.psqh.com/analysis/in-context-extracting-relevance-from-unstructured-medical-data/

8. Mooi, E., Sarstedt, M.: Understanding cluster-analysis. In: A Concise Guide to Market Research. The Process, Data, and Methods Using IBM SPSS Statistics, pp. 259–283. Springer, Heidelberg/Dordrecht (2011)

9. Mourya, S., Gupta, S.: Data Mining and Data Warehousing. Alpha Science International, Ltd., Oxford (2012)

10. Altuntas, S., Dereli, T., Kusiak, A.: Analysis of patent documents with weighted association rules. Technol. Forecast. Soc. Change **92**, 249–262 (2015). Elsevier

11. Han, J., Pei, J., Kamber, M.: Data Mining: Concepts and Techniques. Elsevier, Amsterdam (2011)

12. Gönen, M., Margolin, A.A.: Localized data fusion for kernel k-means clustering with application to cancer biology. In: Proceedings of Advances in Neural Information Processing Systems, pp. 1305–1313. MIT Press, Cambridge (2014)

13. Nunez-Iglesias, J., et al.: Machine learning of hierarchical clustering to segment 2d and 3d images. PLoS One **8**(8), e71715 (2013). doi:10.1371/journal.pone.0071715

14. Tan, P.N., Steinbach, M., Kumar, V.: Data Mining Cluster Analysis: Basic Concepts and Algorithms. Pearson Addison-Wesley, Boston (2006)

15. Pereira, C.M., de Mello, R.F.: Persistent homology for time series and spatial data clustering. Expert Syst. Appl. **42**(15), 6026–6038 (2015). Elsevier

16. Du, H.: Data Mining Techniques and Applications: An Introduction. Cengage Learning, Boston (2010)

17. Nohuddin, P.N., et al.: Keyword based clustering technique for collections of hadith chapters. Int. J. Islamic Appl. Comput. Sci. Technol. (IJASAT) **4**(3), 11–18 (2015)

18. Reddy, V.S., Kinnicutt, P., Lee, R.: Text document clustering: the application of cluster analysis to textual document. In: International Conference on Computational Science and Computational Intelligence. IEEE (2016)

19. Abualigah, L.M., et al.: Text feature selection with a robust weight scheme and dynamic dimension reduction to text document clustering. Expert Syst. Appl. **84**, 24–36 (2017). ACM

20. Onan, A., Bulut, H., Korukoglu, S.: An improved ant algorithm with LDA-based representation for text document clustering. J. Inf. Sci. **43**(2), 275–292 (2017)

21. Introduction to clustering. https://www.datascience.com/blog/introduction-to-k-means-clustering-algorithm-learn-data-science-tutorials

22. Kaufman, L., Rousseeuw, P.J.: Finding Groups in Data: An Introduction to Cluster Analysis. Wiley, Hoboken (2009)

23. Torgo, L.: Data Mining with R: Learning with Case Studies. Chapman and Hall/CRC, Boca Raton (2011)

24. Zainol, Z., et al.: Text analytics of unstructured textual data: a study on military peacekeeping document using R text mining package. In: International Conference on Computing and Informatics, pp. 1–7. School of Computing, UUM (2017)

Analysis of Learning Analytics in Higher Educational Institutions: A Review

Sarraf Rajesh Kumar[1(✉)] and Suraya Hamid[2]

[1] Institute of Postgraduate Studies, University of Malaya,
50603 Kuala Lumpur, Malaysia
sarraf@siswa.um.edu.my
[2] Department of Information Systems, Faculty of Computer Science
and Information Technology, University of Malaya,
50603 Kuala Lumpur, Malaysia
suraya_hamid@um.edu.my

Abstract. Learning analytics is relatively new in the field of research models, assessment/evaluation, and business intelligence. The critical analysis of literature explains that, as a consequence of more and better data, learning analytics gained significant attention in education. This paper emphasized integration of three major components: educational data mining, learning analytics, and academic analytics. It gives the comprehensive background for increasing understanding of the positive aspects of implementing the framework of learning analytics (LA) in higher educational institutions in Malaysia. Besides emphasizing LA, the role of educational data mining (EDM) in adaptive learning is also discussed. It gives an empirical-based overview with the key objectives of adopting the proposed model of LA in generic educational strategic planning by Malaysian HEIs. It examined the literature on experimental case studies, conducted during the last six years (2012–2017) for extracting recently updated information on increasing HEIs performance in Malaysia. The results have highlighted some major directions of LA, EDM, and academic analytics in driving techniques for achieving student retention and enhancing employability.

Keywords: Academic analytics · Learning analytics · Higher education · Educational data mining · Student retention

1 Introduction

The empirical framework implies that learning analytics has become an emerging domain, which seeks to utilize data analysis for making informed strategic decisions at different levels of the education system [12]. Since business analytics assesses consumer data to discover a potential range of consumers, on the other hand, learning analytics is the field involving students for creating better pedagogies [28]. Papamitsiou and Economides (2014) and Phillips et al. (2012) also indicated learning analytics as a successful domain that helps by focusing on student problems and evaluating educational programs [22, 24]. Learning analytics are designed for improving retention issues and maintaining academic attainment effectiveness. The core purpose of this document is to propose and implement the most influential constituent, learning

© Springer International Publishing AG 2017
H. Badioze Zaman et al. (Eds.): IVIC 2017, LNCS 10645, pp. 185–196, 2017.
https://doi.org/10.1007/978-3-319-70010-6_18

analytical model in Malaysia's Higher Educational Institutions (HEIs) for increasing student retention, employability, and academic attainment.

1.1   Key Aims and Objectives

This paper aims at assessing how Learning Analytics can be implemented in the Higher Educational Institutions of Malaysia in order to improve teaching and learning. Moreover, no research has been initiated on this specific research area in the Malaysian education system; therefore, this paper aims at identifying how Learning Analytics can be implemented and what impact it will have on the Malaysian education system. The research objectives are:

- To explore the impact of Learning Analytics on the performance of Higher Educational Institutions of Malaysia
- To identify how Learning Analytics can be implemented in the Higher Educational Institutions of Malaysia
- To determine the challenges and hardships in implementing Learning Analytics in higher education in Malaysia.

1.2   Research Questions

Based on the research objectives aimed at introducing Learning Analytics in Higher Educational Institutions (HEIs) in Malaysia, the following questions will be answered by the study:

1. How do different factors of learning analytics and their adoption influence the learning perspectives in Malaysian higher educational institutions?
2. How do learning analytics impact the factors influencing student retention, attainment and employability?
3. What are the attributes for effective implementation of the learning analytics framework within HEIs in Malaysia?

2   Methodology

For this purpose, the review of articles describing or delineating LA was considered and its methods and tools (including factors affecting learning) in the university context was considered. The paper was structured in two phases: the first one focused on investigating education studies in online databases. The keywords used were learning, learning analytics, learning analytics research, educational factors, data mining, and higher educational institutions. The second phase involved scrutiny of the references in the resulting articles, which allowed discovery of topics and new specific authors related to the search objectives. Inclusion criteria included journal articles that link to LA, articles related to learning, articles related to factors influencing learning from the LA framework. Articles whose publication date does not exceed six years old, that is, from January 2012 to 2017, were considered in order to obtain a completely updated literature review, which gives an account of current field discussions, results, and trends. Papers in peer reviewed journals, by virtue of ensuring scientific rigor and quality standards in the literature, were examined.

2.1 Significance of Report

Based upon the challenging issues arising in the HEIs of Malaysia due to high rate of student absenteeism and insufficient employment opportunities, the paper is intended to conduct an exploratory research on developing an effective learning analytics model. On the theoretical foundation of Dawson et al. (2014), learning analytics demonstrated as the most impactful instrument of increasing significant consideration to converge the concepts of information technology and learning in the fields of promoting higher education, computer services, and most importantly learner personal and professional development [28]. Moreover, the report in connection with the learning aspects depicted a framework involving improving usage of the information and data with a specific end goal of enhancing academic outcomes [13].

Chatti et al. (2012) described that learning analytics is a possible key of future trends in delivering competent learning and teaching, which borrow techniques from different fields – contributing to fulfillment of learning objectives. This report defines how learning analytics will develop the connection between the varying elements of academic analytics, action for research, mining of educational data, recommendation systems, along with personalized adaptive learning system in HEIs of Malaysia.

2.2 Problem Statement

Malaysia is considered as one of the biggest hubs of education providers. The government of Malaysia has always developed effective measures to enhance the education system. Implementing Learning Analytics in the education system is regarded as the new but most important measure to improve the education system. Many challenges exist in implementing Learning Analytics in Malaysia; therefore, this research has been initiated to identify and recommend the most effective ways for Higher Educations Institutions in Malaysia to implement such systems. This fact entails numerous challenges and barriers towards the completion of this research topic. While the education sector in Malaysia is highly supported by the government and university management, obtaining in-depth information is very challenging.

To meet this challenge we intend to carry out interview sessions with university management. The limitation associated with this study is obtaining information regarding the experience of individuals (Macklem, 2015). Since no research has been initiated earlier on implementing Learning Analytics in the Higher Educational Institutions in Malaysia, this might also bring challenges for this study; we thus need to rely on primary data only. Another challenge is to gain a maximum number of participants (international and local) to widen knowledge and information. Because of time constraints, it is possible that limited amount of information will be gathered for this research.

3 Emerging Concept of Learning Analytics

The term Analytics of Learning (Learning Analytics) was coined by Mitchell and Costello in 2000, as an emerging concept in its investigation of the visible opportunities in the international market, in the creation and distribution of educational products through the network [7, 19]. Learning Analytics has been defined as "the use of intelligent data that have been produced by the learner, as well as model analysis, with the aim of discovering information and social connections and predicting and advising on learning." [29] Learning Analytics is entrenched in higher education due to the growing popularity of educational processes taught through the Network [29]. Educational institutions have understood the importance of monitoring their platforms to retrieve information produced by student interactions with the learning system [23]. Despite facing a complex task, statisticians and researchers are constantly working on developing new tools to allow management of these data as input to adapt educational processes and enhance the learning process [10].

According to Wagner and Ice (2012) learning analytics serves as an educational tool that provides the teacher with data on personal, interaction, navigation in the system, with whom or with what resource, and how it interacted, location and context data and data on the texts created. Information provided by LA allows customizing of the training activities and design of learning environments accordance to the needs, interests, and forms of interaction between teachers and students and between students themselves [32]. Learning analytics can also provide students with timely information and recommendations as to their interests with two essential objectives: reflection and prediction [20]. It allows visualizing of interactions and identifying patterns of student behavior. Learning analytics will enable an iterative process of feedback, visual and effective, just-in-time feedback that allows the teacher or student to adopt correct teaching or learning strategies [18]. Having information on how people learn results in improved quality of education [3, 33]. Learning environments customized and designed according to learning styles and disciplines are feasible with LA [10]. Learning analytics can provide individuals and groups with a basis of undeniable value for a much more precise investigation of learning processes [8]. The analysis of institutional learning will allow better decision making [12] in two areas. First, instructors can decide the level of demand for different plans and curricula. Second, the academic field will have information to identify elements affecting student performance to strengthen positive factors and reduce negative factors, hence supporting development of new pedagogical models [19, 30].

4 Positive Impact of Learning Analytics

A number of authors have investigated the positive impact of implementing learning analytics on education and student development. Learning analytics referred to a blend of various scenarios at different universities, introduced by management for implementing a virtual learning environment (VLE) exclusively for utilizing effective learning [23]. Dietz-Uhler and Hurn (2013) regard LA as a research model taking advantage of data analysis to inform on the actions and events taking place during the educational process [11]. It seeks to collect, organize and provide data on student performance, allowing a personalized guide, adapting the contents and activities to their abilities and identifying possible learning problems in time [4]. Analytics can reveal data such as feelings, attitudes, social connections and the wishes of users, as well as evidence of what they know, how they learn and their future actions [9]. This allows applying data collection and study techniques relevant for different fields and in particular for education, since it facilitates customization of educational processes according to student needs [12, 13, 36]. Besides making it possible to diagnose problems and identify strategies for improving a course, LA also provides indicators of educational progress at local, regional and even national or international level [22]. LA supports the education system by allowing curriculum adaptation, personalization, and prediction [3]. It enables direct evaluation of the role of learning analytics in the educational process [17] for improving training processes and increasing learning for improved productivity [24]. Having available indicators such as effectiveness, efficiency or time spent on resources, teachers can understand which educational resources failed or are difficult to understand and which are problematic [7, 34]. Resources for future courses can then be improved [23]. Teachers can better understand students, their evolution over time, their achievements, specific subjects problematic for them, profiles, and so forth. Teachers can then provide more effective feedback for them [2]. Predictive techniques allow teachers to detect students at risk and identify slow and fast learners [5, 6]. Early intervention can thus prevent cases such as dropping out of courses or poor learning [6]. Students can visualize and reflect on information about their own learning, see their profiles and make appropriate changes [24]. Adaptation and customization are enabled according to students' profiles to enhance learning [5]. Thus, different learning paths can be designed to accelerate learning [17].

4.1   Integrating Effective Framework of LA

Figure 1 illustrates the process of learning analytics. It shows learning analytics is based on four major perspectives, which include governance, higher educational institutions, online learning environment, and physical learning environment – all perform to improve the learning abilities of an individual or learner [22].

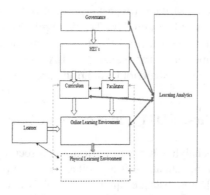

Fig. 1. Process of learning analytics

Governance involves activities related to implementing cross-institutional comparisons, developing benchmarks, informing policy making, and ensuring quality assurance processes [17]. These activities increase productivity, implement a rapid response to critical incidents, and analyze student performance. Phillips et al. (2012) stated that governance predicts high impact on organizational decision-making [24].

As for the second component of the analytic process, West (2012) suggested that HEIs be responsible to analyze processes, optimize resource allocation, meet institutional standards, and compare units across programs and faculties [34]. The model discussed helps in monitoring processes, evaluating resources, tracking enrollment, and analyzing educational outcomes. The functional processes of HEIs in Malaysia predict forecasting techniques, project attrition, model retention rates, goal attainment, employability, and gap identification [6].

The third process consists of curriculum design including the pedagogical model analysis, measuring impact of interventions, and increasing curriculum quality. These activities support education by comparing the learning design, evaluating learning materials, adjusting difficulty levels, and providing resources to learners. Curriculum design involves identifying learning preferences, planning for future interventions, modeling difficulty levels, and developing model pathways [5]. The fourth component of the model is the facilitator who is responsible for comparing the learners, cohorts, and courses, analyzing teaching practices, and increasing quality of teaching. Facilitator activities include monitoring learning progression, creating meaningful interventions, increasing interaction, and modifying content to meet student needs. Facilitators also identify learners at risk, forecast learning progress, and plan interventions [27]. The last fundamental component of learning analytics is the learner who necessitates understanding of learning habits, comparison of learning paths, analysis of learning outcomes, and tracking of progress toward goals. Learners are highly responsible for receiving automated interventions and scaffolds and taking assessments including just-in-time feedback. Recent studies suggest that interest in LA was prompted by the huge amount of data related to education and the increased computer processing power enabling collection of new information from new and different pools of data [9, 35]. Such analytics have stronger impacts by placing productive information for huge numbers of individuals besides ensuring delegated decision-making skills [19]. Besides this, Ali et al. (2013) noted how VLE has become a significant platform incorporating huge amounts of data, for instance, data obtained from academic software [2]. Numerous studies of literature [16, 21, 25] highlighted how learning analytics finds better ways to enhance everyday practice in HEIs. Instead of being hesitant due to privacy concerns, implementers must realize that LA successfully address issues of conflicting interests of different shareholders and the applicable integration [26].

5 Learning Analytics, EDM and Academic Analytics

The process of learning analytics tends to perform as a recurring system of development for the data collection, data analysis as well as interventions mainly derived from different techniques [19]. For instance, quality control is determined as a consistent process for improving teaching and learning perspectives. A close relationship exists between learning analytics, EDM and academic analytics [1, 30]. Pardo and Siemens (2014), consistent with the abovementioned discussion, also asserted the connection of learning analytics with a collection of huge data and representation of the data in the form of useful information [23]. In a similar context, Dawson et al. (2014) also investigated the significance of learning analytics in shaping positive behavior and leading toward the correct direction. Analytical application can extract knowledge in terms of utilizing different techniques of data mining along with the practices of visualization [10].

5.1   Educational Data Mining

While considering the research objective, Dyckhoff et al. (2012) explained Educational Data Mining as a process used in teaching to examine the methods of development to generate information. The process referred to the combination of data collecting techniques that focus on the attainment of student's in-depth understanding in terms of integrating different processes of learning with various settings. However, educational data mining is quite similar to learning analytics, which involves varying processes, procedures, and methodologies aimed at gaining the required information for fulfilling learning objectives [14].

Papamitsiou and Economides (2014) indicated that both fields tend to focus on domains of education and tend to work with potential data generated from the environments. Fidalgo-Blanco et al. (2015) added that processes ensure complete conversion of data into valuable information to purposively improve the learning process. Phillips et al. (2012) reflected that varying techniques are being used in learning analytics in comparison to EDM. Wagner and Ice (2012) argued that the major focus of educational data mining remains the applications developed to ensure techniques of data mining must support learning perspectives of students and teachers. West (2012) noted that these methods should be implemented for data mining and testing of usability in various possible situations. In contrast, Blikstein and Worsley (2016) differentiate data mining with learning analytics by claiming that analytics involves different methods for instance statistics tools, visualization, and techniques of analyzing social networks which ensure compilation of information to transform it into a more effective and informative context.

5.2   Academic Analytics

Blikstein (2013) signifies the role of academic analytics as an imperative aspect to enhance in-depth understanding of learning analytics. As suggested by Scheffel et al. (2014), academic analytics aims at supporting the educational institutions to address the challenging issues hindering students' future success and prosperity. Ali et al. (2013) depicted that analytical analysis also increases the accountability that allows the institutes to perform responsibilities – must be designed for fulfillment of academic objectives or goals. Academic analytics generate a huge amount of data exclusively to predict the level of student retention and the graduation percentage [21].

Meanwhile, Prinsloo and Slade (2013) depicted that academic analytics also combines a particular range of data by utilizing various statistical or inferential techniques for predicting effective models. Ferguson et al. (2014) highlighted how successful implementations of these models help the faculty advisors interpret the challenges faced by students [16]. However, the study of Romero and Ventura (2013) analyzed that academic analytics must be differentiated in a more comprehensive way to allow the educational institutions to draw a fine line among the respective fields.

5.3   Factors Influencing Student Retention

In considering the research questions, it is necessary to examine the concept of student retention as well as analysis of the factors that impact retention. As discussed by Ellis (2013), student retention is based upon core attributes, namely (1) motivation, (2) academic integration, (3) social integration, and (4) financial factors [15].

Daniel (2015) portrayed how the LA framework plays a vital role in motivating students to study and ensure retention by managing student commitment and motivation [31]. Wise (2014) suggested various attributes contribute to increasing student motivation to remain enrolled; course structure, course fee, and educational marketing are key elements to be considered [14]. According to Greller and Drachsler (2012), academic integration is another factor influencing student retention. Academic integration is seen as the involvement of physical and psychological energy that convey individuals an exceptional experience of studying or association with the educational institution [7]. It is also seen as an educational tool, integrated by academics for proper maintenance of individual's time, preparation for assessments, fostering skills and competencies, and ensuring effective critical thinking [14]. It affects student retention through collecting essential information on student progress, which in turn ensures high priority feedback from instructors [10]. Staffing is another characteristic of academic integration that assists in student retention [14]. Besides that, feedback from students enables management to meet student expectations [22]. As indicated by Phillips et al. (2012), social integration is the key component influencing student retention. Studies have supported the impact of social integration on retention, emphasizing on interaction among students, faculty and management in the context of extracurricular activities [14, 22]. Students who feel unwelcome and lack support may drop out [17]. Blikstein and Worsley (2016), in considering financial factors, analyzed that some students from lower socioeconomic groups face financial challenges [6]. These financial hardships might cause them to discontinue their studies [2, 34]. Students from lower income family background experience more critical challenges as compared to their wealthier counterparts. Fee structuring system is another core attribute highlighted by Siemens and Gasevic (2012) who argue that an economical fee structure will attract students [30].

6   Implementation of Learning Analytics Framework in HEIs

In consideration of the literature review and different facts, a new model is proposed that entails as a conceptual framework, where attributes such as motivation, social integration, financial facts, and academic integration are taken as independent variables; with student retention, employability, and attainment being considered as dependent variables (Fig. 2).

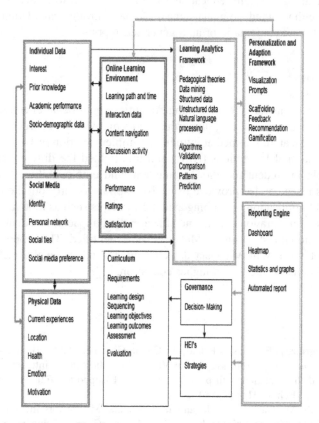

Fig. 2. Learning analytics framework to implement in HEIs in Malaysia.

The variables are selected in such a way because the study of Chatti et al. (2012) suggested that characteristics such as student retention, employability, and attainment are significantly influenced by the financial facts, motivation, academic integration as well as social integration [7]. The model also plays a crucial role in maintaining a consistent level of communication that helps institutes in keeping the functionality of the model manageable and productive. According to the framework, educational institutions need to emphasize three major aspects (1) individual data, (2) social media, and (3) physical data. Moving to the second stage, consistent with the findings of Siemens and Gasevic (2012) these three factors assist in developing an effective online learning environment, based upon interaction, discussion activities, assessment, performance, ratings, and student satisfaction [30]. This component is further directly linked to the learning analytics framework revolving around pedagogical theories, data mining, structured data, unstructured data, and natural language processing. Pardo and Siemens (2014) underscored the significance of personalization and adoption framework, which indicates the functionality of visualization prompts, scaffolding and feedback [23]. After the successful integration of both the structures within the educational system, educational institutions need to critically consider the reporting engine that intends to manage the dashboard through calculating the statistics and graphs and create automatic or auto-generated reports.

7 Conclusion

This paper has demonstrated that Learning Analytics could be an effective strategy for intelligent instructing practice – supporting and empowering instructors to conduct assessment and research. It aimed at introducing implementation of Learning Analytics in Higher Educational Institutions (HEIs) and highlighted the different factors which play a vital role in student retention, attainment, and employability. The framework adopted in this research also provided extensive support to carry out the future studies on the empirical implication of learning analytics. Factors such as motivation, academic integration, social integration, and financial factors that impact on student retention rate in higher educational institutions in Malaysia were identified. The proposed integrated practical model for LA in Malaysia depicts how the educational structure must be implemented to ensure success in higher education.

References

1. Agudo-Peregrina, Á.F., Iglesias-Pradas, S., Conde-González, M.Á., Hernández-García, Á.: Can we predict success from log data in VLEs? Classification of interactions for learning analytics and their relation with performance in VLE-supported F2F and online learning. Comput. Hum. Behav. **31**, 542–550 (2014)
2. Ali, L., Asadi, M., Gašević, D., Jovanović, J., Hatala, M.: Factors influencing beliefs for adoption of a learning analytics tool: an empirical study. Comput. Educ. **62**, 130–148 (2013)
3. Arnold, K.E., Pistilli, M.D.: Course signals at Purdue: using learning analytics to increase student success. In: Proceedings of the 2nd International Conference on Learning Analytics and Knowledge, pp. 267–270. ACM (2012)
4. Bienkowski, M., Feng, M., Means, B.: Enhancing teaching and learning through educational data mining and learning analytics: an issue brief. US Department of Education, Office of Educational Technology. vol. 1, pp. 1–57 (2012)
5. Blikstein, P.: Multimodal learning analytics. In: Proceedings of the Third International Conference on Learning Analytics and Knowledge, pp. 102–106. ACM (2013)
6. Blikstein, P., Worsley, M.: Multimodal learning analytics and education data mining: using computational technologies to measure complex learning tasks. J. Learn. Anal. **3**(2), 220–238 (2016)
7. Chatti, M.A., Dyckhoff, A.L., Schroeder, U., Thüs, H.: A reference model for learning analytics. Int. J. Technol. Enhanc. Learn. **4**(5–6), 318–331 (2012)
8. Clow, D.: The learning analytics cycle: closing the loop effectively. In: Proceedings of the 2nd International Conference on Learning Analytics and Knowledge, pp. 134–138. ACM (2012)

9. Daniel, B.: Big data and analytics in higher education: opportunities and challenges. Br. J. Educ. Technol. **46**(5), 904–920 (2015)
10. Dawson, S., Gašević, D., Siemens, G., Joksimovic, S.: Current state and future trends: a citation network analysis of the learning analytics field. In: Proceedings of the Fourth International Conference on Learning Analytics and Knowledge, pp. 231–240. ACM (2014)
11. Dietz-Uhler, B., Hurn, J.E.: Using learning analytics to predict (and improve) student success: a faculty perspective. J. Interact. Online Learn. **12**(1), 17–26 (2013)
12. Drachsler, H., Greller, W.: The pulse of learning analytics understandings and expectations from the stakeholders. In: Proceedings of the 2nd International Conference on Learning Analytics and Knowledge, pp. 120–129. ACM (2012)
13. Dyckhoff, A.L., Lukarov, V., Muslim, A., Chatti, M.A., Schroeder, U.: Supporting action research with learning analytics. In: Proceedings of the Third International Conference on Learning Analytics and Knowledge, pp. 220–229. ACM (2013)
14. Dyckhoff, A.L., Zielke, D., Bültmann, M., Chatti, M.A., Schroeder, U.: Design and implementation of a learning analytics toolkit for teachers. J. Educ. Technol. Soc. **15**(3), 58 (2012)
15. Ellis, C.: Broadening the scope and increasing the usefulness of learning analytics: the case for assessment analytics. Br. J. Edu. Technol. **44**(4), 662–664 (2013)
16. Ferguson, R., Clow, D., Macfadyen, L., Essa, A., Dawson, S., Alexander, S.: Setting learning analytics in context: overcoming the barriers to large-scale adoption. In: Proceedings of the Fourth International Conference on Learning Analytics and Knowledge, pp. 251–253. ACM (2014)
17. Fidalgo-Blanco, Á., Sein-Echaluce, M.L., García-Peñalvo, F.J., Conde, M.Á.: Using learning analytics to improve teamwork assessment. Comput. Hum. Behav. **47**, 149–156 (2015)
18. Gašević, D., Dawson, S., Siemens, G.: Let's not forget: learning analytics are about learning. TechTrends **59**(1), 64–71 (2015)
19. Greller, W., Drachsler, H.: Translating learning into numbers: a generic framework for learning analytics. J. Educ. Technol. Soc. **15**(3), 42 (2012)
20. Lockyer, L., Heathcote, E., Dawson, S.: Informing pedagogical action: aligning learning analytics with learning design. Am. Behav. Sci. **57**(10), 1439–1459 (2013)
21. MacNeill, S., Campbell, L.M., Hawksey, M.: Analytics for education. In: Reusing Open Resources: Learning in Open Networks for Work, Life and Education, p. 154 (2014)
22. Papamitsiou, Z., Economides, A.A.: Learning analytics and educational data mining in practice: a systematic literature review of empirical evidence. J. Educ. Technol. Soc. **17**(4), 49 (2014)
23. Pardo, A., Siemens, G.: Ethical and privacy principles for learning analytics. Br. J. Educ. Technol. **45**(3), 438–450 (2014)
24. Phillips, R., Maor, D., Preston, G., Cumming-Potvin, W.: Exploring learning analytics as indicators of study behavior. In: World Conference on Educational Multimedia, Hypermedia and Telecommunications, pp. 2861–2867. EDMEDIA (2012)
25. Prinsloo, P., Slade, S.: An evaluation of policy frameworks for addressing ethical considerations in learning analytics. In: Proceedings of the Third International Conference on Learning Analytics and Knowledge, pp. 240–244. ACM (2013)
26. Romero, C., Ventura, S.: Data mining in education. Wiley Interdisc. Rev. Data Min. Knowl. Discov. **3**(1), 12–27 (2013)
27. Scheffel, M., Drachsler, H., Stoyanov, S., Specht, M.: Quality indicators for learning analytics. J. Educ. Technol. Soc. **17**(4), 117 (2014)
28. Sclater, N., Peasgood, A., Mullan, J.: Learning analytics in higher education. JISC, London (2016)

29. Siemens, G., Baker, R.S.: Learning analytics and educational data mining: towards communication and collaboration. In: Proceedings of the 2nd International Conference on Learning Analytics and Knowledge, pp. 252–254. ACM (2012)
30. Siemens, G., Gasevic, D.: Guest editorial-Learning and knowledge analytics. Educ. Technol. Soc. **15**(3), 1–2 (2012)
31. Slade, S., Prinsloo, P.: Learning analytics: ethical issues and dilemmas. Am. Behav. Sci. **57** (10), 1510–1529 (2013)
32. Van Barneveld, A., Arnold, K.E., Campbell, J.P.: Analytics in higher education: establishing a common language. EDUCAUSE Learn. Initiat. **1**(1), 1–ll (2012)
33. Wagner, E., Ice, P.: Data changes everything: delivering on the promise of learning analytics in higher education. Educause Rev. **47**(4), 32 (2012)
34. West, D.M.: Big data for education: data mining, data analytics, and web dashboards. Gov. Stud. Brook. **4**, 1 (2012)
35. Wise, A.F.: Designing pedagogical interventions to support student use of learning analytics. In: Proceedings of the Fourth International Conference on Learning Analytics and Knowledge, pp. 203–211. ACM (2014)
36. Yu, T., Jo, I.H.: Educational technology approach toward learning analytics: relationship between student online behavior and learning performance in higher education. In: Proceedings of the Fourth International Conference on Learning Analytics and Knowledge, pp. 269–270. ACM (2014)

Data-Driven Iterative-Evolution-Participatory Design Model on Motion-Based Science Educational Application for ADHD Learners

Ahmad Fazil Zainal and Halimah Badioze Zaman[✉]

Institute of Visual Informatics, Universiti Kebangsaan Malaysia, Bangi, Malaysia
afazil3@gmail.com, halimahivi@ukm.edu.my

Abstract. Attention Deficit Hyperactivity Disorder (ADHD) learners are identified as having problems in learning due to their distinctive characteristics of hyperactivity and inability to give attention to learning. Gamification technology, especially motion-based gamification application, specifically designed for ADHD learners can have significant promise for individuals with ADHD. This paper focuses on the data-driven iterative design adopted on the development of the motion-based science educational application for ADHD learners (Sains-4SL) and its evaluation based on the effectiveness construct of this motion-based science educational application. The effectiveness of this motion-based science educational application was measured based various indicators such as: its learnability, students' attitude towards the application; and the science literacy aspects of the students after experiencing using the application. The data-driven iterative-participatory design approach which underwent many rounds of iterations, was found to be effective in the design and development of the application as these iterations, contributed to a more accurate specification requirements for the ADHD learners. The evaluation conducted found that the motion-based science educational application (Sains-4SL) was positively effective in supporting ADHD learners learn science.

Keywords: Attention Deficit Hyperactivity Disorder (ADHD) · Science educational application · Motion-based technology · Data-driven iterative-participatory design approach

1 Introduction

The National Institute of Mental Health [1, 2] stated that Attention Deficit Hyperactivity Disorder (ADHD) is a common mental disorder that begins in childhood and can continue through adolescence and adulthood. For children with ADHD, the levels of inattention, hyperactivity and impulsive behaviour are greater than other children in their age group. This deficiency leads to difficulty for them to excel in school activities or show good behaviour at home or in their community. ADHD is a disorder that makes it difficult for a person to pay attention and control impulsive behaviour. Even though hyperactivity tends to improve as a child becomes a teen, problems with inattention, disorganization, and poor impulse control often continue through the teen years and into adulthood [2]. Through meta-analysis, it is estimated that 5.3% of

© Springer International Publishing AG 2017
H. Badioze Zaman et al. (Eds.): IVIC 2017, LNCS 10645, pp. 197–211, 2017.
https://doi.org/10.1007/978-3-319-70010-6_19

children and adolescents worldwide is diagnosed with ADHD [3]. In recent study by Canals et al. [4], indicates that the ADHD prevalence among preschool population in Spain is 5.4%. This is within the range values described by Polanczyk.

The use of information and communication technology (ICT) in learning generally, comes in various forms and various terms are used to describe them such as: computer technology, educational software, computerised program, computer-based interventions, computer-supported learning, computer-assisted instruction and computer-generated instruction. Generally, computer-supported learning can aid students with special needs. Starcic et al. [5] introduced a tangible user interface (TUI) as a computer-supported learning for the development of applications and solutions in teaching geometry concepts to an inclusive class which included learners with special needs. Students with low fine motor skills who were unable to use a pen, were given a combination triangle/protractor and a pair of compass that can be used as TUI for autonomous drawing. Houghton et al. [6] found in their research findings that computer technology in this digital era may afford children with ADHD increased opportunities to be more successful, both academically and socially, and to improve their interactions with peers. Lin et al. [7] discovered that ADHD students could use fusion technologies in their learning process by using mobile augmented reality. The abundance of digital teaching materials, in visual and auditory cues, with easy to comprehend literacy content, would enhance ADHD students' attention and promote learning efficiency. Shaw and Lewis [8] found that participants with ADHD produced the greatest number of accurate responses on the more basic computerised task and exhibited significantly more on-task activity on animated computerised tasks. These findings are encouraging and may have wide reaching practical implications in terms of the design and implementation of educational software aimed at promoting improvements for children with ADHD in terms of both their academic performance and behaviour in the classroom.

2 Literature Review

Due to the ADHD children's high level of impulsivity, hyperactivity and inattention, they are at risk of behavioural as well as familial, socializing and relationship skills [9–12]. On academic and soft skills, ADHD children have difficulty in reading, writing, mathematics, recalling stories and communication and interpersonal skills [11–17]. These difficulties have affected their academic achievement during pre-school, elementary, high school and tertiary [9, 18–21]. Various studies have shown that ADHD young learners are facing academic under achievement when reaching high schools [19, 20, 22–24]. Academic difficulties faced by these ADHD students have affected their performance. There are cases where these ADHD students had to be retained in their previous grade, suspended from school or even failed to complete high school [25, 26].

Many research have explored the use of information and communication technology (ICT) in learning, which comes into various forms and names such as computer technology, educational software, computerized program, computer-based interventions, computer-supported learning, computer-assisted instruction and computer-generated instruction. Generally, computer-supported learning can aid students with special needs. Starcic et al. [5] introduced a tangible user interface (TUI) as a computer-supported learning for the development of applications and solutions in teaching geometry concepts to an inclusive class which included learners with special needs. Students with low fine motor skills who were unable to use a pen, were given a combination triangle/protractor and a pair of compass that can be used as TUI for autonomous drawing. Houghton et al. [6] found in their research findings that computer technology in this digital era may afford children with ADHD increased opportunities to be more successful, both academically and socially, and to improve their interactions with peers. Lin et al. [7] discovered that ADHD students could use fusion technologies in their learning process by using mobile augmented reality. The abundance of digital teaching materials, in visual and auditory cues, with easy to comprehend literacy content, could enhance ADHD students' attention and promote learning efficiency. Shaw and Lewis [8] found that participants with ADHD were able to produce the largest number of accurate responses on the more basic computer based tasks and exhibited significantly more on-task activity, such as animated computer based tasks. These findings are encouraging and may have wide reaching practical implications in terms of the design and implementation of educational applications aimed at promoting improvements of learning for children with ADHD in terms of both their academic performance and behaviour in the classroom.

Previous researches on computer educational programs were conducted to assist ADHD learners in some academic subjects' skills. In the improvement of reading for example, Clarfield and Stoner [27] explored on the use and effectiveness of a Computer-Assisted Instruction (CAI) reading program, Headsprout, on oral reading fluency and task engagement of three students with ADHD. The reading problems involved children at kindergarten and first grade. Headsprout Reading Basics, an internet-based reading program, has explicit instruction in phonemic awareness, fluency building tasks and building sight word recognition. The lessons are automatically adapted to the learner's pace and the program gives learners corrective feedback and encouragement as necessary. Mautone et al. [28], introduced a Computer Assisted Instruction in mathematics for elementary school children with ADHD in a general education classroom. Results of the study showed that ADHD students gained in mathematics and academic engagement during the course of the intervention. Both outcomes of the studies are promising and CAI is thus, effective academic intervention for students with ADHD. Another promising study was one explored by Kang and Zentall [29]. They found that graphic information, presented in computer-generated instruction, is beneficial to learners with hyperactivity and inability to give attention such as ADHD learners, by improving their ability to sustain attention and hold information in-mind. Such learners were found to perform better on advanced geometry problems (e.g., calculation of complex shapes) with visually intense images than with low intense images. The students with both hyperactivity and inattention behavior performed even better than the controlled group that used conventional teaching methods.

Computer technology or what is currently known as assistive technology also has a role on traits improvement of the ADHD individual. Shalev et al. [30] and Reynolds [31], used assistive technology in a form of computerized progressive attentional training program to improve the various attentional function of children with ADHD through direct intensive exercising and technology. They found significant improvements in both academic tests and parents' behavioral ratings of the ADHD children. On another related research, results showed evidence that Computerised Attention Training (CAT) and Computer Assisted Instruction (CAI) using assistive technology, can improve children's attention in the classroom and suggest that computer-based interventions offer a promise for cost-effective early intervention for inattentive, at-risk learners such as ADHD. Learners receiving CAI also showed gains in reading fluency and in teacher ratings of academic performance [32, 33].

Computer Gaming Technology is another significant promise for the education of individuals with ADHD. Shaw et al. [34] and Mathrani et al. [35] found through discussions with parents, that although their children appear to have many difficulties with attention and concentration across environments, their concentration, performance, distractibility and motivation all appear to improve when they play computer games. Their studies confirmed anecdotal reports and their research showed no difference between the inhibitory performances of children with ADHD, compared to typically developing children on two commercially available computer games. It was found by Houghton et al. [6], when tests are attractive (activating), ADHD children are able to sustain attention. Academically, computer games offer teachers, clinicians and parents increased opportunities to assist children with ADHD to maximize their learning potential. Through their study, Zemliansky and Wilcox [36] found that students with ADHD need educational opportunities that are purposeful yet fun and engaging. The advancements in gaming technology, as they relate to the instructional environment, are promising. The empirical observations and findings from Ke and Abras [37] study suggest that educational games, if well designed and used, can promote engagement and learning for students with special learning needs. Learners themselves agreed that gaming approaches to learning can make classroom environments more fun and also make an effective way to grasp some of the difficult concepts in learning. The inclusion of gaming elements with traditional teaching practices will bring about more active learning. This will be beneficial for tutors as well as learners, because games can enable learners to grasp technology based applications quickly in a more enjoyable learning environment [35].

On academic subject, Ota and DuPaul [38] evaluated the effects of a game-based math software program on the performance of ADHD students. They found increased math performance, decreased off-task and disruptive behavior and increased active engagement in the computer-based instruction compared to the traditional classroom lesson. Another research on game based learning was done by Bai et al. [39]. They discovered that game increased mathematical knowledge acquisition in algebra and maintained student motivation to learn. The findings also suggested that the implementation of Dimension in mathematics education can greatly benefit middle school students learning algebra. Providing opportunities for integrating videogame technology into the learning environment is a simple way to address the academic needs of the ADHD students. Findings from the study by Altanis et al. [40], found that immersive environment offers learning experiences through gamification that makes learning experience for ADHD learners fun and meaningful.

Serin [41] suggested that there is a significant increase in the achievements and problem solving skills of the students that received the computer based science and technology instruction. He investigated the effects of the computer-based instruction on the achievements and problem solving skills of the science and technology learners. Study on the use of game technology expands the horizon of learning. Tsai et al. [42] found that most learners find that motion-based technology such as the use of Kinect is effective in delivering teaching and learning materials and find its interactive function easy to conduct, fun and enjoyable. Hsu [43] in his study, found also found that motion-based device such as Kinect has potential to enhance classroom interaction and to spark creativity. Although no study has been conducted to investigate academically the use of Kinect, as a motion based device in learning, it is the assumption that the device can be an effective tool to support and improve teaching and learning of ADHD learners.

3 Problem Statement

As indicated in the literature, many studies has been conducted on the use of computer technology through various assistive technology to help ADHD learners learn effectively. Many of these studies also indicate that the use of these technologies, have shown some improvement in learning on learners with learning problems. Specifically for ADHD learners, the use of the technology has not shown much improvement in ADHD learners who have characteristics such as hyperactivity, high inattention and inability to focus on the subjects being taught. These learners have specific physical as well as mental disabilities that need to be overcome in order that they be able to engage in the learning process. Previous applications using the technologies have not taken into consideration these characteristics, thus there is a need to integrate a technology such as the motion-based technology that will allow ADHD learners to make use of their hyperactivity, high inattention and inability to focus personality to undergo lessons, in line with their natural characteristics. The use of motion-based application means that learners are allowed to be active using fine and hard motor skills to enable them to stay on with the learning process with better concentration and focus on the lessons taught.

In order to ensure that the application is designed and developed to meet the needs of the ADHD learners, the design approach has to be one that is user-oriented which involves the learner from the initial start of the design phase until the final development phase of the application, and must undergo the iterative-participatory method based on the data-driven design of the application. Data on the acceptance test of the active user (that acts as part of the design team), has to be collected iteratively through the 'incidence report', until the user is satisfied that the application is able to meet the objectives of the design and development specifically for ADHD learners. Therefore, the plausible solution to be undertaken is to develop a science educational motion-based application for the ADHD learners that takes into consideration characteristics of the learners, based on the user oriented design using the data-driven iterative-participatory approach to ensure that the application developed really meets the need of the ADHD learners.

4 Methodology

The main objective of this paper is to highlight the design and development of a motion-based application to help ADHD learners learn science through a fun gaming strategy. The strategy used a motion-based device called Kinect to help learners learn more meaningfully, with better focus on the lessons taught. The other objective of this paper, is to evaluate the application based on the effectiveness construct of the application through a test based conducted on seven (7) ADHD learners. The design and development model was the Data- Driven ADHD Iterative-Evolution Participatory Life Cycle model (DD-IP-ADHD-LC) which was designed and developed based on standard Software Development Life Cycle, with the integration of elements from the Rapid Prototyping Model [44], Participatory Design Model [45] and Iterative-Evolution Model [46]. The design model of the application was based on the data-driven iterative-participatory model as indicated in Fig. 1.

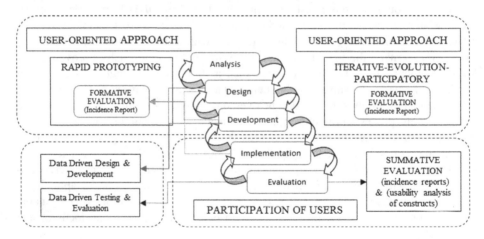

Fig. 1. Data-driven ADHD Iterative-Participatory Life Cycle Model (DD-IP-ADHD-LC)

As can be observed from the model, DD-IP-ADHD-LC comprised five (5) standard software development main phases: Analysis, Design, Development, Implementation and Evaluation. However, each phase has sub phases specifically designed for the purpose of this study. The sub phases in the analysis phase involved aspects such as: requirement analysis, curriculum analysis and analysis planning. Requirement analysis involved identifying user requirements (in this case requirements of ADHD learners) in order to ascertain the Systems Requirement Specifications (SRS), to develop the Sains-4SL application for ADHD learners. In practice, it involves analysis of the nature and behaviour of ADHD learners, as well as appropriate technology to be used and suitable learning techniques and methods to be embedded in the application. This is done through data collected from different focus groups; teachers, parents and ADHD learners. The design phase was the most important and challenging phase, as this involved data-driven approach through various rounds of iterations of design to ascertain the Systems Design Specifications (SDS) based on the SRS acquired during the analysis phase; the interface, the flow of the modules, and the multimedia-fusion tools to be incorporated into the storyboard. The data collected during each iterations were documented in the 'incidence reports' and were taken action appropriately, until the users were satisfied. The data collected and reported in the incidence reports during the iterations were based on cosmetic adequacy, content adequacy, technical adequacy and special user adequacy (user interface suitable for ADHD learners).

The development phase was conducted very closely with the design phase. Guided by storyboard, flow chart and interface, the application was developed using appropriate application development tool that incorporates multimedia-fusion elements to create the modules. The iterations can happen also at this stage when the satisfactory portions of the modules during the design stage is passed to the development phase, and further 'incidence' is discovered by the user and documented in the 'incidence report' for repair and further development until the user was satisfied. The implementation phase ensured that all the modules and sub modules were integrated, run smoothly and met the needs of the user environment. The digital devices and equipment such as notebook, television and the Kinect device to produce a motion- based multimedia-fusion environment, aimed at engaging ADHD learners were prepared and tested at this phase to ensure that there were no hitches when the testing of the application was conducted during the evaluation phase. Learning sessions were held in a room that was conducive and suitable for learning. The final phase was the evaluation phase, conducted through a usability testing based on data-driven constructs.

5 Components of the Instructional Design (ID) Model

The methodology of this study also involved the development of the Cognitive based Instructional Design (ID) model approach of the Sains-4SL application based on the topic 'Living Things' and 'Non-Living Things'. The development of this application was able to enhance learning of science on the topic chosen amongst ADHD learners. The Cognitive based ID model had incorporated four main components as follows:

Component 1: teaching and learning approach
The first component refers to the content delivery and learning methods applied in the application. It involved a combination of several elements such as the integration of the Behaviourist theory, learner-centred learning strategy, errorless learning approach and the thematic instruction. Sains-4SL was designed based on a self-paced application, adopting the Behaviourist theory principles. The learner-centered learning strategies allowed ADHD learners to learn on their own from the beginning until the end of the learning session, whenever they were able to do so. The errorless learning approach was implemented in every evaluation module of the Sains-4SL application. If the learner answered a question correctly, the reinforcement in a form of praise could be heard auditorily. However, for an incorrect answer, a verbal reinforcement could be heard and the correct answer displayed on the screen. The ADHD learner then has an opportunity to answer the questions again. This process can be repeated until the learner has answered all questions correctly. This errorless learning approach helps

make ADHD learners feel at ease and confident to continue and be engaged with the learning process. The choice of science topics in the application was carefully chosen so that it fitted the national curriculum, but also related to real life situations so that they can easily identify with themselves, so that the learning becomes meaningful.

Component 2: Learners' achievement

The second component involves learner's achievement in three domains: cognitive, affective and psychomotor. The cognitive domain refers to new knowledge on living and non-living things exposed to ADHD learners through examples given in the sub module descriptions. They were able to relate new knowledge with their prior knowledge and were able to further expand the knowledge by looking at other examples in real life. For the affective domain, learners were conducting activities that required them to 'feel sorry', 'feel thankful', and 'feel grateful' for life created by the Al-Mighty. They were also observed while conducting their activities and their behaviour and expressions were noted that included behaviour that depicted patience, curiosity, trying, diligent, earnest, happy, active and despair. On the hand, the psychomotor domain involves the kinesthetic use of the fine and hard motors of the ADHD learners to move objects in the motion-based application.

Component 3: Motivation aspect

The third component involves the ARCS model [47, 48], based on the synthesis of concepts pertaining to motivation and its features are encompassed in four (4) categories: attention (A), relevant (R), confidence (C), and satisfaction (S). These four categories represent a set of conditions necessary for an individual to be motivated. The combined use of an animated model, multimedia-fusion elements and the use of Kinect was able to attract the ADHD learners' attention to continue to learn using Sains-4SL. The errorless approach allowed ADHD learners to learn through all five (5) modules according to their own pace and ability. They were also given the option to continue repeating every sub module until they have reached the desired level of understanding in order to gain confidence. Thus, when they succeeded in answering all the questions, they experienced the feeling of satisfaction. The 'praise and encouragement' element embedded in the application, makes ADHD learners perceived acquisition of knowledge as easy, enjoyable, fun and motivating.

Component 4: Teaching media

The teaching media refers to the learning modules, interactivity and multimedia-fusion elements. The multimedia-fusion elements encompass the use of animation, video, sound, text and graphic throughout the application in a virtual motion-based learning environment. The learning modules encompassed five (5) modules: 'Introduction module', 'Being Born module', 'Eat and Drink module', 'Growing Up module' and 'Movement module'. The interactivity within the application refers to the response between the application and the ADHD learners during the learning sessions.

The combination of the ID components and the multimedia-fusion elements embedded in the Sains-4SL application, integrated with the motion-based device, Kinect serve as a unique learning experience aimed at motivating ADHD students to learn.

6   Evaluation of Sains-4SL

The evaluation of the Sains-4SL application was conducted in a private room at two (2) types of environments: school and home environment. A private room was used to ensure that ADHD learners were able to focus during the learning stage. The room was equipped with a computer, a 50 in. television screen and a Kinect device. The ADHD learners were able to start the application by clicking on the icon on the computer. The lessons in the application were projected on a 50 in. television screen where the main menu appeared with greetings and instruction to start the learning process. The ADHD learners were able to choose lessons from the five (5) modules developed to learn any of the modules within the application and to be conducted at their own pace. The motion-based technology through the use of the motion-based device, Kinect was used to initiate interactivity involved in the activities such as: selection of modules, answering of question and moving of objects through 'virtual hands' using Kinect. Each module consists of sub modules namely: Explanation and Exercise Sub Module. Each module has an Explanation Sub Module which the ADHD learners have to undergo, before they proceed to the Exercise Sub Module. During the learning process, observations were made on the response of the ADHD learners and theses responses were captured as part of the evaluation. At the end of the lesson, they were interviewed using the instrument that represents an observational checklist to get their feedback and attitude whilst using the motion-based application.

Samples involved in the Testing of Sains-4SL
The samples involved in the testing of the motion-based application, Sains-4SL, comprised of seven (7) ADHD learners. The number is small due to reasons such as: these learners are protected group of children and thus it is very difficult to get a larger number of samples to conduct a usability study; some of these learners were only involved in the testing, but also in the iterative-evolution participatory phase of the development. Due to the tedious manner in which the development as well as the testing is conducted, the number has to be small in order to be effective; and lastly, this number is more than sufficient to test an application, in order to discover problems with the application so that it can be rectified and improved to meet the needs of users. Neilson [49] suggested that five (5) samples would suffice. The ADHD learners involved in the testing were aged between nine (9) to twelve (12) years old. There were studying in the special education integration program (SEIP), that resides in the mainstream schools. The SEIP has their own syllabus to cater for learners with special needs, such as the ADHD learners. These learners were diagnosed as ADHD learners and were paced in the special classes, equivalent to elementary one (1) in the normal school level. The selections of these students were done by their science teacher as it needs to match with the content of the application. There is a difference of years in terms of academic capabilities between students in SEIP with the normal schools. This is true as indicated in the study by Hardman [50], that in the early school years, students with learning disabilities may find themselves two to four years behind their peers in academic achievement.

Results of testing on Sains-4SL

Testing was conducted on the motion-based application, Sains-4SL, based on two (2) data-driven constructs: learnability and attitude of the ADHD learners towards the application whilst using it. Testing was also conducted on aspects of 'science literacy' after the application was used. This was necessary as the content of the application was designed and developed based on a science subject. The testing was based on the Likert scale in which score 5 indicates "Strongly Agree", score 4 indicates "Agree", score 3 indicates "Mildly Agree", score 2 indicates "Disagree" and score 1 indicates "Strongly Disagree".

Based on the learnability construct, four indicators were measured: interest in learning, understanding, convenience and enjoyment. The indicators comprised of eight (8) elements as can be observed in Table 1. The evaluations on this construct showed the score was between 4–5 for all eight (8) of the study elements. Elements of encouragement and errorless learning technique, obtained an average score of 5; whilst the other elements acquired an average score of 4. In terms of encouragement element, the score was 5 for all learners, except one (1) who scored 4. This resulted with an average score of 5 for the encouragement element. For errorless learning technique element, a total of four (4) ADHD students scored 5, while three (3) ADHD learners scored 4. This resulted in an average score of 5 for errorless learning technique element. However, the overall score for the learnability construct was at level 4 as indicated in Table 1. This shows that the learnability of the Sains-4SL application was high.

Table 1. Test on Sains-4SL: learnability construct

No.	Indicators	Element	ADHD learners' score							Average
			1	2	3	4	5	6	7	
1.	Interest in learning	(a) Media integration	4	4	4	4	4	4	4	4
		(b) Teaching method	4	4	4	4	4	4	4	4
2.	Understanding	(a) Presentation content	4	4	4	4	4	4	4	4
		(b) Errorless learning technique	5	5	4	5	5	4	4	5
3.	Convenience	(a) Navigation	4	4	4	4	4	4	4	4
		(b) Screen design	4	4	4	4	4	4	4	4
4.	Enjoyment	(a) Learning method	4	4	4	4	4	4	4	4
		(b) Encouragement	5	5	5	5	5	5	4	5
		Overall score								4

Testing conducted on the motion-based application, Sains-4SL, taking into consideration the attitude construct, was measured according to indicators such as: attention, relevance, confidence and satisfaction. The indicators comprised of twelve (12) elements as can be observed in Table 2. The results showed that seven (7) ADHD learners chose a score between 3 to 4 for twelve (12) elements in four (4) of the indicators. However, all the twelve (12) elements showed an average score of 4. For the element 'presentation of screen' related to the indicator 'attention', two (2) ADHD learners chose a score of 3, while five (5) ADHD learners chose a score of 4. However, the 'presentation of screen' element still maintained at score 4. Similarly, in terms of 'presentation of content', a total of two (2) ADHD learners chose a score of 3, while five (5) ADHD learners chose score of 4. The 'presentation of content' element still maintained at score 4. Overall, the average score for the attitude construct was at level 4 as indicated in Table 2. This means that the ADHD learners has a positive attitude on the use of Sains-4SL motion-based application.

Table 2. Test on Sains-4SL: attitude construct

No.	Indicators	Elements	ADHD learners' score							Average
			1	2	3	4	5	6	7	
1.	Attention	(a) Presentation of screen	3	4	4	4	4	3	4	4
		(b) Presentation of content	3	4	4	4	3	4	4	4
		(c) Multimedia elements featured	4	4	4	4	4	4	4	4
2.	Relevance	(a) Overall content	4	4	4	4	4	4	4	4
		(b) Relation with existing knowledge	4	4	4	4	4	4	4	4
		(c) Level of understanding	4	4	4	4	4	4	4	4
3.	Confidence	(a) Self	4	4	4	4	4	4	4	4
		(b) Knowledge	4	4	4	4	4	4	4	4
		(c) Future	4	4	4	4	4	4	4	4
4.	Satisfaction	(a) Learning approach	4	4	4	4	4	4	4	4
		(b) Ability	4	4	4	4	4	4	4	4
		(c) End of learning	4	4	4	4	4	4	4	4
		Overall score								4

Tests were also conducted to evaluate ADHD learners' literacy on science through the 'science literacy aspect'. The goal was to ensure that the motion-based application, Sains-4SL, is able to help ADHD learners understand the science lessons incorporated in the application, and also enhance their science literacy skills. Based on the tests conducted, 100% (all seven (7) ADHD learners), scored 4 on all the five (5) modules designed in the Sains-4SL application. This is clearly indicated in Table 3. This means that the science lessons were understood by the learners, and that the application was able to enhance learners' level of science literacy skills.

Table 3. Test on Sains-4SL: science literacy aspect

No.	Science literacy skills [lessons on science]	ADHD learners' score							Average
		1	2	3	4	5	6	7	
1.	Introduction module	4	4	4	4	4	4	4	4
2.	Eat and drink module	4	4	4	4	4	4	4	4
3.	Growing up module	4	4	4	4	4	4	4	4
4.	Being born module	4	4	4	4	4	4	4	4
5.	Movement module	4	4	4	4	4	4	4	4
	Overall score								4

Therefore, it can be observed from Tables 1 through 3, that findings of the study on the motion-based application designed for ADHD learners, designed and developed using the Data-Driven ADHD Iterative-Participatory Life Cycle model (DD-IP-ADHD-LC), and the Cognitive based ID model, had proven to be useful and meaningful to ADHD learners.

7 Conclusion

ADHD learners are learners with special needs. Their characteristics such as slow in understanding, hyperactivity, inattentive and inability to focus needs to be addressed. This means that any software or application designed and developed for these group of learners needs special attention and care in the design and development process. Thus, the reason for adopting the Data-Driven ADHD Iterative-Participatory Life Cycle model (DD-IP-ADHD-LC) in the design and development process of the motion-based application; and the Cognitive-based ID model in the design and development process of the science content. The former, involved very rigorous evaluation and tedious process during iterations that occurred in the design and development phase of the application. All data and information collected (during the initial and the formative evaluations) that underwent iterations during the design and development phase (the number of iterations varied based on the modules), were recorded in the incidence reports. These incidence reports were crucial for the improvements and refinements made to the application based on the approval of the ADHD learners that were selected to be the active participants in the design and development process of the DD-IP-ADHD-LC development model of the application. Improvements and refinements were made based on the cosmetic adequacy, content adequacy, technical adequacy and special user adequacy. All these were evaluated using the incidence reports. The latter, involved the cognitive-based approach to the design of science content which related the content chosen to everyday life. This is important so that topic chosen on: 'living and non-living things' can make ADHD learners learn by identifying with prior knowledge they have in their cognitive process. This makes understanding easier and enhances their science literacy. The delivery strategy chosen in the ID model, which is motion-based using the motion device, Kinect addressed the characteristics of these type learners that enabled them to be engaged and focused in their learning process. Generally, results obtained from the evaluation conducted based on the data-driven constructs, showed that the motion-based science educational application for ADHD learners (Sains-4SL), was effective in supporting these learners learn science.

References

1. National Institutes of Mental Health (NIH): Attention Deficit/Hyperactivity Disorder. Publication No. TR 13-3572 (2013)
2. National Institutes of Mental Health (NIH): ADHD; The Basics. Publication No. QF-16-3572 (2016)

3. Polanczyk, G., de Lima, M.S., Horta, B.L., Biedermen, J., Rohde, L.A.: The worldwide prevalence of ADHD: a systematic review and metaregression analysis. Am. J. Psychiatry **164**(6), 942–948 (2007)
4. Canals, J., Hidalgo, P.M., Jane, M.C., Domenech, E.: ADHD prevalence in Spanish preschoolers. J. Atten. Disord. (2016). doi:10.1177/1087054716638511
5. Starcic, A.I., Cotic, M., Zajc, M.: Design-based research on the use of a tangible user interface for geometry teaching in an inclusive classroom. Br. J. Educ. Technol. **44**(5), 729–744 (2012)
6. Houghton, S., Milner, N., West, J., Douglas, G., Lawrence, V., Whiting, K., Tannock, R., Durkin, K.: Motor control and sequencing of boys with Attention-Deficit/Hyperactivity Disorder (ADHD) during computer game play. Br. J. Educ. Technol. **35**(1), 21–34 (2004)
7. Lin, C.Y., Yu, W.J., Chen, W.J., Huang, C.W., Lin, C.C.: The effect of literacy learning via mobile augmented reality for the students with ADHD and reading disabilities. In: Antona, M., Stephanidis, C. (eds.) UAHCI 2016. LNCS, vol. 9739, pp. 103–111. Springer, Cham (2016). doi:10.1007/978-3-319-40238-3_11
8. Shaw, R., Lewis, V.: The impact of computer-mediated and traditional academic task presentation on the performance and behaviour of children with ADHD. J. Res. Spec. Educ. Needs **5**(2), 47–54 (2005)
9. DuPaul, G.J., McGoey, K.E., Eckert, T.L., Vanbrakle, J.: Preschool children with attention-deficit/hyperactivity disorder: impairments in behavioral, social, and school functioning. J. Am. Acad. Child Adolesc. Psychiatry **40**(5), 508–515 (2001)
10. Coghill, D., Spiel, G., Baldursson, G., Dopfner, M., Lorenzo, M.J., Ralston, S.J., Rothenberger, A.: Which factors impact on clinician-rated impairment in children with ADHD? Eur. Child Adolesc. Psychiatry **15**(1), i30–i37 (2006)
11. Clark, C., Prior, M., Kinsella, G.: The relationship between executive function abilities, adaptive behaviour, and academic achievement in children with externalising behavior problems. J. Child Psychol. Psychiatry **43**(6), 785–796 (2002)
12. Klimkeit, E., Graham, C., Lee, P., Morling, M., Russo, D., Tonge, B.: Children should be seen and heard. Self-report of feelings and behavior in primary-school-age children with ADHD. J. Atten. Disord. **10**(2), 181–191 (2006)
13. Capano, L., Minden, D., Chen, S.X., Schachar, R.J., Ickowicz, A.: Mathematical learning disorder in school-age children with attention-deficit hyperactivity disorder. Can. J. Psychiatry **53**(6), 392–399 (2008)
14. DuPaul, G.J., Morgan, P.L., Farkas, G., Hillemeier, M.M., Maczuga, S.: Academic and social functioning associated with attention-deficit/hyperactivity disorder: latent class analyses of trajectories from kindergarten to fifth grade. J. Abnorm. Child Psychol. **44**(7), 1425–1438 (2016)
15. Graham, S., Fishman, E.J., Reid, R., Hebert, M.: Writing characteristics of students with attention deficit hyperactive disorder: a meta-analysis. Learn. Disabil. Res. Pract. **31**(2), 75–89 (2016)
16. Chan, T., Martinussen, R.: Positive illusions? The accuracy of academic self-appraisals in adolescents with ADHD. J. Pediatr. Psychol. **41**(7), 799–809 (2015)
17. Van Neste, J., Hayden, A., Lorch, E.P., Milich, R.: Inference generation and story comprehension among children with ADHD. J. Abnorm. Child Psychol. **43**(2), 259–270 (2015)
18. Barry, T.D.S., Lyman, R.D., Klinger, L.G.: Academic underachievement and attention-deficit/hyperactivity disorder: the negative impact of symptom severity on school performance. J. Sch. Psychol. **40**(3), 259–283 (2002)

19. Scholtens, S., Rydell, A.N., Wallentin, F.Y.: Development and aging ADHD symptoms, academic achievement, self-perception of academic competence and future orientation: a longitudinal study. Scand. J. Psychol. **54**(3), 205–212 (2013)

20. Taanila, A., Ebeling, H., Tiihala, M., Kaakinen, M., Moilanen, I., Hurtig, T., Yliherva, A.: Association between childhood specific learning difficulties and school performance in adolescents with and without ADHD symptoms. J. Atten. Disord. **18**(1), 61–72 (2012)

21. Gormley, M.J., DuPaul, G.J., Weyandt, L.L., Anastopoulos, A.D.: First-year GPA and academic service use among college students with and without ADHD. J. Atten. Disord. (2016). doi:10.1177/1087054715623046

22. Holmberg, K., Bolte, S.: Do symptoms of ADHD at ages 7 and 10 predict academic outcome at age 16 in the general population? J. Atten. Disord. **18**(8), 635–645 (2012)

23. Sayal, K., Washbrook, E., Propper, C.: Childhood behavior problems and academic outcomes in adolescence: longitudinal population-based study. J. Am. Acad. Child Adolesc. Psychiatry **54**(5), 360–368 (2015)

24. Arnold, L.E., Hodgkins, P., Kahle, J., Madhoo, M., Kewley, G.: J. Atten. Disord. (2015). doi:10.1177/1087054714566076

25. LeFever, G.B., Villers, M.S., Morrow, A.L.: Parental perception of adverse educational outcomes among children diagnosed and treated for ADHD: a call for improved school/provider collaboration. Psychol. Sch. **39**(1), 63–71 (2002)

26. Barkley, R.A., Fischer, M., Smallish, L., Fletcher, K.: Young adult outcome of hyperactive children: adaptive functioning in major life activities. J. Am. Acad. Child Adolesc. Psychiatry **45**(2), 192–202 (2006)

27. Clarfield, J., Stoner, G.: The effects of computerized reading instruction on the academic performance of students identified with ADHD. Sch. Psychol. Rev. **34**(2), 246–254 (2005)

28. Mautone, J.A., DuPaul, G.J., Jitendra, A.K.: The effects of computer-assisted instruction on the mathematics performance and classroom behavior of children with ADHD. J. Atten. Disord. **9**(1), 301–312 (2005)

29. Kang, H.W., Zentall, S.Z.: Computer-generated geometry instruction: a preliminary study. Educ. Tech. Res. Dev. **59**(6), 783–797 (2011)

30. Shalev, L., Tsal, Y., Mevorach, C.: Computerized progressive attentional training (CPAT) program: effective direct intervention for children with ADHD. Child Neuropsychol. **13**(4), 382–388 (2007)

31. Reynolds, J.L.: Can technology help kids with ADHD stay focused? http://health.usnews. com/health-care/patient-advice/articles/2017-05-03/can-technology-help-kids-with-adhd-stay-focused. Accessed 14 Sept 2017

32. Rabiner, D.L., Murray, D.W., Skinner, A.T., Malone, P.S.: A randomized trial of two promising computer-based interventions for students with attention difficulties. J. Abnorm. Child Psychol. **38**(1), 131–142 (2010)

33. Murray, D.S., Rabiner, D.L.: Teacher use of computer assisted instruction for young inattentive students: implications for implementation and teacher preparation. J. Educ. Train. Stud. **2**(2), 58–66 (2014)

34. Shaw, R., Grayson, A., Lewis, V.: Inhibition, ADHD, and computer games: the inhibitory performance of children with ADHD on computerized tasks and games. J. Atten. Disord. **8**(4), 160–168 (2005)

35. Mathrani, A., Christian, S., Ponder-Sutton, A.: PlayIT: game based learning approach for teaching programming concepts. Educ. Technol. Soc. **19**(2), 5–17 (2016)

36. Zemliansky, P., Wilcox, D.: Design and implementation of educational games: theoretical and practical perspectives. Hershey, New York (2010)

37. Ke, F., Abras, T.: Games for engaged learning of middle school children with special learning needs. Br. J. Educ. Technol. **44**(2), 225–242 (2012)

38. Ota, K.R., DuPaul, G.J.: Task engagement and mathematics performance in children with attention-deficit hyperactivity disorder: effects of supplemental computer instruction. Sch. Psychol. Q. **17**(3), 242–257 (2002)
39. Bai, H., Pan, W., Hirumi, A., Kebritchi, M.: Assessing the effectiveness of a 3-D instructional game on improving mathematics achievement and motivation of middle school students. Br. J. Educ. Technol. **43**(6), 993–1003 (2012)
40. Altanis, G., Boloudakis, M., Retalis, S., Nikou, N.: Children with motor impairments play a kinect learning game: first findings from a pilot case in an authentic classroom environment. Interact. Des. Archit. J. **19**, 91–104 (2013)
41. Serin, O.: The effects of the computer-based instruction on the achievement and problem solving skills of the science and technology students. Turk. Online J. Educ. Technol. **10**(1), 183–201 (2011)
42. Tsai, C.H., Kuo, Y.H., Chu. K.C., Yen, J.C.: Development and evaluation of game-based learning system using the microsoft Kinect sensor. Int. J. Distrib. Sens. Netw. **11**(7) (2015)
43. Hsu, H.M.J.: The potential of Kinect as interactive educational technology. Int. J. Inf. Educ. Technol. **1**(5), 365–370 (2011)
44. Wattanagul, N., Limpiyakorn,Y.: Automated documentation for rapid prototyping. In: International Conference on Industrial Engineering, Management Science and Application (ICIMSA), 23–24 May 2016 (2016). doi:10.1109/ICIMSA.2016.7503998
45. Hasdell, P.: Participatory design: re-evaluation as socio-material assembly. In: EPIC Conference, 29 November 2016 (2016). doi:10.1111/559-8918.2016.01092
46. Zaman, H.B.: Simbiosis Seni, Sains Teknologi ke Multimedia-Fusion. Universiti Kebangsaan Malaysia, Bangi (2009)
47. Keller, J.M.: Development and use of the ARCS model of instructional design. J. Instr. Dev. **10**(3), 1–10 (1987)
48. Keller, J.M.: Motivational design for learning and performance: the ACRS model approach. Springer Science and Business Media, Berlin (2009)
49. Neilson, J.: Why You Only Need to Test with Five (5) Users. Neilson Norman Group, New York (2000)
50. Hardman, M.L., Drew, C.J., Egan, M.W.: Human Exceptionality School, Community and Family. 10th Edition. http://books.google.com (2010)

Food Category Recognition Using SURF and MSER Local Feature Representation

Mohd Norhisham Razali[1,2], Noridayu Manshor[1(✉)],
Alfian Abdul Halin[1], Razali Yaakob[1], and Norwati Mustapha[1]

[1] Faculty of Computer Science and Information Technology,
Universiti Putra Malaysia, 43300 Serdang, Selangor, Malaysia
hishamrz@gmail.com, ayu@upm.edu.my
[2] Faculty of Computing and Informatics, Universiti Malaysia Sabah,
88400 Kota Kinabalu, Sabah, Malaysia

Abstract. Food object recognition has gained popularity in recent years. This can perhaps be attributed to its potential applications in fields such as nutrition and fitness. Recognizing food images however is a challenging task since various foods come in many shapes and sizes. Besides having unexpected deformities and texture, food images are also captured in differing lighting conditions and camera viewpoints. From a computer vision perspective, using global image features to train a supervised classifier might be unsuitable due to the complex nature of the food images. Local features on the other hand seem the better alternative since they are able to capture minute intricacies such as interest points and other intricate information. In this paper, two local features namely SURF (Speeded- Up Robust Feature) and MSER (Maximally Stable Extremal Regions) are investigated for food object recognition. Both features are computationally inexpensive and have shown to be effective local descriptors for complex images. Specifically, each feature is firstly evaluated separately. This is followed by feature fusion to observe whether a combined representation could better represent food images. Experimental evaluations using a Support Vector Machine classifier shows that feature fusion generates better recognition accuracy at 86.6%.

Keywords: Food category recognition · MSER · SURF · Bag of features

1 Introduction

Food category recognition deals with the automatic recognition of food objects/types with applications such as personalized dietary assessment, food recommendation services and social media (food) images analytics [1]. This field is becoming a burgeoning research area with the proliferation of smart phones and social media services [1, 2]. Image processing and machine learning are at the heart of such systems with other technologies such as 3D reconstruction also being applied when portion/volume estimation is required to approximate caloric amounts [4].

© Springer International Publishing AG 2017
H. Badioze Zaman et al. (Eds.): IVIC 2017, LNCS 10645, pp. 212–223, 2017.
https://doi.org/10.1007/978-3-319-70010-6_20

Feature representation is crucial in the overall recognition pipeline. Carefully handcrafted features enable trained classification engines to discriminatively categorize food objects into their respective classes. To date, global and local features have been explored depending on the target recognition task. For food category recognition, global features provide a better holistic description of the dishes pertaining to overall color distribution, texture and/or shape. Local features on the other hand capture more minuscule properties such as local gradient directions and interest points locations. Since food objects tend to be inconsistent in appearance, contain non-rigid deformations and overall vary largely across (and even within) foods types [3–7, 10], local features potentially provide a more effective description.

In this paper, we investigate the effectiveness of two local features to recognize food objects in images. Inspired by SIFT (Scale-invariant Feature Transform), we look at two similar local feature descriptors namely SURF (Speeded-up Robust Transform) and MSER (Maximally Stable Extremal Regions). SURF describes interest points in a similar fashion to SIFT, but with the advantage of low computation time. MSER [9] on the other hand has shown promise in scene identification, specifically when dealing with different camera viewpoints and illumination variations.

The rest of the paper is organized as follows. Section 2 discusses related works regarding features, with an emphasis on local feature descriptors. Section 3 explains the experimental setup used in this work for food object recognition. Results are reported in Sect. 4 where we finally conclude our findings in Sect. 5.

2   Related Works

2.1   Feature Representation of Food Images

Food image recognition is a complex computer vision task dealing with highly diverse images. Not only are food dishes' appearances inconsistent, but food images also suffer from extremely low inter-class difference and high intra-class variance [11–14]. Therefore, from a supervised classification perspective, properly handcrafted feature representations are imperative to ensure discriminative recognition and/or matching.

2.1.1   Global Features

Global features describing whole images (e.g. color, texture and shape), either in isolation or fused, have been investigated in the past. Most works use colour and texture as the main consideration in a predominantly supervised classification framework on images that contained minimal food mixtures. For example, [15, 21, 22] performed portion and calories estimation using Support Vector Machines (SVM) where [21, 22] additionally considered size and shape. High classification accuracy was reported ranging from 92%–95%. However, the authors mention future enhancements should cater for mixed food types. Support Vector Clustering was used in [16] to classify nine food categories with some mixed ingredients. Ten global features were considered including HSV colour properties and texture information. Results were a bit lacklustre with only 61% classification accuracy.

2.1.2   Local Features

Local features are able to capture more detailed properties in images. Basically, two steps are involved in local feature generation, namely (i) interest point detection and (ii) description [17]. Local descriptors are hence more compact and descriptive, which is suitable for food images since food objects are invariant to scale, orientation and distortion, while being partially invariant to illumination [18].

Kong and Tan [6] classified food using the SIFT local descriptor with a classification accuracy of 92%. They however highlighted that multi-class and irregularly shaped foods recognitions were poor, mainly due to bad segmentation during pre-processing. In [5], the authors used a multi-view approach based on difference of Gaussian and SIFT. Their mobile phone system performed well on regular shaped foods such as fruits and burgers. However, results were poor for irregularly shaped foods such as steak, sausages and baked potatoes; and multi-class foods such as rice and noodle dishes.

The work in [9] combined local texture and shape information for food categories classification. Specifically, Non-Redundant Local Binary Patterns (NRLBP) and shape context was used on the Pittsburgh Fast Food Image Dataset(PFID) [19] dataset, which consists of 5 food categories. Spatial information was used to cater for the small inter-class difference between food categories that made the frequency of visual words of different categories look identical. SIFT was used to find the interest points and NRLBP was used as a filter to preserve important visual words. The overall accuracy however, was quite low at 63%, where expectedly, the lowest accuracy was for small texture-less food items (e.g. meat pieces and doughnuts).

The authors in [20] trained a linear SVM using local HOG and colour patches. Overall classification accuracy was reported at 79.2% on 100 food categories from the UEC100-Food dataset [20]. Since HOG is not invariant to rotation, the training food images were flipped to create variability in the training data for HOG. In more recent work [21], SURF features were encoded using Spatial Pyramid Matching (SPM) to take account of the spatial information of SURF interest points as well as to tackle the large intra-class difference of food objects. In all, local features have demonstrated to be more efficient than global features.

3   SURF and MSER

This section provides explanations about how the chosen features are used.

3.1   Speeded-Up Robust Feature (SURF)

SURF [22] attempts to locate point correspondences within two images. The four steps of SURF are (i) determining the interest points, (ii) locating major interest points in scale space, (iii) finding the feature direction, and (iv) generating the feature vectors. Among the advantages of SURF over similar algorithms such as SIFT, is the Hessian matrix calculation which is faster and competitively accurate [17]. The descriptor divides the neighboring regions into equally sized sub-regions, where Haar-wavelet responses are then calculated for each region. Food images have very large variations, containing occlusion, diverse illuminations and the image itself can be taken from many angles. SURF can potentially deal with all these challenges and provides a more compact and discriminative representation for food objects [6, 18].

3.2 Maximally Stable Extremal Regions (MSER)

In general, MSER attempts to detect a set of connected regions from an image. Each region (i.e. MSER regions) is defined by an extremal property of the respective region's intensity function to the values of its outer boundaries [23]. Moreover, MSER is computationally inexpensive and can be calculated in linear time [24]. MSER was introduced by Extremal et al. [25] to perform scene recognition under arbitrary viewpoints and illumination conditions. Finding corresponding elements between scenes is a challenging and high-level computer vision task, which in many ways is similar to recognizing food objects. This is because, as with different scenes, non-rigid deformations exist causing food objects to have arbitrary shape and non-uniform texture.

4 Experimental Setup

The number of interest points generated by both SURF and MSER can be very large. Therefore, calculating the similarity between images can become cumbersome. Hence, the Bag of Features (BoF) [26] model is chosen to convert patch-level data (from which features are extracted from) into image-level descriptions so that the image pattern from any category can be better learned by a supervised classifier. As mentioned, SURF and MSER are chosen due to their respective capabilities to capture discriminative feature points from complex appearances of food objects. Both are also fast making them potentially efficient during actual real-world deployment, specifically for faster feature extraction time.

In the experiments, each feature is firstly explored separately. However, we also believe that MSER and SURF have complementary descriptive properties. Therefore, feature fusion of both features is also investigated. The explanation of the stages involved is presented in following section and accompanied by an illustrative depiction of the fusion approach in Fig. 1.

Stage 1: SURF and MSER Extraction
For SURF, interest points are detected from corners, blobs and T-junctions. This minimizes the effect of extracting irrelevant background features since some food images have a multi-class appearance. An integral image algorithm is used as opposed to the Gaussian pyramid construction process in SIFT. SURF basically segments neighbouring regions of each interest point into 4×4 sub-regions. This is followed by calculating the Haar wavelet responses for each sub-region. Since each response has four values, each of the key points is resultantly represented by a 64-dimensional feature vector. MSER on the other hand, discovers a set of connected candidate regions based on the watershed segmentation algorithm. Based on an intensity threshold, pixels are grouped into two sets. The threshold value is changed at each iteration, which changes the cardinality of each set. Finally the extremal regions are generated as connected regions. To describe the extremal region, SURF is used.

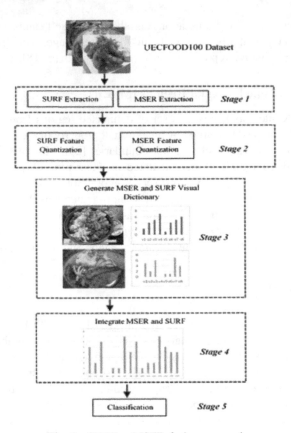

Fig. 1. SURF + MSER fusion approach

Stage 2: Feature Quantization

In this process, interest points are clustered into visual words. The visual words are based on a pre-defined cluster number with K referring to the vocabulary size. A set of interest points are described as $X_1, \ldots, X_n \in \mathbb{R}^D$. To build the visual dictionary, the descriptor space is partitioned using the k-means clustering algorithm with k vectors being the visual words, described as $\mu_1, \ldots, \mu_k \in \mathbb{R}^D$. Each interest point is assigned a visual word: $q_1, \ldots q_2 \in \{1, \ldots K\}$. The vocabulary size is initially set to 500 based on the work done by [8, 21], which seems optimal. A small vocabulary may weaken the discriminative capability as many different patches might be assigned to the similar visual word. On the flipside, a larger vocabulary size may lead to the generation of noise, which reduces generalizability and increases processing overhead [29].

Stage 3: Generate SURF and MSER Visual Dictionary

In this stage, the histogram of every visual word is generated where the occurrence frequency of interest points in each visual word is aggregated. Both SURF and MSER generate 500 feature dimensions.

Stage 4: Integrate SURF and MSER Visual Dictionary

In this final stage, the SURF and MSER visual dictionaries are concatenated (fused). Intuitively, the fusion of multiple features types can provide a more informative and holistic description to improve classification performance [30].

Stage 5: Classification

We trained a Linear-kernel SVM classification engine where 10-fold cross validation was done. The images were randomly split into 10 sets and in each run, one set was used for training and the remaining for testing, until 10 iterations.

5   Results and Discussion

The UEC-FOOD100 [20, 31] dataset is used as the evaluation benchmark. It contains 14,467-JPEG images with different pixel dimensions, containing 100 food categories as shown in Fig. 2.

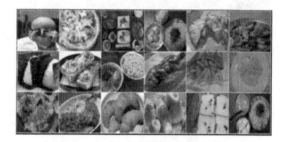

Fig. 2. Samples from the UEC100-FOOD dataset, adapted from [31]

On average, there are 150 images per category. The images in this dataset were collected from the World Wide Web consisting of multiple classes of food categories whose image contrast, lighting and appearances differ greatly.

5.1   Individual Local Features Performance

Table 1 shows the results of using SURF and MSER separately. Note that SIFT is included in the comparison as a baseline comparison. The main observation is feature representation time for detection and quantization.

Table 1. Comparisons of local features performance

Feature	Number of interest points	Feature representation (minutes)			Classification accuracy (%)
		Detection (a)	Quantization (b)	a + b	
SURF	4,407,004	12.80	33.50	**46.30**	62.08
MSER	3,087,664	30.04	19.73	49.77	**73.89**
SIFT	13,912,613	176.74	368.02	544.76	64.65

SURF takes the least amount of time to construct the BoF representation. MSER lags behind by ~3-min and takes lesser time than the others for quantization. This is expected since the number of detected interest points is also low. As expected, SIFT took the longest time as it extracts the most number of interest points.

One interesting observation is that although MSER detects lesser interest points, the overall classification accuracy is highest at 73.89%. Overall time is higher compared to SURF but not that significant. SURF and SIFT have classification accuracies of 62.08% and 64.65%, respectively but the time taken by SIFT is significantly longer due to the high number of interest points. Figure 3 shows sample outputs after running MSER and SURF on three types of food images.

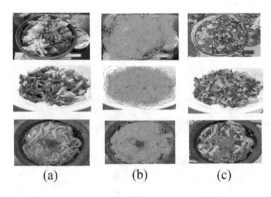

(a)   (b)   (c)

Fig. 3. Original image (a), SURF detection (b), MSER region detection (c)

These images can be considered as the foods that have single object appearance with some mixture of ingredients. The detection using MSER is more selective whereas SURF is denser.

5.2 Feature Fusion Performance

The results of the feature fusion approach are shown in Table 2. Expectedly, classification accuracy improves by combining both features. Note that we also tested the combinations of SIFT + MSER, as SIFT is similar to SURF. Therefore, we believe that combining it with MSER might provide some useful insights.

Table 2. Comparisons of local features fusion performance

Feature	Number of interest points	Feature representation (minutes)			Classification accuracy (%)
		Detection (a)	Quantization (b)	a + b	
SURF + MSER	7,494,668	42.84	53.23	**96.07**	86.60
SIFT + MSER	17,000,277	206.78	387.75	594.53	**87.63**

In terms of overall classification accuracy, the difference is not significant. SIFT + MSER does produce highest classification accuracy but, at the cost of overall computation time where it takes 6-times longer than using SURF + MSER. However, the classification accuracy of SURF + MSER is also quite impressive falling back by only 1.03% compared to SIFT + MSER. This is very promising considering the time saving benefit. Therefore, at this stage of the work we can argue that SURF can also be used as an effective interest point descriptor despite generating lesser interest points than SIFT.

5.3   The Strength of SURF and MSER Feature

Based on our observations, SURF was unable to effectively represent multi-class food objects with high non-rigid deformities as well as foods with strong mixture of ingredients. MSER on the other hand provided better representation for such food objects (Fig. 4).

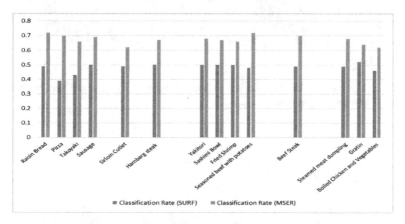

Fig. 4. SURF vs MSER for multi-class food objects with high non-rigid deformities and strong mixture of ingredients

Figure 5 shows sample detection results for three food categories with strong mixtures of various ingredients. This illustrates how MSER provides a more discriminative representation for foods with small and deformed ingredients, as well as exhibiting complicated textures. As can also be observed, SURF detects too many potentially irrelevant points that might contain redundancies.

Due to this observation, SURF seems better suited for texture-less foods such as liquid foods. This is illustrated in Fig. 6 where the classification accuracy for such food objects is higher for SURF. MSER is unable to provide an effective representation due lesser or absence of ridgelines and strong edges, resulting in undetectable extremal regions.

Figure 7 shows sample detection results for both SURF and MSER for Potage, which is a type of thick soup that contains virtually no texture. Observably, more extremal regions are sampled in the background using MSER. SURF samples only few relevant interest points from the Potage region itself.

(a) (b) (c)

Original Images

SURF

MSER Region Detection

MSER Feature Description

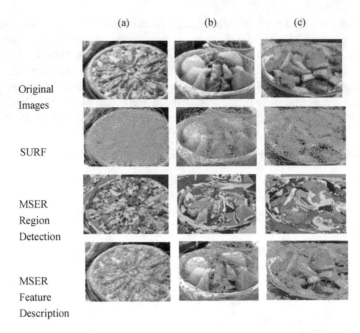

Fig. 5. SURF and MSER detection on mixed foods (a) pizza (b) seasoned beef with potatoes (c) boiled chicken and vegetables

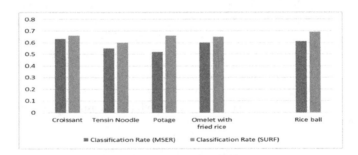

Fig. 6. Performance comparisons between MSER and SURF on texture-less food categories

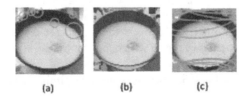

(a)   (b)   (c)

Fig. 7. SURF (a), MSER region detection (b), MSER feature description (c) for Potage.

6 Conclusions and Future Works

In this work, we have explored the use of two local features, namely SURF and MSER for food objects recognition. Specifically, each feature was firstly evaluated separately, followed by evaluating a representation approach that fuses both features. Recognition was ultimately performed by training a SVM based on the highly diverse UEC100-FOOD dataset. We have observed feature detection, computation time as well as recognition accuracy for foods containing strong mixture of ingredients, which included multi-class food objects with high deformations. Our experiments have shown that MSER is an effective feature to represent such images. SURF on the other hand was more effective in represented the less variable and texture-less food types. However, it seemed to complement MSER very well as demonstrated when evaluating the feature fusion approach. Specifically, the recognition accuracy was quite high at 86.6%. Furthermore, although this was achieved only in the feature fusion approach, one of the considerations was SURF, which is a less dense (and perhaps viewed as less descriptive) descriptor compared to SIFT. However, due to the impressive results, SURF can seemingly describe food images well as long as it is being complemented by MSER. In the future, since the recognition accuracy on texture-less food categories are less than 70%, we will investigate other feature representations to improve overall recognition results.

References

1. Yanai, K., Kawano, Y.: Twitter food photo mining and analysis for one hundred kinds of foods. In: Ooi, W.T., Snoek, C.G.M., Tan, H.K., Ho, C.-K., Huet, B., Ngo, C.-W. (eds.) PCM 2014. LNCS, vol. 8879, pp. 22–32. Springer, Cham (2014). doi:10.1007/978-3-319-13168-9_3
2. Farinella, G.M., Allegra, D., Moltisanti, M., Stanco, F., Battiato, S.: Food understanding from digital images. (2015)
3. Xu, R., Jiang, S., Wang, S., Song, X., Jain, R., Herranz, L.: Geolocalized modeling for dish recognition. IEEE Trans. Multimed. 17, 1187–1199 (2015)
4. Pouladzadeh, P., Shirmohammadi, S., Al-maghrabi, R.: Measuring calorie and nutrition from food image. IEEE Trans. Instrum. Measur. 63, 1947–1956 (2014)
5. Kong, F., Raynor, H.A., Tan, J., He, H.: DietCam: multi-view regular shape food recognition with a camera phone. Pervasive Mob. Comput. 19, 108–121 (2015)
6. Kong, F., Tan, J.: DietCam: automatic dietary assessment with mobile camera phones. Pervasive Mob. Comput. 8, 147–163 (2012)
7. Bosch, M., Zhu, F., Khanna, N., Boushey, C.J., Delp, E.J.: Combining global and local features for food identification in dietary assessment. pp. 1789–1792 (2011)
8. Kagaya, H., Aizawa, K.: New Trends in Image Analysis and Processing - ICIAP 2015 Workshops, vol. 9281, pp. 350–357. Springer, Heidelberg (2015). doi:10.1007/978-3-319-23222-5
9. Nguyen, D.T., Ogunbona, P.O., Probst, Y., Li, W., Zong, Z.: Food image classification using local appearance and global structural information. Neurocomputing. 140, 242–251 (2014)

10. Altintakan, U.L., Yazici, A.: An improved BOW approach using fuzzy feature encoding and visual-word weighting. In: IEEE International Conference on Fuzzy System 2015-November, (2015). doi:10.1109/FUZZ-IEEE.2015.7338108
11. Kong, F., Tan, J.: DietCam: Regular Shape Food Recognition with a Camera Phone. In: International Conference on Body Sensor Networks (2011)
12. Anthimopoulos, M.M., Scarnato, L., Diem, P., Mougiakakou, S.G., Gianola, L.: A food recognition system for diabetic patients based on an optimized bag-of-features model. IEEE J. Biomed. Health Inform. **18**, 1261–1271 (2014)
13. Razali, M.N., Manshor, N.: Object detection framework for multiclass food object localization and classification
14. Norhisham, M., Manshor, N., Halin, A.A., Mustapha, N.: Analysis of SURF and SIFT representations to recognize food objects
15. Zhu, F., Woo, I., Kim, S.Y., Boushey, C.J., Ebert, D.S., Delp, E.J., Bosch, M.: The use of mobile devices in aiding dietary assessment and evaluation. IEEE J. Sel. Top. Signal Process. **4**, 756–766 (2010)
16. Oliveira, L., Neves, G., Oliveira, T., Jorge, E., Lizarraga, M., Costa, V.: A mobile, lightweight, poll-based food identification system. Pattern Recogn. **47**, 1941–1952 (2014)
17. Wu, J., Cui, Z., Sheng, V.S., Zhao, P., Su, D., Gong, S.: A comparative study of SIFT and its variants. Meas. Sci. Rev. **13**, 122–131 (2013)
18. Zong, Z., Nguyen, D.T., Ogunbona, P., Li, W.: On the combination of local texture and global structure for food classification. In: Proceedings of 2010 IEEE International Symposium Multimedia, ISM 2010, pp. 204–211 (2010). doi:10.1109/ISM.2010.37
19. Chen, M., Wu, W., Yang, L., Sukthankar, R., Yang, J., Dhingra, K.: PFID: pittsburgh fast-food image dataset. In: Proceedings of the 16th IEEE International Conference on Image Processing. pp. 289–292 (2009)
20. Kawano, Y., Yanai, K.: FoodCam: a real-time food recognition system on a smartphone. Multimed. Tools Appl. **74**, 5263–5287 (2015). doi:10.1007/s11042-014-2000-8
21. Pooja, H., Madival, P.S.A.: Food recognition and calorie extraction using bag-of- surf and spatial pyramid matching methods. Int. J. Comput. Sci. Mobile Comput. **5**, 387–393 (2016)
22. Bay, H., Tuytelaars, T., Van Gool, L.: SURF: speeded up robust features. In: Leonardis, A., Bischof, H., Pinz, A. (eds.) ECCV 2006. LNCS, vol. 3951, pp. 404–417. Springer, Heidelberg (2006). doi:10.1007/11744023_32
23. Donoser, M., Riemenschneider, H., Bischof, H.: Shape guided maximally stable extremal region (MSER) tracking. pp. 1800–1803 (2010). doi:10.1109/ICPR.2010.444
24. Nistér, D., Stewénius, H.: Linear time maximally stable extremal regions. In: Forsyth, D., Torr, P., Zisserman, A. (eds.) ECCV 2008. LNCS, vol. 5303, pp. 183–196. Springer, Heidelberg (2008). doi:10.1007/978-3-540-88688-4_14
25. Extremal, M.S., Matas, J., Chum, O., Urban, M., Pajdla, T.: Robust wide baseline stereo from. In: British Machine Vision Conference, pp. 384–393 (2002). doi:10.5244/C.16.36
26. Csurka, G., Dance, C., Fan, L., Willamowski, J., Bray, C.: Visual categorization with bag of keypoints. In: International Workshop in Statistic Learning and Computer Vision, pp. 1–22 (2004). doi:10.1234/12345678
27. Kawano, Y., Yanai, K.: FoodCam: a real-time mobile food recognition system employing fisher vector. In: Gurrin, C., Hopfgartner, F., Hurst, W., Johansen, H., Lee, H., O'Connor, N. (eds.) MMM 2014. LNCS, vol. 8326, pp. 369–373. Springer, Cham (2014). doi:10.1007/978-3-319-04117-9_38
28. Aizawa, K., Li, H., Morikawa, C., Maruyama, Y.: Food balance estimation by using personal dietary tendencies in a multimedia food log. IEEE Trans. Multimed. **15**, 2176–2185 (2013)

29. Jiang, Y., Yang, J., Ngo, C., Hauptmann, A.G.: Representations of keypoint-based semantic concept detection: a comprehensive study representations of keypoint-based semantic concept detection: a comprehensive study. IEEE Trans. Multimed. **12**, 42–53 (2010)
30. Yu, J., Qin, Z., Wan, T., Zhang, X.: Feature integration analysis of bag-of-features model for image retrieval. Neurocomputing **120**, 355–364 (2013). doi:10.1016/j.neucom.2012.08.061
31. Matsuda, Y., Hoashi, H., Yanai, K.: Recognition of multiple-food images by detecting candidate regions. In: Proceedings of IEEE International Conference on Multimedia and Exposition, pp. 25–30 (2012)

Motivation Design Methodology for Online Knowledge Sharing Interface

Prasanna Ramakrisnan[1,2(✉)] and Azizah Jaafar[3]

[1] Institute of Neo Education (iNED), University Technology MARA,
40450 Shah Alam, Malaysia
prasanna@fskm.uitm.edu.my
[2] Faculty Computer and Mathematical Sciences (FSKM),
Universiti Teknologi MARA (Melaka),
Jasin Campus, 77300 Merlimau, Melaka, Malaysia
[3] Institute of Visual Informatics, National University of Malaysia,
43600 Bangi, Selangor, Malaysia
azizahj@ukm.edu.my

Abstract. Online knowledge sharing interface have been used in many higher learning institutions for online learning. Unfortunately, the students tend to lose their attention quickly and no motivation to participate in the online knowledge sharing activities. Efforts have already been taken by higher learning institutions to encourage student participation for knowledge sharing in the online discussion interface. But still the students were unable to participate fully in the online discussion interface. The current interface design is lacking of motivation factor to sustain students' participation in online knowledge sharing activities. It was found that motivation can be designed in user interface for online knowledge sharing activities. However, there are very few methodology proposals for designing motivation in user interface. Therefore, this study presents a methodology for designing motivation for online knowledge sharing interface. This Motivation Design Methodology is applied in development of online knowledge sharing interface called as i-Discuss and serves to illustrate the proposal.

Keywords: Motivation design methodology · Online knowledge sharing · Interface design

1 Introduction

Knowledge sharing refers to a process in which knowledge is given by one party and received by another [1]. In traditional learning method, knowledge sharing is limited to face-to-face discussion in classroom. But with the advancement of technology now sharing of knowledge can take place regardless of time and place in an online learning environment. This online learning environment contains a number of features that enable learning and communication. Among them are the learning modules, communications, test, assignments submission and so on. Although there are many modules, the use of online discussion interface for communication reported the highest usage in online learning environment [2]. The online discussion interface is used as a

© Springer International Publishing AG 2017
H. Badioze Zaman et al. (Eds.): IVIC 2017, LNCS 10645, pp. 224–232, 2017.
https://doi.org/10.1007/978-3-319-70010-6_21

communication medium in online learning environment by both students and educators for the purpose of sharing knowledge [3]. This interface provides a medium for the students to continue their classroom discussions online. Correspondingly, many studies underscore the advantages of using the online discussion interface since it can provide a platform for the students to share and gain knowledge [4], interact [5], increase discussion and cooperation among other students [6], prepare for cognitive learning and better exploration [7] and improve critical thinking skills [8].

It was identified that the current online discussion interface design need to be further improved to increase the students' intention to use it [9]. Therefore, it is important to review the interface design for online discussion related to education because use of online discussion interface has great potential to enhance the learning experience and learning outcomes [10]. One of the user interface enablers that drives students' knowledge sharing ability in online discussion interface is motivation design [11].

Study shows motivation can be nurtured through an user interface design [12]. Motivation is a theoretical construct used to describe student behavior. It illustrates the cause of student action, desires, and needs. Motivation is also an inducement that one has. It can be a challenging job to give students an inner impetus in the process of sharing knowledge online. Therefore, the discussion interface should be designed based on motivation so that the students will share their knowledge due to internal encouragement. Understanding these importance, our aim is to highlight a specific methodology for designing motivation in user interface.

2 Motivation Design Methodology

Edward Deci and Ryan Richard has developed the general human motivation of Self-Determination Theory (SDT) to emphasize self-determined behavior by the students. The focus on self-determination enables students to perform their goals clearly. Internal motivation comes from within the student and is connected to the understanding that learning is beneficial and meaningful.

The main element of the theory is that the students meet their basic psychological needs; the more they achieve these basic needs, the more their behavior is determined by themselves. Some students can struggle by creating internal motivation during online knowledge sharing activities as they see it as a necessity rather than a meaningful experience. In this case, interface designers can influence students' motivation to share their knowledge by maximizing their autonomy, competence and relatedness.

Therefore, motivation should be effectively designed in the online discussion interface. It is found that the effectiveness of motivation is determined by autonomy, competence, and relatedness with an interface. In addition, the elements used to apply motivation in the interface play an important role. If this aspect is not taken into consideration, the motivational effect may not be as expected, ineffective or not motivating. Thus, to motivate them effectively in the online discussion interface, a method is suggested based on some previous studies [13, 14]. The Motivation Design Methodology is recommended with five simple steps. Figure 1 illustrates the five easy steps to design motivation in the user interface.

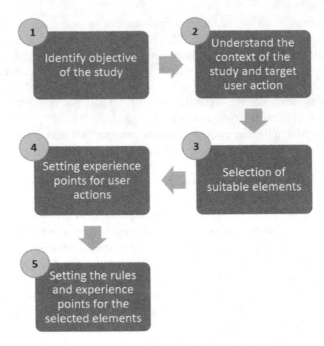

Fig. 1. Steps in Motivation Design Methodology

2.1 Step 1: Identify Objective of the Study

The objective of the study is to enhance online knowledge sharing activities by increasing the intrinsic motivation of students. Enhancing online knowledge sharing activities is a challenge. It is important to ensure the objective of online knowledge sharing and motivation are clear for the success and motivational experiences. This objective helps to determine the scope of the study, while the goal of online knowledge sharing is key to creating meaningful structures. Therefore, this study will develop an interface to enhance intrinsic motivation and user interest (student) in online knowledge sharing activities.

2.2 Step 2: Understand the Context of the Study and Target User Action

In order to gain a better understanding of the context where by intrinsic motivation is applied and the target user action, the interface designer needs to analyze the intrinsic motivational context and target user action. Target user of this study are students. While the context of the study is an online interface where students are intrinsically motivated in knowledge sharing activities. Table 1 shows the context of online knowledge sharing and student actions in the discussion interface for online knowledge sharing.

Table 1. Context and student actions

Context	Student actions
Registration	Completing registration
Knowledge seeking	Reading comments
	Asking questions
Knowledge contribution	Replying comment or questions

2.3 Step 3: Selection of Suitable Elements

Design elements such as game [15] and social [16] can motivate students intrinsically in learning. Therefore, a set of game and social design elements are recommended for designing motivation in user interface [11]. This user interface design is expected to increase students' motivation in knowledge sharing activities. The selection of appropriate game and social elements with the context of online knowledge sharing was identified to support the needs of human motivation (autonomy (A), competence (C) and relatedness (R)). Table 2 shows the game and social elements that have been identified for designing motivation for online knowledge sharing interface.

Table 2. Elements for motivation design

Elements	Context	A	C	R	Purpose	Activities
GAME						
1. Avatar	Registration	A1	.		To provide choice to choose students avatar	When the students wants to change their profile picture
2. Badges	Knowledge contribution and seeking		C1		To provide unexpected responses to the students when they achieve their performance	When students fulfill the target action in online knowledge sharing activities
				R2	To display student ability and level of involvement to other students	When displayed in students profile for view of other students
3. Leaderboard	Knowledge contribution		C2		To provide direct responses to the students about their position	When students total knowledge contribution is related with ranking
				R2	To visualize student ability and their contribution with other students	When wants to create competition among the students

(continued)

Table 2. (*continued*)

Elements	Context	A	C	R	Purpose	Activities
4. Player control	Knowledge seeking	A2			To provide choice in receiving immediate feedback (e-mail)	When the students wants immediate feedback for their knowledge sharing activities
	Knowledge contribution	A3			To provide choice in type of media	When the students or lecturers wants to use various types of media in online knowledge sharing activities
5. Feedback	Knowledge seeking and contribution		C3		To provide positive feedbacks for student effort	When students contribution in online knowledge sharing activities is appreciated
				R3	To show appreciation to other students	When students contribution is appreciated by other students
6. Level	Knowledge contribution		C4		To provide view of student progression	When students progression in online knowledge sharing activities shown in form of growth
				R2	To show students growth to other students	When wants to show status and student growth to other students
SOCIAL						
7. Tagging	Knowledge contribution			R1	To connect students with similar information contribution	When student wants to contribute similar information with other students
	Knowledge seeking				To connect students with similar seeking interest	When student wants to seek information with similar interest with other students

2.4   Step 4: Setting Experience Points for User Actions

Students are awarded with experience points rather than grade points to encourage them to share their knowledge online. This experience point can provide immediate satisfaction that can successfully motivate the students [17]. According to Barata et al., the experience points can be matched with traditional grading systems at universities. Previous studies have found that for every 1000 student experience points, their experience level is increasing and each level has been labelled with a unique title. Students must reach level 10 from maximum 20 level (20,000 experience points) to pass a course [18]. This level is said to be matching with the traditional 20 grading system used in universities.

The range of experience points is allocated for each student action in a motivating interface. Table 3 shows the range of experience points for student actions in online knowledge sharing activities.

Table 3. Allocation of experience point range for student actions

Context	Student actions	Experience points
Registration	Completing registration	5
Knowledge seeking	Reading comments	5
	Asking questions	10
Knowledge contribution	Replying comment or questions	30

2.5   Step 5: Setting the Rules and Experience Points for Selected Elements

At this stage, the identified elements are provided with appropriate rules and experience points. Table 4 shows the allocation.

Table 4. Elements for motivation design

Elements	Context	Activities	Rules	Experience points
	Registration		Student register in	1
1. Avatar	Registration	When the students wants to change their profile picture	Students update profiles with pictures	4
2. Badges	Knowledge contribution and seeking	When students fulfill the target action in online knowledge sharing activities When displayed in students profile for view of other students	Students read discussion topics (Student type: Reader) Students start a discussion topic (Student type: Initiator) Students contribute knowledge in discussion (Student type: Contributors)	5 10 20
			* Upload a picture yourself gets a badge	
3. Leaderboard	Knowledge contribution	When students total knowledge contribution is related with ranking When wants to create competition among the students	* Position on the leaderboard depends on the experience point. Arrangement is from students who earn high experience points to low	

(continued)

Table 4. (*continued*)

Elements	Context	Activities	Rules	Experience points
4. Player control	Knowledge seeking	When the students wants immediate feedback for their knowledge sharing activities	* Player controls are not given experience points as they are related to setting	
	Knowledge contribution	When the students or lecturers wants to use various types of media in online knowledge sharing activities	* Experience points for use of various media in knowledge sharing activities is not provided as 20 points are awarded for any type of contribution	
5. Feedback	Knowledge seeking and contribution	When students contribution in online knowledge sharing activities is appreciated	Appreciation for student contribution (student type: Popular)	10
		When students contribution is appreciated by other students		
6. Level	Knowledge contribution	When students progression in online knowledge sharing activities shown in form of growth	* Level depends on the received experience points. The below 10 levels with experience point range is used	
		When wants to show status and student growth to other students	Level 10 15,000+ Level 9 10,000–14,999 Level 8 5,000–9,999 Level 7 2,500–4,999 Level 6 1,500–2,499 Level 5 500–1,499 Level 4 250–499 Level 3 30–249 Level 2 5–29 Level 1 0–4	
7. Tagging	Knowledge contribution	When student wants to contribute similar information with other students When student wants to seek information with	* Social elements are not provided with rules and experience points as these allocations are only suitable for game elements [19]	
	Knowledge seeking	similar interest with other students		

3   Conclusion

Despite the great impact on online knowledge sharing interface for motivating students in discussion participation, there are lack of specific methodology for designing motivating user interface. This paper, therefore, present a new methodology for motivation design in user interface. With this aim, the methodology proposes five steps: identify objective of the study, understand the context of the study and target user action, selection of suitable elements, setting experience points for user actions and setting the rules and experience points for selected elements.

This proposed Motivation Design Methodology was used to design a motivating user interface. An interface named as i-Discuss was designed by implementing the intrinsic motivation design criteria using the proposed methodology. Further details of the implementation is extended into another paper.

There are two main lines in our future work. Firstly, continue applying this methodology in other context or area for designing a motivating user interface. Lastly to validate the proposed methodology during the user interface development and test the final interface with the actual user to measure their motivation level.

Acknowledgement. We would like to thank the Universiti Teknologi MARA (UiTM) for sponsoring this paper through the iRAGS grant (600-RMI/IRAGS 5/3 (4/2015)). Their support is greatly appreciated.

References

1. Sharratt, M., Usoro, A.: Understanding knowledge-sharing in online communities of practice. Electron. J. Knowl. Manag. **1**, 187–196 (2003)
2. Moore, J.L., Dickson-Deane, C., Galyen, K.: e-Learning, online learning, and distance learning environments: are they the same? Internet High. Educ. **14**, 129–135 (2011)
3. Kearsley, G.: Online Education: Learning and Teaching in Cyberspace. Wadsworth, Belmont (2000)
4. Ardichvili, A.: Learning and knowledge sharing in virtual communities of practice: motivators, barriers, and enablers. Adv. Dev. Hum. Resour. **10**, 541–554 (2008)
5. Whittaker, S., Terveen, L., Hill, W., Cherny, L.: The dynamics of mass interaction. In: Lueg, C., Fisher, D. (eds.) From Usenet to CoWebs CSCW, pp. 79–91. Springer, London (2003). doi:10.1007/978-1-4471-0057-7_4
6. Stodel, E.J., Thompson, T.L., MacDonald, C.J.: Learners' perspectives on what is missing from online learning: Interpretations through the community of inquiry framework. Int. Rev. Res. Open Distance Learn. **7** (2006)
7. Haggerty, N., Schneberger, S., Carr, P.: Exploring media influences on individual learning: implications for organizational learning (2001)
8. Collison, G., Elbaum, B., Haavind, S., Tinker, R.: Facilitating Online Learning: Effective Strategies for Moderators. ERIC (2000)
9. Jaafar, A., Ramakrisnan, P.: Understanding of the students' behavioral intention to use online discussion site (ods) using rasch analysis. In: Stephanidis, C. (ed.) HCI International 2015-Posters' Extended Abstracts, HCI 2015. CCIS, vol. 529, pp. 247–252. Springer, Cham (2015). doi:10.1007/978-3-319-21383-5_42

10. Khoo, E.G.L.: Developing an online learning community: a strategy for improving lecturer and student learning experiences. In: 26th Annual Ascilite International Conference, pp. 528–532. The University of Waikato (2010)
11. Ramakrisnan, P., Jaafar, A.: Usable, aesthetic, sociable and motivating interface for students' online knowledge sharing. In: Zaphiris, P., Ioannou, A. (eds.) LCT 2016. LNCS, vol. 9753, pp. 550–561. Springer, Cham (2016). doi:10.1007/978-3-319-39483-1_50
12. Birk, M.V., Atkins, C., Bowey, J.T., Mandryk, R.L.: Fostering intrinsic motivation through avatar identification in digital games (2016)
13. Aparicio, A.F., Vela, F.L.G., Sánchez, J.L.G., Montes, J.L.I.: Analysis and application of gamification. In: Proceedings of the 13th International Conference on Interacción Persona-Ordenador, p. 17. ACM (2012)
14. Huang, W.H.-Y., Soman, D.: Gamification of Education. Research Report Series: Behavioural Economics in Action (2013)
15. Hamari, J., Koivisto, J., Sarsa, H.: Does gamification work?–a literature review of empirical studies on gamification. In: 2014 47th Hawaii International Conference on System Sciences (HICSS), pp. 3025–3034. IEEE (2014)
16. Oldfather, P., Dahl, K.: Toward a social constructivist reconceptualization of intrinsic motivation for literacy learning. J. Lit. Res. **26**, 139–158 (1994)
17. Natvig, L., Line, S.: Age of computers: game-based teaching of computer fundamentals. ACM SIGCSE Bull. **36**, 107 (2004)
18. Barata, G., Gama, S., Jorge, J.A.P., Gonçalves, D.J.V: Relating gaming habits with student performance in a gamified learning experience. In: Proceedings of the First ACM SIGCHI Annual Symposium on Computer-Human Interaction in Play, pp. 17–25. ACM (2014)
19. Bista, S.K., Nepal, S., Colineau, N., Paris, C.: Using gamification in an online community. In: CollaborateCom, pp. 611–618 (2012)

Review on Data Driven Preliminary Study Pertaining to Assistive Digital Learning Technologies to Support Dyscalculia Learners

Kohilah Miundy[✉], Halimah Badioze Zaman, and Aliimran Nordin

Institute of Visual Informatics, Universiti Kebangsaan Malaysia,
43600 Bangi, Selangor, Malaysia
kohilah@yahoo.com, {hali,aliimran}@ivi.ukm.my

Abstract. Dyscalculia is a specific learning disability amongst learners in underachievement of learning Mathematics, which begins in childhood and is persistent through adulthood. The population of dyscalculia is estimated to range between 3% and 6% of the world population, including Malaysia. In this preliminary study, we highlight a data driven approach, through literature content analysis and interviews conducted upon teachers, to analyse the different terms used on dyscalculia, and the effectiveness of computer-based technologies or assistive learning technologies, which are developed and used for learners with learning problems in mathematics for the past two decades. Current studies show an increasing interest in adopting Augmented Reality (AR) technology in education, and in optimisming to create unique educational setting for special education learners, specifically Dyscalculia learners, to enable them to undergo experiential learning by experiencing learning through the real world, mixed with virtual objects without losing their sense of reality.

Keywords: Dyscalculia · Acalculia · Assistive digital learning technologies · Augmented Reality

1 Introduction

The terms developmental dyscalculia (DD) or acquired dyscalculia and acalculia are used to describe the difficulties on the ability of learners to count or apply numbers and its concepts [1]. Neurologists discovered the existence of dyscalculia in adults after they were exposed to severe head injuries such as stroke, and later was unable to perform calculations [1, 2]. Sometimes, dyscalculia is reserved for less severe problems in specific developmental disorder, which is first required acquisition of mathematical knowledge through observation, while acalculia is used to refer to lack of ability to use mathematical symbols such as addition, subtraction, multiplication and even simple comparison on large and small numbers. Dyscalculia is a study in the field of neurology, particularly related to the brain [3], but later led to investigations within edu cational research known as mathematical achievement or under-achievement [4] of learners.

DD or acquired dyscalculia and acalculia can be affected by young learners in schools. However, studies by various neurologists also showed that dyscalculia

H. Badioze Zaman et al. (Eds.): IVIC 2017, LNCS 10645, pp. 233–246, 2017.
https://doi.org/10.1007/978-3-319-70010-6_22

generally, can also occur in adults, especially after they are exposed to severe head injuries such as stroke, which affects their ability after that to perform calculations [1, 2]. Sometimes, dyscalculia can affect learners with less severe problems, due to specific developmental disorder, which affects the acquisition of mathematical knowledge through observation, while acalculia can occur to those with the lack of ability to use mathematical symbols such as addition, subtraction, multiplication and even simple comparison on large and small numbers. Thus, dyscalculia is a study in the field of neurology, largely affecting the brain [3]. However, today we see research on dyscalculia has become a multidisciplinary study which also integrates educational research pertaining to mathematical achievement and mathematical under-achievement [4] based on their cognitive and creative ability. This has made it necessary to study the history and characteristics of learners that suffer from dyscalculia and how can learning be made more interesting and meaningful for these learners. There is also the need to study on the type of assistive technologies that can help them learn mathematical concepts and mathematical algorithms more effectively.

1.1 Brief History of Dyscalculia

In the twentieth Century, the first research centre on neurological behaviour was set up in Germany. Reseachers have accepted that the Wertheimer Gestalt theory was designed based on the hypotheses in relation to the functions of the brain. Through this theory, the brain is accepted to be a complex organ in processing information. Therefore, specific areas in the brain could be damaged, but the symptoms of injuries was unable to specify the affected area with change of behaviours [1].

It was observed in 1921, that the difficulty in calculation was based on agnosia (understanding on symbols) on basic arithmetic [1]. While, Gerstmann [5], discovered symptoms indication of a brain lesion in the left parietal lobe such as agraphia, acalculia, right-left disorientation and finger agnosia. In the year 1919, Salomon Henschen who was a Swedish neurologist discovered that a person who has normal intelligence, can possibly be undergoing impairment in mathematics abilities. In 1952, Henschen, was the first to use the term acalculia [8] in describing three types of mathematical disorder: visual, acoustical and ideational [7]. Through this discovery, he further investigated and confirmed the existence of acalculia, which later followed by dyscalculia.

1.2 Definition of Dyscalculia

Dyscalculia originates from Greek and Latin words, which mean "counting badly". The prefix "dys" from Greek means "badly" and root "calculia" from Latin "calculare" means "to count". There are several terminologies used to describe the mathematics learning disabilities. There are authors in the field that uses the term "acalculia" and dyscalculia as synonyms [1]. Table the terms used in related studies to describes Dyscalculia and Acalculia (Table 1).

The table shows that the authors had differentiated acalculia from dyscalculia based on different perceptions. Whilst, acalculia was described as inability of the entire system of the individual to calculate [12]; dyscalculia was described as the inability of a

Table 1. Terms used to describe dyscalculia and acalculia

Study	Terms	Description
Bryan et al. (1982) [9]	Dyscalculia	Difficulty in mastering mathematical concepts and/or computations
Dahmen et al. (1982) [10]	Acalculia	Complete or partial inability to deal with numbers due to a focal lesion
Singer, H.D (1933) [11]	Acalculia	Difficulty to perform basic arithmetic operation

part of the system, which led to the impairment of the entire system [13]. Doubtless that dyscalculia is affected by the same deficit in the brain, basically in the intra-parietal sulcus (IPS) [2]. Besides that, a number of dissimilar terms were used to describe mathematics under-achievement by these types of learners. Table 2 shows the terms used to describe mathematics under achievement.

Table 2. Terms used to describe mathematics under achievement

Study	Terms
Kosc (1974) [4]	Development dyscalculia
Geary (1993) [14]	Mathematics disabilities
Lewis et al. (1994) [15]	Specific arithmetic difficulties
Koontz (1996) [16]	Arithmetic learning disabilities
McLean (1999) [17]	Specific arithmetic learning difficulties
Jordan (1997) [18]	Mathematics difficulties
Temple (2002) [19]	Number fact disorder
Urgan et al. (2012) [20]	Mathematics disorder
Butterworth (2003) [21]	Dyscalculia
Butterworth (2003) [21]	Number blindness

Based on the table above, in a nutshell, acalculia and dyscalculia can be described based on various terms or definitions. However, in general can be described or defined as mathematical disability or difficulty faced by a person to perform daily life activities which involved the use of arithmetic.

Preliminary study conducted by the writers on teachers teaching learners with learning difficulties, which was conducted through interviews, found that majority of the teachers (more than 80%) were unaware of the different types of terms used for mathematics under-achievement learners. All of them were also unaware of the difference between acalculia and dyscalculia. This finding is crucial for teachers teaching learners with learning difficulties in order for them to build the appropriate teaching media aids and learning strategy to ensure that these type o learners can benefit from the learning process.

1.3   Classification of Dyscalculia

When a person have difficulty to perform operations involving mathematics, either they themselves or others will normally label them as poor or under-achiever in mathematics. Under-achievement in mathematics very often occur due to lack of motivation, unapproachable teaching method, unsettling classroom environment and inappropriate instruction [2, 22]. However, if these factors are not the causes of difficulty in performing operations involving mathematics, then the person is experiencing a learning disability in mathematics or what is termed as dyscalculia.

Based on the study by Kosc, he classified six (6) formal levels of dyscalculia distinguished by the different terms [4], eventually Rosselli and Ardilla, investigated and validated these terms [23]. It was discovered that, a person can actually have one, a few or all of the following types of dyscalculia [4, 24] as indicated in the Table 3.

Table 3. Classification of sub types of dyscalculia

Name/Study	Definition
Verbal dyscalculia [4]; Aphasia acalculia [23]	A person finds it difficult to name number, symbols or even qualities
Lexical dyscalculia [4]; Alexic acalculia [23]	A person has difficulties in reading mathematical symbols
Graphical dyscalculia [4]; Agraphic acalculia [23]	A person has difficulties in writing mathematical symbols
Operational dysclculia [4]; Frontal acalculia [23]	A person faces difficulties when carrying out mathematical operations and calculations
Ideognostic dyscalculia [4]; Anarithmetia [23]	A person finds it complicated to make mental calculations and operations as well as understanding mathematical concepts
Practognostic dyscalculia [4]; Spatial acalculia [23]	A person has trouble to enumcrate, manipulate, compare and relate objects and figures by themselves

Adapted from [4, 23, 25, 26].

Preliminary study conducted in Malaysia prior to a full fledge study on teachers teaching learners with learning difficulties. The report in Table 4 indicates the preliminary study in interview with teachers, also found that majority (more than 85%) of the teachers were unaware of the levels and types of dyscalculia. This finding is also crucial for teachers teaching learners with learning difficulties, especially those undergoing dyscalculia. It is natural that a person with dyscalculia, would feel that the normal approach or strategy used in the learning process of learning mathematics are unapproachable and ineffective, because they may not fit the learners, as they may belong to different levels or types of dyscaculia. Furthermore, dyscalculia learners need early and appropriate remedial intervention [27]. An early remedial intervention may help to reduce the later impact that would remain in adulthood [28].

Table 4. Preliminary study: interview with teachers on possible assistive technologies for dyscalculia learners

Item no.	Comments	Percentage (%)
1	Teachers are unaware of the levels and types of dyscalculia and therefore require different type of assistive technologies	85
2	Teachers commented on frequent lack of availability of internet access and technical support. They felt that they were overloaded with work; they found themselves disorganised, as they were given too many materials and too many tasks to handle	80
3	Teachers lamented that they faced many barriers when using web based learning approaches such as: constant breakdowns of equipment; and weak access to the internet and web services	60
4	Teachers said that mobile devices such as smart phones and tablets have offered much easier and cheaper access to learning than before	60
5	Teachers stressed that when mobile technology using hand phones and tablets are used for learning, they should focus on long term and short term impact of these learning technologies	20
6	Teachers said that virtual learning environment technologies, were very expensive for most schools or homes. It is important for dyscalculia learners to have the facilities for them to use every day for their studies	70
7	Teachers said that showed that the use of AI based learning applications is a positive thing, because the children today are keeping abreast with new technologies. They can be seen bringing their tablets and smart phones everywhere for search of entertainment	20
8	Teachers said that gaming learning technologies, were ineffective in learning achievement amongst dyscalculia learners	40
9	Teachers said that dyscalculia learners, found gaming fun and enjoyable	60
10	Teachers are not aware of AR technology; assume it must be expensive, assume difficult interfacing with existing systems	85

Note* 30 Teachers were the samples interviewed during the Preliminary Study, prior to the full fledge study conducted.

2 Overview on Assistive Digital Learning Technologies for Dyscalculia

Initiatives on digital divide could be conducted to assist those who are struggling with dyscalculia by indemnifying the deficient skills and abilities with the use of assistive digital learning technologies using media such as audio and/or visual as support to promote independent learning [29, 30].

The USA have acknowledged the importance of integrating assistive digital technology into their education curriculum so that children with learning disabilities will be given equal opportunities. Both the No Child Left Behind (NCLB) and the Individuals with Disabilities Education (IDEA) Act are related to the education of disabled children and mandates that schools implement digital technology devices and services to assist children with disabilities. Meanwhile in Britain, the British Educational Communications and Technology Agency (BECTA), stated that assistive digital technologies is a medium used to remove barriers for a successful learning strategy, and practice towards a positive relationship with both teachers and peers [31]. It was reported that assistive digital technologies also been classified as a remediation tool to help overcome learning disabilities [32].

Assistive digital technologies such as Computer Assist Instruction (CAI), web, mobile, Virtual Reality, Artificial Intelligence and Gaming, have attractive approaches, which are able to remove barriers to increase opportunities in encouraging dyscalculia children with different aspects of learning difficulties including those with mathematics learning difficulties [33]. Regarding the emerging of computer based education such as Six Sifteo cubes [34], CAI, e-learning and Adaptive e-learning [35], Apple Application IPhone Voice memo and Graper [36], Calculator Application [36], MathemAntics [37] and Calculating Aid Tools: KitKanit [38] for Dyscalculia, shows significant preferences from the reviewed studies have a better learning performance and promotes learning motivation.

However, based on the preliminary study conducted through interviews with teachers in Malaysia, the contrary was observed as indicated in Table 4. More than 80% of the teachers complained that there occurred frequent lack of availability of access and technical support. Furthermore, they felt overloaded with work, and were disorganised due to the various amount of materials and tasks that were made available to them. As regards to the emerging of web-based education such, as Dots2Digit and Dots2Track [39], Number Race and Graphogame Math (Computer Games) [40], Calcularis [41] and Number Sense [42, 43] for Dyscalculia, shows significant in mathematical skills. Again, interviews with teachers during the preliminary study in Malaysia, shows a contrary result, where 60% of the teachers indicated that there are barriers faced by such technological based learning approaches as there are constant breakdowns of equipment and weak access to the internet and web services.

Many emerging mobile technology based leaning applications such as MathBoard [44, 45], Long Division [44], Multiplication Genius, Flashcards to Go and Math Magic Mad Math, Pop Math, Flash to Pass, Math Drills, Multiplication [46], Go Play Ball and Go Road Trip [47], Go Math [48] and Calculic Kids [49] for Dyscalculia learners, show better and interesting method to learn, because of the graphical content, interaction and sound embedded in the application that can help to stimulate their brain to learn mathematics more effectively and to help them grasp the concepts more effectively. Preliminary study with the teachers in Malaysia, shows that 80% of the teachers were of the opinion that mobile devices such as smartphones and tablets have offered much easier and cheaper access than before, and 20% of the teachers said that they should focus on both short term and long term impact of these learning technology applications.

This review conducted also found that emerging virtual learning environment technologies such as Hanoi Towers puzzle [50], Tom's Rescue [51], ICT-based dynamic assessment [52, 53] and My vWallet [54] for Dyscalculia learners, also show that it can combine the strength from both behavioural theory and theory of the mind as its underpinning assumption. Preliminary study administered on teachers in Malaysia through interviews conducted, found that 70% of the teachers were of the opinion that virtual learning environment technologies, remain prohibitively expensive for most schools or homes. What is crucial for dyscalculia learners is that facilities should be available to them, every day of their study life, as it involved not only of administrative but content related nature. Therefore, desktop based virtual learning environment technology, are more common place to support special education, including learners with mathematics learning problems such as dyscalculia.

Considerably less studies were conducted regarding the emerging of Artificial Intelligence (AI) based technology, such as Active Math [55], which adapts to the cognitive needs of the learners and allows learners to study based on their own learning environment and Intelligent Tutoring Systems (ITS) [56]; This approach was significant over handwriting, faster, and less prone to error, then typing in mathematics numeric details during the process of learning. The interview conducted with the teachers through a preliminary study conducted, showed that 20% of them claimed that the use of AI based learning applications was very positive due to the fact that children now days are keeping abreast with new technologies, bringing their tablets and smart phones everywhere for search of entertainment.

Effects of emerging gaming learning technologies, such as disMAT [57] for Dyscalculia learners, show that the use of these technologies helped improve learners' mathematics results. On the contrary, preliminary study conducted amongst teachers who were interviewed in Malaysia, showed that 40% of teachers were of the opinion that gaming learning technologies, were ineffective in learning achievement amongst dyscalculia learners. However, 60% of the teachers interviewed said that their experience with dyscalculia learners, found that gaming is fun and enjoyable, and could stimulate interest and excitement in these type of learners.

From the content analysis conducted based on previous studies and the preliminary study conducted on local teachers interviewed, it can be summarised that there are an extensive variety of assistive digital technologies learning solutions available from traditional desktop computers, to more revolutionary technologies that are able to support and assist dyscalculia learners. Multipurpose portable devices such as smartphones and tablet computers may offer opportunities through the use of a conventional device which is customisable through the addition of an extensive variety of available software or applications. Further revolutionary technologies that evolve along the lines of ubiquitous computing or technologies, which are embedded in an everyday environment or along the alternative dimension of Augmented Reality will be the next type of assistive learning technology that could support and assist dyscalculia learners.

3 Augmented Reality (AR) in Learning Environment

In 1990, Augmented Reality (AR) was invented by a former Boeing researcher known as Tom Caudell. The concept of AR was used in late 1960 and 1970 in a number of applications [58]. In 1990, a few large companies began to adapt the purpose of AR in visualisation and training. AR technology provides opportunities to create novel assistive digital learning technologies which able to blend physical real world objects with virtual information [59, 60] for learning purposes. AR allows the users to see the real world with virtual objects composited with the real world [61]. A level of AR can be attained through vision recognition software, smart phones with a camera or through game technologies. Thus, it has potential for more educational innovations to emerge in this domain in the near future. This will help learners to visualise objects for better understanding in their learning process.

3.1   Advantages in Augmented Reality

In an AR world, it does not completely eliminate the real world from users' experience. Hence, users have a more realistic sense of presence in the visualization experiment. In addition, AR provides a convenient interface for constructivism and discovery-based learning, spatial understanding and social interaction, while it allows users to learn through making mistakes without having to fear about real world consequences. AR supports seamless interaction between real and virtual environments and allows the use of tangible interface metaphor for object manipulation [59]. Simultaneously, AR provides instructors in a way, that they are able to strengthen their students' understanding of lessons taught in the classroom using augmented physical learning aids or media with virtual annotations and illustrations [62]. In addition, AR creates a learning experience linked to the formal classroom so that students are able to learn beyond the school limits [60]. Most studies reported that AR in educational setting leads to better learning performance and promotes learning motivation. This is because AR supply the authenticity graphical content and interaction that other learning aids or media cannot do. The use of AR as learning aids or media also allows for deeper students' engagement, improved perceived enjoyment and positive attitudes of AR [63]. For dyscalculia learners, the ideal learning environment must contain as many sensual stimuli as possible. Therefore, lessons prepared for these students must be based on audio, visual, user context-adaptive, and the selection of learning paths should be non-linear and flexible [64].

3.2   Challenges in Using Augmented Reality (AR)

Despite the emerging interest in AR, there are several challenges that needs to be addressed. There are still unattended limitations with AR technology that needs to be overcomed. AR system has to deal with vast amount of information in reality. Therefore, the hardware used should be high end hand held devices such as small, light and easily portable and fast enough to display graphics. However, not all high end hand held devices, have the supporting hardware configuration [65]. Also the battery life used by these complicated AR devices is another limitation for AR users.

Another technical challenge is that AR tracking, needs some system hardware such as GPS and digital compass, to fetch user location. This means that it has to provide accurate marker to be reliable enough to function on all handheld devices [65]. These hardware obstacles need to be resolved for practical AR use. AR systems usually obtain a lot of information and need the right software to filter the information, retain useful information, discard useless data and display it in a convenient way. The lack of cost effective support devices such as display monitors, Head Mounted Displays (HMD) and Tracking Devices are also another challenge. Initially, in research outcomes when it comes to applied applications of AR, one need to consider aspect on the smooth transition of research to practice [66]. Thus, smooth interfacing of AR technology with the already existing system is crucial.

Therefore, AR technology has positive potential to support learning and teaching process of dyscalculia learners, whilst at the same time, many issues should be taken into consideration when implementing AR in the educational setting, particularly that for learners with disabilities, such as dyscalculia. Additionally, direct observation or experiences in the field is needed to design a suitable learning environment to support the adequacy and appropriateness for these learners by considering the challenges that could occur.

3.3   Use of Augmented Reality (AR) in Learning Disabilities (LD)

AR has been exposed to various possibilities that could be used for a diversity of disabilities. There are more to be explored in AR that can help to enhance the lives of those with LD. This is because AR is able bring a new environment for learning. AR also has potential to improve not just learning, but the lives of those with severe LD such as autistic spectrum disorder (Autism), Attention Deficit Hyperactivity Disorder (ADHD) and specific learning difficulties (SLD) such as dyslexia, dyscalculia and dysgraphia as well as visual or auditory impairments. In addition, it could also improve learning opportunities for those with "milder" learning differences through engagement, 3-D immersion and interactivity, calming and prompting, as well as creation and choice.

An example of what is being done to support a variety of disabilities with AR is program such as the "Sixth Sense for Autism", invented by Tim Byrne from Western Washington University. The reason that motivated Tim Byrne for such invention was his brother who is an autistic disorder sufferer, a fact that propelled him to invent "Sixthsense for Autism". It was developed upon MIT's Pranav Mistry's SixthSense technology. The conceptual goal of this project was to provide its user with social cues for everyday situations [67].

Another example is OxSight, which is a smart glasses founded by Dr. Stephen Hicks, a neuroscientist specializing in physical control. OxSight is an aid to make lives easier for the visually impaired, to assist them recognize and navigate objects in their environment. OxSight rely on technologies like see-through displays, camera systems and computer vision techniques that have been developed using AR technology to understand the environment [68]. Interactive TextBook or reading books, based AR for Mild Learning Disability (MLD) are also effective for students with learning difficulties. Interactive TextBook provides assistance in the process of learning to be much easier for MLD learners. This application works in five modules based on video capture, video display, image processing, character recognition and AR [69, 74].

The process of educating students with LD is a great challenge. This is because the 'boundaries' that they create around them, causes attention span to be easily distracted. With the invention of AR assistive learning technologies, they are able to simulate their interest and draw their attention that is needed to ensure an effective learning. With the assistance of learning aids such as AR, teachers are able to combine virtual environment with the real environment to make learning more interesting, engaging and interactive for learners with LD. AR assistive learning technology has also the potential to integrate learning and teaching materials especially for subjects that require students to visualize. Relatively there is limited studies conducted in the field of AR assistive learning technology for LD learners.

3.3.1   Experience of Augmented Reality (AR) in Dyslexic Learners

Dyslexic is known as a common type of learning difficulty that primarily affects the skills involved in reading or spelling of words, letters and other symbols but that do not affect general intelligence [70] of the individual. A pilot study was conducted on dyslexic students to benefit the experience of using AR in transforming a straight learning procedure, into one that is stimulating and entertaining. The first phase of the study, was conducted by giving the students words to memorise in 90 s, the control group underwent the process without the use of AR, whilst the experimental group underwent the process with AR. The second phase, tested them on writing out the words and letters. The results of the study shows that through the use of AR, dyslexic learners were able to learn more easily and effectively [71].

A private company called KanHan Technologies Limited (KanHan), had developed the first AR Learning Chinese characters application for kids with dyslexia in Hong Kong. This application using the AR assistive learning technology, consists of five (5) stories and each story has four (4) stages with voice-over for listening in mission to match accurately the corresponding strokes of the Chinese characters in order to move to the next level with the assistance of cards which provide access to 3D content via AR. This application is to stimulate the interest of children, to awaken their interest and motivate them to learn Chinese Language [72]. In Malaysia, an AR assistive learning application called AR-Baca was designed and developed at the Universiti Kebangsaan Malaysia (UKM) to help down syndrome children learn to read Malay [74]. Like the former, this AR book too was to stimulate interest of these children and to motivate them to learn to read in the Malay language.

Both studies in Hong Kong (on dyslexia) and Malaysia (on down syndrome) show that Augmenting existing school books or creating new books for students with LD can help them in their learning process. For both studies too, the reading and exercises are designed to include both auditory and visual with certain objects augmented for them to manipulate these objects and thus involved 'hands-on'. Both the AR assistive learning applications in the mentioned studies too, can also be accessed through smart phones. Both studies too showed that there was positive attitudes between the teachers and the dyslexic and down syndrome children, respectively [73, 74].

As indicated in item 10, in Table 4, most teachers interviewed during the preliminary study, were not aware of the existence of AR technology as assistive learning technology that can be used to help learning process of children with LD; they were of the assumption that the technology is expensive and that there would be difficulties in trying to integrate the application with existing systems. Both the studies mentioned earlier, are just the beginning steps where difficulties in technology and in learning faced by teachers and dyscalculia learners can slowly be treated with better attention.

4 Conclusion and Future Work

From the content analysis of the literature review conducted, previous studies as well as the preliminary study conducted, dyscalculia could be an inborn disability in an individual. However, it does not mean that those who are born with this disability has to remain as disability learners all their lives. Studies on dyscalculia has since been much less studied, recognised and treated, compared to its more popular cousin, dyslexia [2]. Research on computer-based, Web Based, Mobile, Virtual Environment, Artificial Intelligence (AI) and Gaming examples of assistive learning tools that are successfully used to help children with LD have not been fully studied and explored for dyscalculia learners. Most of the previous studies conducted show that assistive digital learning technologies have potential to assist in making learning more fun, enjoyable and entertaining. The studies also showed that these type of learning aids too, are effective in engaging and motivating LD learners to focus and learn better. Very limited studies has been done on the use of AR to support dyscalculia learners learn. Therefore, it is clear from the data driven preliminary study conducted (through content analysis of literature review, previous studies and interviews conducted), that the direction for future research that should be explored, is on new application and creation of new assistive digital learning technologies, based on AR technologies and devices, which has shown to possess potential possibilities, to assist and support children with LD in Mathematics or dyscalculia.

References

1. Ruth, M.: Measures of Research Predictors for Dyscalculia (Mathematics, Psychology, Tests) (1986)
2. Wilson, A.J., Dehaene, S.: Number sense and developmental dyscalculia. Hum. Behav. Learn. Dev. Brain Atyp. Dev. **2**, 212–238 (2007)
3. Cohn, R.: Dyscalculia. Arch. Neurol. **4**, 301–307 (1961)
4. Kosc, L.: Developmentol dyscalculia. J. Learn. Disabil. **7**, 164–177 (1974)
5. Gerstmann, J.: Some notes on the gerstmann syndrome. Neurology **7**, 866 (1957)
6. Kertesz, A.: Aphasia and Associated Disorders. Taxonomy, Localization and Recovery. Grune & Stratton, New York (1979)
7. Springer, S., Deutsh, G.: Left Brain, Right Brain. W.H. Freeman, San Franciso (1981)
8. Henschen, S.E.: Clinical and anatomical contributions on brain pathology. Arch. Neurol. Psychiatry **13**, 226–249 (1925)
9. Bryan, T., Bryan, J.H.: Understanding Learning Disabilities (1982)
10. Dahmen, W., Hartje, W., Busing, A., Sturm, W.: Disorder of calculation in aphasic patients spatial and verbal components. Neuropsychologia **20**, 145–153 (1982)
11. Singer, H.D., Low, A.A.: Acalculia (henschen) a clinical study. Arch. Neurol. Psychiatry **29**, 467–498 (1933)
12. Nicolosi, L., Harryman, E., Kresheck, J.: Terminology of Communication Disorders: Speech-Language-Hearing, Williams & Wilkins, Baltimore (1978)
13. Košč, L.: Neuropsychological implications of diagnosis and treatment of mathematical learning disabilities. Top. Learn. Learn. Disabil. **1**, 19–30 (1981)

14. Geary, D.C.: Mathematical disabilities: cognitive, neuropsychological, and genetic components. Psychol. Bull. **114**, 345–362 (1993)
15. Lewis, C., Hitch, G., Walker, P.: The prevalence of specific arithmetic difficulties and specific reading difficulties in 9- to 10-year-old boys and girls. J. Child Psychol. Psychiatry **35**, 283–292 (1994)
16. Koontz, K.L., Berch, D.B.: Identifying simple numerical stimuli: processing inefficiencies exhibited by arithmetic learning disabled children. Math. Cogn. **2**, 1–24 (1996)
17. McLean, J.F., Hitch, G.J.: Working memory impairments in children with specific arithmetic learning difficulties. J. Exp. Child Psychol. **74**, 240–260 (1999)
18. Jordan, N.C., Montani, T.O.: Cognitive arithmetic and problem solving: a comparison of children with specific and general mathematics difficulties. J. Learn. Disabil. **30**, 624–634 (1997)
19. Temple, C.M., Sherwood, S.: Representation and retrieval of arithmetical facts: developmental difficulties. Q. J. Exp. Psychol. **55A**, 733–752 (2002)
20. Eroglu, S., Toprak, S., Urgan, O.M., Ozge, E., Onur, M., Arzu Denizbasi, M., Haldun Akoglu, M., Cigdem Ozpolat, M., Ebru Akoglu, M.: DSM-IV Diagnostic and Statistical Manual of Mental Disorder (2012)
21. Butterworth, B.: Dyscalculia Screener. Nelson Publishing Company Ltd., Nashville (2003)
22. Butterworth, B.: Developmental dyscalculia. Handb. Math. Cogn. 455–468 (2013)
23. Ardila, A., Rosselli, M.: Acalculia and dyscalculia. Neuropsychol. Rev. **12**, 179–231 (2002)
24. Kuhl, D.E.: Voices count: employing a critical narrative research bricolage for insights into dyscalculia, pp. 1–135 (2014)
25. Newman, R.M.: The Dyscalculia Syndrome (1998)
26. Munro, J.: Dyscalculia: a unifying concept in understanding mathematics learning disabilities. Aust. J. Learn. Disabil. **8**, 25–32 (2003)
27. Monuteaux, M.C., Faraone, S.V., Herzig, K., Navsaria, N., Biederman, J.: ADHD and dyscalculia: evidence for independent familial transmission. J. Learn. Disabil. **38**, 86–93 (2005)
28. Goswami, U.: Neuroscience and education: from research to practice? Nat. Rev. Neurosci. **7**, 406–411 (2006)
29. Butterworth, B., Varma, S., Laurillard, D.: Dyscalculia: from brain to education. Science **332**, 1049–1053 (2011). doi:10.1126/science.1201536
30. Nagavali, T., Juliet, P.F.P.: Technology for Dyscalculia Children, pp. 1–10 (2015)
31. Becta, (British Educational Communications and Technology Agency): what the research says about ICT supporting special educational needs (SEN) and inclusion (2003)
32. Smith, B.: We have the technology, we can assist them! Using technology to assist students with learning disabilities and difficulties (2016)
33. Rubinsten, O., Henik, A.: Developmental dyscalculia: heterogeneity might not mean different mechanisms. Trends Cogn. Sci. **13**, 92–99 (2009)
34. Lønstrup, J., Denager, T., Christensen, M.B.: Enhancement of 7th-10th Graders' understanding of equations with tangible representations. In: SIDeR 2012, p. 60 (2012)
35. Brunda, A., Bhavithra, J.: Adaptive computer assisted instruction (CAI) for students with dyscalculia (learning disability in mathematics). In: A2CWiC 2010 (2010)
36. O'Connell, T., Freed, G., Rothberg, M., Using apple technology to support learning for students with sensory and learning disabilities. In: The Carl Ruth Shapiro Family National Center for Accessible Media, WGBH Educational Foundation, pp. 1–25 (2010)
37. English, L.D., Mulligan, J.T.: Reconceptualizing Early Mathematics Learning. Advances in Mathematics Education. Springer, Dordrecht (2013). doi:10.1007/978-94-007-6440-8

38. Poobrasert, O., Gestubtim, W.: Development of assistive technology for students with dyscalculia. In: 2013 2nd International Conference on E-Learning and E-Technologies in Education (ICEEE), pp. 60–63 (2013)
39. Butterworth, B., Laurillard, D.: Low numeracy and dyscalculia: identification and intervention. ZDM - Int. J. Math. Educ. **42**, 527–539 (2010)
40. Räsänen, P., Salminen, J., Wilson, A.J., Aunio, P., Dehaene, S.: Computer-assisted intervention for children with low numeracy skills. Cogn. Dev. **24**, 450–472 (2009)
41. Käser, T., Baschera, G.M., Kohn, J., Kucian, K., Richtmann, V., Grond, U., Gross, M., von Aster, M.: Design and evaluation of the computer-based training program calcularis for enhancing numerical cognition. Front. Psychol. **4** (2013)
42. Wilson, A.J., Revkin, S.K., Cohen, D., Cohen, L., Dehaene, S.: Principles underlying the design of "the number race", an adaptative computer game for remediation of dyscalculia. Behav. Brain Funct. **2**, 20 (2006)
43. Pólya, G.: Early Grade Development and Numeracy: The Academic State of Knowledge and How It Can Be Applied In Project Implementation In Socio-Economically Less developed countries, Giz.De. p. 7 (2012)
44. Nagavalli, T., Juliet, P.F.P.: Technology For Dyscalculia Children, SALEM,16, pp. 1–10 (2015)
45. Moomaw, S.: Assessing the difficulty level of math board games for young children. J. Res. Child. Educ. **29**, 492–509 (2015)
46. Kiger, D., Herro, D., Prunty, D.: Examining the influence of a mobile learning intervention on third grade math achievement. J. Res. Technol. Educ. **45**, 61–82 (2012)
47. Alexander, A., Blair, K.P., Goldman, S., Jimenez, O., Nakaue, M., Pea, R., Russell, A.: Go Math! how research anchors new mobile learning environments. In: 6th IEEE International Conference on Wireless, Mobile and Ubiquitous Technologies in Education, WMUTE 2010: Mobile Social Media for Learning and Education in Formal Informal Settings, pp. 57–64 (2010)
48. O'Malley, P.O., Jenkins, S., Wesley, B., Donehower, C., Rabuck, D., Lewis, M.E.B.: Effectiveness of using iPads to build math fluency. In: Paper presented at the Council Exceptiona Children Annuual Meeting, San Antonio, Texas, pp. 1–19 (2013)
49. Ariffin, M.M., Azureen, F., Halim, A., Abd, N.: Mobile application for dyscalculia children. In: Proceedings of 6th International Conference Computing and Informatics, ICOCI 2017 pp. 467–472 (2017)
50. Antonia, P.P., Vlamos, P.M.: Algorithmic problem solving using interactive virtual environment: a case study. In: Iliadis, L., Papadopoulos, H., Jayne, C. (eds.) EANN 2013. CCIS, vol. 383, pp. 433–445. Springer, Heidelberg (2013). doi:10.1007/978-3-642-41013-0_45
51. De Castro, M.V., Bissaco, M.A.S., Panccioni, B.M., Rodrigues, S.C.M., Domingues, A.M.: Effect of a virtual environment on the development of mathematical skills in children with dyscalculia. PLoS One **9**, 1–16 (2014). doi:10.1371/journal.pone.0103354
52. Kopp, K.H., Stowitschek, J.J.: Effects of teachers' planning on mathematics computation skills. Teach. Educ. Sepc. Educ. **5**, 43–50 (1980)
53. Peltenburg, M., Van Den Heuvel-Panhuizen, M., Doig, B.: Mathematical power of special-needs pupils: an ICT-based dynamic assessment format to reveal weak pupils' learning potential. Br. J. Educ. Technol. **40**, 273–284 (2009)
54. Tahan, O., Baraké, F., Seliman, N., Merhi, Z.: My vWallet - a smartphone application for assisting people with math difficulties at point of sale. In: 2015 5th International Conference on Information and Communication Technology Accessibility ICTA 2015, pp. 1–5 (2016)

55. Melis, E., Andrès, E., Büdenbender, J., Frischauf, A., Goguadze, G., Libbrecht, P., Pollet, M., Ullrich, C.: ActiveMath: a generic and adaptive web-based learning environment. Int. J. Artif. Intell. Educ. **12**, 385–407 (2001)
56. Anthony, L., Yang, J., Koedinger, K.R.: Toward next-generation, intelligent tutors: adding natural handwriting input. IEEE Multimed. **15**, 64–68 (2008)
57. Ferraz, F., Costa, A., Alves, V., Vicente, H., Neves, J., Neves, J.: Gaming in dyscalculia: a review on *disMAT*. In: Rocha, Á., Correia, A.M., Adeli, H., Reis, L.P., Costanzo, S. (eds.) WorldCIST 2017. AISC, vol. 570, pp. 232–241. Springer, Cham (2017). doi:10.1007/978-3-319-56538-5_25
58. Caudell, T.P., Mizell, D.W.: Augmented reality: an Application of heads-up display technology to manual manufacturing processes. In: Proceedings of Twenty-Fifth Hawaii International Conference System Sciences, vol. 2, pp. 659–669 (1992)
59. Akçayır, M., Akçayır, G.: Advantages and challenges associated with augmented reality for education: a systematic review of the literature. Educ. Res. Rev. **20**, 1–11 (2017)
60. Azuma, R.: A survey of augmented reality. Presence Teleop. Virt. Environ. **6**, 355–385 (1997)
61. Mekni, M., Lemieux, A.: Augmented Reality : applications, challenges and future trends. In: Applied Computational Science, pp. 205–214 (2014)
62. Sabri, F.N.M., Khidzir, N.Z., Ismail, A.R., Daud, K.A.M.: An exploratory study on mobile augmented reality (AR) application for heritage content. J. Adv. Manag. Sci. **4**, 489–493 (2016)
63. Chen, P., Liu, X., Cheng, W., Huang, R., Popescu, E., Mohamed, K., Khribi, K., Huang, R., Jemni, M., Demetrios, N.C.: A review of using augmented reality in education from 2011 to 2017. Innov. Smart Learn. 13–14 (2017)
64. Käser, T., Busetto, A.G., Baschera, G.-M., Kohn, J., Kucian, K., von Aster, M., Gross, M.: Modelling and optimizing the process of learning mathematics. In: Cerri, Stefano A., Clancey, William J., Papadourakis, G., Panourgia, K. (eds.) ITS 2012. LNCS, vol. 7315, pp. 389–398. Springer, Heidelberg (2012). doi:10.1007/978-3-642-30950-2_50
65. Dunleavy, M., Dede, C., Mitchell, R.: Affordances and limitations of immersive participatory augmented reality simulations for teaching and learning. J. Sci. Educ. Technol. **18**, 7–22 (2009)
66. Vyas, D.A., Bhatt, D.: Augmented reality (AR) applications: a survey on current trends, challenges, & future scope. Int. J. Adv. Res. Comput. Sci. **8**, 5 (2017)
67. Rouli: Augmented Reality for Autism. http://artimes.rouli.net/2010/05/augmented-reality-for-autism.html
68. Williams, F.: OxSight uses augmented reality to aid the visually impaired. https://techcrunch.com/2017/02/16/oxsight-uses-augmented-reality-to-aide-the-visually-impaired/
69. Vinumol, K.P., Chowdhury, A., Kambam, R., Muralidharan, V.: Augmented reality based interactive text book: an assistive technology for students with learning disability. In: 2013 XV Symposium on Virtual Augmented Reality (SVR), pp. 232–235 (2013)
70. Bolhasan, R.A.: A study of dyslexia among primary school students in Sarawak, Malaysia intoduction. Sch. Dr. Stud. (Eur. Union.) J. **1**, 250–268 (2009)
71. Ho, S.S., Lee, K.W., Chui, J.H.-l.: Enhancing learning experience of students with specific learning difficulties with augmented reality: a pilot study. In: Paper Presented at the the Asian Conference on Education (2011)
72. KanHan Technologies Limited: Apps to Support Kids with Dyslexia
73. Persefoni, K., Tsinakos, A.: Augmented reality and dyslexia : a new approach in teaching students. pp. 1–13 (2016)
74. Abas, H., Zaman, H.B.: Digital storytelling design with augmented reality technology for remedial students in learning Bahasa Melayu. In: Global Learn, pp. 3558–3563 (2010)

Engineering and Data Driven Innovation

Image Enhancement Based on Fractional Poisson for Segmentation of Skin Lesions Using the Watershed Transform

Alaa Ahmed Abbas Al-abayechi[1], Hamid A. Jalab[2(✉)],
Rabha W. Ibrahim[3], and Ali M. Hasan[4]

[1] Al-Rusafa of Management Institute, Middle Technical University,
Baghdad, Iraq
alaa.abayechi@gmail.com
[2] Faculty of Computer Science and Information Technology,
University of Malaya, 50603 Kuala Lumpur, Malaysia
hamidjalab@um.edu.my
[3] Modern College of Business and Science, Muscat, Oman
rabha.alwaelli@mcbs.edu.om
[4] School of Computing, Science and Engineering,
University of Salford, Manchester M5 4WT, UK
a.hasan4@edu.salford.ac.uk

Abstract. Image segmentation is considered as a necessary step towards accurate medical analysis by extracting the crucial medical information in identifying abnormalities. This study proposes a new technique for segmentation a malignant melanoma in images. A new filter is proposed for smoothing input images and more accurate segmentation based on fractional Poisson. In the pre-processing step, eight masks of size n × n are created to eliminate noise and obtain a smooth image. The watershed algorithm is used for segmentation with morphological operation to better segment the skin lesion area. The proposed method was capable of improving the accuracy of the segmentation up to 96.47%.

Keywords: Fractional calculus · Fractional Poisson · Watershed algorithm · Skin lesion · Segmentation

1 Introduction

Segmentation is a flexible process in many medical image processing applications. Medical imaging techniques produce images that contain a lot of information. For computer aided medical diagnosis, image segmentation facilitates the extraction of crucial medical information on anatomical structures in identifying abnormalities. Several characteristic features of a skin lesions can be found in dermoscopic images that enables physicians to determine whether the lesion is malignant or benign [1]. Feature extraction of pigmented lesions is used to distinguish between malignant and benign melanoma after the skin lesion region is segmented from healthy skin.

Many approaches for image segmentation are available and can be generally categorized based on threshold, edge and region. Threshold techniques are simple for

© Springer International Publishing AG 2017
H. Badioze Zaman et al. (Eds.): IVIC 2017, LNCS 10645, pp. 249–259, 2017.
https://doi.org/10.1007/978-3-319-70010-6_23

clustering image into two classes, but the major problem is the influencing of changing in illumination and noise across the image [2]. However, the watershed segmentation algorithm uses the concept of edge in the image without using the edge detection methods. The watershed segmentation algorithm is used to define the "watershed lines" in the image in order to divide images into separate image regions.

In this study, a new technique is proposed for image enhancement using fractional Poisson to improve the performance of the watershed algorithm using fractional Poisson. The clinical image dataset used in this study consists of 70 dermoscopic images from different sources made up of 66 melanoma and 4 nevi.

The remainder of this study is organized as follows: in Sect. 2, the relevant literature is introduced; Sect. 3 illustrates the steps of the proposed method; in Sect. 4, experimental results and discussions are presented. Finally, conclusions and possible future work are described in Sect. 5.

2 Related Works

Threshold techniques assign individual pixels to one of two groups based on a similar intensity value in order to obtain two classes of pixels [3]. The watershed algorithm is another image segmentation algorithm which splits the input image into different regions of small areas based on the maximum gradient. The performance of the watershed algorithm is hampered by many factors when it is implemented directly in low-contrast images.

Numerous studies have been undertaken to solve the problem of watershed over-segmentation [4]. The combination of the watershed transform with a hierarchical merging process was used to reduce noise and to preserve edges through application of magnetic resonance (MR) images [5]. In [6] a watershed algorithm was proposed based on connected components to improve watershed segmentation. Moreover, in our previous work [7], a technique was proposed for skin lesions segmentation through a combination of the watershed transform and wavelet filters. The wavelet transform with a level 2 bi-orthogonal was found to obtain the highest accuracy in the segmentation of skin lesions. In [8], watershed was implemented to segment the brain in MRI images. It was a more effective approach than others for clustering pixels with the same intensity values within the same group.

Watershed transformation is suffering from the problems of over-segmentation and sensitivity to noise. However, employing prior shape knowledge has achieved robust segmentation results for medical images [9]. Also, [10] modified the watershed algorithm to segment skin lesions and implemented the B-spline second stage to smooth the border of the segmented region.

Recently, fractional calculus with differential and integral operators are utilized in signal and image processing. The fractional calculation is used to enhance the quality of images in order to preserve edges and for image restoration [11, 12]. Furthermore, fractional calculus is actively applied in design problems of variables and in different types of applications in engineering and science [13, 14].

3   Proposed Method

The proposed algorithm which aims to improve the performance of segmentation accuracy of skin lesions is illustrated in Fig. 1.

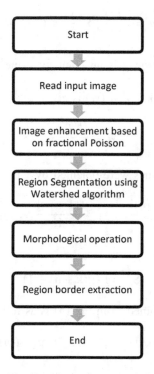

Fig. 1. The flowchart of proposed algorithm

3.1   Image Enhancement

In the image processing stage, image enhancement essentially focuses on making the image more suitable for specific applications. In this stage, the quality of the dermoscopic image is enhanced and rescaled into a new intensity range in order to reduce the similarities between the lesion region and the healthy skin, which is a persistent problem that defeats most segmentation algorithms.

The new image enhancement algorithm introduced in this work is based on fractional Poisson. A Poisson process is a stochastic process that uses random variables to evaluate the number of events. The original homogeneous formula was proposed by [15]:

$$p_\mu(n,t) = \frac{(vt^\mu)^n}{n!} \sum_{k=0}^{n} \frac{(k+n)!}{k!}$$
$$\times \frac{(-vt^\mu)^k}{\Gamma(\mu(k+n)+1)} \tag{1}$$

where, $p_\mu(n,f)$ is the probability of n events. The parameter μ offers new features in comparison with the standard Poisson distribution and it is $0 < \mu < 1$ [15], and Γ is a gamma function. The proposed method is a modification of Eq. (1) and computed as follows:

$$fp = \frac{(vf^\mu)^n}{n!} \sum_{k=0}^{n} \frac{y_k}{S_k} \times (-vf^\mu)^k \tag{2}$$

where, fp is a fractional Poisson, f is an intensity value for one pixel in the image, $n = (1,2,3,\ldots)$, $k = (0,1,\ldots,n)$.

The two dimensional mask $n \times n$ (y_k) is given by:

$$y_k = \frac{(k+n)!}{k!} \tag{3}$$

The terms of non-zero values were obtained by y is as follows:

$$y_0 = \frac{(0+n)!}{0!}, \quad y_1 = \frac{(1+n)!}{1!}, \ldots, y_n = \frac{2n!}{n!} \tag{4}$$

and,

$$S_k = \Gamma(\mu(k+n)+1) \tag{5}$$

The coefficients for S obtained from Eq. (5) is as follows:

$$S_0 = \Gamma(\mu(0+n)+1), \quad S_1 = \Gamma(\mu(1+n)+1), \ldots, \\ S_n = \Gamma(\mu(2n)+1) \tag{6}$$

Each mask is rotated in eight directions using different angles, $0°$, $45°$, $90°$, $135°$, $180°$, $225°$, $270°$ and $315°$, as shown in Fig. 2. Finally, the magnitude of each filter (G) can be obtained as follows:

$$G = \sum_{k=0}^{n} \frac{y_k}{S_k} \times (-vf^\mu)^k \tag{7}$$

The values of G for the various angles are calculated as follows:

$$G_{0°} = \sum_{k=0}^{n} \left(\frac{y_k}{S_k}\right)_{0°} \times (-vf^\mu)^k, \quad G_{45°} = \sum_{k=0}^{n} \left(\frac{y_k}{S_k}\right)_{45°} \times (-vf^\mu)^k, \\ G_{90°} = \sum_{k=0}^{n} \left(\frac{y_k}{S_k}\right)_{90°} \times (-vf^\mu)^k, \quad G_{315°} = \sum_{k=0}^{n} \left(\frac{y_k}{S_k}\right)_{315°} \times (-vf^\mu)^k \tag{8}$$

Then, the fractional Poisson (fp) for one pixel is given by:

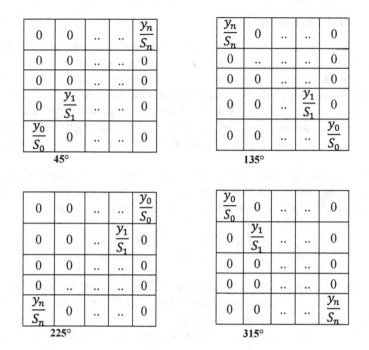

Fig. 2. Sample of fractional Poisson masks.

$$fp(i,j) = \frac{(vf^{\mu}(i,j))^{n}}{n!} \times G_{\theta} \tag{9}$$

Equation (7) is implemented on whole image. The final new intensity image $fp(i, j)$ based on fractional Poisson with two dimensions are computed from the following equation:

$$fp(i,j) = \frac{1}{\theta}\sum_{\theta=1}^{8} \frac{(vf^{\mu}(i,j))^{n}}{n!} \times G_{\theta} \tag{10}$$

In this study, the mask windows are applied in eight directions. For color images the same algorithm used for gray images can be applied but performed separately for each of the R, G and B color components.

Fractional Poisson was applied to reduce noise from the images. The proposed method to enhance grayscale images can be summarized as follows:

(i)   Create a mask window of size $(n \times n)$ and define the fractional powers μ and v.
(ii) Implement the fractional mask convolution operations in eight directions with the gray value of the gradient image.
(iii) Adding all product terms to obtain the weighting average of the eight directions as an approximate value of fractional Poisson for the image pixels.
(iv) Repeat step two for all pixels.

3.2   Watershed Transform

The watershed transform is considered as a morphological approaches used for image segmentation. However, the performance of the watershed algorithm is hampered by problems such as over/under-segmentation of badly contrasted images when it is implemented directly on gradient data for low-contrast images.

The topographical idea behind watershed for two-dimensional grayscale images is that the bright (high intensity) regions are peaks and the dark (low intensity) parts are valleys. If the valley is filled with water, it can meet the water in the neighbouring valleys.

In this study, the rain fall watershed technique was used because it is computationally faster than other available techniques [16]. The maximum value of global threshold was fixed experimentally to be 38 or 255 and given by [17]:

$$c(i,j) = \begin{cases} 38, fp(i,j) \leq \max(fp(i,j) * th) \\ 255, \textit{otherwise} \end{cases} \qquad (11)$$

where, *th* is the global threshold. These operations can remove noise in the form of dark and bright spots from the background. Then, the watershed transform was applied on the enhanced image. This method was very effective as it achieved a large reduction in the number of watershed regions and removed weak edges as shown in Fig. 3 in the last column.

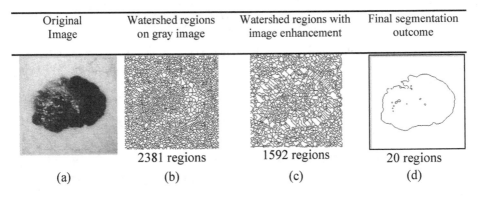

Original Image	Watershed regions on gray image	Watershed regions with image enhancement	Final segmentation outcome
(a)	2381 regions (b)	1592 regions (c)	20 regions (d)

Fig. 3. The number of watershed areas. (a) Original image in grayscale, (b) de-noised image using fractional Poisson, (c) the outcome of watershed transformation with 1693 segments, (d) the watershed segments are reduced to 906 using the proposed method.

3.3   Post-processing

The post-processing was to combine similar watershed areas with a region adjacent list (RAL) [17]. This function is applied to obtain two criteria: region homogeneity and border homogeneity. The regions with similar homogeneity take a value of 1 and those that are dissimilar have a value of 0, in order to obtain a black and white image. The morphological operations, dilation and filling, were implemented to merge the areas of the region around the skin lesion that have a weak border. Then, the biggest area, namely, the skin lesion, was selected. The area of the lesion is the merged area with the pixel value 1, while the black areas of pixel value 0 indicate the healthy skin [18].

4   Experimental Results

In this study, eight masks were created from Eq. (3) to eliminate noise such as hair, light reflection and air bubbles. Equation (8) was implemented, rescaling the grayscale image to a new intensity using the fractional Poisson process and obtaining a smooth image.

The fractional Poisson process was used to minimize the number of watershed regions as shown in Fig. 3. Different values of v (-2, -5, and -8) and μ (0.25, 0.3, 0.35 and 0.45) were implemented to select optimal values that led to obtain more accurate in segmentation. Figure 4 shows the results from different values of v and μ. The optimal value for v was found to be -5 and the optimal value for μ was 0.45. When μ and v were less than 0.35 and -5, respectively, the segmentation covered only the darker parts of the skin lesion. When μ was greater than 0.35, the segmentation process was able to detect only the area outside the skin lesion, i.e. healthy skin.

σ	8		-5		-2	
μ	0.45	0.35	0.45	0.35	0.45	0.35
Manual Border						

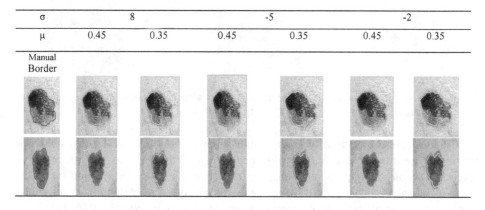

Fig. 4. Comparison of the automatic border and manually labeled border with different values for σ and μ. The first column in the left is the original image with manually drawn border. The best automatic border achieved with σ = −5 and μ = 0.35.

Next, morphological dilation with a structure disk radius of 5 pixels, and filling, were applied in order to combine all small regions around the lesion and fill all the gaps.

The proposed method introduces an image enhancement step that is capable of removing noise. The modified watershed algorithm was implemented to segment the skin lesion. From Fig. 4, it can be seen that the automatically generated border was close to the manually labelled border. The watershed algorithm was refined to combine the regions around the lesion area. Nonlinear and linear filtering with thresholding was combined with the thresholding method in [17] in order to reduce over-segmentation. This enabled greater reduction in the number of regions to less than 20 regions and removal of the weak edges. In addition, the thresholding method in [10] was applied, which determined the edge object value in order to decrease the false positives. When μ was greater than 0.45, the segmentation process was able to detect only the area outside the skin lesion, i.e. healthy skin.

In this study, we computed the threshold value to combine the darker areas that belong to the lesion region rather than the healthy skin. The threshold value is given by:

$$T = [\frac{1}{NM} \sum_{i=1}^{N} \sum_{j=1}^{M} (X(i,j,k)) * 0.25] - 3 \tag{12}$$

$$BW(i,j) = \begin{cases} 1 & if\ ((X(i,j,k)) * 0.25) > T \\ 0 & otherwise \end{cases} \tag{13}$$

where, X is the image with two dimensions M and N, k is the green color channel, T is the threshold value, and $BW(i, j)$ is the label for the black and white image. Figure 5 shows the result of proposed method after applying the threshold value.

Fig. 5. The automatic border before (white color) and after (blue color) image enhancement based on fractional (proposed method) (Color figure online)

Three metrics were used to evaluate the segmentation are: the sensitivity which represents the true positive fraction, the specificity which represents the true negative fraction, and the accuracy of the border extraction of the proposed method on a dermoscopic database consisting of 70 images with two types of melanoma: benign and malignant. These metrics were computed using the following equations [6, 14]:

$$Sensitivity = \frac{TP}{TP + FN} \times 100 \tag{14}$$

$$Specificity = \frac{TN}{TN + FP} \times 100 \tag{15}$$

$$Accuracy = \frac{TN + TP}{TP + TN + FN + FP} \times 100 \tag{16}$$

where:

TP: the overlapping pixels in the lesion, TN: the overlapping pixels outside the lesion, FP: the overlapping pixels between the automatically categorized lesion and those outside the manually categorized lesion, FN: the overlapping pixels between the manually categorized lesion and those outside the automatically categorized lesion.

Table 1 presents the results of the comparison of the proposed method with three other methods from the literature. It can be seen that some techniques have high values of specificity but the results did not include the lighter regions of the lesion. Conversely, some of these techniques have high sensitivity but some regions of the lesion were detected incorrectly. Both the Sarker et al. [17] and Wang et al. [10] methods were used for lesion segmentation but they were unable to detect the lighter region within the skin lesion; the methods were only able to detect the darker regions.

Table 1. The average results of the proposed method with other researchers' methods.

Methods	Wang et al. [10]	Schaefer et al. [19]	Sarker et al. [17]	Combined watershed and wavelet (bior3.3) [7]	Proposed method
Accuracy	95.14	94.77	91.12	94.61	**96.47**
Sensitivity	76.87	89.44	82.84	88.6	95.72
Specificity	98.4	97.79	97.62	98.21	96.41

The proposed method was also compared with our previous method that combined watershed with the bi-orthogonal 3.3 level 2 (bior 3.3) wavelet transform. The results are shown in Fig. 6. The disadvantage of the previous method (second last column) was that it ignored the areas at the boundary of the lesion. However, watershed is sensitive to noise. The new technique with fractional Poisson was able to remove the noise from the image, thus improving the average accuracy of the watershed segmentation. As can be seen from Fig. 6, our proposed method achieved the highest accuracy in comparison to the other methods in the literature.

In Table 2, the proposed method is compared with different state-of-the-art approaches for segmentation of skin lesions, based on the results published in the

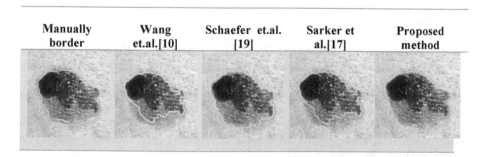

Fig. 6. Comparison of automatic border with the manually labeled border. The automatic border by the proposed method is closer to the manual border, with an average accuracy of 96.47%.

Table 2. Comparison of the proposed method with different segmentation techniques for skin lesion

Method	Sensitivity	Specificity	XOR%
SLIC [20]	93.53	91.30	–
Mean shift [21]	81%	99%	–
Texture analysis [22]	92.61	93.93	15.47
Color space and thresholding [23]	–	–	24.58
Proposed method	95.72	96.47	**6.7**

literature. XOR calculates the overlap of regions identified, hence determining accurate segmentation by obtaining a low value (0% for perfect segmentation). The lowest average of XOR was achieved by the proposed method at 3.53%.

5   Conclusion

A new Image enhancement algorithm based on fractional Poisson is proposed to improve the segmentation of skin lesions using the watershed transform. In the pre-processing stage we used fractional Poisson to rescale the image to a new intensity in order to enhance the image. Eight masks were implemented to remove noise such as hair and light reflection before the skin lesions were segmented. Then, the watershed algorithm was applied to detect the contours of the skin lesion at a lower processing time. The use of this algorithm enhanced the segmentation performance by increasing the average accuracy to 96.47% on a dermoscopic images consisting of both malignant and benign melanoma. In future, we aim to increase the accuracy using other types of skin lesions.

Acknowledgements. The authors would like to thank both Dr. Joaquim M. da Cunha Viana and Mr. Navid Razmjooy for providing the dermoscopic images used in this study. We would also like to thank skin specialist Dr. Mohammed Ahmed, for providing the necessary information for this study. This research is supported by the Fundamental Research Grant Scheme (FRGS), Project: FP073-2015A from Ministry of Higher Education, Malaysia.

References

1. Von Landesberger, T., Andrienko, G., Andrienko, N., Bremm, S., Kirschner, M., Wesarg, S., Kuijper, A.: Opening up the "black box" of medical image segmentation with statistical shape models. Vis. Comput. **29**, 893–905 (2013)
2. Wu, Q., Merchant, F., Castleman, K.: Microscope Image Processing. Academic Press, Cambridge (2010)
3. Garnavi, R., Aldeen, M., Celebi, M.E., Varigos, G., Finch, S.: Border detection in dermoscopy images using hybrid thresholding on optimized color channels. Comput. Med. Imaging Graph. **35**, 105–115 (2011)

4. Jung, C.R.: Multiscale image segmentation using wavelets and watersheds. In: 2003 XVI Brazilian Symposium on Computer Graphics and Image Processing, SIBGRAPI 2003, pp. 278–284. IEEE (2003)
5. Haris, K., Efstratiadis, S.N., Maglaveras, N., Katsaggelos, A.K.: Hybrid image segmentation using watersheds and fast region merging. IEEE Trans. Image Process. **7**, 1684–1699 (1998)
6. Weickert, J.: Efficient image segmentation using partial differential equations and morphology. Pattern Recogn. **34**, 1813–1824 (2001)
7. Ahmed Abbas, A., Tan, W.-H., Guo, X.-N.: Combined optimal wavelet filters with morphological watershed transform for the segmentation of dermoscopic skin lesions. In: Anthony, P., Ishizuka, M., Lukose, D. (eds.) PRICAI 2012. LNCS, vol. 7458, pp. 722–727. Springer, Heidelberg (2012). doi:10.1007/978-3-642-32695-0_63
8. Mustaqeem, A., Javed, A., Fatima, T.: An efficient brain tumor detection algorithm using watershed & thresholding based segmentation. Int. J. Image Graph. Sig. Process. **4**, 34 (2012)
9. Hamarneh, G., Li, X.: Watershed segmentation using prior shape and appearance knowledge. Image Vis. Comput. **27**, 59–68 (2009)
10. Wang, H., Moss, R.H., Chen, X., Stanley, R.J., Stoecker, W.V., Celebi, M.E., Malters, J.M., Grichnik, J.M., Marghoob, A.A., Rabinovitz, H.S.: Modified watershed technique and post-processing for segmentation of skin lesions in dermoscopy images. Comput. Med. Imaging Graph. **35**, 116–120 (2011)
11. Jalab, H.A., Ibrahim, R.W.: Fractional Alexander polynomials for image denoising. Sig. Process. **107**, 340–354 (2015)
12. Jalab, H.A., Ibrahim, R.W.: Texture enhancement based on the Savitzky-Golay fractional differential operator. Math. Probl. Eng. **2013**, 1–8 (2013)
13. Ibrahim, R.W., Jalab, H.A.: Existence of entropy solutions for nonsymmetric fractional systems. Entropy **16**, 4911–4922 (2014)
14. Ibrahim, R.W., Jalab, H.A.: Existence of ulam stability for iterative fractional differential equations based on fractional entropy. Entropy **17**, 3172–3181 (2015)
15. Laskin, N.: Fractional poisson process. Commun. Nonlinear Sci. Numer. Simul. **8**, 201–213 (2003)
16. Stoev, S.L.: A fast watershed algorithm based on rainfalling simulation (2000)
17. Sarker, M.S.Z., Haw, T.W., Logeswaran, R.: Morphological based technique for image segmentation. Int. J. Inf. Technol. **14**, 55–80 (2008)
18. Logeswaran, R., Haw, T.W., Sarker, S.Z.: Liver isolation in abdominal MRI. J. Med. Syst. **32**, 259–268 (2008)
19. Schaefer, G., Rajab, M.I., Celebi, M.E., Iyatomi, H.: Colour and contrast enhancement for improved skin lesion segmentation. Comput. Med. Imaging Graph. **35**, 99–104 (2011)
20. Wu, Y., Xie, F., Jiang, Z., Meng, R.: Automatic skin lesion segmentation based on supervised learning. In: 2013 Seventh International Conference on Image and Graphics (ICIG), pp. 164–169. IEEE (2013)
21. Zhou, H., Schaefer, G., Celebi, M.E., Lin, F., Liu, T.: Gradient vector flow with mean shift for skin lesion segmentation. Comput. Med. Imaging Graph. **35**, 121–127 (2011)
22. He, Y., Xie, F.: Automatic skin lesion segmentation based on texture analysis and supervised learning. In: Lee, K.M., Matsushita, Y., Rehg, J.M., Hu, Z. (eds.) ACCV 2012. LNCS, vol. 7725, pp. 330–341. Springer, Heidelberg (2013). doi:10.1007/978-3-642-37444-9_26
23. Cavalcanti, P.G., Yari, Y., Scharcanski, J.: Pigmented skin lesion segmentation on macroscopic images. In: 2010 25th International Conference of Image and Vision Computing New Zealand (IVCNZ), pp. 1–7. IEEE (2010)

A Simulation Study of Micro-Drone Chemical Plume Tracking Performance in Tree Farm Environments

Kok Seng Eu[✉], Kian Meng Yap, and Wan Chew Tan

Faculty of Science and Technology, Sunway University, Petaling Jaya
Selangor, Malaysia
{12058889,16000150}@imail.sunway.edu.my,
kmyap@sunway.edu.my

Abstract. Chemical plume tracking (CPT) technology is the mean of tracking the flow of specific chemical plume in the air, to locate the source. Nowadays, CPT technology, for instance, a micro-drone based chemical plume tracking robot, has great potential in identifying hidden explosives, illegal drugs and blood for police and military purposes. However, environmental factors such as obstacles on site can change the wind vectors will cause inconsistent odor plume propagation. With most of the previous work conducted from numerous researchers carried out in empty open space, this paper studies the influence of obstacles on site towards CPT's performance, which the simulation focus in one specific environment, a tree farm, with different density of trees or trees' spacing. For this paper, we developed a 3D gas dispersion simulator with mobile robot olfaction (MRO) capability. Through the simulation, correlation between the impacts of tree farm density factor to CPT's performance is found out, where higher tree density (or smaller tree spacing distance) can significantly reduce the performance of CPT. This study is an important fundamental contribution for drone's CPT operation in agriculture application beneficial to future use, such as smell tracking of mature fruits in tree farm.

Keywords: Chemical plume dispersion simulation · Mobile robot olfaction · Chemical plume tracking · Tree farm environment

1 Introduction

In several countries, police and military forces have been training dogs to detect dangerous substances which gives out faint smells such as explosives, illegal drugs or blood. To do so, a police or military dog, also known as detection or sniffer dog is trained to perform chemical plume tracking (CPT). Proudly, Britain manage to train a sniffer dog to search for bodies underwater with maximum range of smell 100 ft away [1]. Nevertheless, there is limitation to this approach of CPT. First, a sniffer dog is not easy to be trained, where the entire process is time consuming and extremely expensive. Second, short serving time and weak physical endurance restricts the capability of a sniffer dog. Lastly, sniffer dogs are not able to perform under hazardous conditions.

© Springer International Publishing AG 2017
H. Badioze Zaman et al. (Eds.): IVIC 2017, LNCS 10645, pp. 260–269, 2017.
https://doi.org/10.1007/978-3-319-70010-6_24

To overcome the disadvantages of a sniffer dog, a flying CPT robot—a micro-drone equipped with an electronic nose is proposed. Theoretically, a micro-drone can do better job than sniffer dog because micro-drone performs 3D CPT tracking, while in the case of sniffer dog CPT is in 2D form due to simple biological vectors. For example, a dog can perform limited 2D odor plume tracking within 30 to 100 m [1], whereas a moth is able to perform 3D odor plume tracking within 1000 m above [2].

Regardless 2D or 3D CPT, a robot's performance relies heavily on environmental factors such as wind direction and speed, humidity of the air, temperature and obstacles on site. Environment with structure obstacles (i.e. tree farm or warehouse) as shown in Fig. 1 could bring significant impact to CPT's performance, as the obstacles will change the wind vectors and alter odor plume propagation. This will affect the robot's CPT performance. Thus, this paper targets on only one specific environment, a tree farm. We want to study how the density of trees in the farm influence a robot's CPT performance.

(a)   (b)

Fig. 1. Environment with structure obstacles affect chemical plume propagation pattern

The problem statement is analyzed through the studying of interaction between robot's CPT performance and different trees density in farm. With the result obtained through the simulation, it is observed that higher tree density with smaller tree spacing distance will drastically reduce the effectiveness of CPT. This study plays a critical role for drone utilization in agriculture field in the future, as suggested the smell tracking of mature fruits in tree farm using drones could be implemented for better timing of plucking ripen fruits.

2 Related Works

In field of CPT, most of the research done by other researchers is performed using 2D CPT simulation. The simulation is built on a 2D graph using Matlab platform, as shown in the work by Liu et al. and Gong et al. [6, 7]. Through 2D CPT simulation, researchers can evaluate the performance of CPT algorithms. One example of 2D CPT simulation as shown in Fig. 2. It shows that the chemical plume propagation varies against time, then robots (represented by red dots) tracking forward chemical source. It may be presented as a simple model, but 2D CPT simulation lays a crucial foundation in CPT simulation research.

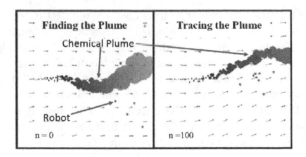

Fig. 2. Example of 2D CPT simulation [3] (Color figure online)

On the other hand, there were only little work done in 3D CPT simulation. One of the great contributions are from Cabrita et al. [5], where a simulator named PlumeSim is developed based on player/stage robotics framework. Besides that, Monroy et al. [8] use the Open Mobile Robot Architecture (OpenMORA) to developed Mobile Robotics Olfaction simulation, while Khaliq et al. [4] apply Robot Operating System, Open-FOAM to simulate a truthful gas dispersion. Example of a 3D CPT simulation is as shown in Fig. 3. The chemical plume dispersion model uses a real-scale model of robot in the simulation. As 3D CPT simulator is considered as one dimension higher than 2D CPT, it is closely related to real-life scenario.

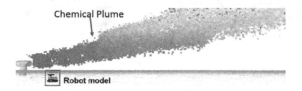

Fig. 3. Example of 3D CPT simulation [4]

Interestingly, most of the CPT simulation studies target in an empty open space [9–11], while only a few covers simple obstacles environment with one to two obstacle blocks [5] as shown in Fig. 4. Standing out from other's work, Morjovi and Marques did a CPT research in a structured environment [12]. They investigate the CPT performance in an environment like warehouse as shown in Fig. 5, which is a complex environment with various obstacles.

In the literature, there is no CPT task done in tree farm environment. The study itself is vital as it would benefit drone's function in agricultural field in future. A no-table example is the drone could be used in a durian tree farm to track mature fruits. This could prevent unwanted accidents from happen to the farmers when picking up ripe durians.

Fig. 4. CPT simulation with two obstacles [5]

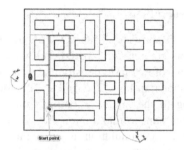

Fig. 5. CPT task in a structure environment similar to warehouse [12]

3 Simulation Setup

Affected by numerous factors, different plantation of tree farm has different trees' density or trees' spacing. To ensure good growth of trees, oil palm trees, for example, is assigned to be planted 10 m from each other [13], so that all the branches has enough space to grow and bear fruits. While coconut trees' recommended tree spacing is around 7.5 m in square planting [14], in contrast to oil palm trees which has long branches, rubber trees' best spacing is around 5 m because it has relatively shorter branches. Thus, there is no need of big space to grow its branches and fruits [15].

In our simulation setups, we test three different tree farm density in square planting with area of 25 × 25 m, range of tree spacing spanning from 5, 7.5 and 10 m as shown in Fig. 6. Under such arrangement, tree spacing with 10 m and 7.5 m can fit a total of 9 trees in an area of 25 × 25 m, whereas tree spacing with 5 m can accommodate a total 25 trees in the same area.

There are two important stages of simulation setups. First, the 3D wind vectors in the simulator is generated by using computational fluid dynamics (CFD) software. Next, the generated 3D wind vectors data is imported into the chemical plume dispersion and mobile robot olfaction (MRO) simulator. With the above two stages fulfilled, we can finally evaluate the robot's CPT performance. The details of these two stages will be discussed in followings subsections.

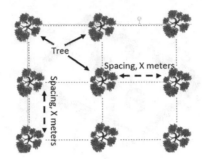

Fig. 6. Tree farm density or tree' spacing in square planting

3.1   3D Wind Vector Generations

We use an open source CFD software, TYCHO [16], to generate 3D wind vectors. Each generated wind vectors contain wind speed and wind direction information. As we test out the three scenarios of tree farm density, the snapshot of 3D wind vectors for each tree farm density are shown in Figs. 7, 8 and 9. The colors of the arrows indicate the wind speed. According to the intensive colors from blue to red, it shows the changing in speed from minimum to maximum. The wind vector is indicated by the arrows' direction. Note that this simulation is an exploration study, we will only consider the trunk of the tree as obstacles and neglect the branches and leaves of tree in the generation of wind vectors.

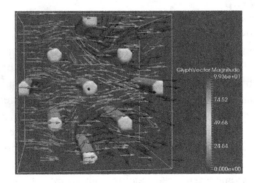

Fig. 7. 3D wind vectors for tree spacing of 10 m (top view)

In Fig. 7, the airflow between tree trunks is smoother. The stream of the flow is also more consistent and less chaotic. In compare to Fig. 7, the wind vector shown in Fig. 8 has comparatively faster wind speed and more chaotic stream of flow. Nevertheless, it is observed that the wind vectors in Fig. 9 has the most chaotic stream of flow in random speed and direction. Our hypothesis of this simulation is: smoother stream of flow will have better CPT performance; random and chaotic stream of flow will reduce the performance of CPT.

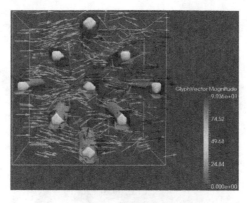

Fig. 8. 3D wind vectors for tree spacing of 7.5 m (top view)

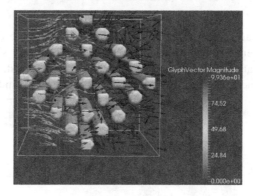

Fig. 9. 3D wind vectors for tree spacing of 5 m (top view)

3.2   Chemical Plume Dispersion (CPD) and Mobile Robot Olfaction (MRO)

Follow on from the first step, the CFD generated 3D wind vectors data will be integrated into our chemical plume dispersion and mobile robot olfaction (MRO) simulator. The simulator used is developed in our previous work [17]. Figure 10 shows one of the CPT example in tree farm environment. The markers in Fig. 10 represent chemical plume filament, with colors to represent the odorant concentration. The trajectory path of the drone is recorded by a black color line. In the simulation, the wind vectors will influence the chemical plume propagation in the tree farm. The simulation will only stop after the sniffer robot armed with gas sensors is able to track towards the chemical plume by using its tracking algorithm and then locate the chemical source.

In this paper, Moths' olfactory tracking strategy (also known as Zigzag algorithm, is used to complete the CPT [19]. When the odor plume is detected, moth will track closely to the odor plume along the wind direction. This action is called the upwind surge. However, the pattern of odor plume is complex and unpredictable in real-life environment, therefore the moth might lose track of the odor plume during the surging

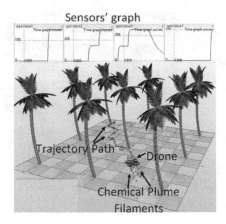

Fig. 10. 3D CPT simulation in tree farm environment

behavior. For this reason, whenever the moth failed to track the odor plume, it will perform zigzag movement orthogonal to the wind direction and slowly increases its zigzag wave length after each iteration. This action is called casting as illustrated in Fig. 11. Once, the moth is back on the track, it performs upwind surge again. The process of switching upwind surge and zigzag casting would continue until the odor source is located.

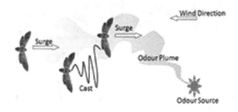

Fig. 11. Moth inspired plume tracing strategies [18]

4   Result and Discussion

The CPT results obtained from the simulation are listed in Table 1. There are two keys of performance indication to evaluate the CPT performance, i.e. distance over-head and elapsed time. Distance overhead is defined as the total travelled distance divided by the distance of the shortest path to the source, where smaller value indicates better performance. In the same way, shorter elapsed time also indicates better performance.

From Table 1, tree spacing of 10 m has smaller distance overhead and elapsed time. This means in this scenario the CPT performance is better than in the other two. As we look at the trajectory path of scenario (a) shown in Fig. 12, it is observed that there is only one upwind surge and without any loss of trace. There is also no zigzag casting performed in scenario (a).

Table 1. CPT results

Scenario	Tree farm density	Distance overhead	Elapsed time (s)
(a)	Tree spacing of 10 m	1.483	259.90
(b)	Tree spacing of 7.5 m	2.314	384.20
(c)	Tree spacing of 5 m	2.504	431.10

Fig. 12. Trajectory path for tree spacing of 10 m

In scenario (b) from Table 1, the CPT performance is poorer than the results obtained from scenario (a). With tree spacing of 7.5 m, the distance overhead and time elapsed has increase. This is caused by the long trajectory path of drone in scenario (b), as the drone lost trace of the chemical plume twice. Thus, the drone had to per-form zigzag casting twice in order to trace back the chemical plume stream. The trajectory path of drone in scenario (b) is shown in Fig. 13.

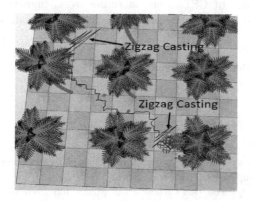

Fig. 13. Trajectory path for tree spacing of 7.5 m

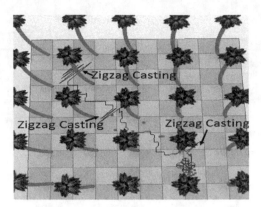

Fig. 14. Trajectory path for tree spacing of 5 m

Finally, the CPT performance in scenario (c) has the worst performance of all, which it gains the highest values in both distance overhead and time elapsed. In scenario (c), the tree spacing of 5 m causes chaotic stream of air flow and brings random propagation of chemical plume around the trees. Hence, it is difficult for the drone to perform CPT. In Fig. 14, it is clearly shown that the drone has lost trace of chemical plume for three times and performed zigzag casting thrice. Therefore, the values gain in both category especially the elapsed time.

5 Conclusion

In summary, the CPT performance in tree farm environment with three different tree farm densities being tested in simulation have been studied. From the result obtained, the impact of tree farm density factor to CPT performance has been correlated. It is concluded that higher tree density or smaller tree spacing distance can significantly reduce the performance of CPT. Thus, in future work, higher number of multiple drones could be used in a complex environment to compensate the performance of robots' CPT.

Acknowledgements. This work was supported by the Sunway Internal Grant Scheme (Grant No: INT-FST-CIS-2016-03) at Sunway University, Malaysia.

References

1. Dog sniffing distance. http://dogspired.com/britains-first-underwater-sniffer-dog-can-find-submerged-bodies-up-to-100ft-away/. Accessed 5 Sept 2017
2. Lindsey, K.: 7 Things You Don't Know about Moths. http://www.livescience.com/21933-moth-week-facts.html. Accessed 5 Sept 2017

3. Jatmiko, W., Sekiyama, K., Fukuda, T.: A mobile robots PSO-based for odor source localization in dynamic advection-diffusion environment. In: 2006 IEEE/RSJ International Conference on Intelligent Robots and Systems, pp. 4527–4532 (2006)
4. Khaliq, A., Pashami, S., Schaffernicht, E., Lilienthal, A., Bennetts, V.H.: Bringing artificial olfaction and mobile robotics closer together – an integrated 3D gas dispersion simulator in ROS. In: 16th International Symposium on Electronic Nose, p. 78 (2015)
5. Cabrita, G., Sousa, P., Marques, L.: PlumeSim-player/stage plume simulator. In: ICRA Workshop on Networked and Mobile Robot Olfaction in Natural, Dynamic Environments (2010)
6. Liu, Z., Lu, T.-F.: A simulation framework for plume-tracing research. In: Australasian Conference on Robotics and Automation, pp. 3–5 (2005)
7. Gong, D.W., Zhang, Y., Qi, C.-L.: Localising odour source using multi-robot and anemotaxis-based particle swarm optimisation. IET Control Theory Appl. **6**, 1661 (2012)
8. Monroy, J.G., Blanco, J.-L., González-Jiménez, J.: An open source framework for simulating mobile robotics olfaction. In: 15th International Symposium on Olfaction and Electronic Nose (ISOEN), pp. 2–3 (2013)
9. Villarreal, B.L., Olague, G., Gordillo, J.L.: Synthesis of odor tracking algorithms with genetic programming. Neurocomputing **175**, 1019–1032 (2016)
10. Gao, B., Li, H., Li, W., Sun, F.: 3D Moth-inspired chemical plume tracking and adaptive step control strategy. Adapt. Behav. **24**, 52–65 (2016)
11. Neumann, P.P., Bennetts, V.H., Lilienthal, A.J., Bartholmai, M.: From insects to micro air vehicles—a comparison of reactive plume tracking strategies. In: Menegatti, E., Michael, N., Berns, K., Yamaguchi, H. (eds.) Intelligent Autonomous Systems 13. AISC, vol. 302, pp. 1533–1548. Springer, Cham (2016). doi:10.1007/978-3-319-08338-4_110
12. Marjovi, A., Marques, L.: Multi-robot olfactory search in structured environments. Rob. Auton. Syst. **59**, 867–881 (2011)
13. FAO Corporate Document Repository. http://www.fao.org/docrep/006/t0309e/T0309E03.htm. Accessed 5 Sept 2017
14. Horticulture: Plantation Crops : Coconut - Spacing and Planting. http://agritech.tnau.ac.in/horticulture/horti_pcrops_coconut_spacing.html. Accessed 5 Sept 2017
15. Rubber Board: Land Preparation. http://rubberboard.org.in/Faq.asp?Id=24&Fid=49. Accessed 5 Sept 2017
16. Colella, P., Woodward, P.R.: The piecewise parabolic method (PPM) for gas-dynamical simulations. J. Comput. Phys. **54**, 174–201 (1984)
17. Eu, K.S., Yap, K.M.: An exploratory study of quadrotor's propellers impact using 3D gas dispersion simulator. In: The International Symposium on Olfaction and Electronic Nose (ISOEN), Canada (2017)
18. López, L.L.: Moth-like chemo-source localisation and classification on an indoor autonomous robot. In: On Biomimetics, pp. 453–466 (2005)
19. Li, W., Farrell, J.A., Cardé, R.T.: Tracking of fluid-advected odor plumes: strategies inspired by insect orientation to pheromone. Adapt. Behav. **9**, 143–170 (2001)

Similarity Assessment of UML Sequence Diagrams Using Dynamic Programming

Alhassan Adamu[1,2] and Wan Mohd Nazmee Wan Zainon[1(✉)]

[1] Universiti Sains Malaysia, Penang, Malaysia
Kofa062@gmail.com, nazmee@usm.my
[2] Kano University of Science and Technology, Wudil, Nigeria

Abstract. Unified Modeling Language is a modelling language used to visualize software system during requirement engineering phase. It was accepted as a standard modeling language for visualizing, specifying and documenting software systems by International Organization for Standardization (ISO) as a standard specification. It contained different type of diagrams for specifying software system, among these diagrams is sequence diagrams which is used to specify the functional behavior of software system. The growing complexity of software systems is one of the motivation behind matching of UML diagrams in order to pave the way of reusing existing software to developed new software systems. Previous works on sequence diagrams matching are based on Graph representation in which there is node whenever there is message sending or received. However, the search space for these approach is very large due to the number of nodes in the graph which makes the matching computationally expensive. This paper employed the use of Dynamic Programming approach in order to improve the efficiency of matching between two or more sequence diagrams.

Keywords: UML matching · Similarity assessment · Model reuse

1 Introduction

The use of UML diagrams in the designing of software system has drastically reduce the complexity of software systems [1]. UML diagrams allow software engineers to capture precisely related aspects of a software system from a given view and at an appropriate abstraction. Initially, UML diagrams are used to describe single software systems. For each software system there is set of diagrams that describe its static, behavioral and functional structure [2]. Sequence diagrams is considered as the representative of the functional structure of software system, this is because use cases can be used to describe the functionality of software systems and each of the use case is typically realized using one or more sequence diagrams that illustrate how objects interact with each other to provide services [2, 3].

Recently, researchers have realized the importance of similarity assessment of software functional requirements, since they specify the fundamental behaviors that should be provided by the software systems [4, 5], and in particular sequence diagrams [3]. Similarity assessment of UML diagrams is the task that correspond to identifying

© Springer International Publishing AG 2017
H. Badioze Zaman et al. (Eds.): IVIC 2017, LNCS 10645, pp. 270–278, 2017.
https://doi.org/10.1007/978-3-319-70010-6_25

the semantic correspondence between elements of two diagrams (e.g. class names) [6]. It is task that is error-prone, because these diagrams while representing similar software system functionalities are used independently by different software engineers, thus creating inconsistencies and design differences among the diagrams. Therefore, a similarity assessment technique that can accurately match and quantified these differences must be used. In this work, the similarity between sequence diagrams is computed using Edit Distance with the aid of Dynamic Programming.

2 Related Works

Significant research has been carried out on UML-based matching. For example, Ali and Du [7] used conceptual graph to aid the retrieval of software models. The similarity computation was based on the estimation of the conceptual distance between terms in the query and the terms in repository models.

On the other hand, Robinson and Woo [8] compute the similarity between sequence diagrams using SUBDUE [9] graph matching algorithm. Sequence diagrams were represented as conceptual graphs in which the object names in the sequence diagrams represents vertices, and the relationships between the diagrams (messages) represented the edges of the graph. The SUBDUE algorithm find the similarity between the graph by comparing the substructures of sequence diagrams in query and repository.

More research in this concern by Park and Bae [10] put forward two-stage framework to retrieve UML artifacts from repository. In the first stage the similarity between class diagrams was computed using structured mapping engine (SME). SME is analogical reasoning mapping technique which allows mapping of knowledge from one domain to another by considering the relational communalities between objects in the domain regardless of the objects involved in the relationships. The subset of the repository UML projects were selected for subsequent comparison using class diagram. In the second stage, sequence diagrams in the shortlisted models were converted to message-order-graph (MOOGs), where nodes denote the location where events occur (message send or received) in sequence diagrams and the edges denote the flow of events between objects and the flow of time inside each object. The similarity between two MOOGs was computed based on the number of nodes and edges in each of the graph using graph matching algorithm.

In more recent study, a similar approach was reported by Salami and Ahmed [3] where sequence diagrams were converted to a directed graph, the similarity between the graphs was determined with the aid of genetic algorithm (GA). The GA helped to terminate the searching process in order to avoid exhaustive comparison. The termination criteria was based on three conditions: first, if the fitness value reached 0, it indicated the maximum similarity between class diagrams, second, if the maximum number of iteration reached, or if the fitness function did not improve within a given number of iterations. In our previous work [11, 12], we proposed a framework for enhancing the retrieval of UML diagrams. State machine diagrams were represented by finite state machine diagram in which (i) every states in the state machine diagrams represents states in the finite state machine, (ii) the transition between one state to another in state machine represents the transition in finite state machine. The similarity between state machines diagrams is computed by means of similarity function table containing the differences between the various types of relationship in UML state machine diagram.

3 Similarity Framework

The problem of sequence diagram similarity computation could be divided into two: structure matching and similarity scoring. The structure matching entails mapping of nodes in sequence diagrams graph representation (e.g. objects, message sending/ received appearing in sequence diagrams). Determination of suitable mapping of sequence diagrams entities may involve examination of large spaces.

The similarity scoring on the other hand is concerned on how to determine the degree of similarity of a given sequence diagrams. Consequently, similarity measured to determine the degree of similarity of two or more sequence diagrams is proposed using Edit Distance. Edit Distance is the minimum number of edits required to transform one string into another string [13]. It had several applications in the areas of bioinformatics such as DNA or protein alignment, file comparison, gas chromatography and speech recognition [14]. The similarity between two sequence diagrams is computed based on the minimum (sequence of messages) of edits required to transformed one sequence diagram to another.

Let s_1 and s_2 be two sequence diagrams having messages of length of $|m_1|$ and $|m_2|$ respectively, the similarity measure of two sequence diagrams was obtained from the length of their common messages. We defined a mapping $Mapping(S_1, S_2)$ from one sequence diagram to another if the source and receiving classes of the two messages are mapped as shown in Eq. (1) as follows:

$$Mapping(S_1, S_2) = \begin{cases} M_1 = M_2 \, \forall \, M_i \in S_i : Ob_{1_{msrc}} = Ob_{2_{msrc}} \text{ and } Ob_{1_{mdest}} = Ob_{2_{mdest}} \\ M_i \neq M_j \qquad\qquad\qquad\qquad\qquad\qquad\qquad\qquad\quad \text{otherwise} \end{cases} \quad (1)$$

$Ob_{i,j}$ were objects in S_i ($Ob_1 \leq Ob_2$), M_i denoted the messages in sequence diagrams S_i and $mrsc$ and $mdest$ were the source and the destination of M_i.

3.1 Dynamic Programming Method

The classic dynamic programming solution problem was invented by (Wagner and Fischer, 1974). In its simplest form, given two sequences x_1 and x_2 having length l_1 and l_2 respectively, the dynamic programming algorithm iteratively built an $l_1 \times l_2$ score matrix M in which $M[i, j]$, $0 \leq i \leq l_1$, $0 \leq j \leq l_2$, was the length of an LCS between two strings $x_1[1,..........,i]$ and $x_2[1,...............,j]$. The score matrix could be defined based on the recursive formula in Eq. (2) as follows:

$$M(i,j) = \begin{cases} 0 \;\; if \;\; i = 0 \, or \, j = 0 \\ M[i-1, j-1] + 1 \; if \; x_1[i] = x_2[j] \\ \max(M[i,j], M[i-1,j] \; if \; x_1[i] \neq x_2[j] \end{cases} \quad (2)$$

Let A and B be two set of sequence diagrams, and let SA and SB denoted the sets of sequence diagrams $(A_1, A_2, A_3......A_{SA})$, $(B_1, B_2, B_3......B_{SB})$ of A and B respectively. Assuming that A contained O_a number of objects $(a_1, a_2, a_3......a_{ca})$ and B contained O_b number of objects $(b_1, b_2, b_3......b_{cb})$. Furthermore, let A_i and B_i denoted the number of messages in A and B respectively, A_i is denoted as $|A_i|$ such that $(1 \leq i \leq SA)$ and B_i was denoted as $|B_i|$ such that $(1 \leq i \leq SB)$. The degree of similarity of similarity of two set of sequence diagrams A and B could be formulated in the following four possibilities:

i.   There was n number of objects O_a in A such that the number of classes in A were at most the number of classes in B and the number of sequence diagrams in SA were at most the number of sequence diagrams in SB $(O_a \leq O_b, SA \leq SB)$.
ii. There was n number of classes O_a in A such that the number of classes in A were at most the number of classes in B and the number of sequence diagrams in SA were greater than the number of sequence diagrams in SB $(O_a \leq O_b, SA > SB)$.
iii. There was n number of classes C_a in A such that the number of classes in A were greater than the number of classes in B and the number of sequence diagrams in SA were at most the number of sequence diagrams in SB $(O_a > O_b, SA \leq SB)$.
iv. There was n number of classes C_a in A such that the number of classes in A were greater than the number of classes in B and the number of sequence diagrams in SA were greater than the number of sequence diagrams in SB $(O_a > O_b, SA > SB)$.

The degree of similarity could be computed using Eq. 3 as follows:

$$FSim(A, B) = 1 - \frac{1}{\min(S_i)} \sum_{i=1}^{S_i} \frac{2 * P[\min(A_i, B_i), \max(A_{Si}, B_{Si})]}{|A_{Si}| + |B_{Si}|} + 2\beta \frac{\max(S_i) - \min(S_i)}{S_1 + S_2} \qquad (3)$$

P was a permutation vector for mapping the classes and sequence diagrams in A and B. max and min were function that return the larger and smaller of its arguments respectively. $\beta \in (0, 1]$ was a constant that determines how the unmatched sequence diagrams affected the degree of similarities. Larger value of β increased the similarity value between A and B and indicated the less similarity between A and B.

P can be calculated using Equation. Let a and b denoted two sequence diagrams having $|a|$ and $|b|$ messages, respectively. We could also assume a involves ca classes $a_1, a_2,.....a_{oa}$ while b involves cb classes $b_1, b_2,....b_{ob}$ $(oa \leq ob)$ as shown in Fig. 1. Let P be a permutation vector such that B maps all classes ca to cb classes. The Edit distance between a and b, given a permutation vector P can be obtained using recursive formula is Eq. (4) as follows:

$$P(i, j) = \begin{cases} 0 & \text{if } i = 0 \text{ or } j = 0 \\ P[i-1, j-1] + 1 & \text{if } i > 0 \text{ and } j > 0 \ Ob(a_{imsrc}) = Ob(b_{imsrc}) \\ & \text{and } Ob(a_{imdest}) = Ob(b_{imdest}) \\ \max(P[i, j], M[i-1, j] & \text{if } x_1[i] \neq x_2[j]) \end{cases} \qquad (4)$$

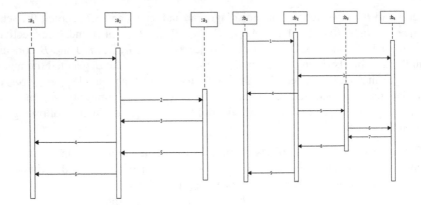

Fig. 1. Two sample sequence diagrams *a* and *b*

Based on this, *max* was a function that return the lager value of its arguments, and a_{imsrc}, b_{jmsrc}, a_{imdest}, b_{jmdest} denoted the message source and destination class respectively.

Table 1 shows the value of Edit distance between the messages in *a* and *b*. The rows and column of the table indicate the message sequence number of *a* and *b*.

Table 1. Values for *P* used in computing *Edit Distance*

c	1	2	3	4	5	6	7	8	9
r	0	0	0	0	0	0	0	0	0
1	0	0	0	0	0	1	1	1	1	1
2	0	0	0	0	0	1	1	1	1	1
3	0	0	0	0	0	1	1	1	2	2
4	0	0	0	0	0	1	1	1	2	3
5	0	0	0	0	0	1	1	1	2	3
6	0	0	0	0	1	1	1	1	2	3

The edit distance between two sequence diagrams can be computed using Eq. (5) as follows:

$$Sim(a, b) = 1 - \frac{2 * ED(a, b)}{|a| + |b|} \tag{5}$$

The value of *P* is obtained from Table 1, |a| and |b| are the message size of *a* and *b* respectively. The possible value of *Sim* should lie in the range of [0, 1], with 0 indicated the maximum degree of similarity and value of 1 indicated the least possible degree of similarity between two sequence diagrams.

3.2   Case Study

This section presents a case study showing how the proposed sequence diagrams matching technique in action. Given two sets of sequence A and B as shown in Fig. 2, the similarity of two sequence diagrams using permutation vector $P = (1, 3, 4)$, $S = (2, 1)$ and $\beta = 0.15$, $C_a = 3$, $C_b = 4$, $SA = SB = 2$, $|A_1| = |A_2| = |B_1| = |B_2| = 4$. Since $O_a < O_b$ and $SA = SB$ then SA would be mapped to SB.

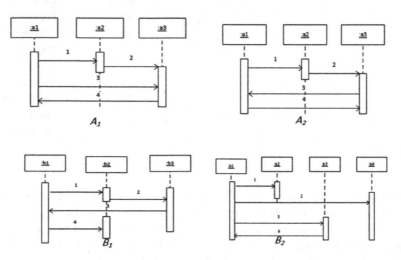

Fig. 2. Two sets of sequence diagrams A and B

The similarity between the two sequence diagrams can be computed using Eq. (6) as follows:

$$1 - \frac{1}{2}\left(\frac{2 * P(A_1, B_2)}{|A_1| + |B_2|} + \frac{2 * P(A_2, B_1)}{|A_2| + |B_1|}\right) + 2\beta \frac{SB - SA}{SA + SB} \tag{6}$$

$$1 - \frac{1}{2}\left(\frac{6}{8} + \frac{6}{8}\right) + 2 * 0.15 \frac{2 - 2}{2 + 2} = 0.25$$

The value of P was obtained using recursive formula in Eq. 4. The similarity obtained shows that the two sequence diagrams A and B were similar. This was indicated by the lower similarity obtained as 0.25, since 0 indicated maximum similarity and 1 indicated maximum dissimilarity.

4   Evaluation

The query and repository diagrams were formed in the manner conducted by Salami and Ahmed [3], We formed ten query sequence diagrams from undergraduate and text book fragment found in Yue et al. [15] and Larman [16]. The summary of the data is described in Table 2.

Table 2. Properties of query sequence diagrams

Sequence diagrams	Number of messages	Number of objects	Source	Domain
q_1	15	7	Yue et al. [15]	Banking system
q_2	7	2	Larman [16]	POS
q_3	8	3	SP[a]	Education
q_4	24	6	SP	GPS
q_5	4	4	SP	Education
q_6	8	3	SP	Education
q_7	11	4	SP	Tracking system
q_8	14	5	SP	Tourism
q_9	8	7	SP	Online retails
q_{10}	8	6	SP	Online shopping

[a]Students project

A repository containing 60 sets of sequence diagrams was formed using six set of queries, each of the query was used to create ten sets of projects such that each query partially matched the repository projects. The projects were created from the query by randomly deleting or adding messages in q_i as follows: (i) randomly deleting the number of messages in sequence diagrams q_i such that $m_i \leq r_i < q_i$, (ii) randomly adding more messages to the sequence diagrams q_i so that $m_i \leq q_i < r_i$. Where $m_i = 0.3$ denoted the percentage of messages added or deleted from q_i to form r_i.

4.1 Results and Discussion

The matching quality was measured using Mean Average Precision (MAP), a measured commonly used to evaluate information retrieval system. Average precision (AP) for a given query was obtained using precision values calculated at each point whenever a new projects was retrieved (i.e. precision = 0 for each of the relevant project that is not retrieved). The Mean Average Precision for a set of query was the mean of the AP scores for each query, also referred as mean precision at seen relevant projects [17]. The formula is given in Eq. (7).

$$MAP = \frac{1}{N} \sum_{j=1}^{N} \frac{1}{Q_j} \sum_{i=1}^{Q_j} P(rel = i) \tag{7}$$

N is the number of queries, Qj is the number of relevant documents for query j and P(rel = i) is the precision at the ith relevant document.

Figure 3 shows the comparison of the values of MAP between the **FSim** method and MOOG method proposed by Park and Bae [10] and GA + MOOG proposed by Salami and Ahmed [3]. It can be observed from Fig. 3 that in both cases **FSim** methods returned

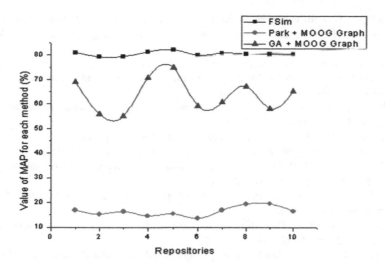

Fig. 3. Comparison of MAP of three retrieval methods

high value of MAP compared to other methods. The method return all relevant repository models as the top ranking diagrams in almost all the cases with MAP of up to 82%.

Park and Bae approach produces low values of MAP, which indicates that the method does not usually return relevant repository diagrams as the top ranking diagrams based on the input query. On the other hand, GA + MOOG also return relevant repository diagrams as the top ranking diagrams with an average value of MAP 60% to 67%. *FSim* and GA + MOOG were able to produce good MAP. However, in all cases the *FSim* gave better MAP compared to the corresponding GA + MOOG.

5 Conclusion

This paper proposed and approach for UML sequence diagrams similarity assessment using dynamic programming. The approach support software developers to easily visualize the similarity and difference between two sequence diagrams during software development. Experimental shows that our approach is able to compute the similarity between two or more sequence diagrams with MAP of up to 82%. In the future we plan to develop a tool in order to allow the software developers to adapt the similar sequence into new software development.

Acknowledgements. This work was supported by the Ministry of Higher Education of Malaysia, under the Fundamental Research Grant Scheme (FRGS: 203/PKOMP/6711533).

References

1. Apel, S., Janda, F., Trujillo, S., Kästner, C.: Model superimposition in software product lines. In: International Conference on Theory and Practice of Model Transformations, pp. 4–19 (2009)

2. Ahmed, M.: Towards the development of integrated reuse environments for UML artifacts. In: The Sixth International Conference on Software Engineering Advances, ICSEA 2011, pp. 426–431 (2011)
3. Salami, H.O., Ahmed, M.: Retrieving sequence diagrams using genetic algorithm. In: 2014 11th International Joint Conference on Computer Science and Software Engineering (JCSSE), pp. 324–330 (2014)
4. Paydar, S., Kahani, M.: A semi-automated approach to adapt activity diagrams for new use cases. Inf. Softw. Technol. **57**, 543–570 (2015)
5. Valderas, P., Pelechano, V.: A survey of requirements specification in model-driven development of web applications. ACM Trans. Web (TWEB) **5**, 10 (2011)
6. Chechik, M., Nejati, S., Sabetzadeh, M.: A relationship-based approach to model integration. Innov. Syst. Softw. Eng. **8**, 3–18 (2012)
7. Ali, F.M., Du, W.: Toward reuse of object-oriented software design models. Inf. Softw. Technol. **46**, 499–517 (2004)
8. Robinson, W.N., Woo, H.G.: Finding reusable UML sequence diagrams automatically. IEEE Softw. **21**, 60–67 (2004)
9. Jonyer, I., Cook, D.J., Holder, L.B.: Graph-based hierarchical conceptual clustering. J. Mach. Learn. Res. **2**, 19–43 (2002)
10. Park, W.J., Bae, D.H.: A two-stage framework for UML specification matching. Inf. Softw. Technol. **53**, 230–244 (2011)
11. Adamu, A., Zainon, W.M.N.W.: Matching and retrieval of state machine diagrams from software repositories using cuckoo search algorithm. In: International Conference on Information Technology Al Zaytoonah University of Jordan, Amman, Jordan (2017)
12. Adamu, A., Zainoon, W.M.N.W.: A framework for enhancing the retrieval of UML diagrams. In: Kapitsaki, G.M., Santana de Almeida, E. (eds.) ICSR 2016. LNCS, vol. 9679, pp. 384–390. Springer, Cham (2016). doi:10.1007/978-3-319-35122-3_25
13. Herman, D.: Asset reuse of images from a repository. Walden University (2014)
14. Begum, A.: A greedy approach for computing longest common subsequences. J. Prime Res. Math. **4**, 165–170 (2008)
15. Yue, T., Briand, L.C., Labiche, Y.: Automatically deriving UML sequence diagrams from use cases. Simula Research Laboratory (2010)
16. Larman, C.: Applying, UML Patterns: An Introduction to Object-Oriented Analysis and Design and Iterative Development. Prentice Hall (2004)
17. Teufel, S.: An overview of evaluation methods in TREC ad hoc information retrieval and TREC question answering. In: Dybkjær, L., Hemsen, H., Minker, W. (eds.) Evaluation of Text and Speech Systems. Text, Speech and Language Technology, vol. 37, pp. 163–186. Springer, Dordrecht (2007). doi:10.1007/978-1-4020-5817-2_6

An Automated Image-Based Approach for Tracking Pedestrian Movements from Top-View Video

Halimatul Saadiah Md. Yatim[1], Abdullah Zawawi Talib[1(✉)], and Fazilah Haron[2]

[1] School of Computer Sciences, Universiti Sains Malaysia,
11800 USM Pulau Pinang, Malaysia
hsmyll_com060@student.usm.my, azht@usm.my
[2] Department of Computer Science, Taibah University, Al-Madinah
Al-Munawwarah, Kingdom of Saudi Arabia

Abstract. In order to gain better and more understanding of pedestrian safety video, better tracking of pedestrian movements is necessary. However, existing works on video tracking of pedestrian movements focus in some specific places or situations, extracted limited data from the video and in some cases, a lot of human interventions are required in handling the data extraction. This paper presents an automated image-based approach for tracking pedestrian movements that takes advantage of the top-view video. The proposed approach consists of several steps namely detection, tracking, image calibration and extracting characteristics of a pedestrian from a video. The methods used in these steps are adapted or enhanced from some of the existing work in this area. These steps also allow automated video monitoring and require less human efforts. Besides, it is also used to estimate the speed of a pedestrian. The results of the experiment for the proposed approach using five videos with different scenario are presented. The pedestrian movement was plotted accurately and the numbers of pedestrians detected in the video were recorded correctly whereas the speed of the pedestrians from the framework was very close to the actual speed. The proposed approach can be used to monitor pedestrians in a sparse environment such as at the entrance of a hall or building or along a corridor.

Keywords: Object tracking · Pedestrian tracking · Crowd monitoring

1 Introduction

Videos have been used for many years for entertainment and surveillance using closed-circuit television video (CCTV). Monitoring for safety and comfort manually through CCTV is not practical and requires constant attention of the safety personnel. As such, there is a growing interest in research on surveillance and monitoring for safety and comfort [1]. In particular, there is need for an automated approach to minimize human effort and intervention on pedestrian monitoring so that the monitoring process can be executed automatically or semi-automatically.

© Springer International Publishing AG 2017
H. Badioze Zaman et al. (Eds.): IVIC 2017, LNCS 10645, pp. 279–289, 2017.
https://doi.org/10.1007/978-3-319-70010-6_26

The monitoring process involves extracting and analyzing the macroscopic and even microscopic data from the images of the video camera. An automated monitoring usually does not require manual inspection on the video and therefore, usually results in less or no human intervention or effort. Research in this area normally revolves around getting the pedestrian characteristics from a video such as the trajectory of moving objects or pedestrians, and density of pedestrians in a specific area. This paper presents an automated approach for pedestrian tracking from top-view video footage. The output from the tracking could be used to validate and calibrate simulation model for crowd safety, improve the design architecture of a building and alert the security personnel on anomaly of events. The automated approach can be used to monitor pedestrians at the entrance of a building or a hall, or along a corridor with minimum or less human effort or intervention.

2   Related Work

Extracting data from a video-footage has been an active area of research. The researches focus on various aspects and targets [1] and include determining the crowd density [2–5], the number of pedestrians [2, 6, 7], and trajectories of a moving object [4, 5, 8, 9]. In detecting trajectories of a moving object, the objects include pedestrian [10], vehicle [11], human fingertip [12] and the methods employed include supervised learning [8], unsupervised learning [13] and clustering of trajectories [14]. The trajectory extracted can be used to determine the movement pattern of the object of interest [14, 15].

Detecting individual pedestrian is quite challenging and existing methods are mostly for specific and controlled situations. One of the methods is background subtraction [16–18] and the method itself, cannot guarantee that a detected object is the object of interest. The method has also been combined with other method [19, 20]. Another method is object classification in which one of the methods belonging to this category classifies the pedestrians based on their color [21, 22].

The next step after pedestrian detection is, tracking of the detected pedestrian throughout the video frames. Tracking algorithms normally focus on specific situations and have some limitations and they include Kalman filter [6, 21], feature-based tracking [9, 22], particle filter [23], and active contour-based tracking [24].

The next step after tracking of pedestrian is extracting the position of a pedestrian. With the information on the positon of the pedestrian, we can obtain other attributes from the video footage such as speed, trajectory and the number of pedestrians in the footage. An accurate measurement is required at this stage. However, this can hardly be achieved due to the placement of the camera and characteristics of the lens. The resulting phenomenon called geometric distortion [25], must be corrected in order to accurately obtain the position of pedestrian. This process is sometimes called image calibration [7]. A conventional way of getting accurate speed of the pedestrian is by manually calculating the speed manually and also by having the pedestrian to carry a GPS device [26].

3 Proposed Approach

In this paper, an automated approach with less human intervention and effort is proposed for the entire process of extracting pedestrian characteristics from video footages. Figure 1 shows the entire process of the proposed approach. The proposed approach is largely based on the proposed preliminary framework of automating pedestrian tracking from a video [27]. However, in this paper, the proposed approach takes advantage of the top-view video for a better and more accurate approach and thus, the proposed approach is more suitable for situations involving placement of the camera at specific location such as at the entrance of a building or a hall, or along a corridor.

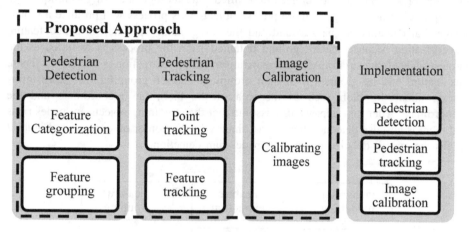

Fig. 1. Proposed approach

The processes involved include pedestrian detection, pedestrian tracking, and image calibration. Pedestrian detection firstly involves getting the background image from the video [28]. Frame differencing method [29] is then applied to extract moving object in the video. In this work, a moving object refers to a pedestrian and there should be no other objects in the background image. Next, image processing techniques is applied to each frame of the video to extract individual objects. The objects need to be filtered in order to remove objects of non-interest (e.g. very small objects). After obtaining the desired objects, the centroid coordinate [16] of each object is identified. Then, each object is grouped and labeled. The same object is tracked between frames by using a hybrid method of point tracking and feature tracking. Point tracking uses coordinate of the object and feature tracking uses feature grouping from the previous frame and thus, the movement vector for each object is extracted. Next, characteristics such as speed, trajectory and also the number of pedestrians detected are extracted from the video footage. The calibration value obtained during the video camera set up will be used in speed measurement to ensure better approximation of the speed. In each step, existing methods are either adapted or enhanced for more effective implementation of the approach.

3.1   Detection

This step which is the first in the proposed approach involves extracting the back-ground image [29] from a video frame. Frame differencing techniques [30] are applied between video frames and the background image in order to extract the objects of interest which are moving objects in the scene. Pixels that change will be group as foreground blobs which are the object present on the image [31]. They are then con-verted to grayscale [32] and threshold by using the method by Otsu [33]. Then, the morphological operations techniques are applied which consist of morphological reconstruction, morphological opening, morphological filtering and morphological closing. The objects on the image might not be filled completely (in the form of a blob), the holes present on each object need to be filled. Morphological closing techniques are also applied in order to get a more precise object. This process will produce a binary image that contains the background and the foreground. This step is called feature categorization because the foreground obtained from the process is assumed as the interest object (pedestrian). After categorization, feature extraction is conducted. Then, this feature will be grouped in feature grouping. Feature grouping will store infor-mation about the blob such as the area of the blob, the x-coordinate and the y-coordinate. After this step, we can assume that the remaining objects are pedestrians and there is no false detection because of shadow, reflection or other reasons. Figure 2 shows the overall detailed process for pedestrian detection.

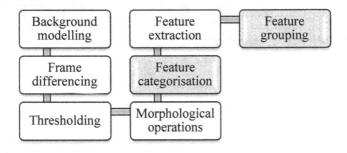

Fig. 2. Overall process for pedestrian detection

3.2   Tracking

The pedestrian tracking method that we have applied in the implementation of the proposed framework are point tracking and feature tracking. These two methods are selected because it is suitable to be used in this proposed approach. In pedestrian detection, feature grouping will return a feature of the object in terms of the area, shape and coordinates of the blob. These parameters passed from pedestrian detection can be very useful in pedestrian tracking. Coordinates of the blob can collaborate with the point tracking while the area and shape of blob can collaborate with the feature tracking. This hybrid tracking method is the enhancement proposed for this approach. Figure 3 shows the block diagram illustrating the proposed hybrid tracking method.

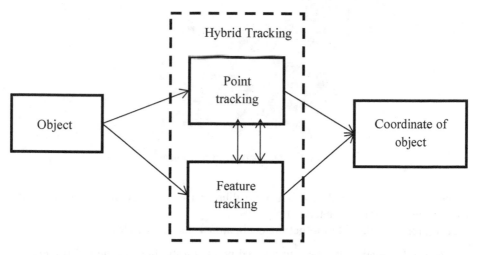

Fig. 3. Overall process for tracking.

In point tracking, Kalman filter algorithm is chosen for the implementation of this method. This algorithm is chosen because it has two steps to track the object in subsequent frames which are prediction and correction. The centroid of the object of interest is used as a point to track the object of interest. In feature tracking, the feature of the object that has been grouped from feature grouping in the initial frame is maintained throughout the video frames. This is to ensure that the same object is tracked successfully and accurately. The features of the object of interest include the shape of the object and the area of the blob. These two parameters act as a template of the object of interest between the video frames. Therefore, the centroid of the object can be maintained in the same shape of the object of interest. This can help reduce the rate of inaccuracy because of the shape changing between frames can result in the change of the centroid position.

The objects in subsequent frames are labeled in such a way that each object has similar label in all frames. The coordinates of the centroid position of each object in each frame are extracted and recorded. It will record in two-dimensional (2D) manners which consist of x-coordinate and y-coordinate. The set of the coordinates of the object recorded from all frames of the video footage is called movement vector.

3.3   Image Calibration

Image calibration is conducted in order to get an accurate and precise position of the pedestrian on the image. This is crucial as the results of the proposed approach depend on the position and movement of the pedestrian. The calibration technique proposed in [2] requires user to choose four points on the image. The four points marked are used to calculate and normalize the pixels on the images. For this proposed approach, instead of choosing four points in the image manually, the video will capture a scene that has four markers that illustrate the square shape on the ground plane (see Fig. 4). The four markers are a precondition during the setup of camera in the particular scene. By taking

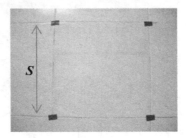

Fig. 4. Four markers in real image

advantage of top-view video, the image calibration can be calculated automatically without the need for user intervention.

The proposed algorithm to get the calibration value is as follows:

1. Capture the image with the four marked points on the floor in the video scene.
2. Detect the four marked points.
3. Get all the length (perimeter) of the square shape in the image.
4. Calculate the mean of the length (in pixels), A.

$$A = \frac{1}{4}\sum_{k=1}^{4} a_k \tag{1}$$

where a_k is the length of each side of the distorted square shape (as captured in the video frame).

5. Calculate the mean of the length (in centimetre), S.

$$S = \frac{1}{4}\sum_{k=1}^{4} s_k \tag{2}$$

where s_k is the length of each side of the actual (real) square shape.

6. Calculate the distorted value.

$$V = S/A \tag{3}$$

where V is a measurement (size) for one pixel in centimetre. This value is used as the calibration value.

3.4   Extracting Pedestrian Parameters

Pedestrian parameters that will be extracted from the proposed method are the number of pedestrians, and trajectory and the speed of pedestrian. The trajectory of pedestrian shows a path that has been passed by the pedestrian. To get the trajectory of the pedestrian, the x-coordinate and y-coordinate which are saved as movement vector is used. These coordinates will be plotted into a graph and this graph will show the movement pattern of the pedestrian. Trajectories of the pedestrians plotted in a graph will illustrate the movement pattern of that specific location.

Speed can be obtained from the distance in which the object has moved in pixel per second. Distance is obtained from the movement of the object of interest from one position to another position. The distance d is calculated using the following equation:

$$d = \sqrt{((x_2 - x_1)^2 + (y_2 - y_1)^2)} \tag{4}$$

where the initial point is (x_1, y_1) and the final point is (x_2, y_2). The distance is calculated for every frames of the video. Therefore, the initial point (x_1, y_1) is taken at the start of the frame rate and the final point (x_2, y_2) is taken at the next frame. The distance is the total distance of the pedestrian in the video.

Speed is recorded from an average of every second of the video in order to get more accurate calculation. This is to avoid getting the movement result of a straight line from the initial to final point as pedestrians might randomly move from one place to another. Thus, the average speed for every second distance is deemed to be practical for more accurate calculation of speed. The average speed is obtained as follows:

$$\text{Average Speed} = (Total\ Distance)/(Total\ Time) \tag{5}$$

The total distance in Eq. 4 will be displayed in pixels. The time that will be used to calculate the average speed can be extracted directly from the video duration in seconds since the video is captured in real time. Therefore, the average speed is presented in pixel per second. The average speed is then calibrated by the following equation:

$$r = \text{average speed x } V \tag{6}$$

where V is the calibration value and r is a calibrated speed in centimetre (cm) per second.

4 Experimental Results and Discussion

For the purpose of doing a testing on the proposed approach, we have captured several videos which were taken from the top view using a single fixed camera. We have used five different scenarios and they were captured at the same place. Table 1 shows the results of the experiment which consists of the trajectories and number of detected pedestrians for the five different scenarios.

The graphs in Table 1 show an accurate movement path of the pedestrian for all the scenarios. In Scenario 4 and Scenario 5, the first pedestrian is indicated by blue color, the second pedestrian by green color and the third pedestrian by red color. The tracking can be said to be successful as the trajectory depicts the pedestrian movement in the video as observed in manual observation. In addition, no overlapping or wrongly assigned of object label are shown in the graph. The trajectory might give an erratic result if the tracking method is not successful such as wrong tracking of object between

Table 1. Results of the experiment (number of detected pedestrians and trajectory)

Scenario	Video information	Description	Sample image of the video	Trajectory	Number of detected pedestrians
1	• 6 sec • 25 fps • Total number of frames: 150	A pedestrian walking in a straight line.			1
2	• 8 sec • 25 fps • Total number of frames: 200	A pedestrian walking as in Scenario 1 but slower.			1
3	• 9 sec • 25 fps • Total number of frames: 225	A pedestrian walking in a zigzag manner.			1
4	• 4 sec • 25 fps • Total number of frames: 100	Two pedestrians walking in a straight line.			2
5	• 8 sec • 25 fps • Total number of frames: 200	Three pedestrians walking one after another with different speed.			3

the video frames. The resulting number of detected pedestrians is the exact number as observed manually for both scenarios.

Table 2 shows the result of the actual speed of pedestrians, speeds in pixels per second, and calibrated and uncalibrated speeds in centimeter per second (cm/s) for the five different scenarios. As shown in the table, the calibrated speed and uncalibrated speed for all scenarios show a different value. However, the calibrated speed (cm/sec) is closer to the speed value from manual calculation compared to the uncalibrated speed. The uncalibrated speeds give huge gap of speed measurement. It can be concluded that the proposed image calibration method for the top-view video is an important aspect to be added in the proposed approach in order to extract the pedestrian data. These small differences recorded show that the calculation method used in setting the calibration value is also reliable. The speeds recorded are acceptable and close to the real speed measurement from manual observation.

Table 2. Results of the experiment (speed)

Scenario	Number of detected pedestrians	Speed			
		Manual	Proposed approach		
			Pixels/sec	Calibrated (cm/sec)	Uncalibrated (cm/sec)
1	1	96.7	141.8667	92.21	85
2	1	63.8	68.9155	59.27	55
3	1	78	83.128	72.07	66.5
4	1	113.9	136.3731	96.44	83.2
	2	127.6	162.4433	107.55	99.1
5	1	151.9	167.19	147.13	137
	2	120	132.05	116.2	108.3
	3	87	98.46	86.6	80.74

5 Conclusion and Future Work

The proposed approach can be used to get the movement path and speed of the pedestrians, and the numbers of pedestrians detected in a video footage based on the top view in an automated manner and with less human effort. In all cases accurate or exact results are obtained. However, for the speed, the result is very close to the actual speed measurement. The steps involved in the proposed approach are implemented by adapting or enhancing some existing methods and techniques in order to reduce and minimize the constraints and limitations of automating the entire processes in the proposed approach. Moreover, the implementation also provides analysis and visualization of the results.

For future work, enhancement can be made to detection, tracking and image calibration techniques. Perhaps, it should be enhanced for dense crowds. Also, to ensure the robustness of the system, a wider variety of videos and scenarios should be used for testing and validation. Focus should also be on occlusion handling and placement of the video camera.

Acknowledgements. The authors would like to acknowledge the support of the Ministry of Higher Education Malaysia for this research under the Fundamental Research Grant Scheme entitled "More Accurate Models for Movements of Pedestrians in Big Crowds".

References

1. Hu, W., Tan, T., Wang, L., Maybank, S.: A survey on visual surveillance of object motion and behaviors. IEEE Trans. Syst. Man Cybern. Part C (Appl. Rev.) **34**(3), 334–352 (2004)
2. Ma, R., Li, L., Huang, W., Tian, Q.: On pixel count based crowd density estimation for visual surveillance. In: Proceedings of IEEE Conference on Cybernetics and Intelligent Systems, pp. 170–173. IEEE (2004)

3. Liu, X., Song, W., Zhang, J.: Extraction and quantitative analysis of microscopic evacuation characteristics based on digital image processing. Phys. A: Stat. Mech. Appl. **388**(13), 2717–2726 (2009)
4. Zheng, J., Yao, D.: Intelligent pedestrian flow monitoring systems in shopping areas. In: Proceedings of 2nd International Symposium on Information Engineering and Electronic Commerce, pp. 1–4 (2010)
5. Steffen, B., Seyfried, A.: Methods for measuring pedestrian density, flow, speed and direction with minimal scatter. Phys. A: Stat. Mech. Appl. **389**(9), 1902–1910 (2010)
6. Celik, H., Hanjalic, A., Hendriks, E.: Towards a robust solution to people counting. In: IEEE International Conference on Image Processing, pp. 2401–2404. IEEE (2006)
7. Conte, D., Foggia, P., Percannella, G., Tufano, F., Vento, M.: A method for counting moving people in video surveillance videos. EURASIP J. Adv. Sig. Process. **2010**, 231–240 (2010)
8. Albusac, J., Castro-Schez, J.J., Lopez-Lopez, L.M., Vallejo, D., Jimenez-Linares, L.: A supervised learning approach to automate the acquisition of knowledge in surveillance systems. Sig. Process. **89**(12), 2400–2414 (2009)
9. Boltes, M., Seyfried, A., Steffen, B., Schadschneider, A.: Automatic extraction of pedestrian trajectories from video recordings. In: Klingsch, W.W.F., Rogsch, C., Schadschneider, A., Schreckenberg, M. (eds.) Pedestrian and Evacuation Dynamics 2008, pp. 43–54. Springer, Heidelberg (2010). doi:10.1007/978-3-642-04504-2_3
10. Makris, D., Ellis, T.: Path detection in video surveillance. Image Vis. Comput. **20**, 895–903 (2002)
11. Zhang, Z., Huang, K., Tan, T., Wang, L.: Trajectory series analysis based event rule induction for visual surveillance. In: Proceedings of IEEE Conference on Computer Vision and Pattern Recognition, pp. 1–8. IEEE (2007)
12. Ren, D.W., Li, J.T.: Vision-based dynamic tracking of motion trajectories of human fingertips. In: Tan, T.J., Chen, S.B., Zhou, C. (eds.) Robotic welding, Intelligence and Automation. LNCIS, vol. 362, pp. 429–435. Springer, Heidelberg (2007). doi:10.1007/978-3-540-73374-4_51
13. Johnson, N., Hogg, D.: Learning the distribution of object trajectories for event recognition. Image Vis. Comput. **14**, 609–615 (1996)
14. Piciarelli, C., Foresti, G., Snidaro, L.: Trajectory clustering and its applications for video surveillance. In: Proceedings of IEEE Conference on Advanced Video and Signal Based Surveillance, pp. 40–45. IEEE (2005)
15. Fernández-Caballero, A., Castillo, J.C., Rodríguez-Sánchez, J.M.: A proposal for local and global human activities identification. In: Perales, F.J., Fisher, R.B. (eds.) AMDO 2010. LNCS, vol. 6169, pp. 78–87. Springer, Heidelberg (2010). doi:10.1007/978-3-642-14061-7_8
16. Yue, H., Shao, C., Zhao, Y., Chen, X.: Study on moving pedestrian tracking based on video sequences. J. Transp. Syst. Eng. Inf. Technol. **7**(14), 47–51 (2007)
17. Hao-li, C., Zhong-ke, S., Qing-hua, F.: The study of the detection and tracking of moving pedestrian using monocular-vision. In: Alexandrov, V.N., van Albada, G.D., Sloot, P.M.A., Dongarra, J. (eds.) ICCS 2006. LNCS, vol. 3994, pp. 878–885. Springer, Heidelberg (2006). doi:10.1007/11758549_117
18. Dedeoğlu, Y., Töreyin, B.U., Güdükbay, U., Çetin, A.E.: Silhouette-based method for object classification and human action recognition in video. In: Huang, T.S., Sebe, N., Lew, M.S., Pavlović, V., Kölsch, M., Galata, A., Kisačanin, B. (eds.) ECCV 2006. LNCS, vol. 3979, pp. 64–77. Springer, Heidelberg (2006). doi:10.1007/11754336_7
19. Bazzani, L., Bloisi, D., Murino, V.: A comparison of multi hypothesis Kalman filter and particle filter for multi-target tracking. In: 11th IEEE International Workshop on Performance Evaluation of Tracking and Surveillance, PETS 2009, pp. 47–55. IEEE (2009)

20. Berclaz, A., Shahrokni, J., Fleuret, F.: Evaluation of probabilistic occupancy map people detection for surveillance systems. In: 11th IEEE International Workshop on Performance Evaluation of Tracking and Surveillance, PETS 2009, pp. 55–62. IEEE (2009)
21. Hoogendoorn, S., Daamen, W., Bovy, P.H.L.: Extracting microscopic pedestrian characteristics from video data. In: Presented at 82nd Annual Meeting at the Transportation Research Board, pp. 1–15 (2003)
22. Ma, J., Song, W., Fang, Z., Lo, S., Liao, G.: Experimental study on microscopic moving characteristics of pedestrians in built corridor based on digital image processing. Build. Environ. **45**(10), 2160–2169 (2010)
23. Ali, I., Dailey, M.N.: Multiple human tracking in high-density crowds. Image Vis. Comput. **30**(12), 540–549 (2012)
24. Yilmaz, A., Javed, O., Shah, M.: Object tracking. ACM Comput. Surv. **38**(4), 1–45 (2006)
25. Lee, S., Lee, S., Choi, J.: Correction of radial distortion using a planar checkerboard pattern and its image. IEEE Trans. Consum. Electron. **55**(1), 27–33 (2009)
26. Bandini, S., Federici, M., Manzoni, S.: A qualitative evaluation of technologies and techniques for data collection on pedestrians and crowded situations. In: Proceedings of the 2007 Summer Computer Simulation Conference, Society for Computer Simulation International, pp. 1057–1064 (2007)
27. Yatim, H.S.M., Talib, A.Z., Haron, F.: A practical and automated image-based framework for tracking pedestrian movements from a video. IERI Proceedia **4**, 181–187 (2013)
28. Cheung, S.S., Kamath, C.: Robust techniques for background subtraction in urban traffic video. In: Proceedings of SPIE, pp. 881–892. SPIE (2004)
29. Karaman, M., Goldmann, L., Yu, D., Sikora, T.: Comparison of static background segmentation methods. In: Li, S., Pereira, F., Shum, H.-Y., Tescher, A.G. (eds.) Visual Communications and Image Processing 2005, vol. 5960, pp. 2140–2151. SPIE, Bellingham (2005)
30. Zhan, C., Duan, X., Xu, S., Song, Z., Luo, M.: An improved moving object detection algorithm based on frame difference and edge detection. In: Proceedings of Fourth International Conference on Image and Graphics, ICIG 2007, pp. 519–523 (2007)
31. Kong, D., Gray, D.: A viewpoint invariant approach for crowd counting. In: 18th International Conference on Pattern Recognition, ICPR 2006, pp. 1187–1190. IEEE (2006)
32. Hussain, N., Yatim, H.S.M., Hussain, N.L., Yan, J.L.S., Haron, F.: CDES: a pixel-based crowd density estimation system for Masjid al-Haram. Saf. Sci. **49**, 824–833 (2011)
33. Otsu, N.: A threshold selection method from gray-level histograms. IEEE Trans. Syst. Man Cybern. **9**, 62–66 (1979)

Exploratory Research on Application of Different Vision System on Warehouse Robot Using Selective Algorithm

Wan Chew Tan[(⊠)] and Kian Meng Yap

Faculty of Science and Technology, Sunway University,
Petaling Jaya, Selangor, Malaysia
16000150@imail.sunway.edu.my, kmyap@sunway.edu.my

Abstract. Warehouse robots rely on navigation algorithm to maneuver in the warehouse. One of the available navigation algorithm includes the use of vision technology. Yet, the technology requires depth cameras to act as "eyes" of the robot. It is known that cameras depend on lighting factor to operate. A sole example includes failure of vision-powered warehouse robots in extreme lighting conditions. Thus, this paper discusses the approach to enable warehouse robot in in-tense lighting conditions with implementation of two vision technology. In this paper, two depth cameras that function on different technology were used. The cameras chosen are stereoscopic camera and infrared based time-of-flight camera. This paper first studies the lighting factor that affects the performance of both cameras. Next, both camera were simulated in extreme lighting condition. The results obtained are further analyzed and constructed into a selective algorithm. This exploratory study is an important fundamental contribution to complete robot functioning warehouse in future.

Keywords: Infrared based time-of-flight vision · Stereoscopic vision · Warehouse robots

1 Introduction

Since year 2012, Amazon.inc propose the idea of using robots to manage their warehouse [1]. With much effort, the technology finally rolled into practice in year 2014. In year 2017, China adopted warehouse robots in courier firms to manage the parcels [2]. However, current warehouse robots can only operate in magnetic tapes, RFID tags or ambient lighting environment [3]. Enhancing navigation system of robots can surmount the restrictions of warehouse robots. This paper focus on navigation using robotic vision as it is more elastic and expandable [4]. Embedding two different vision systems to a warehouse robot can be the solution. The solution allows warehouse robots to function at outdoor and indoor environment. In the experiment, Microsoft Kinect v2 plays the role of infrared based vision system, while ZED from Stereolabs represents stereoscopic vision system. Both devices were operated in intense lighting condition. Based on [5], environment factors such as external radiation and insufficient lighting will affect the quality of vision. This is due to the different principle of operation of both depth cameras. The quality of vision obtained is recorded down

© Springer International Publishing AG 2017
H. Badioze Zaman et al. (Eds.): IVIC 2017, LNCS 10645, pp. 290–296, 2017.
https://doi.org/10.1007/978-3-319-70010-6_27

during the simulation. A selective algorithm based on the logic system and pseudocode is then developed. The algorithm can be applied in real-life scenario in future to achieve a complete robot functioning warehouse.

In this paper, Sect. 2 presents the related works done on navigation system of robots. The next section describes the simulation setup of the paper. Section 4 shows the result and discussion of the experiment conducted. The paper ends with a conclusion on work done to prove the solution proposed is workable.

2 Related Works

There are many proposed ways to enable warehouse robots to navigate around. Prior to topic of paper, this section will discuss navigation system based on vision. Early in year 2014, Zaki et al. proposed a hybrid navigation system that combines the perception (ultrasonic sensors) and dead reckoning (encoder) system. They found both sensors were complement to give a satisfactory navigation system of a mobile robot [6]. Even so, the hybrid system poses tedious sensors setup on the body of robots. Figure 1 displays the prototype of sensors setup by Zaki et al.

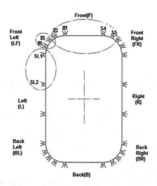

Fig. 1. Sample setup of system proposed by Zaki et al. [6].

Urcola et al. introduced laser scanner to obtain a visual map of the warehouse. At outdoor, differential GPS is suggested for localization of robot. It provides position estimation with only error of few centimeters [7]. Nevertheless, GPS wanes in cloudy condition as the cloud blocked the signal transmission between robot and satellite. Laser scanning is also an expensive technology to embed onto a robot for vision purposes. Figure 2 shows the mapping route obtained from GPS system.

The work done by Akupati is same as Urcola et al., but Akupati embed one extra module to the robot, which is IMU (Inertial Measurement Unit) sensor to find the orientation of robot [8]. The IMU sensor is applied for calculating a way-point angle base on the robot current position and the next destination to be reached by it. This further enhance the noise created by GPS but can only be an extended version of work done by Urcola et al.

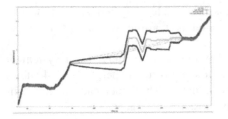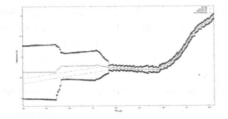

Fig. 2. Example of GPS mapping system [7].

In the literature, there is no work done to refine the vision system through the hybrid of two different vision technology. Vision navigation is easy for maintenance compare to GPS. It does not depend third party technology like satelite. Besides that, the hybrid produces vision result compatible with laser rangefinder sensor. Thus, this paper eliminates the use of expensive technology on a warehouse robot.

Vision system can be used in SLAM (Simultaneous Localization and Mapping) algorithm. SLAM algorithm works with robotic vision to map the surrounding environment [11]. Moreover, further work can combine SLAM with deep learning to realise a complete fobot functioning warehouse. Hence, this study is critical fundamental study for future warehouse.

3 Simulation Setup

Indoor and outdoor environment differs largely in lightning condition. While indoor environment is filled with ambient lights all day long unless switched off by facility department, outdoor environment is more dynamic in lightning condition where there may be cloudy skies or strong sunlight in different timing of a day. Nevertheless, in terms of obstacles, indoor environment poses more difficult pathway for robots to navigate around as there is countless shelves positioned in the warehouse, while out-door environment is usually empty with only several trucks parked in the loading bay.

The simulation progress with Kinect v2 and ZED camera tested under indoor and outdoor environment. Both device will be operating simultaneously in research lab and football field of our university, which resemble the indoor and outdoor environment of the warehouse. The scene is chosen with care, where in the research lab there is several shelves filled with items to duplicate a likely vision obtained in warehouse. In the other hand, football field is chosen due to its broadness and openness, thus the only factor that affects the lightning condition will be by nature itself.

The design of model is to choose both depth cameras that complement each other. In the case of ZED, it provides longer range of sight than Kinect v2. The accuracy of measurement in depth is the reason for choosing Kinect v2. Both camera complement each other in terms of range and measurement.

Research shows that Infrared based vision system does not function well under the influenced of external radiation such as sunlight [5], while stereoscopic vision with two cameras relies heavily on the lightning condition of the situation. Thus, to test the capacity of both vision technology, the devices were being operated in different conditions as specified Table 1.

Table 1. Condition of the environment being tested.

	Outdoor	Indoor
Strong sunlight	$\sqrt{}$	
Ambient light		$\sqrt{}$
No light	$\sqrt{}$ (insufficient light)	

In the simulation, corresponding depth viewing software from both Self Developing Kit (SDK) is used due to the different calculating algorithm both device derive from the raw data obtained to produce the final vision. For Kinect v2, Kinect Fusion Explorer is used while ZED camera uses ZEDfu. Kinect v2 measures the time-of-flight of Infrared pulses to determine the depth of corresponding points for the creation of point cloud data [9]. In the case of ZED camera, triangulation method is used to calculate corresponding depth of pixels acquire from the video stream from both sides of camera to build a depth map [12]. As this is an exploratory study, obstacle avoidance algorithm is not considered where this paper only discusses the usage of different vision system in different condition.

4 Result and Discussion

Comparison of result in Table 2 shows the difference of image obtained from Kinect v2 and ZED camera. The final image acquired from Kinect v2 is preserved notably, as it greatly resembles the scene in real-life. The details on items is not blurred, for example,

Table 2. Result of simulation.

	Outdoor environment with strong sunlight	Indoor environment with sufficient ambient light	Outdoor environment with spotlight in night	Indoor environment without light
Stereoscopic vision			No image obtained	No image obtained
Infrared based time-of-flight vision				

the words printed on the box in indoor environment can be read without much difficulty from the results obtained from Kinect v2. The outline of the object geometry is also sharp, where the edges of the box and shelves can be observed clearly from the results obtained. Nevertheless, the overhead of such precision is the noise delivered from Kinect v2, as shown in outdoor results with flying point clouds hovering above the boxes. Besides, the quality of vision wanes drastically when Kinect v2 is tested in outdoor environment. Thus, heavy computation is needed to maintain the quality of robotic vision.

ZED camera holds the constant vision quality over indoor and outdoor environment, except that it cannot function in the dark as it relies heavily on light to operate. Comparison of results shows that the quality of vision of ZED is better than Kinect v2 when they were operated in outdoor environment with strong sunlight. From the images obtained the field of view of ZED camera is large to capture more objects of the scene, which means earlier detection of obstacle is possible with ZED camera. Despite having larger range of vision, the accuracy of object geometry obtained from ZED camera is rather poor. The sets of results obtained in the test shows discrepancy on shape of object, where the outline of the object is crooked and blurred with no distinction between edges. Thus, vision priority must be given to the Infrared based time-of-flight system, as accuracy is important to prevent miscalculation of route.

The simulation concludes that the accuracy of obtaining precision of measurements by Infrared based time-of-flight system can be designed to govern the robot in indoor environment, whereas long range of stereoscopic vision system that gives high definition vision in even strong lightning condition can be used in outdoor environment. The next step will be designing logic gates and pseudocode for the operation of warehouse robots.

To inform warehouse robot about the existence of specific limiting factors on both vision system, light sensor and ultraviolet sensor can be embedded on the robot to show the presence of sufficient light and sunlight. Table 3 shows the conditions and resulting vision technology to be used. 1 in light sensor signifies that sufficient lightning is detected and vice versa in the case of 0. In the row of ultraviolet sensor 1 stands for the existence of sunlight in the environment while 0 for none. With the result obtained in the row of Kinect and ZED, 1 means active system while 0 means inactive.

Table 3. Condition to use corresponding vision technology.

Light sensor	1	1	0	0
Ultraviolet sensor	1	0	1	0
Kinect	0	1	0	1
ZED	1	1	1	1

The result from Table 3 is further summarized into logic gates as below.

$$K = !U \tag{1}$$

$$Z = L \vee U \tag{2}$$

where

K = Kinect v2,
Z = ZED camera,
U = Ultraviolet Sensor,
L = Light sensor

The pseudocode generated is the selective algorithm to be embedded to the ware-house robot. The pseudocode first checks the presence of sunlight through ultraviolet sensor installed on the robot. Next, the obtained value from ultraviolet sensor is being processed by the logic gate developed as above and stored in variable K. While the value of K is 1, the robot will activate the Infrared based time-of-flight vision system to navigate around. During active time, the robot will have to check for the condition if fulfils the arguments of logic gates. If no, another vision system will be selected. This step will keep looping until the robot is inactive.

```
While warehouse robot is active
   read value from ultraviolet sensor and store into U;
   K = !U;
   While K is equal to 1
     Activate Infrared based time-of-flight vision
system;
     read new value from ultraviolet sensor and store
into U;
     Check K = !U;
   End while
   read value from light sensor and store into L;
   Z = L || U;
   While K is equal to 0 and Z is equal to 1
     Activate stereoscopic vision system;
     read new value from light sensor and store into L;
     Check Z = L || U;
   End while
End while.
```

5   Conclusion

In summary, this paper explores the capability of Infrared based time-of-flight vision and stereoscopic vision in robots. Both vision system was tested in various environment and condition and results were obtained from the simulation to create a workable selective algorithm. The algorithm will be applying on robots so that decision can be made to use suitable vision system to obtain the best quality of vision for SLAM algorithm. In future work, a complement algorithm can be developed to enable warehouse robots to acquire the pro side of corresponding vision technology in different environment and condition.

Acknowledgement. This work was supported by the Small Grant Scheme – Sunway Lancaster (Grant No: SGSSL-FST-DCIS-0115-08) at Sunway University, Malaysia.

References

1. Bhattacharya, A.: Amazon is just beginning to use robots in its warehouses and they're already making a huge difference (2016). https://qz.com/709541/amazon-is-just-beginning-to-use-robots-in-its-warehouses-and-theyre-already-making-a-huge-difference/. Accessed 27 Apr 2017
2. Tracy: Meet 'Little Orange', the cutest warehouse worker: self-charging robots can sort 20,000 parcels an hour at a Chinese courier firm (2017). http://www.dailymail.co.uk/news/article-4401108/Meet-Little-Orange-robot-warehouse-worker-China.html. Accessed 4 Sept 2017
3. Banker, S.: Robots in the Warehouse: It's Not Just Amazon (2016). https://www.forbes.com/sites/stevebanker/2016/01/11/robots-in-the-warehouse-its-not-just-amazon/#790cd3be40b8. Accessed 27 Apr 2017
4. Bélanger-Barrette, M.: Robotic vision systems: what is doable? (2016). http://www.controleng.com/single-article/robotic-vision-systems-what-is-doable/dd4e2be762802d6dce70384b5a0cf257.html. Accessed 17 May 2017
5. Elberink, S.O., Khoshelham, K.: Accuracy and resolution of kinect depth data for indoor mapping applications. Sensors $12(2)$, 1437–1454 (2012). doi:10.3390/s120201437
6. Arafa, O., Amer, A.I., Zaki, A.M.: Microcontroller-based mobile robot positioning and obstacle avoidance. JESIT $1(1)$, 58–71 (2014). doi:10.1016/j.jesit.2014.03.009
7. Lorente, M.T., Villarroel, J.L., Montano, L., et al.: Seamless robot localization and navigation in indoors-outdoors for logistics in warehouses (2015)
8. Akupati, C.R.: Intelligent outdoor navigation of a mobile robot platform using a low cost high precision RTK-GPS and obstacle avoidance system (2015)
9. Endres, F., Hess, J., Sturm, J., et al.: Real-time 3D visual SLAM with a hand-held RGB-D camera (2011)
10. Chang, H.Y., Sarkar, S., Chen, M.N., et al.: An integrated system for 3D pose estimation in cluttered environments. In: 29th Conference on Neural Information Processing Systems (2016)
11. Zhang, J., Tai, L., Boedecker, J., et al.: Neural SLAM. In: 1st Conference on Robot Learning (2016)
12. Lee, S., Choi, O., Horaud, R., et al.: An overview of depth cameras and range scanners based on time-of-flight technologies. MVA $27(7)$, 1005–1020 (2016)

Travel Route Recommendation Based on Geotagged Photo Metadata

Ching May Lee and J. Joshua Thomas[(✉)]

Department of Computing, School of Engineering, Computing and Built
Environment, KDU Penang University College, George Town, Penang, Malaysia
chingmay131@gmail.com, jjoshua@kdupg.edu.my

Abstract. Travellers usually look for two kinds of information when they are
planning a trip to a new destination: the points of interest (POI) and the interesting travel sequences given the POI in the destination. In recent years, due to
the spread of the photo-taking gadgets with the global positioning system
(GPS) functionality and the act of the travellers sharing and contributing photos
on websites, such as Flickr and Panoramio, there are plenty of geotagged photos
available on the Web. Through assembling diverse sets of geotagged photos
shared by the travellers from the Web, the POI and the travel sequences given
the POI in a destination can be mined if the travellers visit several POI in a day
and take photos at each of the visited POI. In this paper, a web-based travel
route recommendation system, namely Travel Route Recommendation System
(TRRS), is presented. The purpose of this system is to generate and recommend
travel route to the travellers who are visiting a destination for the first time and
only for one day based on geotagged photo metadata.

Keywords: Travel route recommendation · Geotagged photo metadata · Travel
pattern generation · Point of interest

1 Introduction

Planning a trip is very time-consuming. There are four main steps to plan a multi-day
trip: choosing a destination, making travel arrangements, finding accommodations, and
planning activities. However, there are only two main steps to plan a one-day trip:
choose a destination and planning activities. Choosing a destination perhaps is the
easiest step among the steps to plan a trip because it highly depends on the traveller's
budget for the trip. By the time a destination has been chosen, the next step would be
planning activities for the trip, which is also the most daunting task for most of the
travellers. The traveller would need to compile a list of sights to see and activities to do
in the destination that they are travelling to by reading printed or online travel guides.
After that, the traveller would need to prioritise the sights to see, as well as the activities
to do, and then followed by plan the trip accordingly with the prioritised sights and
activities while taking the visit durations for each sight or activity and the travel time
between sights and activities into consideration. In short, travellers usually look for two
kinds of information when they are planning a trip to a new destination: the points of
interest (POI) and the interesting travel sequences given the POI in the destination.

© Springer International Publishing AG 2017
H. Badioze Zaman et al. (Eds.): IVIC 2017, LNCS 10645, pp. 297–308, 2017.
https://doi.org/10.1007/978-3-319-70010-6_28

In recent years, due to the spread of the photo-taking gadgets with the global positioning system (GPS) functionality and the act of the travellers sharing and contributing photos on websites, such as Flickr and Panoramio, there are plenty of geotagged photos available on the Web [5]. Through assembling diverse sets of geotagged photos shared by the travellers from the Web, the POI and the travel sequences given the POI in a destination can be mined if the travellers visit several POI in a day and take photos at each of the visited POI [6]. Therefore, many works [4–9] have been proposed by the researchers to build a travel route recommendation system based on the geotagged photos on the Web.

In this paper, a web-based travel route recommendation system, namely Travel Route Recommendation System (TRRS), is presented. The purpose of this system is to generate and recommend travel route to the travellers who are visiting a destination for the first time and only for one day based on geotagged photo metadata in five steps after a destination is selected. Firstly, a set of geotagged photos are clustered based on the coordinates of the photos. Secondly, a list of POI of a destination will detect from the geotagged photo clusters. Thirdly, a list of travel sequences will create from the geotagged photo metadata. Fourthly, a list of frequent travel patterns will extract from the created travel sequences. Lastly, a travel route will create from the extracted frequent travel patterns and detected POI.

The rest of this paper is organised as follows. Section 2 discusses the related work. Section 3 describes the methodology used to develop the system. Section 4 describes the implementation and experiment conducted on the system. Section 5 discusses the results obtained in the experiment. Section 6 concludes this paper.

2 Related Work

In recent years, the researchers have implemented various methods in their presented travel route recommendation systems. However, all the presented systems have only one purpose: recommend travel routes to travellers based on geotagged photo metadata.

Prior to recommending travel route of a destination based on geotagged photo metadata, firstly the POI in the destination need to be detected from geotagged photos. Detecting POI from geotagged photos can be considered a clustering problem of identifying POI that are often captured as photos in a destination. Clustering algorithms such as density-based spatial clustering of applications with noise (DBSCAN) [2] and mean shift [1] algorithms have been used in many works to cluster the photos of POI using the associated GPS coordinates in order to detect POI from the photos.

DBSCAN algorithm has been used in many works such as the works in [5, 7], whereas mean shift algorithm has been used in many works such as the works in [4, 9]. According to the authors of [9], there are several criteria should be satisfied during the clustering. Firstly, all the neighbouring points should be grouped together. Secondly, the clustering should be capable of accommodating arbitrary shapes. Lastly, the parameters for the clustering should be established according to the system scenario.

On the other hand, researchers for their systems to recommend travel routes to travellers often use two methods. The first method would be frequent travel pattern ranking, in which the frequent travel patterns will be extracted from geotagged photos, followed by ranking of the patterns, and finally recommend travel routes to travellers. The second method would be usage of Markov model, in which the frequent travel patterns will be extracted from geotagged photos, followed by modelling of the patterns, and finally recommend travel routes to travellers.

Based on the works in [5, 9], after the clustering of the geotagged photos taken in a destination is completed, the travel sequences based on the visiting sequence of the POI will then be created. The prefix-projected sequential pattern mining (PrefixSpan) algorithm [3], which is often used in mining frequent sequential patterns from a set of sequences, will be used to extract the frequent travel patterns from the created travel sequences. In other words, the algorithm will be used to extract all the travel patterns in which the frequency of each travel pattern is equal to or greater than the minimum support threshold. The number of travel sequences containing a travel pattern defines the frequency of the pattern.

After the frequent travel patterns are extracted from the travel sequences using the algorithm, the patterns will then be ranked by their frequencies. In this case, the authors of [5] did not propose any algorithms on frequent travel pattern ranking. On the other hand, according to the authors of [9], although the important POI might already have been covered by the top frequent travel patterns, the patterns are not informative because travellers pay more attention to the sequence of the POI. Therefore, they proposed a ranking algorithm, based on the assumptions they made about the relationship among users, locations, and travel sequences in geotagged photos.

Furthermore, Markov model is a probabilistic model that is often used in handling sequential information. Thus, the model has been used in many works such as the works in [4, 7, 8] to mine travel patterns from geotagged photos, followed by recommendations of travel route to travellers. The authors of [4] combined Markov model with topic model to build a model that can be used to predict the next POI based on the current location as well as the interest of the user. The authors of [7] used Markov chain to mine travel patterns from geotagged photos, followed by recommendations of travel route to travellers based on the country of origin of the traveller with the assumption that travellers from different countries tend to have different travel preferences. The authors of [8] generated a model from Markov model, in which the model can be used to recommend travel routes to travellers by taking the season as well as the time of the day into account.

3 Methodology

3.1 Filtering Geotagged Photos Based on Metadata of the Photos

The availability of proper geotagged photo datasets is relatively limited on the Internet. For example, a geotagged photo dataset, which is supposed to contain the metadata of geotagged photos taken in Barcelona, might contain some metadata of geotagged photos taken in London. Therefore, the filtering of geotagged photos based on the photo metadata is needed for the situation. In this case, a photo metadata consists of four attributes, which are the ID of the photo, ID of the user who captured the photo, latitude, longitude, and date taken of the photo. To facilitate the filtering of geotagged photos taken in a destination, firstly a bounding box is defined for the destination. Each bounding box contains the minimum latitude, minimum longitude, maximum latitude, and maximum longitude, which is represented by min_lat, min_lon, max_lat, and max_lon respectively. After that, for each photo coordinate which consists of a latitude and a longitude. If the latitude is lesser than or equal to max_lat and greater than or equal to min_lat, whereas the longitude is lesser than or equal to max_lon and greater than or equal to min_lon, the photo is said to have been taken in the destination. The metadata of the photo will then be used for travel route recommendation.

3.2   Clustering Geotagged Photos for POI Detection

DBSCAN algorithm is used to cluster geotagged photos based on the coordinates of the photos. This algorithm requires three parameters: a set of points, the radius, and the minimum number of points to form a cluster. Firstly, a cluster is created for grouping all noise points, and a list is created for grouping all visited points. Then, for each point in the set of points, if the point is not in the list for visited points, it will be added to the list and used to find all neighbouring points within the given radius to form a cluster. After that, if the number of neighbouring points is less than the minimum number of points to form a cluster, the visited point will add to the cluster for noise points, whereas if the number of neighbouring points is equal to or more than the minimum number of points to form a radius, a new cluster will be created. The visited point, its neighbouring points, the new cluster, the radius, and the minimum number of points to form a cluster will use to expand the cluster by finding more neighbouring points and finally form a cluster.

After all geotagged photos are clustered based on the coordinates of the photos, the coordinates of each cluster centroid will be identified. In this case, the centroid of each geotagged photo cluster is a POI in a destination, and thus a list of coordinates will create from the clusters. The list of coordinates will be retrieve the information about the POI from Google Places API Web Service.

3.3   Creating Travel Route from Geotagged Photo Metadata

There are three steps to create travel route from geotagged photo metadata. First, create travel sequences from geotagged photo metadata. Second, extract frequent travel patterns from the created travel sequences. Last, create travel route from the extracted frequent travel patterns and detected POI.

Prior to creating travel sequences from the geotagged photo metadata, all photos taken by the same user need to be grouped together. After the grouping of the photos is done, all users' photos will be sorted by date taken in order to create the travel sequences of all users. During the creation of travel sequences, if the user took more than one photo, the photo coordinates will be extracted from the photo metadata to form an ordered list of photo coordinates. In this case, the ordered list of coordinates of the photos taken by the user is the travel sequence of the user in a destination. However, some duplicate coordinates are found in the created travel sequence, and thus the removal of duplicate coordinates is needed for this situation.

PrefixSpan algorithm is used to extract frequent travel patterns from the created travel sequences. To facilitate the extraction of frequent travel patterns, a sequence-match matrix is created from a list of travel sequences. For example, given five travel sequences, the matrix will be [(0, 0), (1, 0), (2, 0), (3, 0), (4, 0)], in which each element in a sequence-match matrix consists of the index of each sequence and a starting index of zero. On the other hand, this algorithm requires three parameters: sequence pattern, minimum support threshold, and sequence-match matrix. In this case, the length of a sequence-match matrix is the frequency of a sequential pattern. Firstly, for each element in the matrix, the system will find the sequence based on the sequence index from the matrix element. Then, for each index in the range between the starting index from the matrix element and the length of the sequence, the sequence object and an empty list will add to a dictionary as key and value respectively based on the index. If the list for matrix elements is empty or if the sequence index in the last element of the list is not equal to the current sequence index, the matrix element that consists of the current sequence index and index + 1 will be appended to the list. After that, for each set of a sequence object and its frequency, if the frequency of the sequence object is greater than or equal to the minimum support threshold, a new pattern will be create by adding the sequence object to the previous pattern. Finally, the algorithm will execute again with the new pattern, same minimum support threshold, and frequency of the sequence object as parameters.

Prior to creating a travel route, firstly the extracted frequent travel patterns are sorted by the frequency, followed by the length. Then, the first pattern in the sorted list is identified as the travel route. However, most of the coordinates in the travel route are not the exact coordinates of a POI of the destination. Therefore, the distance between the coordinate in the travel route and the coordinate of each detected POI is calculated in order to identify the nearest POI to the coordinate in the travel route. After the nearest POI to the coordinate in the travel route is identified, the information about the nearest POI will be retrieved and displayed along with the travel route on the map embedded on the system.

Definition 1 (Travel Sequence). The sequence of POI visited by a traveller. For example, the travel sequence of a traveller in Kuala Lumpur is Merdeka Square – Petronas Twin Towers – KL Tower – Chinatown.

Definition 2 (Frequent Travel Pattern). The sequence of POI that are often visited by travellers. For example, the frequent travel pattern of the travellers in Kuala Lumpur is Petronas Twin Towers – KL Tower given three travel sequences as follows.

- Petronas Twin Towers – KL Tower – Merdeka Square – KL Bird Park
- Batu Caves – Petronas Twin Towers – KL Tower – Merdeka Square
- Merdeka Square – Petronas Twin Towers – KL Tower – Chinatown.

4   Implementation

There is a total of six functionalities of TRRS which are stated as follows.

- Select destination to get travel route recommendation
- Cluster geotagged photos based on coordinates of the photos
- Detect POI from geotagged photo clusters
- Create travel sequences from geotagged photo metadata
- Extract frequent travel patterns from travel sequences
- Create travel route from frequent travel patterns and detected POI.

The above functionalities are developed in Python programming language, whereas the user interface of the system is developed in JavaScript programming language.

4.1   Software and API Used

Sublime Text, Mapbox API, and Google Places API Web Service are used to develop the front-end of TRRS. On the other hand, Anaconda and Spyder[1] are used to develop the back-end of TRRS.

The purposes of the above software and API are described in the following Table 1.

Table 1. Purposes of the software and API used

Software/API	Purpose
Sublime Text	A source code editor for developing the user interface of the system
Mapbox API	A mapping API for developing the map embedded on the system
Google Places API Web Service	A web service for retrieving the information about the POI of a destination
Anaconda	A Python distribution for data processing and algorithm implementation
Spyder	A Python integrated development environment (IDE) for developing the functionalities of the system

4.2   Select Destination to Get Travel Route Recommendation

The destination drop-down list in TRRS currently only offers six destinations, which are Barcelona, Berlin, London, Paris, Rome, and Kuala Lumpur.

Upon selecting a destination from the drop-down list, the dataset containing 1000 metadata of geotagged photos taken in the destination will be loaded to the system for generating travel route recommendation. Each geotagged photo metadata usually consists of the ID of the photo, ID of the user who captured the photo, latitude, longitude, and date taken of the photo.

4.3   Cluster Geotagged Photos Based on Coordinates of the Photos

All geotagged photos will be clustered based on the coordinates of the photos using DBSCAN algorithm.

---

[1] Upon installation, Anaconda comes with Spyder, as well as the latest version of Python.

Prior to clustering the geotagged photos using the algorithm, three parameters are required, which are a set of points, the radius, and the minimum number of points to form a cluster. In this case, a list of geotagged photo coordinates is provided to the first parameter, while the second and third parameters are set to 0.0015 and 15 respectively.

4.4   Detect POI from Geotagged Photo Clusters

After the clustering of the geotagged photos, a list of POI will be detected from the geotagged photo clusters. Firstly, the centroids of the clusters will be identified, and the coordinates of the centroids will be used to search nearby POI using the function for nearby search from Google Places API Web Service with search radius of 100 m. Then, the nearest POI to the coordinates of the centroids will be identified, and all the place ID of the nearest POI will be used to retrieve the information, which are the name, type, address, opening hours, phone number, website, and coordinates of the POI, as well as the photos of the POI from Google Places API Web Service. Finally, all the POI detected from the clusters will be displayed on the map embedded on the system.

4.5   Create Travel Sequences from Geotagged Photo Metadata

A list of travel sequences will be created from the geotagged photo metadata. Firstly, all geotagged photos taken by the same user will be grouped. Then, the geotagged photos will be sorted by the date taken of the photos. After that, the coordinates of the geotagged photos will be extracted to create the travel sequence of the user. Furthermore, the duplicate coordinates will be removed from the travel sequence. Finally, the travel sequence will be displayed on the map embedded on the system.

4.6   Extract Frequent Travel Patterns from Travel Sequences

A list of frequent travel patterns will be extracted from the created travel sequences using PrefixSpan algorithm.

Prior to extracting frequent travel patterns from travel sequences using the algorithm, two parameters are required, which are a sequence database and the minimum support threshold. In this case, a list of travel sequences is provided to the first parameter, while the second parameter is set to 2.

4.7   Create Travel Route from Frequent Travel Patterns and Detected POI

A travel route will be created from the extracted frequent travel patterns and detected POI. Firstly, the extracted frequent travel patterns will be sorted by the frequency, followed by the length of the patterns. Then, the first pattern in the sorted list will be the travel route for the selected destination. After that, the coordinates in the travel route will be used to identify POI from the list of detected POI. Finally, the travel route will be displayed along with the POI on the map embedded on the system.

5 Experiments and Results

As mentioned earlier, there are five steps to generate travel route recommendation, which are the clustering of geotagged photos based on coordinates, detection of POI from geotagged photo clusters, creation of travel sequences from geotagged photo metadata, extraction of frequent travel patterns from created travel sequences, and creation of travel route from extracted frequent travel patterns and detected POI.

The experiment and result obtained in each step for each destination will be described as follows.

5.1 Cluster Geotagged Photos Based on Coordinates of the Photos

Based on Table 2, there are, averagely, 24 geotagged photo clusters that are created from the dataset of each destination. The total geotagged photo clusters for each destination are shown in the following Table 2.

Table 2. Total geotagged photo clusters for each destination

Destination	Total geotagged photo clusters
Barcelona	24
Berlin	30
London	22
Paris	25
Rome	26
Kuala Lumpur	14

5.2 Detect POI from Geotagged Photo Clusters

Based on Table 3, the POI in each destination are able to be detected from most of the geotagged photo clusters which are created from geotagged photo datasets. The total POI detected from geotagged photo clusters for each destination are shown in the following Table 3.

Table 3. Total POI detected from geotagged photo clusters for each destination

Destination	Total POI detected from geotagged photo clusters
Barcelona	24
Berlin	29
London	23
Paris	25
Rome	27
Kuala Lumpur	14

5.3   Create Travel Sequences from Geotagged Photo Metadata

Based on Table 4, there are, averagely, 89 travel sequences that are created from the metadata of geotagged photos taken in each destination. The total travel sequences for each destination are shown in the following Table 4.

Table 4. Total travel sequences for each destination

Destination	Total travel sequences
Barcelona	89
Berlin	92
London	87
Paris	86
Rome	98
Kuala Lumpur	84

5.4   Extract Frequent Travel Patterns from Travel Sequences

Based on Table 5, there are, averagely, 28 frequent travel patterns that are extracted from the travel sequences of the travellers in each destination. The total frequent travel patterns for each destination are shown in the following Table 5.

Table 5. Total frequent travel patterns for each destination

Destination	Total frequent travel patterns
Barcelona	72
Berlin	26
London	21
Paris	22
Rome	9
Kuala Lumpur	17

5.5   Create Travel Route from Frequent Travel Patterns and Detected POI

Basically, the travel route of a destination is created by ranking the frequent travel patterns according to the frequency followed by the length of the patterns, and then identifying the POI in the travel route. The travel pattern with the highest frequency or most number of POI coordinates will be the recommended travel route for the destination.

Based on Table 6, although all the travel patterns in London has the same frequency, the first travel pattern has the most number of POI coordinates, which is six, among the patterns. Therefore, the travel pattern will be the recommended travel route for London with a total of six POI (see Fig. 1).

Table 6. Ranked frequent travel patterns in London

Travel pattern	Frequency
(51.51189, −0.13373), (51.50399, −0.118073), (51.503732, −0.128724), (51.513821, −0.101679), (51.481886, −0.007177), (51.505875, −0.076202)	2
(51.496413, −0.138838), (51.505355, −0.075803), (51.504992, −0.085905), (51.511624, −0.135455), (51.506207, −0.074718)	2
(51.496413, −0.138838), (51.505355, −0.075803), (51.504992, −0.085905), (51.511624, −0.135455), (51.505389, −0.154672)	2

Fig. 1. Recommended travel route for London with six POI

In addition, based on Table 7, there are, averagely, five POI in a travel route for one-day trip to each destination. The total POI in the travel route for each destination are shown in the following Table 7.

Table 7. Total POI in the travel route for each destination

Destination	Total POI in the travel route
Barcelona	4
Berlin	6
London	6
Paris	5
Rome	5
Kuala Lumpur	6

5.6 Summary of Experiments and Results

Overall, the travel route of each destination is successfully generated by the system in five steps based on the metadata of geotagged photos taken in each destination.

The first step – cluster geotagged photos based on coordinates of the photos – returned, averagely, 24 geotagged photo clusters for all destinations.

In the second step – detect POI from geotagged photo clusters, the POI are able to be detected for all destinations from most of the geotagged photo clusters.

The third step – create travel sequences from geotagged photo metadata – returned, averagely, 89 travel sequences for all destinations.

The fourth step – extract frequent travel patterns from travel sequences – returned, averagely, 28 frequent travel patterns for all destinations.

The last step – create travel route from frequent travel patterns and detected POI – returned, averagely, five POI in the travel routes for all destinations.

6 Conclusion and Future Work

Although all the features of TRRS are working as intended, the detection of POI relies heavily on the centroid of the clusters because restaurants, bars and hotels may be detected from the cluster centroids. In addition, the detection of POI from geotagged photo clusters may be time-consuming because the information of all detected POI need to be retrieved upon sending requests from the system to Google Places API Web Service and then followed by returning results from Google Places API Web Service to the system. Furthermore, the photos of all detected POI to be used in creating markers on the map and displaying in the popup need to be retrieved separately from Google Places API Web Service, and thus the detection of POI may be prolonged.

The travel route created from extracted frequent travel patterns and detected POI is currently displayed on the map with a few numbered markers. In other words, the marker which is labelled as 1 is the first POI that people normally visit when travelling in the destination. The travel route could be displayed on the map with not only a few numbered markers, but also lines to connect all markers from the first marker to the last marker to create a sequence of markers on the map. In addition, the distance between the markers and estimated travelling time taken from one point to another could be calculated and displayed above the line connecting the markers. By manoeuvring the mouse over the line, users can improvise their itinerary in terms of transportations arrangement and time spent at each place.

References

1. Cheng, Y.: Mean shift, mode seeking, and clustering. IEEE Trans. Pattern Anal. Mach. Intell. **17**(8), 790–799 (1995)
2. Ester, M., Kriegel, H.P., Sander, J., Xu, X.: A density-based algorithm for discovering clusters in large spatial databases with noise. In: 2nd International Conference on Knowledge Discovery and Data Mining, Portland, Oregon, USA, pp. 226–231. AAAI (1996)
3. Pei, J., Han, J., Mortazavi-Asl, B., Pinto, H., Chen, Q., Dayal, U., Hsu, M.C.: PrefixSpan: mining sequential patterns efficiently by prefix-projected pattern growth. In: 17th International Conference on Data Engineering, Heidelberg, Germany, pp. 215–224. IEEE (2001)

4. Kurashima, T., Iwata, T., Irie, G., Fujimura, K.: Travel route recommendation using geotags in photo sharing sites. In: 19th ACM International Conference on Information and Knowledge Management, Toronto, ON, Canada, pp. 579–588. ACM (2010)
5. Majid, A., Chen, L., Mirza, H.T., Hussain, I., Chen, G.: A system for mining interesting tourist locations and travel sequences from public geo-tagged photos. Data Knowl. Eng. **95**, 66–86 (2015)
6. Okuyama, K., Yanai, K.: A travel planning system based on travel trajectories extracted from a large number of geotagged photos on the web. In: The Era of Interactive Media, pp. 657–670 (2013)
7. Vu, H.Q., Li, G., Law, R., Ye, B.H.: Exploring the travel behaviors of inbound tourists to Hong Kong using geotagged photos. Tour. Manag. **46**, 222–232 (2015)
8. Yamasaki, T., Gallagher, A., Chen, T.: Personalized intra-and inter-destination travel recommendation using large-scale geotags. In: 2nd ACM International Workshop on Geotagging and its Applications in Multimedia, Barcelona, Spain, pp. 25–30. ACM (2013)
9. Yin, Z., Cao, L., Han, J., Luo, J., Huang, T.S.: Diversified trajectory pattern ranking in geo-tagged social media. In: 2011 SIAM International Conference on Data Mining, Mesa, Arizona, USA, pp. 980–991. SIAM (2011)

Predicting Traffic Flow Based on Average Speed of Neighbouring Road Using Multiple Regression

Bagus Priambodo[1,2(✉)] and Azlina Ahmad[1]

[1] Institute of Visual Informatics, Universiti Kebangsaan Malaysia,
Bangi, Malaysia
bagus.priambodo@mercubuana.ac.id,
azlinaivi@ukm.edu.my
[2] Information System, Universitas Mercu Buana, Jakarta, Indonesia

Abstract. The prediction of traffic flow is a challenge. There are many factors that can affect traffic flow. One of the factors is an inter path relationship between neighbouring roads. For example, an individual incidents (such as accidents) may cause ripple effects (a cascading failure) which then spreads and creates a sustained traffic jam the neighbouring area. To know the relationship between road segments we propose multiple regression method to predict the traffic based on the nearby surrounding roads. The prediction factor is chosen from a high-relation road with the path to be searched. To know the relationship between roads we calculate their correlation among neighbouring roads. The results are then displayed on the map for further observation. From this study, we demonstrate that multiple regression method can be used to predict impact of speed of vehicles on neighbouring roads on traffic flows.

Keywords: Traffic flow prediction · Multiple regressions · Traffic flow propagation

1 Introduction

Traffic congestion is a condition in which road users exceed the capability of the road. Characteristic features of road congestion are slow speed, longer travel time, and the length of the queue of cars on the road. During past few years, numerous algorithms for traffic flow prediction have been proposed to predict traffic flow. One interesting research is about impact of road flow of neighbouring road. Previous research in analysis of traffic flow shows when there is a traffic jam or slow speed situation on a road, it will impact other roads [2, 3, 15]. This finding is important for road users as they can avoid impacted roads with slow traffic or traffic jam by providing alternative roads.

2 Related Work

Time series models are widely used to predict traffic flow and traffic congestion. Time series predictions are based on historical data on the same road location. The Arima method [1, 7, 16] is often used for time series prediction. The seasonal Arima model

© Springer International Publishing AG 2017
H. Badioze Zaman et al. (Eds.): IVIC 2017, LNCS 10645, pp. 309–318, 2017.
https://doi.org/10.1007/978-3-319-70010-6_29

shows high performance in traffic flow forecasting [1], performance improvement using Arima method can also be done with addition of day classification [7]. In addition to Arima and regression [6], neural networks are also commonly used for traffic flow prediction [10] and traffic congestion based on time series, among others: [5] using linear fuzzy for short time prediction on toll roads to design a number of sensors on the highway, [8] based on the similarity of space and time. Considering many factors that can affect the flow of traffic than many traffic flow predictions is done using multivariate methods. Among them are predicting the traffic road safety level based on the licensed drivers, factor, Gross Domestic Product and accident using multilevel regression and predicting traffic [12] based on weather data using neural networks [11]. Short time prediction use neural networks based on speed data from various vehicles, days, and traffic density.

Aside from predictions using both linear and nonlinear methods, there are also other methods used to predict traffic flow. The road congestion prediction is based on the slices of the crossroads using the BML model [9]. Traffic prediction is based on similarity of traffic congestion pattern [13] but the result is not satisfactory.

In predicting traffic flow and traffic congestion on a road, many factors are involved which include previous data, [16] vehicle speed [11], weather [12], and accidents [3]. Another factor that affects traffic congestion on a road is congestion at neighbouring road. Previous research in this aspect of road congestion are the inter-road relationship extracted using of the 3D Markov model [2], visualizing and highlighting impact traffic seen as affecting adjacent roads [3], the visualization of traffic jam which reflects the spread of traffic flow [15], the detection of traffic jam based on the slices between the intersections which indicates an inter path relationship [9] and mining congestion between road segments [14].

3 Problem

Many factors influence traffic flow. Factors such as history [16], vehicle speeds [11], weathers [12], accidents [3], and special days or events can be used to predict traffic flows. In addition to the factors we have mentioned, the congestion level factor on neighbouring roads greatly affects road congestion. Previous research which involves extracting inter-road relationship [2], visualizing traffic accident impact with high lights [3], spreading of traffic flow when visualizing traffic jam [15], detection of traffic congestion based on intersection [9], and mining congestion between road links [14], have assumed that in the traffic flow there is a relationship between neighbouring roads.

The strong relationship between one road and the other roads around it makes the road a strong candidate for factor input in predicting speed on the road. This type of prediction can help in predicting road speed on roads that have damaged sensor or missing data. The surrounding road traffic can be used as a tool to predict traffic flow propagation. As we can see in Fig. 1, road 158324 is influenced by the road that surrounds it. If there is traffic jam or road congestion on the neighbouring road it will affect the average speed on the road 158324.

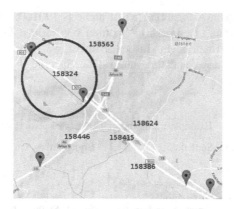

Fig. 1. Road 158324 and its neighbouring road.

4 Methodology

Our research methodology is described as follows:

1. Data set.
2. Determining relationship between road segments using correlation method between road segments among neighbouring roads.
3. Predicting the speed using multiple regression method.

4.1 Data Set

Our data set is taken from IoT traffic sensor in Aarhus, Denmark [17, 18]. The total number of IoT sensors are 449 sensors as we can see in Fig. 2.

Fig. 2. Map of 449 Iot traffic sensors in city of Aarhus, Denmark.

An example sensors in A location, sensor name is 190100. This sensor are placed from Nørreport 93 Aarhus, Denmark to Spanien 63 Aarhus, Denmark, the distance between points is 1490 meters. In this experiment we only use average speed as representation of traffic flow, and timestamp data. Specific details of this sensor are described in Tables 1 and 2.

Table 1. Example traffic data taken from sensor 190100.

Duration from	Duration to	Start point	End point	Cross observation point data
2014-10-01 01:45:00	2014-11-13 10:40:00	City: Aarhus Street: Nørreport 93 Postal Code: 8000 Coordinates (lat, long): 56.161017815103236, 10.21197608217426	City: Aarhus Street: Spanien 63 Postal Code: 8000 Coordinates (lat, long): 56.14892750591274, 10.209599775463175	Distance between two points in meters: 1490 Duration of measurements in seconds: 202 NDT in KMH: 27 EXT ID: 359 Road type: MAJOR_ROAD

Table 2. Example traffic data taken from sensor 190100.

Status	avg Measured Time	avg Speed	Ext ID	median Measured Time	TIMES TAMP	Vehicle count	_id	REPORT_ID
OK	376	14	1051	376	2014-08-01T08:30:00	4	20749724	190100
OK	225	23	1051	225	2014-08-01T08:40:00	3	20750622	190100
OK	285	18	1051	285	2014-08-01T08:50:00	2	20751520	190100

4.2 Determining Relationship Between Road Segments Among Neighbouring Roads

To predict average speed using neighbouring road, we need to find the highest correlation among all roads in neighbouring roads. We consider a neighboring road is a road that has a distance approximately four kilometers from the road location. We calculate correlation among all neighbouring roads using formula (1).

$$Cor_{xy} = \frac{\sum_{i=1}^{n}(x_i - \bar{x}) \cdot (y_i - \bar{y})}{\sqrt{\sum_{i=1}^{n}(x_i - \bar{x})^2 \cdot \sum_{i=1}^{n}(y_i - \bar{y})^2}} \tag{1}$$

We calculate correlation of all neighbouring roads based on the median value of average speed at 11.00 am to 13.00 pm from 01-08-2014 until 28-09-2014. We choose 11:00 am to 13:00 pm because at the time vehicles are always passing through the sensor or vehicle count > 0. In this paper, we only discuss the results of two roads which is road 158324 and road 158744. The neighbouring road of correlation of road 158324 is shown in Fig. 3 and the result of correlation of road 158324 is described in Table 3. The neighbouring road of correlation of correlation of road 158744 is shown in Fig. 4 and the results of correlation of road 158744 is described in Table 4.

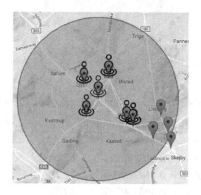

Fig. 3. Neighbouring road 158324 and correlation results.

Table 3. Correlation result of road 158324.

Roads	Correlation results	Distance (km)
158624	**0.789**	1.104
158386	**0.770**	1.867
158595	**0.757**	2.197
158415	**0.715**	0.975
158475	**0.701**	1.104
158446	**0.686**	1.143
158536	**0.637**	2.197
158355	**0.629**	1.104
171969	**0.641**	1.104
172329	0.514993548	1.867

4.3 Predicting the Speed Using Multiple Regression Method

First, we predict average speed on road 158324. We choose the road that has correlation values > 6, obtained nine roads to become independent variables. Nine independent variables are road 158624, road 158386, road 158595, road 158415, road 158475, road 158446, road 158536, road 158355 and road 171969. One dependent variable is road 158324 (Y). The data was taken from 01-08-2014 to 28-09-2014 15:00 pm. We obtained the coefficients of multiple regressions as follow:

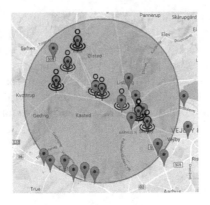

Fig. 4. Neighbouring road 158744 and correlation results.

Table 4. Correlation result of road 158744

Roads	Correlation results	Distance (km)
158954	**0.436660191**	1.157
158446	**0.425732191**	2.629
158505	**0.414264573**	2.196
158475	**0.393660707**	2.382
159014	**0.378868354**	2.826
158595	**0.378515879**	0.018
158565	0.34790664	2.629
158924	0.342129916	0.349

$$Y = -1.412068 + 0.060048X_1 + 0.281535X_2 + 0.184692X_3 + 0.020628X_4$$
$$- 0.002242X_5 + 0.123846X_6 + 0.071511X_7 + 0.039800X_8 + 0.047805X_9 \quad (2)$$

Results of prediction and deviation of error rate are described in Table 5 below.

Table 5. Results of 158324 traffic flow prediction.

Time	Prediction	Actual	MAD	MSE	RMSE	MAPE
15:05	61.0715	60	1.07	1.15	1.07	1.75
15:10	63.0549	68	3.01	12.80	3.58	4.80
15:15	63.2426	68	3.59	16.08	4.01	5.71
15:20	64.3689	65	2.85	12.16	3.49	4.53
15:25	62.4896	60	2.78	10.97	3.31	4.42
15:30	61.0362	60	2.49	9.32	3.05	3.96

Second, we predict the average speed on road 158744. We choose the road that has correlation values > 3.5 since there is no road that has correlation value with road 158744 above 0.6, obtained six roads to become independent variables. Independent variables used to find dependent variable of road 158744 (Y), were road 158954, road 158446, road 158505, road 158475, road 159014 and road 158595. The data taken from 01-08-2014 to 28-09-2014 15:00 pm. We get the coefficients of multiple regressions as follows:

$$Y = 56.432470 + 0.115115X_1 + 0.005259X_2 + 0.084683X_3$$
$$- 0.151605 X_4 + 0.285097X_5 - 0.004562X_6 \tag{3}$$

Results of prediction and deviation of error rate are described in Table 6 below.

Table 6. Results of road 158744 traffic flow prediction.

Time	Prediction	Actual	MAD	MSE	RMSE	MAPE
15:05	92.01	84	8.01	64.22	8.01	8.71
15:10	84.63	87	5.19	34.91	5.91	5.75
15:15	82.87	82	3.75	23.53	4.85	4.19
15:20	89.16	79	5.35	43.45	6.59	5.99
15:25	90.40	79	6.56	60.75	7.79	7.31
15:30	91.40	81	7.20	68.66	8.29	7.99

5   Results and Discussion

After conducting the experiments, we calculate the error of prediction using mean absolute deviation (MAD), mean square error (MSE), root mean square error (RMSE), and mean absolute percentage error (MAPE). Using result from Tables 5 and 6. and using line chart shown in Figs. 5 and 6, results indicate that prediction average speed in road 158324 is more accurate than prediction in road 158744. Deviation error between predicted value and actual value in road 158744 is higher in road 158324.

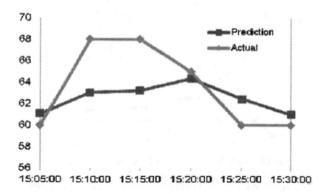

Fig. 5. Average speed prediction in 158324

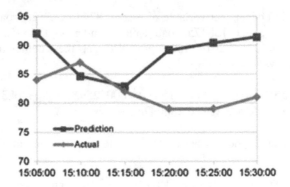

Fig. 6. Average speed prediction in 158744

A clearer result can be seen using line chart as shown in Figs. 7 and 8. Both figures show clearly that the results of predicted value in road 158744 is less accurate compared to predicted value in road 158324. The error trend on road 158744 is greater for long interval. While at road 158324, result is positive since the error trend is lower. From Tables 3 and 4 it can be seen that the correlation neighbouring road 158324 has a higher value than the correlation value of neighbouring road 158744, since all road correlation values are above 0.6. This is different from the correlation values at road 158744, which all correlation values are below 0.6. The high correlation value indicates that the prediction of average speed at road 158324 is better or more accurate than prediction of average speed at road 158744. The question is what factors caused the correlation value in road 158744 lower than road 158324 since there are also correlation on other paths which value is below 0.6. This is probably due to location of the roads, the average speed on the roads, and the number of vehicles passing through the roads which leads to the differences in the value of correlation.

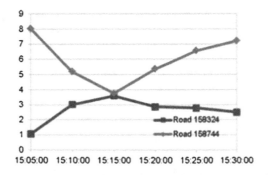

Fig. 7. Line chart MAD between road 158324 and 158744

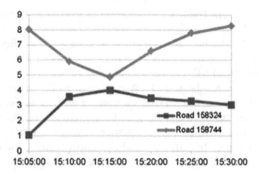

Fig. 8. Line chart RMSE between Road 158324 and 158744

6 Conclusion

Our research aims to investigate the impact of traffic flow of one road on traffic flow of neighbouring roads. The experiments conducted shows that there is a relationship between a road and its neighboring roads. The strong relationship between one road and the other road around it, makes it an important factor for predicting traffic flow. The experiments show that high correlation roads can be used to predict the value of average speed for short time prediction. However, not all roads have high correlation value with their neighbouring roads. The location of roads, the average speed on the roads, the number of vehicles passing through the road are possible factors that lead to the difference in correlation value of the road.

References

1. Abadi, A., Rajabioun, T., Ioannou, P.A.: Traffic flow prediction for road transportation networks with limited traffic data. IEEE Trans. Intell. Transp. Syst. **16**, 653–662 (2015). doi:10.1109/TITS.2014.2337238
2. Ahn, J., Ko, E., Kim, E.Y.: Highway traffic flow prediction using support vector regression and Bayesian classifier. In: 2016 International Conference on Big Data Smart Computing, pp. 239–244 (2016). doi:10.1109/BIGCOMP.2016.7425919
3. Anwar, A., Nagel, T., Ratti, C.: Traffic origins: a simple visualization technique to support traffic incident analysis. IEEE Pacific Visualization Symposium, pp. 316–319 (2014). doi:10.1109/PacificVis.2014.35
4. Cai, H., Yan, L., Zhu, D.: Traffic Safety Level in China, pp. 363–369 (2015)
5. Chan, K.Y., Dillon, T.S.: Traffic flow prediction using orthogonal arrays and Takagi-Sugenoneural fuzzy models (2014)
6. Dai, H., Yang, Z.: Real-time traffic volume estimation with fuzzy linear regression. In: 2006 6th World Congress on Intelligent Control and Automation, pp. 3164–3167 (2006). doi:10.1109/WCICA.2006.1712950
7. Dong, H,, Jia, I , Sun, X,, Li, C., Qin, Y.. Road traffic flow prediction with a time-oriented ARIMA model, pp. 1649–1652 (2009). doi:10.1109/NCM.2009.224
8. Hu, C., Xie, K., Song, G., Wu, T.: Hybrid process neural network based on spatio-temporal similarities for short-term traffic flow prediction, pp. 253–258 (2008)

9. Hu, W., Yan, L., Wang, H.: Traffic jams prediction method based on two-dimension cellular automata model (2014)
10. Kumar, K., Parida, M., Katiyar, V.K.: Short term traffic flow prediction for a non urban highway using artificial neural network. Procedia - Soc. Behav. Sci. **104**, 755–764 (2013). doi:10.1016/j.sbspro.2013.11.170
11. Lee, J., Hong, B., Lee, K., Jang, Y.-J.: A prediction model of traffic congestion using weather data. In: 2015 IEEE International Conference on Data Science and Data Intensive Data Science and Data Intensive Systems, pp. 81–88 (2015). doi:10.1109/DSDIS.2015.96
12. Lee, K., Hong, B., Jeong, D., Lee, J.: Congestion pattern model for predicting short-term traffic decongestion times. In: 2014 17th IEEE International Conference on Intelligent Transportation Systems, ITSC 2014, pp. 2828–2833 (2014). doi:10.1109/ITSC.2014. 695814313
13. Wang, Y., Cao, J., Li, W., Gu, T.: Mining traffic congestion correlation between road segments on GPS trajectories. In: 2016 IEEE International Conference Smart Computing, SMARTCOMP 2016 (2016). doi:10.1109/SMARTCOMP.2016.7501704
14. Wang, Z., Lu, M., Yuan, X., Zhang, J., Van De Wetering, H.: Visual traffic jam analysis based on trajectory data. IEEE Trans. Vis. Comput. Graph. **19**, 2159–2168 (2013)
15. Xiong, W., Yu, Z., Eeckhout, L., Bei, Z., Zhang, F., Xu, C.: SZTS: a novel big data transportation system benchmark suite. In: Proceedings of the International Conference on Parallel Process, pp. 819–828, December 2015. doi:10.1109/ICPP.2015.91
16. Zhang, R., Shu, Y., Yang, Z., Cheng, P., Chen, J.: Hybrid traffic speed modeling and prediction using real-world data. In: 2015 Proceeding of IEEE International Congress on Big Data, BigData Congress 2015, pp. 230–237 (2015). doi:10.1109/BigDataCongress.2015.40
17. Tönjes, R., Barnaghi, P., Ali, M., Mileo, A., Hauswirth, M., Ganz, F., Ganea, S., Kjærgaard, B., Kuemper, D., Nechifor, S., Puiu, D., Sheth, A., Tsiatsis, V., Vestergaard, L.: Real time IoT stream processing and large-scale data analytics for smart city applications. Poster Session European Conference on Networks and Communications (2014)
18. Bischof, S., Karapantelakis, A., Nechifor, C.-S., Sheth, A., Mileo, A., Barnaghi, P.: Semantic modeling of smart city data. Position Paper in W3C Workshop on the Web of Things: Enablers and Services for an Open Web of Devices, 25–26 June 2014, Berlin, Germany (2014)

People Detection and Pose Classification Inside a Moving Train Using Computer Vision

Sergio A. Velastin[1,2(✉)] and Diego A. Gómez-Lira[3]

[1] Department of Computer Science, Universidad Carlos III de Madrid,
Colmenarejo 28270, Madrid, Spain
sergio.velastin@ieee.org
[2] Queen Mary University of London, London, UK
[3] Department of Informatics Engineering, Universidad de Santiago de Chile,
Santiago, Chile
diegog.asd@gmail.com

Abstract. The use of surveillance video cameras in public transport is increasingly regarded as a solution to control vandalism and emergency situations. The widespread use of cameras brings in the problem of managing high volumes of data, resulting in pressure on people and resources. We illustrate a possible step to automate the monitoring task in the context of a moving train (where popular background removal algorithms will struggle with rapidly changing illumination). We looked at the detection of people in three possible postures: Sat down (on a train seat), Standing and Sitting (half way between sat down and standing). We then use the popular Histogram of Oriented Gradients (HOG) descriptor to train Support Vector Machines to detect people in any of the predefined postures. As a case study, we use the public BOSS dataset. We show different ways of training and combining the classifiers obtaining a sensitivity performance improvement of about 12% when using a combination of three SVM classifiers instead of a global (all classes) classifier, at the expense of an increase of 6% in false positive rate. We believe this is the first set of public results on people detection using the BOSS dataset so that future researchers can use our results as a baseline to improve upon.

Keywords: People detection · Posture classification · People monitoring · On-board surveillance · Machine learning

1 Introduction

The use of surveillance cameras for the prevention and management of criminal incidents is becoming increasingly common. Santiago de Chile saw in 2010 an increase of 78% in the number of cameras (313 extra cameras in 24 city districts) with an investment of over 800 thousand US dollars [1]. Furthermore, in 2013 Metro Santiago announced that it will install surveillance cameras in the more than 185 new trains to become operational in the next few years. Elsewhere, the UK is one of the world leaders in this field, [2] cites a report from Big Brother Watch claiming that there are about 51,000 police-run cameras in urban areas, with an investment of 807 million euros in the last four years and the country estimated to have 20% of the security

© Springer International Publishing AG 2017
H. Badioze Zaman et al. (Eds.): IVIC 2017, LNCS 10645, pp. 319–330, 2017.
https://doi.org/10.1007/978-3-319-70010-6_30

cameras in the world. Nevertheless, it has been reported that only one crime is solved for every 1,000 cameras [3] highlighting the need for automatic means of detecting unusual situations and where computer vision can assist. It is assumed here that the reader is reasonably familiar with computer vision and image processing techniques. In the context of this work, we focus on machine learning techniques, specifically Support Vector Machines (SVMs), e.g. see [4, 5] and pedestrian detection using Histograms of Oriented Gradients [6]. Learning machines are used to recognize patterns typically using labeled examples [7]. Popular learning machines in computer vision include SVMs [8], Adaboost [9] and neural networks (including the increasingly successful "deep" learners [10–12]). There are surprisingly little reports on the use of BOSS [13]. Truong Cong et al. [14, 15] report a foreground estimation and person re-identification approach, but it is not clear how it can deal with stationary people, nor they consider different postures. More recently Coniglio et al. [16] present an interesting approach based on shape priors, HOG and multiple SVMs but it is not clear how they deal with different poses.

In this work, we look at the classification performance of the HOG descriptor combined with a binary SVM. In our case, the observed people are contained within a normalized window of 128×256 pixels with a block size of 16 pixels, with an overlap of 8 pixels, cells of 8×8 pixels, 4 cells/block and 9 bins. Therefore, the HOG descriptor is of size 16740 (floating point numbers). The overall idea is to collect sufficient samples of people (at the different poses that need to be classified) and of *not people* (negative samples), compute the corresponding descriptors and train a classifier to separate such sample populations. In the sections that follow, we will first describe the dataset and the procedure to obtain such samples and then the results of the classification process.

2 The Dataset

For this work, we used the public BOSS dataset as it contains a series of semi-realistic videos of people acting out incidents (such as thefts, fights, fainting, etc.) as well as normal behavior inside a moving train (thus with sometimes rapidly changing illumination), using 9–10 cameras. The dataset has a sixteen video sequences (the language refers to the audio that was also recorded), including:

1. Cell phone Spanish: struggle between two people and theft of a cell phone.
2. Checkout French: appearance of three people, in which a fight between two of them occurs.
3. Disease: Person fainting.
4. Disease public: Person fainting, plus six people helping.
5. Faces (4 sequences): different people walking along the train corridor.
6. Harass French: harassment of a passenger by another.
7. Harass Spanish: harassment of a passenger by another.
8. Harass French 2: harassment of a passenger by another plus 5 witnesses.
9. Newspaper French: fight between two passengers over a newspaper with 4 witnesses.

10. Newspaper Spanish: fight between two passengers over a newspaper with 4 witnesses.
11. No event (2 sequences): Between seven to ten people talking or greeting each other.
12. Panic: Eleven people fleeing the train.

Ultimately, it will be useful to investigate human action/interaction recognition algorithms that could identify the above situations. However, there are not enough examples on this video set to train such systems and in any case, before actions/interactions could be detected a system would typically need first to detect/track each individual in the images and their postures. As this is still a challenging problem (especially when dealing with multiple postures and rapid illumination changes), that is what we concentrate on in this paper. For our experiments, we used data from camera 1, an example of which is shown in Fig. 1.

Fig. 1. View from camera 1 (BOSS dataset)

The BOSS dataset only provides annotations at the level of actions/interaction and not of the position and posture of each person, so we had to create such ground truth (this is available upon request from the authors). We used the VIPER-GT [17] annotation tool, using three attributes for each person every eight frame (to save some effort): ID (a unique identifier assigned to a person when he/she appears for the first time in the scene), Body (a rectangular bounding box) and Status (the posture class coded as 0: Sat down, 1: Sitting (half-way between Sat down and Standing), and 2: Standing).

2.1   Ground-Truthing

The ground-truthing process consists of five sequential stages:

Video Labeling.
This process consists on using VIPER-GT to manually localize and label each person in each frame of the video (this is therefore the most time-consuming part) as illustrated in Fig. 2a.

Pre-processing.
Once the frames have been labeled, the images for each labeled pedestrian are extracted to be used later as positive training samples for the classifiers. This is illustrated in

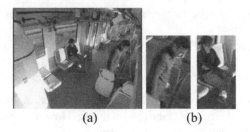

(a)   (b)

Fig. 2. (a) Labeling each person in the video (ID, bounding box and status), (b) extracted pedestrians

Fig. 2b. It should be noted that in fact, we extract an additional border of 10% of the annotated bounding boxes, following the finding in [6] that the inclusion of some background improves the performance of the classifier. These are referred as *expanded* bounding boxes/images.

Under the hypothesis that we want to avoid too much occlusion in the positive training samples, a further check is done on bounding boxes in each frame. For a given *expanded* bounding box, its intersection I_{eu} with other non-expanded bounding box in the same frame is calculated by:

$$I_{eu} = \frac{A_e \cap A_u}{A_e \cup A_u} \tag{1}$$

where A_e is the area of the expanded box and A_u the area of an unexpanded box. If the intersection is *greater* than a given threshold (τ_{ov}) then the candidate expanded sample is *discarded*. An illustration of intersection is shown in Fig. 3 To evaluate the effect of this process of positive samples selection, we have conducted tests for values of $\tau_{ov} = 1.0$, 0.5 and 0.2 yielding 16323, 13852 and 6698 positive samples respectively. Note that a value of 1.0 means that all samples arc accepted even if they are fully occluded.

Fig. 3. Intersection of bounding boxes

Extraction of Positive Images.
This consists on using the ground truth annotation and the intersection rule to extract positive samples (including the additional border). An illustrative example is shown in Fig. 4.

Fig. 4. An image and the corresponding extracted positive sample (in this case of status "Sat down")

Image Normalization.

A restriction with most learning machines (including SVM) is that the feature vectors for all samples (positives and negatives) need to be of the same dimension. An additional restriction in our case is that the OpenCV implementation of HOG needs the size (horizontal and vertical) of the images to be a multiple of 8. As pedestrian images in the original annotations vary in size, we have used OpenCV's *resize* function to resize all positive samples obtained after stage 3 above, to a size of 128×256 (these are close to the mean sizes of the annotated images).

Extraction of Negative Examples.

Negative samples are image regions (normalized as explained above) that contain no people. Given the ground truth, we know where people are and so what can be done is to sample the video images randomly making sure that such samples do not overlap regions containing people. In this way, a very large number of negative samples (compared to the number of positives) can be obtained. To reduce the size of such population, we use the following rules (in each case the resulting negative samples are then size normalized to 128×256):

- For each frame without people, we obtain five random (location and size) negative images (the literature tells us that a ratio of five negatives for one positive is popular).
- In frames with people, for each person we get a random sample of the same size and checking that it does not overlap more than a given fraction (as above) with any annotated person.

In this way, a total of 23990 negative samples were obtained. That population of negative samples is maintained constant for all the experiments so as not introduce a random element. This will also allow a better comparison of algorithms should other researchers wish to use the same data (available upon request from the authors).

2.2 Sample Groups and Sizes

To evaluate the performance of various machines, different groups of positives, depending on the position of people and the intersection with others were used:

By Posture.
We separated the positive samples into four groups. The three first groups correspond to samples in each of the posture categories (Sat down, Sitting, Standing) while the last group contains all samples irrespective of their posture and we called this **Full**.

By Intersection.
These correspond to the groups obtained by varying the maximum allowed overlap as explained earlier and called "**1.0**", "**0.5**" and "**0.2**".

The above groupings resulted in the following numbers of positive samples (Table 1):

Table 1. Positive samples groupings

1.0 (100%)	0.5 (50%)	0.2 (20%)
Sat down: 11218	Sat down: 9232	Sat down: 3428
Sitting: 1198	Sitting: 1079	Sitting: 640
Standing: 3907	Standing: 3541	Standing: 2630
Full: 16323	Full: 13852	Full: 6698

3   Experimental Classification Results

The descriptors for each of the negative and samples can be calculated using OpenCV's *compute()* method in its *HOGDescriptor* class. The different groupings outlined above form the basis for different experiments. In each case, we use OpenCV's SVM implementation to train classifiers. We use 10-fold cross validation meaning that in each group we take 10% of the samples as a testing set and the remaining 90% as a training set, computing results (mean, variances) for 10 possible 10%:90% partitions. We compute *sensitivity (S)* and *false positive rate (FPR)*:

$$S = \frac{TP}{TP + FN}, \quad FPR = \frac{FP}{TP + FP} \tag{2}$$

where *TP* is the number of true positives, *FN* the number of false negatives and *FP* the number of false positives.

3.1   Global vs. Specific SVM

The first test is to evaluate the performance of a classifier that considers all postures and compare it with classifiers trained on specific postures to see if such specialization is useful for the purposes of pedestrian detection (independently of postures). The aggregated cross-validation results for sensitivity and FPR are shown in Table 2.

These indicate that in all cases, the global classifier has a poorer performance than the more specialized classifiers. The results for the other two intersections are given in Tables 3 and 4 that confirm this finding and show that results tend to improve with less occluded training samples (but this effect might be due to the smaller variability in the less occluded samples, recalling that these resulted from discarding positive samples).

Table 2. Mean sensitivity and FPR for intersection 1.0 (ERROR is standard deviation)

	Sensitivity	ERROR	FPR	ERROR
Global	0.790	0.053	0.253	0.109
Sat down	0.817	**0.037**	0.128	0.052
Sitting	0.830	0.043	**0.056**	**0.017**
Standing	**0.850**	0.043	0.132	0.026

Table 3. Mean sensitivity and FPR for intersection 0.5

	Sensitivity	ERROR	FPR	ERROR
Global	0.810	0.035	0.205	0.095
Sat down	0.857	0.057	0.124	0.066
Sitting	0.868	0.037	**0.045**	**0.009**
Standing	**0.889**	**0.020**	0.097	0.017

Table 4. Mean sensitivity and FPR for intersection 0.2

	Sensitivity	ERROR	FPR	ERROR
Global	0.860	0.031	0.158	0.070
Sat down	**0.941**	**0.021**	0.058	0.022
Sitting	0.877	0.045	**0.039**	0.014
Standing	0.907	0.022	0.073	**0.011**

Overall, the more specific classifiers show an improvement of between 1–8% in sensitivity and 8-20% in FPR.

3.2 Use of Cross-Negatives

By "cross" negatives we mean people samples from a different class that are used as negative training samples (e.g. using "Sat down" positive samples as negative samples to train a "Standing" classifier). We have experimented with adding different proportions of such samples (10%, 20% and 50% taken equally from the remaining two classes), obtaining the results shown in Tables 5, 6 and 7. In none of these cases the addition of this type of negative samples improved the performance of the individual of these classifiers.

Table 5. Mean sensitivity and FPR for "Sat Down" classifier, using cross negatives

	Sensitivity	ERROR	FPR	ERROR
Sat down	**0.941**	**0.021**	**0.058**	**0.022**
Sat down + 10%	0.914	0.032	0.066	0.023
Sat down + 25%	0.880	0.028	0.077	0.031
Sat down + 50%	0.859	0.031	0.084	0.036

Table 6. Mean sensitivity and FPR for "Sitting" classifier, using cross negatives

	Sensitivity	ERROR	FPR	ERROR
Sitting	**0.877**	**0.045**	**0.039**	**0.014**
Sitting + 10%	0.777	0.066	0.067	0.016
Sitting + 25%	0.719	0.108	0.082	**0.014**
Sitting + 50%	0.730	0.058	0.106	0.019

Table 7. Mean sensitivity and FPR for "Standing" classifier, using cross negatives

	Sensitivity	ERROR	FPR	ERROR
Standing	**0.907**	**0.022**	**0.073**	**0.011**
Standing + 10%	0.886	0.032	0.103	0.022
Standing + 25%	0.847	0.062	0.111	0.026
Standing + 50%	0.829	0.034	0.122	0.020

3.3   General vs. Combined Classifier

In this experiment, we investigate if the better performance we have seen in the individual classifiers could be maintained by combining them as an alternative to the global classifier. The steps in this experiment are:

- Separate training: Each classifier is independently trained as reported earlier (using an intersection of 0.2). The negative samples set is the same for each classifier.
- Separate testing: For each test image, each classifier is evaluated.
- Combination by voting: if at least one classifier indicates the presence of a person, then a person is deemed to have been detected. If no classifier detects a person, then no person is detected.

The results of this type of combination are shown in Table 8. There is an improvement in sensitivity of 11.8%, but at the expense of an increase in FPR of 6.3% (as it might be expected given the combination rule).

Table 8. Sensitivity and FPR for the global and the combined classifiers (intersection = 0.2)

	Sensitivity	ERROR	FPR	ERROR
Global	0.860	0.031	**0.158**	0.070
Combination	**0.978**	**0.007**	0.221	**0.058**

3.4   Using the Distance to the Hyperplane

In all the above experiments, we have used the default behavior of the SVM software, which returns the distance to the hyperplane. If this distance is negative the result is taken as a person detection, otherwise a no person detection. In other words, the decision boundary is at zero. It might be useful to explore if performance could be improved by changing this boundary. Figure 5 shows the distribution of the distance to

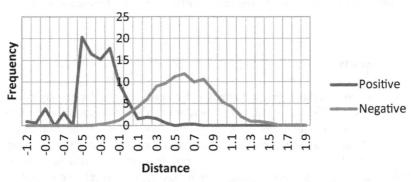

Fig. 5. Distribution of distance to hyperplane for positive and negative samples ("Sat down")

the hyperplane for positive and negative samples for the "sat down" class. Table 9 shows the results obtained when the decision boundary is −0.1, −0.2 and −0.3 compared to the original 0.0. Similarly (to save space we omit here the distance frequency graphs), Tables 10 and 11 show the results for classes "sat down" and "sitting", respectively. It is clear than in all cases there is an increase in sensitivity but at the expense of a noticeable larger increase in the FPR (effectively the operating point in a

Table 9. Sensitivity and FPR ("Sat down") for varying distances to hyperplane

	Sensitivity	ERROR	FPR	ERROR
Original	0.941	0.021	**0.058**	**0.022**
0.1	0.972	0.011	0.110	0.036
0.2	0.988	0.007	0.192	0.052
0.3	**0.999**	**0.002**	0.413	0.082

Table 10. Sensitivity and FPR ("Sitting") for varying distances to hyperplane

	Sensitivity	ERROR	FPR	ERROR
Original	0.877	0.045	**0.039**	**0.014**
0.1	0.975	0.023	0.148	0.033
0.2	0.981	**0.021**	0.237	0.046
0.3	**0.992**	0.447	0.345	0.186

Table 11. Sensitivity and FPR ("Standing")

	Sensitivity	ERROR	FPR	ERROR
Original	0.907	0.022	**0.073**	**0.011**
0.1	0.959	0.015	0.142	0.020
0.2	0.982	0.010	0.241	0.028
0.3	**0.996**	**0.003**	0.360	0.040

Receiver Operating Curve, ROC, changes in a typical manner at the top end of sensitivity). Should it be necessary to minimize FPR, a decision boundary of zero would work best.

4 Conclusions

As far as we are aware, this is the first attempt at investigating and assessing pedestrian detection using the BOSS dataset and in particular in an environment subject to rapidly changing illumination conditions because of the movement of the train. A time-consuming manual ground-truthing process has been carried out and the resulting data is made available to the research community upon request for further progress in this field. We verified, through cross-validation, that classification is relatively stable as the standard deviations are within 0.1.

We also showed that the use of specialized classifiers (trained for each posture class) produce better results, in terms of sensitivity and FPR, than a classifier trained just for pedestrian presence. We also looked at the effect of fine-tuning the positives training sets by discarding samples that presented occlusion and saw that "cleaner" samples (with a stricter intersection rule) resulted in better classification performance. We rejected the hypothesis that negative samples containing pedestrians in different postures would improve posture-specific classification. This seems to indicate that although the samples are of different postures, they are sufficiently close to the positives and far from the negatives to create confusion in the classifier. We also looked at a combined classifier used to classify people presence. The motivation here being to exploit the higher sensitivity of the specialized classifiers to solve a "global" (posture-independent) pedestrian classification problem. Although sensitivity improved noticeably, so did the FPR, indicating that we moved too far to the right on the operating curve. As the combination rule is relatively simple, there is significant scope for improvements. For example, it would be possible to use the distance output of each classifier (we also saw how using this distance as a decision boundary changed the operating point of a classifier) as an indication of confidence to be used as weighted vote (better still, the output of each SVM could be converted to a pseudo-probability [18] which is a better indication of normalized confidence than an absolute distance). We hope that we have established a good baseline using a public dataset so that researchers elsewhere can compare their results to improve performance in this field. It should be noted that here we have concentrated on the classification problem i.e. given an image extract (of the same size as used for training) what is the probability that a classifier will correctly label it as a pedestrian (what we called the "global" classification) or as a pedestrian in each posture (the specific classification). Once a classifier has been evaluated, there remains the localization problem i.e. given a complete image, where are the people and in what posture. This is traditionally solved using a sliding window to scan the image in all possible locations and at different scales (because people would have different sizes as the ones used for training). This is not a trivial problem because as the sliding window starts approaching a person, the classifier would typically start responding positively and that will generate multiple hits that have be "cleaned up" (typically using non-maximal suppression). In [18] we show how this problem is significantly eased by first characterizing the response of a classifier in terms of probability.

Acknowledgments. The work described here was carried out as part of the OBSERVE project funded by the Fondecyt Regular Program of Conicyt (Chilean Research Council for Science and Technology) under grant no. 1140209. S.A. Velastin is grateful to funding received from the Universidad Carlos III de Madrid, the European Union's Seventh Framework Programme for research, technological development and demonstration under grant agreement no. 600371, el Ministerio de Economía y Competitividad (COFUND2013-51509) and Banco Santander.

References

1. La Tercera: Cámaras de seguridad en la Región Metropolitana aumentarán en un 78% (2010). http://www.latercera.com/noticia/camaras-de-seguridad-en-la-region-metropolitana-aumentaran-en-un-78. Accessed 24 June 2017
2. Evans, I.: Report: London no safer for all its CCTV cameras (2012). http://www.csmonitor.com/World/Europe/2012/0222/Report-London-no-safer-for-all-its-CCTV-cameras. Accessed 24 June 2017
3. BC News: 1,000 cameras 'solve one crime' (2009). http://news.bbc.co.uk/2/hi/8219022.stm. Accessed 24 June 2017
4. Burges, C.J.: A tutorial on support vector machines for pattern recognition. Data Min. knowl. Discov. **2**(2), 121–167 (1998)
5. Nowozin, S., Lampert, C.H.: Structured learning and prediction in computer vision. Found. Trends® Comput. Graph. Vis. **6**(3), 185–365 (2011)
6. Dalal, N., Triggs, B.: Histograms of oriented gradients for human detection. In: IEEE Computer Society Conference on Computer Vision and Pattern Recognition CVPR 2005, vol. 1, pp. 886–893 (2005)
7. Chen, G., Hou, R.: A new machine double-layer learning method and its. In: International Conference on Mechatronics and Automation ICMA 2007, pp. 796–799 (2007)
8. Wang, Z., Yoon, S., Hong, C., Park, D.S.: A novel SVM based pedestrian detection algorithm via locality sensitive histograms. In: Proceedings of the International Conference on Image Processing, Computer Vision, and Pattern Recognition (IPCV), vol. 2, p. 1, The Steering Committee of The World Congress in Computer Science, Computer Engineering and Applied Computing (WorldComp) (2014)
9. Wang, Z., Yoon, S., Xie, S.J., Lu, Y., Park, D.S.: A high accuracy pedestrian detection system combining a cascade AdaBoost detector and random vector functional-link net. Sci. World J. **2014**, 7 p. (2014). doi:10.1155/2014/105089. Article ID 105089
10. Cuyang, W., Wang, X.: Joint deep learning for pedestrian detection. In: 2013 IEEE International Conference on Computer Vision (ICCV), pp. 2056–2063. IEEE (2013)
11. Zeng, X., Ouyang, W., Wang, M., Wang, X.: Deep learning of scene-specific classifier for pedestrian detection. In: Fleet, D., Pajdla, T., Schiele, B., Tuytelaars, T. (eds.) ECCV 2014 Part III. LNCS, vol. 8691, pp. 472–487. Springer, Cham (2014). doi:10.1007/978-3-319-10578-9_31
12. Fukui, H., Yamashita, T., Yamauchi, Y., Fujiyoshi, H., Murase, H.: Pedestrian detection based on deep convolutional neural network with ensemble inference network. In: 2015 IEEE Intelligent Vehicles Symposium (IV), pp. 223–228. IEEE (2018)
13. https://www.multitel.be/projets/boss/. Accessed 05 Sept 2017

14. Cong, D.N.T., Achard, C., Khoudour, L.: People re-identification by classification of silhouettes based on sparse representation. In: 2010 2nd International Conference on Image Processing Theory Tools and Applications (IPTA), pp. 60–65. IEEE (2010)
15. Cong, D.N.T., Khoudour, L., Achard, C., Flancquart, A.: Adaptive model for object detection in noisy and fast-varying environment. In: Image Analysis and Processing–ICIAP 2011, pp. 68–77 (2011)
16. Coniglio, C., Meurie, C., Lézoray, O., Berbineau, M.: People silhouette extraction from people detection bounding boxes in images. Pattern Recog. Lett. **93**, 182–191 (2017)
17. University of Maryland.: ViPER: The Video Performance Evaluation Resource (2003). http://viper-toolkit.sourceforge.net/docs/. Accessed 24 June 2017
18. Quinteros, D., Velastin, S.A., Acuna, G.: Characterisation of the spatial sensitivity of classifiers in pedestrian detection. In: 6th LatinAmerican Conference on Networked Electronic Media, Medellin, Colombia (2015)

A Conceptual Design of Spatial Calibration for Optical See-Through Head Mounted Display Using Electroencephalographic Signal Processing on Eye Tracking

Azfar Tomi and Dayang Rohaya Awang Rambli[✉]

Department of Computer Information Sciences,
Universiti Teknologi PETRONAS, Bandar Seri Iskandar, Perak, Malaysia
{azfar.tomi_g03125,dayangrohaya.ar}@utp.edu.my

Abstract. One of vital issue in Optical See-Through Head Mounted Display (OST HMD) used in Augmented Reality (AR) systems is frequent (re)calibrations. OST HMD calibration that involved user interaction is time consuming. It will distract users from their application, which will reduce AR experience. Additionally, (re)calibration procedure will be prone to user errors. Nowadays, there are several approaches toward interaction-free calibration on OST HMD. In this proposed work, we propose a novel approach that uses EEG signal processing on eye movement into OST HMD calibration. By simultaneously recording eye movements through EEG during a guided eye movement paradigm, a few properties of eye movement artifacts can be useful for eye localization algorithm which can be used in interaction-free calibration for OST HMD. The proposed work is expected to enhance OST HMD calibration focusing on spatial calibration formulation in term reducing 2D projection error.

Keywords: Optical See-Through Head Mounted Display · Spatial calibration · Electroencephalographic · Eye-tracking

1 Introduction

In early days, Optical See-Through Head Mounted Display (OST HMD) can be considered as a component of the Augmented Reality (AR) framework's settings [1–6]. Accurate spatial registration in OST HMD AR system implementation can be done if we have a proper OST HMD calibration procedure [31]. There are a few existing calibration algorithms that have been formulated all through years. Technically, the OST HMD calibration principle goal is to acquire eye position data [8]. Interaction from user during calibration procedure is a common method in early days. These methods can be identified as manual calibration. However, manual calibration methods inclined to user error, which later prompts to reduce spatial registration accuracy. Nowadays, automated calibration approaches are presented by acquiring eye's data from user using portable eye tracking system [16, 36] which permit OST HMD calibration without user interaction. But, there are a few issues in recent automated calibration methods which are virtual display calibration related issues and eye tracking

© Springer International Publishing AG 2017
H. Badioze Zaman et al. (Eds.): IVIC 2017, LNCS 10645, pp. 331–339, 2017.
https://doi.org/10.1007/978-3-319-70010-6_31

related issues. As mentioned, eye tracking system has been utilized as a part of automated calibration procedure, which we can be identify it as Video-Oculography (VOG), a system where eye is tracked using camera pointed to it. This method is inherently noise due to the issues between the eye and the camera, which related with varying light condition and occlusion [32]. Recently, the most promising method in gaze tracking is using brain signal processing via EEG [29]. Moreover, there have been few commercial portable EEG devices which is suitable to combine with OST HMD.

In this proposed work, we proposed a novel approach towards interaction-free OST HMD calibration by exploring and investigate the potential of EEG signal processing on eye movement as to improve recent studies on interaction-free calibration methods. Several approaches focusing on interaction-free OST HMD calibration and EEG signal processing on eye movement techniques, will be presented in the next section.

2   Related Work

Basically, this proposed work combines research from several areas which are display calibration and EEG eye movement. The primary objective in OST HMD calibration is to distinguish the virtual camera system that consists of the user's eye and the screen of an OST HMD, which will formulate projection of the real world through it. Subsequently, the projection contains geometric data of user's eye, since the user's eye data acquisition is a part of the framework. There are already several approaches that have been introduced generally to formulate the eye to the screen projection for OST HMD calibration.

2.1   Display Calibration

Most convenient method was presented by Tuceryan et al. called Single Point Active Alignment Method (SPAAM) [10]. SPAAM permits head movement without restrictions inside the physical environment. By using SPAAM, users must align a cross hair that has been drawn randomly on their HMD screen to a given physical point of interest at a known world position for multiple time. 6 2D-3D correspondences are enough to completely determine the projection matrix as the recommended correspondences are no less than 12, due to preserve enhancement calibration formulation in contradiction of user errors. All through years, SPAAM has turned into a broadly utilized strategy in OST HMD calibration for AR applications.

Several calibration approaches that aimed to reduce user interaction have been presented throughout years. Furthermore, an extended version of SPAAM called Easy SPAAM [14, 30] has been presented. This method reuses previous SPAAM projection matrix followed by the alignment of that projection matrix with an updated user's eye position. The 2D-3D correspondences that are needed for online calibration in Easy SPAAM are no less than 2, which leads to reduction of the alignment task. Moreover, Owen et al. proposed Display-Relative Calibration (DRC) [15], which separates display screen properties and eye tracking properties into separate parameters. In DRC, there are two stages calibration procedure which are offline calibration for the display parameters utilizing mechanical jigs and online calibration which consists of 5 different options, including online calibration using fewer parameters of eye localization estimation, and online calibration that needs 6 Degree-of-Freedom (Dof) of eye localization estimation.

Recent approaches allow no interaction from user during OST HMD calibration procedure which can be identify as automated calibration. Itoh et al. proposed Interaction Free Display Calibration (INDICA), a method that utilizes dynamic 3D eye position estimations from an eye tracker combined with static display calibration parameters [10]. Schematic of the overall INDICA setup can be seen in Fig. 1. But still, it did not outperformed SPAAM in term of 2D projection error. This probably happen due to two conceivable reasons such as the offline calibration parameter estimation quality and eye tracking error related. Furthermore, details information about the anatomical parameter of human eyeball is needed as eye of each individual should be different [16, 36]. Thus, a simple 3D eye model is not sufficient for INDICA implementation.

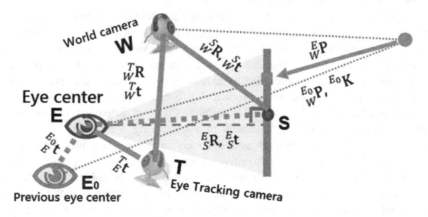

Fig. 1. Schematic overview of the automated OST-HMD calibration [16, 36].

Plopski et al. then proposed Corneal Imaging Calibration (CIC), an OST-HMD calibration based on cornea position estimation using corneal imaging to obtain correspondence pairs from a calibrated HMD-screen and its content reflection on the cornea in an eye image [36]. This approach is more practical as to compare with INDICA. However, SPAAM still outperformed CIC approach in term of 2D projection error due to CIC uses a similar approach as INDICA in term of computation between the OST HMD to the eye relationship. Thus, it will still limit the upper bound of calibration accuracy as CIC and INDICA could achieve. Furthermore, SPAAM inaccuracies is technically based on 2D-3D alignment errors done by users during calibration, as to compared with CIC and INDICA.

Thus, we can conclude that most of the issues in OST HMD, ranging from manual calibration to automated calibration, is eye tracking related issues. Moreover, first step that needed to take care of before we can proceed with the calibration formulation is the eye data acquisition. Further related work on eye tracking approaches will be discuss in the next sub-section.

2.2   Eye Tracking

Eye tracking can be defined as estimating a person's eye movement and focus of foveal attention [33–35]. Eye movement types can be categorized as saccades, smooth pursuit, fixation and blinking. Generally, eye tracking techniques can be classified into two categories which are VOG approaches and non-optical approaches.

VOG is an eye tracking techniques that has widely being used especially in gaze tracking system. There are already several approaches on wearable head-mounted eye tracking system [17–21]. Mostly, these systems are used to collect and analyze user's viewing direction for gaze analysis. Most known non-optical eye tracking techniques are Electrooculography (EOG) and EEG signal processing on eye movement. In this paper, we will be more focusing on acquiring eye movement data from EEG. There are several approaches on EEG eye movement studies which use non-invasive Brain Computer Interface (BCI) to track eye movement [23–27]. Mostly, these studies involving with eye movement artefacts removal from EEG signal for robust eye tracker that would be beneficial to gaze tracking.

To overcome error related to the eye tracking on recent interaction-free OST HMD calibration, we propose to use EEG signal processing to track eye movement as to replace the eye tracking system that has been used in the recent implementation, which has been reported as possible error due to insufficient information of the eye parameter. This eye information can be provided by extensive investigation and revision on eye movement artefacts, including cornel-retinal dipole changes, saccadic spike potentials and eyelid artefacts as well as their interrelations during different types of eye and eyelid movement [24]. Recent advances in eye-tracking technology have allowed researchers to use eye movements as the means of segmenting the ongoing brain activity into episodes relevant to cognitive processes in scene perception, as well as visual search [26]. This kind of information is important as the calibration depends on eye projection to the HMD screen. Moreover, the prevalent method for eye tracking in current implementation of automated calibration is related with VOG. Eye image capture can be considered noisy due to the issues between the eye and the camera, which related with varying light condition and occlusion [32].

Then, the calibration technique will be based on formulated eye position relative to world camera and screen display. It can be investigated by conducting a complete virtual display calibration. DRC can be an option for the investigation, as to perform offline and online calibration based on formulated eye position from processed EEG signal on eye movement. The conceptual design of the proposed work will be presented in the next section.

3   Proposed Work

In this section, we will present the conceptual design of the proposed work. It can be divided into 2 sub-sections which are display calibration and EEG signal processing on eye movement.

3.1 Display Calibration

Figure 2 shows our proposed model of spatial calibration for OST HMD that utilizes eye movement based on EEG signal processing from E to produce an estimated eye position measurement E_T. This proposed display calibration formulation can be divided into three stages.

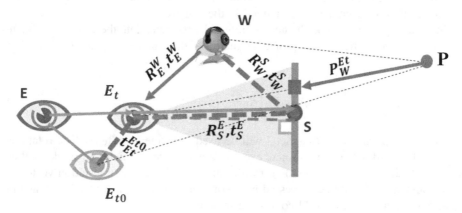

Fig. 2. Schematic overview of the proposed display calibration formulation.

The first stage is by considering a virtual camera which can been defined by the eye and the virtual screen of the OST HMD. The virtual screen will has its coordinate system S and it is located at translation vector $t_{SEt0} = [s_x, s_y, s_z]^T$ in the camera coordinate system E_{T0}. This camera coordinate system can be referred as a pinhole camera. Thus, it can be written as intrinsic camera matrix K_{Et0}:

$$K_{ET0} = \begin{bmatrix} a_x & & \\ & a_y & \\ & & 1 \end{bmatrix} \begin{bmatrix} s_z & & -s_x \\ & s_z & -s_y \\ & & 1 \end{bmatrix} = AS(t_{SEt0}) \tag{1}$$

while assuming that the E_{T0}'s z-axis is perpendicular with screen. Based on Eq. (1), A is a diagonal matrix that transforms projected screen points into image pixel points by scaling factor a_x and a_y, while $S(t_{SEt0})$ is a transformation of 3D points in E_{T0} to the screen in real scale. The image pixel plane origin can be determined by $S(t_{SEt0})$, while t_{SEt0} will dependent on estimated eye position E_T in the next stage.

The second stage is considering a new eye coordinate system E_T, which is based on eye position data acquisition that can be obtained from E. Based on the same idea in first stage (by referring this new camera coordinate system E_T as a pinhole camera), E_T's z-axis can be assumed as perpendicular to the screen. Based on transformation from E_{T0} to E_T, we can be defined the translation vector $t_{Et0Et} = [t_x, t_y, t_z]^T$ which will determined the screen position in E_T as:

$$t_{SEt} = t_{EtOEt} + t_{SEt0} \tag{2}$$

Intrinsic camera matrix K_{Et} can be expressed similarly as in Eq. (1):

$$K_{Et} = AS(t_{SEt}) \tag{3}$$

Based on Eq. (3), another new camera coordinate system based on new eye position data acquisition measurement can defined in the same way.

In third stage, all new coordinate system will be relocated into the world coordinate system W. By referring to basic projection matrix of the pinhole camera model, we can define:

$$p_{Et} = K_{Et}[R_{WEt} \quad t_{WEt}] \begin{bmatrix} p_w \\ 1 \end{bmatrix} \tag{4}$$

The extrinsic parameters $[R_{WEt} \, t_{WEt}]$ will be used to define $P_{WEt}(t_{WEt})$. The rotations from world coordinate system to new eye coordinate system which will be defined as R_{WEt} can be determined by rotation screen to the world R_{WS}. The translation vector of screen position in E_T can be expressed based on translation vector world coordinate in E_T and translation vector world coordinate in screen as:

$$t_{SEt} = t_{WEt} - t_{WS} \tag{5}$$

Thus, based on Eqs. (3) and (4), the projection matrix $P_{WEt}(t_{WEt})$ can be written as:

$$P_{WEt}(t_{WEt}) = AS(t_{WEt} - t_{WS})[R_{WS} \quad t_{WEt}] \tag{6}$$

There are several parameters that Eq. (6) needed such as a complete set of display parameters of t_{WS} (which can be done in offline calibration), the pixel scaling factor a_x and a_y (refer to Eq. (1)), rotation R_{WEt} (which can be defined based on rotation R_{WS}), and translation vector t_{WEt}.

Moreover, E_{T0} and E_T values will be obtained based on EEG signal processing to acquire estimated eye movement which later falls into the next step of our proposed method. This second step can be defined as an eye tracking technique which utilizes EEG signal processing on eye movement. We then formulate the data acquisition for eye position measurement, which later will be used as eye coordinate system E_{T0} and E_T.

3.2 EEG Signal Processing on Eye Movement

There are several approaches on EEG eye movement studies which use non-invasive Brain Computer Interface (BCI) to track eye movement [23–27]. In current implementation, this proposed work will use EEG signal processing in eye tracking based on Samadi et al. work [29].

The current proposed work implementation will use EEG eye position measurement in relation to the visual field from Steady State Visually Evoked Potential

(SSVEP) response detection, which technically based on the positions of stimuli in the visual field. Figure 3 shows the overall stages of our proposed work on EEG signal processing on eye movement.

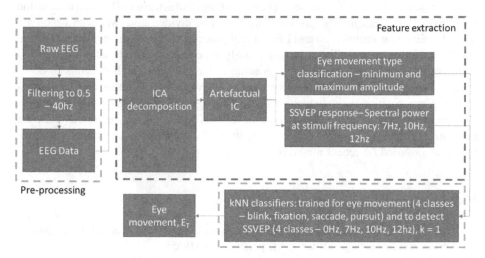

Fig. 3. Overall stages of the proposed work on EEG signal processing on eye movement.

Based on Fig. 3, there are few stages will be included in the proposed work which are:

(1) *Pre-processing:* Band-pass filtered the EEG channels to remove the slow drifts and high-frequency noise.
(2) *Independent Component Analysis:* The source component will be extracted from channels using Blind Source Separation (BSS) algorithm.
(3) *Feature Extraction:* Feature from the pre-processed EEG channels are extracted by referring to SSVEP response estimation. The extracted features from all channels will be concatenated.
(4) *Classification:* Current implementation is using k-Nearest Neighbour (kNN) classifier. This classifier is trained for eye movement type and to detect SSVEP using the feature extracted from ICA components.

From here, we can determine eye focus of foveal attention which later will be matched synchronously with the eye position estimation for camera-eye calibration, and then will be used as E_T. Further investigation on this proposed EEG signal processing on eye movement will be conducted to formulate high accuracy estimated eye position measurement.

4 Conclusion and Future Work

In this paper, we have presented a conceptual design of spatial calibration for OST-HMD using EEG signal processing on eye tracking. The proposed work is based on combination of research from several different areas which are OST HMD calibration and EEG eye movement. The proposed work can be divided into two steps which are display calibration formulation and EEG signal processing on eye movement. In current implementation, we are still conducting a study on eye position estimation using EEG signal processing as to formulate an algorithm for use of the overall calibration.

For future work, further extensive studies on various algorithms and techniques focusing eye position estimation based on EEG signal processing on eye movement will be conducted. A prototype will be developed based on the proposed work for evaluation purposes. A set of experiments will be conducted as to evaluate the proposed work based on recent methods.

References

1. Sutherland, I.: The ultimate display. In: Congress of the International Federation of Information Processing (IFIP), vol. 65, pp. 506–508 (1965)
2. Caudell, T.: Augmented reality: an application of heads-up display technology to manual manufacturing processes. In: Hawaii International Conferences on Systems Sciences, pp. 659–669 (1992)
3. Feiner, S.: Knowledge-based augmented reality. Commun. ACM **36**, 53–62 (1993)
4. Rolland, J.: A comparison of optical and video see-through head-mounted displays. In: SPIE Telemanipulator and Telepresence Technologies, pp. 293–307 (1994)
5. Azuma, R.: Predictive tracking for augmented reality. Ph.D. thesis. University of North Carolina, Chapel Hill, NC (1995)
6. Reiners, D.: Augmented reality for construction tasks: doorlock assembly. In: IWAR (1998)
7. Itoh, Y.: Calibration of head-mounted finger tracking to optical see-through head mounted display. In: ISMAR (2013)
8. Zhou, J.: Calibration of optical see through head mounted displays for augmented reality. Ph. D. thesis. Michigan State University (2007)
9. Klinker, G.: Augmented reality: a balancing act between high quality and real-time constraints. In: ISMR1999, pp. 325–346 (1999)
10. Tuceryan, M.: Single point active alignment method (SPAAM) for optical see-through HMD calibration for AR. In: ISAR, pp. 149–158 (2000)
11. Genc, Y.F.: Optical see-through HMD calibration: a stereo method validated with a video see-through system. In: ISAR, pp. 165–174 (2000)
12. Axholt, M.: Optical see-through head mounted display direct linear transformation calibration robustness in the presence of user alignment noise. In: Human Factors and Ergonomics Society 54th Annual Meeting, pp. 2427–2431 (2010)
13. Axholt, M.: Parameter estimation variance of the single point active alignment method in optical see-through head mounted display calibration. In: VR, pp. 27–34 (2011)
14. Genc, Y.M.: Practical solutions for calibration of optical see-through devices. In: ISMAR, pp. 169–175 (2002)
15. Owen, C.: Display-relative calibration for optical see-through head-mounted displays. In: ISMAR, pp. 70–78 (2004)

16. Itoh, Y.K.: Interaction-free calibration for optical see-through head-mounted displays based on 3D eye localization. In: 3D User Interfaces (3DUI), pp. 75–82. IEEE (2014)
17. Tsukada, A., Shino, M.: Illumination-free gaze estimation method for first-person vision wearable device. In: ICCV Workshops, pp. 2084–2091 (2011)
18. Tsukada, A., Kanade, T.: Automatic acquisition of a 3D eye model for a wearable first-person vision device. In: Eye Tracking Research and Applications (ETRA), pp. 213–216 (2012)
19. Ishiguro, Y.: Aided eyes: eye activity sensing for daily life. In: Augmented Human International Conference, p. 25. ACM (2010)
20. Schneider, E.: EyeSeeCam: an eye movement-driven head camera for the examination of natural visual exploration. In: Annuals of the New York Academy of Sciences, pp. 461–467 (2009)
21. Nitschke, C.: Corneal imaging revisited: an overview of corneal reflection analysis and applications. IPSJ Trans. Comput. Vis. Appl. 5, 1–18 (2013)
22. Nitschke, C., Nakazawa, A.: Image-based eye pose and reflection analysis for advanced interaction techniques and scene understanding. In: Computer Vision and Image Media (CVIM), pp. 1–16 (2011)
23. Gao, J.: Automatic removal of eye-movement and blink artifacts from EEG signals. Brain Topogr. 23, 105–114 (2010). Springer
24. Plöchl, M.: Combining EEG and eye tracking: identification, characterization, and correction of eye movement artifacts in electroencephalographic data. In: Frontiers in Human Neuroscience, p. 278. Frontiers Media S.A. (2012)
25. Noureddin, B.: Online removal of eye movement and blink eeg artifacts using a high-speed eye tracker. Biomed. Eng. 59, 2103–2110 (2012). IEEE
26. Nikolaev, A.R.: Eye movement-related brain activity during perceptual and cognitive processing. In: Frontiers in Systems Neuroscience, p. 62. Frontiers Media S.A. (2014)
27. Kim, M.: Quantitative evaluation of a low-cost noninvasive hybrid interface based on EEG and eye movement. In: Neural Systems and Rehabilitation Engineering, pp. 159–168. IEEE (2015)
28. Swirski, L., Bulling, A., Dodgson, N.: Robust real-rime pupil tracking in highly off-axis images. In: Eye Tracking Research and Applications (ETRA), pp. 173–176 (2012)
29. Haji Samadi, M.R., Cooke, N.: EEG signal processing for eye tracking. In: 2014 Proceedings of the 22nd European Signal Processing Conference (EUSIPCO), pp. 2030–2034 (2014)
30. Navab, N.: An on-line evaluation system for optical see-through augmented reality. In: VR, pp. 245–246 (2004)
31. Grubert, J.: Comparative user study of two see-through calibration methods. In: VR, pp. 269–270. IEEE (2010)
32. Hansen, D.: In the eye of the beholder: a survey of models for eyes and gaze. Pattern Anal. Mach. Intell. 35, 478–500 (2010). IEEE
33. Kim, K.-N.: Vision-based eye-gaze tracking for human computer interface. In: Systems, Man, and Cybernetics, pp. 324–329. IEEE (1999)
34. Smith, K.: Tracking the multi person wandering visual focus of attention. In: 8th International Conference on Multimodal interfaces, pp. 265–272. ACM (2006)
35. Morimoto, C.H.: Eye gaze tracking techniques for interactive applications. Comput. Vis. Image Underst. 98, 4–24 (2005)
36. Plopski, A., Itoh, Y., Nitschke, C., Kiyokawa, K., Klinker, G., Takemura, H.: Corneal-imaging calibration for optical see-through head-mounted displays. IEEE Trans. Vis. Comput. Graph. 21(4), 481–490 (2015)

Review of Spatial and Non-spatial Data Transformation to 3D Geovisualization for Natural Disaster

Muhammad Yudhi Rezaldi[1,2]([✉]), Rabiah Abdul Kadir[1],
Mohamad Taha Ijab[1], and Azlina Ahmad[1]

[1] Institute of Visual Informatics, The National University of Malaysia,
Bangi, Malaysia
rezaldi1106@gmail.com
[2] Research and Development Division for Technology Information,
Indonesian Institute of Sciences, Bandung, Indonesia

Abstract. Climate change is a pressing issue that has taken many countries to task in addressing this global concern. The public need an effective information channel in enhancing their awareness pertaining to the impacts of climate change. One of the most appropriate ways to convey such information is through the optimisation of 3D visualization media. This paper reviews extant work on the use of 3D visualization media with regards to severe floods, argued here as one of the immediate and observable impacts of climate change. The analysis of literature shows that 3D geovisualization is often used to transform spatial and non-spatial data into a 3D visual using software data transformation tools such as ArcGIS, Feature Manipulation Engine (FME) or Google Sketchup. The data transformation process is often followed by the process of creating 3D visuals using Google Sketchup, thus producing a complete 3D visualization project. This is done through a process called the Building Information Modeling (BIM). This process is able to calculate number of elements, can determine the size (magnitude and scale) of an element, check or prove the accuracy of information, and also to create a realistic visualization. With the many advantages of the BIM process, it can be also used to calculate the amount of material losses caused by the flood. However this process is new and quite complicated to use resulting in its limited use by the practitioners. From the study, 3D visualization using BIM process will improve visualization outcomes compared to the deployment of conventional multimedia design process.

Keywords: 3D visualization · Geovisualization · Multimedia design · Media information

1 Introduction

Climate change is the change in the average weather, such as changes in average precipitation, annual average temperature change, change of seasons of a region, city, and state [4, 12, 14, 23].

© Springer International Publishing AG 2017
H. Badioze Zaman et al. (Eds.): IVIC 2017, LNCS 10645, pp. 340–351, 2017.
https://doi.org/10.1007/978-3-319-70010-6_32

With the onset of climate change, a number of serious implications are expected to bring impacts including rise in sea levels, rise in sea temperature causing the melting ice in the North Pole, increase in air temperature, increase in rainfall, increase in evaporation, and increase in the occurrence of tropical storms. Further, climate change is claimed by climate scientists as the cause of various natural disasters such as severe floods, major landslides, prolonged droughts, massive forest fires, the sinking of small islands, and so forth [12, 14, 23].

Although the effects of climate change take a very long time to be observed, the increasing frequency of the natural disasters stated earlier provide evidence supporting the theory of climate change [12]. It is posited that various natural disasters will be more frequently happening, in particular the severe floods which threatened urban and rural areas in many countries.

With regards to conveying information on natural disaster, there are some conventional mediums that can be used in facilitating information, namely: television, radio, print media, and international news agency. In addition to that, computer-based media can also be used and found to be more effective in conveying the message across in a faster and more efficient manner [4].

3D visual effect is part of the computer-based media that can be harnessed to communicate an idea, a message, an event or fact, it is also often used as a media presentation. For example, animated movie developed using 3D visual effect is used to achieve a special effect that cannot be achieved by a live film technique using normal camera shooting [11].

3D visual effects generally include 3D graphics, 3D rendering, and computer generated imagery *(CGI)* [10, 11, 16, 20]. In essence, it is a process in which graphiccontent created using 3D software to produce high quality digital content. This study will analyze the use of 3D modeling as a computer-based media to convey information on severe flood. This is done by analyzing the literature on how to transform spatial- and non-spatial data into a 3D visual effect.

From the results of a review of some previous research, typical data that they use is the spatial data, which is a geographically-oriented data *(i.e., the real picture of a region)* and has a coordinate system specified as a basic reference, have an important part made differently from other data such as location information *(spatial)* and descriptive information/attributes *(non-spatial)* [19]. The common example of spatial data includes graphs, maps, and images in raster format and shaped with a certain value.

A review of how the transformation of spatial data into 3D modeling is necessary in producing better 3D visualization modeling than methods used previously and the results of these studies are reviewed in this paper.

The design of this study will use qualitative methods by exploring a problem as the focus of the research, in the form of review on how to change spatial and non spatial data to 3D geovisualization. The process of data collection and analysis, triangulation, and discussion is shown in Fig. 1.

The first phase commences by conducting a study of the literature by reviewing extant works on 3D modeling of floods. Analysis of the methods used by researchers in performing 3D visualization of the floods such as what data is needed, the software applications used in performing 3D modeling, and their main purpose in doing 3D visualization on floods was conducted.

Fig. 1. Flow of review

In the second phase, mapping of the actual data used in the previous studies and classifying them into two parts in the form of spatial data and non-spatial. This is followed by studying each software on the process of transforming the data into 3D visualization by conducting how to use software from existing data in previous research. Analysis captured every step of the process in the form of a chart and then matched it with the visualization process obtained from literature review, and then summed up how the actual process is to be applied.

In the third stage, analysis of the visual results of each 3D modeling software was conducted using SWOT analysis to determine the strengths, weaknesses, opportunities, and threats of these softwares. The first author tried the software on the computer by reviewing the functionalities and features of the software (ArcGIS, FME and Google Sketchup), and by reading technical books of each software in order to fully understand how the process of making 3D modeling visualization of floods can be implemented under these software environments.

The final phase of the review provides recommendation on the best way to perform the visualization of 3D modeling for the flood modeling. This conclusion is based on the results of analysisconducted from the first stage to the third stage. The detail findings will be explained in Sect. 4 of the paper.

2 Theoretical Background of 3D Geovisualization

In an effort to provide background knowledge to the research and to explore the extant work done on 3D media modeling in the context of severe floods, a review of literature was conducted. The findings of the literature analysis contribute to the development of the theoretical framework (refer Fig. 2) of this research. The literature findings cover the main topics discussion of spatial and non spatial data, transformation of data into 3D geovisualization and 3D software used in geovisualization.

2.1 Spatial and Non-spatial Data

Data is a collection of facts obtained from a measurement and good decision is the result of the conclusion based on accurate data [3]. To obtain accurate data require a reliable and valid measuring instrument, a geological mapping tool such as GPS and others.

The location information *(spatial)* is information relating to geographic coordinates *(latitude and longitude)* or rectilinear *x y z (Cartesian) coordinate* of abscissa, coordinates and altitude, including projection systems from dimension of the Earth. While descriptive information/attributes *(non-spatial)* is the information of a location that has some information related to the location, for example, the type of vegetation, population, area, zip code, and so on. Attribute information is sometimes used to express the condition of the location [27].

2.2 3D Geovisualization

The 3D model is preferred because of the interactive capabilities and ability to visual in conveying information about the risk of flooding [1, 2, 9, 10, 12]. GIS is recommended in producing good visualization results and provide a better platform for visualizing flooding [1].

3D geovisualization is a term used for 3D visualization display from the surface of the Earth overall or only partially [5]. 3D geovisualization has the ability to attract attention to everyone who sees it, allows people to focus in receiving the information that have been portrayed. Therefore, 3D geovisualization can be implemented to illustrate the flooding risks and be considered as an efficient technology to support discussion and collaborative thinking in an area of flood risk management [13].

In making 3D geovisualization, there is some research which uses the concept of BIM. This is a process of making 3D buildings virtually, equipped with detailed information, commonly used for planning, design, implementation of development, and maintenance of buildings [7]. Using software GIS, is a software which is capable of producing visual geodatabase, geovisualization, and geoprocessing, This view can be a 2D or 3D visualization [25–27].

Conclusion results show that 3D geovisualization especially those that use the concept of BIM, can be used to assess in detail the cost of building damage caused by flooding. However, the results of the study by [2] is still limited to a small scale area consisted one or a few buildings and have not been able to scale to the size of a big city [2].

2.3 Transformation of Data to 3D Geovisualization

Transformation of data is a process of transforming data in order to make it more useful and for further manipulation. The steps taken are reading the data, perform the transformation, and turn it into a new form [10].

Bogetti Sam, has done research using spatial data to perform topography such as LIDAR (light detection and ranging), is optical long distance touch technology which measures the properties of light to find distance or other information from distant targets, bathymetric point is the process of drawing waters base from a stream of water, and ESRI files is the data file format produced by GIS software [6].

The software they use is ESRI ArcGIS 10, package FME 2011, and Google Sketchup. ESRI ArcGIS is used to describe the research area, preprocess topographic data, and to prepare the building and retaining floods to form a layer of the modeling process. FME 2011 is used to convert the terrain, buildings, and other information, into a CAD file that can be opened in Google Sketchup [6].

In another study conducted by [1], exploration of LIDAR data and 3D modeling applications to provide flood risk analysed the combination of 3D GIS applications and Google SketchUp. The aim was to make the simulation and to predict flooding and its impact on utility providers as a powerful visual representation for basis of good decision-making in the event of flooding. The study looked for accurate and high planimetry geoidal coordinates to be processed in finding LIDAR strip at the location, bare earth DEM soil extract, extract building footprints, edit footprints by comparing cadastral data, then the data for the 3D modeling of the flood [1].

A study of 3D visualization as a medium of information and evaluation to measure due to flood damage to buildings was reported in creating 3D modeling using the BIM process concept with GIS [2]. The purpose of the research was to create a 3D geovisualization that is able to analyze in detail the damage to buildings caused by floods, making it useful for owners and users of buildings, insurance companies, and others. This study also aims to increase community resilience to flooding and the adverse impacts on them by understanding the risks and to enable them to take the best decisions and policies [2].

2.4   Building 3D Geovisualization

Researchers and practitioners in the area of 3D modeling and visualization used a number of tools to help them make the most out of their spatial data. These tools include ESRI ArcGIS 10, FME 2011, and Google Sketchup [1, 6]. In terms of the visualization process, a method called Building Information Modeling *(BIM)* is commonly used [2, 15, 22].

3D modeling is defined as a process of making 3-dimensional shapes of an object, character, or other form which is desired and this process uses 3D modeling software which is installed on a computer [20]. Visualization is defined as a process of changing the form of data or information into visual, allowing people to recognize the situation, structure, and behavior of the form. Generally, visualization is different with geovisualization [16].

Geovisualization is organize information about location surface of the earth view which are interesting, and informative, in 2D and 3D visualize. While visualization is image making techniques, diagrams or animations for the appearance of an information [16].

Figure 2 below illustrates the process of 3D geovisualization, by transforming spatial data, and then processed into a visual form with ESRI software ArcGIS, FME, or Google Sketchup. After creating the visualization using the BIM process, then the result called geovisualization, functioning to inform about the flood [2, 9, 18, 19, 26].

Fig. 2. The process of 3D geovisualization

Geographic information system (GIS) is a computer system for the management, analysis, and display of geographic information [1, 6, 25, 26]. GIS uses geographic data in the form of spatial data and non-spatial data then changed into 2D or 3D visual form, so it generates base geodata, (see the *process of 3D geovisualization in Fig. 2*). One of the software that can be used to translate and transform data to solve data interoperability issue is FME *(Feature Manipulation Engine)*. Interoperability here refers to communication, sharing and distribution of data, as well as the ability to use transparent data, sometimes classified as spatial ETL *(Extract, Transform, and Load)* across applications. FME is often used to store and extract data from its source, then change it according to user needs and put it in the data warehouse. The software supports different types and formats of data, such as: GIS, CAD, 3D, database, etc. [8].

Google Sketchup is used by many practitioners in designing 3D geovisualization. This software also often used in the field of multimedia design and architecture. Since its inception in 2006, this application has improved its performance by adding plug-ins that can give more realistic effects. This application integrated with data warehouse and allows users to get a variety of 3D objects and additional plugins easily [17].

Building Information Modeling (BIM) is a process for building virtual structure by creating 3D digital models. It also contains all building information which serves as a means for planning, designing, developing, implementing, maintaining buildings and other infrastructure. Using the BIM process the resulting 3D modeling become easier and clearer, making it easier detecting if an error occurs and will help to evaluate also at the moment make decisions in designing [7].

This BIM process has quite a number of capabilities such as: storing information, counting the number of elements, performing quality control, modeling information, determining the needs and choosing elements, determining the size of an element, simulating and predicting financial modeling performance, checking or proving the accuracy of information, creating a realistic visualization, modifying information and translating it in order to be processed in another program, creating a symbol representation of the modeling, making records of information in the form of narration, and enabling a rapid prototype development.

This process is more widely used in the field of architecture. In geovisualization, this process is only used to calculate how much the amount of loss as a result of damage to buildings caused by natural disasters such as floods, but the ability of this process can be used to count only one building, not yet usable in larger quantities such as counting damage of an entire village or town [2, 7].

3 3D Geovisualization Modeling

The data required to create flood modeling is divided into two parts:

- Sample data of location information *(spatial)* such as the limit territory, population, gender, coordinates of the zone, digitized maps, and attribute data.
- Sample data of descriptive information/attributes *(non-spatial)* such as administrative map, soil map, map of soil types, slope maps, land use maps, rainfall maps, maps of land units, and hydrology.

To develop 3D modeling of flood, the first step is to collect all the necessary data such as spatial and non spatial data, as described above. Next is by creating a flood location map of the area set in 2D form and use ArcGIS for data preprocessing. The final stage is to import files on flood maps from ArcGIS format into Google Sketchup, and further processed and developed into 3D modelling file format. Figure 3 shows the flow of developing 3D modeling using ArcGIS and Google Sketchup [2, 6, 26, 27].

Fig. 3. 3D modeling flow with ArcGIS/FME and Google Sketchup

GIS is commonly used to change spatial data and non spatial from a flooded location, with purpose to do the mapping, give coordinates, annotate, create a layout map, and then export the AutoCAD file format which can be further processed using Google Sketchup. The detail of each stage of GIS process can be seen in Fig. 4 [2, 19, 25, 27].

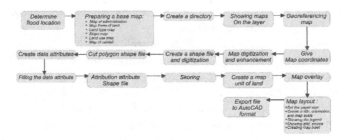

Fig. 4. Data transformation flow using GIS

Another software is known as FME *(Feature Manipulation Engine)* and its function is similar to the GIS, which is to transform the initial data and do a further processing into a 3D visualization. The data transformation process for FME can be seen in Fig. 5 [9].

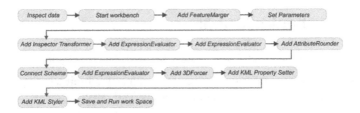

Fig. 5. Transformation data flow using FME

Google Sketchup is used to create 3D modeling from the initial data that has been processed previously using GIS or FME. The output files that have been saved in AutoCAD format or other relevant formats will be imported to Google Sketchup for the modeling by processing or adding after effects and materials as needed, so that it becomes a form of 3D geovisualization. The modeling process can be seen in Fig. 6 [11, 13, 16, 18]:

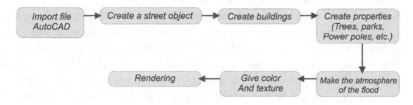

Fig. 6. Using Google SketchUp 3D modeling

Finally, the output file will be saved in the form of image with file format JPG, PNG, TIFF, etc., or it also can be saved in a movie form with a file format avi, quick time, etc. Figure 7 shows some of the examples of 3D visualization created by Bogetti [1, 2, 6], by implementing a series of the 3D modeling process as the above described.

Fig. 7. Example of 3D geovisualization

4   SWOT Analysis on 3D Geovisualization Software Tools

This section discusses the use of SWOT analysis in examining the advantages and disadvantages of each of the software tool involves in developing the 3D geovisualization. This analysis carried out by reading literature and software testing There are four elements in SWOT analysis to identify the strengths and weaknesses, as well as opportunities and threats for every single software tools of 3D geovisualization development. Below are the description of the SWOT analysis [8, 21, 24]:

- ESRI ArcGIS

  1. *Strength:* Can export file format: BSQ, BIL, BIP, JPEG, TIFF, BMP, GeoTIFF or grid data derived from ARC/INFO,and others. Having a more structured data management and easy to use in the mapping process. Having the data online from all over the world, such as: weather data, forestry, marine, climate and

others. There are free and paid plugins, in vector and raster format. In making the map, the statistics complicated calculations can be executed with a simple and easy. Using network analysis to calculate the shortest distance and so on as well as the model builder to create a model of spatial data calculation is very easy to use in ArcGIS. Capable of displaying 3-dimensional data that is directly connected to the internet, and assist in making the display processing 3 D, to do further editing of the data, edit data such as trim, fillet, extending curves. Able to produce visualizations with jpg format and video *(avi)*.

2. *Weakness:* It takes a high spec computer hardware, by default does not support multi-view and multi-layout, it is very difficult to make mass map like GNRHL activity map. The use of ArcGIS will not be efficient if it does not use some other software besides ArcMap opened together, such as ArcCatalog, Windows Explorer and Notepad. ArcGIS is not 100% compatible with ArcView 3x. The migration process will be very greatly change, such as migration from MS Word 2003 or MS Word 2007. In ArcGIS there Xtool and ET but paid.

3. *Opportunity:* Visual results were supported by the data is accurate and visual results were able to be exported in a video format, enabling the visualization of ArcGIS can be used as movie content for further processing as an information media.

4. *Threat:* Still less efficient because it must be supported by other software, resulting in users switching to other software that is more practical.

- FME *(Feature Manipulation Engine)*

  1. *Strength:* Supports a variety of types and data formats, such as: GIS and CAD to BIM, Point cloud via XML, raster, database, non-spatial, 3D, and others. Being able to create a realtime map. Can take a satellite image data. Users are able to share resources through the translation of the FME server repository. Being able to connect directly to virtual machines through a web service with tools FME Cloud. Able to translate and transform data into a graphical interface. Can ensure that the information received is correct with the data inspection. Has more than 400 functions change data. Having the ability to do geoprocessing and translate it into 3D Visual.

  2. *Weakness:* Too many steps in the data-processing causing users who are not adept will have difficulty in using this software.

  3. *Opportunity:* This capability supports a variety of file formats, opening up opportunities for this software to be combined with multimedia software, so it is possible to use into a movie content to serve as a media of information. Ability to process geoprocessing, not shared by other ETL software, allowing the software to be used in work geovisualization.

  4. *Threat:* How to use is quite complicated, thus making it difficult to learn it themselves without the guidance of an instructor, that makes people hesitate to learning more.

- Google Sketchup

  1. *Strength:* Ability to create 3D images fast and practical. Can process file format 2D into 3D. Software is lighter and easier to learn. There are many open source

plugin. Results able to replicate the real picture when coupled with the plug-in renderer like VRay, and Maxwell. Able to support file to 3ds max, AutoCAD, and Google Earth, with 3ds file format, DWG, kmz, pdf, jpg, bmp, DVX, and others.

2. *Weakness:* For advanced modeling, there are still many limitations despite being aided with plugins. Frequent crashes when creating objects that are using vertex and patches. When not coupled with plugin then the results will be less satisfactory.

3. *Opportunity:* The software is open source, easy to use, and rendering results which is supported by plug-in application.

4. *Threat:* Frequent crashes in the manufacture of advanced modeling, will be considered whether to continue or replace the software with other software that is more stable.

ESRI ArcGIS and FME are software used to configure data into a visual form. From the SWOT analysis performed above, the authors conjectured that the use of ArcGIS is preferable as the software is more familiar compared to FME. File results from this data conversion software will be further processed using Google Sketchup by making models, adding effects, create animation, and etc. for the eventual 3D geovisualization modeling.

5 Conclusion and Future Research

One of the most appropriate ways to deal with problems of severe flooding due to climate change is by providing information through the media of 3D visualization. Most extant research make use of media information and flood simulation using 3D media geovisualization by transforming spatial data and non-spatial using ArcGIS or FME. It is then processed again into 3D shape modeling using Google Sketchup software.

3D modeling is preferred because of its ability to interact in visualizing information, providing a better platform than the previous media such as 2D maps. 3D modeling capability is able to captivate the attention of the target audience, allowing people to focus on getting the flood information given, thereby 3D geovisualisation of the risk of flooding can be considered as an efficient technology in flood risk management.

SWOT analysis of 3D visualization software was conducted to determine the advantages and disadvantages of each software in generating 3D geovisualization. The results of the analysis indicate that the manufacture of 3D visualization using BIM process visualization able to have an accuracy level of size, shape, and the coordinates which are close to perfect.

The results of this analysis have also shown not all 3D geovisualisation need to use BIM process, only 3D geovisualization which aims to calculate the amount of losses and damage to buildings caused by the flood need to use BIM process. As for 3D geovisualization which aims to make simulated flood, it should not be necessary to use the BIM process just doing transforming the data into visual using GIS or FME software, which combined with google sketchup.

Therefore, it is highly recommended for future research that the combination of both of these methods *(BIM and Multimedia design)*, to create 3D geovisualization which aims to calculate the amount of loss caused by severe floods. As for 3D geovisualization with the aim of flood simulation, it can incorporate geovisualisation software and software maker of multimedia products, like 3DS Max, Maya, Adobe After Effects, etc. such that it can create an accurate 3D flood visualization and resembles the original object.

Further, 3D modeling visualization of flooding can be used as a media of visualization for the government to make a decision in adopting measures such as: termination of electric current, turning off the water channel, closure of public facilities, roads and buildings, evacuation, arrange the system disposal waste, and estimating the amount of property damage caused by flooding.

References

1. Addaa, P., et al.: Flood-risk 3D models of government infrastructure. Commission VI, WG VI/4. Department of Geodesy and Geomatics Engineering, University of New Brunswick, Fredericton NB Canada E3B 5A3 (2010)
2. Amirebrahimi, S., Rajabifard, A., Mendis, P., Ngo, T.: A Data Model For Integrating GIS and BIM for Assessment and 3D Visualisation of Flood Damage to Building. The paper's authors. Copying permitted only for private and academic purposes. In: Veenendaal, B., Kealy, A. (eds.): Research@Locate 2015, Brisbane, Australia, 10–12 March 2015 (2015). http://ceur-ws.org. Research@Locate 2015
3. Amin, I., Aswin, A., Fajar, I., Isnaeni Iwan, S., Pudjirahaju, A., Sunindya, R.: Statistics for Health Practitioners. Graha Ilmu, Yogyakarta (2009)
4. Arroyo Barrantes, S., RodrIguez, M., Perez, R.: Information management and communication in emergencies and disasters: manual for disaster response teams. Area on Emergency Preparedness and Disaster Relief, Pan American Health Organization, Washington, DC (2009)
5. Bleisch, S.: 3D geovisualization–definition and structures for the assesment of usefulness. In: ISPRS Annals of the Photogrammetry, Remote Sensing and Spatial Information Sciences, 2012 XXII ISPRS Congress, Melbourne, Australia, 25 August–01 September 2012, vol. I-2 (2012)
6. Bogetti, S.: Three-Dimensional (3D) Modeling For Flood Communication. Examensarbete, Kandidatniva, 15 hp Geomatik Programmet. Akademin For Teknik Och University of Gävle, Faculty of Engineering and Sustainable Development, Department of Industrial Development, IT and Land Management (2012)
7. Cad Media: Understanding of BIM (Building Information Modeling). Cad Training Solution (2017). http://cad-media.blogspot.my/2016/08/pengertian-tentang-bim.html. Accessed 1 Apr 2017
8. Dartmouth UMass: Strategic Plan for Information Technology 2010–2015, University of Massachusetts Dartmouth (2010)
9. Desktop Training Manual: FME Desktop Training Manual (2015). © 2005–2015 Safe Software Inc. All rights are reserved
10. Green, J.: What Is 3D Visualization, Who Does It & Why Do You Need It? (2015). https://www.upwork.com/hiring/design/what-is-3d-visualization-who-does-it-why-do-you-need-it/. Accessed 23 Feb 2017

11. Hamidon, Z., Ho, K., Noor, A.M.: Embedding visual effect in 3D animated environment design for short movie. Online J. Art Des. **1**(2) (2013)
12. Iqbal, M.J., Ali, F.M., Khursheed, M.B.: Analysis of role of media in disaster reporting in Pakistan. Eur. Sci. J. **10** (2014). 2014/SPECIAL/edition, ISSN: 1857-7881 (Print) e - ISSN 1857-7431
13. Jacquinodi, F.: 3D Geovisualizations for Flood Mitigation Planning: a Tool to Enhance Collaboration Between Praticioners, Elected Representatives and Citizens. Posters - C7 - Inondation & Societe/Floods & Societe. Is Rivers. funded by the European Union and the Plan Rhone (2015)
14. Kakade, O., Hiremath, S., Raut, N.: Role of media in creating awareness about climate change – a case study of Bijapur City. IOSR J. Human. Soc. Sci. (IOSR - JHSS) **10**(1), pp. 37–43 (2013). e-ISSN: 2279-0837, p-ISSN: 2279-0845. www.Iosrjournals.Org
15. Kreider, R.G., Messner, J.I.: The Uses Of BIM Classifying and Selecting BIM Uses. Penn State, Computer Integrated Construction (2013)
16. Lang, U.L., et al.: 3D Visualization and Animation – An Introduction. Photogrammetric – Week 2003. Dieter Fritsch (ed.). Wichmann Verlag, Heidelberg (2003)
17. Masufu: Sketchup Course (2015). http://mufasucad.com/apa-itu-sketchup/. Accessed 1 Apr 2017
18. Manullang, R.: 3D Home Drawing Techniques With AutoCad and Google Sketchup. PT. Alex Media Komputindo, Kompas Gramedia, Jakarta-Indonesia (2016)
19. Nuarsa, I.W.: Analyze Spatial Data with Arcview GIS 3.3 for Beginners. Gramedia. Jakarta (2005)
20. O'Malley, S.: 3D Modeling and Animation. University of Michigan 3D Lab Digital Media Commons, Library (2015). http://um3d.dc.umich.edu
21. Ommani, A.R.: Strenghts, weaknesses, opportunities and threats (SWOT) analysis for farming system businesses management: case of wheat farmers of Shadervan District, Shoushtar Township Iran. Afr. J. Bus. Manag. **5**(22), 9448–9454 (2011). Academic Journals
22. Rahman, A.: Guidelines on Implementation and Adoption of BIM for Construction and Engineering Industry. The Big 5 Construct. International Building & Construction Show. 9–11 November 2016. Jakarta Convention Center (2016)
23. Sandra, M.: What Are Climate Change (2015). https://www.nasa.gov/audience/forstude-ts/5–8/features/nasa-knows/what-is-climate-change-58.html. Accessed 10 Jan 2017
24. Sammut Bonnici, T., Galea, D.: SWOT Analysis. Wiley Encyclopedia of Management, edited by Professor Sir Cary L Cooper, John Wiley & Sons, Ltd (2014)
25. Wahana Komputer: GIS Modeling For Disaster Mitigation, Geographic Information Distribution To Make Disaster Area Distribution. PT. Alex Media Komputindo, Kompas Gramedia, Jakarta, Indonesia (2015)
26. Wahana Komputer: Complete Tutorial Master ArcGIS 10. ANDI, Yogyakarta, Indonesia (2017)
27. Yousman, Y.: Geographic Information System with ArcView 3.3 Professional. Yogyakarta: Andi Offset (2004)

Face Recognition with Real Time Eye Lid Movement Detection

Syazwan Syafiqah Sukri, Nur Intan Raihana Ruhaiyem$^{(\boxtimes)}$,
and Ahmad Sufril Azlan Mohamed

School of Computer Sciences, Universiti Sains Malaysia (USM),
11800 Gelugor, Penang, Malaysia
ssyafiqah.ucom13@student.usm.my,
{intanraihana, sufril}@usm.my

Abstract. The enhancement of current face recognition system used in attendance system is proposed to fulfill the motivations for this project which are to encounter the shortcomings from the existing systems, to put an innovation into the existing system and to make the system smarter by using real-time functionality. There are three objectives in this project which are to make the system able to differentiate between real face and a photo, to make the system works on desired speed and important key is to make a user-friendly system in term of its interface and functions. Techniques that will be used to achieve the objectives are by using average standard deviation of depth or pulse magnification, using JAVA programming language and develop using simple and standard user interface components and functions. At the end, this system is expected to fulfill the objectives stated and can encounter the problem arise in existing system. As the conclusion, there is no perfect system and still need to be enhanced from time to time.

Keywords: Attendance system · Face recognition system · Innovation · Real-time

1 Introduction

Biometric recognition system has been acknowledged by many sectors especially for those who are practicing the safety precautions like immigration department, police department and custom department to prevent and minimize crimes. Nowadays, even the attendance system is using biometric recognition system. Attendance system is started by using signature system where this is no longer effective as one person can copy the other person's signature. Then, it moves to card scanning where nowadays there are still sectors that implementing this system. However, this method still not effective enough as the scanner often depends on the electricity and the card can be transferred from one person to another. There is still possibility that the card is not in the owner's hand. Next, it moves to biometric recognition system. From all biometrics like fingerprint, iris and face, face recognition system is the optimal but it still has several shortcomings that need to be improved. People may use a photo instead of the person himself to be recognized and this will lead to the false acceptance thus create negative consequences.

© Springer International Publishing AG 2017
H. Badioze Zaman et al. (Eds.): IVIC 2017, LNCS 10645, pp. 352–363, 2017.
https://doi.org/10.1007/978-3-319-70010-6_33

The highlight of this system is the real-time functionality that will be implemented. Most of processes involved in this face recognition system will be operated in real-time starting from detection and tracking face to recognition. Furthermore, this system also is operated without human presence or human monitoring. In other word, this system will be a stand-alone face recognition system.

1.1 Problem Statement

Attendance system has been started with a simple manual way which a student or an employee needs to sign for their attendance. This way has many shortcomings as a person can simply cheat on the signature. Another person can easily copy their friends' signature to help them fulfill the attendance. Next, punch card and card scanning has been introduced to people. At first, this seems to be an effectively way to avoid any false attendance and it is easy to implement as nowadays there are sectors still implementing this method. However, the disadvantage of this system is one person can use the other's card to have the permission. This is worrying as it will affect the security measures. Sometimes when there is no electricity, it is also such a troublesome as the card scanner cannot function.

Then, the biometric system has been developed with using fingerprint. Unfortunately, this method comes with several disadvantages to the user. The devices needed to operate this system can be expensive to afford, thus it makes the use of this fingerprint system is limited. Other than the cost, this system will not function well as the devices not only detect the image of the finger but also contamination found on the finger such as dust and other dirty that will lead to incomplete image of fingerprint being detected. Therefore, there are chances of being rejected by the system. Besides that, by using external devices for operating the system, fingerprint system is complex where it needs physical contact between users and devices. Some users might think that it is distressed to use the system. Next, face recognition attendance system has been developed but there are still several issues regarding this system such as the quality of the image processed, the system and its maintenance are expensive and accuracy rate is low. On the other hand, there is possibility where a person might use a picture instead of the person himself to be recognized. This can lead to false acceptance. Real-time based system is not very common yet among users as most of the system available still need the human-control where a person in charge need to be in place with the system to monitor it. The common consequence from this behavior is bias problem and time waste just to monitor the system.

1.2 Proposed Solutions

With the wide availability of existing system, this system will be enhanced by taking the deficiency of the current work and innovates on that part so that the deficiencies can be at least minimized. The proposed system will operate in real-time as it is the main highlight of this system. The face of user will be detected and tracked in real-time using camera integrated with the system and the face detected will also be recognized in real-time and automatically. In this case, the specifications of the camera used is not taken into consideration as for now the camera input source can be any. Next, the other innovation will be done on the recognition part where based on the problem which the user can use a picture instead of the person himself to be recognized. Eye blink detection [1] will be implemented and tested in this system as the solution to make the system to detect whether it is real face or photo attack. Based on scientist research, the average a person blinks are 15-20 times per minute or every four seconds [2], thus it can be one of the indicator to detect it is the real face.

There are existing techniques or algorithms that have been used by other developer to develop this kind of recognition. Some of them are Local Binary Pattern (LBP), Linear Discriminant Analysis (LDA) and Neural Network. The algorithm proposed for this Real-Time FRS is Principal Component Analysis (PCA) which is the simplest of the true eigenvector-based multivariate analyses. The use of PCA in this system is because compared to other algorithms, PCA is using less time to train the data compared to LDA which require more training time than PCA because it generally uses PCA as a preprocessing step to avoid the small sample size problem.

This system is integrated with the attendance database by updating the tables in the database. In this case, there is no attendance system involved but only the database that shows similar attributes as attendance system to show that this system can work well with the attendance database. Attendance database created for this system acts as a support function to show the system is well-functioning and meet its requirements.

2   Background and Related Work

This research project is the enhancement of the developed project done previously. There are functions that newly added and some functions are changed. One of them is this system involves real time photo taken instead of static photo that manually inserted into the system to be recognized from database from previous work.

Face recognition or facial recognition system has captured government's attention such as the immigration department as they are dealing with various people from various corner of the world. From their perspective, it is the security aspect that leads to implementation of face recognition system. NEC Corporation of Malaysia introduces Neoface® facial recognition solutions for the first time in Malaysia as part of public safety capabilities [3].

There is a system that runs face recognition which is KeyLemon. This system is used generally for locking and unlocking a system. However, this existing system is not secured. It is because even the face recognition accuracy settings are set at high accuracy, it provides less security than a password. This face recognition software has a high false acceptance rate such that it is easy to be hacked by anyone having only basic photo editing skills according to a review site on Internet [4]. Some of the existing algorithms that always been used in this type of recognition system are Principal Component Analysis (PCA) and Local Binary Pattern (LBP).

PCA is based on the information theory approach. The relevant information in a face image is extracted and encoded efficiently as possible. It is also widely used for dimensionality reduction which in 1991, Eigenfaces is introduced by Turk and Pentland. By using this dimensionality reduction, the dimensionality of a face model can be reduced from image pixel size to several principle bases. The information may be encoded by the bases sufficiently. The subspace of the image space spanned by the training face image data is identified by PCA and decorrelates the pixel values [5, 6].

LBP was proposed by Ahonen. The method provides information about the shape and texture. The original LBP operator labels the pixels of an image by thresholding the 3 * 3-neighbourhood of each pixel with the center value and consider the results as a binary number, thus a histogram is made to describe the image. A LBP is called uniform if it contains at most two bitwise transitions from 0 to 1. With this criterion, the number of bins of different patterns reduced from 256 to 59, 58 bins for different uniform patterns and one bin for non-uniform patterns [5, 6].

The code for detecting and tacking face is already available on the internet done by other developers but the existing code itself is still having deficiency to differentiate between real face and photo attack. Although the user is scanning using photo, the system still detects and tracks the photo as it is the real face. This shows that this code needs to be enhanced so that the system will be able to detect and track only the real face.

3 Methodology

Information gathering is carried out by making comparison between the algorithms available for face recognition system which are Principal Analysis Component (PCA), Local Binary Pattern (LBP) and Linear Discriminant Analysis (LDA) [7]. Through the comparison, the differences between the algorithms can be pointed out, thus the suitable algorithm to be used is chosen. Moreover, information gathering also is carried out by storing and testing with various dataset. This is because by using various dataset; the results achieved are more accurate compared to single dataset. In addition, when it involves the face recognition, it is very complex to be analyzed using single dataset.

Face recognition system is consisting of four main components which are user, camera, the system and database. In this system, the user will be a student or a staff that wants to get his or her attendance marked as present. They need to look at the camera to get his or her face to be detected and recognized. Next, the system will detect and track the face before it captures the face detected to be processed in recognition phase. After the face has been captured, the system will do recognition process by comparing the face with the dataset in database. The dataset is stored in various conditions and poses such as frontal face, side face and conditions of light so that the changes of getting accurate result is high. Meanwhile, for the unrecognized face, the detected face will be stored in the database as a new database such that it can be used in the future if there is a case where the person is detected again. Below is the network diagram that illustrates the components involved in this system.

The figure below shows the algorithm of Principal Component Analysis (PCA) which will be implemented and tested in this system. The algorithm shows the processes of getting the features analysis and recognizing the face (Fig. 1).

This system uses webcam to acquire face image of a user, hence this system is a real-time system. In the webcam video, the system will detect and track the face and eyes position of user before it captures the face for further process. At this stage, blink detection is executed for validating between real face and photo attack where if blink is detected, then it is real face but if there is no blink, then it is not real face and can be

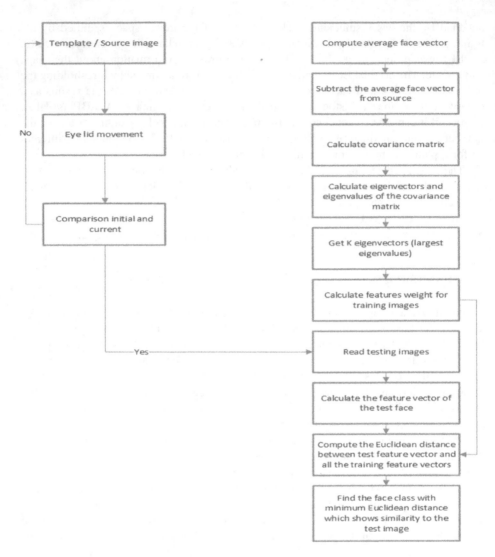

Fig. 1. Principal Component Analysis (PCA) Flow

concluded to be a photo attack. When the system has identified that it is a real face, the face will be captured. After that, the face captured will be pre-processed by the system. The pre-processes include creating eigenvectors or eigenvalues bundle for the specified training images and save each eigenfaces (eigenvectors) as an image file. The array of training images is converted into a matrix where each row is an image and the number of columns is the number of pixels in the image. Then, the array is normalized. As the result, each row in the matrix is a normalized image. Next, the mean face vector is calculated as an array from the average of each matrix column. After that, the mean of each column is subtracted from each matrix row. Each row now contains only distinguishing features from a training image. The covariance matrix is then calculated by multiplying the normalized matrix and its transpose. Eigenvalues and eigenvectors for covariance matrix is the calculated before it is sorted into descending order by eigenvalues. The result is added to a table so the sorting of the values adjusts the corresponding vectors. In the table, the eigenvalues act as the key while the eigenvectors act as the value. The sorted key list is converted into an array and it is used to update the eigenvalues array. The eigenfaces for the training images also are normalized by multiplying the eigenvectors to the training images matrix. After all these calculations were made, the eigenfaces are saved as images. It is an optional to reconstruct the eigenfaces back to original. The face captured will be changed into an array and converted into normalized one-dimensional array. Next, the mean of the image is subtracted from the image array and the image is mapped into eigenspace, returning its coordinates which is its weights. After that, the smallest Euclidean distance between image and training images is calculated and the closest training image is chosen. Based on the above result, the face captured will be classified as either known or unknown. The following figure shows the architecture of Real-Time FRS (Fig. 2).

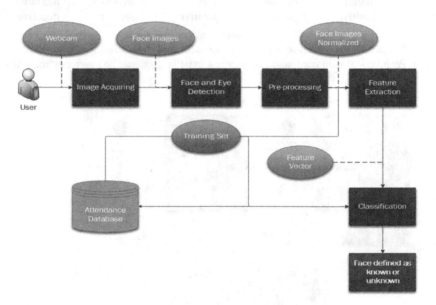

Fig. 2. Real-Time FRS architecture

3.1 Recognition Testing

For recognition module, several test cases have been carried out to evaluate the system accuracy. The method used for evaluation is ROC (Receiver Operating Characteristic) Curve. Table 1 and Fig. 3 show the several test cases that have been carried out.

Based on this information, the ROC Curve is drawn. The data format chosen is Format 1 which is Ordinal Rating Scale. For this format, each line is representing one test case. On each line, there will be two numbers where the first number is either "0" or "1", depending whether the test case is truly positive ("1") or truly negative ("0") and the second number is any integer (1, 2, 3, …) representing the confidence rating of

Table 1. Test cases and scenarios for recognition testing in Real-Time FRS

User	Test 1	Test 2	Test 3	Test 4	Test 5
#1	Not found in database	Not found in database	Positively recognized	Falsely recognized	Falsely recognized
**Remark	**Truly and definitely negative**	**Truly and definitely negative**	**Truly and definitely positive**	**Truly and definitely negative**	**Truly and definitely negative**
#2	Positively recognized	Falsely recognized	Falsely recognized	Positively recognized	Positively recognized
**Remark	**Truly and definitely positive**	**Truly and definitely negative**	**Truly and definitely negative**	**Truly and definitely positive**	**Truly and definitely positive**
#3	Not found in database	Not found in database	Not found in database	Not found in database	Found in database
**Remark	**Truly and definitely positive**	**Truly and definitely positive**	**Truly and definitely positive**	**Truly and definitely positive**	**Truly and definitely negative**

**User 1 and User 2 are in database while User 3 is not in database.
**Truly Negative – Person not found (for user existed in database) and falsely recognized.
**Truly Positive – Person not found (for user not exist in database) and correctly recognized.

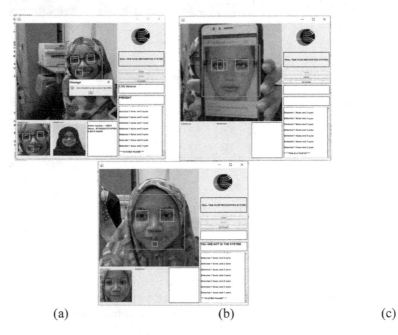

(a)   (b)   (c)

Fig. 3. (a) Test result 1 of 'correctly recognized', (b) Test result 2 of 'photo attack detected' and (c) Test result 3 of 'not in database'

each test cases. The higher number indicates greater positivity. For these test cases, the categories would have the following meaning; (a) definitely negative, (b) either negative or positive, and (c) definitely positive (Fig. 4).

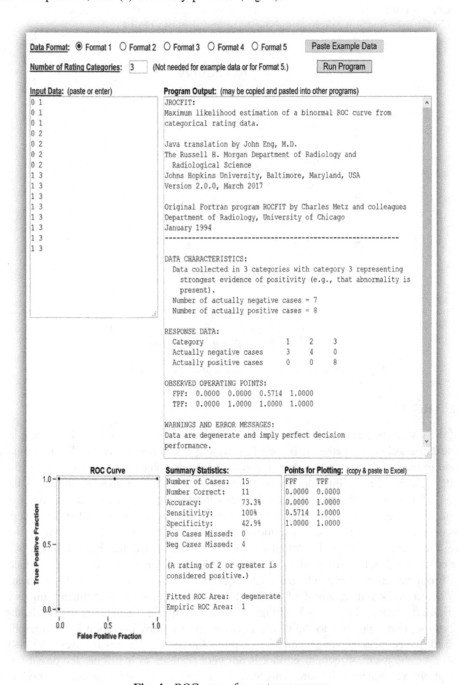

Fig. 4. ROC curve for system accuracy

Based on the above figure, the result given is based on the data in Table 1. For given test cases, the system accuracy is approximately 73.3 percent (73.3%) accurate. However, the accuracy is different when there are other test cases. The testing has been carried out for different users' category. The categories are user that exists in the database, user that not exists in the database and a photo (Fig. 5).

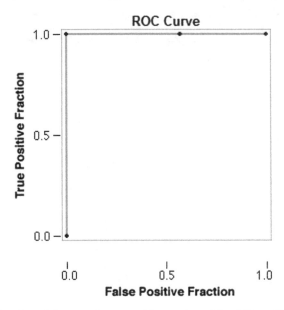

Fig. 5. ROC curve for recognition testing of Real-Time FRS

3.2   Results

All the test cases are carried out based on the use case of Real-Time FRS. For example, to test the webcam whether it is well-functioning and work correctly, the user must stand in front of the webcam and see the video of the person displayed in the box on the system main screen. In this situation, the video is tested whether it can display back the video of user smoothly and well. Like the other function like tracking and detecting eye blink. For face tracking, it is being tested whether the system can track the position of the user's face whenever he or she moves the face either right or left. Meanwhile for eye blink detection, it is being tested whether the system can detect eye blink as this is the criterion taken to distinguish or validate whether the user is using photo or real face.

From the unit testing conducted, each requirement is functioning well. The webcam can detect, track and capture the face. The blink detection also is well-functioning as it can detect whether the user is blinking within a specific time range. As the result, the system will only proceed to the next process when the blink detection is successfully passed. Every message is also correctly displayed in the right boxes for user reference. However, the result of recognized face is not very accurate as it still has the possibility of falsely recognize a person. This can be improved by refining the method of calculating the eigenvalues of training images and increasing the number of training images with different illuminations and styles.

One of the weaknesses of existing solution is that for validating real face, it does not have restrictor in detecting eye blink. Although the eye blink detection is implemented, without a restrict conditions, user can manipulate the function easily by using some photo editing using various editing software. Thus, the integrity of the system can be questioned and the result of recognition process can be tainted. In Real-Time FRS, eye blink detection is also being implemented but with a restrict condition where the user need to blink a few times continuously in a specific time range. If the user really uses real face, this condition will be easily being passed without any error warning from the system.

Furthermore, this system utilizes the real-time functionality where it is now one of the demand functionality due to its benefits to human being. By using real-time functionality, the information gathered is always up-to-date without any delay. For example, in this system that involves the attendance, the remark whether he or she is present or not is stored on the spot when he or she has been recognized. Meanwhile, if a person is not recognized by the system, the organization can be immediate notified about the situation for further process or action. One of the constraint of this system is it can only process one person at a time. Only one person at a time can stand in front of the camera attached to this system. However, this constraint can be improved in future work of this system.

4 Conclusion and Future Work

The idea of Real-Time Face Recognition System (Real-Time FRS) is proposed for solving the problems faced by the related authority and organizations in Universiti Sains Malaysia as the initial target. It is believed that this proposed solution will sustain and improve students' and staffs' attendance performance by decreasing the chances of false attendance made by the students of staffs. It is because with the current method of taking an attendance which is using signature, it has high percentage of students giving false signature. For example, students can just sign the attendance for their friends who did not attend the class. Hence, this system can minimize this false attendance because it is using real-time function, real face validation and it compares with the database. With these restrictions, it is believed students cannot cheat about the attendance. This recognition system utilizes the real-time function, real face validation and database comparison and then displays the related information corresponding to the user but the information will only be shown if the person is recognized by the system when comparing with the database. The expected outcome of this solution is to check whether the user is using real face or photo besides whether the person is being recognized by the system correspond to the database.

The development process of Real-Time FRS had faced many challenges which one of it is the accuracy of the detection algorithm; in this case the system used haarcascade classifiers which are haarcascade_frontalface_alt.xml for face detection and haarcascade_eye_tree_eyeglasses.xml for eye detection. Although the available detection tool is used, it can also make mistake in detecting the face and eye. Many technologies are being used in this project such as SQL which is the fundamental of Real-Time FRS and it is where all the data are retrieved and stored. Besides that, Java programming language is used for coding the system and Eclipse Neon is the Integrated Development Environment (IDE) platform. At the end, the result met the main objectives which are to verify the person is in database through several processes, classify unverified face, increase security level and innovate attendance system by using biometric and real-time function.

The Real-Time FRS has a spacious room for improvement as it utilizes the technologies that rapidly improving, for example, the biometric element which in this case is the face of a user. Apart from face, there are many biometric elements that can be used or integrated in this system. Thus, this system is not limited to only face. Furthermore, although this system can only process one face at a time, it can be modified to multiple faces being processes at a time in the future with more details development. Using this technology, the system can give a better result and accuracy in identifying and verifying a person with the organization's database to secure the security of the organization. Nowadays, there are a lot of security breaches that can contaminate the integrity of an organization. As a result, the organization can have a better security level with less caution on security breach.

In the future, instead of processing one face at a time, processing multiple faces at a time can be done with more details development work. Image tracking [8] could be one of the best choices for this implementation. The benefit of processing multiple faces at a time is it can reduce time consuming to identify and verify a person with the database. Other than that, other biometric elements such as retina scan and body temperature detection can be integrated with this system [9]. The benefit of these additional elements is they can give more accurate result on person verification because there are more criteria that being considered and processed by the system, which could also include other improved image processing and segmentation such which have been proven and applied on more complex images [10–15]. Several people might have one common feature for one criteria, but when there are several criteria are being processed, the chances of group of people have common feature is low. It is believed that these future works can be done successfully by giving more efforts, suitable technologies both software and hardware and detailed research need to be done.

Acknowledgments. The authors wish to thank Universiti Sains Malaysia for the support it has extended in the completion of the present research through Short Term University Grant No: 304/PKOMP/6313259.

References

1. Cornelissen, F., Peters, E., Palmer, J.: The Eyeblink Toolbox: eye tracking with MATLAB and the Psychophysics Toolbox. Behav. Res. Methods Instrum. Comput. **34**(4), 613–617 (2002)
2. How often and why do people's eyes blink? - The Boston Globe. http://archive.boston.com/news/science/articles/2007/05/14/how_often_and_why_do_peoples_eyes_blink/

3. NEC Corporation of Malaysia introduces Neoface® facial recognition solutions for the first time in Malaysia. http://sg.nec.com/en_AP/press/201408/ap_20140812_01.html
4. Review KeyLemon: Biometric-solutions.com (2016). http://www.biometric-solutions.com/software/reviews.php?story-keylemon
5. Makwana, H., Singh, T.: Comparison of different algorithm for face recognition. Glob. J. Comput. Sci. Technol. Graph. Vis. **13**(9), 17 (2013)
6. Ahonen, T., Hadid, A., Pietikäinen, M.: Face recognition with local binary patterns. In: Pajdla, T., Matas, J. (eds.) ECCV 2004. LNCS, vol. 3021, pp. 469–481. Springer, Heidelberg (2004). doi:10.1007/978-3-540-24670-1_36
7. Singh, A.: Comparison of face recognition algorithms on dummy faces. Int. J. Multimed. Appl. **4**(4), 121–135 (2012)
8. Mohamed, A.S.A., Ritchings, T., Pearson, S.: Image tracking using normalized cross-correlation to track and analyse mechanical tendon properties. In: Proceedings of the Salford Postgraduate Annual Research Conference (SPARC 2011), Manchester, United Kingdom, vol. 2, pp. 10–11 (2011)
9. Shanmugasundaram, K., Mohamed, A.S.A., Venkat, I.: An overview of multimodal biometrics using meta-heuristic optimization techniques for F2R system. Int. J. Soft Comput. Eng. (IJSCE) vol. 5(5) (2015)
10. Ruhaiyem, N.I.R., Mohamed, A.S.A., Belaton, B.: Optimized segmentation of cellular tomography through organelles' morphology and image features. J. Telecommun. Electron. Comput. Eng. (JTEC) **8**(3), 79–83 (2016)
11. Halim, M.A.A., Ruhaiyem, N.I.R., Fauzi, E.R.I., Mohamed, A.S.A.: Automatic laser welding defect detection and classification using sobel-contour shape detection. J. Telecommun. Electron. Comput. Eng. (JTEC) **8**(6), 157–160 (2016)
12. Veeraputhara Thevar, V., Ruhaiyem, N.I.R.: Concept, theory and application: hybrid watershed classic and active contour for enhanced image segmentation. In: The Visual Informatics International Seminar, Bangi, Selangor (2016)
13. Ruhaiyem, N.I.R.: Semi-automated cellular tomogram segmentation workflow (CTSW): towards an automatic target-scoring system. In: Proceedings of the International Conference on Computer Graphics, Multimedia and Image Processing, Kuala Lumpur, Malaysia, pp. 38–48 (2014)
14. Ruhaiyem, N.I.R.: Boundary-based versus region-based approaches for cellular tomography segmentation. In: Proceedings of 1st International Engineering Conference, Erbil, Iraq, pp. 260–267 (2014)
15. Ruhaiyem, N.I.R.: Multiple, object-oriented segmentation methods of mammalian cell tomograms, Ph.D. thesis, Institute for Molecular Bioscience, The University of Queensland (2014). doi:10.14264/uql.2014.554

Action Key Frames Extraction Using L1-Norm and Accumulative Optical Flow for Compact Video Shot Summarisation

Manar Abduljabbar Ahmad Mizher[1], Mei Choo Ang[1](✉),
Siti Norul Huda Sheikh Abdullah[2], and Kok Weng Ng[3]

[1] Institute of Visual Informatics, Universiti Kebangsaan Malaysia,
Bangi, Malaysia
manar@siswa.ukm.edu.my, manar_mizher@yahoo.com,
amc@ukm.edu.my
[2] Faculty of Information Science and Technology,
Universiti Kebangsaan Malaysia, Bangi, Malaysia
snhsabdullah@ukm.edu.my
[3] Industrial Centre of Innovation in Industrial Design,
Sirim Berhad, Bukit Jalil, Malaysia
kwng@sirim.my

Abstract. Key frame extraction is an important algorithm for video summarisation, video retrieval, and generating video fingerprint. The extracted key frames should represent a video sequence in a compact way and brief the main actions to achieve meaningful key frames. Therefore, we present a key frames extraction algorithm based on the *L1-norm* by accumulating action frames via optical flow method. We then evaluate our proposed algorithm using the action accuracy rate and action error rate of the extracted action frames in comparison to user extraction. The video shot summarisation evaluation shows that our proposed algorithm outperforms the-state-of-the-art algorithms in terms of compression ratio. Our proposed algorithm also achieves approximately 100% and 0.91% for best and worst case in terms of action appearance accuracy in human action dataset KTH in the extracted key frames.

Keywords: *L1-norm* · Optical flow · Colour histogram · Frame differences · Blocks differential

1 Introduction

Key frames extraction is the first step in several computer vision fields such as video summarisation, video retrieval, and video forgery detection based on the fingerprint. Generally, the algorithm for key frame extraction should provide a compact video representation, but it should not be a complex and time consuming process. There are several visual features were used for key frame extraction including static features and motion features such as colour, texture, shape, and camera movement and object motion [1]. The motion feature is used to generate a compact video representation while protecting the important actions of the original video. The motion feature is

© Springer International Publishing AG 2017
H. Badioze Zaman et al. (Eds.): IVIC 2017, LNCS 10645, pp. 364–375, 2017.
https://doi.org/10.1007/978-3-319-70010-6_34

calculated by a motion estimation technique such as optical flow to describe the visual contents with temporal differences inside a video [2]. The Lucas–Kanade method [3] is widely used in differential methods for optical flow estimation and computer vision by calculating the motion feature between two frames which are taken at a specific time. Lu, et al. [4] proposed a real time motion detection algorithm based on the integration of accumulative optical flow and twice background filtering technique. The Lucas-Kanade method was employed to compute frame-to-frame optical flow to extract a 2D motion field. The accumulative optical flow method was used to cope with variations in a changing environment and to detect movement pixels in the video. The advantages of the algorithm [4] are: avoiding the need to learn the background model from a large number of frames, and it can handle frame variations without prior knowledge of the object shapes and sizes. The algorithm was reported to be able to detect tiny objects and even slow moving objects accurately. Many authors focused on motion estimation and analysis to extract key frames to keep important information about actions of the original video and to provide a compact video representation [5–7].

A variety of different key frame extraction algorithms were developed in recently to extract key frames to segment video into shots or scenes. The simplest was the selection of key frames by calculating the colour histogram difference between two consecutive frames [8], then computing the threshold based on the mean and the standard deviation of absolute difference. After that, comparing the difference with the threshold if the difference is larger than the threshold. Then select the current frame as a key frame. Steps were repeated until the end of the video to extract all key frames. In another typical method [9], key frames were extracted by comparing the consecutive frame differences with a pre-determined threshold value. The algorithm read each frame in a video and converted them into the gray level, and calculated their differences between two consecutive frames. Then it calculates the mean and standard deviation values simultaneously and sets the threshold value similar to standard deviation multiply by a constant number. If the difference is larger than the threshold, then the current frame will be saved as key frame. Cao, et al. [10] proposed a key frame extraction algorithm based on frame blocks differential accumulation with two thresholds. In their algorithm, the first frame in a video was considered as a first reference frame. The remaining video frames were then partitioned into equal sized image blocks. The created image blocks were used to detect any local motion in the video. The colour mean differences were computed in RGB colour space of the corresponding blocks in the reference frame and the current frame. The algorithm counted the blocks changing in the current frame in relation to the block changing in the reference frame. If the count number was greater than the global threshold, this means the current frame had more changes than the reference frame. Then, the algorithm used the current frame as key frame instead of the reference frame and similar steps were repeated until the last frame. The algorithm [10] was able to identify the movements in high efficiency and to extract key frames with strong robustness in different types of video.

The majority of key frame extraction algorithms was developed to segment videos into shots or scenes. There are very few researchers as [8] focused on extracting key frames within the video shots. However, it is considered important in some fields which need a compact presentation of video shots such as in video forgery detection system based on fingerprint [11], for video copyright protection [12], and it may give a good benefit in the field of improving the hallucination of probes in the videos [13].

In Sect. 2, key frames extraction algorithm within the video shot is presented and discussed; Sect. 3 argues the experiments, analysis the result, and shows the quantitative evaluation of the proposed algorithm. Finally, Sect. 4 concludes the work and suggests future work.

2   Action Key Frames Extraction Algorithm

The key frames extraction within a scene is an easier task than extracting them inside a shot. A scene has a transition between two sequential shots and different views from shot to shot, while the shot is a sequence of successive frames captured without interruption by the same camera. In order to derive an algorithm to perform key frame extraction effectively inside shots is a challenging task because video frames are attributed to many visual features such as motion and colour. The most important key frames which contain critical action of objects and extracted with a compact limited number make them easier to use in different systems such as video retrieval and video fingerprint. The basic action was defined by [14] as the unit into which human behavior shall be classified, and the amount of information which needs to be accumulated depends on the complexity of the action such as a high jump needs more frames rather than running and jumping. Schindler and Gool [14] claimed that the one to seven frames are sufficient for basic action recognition from a very short shot. They extracted the local shape and optic flow features for each frame and achieved a good averaging of correct recognitions around 90%. The frames were between five to seven and about 0.3 to 0.5 s of the video. Therefore, we chose ten as an average for accumulative action frames to be moderate and suitable for detecting more complex actions such as moving objects with a static camera either with a static or dynamic background, moving objects with a moving camera or a shaky camera.

At the beginning, our proposed algorithm read ten consecutive frames from the video shot, and used the optical flow to estimate objects' velocities from each frame based on Lucas-Kanade method. If the objects' velocities of any frame equal zero, the frame was discarded and read the following frame. Each selected ten frames were organized as a window. Later, the algorithm generated an absolute difference image *AbsDiff* from optical flow frames Of_i and Of_{i-1}, where Of_i is the first frame in the current window, and Of_{i-1} is the last frame in the previous window as shown in Eq. (1). Features extraction usually used to extract the information that represents the objects [15]. Thus, to inspect the sparsity of the motion information in *AbsDiff* images, the *L1-norm* (least absolute error) was used in Eq. (2). *L1-norm* was proposed by Claerbout and Muir [16] for data modeling and used by Schindler and Gool [14] to extract motion features.

$$AbsDiff = |Of_i - Of_{i-1}|, \tag{1}$$

$$L1\_norm = \sum_1^j \sum_1^k (AbsDiff) \tag{2}$$

where j and k are the *AbsDiff* number of columns and rows respectively. *L1-norm* is the sum of the absolute differences between *Ofi* and *Ofi–1*, and it returns motion information about the current *AbsDiff* frame. Different threshold values were examined to pick out the optimal value able to detect the accurate action frames *Af* generated by Eqs. (1) and (2) to filter the frames were selected via *L1_norm*, and to discard *Af* with none or tiny motion information, refer to Sect. 3. In [17], the sum of absolute differences (SAD) was calculated from image blocks to create a block similarity while in our proposed algorithm the SAD was calculated from action frames to create action frames summations, as shown in Eqs. (3) and (4).

$$Action\_FrDiff = |Af_i - Af_{i-1}|, \tag{3}$$

$$Action\_FrSum = \sum\nolimits_{m=1}^{10} (Action\_FrDiff(m)) \tag{4}$$

where *Action_FrDiff* is the absolute difference frame between the two consecutive action frames, Af_i is the current action frame, Af_{i-1} is the previous action frame. *Action_FrSum* was defined as candidate key frames generated by accumulating ten of action frames, m is the current *Action_FrDiff* frame. The selection of key frames depended on three cases. In the first case, if the candidate key frames were between six to ten, they were acceptable and saved as the final key frames. In the second case, if the candidate key frames had extra keys less or equal ten, it means the shot has little dynamic texture and/or small motion objects need to be detected. Therefore, the difference between each two consecutive candidate key frames was calculated, then the candidate key frames with maximum differences were selected. In the third case, if the candidate key frames had extra keys more than ten, the candidate key frames were converted to a binary image using Otsu's method [18]. The reason of using Otsu's method because it can computes a global threshold that can be used to convert an intensity image to a binary image. Then the difference words counts between each two consecutive candidate key frames were founded. After that, the ten candidate key frames with maximum differences were selected. The pseudo code of the proposed algorithm steps is shown in Fig. 1.

3   Experiments and Result Analysis

Our experiments were performed on a laptop, Toshiba Satellite C850-B098 with CPU-Intel (R) Core (TM) i3-2312 M CPU @ 2.10 GHz, memory RAM-2 GB, system type 32-bit. Our system was programmed with Matlab2013a using Windows 7. Our proposed algorithm was implemented under KTH human action dataset which presented in [19]. KTH contains 599 video shots - we used the term of video shot instead of video because each video in KTH has the same view without transition - of six types of human actions: boxing, hand clapping, hand waving, jogging, running, and walking. The actions were performed by 25 actors and actresses in four different scenarios: outdoor d1, outdoor with scale change d2, outdoor with different clothes d3, and indoor d4. KTH video shots were taken over a homogeneous background, frame rate equal to 25 frames per second, resolution 160×120 pixels per frame, and a length less than

Input : Video V, with number of frames n
Output : Set of key frames K for input video V

K – Key Frames Extraction Algorithm (V)
{
Step-1: Read ten consecutive frames from V
 Estimate objects' velocities *Of* from each frame
 Create a window of each 10 frames if frame velocities Not (Zero)
Step-2: Generate an absolute difference image *AbsDiff* from *Ofi* and *Ofi-1*, where *Ofi* is the first
 frame in the current window, and *Ofi-1* is the last frame in the previous window.
Step-3:Claculate L1-norm = Sum (*AbsDiff* images between *Ofi* and *Ofi-1*).
Step-4: Action Frames *Af* = Threshold (frames selected by L1-norm)
Step-5: Calculate *Af differences*= *Afi* - *Afi-1* where, *Af_i* is the current action frame, *Af_{i-1}* is the
 previous action frame.
Step-6: Candidate key frames *CF* = Sum (10 of *Af differences*), discard if has none or tiny motion
 information.
Step-7: For each candidate key frames
   { if *CF* >= 6 and <=10
   K = *CF*
   }
   { if *CF* has Extra keys <=10
   Calculate difference between each two consecutive *CF* frames
   K= 10 maximum differences frames
   }
   { if *CF* has Extra keys >10
   Convert to binary image (*CF*)
   Calculate the difference words counts between each two consecutive CF
   K = 10 maximum differences frames
   }
}

Fig. 1. The pseudo code of the proposed key frame extraction algorithm steps.

one minute. We divided KTH into two different sets. The five selected video shots in [8] from KTH as a training set, and all 300 video shots in the jogging, running, and walking as a validation set.

L1-norm threshold is a global threshold since its value is defined using the whole frame and need not segment the whole frame to blocks. The global threshold is easier to implement than the local threshold with less computation time [20]. *L1_norm* action frames were compared with the action frames selected by a user using a comparison of user summaries (CUS) evaluation method [8], more details about CUS method were discussed in Sect. 3.1. As shown in Fig. 2, the user selected four sequence groups for the same action in the same video shot.

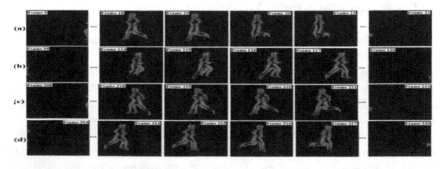

Fig. 2. The action frames of the target selected by a user (a) the first appearance (b) the second appearance (c) the third appearance (d) the fourth appearance.

The accuracy rate and error rate were used to evaluate the quality of the auto-matically extracted key frames compared with user extraction in [21]. In this work, the action accuracy rate (*ActionA*) in Eq. (5) and action error rate (*ActionE*) in Eq. (6) were used to evaluate the quality of the detected action frames by *L1-norm* threshold comparing with selected user action frames.

$$ActionA = \frac{\#Matching\ action\ frames}{\#user\ action\ frames} \tag{5}$$

$$ActionE = \frac{\#Non - Matching\ action\ frames}{\#user\ action\ frames} \tag{6}$$

where *Matching action frames* means the extracted action frames based on *L1-norm* matched the action frames set which selected by the user. *Non-Matching action frames* means the extracted action frames based on *L1-norm* not matched the action frames set which selected by the user. The line graphs in Figs. 3 and 4 show the effects of implementing different values of *L1_norm* threshold from 600 to 5400. The *ActionA* of *L1-norm* goes down after 2600 between 0.003 to 0.042, while the *ActionE* of *L1-norm* stability begins from 4600 with least action error rates between 0.005 to 0.011. The *ActionA* and the *ActionE* are complementary, the highest quality being when *ActionA* equal one and *ActionE* equal zero that means all detected action frames by *L1-norm* and the user are exactly matched. Therefore, the 4600 value was chosen of *L1-norm* because it has an *ActionA* equal one except the last video shot which has an *ActionA* approximately 0.99 with minimum *ActionE*.

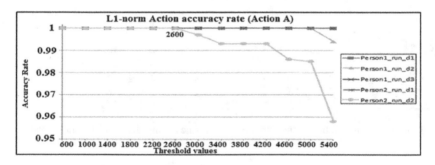

Fig. 3. Action accuracy rate using different *L1-norm* threshold values.

The compactness measure of video shots contents due to the extracted key frames was computed using the compression ratio (CR) to evaluate the performance of key frame extraction algorithms. The higher value of CR of an algorithm indicates that the algorithm is good [8]. The CR was calculated using the Eq. (7) from [8].

$$CR = \frac{\#Video\ frames}{\#Extracted\ key\ frames} \tag{7}$$

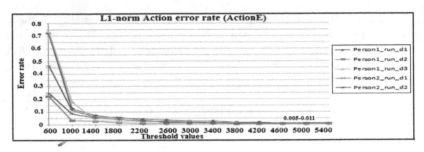

Fig. 4. Action error rate using different *L1-norm* threshold values.

The CR results of the absolute colour histogram difference were described in [8], while the CR results of our proposed algorithm, the grey level consecutive frame differences with threshold [9], and RGB colour space frame blocks differential accumulation with two thresholds were obtained by experiments using the training set video shots from KTH as described in [8]. To determine the acceptable values for frame blocks differential thresholds variables a and b [10] on KTH training set video shots, different experiments were executed in Eq. (8) and Eq. (9). As shown in Fig. 5, frame blocks differential threshold [10] had the best CR when a = 1 and b = − 6.

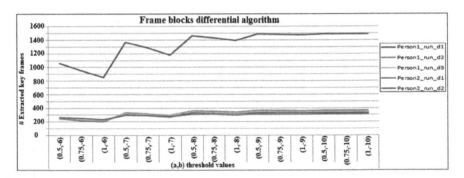

Fig. 5. The total number of the extracted key frames using different thresholds value's.

$$Threshold1 = a \times mValue \tag{8}$$

$$Threshold2 = b + (m \times n) \times \propto where \propto = 0.6 \tag{9}$$

where the *mValue* is the mean differences of all blocks in each frame, *m* and *n* are the numbers of columns and rows respectively in the frame. Variable *a* range is [0,1] and variable *b* range is [−10,10]. The main disadvantage of [10] is the difficulty of determining the threshold value, and several experiments need to be attempted to find the appropriate threshold value.

Table 1 gives the CR value of the training set video shots in KTH dataset. All selected video shots were represented as individual action in a single video shot. As shown in Table 1, our proposed algorithm had the best CR of extracting key frames for the five video shots comparing with the-state-of-the-art algorithms, the absolute colour histogram difference [8], the grey level consecutive frame differences with threshold [9] and RGB colour space frame blocks differential accumulation with two thresholds [10] respectively.

Table 1. CR for our key frames extraction algorithm and the-state-of-the-art algorithms.

Training set video shots	Frames count	Compression ratio of the extracted key frames			
		Our alg.	Colour his. diff.	Con. frame diff.	Frame blocks diff. (1,−6)
Person1_runing_d1	335	41.88	5.68	4.14	1.58
Person1_ runing_d2	365	36.50	8.90	2.92	1.79
Person1_ runing_d3	350	38.88	6.48	3.72	1.57
Person2_ runing_d1	314	31.40	6.83	2.51	1.35
Person2_ runing_d2	1492	149.20	7.54	1.79	1.75

3.1 Quantitative Evaluation of the Proposed Key Frame Extraction Algorithm

Video summarisation is a technique to generate a short summary of a video. The summary can either be an order of static images called key frames or moving images called video skims. A good video summarisation should return a maximum information about the video in an identified time limitation or adequate information in the minimum time [22]. To evaluate any proposed algorithm for video summarisation, the best choice is comparing it against existing algorithms. Nevertheless, a stable evaluation framework is absent for key frame extraction and video skims. Currently, every key frame extraction algorithm has its own evaluation methodology and regularly presented without any performance comparison with existing algorithms. This occurs because the definition of what should be considered as an exact detection is not an explicit task [23, 24]. Therefore, the existing evaluation methods for video summarisation by extracting key frames algorithms are grouped into three different categories [22]. These categories are the result description which does not require any comparison with other algorithms, and used to discuss the effect of the system parameters or visual dynamics of the video sequence on the extracted key frames. The objective metrics are used to compare the key frames extracted by different algorithms or by changing parameters for the same algorithm. The user studies require independent users to judge the quality of video summary or extracted key frames. Therefore, a novel evaluation method to evaluate video summaries was proposed [23, 24]. This evaluation method called the comparison of user summaries (CUS), the video summary is built manually by a number of users from the sampled frames. The user summaries are taken as a reference to be compared with the summaries obtained by different methods.

Ideally we should use the same data sets and same metrics to compare our proposed algorithm with the state of the art algorithms. However, most of the previous algorithms that used the KTH data set focused on human action recognition and this made direct comparisons almost impossible. For this reason, to verify our key frames extraction algorithm, we used the jogging, running, and walking scenarios amounting to a total of 300 video shots from KTH as a validation set. The validation set has several human appearances from the right and the left sides for each action. The key frames in [25] were extracted by searching the human appearances inside the video shots in KTH dataset as the first step in human action recognition system. Therefore, to study if our key frames - called action key frames - extraction algorithm can detect all human appearances in KTH. We presented Eq. (10) to study the accuracy of our action key frames extraction algorithm in detecting the different appearances for the same action in the same video shot. The best value for Action_appearance$_{acc}$ equals one, that's mean each different action appearance is detected by one key frame or more.

$$Action\_appearance_{acc} = \frac{\#Detected \text{ action appearances}}{\#Action \text{ appearances}} \tag{10}$$

Our proposed algorithm is able to extract the action key frames in sorted order to enable the visual understanding of the result as shown in Fig. 6. In addition, the extracted action key frames were able to detect and extract video shots with different scale appearances as shown in Fig. 7, and partial appearances as shown in Fig. 8.

Fig. 6. Six sorted appearances from video shot person12-jogging-outdoor with their saved names.

Fig. 7. Four different scale appearances from video shot person23-walking-outdoor.

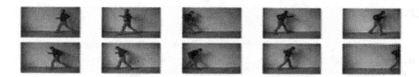

Fig. 8. Four partial appearances from video shot person2_running_indoor.

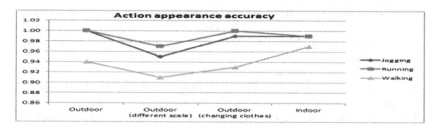

Fig. 9. Comparison of action appearance accuracy under validation set video shots.

In Fig. 9, the running action has the best Action_appearance$_{acc}$ in a different camera and environment conditions while the walking action has the least Action_appearance$_{acc}$. On average, indoor has the best Action_appearance$_{acc}$ comparing with other conditions; nevertheless, outdoor has a complete Action_appearance$_{acc}$ equal one in jogging and running actions. In general, the highest accuracy in the best cases equal one and in the worst case equal 0.91%. The jogging and running actions have the same standard deviation equal six while walking action has twelve.

4 Conclusion and Future Work

The extracted key frames can be used to represent the video as a whole and summarize the important actions of the video. The optimal number of extracted key frames is mainly dependent on video complexity, such as camera motion, shot visual contents, or the dynamicity of foreground or background. Our proposed algorithm focused on estimating motion by using an accumulative number of optical flow frames based on *L1-norm*. In comparison with the-state-of-the-art algorithms tested in our experiments, our proposed algorithm detected the important actions in the video shots with a compact controlled number of key frames between six and ten. For all video shots, our proposed algorithm was able to extract action key frames automatically which makes it suitable for full automatic application in future for video fingerprint generation, detecting video forgery system, video retrieval and searching system, and video summarisation. For future work, we need to eliminate the wrong detection that appeared in video shots with shadow appearances instead of a person or empty key frames caused by sudden shaking camera. We would like to acknowledge that this paper has been supported by the Ministry of Higher Education under the Prototype Research Grant Scheme PRGS/1/2016/ICT02/UKM/02/1 entitled "Intelligent Vehicle Identity Recognition for Surveillance".

References

1. Hu, W., Xie, N., Li, L., Zeng, X., Maybank, S.: A survey on visual content-based video indexing and retrieval. IEEE Trans. Syst. Man Cybern. Part C (Appl. Rev.) **41**(6), 797–819 (2011)
2. Sujatha, C., Mudenagudi, U.: A study on keyframe extraction methods for video summary. In: International Conference on Computational Intelligence and Communication Networks (CICN), pp. 73–77. IEEE (2011)
3. Lucas, B.D., Kanade, T.: An Iterative Image Registration Technique with an Application to Stereo Vision, vol. 81, no. 1, pp. 674–679 (1981)
4. Lu, N., Wang, J., Yang, L., Wu, Q.H.: Motion detection based on accumulative optical flow and double background filtering. In: World Congress on Engineering (WCE), IWCE 2007, London, U.K., pp. 602–607. Citeseer (2007)
5. Zheng, R., Yao, C., Jin, H., Zhu, L., Zhang, Q., Deng, W.: Parallel key frame extraction for surveillance video service in a smart city. PLOS One **10**, 1–8 (2015)
6. Raikwar, S.C., Bhatnagar, C., Jalal, A.S.: A framework for key frame extraction from surveillance video. In: International Conference on Computer and Communication Technology (ICCCT), Allahabad, India, pp. 297–300. IEEE (2014)
7. Sosa, J.C., Rodríguez, R., Ortega, V.H.G., Hernández, R.: Real-time optical-flow computation for motion estimation under varying illumination conditions. Int. J. Reconfigurable Embed. Syst. (IJRES) **1**(1), 25–36 (2012)
8. Sheena, C.V., Narayanan, N.K.: Key-frame extraction by analysis of histograms of video frames using statistical methods. Procedia Comput. Sci. **70**, 36–40 (2015)
9. Thepade, S.D., Tonge, A.A.: An optimized key frame extraction for detection of near duplicates in content based video retrieval. In: International Conference on Communications and Signal Processing (ICCSP), pp. 1087–1091. IEEE (2014)
10. Cao, C., Chen, Z., Xie, G., Lei, S.: Key frame extraction based on frame blocks differential accumulation. In: 24th Chinese Control and Decision Conference (CCDC), pp. 3621–3625. IEEE (2012)
11. Mizher, M.A., Ang, M.C., Mazhar, A.A., Mizher, M.A.: A review of video falsifying techniques and video forgery detection techniques. Int. J. Electron. secur. digit. **9**(3), 191–209 (2017). Publisher: Inderscience online
12. Shi, Y., Yang, H., Gong, M., Liu, X., Xia, Y.: A fast and robust key frame extraction method for video copyright protection. J. Electr. Comput. Eng. **2017**, 1–7 (2017). Article no. 1231794
13. Zamani, N.A., Zahamdin, A.D.M., Abdullah, S.N.H.S., Nordin, M.J.: Sparse representation super-resolution method for enhancement analysis in video forensics. In: 12th International Conference on Intelligent Systems Design and Applications (ISDA), pp. 921–926. IEEE (2012)
14. Schindler, K., Gool, L.V.: Action snippets: how many frames does human action recognition require? In: Conference on Computer Vision and Pattern Recognition (CVPR), pp. 1–8. IEEE (2008)
15. Abdulameer, M.H., Abdullah, S.N.H.S., Othman, Z.A.: Support vector machine based on adaptive acceleration particle swarm optimization. Sci. World J. **2014**, 1–8 (2014). Publisher: Hindawi Publishing Corporation
16. Claerbout, J.F., Muir, F.: Robust modeling with erratic data. Geophysics **38**(5), 826–844 (1973). Publisher: Society of Exploration Geophysicists
17. Richardson, I.E.: H. 264 and MPEG-4 Video Compression: Video Coding for Next-Generation Multimedia. Wiley, Hoboken (2004)

18. Otsu, N.: A threshold selection method from gray-level histograms. IEEE Trans. Syst. Man Cybern. **9**(1), 62–66 (1979)
19. Schuldt, C., Laptev, I., Caputo, B.: Recognizing human actions: a local SVM approach. In: Proceedings of the 17th International Conference on Pattern Recognition (ICPR), vol. 3, pp. 32–36. IEEE (2004)
20. Hussein, W.A., Sahran, S., Abdullah, S.N.H.S.: A fast scheme for multilevel thresholding based on a modified bees algorithm. Knowl.-Based Syst. **101**, 114–134 (2016)
21. Dang, C., Radha, H.: RPCA-KFE: key frame extraction for video using robust principal component analysis. IEEE Trans. Image Process. **24**(11), 3742–3753 (2015)
22. Truong, B.T., Venkatesh, S.: Video abstraction: a systematic review and classification. ACM Trans. Multimed. Comput. Commun. Appl. (TOMM) **3**(1), 3 (2007)
23. de Avila, S.E.F., Lopes, A.P.B., da Luz Jr., A., de Albuquerque Araújo, A.: VSUMM: a mechanism designed to produce static video summaries and a novel evaluation method. Pattern Recogn. Lett. **32**(1), 56–68 (2011). Publisher Elsevier B.V.
24. de Avila, S.E.F., da Luz Jr., A., de Albuquerque Araújo, A., Cord, M.: VSUMM: an approach for automatic video summarization and quantitative evaluation. In: XXI Brazilian Symposium on Computer Graphics and Image Processing, Campo Grande, Brazil, pp. 103–110. IEEE (2008)
25. Vishwakarma, D.K., Rawat, P., Kapoor, R.: Human activity recognition using gabor wavelet transform and ridgelet transform. Procedia Comput. Sci. **57**, 630–636 (2015)

Mandarin Language Learning System for Nasal Voice User

Thagirarani Muniandy[1(✉)], Thamilvaani Arvaree Alvar[1,2], and Chong Jiang Boon[1]

[1] Nilai University, Persiaran University,
71800 Nilai, Negeri Sembilan, Malaysia
rani@nilai.edu.my, Thamil.Vaani@nottingham.edu.my
[2] University of Nottingham Malaysia Campus,
Jalan Broga, 43500 Semenyih, Malaysia

Abstract. Since the technology is growing rapidly, a lot of people nowadays start to learn the foreign language by using computer or mobile phone where they can simply download the language learning software into their phone or computer, and learn it without attending the traditional class room. However, most of the language learning software on the market does not support the nasal recognition. If a user contains nasal voice, the system may not able to recognize and determine his/her voice. Thus, nasal user may find it difficult in using this kind of language learning system. In this research, a new Mandarin Language Learning System is developed for nasal voice user. This Mandarin Language Learning System able to understand the nasal pronunciation which allows the nasal voice user to learn Mandarin without facing any problems. Once the system able to recognize the nasal pronunciation, it will increase the accuracy of recognition and also the efficiency of the system. In this research, Mel Frequency Cepstral Coefficient (MFCC) features are extracted from nasal speech signal and normal voice signal. Later extracted signals are studied the difference and matching using Dynamic Time Warping (DTW) techniques. Results obtain are compared with Hidden Markov Model (HMM). The accuracy of Nasal Voice is much higher by Combining MFCC features and DTW.

Keywords: Nasal voice · Mel Frequency Cepstral Coefficient (MFCC) · Dynamic Time Warping (DTW) · Hidden Markov Model (HMM)

1 Introduction

This research explains the development of the Mandarin Language Learning System for Nasal Voice Users. Mandarin language learning system for nasal voice users is a system that used to detect the accuracy of Mandarin pronunciation with the aid of voice recognition system. Thus, this system assists users in their Mandarin language learning process by allowing users to realize their problems in pronunciation of Mandarin.

Nowadays, China is considered as the world's second largest economy by attracting abundant of foreigners entering the market for investment [1]. Therefore, it attracts a lot of foreigners starting to teach Mandarin as their second language in order to communicate and interact with Chinese for sharing and exchange of information or ideas.

© Springer International Publishing AG 2017
H. Badioze Zaman et al. (Eds.): IVIC 2017, LNCS 10645, pp. 376–388, 2017.
https://doi.org/10.1007/978-3-319-70010-6_35

In accordance to a survey of Dalian University, it is found that the number of foreign mandarin language learners has increased to 100 million in 2014 as compared to 30 million in 2004 [2]. As such, it is obvious that the role of Mandarin is kept increasing as time goes on. In order to allow foreigner to learn Mandarin in a more effective way, the development of a Mandarin language learning system is vital in current era.

In the process of learning Mandarin language, the most common problems faced by learners are their nasal voice made in pronunciation [3]. According to a research, nasal voice always occur when abnormal coupling of oral and nasal cavities during speech, especially with vowel productions [4]. As we know, nasal voice is a disorders and it hard to be controlled by the patients. It is because the nasal voice will be occurred unconsciously, and the patient will not aware of it. In this case, when the patients try to communicate with other people, the nasal voice will directly affect pronunciation of the patient. Thus, this system will help to detect the nasal voice of the users. With the system, the users able to learn the Mandarin Language by listening to certain Mandarin words that pronounced by the system and then pronounce the words through the microphone to allow the voice detection system to access the pronunciation of the users. As such, the system will recognize the nasal pronunciation of the learner. By understanding the nasal pronunciation, the users are able to proceed with making correction on their Mandarin pronunciation.

1.1 Problem Statement

With the technology advancement nowadays, most of the people start to use the language learning software to learn mandarin as their second language such as Rosetta Stone, TellMeMore, eLanguage, RocketLanguage and etc. These mandarin language learning software allow the learner to learn the Mandarin in a more simple way without attending the formal language learning classes. However, all of the existing Mandarin language learning software in the market does not help to recognize the nasal tone from the learner, especially those with nasal voice.

Nasal voice is a disorder that learner's voice contains nose sound. As there is too much sound resonating in the nasal cavity during speech, nasal voice will occur [5]. The nasal voice learner find it difficult in learning Mandarin language by using the existing language learning software as they has difficulties in pronouncing Mandarin tone correctly [6]. The nasal voice may affect the user while they are pronouncing the Mandarin tone. Meanwhile, the nasal voice may also influence the recognition rate and accuracy of the software. When the learner speak with nasal voice, the existing language learning software is hard to recognize the voice of learners.

The majority of existing language learning software does not have the nasal voice detection function. Thus, if the nasal voice user speaks to the software, the software function can only determine the user pronunciation but it is unable to detect nasal voice from the user. The learner find very difficult in pronouncing Mandarin when they using the existing language learning software as the learner does not know their nasal voice that will affect their pronunciation.

In language learning process, the first language may influence the target language of learners. This can be reflected in the case that most learners will find it difficult to pronounce because some Chinese sounds is similar with their first language sounds, but they are totally different from each other [7]. In addition, nasal sounds also are one of the reasons that cause the learner unable to pronounce mandarin correctly. Nasal sound will prevent the occurrence of certain combinations of consonant sound, thereby limit the Mandarin language learner's ability in proper pronunciations [8]. Due to the reason above, nasal voice learner find it more difficult in pronouncing the correct mandarin.

The purpose of this research is to allow the entire nasal voice user to simply use the language learning software to learn Mandarin and reduce their nasal voice pronunciation to ensure that they can pronounce the correct Mandarin. This project will proposed a learning tool for nasal voice user to learn Mandarin and allow them to pronounce Mandarin with correct tone. This learning tool will encourage more nasal voice user to use this learning tools to learn Mandarin. In addition, this learning tools will include the nasal pronunciation detection function to accuracy detect user nasal voice to help the user reduce their nasal voice and allow the nasal voice user can pronounce the Mandarin with correct tone.

1.2   Research Objectives

The purpose of this research is to develop a mandarin language learning system for nasal voice user. The system will analyse the pronunciation and intonation of the speaker, and determine the correctness of the pronunciation of the user. The following objectives are set to achieve the main aim to recognize and analyse the nasal pronunciation from nasal voice user by using Mel Frequency Cepstral Coefficient (MFCC) and Dynamic Time Warping (DTW).

1.3   Scope

This research focus on the implementation of the Mandarin language learning system and also the nasal pronunciation detection function. As this Mandarin language learning system includes the nasal pronunciation detection function, it may allow the nasal voice user to learn the new language and help to reduce their nasal voice to ensure that they can pronounce the correct Mandarin tone. By using this new nasal pronunciation detection function, it will recognize the nasal pronunciation from user and efficiently to help them to reduce their nasal voice.

However, there still have some problems for the nasal pronunciation detection function. For example, if some mandarin words are containing with nasal end, this kind of words will cause the detection function cannot determine the nasal level of user and it will influence the operation of system.

2   Speech Recognition

In this section, the information regarding to the speech-recognition system of language learning system, MFCC feature extraction, Dynamic Time Warping and Hidden Markov Model is discussed. The implementation of each techniques and also the comparison between two matching techniques Dynamic Time Warping (DTW) and Hidden Markov Model (HMM) will be discussed.

2.1 Speech–Recognition System

Figure 1 has shown that how is the speech-recognition system work. Application's interface with the decoder is applied to gain recognition results which will be adopted to adapt other components within the system. The representation of knowledge about phonetics, acoustics, gender, microphone, environment variability and dialect differences among speakers are included in the acoustic models. Language models is referring to the knowledge of a system of what forms a possible word, what word is likely to be co-occurred, and in what sequence.

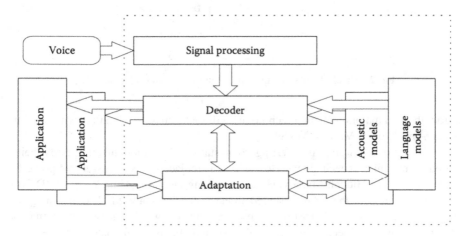

Fig 1. System architecture of speech-recognition system

2.2 Feature Extraction

There are many feature extraction techniques being used by speech/speaker recognition system, such as LPCC, KNN, MFCC and etc. Following sections, will discuss on MFCC feature extraction and the implementation into Mandarin language learning system.

2.2.1 Mel-Frequency Cepstral Coefficients (MFCC) Features Extraction

Mel-Frequency Cepstral Coefficients (MFCC) is the most common features extraction technique that being used by the speech/speaker recognition system. This features extraction method was introduced by Bridle and Brown in 1974. MFCC is regarded as the coefficients that being used to represent the sound based on the human speech perception. The derivations of MFCC are made by taking the signals' Fourier Transform and warp it by applying the Mel-filter bank to mimic the Mel-scale. The last step is to perform Discrete Cosine Transform on the logarithm power of the speech frame from the Mel-scale output (Fig. 2).

There are many matching techniques being used by the speech/speak recognition system, such as Gaussian Mixture Models (GMM), Support Vector Machine (SVM), Dynamic Time Warping (DTW), Hidden Markov Models (HMM) and etc. In this

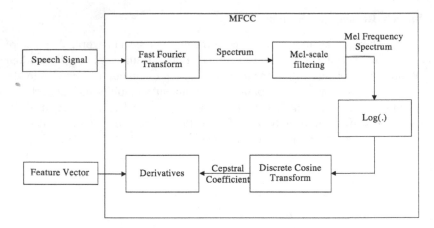

Fig 2. Block diagram of the MFCC algorithm and reference [9]

section, the two majors matching techniques will be discussed, which is Dynamic time warping and Hidden Markov Model.

Dynamic time warping is referring to a statistical method that normally being applied to recognize speech signal. However, it is replaced by successful and powerful techniques such as Hidden Markov Model. By using Dynamic Time Warping (DTW), different type of data that is represented linearly can be analysed. The advantage of using DTW algorithm is in measuring similarity between two time series which may be different in time or speech. For example, to find the optimal match between two sequence, the input and reference template. DTW main principle is to differentiate between two dynamic patterns and measure the similarity and calculate the minimum distance between the two patterns. A formula is used to find the minimum cost between input frame (fi) and transition cost (Txy) by calculating the distance between the reference frame and the input frame.

$$D(i,j) = d(i,j) + \min(D(i,j) + T_{10}, D(i,j) + T_{11}, D(i,j) + T_{01})$$

Where $D(i,j)$ **is lowest cost to** i,j (1)

$D(i,j)$ **is lowest match cost**

The steps included in Dynamic time warping are as follow:

- Recording, Parameterizing and storing reference words' vocabulary.
- Recording test word to be parameterized and recognized.
- Measuring the distance between test word and each reference words.
- Choosing reference words closest to test word.

2.2.2   Hidden Markov Model

The difference between Hidden Markov Model (HMM) and Markov Chain is that HMM is a finite-state machine with probabilistic transitions between states and also a set of observation probabilities associated to the states. For Markov chain, the states are directly visible to the observer but for HMM are not directly visible but the observations are visible. HMM is widely used in temporal pattern recognitions application such as speech recognition, handwriting recognition and part of speech tagging (Fig. 3).

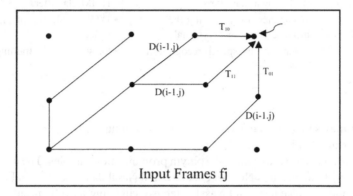

Fig 3. Optimal alignment between input frame and reference [10]

For the standard Hidden Markov Model, the state space is discrete, while the observations can either be discrete or continuous. The parameters of interest comprise the state transition probabilities and observation probabilities. The state transition probabilities control the way the hidden state at time t + 1 is chosen given the hidden state at time t. On the other hand, the observation probabilities govern the distribution of the observations at a particular time given the state at that time (Fig. 4 and Table 1).

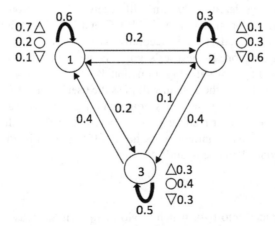

Fig 4. Example of a three-state Hidden Markov Model with discrete observation symbols

Table 1. Comparison of DTW and HMM

Classifier	Pros	Cons
Hidden Markov Model (HMM)	• Accuracies for speech recognition tasks that are comparable to other well-known classifiers	• A lot of design issues related to the structure and training of the HMM classifier
Dynamic Time Warping (DTW)	• Accuracies for measuring the distance between two signals	• DTW need a lot of memory space
	• Often used by speech recognition system	• Slow during the training section

2.2.3 Comparison Between Dynamic Time Warping and Hidden Markov Model

The function of database is to collect the pinyin pronunciation samples. The database will be separated by two, which is Normal database and Nasal database. Normal database is used by the normal voice user, and Nasal database will being used by nasal voice user.

Mel-frequency cepstral coefficients (MFCC) features extraction and Dynamic time warping (DTW) pattern matching will be the main techniques that being used in this Mandarin language learning system. Based on the research conducted by Fan and Liu (2010), the efficiency and accuracy of the combination of MFCC and DTW is higher than the combination of MFCC and Hidden Markov Model (HMM). Therefore, the efficiency and accuracy of Mandarin language learning system will become higher if the combination of MFCC and DTW is applied into this system.

3 Methodology

The Mandarin language learning system will receive a voice from user. After that, system will establish the connection with MFCC and DTW functions to ensure that these two functions are ready to use. Secondly, system will start to verify the user's voice, and make a decision. If the user's voice is not valid, the system will display "voice not valid" and system will stop immediately.

If the voice is valid, then the system will pass the user's voice to MFCC for feature extract and DTW for compare the user's voice with the database samples. Lastly, the system will determine the user result is good or no good. If the result is good, then the system will display "Good! Continue work hard!". If the result is no good, the system will display "No good! Practice again!".

3.1 Database

The database is divided into two, which is Normal pinyin database and Nasal pinyin database. The purposes of database are used to compare the user pronunciation. If the voice is from the normal user, then the system will compare their voice with the normal database. If the voice is from the nasal user, then the system will compare their voice with the nasal database.

The samples of pinyin database are retrieved from an open source website and each pinyin letter is pronounced by different speaker. As such, the samples of nasal pinyin database are recorded by different nasal speakers.

For normal database 23 pinyin initials pronunciation will be stored in the normal database. Each pinyin initial have 4 simples, and all the samples is pronounced by different people. The main purpose of the database is used for training, matching and comparing. Whereas for nasal database, 23 nasal pinyin initials pronunciation will be stored in the nasal database. Each nasal pinyin initial also have 4 simples, and all the samples is pronounced by different nasal people. The main purpose of the database is used for training, matching and comparing.

3.2 Signal Processing

The first step is to extract MFCC features from normal and nasal Pinyin speech signal. This file is saved as .mat (Fig. 5).

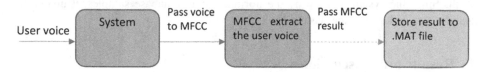

Fig 5. Flow chart from user's voice to MFCC

The extracted features are supplied to DTW algorithm to compare the pattern of nasal and normal pinyin speech signal. The result of the comparison will be stored into. MAT file (Fig. 6).

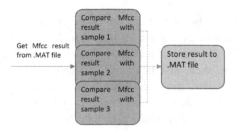

Fig 6. Flow chart for DTW implementation in this system

Subsequently, a baseline sample is formed to use for comparing against the DTW results. This baseline sample is formed through matching the best two samples from normal pinyin database. Lastly, system will select the result with least distance from 3 pairs of DTW results and compare it with the baseline. A final output is prompt with a condition, if the result is higher than 60%, it is considered acceptable (Fig. 7).

The method for detection of nasal pronunciation is basically similar with method for detecting the normal pronunciation.

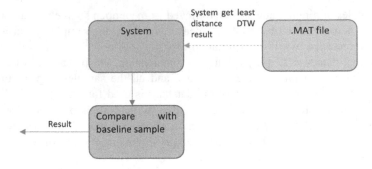

Fig 7. System for comparing least distance DTW result with baseline sample

Most of the existing language learning system in the market only has one database, which is the normal pinyin database. By using one database, the system will face difficulty when analyze the nasal user voice and it also will reduce the accuracy of the result. Since the system is train by the normal pinyin database samples, it unable to analyze and understand the nasal voice.

4   Results and Discussion

Testing has been conducted with 10 subjects. Five subjects tested for "Normal Voice Lesson" and another five subjects tested for "Nasal Voice Lesson". Each group of five subjects contains two females and three males. All the subjects are briefed before the testing take place. Each subjects are tested for all 23 Pin Yin letters (Table 2).

4.1   Normal Voice Pin Yin Result

The result table below has shown that the lowest pinyin pronunciation letters are b, f, and l. It means that the normal voice user may found it difficult to pronounce those pinyin letters correctly. The reason that they facing difficulty in pronouncing those pinyin letters is because their first language is affecting them while they are pronouncing those pinyin letters. Since the pinyin pronunciation of b, f and l is quite similar with some of their first language word, but they are exactly difference. Therefore, it will cause the normal voice user hard to pronounce b, f and l correctly.

The highest pinyin pronunciation letters on the result table above is k, z and j. It means that the normal voice user has high accuracy while they are pronouncing those pinyin letters. Since the pronunciation of k, z and j is totally similar with some of their first language pronunciation. Therefore, they user may found it very easy while they are pronouncing the letters k, z and j.

4.2   Nasal Voice Lesson Result

From the result tabulated in Table 3, it shows that the lowest pinyin pronunciation letters are q and x. The nasal voice user may found it difficult to pronounce this two

Table 2. Result of Normal Voice Lesson

Initials	A	B	C	D	E	Average
b	67.5613%	79.6382%	70.5638%	60.3878%	19.8277%	**59.5957%**
P	79.4303%	100%	91.4674%	69.5730%	49.3536%	**77.9648%**
m	96.6323%	100%	75.3485%	73.0304%	81.1713%	**85.2365%**
f	60.5758%	99.7235%	66.0969%	38.3328%	64.0463%	**65.7550%**
d	92.3434%	100%	83.8376	71.3749%	98.4281%	**89.1960%**
t	93.3718%	73.2548%	68.4516%	57.9791%	85.0009%	**75.6116%**
n	83.8201%	79.2424%	80.3266%	75.0968%	78.2784%	**79.3528%**
l	77.3567%	83.2698%	62.3557%	38.5855%	84.2051%	**69.1546%**
g	100%	75.7297%	74.1475%	78.1650%	91.3328%	**83.8750%**
k	100%	100%	98.0979%	80.5739%	89.3738%	**93.6091%**
h	100%	84.4021%	93.9986%	73.0484%	71.2149%	**84.5328%**
z	93.2184%	100%	96.3355%	85.2849%	100%	**94.9678%**
c	87.9842%	90.4638%	100%	64.6385%	84.2739%	**85.4721%**
zh	83.2427%	99.1734%	96.8326%	70.0015%	90.0193%	**87.8539%**
ch	97.5848%	86.5296%	100%	76.2918%	77.1427%	**87.5098%**
sh	100%	87.5785%	100%	63.0165%	81.9881%	**86.5166%**
r	79.7049%	85.4759%	66.8455%	81.6679%	68.1320%	**76.3652%**
j	98.1845%	100%	94.6401%	90.1284%	75.2839%	**91.6474%**
q	88.7584%	100%	100%	67.3473%	88.1273%	**88.8466%**
x	94.8459%	96.9462%	83.7549%	77.7392%	61.3847%	**82.9342%**
y	69.9033%	79.1029%	73.1038%	100%	98.8726%	**84.1965%**
w	79.8634%	88.2179%	80.3290%	82.7823%	100%	**86.2385%**
s	82.2840%	90.4739%	71.3834%	80.3845%	65.7218%	**78.0495%**
Total Average						**82.5651%**

pinyin letters with the lowest percentage, 70%. The reason that could be inferred from the result is may be the nasal voice user found difficult to pronounce q and x Therefore, the nasal voice will definitely cause the user unable to pronounce the pinyin tone correctly.

Further, from Table 3, it can be seen that the highest accuracy of pinyin pronunciation letters is from k and w which are above 90%. This further indicates that the nasal user has high accuracy in pronouncing the pinyin letters k and w. Since the pronunciation of k and w is containing some nasal end, so the nasal voice will not affecting them while they are pronouncing k and w.

4.3 Discussion

The proposed system has successfully developed for normal and nasal voice users who wish to learn Mandarin. The result shows that the system has effectively recognized the user pronunciation with normal or nasal voice. For normal voice lesson, the total

Table 3. Result of Nasal Voice Lesson

Initials	F	G	H	I	J	Average
b	69.7123%	76.2706%	81.8474%	85.8334%	59.6685%	**74.6664%**
P	89.9353%	83.0231%	76.7127%	70.4849%	66.5598%	**77.3432%**
m	89.3505%	36.0634%	90.8349%	89.4590%	73.7340%	**75.8884%**
f	82.0851%	62.2384%	75.4658%	90.5897%	88.9964%	**79.8751%**
a	100%	79.4108%	67.3723%	72.6859%	100%	**83.8938%**
t	89.4638%	100%	70.0938%	98.1200%	80.8032%	**87.6962%**
n	89.7919%	70.7244%	75.3248%	80.7635%	64.1003%	**76.1410%**
l	79.4739%	86.7189%	73.0093%	72.3323%	90.8976%	**80.4864%**
g	68.7148%	100%	61.6758%	100%	100%	**86.0781%**
k	98.2695%	84.8594%	78.7584%	100%	88.6524%	**90.1079%**
h	95.1480%	82.2317%	64.5854%	67.3699%	100%	**81.8670%**
z	100%	96.9955%	80.5447%	89.9328%	75.7733%	**88.6493%**
c	74.8473%	81.8329%	59.3369%	63.7786%	93.4743%	**74.6540%**
zh	83.3019%	72.5859%	77.3990%	92.7062%	100%	**85.1986%**
ch	100%	58.7482%	60.8243%	71.7464%	78.9557%	**74.0549%**
sh	87.4357%	65.9477%	91.8574%	89.9856%	78.3322%	**82.7117%**
r	79.3728%	70.6478%	63.5948%	60.2238%	82.7666%	**71.3212%**
j	61.7605%	77.7898%	83.4627%	79.9178%	85.3343%	**77.6530%**
q	87.9854%	70.2985%	95.0937%	66.5698%	32.5774%	**70.5050%**
x	78.7858%	63.5740%	55.4990%	84.4436%	67.8423%	**70.0289%**
y	91.4358%	86.4233%	67.3238%	80.5588%	89.0064%	**82.9496%**
w	82.3473%	89.8876%	86.9548%	100%	100%	**91.8379%**
s	78.4637%	88.1929%	100%	72.7481%	81.4755%	**84.1760%**
Total Average						**80.3384%**

average result is 83%. It indicates that the system has high ability to recognize and analyze the normal pinyin pronunciation from the user. In addition, the result of nasal voice lesson is 80%. The result is a good evidence to prove the system can understand and recognize the pinyin pronunciation from nasal user. Also, this system result is not affected by the users' gender. It is because the system is using dynamic time warping (DTW) matching technique. This is because DTW technique is measuring the distance between two sample audio, so that the high pitch and high energy from the female is hard to affect the decision of DTW. Finally, this system definitely increases the confident of the nasal user while they are using it.

5   Conclusion

Although the objective of this research project is achieved, the system still has some limitations which can be improved in future. For example, if the user pronunciation consisting some background noise, it will simply affect the result and decision of the system. It is because the system assumes the background noise is part of the user voice and calculates together with the user's voice. Therefore, the background noise affects the system's accuracy and confuses the system further.

However, it is believed that Mandarin language learning system will benefitted the people who wish to learn Mandarin, especially the nasal voice user. It is because the system is designed for nasal voice user. Since this system has the ability to understand and recognize the nasal pronunciation from nasal user. Thus, will reduce the problem that user will face when using other language learning system.

Some of the future direction can be work on this current work will be by improving the interface, including more samples into both databases and by adding noise filtering techniques.

References

1. Valoes, L.D.: The Importance of Language - Why Learning a Second Language is Important (2014). http://www.trinitydc.edu/continuing-education/2014/02/26/importance-of-language-why-learning-a-second-language-is-important/. Accessed 22 Nov 2015
2. Wantchinatimes: Number of Mandarin Chinese learners hits 100 million (2014). http://www.wantchinatimes.com/news-subclassnt.aspx?id=20140901000011&cid=1104%20/. Accessed 22 Nov 2015
3. Merritte, A.: Why learn a foreign language? Benefits of bilingualism (2013). http://www.telegraph.co.uk/education/educationopinion/10126883/Why-learn-a-foreign-language-Benefits-of-bilingualism.html. Accessed 22 Nov 2015
4. Berger, M.K.: Instrumental Assessment of Velopharyngeal Dysfunction: Multi-View Videofluoroscopy vs. Nasopharyngoscopy (n.d.). http://www.ohioslha.org/pdf/Convention/2011%20Handouts/SC18VoiceBergerC.pdf. Accessed 24 Nov 2015
5. Kummer, A.: Handout-Resonance-Disorders (2014). http://www.smiletrain.org/medical/for-patients/speech-services/Handout-Resonance-Disorders.pdf
6. Tsai, R: Teaching and learning the tones of Mandarin Chinese (2011). http://www.scilt.org.uk/portals/24/library/slr/issues/24/24_5_tsai.pdf. Accessed 21 Mar 2016
7. Zhang, F., Yin, P.: A study of pronunciation problems of English learners in China. Asian Soc. Sci. 5(6), 141–146 (2009)
8. Finegan, E., Rickford, J.R.: Language in USA: Themes for the Twenty First Century. Cambridge University Press, Cambridge (2004)
9. Lutter, M.: Mel-Frequency Cepstral Coefficients (2014). http://recognize-speech.com/feature-extraction/mfcc. Accessed 20 Mar 2016
10. Kaur, P., Singh, P., Garg, V.: Speech recognition system; challenges and techniques. Int. J. Comput. Sci. Inf. Technol. 3(3), 3989–3992 (Online)
11. Huang, X., Deng, L.: An overview of modern speech recognition. Accessed 26 Nov 2015
12. Lin, Y.C., Wang, H.C.: Nasal Detection in Continuous Mandarin Speech (n.d.). http://slam.iis.sinica.edu.tw/NGASR/paper/O-Cocosda2005-HCW.pdf. Accessed 26 Nov 2015
13. Schuller, B., Rigoll, G., Lang, M.: 'Hidden Markov Model Based Speech Emotion Recognition'. In: IEEE ICASSP, pp. 1–3 (2003)
14. Rabiner, L.R., Juang, B.: Fundamentals of Speech Recognition, 2nd edn. Pearson Education Press, Singapore (2005)
15. Tiwari, V · "MFCC and its applications in speaker recognition". Deptartment of Electronics Engineering, Gyan Ganga Institute of Technology and Management, Bhopal, MP, India, (Received 5 Nov 2009, Accepted 10 Feb 2010)

16. Dhingra, S.D., Nijhawan, G.: Speech recognition using MFCC and DTW. International Journal of Advanced Research in Electrical, Electronics and Instrumentation Engineering (An ISO 3297: 2007 Certified Organization), vol. 2, issue 8, August 2013. (Copyright to IJAREEIE)
17. Kong, J.: Speech Multi-Mode Research and Diversified Phonetics in Voice of China. Commercial Press, Beijing (2008)
18. Dang, J., Honda, K., Suzuki, H.: Morphological and acoustical analysis of the nasal and the paranasal cavities. J. Acoust. Soc. Amer. **96**, 2088–2099 (1994)
19. Hawkins, S., Stevens, K.: Acoustic and perceptual correlates of the non nasal-nasal distinction of vowels. J. Acoust. Soc. Amer. **77**, 1560–1575 (1985)
20. Gold, B., Morgan, N.: Speech and Audio Signal Processing. Wiley, New York (2000)
21. Becchetti, C., Ricotti, L.P.: Speech Recognition. Wiley, England (1999)

Data Driven Societal Well-being and Applications

User Experience of Autism Social-Aid Among Autistic Children: AUTISM Social Aid Application

Iman Nur Nabila Ahmad Azahari, Wan Fatimah Wan Ahmad$^{(\boxtimes)}$,
Ahmad Sobri Hashim, and Zulikha Jamaludin

Department of Computer and Information Sciences,
Universiti Teknologi Petronas, Bandar Seri Iskandar, Perak, Malaysia
nabilaazahari92@gmail.com,
{fatimhd, sobri.hashim}@utp.edu.my, zulikha@uum.edu.my

Abstract. Autism is a developmental disability that influences a significant number of daily skills, which includes social, communication and behavioural challenges. Technology has proven as one of the prompt intermediation and efficient educational method that leads to infinite improvement especially for children. Autistic children seem to have difficulties in communication and social skills and as a result of this need their teachers and parents' support with their social interaction. Numerous educational practices and approaches have been carried out in order to assist as well as develop these children. This paper presents the results of user experience testing of Autism Social-Aid mobile application to children with autism. The session was conducted to children with medium functioning Autism Spectrum Disorder, from two different age groups that include 5–14 years old and 14–18 years old. The children's reactions were observed and scored by a moderator. Results have shown that majority of the children with autism are more confident and satisfied when using the application. The application does need to be improved in ways that could capture the child's attention towards the mobile activities.

Keywords: Autistic children · User experience · Social communication · Mobile application

1 Introduction

Autism is a developmental disability that naturally happens in the first three years when a child is born. Understanding the behaviour of these children can be a challenge, as each of them are unique and diverse in their own qualities [1]. Autism Spectrum Disorders (ASD) is mutual youth neuron developmental disorder [2]. Core features comprise social and verbal impairments, sensory restriction and monotonous stereotype behaviour. Although auditory skills are known as their biggest flaw, visual sensory abilities are generally their main quality [3]. It is known that various learning theories have been conducted to aid and improve the everyday skills of children with autism. Mobile technologies are a well-known trend today. Mobile technology offers a simpler and effective access compared to computers. For a child with autism, it is vital to

© Springer International Publishing AG 2017
H. Badioze Zaman et al. (Eds.): IVIC 2017, LNCS 10645, pp. 391–397, 2017.
https://doi.org/10.1007/978-3-319-70010-6_36

sustain their interest, as they are unable to focus for a long period of time. Hence, the assistance of mobile devices like tablets or iPad could enhance their learning concentration and motivation. Although the technology is occasionally problematic, mobile devices were proven effective for children with autism than without any gadget [4].

The current teaching materials lacks therapeutic effect that is essential for the students. Children with autism's find it difficult to participate in behavioural and emotional skills since they need to familiarize themselves in a varied social context. Therefore, this reduces their capability to study and interact properly with other children [5]. Knowing that these children are particularly strong in their visual skill, many educators implement one of the newest theories, which is the visual approach. According to [6], visual approach is the most recent method in teaching children with autism, which can be applied by using images, videos or other visual items to educate. They commonly show potencies in tangible intellectual, memorization, sympathetic of graphic associations, battles in nonconcrete thinking, communal observant, communication, and attention [7]. Hence the objective this paper is to evaluate the learning experience of children with autism while using Autism Social-Aid application. At the same time, this paper aims to compare the learning experience between two different autistic age groups.

2 Literature Review

Autism is an eternal neuro developmental incapacities categorized with the following characteristics; impairments in social interactions, deficiencies in verbal and non-verbal communication, stereotyped manners and routine [8]. All around the globe, approximately 35 million people are born with autism. In Malaysia, one in every 600 children is affected by autism. Latest records indicate that about 47,000 of the citizen in this nation are autistic [9]. It is a challenge to develop the skill of children with autism, as each of them is special in their individual habits. However, the continuous practices and support by parents, teachers including experts is crucial to improve every child's performances and strong point. Their characteristics can be categorized into 3 main areas, which includes speech impairments, challenging behaviors, and their social skills [10].

Children with autism encounter limitless complications day-to-day. Conversely, their problem of socializing in a public setting is their greatest challenge. Social interaction problems could include disadvantage in peer interaction, disadvantage in using and accepting nonverbal communication, and constrained imitation of other's actions [11]. As a result, they have a tough time in building relationships and may not seem eager to do so. On top of that, they are unable to recognize people's feelings and actions and may express little or no facial expressions in response to others [12]. As a result, this will reduce their independence routine. Their limited social attention may decrease entire impulsiveness in skill performance, thus increasing the necessity of adult supervision.

The novel and effective method in teaching children with autism is the visual approach that uses videos, images or other visual items to communicate with their environment [13]. This could definitely help these children as they have the ultimate capability with their visual strength. Based on [14], the visual approach is known as the most effective method in catering for students with autism. An increase in acceptance of visual education for children with autism is becoming a practice in the academic sector [15]. Hence, with the assistance of visual approach, autistic children became more interested and are able to grow more as their strong points is honed every day. Real or actual pictures are the most effective teaching tools that can be applied for the purpose of supporting these children. Therefore, a mobile application, Autism Social-Aid has been developed using videos and games to support the Autistic children to teach on communication skills.

2.1   Autism Social-Aid

Autism Social-Aid is a mobile application developed for the children with autism, focusing on social learning. The objective of Autism Social-Aid is to assist the children with autism to learn and apply basic social interaction skills. The development of Autism Social-Aid aims to provide a platform where children could experience virtual learning anytime and anywhere. The contents are adapted from the modules given by Ministry of Education. Autism Social-Aid offers an option to select between two languages, English Language or Bahasa Malaysia Language.

The application consists of two different features that are 'Lesson' and 'Activity'. Under the 'Lesson' feature, the application displays a set of different video modules to teach basic social interaction skill, which includes; 'Introducing Yourself', 'Emotions' and 'Gestures'. 'Introducing Yourself' module educates the children on how to answer basic questions about yourself. 'Emotion' module displays the basic human emotions, which are Happy, Sad and Anger. Lastly, the 'gesture' module introduces some basic gestures in daily social communication such as waving hand, nodding head and clapping hands. Figure 1 displays an interface of a video module that is embedded in the application.

Fig. 1. Interface of video module

Every video module shows a distinctive way on how to carry out every day social activities including acting scenes on when you should apply the social skill. Another feature that is available in the "Video Module" is the replay button. The user can click on the replay button at the bottom right of the screen to repeat the video session or they can proceed to the next video by clicking the number buttons at the bottom screen. Another function is the "Record and Playback" button. It provides a user with a feature that could record their voice while holding the button and when it is released, the application will playback the user's voice. This function aims to train their pronunciation and conversation. They could replay their voice and try pronouncing the word again in order to convey it correctly.

Figure 2 displays the "Activity" feature that consists of two activities, which include "Quiz Me!" and "Listen". "Quiz Me!" is an activity where children have to match different type of emotions to the correct picture. This is to evaluate whether they understand the different emotion expression. Next, the "Listen" activity displays different emotions and the child could record their voice to properly practice they pronunciation of each emotion.

Fig. 2. Activity feature

3 Methodology

User experience testing was conducted for two special needs class from the National Autism Society of Malaysia (NASOM) centre in Butterworth, Penang. A total of 12 students with medium functioning ASD were involved, from two different age groups. The first is a primary class, which involves student aged 5 to 14 years old and a technical class that involves children aged 14 to 18 years old. The children were given the opportunity to play and learn Autism Social-Aid application and they were evaluated based on their reactions towards the application. The child was assisted by a teacher to make them feel comfortable in the observation room. The observations were adopted from the ARCS Model of Motivational Design [16]. The evaluation criteria contains attention, relevance, confidence and satisfaction. The "Attention" criteria is analysed based on their enjoyment, happiness, eagerness and excitement while using the application. The "Relevance" criteria is analysed based on their ability to under-stand easily and familiarized application. The "Confidence" criteria is analysed according to their happiness while using the application without being forced, ability to explore the application without any assistance and also their motivation to use the application thoroughly. Finally, the "Satisfaction" was analysed conferring on their satisfaction if they choose a correct answer and also the ability to do the activities provided correctly. The criteria were rated on scale 1 to 5 (1 = strongly disagree, 5 = strongly agree).

4 Results and Discussions

This section discusses the results of the observation evaluation. Figure 2 shows the results from the user experience testing for both age groups of children with autism. The results show the average of the tests from evaluation forms during the user experience testing session.

All students show different reaction towards the modules. Some were captivated in watching, while others were very passive and avoids eye contact. 80% of them were fascinated by the modules displayed. They were curious with the medium used. Only a few students are unable to concentrate with the video, as there are many distractions that caught their attention. Based on Fig. 3, the results show that children aged 5–14 years old are able to score higher compared to children aged 14–18 years old. Children

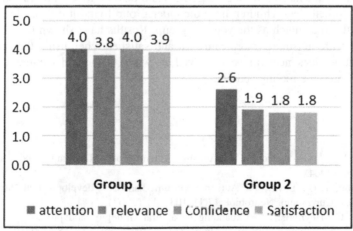

Group 1: Children aged 5-14 years old
Group 2: Children aged 14-18 years old

Fig. 3. User experience result

from the younger age group are more eager and interested to try all activities in the application. They are more interested and are able to accept and familiarise themselves to the new application. Even if some were easily distracted, they are able to focus again when prompted.

On the other hand, children aged from 14–18 years old are harder to manage as the activity requires them to alter their routine. If a child is familiar with any mobile application from an early age, he/she is able to accept application. However, in this case, the older children were so focused and consumed by their original routine, it is difficult for them to be introduced to new activities. They seem inexperienced with the technology but are fascinated when it started. However, their attention do not last long. From the observation, only 50% of them are eager to play throughout the whole activity.

The study also showed that there is a gap between the children in 5–14 years old and 14–18 years old class. The older children are having difficulties in adapting to the new learning platform as they are used to their traditional routine. It takes time for them to understand and alter what has been taught to them. This result seems to be consistent with the findings from [15]. However, the children from the younger age group are more enthusiastic and motivated to learn as they have not yet adapted to a routine. Most of them are able to understand and enjoy the session compared to their previous learning materials such as flash cards and books. Thus, it is established that prompt education or excellent intervention could help in assisting children to lessen their autistic effect.

5 Conclusion

In conclusion, the results of the existing study have showed that the mobile application is suitable for children with autism using visual approach to train social interaction skills. Most students had shown their eagerness and passion to learn more using mobile application. Nonetheless, children from the older group found it difficult to accept the learning platform as much as the younger group. Results have shown that majority of the children with autism are more confident and satisfied when using the application. The application does need to be improved in ways that could capture the child's attention towards the mobile activities.

References

1. Zander, E.: An Introduction to Autism. Autismforum Handikapp and Habilitering, Stockholm (2004)
2. Geschwind, D.H., Levitt, P.: Autism spectrum disorders: developmental disconnection syndromes. Curr. Opin. Neurobiol. 17(1), 103–111 (2007)
3. Schmidt, C., Heybyrne, B.: Expanding behavioral strategies and promoting success. In: Autism in the School-Aged Child. Autism Family Press, pp. 71—78 (2004)
4. Family center on technology and disability: Autism and the ipad : finding the therapy in consumer tech. Technol. Voices 130, 1–13 (2011)

5. Bauminger, N.: Brief report: group social-multimodal intervention for HFASD. J. Autism Dev. Disord. **37**(8), 1605–1615 (2007)
6. Loring, W., Hamilton, M.: Visual Supports and Autism Spectrum Disorders (2011). Available from Autism Speaks www.autismspeaks.org/docs/sciencedocs/atn/visual_supports.pdf
7. Ministry Of Education Special Programs Branch: Teaching Students with Autism: A Resource Guide for Schools. British Columbia, Victoria BC (2000)
8. Centre for Developmental Disability Health Victoria: Autism Spectrum Disorders, Notting Hill, Victoria (2010)
9. Bernama: With support, autistic children can move on. The Malaysian Times, pp. 8–10 (2014)
10. Goin-Kochel, R.P., Myers, B.J.: Parental report of early autistic symptoms: differences in ages of detection and frequencies of characteristics among three autism spectrum disorders. J. Dev. Disabil. **11**(2), 21–39 (2004)
11. Poliakova, N., Palkhivala, A., Johnson, J.: Social impairment in children with autism spectrum disorder. Abilities **14**, 50–51 (2008)
12. Brereton, A.: Core features of autism: social skills. Act Now, pp. 1–3 (2011). http://www.med.monash.edu.au/assets/docs/scs/psychiatry/autism-social-skills-en.pdf
13. Anderson, L.W.: Objectives, evaluation, and the improvement of education. Stud. Educ. Eval. **31**, 102–113 (2005)
14. Gray, C.: The New Social Story Book, Illustrated edn. Future Horizons Inc., NewYork (2000)
15. Hodgdon, L.A.: Visual Strategies for Improving Communication: Practical Supports for Autism Spectrum Disorders. Quirk Roberts, Brandon (2011)
16. Keller, J.: An integrative theory of motivation volition, and performance. Technol. Instr. Cogn. Learn. **6**, 79–104 (2008)

Guideline for the Development of Instructional Media with DST Concept on Touch Screen Tablet

Hashiroh Hussain[1(✉)] and Norshuhada Shiratuddin[2]

[1] IPG Kampus Sultan Abdul Halim, 08000 Sungai Petani, Kedah, Malaysia
hashiroh@gmail.com
[2] College of Arts and Sciences, UUM, 06010 Sintok, Kedah, Malaysia
shuhada@uum.edu.com

Abstract. The aim of this study is to create a standard guideline for the development of instructional media (apps) with digital story telling (DST) concept for touch screen tablet. High demand for apps with mobile interaction has boosted the need to create tablet-based teaching products. Nevertheless, guidance to create such products is lacking. Content and comparative analyses were employed based on the previous studies on digital media guidelines to formulate the components of the guidelines. A total of 13 experts, representing the Institute of Teacher Education (ITE) and the Institute of Higher Education (IPTA), were appointed as panel of experts to validate the guideline. Expert review checklist and interviews were used as data collection methods. The guideline should ease novice designers cum teachers to develop apps with mobile technology. Besides, students too can benefit from the new teaching strategy with DST concept.

Keywords: Digital storytelling · Expert review · Guideline

1 Introduction

The rapid growth of Information and Communication Technology (ICT) stimulates the application of technology in education. It has inspired teachers to transform teaching strategy via storytelling and set a new shift of conveying information. Thus, the combination of storytelling and multimedia technology which was introduced by Lambert (2006) and Dana Atchley (pioneers of DST) had caused the delivery of information to become more effective as the narrative was transformed into digital form, better known as the Digital Storytelling (DST) (Lambert 2006; Porter 2004; Signes 2008). Thus, the need for better learning instruction with technology will ease teachers to tailor lessons in the learning based technology (Siemens 2002; Yao et al. 2012). Teaching strategy could be improved with the development of teaching products (apps) in the teaching and learning. This article includes background study for guideline which involves the guidelines components namely the development process, DST elements and mobile technology. The next section will cover the methodology to obtain result of this study and the latter includes the conclusion to summarize the findings.

© Springer International Publishing AG 2017
H. Badioze Zaman et al. (Eds.): IVIC 2017, LNCS 10645, pp. 398–411, 2017.
https://doi.org/10.1007/978-3-319-70010-6_37

2 Background Study

The introduction of DST concept in the teaching strategy has resulted positive impact because it is in line with the need of latest technology (Yahya and Dayang Raini 2011). High demand of teaching products (apps) with mobile interaction has boosted the need to create tablet-based teaching products. Recent studies indicate that many users do not know how to interact with mobile devices (touchscreen) although these interactions are easy to learn (Malizia and Bellucci 2012; Montague et al. 2011). This is due to the lack of standards for determining the interaction of the touch screen and established guidelines (Norman and Nielsen 2010). The proposed guideline is to ensure that the development of instructional media will comprehend the concept of DST and interaction with touch screen tablet. It is a standard guide for novice designer cum teacher to instill DST concept in the development of digital media. The next section discusses thoroughly the suggested components for the proposed guideline.

2.1 Guideline Components

Prior to proposing the guideline for development of instructional media with DST concept for touch screen tablet. A critical analysis is employed. In order to explore issues and create ideas for shaping the components to the desired guideline of this study, a total of 10 existing models of digital media guideline from previous studies are selected. They are used as a basis to seek for commonalities of components of the proposed guideline based on the justification details in Table 1.

2.2 DST Elements

Concept of DST is recognised by elements to distinguish DST from other types of media such as film, television, video and blog (Lowenthal 2006). Furthermore, in order to draw audience's attention in listening to stories, designer is to rely on its element. Comprehensive study by Tenh et al. (2012) suggested 14 key interactive DST elements, which are perspective, intention, personal, dramatic question, engagement, articulation, sound track, tempo, story map, expression, significant content, collaboration, user contribution and minimal. The elements are validated by 7 prominent DST experts such as Robin, Porter, Ohler, Lambert, Sapeter, Paul and Fiebich and Schafer. However, the elements are scarce and do not emphasis on types of technology applied. Mobile devices and softwares are suggested tools of technologies for editing and recording stories which will ease the development process of storytelling (Green 2011). Detail description of the DST elements on touch screen tablet are presented in Table 2.

2.3 Mobile Technology

Students are active users of the new technology, hence design for an innovative teaching strategy in delivering knowledge is required to capture students' interest in learning. Therefore, the concept of DST is designed in line with mobile technology to stimulate the rapid changes in education. Transformation from revolutionary devices to mobile devices such as laptops, smartphones and tablets have brought about to higher

Table 1. Justification for selecting models with content analysis

Source	Justification of selecting guideline model	Component
Rubegni et al. (2013)	Provide a set of user design requirements to design tool for DST with tablet-based with reference to Narrative Application Model (NAM). The model supports collaboration on a key element in educational practices	• DST element • Tool features • System requirement • Development process • Theory and model
Robin and McNeil (2012)	Propose a general guideline with the integration of DST in teaching and learning process in the classroom according to ADDIE Model	• DST element • Tool features • System requirement • Development process • Theory and model
Tenh et al. (2011)	Propose DST interactive and non-interactive key elements as guidance for designers to develop DST without emphasising the development process and mobile technology aspects	• DST element • System requirement • Development process • Theory and model
Ma et al. (2012)	Provide guidance for designer in depicting emotions based on story situations in order to create a story idea in a storyboard	• DST element • Tool features • System requirement • Development process
Kelvin and Norshuhada (2006)	Provide guidance for the designer in adapting media technology in the development process of digital materials	• DST element • Tool features • System requirement • Development process • Theory and model
Häkkilä and Mäntyjärvi (2006)	Provide design guideline on human-computer interaction with context-aware mobile handheld devices without considering interaction design	• Tool features • System requirement • Development process
Jumail et al. (2010)	Provide a DST prototype system to guide children in creating stories in a flashcard form	• Tool features • System Requirement • Theory and model
Landoni and Rubegni (2014)	Propose a guide to help designers in creating eBook for mobile learning with	• DST element • Tool features

(*continued*)

Table 1. (*continued*)

Source	Justification of selecting guideline model	Component
	users' collaboration (participatory approach)	• System requirement • Development process
Ariffin and Faizah (2010)	Adoption of Nielsen heuristics in the process of developing guidelines for Assistive Technology	• DST element • System requirement • Development process
Fadhl et al. (2009)	Identify the usability issues and develop guideline for mobile devices	• DST element • System requirement • Development process

Table 2. DST elements for touch screen tablet

No	Element	Description
1.	Story objective	Objective of the story with a specific focus so that the information is delivered clearly
2.	Story content	Story includes a headline, type of story and adequate learning support materials for learning based on structure and story map
3.	Story style	Style of story is presented by narrator for audience's awareness by encouraging questions and dramatical views
4.	Character	An image for interaction via two-way communication to draw audience's attention through facial expressions or body language
5.	Editing media	Editing media (text and images) by changing size and format, move and delete in order to manipulate the media in accordance with the story line
6.	Authenticity	An appropriate background or image to describe a real situation with the correct angle of view
7.	Interactivity	Interaction with audience to navigate on the touch screen via finger input based on the size of media
8.	Screen display	A suitable working area on the screen so that the audience can interact smoothly on touch screen
9.	Collaboration	Audience and designer are engaged to contribute and share stories to enclose gap via interaction with story's system
10.	Articulation	Narration or voice recording and combination of text and voice are played together with effective background music for a better impact in delivering message
11.	Story beat	Image is displayed at a certain time according to the story line. Each scene uses transition and animation to demonstrate the continuity of the story

quality of information delivery, tablets. The high demand for the mobile devices in education is due to its low price, ease of use and touch screen interaction (Druin et al. 2009). According to the analysis of Ericsson Consumer Lab in South-East Asia, there is an increase of tablet users, which almost tripled the use from 14% in 2012 to 39% in 2013 (Xiung 2013). Compared to other mobile devices, tablet features such as light, fast start up, high performance graphics and efficient memory have fascinated many users (Milne et al. 2010). The touch screen technology has taken over the role of the control device input (keyboard and mouse) for better interaction with the touch of a finger on screen information and manage to convince users to control their interactions (Yao et al. 2012). In producing authenticity in media, special editing functions are used to resize and edit images by enabling designers to enlarge, shrink and move images to the desired locations. With touch screen technology, these tasks can be done by flicking, flinging, pinching and spreading to complete certain tasks and reduce errors quickly (Jennings et al. 2013). Thus, developing apps and editing activities becomes fun and interesting tasks for designers. A study conducted by Multimedia Super corridor (MSC) on the development of apps found that the quality of the teaching products is low, particularly the pedagogy and contents of which are less attractive. Thus, the needs to create tablet-based teaching products have increased. Nevertheless, guidance to create such products (apps) is lacking (Malizia and Bellucci 2012; Montague et al. 2011; Norman 2010; Rafiza and Maryam 2013). Therefore, the aim of this study is to create a standard guideline for the development of instructional media (apps) with DST concept on touch screen tablet.

3   Methodology

In proposing the desired outcome, this study was implemented with three phases as shown in Fig. 1. In the first phase, a total of 10 sample of digital media guidelines and seven sample of DST tool from past studies were identified and used as a basis to get

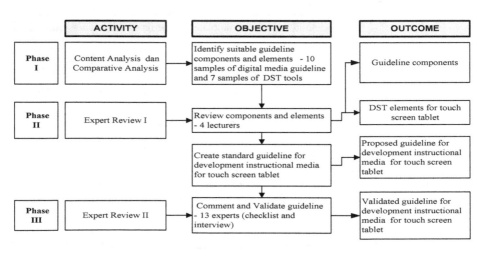

Fig. 1. Summary of activity

the generic components of the proposed guideline. Content analysis was to justify and identify generic components. Meanwhile, a comparative analysis was carried out to seek for the commonalities among the components, whereby other studies were compared against each other in order to formulate a standard guideline. In the second phase, experts would review the proposed guideline components and DST elements for touch screen tablet. The proposed guideline was then validated in the third phase using an expert's checklist and interview with the experts.

4   Results and Discussion

Based on the methodology of this study, a guideline was developed and validated by experts. A comparative analysis was conducted to formulate a standard guideline based on components derived from the content analysis as discussed earlier (Table 1). The components was designated through comparative analysis based on the majority scores on components applied in other studies as shown in Table 3.

Table 3. Comparative analysis for guideline components

Component	A	B	C	D	E	F	G	H	I	J	Total score
Development process	✓	✓	✓	✓	✓	✓	✗	✓	✓	✓	9
DST dimension	✓	✓	✓	✗	✗	✗	✗	✓	✗	✗	4
DST element	✓	✓	✓	✓	✓	✓	✓	✓	✓	✓	10
Theory and model	✓	✓	✓	✓	✓	✓	✓	✓	✓	✓	10
DST heuristic	✗	✗	✗	✗	✓	✓	✗	✓	✓	✓	5
System requirement	✓	✓	✓	✓	✓	✓	✓	✓	✓	✓	10
Tool feature	✓	✓	✓	✓	✓	✓	✓	✓	✓	✓	10

✓: the component is applied	✗: the component is not applied
A: Rubegni et al. (2013)	F: Häkkilä and Mäntyjärvi (2006)
B: Robin and McNeil (2012)	G: Jumail et al. (2010)
C: Tenh et al. (2011)	H: Landoni and Rubegni (2014)
D: Ma et al. (2012)	I: Ariffin and Faizah (2010)
E: Kelvin and Norshuhada (2006)	J: Fadhl et al. (2009)

4.1   The Proposed Guideline

The findings was analyzed according to the condition for classification of generic components as presented in Table 4 (Azizah et al. 2015). If the score is between 8 to 10, this indicates the component is highly recommended, but if the score is between 4 to 7, these component is recommended. On the other hand, if the score is less than 3, the component is discarded. This is important to attain an accurate result and appropriate components for the proposed guideline.

Table 4. Conditions for classification of generic components.

Condition (Total score)	Indicator
8 to 10	Compulsory
4 to 7	Recommended
0 to 3	Discarded

Based on the results, all components were sustained because they have scores of more than 4. Having all components recommended in the proposed guideline, a model of the guideline is formed. A brief design of the guideline with the integration of all components was developed as illustrated in the Fig. 2. The guideline was then validated by experts before it was implemented by respondents to create an instructional media (apps).

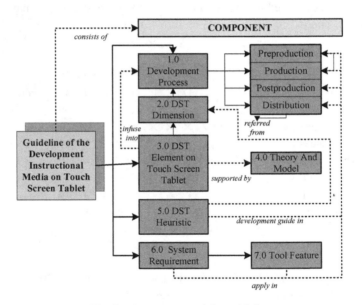

Fig. 2. Components of the guideline

The proposed guideline has identified seven components based on the format of the guidelines proposed by Kelvin and Norshuhada (2006), comprised of basic concepts, development process and technology. Thus, there were three main components in this study, namely process development, DST element and system requirement. Other four components were DST dimension, theory and model, DST heuristic and tool features. Designers would implement activities from four phases (preproduction, production, postproduction and distribution) in the development process. DST elements was infused into the development process in an attempt to produce apps with the concept of DST. The elements were supported by theory and model, while DST heuristic was applied in the development guide. Tool features were referred by designers for selecting DST tools in the development of the apps. In order to conform to the proposed guideline, experts were to check and validate the guidelines to ensure the smooth process in developing the apps.

4.2   Expert Review

This process was implemented through iterative methodology until the experts were satisfied. They would validate the proposed guideline to the correct procedures based on their expertise through two cycles of expert review method. Table 5 lists the demographic profile of experts based on the information obtained in the expert's checklist such as gender, post, affiliation and experience, to support the reliability of the experts. Thirteen experts involved in the study represented academic lecturers (six men

Table 5. Demographic expert profile

Expert	Gender	Post	Affiliation	Expertise	Experience (year)
A	Male	Ass.Prof./Dr.	USM	Multimedia in education	20
B	Female	Ass.Prof./Dr.	USM	Instructional design/DST	10
C	Female	Senior Lecturer/ Dr	MMU	Multimedia	15
D	Female	Senior Lecturer/ Dr	UiTM	Multimedia in education/ DST	8
E	Male	Lecturer	IPGK Darul Aman	Multimedia in education	15
F	Male i	Senior Lecturer	IPGK Darul Aman	IT	20
G	Male	Senior Lecturer	IPGK Darul Aman	Multimedia in education	15
H	Male	Senior Lecturer	IPGK Sultan Abdul Halim	IT	13
I	Female	Senior Lecturer/Dr.	UUM	IT	13
J	Female	Senior Lecturer/Dr.	UUM	Multimedia in education	15
K	Female	Senior Lecturer/Dr.	UUM	Multimedia	9
L	Female	Senior Lecturer/Dr.	UiTM	Multimedia/usability	10
M	Male	Lecturer	UMK	Multimedia/ DST	6

UUM: Universiti Utara Malaysia.
MMU: Multimedia Malaysia University.
USM: Universiti Sains Malaysia.
UiTM: Universiti Teknologi MARA.
UMK: Universiti Malaysia Kelantan.
IPGK: Institut Pendidikan Guru Kampus.

and seven women) from the Institute of Teacher Education (ITE) and universities (USM, UM, MMU, UiTM). They have relevant expertise such as Digital Storytelling, Information Technology, Instructional Design and Multimedia. Experts contributed constructive comments and suggestions for the improvement in the proposed guideline.

Expert Checklist

The information obtained from expert's checklist was analyzed by frequency, mean and percentage scores (Wesiak et al. 2012). The checklist consisted of

- the relevance of the proposed guidelines and dimension component
- the understanding of DST elements for touch-screen tablet
- the applicability of MPBPD development guidelines for touch-screen tablet

They were given the proposed guideline model for validation and making comments. As a result, the majority of the experts agreed that the guidelines (75.82%), the DST dimensions (80.80%) and DST elements on touch-screen tablet (76.92%) are relevant and understandable. In determining the relevance of the proposed guidelines, all experts (100%) agreed that the development process is the most relevant component in the guideline as shown in Fig. 3. The majority of experts agreed with 76.92% for DST heuristic, 69.23% for system requirement, 61.54% for DST tool features, 69.23% for theory and model. Meanwhile, majority of the experts (84.60%) agreed that the relevance of the DST dimensions for the narrative, interface and multimedia tablet and 69.20% for functional. Figure 4 represents information on understanding of DST on touch screen tablet. The majority of the experts (76.92%) have a clear understanding, 22.38% experts require a little explanation and only one expert (0.70%) requires some explanations on screen display.

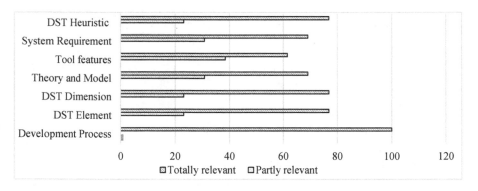

Fig. 3. Percentage from expert feedback on the relevance of the component

Next, for the latter section of the checklist, majority of the experts (79.12%) agreed to the applicability of the guideline as shown in Fig. 5. Majority of experts agreed that:

1. P1: (84.62%) for the guideline is clearly understood,
2. P2:100% for the DST elements is identified,

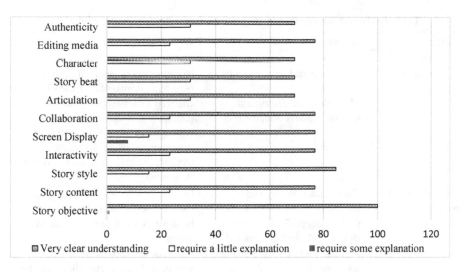

Fig. 4. Percentage from expert feedback on understanding of the DST element

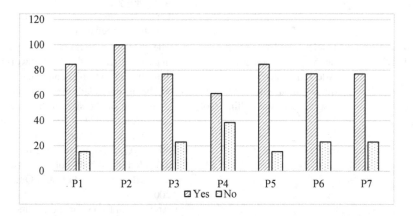

Fig. 5. Percentage from expert feedback on applicability of the guideline

3. P3:76.92% for the guideline is very systematic,
4. P4:61.54% for the use of the correct term and the statement is very clear,
5. P5:84.62% for the clear sequence in the relation of each guideline component,
6. P6:76.92% for the technology (hardware and software) that is used to ease the development process and
7. P7:76.92% for the guideline is easy understood.

Apart from experts' comments, transcribe of the interview was used to triangulate data in order to improve the proposed guideline. The interview with experts was repeated three or four times until data was saturated. The summary of expert comments and suggestions are analyzed according to the theme and subthemes to justify expert comments as shown in Table 6.

Table 6. Expert comments and suggestions based on theme and subthemes

Theme	Subtheme	Expert suggestion
Use correct statements and terms	• Unclear description • Confusing and wrong use of terminology • More detailed description • Use of negative statement	• The terminology for technology (component) is changed to system requirement, realistic(element) is changed to authenticity, screen (element) is changed to screen display • All negative statements in the development of guideline are reorganized and changed to positive statements
Applicability of theory and model	• Only related theory and model, heuristic PD included • Only appropriate and useful theory and models included • Require more detailed theory and model	• Do not include all the components such as theory, model and heuristic because they are not essential to designers • Instructional Design Model is sugggested in the guideline because the analysis of audience's background is important in the selection of technology • Character element is moved into the narrative dimension
Clear design of technology	• Unclear guidance for the development process • Add more specific development guideline • Use generic storytelling tool	• The guideline should be more specific in terms of size of the display working area, size of the object and size of the file being uploaded, therefore, the suggestion of the size of the screen resolution is 1024 × 786 pixels, the font size is 17 pt, the object size is 40 × 40 pixels and the size of uploaded file should not exceed 2 GB to 4 GB (Sun, Plocher, and Qu, 2007). • Android and iOS for tablets and Windows for personal computers are suggested operating system (OS) • DST tool should be categorized according to its functional
Readability and layout components	• The flow of the wrong direction in the development process • Wrong numbering system in the flow of the development process • Show the correct indicator of the guideline	• The flow of the correct direction in the development process should be arranged from left to right according to the normal readings • Accurate numbering system of each component is arranged according to the preference of the development process • The indicator should show the differences between types of arrows, type and color of the boxes

Experts have suggested some improvements to be considered in the proposed guideline so that designers cum teachers could comprehend and follow the correct procedures. The validation of the guideline based on their expertise judgement was to provide justification for the designers who would implement the guideline and create the apps according to the objective of this study as illustrated in Fig. 6.

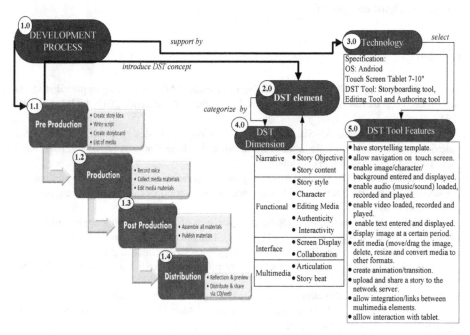

Fig. 6. Guideline for development of instructional media with DST concept on touch screen tablet

5   Conclusion

The guideline is designed for the development of instructional media with DST concept on touch screen tablet for designers cum teachers who are keen in the developing apps. A critical analysis (content and comparative analysis) is employed for better justification on the components of the guideline. There are seven components of the guideline, namely process development, DST element, system requirement, DST dimension, theory and model, DST heuristic and tool features. However, DST heuristic, theory and model are not displayed in the model due to experts comments' as they are irrelevant for designers' reference. The experts' validation and comments have successfully confirmed the correct procedure of the guideline and improved the proposed guideline. With the rearrangements of the components and process flow, the development process can then be implemented appropriately by designers. The novelty of the guideline for the development of instructional media with DST concept on touch screen tablet is the DST element that is infused in the development process. Therefore, the development of compelling apps with DST concept can be created with a systematic guide. There is also potential for a greater emphasis to incorporate end user evaluation with the apps on touch screen tablet during future research. However, the new educational interventions need time to become embedded in classroom practice. Hence, stakeholders such as school leaders and researchers should acknowledge that the benefits of a new technology might not be immediate and will take time to be accepted in school curriculum.

References

Ariffin, A.M., Faizah, M.: Guidelines of assistive courseware (AC) for hearing impaired students. In: Proceedings of Knowledge Management International Conference 2010. UUM, pp. 186–191 (2010)

Azizah, C.O., Norshuhada, S., Siti Mahfuzah, S.: Conceptual design model of interactive television advertising: towards influencing impulse purchase tendency. ARPN J. Eng. Appl. Sci. **10**(3), 1427–1437 (2015)

Druin, A., Bederson, B.B., Quinn, A.: Designing intergenerational mobile storytelling. In: Proceedings of the 8th International Conference on Interaction Design and Children, pp. 325–328. ACM (2009)

Fadhl, H., Halina, D., Basheer, A.X.: Usability guidelines of mobile learning application. J. Inf. Syst. Res. Innov. **5**(special issue), 71–77 (2009). http://seminar.utmspace.edu.my/jisri/

Green, M.R.: Teaching the writing process through digital storytelling in pre-service education. Texas A&M University, Ann Arbor (2011). http://eserv.uum.edu.my/docview/885229630?accountid=42599

Häkkilä, J., Mäntyjärvi, J.: Developing design guidelines for context-aware mobile applications. In: Proceedings of the 3rd International Conference on Mobile Technology, Applications and Systems, pp. 1–7. ACM, New York, USA (2006)

Jennings, A., Ryser, S., Drews, F.: Touch screen devices and the effectiveness of user interface methods. In: Proceedings of the Human Factors and Ergonomics Society Annual Meeting, vol. 57, pp. 1648–1652 (2013). https://doi.org/10.1177/1541931213571366

Jumail, W., Dayang Rohaya, A.R., Suziah, S.: A guided digital storytelling prototype system using illustrated flashcards. In: Proceedings 2010 International Symposium on Information Technology — Visual Informatics, ITSim 2010, vol. 1 (2010). https://doi.org/10.1109/ITSIM.2010.5561377

Kelvin, B.W.K., Norshuhada, S.: Building knowledge resource of current state of the digital rights management implementation in epublication. In: Knowledge Management International Conference and Exhibition 2006 (KMICE 2006) (pp. 266–272). Universiti Utara, Kuala Lumpur, Malaysia (2006). https://doi.org/ISBN983-3282-90-3

Lambert, J.: Digital Storytelling: Capturing Lives, Creating Community, 2nd edn. Digital Diner Press, Berkelay (2006)

Landoni, M., Rubegni, E.: Design guidelines for more engaging electronic books: insights from a cooperative inquiry study. In: Proceeding IDC 2014 Conference on Interaction Design and Children, pp. 281–284. ACM, Denmark (2014). https://doi.org/10.1145/2593968.2610472

Lowenthal, P.: Digital storytelling : an emerging institutional technology? In: Story Circle: Digital Storytelling Around the World. Wiley-Blackwell, pp. 297–305 (2006)

Ma, X., Forlizzi, J., Dow, S.: Guidelines for depicting emotions in storyboard scenarios. In: Brassett, J., McDonnell, J., Malpass, M. (eds.) Proceedings of 8th International Design and Emotion Conference, pp. 11–14, London (2012)

Malizia, A., Bellucci, A.:Viewpoint: the artificiality of natural user interfaces toward user-defined gestural interfaces. Commun. ACM **55**(3), 36–38 (2012). https://doi.org/10.1145/2093548. 2093563

Milne, I., Bayer, M., Cardle, L., Shaw, P., Stephen, G., Wright, F., Marshall, D.: Tablet-next generation sequence assembly visualization. Bioinf. Appl. Note **26**(3), 401–402 (2010). https://doi.org/10.1093/bioinformatics/btp666

Montague, K., Hanson, V., Cobley, A.: Evaluation of adaptive interaction with mobile touch-screen devices. Digital Engagement Conference, United Kingdom (2011). http:// de2011.computing.dundee.ac.uk/wp-content/uploads/2011/10/Evaluation-of-Adaptive-Interaction-with-Mobile-Touch-Screen-Devices.pdf

Norman, D.A.: The way I see it: natural user interfaces are not natural. Interactions (2010). https://doi.org/10.1145/1744161.1744163

Norman, D.A., Nielsen, J.: Gestural interfaces: a step backward in usability. Interactions **17**(5), 46–49 (2010)

Porter, B.: Digitales: The Art of Telling Digital Stories. BJP Consulting, Sedalia (2004)

Rafiza, A.R., Maryam, A.R.: Pembinaan media pengajaran berasaskan multimedia di kalangan guru ICTL. Jurnal Kurikulum Pengajaran Asia Pasifik **1**(2), 20–31 (2013)

Robin, B.R., McNeil, S.G.: What educators should know about teaching digital storytelling. Digit. Educ. Rev. **22**, 37–51 (2012)

Rubegni, E., Colombo, L., Landoni, M.: Design recommendations for the development of a digital storytelling mobile application. In: Proceedings of the 27th International BCS Human Computer Interaction Conference (HCI 2013) (2013). http://dl.acm.org/citation.cfm?id= 2578096

Siemens, G.: Instructional design in e-learning (2002). http://www.elearnspace.org/Articles/ InstructionalDesign.htm. Accessed 20 Feb 2014

Signes, C.G.: Integrating the old and new : digital storytelling in the EFL language. Revista Para Profesores de Inglés **16**(1&2), 43–49 (2008). http://www.uv.es/gregoric/DIGITALSTORY TELLING/DS_files/DST_15_ene_08_final.pdf

Tenh, H.K., Norshuhada, S., Harryizman, H.: Digital storytelling's conceptual model: a proposed guide towards the construction of a digital story. In: International Conference on Teaching and Learning in Higher Education (ICTLHE 2011), Melaka (2011)

Tenh, H.K., Norshuhada, S., Harryizman, H.: Core elements of digital storytelling from experts' perspective. In: Knowledge Management International Conference (KMICe), pp. 397–402, Johor Bahru, Malaysia (2012)

Wesiak, G., Al-Smadi, M., Gutl, C.: Towards an integrated assessment model for complex learning resources: findings from an expert validation. In: 15th International Conference on Interactive Collaborative Learning, ICL, pp. 1–7. IEEE, Villach, Austria (2012). https://doi. org/10.1109/ICL.2012.6402093

Xiung, C.J.: Smartphone penetration hits 63% in Malaysia. The Star Online. Star Publications (M) Bhd, Kuala Lumpur. http://www.thestar.com.my/Tech/Tech-News/2013/09/12/ Smartphone-and-tablet-penetration-hits-63-percent.aspx/. Accessed 12 Sept 2013

Yahya, O., Dayang Raini, P.: Kesan aplikasi perisian cerita interaktif semasa mengajarkan kemahiran bacaan dan kefahaman dalam kalangan murid tahun 4 di Brunei Darussalam. Jurnal Pendidikan Bahasa Melayu **1**(1), 27–49 (2011)

Yao, J., Fernando, T., Wang, H.: A multi-touch natural user interface framework. In: 2012 International Conference on Systems and Informatics (ICSAI), pp. 499–504 (2012). https:// doi.org/10.1109/ICSAI.2012.6223046

Preliminary Investigations on Augmented Reality for the Literacy Development of Deaf Children

Aziza Almutairi and Shiroq Al-Megren[✉]

Information Technology Department,
King Saud University, Riyadh, Saudi Arabia
aziza.m.m@hotmail.com, salmegren@ksu.edu.sa

Abstract. This paper reports on ongoing research on the development of an Augmented Reality (AR) application for the literacy development of hard of hearing children, particularly deaf children that rely on Arabic Sign Language (ArSL). This research is intended to help deaf children learn how to read by enhancing current elementary courseware with visual augmentation. Elicitation from literature reveals the profound value AR can provide for deaf learners, i.e. visual learners. Nevertheless, this approach is rarely undertaken for ArSL. Preliminary studies were conducted to determine the visual needs of deaf Arabic learners using three different instruments and targets: interviews with teachers and interpreters, observation of deaf children, and questionnaire for parents of deaf children. The results from teachers and parents of deaf children indicate a preference for multiple resources, primarily ArSL, photos, and videos. Students, in the other hands, performed better with finger-spelling and poorly in SL. This disconnect highlights the importance of considering various perspectives in the development of applications that target literacy in younger children.

Keywords: Augmented Reality · Deaf · Hard of hearing · DHH · Arabic Sign Language · ArSL

1 Introduction

Literacy is critical for children's growth as it significantly impacts educational, vocational, and social development. The reading process requires two related factors: language familiarity and decoding. Decoding is the process that leads to understanding the mapping between the language and the printed text [1]. A hearing child is exposed to spoken language early in their developments, i.e. their native language, and this early exposure builds familiarity. To learn how to read, a hearing child must learn to map the familiar spoken language to the printed word. Deaf children are clearly disadvantaged on both factors; no access to familiar language early in their development and a lack of phonemic awareness via decoding [2].

Deafness is categorised by educators in functional terms as hard of hearing or deaf, where the former is able to function auditorially with amplification (e.g. by using hearing aid) and the latter is not [3]. Recent statistics from the General Authority for Statistics in Saudi Arabia declared 76,902 registered individuals that are deaf or hearing

© Springer International Publishing AG 2017
H. Badioze Zaman et al. (Eds.): IVIC 2017, LNCS 10645, pp. 412–422, 2017.
https://doi.org/10.1007/978-3-319-70010-6_38

impaired [4]. While Arabic is the native language of many of the country's population, Arabic Sign Language (ArSL) is the native language of deaf and hard of hearing people. Sign language is realised in the visual modality. While a hearing person would decode a printed word into speech, a deaf person decodes the printed word into other forms: decoding into articulation (e.g. lip reading), fingerspelling (or dactylology), or signing using SL [5]. Of the three approaches, decoding into SL was found to be the most effective and preferred options for deaf readers. This approach is further supported by various reading techniques, such as chaining or sandwiching [6], using finger-spelling.

Visual literacy is the ability to understand ideas that are represented visually in static or dynamic forms [7]. Deaf children visual literacy can be developed with the support of Augmented Reality (AR) [8]. AR enriches its user's real environment with virtual object to enhance perception. Unlike virtual reality, AR does not completely replace the real world thus the user remains grounded to the various resources being augmented. AR is able to convert static image in book and newspapers into 3-dimensional interactive graphics or videos. There are several benefits to AR in education, that includes: seamless integration with real objects, increased motivation and attention, information accessibility, and creativity [9].

In this paper, we describe the preliminary investigation conducted to identify the visual needs of deaf student to develop literacy competence. Current practices in classrooms utilises picture and videos to support the mapping process between printed text from various subjects to ArSL. This paper aims to make informed decisions regarding various media and their support for elementary grade reading. Qualitative assessments are conducted with those that play a vital role in a deaf child's literacy, including: the child, parents, and teachers. The scope of this paper is limited to ArSL, Arabic courseware for literacy, and elementary school children.

The remainder of this paper is organised as follows: The related work section reviews work that adopts AR for the education of deaf students via visual learning. The following section describes the various instruments used in the requirement gathering methodology to identify the visual needs of deaf readers. These instruments include interviews, observations, and questionnaire; each is described and their outcomes analysed. The next section discusses the cumulative results from the requirement gathering phase of this research. The final section concludes the paper and briefly summarises future directions.

2   Related Work

Various studies have been conducted in the field of ArSL systems and application. However, the majority of works is concerned with Arabic language processing (e.g. [10]), ArsL representation (e.g. [11], gesture and speech recognition (e.g. [12, 13]). Up to now, there has been little work to support the visual literacy of deaf students using AR. The rest of this section review work that utilises AR for the education of deaf children and adults in various SLs.

An AR application was developed as a mobile phone application for the 3-dimensional representation of Indonesian SL [14]. Utilising a marker-less detection techniques, the AR application augmented printed letters with its corresponding SL. The application can assemble the various alphabet card to form words that are finger-spelled using the application. While the application was mainly intended for SL learners, in general, its benefits can be extended to deaf visual learners. Particularly children for the purpose of advancing their literacy development. Cards as AR input was also explored for integrating printed text with Chinese SL on a desktop, however the exploration merely explored the concept [15].

PekAr-Mikroogranisma is a science courseware development for older deaf students that is augmented with AR via web-based application [16]. The enhanced courseware is augmented with 3-dimensional models of organisms, while also being supported with Malaysian SL visual description. The courseware and application were heuristically evaluated with education courseware experts and feedback was encouraging. The development of this application and courseware was based on a preliminary study to determine the need of deaf science students [17]. Observations were carried out with three deaf students in various tasks, where common characteristics were identified. Interviews were also conducted with education officers to further explore the difficulties facing deaf learners.

A sign language teaching model (SLTM), multi-language cycle (MuCy), was developed with AR technology to supplement sign language pedagogical material (SLPMs) with visual and interactive digital content [18], visual reference, and printed word; then vocalising the printed word. The SLPMs are augmented with avatars that use American SL. An experimental study showed improvement when using the augmented SLPMs and verified it complementary effectiveness when teaching deaf children.

More recently the efficiency of using an AR application when learning SL was assessed and examined [19]. An AR application was developed for Slovenian SL to compare its performance against picture and physical SL interpretation. The application detects a sign language interpreter and augments the image with videos. The experimental results showed that users performed better when using the AR applications compared to the photo, but did not perform as well as an SL from a sign language interpreter. It was suggested that AR application can be a complementary education tool along with a sign language interpreter when teaching deaf children.

3   Gathering Requirements

This study uses several qualitative approaches to determine the literacy development needs of deaf children from the perspective of teachers, interpreters, parents of deaf children, and deaf children. It was important to collect feedback from all those that play a role in the development of a deaf child's reading skill. For each of these vital roles, a suitable instrument was used.

3.1   Interviews

Semi-structured interviews were utilised for the extraction of exhaustive information from teachers and interpreters. This instrument was used due to its flexibility, yet still offering guidance throughout the interview sessions. They allow the interviewer to probe and explore different elements in a subject matter that helps elucidate that subject.

Method. Three female teachers and two interpreters were interviewed. Teachers had a mean age of 44 years with a standard deviation of 7.93 years. All three teachers are current teaching professionals from Al-Amal deaf institute in Riyadh, Saudi Arabia. Al-Amal institute caters to all the instructional stages of deaf and hard of hearing female students from elementary to high school. While all three teachers taught children at the elementary level at the institute, one teachers expertise was in science education. At the elementary level, the institute had students ranging from the age of 8 to 18 years old. Both interpreters were 30 years old and were recruited from the College of Education, King Saud University. The university provides assistance to disabled university students (typically aged 18 to 30 years old) through interpreters from the college. The interviews were conducted over several sessions that spanned two days. Each session lasted approximately two and a half hours and were held at the interpreters and teachers place of work. Interviews with teachers were conducted individually. The two interpreters were interviewed in the same session due to difficulties in schedule one-on-one sessions. Therefore, their answers were combined as one. All interviews were audio recorded and conducted in Arabic.

Interview Protocol. An interview protocol was devised to list the issues that are to be explored and to ensure that the same basic line of inquiry is being pursued in each interview. Throughout the session the protocol serves as a guide or a check-list to guarantee that all relevant topics were covered. The interview protocol was as follows (the protocol slightly varied with the interpreters and will be highlighted):

- Introductions and the presentation of the purpose of the research. The confidentially of the interviewee's responses was also clarified.
- A consent form is presented and signed by the interviewee.
- General information is collected. This includes: age, expertise, years of experience, and job description. Teachers and interpreters are also asked about the age of the deaf and hard of hearing students they work with and grade level.
- Questions about current practices: this was intended to investigate current
- Practices utilised by teachers when working with deaf student. Interpreters were asked similar questions regarding university-level deaf students.
- Questions about text representation: the literature exhibited a range of media used to visualise printed text or concepts. This part of the interview investigated appropriate media for visual learning and students' preferences from the teachers' or interpreters' perspectives.
- Two AR applications were demonstrated to the interviewees to clarify the idea behind the research. The demonstrated AR applications were: Magic Camera [20] and Anatomy 4D [21].
- Recommendation for the proposed AR application: the final set of questions probed the interviewees for recommendations for AR input, methods to avoid distraction, and potential support that can be implemented.

Results. The audio recorded interviews were first transcribed and then translated into English. Thematic analysis was used to elicit meaning from the transcribed interviews. This approach is popularly utilised in various fields and aims to identify, analyse, and report themes within the data via organisation and description [22]. The approach undertaken involved a mix of inductive and deductive means of interpretation. The following steps were used to identify themes [22]: data familiarisation by reading the transcripts, coding and collating important features, searching for themes and selecting candidates, reviewing candidate themes, defining the scope of the themes, and finally contextualising the analysis. The thematic analysis resulted in the following themes:

Text Representation. Teachers and interpreters were asked for their preferred media to use to clarify printed concepts or new vocabulary. All interviewees advocated for SL as the main media to use, preferably combined with picture and/or video. One teacher also utilised sound for students that were hard of hearing.

Vocabulary. Teachers were asked about the difficulties facing deaf students when reading, and they unanimously agreed that students had problem identifying word in context or its connotations. One teacher stated students' difficulties in understanding synonyms and antonyms. Interpreters did not agree with this point but instead highlighted problems that university-level deaf students had with adjectives and adverbs. This contradiction between teachers and interpreters was expected given the age of deaf students they typically interact with [23].

Sign Language. Interpreters agreed that SL is their primarily means of communication with deaf students. This was also agreed upon by teachers as well. Teachers pointed out the difficulties some students face with learning SL, which includes being raised in a deaf or hearing households. The latter seems to struggle more with SL than the former. This is further confirmed in the literature, where developmental delays are more noticeable with deaf children in hearing households.

Teaching Techniques. Surprisingly, the teachers all agreed that no particular teaching methods (e.g. sandwiching or chaining) is used when teaching reading.

Technical Resources. Interviewees were probed for information regarding the use of technology in their teaching or interpretation process. Teachers utilised projectors to display video and pictures to clarify the meaning of words or concepts being taught. Interpreters utilise applications such as Facetime to communicate with deaf students. No other application or technologies were noted by the teachers and interpreters. In fact, one teacher was discouraged by the lack of ArSL application that can help her during teaching.

AR Input. The interviewees presented several potential options for the AR input: printed book, electronic book, or printed cards. Two teachers advocated for the printed book for elementary deaf students as it would be harder to lose. An interpreter and a teacher preferred the use of an electronic book.

3.2 Observations

A guided observational study was carried out with deaf student. This approach was utilised to confirm and observe the difficulties facing deaf student when associating a printed text with various media. The observations were guided by using tasks to encourage the identification of problem areas and to collect objective and subjective information about the students' experience while reading.

Method. Six students were recruited from Al-Amal institute. All students were female with moderate to severe hearing loss. Three students were in fifth grade and the other three were in first grade. The fifth graders had an average age of 14 years old with a standard deviation of 3.46 years. First grades age ranged from 8 to 13 years old, with a standard deviation of 2.64 years. Typical ages for first and fifth graders are 7 and 10, respectively. This in itself could be indicative of the effect of their disability on their educational development. The observation was carried out in two sessions: one with the fifth graders and the other for the first graders. The observations were documented in text and photos and each session last approximately 2 h.

The observations were carried out as follows:

- The observer introduced herself to the deaf student while the teacher interpreted this interaction.
- General information was collected about the students.
- The students were assigned tasks that associates printed text with various
- media.
- The students were exposed to an AR application (Magic Camera [20]) and
- Let's Read [24], an application the interprets a story using SL, sound, and images.

Task. The purpose of the task was to witness students reading performance when associated with various media. The media investigated were based on the interviews previously carried out in Sect. 3.1 and include: video, pictures, sign language, and finger-spelling. For each task, the students were asked to associate a printed text with a certain media. The text was chosen from the original courseware for elementary students in Saudi Arabian schools and was a mix of adjectives and nouns.

- Link picture to text: in this task, photos and text cards were spread out in a mixed order on a table and the students were asked to associate the text card with the correct image (see Fig. 1). Photos include: two realistic photos and two cartoon photos. The purpose for this was to identify preference for realistic or animated representations in photos and videos.
- Link video to text: in this task, text card were spread out on a table. The student was shown a video on a mobile phone and asked to associate it with the correct printed word. Similar to the photos task, students were presented with two realistic videos and two cartoon videos.
- Link sign language to text: this task presented the students with five videos of ArSL signs. For each video, the students were asked to assign the SL to printed text. The videos included two realistic and two animated (or avatar) interpreters that were shown full-bodied. Another video displayed only the hands of a realistic human interpreter.

Fig. 1. A deaf student associating a realistic image of a camel with the corresponding printed text.

Fig. 2. A deaf student imitating the sign for an Arabic alphabet using finger-spelling.

- Link finger-spelling to text: the final task had photos of finger-spelled words and text card that were spread out in a mixed order (see Fig. 2). The students were asked to associate the finger-spelling with the correct word.

For each task, the students were given two chances to answer correctly. If the students did not get the correct answer, the teacher is asked to interpret the printed text or image using ArSL. At the end of each task the students were asked for their preferred media.

Results. Table 1 summarises the performance on the six observed students during the link media to text task. As expected, students from fifth grade (session one) performed better than those in the first grade (session two). The results of each task were as follows:

Text to Picture. All fifth graders were able to associate the right photo with its corresponding printed text. This was not the case for first graders, where only one student was able to link all photos to their text. One first grade student was only able to associate one out of 4 photos to its correct text. Preference for photos were equally split between realistic and cartoon photos.

Text to Video. Students had more difficulty with videos than they did with the photos, where only one student from the fifth grade was able to complete the association correctly. The performance in both session was somewhat level. Similar to photos their preference for realistic or animated videos was equally split between the two versions.

Text to Sign Language. All students struggled with ArSL which was unexpected. Two first graders failed in completing any of the subtasks, while the last student was only able to answer one subtask correctly. Fifth graders fared slightly better, but generally did not perform as well as they did in the picture and video tasks.

Text to Finger-Spelling. Finger-spelling proved easy for fifth graders where all students completed the tasks successfully. First graders were observed signing the letter along with the photos to help them associate them with the printed text and performed relatively well.

Table 1. Deaf students' task completion in both sessions.

Tasks	Session one			Session two		
	C1	C2	C3	C4	C5	C6
Realistic photo 1	✓	✓	✓	✓	✓	✓
Realistic photo 2	✓	✓	✓	✓	✓	×
Cartoon photo 1	✓	✓	✓	×	✓	×
Cartoon photo 2	✓	✓	✓	✓	✓	×
Realistic video 1	✓	✓	×	✓	✓	×
Realistic video 2	✓	×	×	×	×	×
Cartoon video 1	✓	✓	✓	✓	✓	✓
Cartoon video 2	✓	✓	✓	✓	✓	×
Human interpreter 1	✓	×	×	×	×	×
Human interpreter 2	✓	✓	✓	×	✓	×
Animated interpreter 1	×	×	×	×	×	×
Animated interpreter 2	×	×	×	×	×	×
Hand sign	✓	✓	×	×	×	×
Finger-spelling 1	✓	✓	✓	✓	✓	×
Finger-spelling 2	✓	✓	✓	×	✓	×
Finger-spelling 3	✓	✓	✓	✓	✓	✓

At the end of the linking tasks, the students were shown two applications that utilises SL and printed text. The first application, Let's Read [24], used ArSL to interpret a story that is visualised and presented in Arabic. The second application, Magic Camera [20], uses AR to animate a baby avatar to sign English words in American SL. Fifth graders preferred Let's Read, while first graders were intrigued by Magic Camera. Of course in the latter case, students did not know American SL and likely were impressed with the novel application.

3.3 Questionnaire

Parents of deaf children play a vital role in developing the child's reading ability. A questionnaire was used to collect information about deaf children's literacy from a parent's perspective. The questionnaire used both open- and close-ended questions to gather information pertaining to a deaf child's literacy development. The questionnaire was divided into four main sections:

- A general information section gathered details about the deaf child such as age, sex, loss of hearing, school grade, and school performance.
- The reading and SL section asked questions relating to ArSL and reading proficiency and difficulties. It also enquired about
- The third section asked questions pertaining to a deaf child's technological competence and preference. It also enquired about application preferred by deaf children.
- The final questions probed parents of deaf children for media recommendations for the proposed AR application.

The questionnaire was published on-line and distributed in various platforms including Twitter, Facebook, various forums for deaf societies, and Whatsapp. Thirty-seven responses were received, but only 14 of those were from parents of deaf children.

Results. Parents of deaf children provided general information about their children including sex (57% male and 43% female) and age (ranged from 7 to 17 years old). The majority of the children had profound hearing loss at 57%. Half of the children were born deaf and 36% lost their hearing during the first vital two years, and the rest after their second year. Parents judged their children's school performance as good (57%), while 29% states poor performance. None of the parents declared excellent school performance.

The following section in the questionnaire enquired about reading and SL proficiency. 65% of the children knew SL, specifically ArSL, and 71% could read. However, 36% of those children reading skill was judged purely by their parent. The questionnaire also asked parents about places of learning that play a role in developing a child's reading and SL (see Fig. 3(a) and (b)), where family and schools for the deaf play the prominent roles. Parents of deaf children also listed some of the difficulties their children face when reading, this list included: a weak inquisition crop, difficulty in comprehending the meaning of a word, difficulty associating a word with SL, and the child's inability to associate the alphabet to SL.

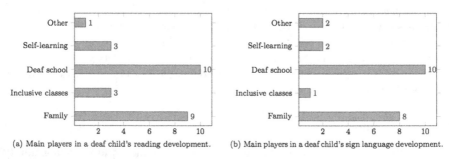

(a) Main players in a deaf child's reading development.   (b) Main players in a deaf child's sign language development.

Fig. 3. The role of family, schools, and self-learning in the development of a deaf child's reading and SL skills.

Parents of deaf children stated the technological competence of their children, where all were familiar with touch smartphones and/or tablets. Children mainly used the device for entertainment, while only 43% used it for educational purposes. Parents were also asked about what they think mostly attracts their children in an application, their responses ranked videos as a favourite, followed by pictures and then animation. SL and finger-spelling had a week preference at 29% and 15%, respectively.

The final section asked the parents for their recommendations for an application intended for deaf children. Their responses ranked pictures and videos as the most preferred method of representation, followed by SL and finger-spelling.

4 Discussion

Three instruments were used to collect data for the design and development of an AR application for the literacy development of deaf children. Interviews conducted with teachers of deaf elementary school children advocated for the use of ArSL to represent written text. They suggested further supplementing this mapping with picture and/or videos. They also recommended the inclusion of sounds to support hard of hearing students. Difficulties relating to vocabulary were also noted by teachers to include synonyms and antonyms, while interpreters reported difficulties with adjectives and adverbs when working with university deaf students. Observations of deaf students identified a weakness in ArSL, but the students fared better with finger-spelling. The observations also demonstrated the importance of showing the interpreter's face and body. The majority of students seemed to also struggle with animated interpreters. Questionnaire results from parents of deaf children supported the suggestion of teachers with the inclusion of photo and/or videos, but gave them a higher priority over SL. Surprisingly finger-spelling was neither suggested by parents or teachers, where the observation indicates its utility to demonstrate vocabulary and also SL. While teachers pushed for SL as the best form of representation, the observed students struggled with mapping the sign with its corresponding written words. This clearly indicates a weakness of deaf student in decoding SL to written text.

5 Conclusion

This research aims to develop an AR application and book to support the development of deaf children's literacy. Preliminary qualitative studies were conducted to determine the visual needs of deaf children from their personal perspectives, the perspective of their teachers and parents. The qualitative results demonstrate the difficulties deaf students face with vocabulary and SL. For future work, a participatory design approach will be adopted to develop the AR application for the literacy development of deaf children. The design will consider the perspective of all those involved in a child's reading progress: teachers, interpreters, parents of deaf children, and deaf children.

References

1. Goldin-Meadow, S., Mayberry, R.I., Read, T.O.: How do profoundly deaf children learn to read? Learn. Disabil. Res. Pract. **16**, 222–229 (2001)
2. Hanson, V.L.: Phonology and reading: evidence from profoundly deaf readers. Phonol. Read. Disabil. Solving Read. Puzzle **6**, 67–89 (1989)
3. Musselman, C.: How do children who can't hear learn to read an alphabetic script? A review of the literature on reading and deafness. J. Deaf Stud. Deaf Educ. **5**, 9–31 (2000)
4. Kingdom of Saudi Arabia General Authority of Statistic: Demographic survey. https://www.stats.gov.sa/en/852
5. Treiman, R., Hirsh-Pasek, K.: Silent reading: Insights from second-generation deaf readers. Cogn. Psychol. **15**, 39–65 (1983)

6. Humphries, T., MacDougall, F.: Chaining and other links: making connections between American sign language and English in two types of school settings. Vis. Anthropol. Rev. **15**, 84–94 (1999)
7. Elkins, J.: The concept of visual literacy, and its limitations. In: Visual Literacy. Routledge (2008)
8. Uluyol, Ç., Sahin, S.: Augmented reality: a new direction in education (2016)
9. Diegmann, P., Schmidt-kraepelin, M., Van Den Eynden, S., Basten, D.: Benefits of augmented reality in educational environments – a systematic literature review. Wirtschaftsinformatik **3**, 1542–1556 (2015)
10. Halawani, S.: Arabic sign language translation system on mobile devices. IJCSNS Int. J. Comput. Sci. Netw. Secur. **8**, 251–256 (2008)
11. Al-Dosri, H., Alawfi, N., Alginahi, Y.: Arabic sign language easy communicate ArSLEC. In: International Conference in Computer Information Technology, pp. 474–479 (2012)
12. El-Bendary, N., Zawbaa, H.M., Daoud, M.S., Hassanien, A.E., Nakamatsu, K.: ArSLAT: Arabic sign language alphabets translator. In: International Conference on Computer Information Systems and Industrial Management Applications, pp. 590–595 (2010)
13. Halawani, S.M., Daman, D., Kari, S., Ahmad, A.R.: An avatar based translation system from Arabic speech to arabic sign language for deaf people. Int. J. Inf. Sci. Educ. **2**, 13–20 (2013)
14. Oka Sudana, A.A.K., Aristamy, I.G.A.A.M., Wirdiani, N.K.A.: Augmented reality application of sign language for deaf people in Android based on smartphone. Int. J. Softw. Eng. Appl. **10**, 139–150 (2016)
15. Jiang, J., Kuang, Y.: The implementation of literacy and sign language learning system for deaf children based on the augmented reality. In: IEEE Workshop on Advanced Research and Technology in Industry Applications, pp. 911–913 (2014)
16. Zainuddin, N.M.M., Zaman, H.B., Ahmad, A.: Heuristic evaluation on augmented reality courseware for the deaf. In: International Conference on User Science and Engineering, pp. 183–188 (2011)
17. Zainuddin, N.M.M., Zaman, H.B., Ahmad, A.: Learning science using AR book: a preliminary study on visual needs of deaf learners. In: International Visual Informatics Conference, pp. 844–855 (2009)
18. Cadeñanes, J., Arrieta, A.G.: Development of sign language communication skill on children through augmented reality and the MuCy model. In: Mascio, T.D., Gennari, R., Vitorini, P., Vicari, R., de la Prieta, F. (eds.) Methodologies and Intelligent Systems for Technology Enhanced Learning. AISC, vol. 292, pp. 45–52. Springer, Cham (2014). doi:10.1007/978-3-319-07698-0_6
19. Kožuh, I., Hauptman, S., Kosec, P., Debevc, M.: Assessing the efficiency of using augmented reality for learning sign language. In: Antona, M., Stephanidis, C. (eds.) UAHCI 2015. LNCS, vol. 9176, pp. 404–415. Springer, Cham (2015). doi:10.1007/978-3-319-20681-3_38
20. Baby Sign and Learn: Magic Camera - American Sign Language Edition. https://itunes.apple.com/us/app/magic-camera-american-sign-language-edition/id662781080?mt=8
21. DAQRI: Anatomy 4D. http://anatomy4d.daqri.com/
22. Braun, V., Clarke, V.: Using thematic analysis in psychology. Using Qual. Res. Psychol. **3**, 77–101 (2006)
23. Goldin-Meadow, S., Feldman, H.: The creation of a communication system: a study of deaf children of hearing parents. Sign Lang. Stud. **8**, 225–233 (1975)
24. Kids App: Let's Read. https://itunes.apple.com/us/app//id1205247520?mt=8

Understanding the Atmospheric Cues Effects on Consumer Emotions: A Case Study on Lazada Malaysia

Saliza Aksah, Jamaliah Taslim$^{(\boxtimes)}$, Maslina Abdul Aziz,
Paezah Hamzah, Norehan Abdul Manaf, and Zan Azma Nasruddin

Faculty of Computer and Mathematical Sciences,
Universiti Teknologi MARA Malaysia, Shah Alam, Malaysia
zalliza12@gmail.com, {jamaliah,maslina,paezah,
norehan,zanaz}@tmsk.uitm.edu.my

Abstract. The effectiveness of atmospheric cues on consumer's emotion has a significant impact on online businesses. The usability issues with regards to atmospheric cues especially while browsing electronic commerce (e-commerce) websites are very important. This paper aims to identify the common atmospheric cues, usability issues and their effects on consumer emotions while browsing e-commerce websites. Usability testing techniques was conducted to five (5) participants from different backgrounds by using qualitative methods. The outcome of this preliminary study will help e-commerce websites specifically Lazada Malaysia to reduce usability gap of online shopping experience. The result highlights the atmospheric cues and their influence on the website. These initial findings motivated the current study, which extends our previous work by proposing other key variables and several new recommendations for improvement to generate more effective usability issues.

Keywords: Atmospheric cue · Usability · E-commerce · Consumer emotions

1 Introduction

Malaysia has shown robust development and opportunities of electronic commerce (e-commerce) market. Recent e-commerce report published by Lifting the Barriers to E-Commerce in ASEAN (2015) revealed that the online retail market in the Association of Southeast Asian Nations (ASEAN)[1] is worth an estimated $7 billion. ASEAN's e-commerce market is projected to grow at least twice as fast as the e-commerce market in the United States, Europe, and Japan [1]. This indicates great potential for all e-commerce businesses, across all sectors and industries to embark onto online shopping. E-commerce website is widely used by companies as a key marketing and sales vehicle for their goods or services [2]. Lazada is one of the leading e-commerce website, offering a wide range of the world's most famous brands with operations across Southeast Asia.

---

[1] https://www.atkearney.co.uk.

© Springer International Publishing AG 2017
H. Badioze Zaman et al. (Eds.): IVIC 2017, LNCS 10645, pp. 423–432, 2017.
https://doi.org/10.1007/978-3-319-70010-6_39

Atmospherics are the components of retail in the atmosphere, which in this context is web atmospheric environment of a retail environment that trigger emotional reactions in potential consumers, encouraging them to stay cues [3]. Consumers' emotions to e-commerce environment are about their willingness to spend time and money, review, evaluate, and proceed with transaction [4]. In Malaysia, there are several studies conducted to evaluate the accessibility level of various websites [5, 6].

However, studies of usability level for e-commerce website in Malaysia is still lacking. Usability testing to assess e-commerce website is important as one of e-commerce strategy to survive in the retail businesses [7–9]. It helps to gain a comprehensive understanding of consumer's needs and to improve products and services to provide better user experience [7]. However, many e-commerce websites still do not meet consumers' usability requirements. Therefore, this study conducts usability testing (atmospheric cues) to analyze and identify a user interface while browsing e-commerce websites.

2 Literature Review

Nowadays, e-commerce offers a lot of things from different perspective of consumers. It provides a range of services that consumers themselves can execute without direct human intervention. It has become a main component for companies to market their products and services via online. One of the pioneer in e-commerce website across the fastest growing countries in the world is Lazada. Lazada Group founded in 2012 by Samwer brothers is one of the preferred websites by Malaysian to shop online [10]. It offers a fast, secure and convenient online shopping experience aligned with its tagline 'effortless shopping' with a wide range of products from fashion to automotive. Atmospheric for website is defined as any cues that are consciously designed and visible to the online consumers in online shopping environment. These include all the cues used to design the website and its layout, for instance, the background pattern and color, links, icons, overall color structure, font and web structures [11].

A well-known framework, S-O-R framework and Pleasure-Arousal-Dominance (PAD) model are two important concepts with regards atmospheric cues and emotions studies in retail environment. The S-O-R theory stated that a stimulus (S) spurs people's internal affective evaluations, organisme (O), which in turn leads to approach or avoidance responses (R). PAD model is a functional theory to investigate consumers' internal states and predict their responses in the shopping process[13]. However, the role of dominance is not intensely examined and has been neglected in most of existing studies [3, 12, 13].

Some of the feelings that consumers experienced when shopping online are under retailer's control. Thus, the atmospheric cues of the web e-commerce are often designed in such a way as to induce emotions in consumers [14]. Usability is quality attribute or characteristic of a product that measures how easy to use the user interfaces [8]. The broad goal of usability in e-commerce from a user's perspective is to acquire acceptable effectiveness, efficiency and satisfaction [7]. Usability, therefore, considered being one of the most vital quality factors for web applications.

From web perspective, usability is a crucial condition for survival. If the main page failed to clearly mention what the company offers and what consumers can perform further, consumers will leave the website [8]. If customer experience difficulties in finding a product, there is a high chance he or she will cancel the whole transaction.

There are various evaluation methods used in product evaluation. The selection of the evaluation methods depends on the usability goals and usability dimension that need much more concern in the specific context of study [16]. Among all, user testing and heuristic evaluation method are commonly used for e-commerce website [7, 8]. In conducting usability testing, most common data gathering techniques used are; observation, interview (part of inquiry method technique), think aloud, eye tracking, questionnaires (part of inquiry method technique), and remotely conducting the testing.

3   Methodology

This study used qualitative method approach in conducting usability testing on Lazada Malaysia website to identify usability issues. In this study, the approaches used is a combination of user testing techniques, which are observation, interview and think aloud. A set of task-scenario was given during the user testing. Different techniques were used to collect different type of data. For instance, interview which is considered an efficient way of collecting the data [17]. Interview is used to collect demographic data, participant general interest and user feedback on atmospheric cues and emotions, as well as their recommendations to improve the identified atmospheric cues the Lazada Malaysia website. Observation technique is done while user performing the assigned tasks used to provide realistic situation to the participants while they were browsing Lazada Malaysia website. Whilst, think aloud is used to acquire participant's thought while they are completing a given task. This method is a best way to encourage participants to articulate their feelings [18].

4   Results and Analysis

Demographic data and information about participants' experiences using Lazada Malaysia website will be discussed in this section. The one-to-one usability testing was conducted from 21st November 2015 to 11th December 2015.

(A)   Pre-test Result
Five (5) participants with IT background aged between 20 to 39 years old involved in this usability testing; four (4) female participants and one (1) male participant. The participants were randomly selected from public with different education backgrounds. Participants have experienced purchasing from Lazada website, at least once. Figure 1 below is the result of the participant's preferences.

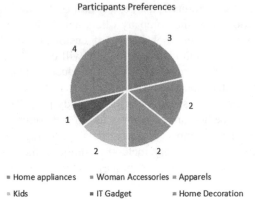

Fig. 1. Participant's preferences

(B) Testing

Participants were observed while performing the five tasks-scenarios and they are encouraged to articulate their thinking and loudly expressed their feelings during the testing. Table 1 below is the result of the tasks-scenarios method.

Table 1. Task scenarios result

Task-scenario	Observation result	
	Positive	Negative
Task 1: Product search	Participants successfully completed the task	One (1) participant had problems using filtering option for price range (the range is too small)
Task 2: Product search (think aloud technique)	Most of the participants expressed their excitement when they looked at the promotional product. One (1) participant read the description of the products	No negative comments
Task 3: Purchase the product	The process went smooth and satisfying. Only (1) participant read the product specifications. Only (1) participant compare the products before adding the product to the 'Cart	The product description were ambiguous, lengthy with the image displayed
Task 4: Profile update	All participants able to find the menu, as it is located at the top right of the page	No negative comments
Task 5: System log off	Participants successfully completed the task	No negative comments

Task 1: Product Search
The first task required participants to search using search bar. The purpose of this task is to observe how participants navigate the website in general, and to find any usability issue with regards the atmospheric cues of graphics and colors on overall website

Task 2: Product Search (Think Aloud)
This task aimed to see how participants used think aloud technique to express their emotions while browsing the website.

Task 3: Purchase the Product
The purpose of this task is to identify any usability issue with regards atmospheric cues links and menu during purchasing process.

Task 4: Profile Update
The purpose of this task is to identify any usability issue with regards atmospheric cues links and menu.

Task 5: System Log Off
The final task aimed to identify usability issue with regards atmospheric cue menu similar to previous task.

(C) Post-test Result
Post-Test Result objective is to gather participant's feedback and recommendation on Lazada Malaysia website. Post-test questions are divided into three (3) parts which are Part 1: Atmospheric Cues, Part II: Emotions and Part III: General Opinion.

Table 2. Atmospheric cues result

Atmospheric cues	Positive	Negative
Graphic	All participants agreed that graphic designs such as product image, animation on the website are fun and visually comforting	Three (3) participants commented the graphics on website are just nice
Colour	Majority agreed the colors used in the website are visually appealing Majority agreed with the use of visually appealing colours to distinguish important contents	Three (3) participants disagree with newly displayed merchandises with distinctive colours
Menu	All participants agreed that the website menus were recognizable and easy to use All participants agree the segmentations and design in the website are satisfying, suitable and consistent with the overall website style	No negative comment

(*continued*)

Table 2. (*continued*)

Atmospheric cues	Positive	Negative
Links	All participants agreed that the website provides buttons and shortcut paths to ease the consumers to find products All participants agreed that the website able to find out what customers want within three clicks from the first page	One (1) participant was unsure with the useful links to move into the sub-sites provided

Part 1: Atmospheric Cues (Graphics, Colors, Menu, Links)
Based on previous research, it is understandable that atmospheric cues are the important part of website design, which can trigger a pleasurable online shopping experience, and eventually induce purchase intentions. Participant's feedback on the four (4) chosen atmospheric cues are shown in Table 2 above.

Part 2: Emotions (Pleasure and Arousal)
The result from the Post-Test interview indicates that all participants have expressed their positive emotions while they browsing and using Lazada Malaysia website. This part aimed to collect feedback on participant's best emotions while browsing Lazada Malaysia website and purchase from the website. Surprisingly, all participants demonstrated positive emotions for both Pleasure and Arousal elements.

(A) Pleasure
The result from the Post-Test interview indicates that all participants have expressed their positive emotions while they browsing and using Lazada Malaysia website. This part aimed to collect feedback on participant's best emotions while browsing Lazada Malaysia website and purchase from the website. Feedback on pleasure was gathered using ten (10) measures, both positive and negative, by asking them what kind of feeling that best described them when using Lazada Malaysia website to shop [19]:

- Contented/Depressed;
- Happy/Unhappy;
- Satisfied/Unsatisfied;
- Pleased/Annoyed; and
- Free/Restricted.

Surprisingly, all participants demonstrated positive emotions using Lazada Malaysia website to shop.

(B) Arousal
For arousal, there are eight (8) measures as well, both emotions; positive and negative feedback were gathered when purchasing through Lazada Malaysia website:

- Aroused/Not aroused;
- Wide Awake/Sleepy;
- Excited/Calm; and
- Frenzied/Sluggish.

Similarly, participants feel aroused, wide-awake, excited, frenzied when they purchased from Lazada Malaysia website with the big discount offered, nice graphics and colours, and so forth. The detail result is shown in Table 3 below.

Table 3. Emotions post-test result

Emotions	Positive	Negative
Pleasure	All participants felt content happy, satisfied, pleased and free when shopping at Lazada website	No negative comments
Arousal	Majority agreed they feel aroused, wideawake, excited, frenzied when they purchased from Lazada website with the big discount offered, nice graphics and colors, and so forth	No negative comments

Part 3: General Opinion

In general, all participants agreed that it is easy to navigate around Lazada Malaysia website. They also emphasized that they will continue purchase from Lazada Malaysia website due to the convenient it offers, eases of use and less hassles. Apart from the issues highlighted during actual testing, participant also provided feedback on other issues on overall website. Among others are, the website is too crowded with promotional items, searching retrieved irrelevant products and shipping cost that only available during checkout process. Other feedback are product images do not represent the actual product, for example the size of kid's apparel, the promotion link is still available even though the promotion period already ended, invalid voucher claim link and product descriptions do not represent the actual product. Apart from the issues during actual testing, participant also highlighted other issues about the website. Table 4 are the findings of Lazada website.

Table 4. Opinion and general observations about Lazada website

General opinion	
1	Easy to navigate around Lazada Website
2	The website is too crowded with promotional items
3	Search result retrieved irrelevant products
4	Product images do not represent the actual product. Some promotions have expired
5	Shipping cost were not clearly mentioned at early stage
6	Invalid voucher claim link
7	Product descriptions do not represent the actual product

Based on the findings, there are eight (8) ways to improve the user experience of Lazada Malaysia website shown in Table 5 below. The main point is visitors can easily and quickly find the information that interests them. In general, there are several important issues that need to be improved; navigation, display, design and user experience. For example, the main page should not be too crowded with unnecessary promotional items. This promotional item are disturbing and distracting customers. The customers lose interest if this trend increases.

Table 5. Improvements suggestions for Lazada Malaysia website

Improvements	
1	Main page should not be too crowded with unnecessary promotional items
2	Filtering option for price range should be more flexible and easy to use
3	Product color is coded based on consumer's preferences
4	Product searching mechanism need to be refined
5	Shipping cost need to be mentioned before the checkout process
6	Product images should represent the actual size or provide size information
7	Promotion link should be frequently updated
8	The sales product should be highlighted and must be aligned with the description

Usability testing was conducted by applying usability testing techniques including observation, interview and think aloud in three (3) different stages; Pre-test, Test and Post-test. The data gathered during the actual testing were then analyzed and interpreted. The findings, which are the usability issues are classified into three (3) categories with respective elements as shown in Table 6. Table 6 summarizes usability testing results with the core elements of atmospherics cues and emotions.

Table 6. Summary of usability testing results

Category	Element	Usability issues/Explanation
Atmospheric cues	Graphics	• Product image does not represent actual size (kid apparel); and • Product image does not highlight actual product offer (ambiguous product description)
	Colors	• Hardly distinguish the colors of apparel
	Menu	• No issue highlighted
	Links	• Invalid promotion link (expired, but the link still there); and • Unable to redeem entitled voucher
Emotions	Pleasure arousal	• Relatively positive respond received
Others		• Hard to drag filtering option for price range; • Homepage crowded with promotional items, sometimes quite distracting; • Product search function is not well-defined as it resulted of unnecessary products based on the keyword inputted; and • Shipping cost only stated during checkout stage

5   Conclusions

Overall, Lazada Malaysia website is a usable e-commerce website in terms of overall design especially on the four (4) atmospheric cues. However, there are minor issues that need to be improved from perspectives of atmospheric cues graphics, colors and links, and as well as overall Lazada Malaysia website. The contribution for usability practice and future research are explained based on two (2) disciplines (i) e-commerce; theory building process in minimizing the existing gaps in the online atmospheric literature, and companies should take into consideration of human aspects, in this case is consumers' emotion in designing a good e-commerce website to induce consumer's satisfaction while using the website, and, in return, will generate more revenues and increase the profits, which are the ultimate goals and strategies for most of the companies, and from (ii) HCI discipline; promoting the practice of HCI in Malaysia context, and may help the companies to reduce the gap of finding website issues from the earlier stages.

There are several limitations acknowledged in this study whereby this study (i) only focusing on four (4) atmospheric cues only, and two (2) emotion elements, namely pleasure and arousal. The testing is done (ii) in general, applying usability testing method, based on observation, interview and think aloud techniques, which the identified usability issues are solely from user's perspectives. This study is using Lazada Malaysia website as a case study and the usability issues identified may not represented the overall e-commerce business activities, which nowadays, consumers rely on various Internet sources to perform online purchase activities (iii).

There are three (3) relevant areas to conduct further research, (i) to evaluate usability on other key variables of web atmospheric cues, and another emotion (PAD) element which is dominance that has been left out in previous research, (ii) involvement expert views, for example using Heuristic Evaluation method and using different technique, such eye-tracking, which would potentially improve the current website design from different perspectives and the last recommendation (iii) is to extend this study by conducting usability study on social media platforms, for example Facebook or Instagram that would generate a comprehensive understanding of usability role when consumers and companies interact with these new technologies.

References

1. Kearney, T.: Lifting the barriers to e-commerce in ASEAN. https://www.atkearney.com/documents/10192/5540871
2. Smith, T.J., Spiers, R.: Perceptions of e-commerce web sites across two generations. Inf. Sci.: Int. J. Emerg. Transdiscipl. **12**, 159–180 (2009)
3. Yani-de-Soriano, M.M., Foxall, G.R.: The emotional power of place: the fall and rise of dominance in retail research. J. Retail. Consum. Serv. **13**(6), 403–416 (2006)
4. Foxall, G.R., Greenley, G.E.: Consumers' emotional responses to service environments. J. Bus. Res. **46**(2), 149–158 (1999)

5. Aziz, M.A., Isa, W.A.R.W.M., Fadzir, N.S.M.: Accessibility of websites for people with disabilities (PWD) in Malaysia: an empirical investigation. Int. J. Adv. Sci. Eng. Inf. Technol. **1**(2), 221–226 (2011)
6. Aziz, M.A., Isa, W.A.R.W.M., Nordin, N.: Assessing the accessibility and usability of Malaysia higher education website. In: 2010 International Conference on User Science and Engineering (i-USEr), pp. 203–208. IEEE (2010)
7. Goh, K.N., Chen, Y.Y., Lai, F.W., Daud, S.C., Sivaji, A., Soo, S.T.: A comparison of multiple usability testing methods to evaluate and analyze an e-commerce website: a malaysian case study on an online gift shop. In: Tenth International Conference on Information Technology-New Generations (2013)
8. Nielsen, J.: Usability 101: Introduction to Usability (2003)
9. Belanche, D., Casaló, L.V., Guinalíu, M.: Website usability, consumer satisfaction and the intention to use a website: the moderating effect of perceived risk. J. Retail. Consum. Serv. **19**(1), 124–132 (2012)
10. San, L.Y., Omar, A., Thurasamy, R.: Online purchase: a study of generation Y in Malaysia. Int. J. Bus. Manag. **10**(6), 298 (2015)
11. Eroglu, S.A., Machleit, K.A., Davis, L.M.: Atmospheric qualities of online retailing: a conceptual model and implications. J. Bus. Res. **54**(2), 177–184 (2001)
12. Mehrabian, A., Russell, J.A.: The basic emotional impact of environments. Percept. Mot. Skills **38**(1), 283–301 (1974)
13. Floh, A., Madlberger, M.: The role of atmospheric cues in online impulse-buying behavior. Electron. Commer. Res. Appl. **12**(6), 425–439 (2013)
14. Machleit, K.A., Mantel, S.P.: Emotional response and shopping satisfaction: moderating effects of shopper attributions. J. Bus. Res. **54**(2), 97–106 (2001)
15. Fernandez, A., AbrahãO, S., Insfran, E.: Empirical validation of a usability inspection method for model-driven web development. J. Syst. Softw. **86**(1), 161–186 (2013)
16. Quesenbery, W.: Balancing the 5Es of usability. Cutter IT J. **17**(2), 4–11 (2004)
17. van Kuijk, J., van Driel, L., van Eijk, D.: Usability in product development practice; an exploratory case study comparing four markets. Appl. Ergon. **47**, 308–323 (2015)
18. Hackos, J.T.: Handbook of Usability Testing (1995)
19. Koo, D.M., Ju, S.H.: The interactional effects of atmospherics and perceptual curiosity on emotions and online shopping intention. Comput. Hum. Behav. **26**(3), 377–388 (2010)

Integrating Learning Techniques into iCAL4LA-*Bijak Matematik* Courseware to Motivate Low Achieving Children in Learning

Siti Zulaiha Ahmad[1(✉)] and Ariffin Abdul Mutalib[2]

[1] Universiti Teknologi MARA Perlis, 02600 Arau, Perlis, Malaysia
sitizulaiha@perlis.uitm.edu.my
[2] Universiti Utara Malaysia, Sintok, Kedah, Malaysia
am.ariffin@uum.edu.my

Abstract. Children with learning difficulties require support during teaching and learning process. This study looks into the solution of learning difficulties confronted by the low achieving (LA) children who particularly have problems in literacy (reading) and numeracy (calculating). This study proposed the suitable learning techniques integrated into a learning courseware in order to ensure the children are engaged during the learning process as well as able to accomplish the whole learning content. The main objective is achieved through three research activities, which are (i) learning techniques selection, (ii) design and development of courseware, and (iii) user experience testing. As the result, this study initially found three learning techniques that are suitable for LA children. They are deployed into a courseware, iCAL4LA-*Bijak Matematik* in motivating the LA children to learn mathematics. The user experience testing revealed that it was motivating the LA children with percentage of mean, 97% as the ability in accomplishing overall sub-modules, as they can choose specific learning technique based on their preference.

Keywords: Low achieving · Learning techniques · User experience

1 Introduction

Learning abilities varied among children with some of them demonstrating an excellent performance, while others may face specific difficulties, which implicate their academic achievement [1]. Generally, learning difficulties refers to those who academically and practically have problems to absorb what is being thought in schools. Several outlines [2–4] agree that learning difficulties can be observed in those who are unable to perform in academic and examination evaluation. Similarly, [5] suggest that learning difficulties should be categorized from general to specific learning difficulties by implying the term 'moderate learning difficulties' to those who are incompetent in their study. These children are quite tormented in the mainstream education system, as they struggling with their difficulties and need to cope with the learning content.

© Springer International Publishing AG 2017
H. Badioze Zaman et al. (Eds.): IVIC 2017, LNCS 10645, pp. 433–444, 2017.
https://doi.org/10.1007/978-3-319-70010-6_40

Accordingly, this study refers them as low achieving (LA) children who require an attentive learning approach or technique in motivating them to learn.

Proper learning techniques are required in order to provide them with a better learning concept. The learning process could cultivate their interest by blending the learning techniques and interactive computer assisted learning (iCAL) in a learning courseware. Referring to the previous studies by [6], they justified the learning requirements and concept that are vital to be included in the digital learning material for LA children, in which interactive multimedia are most appropriate. Therefore, this study proposed the incorporation of learning techniques and interactive multimedia learning courseware in the conceptual model of iCAL4LA (interactive computer assisted learning for low achiever). The main objective of this study is to propose the appropriate learning technique that suitable for LA children based on the previous studies and to integrate them into a learning courseware with the intention of motivating the LA children in completing the learning process. In line with that, this paper is outlined into four main sections: (i) literature review, (ii) methodology (iii) finding and discussion, and (iv) conclusion.

2 Literature Review

2.1 Learning Technique

Learning technique is a specific approach to support pedagogical activities for a particular lesson. In traditional classrooms, teachers usually implement various learning techniques in order to enhance learning performance especially with those with learning difficulties [7, 8] such as LA children. In line with that, to propose a conceptual model of iCAL4LA, the consideration of learning techniques is essential because LA children require specific technique to facilitate them during the learning process. Therefore, the following subsections discuss three learning techniques that are suitable for different learning content such as mathematics and language. They are (i) e-flashcard, (ii) phonic reading, and (iii) mental arithmetic.

E-flashcard. In a traditional way, flashcard refers to a learning tool that utilizes visual representation of paper-based materials consisting of specific learning contents such as characters, vocabulary or math facts on either one side or both [9–11]. The initial concept of flashcard is to enable learners, especially children to memorize or study facts [12, 13] in different range of complexity which can be presented from easy to a hard level [14]. In fact, Wissman and friends [15] found that learners prefer to use flashcard as it is helpful in providing an easier way of learning. However, with the advancement of digital technology, utilizing flashcards as a learning technique has shifted to the implementation of digital flashcard or e-flashcard. E-flashcard is a digital version of flashcards implemented in the form of computer-based or mobile-based application with the incorporation of multimedia elements [11, 16]. The inclusion of innovative and creative concept of e-flashcard has been proven effective [17] as it enables learners to get prompt response from digitally designed learning materials [18]. It is suggest that e-flashcard is applicable for all range of age and suitable to assist children with learning difficulties [16], which is related to iCAL4LA study.

Mental Arithmetik. Mental arithmetic is a specific technique for mathematical learning. Mental arithmetic is basically based on the working memory utilization on how to perform simple addition mentally within the range of 'whole number fact' [19, 20], which is useful for elementary level children. In fact, Price and the team [21] revealed that inability to mentally perform arithmetic operation during elementary level could implicate their mathematical performance at high school level. In addition, Wu and his colleagues found that LA children rely on the central execution of working memory [22], which works as a supervisory control system to choose and apply particular strategies in solving arithmetic problems such as addition problem. One of the strategies is mental arithmetic strategy that employs working memory capacity to perform addition of two numbers such as 8 + 3. Unfortunately, to rely only on the working memory capacity alone is challenging for LA children as they have low ability to memorize many numbers at once. On contrary to that, [23] have studied the finger-based representation to perform arithmetic calculation such as German and Chinese finger counting techniques. They found that this technique is proven to stimulate mental arithmetic skill among not only children but also adults' learners. In short, to simplify the application of mental arithmetic technique only one digit will be stored in the working memory [20, 22] and the other numbers will be counted using fingers [23].

Phonic Reading. Phonic is "*a type of reading instruction that is intended to promote the discovery and understanding of the alphabetic principle, the correspondences between phonemes and graphemes, and phonological decoding*" [24, p. 326]. In a simple concept, phonic reading technique emphasizes the reader to pronounce a single letter-sound and incorporate it with other vowel/consonance letter-sounds to form a syllable. Even though this technique is commonly used for the English language [25, 26], it is also applicable for the Malay language [27, 28]. In the Malay language for example, the letter 'b' is decoded as "beh" and letter 'a' is decoded as 'aaa', in which the combination of both letters forms a syllable 'ba' [27, 29]. In fact, previous studies have proven the effectiveness of phonics reading technique to develop reading proficiency [26, 30, 31]. This technique is not only useful as an early stage of reading process but can also be utilized as an intervention program for children with reading difficulties [32, 33] such as LA children that are related to iCAL4LA study.

2.2   The Motivating Aspect in User Experience

Positive experiences encourage users to do something and they become more energized than the prior state. In a broad point of view, [34] stated that "*motivation is indicated by the intensity (or energy), direction, and persistence of a goal-directed behavior or action*" (p. 11), which are related to the effort of a particular person. However, in specific user experience definition, [35] emphasize that motivation is one the value that obtained from the interaction with software, which reflect to the internal state of the user. It shows that, motivation is a process to enhance user capability and interests in a particular field for example in education field. Basically, in order to capture motivational significance of users, they have to be exposed to the interactive software [36] by fostering generative processing [37] for example, in interactive multimedia software

[38]. Numbers of studies have look into this by associating motivating aspect with user engagement in using an interactive software [39, 40] and game based software [41]. It measures the user experience in form of engagement aspect or in short, to which extend user are motivated to engage to an application. Period of engagement can be quantify by observing users' ability to complete the whole learning module within specific time [42, 43], which is suitable to level of user especially children.

2.3   The iCAL4LA

The motivation of constructing the conceptual model of iCAL4LA is based on the existing studies with enhancement on the interaction design component and its principles that are specifically designed for LA children that focus on providing fun, helpful, and motivating experience. The conceptual model of iCAL4LA is expected to expose the LA children with learning concept that comprises comprehensive components with utilization of interactive learning assistance technology and comparison of previous studies. The components were determined based on iCAL perspective, which embraces pedagogical context such as learning theories, learning approaches, learning techniques and instructional design model by specifying structure, content, and technology incorporated in it. The model provides a complete design guideline for designers or developers of digital learning contents such as teachers, courseware developers, and instructional designers to create digital learning material for LA children. However, this paper only discussed on the motivating perspective within the application of learning techniques. Figure 1 summarizes the basic concept of the conceptual model of iCAL4LA [44].

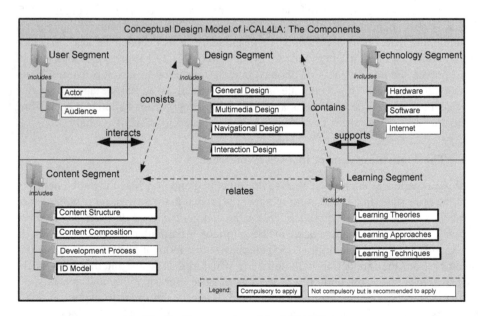

Fig. 1. Conceptual model of iCAL4LA.

3   Methodology

This study involves three steps of research activities, which are selection of the component, design and develop of the courseware, and testing of user experience. First, this study determines and selects the component of learning techniques based on the discussion from the literature review section. Next, during the design and development process, this study integrates the selected techniques into the courseware known as iCAL4LA-*Bijak Matematik*. Based on the outcome of the previous process, iCAL4LA-*Bijak Matematik* undergo user experience testing in investigating the motivating aspect. In order to gather the user motivating aspect, this study utilizes interaction log using specialize software, Free Studio that provides a screen video recording while the user interacting with the prototype. Using the software, the recorded video can be stored and retrieved later for analysis purposes. Finally, this study analyzes the results and justifies them based on the ability of the LA children in accomplishing the whole content of iCAL4LA-*Bijak Matematik*. Figure 2 summarizes the whole process of this study.

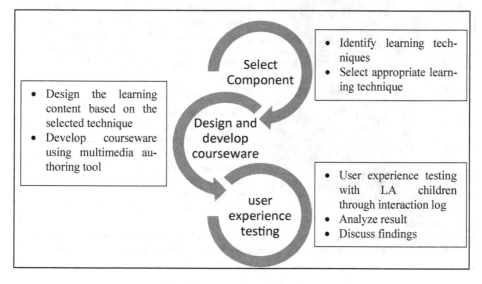

Fig. 2.   Research methodology.

3.1   Selection of Learning Segment of iCAL4LA

The adaptation of existing learning theories and approaches in this study are beneficial with the inclusion of the learning techniques for specific learning content. Thus, this study suggests the utilization of phonic reading for literacy content and the inclusion of mental arithmetic for numeracy content respectively. In addition, flashcard technique is also useful to memorize a chunk of basic learning contents. The implementation of those components is applicable for LA children as the Conceptual Model of iCAL4LA concerns on providing them with the comprehensive learning support.

3.2   Application of Learning Technique Component

The iCAL4LA-*Bijak Matematik* utilizes the learning techniques that are related to the mathematical lesson content. As a formal learning content, it covers the topics of numbers, addition, and subtraction, in which are subsequently presented with simple introduction, followed by lesson contents, interactive assessment module, and cheerful closing for each topic. It is expected that the LA children are able to follow the delivery of each module. As for the learning technique, mental arithmetic is the main technique that has been incorporated into the learning content to deliver the addition operation topic. Meanwhile, flashcard and phonic reading techniques are appropriately adapted within the lesson content in order to provide learning support for LA children. The utilization of those techniques is depicted in Figs. 3, 4 and 5.

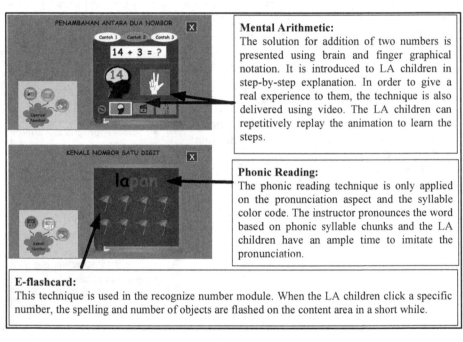

Fig. 3. Sample of iCAL4LA-*Bijak Matematik* screenshots that apply the learning techniques (e-flashcard and mental arithmetic using animation).

This study refers the motivating aspect as the willingness of the LA children to engage in the learning content in iCAL4LA-*Bijak Matematik*. It is obtained by delivering the contents with inspiring modes that enables the LA children to focus in the learning process. These children require positive words that praise for accomplishment of every single module or token of appreciation as a reward for engaging in the interactive activities. Accordingly, the motivating aspect is bounded in iCAL4LA-*Bijak Matematik* by utilizing the principles of multimedia elements. It contains (i) easy to read texts, (ii) attentive video and animation of tutorials, (iii) attractive and familiar

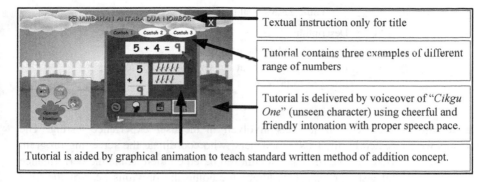

Fig. 4. Sample of addition technique alternative using animation.

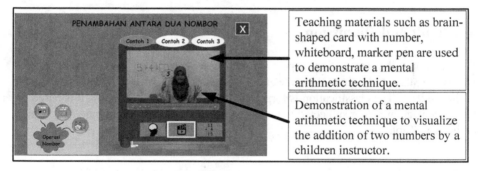

Fig. 5. Sample of learning content in iCAL4LA-*Bijak Matematik*

graphics and (iv) a clear and pleasing audio that leads to the engagement of the LA children. Besides that, color plays important roles in providing them with familiar and alluring metaphor with consideration of specific themes. It provides attraction during the learning process that could establish an engagement with iCAL4LA-*Bijak Matematik*.

3.3   User Experience Testing of ICAL4LA-*Bijak Matematik*

Testing Instrument and Procedure. The instrument for the interaction log is in a form of a checklist. The interaction log of motivating aspect are based on the user engagement and interaction [45] with the prototype. The instrument is a simplified form adapted from Tullis and Albert [46]. For this study, the instrument is structured into a checklist form on a piece of paper. It contains a list of modules and sub-modules in the iCAL4LA-*Bijak Matematik* and the engagement score column for each participant as well as a remark column. A three-point scales is used for the instrument, as recommended by Spencer and Usher [47] as seen in Table 1. Later, observers are required to input the score based on the user's engagement for analysis purpose.

Table 1. Motivating indicator.

Score	Description
0	Did not complete the content at all
1	Engaged to the content but partially completed
2	Engaged to the content and fully completed

Participant. There were 30 subjects involved in the user experience testing. The subjects were selected by the LINUS teachers, who coordinate the screening program in school. They were also verified as LA children based on their academic performance in the most recent test (for year 1 children) including the previous year of the final examination results. The permission to involve the subjects in this study was obtained from their guardians using an agreement form witnessed by their class teacher.

4   Result and Discussion

In evaluating the motivating aspect of the user experience for iCAL4LA-*Bijak Matematik*, this study, first, elaborates the findings in terms of the overall engagement of the subjects. The classification is formulated specifically for this study. It is based on the percentage indicator subjected to the target goal of task completion rate [46], which is listed in Table 2.

Table 2. Motivating classification.

Percentage	Classification	Description for classification
80–100	Motivating	Subject completes more than 10 sub-modules
60–79	Fairly Motivating	Subject completes between 7 to 9 sub-modules
40–59	Average	Subject completes between 5 and 6 sub-modules
20–39	Fairly Low Motivating	Subject completes between 3 and 4 sub-modules
0–19	Low Motivating	Subject completes below than 2 sub-modules

This study classifies that the iCAL4LA-*Bijak Matematik* is perceived as motivating if the percentage of the overall completion modules is more than 80%. The prototype contains four main modules, which are Let's Sing, Recognize Number, Number Operation, and Mastery Activity with a total of 12 sub-modules. As for Addition module, it consists of three different techniques. This study considers that the subject completed the sub-module if they choose any one of the learning techniques. Based on the condition and having analyzed the data, Table 3 tabulates the results.

Based on the percentage of the mean score in Table 3, it is clearly proven that the iCAL4LA-*Bijak Matematik* is perceived as motivating. This is proven as 97% (N = 29) of the subjects were able to accomplish at least 80% of the overall sub-modules. The remaining 3% (N = 1) is indicated as fairly motivating as the subjects were able to complete 60% to 79% of the overall sub-modules.

Table 3. Mean score based on motivating classification.

Classification	N	Mean score (percentage)
Motivating	29	97%
Fairly motivating	1	3%
Average	0	0%
Fairly low motivating	0	0%
Low motivating	0	0%
Total	30	100%

Additionally, in order to extract the detailed results, Table 4 presents the frequency based on each motivating completion indicator (stated in Table 1). The total recorded responses (N) are 360. It refers to the total number of sub-modules (12 sub-modules) recorded for each subject (30 subjects). The finding exhibits the highest percentage of complete responses, which is 94.44% (N = 340) of the overall frequencies. It indicates that a majority of the subjects was able to fully complete the sub-modules and adhere to the content. Through the observation, this study found that most of the subjects repeated the sub-modules several times based on their preferences. It was also observed that the subjects were likely to engage in the most preferred techniques of addition operation's examples through either video or animation. In contrast, only 2.22% (N = 8) responses were recorded as partially completed and 3.33% (N = 12) as incomplete. Particularly, the occurrences caused by their preferences of the availability of several examples in addition and subtraction sub-modules.

Table 4. Summary of motivating of user experience testing for iCAL4LA-*Bijak Matematik*.

Motivating frequency		Response	
		N	Percent
Motivating[a]	Incomplete	12	3.33%
	Partially complete	8	2.22%
	Fully complete	340	94.44%
Total		360	100.0%

[a]Group

Accordingly, this study found that the user perceived motivating, as they could accomplish most of the iCAL4LA-*Bijak Matematik* contents with the low incomplete and partially complete percentage.

5 Conclusion and Future Work

This study focuses in integrating the learning techniques proposed for the conceptual model of iCAL4LA into an interactive learning courseware for LA children. The main elements of learning technique that have been integrated in the courseware are mental arithmetic, e-flashcard, and phonic reading that found suitable for LA children. Those techniques are integrated with multimedia approach with interactive and instructive learning concept. This concept is implemented in the courseware known as iCAL4LA-*Bijak Matematik*. It contains basics mathematical learning content that suitable for a year 1 to year 3 primary school students who have learning difficulties especially in numeracy and literacy. Having conducted the user experience testing with the LA children, this study found that majority of the participants could engage to the whole content of iCAL4LA-*Bijak Matematik*. They were obviously attached to the learning content during the learning session with the availability of several learning techniques that can be chosen based on their preference. In order to triangulate and confirm the result, this study will look forward to interviewing the LA children for the future works.

References

1. Nandhini, K., Balasundaram, S.R.: Math word question generation for training the students with learning difficulties. In: Proceedings of the International Conference & Workshop on Emerging Trends in Technology - ICWET 2011, pp. 206–211 (2011)
2. Hock, T.T., Chang, W.S., Muhamad Rais, A.: Clinical diagnosis and non-verbal ability of primary-one school children with LD. Int. J. Public Health Res. 33–40 (2011). Special Issue 2011
3. Compton, D.L., Fuchs, L.S., Fuchs, D., Lambert, W., Hamlett, C.: The cognitive and academic profiles of reading and mathematics learning disabilities. J. Learn. Disabil. **45**(1), 79–95 (2012)
4. Adam, T., Tatnall, A.: Use of ICT to assist students with learning difficulties: an actor-network analysis. In: Reynolds, N., Turcsányi-Szabó, M. (eds.) KCKS 2010. IAICT, vol. 324, pp. 1–11. Springer, Heidelberg (2010). doi:10.1007/978-3-642-15378-5_1
5. Norwich, B., Ylonen, A., Gwernan-Jones, R.: Moderate learning difficulties: searching for clarity and understanding. Res. Pap. Educ. **29**(1), 1–19 (2012)
6. Siti Zulaiha, A., Ariffin, A.M.: Exploring computer assisted learning for low achieving children: a comparative analysis study. J. Teknologi **77**(29), 1–7 (2015)
7. Dunn, R., Honigsfeld, A.: Learning styles: what we know and what we need. Educ. Forum **77**(2), 225–232 (2013)
8. Dunlosky, J., Rawson, K.A., Marsh, E.J., Nathan, M.J., Willingham, D.T.: Improving students' learning with effective learning techniques: promising directions from cognitive and educational psychology. Psychol. Sci. Public Interest **14**(1), 4–58 (2013)
9. Byram, M.: Flashcard. In: Encyclopedia of Language Teaching & Learning, pp. 217–218. Routledge, Abingdon (2000)
10. Bryson, D.: Using flashcards to support your learning. J. Vis. Commun. Med. **35**(1), 25–29 (2012)
11. Srithar, U.: Learning at your own pace: M-learning solution for school students. Int. J. Inf. Electron. Eng. **5**(3), 216–224 (2015)
12. Kornell, N., Bjork, R.A.: Optimising self-regulated study: the benefits - and costs - of dropping flashcards. Memory **16**(2), 125–136 (2008)
13. Skarr, A., Williams, R.L., Mclaughlin, T.F.: The effects of direct instruction flashcard and math racetrack procedures on mastery of basic multiplication facts by three elementary school students. Educ. Treat. Child. **37**(1), 77–93 (2014)

14. Browder, D.M., Roberts, M.L.: Guidelines for flash card instruction. J. Behav. Educ. **3**(3), 235–245 (1993)
15. Wissman, K.T., Rawson, K.A., Pyc, M.A.: How and when do students use flashcards? Memory **20**(6), 568–579 (2012)
16. Aryati, B., Nor Hawaniah, Z., Siti Nazirah, M.Z., AbuSafia, A.H.: A conceptual model of Al-Furqan courseware using persuasive system design for early learning childhood. In: 8th Malaysian Software Engineering Conference, Langkawi, pp. 336–341. IEEE (2014)
17. Saatz, I., Kienle, A.: Learning with e-flashcards – does it matter? In: Hernández-Leo, D., Ley, T., Klamma, R., Harrer, A. (eds.) EC-TEL 2013. LNCS, vol. 8095, pp. 629–630. Springer, Heidelberg (2013). doi:10.1007/978-3-642-40814-4_85
18. Schmidmaier, R., Ebersbach, R., Schiller, M., Hege, I., Holzer, M., Fischer, M.R.: Using electronic flashcards to promote learning in medical students: retesting versus restudying. Med. Educ. **45**(11), 1101–1110 (2011)
19. Ashcraft, M.H.: The development of mental arithmetic: a chronometric approach. Dev. Rev. **2**(3), 213–236 (1982)
20. Hitch, G.J.: The role of short-term working memory in mental arithmetic. Cogn. Psychol. **10** (3), 302–323 (1978)
21. Price, G.R., Mazzocco, M.M.M., Ansari, D.: Why mental arithmetic counts: brain activation during single digit arithmetic predicts high school math scores. J. Neurosci. **33**(1), 156–163 (2013)
22. Wu, S.S., Meyer, M.L., Maeda, U., Salimpoor, V., Tomiyama, S., Geary, D.C., Menon, V.: Standardized assessment of strategy use and working memory in early mental arithmetic performance. Dev. Neuropsychol. **33**(3), 365–393 (2008)
23. Klein, E., Moeller, K., Willmes, K., Nuerk, H.C., Domahs, F.: The influence of implicit hand-based representations on mental arithmetic. Front. Psychol. **2**, 1–7 (2011)
24. Scarborough, V., Brady, S.: Toward a common terminology for talking about speech and reading: a glossary of the 'Phon' words and some related terms. J. Lit. Res. **34**(3), 299–336 (2002)
25. Wyse, D., Goswami, U.: Synthetic phonics and the teaching of reading. Br. Edu. Res. J. **34** (6), 691–710 (2008)
26. Davis, A.: To read or not to read: decoding synthetic phonics. Impact **2013**(20), 1–38 (2013)
27. Ahmad, S.Z., Nik Ludin, N.A.A., Ekhsan, H.M., Rosmani, A.F.: Bijak Membaca - applying phonic reading technique and multisensory approach with interactive multimedia for dyslexia children. In: IEEE Colloquium on Humanities, Science & Engineering Research (CHUSER 2012), Kota Kinabalu, pp. 554–559. IEEE (2012)
28. Ismail, S.S., Mohd Mahidin, E.M., Umar, I.R., Mohd Yusoff, M.Z.: E-Z-disleksia for dyslexic children. In: Proceedings of Regional Conference on Knowledge Integration in ICT, pp. 435–444. KUIS, Selangor (2010)
29. Sidhu, M.S., Manzura, E.: An effective conceptual multisensory multimedia model to support dyslexic children in learning. Int. Inf. Commun. Technol. Educ. **7**(3), 34–50 (2011)
30. Stahl, S.A.: Teaching children with reading problems to decode: phonics and 'not-phonics' instruction. Read. Writ. Q. **14**(2), 165–188 (1998)
31. Chard, D.J., Osborn, J.: Phonics and word recognition instruction in early reading programs: guidelines for accessibility. Learn. Disabil. Res. Pract. **14**(2), 107–117 (1999)
32. Hornery, S., Seaton, M., Tracey, D., Craven, R.G., Yeung, A.S.: Enhancing reading skills and reading self-concept of children with reading difficulties: adopting a dual approach intervention. Aust. J. Educ. Dev. Psychol. **14**(2014), 131–143 (2014)
33. Saine, N.L., Lerkkanen, M.K., Ahonen, T., Tolvanen, A., Lyytinen, H.: Computer-assisted remedial reading intervention for school beginners at risk for reading disability. Child. Dev. **82**(3), 1013–1028 (2011)

34. Dai, D.Y., Sternberg, R.J.: Beyond cognitivism: toward an integrated understanding of intellectual functioning and development. In: Motivation, Emotion, and Cognition: Intergrative Perspectives on Intellectual Functioning and Development, Laawrence Erlbaum Associates, New Jersey (2004)
35. Hassenzahl, M., Tractinsky, N.: User experience - a research agenda. Behav. Inf. Technol. **25**(2), 91–97 (2006)
36. Ariffin, A.M., Norshuhada, S.: Conceptual design model of reality learning media (RLM). In: Proceedings of IADIS International Conference e-Society 2009, pp. 353–360 (2009)
37. Mayer, R.E.: Incorporating motivation into multimedia learning. Learn. Instr. **29**(2014), 171–173 (2014)
38. Lee, S.H., Boling, E.: Screen design guidelines for motivation in interactive multimedia instruction: a survey and framework for designers. Educ. Technol. **39**(3), 19–26 (1999)
39. Attfield, S., Kazai, G.: Towards a science of user engagement. In: WSDM Workshop on User Modelling for Web Application. ACM (2011)
40. Chapman, P., Selvarajah, S., Webster, J.: Engagement in multimedia training systems. In: Proceeding of 32nd Annual Hawaii International Conference System Science, pp. 1–9 (1999)
41. Ronimus, M., Kujala, J., Tolvanen, A., Lyytinen, H.: Children's engagement during digital game-based learning of reading: the effects of time, rewards, and challenge. Comput. Educ. **71**(2014), 237–246 (2014)
42. Aznoora, O., Wan Ahmad, W.J., Aznan, C.A.: Educational multimedia app for dyslexia literacy intervention: a preliminary evaluation. Procedia – Soc. Behav. Sci. **176**(2015), 405–411 (2015)
43. Said, S.N.: An engaging multimedia design model. In: Proceeding - Interaction Design and Children Building a Community, IDC 2004, pp. 169–172 (2004)
44. Siti Zulaiha, A., Ariffin, A.M.: Conceptual model of iCAL4LA: proposing the components using comparative analysis. In: AIP Conference Proceeding, vol. 1761 (2016)
45. Ulhq, H., Odlqh, D.Q.G.: What is user engagement? A conceptual framework for defining user engagement with technology. J. Am. Soc. Inf. Sci. Technol. **59**(6), 1–37 (2008)
46. Tullis, T., Albert, B.: Measuring the User Experience. Morgan Kaufmann, Burlington (2010)
47. Spence, D., Usher, E.: Engagement with mathematics courseware in traditional and online remedial learning environments: relationship to self-efficacy and achievement. J. Educ. Comput. Res. **37**(3), 267–288 (2007)

MyRedList: Virtual Application
for Threatened Plant Species

Norul Maslissa Ahmad[1,2(✉)], Nazlena Mohamad Ali[1],
and Hanif Baharin[1]

[1] Institute of Visual Informatics, Universiti Kebangsaan Malaysia,
Bangi, Malaysia
{nazlena.ali,hbaharin}@ukm.edu.my
[2] Forest Research Institute Malaysia, Kepong, Malaysia
lissa@frim.gov.my

Abstract. In this paper, we consider the use of a virtual forest environment to increase the awareness of conservation of the endangered plants by developing a web application. Tropical rainforest in Malaysia consists of unique ecosystems, however, the population of Dipterocarpaceae, the most numerous family of flora in the tropical forest in Peninsular Malaysia, is decreasing. Some of the species in this family are listed as endangered and threatened plant in Malaysia Plant Red List. We argue that increasing stakeholder awareness of conservation activities of these endangered species through experiencing an immersive virtual forest environment in the efforts to conserve the species.

Keywords: Virtual environment · Web application · Forest conservation · Threatened plant

1 Introduction

In this study, we propose the design of a virtual application for species of threatened plants in Peninsular Malaysia with the aim to increase the awareness on conservation of threatened plant species. Malaysia is among one of the countries with the highest biodiversity in the world. The tropical rainforest in Malaysia consists of approximately 8,500 species of vascular plants in Peninsular Malaysia and Sabah and 15,000 in Sarawak [1].

The main types of forest vegetation in Peninsular Malaysia consist of dipterocarp forest below ground, hill dipterocarp forest, dipterocarp forest hill tops, oak-laurel forest, montane ericaceous forest, peat swamp forests and mangroves. There are also smaller areas of swamp forest, freshwater swamp forest, forest in limestone and quartz ridge [2]. Dipterocarp family is the largest group in the Tropical Rainforest in Peninsular Malaysia. It contains more than 80% growth of individuals and more than 40% tree canopy. This growth factor is due to the type of soil and the weather is perfect on this earth, Malaysia [3].

The rapid socioeconomic development gives an impact to forest biological diversity. From the 1970s, dipterocarp family is a source of tropical hardwood in international and national hardwood trade [4], thus, making it susceptible to become endangered. Various

© Springer International Publishing AG 2017
H. Badioze Zaman et al. (Eds.): IVIC 2017, LNCS 10645, pp. 445–454, 2017.
https://doi.org/10.1007/978-3-319-70010-6_41

reactions of the public to express concern about the current state of the forest that have shown the risk of extinction of forests in Peninsular Malaysia [5–7].

This paper is divided into several sections. Section 2 explains the background work on decreasing forest population, Sect. 3 describes the Materials and methods used in the development of the application.

2 Background Work

2.1 Decreasing Population of Forest in Peninsular Malaysia

There is a need to educate the public in general and the stakeholders in particular, to "urge" the parties responsible for conservation action in Malaysia. We argue that awareness in the conservation of endangered plants in Malaysia is very important for reducing the risk of extinction of these plants, especially the dipterocarp family. This is because, in Peninsular Malaysia, the dipterocarp family population has been reduced due to the development and harvesting activities. Forest areas were massively reduced due to the usage of forest land for agriculture and development since the 1960s and 1980s [4]. Census of forest areas over the years have been made by various agencies indicate the percentage of forest areas in Peninsular Malaysia has declined. Figure 1 shows the statistical data for forest area collections made from years before 1972 to 2002 [4]. No census was made after 2002 and the reduction of forest areas is very worrying.

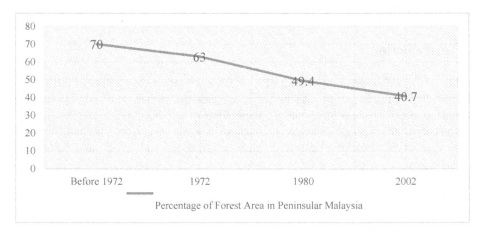

Fig. 1. Shows the reduction of forest areas in Peninsular Malaysia. Source: Chua et al. [4]

According to Mohd [7], threatened plant populations in forests of Peninsular Malaysia is 36.8% as can be seen in Fig. 2.

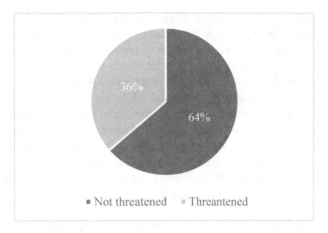

Fig. 2. Categories of plant species in the forests of Peninsular Malaysia. Source: Mohd [7]

2.2 Application of Red List

The urgency in dealing with forest conservation should be a priority. This issue is a global problem not only in Malaysia but also worldwide. In order to ensure the conservation of flora and fauna on the ongoing basis, the International Union for Conservation of Nature (IUCN) has developed the Red List of threatened species of flora and fauna worldwide. Figure 3 shows the level of extinction risk ladder where the bottom represents less risk level and the upper level represents the most at risk.

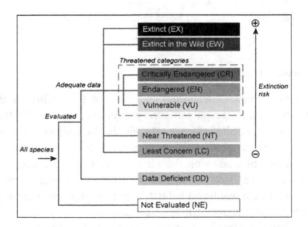

Fig. 3. Category endangered plant developed by IUCN. Source: IUCN

The Read List is classified into 9 categories according to the priority of the risk of extinction - Lease Concern (LC), Near Threatened (NT), Vulnerable (VU), Endangered (EN), Critically Endangered (CR) and a further category Extinct in the Wild (EW), and Extinct (EX) [4].

In 1998, The Malaysian Malaysia Policy on Biological Diversity has been formulated to establish the agenda and direction of the government in implementing strategies and action plans in the conservation of forests and preserve endangered plant species [4]. With this, in 2010, the Forest Research Institute Malaysia (FRIM) has taken the initiative to develop the Malaysia Plant Red List and it is a complete list of the risk of extinction of plants in Peninsular Malaysia and focus Dipterocarpaceae family as it is the largest forest types in Peninsular Malaysia. Malaysia Plant Red List is developed to assist in the monitoring of conservation of critically threatened plant species of the families Dipterocarpaceae. Table 1 is the summary for quick reference on species in Dipterocarpaceae family that has been categories from IUCN category. A total of 164 taxa comprising 155 species of Peninsular Malaysian Dipterocarpaceae were assessed in the Malaysia Plant Red List.

Table 1. The number of taxa in Peninsular Malaysia, grouped according to genus, under respective IUCN categories. Source by Malaysia Plant Red List.

Genus	EX	CR	EN	VU	NT	LC	DD	Total
Anisoptera	0	0	1	4	0	1	0	6
Cotylelobium	0	0	1	0	1	0	0	2
Dipterocarpus	0	3	7	10	7	4	1	32
Dryobalanops	0	0	1	0	1	1	0	3
Hopea	0	4	6	11	9	3	0	33
Neobalanocarpus	0	0	0	0	1	0	0	1
Parashorea	0	1	0	0	1	1	0	3
Shorea	1	5	12	12	19	12	1	62
*Vatica**	0	2	7	5	7	1	0	22
Total	1	15	35	42	46	23	2	164

*Note: Vatica sp. was not evaluated.

2.3   Virtual Forest Environment

With the rapid development of technology, no doubt the ability of the Internet in disseminating information to the public is very effective. As we all know, the use of web applications can spread the information quickly. In addition, use of virtual technology to learn about endangered species can help in the management of forests [8].

There are a number of studies on the virtual forest in the context of forest management already been done. This virtual reality display computer graphics that can be seen, heard and touch like a real forest habitat is an important breakthrough in usability collaboration with forest management [8]. A simulation study of growth and development as Sibyl - Fabrika Slovakia that uses augmented reality technology virtual of forest habitat, is one of the important components in the forecast in the management of forest development in Slovakia [9] as well as for other countries [10, 11].

Various researches also were conducted to study the effect of users in a virtual environment application system. The factors influencing the sharing of information by users in virtual learning [12] and the factors that affect users in virtual learning traditional architectural heritage house [13] are among of the studies.

However, in Malaysia, there are no studies combining virtual technology and forest. The applications that have previously developed with the display of static images only. In this study, we will develop a virtual application, MyRedList with the addition of interactive technologies such as virtual reality, 360° panoramic images and immersive technology of forest areas (in particular the actual habitat for threatened plant species in Malaysia). This virtual environment will show the graphic multimedia as if the user is in the natural habitat of the forest area concerned. The factors influencing the user that has been identified in these studies through the use of virtual environments will be taken into account in building the MyRedList in increasing the awareness of forest conservation. In the future, an experiment will be conducted to measure the ability of this virtual application to increase the awareness of conservation of threatened plant species in Malaysia.

3   Material and Method

3.1   Initial Analysis

The public and government can play a role in protecting the forest [14]. Knowledge of the importance of forests needs to be disseminated to the public so that they are aware of the danger of the extinction risk of forest plants. The involvement of all stakeholders in the conservation of forests is important [15].

We argue that the existence of awareness of the public can be gauged via the Google Trends website which shows the trend of keywords search on Google search engine. Nghiem et al. mentioned that Google Trends data are a powerful tool to monitor and evaluate the public interest in conservation [16]. It can be used as a benchmark to show the level of public interest in the endangered plant. If the number of search keywords in the data on the Google Trends is high, by common sense, then there is awareness of the issue of the keywords.

Figure 4a and b show search statistics for the keyword "Tumbuhan Terancam" (Endangered Plants in Malay) and "Endangered Plants" used in Google search worldwide for the past five years. This view was taken on April 27, 2017. From Fig. 4, residents of the United States and in Indonesia used these keywords but there are no statistics for Malaysia because the data is too low to display.

As in Fig. 5a and b are statistical search the same keywords but focused on Malaysia. The displays show incomplete data can generate a map display for the keyword "Endangered Plant" and only one state of Kelantan has shown there is a search for the keyword "Tumbuhan Terancam".

3.2   Application Development

We argue that a web-based virtual application tool may be used to increase public awareness on critical conservation of endangered plant. Thus we proposed an application called 'MyRedList'. Figure 6 shows a diagram of application architecture for the MyRedList application.

(a)

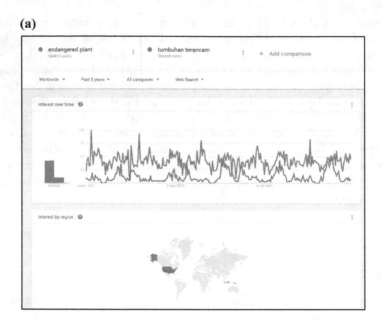

(b)

Fig. 4. (a) Display Google Trends search for the whole world. (b) Display Google Trends search for the whole world (2nd page).

Thus, the virtual environment technology will be used in this study by using the equipment as shown in Fig. 7.

(a)

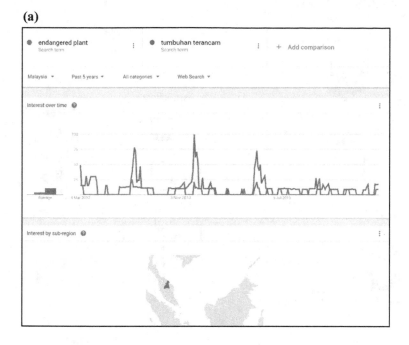

(b)

Fig. 5. (a) Display Google Trends search for Malaysia. (b) Display Google Trends search for Malaysia (2nd page).

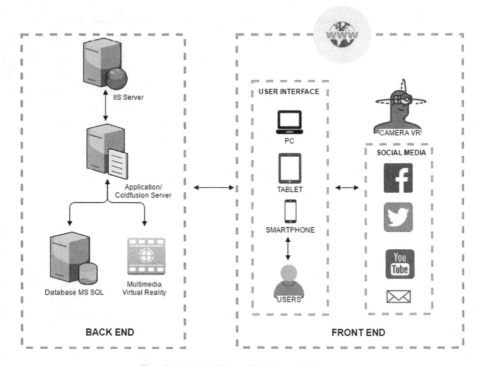

Fig. 6. MyRedlist application architecture

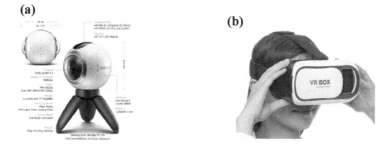

Fig. 7. (a) Camera 360. Source: Samsung.com. (b) Virtual reality glasses. Source: VR Box

Development of the proposed application will be based on phases as follows:

Phase One: Needs Analysis

This phase is drawing up research activities in a systematic manner. List of activities in detail, including the period for each activity. In this phase also, a literature review will be conducted, including reviewing the systems that have been developed previously in the domain of the same scope. There is also a focus of study that influence of different users in the system and then the reviews of measurement of awareness will also be conducted in adapting the questionnaire to be adopted in the next study.

This phase will also conduct information gathering activities. Information available in Malaysia Plant Red List will be used in the development of this application. Information available in book form will be converted to digital format. This valuable knowledge will be organized in a database that will be developed in the next phase. In this phase also, sites of ex-situ or in-situ will be identified through recommendations from experts in FRIM to produce virtual videos in the next phase.

Phase Two: Application Development
This study proposed to use a development method called Faster Application Development (RAD) framework through iterations. The method is selected because it enables applications to be developed in a short time.

This phase begins with the development of the database scheme for the information obtained from the previous phase. The schema will be developed using the Microsoft SQL Server Management Studio. After that, the information obtained in the previous phases will be included in the database. Then, the system design will be developed and further development of the system will use Adobe Coldfusion programming and Bootstrap. Development is based on a literature review has been made of the influence of advance towards using virtual applications. The application will be linked to a database by using Microsoft IIS Server.

Next, for the development of multimedia components, some components of which are identified are a virtual environment, 360-degree panoramic images and immersive technology with consumer gadgets. The equipment which will be used are Smartphone Samsung Edge S7, Samsung Camera Gear 360 and VR-Box Virtual Reality Glasses. The software that will be used in developing the multimedia components are Adobe Photoshop, Apps Samsung Gear 360 and Gear 360 Action Direction. The application will then be evaluated to see if it can increase on the awareness about endangered plant species among the sample respondents.

4   Conclusion

This research is expected to generate increased awareness in the conservation of endangered plant species in Malaysia. With the socioeconomic growth in Malaysia, especially in Peninsular Malaysia, there are reductions in forest area over the years and led to the extinction risk of species of dipterocarp family, the largest component in Peninsular Malaysia. To assist in the improvement of public awareness and national policy makers on the issue, this study proposes to develop an application, Virtual Application for Threatened Plant Species (MyRedlist). MyRedlist will be implemented with the latest multimedia components such as virtual environment, technology and immersive 360-degree panoramic photos that will make the starting point of extinction risk of forest users feel the need to be addressed immediately and awareness in conserving this endangered species of plants can be improved. An assessment of the level of awareness will also be carried out in the next study after initial MyRedlist has been developed.

References

1. Saw, L.G., Chung, R.C.K.: Towards the flora of Malaysia. In: Chua, LS.L., Kirton, L.G., Saw, L.G. (eds.) Proceedings of the Seminar and Workshop on the Status of Biological Diversity in Malaysia & Threat Assessment of Plant Species in Malaysia, pp. 203–219. Forest Research Institute of Malaysia, Kepong, Malaysia (2007)
2. Saw, L.G.: Flora of Peninsular Malaysia. In: Kiew, R., Chung, R.C.K., Saw, L.G., Soepadmo, E., Boyce, P.C. (eds.) Floral of Peninsular Malaysia, Vegetation of Peninsular Malaysia, pp. 21–45. Forest Research Institute of Malaysia, Kepong, Malaysia (2010)
3. Saw, L.G., Chua, L.S.L., Suhaida, M., Yong, W.S.Y., Hamidah, M.: Conservation of some rare and endangered plants from Peninsular Malaysia. Kew. Bull. **65**(4), 681–689 (2010). doi:10.1007/s12225-011-9251-6
4. Chua, L.S.L., Suhaida, M., Hamida, M., Saw, L.G.: Malaysia plant red list: Peninsular Malaysian dipterocarp, 210 p. Forest Research Institute Malaysia (FRIM), Malaysian (2010)
5. Rosman, S.: Forest Reserve Endangered Bikam. Daily News (North) (2010)
6. Yip, Y.T.: Sniffing out the illegal trade. The Star Online (2014)
7. Mohd, N.A.I.: Plant species less and less. Utusan Malaysia (2016)
8. Fabrika, M.: Virtual forest stand as a component of sophisticated forestry educational systems. J. Forest Sci. **49**(9), 419–428 (2003)
9. Pretzcsh, H., Biber, P., Dursky, J.: The single-tree stand based simulator SILVA: construction, application and evaluation. For. Ecol. Manag. **162**, 3–21 (2002)
10. Chen, I.Y.L., Chen, N.S., Kinshuk: Examining the factors influencing participants' knowledge sharing behavior in virtual learning communities. Educ. Technol. Soc. **12**(1), 134–148 (2009)
11. Abe, M., Yoshimura, T., Koizumi, S., Hasegawa, N., Osaki, T., Yasukawa, N., Koba, K., et al.: Virtual forest: design and evaluation of a walk-through system for forest education. J. Forest Res. **10**(3), 189–197 (2005)
12. Nazrita, I., Nazlena, M.A., Noor, F.M.Y.: Factors facilitating cultural learning in virtual environments architectural heritage. J. Comput. Cult. Herit. **8**(2), 1–20 (2015)
13. Tomaszewski, B.: Situation awareness and virtual globes: applications for disaster management. Comput. Geosci. **37**(1), 86–92 (2011)
14. 5th National Report to the Convention on Biological Diversity. Ministry of Natural Resource and Environment, Malaysia (2015)
15. Pawar, K.V., Rothkar, R.V.: Forest conservation & environmental awareness. Procedia Earth Planet. Sci. **11**, 212–215 (2015)
16. Nghiem, L.T.P., Papworth, S.K., Lim, F.K.S., Carrasco, L.R.: Analysis of the capacity of Google trends to measure interest in conservation topics and the role of online news. PLoS ONE **11**(3), e0152802 (2016). doi:10.1371/journal.pone.0152802

Reward Conditions Modify Children's Drawing Behaviour

Siti Rohkmah Mohd Shukri[1][✉] and Andrew Howes[2]

[1] Computer and Information Sciences Department,
Universiti Teknologi PETRONAS, 31750 Perak, Malaysia
sitirohkmah.mshukri@utp.edu.my
[2] School of Computer Science, University of Birmingham,
Birmingham B15 2TT, UK
a.howes@cs.bham.ac.uk

Abstract. Children like to draw, but how do they draw on a touch-screen device and to motivational context for action? Despite the fact that many children choose to draw on tablets there have been few studies about their drawing behaviour. To answer this question, we conducted an empirical study to examine how children aged between 5 to 11 years old adjust their drawing actions on touch surfaces according to extrinsic rewards. The present study suggests that drawing with reward conditions modify drawing behaviour. In essence, we are proposing that children are more motivated to draw better when the reward is harder to achieve than when it is easier. This shows that traces and marks left on screen could be quantified more accurately to understand children's behaviour better. The purpose of the study is to emphasize the benefit of rewarding effect as feedback to children's performance when using touch-based tool.

Keywords: Children's drawing · Reward · Motivation · Touchscreen

1 Introduction

Children these days make increasing use of mobile devices for entertainment and learning activities. With the current advancement of technologies, touch-based applications are now easily available and accessible by teachers, parent or children themselves whether at home or at school. These applications have becoming more interesting with gamification styles and reward-based system to engage children more. The reward-based system specifically has been used in many touch-based applications for feedback and assessment. While rewarding system can be motivating for children, there is still less work on the effect of rewarding condition towards children behaviour. There are even some concerns on the negative impact of rewarding condition that can bring to children especially on their intrinsic motivation. Although there could be differential effects on children motivational behaviour, the work have been inconclusive so far [11]. As touch-screen devices are commonly use nowadays, there is a need among re-searchers and developers to study the benefit of rewarding effect as feedback to children's performance when using such application.

© Springer International Publishing AG 2017
H. Badioze Zaman et al. (Eds.): IVIC 2017, LNCS 10645, pp. 455–465, 2017.
https://doi.org/10.1007/978-3-319-70010-6_42

One of the natural task that children seems to enjoy doing is drawing. There is an established literature on children's drawing that studies children psychological and developmental growth to understand children behaviour better. Since children nowadays have started to frequently use drawing touch tools for drawing activity apart from drawing using pencil and paper, there is a need to under-stand children's drawing from the technology perspective. One of the differences between the traditional way of drawing on paper and drawing on touch screen would be the use of finger tips to draw than holding a pen. Even with a drawing tool, children can receive feedback from their work which otherwise has to be achieved socially if drawing on paper. Although drawing on a touch screen could yield similar result to drawing on paper, traces and marks left on screen could be quantified more accurately [12, 16, 19]. Current research suggests that children's drawings on a touch screen or a computer convey far quicker and richer information than had often been claimed in the past (e.g., [6, 13, 21]). Thus, there is still less work that study children's drawing actions on a touch screen and how feedback in drawing could affect their behaviour.

This paper addressed on how rewarding condition modifies children's drawing behaviour when drawing on a touch screen. The work look into children movement sequencing of drawing action with different reward functions. According to Bijleveld et al. [3], people tend to put more e ort when the reward is more valuable. The higher the reward, the more e ort is attained to gain the reward [5]. Therefore, the purpose of this work is to examine how children would re-act given two different reward conditions from their drawing actions. Do they perform better if the reward is harder to achieve than if it is easier? Specifically, our work finds how children alter their drawing actions in response to the re-ward functions introduced when drawing on a tablet. Following Mohd Shukri and Howes [14], the idea was to see how children adapt to the reward conditions when tracing trajectories through the dots on touch screen surfaces using the tip of their finger or a pen. The study consisted of drawing tasks that mimic the conventional way of joining the dots on paper but with reward feedback, a significant advantage when drawing on a tablet. At the end, we hope to conclude that different reward conditions do alter children's drawing behaviour.

2   Background

Children are more motivated to complete a task that is extrinsically rewarded [7]. One of the substantial effect when giving a reward to children is that they tend to spend more time on a task given. In a study that involves motor task with children aged 3 to 4, the task with more trials were completed in higher numbers due to the reward than the task without the reward [1]. 7 years old children were found to spend more time learning language and doing reading work when there was a reward than none [17]. In another study, children with low-performing were found to persist longer in learning fraction when there was a reward effect [15]. Thus, these show that a reward system can act as an external motivation for children to not only engage in a task for longer but also increase their behavioural performance better. But how can we know whether giving a reward can affect children intrinsic or extrinsic motivation?

Cerasoli et al. [4] work reviewed the relationship of intrinsic and extrinsic motivation towards human performance. According to them, a task that is intrinsically motivated is mostly enjoyable, purposeful, well-being and give happiness, which provide sufficient reason for one to persist whether with or without reward. This type of task often indirectly yield towards the quality of one's performance. An extrinsic motivated task is more likely to be repetitive and non-complex, which requires a reward feedback as a driving mechanism to complete the task. This type of task on the other hand, plays more directly in dominance towards the prediction of a person behavioural performance. While both do have an effect towards performance in context, the former is more related to quality while the latter related to quantity. Quality type of task generally requires higher complexity skills rather than the quantity type of task that tends to be lower in complexity. As motivation is partly an important element in children's drawing, it is not unreasonable to suppose that their perception of the quality of what they draw is influenced by their assessment of a drawing fitness. Rather, reward that informs drawing feedback could be used to compare, evaluate and simply describe children performance. This can give a variance in the quantity performance of children from different ages. Since our drawing task are built upon less complexity, straightforward and are highly repetitive, the reward system is therefore closely linked to the extrinsic motivation of children's behaviour.

In a technological learning environments, a reward can be a simple feedback that can support the achievement and appropriate behaviour of a correct response. According to Shadmehr et al. [18], imposing a reward can change the state of the body to make movement that feels more valuable. Kluger and DeNisi [8] proposed an overarching theory regarding how different effects of feedback can adjust a behaviour's person by comparing to a standard goal. The feedback can distinct the effects on motivation that yields to performance. People become more motivated and therefore tend to invest e ort when they are sensitive to the value of rewards [3]. Rewards are provided under the assumption that a person will modify its behaviour in order to achieve higher performance. The present study suggests that meaningful drawing with reward conditions modify drawing behaviour, in accordance to movement sequencing in the organization of the drawing action. In essence, we are proposing that children are more motivated to draw better when the reward is harder to achieve than when it is easier to achieve.

3 The Experiment

This study investigated the effect of different reward functions on drawing tasks for children. The first reward function, High reward, measured on how accurately the children hit the dots. The scoring for High reward is according to the accuracy of the contact points in drawing lines (see Fig. 1a). It is calculated based on the weighted function of least squared errors, where drawing lines need to accurately go through a series of dots to get a perfect score. The contact points distance of the drawing lines were calculated based on the minimal distance of the drawing lines to the numbered dots. If the distance of the drawing lines are far o from the contact points, the number of stars awarded will be low. The second reward function, Low reward, measured how accurately they generated the shape of the drawing. The scoring for Low reward on the other hand, is according to the shape maintenance of drawing figure (see Fig. 1b). Children's drawing lines were examined whether they retain the original shape of the drawing figure by measuring with sum-squared error. Under this Low reward condition, more stars could be gained for the right shape even if the distance of the drawing lines from the contact points were o by some amount.

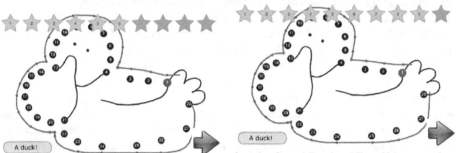

a: A *High* Reward Function on the Accuracy-of-the-Contact-Points where if the distance of the contact points are off, the rating star is low.

b: A *Low* Reward Function of Shape-Maintanence where if the distance of the contact points are off but the shape of the drawing lines retain the shape of the drawing figure, the rating star is high.

Fig. 1. Reward conditions in join-the-dots drawing task.

The purpose of the reward manipulation was to examine how children's drawing behaviour differs under two different reward functions with Low reward gives easy access to ten stars and High reward makes it more di cult to attain ten stars. Do children who draw with High reward function are more motivated to draw better than children who draw with Low reward function? We derived our hypothesis according to the following; children are motivated to draw more accurately given High reward than Low reward. The study proposes that when the reward of high number of stars are harder to achieve, children would be more motivated to draw better by drawing more accurately to get high number of stars. However, when the reward of higher number of stars are easy to achieve although children draw less accurately, they can become less motivated affecting their drawing performance. The study also investigated the difference performance when drawing with a finger and a pen. Do children who draw using a pen draw more accurately than those using their fingers? The second hypothesis is derived; children who draw using a pen can draw more accurately than those who draw using their finger.

3.1   Method and Stimulus

Apparatus. The experimental setup used was an iPad Air tablet device with 10.1-inch wide screen that was connected to an Apple MacBook-Pro 13-inch laptop through a USB cable. The drawing application was loaded by a Safari web browser on the tablet device via a stable internet connection. Join-the-dots drawing application was developed using HTML5 and JavaScript. Two drawing applications were built; both having similar tasks but two different reward functions, High and Low rewards. There were 20 common drawings comprised of 10 vehicles and 10 animal shapes displayed in random order. The number of dots in each drawing are ranged from a minimum of 15 dots to a maximum of 35 dots. Each dot were numbered based on their order. The size of the rst dot is slightly bigger than the rest of the dots and unlike other dots, it had a grey background to be conveniently located by the subjects. Upon completing all the tasks successfully, an overall reward of ten stars would be displayed on top of the page with scores obtained by a subject is shown in golden stars.

Procedure. In the drawing task, subject would need to draw the lines from one dot to the next dot based on their order. The drawing time was recorded starting when the finger/pen was tapped on the first dot until the final dot was touched. Once one drawing task completed, the screen would halt and the number of stars would be displayed together with a text describing the object drawn at the bottom-left of the page. The next page was a rest page which appeared after every drawing task for subject to take a break after each drawing task. Altogether there were 20 drawing tasks to complete in the experiment. At the end of the session, a page with detail scoring for every drawing task would be shown together with the overall score. The last page thanks subjects for their participation. (Refer Fig. 2). On average, the experiment lasted about 40 min to 1 h per subject.

a: Front page.
b: Instruction page.
c: Drawing task 1 (a spaceship).
d: User drawing strokes and score.
e: Rest page with current score.
f: Drawing task 2 (a fish).
g. User drawing strokes and score.
h: Score board.
i: End page.

Fig. 2. Drawing application join-the-dots.

Experimental Design. The experiment was between participants design with two independent variables: reward manipulation (High and Low) and medium input (Finger or Pen). There were 4 experimental groups; High Reward with Finger (A1B1), Low Reward with Finger (A1B2), High Reward with Pen (A2B1) and Low Reward with Pen(A2B2). It was a one data point per participant, a two-by-two analysis of whether subject's drawing action was affected by using Finger or Pen and whether it was affected with a Low or High rewarding score.

Pilot Study. Apilot study was conducted on 4 children participants of 2 boys and 2 girls, aged of 5, 6, 8 and 9 years old. The first three pilot child-users did very well in completing the drawing tasks. The fourth pilot child-user could not attempt the drawing task as she was not familiar with numbering order. To ensure child-user understand the numbering order, Join-the-dots activity on paper need to be introduced before the main experiment.

Subjects. Thirty four children participated (15 boys and 19 girls) with age rang-ing from 5 to 11 years old. One participant was discarded from the analysis due to not following the order of the task, thereof, thirty three children participants were involved with a mean age of 7.76 years (SD = 2.0 years) (Refer Fig. 3). The children were from a mix of Asian backgrounds and they all attend primary schools in Birmingham, UK. These children participants on an average used two hours of touch screen devices daily.

Children Age Distribution

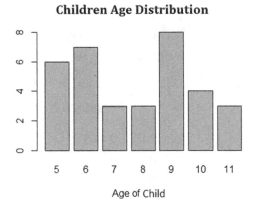

Age of Child

Fig. 3. Age distribution for children participants.

Instruction. All parents had given their informed consent to allow their children to participate in the study. Participants also gave their informed consent verbally and in writing prior to the session conducted during the experiment. They were briefly informed on how the task should be completed and were then asked whether they had any experience using touchscreen devices. Those without or having less experience were given a tablet to familiarize themselves using the touchscreen device for about ten minutes. Later, they had a warm-up session of join-the-dots task on paper using a pen or pencil. Once they completed the tasks on paper, they were assigned to one of four groups. The group assignment was based on the order of participants. The first subject was assigned to A1B1; second subject assigned to A1B2; third subject assigned to A2B1; fourth subject assigned to A2B2; fifth subject was again assigned to A1B1 and the pattern continued for the rest of the subjects. All were unaware of the hypotheses under test. When subjects completed the tasks, they were each given a form to ll in and provided information on their background and the amount of time spent drawing on paper and tablet daily. At the end of the session, they were each given a token of appreciation for their participation.

4   Results

A two-way between-group analysis of variance was conducted to examine the effect of reward functions and drawing medium towards the score of the drawing tasks. There were 33 participants (n = 33) data. There was a statistically significant main effect for the reward functions; $F (1,29) = 18.485$, $p < 0.0001$ with High reward having a mean score of 89.25 for finger, 86.31 for pen and Low reward having a mean score of 68.79 for finger, 77.15 for pen (see Fig. 4) with a large effect size; partial eta squared = 0.389. There was no main effect for drawing mediums; $F (1,29) = 0.619$, $p = 0.438$ and no interaction effect between the reward functions and drawing mediums, $F (1,29) = 2.687$, $p = 0.112$. The result shows that child users whether they were drawing using a finger or a pen, scored higher in High reward than in Low reward but there was no effect on the scoring due to the selection between the two medium inputs.

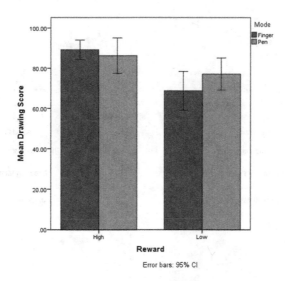

Fig. 4. Participant's average drawing score according to the reward function (High/Low) and mode of drawing (Finger/Pen).

The relationships on children's drawing behaviours such as drawing scores, drawing time, pen-lifts, speed and mistakes among children were also investigated using Pearson product-moment correlation coefficient. Preliminary analyses were performed to ensure no violation of the assumptions of normality, linearity and homoscedasticity. There was a strong positive significant correlation between the age of children and number of stars, $r = 0.67$, $p < 0.0001$ where older child users scored higher than younger child users (see Fig. 5a). There was a moderate significant negative correlation between age of children and number of penlifts, $r = -0.419$, $p = 0.019$ (see Fig. 5c) and a strong positive significant correlation between age of children and drawing speed, $r = 0.597$, $p < 0.0001$ (see Fig. 5b). Younger child users made more number of penlifts and drew slower than older child users when performing the drawing tasks. Younger child users would probably take more time to draw accurately than older child users due to their generally slower speed. Drawing time however did not show any correlation with age of children although older child users drew faster than younger child users. However, during the experiment, some of the child users were observed to pause drawing at the contact points without lifting their finger or pen before making the next drawing move. When child users pause between contact points, the drawing time was still recorded. Therefore, this contributed to making the overall drawing time for younger and older children about the same. The most significant mistakes that child users committed were trailing their non-drawing fingers while drawing and drawing the lines not according to the numbering order.

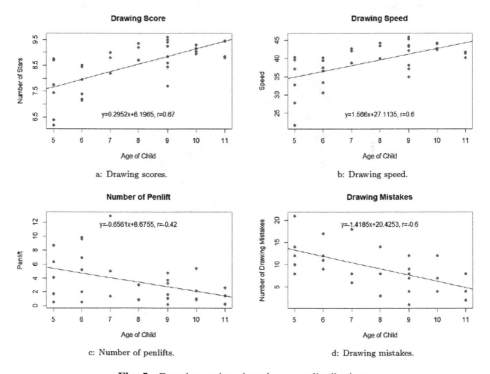

a: Drawing scores.   b: Drawing speed.

c: Number of penlifts.   d: Drawing mistakes.

Fig. 5. Drawing actions based on age distributions.

There was a strong negative significant correlation between age of children and number of drawing mistakes, $r = -0.603$, $p < 0.0001$ which indicated that younger child users make more mistakes when drawing on a tablet than older child users (see Fig. 5d).

5 Discussions

The aim of the work reported here is to understand the effects on children's drawing strategies to the reward functions introduced and how they would per-form when drawing on a tablet using two different medium inputs, a finger and a pen. The result suggested that child users were more motivated to draw better when the number of stars or reward were harder to obtain rather than when it is easier to do so. The selection on the medium of drawing input whether with a finger or a pen did not make any significant difference to the drawing star scores. According to Tu et al. [19], drawing with a pen mostly outperformed finger in smaller surface of detailed area. The fact that the drawing tasks in this study measured the lines of contact points that are basically the outline of a whole drawing figure, no differences occurred between the two medium inputs.

How could we be sure that children who did the High reward were more motivated to draw better than those who did the Low reward? Perhaps children in both conditions had understood that they need to hit the dots as accurate as they could and that the same scoring system should quantified the differences between the group. Additional analysis had been made where both groups were tested for each separate scoring function of High reward (accuracy of hitting the dot), Low reward (shape of the drawing) and a combination of both type of rewards where High and Low rewards are embedded together to test the performance of the drawing lines. All tests have shown that there were no significant differences in the result with both High's, $F(1,29) = 4.057$, $p = 0.053$; both Low's, $F(1,29) = 0.32$, $p = 0.576$ and both combination of High-Low are $F(1,29) = 1.999$, $p = 0.168$. However, the result for High reward function to both groups is showing close to significant where the High group scored higher in both medium of drawing than the Low group. This shows that children participants in High group were motivated to draw more accurately in hitting the dots than those in the Low group. Since children participants in the Low group were not punished according to how accurately they hit the dots, they were less likely to draw the lines closer to the dots. This t the purpose of the main objective of the experiment, where children were adapted to the reward functions introduced. The result for Low reward function tested toward both groups shows that children in overall tried to maintain the shape of the drawing lines. The black dots as reference of the drawing figure are closed to each other making it hard for children to deviate their drawing lines from the point of reference. When both High-Low functions were combined to test their performance, both average score were about the same yielding no significant differences showing a balance score between the first two additional tests. The main result earlier showing highly significant differences among the two groups with different reward functions introduced can be firmly concluded that children do adapt to the reward functions introduced. Specifically, children in High group were more motivated to draw more accurately than those in the Low group.

Children's drawing behaviours and attributes were also investigated apart from the main finding. Younger child users tend to make more penlifts when drawing and attempted more drawing mistakes than older child users. They made unintentional touches with trailing fingers and thumbs [2, 13] and drew line segments in out of order. Older child users generally scored better than younger child users. Although they draw faster than younger child users, they were observed to stop at the contact points without lifting their finger or pen when drawing before making the next drawing move. The precaution of stopping on the dots reflects more on the cognitive aspect of drawing rather than ne motor skill [9]. This would yield about the same drawing completion time overall with younger child users that made pen lift. The overall result regarding children's drawing behaviour is supported by Vatavu et al. [20] that reported children's touch screen performance in task completion time and accuracy improved with age; and that due to increased motor maturation and improved drawing proficiency, older children tend to draw faster than younger children [10, 12]. The result strengthened and supported the existing attributes regarding children's drawing behaviour from an empirical approach and an external reward function.

6 Conclusion and Future Work

Drawing itself is a rewarding task to children whether the reward system is present or absent. By imposing an external reward function in drawing, the task can help researchers gauge children's competency and performance in drawing more confidently. The main purpose of our work is to highlight that rewarding conditions can modify children's drawing behaviour relating to their motivation and behavioural performance. The result has shown that children alter their drawing actions in response to the reward conditions introduced. The experiment provided encouraging evidence that children do adjust their drawing actions to the reward functions. However, can they adapt optimally? What if besides gaining rewards of higher number of stars, there is also a penalty effect nearby? How do they adapt their drawing actions to perceive cost and risks of drawing errors? Would children be able to plan their drawing to gain higher rewards within some limitations? While these questions are interesting to answer, it could be a possibility for future work to study the challenges when children draw on a touch screen.

References

1. Alvarez, A.L., Booth, A.E.: Motivated by meaning: testing the effect of knowledge-infused rewards on preschoolers' persistence. Child Dev. **85**(2), 783–791 (2014)
2. Anthony, L., Brown, Q., Nias, J., Tate, B., Mohan, S.: Interaction and recognition challenges in interpreting children's touch and gesture input on mobile devices. In: Proceedings of the 2012 ACM International Conference on Interactive Tabletops and Surfaces, pp. 225–234. ACM (2012)

3. Bijleveld, E., Custers, R., Aarts, H.: Adaptive reward pursuit: how effort requirements affect unconscious reward responses and conscious reward decisions. J. Exp. Psychol. Gen. **141**(4), 728 (2012)
4. Cerasoli, C.P., Nicklin, J.M., Ford, M.T.: Intrinsic motivation and extrinsic incentives jointly predict performance: a 40-year meta-analysis. Psychol. Bull. **140**(4), 980 (2014)
5. Gollwitzer, P.M., Bargh, J.A.: The Psychology of Action: Linking Cognition and Motivation to Behavior. Guilford Press, New York (1996)
6. Helbig, H.B., Ernst, M.O.: Optimal integration of shape information from vision and touch. Exp. Brain Res. **179**(4), 595–606 (2007)
7. Kelley, H.H., et al.: Causal Schemata and the Attribution Process. General Learning Press, Morristown (1972)
8. Kluger, A.N., DeNisi, A.: The effects of feedback interventions on performance: a historical review, a meta-analysis, and a preliminary feedback intervention theory (1996)
9. Lange-Küttner, C., Reith, E.: The transformation of figurative thought: implications of Piaget and Inhelder's developmental theory for children's drawings. Harvester Wheatsheaf (1995)
10. Laszlo, J., Bairstow, P.: Kinaesthesis: its measurement, training and relationship to motor control. Q. J. Exp. Psychol. **35**(2), 411–421 (1983)
11. Lin, L., Atkinson, R.K., Christopherson, R.M., Joseph, S.S., Harrison, C.J.: Animated agents and learning: does the type of verbal feedback they provide matter? Comput. Educ. **67**, 239–249 (2013)
12. Lin, Q., Luo, J., Wu, Z., Shen, F., Sun, Z.: Characterization of NE motor development: dynamic analysis of childrens drawing movements. Hum. Mov. Sci. **40**, 163–175 (2015)
13. McKnight, L., Fitton, D.: Touch-screen technology for children: giving the right instructions and getting the right responses. In: Proceedings of the 9th International Conference on Interaction Design and Children, pp. 238–241. ACM (2010)
14. Mohd Shukri, S.R., Howes, A.: How do children adapt strategies when drawing on a tablet? In: Proceedings of the Extended Abstracts of the 32nd Annual ACM Conference on Human Factors in Computing Systems, pp. 1177–1182. ACM (2014)
15. O'Rourke, E., Haimovitz, K., Ballweber, C., Dweck, C., Popovic, Z.: Brain points: a growth mindset incentive structure boosts persistence in an educational game. In: Proceedings of the SIGCHI Conference on Human Factors in Computing Systems, pp. 3339–3348. ACM (2014)
16. Price, S., Jewitt, C., Crescenzi, L.: The role of ipads in pre-school children's mark making development. Comput. Educ. **87**, 131–141 (2015)
17. Ronimus, M., Kujala, J., Tolvanen, A., Lyytinen, H.: Children's engagement during digital game-based learning of reading: the effects of time, rewards, and challenge. Comput. Educ. **71**, 237–246 (2014)
18. Shadmehr, R., de Xivry, J.J.O., Xu-Wilson, M., Shih, T.Y.: Temporal discounting of reward and the cost of time in motor control. J. Neurosci. **30**(31), 10507–10516 (2010)
19. Tu, H., Ren, X., Zhai, S.: Differences and similarities between finger and pen stroke gestures on stationary and mobile devices. ACM Trans. Comput.-Hum. Interact. (TOCHI) **22**(5), 22 (2015)
20. Vatavu, R.D., Cramariuc, G., Schipor, D.M.: Touch interaction for children aged 3 to 6 years: experimental findings and relationship to motor skills. Int. J. Hum.-Comput. Stud. **74**, 54–76 (2015)
21. Zhai, S., Kristensson, P.O., Appert, C., Andersen, T.H., Cao, X.: Foundational issues in touch screen stroke gesture design-an integrative review. Found. Trends Hum.-Comput. Interact. **5**(2), 97–205 (2012)

Advances in Mobile Augmented Reality from User Experience Perspective: A Review of Studies

Shafaq Irshad[✉] and Dayang Rohaya Awang Rambli

Department of Computer and Information Sciences,
Universiti Teknologi PETRONAS, Bandar Seri Iskandar, Malaysia
shafaqirshad223@gmail.com

Abstract. Augmented Reality (AR) is maturing with the evolution in fields of computer and interactive graphics. Rapid advancements and growth of the mobile industry have allowed AR experiences to be delivered on mobile devices as well. When camera fitted mobile devices point towards a digital object to deliver AR experiences it creates design challenges due to Unique interaction style and Information presentation on Mobile Augmented Reality (MAR) applications. In order to overcome these design challenges, one needs to understand the User Experience (UX) of MAR. This paper reviews the advances in mobile augmented reality from UX perspective. This study aims to present a comprehensive and detailed review and will help in guiding the developers of MAR to focus on areas that need improvement.

Keywords: Augmented reality · Mobile augmented reality · User studies · User experience · Interaction · Human computer interaction

1 Introduction

1.1 Augmented Reality

Augmented Reality (AR) is a leading-edge technology that provides a digitally amplified view of the real world, presenting end users with useful and informative content in different situations. According to Azuma et al. [3] when a system combine existing and virtual environments, provide interaction in the real time and allow end user to observe the real world in 3D, the system is termed as AR system. Although Azuma's definition of AR is a substantial standard AR is also termed as "a system that combines real and computer generated information in a real environment, interactively and in real time, and align virtual objects with physical objects [16]".

1.2 Mobile Augmented Reality

Fast-paced development in mobile industry has bought AR experiences to mobile devices. Researches show how mobile devices can be utilized in computer-vision based Augmented Reality tracking and registration [51, 60], analogue video transmission [8], context supported interaction, browser oriented interaction [38] and other technologies.

H. Badioze Zaman et al. (Eds.): IVIC 2017, LNCS 10645, pp. 466–477, 2017.
https://doi.org/10.1007/978-3-319-70010-6_43

MAR systems allow user to communicate, connect and interact through computer supported information from databases or remote experts, without getting distracted from the real task. Mobile Augmented Reality (MAR) is a leading technology that provides a digitally improved and enhanced 3D view of the physical world through a mobile device, connecting users with useful virtual content that cannot be detected with human senses [4]. AR systems demonstrate virtual information that can help the users perform di cult projects such as giving directions to workers through electrical wires in airplanes by showing digital information through headsets [6], assist in educational purposes or provide entertainment (such as playing AR games [56]).

The current generation of smart phones with high image processing ability, high definition display screens and cameras, sensor technologies such as GPS and orientation, wireless communications, networking, computational abilities and dedicated 3D graphic chips allow mobile devices to execute AR experiences [16]. Combination of such technologies integrated in one device make smart phones capable of doing much more than expected and thus, it is a suitable platform for building AR applications and services [15, 54].

MAR is providing new commercial enterprise and business activities around areas that can draw on digital information from navigation of places or objects, exploration, adventure, gaming, retail and advertising [6]. It is widely used for advertising and marketing by companies around the globe [7, 50]. The adoption of MAR services is expected to increase at a Compound Annual Growth Rate (CAGR) of 135.35% over the period of 2015–2019 [57]. However, when camera-fitted mobile device points towards a digital object to access information, it creates design challenges for the end users [23]. In order to overcome these design challenges and deliver positive MAR experiences to the target audience, one needs to understand the overall user experience of MAR [24].

1.3 User Experience

Irrespective of its conceptual obscureness, the term User Experience has gained a huge acceptance as a leading concept in Human Computer Interaction (HCI) domain [37]. Usability and User centered design (UCD) are modified with the concept of UX [30]. In the past few years, Computer Human Interaction (CHI) community has helped to systematize and conceptualize the diversified field of UX with the help of special interest groups, panels and workshops [31].

UX involves an individual's attitude, behavior and emotions towards a specific artifact, product or service. The International Organization for Standardization (ISO) defines UX as "A person's perceptions and responses resulting from the use and/or anticipated use of a product, system or service" [26].

From the historical background, UX was first defined in 1996. Lauralee Alben states that UX is an all-inclusive terminology that describes how an interactive product look, feels, serve and contributes to the context and quality of one's life [1]. In addition to the traditional usability aspects, UX involves value-sensitive design, social and cultural interaction, and emotional impact encompassing interaction experiences such as joy of using a product, aesthetics, excitement and pleasure [36]. Elements of instrumental, emotional, sensory, social and aesthetic experiences have also been identified and studied [5, 10] in the past in order to understand UX.

In 2015, Mirnig and colleagues proposed recommendations for improving existing version of ISO UX definition using methods from formal logic. Mirnigs definition recommends that "UX is a four-digit predicate UX 4 in which [User] has a UX of [contents of UX] via [system] at [time]". He further suggests that user and system associated factors should be specified including the object of UX [41]. Overall, UX is considered as context-dependent and universal concept.

Furthermore, UX is basically subjective, as it occurs only in users mind and change as users experience of a particular product change with time. UX is widely characterized as an umbrella term for designing, evaluating and studying the experiences that users feel while using any product, system or service in a particular context [52].

Currently, there is an increasing interest in understanding the knowledge and characteristics of UX in fields such as Mobile Augmented Reality [46]. One limitation in the path of revolutionizing MAR is the lack of research understanding of the User Experience (UX) resulting from the unique interaction style and the mixing of real and virtual environments that MAR embodies [19, 21]. The re-search study presents an overview of the advances in MAR from UX perspective. In this paper a detailed review on UX of MAR applications is presented. The aim of this review is to present an overview of the current knowledge about UX in context of MAR. The research findings aim to provide resources that can be used by MAR research community to understand the knowledge gap between MAR and UX.

2   Methodology

To review the research publications, our methodology was categorized by iterative assortment, filtering and classification method. For the first step, preliminary literature survey was selected from pertinent sources. For the second step, filtering on the selected literature was performed by using specified keywords. False positive results were removed from the search. For the next step MAR articles containing UX studies were selected. Finally, the results were categorized based on four major UX fields of study in MAR.

Prominent databases and digital libraries were searched from World Wide Web. Over 3500 publications were identified from year 2005 to 2016. There were nearly no publications regarding MAR in context of UX before year 2005. A few publications that were identified before year 2005 were not related to UX so they were eliminated. For the detailed list of database libraries refer to 1 below. Databases are plotted along the x-axis and No. of publications along y-axis (Fig. 1).

2.1   Classification of MAR Publications Based on UX Studies

Prominent research contribution has been made in user studies regarding MAR and there is a growing interest in understanding this technology further. To gain an overview of the present knowledge about UX and MAR collectively, we classified the selected MAR publications into four major fields namely user interface, UCD studies, UX studies and UX frameworks for MAR. These MAR publications have been presented in the form of Table 1.

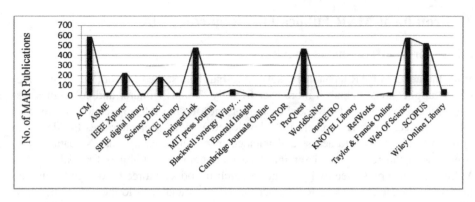

Fig. 1. MAR publication of well-known digital libraries from year 2005–2016

Table 1. Prominent MAR contributions from UX perspective

Context	Author	Research topic
User interface of AR	Hollerer et al. [18]	Interface of indoor and outdoor AR
	Hollerer et al. [17]	UI management techniques for collaborative MAR
	Joslin [28]	Augmented reality based user interface for mobile applications and services
UCD studies of AR	Gabbard and Hix [13]	Design guidelines for general AR systems
	Dunser et al. [12]	Aspects of AR design
	Siltanen et al. [55]	UCD of AR interior design service
UX studies of AR	Olsson et al. [44]	User expectations of MAR
	Olsson et al. [46]	User survey on MAR applications
	Olsson and Salo [47]	User expectations of MAR
	Arol [2]	MAR supporting marketing
	Kamilakis et al. [29]	Mobile UX in AR vs Maps Interfaces: A Case Study in Public Transportation
	Olsson et al. [45]	UX evaluations on different MAR application scenarios
	Olsson and Salo [48]	Types of MAR experiences
	Olsson et al. [46]	Influence of MAR elements on UX
	Dhir and Al-kahtani [11]	Case study on UX evaluation
UX frameworks for MAR	Jaasko and Mattelmaki [27]	Framework for measuring MAR features
	Hassenzahl [14]	Model of UX for marketing products
	Perritaz et al. [49]	Interaction framework for enhancing UX
	Olsson [43]	Layers of user expectations of future technologies

3   Prominent MAR Publications Regarding UX

3.1   User Interface Studies on AR

With the advent of AR technology, several researchers started to work on the interface of AR applications making it more user friendly. Tobias Hollerer and colleagues was one of the researchers who worked on indoor and outdoor AR applications to improve their interface. Some researchers [18] developed various user interfaces to allow outdoor and indoor users to access and manage information easily, that is spatially registered with the real world. User interface management techniques for collaborative MAR were also presented by [17]. The research introduced three UI design techniques that were intended to make AR interfaces as obvious and clear to the user as possible. His research also improved information filtering, UI component design, and view management.

Research on AR based UI for mobile applications and services is done by [28]. Methods for improving the UI of mobile devices by implementing human-centered design have been introduced. Researcher suggests combining augmented reality techniques with image recognition so that users can access the visualized interface. Combination of virtual buttons and hand gestures has been implemented in order to achieve this. The research contributes by evaluating AR interfaces and this technique useful in improving the UIs of mobile devices.

3.2   User Centered Design Studies on AR

UCD of AR interior design services was examined by [55]. Research presents benefits and challenges of applying user-centered approach with three target user groups i.e. consumers, pro-users and professionals. Desired features of AR interior design service with their technical and practical feasibility are also discussed. User expectations for AR interior design services were studied with a scenario-based survey, co-design sessions and focused interviews. Results of this study indicated that there is a demand for easy-to-use AR design tools for consumers and professional users however, both target users and professional interior designers have different requirement in terms of design tools and need to be considered in the future.

Various researchers worked on the user related aspects of AR technology. In 2001, Gabbard and Hix surveyed the design guidelines for general AR systems focusing on human factors to increase the users' engagement. He proposed general methodologies and considerations based on user centered design [13]. Similarly, [12] presented eight aspects of AR design by combining the user-centered design principles with the context and particularities of AR system. He further argued that one reason for the lack of UX research on AR systems could be lack of knowledge on how to conduct the evaluations and what kind of methods and metrics to use. Similarly, Panos [35] presents interaction design principles for MAR applications.

3.3 User Experience Studies on AR

Olsson and colleagues tried to understand the potential of MAR technology and identified diverse user expectations to be the actual factor that affect UX in AR [44]. Their findings highlighted an extensive set of user-oriented issues to be considered in developing the MAR applications. Online User Survey on Current Mobile Augmented Reality Applications was also conducted by [47]. Olsson, in his online user survey, also evaluated the acceptance of very different MAR scenarios.

Furthermore, in his work, [48] identified various types of MAR experiences and performed a qualitative analysis of 84 users to observe their satisfying and unsatisfying experiences. First generation location-based AR browsers and image recognition AR applications were used in the study. The results uncovered a number of experiences such as awareness of surroundings, empowerment, positive surprise, amazement and fascination from the novelty value, as well as a sense of immersion and social connectivity. The result analysis indicated MAR applications have not reached their potential to evoke a positive UX. This study helped in understanding the experimental design needs of mobile augmented reality and UX issues that needs to be addressed in order to improve MAR technology.

Olsson [46] also conducted a preliminary user study in order to understand the end user expectations for MAR applications. The study presents insight on how the different elements of future MAR services influence UX. The expected UX characteristics and crucial user requirements related to MAR were also discovered. The author further highlighted broad set of diverse experience characteristics that MAR services are expected to produce [19].

Another important contribution in the field of MAR is the case study on UX evaluation performed by Dhir and Al-kahtani [11] performed prominent case study on MAR. He performed UX evaluation on several MAR prototypes by using 3 different methods. He identified users' expectations for MAR and presented methodological insight evaluation methods for UX. The results from his study revealed that users value concreteness, reliability, personalization, novelty, intuitiveness and the usefulness of given information. Improving these factors can help develop more satisfactory MAR services.

Health and Biomedical Informatics Research Unit also conducted UX evaluations on MAR medical applications. This design based research was envisioned to improve biomedical research [33]. Other researchers worked on MAR investigative tools for context immersion utility [34], MAR manuals [42], UX evaluation of real-time MAR feedback [40] and UX evaluation for MAR architectural planning.

Xin and Kwang proposed a very proficient, robust and distinct binary descriptor called Local Difference Binary (LDB) to enhance the user experience of MAR applications [59]. Keating et al. [32] outlines the limitations of existing user centered design (UCD) methodologies for UX studies on MAR. An innovative cloud-based mobile panorama view was designed by Li and Zhu [39]. This cloud based system improved the effectiveness of MAR applications. An OSGi (Open Service Gateway initiative) based prototype called cloudlet was implemented by Android platform and evaluated using MAR use case [58] to optimize the end user experience.

Findings and guidelines on an ongoing design project were presented by re-searchers in context of MAR. The research highlighted benefits and drawbacks of low fidelity, mixed fidelity and high fidelity prototypes for MAR by framing them into a set of analytic categories extracted from the existing literature on prototyping and design [9]. The research also drafts several reasons of creating a persuasive MAR experience with competent formative design [53].

3.4   UX Frameworks on AR

The above literature focuses more on the UX studies related to the design and evaluation of MAR applications. In order to gain more insight on the concept, it is important to discuss the existing UX frameworks for AR applications.

In order to support UCD concepts, Jaasko and Mattelmaki [27] proposed a framework of user experience qualities. It highlighted the MAR product features that can be measured. In addition, researchers' paid attention to the interaction, the environment (context) and users' personality (e.g. life-style, attitudes and values) as factors affecting the comprehensiveness of UX. The framework was based on the point of view of concept design.

Hassenzahl [14] presents a user experience model that points out general product features such as content, presentation, functionality and interaction that ascribe certain apparent product attributes. These product features are selected and combined by the product designer to convey intended product characteristics. The product characteristics summarize the products attributes i.e. a product can be useful, novel, interesting, attractive, efficient and so on. When an individual use a product they first perceive the product features and based on their experience construct personal opinion about the product characteristics. Experience with technological product or service is always unique and exclusive to every user. Therefore, the consequences or outcomes of these attributes vary from user to user. His model of UX is widely accepted in HCI community.

Perritaz et al. [49] and his fellows worked on identifying the important variables that impact UX and proposed a model to link the effect of these variables with the Quality of Experience metrics. The author studied end UX of AR applications in real time and presented a general framework for maximizing UX by improving the MAR interaction in real time. Other researchers [43] proposed an initial UX framework for understanding user expectations towards the MAR technology. The framework provided understanding of user expectations of MAR for user evaluations.

4   Discussion and Future Work

This study aims to explore MAR from UX perspective. From the literature discussed in the proceeding sections it is evident that the dynamic and subjective nature of UX, its different characteristics (such as emotional, aesthetics, pragmatic, hedonic), context of use and time are important facets to be considered in UX research. Because it is a relatively new concept, it is important to conduct empirical research in order to further re ne the methods and tools used in UX research.

The potential use of MAR in various application domains is unlimited. Using MAR allow end users to have more interactive experiences. MAR stimulate unique experiences when end users interact with 3D content through their mobile devices and interact digitally with the presented content. As MAR is maturing as a technology, various services and methods (e.g. user research) utilizing MAR, are still evolving. Despite the rapid growth in MAR, it is evident that there is a need of UX research frameworks that address the design and evaluation aspects of MAR in particular application domains.

From the literature it is evident that there is lack of user research on MAR regarding the user experience, unique interaction, ways of browsing, creating and sharing AR information and its context of use. Despite the unlimited potential of MAR, challenges are faced while designing a rich and emotionally satisfied UX for MAR services. The challenges arise due to the novel interaction with the augmented information AR offers through mobile devices. MAR seems to lack proper user centered design and evaluation methodologies [25]. From the literature review, a noticeable lack of UX research frameworks that address the design and evaluation aspects of MAR applications. In order to improve MAR experiences for end users the technology needs to be understood in its specific domain. After going through the literature we can argue that it is important to design domain specific UX frameworks [20, 22] that address the issues in MAR and end user experiences invoked when using MAR applications.

5 Conclusion

Although AR is well developed technology but researchers have highlighted the need of studies on how user perceives this technology especially in specific domains. Despite the unlimited potential of MAR, challenges are faced while de-signing a rich and emotionally satisfied UX for MAR services. The challenges arise due to the novel interaction with the augmented information AR offers through mobile devices. MAR seems to lack proper user centered design and evaluation methodologies. From the literature review, a noticeable lack of UX research frameworks that address the design and evaluation aspects of MAR applications is observed. The research gap highlighted in this study can be used by future researchers to bridge knowledge gap between MAR and UX.

References

1. Alben, L.: Defining the criteria for effective interaction design. Interactions 3(3), 11–15 (1996)
2. Arol, K.P.: Mobile augmented reality supporting marketing, using mobile augmented reality based marketing applications to promote products or services to end customers. Ph.D. thesis, Lahti University of Applied Sciences (2014)
3. Azuma, R.T., et al.: A survey of augmented reality. Presence 6(4), 355–385 (1997)
4. Barfield, W.: Fundamentals of Wearable Computers and Augmented Reality. CRC Press, Boca Raton (2015)

5. Buccini, M., Padovani, S.: Typology of the experiences. In: Proceedings of the 2007 Conference on Designing Pleasurable Products and Interfaces, DPPI 2007, pp. 495–504. ACM, New York (2007)

6. Carmigniani, J., Furht, B.: Augmented reality: an overview. In: Furht, B. (ed.) Handbook of Augmented Reality, pp. 3–46. Springer, New York (2011). doi:10.1007/978-1-4614-0064-6_1

7. Craig Foster, C.W.: Augmented Reality for Mobile Devices. Technical report, August 2015

8. Dempski, K.L.: Arbitrary object tracking augmented reality applications, 23 May 2006. US Patent 7,050,078

9. De Sá, M., Churchill, E.: Mobile augmented reality: exploring design and prototyping techniques. In: Proceedings of the 14th International Conference on Human-Computer Interaction with Mobile Devices and Services, MobileHCI 2012, pp. 221–230. ACM, New York (2012)

10. Desmet, P.M.A., Hekkert, P.: Framework of product experience. Int. J. Des. 1(1), 57–66 (2007)

11. Dhir, A., Al-kahtani, M.: A case study on user experience (UX) evaluation of mobile augmented reality prototypes. J. UCS 19(8), 1175–1196 (2013)

12. Dunser, A., Grasset, R., Seichter, H., Billinghurst, M.: Applying HCI principles to AR systems design (2007)

13. Gabbard, J., Hix, D.: Researching usability design and evaluation guidelines for augmented reality (AR) systems. Laboratory for Scientific Visual Analysis, Virginia Tech, USA (2001)

14. Hassenzahl, M.: The thing and I: understanding the relationship between user and product. In: Blythe, M., Overbeeke, K., Monk, A., Wright, P. (eds.) Funology, Human-Computer Interaction Series, vol. 3, pp. 31–42. Springer, Dordrecht (2005). doi:10.1007/1-4020-2967-5_4

15. Henrysson, A.: Bringing augmented reality to mobile phones (2007)

16. Hollerer, T., Feiner, S.: Mobile augmented reality. In: Telegeoinformatics: Location-Based Computing and Services. Taylor and Francis Books Ltd., London, UK 21 (2004)

17. Hollerer, T., Feiner, S., Hallaway, D., Bell, B., Lanzagorta, M., Brown, D., Julier, S., Baillot, Y., Rosenblum, L.: User interface management techniques for collaborative mobile augmented reality. Comput. Graph. 25(5), 799–810 (2001)

18. Hollerer, T., Feiner, S., Terauchi, T., Rashid, G., Hallaway, D.: Exploring mars: developing indoor and outdoor user interfaces to a mobile augmented reality system. Comput. Graph. 23 (6), 779–785 (1999)

19. Irshad, S., Awang, D.R.B.: User perception on mobile augmented reality as a marketing tool. In: 2016 3rd International Conference on Computer and Information Sciences (ICCOINS), pp. 109–113, August 2016

20. Irshad, S., Rambli, D.R.A.: Preliminary user experience framework for designing mobile augmented reality technologies. In: 2015 4th International Conference on Interactive Digital Media (ICIDM), pp. 1–4, December 2015

21. Irshad, S., Rambli, D.R.B.A.: User experience of mobile augmented reality: a review of studies. In: 2014 3rd International Conference on User Science and Engineering (i-USEr), pp. 125–130, September 2014

22. Irshad, S., Awang Rambli, D.R.: Multi-layered mobile augmented reality framework for positive user experience. In: Proceedings of the 2nd International Conference in HCI and UX Indonesia 2016, CHIuXiD 2016, pp. 21–26. ACM, New York (2016). http://doi.acm.org/10.1145/2898459.2898462

23. Irshad, S., Rambli, D.R.A.: User experience evaluation of mobile AR services. In: Proceedings of the 12th International Conference on Advances in Mobile Computing and

Multimedia, MoMM 2014, pp. 119–126. ACM, New York (2014). http://doi.acm.org/10. 1145/2684103.2684135

24. Irshad, S., Rambli, D.R.A.: User experience satisfaction of mobile-based AR advertising applications. In: Badioze Zaman, H., Robinson, P., Smeaton, A.F., Shih, T.K., Velastin, S., Jaafar, A., Mohamad Ali, N. (eds.) IVIC 2015. LNCS, vol. 9429, pp. 432–442. Springer, Cham (2015). doi:10.1007/978-3-319-25939-0_38

25. Irshad, S., Rambli, D.R.A.: Design implications for quality user eXperience in mobile augmented reality applications. In: Sulaiman, H.A., Othman, M.A., Othman, M.F.I., Rahim, Y.A., Pee, N.C. (eds.) Advanced Computer and Communication Engineering Technology. LNEE, vol. 362, pp. 1283–1294. Springer, Cham (2016). doi:10.1007/978-3-319-24584-3_ 110

26. Ergonomics of human system interaction - part 210: Human-centered design for interactive systems. Standard, International Organization for Standardization, Technical report International (2010)

27. Jaasko, V., Mattelmaki, T.: Observing and probing. In: Proceedings of the 2003 International Conference on Designing Pleasurable Products and Interfaces, pp. 126–131. ACM (2003)

28. Joslin, P.: Augmented reality based user interface for mobile applications and services. Ph.D. thesis, P.O. Box 3000, FIN-90014 University of Oulu, Finland (2005)

29. Kamilakis, M., Gavalas, D., Zaroliagis, C.: Mobile user experience in augmented reality vs. maps interfaces: a case study in public transportation. In: De Paolis, L.T., Mongelli, A. (eds.) AVR 2016. LNCS, vol. 9768, pp. 388–396. Springer, Cham (2016). doi:10.1007/978-3-319-40621-3_27

30. Karapanos, E.: User experience over time. In: Karapanos, E. (ed.) Modeling Users' Experiences with Interactive Systems, pp. 57–83. Springer, Heidelberg (2013). doi:10.1007/978-3-642-31000-3_4

31. Kaye, J.J., Buie, E., Hoonhout, J., Höök, K., Roto, V., Jenson, S., Wright, P.: Designing for user experience: academia & industry. In: CHI 2011 Extended Abstracts on Human Factors in Computing Systems, CHI EA 2011, pp. 219–222. ACM, New York (2011). http://doi.acm.org/10.1145/1979742.1979486

32. Keating, G., Guest, D., Konertz, A., Padovani, N., Villa, A.: Designing the AR experience: tools and tips for mobile augmented reality UX design. In: Marcus, A. (ed.) DUXU 2011. LNCS, vol. 6770, pp. 135–141. Springer, Heidelberg (2011). doi:10.1007/978-3-642-21708-1_16

33. Kilby, J., Gray, K., Elliott, K., Waycott, J., Sanchez, F.M., Dave, B.: Designing a mobile augmented reality tool for the locative visualization of biomedical knowledge. Stud. Health Technol. Inf. **192**, 652–656 (2012)

34. Kim, M.J.: A framework for context immersion in mobile augmented reality. Autom. Constr. **33**, 79–85 (2013)

35. Kourouthanassis, P.E., Boletsis, C., Lekakos, G.: Demystifying the design of mobile augmented reality applications. Multimedia Tools Appl. **74**(3), 1045–1066 (2015)

36. Kuniavsky, M.: Observing the User Experience: A Practitioner's Guide to user Research. Morgan Kaufmann, Burlington (2003)

37. Kuutti, K.: Where are the Ionians of user experience research? In: Proceedings of the 6th Nordic Conference on Human-Computer Interaction: Extending Boundaries, NordiCHI 2010, pp. 715–718. ACM, New York (2010). http://doi.acm.org/10.1145/1868914.1869012

38. Lee, J.Y., Seo, D.W., Rhee, G.: Visualization and interaction of pervasive services using context-aware augmented reality. Expert Syst. Appl. **35**(4), 1873–1882 (2008)

39. Li, H., Zhu, W.: mPano: cloud-based mobile panorama view from single picture. In: SPIE Optical Engineering + Applications, p. 88560D. International Society for Optics and Photonics (2013)

40. Liu, C., Huot, S., Diehl, J., Mackay, W., Beaudouin-Lafon, M.: Evaluating the benefits of real-time feedback in mobile augmented reality with hand-held devices. In: Proceedings of the SIGCHI Conference on Human Factors in Computing Systems, pp. 2973–2976. ACM (2012)

41. Mirnig, A.G., Meschtscherjakov, A., Wurhofer, D., Meneweger, T., Tscheligi, M.: A formal analysis of the ISO 9241–210 definition of user experience. In: Proceedings of the 33rd Annual ACM Conference Extended Abstracts on Human Factors in Computing Systems, CHI EA 2015, pp. 437–450. ACM, New York (2015). http://doi.acm.org/10.1145/2702613.2732511

42. Müller, L., Aslan, I., Krüßen, L.: GuideMe: a mobile augmented reality system to display user manuals for home appliances. In: Reidsma, D., Katayose, H., Nijholt, A. (eds.) ACE 2013. LNCS, vol. 8253, pp. 152–167. Springer, Cham (2013). doi:10.1007/978-3-319-03161-3_11

43. Olsson, T.: Layers of user expectations of future technologies: an early framework. In: CHI 2014 Extended Abstracts on Human Factors in Computing Systems, pp. 1957–1962. ACM (2014)

44. Olsson, T., Ihamäki, P., Lagerstam, E., Ventä-Olkkonen, L., Väänänen-Vainio-Mattila, K.: User expectations for mobile mixed reality services: an initial user study. In: European Conference on Cognitive Ergonomics: Designing Beyond the Product Understanding Activity and User Experience in Ubiquitous Environments, p. 19. VTT Technical Research Centre of Finland (2009)

45. Olsson, T., Karkkainen, T., Lagerstam, E., Venta-Olkkonen, L.: User evaluation of mobile augmented reality scenarios. J. Ambient Intell. Smart Environ. 4(1), 29–47 (2012)

46. Olsson, T., Lagerstam, E., Karkkainen, T., Vaananen-Vainio-Mattila, K.: Expected user experience of mobile augmented reality services: a user study in the context of shopping centers. Pers. Ubiquit. Comput. 17(2), 287–304 (2013)

47. Olsson, T., Salo, M.: Online user survey on current mobile augmented reality applications. In: 2011 10th IEEE International Symposium on Mixed and Augmented Reality (ISMAR), pp. 75–84. IEEE (2011)

48. Olsson, T., Salo, M.: Narratives of satisfying and unsatisfying experiences of current mobile augmented reality applications. In: Proceedings of the SIGCHI Conference on Human Factors in Computing Systems, pp. 2779–2788. ACM (2012)

49. Perritaz, D., Salzmann, C., Gillet, D.: Quality of experience for adaptation in augmented reality. In: IEEE International Conference on Systems, Man and Cybernetics, SMC 2009, pp. 888–893. IEEE (2009)

50. Rambli, D.R.A., Irshad, S.: UX design evaluation of mobile augmented reality marketing products and services for Asia pacific region. In: Proceedings of the Asia Pacific HCI and UX Design Symposium, APCHIUX 2015, pp. 42–45. ACM, New York (2015). http://doi.acm.org/10.1145/2846439.2846450

51. Reitmayr, G., Drummond, T.W.: Going out: robust model-based tracking for outdoor augmented reality. In: IEEE/ACM International Symposium on Mixed and Augmented Reality, ISMAR 2006, pp. 109–118. IEEE (2006)

52. Roto, V., Law, E., Vermeeren, A., Hoonhout, J.: User experience white paper. Bringing clarity to the concept of user experience (2011)

53. de Sa, M., Churchill, E.F., Isbister, K.: Mobile augmented reality: design issues and opportunities. In: Proceedings of the 13th International Conference on Human Computer Interaction with Mobile Devices and Services, MobileHCI 2011, pp. 749–752. ACM, New York (2011)

54. Schmalstieg, D., Langlotz, T., Billinghurst, M.: Augmented reality 2.0. In: Brunnett, G., Coquillart, S., Welch, G. (eds.) Virtual Realities. Springer, Vienna (2011). doi:10.1007/978-3-211-99178-7_2
55. Siltanen, S., Oksman, V., Ainasoja, M.: User-centered design of augmented reality interior design service. Int. J. Arts Sci. 6(1), 547 (2013)
56. Squire, K.D., Jan, M.: Mad city mystery: developing scientific argumentation skills with a place-based augmented reality game on handheld computers. J. Sci. Educ. Technol. 16(1), 5–29 (2007)
57. TechNavio: Mobile augmented reality market for marketing and advertising in APAC 2015–2019. http://www.researchandmarkets.com/research/xqjh2d/mobileaugmented
58. Verbelen, T., Simoens, P., De Turck, F., Dhoedt, B.: Adaptive deployment and configuration for mobile augmented reality in the cloudlet. J. Netw. Comput. Appl. 41, 206–216 (2014)
59. Yang, X., Cheng, K.T.: LDB: an ultra-fast feature for scalable augmented reality on mobile devices. In: 2012 IEEE International Symposium on Mixed and Augmented Reality (ISMAR), pp. 49–57. IEEE (2012)
60. Zhou, F., Duh, H.B.L., Billinghurst, M.: Trends in augmented reality tracking, interaction and display: a review of ten years of ISMAR. In: Proceedings of the 7th IEEE/ACM International Symposium on Mixed and Augmented Reality, pp. 193–202. IEEE Computer Society (2008)

Exploring Malay Older User Motivation to Play Mobile Games

Fariza Hanis Abdul Razak[✉], Nor Haizam Che Azhar,
Wan Adilah Wan Adnan, and Zan Azma Nasruddin

Faculty of Computer and Mathematical Sciences,
Universiti Teknologi MARA (UiTM), 40450 Shah Alam, Selangor, Malaysia
{fariza, adilah, zanaz}@tmsk.uitm.edu.my,
nhaizam69@gmail.com

Abstract. Recent studies show that playing games brings cognitive and psychological benefits to the older adults. In Malay culture, any older adults who play games will be perceived negatively. This is due to our belief that games are only meant for children and older adults should spend their time on spiritual or religious activities. There is evidence from our previous study that our older adults do play games, thus, we were motivated to find out why and how they played games. We tested a mobile game with five (5) older adults who are gamers aged between 56 and 63. From our study, we learned that gaming motivation among older adults can be described as intrinsic: psychological benefits and enjoyment. Like other young gamers, our older adults were seen immersed and enjoying themselves when playing with the game, however, unlike young gamers, they preferred to play alone and played it short but frequent. Aware of the negative perception towards them, some of the older adults have approached the game creatively: playing and chanting zikir (dzikr) at the same time. The findings from this study can provide opportunities for the game developers to innovate and create competitive advantage in gaming industry and consequently help older adults in improving their quality of life.

Keywords: Older adults · Gaming · Motivation · Playability evaluation · Creative interaction

1 Introduction

In 2015, a survey of gamers was conducted by [7] in United States of America, it was found that 27% of the gamers was from the age group above 50 years old. It was a surprise to discover that number of older adults who play casual games is quite high. Casual games refer to the digital games that are simple, easy to learn and targeted the mass market especially for non-gamers [17]. The games can be played in a short time period at home, office and public places and during waiting or travelling in public transports. Nowadays, they are more commonly played on mobile devices rather than console because they can be easily connected to the Internet and can be played on multi player mode. Casual games are now becoming increasingly popular among older adults above 50 years old due to the perceived benefits particularly to improve their cognitive

H. Badioze Zaman et al. (Eds.): IVIC 2017, LNCS 10645, pp. 478–488, 2017.
https://doi.org/10.1007/978-3-319-70010-6_44

skills [28, 29], decrease stress and increase positive mood [19] as well as improve their psychological functioning [1]. These benefits show that by playing casual games can help achieve healthy aging. The success of a particular game is highly dependent on player motivations and the playability of the game [4]. In the game design, the game designer must first understand the target audience motivational factors, which make them feel attracted and want to continue to play the game. Good characteristics of a successful game are that it should be easily playable, fun, learnable and reliable [18]. These characteristics are termed as playability. Up to present, most studies on the playability and older adults have come from western countries. From our previous study with older people [26], we found evidence that some of our older adults do play casual games. Unlike in western countries where their society can easily accept the fact that older adults play games, our older adults who play games at their old age will be somehow perceived negatively by our society. Due to this, we were motivated to find out why older people still play games despite this negative perception. Thus, this paper will discuss the older adults' motivation and describe their playability experience. This study hopes to provide knowledge and understanding towards healthy ageing.

2   Related Work

2.1   Gaming Motivation Among Older Adults

Gaming motivation refers to the motivation that leads people to play games [4]. It is most important to know who are the players and why they want to play the game. As a normal human being, the interest, desires and satisfaction are mainly for self-achievement, recognition and satisfaction. When any of these basic human needs are fulfilled, humans feel that they are being rewarded by either achieving the target of the game, congratulated by the fellow players or simply enjoying the game as a basic entertainment of living [4].

[24] conducted an explorative study by using semi-structured interviews and observations to investigate the meaning of digital games in older adults live. A total of 35 older adults ranging from 50 to 72 years of age participated in their study. Their study found that the most important motivational factors for older adult to play games were competition, loneliness and social interaction. Their interviewees reported that:

- "Digital games are fun way to compete with my partner and my friend";
- "Digital games are something that I do alone"; and
- "Digital games are a way to meet new people".

Meanwhile, [23] showed that the most popular motivation of older adults in playing games was the challenge motive. In his study, challenges had been a motive that forced the respondents to overcome them and reach the next and higher level. Social interaction motives received low mean scores because most of his respondents reported that they seldom play with other players.

A quantitative study that was conducted by [15] among 12 Brazilian gamers identified that the most important elements that attracted players to play casual games on Facebook i.e. a puzzle match of three games were the activities and reward system. They also found that the scores for socialization elements (competition and social status) were lower.

[29] conducted online survey among 10,308 adults with age ranged from 18 to 80 years old to find out the reason for playing a particular casual game named Bejeweled Blitz (BJB). They found that older adult respondents (50 to over 60 years old) reported that their main reasons were to seek challenge and to find stress relief. Only minority of them indicated that they play because they enjoy the graphics and effects and for competition. Most of the older adult respondents reported that the game's cognitive effect was to help them feel sharper and perform task-timed task more quickly.

2.2   Playability Evaluation

[21] defined playability as *"the degree to which specified users can achieve specified goals with effectiveness, efficiency and especially satisfaction and fun in a playable context of use"*. They proposed a set of seven attributes to characterise playability: effectiveness, learnability, immersion, satisfaction, motivation, emotion and socialization.

Effectiveness: refers to the player's ability to achieve the game's goals within specific time and resources.

Learnability: refers to the player's ability to understand and master the game's system. The learning curve of a video game can be either steep learning curve or learn step-by-step in a guided way.

Immersion: refers to the capacity of the video game that influences the involvement of the players in the virtual game world.

Satisfaction: refers to the pleasure experience derived from playing video games. It is very difficult to measure the satisfaction because it depends on the preferences of the players.

Motivation: refers to the game characteristics that motivates player to play the game until they are completed.

Emotion: refers to the ability of a video game to generate different emotional states such as happiness, sadness, fear, etc. in order to help the players to achieve *optimum experience.*

Socialization: promotes new social relationship when the player plays with other players and offers different game experience to the players.

In order to measure the degree of player experience offered by the game, they proposed a number of properties for each attribute.

3   Playability Evaluation Methods

The study was conducted qualitatively as we wanted to understand why and how our older adults played games. Playability evaluation methods such as playtesting, observation and interview were used in the study.

3.1   Older Adult Participants

A total of five older adults were recruited to participate in this study. Two of them were recruited through phone calls, while the remaining participants were recruited via the referral sampling. There are four female participants and one male participant from various parts in Malaysia. They were chosen because they played mobile games. The oldest participant was a female aged 63 years old, while the youngest was a male, aged 56. All of them are married and their health status regarding self-assessment was "Good". Two participants are pensioners and the remaining participants are still working as a clerk, a doctor and a manager. All of them spent more than one hour per week playing games.

3.2   Candy Crush Soda Saga (CCSS)

This study chose one casual game known as Candy Crush Soda Saga (CCSS) for the playtesting session as recommended by one of key participants. All participants have downloaded this game into their smartphones. This game is one of the most successful and popular games nowadays and it is suitable for a test session that is no longer than 20 min. Figure 1 shows CCSS game interface.

Fig. 1. Candy crush soda saga (Credit Google Android)

3.3   Playtesting

Form the literature, it was understood that playtesting is one of the most popular methods used in evaluating the playability of released games such as CCSS. Playtesting was conducted to gain an insight whether the participants were satisfied or not with their playing experience. Playtesting adapts the principles of usability [14] in the evaluation of a game. Each participant was asked to play CCSS in a free form, where they were free to play the game as they wished and were not instructed to play any level. They were free to ask any questions and give their insights about the game. Each playtesting session took place approximately 15 to 20 min. It was a one-on-one testing where an evaluator played a role as a complete observer who sat down with the individuals, watched over their shoulder and reported their achievement on the effectiveness attributes of the CCSS.

There are three stages of evaluation process with respect to the playtesting session, which are known as pre-playtesting, playtesting and post-playtesting.

Pre-playtesting: Before playtesting session, the evaluator conducted a first interview as a warm-up interview to find out their reasons for playing digital games and CCSS game.

Playtesting: Playtesting was conducted in one-on-one testing, where the evaluator sat down with participants and watched them from behind while their gameplay being video-recorded. The purpose of the video recording was to observe their playing behavior and their emotions while playing.

Post-playtesting: After the playtesting sessions, the evaluator sat down face-to-face with the participants and gave them a second interview. The purpose of this interview was to gain an insight of their motivation and experience in the game, and to verify the playtesting and observation results.

4   Results and Discussion

4.1   Gaming Motivation

Gaming motivations refers to the reasons that stimulate the participants to play digital games [23]. The results from the interviews demonstrated that the participants play games for a range of reasons such as follows:

They are Gamers
The first theme that arose in the interviews was that they are gamers. It was based on their experience in playing digital games, their time spent for gaming per week and the frequency of their gameplay. All participants are baby boomers where their ages ranged from 55 to 63 years old. They were categorized as regular gamers because they have been playing games since they were younger and spent almost more than 3 h per week of their times playing games. Participant 3 spent the longest time for gaming; approximately 14 h per week, whereas, Participant 1 spent the shortest time for gaming, approximately 4.5 h per week. They play games everyday and they spend approximately 15 min to 30 min per session.

They See Benefits for Their Well-Being

Cognitive Benefits
The theme of cognitive benefits arose from their psychological needs to maintain and improve their cognitive functions as they realized that their basic cognitive functions such as attention and memory [9] were most affected by their age. According to the participants, they play CCSS because it is one of the activities that helped them to exercise and sharpen their mind, as they grow older. *"This game teaches me to think and be patience. It can help me sharpen my mind at this age of mine"* (Participant 3, 58, female).

As a doctor, Participant 4 said that they need to prevent themselves from Parkinson's disease, which has been known as movement disorder. Parkinson's disease has been characterized by tremor and slow movement and recognized as cognitive difficulties due to ageing factor [5]. She added that people with Parkinson's has slow movement such as finger movement due to their slow thinking ability. Playing CCSS could help them in coordination of brain activity and finger movement. She said that CCSS is a mentally challenging game that helps her to think, plan and employ strategies to win the game and compete with other players. *"The game is a bit challenging when it reaches certain levels and make me continue playing the particular mobile games...Strategically you should aim to match 5 candies either in the form of "T" or "L". You have to think one or two steps forward. You have to imagine that if you were to move a certain candy to make it 3 in a row, which candies will go up or down. You have to decide whether to select the vertical or horizontal candies. When the candy falls down, which candy will it hit it."* (Participant 5, 56, male).

Emotional Benefits
From the interviews, it was found that loneliness is one of the strong factors that motivate the participants to play games. Participant 4 said that she felt lonely when she was at home with nothing to do since her husband passed away five years ago. Her daughters are married and live away from her while her son is still studying and lives at the university. The main reason for her to play games is to combat her loneliness. *"I am a single mother, living alone, so I play to fill my time and to get rid of loneliness and boredom; that is my main reason"* (Participant 4, 59, female).

Another emotional benefit is that playing games is a stress reliever. Three of the participants said that they were motivated to play game to relieve their stress. Playing game is a great way to release stress from the demand of everyday life. They found that CCSS is a relaxing casual game that can release their work stress after a tiring working day. According to them, playing games upon coming home after work helps them to divert their thoughts away from work. Similarly, it also keeps them away from stressful things.

They are Attracted to the Game Features

Five free live and extra live: According to the participants, CCSS encourages the players to play by giving five free lives in the beginning of the game to complete a level. If they fail to pass a level, they will lose one life. Therefore, they are given a chance to pass a level with five times trial. The game also allows them to get extra lives by asking help from their Facebook friends. For those players who play without connecting through Facebook, they could get extra lives by asking help from the other players. When the given extra lives are finished, they have to wait for a few minutes to get back one new life. *"When I lose and couldn't get pass through a level, I never gave up. I will keep trying until I could get pass though it. If my lives number is finished, I will get help from friends to get extra "live". If this extra "live" is also finished, I will need to wait a little bit before I get a new live"* (Participant 3, 58, female).

Positive reward: Apart from that, CCSS provides constant positive feedback when they play well. The positive reward words pop up on their screen according to level of their achievement, accompanied by a voice such as *"Devine"*, *"Sweet"*, *"Juicy"* and *"Sodalicious"*. Participant 3 said that those amazing positive rewards motivate her to continuously play CCSS.

Diversity of game elements: Four participants said that CCSS was an interesting game to play because they were interested with colourful candies and different elements of CCSS that appeared in each level. These elements make the game interesting and motivate them to continue playing CCSS. *"There are actually a lot of different levels in this game. Look at this (while showing her hand phone screen) In one episode, there are 15 levels, and in these 15 levels, there is a mix of elements like chocolates, bears, bottles, etc. So it is interesting because there is a variation"* (Participant 4, 59, female).

4.2 How Older Adults Play It and Their Playable Experience

They Like to Play in Silence
There were four participants who said that they preferred to play in silence. They muted the sound for two reasons: they did not want to disturb others and they did not like the music sounds.

They Know How to Play Game
All participants had gaming experience ranging from two to six years and they play games every day. They played games such as Fruit Bunny Mania, Farm Hero Saga, Bubble Witch Saga, Flick Shot US, Total Snooker, Chess Free, and Real Racing. In addition, they also had game knowledge from previous version of Candy Crush which is Candy Crush Saga. Therefore, they found it easier to assimilate new concepts and understand how to play. *"I have played Candy Crush Saga before. So this CCSS is very similar except for the new fish and a few other things"* (Participant 5, 56, male).

Three participants learnt to play CCSS games by themselves from the guide provided in the game. However, two participants learnt about this game from her friends. They even referred to YouTube to learn how to play the game and how to pass the hard levels. *"I started playing when I met some friends while working during a netball tournament. They were the ones who taught me this game"* (Participant 2, 63, female).

The interview answers also emphasised that all participants understood the game concept very well where they have to match three candies in a line. In addition, they also knew a lot of tips and trick to win the levels with high scores. *"We must target to get these 5 candies. Try to get the most candies (referring to special candy) but hold on, don't swipe yet. Collect those special candies as many as you can and only then you swipe the candies. This will trigger a chain reaction that will explode the other special candies. If we have a candy with a big and dotted chocolate (referring to colour bomb) and immediately swipe it, it is not powerful. I usually combine colour comb with "L" or "T" shape candy (referring to wrapped candy). My strategy is to collect as many special candies as possible and leave them there. Don't immediately swipe them, unless you have no choice. Combine the colour bombs with wrapped candies and when it explodes all of them "poom, poom, poom, poom, poom". That's my trick"* (Participant 5, 56, male).

They are Engrossed in the Game But Consciously Aware of Their Actions

According to [12], as the player becomes more immersed in a game, their eyes movement will decrease. From the observations, it was found the participants' attention was more on the game as their eyes stayed on the visual components of CCSS. Most of them were talking to themselves during the playtesting session. Their verbal expression reflected a sense of being in the game. For instance, Participant 1 was asking herself *"where are the other bears, I can't find the bears"* when she cannot find the bears that were trapped in the ice. When she found the bear, she said *"kau kau kau kau kau kau, look there's a bear"*. She also read the positive reward that popped up on her screen *"Juicy, Juicy"*. Those verbal expressions showed that she was immersed in the game. The other participant sometimes counted the number of chocolates left as he feels that he had a chance to win in a matter of time.

Body movement is one of the attributes of immersion; players who were immersed showed more focused behaviour with a forward still leaning body and still head [2]. In the beginning, they played the game easily. However, as they came to the higher level of difficulty, they looked very immersed in the game. Participant 1 looked pensive with her left hand on her chin and right hand on her elbow while thinking to achieve the goal. She changed her sitting position as soon as she achieved the goal of the level. This body movement indicated the transition of her feelings [8] from being very immersed to very good. While waiting for her score calculation and rating, she grasped and moved her fingers as a relaxation movement [3].

From the interviews, we understood that most of them were really focused on solving the problems to achieve the goal and to obtain the highest score for each level. They usually engrossed during the critical time to achieve the goal. *"I will focus on solving the problem; for example, in order to save the bears, I will need to know where the bears are"* (Participant 1, 62, female) However, Participant 3 shared her experience where she lost awareness of her surroundings when she was totally immersed in the game. *"I don't really pay attention to other people around me when I am playing this game. If they are talking to me, I will just nod my head or answer "emm""* (Participant 3, 58, female).

Although CCSS is not specifically oriented to older adults, four participants said that CCSS is a suitable game for their age group. However, the eldest participant said that people at her age should always perform zikr (remembering God) rather than playing games. Initially, she considered the game as distracting. In the end, she compromised to perform zikr while playing the game so that she could get benefits from that activity. She suggested that people at her age should always perform zikr while swiping the candies. *"Not very suitable for older people like me, because it is distracting and engrossing except if you remember God while you are swiping the candies, like what I am practicing now"* (Participant 2, 63, female).

They Prefer to Play Alone

The participants stated that CCSS is a single player game with a social connection through Social Network Sites i.e. Facebook. All participants have their own Facebook account, however only one participant plays CCSS through Facebook. From the interviews, we learned that some of them were shy to admit that they play games. *"Actually I am a bit ashamed to admit that I play games, but I play this game to fill my free time."* (Participant 4, 59, female).

Participant 5 used to ask for extra lives from his Facebook friends however failed to get any response. He expressed his frustration as follows. *"I did ask for help from friends, once or twice, but none of them responded. I also sent lives to other players 2 or 3 times, whenever the screen prompts it"* (Participant 5, 56, male).

Two participants never asked for help because they believed that some of their Facebook friends felt annoyed when being asked for lives and invited to play the game. So, they played CCSS alone without connecting to Facebook and never asked help from other players as well. *"Socially, we could request live from friends. But sometimes when we request the lives not everyone will like it. Also, when we invite people to play it, there are some people who don't like it; sometimes it could make them angry. Hahaha"* (Participant 4, 59, female).

They Enjoy But Get Frustrated with the Game Just Like Young Gamers

Excited: From the observations, it was found that the context of candy primarily special candies such as fish, stripped, wrapped candies, colouring and lighting bombs have triggered the participants' enjoyment. Participant 2 was so excited when there were so many fish candies appeared on the screen and said *"uuuu there's a lot of fish!, I've already got a lot of fish!, can you see them? hahahaha"*. Participant 4 was so excited with the appearance of graphical animations when she matched the colouring bombs with purple fish where all the purple candies were turned into fish candies and popped the bottles. They reported very excited when they managed to win the game. They said that achieving the target with a high score made them feel very satisfied. The feeling was even better especially when they could beat younger or more experienced players. As Participant 4 said, *"...just feel "great" because as an older person, I can still play this game and beat the younger player."* *"I enjoy it, especially when I can beat any friends who play earlier than me. I'm now above 400 levels, but my friends are still below my level."* (Participant 1, 63, female).

Frustrated: They were so frustrated when they failed to pass the level. Participant 1 shouted *"Arghh"* and clapped her right hand on her thigh when she lost the game. Sometimes, she expressed her frustration with a frowning mouth and disappointed eyes and said, *"game over"*. Participant 5 expressed his frustration by taking a deep breath and sighed when he lost the game. *"I've achieved level 45 a few times, but could not proceed to level 46 because of time bar. I have to wait for about 3 days before I can play that level 46. I can ask for help from friends, but I don't want to."* (Participant 5, 56, male).

Annoyed: However, Participant 4 felt annoyed when she saw those emotional cartoon characters especially the sad face shown by the cartoon when she failed the level. *"Sometimes I hate to see that cartoon (while laughing). If it wasn't there, it's probably better. It's like it's jeering at us"* (Participant 4, 59, female).

They Play It Short But Frequent

All of the participants said that they only spent like 15–30 min per game session but play the game for a few times in a day. Since a game session in CCSS can be completed in 20 min, CCSS seems suited for the older adults to play.

5   Conclusion

The main reason for older adults to play games is for their psychological benefits. They play CCSS because it is a mentally challenging game that helps them to think, plan and employ strategies to win the game. The CCSS's cognitive effect helps them to exercise and sharpen their mind. Indirectly by playing games, it helps them feel less lonely. The CCSS game features are also able to attract them to play and provide them with an enjoyable experience. The older participants in this study are all gamers. They still play games despite old age. Like young gamers, they often enjoy playing games. However, unlike young gamers, they prefer to play games alone. They rather seek help from unknown players when they are really in trouble. They also have short play time but play it frequently. Aware of the negative perception towards them, they interact with the game creatively: playing and performing zikr (chanting) at the same time. In order to encourage older adult non-gamers to play games, further study should be conducted among older adult non-gamers so that their motivational elements and their experience could provide more input requirements to improve the design of casual game.

References

1. Allair, J.C., McLaughlin, A.C., Trujillo, A., Whitlock, L., LaPorte, L.: Succesful aging through digital games: sociomotional differences between older adults gamers and non-gamers. Comput. Hum. Behav. 1302–1306 (2003)
2. Bernhaupt, R.: User experience evaluation methods in the games development life cycle. In: Bernhaupt, R. (ed.) Game User Experience Evaluation. HIS, pp. 1–8. Springer, Cham (2015). doi:10.1007/978-3-319-15985-0_1
3. Berthouze, N.B.: Understanding the role of body movement in player engagement. Hum.-Comput. Interact. 28, 40–75 (2013)
4. Cota, T., Ishitani, L., Vieira Jr., N.: Mobile game design for the older adults: a study with focus on the motivation to play. Comput. Hum. Behav. 51, 96–105 (2015)
5. Dastipour, K.: Do genetic factors protect against Parkinson's disease? What I can learn from my healthy grandma. Med. Hypotheses 38(6), 637–639 (2014)
6. Desurvire, H., El-Nasr, M.S.: Methods for game user research. Comput. Soc. 82–87 (2013)
7. Entertainment Software Association: 2015 Essential facts about the computer and video game industry, Entertainment Software Association (2015)
8. Fulton, B., Lazzaro, N.: Playtesting. In: Fullerton, T. (ed.) Game Design Workshop – A Playcentric Approach on Creating Innovative Games, pp. 248–271. CRC Press (2014)
9. Glisky, E.L.: Changes in cognitive function in human aging. In: Riddle, D.R. (ed.) Brain Aging: Models, Methods, and Mechanisms, pp. 4–20. Taylor & Francis Group, LLC, United States of America (2007)
10. Hansegard, J.: Tech: Wall Street Journal. http://www.wsj.com/articles/the-drama-behind-candy-crush-soda-saga-creating-new-levels-1428422303

11. Hwang, M., Hong, J., Hao, Y., Jong, J.: Elder's usability, dependability, and flow experiences on embodied interactive video game. Educ. Gerontol. **37**(8), 715–731 (2011)
12. Jennetta, C., Coxa, A.L., Cairnsb, P., Dhopareec, S., Eppsc, A., Tijsd, T.: Measuring and defining the experience of immersion in games. Int. J. Hum.-Comput. Stud. **66**, 641–661 (2008)
13. Korhonen, H., Koivisto, E.M.I.: Playability heuristics for mobile games. In: Proceedings of 8th conference on Human-Computer Interaction with Mobile Devices and Services, pp. 9–16. ACM, New York (2006)
14. Nielsen, J.: Usability 101: Introduction to Usability. https://www.nngroup.com/articles/usability-101-introduction-to-usability/
15. Omori, M., Felinto, A.: Analysis of motivational elements of social games: a puzzle match 3-games study case. Int. J. Comput. Games Technol. 1–10 (2012)
16. Palacio, R., Acosta, C., Cortez, J.M.: Usability perception of different video game devices in older adults users. Univ. Access. Inf. Soc. **16**(1), 103–113 (2015)
17. Raffaele, R., Alencar, R., Júnior, I., Colley, B., Pontes, G., Carvalho, B., Soares, M.M.: *Doctor Who:* legacy, an analysis of usability and playability of a multi-platform game. In: Marcus, A. (ed.) DUXU 2015. LNCS, vol. 9188, pp. 283–291. Springer, Cham (2015). doi:10.1007/978-3-319-20889-3_27
18. Razak, F.H.A., Sulo, R., Adnan, W.A.W., Ahmad, N.: Elderly mental model of reminder system. In: APCHI 2012 Conference Proceedings, Matsui, Japan. ACM (2012)
19. Russoniello, C., O'Brien, K., Parks, J.: The effectiveness of casual video games in improving mood and decreasing stress. J. CyberTheraphy Rehabi. **2**(1), 53–66 (2009)
20. Saarenpaa, H.: Data gathering methods for evaluating playability, Finland (2008)
21. Sanchez, J.L.G., Vale, F.L.G., Simarro, F.M., Zea, N.P.: Playability: analysing user experience in video games. Behav. Inf. Technol. **31**(10), 1033–1054 (2012)
22. González Sánchez, J.L., Padilla Zea, N., Gutiérrez, F.L.: From usability to playability: introduction to player-centred video game development process. In: Kurosu, M. (ed.) HCD 2009. LNCS, vol. 5619, pp. 65–74. Springer, Heidelberg (2009). doi:10.1007/978-3-642-02806-9_9
23. Schutter, B.D.: Never too old to play: the appeal of digital games to an older audience. Games Cult. **6**(2), 155–170 (2011)
24. Schutter, B.D., Abeele, V.: Designing meaningful play within the psycho-social context of older adults. In: Proceeding of 3rd International Conference on Fun and Games, pp. 84–93. ACM (2010)
25. Social Welfare Department Malaysia: Country Report Malaysia. Social Welfare Department Malaysia (2012)
26. Soomro, S., Wan Ahmad, W.F., Sulaiman, S.: Evaluation of mobile games using playability heuristics. In: Zaman, H.B., Robinson, P., Olivier, P., Shih, T.K., Velastin, S. (eds.) IVIC 2013. LNCS, vol. 8237, pp. 264–274. Springer, Cham (2013). doi:10.1007/978-3-319-02958-0_25
27. Sykes, J., Federoff, M.: Player-centred game design. In: CHI 2006 Workshop, Canada, pp. 1731–1734. ACM (2006)
28. Thompson, O., Barrett, S., Patterson, D., Craig, D.: Examining the neurocognitive validity of commercially available, smartphone-based puzzle games. Psycholog **3**(7), 525–526 (2012)
29. Whitbourne, S., Ellenberg, S., Akimoto, K.: Reasons for playing casual video games and perceived benefits among adults 18 to 80 years old. Cyberpsychol. Behav. Soc. Netw. **16** (12), 892–897 (2013)

Utilizing Mobile Application for Reducing Stress Level

Aslina Baharum[1(✉)], Nurhafizah Moziyana Mohd Yusop[2],
Ratna Zuarni Ramli[3], Noor Fazlinda Fabeil[4], Sharifah Milda Amirul[4],
and Suhaida Halamy[5]

[1] Faculty of Computing and Informatics, Universiti Malaysia Sabah,
88400 Kota Kinabalu, Sabah, Malaysia
aslinabaharum@gmail.com
[2] Faculty of Defence Science and Technology,
National Defence University of Malaysia, 57000 Kuala Lumpur, Malaysia
[3] Faculty of Computer, Universiti Teknologi MARA,
Kuala Pilah Campus, 72000 Kuala Pilah, Negeri Sembilan, Malaysia
[4] Faculty of Business, Economics and Accountancy, Universiti Malaysia Sabah,
88400 Kota Kinabalu, Sabah, Malaysia
[5] Faculty of Information Management, Universiti Teknologi MARA,
Sarawak Campus, 94300 Kota Samarahan, Malaysia

Abstract. In these modern days, conflicts, negative revolution, suicides and other common crime had been occurred in the worldwide. After several studies and investigations, its have been found out the one of the root cause – stress. Although stress can make someone to improve work performance and awareness, the desperate situation would happen if someone unable to cope with it. To decrease this kind of unfavourable situation from continuing, several methods had been proposed such as listening to music, physical activities, doing desired activities, surfing, and others. In this study, music will be the main concern as distress purpose. Here, a product of this study will be a mobile application. It will be presented in health and fitness category of mood music based mobile application. The methodology used here are the quantitative method survey, in order to identify the music and mood categories. The expected outcome of this study would be features of music and mood categories for a mobile application. With this app, it might greatly help in decreasing and eliminating the tension, unsatisfaction, and others negative feelings of users in their daily life. Thus, this study hopes that mobile application based on music and mood can be one of the alternative ways to relief stress.

Keywords: Mobile application · Stress · Music · Mood

1 Introduction

In this fast growing and steampunk era of innovation, "stress" is always the main concern for every community and country. Stress is situation of fear or negative feelings such as anxiousness and frustration [1]. It happens to make us know that stress and mood could affect each other at the same time, concluded from the statistical

© Springer International Publishing AG 2017
H. Badioze Zaman et al. (Eds.): IVIC 2017, LNCS 10645, pp. 489–499, 2017.
https://doi.org/10.1007/978-3-319-70010-6_45

models about the stress effects on mood in daily life [2]. With this relationship, [3] stated that a positive emotion in daily life is enough to moderate the major and minor stress from reactivate. Hence, a study was carried out to determine how far the music is capable of constructing a positive mood by using a mobile phone.

Stress can be felt or experienced from the environment, physiological, social stressors, and thoughts. Some of stressor's example, there are financial demands, conflicts among people, family issues, and others that could influence all aspects of human daily behaviour and human functioning respectively. In order to decrease the stress level among the society, music is one of the choices. Listening to different types of music can decrease health issues that caused by high level of stress hormones [4]. However, one music is not enough to satisfy everyone. [5] stated that how could someone from different cultural background listening to the same music in moods that are different with others. Hence, the relationship between music and moods that are acceptable will be the main concern in this study.

In the conclusion, stressors mainly raise up from the aspects of environmental, physiological, social stressors, and mind thoughts. In order to reduce the level of stress, a positive thinking or positive emotion is urgent to every single individual. To maintain a peaceful, positive mood or convert a negative mood to positive one, music will be the medicament in this healing process. This study aimed to match music with the right mood type, and thus create a favourable music mood application, DeMuse to verify this relationship. The result will be collected after tested by the selected samples. The selected sample will be the university student from Universiti Malaysia Sabah (UMS).

2 Related Studies

Many studies showed different methods in handling the stress level. However, most of the results depend on the samplings taken. According to the study conducted by [6], common stressors that affect the university students are normally came from education, financial problems, and surrounding environment. As university students frequently expose to these kind of negative stressors, this greatly twisted a student's daily lifestyle, in which the bonding among family members and friends, academic and physical performance could be ended up in negative way. A research conducted by [6] which is a cross sectional study among study samples in Pakistan, which include Pharm-D junior students (first year students) and senior students (fifth year students). The questionnaire applied considered two parts, demographic characteristics, and perceived stress scale (PSS) that consists of 14 questions about stressors and strategies to cope the stressors.

The result in Fig. 1 shows that most of the students willing to share and discuss the problems with their family or friends in order to relief stress. According to the observation and result of PSS, [6] concluded that different stressors is handled with different strategies. Hence, the students' responses towards some coping strategies would be different than others (Fig. 2).

According to the study of [7], the stressors that university students in UMS are mainly came from academic studies that are tremendously high in workload. A set of questionnaire had been distributed among the study samples of 30 students. It

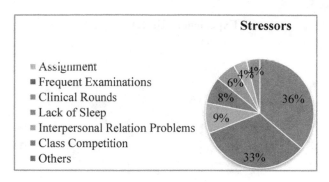

Fig. 1. Frequencies of stressors [6]

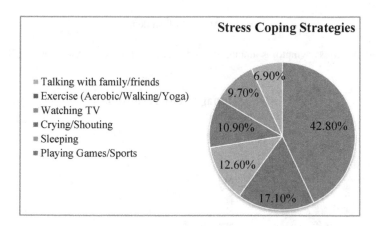

Fig. 2. Stress coping strategies [6]

comprises three parts, which includes demographic, symptoms of stress, and stress management techniques. The related result had shown in the following figures (Figs. 3 and 4).

Based on the result analysed, a large number of study subjects would feel tired and fatigued since this particular symptom ranked top among others with 22 (Fig. 3). According to Fig. 4, most of the sample subjects chose surfing Internet and go online as their primary stress management technique, which achieved 26. Listening to music and playing video game have achieved 25 and 24 respectively in which makes both ranked second and third place.

In the conclusion, listening to music would be the key of this study. This decision had made based on some reasons. First, the target sample subjects applied. The target study subjects were university students from UMS and it is equal same as the study sample of [7] research. Since the characteristics such as aged group, cultural background, and academic environment are same; it would greatly increase the accuracy if the identification of stress management technique refers to the result provided. According to the result of stress management techniques [7], listening to music is a

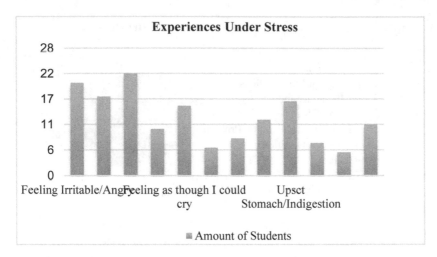

Fig. 3. Stress symptoms among 30 study samples (Sources: Aslina et al. [7])

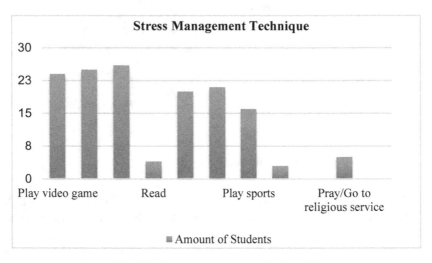

Fig. 4. Stress management technique [7]

choice after the surfing Internet. [8] stated that many Internet users enjoy with its positive aspects, such as informative stuff, convenient, entertainment, and resourcefulness. As the result, surfing Internet or go online might be an action that is too general or common, and this atmosphere causes hard to focus in studying. As an individual listening to music, it could assist in alleviate the anxieties and stress, and thus relief the pain [9]. Furthermore, anyone who listen to the music able to regulate their emotion in order to get rid of stress [10]. Hence, the case that "listening to music" has become the primary option in this study.

According to Google, the most popular mobile application in the year of 2014 was the category in terms of health and fitness [11]. This is a concluded result after collected the data from Google Play Store, and health and fitness categorised applications have been chose after conducted an end-of-year rundown. Since the meditation and stress relieved type mobile application is being categorised in the theme of health and fitness, a mobile application named DeMuse would be developed throughout this study, with the analysed result of features and relationship between music and mood.

3 Methodology

To comprehend and determine the suitable music and mood categories, the quantitative method were applied in order to collect the related data among university students in UMS. In this study, questionnaires were designed in purpose and distributed in order to study their habits, relationship between music and emotion, and the influences level of their favourite genre of music in daily life.

A set of questionnaire is the quantitative method used on the target samples, in order to obtain and record some useful information on the particular issue of interest [12]. Based on the view of [13], the reason questionnaire known as one of the effective analytic way is that the condition of face-to-face and target sample to complete the questionnaire section independently could be achieved. Hence, this condition turns to construct a structured interview basis. Indeed, this would promise a list of worded and structured questions in the priority of balancing the requirements asked, either in paper or electronic form.

Based on the study of [12], the "piloting questionnaire" will be the most qualified and suitable questionnaires' style. This is because the only target was come from a university, named UMS. At the same time, the samples that stayed in the range among 19 to 24 aged groups will be an element that takes into consideration. Thus, these specifications were the meaning of piloting properties doubtlessly, which consider small group of respondent samples. This method will be operated in paper form. In the process of face-to-face reviews, the rate of misunderstanding error would be minimized as well as responding time. In addition to increase the accuracy of result, a number of different faculties in UMS will be involved.

3.1 Participants

The study samples will be taken randomly from university students of UMS. The number of study samples had achieved 148 students, which consists of 71 male and 77 female. Among these students, there are 34 first years, 49 second year, 43 third years, and 22 fourth year students respectively had participated in this questionnaire section.

4 Analysis and Results

According to the results of the quantitative methods applied on 148 study samples, almost all respondents felt that music greatly affects respective emotional status. Target samples believed that music only would benefits daily activities and life. This phenomenon also could be explained by the study of [4] on the relationship among different music types and different mood status based on the Personal Feelings Survey (PFS) results, which indicated that a same person could be stayed in different varieties of emotional status after listened to different music genre.

Meanwhile, respondents would like to listen to certain music in order to switch respective emotional status to the positive level. Since [3] stated the existence of the relationship between positive emotion and the way in minimizing negative stress level, related questions would be applied on the study samples in order to understand respective musical behaviour.

According to the results analysed that showed in Figs. 5 and 6 respectively, pop music took the highest popularity among the study samples, in corresponding of 68 numeric numbers or 46% study samples listening to pop music daily, and 49 numeric numbers or 33% study samples listening to pop music for stress relieving purpose. These results certainly define the pop music as the master key in increasing the positive level of emotion and mind behaviour, and directly decrease the level of negative stress. This might respond to the reason that most of the UMS students listening to the pop music in daily life. Based on the study of [14], two thirds of local students experienced stressful life as long as educate in the local university. Thus, there is no doubt that UMS student using the power of music in the purpose of reducing stressful life respectively. According to the study result of [4], the reports mentioned that adult of the 25–54 aged group would likely listening to the music genre of country and new age in increasing relaxation and decreasing tension purpose. Thus, the variation of music genre would occur according to the changing trend of aged group.

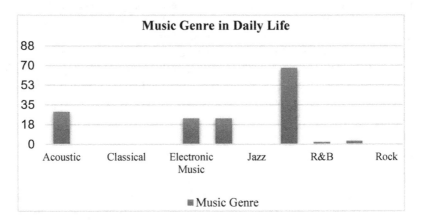

Fig. 5. Statistical result of music genre that listening most in everyday life

Although the target samples highly voted the pop music, music still can be categorised into various ways. One of the ways is the lyrics song and the vocal on or off does matter in listening. The related question had been applied in this quantitative method. After interview conducted well, 70% of respondents prefer music with lyrics and hence vocal music (Fig. 7).

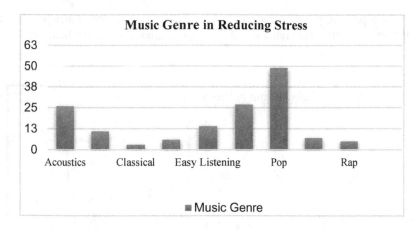

Fig. 6. Statistical result of music genre that listening most in relieving stress

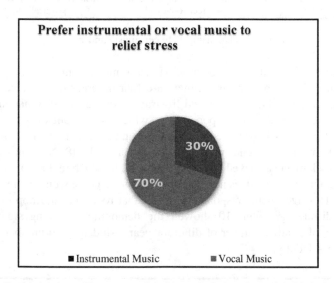

Fig. 7. Determination of instrumental (without lyrics) and vocal (with lyrics) music

Again based on the study of [4], the study samples could affect respective emotional status when listening to the music. According to the Figs. 8 and 9, the effects of the relationship between music and mood in the aspect of emotional memories, someone to feel conveyed, and someone tends to physically move; the similarity is that the agree option voted as the highest number. In this case, these trends are greatly showed that different music types with different tempo or beats per minute (bpm) would affect the level of physiological effects applied on the body. Music with fast tempo, 120 to 130 bpm could increase heartbeat rate and blood pressure, whereas music with slow tempo, 50 to 60 bpm could decrease heartbeat rate and blood pressure

[15]. In the aspect of physical movement, previous research recommended that the higher the music tempo, the higher the physiological arousal level and hence causes an increment of active rate [16].

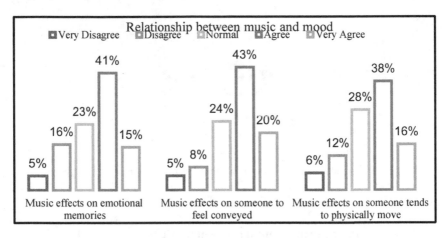

Fig. 8. Relationship between music and mood

Furthermore, [4] stated that different variation of music genre could cause different emotional status. Based on the Fig. 9, there are four different mood behaviour stated, which are happiness, sadness, anger, and frustration. In the aspect of happiness status, most of the study samples chose pop music, which are 74 out of total 148. In the sadness aspect, jazz music occupied the highest number, which is 64 out of total 148; and then blues music in second, which are 27 out of total 148. Next, in the aspect of anger status, rock music achieved 50 out of total 148, in which ranked top. Lastly, there are quite a lot of respondent does not aware which music genre would annoy the feeling respectively. However, some respondent's feels that rock, and hip hop or rap music genre quite disturbing. Figure 10 showed the demographic among study samples, which consists of gender, number of different year's students and number of students among different faculty.

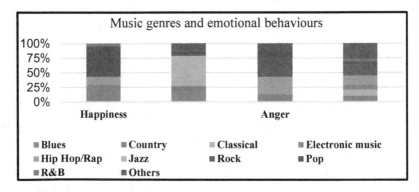

Fig. 9. Effects of music genres towards emotional behaviours

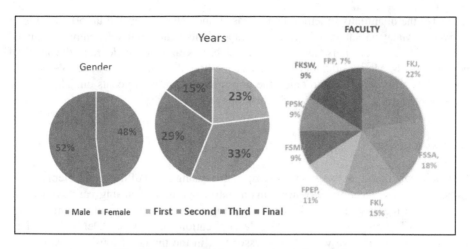

Fig. 10. Demographic among the study samples

5 Discussion

Based on the sections mentioned before, it could be summarized that listening to the pop, vocal music would be the favour of UMS students in coping daily stressful life. Hence, a representative app, which is known as "DeMuse" will be developed for the target users.

Indeed, [17] defined that, "Stress is often described as a feeling of being overloaded, wound-up tight, tense and worried". This statement had informed that stress would be anywhere, anytime as long as people moving toward negative emotion status. Ironically, this phenomenon will always be there only if certain situations occurred had altered the emotional behaviour of somebody. Normally, these kinds of situations are tougher enough to handle. Most of these condition able to depress an individual and turns to become a stressful obstacle. If any high authorization, jurisdiction, government or even a smaller scale of societies, family and personal individual are try shutting eyes to these sickness, it will be not a stranger anymore but a fallen angel that could threaten the pure Mother Nature's humanities and life.

However, many studies have found out a number of ways in order to calm down the outrage of "stress", such as regular exercise, communicating with family and friends, shouting, playing video games, watching television, surfing Internet, and listening to music [6, 7]. Since there are numerous ways to relief stress, "listening to music" will be the bible of this study in order to proof its value of authenticity. In order to maintain a positive mood to cope with the stressful situation, music is one of the choices to get rid of negative mood. Obviously, music often used to change the emotion status or become better, and also afford to make certain people in accomplishing the current works [10]. Based on several studies, [18] found out the ability of music to function as a stress management tools. Patients were deceasing the anxiety and stress level, and a lower blood pressure result was showed during the patients listening to music in order to wait for surgery subjectively [18].

After the quantitative method had released and interviewed a total 50 students of Universiti Malaysia Sabah (UMS), many respondents believed that listening to suitable music able to soothe personal individual's feelings and hence degrade the level of negative stress. Meanwhile, this quantitative method also finds out that people in 19 to 24 aged groups were likely to enjoy the pop music genre with vocals on. This will be the key element in this application's development.

6   Conclusion

In conclusion, based on the previous studies, increasing trend of health problem mainly came from stress faced in daily life. This negative symptoms causing various methods to minimize this negative trend, such as surfing Internet, playing video games, exercising, and listening to music. A Mobile application, namely as "DeMuse" will be develop as an alternative way of de-stressor that in the theme of music. DeMuse will consists of meditation properties, some sentences of guidance instruction would applied to ease users in understanding the steps. Furthermore, some different relaxation types would applied for users to choose as the relieving stress purposes. A sentence of inspiration quote would show at the bottom position of DeMuse application. Since DeMuse is a music mood application, the general features of a music media player such as option lists of music, and create personal playlists should be added. Through the development of DeMuse, users may able to reduce their stress in everywhere. Since the overall music and emotion categories are mainly concern with the UMS students, these arrangements and relationships will be again obtained from users as further improvement purpose. Furthermore, the features applied in "DeMuse" will be modified in order to make users experience it in more simple way. Lastly, "DeMuse", which is the product of this study, is willingly to be an alternative way in coping with this negative stress.

References

1. Klinic Community Health Centre: Stress & Stress Management (2010). http://hydesmith.com/de-stress/files/StressMgt.pdf. Accessed 23 June 2017
2. Bolger, N., DeLongis, A., Kessler, R.C., Schilling, E.A.: Effect of daily stress on negative mood. J. Pers. Soc. Psychol. 57(5), 808–818 (1989)
3. Ong, A.D., Bergeman, C.S., Bisconti, T.L., Wallace, K.A.: Psychological resilience, positive emotions, and successful adaptation to stress in later life. J. Pers. Soc. Psychol. 91, 730–749 (2006)
4. McCraty, R., Barrios-Choplin, B., Rozman, D., Atkinson, M., Watkins, A.D.: The impact of a new emotional self-management program on stress, emotions, heart rate variability, DHEA and cortisol. Integr. Physiol. Behav. Sci. 33(2), 151–170 (1998)
5. Lee, J.H., Hu, X.: Cross-cultural similarities and differences in music mood perception. In: iConference 2014 Proceedings, pp. 259–269 (2014)
6. Yasmin, R., Asim, S.S., Ali, H., Quds, T., Zafar, F.: Prevalence of perceived stress among pharmacy students in Pakistan. Int. J. Pharm. Sci. Rev. Res. (55), 343–347 (2013)

7. Aslina, B., Minshen, C., Siti Hasnah, T., Nurul-Hidayah, M.Z., Mohd-Nabil, Z., Emelia, A.R., Muhammad, O.: Stress monitoring using mobile phone and wearable technology: stress catcher. J. Telecommun. Electron. Comput. Eng. (JTEC) (2017). Special Issue (ISSN 2180 1843, e-ISSN 2289 8131), Universiti Teknikal Malaysia Melaka (UTeM), Melaka, Malaysia

8. Alam, S.S., Hashim, N.M.H.N., Ahmad, M., Wel, C.A.C., Nor, S.M., Omar, N.A.: Negative and positive impact of internet addiction on young adults: empirical study in Malaysia. Intang. Cap. **10**(3), 619–638 (2014)

9. Nilsson, U.: The anxiety- and pain-reducing effects of music interventions: a systematic review. AORN J. **87**(4), 780–807 (2008)

10. Chami, A.: Daily uses of music in mood management. MSc in music psychology, module 2, option 5 (2003)

11. Boxall, A.: Is the year of health and fitness apps, says Google (2014). http://www.digitaltrends. com/mobile/google-play-store-2014-most-downloaded-apps/. Accessed October 2016

12. Kirklees, C.: Research and consultation guidelines: focus groups (2014). https://www. kirklees.gov.uk/community/yoursay/questionnaires.pdf. Accessed November 2016

13. Roddy, K., Allsop, L.: Creating Effective Questionnaires and Surveys and Analyzing the Data (2006). https://www.google.com/url?sa=t&rct=j&q=&esrc=s&source=web&cd=2&cad rja&uact=8&ved=0ahUKEwjcgveu-tDQAhWDFZQKHZiBCCYQFgglMAE&url=http%3A %2F%2Fwww.lse.ac.uk%2Flibrary%2Fversions%2FCreating%2520effective%2520questio nnaires%2520and%2520surveys.pdf&usg=AFQjCNGbEu0BDySn_fqkZCgC7mW_rCQQ8 Q&sig2=reojrubM6aOUGZg6cF2mtQ&bvm=bv.139782543,d.dGo. Accessed November 2016

14. Borg, C., Cefai, C.: Stress, health and coping among international students at the University of Malta (2014). https://www.um.edu.mt/__data/assets/pdf_file/0005/223583/International students_monograph_final_version.pdf. Accessed November 2016

15. Edworthy, J., Waring, H.: The effects of music tempo and loudness level on treadmill exercise. Ergonomics **49**(15), 1597–1610 (2006)

16. Karageorghis, C.I., Jones, L., Low, D.C.: Relationship between exercise heart rate and music tempo preference. Res. Q. Exerc. Sport **77**(2), 240–250 (2006)

17. Australian Psychological Society: Understanding and managing stress, Melbourne, Australia (2012). https://www.psychology.org.au/assets/Files/StressTipSheet.pdf. Accessed January 2016

18. Kent, D.: The Effect of Music on the Human Body and Mind (2006). https://www.google. com/url?sa=t&rct=j&q=&esrc=s&source=web&cd=1&cad=rja&uact=8&ved=0ahUKEwi11 LbZ5djPAhVCRo8KHWRrA9YQFggcMAA&url=http%3A%2F%2Fdigitalcommons.libert y.edu%2Fcgi%2Fviewcontent.cgi%3Farticle%3D1162%26context%3Dhonors&usg=AFQj CNFlTtN0FQeH2XG4HNlUXdoqY8h5Dw&sig2=CW_MPtDK7yJqYtE04FLXtQ&bvm= bv.135475266,d.c2I. Accessed October 2016

Game Interface Design: Measuring the Player's Gameplay Experience

Ibrahim Ahmad[1(✉)], Erman Hamid[1], Nazreen Abdullasim[1],
and Azizah Jaafar[2]

[1] Universiti Teknikal Malaysia Melaka,
76100 Durian Tunggal, Melaka, Malaysia
{ibrahim,erman,nazreen.abdullasim}@utem.edu.my
[2] Institute of Visual Informatics, UKM, 65000 Bangi, Selangor, Malaysia
azizahj@ukm.my

Abstract. The objective of this study is to investigate the effects of user's gameplay experience on the generated game interface design. This paper focuses only on the findings from a conducted questionnaire involving 94 users who utilized the game interface design of "A Garuda". The seven factors observed from the gaming experience are immersion, flow, challenge, tension, competence, positive and negative affect adapted from the Game Experience Questionnaire (GEQ). The results showed that the game interface design produced has showed a lot of positive factor where the positive affect factor gave a higher mean value compared to the other factor of the gaming experience. The results from the t-test showed the effect of positive factors and the negative factors of the user's game experience, where there is a significant impact towards both aforementioned factors. However, there is also a high impact on the negative factor resulting from the effect of user's interaction on the related game interface design. This shows that the related interface design still needs to be improved in the future. The outcome of this study gives significance to game designers that they should take into account of the user's affective effect towards any game interface designs that they produced.

Keywords: Game experiences · GEQ · Game interface design

1 Introduction

Famous researcher in the field of affective computing, Picard [1] defined affective computing as "computing related to, 'arises from emotion' or 'deliberately influencing emotions'. Affective computing is a field in which its disciplines include computer science, psychology, and cognitive science [2]. Picard explained that the affective computing system must have several capacities: 1. recognition, 2. expressing, or 3. having emotions [3]. The aim of this is to focus on creating a computing system that has the ability to significantly detect, recognize and understand after a positive intervention from the state without intervention [4].

The first step in designing a good computer game is to understand how to design user emotions that can be produced from the game Lazzaro in Bateman [5]. Numerous

© Springer International Publishing AG 2017
H. Badioze Zaman et al. (Eds.): IVIC 2017, LNCS 10645, pp. 500–509, 2017.
https://doi.org/10.1007/978-3-319-70010-6_46

studies on the design and development of computer game applications have been carried out. However, studies related to basic computer game design that particularly involve the user affective elements are less likely to be received. This is because it requires detailed research on the aspects of social, emotional and other relevance to human life. When designers want to use the appropriate method or technique to design computer games that are associated with human social needs, they have special constraints to make it work. They lack the appropriate methods and techniques for developing complex user-centered designs other than conducting tests and assessments [6, 7].

2 Affective and Game Design

In the case of affective studies, Pagulayan et al. [8] and IJsselsteijn et al. [9] has discussed some of the differences between entertainment and productivity-oriented applications in detail.

- First, in productivity-oriented applications, constraints are eliminated as much as possible, but obstacles in entertainment games are created deliberately in order to challenge the player.
- Second, in games, the process of playing moves on its own, the rewards received are intrinsic in nature, and do not rely on yeild-based rewards that are always applied in productivity-oriented applications.
- Third, productivity-oriented applications strive for constant consistency; this is different to entertainment application like games that drives more towards creating various gameplay experiences.
- Fourth, there are various input devices to interact with game (such as simulated weapons, computer vision input like Sony Eye Toy or acceleration and sensation positioning like Nintendo Wii) than in productivity application that usually only use the keyboard and mouse.
- Fifth, the use of sound and graphics in productivity applications serves to communicate the function, while in games it works to create a fascinating environment as well as to support the narrative of the game and users to trigger immersive senses.

As a game designer, we cannot design the game interface in a direct manner. We can only design the rules that cause the experience to occur. Game designers are capable of producing experience but only indirectly [10, 11]. This is due to the reason that emotions are directly related to a person's goals, it is always involved in the player's experience, regardless of whether the designer is aware of it or not [5].

A design can be made to support different game activities but it is more difficult to trigger accurate reactions or restrict specific game patterns. In its inherent nature, the design does not have a logical outcome, therefore, no sequence of operations will guarantee the end result [11, 12].

Gilleade et al. [13], Ermi and Mäyrä [14] in De Castell and Jenson [15] and IJsselsteijn et al. [16] agree to the statement that explained that there are differences between frustration to the game and in the game, where the frustration towards the game essentially involves difficulty with the user interface, for example unresponsive to input devices, unimpressive and weak interactions with tools that are used.

Frustration to the game clearly breaks the player flow, and it should be improved by applying user-centered design principles to the game interface design.

Most of the studies in the field of gaming experience, in which it can be observed as a subjective relationship between the players and the game itself, are carried out in a controlled environment [17, 18]. Despite an increase in the field of game research, the actual experience of playing digital games is still poorly represented in literature review of games. Existing researches in gameplay experience are mostly centered on one dimension of gaming experience, such as flow or immersive. As such, the writing of current literature reviews of gameplay experiences are split up [19].

Therefore, we see the need to develop a "self-report" measurement for gameplay experiences, covering the wide spectrum for experiences caused by digital games [16]. Even so, Poels et al. [19] viewed that it is impossible to develop any instrument without a comprehensive conceptual for gameplay experiences that can act as a framework to formulate the mentioned "self-report".

Aside from looking at the emotional aspect of users in evaluating the effect of he generated computer game interface design, the need to observe from user's affective angle, especially from the gameplay experience aspect can also be used as an indicator for the competence of interface design produced.

From the aspect of gameplay experience shown by the users, this study uses seven factors: immersive, flow, competencies, tension, challenge, positive affective and negative affective. Based on the questionnaires adapted from the game experience questionnaire (GEQ), the results of user affective towards the design of the computer game interface produced have been able to make a significant impact in this study. Because, according to Poels et al. [20], most researchers lack the appropriate methods to measure specific entertainment experiences in determining the accurate emotional level, the approach to analyzing user game experiences can also help researches to reinforce the findings obtained from studies related to the user's emotional effect on a design that is produced.

Another method that can be used to detect emotional presence is through the changes in voice and facial expressions [21]. For example, the views expressed in the study of Gilleade et al. [13] mentioned, if the user is playing RPG games, and the player's frustration increases, the researcher should

- identify the probable causes that cause intrinsic frustration towards the game design,
- evaluate the current status of the player in the game,
- then pick the cause that most possibly is the cause if frustration and,
- adjust the game to correct the fault (for example, if the frustration starts to rise and the game finds that the user is still trying to find the suitable antidote, it will drive the player with an indication to the cause of the frustration.

Brown and Cairns [22], Al Mahmud et al. [23] and Johnson et al. [24] said one of the dimensions of user experience, which is immersive, can be defined as the level of player engagement in the game. A player responded as follows in their qualitative interviews; "The game allow me to connect deeper with myself and I think I went deeper into the game".

Jennett et al. [25], Nacke [26], Cox et al. [27] and Kappen et al. [28] describes flow as an optimum process of experience, which is the situation in which individual involved engaged in an activity that feels nothing else is more interesting than the said activity.

In the year 1990, Csikszentmihaly has presented all eight components of flow, which are a clear goal; high level of concentration; loss of self-awareness (feeling calm); feel distorted by time; direct and immediate feedback; balance between skill levels and challenges; feel of satisfying personal intrinsic control [25, 26, 29, 30].

To measure the level of user gameplay experience, IJsselsteijn et al. [16] has developed and performed a validation to a questionnaire that was named Game Experience Survey (GEQ). This questionnaire was used to identify the differences between the seven dimensions that differ on the level of user gameplay experience, namely sensory and imaginative immersive, Tension, Competencies, Flow, Negative Affective, Positive Affective, and Challenges [16, 19, 31–33].

Based on studies conducted by previous researchers on use of technology and its effect on user emotions, it would be appropriate if the study was conducted on a computer game interface design and observation on the emotional aspects of the user is done while looking at the design impact on the field of human computer interaction, such as usability, effectiveness, satisfaction and efficiency.

At the same time, the weaknesses in the field of computer game design can be supported with the involvement of the affective computing field through this study can give a positive impact to the world of computer games.

3   Research Design

The entire study in this project uses the User Centered Game Design (UCGD) model pioneered by Rankin et al. [34] as the methodology of the study. The original model for UCGD was founded by Fullerton et al. [35] which was then improved by Rankin and his colleagues. In the fourth phase of the playtesting phase, testing was performed to determine the effectiveness of the design of the game interface produced.

3.1   Methods

A study was conducted on 94 users who have utilized the designated game interface. The game, named "A Garuda", is a RPG genre game where the main character carried a responsibility to save his kidnapped child.

The criteria of RPG game that were implemented into the game design such as dialogue, combat, mini map and etc., with the purpose for allowing user to be able to interact with the whole respective game design.

Figure 1 displays a screen capture and the user's face while interacting with the game interface design. Apart from the study to identify game experience factors, this study also examines the effect of user's emotions on game interface design. However, the focus of this paper is simply to illustrate the findings of the game experience aspect only.

For the purpose of obtaining data about the gameplay experience for users using the prototype design of the game interface produced, a set of questionnaire called Game Experience Questionanaire (GEQ) was used in this study. This questionnaire was

Fig. 1. Screen capture from video recorded while user play the games

adapted from Al Mahmud et al. [23], Nacke [26], Brockmyer et al. [36], IJsselsteijn et al. [37] and Nacke [30] in their study. This questionnaire contains seven factors related to immersive, flow, competencies, tension, challenge, positive affective and negative affective.

The Likert measurement scale has been used in this questionnaire and it is divided into 5 sections which are 1 to 5. The part or scale 1 represents the "none at all" and the 5 scale represents the "very likely" statement of each item in the aforementioned questionnaire.

3.2   Gathering Data

To analyze the gameplay experience of a user that uses the computer game interface design produced, the quantitative data obtained through the gameplay experience questionnaire has been analyzed descriptively. This is done by looking for the mean and standard deviation values according to the seven specified factors. Data that has been analyzed is then presented in the data table.

Based on the data analysis obtained, the discussion then focuses to the factors that have the highest mean and lowest mean value. In addition, the items of factors are analyzed and seen in two angles of factors, namely positive and negative factors. Next, the conclusion about each factor that are tested will be summarized.

4 Result and Discussion

4.1 Result

From the questionnaire for the demographic section, 94 respondents were involved, in which 28 respondents were men and the remaining were 66 women. Of these numbers of respondents, 10 respondents were aged between 15 and 17 years old, 67 were aged between 18 and 23, 11 were between 24 and 27 years and the remaining 6 were between 28 and 35 years old. The findings also found that 27 respondents played games on a daily basis. 16 people play once a week, while a total of 43 people play occasional and 8 respondents rarely play.

The results of data analysis related to the level of user gameplay experience are obtained through user game experience questionnaire. Tables 1 and 2 show the mean value and the standard deviation for the findings obtained from the related questionnaire.

Table 1. Mean value for positive factor

Factor	Mean	SD
Immersive	3.28	0.16
Flow	3.16	0.46
Competencies	3.29	0.21
Positive affective	3.40	0.21

Table 2. Mean value for negative factor

Factor	Mean	SD
Challenge	2.28	0.41
Tension	2.45	0.14
Negative affective	2.33	01.7

In this user's gameplay experience questionnaire, there are two different factors which is a factor that looks similar to a positive-form factorare Immersive, Flow, Competencies, Challenge and Positive Affective, meanwhile there are two factors that are seen as negative factors which are Tension and Negative Affective.

Based on Table 1, it is notable that the highest mean value is for positive affective factor with the value of 3.40 while the lowest mean value is 2.33 which is the mean value of the negative affective factor. Other positive factors also show a high mean value compared to the negative factors.

The mean value of the Immersive factor is 3.28, the mean value of the Flow factor is 3.16, the mean value of the Competencies factor is 3.29 while the mean value of the Challenge factor is 3.28. All these factors have a mean value of more than 3.00 which means the factors being above the moderate level (in the designated Likert scale) for their opinion on the user's gameplay experience rather thanthe design of the computer games being played.

For negative factors, apart from negative affective factors, the mean value obtained is 2.45 which is for tensile factor, that indicate a small value (in the designated likert scale) for their views on user gameplay experience rather than the computer game design being played. The t-Test was conducted on all the analyzed factors, the results showed that there was a significant difference between the two factors that were seen, such as the positive factor and negative factor. Table 2 shows the data analysis that has been obtained.

Table 3. t-Test analysis

Factors	Mean	P
Positive	3.27	0.000
Negative	2.34	

Based on Table 3, it can be seen that the overall mean of the positive factor is 3.27 while the mean value of the overall negative factor is 2.34. From Table 3, there were significant differences between positive factor (M = 3.27, SD = 0.098) and negative factor (M = 2.34, SD = 0.087) given that: t (92) = 0.801, P = 0.00. The results show that the significant value obtained (P = 0.000) is less than the prescribed value of significance (P < 0.05). This shows that the computer game interface design created poses more positive effects on user's gameplay experience.

4.2   Discussion

To analyze the data for the findings from the player experience questionnaire. It can be seen from two factors which are the positive and negative factors. Positive factors consist of five factors, namely immersive, flow, competencies, challenge and positive affective, while negative factors are tension and negative affective factors.

Based on Table 1, it is found that the positive characteristic value has a mean value greater than 3.00 while the negative factor has a value less than 3.00. For positive factors, the value obtained is 3.28 for immersive factors, 3.16 for flow factor, 3.29 for competencies factor, 3.28 for challenge factor and 3.40 for positive affective factor. For the negative factor, the mean value obtained is 2.45 for tension factor and 2.33 for negative affective factor. The findings of this study are consistent with what IJsselsteijn et al. [16] and Nacke et al. [38] who looked at all these factors in their study. They found that the impact of positive factors has a high mean value of which the generated game design has a positive impact on user gameplay experience. In a study conducted by Nacke et al. [38], comparisons were made with a study made by Shilling et al. [39]. He finds that the results of his studies are contrary to the study conducted by Shilling et al. [39] who found that the mean value of a positive factor was not necessarily high as was obtained by Nacke et al. [38]. However, the study by Nacke et al. [38] is in line with the findings of previous studies such as Ravaja et al. [40], Lindley et al. [41], IJsselsteijn et al. [16] and Livingston et al. [42].

In addition, a study conducted by Poels et al. [19] and Poels et al. [20] on children as well as the enjoyment of the user on the computer game interface design found that there was significant high mean value with positive factors such as immersive, flow, competencies and positive affective in their research findings. The mean value obtained for the positive factor exceeded the mean value of 4.00, which indicated a sign of agreement on the relationship between the game used and the tendency for positive user gameplay experience. This was then reinforced by the study conducted by Nacke et al. [38] and IJsselsteijn et al. [37]. They have discovered that there was a significant relationship between the user gameplay experience and the positive factors found in the questionnaire through their study.

Based on the discussion that has been made, it can be said that the user's gameplay experience that is categorized as a positive factor has a greater effect on the design of the interface produced.

5 Conclusion

Relevancy between interface design and game experience gives the designers a bigger impression to think of something meaningful. Based on the findings, players are very concerned about the immersive and the flow of which gives the player a sense of mood to better feel while playing the game.

Apart from research related to game experience, research is also suggested to look at the effects of game design on user emotions. This is also very important from the point of play satisfaction to the user.

References

1. Picard, R.W.: Affective Computing (1995)
2. Tao, J., Tan, T.: Affective computing: a review. In: Tao, J., Tan, T., Picard, R.W. (eds.) ACII 2005. LNCS, vol. 3784, pp. 981–995. Springer, Heidelberg (2005). doi:10.1007/11573548_125
3. Chen, G.-S., Lee, M.-F.: Detecting emotion model in e-learning system. In: 2012 International Conference on Machine Learning and Cybernetics (ICMLC), pp. 1686–1691 (2012)
4. Rezazadeh, I.M., Wang, X., Firoozabadi, M., Golpayegani, M.R.H.: Using affective human–machine interface to increase the operation performance in virtual construction crane training system: a novel approach. Autom. Constr. **20**, 289–298 (2011)
5. Bateman, C.: Beyond Game Design: Nine Steps Toward Creating Better Videogames. Cengage Learning (2009)
6. Karat, J., Karat, C.-M.: The evolution of user-centered focus in the human-computer interaction field. IBM Syst. J. **42**, 532–541 (2003)
7. Nielsen, J., Christiansen, N., Levinsen, K., Nielsen, L., Yssing, C., Ørngreen, R., Clemmensen, T.: The human being in the 21. st century,-design perspectives on the representation of users in IS development. In: Proceedings of OZCHI 2004 (2004)
8. Pagulayan, R.J., Keeker, K., Wixon, D., Romero, R.L., Fuller, T.: User-Centered Design in Games. CRC Press, Boca Raton (2002)
9. IJsselsteijn, W., De Kort, Y., Poels, K., Jurgelionis, A., Bellotti, F.: Characterising and measuring user experiences in digital games. In: International Conference on Advances in Computer Entertainment Technology, p. 27 (2007)

10. Kuittinen, J., Kultima, A., Niemelä, J., Paavilainen, J.: Casual games discussion. In: Proceedings of the 2007 Conference on Future Play, pp. 105–112 (2007)

11. Kultima, A., Stenros, J.: Designing games for everyone: the expanded game experience model. In: Proceedings of the International Academic Conference on the Future of Game Design and Technology, pp. 66–73 (2010)

12. Drachen, A.: Behavioral telemetry in games user research. In: Bernhaupt, R. (ed.) Game User Experience Evaluation. HIS, pp. 135–165. Springer, Cham (2015). doi:10.1007/978-3-319-15985-0_7

13. Gilleade, K., Dix, A., Allanson, J.: Affective videogames and modes of affective gaming: assist me, challenge me, emote me. In: DiGRA 2005: Changing Views–Worlds in Play (2005)

14. Ermi, L., Mäyrä, F.: Fundamental components of the gameplay experience: analysing immersion. In: Worlds in Play: International Perspectives on Digital Games Research, vol. 37 (2005)

15. De Castell, S., Jenson, J.: Worlds in Play: International Perspectives on Digital Games Research, vol. 21. Peter Lang (2007)

16. IJsselsteijn, W., Van Den Hoogen, W., Klimmt, C., De Kort, Y., Lindley, C., Mathiak, K., Poels, K., Ravaja, N., Turpeinen, M., Vorderer, P.: Measuring the experience of digital game enjoyment. In: Proceedings of Measuring Behavior, pp. 88–89 (2008)

17. Moser, C., Fuchsberger, V., Tscheligi, M.: Rapid assessment of game experiences in public settings. In: Proceedings of the 4th International Conference on Fun and Games, pp. 73–82 (2012)

18. Oksanen, K.: Subjective experience and sociability in a collaborative serious game. Simul. Gaming **44**, 767–793 (2013)

19. Poels, K., De Kort, Y., Ijsselsteijn, W.: It is always a lot of fun!: exploring dimensions of digital game experience using focus group methodology. In: Proceedings of the 2007 Conference on Future Play, pp. 83–89 (2007)

20. Poels, K., Ijsselsteijn, W., de Kort, Y.: Development of the kids game experience questionnaire. In: Proceedings of Meaningful Play (2008)

21. Merkx, P., Truong, K.P., Neerincx, M.A.: Inducing and measuring emotion through a multiplayer first-person shooter computer game. In: Proceedings of the Computer Games Workshop, pp. 6–7 (2007)

22. Brown, E., Cairns, P.: A grounded investigation of game immersion. In: CHI 2004 Extended Abstracts on Human Factors in Computing Systems, pp. 1297–1300 (2004)

23. Al Mahmud, A., Mubin, O., Shahid, S., Martens, J.-B.: Designing and evaluating the tabletop game experience for senior citizens. In: Proceedings of the 5th Nordic Conference on Human-Computer Interaction: Building Bridges, pp. 403–406 (2008)

24. Johnson, D., Nacke, L.E., Wyeth, P.: All about that base: differing player experiences in video game genres and the unique case of moba games. In: Proceedings of the 33rd Annual ACM Conference on Human Factors in Computing Systems, pp. 2265–2274 (2015)

25. Jennett, C., Cox, A.L., Cairns, P., Dhoparee, S., Epps, A., Tijs, T., Walton, A.: Measuring and defining the experience of immersion in games. Int. J. Hum.-Comput. Stud. **66**, 641–661 (2008)

26. Nacke, L.: Affective ludology: scientific measurement of user experience in interactive entertainment. Blekinge Institute of Technology (2009)

27. Cox, A., Cairns, P., Shah, P., Carroll, M.: Not doing but thinking: the role of challenge in the gaming experience. In: Proceedings of the SIGCHI Conference on Human Factors in Computing Systems, pp. 79–88 (2012)

28. Kappen, D.L., Mirza-Babaei, P., Johannsmeier, J., Buckstein, D., Robb, J., Nacke, L.E.: Engaged by boos and cheers: the effect of co-located game audiences on social player experience. In: Proceedings of the First ACM SIGCHI Annual Symposium on Computer-Human Interaction in Play, pp. 151–160 (2014)

29. Csikszentmihalyi, M., Csikszentmihalyi, I.S.: Optimal Experience: Psychological Studies of Flow in Consciousness. Cambridge University Press, Cambridge (1992)

30. Nacke, L.E.: An introduction to physiological player metrics for evaluating games. In: Seif El-Nasr, M., Drachen, A., Canossa, A. (eds.) Game Analytics, pp. 585–619. Springer, London (2013). doi:10.1007/978-1-4471-4769-5_26

31. De Kort, Y.A., IJsselsteijn, W.A., Poels, K.: Digital games as social presence technology: development of the Social Presence in Gaming Questionnaire (SPGQ). In: Proceedings of PRESENCE, vol. 195203 (2007)

32. Bellotti, F., Kapralos, B., Lee, K., Moreno-Ger, P., Berta, R.: Assessment in and of serious games: an overview. Adv. Hum.-Comput. Interact. **2013**, 1 (2013)

33. Mirza-Babaei, P., Nacke, L.E., Gregory, J., Collins, N., Fitzpatrick, G.: How does it play better?: exploring user testing and biometric storyboards in games user research. In: Proceedings of the SIGCHI Conference on Human Factors in Computing Systems, pp. 1499–1508 (2013)

34. Rankin, Y.A., McNeal, M.M., Shute, W., Gooch, B.: User centered game design: evaluating massive multiplayer online role playing games for second language acquisition. In: Proceedings of the 2008 ACM SIGGRAPH Symposium on Video Games, pp. 43–49 (2008)

35. Fullerton, T., Swain, C., Hoffman, S.: Game Design Workshop: Designing, Prototyping, & Playtesting Games. CRC Press, Boca Raton (2004)

36. Brockmyer, J.H., Fox, C.M., Curtiss, K.A., McBroom, E., Burkhart, K.M., Pidruzny, J.N.: The development of the game engagement questionnaire: a measure of engagement in video game-playing. J. Exp. Soc. Psychol. **45**, 624–634 (2009)

37. IJsselsteijn, W., De Kort, Y., Poels, K.: The game experience questionnaire: development of a self-report measure to assess the psychological impact of digital games (2013, manuscript in preparation)

38. Nacke, L.E., Grimshaw, M.N., Lindley, C.A.: More than a feeling: measurement of sonic user experience and psychophysiology in a first-person shooter game. Interact. Comput. **22**, 336–343 (2010)

39. Shilling, R., Zyda, M., Wardynski, E.C.: Introducing emotion into military simulation and video game design America's army: operations and VIRTE. In: GAME-ON (2002)

40. Ravaja, N., Saari, T., Turpeinen, M., Laarni, J., Salminen, M., Kivikangas, M.: Spatial presence and emotions during video game playing: does it matter with whom you play? Presence: Teleoperators Virtual Environ. **15**, 381–392 (2006)

41. Lindley, C., Nacke, L., Sennersten, C.: Dissecting play–investigating the cognitive and emotional motivations and affects of computer gameplay. In: 13th International Conference on Computer Games (CGames 2008) (2008)

42. Livingston, I.J., Nacke, L.E., Mandryk, R.L.: The impact of negative game reviews and user comments on player experience. In: ACM SIGGRAPH 2011 Game Papers, p. 4 (2011)

Measuring the Variabilities in the Body Postures of the Children for Early Detection of Autism Spectrum Disorder (ASD)

Ahmed Danial Arif Yaakob and Nur Intan Raihana Ruhaiyem[✉]

School of Computer Sciences, Universiti Sains Malaysia (USM),
11800 Gelugor, Penang, Malaysia
danial.ucom13@student.usm.my, intanraihana@usm.my

Abstract. Presently, the number of children with autism appears to be growing at disturbing rate. Unfortunately, the awareness of early sign of Autism Spectrum Disorder (ASD) is still insufficiently provided to the public. Arm flapping is a good example of a stereotypical behavior of ASD early sign. Typically, a standard Repetitive Behavior Scale-Revised (RBSR) - set of questionnaire - used by clinicians for ASD diagnosis usually involved multiple and long sessions that apparently would delay and may have nonconformity. Thus, we aim to propose a computational framework to semi-automate the diagnosis process. We used human action recognition (HAR) algorithm. HAR involved in human body detection and the skeleton representation to show the arm asymmetrical in arm flapping movement which indicates the possibility of ASD signs by extracting the body pose into stickman model. The proposed framework has been tested against the video clips of children performing arm flapping behavior taken from public dataset. The outcome of this study is expected to detect early sign of ASD based on asymmetry measurement of arm flapping behavior.

Keywords: Autism Spectrum Disorder · ASD early detection · Body postures · Arm flapping · HAR algorithm · Skeleton representation

1 Introduction

Lately, the number of children that had being diagnosed with Autism Spectrum Disorder (ASD) has increased dramatically. According to Centre for Disease Control (CDC) in United States, the rate of occurrence of autism is 1 in 68 children. ASD is a type of neurodevelopmental interference that will affects the mental, emotion, learning and memory of person [1]. It can be characterized by three features which are impairment of social interaction, impairment in communication, and restricted, repetitive and stereotyped pattern of behavior, interests and activities. Due to neurological disorder, autism is a complex developmental disability that interferes with the functioning of the brain [2].

Recently, research shows that children can be diagnosed with autism at least at the age of three [3] and therefore earlier detection is necessary – as early as age of 18 months [4]. Currently, there is no confirmation regarding how autism can affect someone either based on specific race or socioeconomic class because autism can be

© Springer International Publishing AG 2017
H. Badioze Zaman et al. (Eds.): IVIC 2017, LNCS 10645, pp. 510–520, 2017.
https://doi.org/10.1007/978-3-319-70010-6_47

found within both of them [5]. Furthermore, the reason of how autism caused also has not been determined yet. The factor of biological conditions such as biochemical imbalances, neurological damages or genetic accidents might be the cause of autism occur [6]. Therefore, early detection of ASD among children is needed to help in increasing quality of their life and families.

This research will be focusing on the general of autism in children and disorder on upper part of body of children who being diagnosed with autism. At the same time, research on how to detect early signs of autism on upper part of body among children also will be given further analysis. By using video analysis from publicly available unconstrained videos to detect early signs of autism on upper part of body as a method, this research will try to provide a better result on early signs of autism among children particularly on upper part of body postures.

2 Related Work

Several studies have been made regarding the analysis of autistic behaviors in children with ASD using different kind of method or algorithm. The study that has been conducted in by Watson and his colleagues examined the emergence of gesture in 9–12 month old infants, using retrospective analysis of home videotapes [7]. The subject data in this study included one group gathered infants later diagnosed with autism, a second group of infants later diagnosed with other development disabilities; and a third group of typically developing infants in their preschool years. The videotapes used as method were divided into 1-min intervals for the intention of rating gestures. In order to reflect both the quantity and diversity of gestures used in each interval, a rating scale was developed and follows few rules: no clear gestures observed; one gesture used one time; one gesture used more than one time; two or more different gestures, used at least once. In the end, the results of this study propose that it is not possible to differentiate infants who will be later diagnosed with autism based on the quantitative ratings of gesture used.

Furthermore, Goodwin and colleagues developed a system that used wrist-worn accelerometers for recognizing stereotypical movements in individuals with autism [8]. The function of accelerometers is for recording data on movements of the limb. The result shown two types of stereotypical movements which were hand flapping and body rocking was performed with satisfying accuracy in two different environments (classroom and laboratory). Another study from Westeyn and colleagues also used accelerometers with pattern recognition algorithms in pilot work to detect stereotypical motor movements [9]. Results from this study proved that 69% of hand flapping events were automatically and accurately detected in this work by using Hidden Markov Models. However, this work did not observe the children with ASD actually performing the behaviors.

Lastly, Azizul et al. use Human Action Recognition (HAR) techniques to detect the arm flapping in children with ASD by measuring the asymmetry score between both upper arms and forearms of the children [10]. The study has been tested using public dataset that shows arm flapping behavior among children. Results shows that the method combination of human poses estimation and skeleton representation were enough to detect arm asymmetry with the score of accuracy 45°.

3 Research Methodology

Here we propose a computational method to automate the diagnose process of arm flapping for ASD detection by using human action recognition (HAR) techniques also known as human body detection and skeleton representation approach. This technique is a combination of both human body detection and skeleton representation to extract a stickman model on subjects that shows arm flapping movement from public dataset of videos. By using this technique, it can show how a child is considered to possibly showing the early signs of ASD if the arm symmetry score of the child is above required threshold. There are 5 main processes in this technique namely; (1) Extract Frame process, (2) Initial Frame Search Criteria process, (3) Human Body Detection process, (4) Skeleton Graph process and (5) Arm Asymmetry Measurement Process. Figure 1 below shows the methodology.

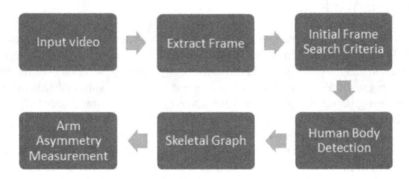

Fig. 1. Human body detection and skeleton representation methodology

3.1 Extract Frame Process

Since the data for this study is obtained from public dataset in term of video clips, so it needs to go through the pre-processed first. This process involves in converting video clips into frames by using cut frame method. We develop the software using Matlab to perform this process. The cutting process takes about 24 s per frame and it cropped to the size of 480×360px by using a laptop with an Intel Core i5 running at 2.5 GHz and 6 GB of RAM. In addition, each frame is cut at every 5 s interval and for each frame; we need to maintain the RGB mode because no filtering can be done to allow consistency in every videos that we choose as our data.

3.2 Initial Frame Search Criteria (IFSC) Process

IFSC is used to search the suitable subject in the frame which is the body pose of children. The further filtering process took place in this process after we obtained all the frames from the video clips. Since we are focusing on detecting arm flapping movement, we need to make sure that the hand of the children is in the part of the frame. Then, the next process is to filter the image frames in order to select the suitable criteria based on the following criteria:

i. We need to make sure that both arms of the subject in the frames are clearly portrayed
ii. We need to choose frames that shows the children performing arm flapping at the highest rate
iii. The subject must be in the frontal view only
iv. Less Gaussion blur discovered in the image
v. RGB mode must be controlled
vi. Need to obtain 5 frames after each selection

3.3 Human Body Detection Process

The function of this process is to ensure human body detection consists in the frame. Since this study will be focusing on upper part of children body to compute arm asymmetry, the body part that must be depicted are the head, torso, left and right upper arms, left and right forearms [11]. In order to define the human body inside the frame, the pictorial structure model is used. Here we briefly review the general framework of pictorial structures for human body detection. Basically, a person's body parts are described by a conditional random field. According to Buehler et al. [12] rectangular image patches can be represented by parts li and their position is parametrized by the location (x, y), orientation θ, scale s, and sometimes foreshortening. Below shows the posterior of a configuration of parts $L = \{li\}$ given an image I is:

$$P(L|I, \Theta) \propto \exp \sum_{(i,j) \in E} \Psi(li, lj) + \sum_i \Phi(I|li, \Theta) \qquad (1)$$

where $\Phi(I|li, \Theta)$ complement to the local image evidence for a part in a particular positon while $\Psi(li, lj)$ corresponds to the prior on the relative position parts such as upper arms must be attached to the torso.

The upper body pictorial structures model subsist of 6 body parts which are torso, head, upper and forearms connected in a tree structure by the kinematic priors $\Psi(li, lj)$. We extend the Eq. 1 above by adding priors' Υ (*lhead*), Υ (*ltorso*) for the orientation of the torso and head:

$$P(L|I, \Theta) \propto \exp \sum_{(i,j) \in E} \Psi(li, lj) + \sum_i \Phi(I|li, \Theta) \qquad (2)$$

where Υ $(\cdot)$ gives uniform probability to the value of θ around vertical and zero probability to other orientations.

3.4 Skeleton Graph Process

In this process, we use the Eshkol-Wachman Notation (EWMN) to adjust the skeleton representation onto the subject's body [13]. It is done manually on each video frame before we proceed to the analysis. The purpose of this method is to extract body pose from the arm asymmetry movement during the arm flapping. The EWMN that we use in this process assumes one general from in human body. In addition, each limb is diminished to its longitudinal axis which is an imaginary straight line with unchanging length. The movement of a single axis of constant length is free to move about one (fixed) end will be confined by a sphere, which means the free end will define a curved path on the surface of this sphere. Furthermore, every limb segment can be described as an axis. Commonly, the curves that are consists on the surface of the sphere will be circles or parts of circles. From the human body representation, we compute a skeleton graph in the frame for analysis. We take the head as our starting point to extract the skeleton graph as we assume the person is in upstanding position. Then, we use the graph matching algorithm as our method to determine the branches and nodes in human joints [14]. The branches can be described in the skeleton point where it possess endpoint and described as junction point. Hence, the connected skeleton point can be defined as a skeleton branch (Fig. 2). There are two ways to build the skeleton graph that being discussed [14]:

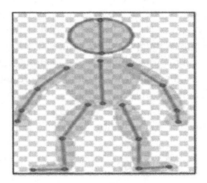

Fig. 2. Skeleton graph with nodes and branches

    i. Both the endpoints and junction points are selected as the nodes for the graph and all the skeleton branches between the nodes are the edges between the nodes.

    ii. The endpoint represent in the skeleton graph is labeled as an end node while the junction point is called a junction node.

3.5   Arm Asymmetry Measurement Process

Based on the study from Esposito et al., he found that autistic children often shown the asymmetric arm positions [15]. It means that the arms are not held in a symmetrical position. As described in RBSR, arm flapping is the more preferred symptoms to show autism tendency in clinical evaluation. Here, symmetrical position of the arm position when arm flapping can be described when the corresponding limbs (an arm and the other arm) are showed with an accuracy of 45° [16]. The example of asymmetrical position when arm flapping can be shown when: (a) an arm is fully extended down-wards while the other arm is held in horizontal position and pointing forward and (b) at least one elbow is in an irregular position (in high position). We compute the arm asymmetry from the human skeleton representation in each frame for analysis. For computing the asymmetry score, we describe the following normalized asymmetry score for each arm segment:

$$AS = \frac{2.0}{1.0 + \exp\left(\frac{-a-\tau}{\sigma_\tau}\right)} \tag{3}$$

where α is the difference between global or relative 2D angles retrieved from left/right arm segments, τ is an asymmetry threshold, and σ_τ is a parameter set to control the acceptable asymmetry values. According to EWMN's accuracy, we set the value of given threshold $\tau = 45°$. We also have concluded that $\sigma_\tau = \frac{\tau}{3}$ helps in measuring the value of asymmetry score.

For the upper arm asymmetry score AS_u, we set the value of α in Eq. 3 with $\alpha_{u=|\dot{v}_l - \dot{v}_r|}$ which is the difference between global angles $\dot{v}_l$ and $\dot{v}_r$ formed between the left and right upper arms with the vertical axis. While for the forearm asymmetry score AS_f, the value of α is similarly defined by $\alpha_{f=|\hat{e}_l - \hat{e}_r|}$, where $\hat{e}$ is the relative forearm angle with respect to the upper arm formed by the elbow. Finally, the asymmetry score for the entire arm is finally characterized as $AS^* = \max\{AS_u, AS_f\}$. The reason behind AS^* is that if the children's upper arm are pointing to different directions, then the arms are probably shown as asymmetric and that means AS_u and AS_f should be high $(AS_u \geq 1.0$ and $AS_f \geq 1.0)$. Based on this equation, we can conclude that if the asymmetry score for both upper or forearm during the arm flapping is greater than the value of threshold $AS_u \geq 1.0$ and $AS_f \geq 1.0)$ a child is considered to possibly showing the signs of ASD (Fig. 3).

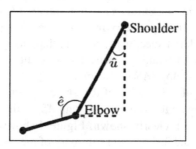

Fig. 3. Angles used to compute arm asymmetry values

4 Implementation

In this study, the data that will be using is in form of video analysis that collected from a public dataset called the 'Self-Stimulatory Behaviors in the Wild for Autism Diagnosis Dataset (SSBD) [17]. First of all, we filtered the dataset from SSBD that only shows footages or clips that the children performing the arm movements. Our data involves 5 subjects from different clips, consists of both males and females. All subjects were given specific ID and with their gender, frequency of arm flapping shown in the video (in seconds) and the length of the clips (in seconds). Table 1 below shows the summary regarding our subject. Note that we assume all the subjects are not clinically

Table 1. Sample data from SSBD dataset

Subject ID	Gender	Frequency of arm flapping	Length of the video clips (in seconds)
#1	Male	22	45
#2	Male	25	60
#3	Female	17	134
#4	Female	18	91
#5	Male	23	89

diagnosed with autism because since we are using data that collected from public dataset, so we do not get any specific information from the description of the video except for subject #5 who we got the information from the description of the video that he has been diagnosed with ASD. Even though our subjects are fewer and our sequences shorter, it is still relevant because; (1) since we are using data from public dataset, not all our subjects are appraised by clinicians and (2) the data that we used took place in a video mode. Thus, we used our symmetry estimation algorithm to screen our dataset for video segments instead of considering each child's case.

5   Results and Discussion

In this section, we summarize our results using HAR algorithm for 5 subjects. Since we are using data that we obtained from public dataset that do not show any presence of autism or absence of autism in a child except for subject #5, so used this algorithm to evaluate the result for the arm asymmetry measurement to detect the presence of early signs of autism among children specifically for arm flapping behavior. We set the value of threshold to the value of 1.0 and we measure the result based on at least one frame show the value of AS_u and AS_f ($AS_u \geq 1.0$ and $AS_f \geq 1.0$) to assume a child is considered to show the signs of ASD or not if the value of both AS_u and AS_f is above the threshold. In order to compare the value of AS_u and AS_f with the value of threshold, we plot the line graph to make it clearly shown. Figure 4 shows the experiment done on subject #5 while Tables 2 and 3 shows the summary of the result of the arm asymmetry measurement for both upper arm and forearm in subject #5. Figure 5 shows the asymmetrical graph that we compute based on the value of AS_f and AS_u to compare with the threshold value.

According to Fig. 5 below, the graph shows at least one frame from 5 frames selected which is in Frame 1446, the value of both AS_f and AS_u are above the threshold value where it indicates a high potential for the autistic arm flapping movement. It also shows the asymmetrical arm movement of the child in Frame 1446 during arm flapping between the left and right forearm. Since we already know that subject #5 had been diagnosed with autism, so it clearly showed that this framework can be used to detect the early signs of ASD among children and demonstrating the accuracy of this proposed methodology where the children consider having autistic arm flapping if the asymmetry scores for one of the frame selected is above the threshold. The results for

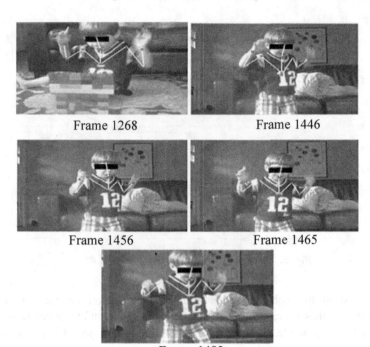

Frame 1268   Frame 1446

Frame 1456   Frame 1465

Frame 1483

Fig. 4. Stickman computed for 5 frames on subject #5

Table 2. Summary of asymmetry score AS_f for subject #5

Frame	Value of $\hat{e}_l$	Value of $\hat{e}_r$	Value of α_f	AS_f
1268	25.92	55.76	29.84	0.9439
1446	68.23	22.21	46.02	1.0038
1456	54.17	15.31	38.86	0.9773
1465	56.36	41.07	15.29	0.8904
1483	67.19	36.14	31.05	0.9484

Table 3. Summary of asymmetry score AS_u for subject #5

Frame	Value of $\acute{v}_l$	Value of $\acute{v}_r$	Value of α_u	AS_u
1268	21.30	50.59	29.29	0.9419
1446	11.80	57.52	45.72	1.0027
1456	13.15	26.49	13.34	0.8833
1465	24.26	39.44	15.18	0.8900
1483	31.77	38.27	6.5	0.8584

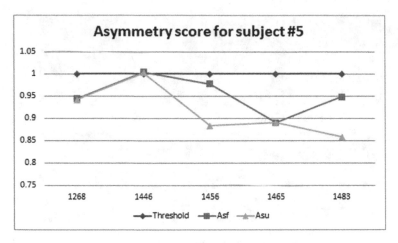

Fig. 5. Asymmetry score graph for subject #5

other subjects show that subject #2 denote asymmetric movement for our manually computed skeleton thus we can consider that the arm movement in subject #2 is autistic arm flapping behavior while for subject #1, subject #3 and subject #4 do not show the autistic arm flapping movement.

Based on our arm asymmetry measurement for 5 subjects, we can simply concluded that our human body detection and skeleton representation are very convenient to detect early signs of ASD specifically arm flapping behavior that mostly occur in children. In addition, the accuracy for arm flapping detection is highly determined by value of asymmetry score that calculated between upper arm (shoulder to elbow) and forearm (elbow to wrist). The asymmetry score also is highly influenced by the selection criteria of optimal frame that we chose which is (a) the subject must be in frontal view (b) left and right arm are both visible and lastly (c) arm flapping movement must be at highest rate in each frame. Furthermore, since we are using public dataset that do not show any presence or absence of autism except for subject #5, the accuracy of this method is really acceptable where it can prove that the subject #5 has performing autistic arm flapping behavior based on the asymmetry score for both AS_f and AS_u that exceed the threshold value $(AS_f \geq 1 \ and \ AS_u \geq 1)$ in at least 1 frames out of 5 frames chosen.

6   Conclusion and Future Work

In this study, we have developed a semi-automatic method to detect the arm asymmetry measurement of arm flapping behavior to obtain the asymmetry score for early ASD detection. We show that how children are considered to show early signs of autism in the arm asymmetry score is above the threshold value. We derived our method into performing the human body detection and skeleton representation in videos taken from public dataset on children performing the arm flapping behavior without showing any presence or absent of autism. As a result, our method shows can be useful in detecting early signs of ASD specifically for arm flapping behavior which is a possible risk sign of autism based on the arm asymmetry score that we obtained on 5 different subjects. In future, we plan to extend this study by computing fully automatic design for repetitive behavior recognition for ASD detection. Furthermore, we also plan to extend this study in detecting not only based on upper part of body, but also other repetitive (stimming) behavior that includes of whole body such as spinning and toe walking which are also an important signs to ASD in unconstrained video [18]. Furthermore, we also plan to increase the number of data collection to a bigger size by analyzing other signs of ASD behavior, as well as integrate these plan with different types of games including improved and intelligent retro game [19] and sensor based simulation game [20].

Acknowledgments. The authors wish to thank Universiti Sains Malaysia for the support it has extended in the completion of the present research through Short Term University Grant No: 304/PKOMP/6313259.

References

1. McCary, L.M., Grefer, M., Mounts, M., Roberts, J.E.: The Importance of Differential Diagnosis in Neurodevelopmental Disorders: Implications for Idea. American Psychological Association, Washington, D.C. (2012)
2. Mesibov, G., Adams, L., Klinger, L.: Autism: Understanding the Disorder. Plenum Press, New York (1997)
3. Schertz, H.H., Baker, C., Hurwitz, S., Benner, L.: Principles of early intervention reflected in toddler research in autism spectrum disorders. Top. Early Child. Spec. Edu. **31**(1), 4–21 (2011)
4. Liaw, L.C.B.@.A.: Phenomenological Study an Explanatory on Parents of Autistic Children in Kuching, Sarawak (2008)
5. Boyd, B.A., Shaw, E.: Autism in the classroom: a group of students changing in population and presentation. Prev. Sch. Fail. **54**(4), 211–219 (2010)
6. Susan, L.H., Patricia, M.R., Davidson, P.: Pervasive developmental disorders in young children. J. Am. Med. Assoc. **285**, 3141–3142 (2001)
7. Watson, L.R., Baranek, G.T., Crais, E.R., Hughes, C., Kristof, M.L., Zanzot, E.: Gesture use of infants with autism at 9–12 months. In: The American Speech-Language-Hearing Association Convention (2000)
8. Goodwin, M.S., Intille, S.S.: Recognizing stereotypical motor movements in the laboratory and classroom: a case study with children on the autism spectrum. In: Proceeding of the 11th International Conference on Ubiquitous Computing (2009)
9. Westeyn, T., Vadas, K., Bian, X., Starner, T., Abowd, G.D.: Recognizing mimicked autistic self-stimulatory behaviors using HMMs. In: Proceedings of ISWC, pp. 164–169 (2005)
10. Azizul, Z., Muty, N.: Detecting arm flapping in children with autism spectrum disorder using human pose estimation and skeletal representation algorithms. In: International Conference on Advanced Informatics: Concepts, Theory and Application (2016)
11. Sigal, L.: Human pose estimation. In: Ikeuchi, K. (ed.) Computer Vision, pp. 362–370. Springer, New York (2014). doi:10.1007/978-0-387-31439-6_584
12. Buehler, P., Everingham, M., Huttenlocher, D.P., Zisserman, A.: Long Term Arm and Hand Tracking for Continuous Sign Language TV Broadcasts (2008)

13. Teitelbaum, O., Benton, T., Shah, P.K., Prince, A., Kelly, J.L., Teitelbaum, P.: Eshkol–Wachman movement notation in diagnosis: the early detection of Asperger's syndrom. Proc. Natl. Acad. Sci. U.S.A. **101**, 11909–11914 (2004)
14. Bai, X., Latecki, L.J.: Path similarity skeleton graph matching. IEEE Trans. Patt. Anal. Mach. Intell. **30**(7), 1282–1292 (2008)
15. Esposito, G., Venuti, P., Apicella, F., Muratori, F.: Analysis of unsupported gait in toddlers with autism. Brain Dev. **33**, 367–373 (2011)
16. Hashemi, J., Spina, T.V., Tepper, M., Esler, A., Morellas, V., Papanikolopoulos, N., Sapiro, G.: Computer vision tools for the non-invasive assessment of autism-related behavioral markers. In: Development and Learning and Epigenetic Robotics, pp. 1–7 (2012)
17. Rajagopalan, S.S., Dhall, A., Goecke, R.: Self-Stimulatory Behaviours in the Wild for Autism Diagnosis (2013)
18. Muhammad, A., Surip, S.S., Harris, B., Mohamed, A.S.A.: Interactive sign language interpreter using skeleton tracking. J. Telecommun. Electron. Comput. Eng. (JTEC) **8**, 137–140 (2016)
19. Ravi, P.L., Ruhaiyem, N.I.R.: Intelligent gameplay for improved retro games. J. Telecommun. Electron. Comput. Eng. (JTEC) **8**(6), 23–26 (2016)
20. Noor Muhammad, M.A., Ruhaiyem, N.I.R., Mohamed, A.S.A.: Keeping curiosity in local historical knowledge alive by sensor based simulation game using flash actionscript 3. In: Proceedings of the International Conference Local Knowledge (2016)

EduNation Malaysia: Closing the Socio-Economic Educational Achievement Gap Through Free Online Tutoring Videos

Jasbirizla Ilia Zainal Abidin[1] and Hanif Baharin[2(✉)]

[1] EduNation Malaysia, Petaling Jaya, Malaysia
jas@edunation.my
[2] Universiti Kebangsaan Malaysia, Bangi, Malaysia
hbaharin@ukm.edu.my

Abstract. Research shows that one of the major factors contributing to the educational achievement gap between the have and have-nots in Malaysia is the ability of parents to spend money on extra tuition outside school. EduNation is a platform that provides free online tutoring videos catering to Malaysian school syllabus. This paper reports a survey conducted to gather information on Edu-Nation users. Data from YouTube Analytics supplements this survey. The results show that the users find EduNation's videos useful because they are accessible, meaning that they are free and allows the students to learn at their own time and pace. However, internet usage trend in Malaysia shows that digital gap still hinders some students with socio-economic disadvantages from accessing EduNation's videos. In the future, we will explore the use of rural telecentres as a mean to widen EduNation's videos accessibility.

Keywords: Online tutoring videos · Online learning · Education for all

1 Introduction

This paper presents the findings from a survey; conducted on the users of a free online video tutoring service provided by EduNation Malaysia; with the objectives of understanding the demographic of the users, their media usage behaviours and their perception on EduNation's videos and its usefulness. EduNation is a philanthropic organisation that provides free online videos to supplement the subjects being taught in primary and secondary schools in Malaysia [1]. The videos are meant to be a form of online tuition and not to replace the full lessons provided at school.

We argue that free online videos as a substitute to paid tuition class outside school is essential to close the educational achievement gap between the haves and have-nots, and between the students in rural and urban areas in Malaysia. This is because, research has shown that parents with higher economic status are able to spend more of their incomes on extra tuition for their children, and this in turn has been shown to produce better examination results [2]. We argue that providing free online tuition using videos will give a head start for those who cannot afford extra tuition and reduces the burden of parents' expenditure on children's education.

© Springer International Publishing AG 2017
H. Badioze Zaman et al. (Eds.): IVIC 2017, LNCS 10645, pp. 521–530, 2017.
https://doi.org/10.1007/978-3-319-70010-6_48

Although the videos are provided for free, there are cost involved to access the videos, namely the cost of procuring devices and internet data usage cost. This paper will analyse the usage trend and accessibility of EduNation's videos and discuss the need to further close the digital divide to make free online tutoring videos accessible to all students, which may reduce the educational achievements gap caused by socio-economic differences.

2 Related Work

EduNation was founded in 2012 with the aim to provide free education resource to all school students in Malaysia [1], by providing online videos, exercises, and test papers where students can track their progress. The learning materials provided by EduNation are based on subjects taught in Malaysian schools. Currently, EduNation's videos cater to all levels of students in primary and secondary schools, although not all subjects are available. EduNation concept is very similar to Massive Online Open Course (MOOC) concept [3] and Khan Academy [4].

Although what constitute MOOCs are diverse [5], essentially, MOOCs are free courses offered to the public through the internet. It gained popularity in 2011 when Stanford University offered three courses which was signed up by 450,000 students [6]. Learning objects can be defined as "any entity, digital or non-digital, which can be used, reused, or referenced during technology-supported learning" [5]. MOOCs offer enough learning objects which can be used by learning institutions to give our certification. In this sense, EduNation platform is more like Khan Academy because it provides learning objects as supplement to learning materials provided at schools. Salman Khan started making tutoring video full time and started Khan Academy in 2009 [7]. The simple voice over drawing methods for teaching concepts and question-drilling method prove to be very popular and effective in making students learn at their own pace which led to investment by Bill & Melinda Gates Foundation and Google. Khan's videos have been used by teachers in flipped classrooms, where students learnt by watching the videos at homes and work on problem-solving and doing discussions in the classrooms [7].

EduNation's motivation to provide free tutoring videos that tailored to the syllabus of Malaysian school stems from the fact that students who receive one-to-one tutoring are more likely achieve better academic results than those who do not. Bloom has shown that average students who received one-to-one tutoring using mastery learning can achieve two standard deviations better than students in conventional classrooms, however, it is too costly to give every student one-to-one learning – this is known as the 2 Sigma problem [8]. With the success of Khan Academy, video tutoring technique is perhaps an effective method to deliver one-to-one masterly learning without the burden of the cost. It has also been observed that in Malaysia, parents with a higher income and educational attainment from the urban areas are more likely to spend money on extra tuition for their children which has a direct impact on students' educational attainment [2]. It is widely acknowledged that in Malaysia, urban schools tend to perform better than rural schools [9]. Hence, EduNation is providing a platform that offers free tutoring videos to Malaysian students to close the academic achievement gap that is caused and has been perpetuated by socio-economic inequality.

EduNation provides two types of videos, 'chalk and talk' or Khan style videos, and talking head videos. There are many types of videos of online learning, classified the videos into 18 types of production styles, as shown in Table 1 below [10]:

Table 1. Video production style

Video production style	Description
Talking head	A presenter presents the content and is recorded from the chest upward
Presentation slides with voice-over	Slides are shown on the video with voice overlay to explain the slides
Picture-in-picture	Talking head video of the presenter is shown on the corner of the slides
Text-overlay	Text summary is shown over talking head video
Khan-style tablet capture	Or known as 'chalk and talk' where the presenter draw on the tablet with voice overlay instruction
Udacity style tablet capture	Similar to Khan Style but on a digital whiteboard that shows the hand writing with the instructor voice over
Actual paper/Whiteboard	Instructor using actual paper or whiteboard is recorded
Screencast	Instructor's voice is overlaid on the recordings of a computer screen
Animation	Computer animation is used - ranging from simple line drawn animation to 3D animation
Classroom lecture	Classroom lecture is recorded
Recorded seminar	Seminar is recorded
Interview	Experts on subject matter are interviewed
Conversation	Informal conversation between instructor and a guest is recorded
Live video	Instructor using live video to teach remote students
Webcam capture	A talking head video shot using a webcam, more informal style of presentation used
Demonstration	Instructor demonstrate a concept or process using actions
On location	Instructor take viewers to a place to discuss about it
Green screen	Green screen is used on the background instead of being recorded in a real place

3   Methodology

A questionnaire was used in this study to understand the demographic of EduNation's users, their media usage behaviours and their perception on EduNation's videos and its usefulness. The survey was conducted from 4 November 2015 until 21 January 2017. The sample size of this survey is 1050, which is representative of 20,000-population size, 3% margin error with 95% confidence level.

The questionnaire was programmed using services provided by Google. On the 4th of November 2015, EduNation sent an email to a list of students' emails registered under the company's mailchimp mailing list and posted a message on EduNation's Facebook page. The message contained an embedded link to the survey; respondents were informed that they could start answering the questionnaire by clicking on the link. A total of 1050 people have responded to the survey (up to the 21st of January 2017). More people are answering the survey as the survey is still live online. YouTube Analytics is also used to complement the data collected from the survey.

Qualitative data is also used in the survey in the form of comments from the respondents. The comments or feedbacks were then analysed using thematic analysis to examine the pattern emerges from them. The patterns were then coded with "names" given to each pattern (later referred as theme). Percentage for each pattern was calculated by dividing it to the total number of responses received. Qualitative data is also collected from the comments in EduNation's YouTube channel comments' section and comments sent by EduNation's users to chitchat@edunation.my.

4 Results

4.1 Descriptive Analysis

1050 people responded to the survey, 65% female and 35% male. 97% of the respondents are 13 years of age and above. 92% of the respondents accessed EduNation's videos from home, while 9% from school and 5% from other places. Table 2 shows the self-reported frequency of watching EduNation's videos in a week among the respondents.

Table 2. Respondents' frequency of watching EduNation's videos per week

Frequency of watching EduNation's videos	Percentage
1 to 3 times	51%
4 to 6 times	17%
7 to 9 times	5%
More than 9 times	8%
Never	18%

Figure 1 shows the percentage of the preferred subjects to be watched by EduNation users. The respondents can choose more than one favourite subjects in the questionnaire. The most favourite subject is History, followed by Additional Mathematics and Chemistry. Khan-style video presentation is used for these three subjects. In terms of preferred language for the videos and learning purposes, the majority prefers the Malay language (79%), followed by Mandarin (14%), Tamil (2%), and other languages (3%). Only 1% of the users prefer the use of English language for EduNation's lesson videos.

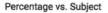

Percentage vs. Subject

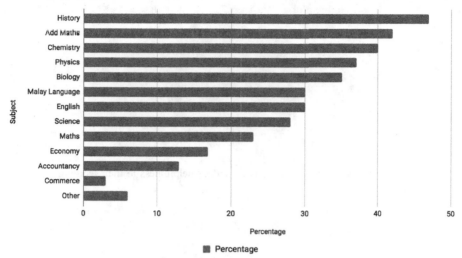

Fig. 1. Respondents' preferences of subjects to watch

The majority of EduNation users views the videos using computers (45% of total views) and mobile phones (40% of total views). Until 26 July 2017, all EduNation's videos have been viewed 6,169,378 times. Figure 2 shows the percentage of total views of all EduNation's videos based on the type of device used, retrieved from YouTube Analytics on 26 July 2017.

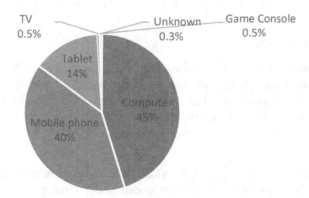

Fig. 2. The percentage of devices used to view EduNation's videos

Figure 3 shows the perceptions of the videos helpfulness by the respondents. Majority of the respondents (91% rated fairly helpful and very helpful to their learning) have the perception that videos from EduNation are helpful to their learning. Figure 4 shows the respondents' perception on the likeliness to share EduNation's videos with others. 62% of the respondents says they are very likely to share the videos with others.

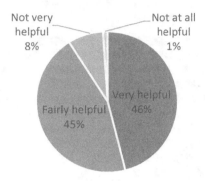

Fig. 3. Respondents' perceptions on videos helpfulness to their learning

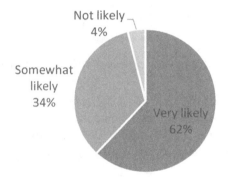

Fig. 4. Respondents' likeliness to share EduNation's videos to others

4.2   Qualitative Results

An open ended optional question was also asked to the respondents; which was, "Why would you recommend EduNation's site to someone?" The survey collected 248 comments from the respondents. The themes emerged from the data based on the feedbacks from respondents were *Usefulness* (83%), *Accessibility* (19%), *Goodwill* (21%), *Personalization* (1%) and *General Comments* (32%).

Usefulness

Most of the respondents indicate that the videos and the site are generally helpful to their learning. The respondents' responses coded under *Usefulness* focuses on the videos' ability to help them or others learn better, improve their knowledge and understanding or improve their academic performances. Below are some comments made under the *Usefulness* theme:

> *I improved my results from 2As 5B + 1G to 6As 2A - 1B. Also, the maths tutorial made me improve my math from a fail to a B. The history tutor is the best. I'm addicted.*

> *Because I scored A in certain subjects and for my whole life I've never gotten an A.*

Because EduNation really helps the students to understand the concept of the subjects. It explains a lot & the videos can be easily understood by the students.

As I am a visual learner I tend to learn better with graphics and detailed explanation. I enjoy the method of learning through videos so with that I could easily rewind or re-watch whenever necessary. The idea is great and I feel that these videos has been a huge help to students like me. Thanks, EduNation!

Because it's very useful for student who didn't go for tuition class. I also can catch up the chapters that I missed from school or my teachers couldn't finish. And... the seminar is very useful! But I hope there are some teachers who can help us personally. Like giving us their contact numbers. When I told my friend about this website, she asked me why didn't I told her earlier.

It helps us to understand better, (especially when) the topics (have not been taught) by the teachers.

Accessibility

The *Accessibility* theme emerges when the respondents' comments indicated that the use of videos as learning tools has made learning easier and more accessible. Some of the comments that fall under the theme of *Accessibility* are:

We can learn everywhere and at any time.

It has all the subjects that a student needs and best of all, it's free, meaning even the poor get free tuition which I think is a great idea.

It's like tuition but minus the effort of showering.

It is very helpful especially for those who don't go to tuition or can't afford one like me, and I really gain what I need to know through the video that were posted.

Personalization

The *Personalization* theme emerges when the respondents' comments indicated that the reason why they use videos by EduNation is because the videos' contents are based on the Malaysian Syllabus, this shows that the videos are personalized to their current learning needs. The comments that fall under *Personalization* are:

It is based on SPM syllabus.

It's rather well tailored specifically to our SPM, instead of more commonly found videos that are either for the IGCSE or AP syllabus.

It's the only free tuition website which follows Malaysian syllabus.

Goodwill

Feedbacks and comments that fall under the category of Goodwill are comments that indicate the intention of the respondents in wanting to spread something that they think is good to others. Comments that fall under this category are:

To help others score in SPM.

To help others who cannot afford tuition to get free tutoring so that they can excel in their exams.

To share the secret of success.

Untuk membantu supaya berjaya bersama. (It can help[us] to succeed together)

Untuk perkongsian ilmu bersama rakan-rakan. (To share knowledge with friends)

General Comments

Feedbacks and comments that fall under the category of *General Comments* are general comments made on the platform or site. Comments that fall under this category are:

It's FREE! And Malaysian likes free stuff.

It's simply awesome!!!

Kerana laman ini percuma tetapi saya sangat berharap agar pihak EduNation membuat sari kata bahasa melayu bagi memudahkan lagi pembelajaran subjeksubjek yang menggunakan bahasa Inggeris. Walaubagaimanapun terima kasih kepada pihak edunation kerana sudi membantu pelajar SPM dan semoga semakin maju jaya. (Because this webpage is free and I really hope EduNation will provide subtitles in Malay to ease the learning of subjects taught in English. However, thank you EduNation for willing to teach SPM students and good luck.)

5 Analysis

5.1 Usage Trend

The demographic of the people responded to the survey shows that most of the respondents are at the median and mean age of 17. The mean age and where they access the lesson videos indicate that these respondents are school students that have taken the initiatives to learn independently at home. Our findings are in line with a survey by the Malaysian Communications and Multimedia Commission (MCMC) in 2016 that shows that among internet users in Malaysia, 97.4% school-goers reported that they use the internet to study, and the school-goers is the group that spent the most time on the internet amongst all internet users, up to three hours a day [11]. Hence using free online videos to reach this demographic is a suitable mean to provide one-to-one tutoring which allow learners to learn at their own pace.

Another important point to note is the trend on the types of videos viewed by the respondents; it is noted that the trend has significantly changed. In our previous survey results (dated 4 November 2015 to 10 November 2015), we have noted that the top three subjects watched by the respondents were Physics, Biology and Chemistry but now the top three subjects viewed online are History, Additional Mathematics and Chemistry. This trend might have emerged due to the increase of the number of videos for those subjects and/or because the videos are now in the preferred language of the respondents, which is Malay language. This may also reflect the general low level of English language mastery among Malaysian students [12].

5.2   Accessibility

As shown on YouTube Analytics, majority of EduNation users (85%) viewed our videos on computers and mobile phones. The users perceived that accessibility of the videos as one of the main factors for them to use the videos, since they can learn at their own time and pace. Some respondents commented that they cannot afford to get extra tuition thus the videos helped them to get free learning tutorials. Since school-goers are already using the internet to study, we argue that if they could access EduNation's videos they can have a form of one-to-one learning which, thus far, has been in form of extra tuition. Research shows that, the second biggest expenditure on schooling children in Malaysia is extra tuition [2]. Thus, parents in Malaysia with higher socio-economic status are more likely to spend on extra tuition which has a positive impact on their children's academic achievement [2]. Although parents in the urban areas are more likely to spend on extra tuition for their children, they are more likely to feel that it is a financial burden to them compared to rural parents, perhaps because the cost of living in urban areas is much higher, and rural parents receive more financial help from the Malaysian government [2].

So, even though EduNation's videos are meant to break the socio-economic barrier through one-to-one learning, and as a possible solution to the 2-sigma problem, accessing the videos stills come at a cost – mainly, the cost of owning a device and the cost of accessing the internet. In term of device ownership, the trend in Malaysia is showing a promising trajectory in closing the digital gap, with the rapid increase in the ownership of smartphones [11]. However, those who have smartphones still cite the cost as one of the main reasons preventing them from having an internet connection [11], and Malaysia follows a worldwide trend where people who are more educated and wealthier are more likely to own smartphones [13]. There is still a rural and urban divide in internet usage, with only 37.9% people who used the internet as surveyed by MCMC stated that they are living in rural areas [11]. Hence, EduNation platform is still not reaching the users who probably need it most – those in the rural areas who are already being academically disadvantaged compared to their urban contemporaries, whose parents tend to spend a higher percentage of their income on extra tuition and books, which leads to a better education achievement in urban students compared to rural students [2]. Although the government is confidence in their effort of opening telecentres [14] in rural areas as a mean to close the rural-urban digital gap, more research is needed on how these telecentres can increase EduNation platform accessibility when the most popular way to access the internet in Malaysia is through smartphones via mobile broadband (89.3% people surveyed by MCMC used smartphones to access the internet and 87.3% has mobile broadband connection) [11].

While MCMC survey shows a significant number of people use the internet for online video (69.5%), most people (more than 80%) used the internet for social media [11]. Perhaps, this is because some internet providers provide unlimited data for social media, while online video consumed more data than texting through social instant messaging. Although competition among mobile internet providers results in the decrease in the price of mobile internet data recently, we argue that mobile broadband, which is more popular in Malaysia than home broadband, still provide a limiting factor to viewing online tutoring videos especially when students need to view them repeatedly in a large time span to understand and to do revision on a subject matter.

6 Conclusion and Future Work

EduNation aims to provide free tuition for all Malaysian primary and secondary school students because one of the major factors contributing to academic achievement inequality is the availability of one-to-one learning. The outcomes from the survey shows that EduNation users used the online tutoring videos because they perceived them as useful in helping them to revise their lessons. Accessibility, in terms of the ability to study at their own time and pace, the perceived zero costs of accessing the videos (as compared to paid extra tuition) is a major factor contributing to the usefulness of EduNation's videos. However, based on internet usage trend in Malaysia, we conclude that although the videos are free, there are still barriers to access the videos especially in the rural areas. The barriers are cost of device ownership and internet data usage cost. Therefore, for future work we will investigate how to make use of telecentres to make EduNation's videos accessible to rural areas. We will also liaise with schools and teachers to encourage students to access the videos from schools.

References

1. EduNation Malaysia - Free Tuition for All. http://www.edunation.my
2. Hassan, O.R., Rasiah, R.: Poverty and student performance in Malaysia. Int. J. Inst. Econ. **3**, 61–76 (2011)
3. Baggaley, J.: MOOC rampant. Distance Educ. **34**, 368–378 (2013)
4. Khan Academy | Free Online Courses, Lessons & Practice. https://www.khanacademy.org
5. Kay, J., Reimann, P., Diebold, E., Kummerfeld, B.: MOOCs: so many learners, so much potential. IEEE Intell. Syst. **28**, 70–77 (2013)
6. Vardi, M.Y.: Will MOOCs destroy academia. Commun. ACM **55**, 5 (2012)
7. Thompson, C.: How Khan Academy is changing the rules of education. Wired Mag. **126**, 1–5 (2011)
8. Bloom, B.S.: The 2 sigma problem: the search for methods of group instruction as effective as one-to-one tutoring. Educ. Res. **13**, 4–16 (1984)
9. Sua, T.Y.: Democratization of secondary education in Malaysia: emerging problems and challenges of educational reform. Int. J. Educ. Dev. **32**, 53–64 (2012)
10. Hansch, A., Hillers, L., McConachie, K., Newman, C., Schildhauer, T., Schmidt, P.: Video and online learning: critical reflections and findings from the field. SSRN Electron. J. **2**, 1–31 (2015)
11. Internet Users Survey 2016 Statistical Brief Number Twenty (2016)
12. Jalaluddin, N.H., Norsimah, M.A., Kesumawati, A.B.: The mastery of English language among lower secondary school students in Malaysia: a linguistic analysis. Eur. J. Soc. Sci. **7**, 106–119 (2008)
13. Poushter J.: Smartphone ownership and internet usage continues to climb in emerging economies but advanced economies still have higher rates of technology use. Pew Research Centre, Washington, DC (2016)
14. Tahir, Z., Malek, J.A., Ibrahim, M.A.: Developing smart ICT in rural communities in Malaysia through the establishment of telecenters. e-Bangi **11**, 227–242 (2016)

Development of Questionnaire to Measure User Acceptance Towards User Interface Design

Aslina Baharum[1(✉)], Sharifah Milda Amirul[2],
Nurhafizah Moziyana Mohd Yusop[3], Suhaida Halamy[4],
Noor Fazlinda Fabeil[2], and Ratna Zuarni Ramli[5]

[1] Faculty of Computing and Informatics, Universiti Malaysia Sabah,
88400 Kota Kinabalu, Sabah, Malaysia
aslinabaharum@gmail.com, aslina@ums.edu.my
[2] Faculty of Business, Economics and Accountancy, Universiti Malaysia Sabah,
88400 Kota Kinabalu, Sabah, Malaysia
[3] Faculty of Defence Science and Technology,
National Defence University of Malaysia, 57000 Kuala Lumpur, Malaysia
[4] Faculty of Information Management, Universiti Teknologi MARA,
Sarawak Campus, 94300 Kota Samarahan, Malaysia
[5] Faculty of Computer, Universiti Teknologi MARA, Kuala Pilah Campus,
72000 Shah Alam, Negeri Sembilan, Malaysia

Abstract. This study develops a questionnaire that can be used to measure user acceptance of web user interface (UI), particularly web object locations. It explored ASEAN users' expectations based on constructs in Expectation-Confirmation Theory (ECT). There were eight constructs, namely Expectation(E), Perceived Usefulness (PU), Perceived Ease of Use (PEU), Perceived Performance (PP), Confirmation (C), Satisfaction (S), Continuance Intention (CI), and Interface Quality (IQ). A total of 160 respondents from the ASEAN community were surveyed for their acceptance of web-based prototype. The results provide an exploratory factor analysis of the model, demonstrate satisfactory reliable and valid scales of the model constructs, and suggest further analysis to confirm the model as a valuable tool to evaluate the user acceptance towards informational website. Hopefully, the results of the study will fulfill the need for developing a sustainable web design, particularly in user-centric website which is based on user expectation for web object locations.

Keywords: Mental model · Expectation-confirmation theory · User interface · User acceptance

1 Introduction

In recent years, significant progress has been made in the development of user-centric or standardized websites for info sharing and distribution. The amount of information and public services that are delivered online grow constantly, with many benefits for organizations, businesses, and governmental institutions, especially for standardization. In this context, it is crucial to implement methods to measure, maintain, and optimize the quality user interface (UI) website. User acceptance is often measured by

© Springer International Publishing AG 2017
H. Badioze Zaman et al. (Eds.): IVIC 2017, LNCS 10645, pp. 531–543, 2017.
https://doi.org/10.1007/978-3-319-70010-6_49

implementing online questionnaires. Hence, this study attempts to develop a questionnaire that can be used to measure user acceptance of web UI, particularly web object locations. The study applies Expectation-confirmation theory (ECT) is widely used in the consumer behavior literature to study consumer satisfaction, behavior, and service marketing in general [1–6]. The predictive ability of this theory has been demonstrated over a wide range of product repurchase and service continuance contexts. Figure 1 illustrates key constructs and relationships in ECT.

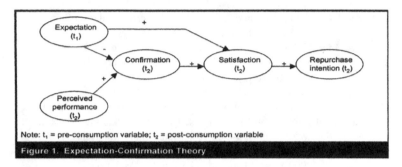

Fig. 1. Expectation-confirmation theory (Oliver [6])

This theory was first introduced by Oliver [6, 7] to construct four major constructs, namely expectations, perceived performance, confirmation, and satisfaction and thus the construct of Repurchase Intention was added later (Fig. 1) [1–9]. The information system (IS) continuance model (Fig. 2) proposed by Bhattacherjee [1] and generated from the original adaptation of ECT (Fig. 1) by Oliver [6] was chosen to be adapted to develop the model of this study due to the significant area of study in IS, Website and Continuance Intention construct, which is believed to be key to the success of a website [1] that later formed the proposed web continuance model.

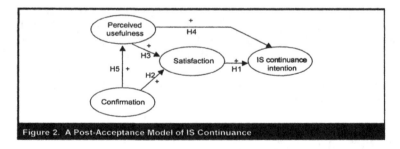

Fig. 2. Model of IS continuance (Bhattacherjee [1])

Bhattacherjee [1] studied users of an online banking system in order to examine the cognitive beliefs and effect influencing the individual's intention to continue using the IS. In the present study, eight hypotheses derived from the ECT model were empirically validated using a field survey of users' expectation of an informational website, a prototype of the ASEAN biodiversity website [11, 12].

2 Methodology

The quantitative phase of the current research focuses on empirically retesting the ECT model in a different setting with newly gathered data. The study used eight constructs, namely expectation, perceived usefulness, perceived ease of use, perceived performance, satisfaction, interface quality, confirmation, and continuance intention. The operationalization of the constructs is summarized in Table 1.

Table 1. Operationalization of constructs

Construct	Operational definition	Items	Source
1. Perceived usefulness (PU)	Users' perceptions of the expected benefits of using the ASEAN biodiversity website	PU1. The interface helps me be more effective PU2. The interface helps me be more productive PU3. The interface is useful	[1–3, 18–26]
2. Perceived ease of use (PE)	Users' perceptions of the ease and convenience of using the ASEAN biodiversity website	PE1. The interface is easy to use PE2. The interface is simple to use PE3. The interface is easy to remember to use it	[19, 25, 27–30]
3. Perceived performance (PP)	Users' perceptions of orientation on the ASEAN biodiversity website	PP1. The interface is easy to navigate through the objects of the website PP2. All the objects in the Web interface are well organized PP3. The interface is easy to read the website's content	[25, 32–34]
4. Expectation (E)	Users' expectations for the location of Web and interface objects on the ASEAN biodiversity website	E1. The Web objects in the interface fit my expectation E2. The Web object's location operation fits my expectation E3. The interface fits my expectation E4. My experience using the interface was better than what I expected E5. I am able to expect the location of the objects easily	[29, 32–34]

(continued)

Table 1. (*continued*)

Construct	Operational definition	Items	Source
5. Confirmation (C)	Users' perceptions of the congruence between expectations of the ASEAN biodiversity website use and its actual performance	C1. The interface meets my needs C2. The interface fits my needs	[2, 10, 20, 24–27, 29, 34, 35]
6. Satisfaction (S)	Users' affect regarding (feelings about) prior use of the ASEAN biodiversity website	S1. The interface is pleasant to use S2. I am satisfied with the use of the interface S3. I am satisfied with the interface	[1, 2, 10, 22–27, 29, 34, 35]
7. Continuance intention (CI)	Users' intention to continue using the ASEAN biodiversity website	CI1. I feel comfortable using the interface CI2. I would recommend it to a friend CI3. I like working with the interface	[2, 21, 22, 24–26, 34–36]
8. Interface Quality (IQ)	Users' affect (feelings) regarding the attractiveness of the user interface design on the ASEAN biodiversity website	IQ1. The interface is appealing IQ2. The interface is pleasant IQ3. The interface has a clear design IQ4. The interface has a clear design IQ5. The interface is user-friendly	[1, 2, 23, 29]

2.1 Development of Instrument

Based on the screening of theory and empirical data from the literature, the first instrument with items was generated. This item has been filtered and combined for the first draft recommendation. The research results show the long list of questionnaires containing 42 items to measure consumer perceptions to design the UI. A pre-test was conducted for the reliability of the instrument. Feedback on the questionnaires and questions related to ambiguity layout was obtained. Some changes were made to the questionnaire as deemed appropriate. The revised questionnaire was distributed through online. There were 24 returned responses, with the overall response rate of 75%. Of these participants, 2 responses were not valid which have been issued prior to data analysis. Thus, only 22 random responses from ASEAN were analyzed. After gone through the validation and reliability process, finally, there is 27 items with 8 constructs were selected (Table 2) for the final version. These items represent the variables utilized in the current study. To ensure high reliability and validity all items were measured on a five-point Likert scale [13, 14], where 1 = completely disagree, 2 = disagree, 3 = neutral, 4 = agree, and 5 = completely agree.

Table 2. Final version of questionnaire

PU1	The interface helps me be more effective
PU2	The interface helps me be more productive
PU3	The interface is useful
PEU4	The interface is easy to use
PEU5	The interface is simple to use
PEU6	The interface is easy to remember to use it
PP7	The interface is easy to navigate through the objects of the website
PP8	All the objects in the web interface are well organized
PP9	The interface is easy to read the website's content
E10	The web objects in the interface fit my expectation
E11	The web object's location operation fit my expectation
E12	The interface fits my expectation
E13	My experience using the interface was better than what I expected
E14	I am able to expect the location of the objects easily
C15	The interface meets my needs
C16	The interface fits my needs
S17	The interface is pleasant to use
S18	I am satisfied with the use of the interface
S19	I am satisfied with the interface
CI20	I feel comfortable using the interface
CI21	I would recommend it to a friend
CI22	I like working with the interface
IQ23	The interface is appealing
IQ24	The interface is pleasant
IQ25	The interface has a clean design
IQ26	The interface has a clear design
IQ27	The interface is user-friendly

The final version of the questionnaires was then distributed to the sample of study, which comprised 160 participants. The sample was almost equally balanced between genders, with 46% of the participants being male (n = 74) and 54% female (n = 86). All the participants were citizens or residents of an ASEAN country (Brunei, Myanmar, the Philippines, Indonesia, Lao PDR, Malaysia, Singapore, Thailand, and Vietnam). Most of the participants (82%) used English as their second language. This indicates that they were familiar with international websites and used English language websites. The majority of the participants (85%) visited the Web every day. To ensure that the participants represented the culture of each country, it was determined that each participant must have resided in their country of origin longer than in any other country and that their native language was their main language of communication. Data collection took place online and in person (at universities, institutes, and companies). Most of the participants had more than six years' experience in the field of technology and the Web.

3 Results and Findings

To test the hypotheses, the structural equation modeling using the partial least squares approach (PLS-SEM) was applied using SmartPLS (Version 3) to analyze the data in three steps: (1) measurement model, (2) structural model, and (3) mediation effect test.

3.1 Measurement Validity

Using SmartPLS, the measurement model was used to test the validity of measurement (Fig. 3). The results of the study showed that all the formative indicators were significant (Table 3).

Table 3. Measurement model assessment

Indicators	Weight		Loading		
	OW	T Statistics	OL	P	VIF
C1 -> Confirmation	0.226	2.367	0.851	0	2.4
C2 -> Confirmation	0.816	9.748	0.989	0	2.4
CI1 -> Continuance intention	0.41	4.124	0.882	0	2.1
CI2 -> Continuance intention	0.206	2.077	0.804	0	2.0
CI3 -> Continuance intention	0.514	4.996	0.919	0	2.1
E1 -> Expectation	0.344	2.99	0.876	0	2.5
E2 -> Expectation	0.334	3.549	0.779	0	1.6
E3 -> Expectation	0.216	1.805	0.833	0	2.4
E4 -> Expectation	0.179	2.021	0.783	0	2.0
E5 -> Expectation	0.18	1.782	0.655	0	1.5
EU1 -> Ease of use	0.452	2.098	0.898	0	2.0
EU2 -> Ease of use	0.501	2.345	0.924	0	2.2
EU3 -> Ease of use	0.187	1.042	0.698	0	1.5
IQ1 -> Interface quality	−0.009	0.065	0.8	0	3.1
IQ2 -> Interface quality	0.804	5.598	0.958	0	3.3
IQ3 -> Interface quality	0.222	1.257	0.539	0	5.3
IQ4 -> Interface quality	−0.337	1.661	0.451	0	5.1
IQ5 -> Interface quality	0.364	2.811	0.743	0	2.1
P1 -> Performance	0.427	2.958	0.84	0	1.6
P2 -> Performance	0.444	3.24	0.817	0	1.4
P3 -> Performance	0.361	2.431	0.773	0	1.4
S1 -> Satisfaction	0.738	7.176	0.941	0	1.4
S2 -> Satisfaction	0.186	1.337	0.703	0	2.8
S3 -> Satisfaction	0.228	1.275	0.763	0	3.1
U1 -> Usefulness	0.397	2.794	0.855	0	1.9
U2 -> Usefulness	0.476	4.173	0.871	0	1.7
U3 -> Usefulness	0.297	2.245	0.83	0	1.9

*Note: OW (outer weights), OL (outer loadings).

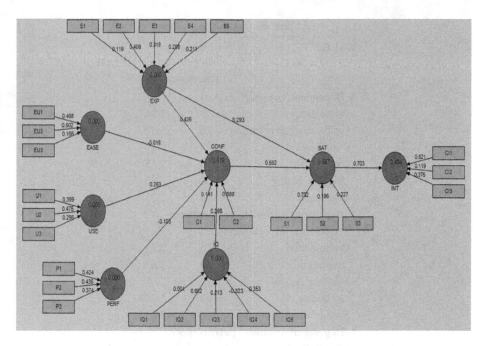

Fig. 3. Measurement model

Based on the rule of thumb, it is recommended that all VIF values are less than 2; however, a VIF value less than 5 is still not violent of collinearity [15]. In this study, the collinearity between each predictive construct with other predictors has been assessed by calculating tolerance and VIF using SPSS version 22. The results (Table 5) showed that the VIF values for all the predictor sets were below 4 (below the threshold) and all the constructs' tolerance values were higher than the recommended threshold (0.2). Therefore, there were no significant levels of collinearity between each set of predictor variables (constructs) (Table 4). Hence, seven separate ordinary least squares (OLS) regressions have been performed as detailed:

Table 4. Collinearity test

Model	Collinearity statistics	
	Tolerance	VIF
1. Dependent variable: usefulness		
Ease of use	.429	2.3
Performance	.265	3.8
Performance expectation	.290	3.451
Confirmation	,509	1.96
Satisfaction	.379	2.63
Interface quality	.307	3.26

(continued)

Table 4. (*continued*)

Model	Collinearity statistics	
	Tolerance	VIF
2. Dependent variable: ease of use		
Performance	.309	3.24
Performance expectation	.276	3.63
Confirmation	.477	2.1
Satisfaction	.395	2.53
Interface quality	.300	3.33
Usefulness	.444	2.25
3. Dependent variable: performance		
Performance expectation	.293	3.41
Confirmation	.475	2.1
Satisfaction	.383	2.61
Interface quality	.374	2.67
Usefulness	.441	2.267
Ease of use	.496	2.015
4. Dependent variable: performance expectation		
Confirmation	.505	1.98
Satisfaction	.386	2.59
Interface quality	.302	3.32
Usefulness	.473	2.11
Ease of use	.435	2.296
Performance	.288	3.47
5. Dependent variable: confirmation		
Satisfaction	.426	2.34
Interface quality	.303	3.30
Usefulness	.471	2.12
Ease of use	.427	2.34
Performance	.265	3.78
Performance expectation	.287	3.49
6 Dependent variable: satisfaction		
Interface quality	.357	2.80
Usefulness	.443	2.25
Ease of use	.446	2.24
Performance	.269	3.72
Performance expectation	.277	3.62
Confirmation	.538	1.86
7. Dependent variable: interface quality		
Usefulness	.452	2.21
Ease of use	.428	2.34

(*continued*)

Table 4. (*continued*)

Model	Collinearity statistics	
	Tolerance	VIF
Performance	.332	3.01
Performance expectation	.273	3.67
Confirmation	.482	2.07
Satisfaction	.451	2.22

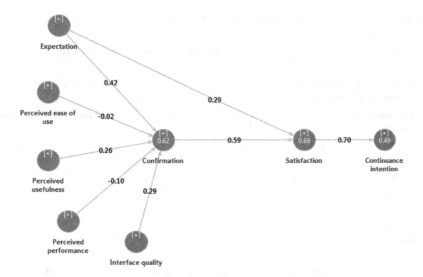

Fig. 4. Structural model

3.2 Structural Model Results

The path coefficients for the structural model are shown in Fig. 4. The path coefficient was calculated in order to assess the accuracy of the predictors in the proposed model. Table 5 presents the Structural Model Results of the study:

Table 5. Structural model results

	Regression weight	T statistics	P values
Confirmation -> Satisfaction	0.59	6.4	0
Expectation -> Confirmation	0.42	4.15	0
Expectation -> Satisfaction	0.29	3.1	0
Interface quality -> Confirmation	0.29	3.23	0
Perceived ease of use -> Confirmation	−0.02	0.25	0.8
Perceived performance -> Confirmation	−0.1	1.08	0.28
Perceived usefulness -> Confirmation	0.26	3.13	0
Satisfaction -> Continuance intention	0.7	11.5	0

3.3 Hypothesis Testing

Table 6 presents the hypotheses testing results of the study.

Table 6. Hypothesis results

Hypothesis	β	Result
H1 Satisfaction is connected positively and significantly to Continuous Intention	−0.7	Accepted
H2 Confirmation has a positive and significant impact on Satisfaction	−.59sig	Accepted
H3 Perceived Usefulness has a positive and significant relation with Confirmation	=−.26sig	Accepted
H4 Perceived Ease of Use has a positive and significant relation with Confirmation	−.02not.sig	Rejected
H5 Perceived Performance has a positive and significant relation with Confirmation	−.1not.sig	Rejected
H6 Expectation has a positive and significant relation with Confirmation	−.42sig	Accepted
H7 Expectation has a positive and significant impact on Satisfaction	−.29sig	Accepted
H8 Interface Quality has a positive and significant impact on Confirmation	−.29sig	Accepted

4 Discussion

Overall, based on the results of the hypotheses testing (Table 6), the theory-based model was supported by the data and thus showing that the proposed model can predict satisfaction and intention to continue surfing or browsing the Web with the developed UI (prototype). To reduce the rejection of websites by users, these findings can be taken into account in the development of sustainable UI design guidelines. The coefficient of determination (R2) results shows that the proposed model predicted 49% of Web viability (R2 = 0.49) (Table 7). In addition to evaluating the R2 values of all the endogenous constructs, the change in the R2 value when a specified exogenous construct is omitted from the model can be used to evaluate whether the omitted construct has a substantive impact on the endogenous constructs. This measure is referred to as the f2 effect size [14].

Table 7. The coefficient of determination, R^2

	R square
Confirmation	0.62
Continuance intention	0.49
Satisfaction	0.69

In this study, the f2 value of confirmation on satisfaction was 0.16 (indicating medium effect size); the f2 value of expectation on satisfaction was 0.53 (indicating large effect size); the f2 value of expectation on confirmation was 0.16 (indicating medium effect size); the f2 value of interface quality on confirmation was 0.08 (indicating small effect size); the f2 value of perceived ease of use on confirmation was 0 (indicating small effect size); the f2 value of perceived performance on confirmation was 0.01 (indicating small effect size); and the f2 value of perceived usefulness on confirmation was 0.07 (indicating small effect size) (see Table 8).

Table 8. Effect size

	Confirmation	Continuance intention	Satisfaction
Confirmation			0.53
Continuance intention			
Expectation	0.16		0.13
Interface quality	0.08		
Perceived ease of use	0		
Perceived performance	0.01		
Perceived usefulness	0.07		
Satisfaction		0.97	

5 Conclusion

In conclusion, an analysis of the measurement model and structural model produced a valid and reliable model. The original model contained eight constructs and 27 items that could be used to guide and assess the UI design. In the results, six items were removed, namely perceived ease of use (PE1, PE2, PE3) and perceived performance (PP1, PP2, and PP3). The remaining constructs facilitate the development of a UI that feels easy to use, is simple, and easy to remember. In addition, the information is conveyed on the website efficiently, as the user experiences the interface as easy to navigate, organized, and easy to read [16, 17]. Even though some items were removed, the model provides an essential guideline for enhanced usability in interface design.

References

1. Bhattacherjee, A.: Understanding information systems continuance: an expectation-confirmation model. MIS Q. **25**(3), 351 (2001)
2. Bhattacherjee, A.: An empirical analysis of the antecedents of electronic commerce service continuance. Decis. Support Syst. **32**, 201 (2001)
3. Bhattacherjee, A., Premkumar, G.: Understanding changes in belief and attitude toward information technology usage: a theoretical model and longitudinal test. MIS Q. **28**(2), 229–254 (2004)
4. Anderson, E.W., Sullivan, M.W.: The antecedents and consequences of customer satisfaction for firms. Mark. Sci. **12**(2), 125–143 (1993)

5. Dabolkar, P.A., Shepard, C.D., Thorpe, D.I.: A comprehensive framework for service quality: an investigation of critical conceptual and measurement issues through a longitudinal study. J. Retail. **76**(2), 139–173 (2000)
6. Oliver, R.L.: A cognitive model for the antecedents and consequences of satisfaction. J. Mark. Res. **17**(4), 460–469 (1980)
7. Oliver, R.L.: A conceptual model of service quality and service satisfaction: compatible goals, different concepts. In: Swartz, T.A., Bowen, D.E., Brown, S.W. (eds.) Advances Inservices Murketing and Management, vol. 2, pp. 65–85. JAI, Greenwich, CT (1993)
8. Patterson, D., Anderson, T., Cardwell, N., Fromm, R., Keeton, K., Kozyrakis, C., Thomas, R., Yelick, K.: A case for intelligent RAM. IEEE Micro **17**, 34–44 (1997)
9. Tse, D.K., Wilton, P.C.: Models of consumer satisfaction formation: an extension. J. Mark. Res. **25**, 203–212 (1988)
10. Spreng, R.A., MacKenzie, S.B., Olshavsky, R.W.: A reexamination of the determinants of consumer satisfaction. J. Mark. **60**, 15–32 (1996)
11. Aslina, B., Azizah, J.: Investigating adaptive ASEAN cultural diversity through users' mental models for user interface design. J. Theor. Appl. Inf. Technol. (JATIT) **61**(3), 617–629 (2014)
12. Baharum, A., Jaafar, A.: Users' expectation of web objects location: case study of ASEAN countries. In: Zaman, H.B., Robinson, P., Olivier, P., Shih, T.K., Velastin, S. (eds.) IVIC 2013. LNCS, vol. 8237, pp. 383–395. Springer, Heidelberg (2013). doi:10.1007/978-3-319-02958-0_35
13. Borg, I.: Mitarbeiterbefragungen. In: Schuler, H. (ed.) Lehrbuch der Personalpsychologie. Hogrefe, Göttingen (2001)
14. Hair, J.F., Hult, G.T.M., Ringle, C., Sarstedt, M.: A Primer on Partial Least Squares Structural Equation Modeling (PLS-SEM). Sage Publications, Inc, US
15. O'brien, R.M.: A caution regarding rules of thumb for variance inflation factors. Qual. Quant. **41**(5), 673–690 (2007). doi:10.1007/s11135-006-9018-6
16. Nurul Hidayah, M.Z., Azizah, J., Fariza Hanis, A.R.: Severity scoring of symptoms associated with carpal tunnel syndrome based on recall of computer game playing experiences. J. Theoret. Appl. Inf. Technol. **63**(1) (2014)
17. Mat Zain, N.H., Abdul Razak, F.H., Jaafar, A., Zulkipli, M.F.: Eye tracking in educational games environment: evaluating user interface design through eye tracking patterns. In: Zaman, H.B., et al. (eds.) IVIC 2011. LNCS, vol. 7067, pp. 64–73. Springer, Heidelberg (2011). doi:10.1007/978-3-642-25200-6_7
18. Davis, F.D., Bagozzi, R.P., Warshaw, P.R.: User acceptance of computer technology: a comparison of two theoretical models. Manag. Sci. **35**(8), 982–1003 (1989)
19. Brown, S.A., Venkatesh, V., Kuruzovich, J., Massey, A.P.: Expectation confirmation: an examination of three competing models. Organ. Behav. Hum. Decis. Process. **105**(1), 52–66 (2008). doi:10.1016/j.obhdp.2006.09.008
20. Limayem, M., Cheung, C.M.K.: Understanding information systems continuance: the case of Internet-based learning technologies. Inf. Manag. **45**(4), 227–232 (2008)
21. Nalysis, S.U.A.: Expectation disconfirmation and technology adoption: polynomial modeling and response. MIS Q. **34**(2), 281–303 (2010)
22. Shih, C.-H., Shiau, W.-L., Huang, L.-C.: Understanding the bloggers' continuance usage: integrating flow into the expectation-confirmation theory information. pp. 1680–1686 (2010)
23. Sonderegger, A., Sauer, J.: The influence of design aesthetics in usability testing: effects on user performance and perceived usability. Appl. Ergon. **41**(3), 403–410 (2010). doi:10.1016/j.apergo.2009.09.002

24. Stone, R.W., Baker-Eveleth, L.: Students' expectation, confirmation, and continuance intention to use electronic textbooks. J. Comput. Hum. Behav. **29**(3), 984–990 (2013). doi:10.1016/j.chb.2012.12.007
25. Tao, Y.-H., Cheng, C.-J., Sun, S.-Y.: What influences college students to continue using business simulation games? The Taiwan experience. Comput. Educ. **53**(3), 929–939 (2009). doi:10.1016/j.compedu.2009.05.009
26. Wu, S., Lin, C.S., Tsai, R.J.: Integrating perceived playfulness into expectation-confirmation model for web portal context. Inf. Manag. **42**, 683–693 (2005)
27. Vela, J.D.: Combining eye-tracking technologies with web usage mining for identifying website key objects. J. Eng. Appl. Artif. Intell. **26**, 1469–1478 (2013). doi:10.1016/j.engappai.2013.01.003
28. Venkatesh, V., Davis, F.D.: A theoretical extension of the technology acceptance model: four longitudinal field studies. Manag. Sci. **46**, 186–204 (2000)
29. Chin, W.W., Lee, M.K.O.: On the formation of end-user computing satisfaction: a proposed model and measurement instrument. pp. 1–16 (2000)
30. Nantel, J., Glaser, E.: The impact of language and culture on perceived website usability. 1–23 (2008)
31. Leuthold, S., Schmutz, P., Bargas-Avila, J.A., Tuch, A.N., Opwis, K.: Vertical versus dynamic menus on the world wide web: eye tracking study measuring the influence of menu design and task complexity on user performance and subjective preference. J. Comput. Hum. Behav. **27**(1), 459–472 (2011). doi:10.1016/j.chb.2010.09.009
32. McKinney, V., Yoon, K.: Measurement of web-customer satisfaction: an expectation and disconfirmation approach. Inf. Syst. Res. **13**(3), 296–315 (2002)
33. Susarla, A., Barua, A., Whinston, A.B.: Understanding the service component of application service provision: an empirical analysis of satisfaction with ASP services. MIS Q. **27**(1), 91–123 (2003)
34. Wang, W.: Supply chain management systems benefits: the expectation-confirmation theory perspective (2012)
35. Chen, C.-Y., Li, Y.-H.: A study on cognitive-affective model of sport consumer satisfaction in the event of Taipei 101 run-up race. pp. 45–62 (2010)
36. Mathieson, K.: Predicting user intentions: comparing the technology acceptance model with the theory of planned behavior. Inf. Syst. Res. **2**(3), 173–191 (1991)

The Effect of Time Manipulation on Immersion in Digital Games

Mohd Hafiz Abd Rahman[1], A. Imran Nordin[1(✉)],
and Alena Denisova[2]

[1] Institute of Visual Informatics (IVI), The National University of Malaysia,
UKM, Bangi, Selangor, Malaysia
P87406@siswazah.ukm.edu.my, aliimran@ukm.edu.my
[2] Swansea University, Swansea, UK

Abstract. Many empirical studies look into identifying factors that influence the quality of experience in video games. In this paper, we present research into the effect of playing time and players' perception of the time on their immersion in the game. We invited 20 participants to play a puzzle game *Bejeweled 2* for 7 min. They played the game in two conditions, namely, correct time (timer was programmed to be exactly 7 min) and wrong time (the countdown was set to be for 6 min, but was presented as a 7 min timer to the player). Players' immersion scores were measured after the game using the IEQ. The results show no significant difference in immersion scores between the two conditions and participants' comments also revealed that they perceived no difference in playing time between the conditions. This suggests that there is a dissociation between gaming time and subjective experience of gaming. Further research is required to investigate the relationship between playing time and positive gaming experiences.

Keywords: Player experience · Immersion · Playing time · Digital games · User experience

1 Introduction

Video games are now one of the most popular types of entertainment since the first video game was introduced several decades ago. The Electronic Software Association (ESA) reported that 65% of U.S. households own a device used to play videogames (ESA 2016). Similarly, the Association for UK Interactive Entertainment (UKIE) reported that in the year 2016, the overall UK games market value was GBP4.33 billion (UKIE 2017). Similar pattern can be seen in the Asia where the revenue from the games market in 2017 is calculated to be amounted USD51.2 billion (ISFE 2017).

This wide acceptance of video games has opened the opportunity for researchers to further investigate the use and application of video games in other fields, such as healthcare (Kato 2010), education (Griffiths 2002), and military (Smith 2009) amongst other fields. Moreover, research into player experience (PX) has become more prominent in recent years, focusing not only on what makes games attractive to the players, but also how positive experiences are formed.

© Springer International Publishing AG 2017
H. Badioze Zaman et al. (Eds.): IVIC 2017, LNCS 10645, pp. 544–551, 2017.
https://doi.org/10.1007/978-3-319-70010-6_50

Several terms have been used to describe positive experiences of playing video games. These terms include fun (Huizinga 2003), flow (Chen 2007), presence (Slater et al. 1994), and immersion (Brown and Cairns 2004) amongst others. These experiences are often used interchangeably to discuss the experience of playing digital games. In this paper, we do not aim to push the boundaries of distinguishing these experiences, instead we focus on the widely-used term, namely, immersion to describe players' involvement with video games that results in real world dissociation and loss of time- and self-awareness.

Fun, flow, presence, and immersion are distinct experiences in theory, there is a common element that connects these experiences. This element is time. Gamers feel that they lose track of time (Luthman et al. 2009), they experience time distortion (Rau et al. 2006), and frequently underestimate the time they spend playing the games (Tobin and Grondin 2009). This has been looked as an important factor in gaming in order to understand how video game players perceive time allows game designers and game user researchers to gain deeper insight into player experience (Nordin 2014).

Looking at specific studies on immersion and time, Sanders and Cairns (2010) conducted an experiment that suggests that players underestimate the amount of time they engage in the game for when there are immersed in the game. Nordin (2014) extend this study to further investigate the relationship of immersion and time perception. However, Nordin (2014) argues that time has no direct effect to immersion during short playing sessions.

In a Flow theory, players were having a distortion of temporal experience – a sense that time has passed faster than normal when the players were being "in flow". (Nakamura and Csikszentmihalyi 2009). To gain further insight into why players lose track of time while gaming, Wood et al. (2007) conducted a study, which reports that 99% of the players' experiencing "time loss" whilst playing video games while Luthman et al. (2009) reported that gamers claimed to "lose track of time" in the studies conducted. Tobin and Grondin (2009) also observed players reporting that their perception of session duration was shorter than the actual time they played the game for. These studies provide some evidence that suggests that time, as perceived by players, is not always accurate and appears to be distorted when being engaged in video game playing. However, outside Nordin (2014), little research has gone into studying how time perception influences player experience, such as immersion. Therefore, we aim to gather some preliminary results that would allow us to shed some light on this interesting problem.

2 Relevant Studies

2.1 Experiences of Playing Videogames

Huizinga (2003) argues that the element of fun is important in video games – games allow players to make believe of another reality whilst playing. Juul (2005) adds that the agency in video games allows players to interact with the games, which is not typical of other types of entertainment, for example watching a film or reading a book. Having this agency while interacting with a game world allows players to experience fun.

Moreover, Chen (2007) had concluded four-step methodology to provide an enjoyable interactive experience for the widest variety and number of users, a game's, and more generally any end-user technology's based on the psychology theory of flow that has been investigated by Nakamura and Csikszentmihalyi (2009). This method has been used in exergaming by Sheehan and Katz (2012) to provide an enjoyable interactive experience for the widest variety and number of users. The theory of flow can be described as an optimal state in which the player experiences total absorption and enjoyment while interacting with the game. The theory of flow is important as it has been used as a base platform specifically to understand more of a player's interaction with a game (Cowley et al. 2008).

Presence in gaming has also been discussed to be one of the engagement experiences in playing videogames. Slater et al. (1994) defined presence as a player's psychological sense of being in a virtual environment while realizing that they physically remain in the real world. Presence can be divided into six different forms (Lombard and Ditton 1997). According to Nordin (2014), the first three forms of presence are related to social presence and the other three forms relate to spatial presence. The interaction between players with other players or in a team when playing games creates an experience of social presence while the games that the players play especially games that provides a high sense of realism in graphics creates a spatial presence that has been define as sense of realism, sense of "transportation" (otherwise described as the sense of "being there"), and the psychological and sensory immersion (Nordin 2014). Hudson and Cairns (2016) investigate on this further and suggest that players can either be competitively or collaboratively present in video games.

In addition, immersion is also frequently used to describe a positive experience of playing video games. The term "immersion" is used to describe a person's degree of involvement with a computer game. (Jennet et al. 2008). Immersion is a commonly used term by gamers, as well as game designers and developers to describe the experience of playing digital games. Brown and Cairns (2004) has conducted a grounded theory that suggested different level of immersion: engagement, engrossment and total immersion.

2.2   Immersion and Time

Immersion lead to loss of one's awareness of their surroundings and decreased awareness of time. The player becomes so involved with the game that the game becomes the only thing that matters (Brown and Cairns 2004). Brown and Cairns (2004) describe immersion as a graded experience with three stages. The first stage is engagement, which is achieved if the player likes the game and the controls and the feedback provided by the game correspond in an appropriate manner. The second stage is engrossment. To enter this stage, players need to like the atmosphere of the game and to empathize with the characters in the game. Once on this stage, they can enter the final total immersion stage. Total immersion leads to the separation between the real and virtual worlds, much like presence – at this stage the game is all that matters to the player.

Based on the theory of flow, cognitive absorption, and presence, Jennett et al. (2008) have developed a questionnaire to measure immersion, which is based on five constructs, namely, cognitive involvement, emotional involvement, real world dissociation, challenge, and control. It is used to measure the immersive experience of players in a game. This self-reported measurement tool has been used widely for research on immersion in games. Nacke et al. (2010) has been using this measurement tools in validate good gameplay experiences (GX) while Molins-ruano et al. (2014) had conducted experiments to increase motivation and learning rate of students using games as new platforms in learning.

3 Methodology

3.1 Aim

The study is aimed at researching the effect of time manipulation and time perception on immersion whilst playing a video game. Our hypothesis is that the players experience one from two sessions of the gaming session to be longer in terms of time while playing the same game without knowing that one of the gaming session has been set up with a manipulated timer (tweaked to perform faster than normal timer).

The experiment was conducted with a counterbalanced measures design. In this study, which was a within-subject design, we also explore whether players' perception of time differs based on the perceived length of the gaming session, i.e. playing a game with a timer displaying real time vs. playing the game when the countdown is deceptively sped up.

3.2 Experimental Design

This experiment is within-subject design, where playing time is the independent variable (IV) and immersion scores, as measured by the IEQ (Jennett et al. 2008) is the dependent variable (DV). Using a psychometric questionnaire allows for the rigorous measurement and assessment of players' subjective emotion and cognition during game play by asking them structured questions post-gaming (Nacke and Lindley 2010).

3.3 Participants

20 participants were recruited for the study (9 male, 11 female) from the student population at UNITAR International University, Malaysia. The age range was between 19 and 25 years (mean = 22.05, SD = 7.58). All participants played video games at least once a week and all of them were familiar with *Bejeweled 2* – the game we used for this study.

3.4 Game: Bejeweled 2

For this study, we chose *Bejeweled 2* – a sequel to a tile-matching puzzle game *Bejeweled*, which was developed and published by PopCap Games. The main objective of the game is to gain points by 'popping' as many jewels on the screen within a certain timeframe by forming 'chains' of jewels. The player can form a chain of three or more gems of the same color by swapping one gem with an adjoining one. The game was chosen due to its relative popularity, ease of controls, and relatively steep learning curve.

3.5   Materials

The time was displayed to the players during the game on a separate screen next to the screen on which the players interacted with the game during the experiment. Two versions of the timer were used: both were set to display 7 min to the player, however one of them was modified to count down faster than the other. To be specific, one timer had a countdown of 7 min (real-time) and the other one 6 min (sped up). Participants were not aware of the modifications. Participants also did not have any personal items on them during the experiment that would allow them to track the time in real time. The reason why we used manipulated timer is because we want to see whether time significantly has an effect on the level of player's immersion.

3.6   Procedure

At the start of the experiment, each participant was briefed about the aim of the experiment. After that they read and signed an informed consent form if they agreed with all the terms. After that, they received an instruction sheet detailing the experiment procedure. Participants then played the first level of Bejeweled 2 to familiarize themselves with the controls and the environment. At this point, no timer had yet been set. When the player was comfortable with the controls, they played bejeweled for 7 min, which was displayed real time on the timer. They were then interrupted and given a demographics and immersive experience questionnaires to fill out.

After completing the questionnaires, each participant engaged with the game once again, but this time the modified timer was set. Even though the timer was displayed as 7 min, the modified timer has been tweaked faster than the normal timer. The participants had no clue that there were not the same 7 min' normal timer. The players were interrupted once the timer stopped, followed by another set of the IEQ with two additional questions about players' perception of time while playing the game in the second session compared to the first session, as well as some open questions asking to elaborate on that comparison. Each participant was then debriefed and provided with a Kinder Bueno chocolate bar as a token of appreciation.

4   Results

Table 1 shows the means and standard deviations of the immersion scores in the two conditions. Interestingly, the results from paired-sample t-test shows no significant difference in immersion scores between the conditions $t(19) = -0.21$, $p > 0.05$ with effect size Cohen's $d = -0.002$. Participants' answers gathered using additional questions at the end of the second session suggest that participants perceived no difference between the two sessions in terms of time they spent playing them: $t(19) = 0.00$, $p < 0.05$. Participants' scores achieved in the game while playing for 6 and 7 min were not significantly different: $t(19) = 1.586$, $p > 0.05$ with medium effect size Cohen's $d = 0.48$.

Table 1. Mean and standard deviation values for immersion scores for each condition.

Wdc	Correct time	Wrong time
Immersion score	103.65 (19.92)	103.70 (21.43)
Game scores	5347.56 (9361.13)	2137.70 (1521.81)
Did the first session feel longer than second session	3.00 (1.07)	

5 Discussion

The results show that time has no significant effect on time perception of players on their levels of immersion whilst playing a video game. Brown and Cairns (2004) argue that participants need to achieve three level of involvement in order to get a total immersion in playing games: engagement, engrossment, and total immersion. However, the data shows that participants most probably lost of interest towards the genre of the games hence effecting the results. From out of 20 participants, the data showed only four indicated liking casual games, such as Bejeweled, while the rest of the participants stated their interest in playing other genres, such as Role-Playing Games (RPG), First Person Shooters (FPS), online or multi-player games, sports and action games.

Seven players out of the 20 stated that they did not notice or paid attention to the time difference between sessions, because they felt that they were enjoying playing the game and invested much effort into achieving higher scores in the second session. Whereas two players reported feeling no time difference at all between the two sessions. Both were regular gamers usually playing games that require much longer time investment, such as multi-player and RPG games. Interestingly though, one player reportedly experienced the time differences between the two sessions, which they explained as feeling unmotivated due to the repetitive nature of the game.

Nordin (2014) argues that time has no direct effect to immersion during short playing sessions. Based on this experiment, the 7-min time used may also be one of the factors contributing to the lack of immersion by the players. Longer time is required in achieving immersion because it is important in ensuring players can achieve the full immersion as described by Brown and Cairns (2004) through the second stage - engrossment and third stage - total immersion.

6 Conclusion

The aim of the paper was to investigate the effect of play duration and players' time perception on their immersion in the game. According to our data, there was no significant effect of time on players' levels of immersion when playing a casual video game, *Bejeweled 2*. It is an interesting finding, considering that the difference in time was substantial for a video game of this kind. However, more research needs to be done using different video games genres in order to explore whether the amount of time players engage with a game for have an effect on their immersive experience, and whether their perception of the time differs based on the different lengths of gaming sessions and video game genres.

References

Essential Facts About the Computer and Video Game Industry (2016). http://www.isfe.eu/industryfacts/statistics

UK Video Games Fact Sheet (2017). https://ukie.org.uk/sites/default/files/UKGamesIndustryFact Sheet07July2017_0.pdf

Gaming in Asia - Statistics & Facts. The Statistics Portal (2017). https://www.statista.com/topics/2196/video-game-industry-in-asia. Accessed 26 July 2017

Kato, P.M.: Video games in health care: closing the gap. Rev. Gen. Psychol. **14**, 113–121 (2010). doi:10.1037/a0019441

Griffiths, M.: The educational benefits of videogames. Educ. Health **20**, 47–51 (2002)

Smith, R.: The long history of gaming in military training. SAGE J. **41**, 6–19 (2009). doi:10.1177/1046878109334330

Chen, J.: Flow in games (and everything else). Commun. ACM **50**, 31–34 (2007)

Nakamura, J., Csikszentmihalyi, M.: The concept of flow, pp. 89–105 (2009)

Cowley, B.E.N., Charles, D., Black, M., Ireland, N.: Toward an understanding of flow in video games. Comput. Entertain. (CIE) **6**, 1–27 (2008)

Lombard, M., Ditton, T.: At the heart of it all: the concept of presence. Comput. Commun. **3** (1997). doi:10.1111/j.1083-6101.1997.tb00072.x

Nordin, A.: Immersion and Players' Time Perception in Digital Games (2014)

Hudson, M., Cairns, P.: Computers in human behavior the effects of winning and losing on social presence in team-based digital games. Comput. Hum. Behav. **60**, 1–12 (2016). doi:10.1016/j.chb.2016.02.001

Jennett, C.I., Cox, A.L., Cairns, P.: Being "In the Game". In: Proceedings of Philosophy of Computer Games, pp. 210–227 (2008)

Brown, E., Cairns, P.: A grounded investigation of game immersion, pp. 31–32 (2004)

Luthman, S., Bliesener, T., Frithjof, S.-M.: The effect of computer gaming on subsequent time perception. Cyberpsychol. J. Psychosoc. Res. Cyberspace **3**, 1–11 (2009)

Nacke, L.E., Drachen, A., Göbel, S.: Methods for evaluating gameplay experience in a serious gaming context. Int. J. Comput. Sci. Sport **9**(2/Special Issue), 1–12 (2010). ISSN 1684-4769

Molins-ruano, P., Sevilla, C., Santini, S., Haya, P.A., Rodríguez, P., Sacha, G.M.: Designing videogames to improve students' motivation. Comput. Hum. Behav. **31**, 2007–2009 (2014)

Sanders, T., Cairns, P.: Time perception, immersion and music in videogames. In: Proceedings of 2010 British Computer Society Conference Human-Computer Interaction (2010)

Sheehan, D., Katz, L.: The practical and theoretical implications of flow theory and intrinsic motivation in designing and implementing exergaming in the school environment. Load. J. Can. Game Stud. Assoc. **6**, 53–68 (2012)

Huizinga, J.: Homo Ludens: A Study of the Play-Element in Culture, vol. 3. Taylor & Francis (2003)

Slater, M., Usoh, M., Steed, A.: Depth of presence in virtual environments. Presence-Teleoperators Virtual Environ. **3**(2), 130–144 (1994)

Rau, P., Peng, S., Yang, C.: Time distortion for expert and novice online game players. CyberPsychol. Behav. **9**(4), 396–403 (2006)

Tobin, S., Grondin, S.: Video games and the perception of very long durations by adolescents. Comput. Hum. Behav. **25**(2), 554–559 (2009)

Wood, R., Griffiths, M., Parke, A.: Experiences of time loss among videogame players: an empirical study. CyberPsychol. Behav. **10**(1), 38–44 (2007)

Juul, J.: Half-real: Video games between real rules and fictional worlds (2005)

Nacke, L.E., Lindley, C.A.: Affective ludology, flow and immersion in a first-person shooter: measurement of player experience. arXiv preprint arXiv:1004.0248 (2010)

Understanding Hospitalized Pediatric Cancer Patients' Activities for Digital Games Design Requirements

Irna Hamzah[1], A. Imran Nordin[1(✉)], Nadhirah Rasid[1],
and Hamidah Alias[2]

[1] Institute of Visual Informatics (IVI), The National University of Malaysia,
43600 Bangi, Selangor, Malaysia
irna.hamzah@yahoo.com, aliimran@ukm.edu.my
[2] Department of Pediatric, Faculty of Medicine, The National University of
Malaysia, 56000 Cheras, Kuala Lumpur, Malaysia

Abstract. This research aims to understand activities performed by pediatric cancer patients at the pediatric oncology ward. The focus of this study is to identify activities performed by patients during their stay in the hospital. 10 parents/guardians of the patients were interviewed to collect the information and description of activities performed by patients under their care. A thematic analysis was conducted to analyze all collected and transcribed interviews. The result shows that pediatric cancer patients express either positive or negative feeling. This feeling is based on their actions in the ward. The consequences from this are alarming: pediatric cancer patients are in high stress and depressed which would not be good for their health. The understanding of their activities in the ward can be transformed into design requirements for designing patient support games. Moreover, designers and developers of games can refer to this finding to compare their current existing games for cancer patients to the actual of the activities performed by the patients.

Keywords: Game design development · Thematic analysis · Pediatric cancer patients · Positive engagement · Qualitative research

1 Introduction

Being diagnosed with cancer can be difficult. It is even harder for a young patient to deal with the illness. Some patients who have been diagnosed with cancer must go through the treatment for a long time because depending on their treatment protocols, it can take years to complete the treatment circle. In 2017, there is an estimated of 1,688,780 new cancer cases diagnosed and 600,920 cancer deaths in the US [1]. Furthermore, the same report shows that nearly 13% of all cancers diagnosed in adults ages 20 and older will be rare cancers, defined in this report as a cancer with fewer than 6 cases per 100,000 people per year.

Cancer can be defined as a different disease with the common characteristic of uncontrolled malignant cell growth. Cancer is also known as one of the most severe illness. It is a leading and growing cause of death worldwide, with the total number of

© Springer International Publishing AG 2017
H. Badioze Zaman et al. (Eds.): IVIC 2017, LNCS 10645, pp. 552–558, 2017.
https://doi.org/10.1007/978-3-319-70010-6_51

death worldwide, with the total number of cases globally increasing, as the world population grows and ages [2]. It is a disease related with an imbalance of replication and cell response in the body. Normally, the cells multiply (replicate) in accordance with the rules to allow the body to grow and heal after an injury. But there are times when these cells grow abnormally causing abnormal growths or also known as a tumor [3].

For children, the common types of cancer include acute lymphocytic leukemia (ALL), brain and other central nervous system (CNS) tumors, and neuroblastoma in those ages 0 to 14 years old. Others include lymphoma, rhabdomyosarcoma, Wilms tumor, bone cancer, and retinoblastoma. The types of treatment that a child with cancer receives will depend on the type of cancer and how advanced it is. Common treatments include: surgery, chemotherapy, radiation therapy, immunotherapy, and stem cell transplant. Treatment is commonly over a longer period of time (usually 2 to 3 years).

The period of disease and treatment is physically and emotionally stressful for the children and the families, who must adapt to a hospital environment with not only physical but also psychosocial challenges. Therapy often leads to disruption in normal family, social, and school life, separating the child from siblings, friends, and peers. The early days of treatment, when the child is often in the hospital, are usually the most stressful for the child and the family. The child may be anxious about being away from home and receiving new treatment. Having cancer and receiving treatment that could affects the central nervous system (brain and spinal cord) may increase the risk of social, emotional, or behavioral problems. Prolong stay in the ward could exaggerates any issue with emotional or behavioral problems.

2   Related Work

2.1   Effects from Cancer Treatments

From those treatments for cancer mentioned earlier, there are several common side effects including appetite loss, constipation, fatigue, hair loss, nausea and vomiting and also concentration problem amongst others [4]. Other cancer treatment effects are low platelet count, low red blood cell count and low white blood cell count [5]. These side effects will increased risk of infections and bruising and bleeding easily.

Chemotherapy have many toxic effects for example the treatment of ALL uses combinations of several chemo drugs like Vincristine, Daunorubicin, Doxorubicin, Cytarabine, L-asparaginase, 6-mercaptopurine, Methotrexate, Cyclophosphamide and Dexamethasone.

2.2   Video Games for Cancer Patients

Videogames can have a positive impact on their users. Videogames are part of the lives of almost all children and teenage lives, with a percentage of 97% children playing video games for at least one hour each day in the United States. Most research indicates that video games are more beneficial and balanced to be used for the benefit of players. A decade ago, it is important to consider the potential benefits of video games as these video games have dramatic, complex, diverse and realistic changes that allow children to interact with it [6].

Video games that are specifically designed for patients can alter the behavior of the patient. Video games designed for health can entertain patients and can alter the behavioral health of every patient. Behavioral principles can guide the development of a video game that focuses specifically on the changes in the various health behaviors of each patient. The guidelines proposed in this study are a step-by-step process for developing video games that provide a solid foundation for behavior change by emphasizing the enhancement of player knowledge and skills. They also suggest game characters and avatars can create personal mastery in a video game environment to promote learning and achieve balance between gaming and learning [7].

Virtual games can be used to decrease patients' negative emotions and stimulated patients' positive self-experienced. During a treatment session, adult cancer patients are motivated to be physically active by playing Nintendo Wii game console. The study was conducted at the Department of Radiation Oncology at the University Hospital in Halle (Saale) in Germany by involving physical training for five days for each patient. Patients spent playing Nintendo Wii for 30 min per day. The result form this study suggests that an elevated level of acceptance by patients to play videogames to increase their physical activity. Patients feel stimulated to become physically active when admitted to hospital by exploring Nintendo Wii console game. All patients were distracted from the normal routine of the hospital when they were playing the console game. Most of the patients at the ward experienced better mood situations after game sessions. The finding suggest that patients feel relax when playing virtual physical activity games [8].

Videogames contribute many opportunities for personalized health care by capturing players' attention. It is being suggested to be used to boost patient's psychological state to help patients overcome their stress with cancer. Looking at mental empowerment, it can cultivate the motivational metaphoric visualization through therapeutic interactive technologies. The major finding of this study shows that video games such as Bronkie the Brachiosaurus, Re-Mission and Packy and Marlon can create awareness and improve patient's related knowledge as well as communication and self-care behaviors. Some type of videogames such as Wii Virtual Reality, Wii Fit and PE Game can improve patients' motor function and static and dynamic balance. Patient Empowerment Exercise Video Game (PE Game) can be developed by interactive technology concept that specifically designed to empower pediatric oncology patients and help them fight cancer [9].

Children with a prolonged illness can use technology to preserve their routines. Growing up can be harder for children who are diagnosed with a chronic illness such as cancer as they are facing with many challenges in keeping up with their social circle. Patients may feel isolated as they missed school when they were admitted into the hospital. The study found that patients are struggling with health aspects as they are suffering from the chronic illness. Patients are also feel missing out due to their health condition. The study also found out that patients have struggle to fitting in soon after they have been diagnosed with their illnesses. Patient also feel rejected after they have missed days in school because of their commitment to the treatment process [10].

For patients to experience less abnormality in their routines, the study suggests various methods by letting the patients to stay connected through connecting online with their friends using social media such as Facebook and Instagram. Patient can use the social media to interact with their friends while they been admitted in the hospital. The study also suggests that through technology patients can feel present with their friends without physically being present. Patients can use video chat to connect with their friends. Patients also played online games with their friends such as Mine Craft video game and Face Time to chat with their friends. The study suggest that patients must get use to their new form of normalcy after they have been diagnosed with chronic illness and communication tools such as social media can helps patients feel normal again [10].

3 Methodology

The research applies open ended interviews with patients' parents or guardian. The aim of this interviews is to understand about the activities performed by pediatric cancer patient when they are hospitalized in the pediatric oncology ward. The interview questions were crafted based on our previous findings through ethnography study conducted for two months at the pediatric oncology ward. During the ethnography study, they only observed patients without having any direct interaction with them [11]. Hence, in this study we will ask the parents or guardians of the patients on our observation. This is to ensure that we understand on what is going on.

Participant. Ten (10) parents or guardians of the pediatric patients were invited to participate in the interview. All the participants in this interview are mother (10/10 participants) to the patients. Their age ranges from thirty five (35) year old to fifty two (52) year old. All the participants were with patients during their entire stay in the hospital.

Procedures. The interviews were conducted at the pediatric oncology ward, Faculty of Medicine, The National University of Malaysia (UKM). Each of the interview held at separate times. The interview for each session took about thirty minutes to one hour. Each interview includes separate set of question. The feedback received from the current interview are used as an information for the question for next interviews. We used a voice recorder to record the answer that came up from the participants. Before the interview started, each participant was given a consent form to ensure that they were happy about the interview are being recorded. The data that has been collected from the interviews has been extracted into themes called thematic analysis. After the interview has ended, the data from the voice recorder were transferred into text transcript. The text transcript was used for the preparing the question for the next interview ahead. This process was used since the interview one until the final interview.

Thematic Analysis. Thematic analysis is a method for identifying, analyzing and reporting themes in the data. Thematic analysis of data compiled by the minimum and describe in detail the data set. Themes indicates attribute, element, descriptor and concept that includes code which have a similar point of reference. Themes also been used as an organized group of ideas that has been collected [12].

4 Result

Table 1 shows the main themes and sub-themes of pediatric cancer patients' feelings and actions performed while they have been hospitalized in the pediatric oncology ward.

Table 1. Main themes and sub-themes of pediatric cancer patients' feelings and action in the ward.

Themes	Code	Feelings	Actions
Internal action (inside the ward)	Positive behavior	Likes, loves, interest, passion	Patients play video games, play Lego, drawing, painting, watching television, mathematical exercise
	Negative behavior	Bored, lonely, stress, depressed, sad, angry, empty, emotional	Patients cries, wants to go home, does not want to eat, refuse to undergo treatment
External action (outside the ward)	Before treatment (before diagnosed)	Active, energetic	Patients play football, bicycle, sports, outdoor
	After treatment (after discharged)	Happy, comfortable	Patients play with siblings, play online video games with friends but patients have limited movement due to health condition

5 Discussion

Patients' feelings and activities can be divided into internal and external engagement. Internal engagement refers to actions performed by people in the ward. Whereas external engagement refers to activities conducted by people from the outside of the ward. From the interviews, we can divide the internal emotions into two sub-themes. These sub-themes were coded as positive behavior and negative behavior.

In Positive Behavior code, patients show their feeling in a different form of event. *"Patients likes to play video game called Mine Craft and Sim-P3"*. Based on the interviews, patients show their positive feelings in the form of passion and interest each time they perform activities such as playing video games, playing toys named Lego, drawing an object, watching television and surfing You Tube. After patients has been admitted into hospital, some of the patients still perform their favorite activities because they brought their toys to the ward. *"There are two things that are very admired by my child which are Lego and Thomas. I also carried all my child favorite toys to the hospital-P1"*. Apart from playing with their toys, according to patients' guardian, patients also played video games. *"At the ward, patients played video games on the mobile phone-P2"*.

The interview also found that video games might help patients while they receive their treatment at the ward. *"Video games helps patients in the present situation-P3"*. This statement proved that video games might help patients' emotions while they go through the process of their treatment. Patients that received chemotherapy treatment have unstable emotions. *"Patient must have suffered emotional distress if after undergoing chemotherapy-P6"*. To handle the situation, patient play video game to conquer boredom and stress. *"Patient played video games to relieve emptiness-P10"*. Some of the guardian tried to cheer up their child using a few mediums such as video games and they give patients play video games because of many reason and one of them is to make patient happy. The result from the interviews shows that patients' guardian also tried to fill the long waiting period of treatment by giving their child to play video games *"I feel that video games are needed at the ward because video games make my child happy. As you can see, all these kids here holding cell phone. While waiting for the queue to perform procedures such as chemotherapy treatment, bone marrow and so on, things done by patient is likely to play video games-P6"*.

While in Negative Behavior code, patients behaved negatively when they feel bored, lonely, stress, depressed, sad, angry, empty and emotional. *"Patient cannot play with anyone because he has no friends at the ward-P1"*. Patients' guardian claimed that patient feels lonely because they were limited interaction in the ward. Based on the interviews, we have found that patient feels depressed during the treatment. *"Patient was worried and scared about the treatment. Patient also think negatively-P4"*. Each of the treatment received by patients at the ward took a plenty period of times. *"Patient complained that he was bored because the process of treatment takes a long time-P10"*. Patient also feel depressed and angry about their health condition during their admission into hospital. Some of the guardian gave patients sometimes for them to relax when they feel depressed. *"I did not give patient play video game when his emotion is not stable. This is because he does not want to play video when he is emotionally disturbed-P6"*.

For the external emotions, we discovered that patients are active and energetic before they were diagnosed with cancer. Most activities performed by patients before they were sick are outdoors activities such as play football, play bicycle and they also like to perform sports activity. *"Patient loves to play football. He actively playing football for the football club and play football at his scholl-P5"*. After patients have been admitted into hospital, their feelings have changed just like we have explained in the internal engagement. Once patients can go home, we noticed that they became happier and comfortable at home. *"Patient feels happy when allowed to go home because it was a chance to play video games online with friends-P4"*. This explained that each time patients were discharged from the ward, their feelings turn into excitement because they feel like they will never be alone anymore.

From the interviews, we have found that patients feel happy at home because they can play with their siblings, perform more daily activities such as playing in the bedroom and play online video games with friends even though patients have limited movement now due to his health condition. Happiness sparks in patients' face when they knew that they can go home. Patients feel so happy as soon as doctors give the permission to discharge from the ward.

6 Conclusion

The study may also help pediatric cancer patients through the recovery process in the presence of the disease effective video game that meet the criteria for pediatric cancer patients.

Video games encourages well-being. Therefore video game may also help treatment for youth that suffers from mental health. The study suggest that expert from different field namely psychologists, clinicians, and game designers can cooperate in developing an advanced methods for mental health as the study found that children and adult are fascinated with video games [6].

References

1. American Cancer Society. https://www.cancer.org
2. World Physical Therapy Day 2012 (2012)
3. Chye, G.L.C.: My Health Kementerian Kesihatan Malaysia. www.myhealth.gov.my
4. National Cancer Institute. https://www.cancer.gov
5. CureSearch for Children's Cancer. https://curesearch.org/
6. Granic, I., Lobel, A., Engels, R.C.M.E.: The benefits of playing video games. Am. Psychol. **69**, 66–78 (2014). doi:10.1037/a0034857
7. Thompson, D.: Designing serious video games for health behavior change: current status and future directions. J. Diabetes Sci. Technol. **6**, 807–811 (2012). doi:10.1177/193229681200600411
8. Jahn, P., Lakowa, N., Stoll, O.: InterACTIV: an exploratory study of the use of a game console to promote physical activation of hospitalized adult patients with cancer (2012). doi:10.1188/12.ONF.E84-E90
9. Bruggers, C.S., Altizer, R.A., Kessler, R.R., Caldwell, C.B., Coppersmith, K., Warner, L., Davies, B., Paterson, W., Wilcken, J., Ambrosio, T.A.D., German, M.L., Hanson, G.R., Gershan, L.A., Korenberg, J.R., Bulaj, G.: Patient-empowerment interactive technologies. Patient-Empowerment Interactive Technol. **4**(152), 2–5 (2012)
10. Liu, L.S., Inkpen, K., Pratt, W.: "I'm not like my friends": understanding how children with a chronic illness use technology to maintain normalcy, pp. 1527–1539 (2015)
11. Hamzah, I., Nordin, A.I., Alias, H., Baharin, H.: Game design requirements through ethnography amongst pediatric cancer patients (2017, to appear)
12. Jones, J., Vaismoradi, M., Jones, J., Turunen, H., Snelgrove, S.: Theme development in qualitative content analysis and thematic analysis (2016). doi:10.5430/jnep.v6n5p100

Designing Persuasive Stroke Rehabilitation Game: An Analysis of Persuasion Context

Mohd Yusoff Omar[1](✉), Dayang Rohaya Awang Rambli[1],
and Mohd Fairuz Shiratuddin[2]

[1] Computer and Information Sciences Department, Universiti Teknologi
PETRONAS, Seri Iskandar, Malaysia
{yusoff_16002296,dayangrohaya.ar}@utp.edu.my
[2] School of Engineering and Information Technology,
Murdoch University, Perth, Australia
f.shiratuddin@murdoch.edu.au

Abstract. Stroke patients suffering limbs deformity or immobility require long and arduous rehabilitation as part of treatment. Many not able to adhere to it due to various reasons such as being depressed after stroke, uninteresting rehabilitation sessions, logistic problems, scarce rehabilitation sessions due to increasing stroke cases and many more. While there are many home based rehabilitation incorporating game technology available, they are still at a proof of concept level and developed in an ad hoc manner. The goal of this study is to develop a home based stroke rehabilitation game with persuasion technology based on Health Behavior Change Support System (HBCSS) concept and Persuasive System Design model (PSD) which will incorporate persuasive feature and targeted voluntary outcome (attitude change) from the patients towards rehabilitation process. This paper presents the persuasion context analysis produced from PSD model that can be used for system designer and developer.

Keywords: Stroke rehabilitation · Home based rehabilitation · Health Behavior Change Support System · Persuasive system development · Gamification

1 Introduction

Stroke patient often needs rehabilitation in order to recover. Ideally, the more frequent rehabilitation sessions they do, the better their motor relearning will be. Many healthcare institutions provide rehabilitation facilities with the assistance of physical therapists. However, frequent rehabilitation require high intensity of repetitive exercise making rehabilitation such a boring, mundane and depressing tasks for the patients. Moreover, 85% of patients prefer to do rehabilitation at home as it allows the patient ability to train more frequently and comfortably [2]. This signifies that home based rehabilitation needs enhancement and further development.

As envisioned by Reed et al. [12], rehabilitation in the future is a mix of home based therapy and regular but less frequent clinic visits. The regular clinic visit would involve consultation and also evaluation by a functional assessment device to evaluate

H. Badioze Zaman et al. (Eds.): IVIC 2017, LNCS 10645, pp. 559–569, 2017.
https://doi.org/10.1007/978-3-319-70010-6_52

the patient's abilities. An appropriate home based therapy would then prescribed for the patient to follow every day. The suggested home based therapy may include an engaging and interactive game to monitor the patient's performance for clinical assessment. Current advancement of computer technology and sensors may enable this vision, but there is a lacking of effective and clinically validated home based rehabilitation methods especially for patients with moderate impairment. There is a growing body of literature utilizing computer technology to explore and improve rehabilitation with games but a lot of them are questionable for practical effectiveness because lacking of clinical evaluations [9, 12].

This study will focus on the development of home based stroke rehabilitation video game with persuasive technology by following the Persuasive Systems Design (PSD) model and Health Behavior Change Support System (HBCSS) concept. The objective of the game is to persuade stroke patients to perform their home based rehabilitation more frequently by providing a conducive, fun and more engaging experience with specific target of attitude and behavioral change of the patients. This paper is structured as follows: Sect. 2 will describe the stroke background and its rehabilitation. Section 3 will introduce gamification of HBCSS and PSD Model approach in detail. Section 4 will elaborate on the implementation of gamified HBCSS through its persuasion context analysis from PSD model and game scenario description and Sect. 5 will conclude this paper.

2 Stroke Background and Rehabilitation

Stroke is a brain attack that occurs when the blood supply carrying oxygen and nutrients to the brain is disrupted due to bursts or clogged of blood vessels [4]. This effected part of brain will start to die silently and may lead to various damages. The common effects by stroke include physical deficits (poor body coordination and/or abnormal posture), cognitive deficits (becoming anxious, disorganized and/or easily depressed) and spatial-perceptual deficits (inability to judge distance, size, position, one sided paralysis) [5].

Stroke has remained as second rank killer in top 10 causes of death in the world since 2000 to 2015 [3]. Untreated living stroke patients that continue living with multiple motor sensory impairments may lead to permanent disabilities, high dependency and exposed to more chronic stage. However, it helps to remember that the patients are able to cure by going under recovering processes that include treatment in hospital with acute care, spontaneous recovery and continuous rehabilitation. Many healthcare institutions are available to provide rehabilitation service with the assistance of physical therapist [5].

2.1 Stroke Rehabilitation

The main purpose of rehabilitation is to effect a relatively permanent change in the brain that allows continued use of the affected limb(s). This is done in series of specific exercise sessions where patients are assisted by therapist/clinician(s) to relearn or find new ways of doing activities or functions lost because of stroke. It is highly recommend that the more frequent rehabilitation sessions they do, the better their motor relearning will be. However, the patient's ability to tolerate intensity of rehabilitation (hours/stamina) and degree of disability must be taken into consideration. An ideal duration of rehabilitation is to start as early as possible after being discharged from the hospital and to be continued at home. This can take months or years as the condition improves. By the end of rehabilitation, the patients may keep current abilities and gain back their lost abilities, becoming more independent and live with community with necessary adjustments of their post stroke life [5, 6].

2.1.1 Traditional Rehabilitation Therapy

Most early rehabilitation activities are conducted in specialized facilities such as a special unit in the hospital, rehab centres or nursing home. These centres are adequately equipped with facilities and specialized team of staffs (doctor/therapist/clinician) for physiotherapy intervention services like activities of daily living (ADL) training, wheelchair training, fine motor/hand function training, gross motor/functional mobility, play and leisure (exploration and training), mental activity therapy (cognitive and perceptual, compression, creative, behavioral) and others. In here, stroke patients will be properly trained physically by using equipment provided under the assistance, guidance or monitored to avoid injuries and to optimize recovery.

Among the common method of conventional therapies being practiced widely are Bobath method and proprioceptive methods. The recently developed are forced use and Constraint-Induced Movement Therapy that binds the unimpaired arm and forces the patient to use only the paretic limb, in order to aid in cortical re-mapping of neurons from damaged to functional brain cells. This forced use is limited to high motor function patients as it is unable to provide assistance to paretic limb. The advantage of this is the learning occurs directly while performing the designated tasks and can be practiced in home therapy [12].

2.1.2 Robotic Therapy

A leverage on modern technology can be done by building robot devices specifically to assist rehabilitation purpose so longer and more frequent rehabilitation sessions can be can be offered to patients.

MIT-Manus is among the earliest and successful robotic upper limb rehabilitation systems that can operate in several planar reaching modes: assisting users, passively sensing/responding to patient's motions. ARMin is 7-DOF upper limb exoskeleton developed from University in Zurich that provides visual, acoustic and haptic interfaces together with cooperative control strategies. Many robotic or robot-assisted rehabilitation devices were developed like Pneu-WREX, T-WREX, RUPERT and more. Some of the robotic therapies are built to be used with game.

The development and deployment of robotic assistive therapy often require significantly high cost making it not widely available in many rehabilitation centres. In contrast of developing more complicated and expensive robots, some efforts should be emphasized on looking for methods that provide 90% of the benefit at the 10% cost [2].

2.1.3 Game Based Rehabilitation

An alternative of therapy which offers fun interaction is in game based therapy. This approach offers low cost of development and provide more engaging interaction between patient and rehabilitative physical activity by utilizing virtual reality technology.

The arrival of game peripheral device, Microsoft Kinect[1] has opened possibilities for game based rehabilitation utilizing gestures. Some game based products for rehabilitation purposes by JINTRONIX[2] and MIRA[3] are commercially available. Many studies and experiments developing games (also known as exergames/serious games/exercise games) targeting to help rehabilitation aspects are built and reviewed as an acceptable tool for rehabilitation due to its low cost and ability to provide adequate accuracy. However, these studies invite questionable practical effectiveness due to the lack of clinical validation [9] and also were built more on ad hoc manner [13].

As the number of stroke cases escalating every year, the resources for stroke rehabilitation has become limited. Healthcare institutions are experiencing under-staffing for not being able to accommodate one-to-one session due to overwhelming demands of rehabilitation services. Many appointments for rehabilitation session are made lower than recommended frequency and thus delaying the recovery process. Moreover, many of traditional rehabilitation requires repetitive of boring, mundane and uninteresting exercises causing depression for many patients. Robot-assisted therapy is deemed expensive and many game rehabilitation experiments are questionable for practical effectiveness.

To overcome these problems, home based rehabilitation must be improved and utilized. This study suggests a more extensive approach in designing home based stroke rehabilitation game with persuasive technology by following Health Behavior Change Support System (HBCSS) concept and Persuasive Systems Design model (PSD). With this game, the patients may optimize their recovery progress by enjoying more immersive experience of home based rehabilitation at their convenient and the overwhelming demands at rehabilitation centres will be better managed. Its economic development involving low cost hardware such as the Microsoft Kinect device would make it more affordable.

3   Health Behavior Change Support System Background

As defined by Oinas-Kukkonen [11], a behavior change support system (BCSS) is a sociotechnical information system with psychological and behavioral outcomes designed to form, alter or reinforce attitudes, behaviors or an act of complying without using coercion or deception. BCSS offers an information system that is transformative and attempting to cause a change of cognitive, emotional and behavior change in the user's current mental state to another planned state. This useful feature is what makes it a suitable concept for designing a persuasive stroke rehabilitation game.

---

[1] http://www.xbox.com/en-US/xbox-one/accessories/kinect.

[2] http://www.jintronix.com/.

[3] http://www.mirarehab.com/.

3.1 Outcome/Change Design Matrix

BCSS suggests the Outcome/Change design matrix as presented in Table 1 to describe the three target potential, successful voluntary outcomes from the user which are the formation, alteration or reinforcement of attitudes, behaviors, or complying.

Table 1. Outcome/Change design matrix [11].

Outcome/Change	C-Change	B-Change	A-Change
F-Outcome	Forming an act of complying (F/C)	Forming a behavior (F/B)	Forming an attitude (F/A)
A-Outcome	Altering an act of complying (A/C)	Altering a behavior (A/B)	Altering an attitude (A/A)
R-Outcome	Reinforcing an act of complying (R/C)	Reinforcing a behavior (R/B)	Reinforcing an attitude (R/A)

BCSS ideally would offer long-lasting support to the user, and the specific intended change in the target user would affect the design and architecture of a BCSS. With the clear target of behavior change being set in the O/C Design Matrix, the system can be designed and evaluated much more efficiently. Langrial et al. [14] showed a practical examples of this matrix usage in the past BCSSs and highlighted its usefulness in future use of BSSCs that is involving social networking.

The health prefix is usually added by researchers to identify their target of study in using BCSS to become HBCSS in order to tailor the implementation within its healthcare context. Many application domains under the application of BCSS have been studied such as exercise with using heart rate monitors, alcohol interventions, weight loss websites, smoking cessation, hazardous drinking, diabetes, stress, and substance abuse.

HBCSS also is a highly potential area for game applications. Alahäivälä and Oinas-Kukkonen [13] had reviewed on 15 gamified health intervention papers and argued that the step of persuasion context analysis is essential in further research of gamified HBCSS.

3.2 PSD Model

Fogg [1] has described persuasion is an attempt to change attitudes or behaviors or both (without using coercion of deception) and further describe the first conceptualization of persuasive feature in computer software in his seminal book. Persuasive Systems Design (PSD) Model was then the state-of-the-art design and evaluation tool created by Oinas-Kukkonen and Harjumaa [10] stated that the development of persuasive systems requires three steps: understanding the key design issues related to persuasive systems, analyzing the persuasion context, and designing the system qualities as illustrated in Fig. 1.

According to PSD Model, the first step is to understand that the seven premises design issues must be addressed in relation to designing the persuasive stroke

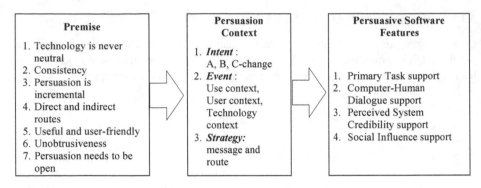

Premise	Persuasion Context	Persuasive Software Features

1. Technology is never neutral
2. Consistency
3. Persuasion is incremental
4. Direct and indirect routes
5. Useful and user-friendly
6. Unobtrusiveness
7. Persuasion needs to be open
	1. *Intent* :
	   A, B, C-change
	2. *Event* :
	   Use context,
	   User context,
	   Technology context
	3. *Strategy:*
	   message and route
		1. Primary Task support
		2. Computer-Human Dialogue support
		3. Perceived System Credibility support
		4. Social Influence support

Fig. 1. Persuasive system design model [8]

rehabilitation game. These premises are however not to be followed as concrete instructions but more as basic guidelines. For this study, the most important premise is the "useful and user friendly" premise whereby the game design and interaction must be easy for the patient to use. For instance, the game must have a smooth navigation between menus, texts and/or icons presented must be readable and clear.

The second step which is to carefully analyse the persuasion context. This can be done by describing the *persuasion intent* (recognizing the persuader and intended outcome/change), the *persuasion event* (defining the use context, user context and technology context) and the *persuasion strategy*. This analysis will be further described in the following section.

The third step is selecting persuasive software features to be implemented in the game. PSD model includes all 28 potential system features which are divided into 4 categories: primary task support (e.g: tailoring, tunnelling, self-monitoring), dialogue support (e.g: verbal praise, timely suggestions, virtual rewards, real-time reminders), credibility support (e.g: showing expertise or referring to authority and endorsements) and social support (e.g: social learning, comparison, facilitation). It should be noted that not to include all design principles in one system as it may decrease its overall persuasiveness [11].

Past studies of HBCSS has shown that it may be effective in changing its user's behaviour. A video game named iLift [8] was developed for nursing personnel to train them in proper lifting and transfer techniques to avoid lower back problems. This study concluded that HBCSS can be effective and the result also showed that cultural aspects especially in regard to technology acceptance must be well addressed. Another HBCSS example is the web based information portal, Onnika [7] was developed as a lifestyle intervention for participants who were at risk of developing a metabolic syndrome. The result showed the persuasive software features like self-monitoring, reminders, and tunnelling were perceived as beneficial and showed the need for social support appeared to grow along the duration of the intervention and unobtrusiveness was found to be very important in all stages.

4 HBCSS Implementation

The following section discusses the implementation of HBCSS in designing the persuasive stroke rehabilitation game. This is done by recognizing the *intent* according to the O/C Design Matrix and following the second and third step in PSD model.

4.1 Persuasion Context Analysis

This section focuses on the analysis of persuasion context related to stroke rehabilitation game design. In the persuasion context analysis step, the *intent*, the *events* and the *strategy* will be analysed.

In this game, the *persuader* will be the rehabilitation centre and the caregiver because they will introduce and encourage the patients to use the game. The *intended outcome/change* are recognized as three main outcomes which are (i) to form a compliance (F/C), (ii) to altering the compliance (A/C) and (iii) to reinforce the compliance of exercising regularly by following specific rehabilitation session.

The *events* will then be further recognized according to *use context*, *user context* and *technology context*. The *use context* is mainly to provide rehabilitation exercise with game technology incorporated. Game features such as goal settings, performance tracking, and achievements record are made available for the stroke patients. The *user context* can be recognized as the patient's profile and the specific stroke rehabilitation treatment. This is normally identified when the patient considered as outpatient and when home based rehabilitation is recommended. One usefulness of user profile is it may load the game setting according to patient's preference making the game more adaptive towards its user.

For *technology context* analysis, the game will use Kinect as low cost motion sensing technology to track patient's exercise. Internet connection should be available in the game for communicating game results to the rehabilitation centre.

The *message* for the patient is to instruct the patient to perform the specific rehabilitation session regularly. While the *direct strategy* used is the patient must comply with rules in the game and *indirect strategy* used is the game interaction persuades the patients to perform rehabilitation with its interactive environment. The results of the analysis of this persuasion context are summarized in Table 2.

4.2 Selection of Persuasive Principles

Final step in PSD model is to select the persuasive systems design principles to be used as the game design features. Table 3 shows the selected persuasive system design principles according to their categories.

The game should be recommended as home based rehabilitation after the stroke patient is considered as outpatient. The game must be pre-loaded with the patient profile such as age, sex and rehabilitation treatment and patient's preference setting. If the patient's technology literacy is too low, he/she might not be able to use the game since it is unfamiliar for patients to use. The care taker might be needed to learn about the game too in order to assist the patient. A small hands-on session or tutorial might be conducted to expose the game to both the care taker and patient.

Table 2. Persuasion context analysis for stroke rehabilitation game

The intent	Description
Persuader	• The rehabilitation centre and caregivers are being the persuader as they will introduce the game for stroke patient to use • The game designed to be autogenous as the patient will play the game on his/her own
Intended Outcome/Change	• Three main outcome are identified which are: (i) to form a compliance (F/C), (ii) to altering the compliance (A/C) and (iii) to reinforce the compliance of exercising regularly by following specific rehabilitation session
The event	**Description**
Use context	• The main purpose of the game is to provide an immersive, fun, and engaging experience for the patient to perform rehabilitation exercise at home • At the beginning rounds, the caretakers might have to force the patients to use it • The game offer features of goal setting and content management system for handling various formats of files • The game also include online capabilities as a mean of communication between home and rehabilitation centre
User context	• An early assessment of the patient's condition shall be made in order to tailor and personalize the game in order to have more focused game. The game will suggest necessary gesture in order to optimize the exercise
Technology context	• The game is based on motion sensing technology to detect gesture • The game also equipped with internet access to facilitate data transfer to/from the rehabilitation centre for further assessment by therapist. It will also facilitate any transfer of any necessary files to the game like videos, documents and others
The Strategy	**Description**
Message	• Patient must perform rehabilitation session
Route	• Direct – The rules in the game requires the patient to perform specific gesture as suggested by the rehabilitation session • Indirect – The game interaction environment will indirectly persuade the patient to perform rehabilitation session

Table 3. Selected persuasive system design principles

Primary task support	Computer-human dialogues support	Perceived system credibility support	Social influence support
Reduction	Praise	Trustworthiness	Cooperation
Tunnelling	Rewards	Expertise	
Simulation	Suggestion	Real world feel	
Tailoring	Liking		
Personalization	Social Role		
Self-monitoring			

The starting point of the game will be the dashboard. Here the patient can access his/her profile detail, track records (if any) and able to set target. For a start, the target maybe recommended by the therapist first. The patient will follow the game according to the target set and try to achieve it under recommended time given. The score will be recorded when the game is completed and kept as an achievement.

The achievement will then be graded and medals or trophy might be awarded for the patient. The patient must be able ability to keep these achievements in the game dashboard and also able to share them with the therapists/other patients or family members by social interaction and accept praises or comments. This social support gained by the patients will then motivate them to set a new/next target and achieve them.

For instance, a patient with paralyzed left arm rehabilitation can start with major muscle group (shoulder and elbow) exercise to improve muscle plasticity and range of movement followed by fine motor rehabilitation (hand and fingers) exercise. The first recommended goal might be is to perform exercise game concentrating on shoulder movements for an adequate number of times. The game also allows video recording while performing the exercise for assessment purpose. If the goal is achieved, an assessment should be done by the therapist first before setting another goal which is about elbow movement. An assessment is necessary as to protect the patient from over train and resulting to injury. Rewards gained from each of goals accomplished will be displayed in the patient's dashboard.

4.3 Game Scenario

The following scenario will illustrate the usage of the selected persuasive features in the proposed game. A male patient who suffered a paralyzed left arm is undergoing a rehabilitation treatment. The game suggested to him by the therapist will be a metaphorical fishing game namely "Fishing trip with Mat". First, the therapist will ask the patient's detail to key in to the game and then assigned a special name preferred by the patient (e.g.: Pak Atan). The therapist also customize the avatar to the patient's liking. While implementing this setting, the caretaker is guided by the therapist so that assistance can be provided at home later. At this stage, the game offers a *personalization* and *liking* design principle whereby the customization is available for the patient. Logo of rehabilitation centre may appear in the game's main menu to show *trustworthiness* and *expertise*.

When this initial game setup is done, the game will start by meeting with an avatar named 'Mat' in a small boat by a jetty. Mat is going to be the patient's virtual friend to show the patient on how to play this game. Mat will provide guidance on what are the necessary hand movements involved like how to paddle the boat, how to setup a bait and lines on fishing rod and how to start fishing. He praises the patients on every correct gestures and also suggest simpler gestures if the patients unable to comply with the game whenever necessary (e.g.: using normal arm to help impaired arm to perform specific gestures). Besides Mat interaction, visual cues are also provided in the game such as a pop up window showing simple animated instructions to aid patient. The main exercise for rehabilitation happens here whereby many persuasive design principles such as *reduction*, *tunnelling* and *tailoring*, *self-monitoring* can be seen. The virtual environment like the lake, boat, fishing gears in the game *simulates* the real fishing trip experience to provide. In addition, Mat virtual presence is offering *social role, praise, suggestion*, and *cooperation* for the patient. Every correct gestures that have to be performed by the patient must be specific according to the real rehabilitation exercise to provide *real world feel* of the real and correct exercise.

If the patient is able to catch a fish at the end of the game, it will be as a reward or trophy for the patient. To promote early usage for the patient, the game difficulty should be adjusted to low as to promote further usage of the game in later session. More interesting gameplay feature such as variety of fish to catch in various locations, attractive fishing gears and more challenging difficulties might provide immersive gaming experience for the patient and indirectly affecting the patient's motivation to exercise.

5 Conclusions

This paper has described the application of persuasion technology in designing stroke rehabilitation game according to Health Behavioral Change Support System concept and following PSD model. The proposed game is intended to provide more immersive, engaging and fun experience for stroke patients to exercise while achieving its main goal which is to affect the attitude of stroke patient in performing rehabilitation. The major implication of this study is to provide a comprehensive persuasion context analysis in PSD model approach for designing the persuasive stroke rehabilitation game. The game scenario described has helped to actualize the usage of selected persuasive design principles. The next necessary step is to develop a prototype for usability testing and evaluation based from the design. By following the PSD model and HBCSS framework, this approach will avoid the black-box thinking approach in research and development of any health intervention information systems.

References

1. Fogg, B.J.: Persuasive Technology: Using Computers to Change What We Think and Do. Morgan Kaufmann, San Francisco (2003)
2. Gregory, P., Edwards, L., Faurot, K., Williams, S.W., Felix, A.C.G.: Patient preferences for stroke rehabilitation. Top. Stroke Rehabil. 17(5), 394–400 (2010). doi:10.1310/tsr1705-394
3. Global Status Report on Noncommunicable Diseases (2014). http://who.int/nmh/publications/ncd-status-report-2014/en/
4. Stroke in Malaysia. http://www.nasam.org/english/prevention-what_is_a_stroke.php
5. Hope: A Stroke Recovery Guide. http://www.stroke.org/stroke-resources/library/hope-stroke-recovery-guide
6. Recovering After a Stroke: A Patient and Family Guide. http://www.strokecenter.org/wp-content/uploads/2011/08/Recovering-After-a-Stroke.pdf
7. Karppinen, P., Oinas-Kukkonen, H., Alahäivälä, T., Jokelainen, T., Keränen, A.-M., Salonurmi, T., Savolainen, M.: Persuasive user experiences of a health behavior change support system: a 12-month study for prevention of metabolic syndrome. Int. J. Med. Inf. 96, 51–61 (2016). doi:10.1016/j.ijmedinf.2016.02.005

8. Kuipers, D.A., Wartena, B.O., Dijkstra, B.H., Terlouw, G., van't Veer, J.T.B., van Dijk, H. W., Prins, J.T., Pierie, J.P.E.N.: iLift: a health behavior change support system for lifting and transfer techniques to prevent lower-back injuries in healthcare. Int. J. Med. Inf. **96**, 11–23 (2016). doi:10.1016/j.ijmedinf.2015.12.006

9. Mousavi Hondori, H., Khademi, M.: A review on technical and clinical impact of microsoft kinect on physical therapy and rehabilitation. J. Med. Eng. **2014**, 16 (2014). doi:10.1155/2014/846514

10. Oinas-Kukkonen, H., Harjumaa, M.: Persuasive systems design: key issues, process model, and system features. Commun. Assoc. Inf. Syst. **24**(1), Article 28 (2009)

11. Oinas-Kukkonen, H.: A foundation for the study of behavior change support systems. Pers. Ubiquit. Comput. **17**(6), 1223–1235 (2013)

12. Reed, K.B., Handžić, I., McAmis, S.: Home-based rehabilitation: enabling frequent and effective training. In: Artemiadis, P. (ed.) Neuro-Robotics: From Brain Machine Interfaces to Rehabilitation Robotics, pp. 379–403. Springer, Dordrecht (2014). doi:10.1007/978-94-017-8932-5_14

13. Alahäivälä, T., Oinas-Kukkonen, H.: Understanding persuasion contexts in health gamification: a systematic analysis of gamified health behavior change support systems literature. Int. J. Med. Inf. **96**, 62–70 (2016). doi:10.1016/j.ijmedinf.2016.02.006

14. Langrial, S., Stibe, A., Oinas-Kukkonen, H.: Practical examples of mobile and social apps using the outcome/change design matrix. In: First International Workshop on Behavior Change Support Systems, CEUR Conference Proceedings, vol. 973, pp. 7–13 (2013)

Designing an Interactive Mural for Cultural Reflections

Wei Hong Lo and Kher Hui Ng[✉]

School of Computer Science, University of Nottingham Malaysia Campus,
Jalan Broga, 43500 Semenyih, Selangor, Malaysia
{khcy4lwo, Marina.Ng}@nottingham.edu.my

Abstract. While many cultural heritage projects currently exist, few explore how to record and transform intangible heritage into a publicly accessible collection. This paper presents an interactive system combining the Web and Internet of Things (IoT) technologies to create an internet-linked interactive mural that allows visitors to listen and interact with crowdsourced life stories. Our findings highlight positive user reactions and some evidence of the interactive system being able to support cultural reflections. While the life stories appeal to most of the adults, younger children were less patient and interested in listening to them. Instead they were attracted to visual projections and the unobtrusive technology. We propose a design framework, outlining three design aspects necessary to understand and design engaging and immersive user experience. The use of interactive mural enabled us to understand the challenges of preserving and sharing intangible heritage so that they are heard and can be reflected upon in greater depth. The paper also outlines recommendations for future work to include a long term longitudinal study and to introduce mechanism for reviewing crowdsourced content.

Keywords: Interactive mural · Intangible cultural heritage · Internet of Things · Cultural reflection · Design guidelines

1 Introduction

The role of museums has changed over the years - learning is not the only goal of museum visitors [1]. As well as their traditional role of collecting, preserving and sharing rich collections, museums now find that they play an increasing role in helping shape cultural identity and bringing different community groups together. Through access to objects, information and knowledge visitors can see themselves and their culture reflected in ways that encourage new connections, meaning making and learning [2]. With the emergence of the concept of an important intangible cultural heritage to be considered and supported alongside the physical and tangible heritage, the concept of cultural identity as the result of a collective historic experience in all fields become closely linked to this living heritage [3]. The 2003 UNESCO Intangible Heritage Convention defines the Intangible Cultural Heritage as the: "...*means the practices, representations, expressions, knowledge, skills – as well as the instruments, objects, artefacts and cultural spaces associated therewith – that communities, groups*

© Springer International Publishing AG 2017
H. Badioze Zaman et al. (Eds.): IVIC 2017, LNCS 10645, pp. 570–581, 2017.
https://doi.org/10.1007/978-3-319-70010-6_53

and, in some cases, individuals recognize as part of their cultural heritage. This intangible cultural heritage, transmitted from generation to generation, is constantly recreated by communities and groups in response to their environment, their inter-action with nature and their history, and provides them with a sense of identity and continuity, thus promoting respect for cultural diversity and human creativity."

Within contemporary museology, personal memoirs and reminiscences of all kinds are now recognized as forming a significant part of the intangible cultural heritage, within which the individual experience forms a part of the common and shared memories that make up the identity of a community. In the subsequent years, many different kinds of public and private organisations and projects have called upon the public to tell their story, share their memories and offer their life stories for social action through an increasing use of digital media. For example, the Museu Da Pessoa in Brazil is a virtual and collaborative museum of life stories that aims to record, preserve and transform life stories into a source of information and connection between people around the world [4]. The main question then is how to create a simple and easily re-applicable way to allow any community and organization to create its own historical narrative as a tool of social change. The second question then was to consider how to help all these organisations to share these narratives so that they are heard in order to exist socially. While a large number of organisations practiced the recording of stories, very few tools exist to process and transform them into a publicly accessible collection.

This paper is thus motivated by the desire to explore the full potential of Internet of Things (IoT) technology to help address this challenge. We have focused our work on the design and development of a surface-based public interactive installation linked to the web, with the aim of promoting understanding of a shared history and culture in Malaysia within a Peranakan framework. Peranakan people, also known as Babas and Nyonyas, were usually local-born child with a foreign parent whom most likely is at the Straits of Malacca for trading [5]. Current visits to most local museums in Malaysia including the Baba Nyonya Heritage Museum in Malacca still rely on self or personal guided tours. We present results concerning the use of crowdsourced life stories and visitors' experiences of interacting with them through an interactive mural. We syn-thesise our experience into a general design framework for guiding future designers wishing to develop similar public interactive exhibits.

The paper begins by reviewing related work to provide necessary background and describing the method, study participants and findings. We then propose the design framework and discuss design implications before concluding.

2   Related Work

Cultural heritage is an important topic of research in the area of Human Computer Interaction. Current digitisation strategies to increase visitor engagement in museums include the use of augmented reality [6] as they are proven to help in education [7], virtual reality paired with audio outputs for immersive virtual tours [8] and surface-based technologies. There have been many examples of surface-based tech-nology used in museums with the most popular being the multi-touch table top interactive exhibits [9, 10]. They include examples such as Churchill Lifeline,

Illuminated Manuscript, Tilty Table and many more as reviewed in an article by Geller [11]. These table top exhibits feature either touchscreen or projections on to different surfaces such as canvas [12] or a blank book [13] with sensors to detect input and usually features some activity such as trivia questions or electronic quests. However, these interactive table top studies usually focus on the technology itself and less on the content used [14]. Most of these studies used only facts and trivia as their content.

Life stories and reminiscences can be considered a significant category of the intangible cultural heritage which value or importance cannot be denied. New technologies represent an enormous possibility for the dissemination of personal narratives across and between scales. For example, the StoryBeads project created an interactive system that incorporates physical objects and modern technology for recording and replaying oral stories that can preserve the meaning of the handcrafted beadwork of the BaNtwane people [15]. Mobile technologies have also been explored as a mechanism for preserving intangible heritage [16]. I-Treasures project proposes the use of a variety of sensors such as facial expression analysis and vocal tract sensing technologies to document the singers' expressions and singing techniques [17]. The communication of these intangible heritage via technologies presents both a challenge and an opportunity for communities and museums. This paper fills the gap by presenting a technique using a visual illusion surface-based exhibit to bring cultural reflection to users. This is further supported by crowdsourcing the content - transformative life stories to be experienced by visitors.

3 Development Process

3.1 Project Design and Iteration

The setting for our interactive visitor experience was the Baba Nyonya Heritage Museum in Malacca, a place where visitors get to learn about the Peranakan culture through existing self and personal guided tours. Our early exploration over a six-month period involved conducting ethnographic studies and brainstorming sessions with museum curators to identify requirements for the interactive experience. The focus on collecting and making public life stories around the Peranakan culture [5, 18, 19] was identified, in line with the museum's role and interest to document intangible cultural heritage in the form of life stories among older Peranakan generations for future generations.

The research project was conducted in 2 phases: (1) the first phase involved the design and development of a basic interactive mural as proof of concept, and (2) then a more advanced prototype version with additional features was developed. The

Fig. 1. Interactive mural prototype

content of the interactive mural highlighted the stories of the Peranakan people where they talked about their ancestry roots and cultural history. As culture can be sustained by constant practice [20], the interactive mural, built on IoT technology allows visitors to listen and connect to life stories crowdsourced among Peranakan people, even of those whom may have moved away from Malacca to different parts of the country or world. This technique is vital to preserve the intangible heritage of the Peranakan culture.

The physical design of the basic prototype of interactive mural consists of visuals printed on a big foam board (Fig. 1). Touch sensitive points on the board were created using conductive paint [21]. The touch points were connected to a Bare Conductive touch board which is a variant of Arduino [22, 23] using cables, with all hardware hidden at the back of the board. Then, users can listen to the crowdsourced audio stories upon touching the touch points. This basic prototype was initially trialled in a public exhibition at the museum by 20 participants of different ethnic groups including 2 children below the age of 12. Positive feedback was gathered whereby all participants lauded the idea of an online platform for people to upload and share their life stories through the web and the majority of them (80%) preferred the interactive mural, as an unobtrusive exhibit compared to a touch screen exhibit. There was also some high degree of success (85%) in getting participants to experience cultural reflections. However, a few participants recommended adding more indication to show that it is an interactive exhibit, for example, using a more prominent sign. It was observed that the level of user engagement with the exhibit could be further improved.

As such, the second iteration of the interactive mural involved digital projection directly onto the board surface for additional visual output in correspondence with associated audio stories. For example, the projector projects vibrant illustrations onto areas of board that is empty except for some objects pre-painted with conductive paint. This allows the background scene to be changed depending on the audio story from which category of Peranakan ethnicities – Kristang, Chitty, Chinese, Baba Nyonya and others/mix it has been selected and playing from. The second iteration also features usage of IoT to download new audio files from the server to the mural (Fig. 2).

Fig. 2. Welcome screen and one of the ethnic group (during trial) of the final product

3.2   Project Implementation

We had developed the interactive mural for public interaction and a website for users to submit their own online stories as a crowdsourcing method. The interactive mural uses a Raspberry Pi 3 [24] which is equivalent to a mini computer and a Bare Conductive PiCap adapter that attaches to the Raspberry Pi 3 to allow touch input. It is coded via Python and provides audio for the interactive mural through the PyGame library (Fig. 3). The graphical interfaces that are projected by the projector are designed via Adobe Illustrator.

The website is coded via WordPress [25] on the Baba Nyonya Heritage Museum domain with the aid of a CPanel server. It allows users to submit their own audio stories which the Raspberry Pi 3 can periodically download through Wi-Fi connection and play through the interactive mural, allowing the content to be crowdsourced and dynamic (Fig. 4).

```
# Starting screen function        def babanyonya():
def scene1(i):                        print ("User selected Baba Nyonya")
    # Define dictionary for scene1   chgImage('fyp-art/5BabaNyonya-01.png')
    select = { 0 : displayHelp,
               1 : kristang,         light_rgb(1, 0, 0)
               2 : others,           light_rgb(0, 0, 0)
               3 : babanyonya,
               4 : chitty,           pygame.mixer.music.load('Audrey_Lim.mp3')
               5 : malay,            pygame.mixer.music.play()
               6 : how,
               }
    select[i]()                       chgScene()
```

Fig. 3. Snippet of code (dictionary definition in Python and one of its sample function)

Fig. 4. Webpage for users to upload their audio stories

4 Evaluation

4.1 Participants

To evaluate the final interactive mural, a public user trial was conducted at the Baba Nyonya Heritage Museum over the course of three days. In total, 25 participants participated in the survey. About 30% of the participants were children (accompanied by adults). About 25% of the participants were tourists from another country.

4.2 Methodology

After signing the consent form and having received a brief explanation about the exhibit, the participants were free to explore and interact with the interactive mural. No assistance was provided at the beginning unless requested or required. Participants were also allowed to look at the back of the interactive mural to get an idea of how it works. At the end of the experience, questionnaires were administered to the participants to gain feedback on the usability of the interactive mural and to determine how well it supports cultural reflection. It is not simply enough to make invisible stories visible. As the interactive system aims to promote personal and social transformation through reflection, we were interested to gain evidence on whether, for example, by listening to a life story, participants could feel, to understand and to experience another existence - to realise how much of the other could be inside themselves and how much of themselves could be in the other. In order to evaluate these, direct user observations were also made on how participants interact with the exhibit along with video recordings of it. Other than questionnaires, interviews were conducted for some participants who were willing to share more.

5 Results

5.1 Results of Survey on Usability Aspects

Based on the results of questionnaire in relation to the usability of the interactive mural, a summary of key findings is as found below:

- When asked if participants prefer touch screen exhibits or the interactive mural, 48% of the participants preferred the interactive mural compared to a touch screen and another 48% preferred both.
- When asked if the interactive mural is engaging enough to catch and retain their attention, a high majority of participants (84%) agreed.
- When asked if the audio stories were interesting enough to hold their attentions, all the participants agreed by giving a score of 5 out of 10 or more.
- On evaluating the educational value of the interactive mural, more than half the participants strongly agree giving a score of 9 or 10 out of 10.

Through interviews and user observations, it was found that the projector placed directly in front of the interactive mural presented a usability issue when participants tended to stand in front of the exhibit blocking the line of light projection. We foresee this could be easily improved by using short-throw projector mounted from the ceiling. There were also issues with language compatibility as many visitors to the museum were non-English speaking tourists, thus could not participate in the trial.

5.2 Results of Analysis

Based on the results obtained from both user trials, further analysis of the data is done to gain more valuable insights. The results of data analysis are classified into several categories which will be explored below.

Age Group

The interactive mural is not limited to any specific age groups. However, it was observed that children usually tend to lose interest in the audio stories before they end, suggesting that current content needs to be modified to suit younger children. This might be in the form of shorter audio clips or accompanied with animations.

Cultural Reflection

In response to the survey question on the level participants experienced cultural reflection when interacting with the content on a scale of 1 (very low) to 10 (very high), the average scores given by participants were 7.15 and 7.2 out of 10 for the basic and advanced prototype respectively. The consistent results suggest the effectiveness of using real peoples' stories as intangible heritage content for supporting reflection. However, it is important to note the quality of the audio stories are vital as well and must be moderated when users upload to the internet which was not done in this research.

Crowdsourcing

Most people supported the idea of having the audio stories crowdsourced as it was said to provide a personal touch and more intimate connection with the listener. Participants liked that the stories were crowdsourced although the sample size of content (6 crowdsourced audio stories) for this research project is minimal. However, it is unsure of how many people would participate in contributing to the audio stories, as this would require marketing strategies to engage online users, which is outside the scope of current research.

Ambience Noise

There were many complaints about audio volume especially in the prototype where it was near a busy street. The final interactive mural has improved ambience and a louder volume but some participants still found it hard to hear the audio stories especially when there were many people around. Potential solutions to the problem include to provide headphones or earbuds in addition to the speaker or to implement usage of directional speakers.

Educational Value

Most of the participants were interested to know how the technology works, for example by looking behind the board. The majority of them appreciated a tutorial functionality explaining how the conductive pain works by interacting with the interactive mural directly (rather than on paper). Mostly, younger children tend to be more interested to learn about the technology rather than the educational content.

6 Discussion

Throughout the process of developing and testing the interactive mural, it is evident that although the overall interactive visitor experience was positive, it lacked certain level of immersion. Having reflected on the design process, findings and current literature on how to design immersive technologies [26], we synthesised lessons learned into a design framework for understanding and planning the design and development of similar interactive exhibit. Firstly, future designers should consider three important design aspects to create an engaging user experience: (1) Balancing physical and digital interactions to support natural user interactions, (2) Creating multisensory input/output interactions, and (3) Increasing the level of immersion.

As shown in Fig. 5, one of the design considerations is to determine the physical and/or digital technology to be used to achieve earlier defined design goals. In this project, a tangible exhibit was developed for visitors to experience audio stories where users could touch the electric paint and get audio and visual feedback. It could be a completely virtual experience such as virtual reality (VR), a physical exhibit such as a physical simulator or a mix of both physical and digital technologies to create a mixed reality application. Our results showed that an interactive exhibit that is able to support natural user interaction will better catch and retain the attention of users.

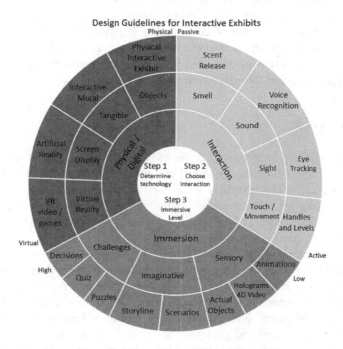

Fig. 5. Design guidelines for interactive exhibits based on immersive interaction design [26]

The method of interaction is another design aspect that will affect the immersion level to a certain extend. During the user trials of the interactive mural, it was observed that visitors enjoyed physically interacting with the exhibit. When the interactive mural was improved with output digital projections, users especially children became even more fascinated by the unobtrusive technology and seeing the digital projections changed when touched. As such, we believe that multisensory interactions could further increase user engagement and may be achieved through the use of scent, physical movements of body, touching, hearing of sound and seeing. It is also possible to include taste as an interaction method, though less popular and developed. It can be anticipated that with increased active interactions, to include physical discovery such as turning of handles and opening flaps/boxes to reveal additional information, users will feel more engaged and have improved user experience.

The final design aspect is the immersion level, which we have stated can be affected by the amount and quality of interaction. More sensory usually means a better immersion but the quality counts as well [26], for example a well written story may be more immersive than a low-quality animation or VR. The other factors affecting immersion are our imagination and cognitive challenges. By using scenarios and settings where user uses their imagination and explore their feelings, better learning and understanding ensues [27]. The interactive mural does provide audio stories for listeners to imagine being in another's shoe, but it highly depends on the audio content. With addition of more images or animation, we postulate more could be felt and imagined by the users, further stimulating the reflective experience. Challenges could also be posed as part of an interactive surface design to encourage users to think of solutions and make decisions, allowing stronger engagement with the content.

In summary, designing for a high level of immersion in the user experience of a surface-based exhibit is essential. A combination of physical/digital technology, multisensory feedback and suitable immersive method and content will determine the level of success of an interactive exhibit. The interactive mural managed to fair well but could be improved further through future work.

7 Future Work

The first thing that can be improved is the overall physical quality of the interactive mural. It is vital that the interactive mural can handle daily interaction without much degradation in quality. This translates to the need to use better material such as canvas, directional speakers for optimal sound quality and ultra-short throw projector for a better viewing experience. This plays an important part in creating immersion as quality of aesthetic promotes extended user interactions.

Based on participant feedback, it was found that crowdsourced content seems to be favourable and valuable in invoking memories and/or reflections among visitors. Due to time limitations, a more comprehensive trial on crowd sourcing could not be done. With that said, all current stories were crowdsourced from contacts with the Baba Nyonya Heritage Museum. Future works may include a longitudinal study and to explore on the effectiveness and guidelines for crowdsourcing content such as how to control and review crowdsourced content. For example, any content that contains inappropriate languages can be filtered out via a speech recognition program to semi-automate and shorten the review process. The rest of the remainder audio stories could then be manually reviewed by a reviewer to ensure it is of appropriate content and of utmost audio quality.

Finally, with certain modifications to the interactive mural, more possibilities of interaction could be achieved. For example, using objects coated with conductive paint to interact with the interactive mural could have diverse interactivity. The interactive mural could turn into a map where users "drive" a toy car coated with electric paint and triggers event as they pass through the landmarks on the map.

8 Conclusion

In conclusion, the project contributes towards understanding how IoT technologies may use to collect and make public intangible cultural heritage stories. It provided a prototype demonstrator in the form of an interactive mural which was trialled in a series of public user trials. Our findings show the potential of interactive mural to enhance visiting experience in museums and most importantly, invoke reflections among visitors by using crowdsourced life stories collected through the web. We have summarised the lessons learned from the design and evaluation process as a design framework enabling the visual informatics and wider HCI community to understand the opportunities as well as gaps that need to be addressed in designing immersive museum exhibits to preserve intangible cultural heritage. The design framework allows designers to look at the design space in a holistic manner in order to seek solutions that will engage users deeply.

When an interactive exhibit supports a high level of user immersion, the knowledge content and transformative message to be reflected upon by users can be easily done. The crowdsourcing method could provide more diverse content with different point of views. In addition to that, an increasing number research in the field of digitalisation of intangible heritage would also greatly benefit the community and promote an understanding of a shared culture among the people.

Acknowledgments. We would like to thank Ms. Melissa Chan from the Baba Nyonya Heritage Museum for allowing us to conduct the evaluation study at the museum and for supporting this research project with constructive feedbacks.

References

1. Kaplan, F.S.: Museums and the making of "ourselves": the role of objects in national identity. Leicester University Press, Leicester (1994)
2. Kelly, L.: Visitors and learners: adult museum visitors' learning identities. na (2007)
3. Solanilla, L., et al.: The internet as a tool for communicating life stories: a new challenge for memory institutions. Int. J. Intang. Herit. 3, 103–116 (2008)
4. Worcman, K., Garde-Hansen, J.: Social Memory Technology: Theory, Practice, Action. Routledge, Abingdon (2016)

5. Lee, S.K.: The Peranakan Baba Nyonya culture: resurgence or disappearance? SARI J. Alam dan Tamadun Melayu **26**, 161–170 (2008)
6. Ng, K.H., Huang, H., Selvamurthy, S., Juzar, M., Sabri, N.A.A., O'Malley, C.: Augmenting learning from physical museum exhibits with personal mobile technology. Transform. Learn. Empower. Learn. **33**, 711–732
7. Di Serio, Á., Ibáñez, M.B., Kloos, C.D.: Impact of an augmented reality system on students' motivation for a visual art course. Comput. Educ. **68**, 586–596 (2013)
8. Song, M., Elias, T., Müller-Wittig, W., Chan, T.K.Y.: Interacting with the virtually recreated Peranakans. In: Proceedings of the 1st International Conference on Computer Graphics and Interactive Techniques in Australasia and South East Asia, p. 223–ff. ACM, New York (2003)
9. Hornecker, E.: "I don't understand it either, but it is cool" - visitor interactions with a multi-touch table in a museum (2008)
10. van Dijk, E.M.A.G., Lingnau, A., Kockelkorn, H.: Measuring enjoyment of an interactive museum experience. In: Proceedings of the 14th ACM International Conference on Multimodal Interaction, pp. 249–256. ACM, New York (2012)
11. Geller, T.: Interactive tabletop exhibits in museums and galleries. IEEE Comput. Graph. Appl. **26**, 6–11 (2006)
12. Reeves, S., Benford, S., O'Malley, C., Fraser, M.: Designing the spectator experience. In: Proceedings of the SIGCHI Conference on Human Factors in Computing Systems, pp. 741–750. ACM, New York (2005)
13. Small Design Firm: Illuminated Manuscript. http://smalldesignfirm.com/project/illuminated-manuscript/#illuminated-manuscript
14. Correia, N., Mota, T., Nóbrega, R., Silva, L., Almeida, A.: A multi-touch tabletop for robust multimedia interaction in museums. In: ACM International Conference on Interactive Tabletops and Surfaces, pp. 117–120 (2010)
15. Smith, A., Reitsma, L., van den Hoven, E., Kotzé, P., Coetzee, L.: Towards preserving indigenous oral stories using tangible objects. In: 2011 Second International Conference on Culture and Computing (Culture Computing), pp. 86–91 (2011)
16. Papangelis, K., Chamberlain, A., Liang, H.-N.: New directions for preserving intangible cultural heritage through the use of mobile technologies. In: Proceedings of the 18th International Conference on Human-Computer Interaction with Mobile Devices and Services Adjunct, pp. 964–967 (2016)
17. Cozzani, G., Pozzi, F., Dagnino, F.M., Katos, A.V., Katsouli, E.F.: Innovative technologies for intangible cultural heritage education and preservation: the case of i-Treasures. Pers. Ubiquitous Comput. **21**, 253–265 (2017)
18. Henderson, J.: Ethnic heritage as a tourist attraction: the Peranakans of Singapore. Int. J. Herit. Stud. **9**, 27–44 (2003). doi:10.1080/1352725022000056613
19. Worden, N.: National identity and heritage tourism in Melaka. Indones. Malays World **31**, 31–43 (2003)
20. Chai, L.T.: Culture heritage tourism engineering at Penang: complete the puzzle of "The Pearl of Orient." Syst. Eng. Procedia **1**, 358–364 (2011). doi:http://dx.doi.org/10.1016/j.sepro.2011.08.054
21. Bare Conductive Electric Paint Technical Sheet. http://www.bareconductive.com/wp-content/uploads/2016/05/ElectricPaint_TechDataSheet.pdf
22. Banzi, M., Shiloh, M.: Getting Started with Arduino: the Open Source Electronics Prototyping Platform. Maker Media, Inc., San Francisco (2014)
23. Badamasi, Y.A.: The working principle of an Arduino. In: 2014 11th International Conference on Electronics, Computer and Computation (ICECCO), pp. 1–4 (2014)
24. Pi, R.: Raspberry pi. Raspberry Pi **1**, 1 (2013)

25. About WordPress. https://wordpress.org/about/
26. Vidyarthi, J.: Sonic Cradle: evoking mindfulness through 'immersive' interaction design (2012)
27. Dirkx, J.M.: The power of feelings: emotion, imagination, and the construction of meaning in adult learning. New Dir. Adult Contin. Educ. **2001**, 63–72 (2001)

Visual Object Interface Signifier of Museum Application for Large Display

Fasihah Mohammad Shuhaili$^{(\boxtimes)}$, Suziah Sulaiman$^{(\boxtimes)}$,
Saipunidzam Mahamad, and Aliza Sarlan

Department of Computer and Information Sciences,
Universiti Teknologi PETRONAS,
32610 Seri Iskandar, Perak Darul Ridzuan, Malaysia
{fasihah_g03599,suziah}@utp.edu.my

Abstract. The use of signifiers, commonly known as affordances, in designing an interface should be given a careful attention since signifiers have been poorly applied especially for large multitouch display. The huge interactional space creates a challenge to the design process. This paper investigates visual object interface signifiers of museum application for a large display in order to support navigation. A user study was conducted with ten of participants interacting with the museum interface, running on a Microsoft SUR40 tabletop. The study findings revealed information on (i) suitable signifiers for a large display and, (ii) features of visible object interface signifiers. Among the suitable signifiers for navigation in the environment are arrow, text or numbers, menu button, and floor map. These findings could be useful for the development of museum interfaces on a large display.

Keywords: Virtual museum · Design interface · Signifier · Affordance · Multitouch tabletop display · Navigation

1 Introduction

Signifier is a term used by researchers to refer to a perceivable signal of the input interaction in designing an interface. The term was recently introduced as previously the term "affordance" was used instead. The term affordance has been heavily criticized because it generates confusion [1] to the virtual world as it is more likely applied for physical control such as door knob and handle rather than for touch devices [2].

Figure 1 shows the transition of the term used in referring the important element in designing interface from affordance to signifier. Affordance is a relationship between specific agents with the object where the agent shall apply possible actions towards the object. It is natural and simply existed where it does not have to be perceivable when it is first introduced by Gibson. After some time, the term was reintroduced by Don Norman but he introduced the term into the design which he was actually referring the term of perceivable affordance. However, many academic scholars misused the term and become confused when it comes to writing an article about the term [3]. Considering the confusion issued, he suggested the term to be replaced by signifier which he briefly provided difference between the two terms affordance and signifier.

© Springer International Publishing AG 2017
H. Badioze Zaman et al. (Eds.): IVIC 2017, LNCS 10645, pp. 582–591, 2017.
https://doi.org/10.1007/978-3-319-70010-6_54

Fig. 1. Transition of term signifier

Affordance in the virtual world refers to any possibilities of action that people explore while signifier refers to signs or perceptible signal of actions that can be done through the discovered possibilities. From this point onwards the term signifier will be used instead of affordance.

Signifier is considered as a critical item in designing interface because it will ensure a user will handle the device properly and allow interaction to happen. The signifier is a core element needed in designing interface where good signifiers can actually keep the users' focus on learning while weak interface design could affect the learning by lagging the progress, causing complication and problem in navigating the interface. There are few common signifiers likely used by users; that are a clickable buttons, underlined text signals [4] and arrows as navigation for the users to interact with the surface [5].

Past research did cover the aspect of signifier but its characteristics has not been fully understood. This leads to the misuse of the term and confusion among researchers. The main element covered by a signifier is the touch ability part which is the main signifier for the touch technology. Meanwhile, the signifier most researchers explored on are the text and menu buttons. Since signifiers are poorly done with multitouch devices [2] and the main focus of this research is to investigate the signifiers, it shows that there are still a lot of signifiers that can be further explored such as arrow signs for navigation and numbers for labeling. These signs and labels are the mapping tools that have been claimed as important in the design and layout of controls and display [5]. Hence, this concludes the need to investigate further on visible object interface signifiers.

In this paper, visible object interface signifier will be identified in designing a virtual museum interface of a large display i.e. a multitouch tabletop. This device supports a more "fluid" collaborative interaction [6] but its large display poses a more challenging task to designers as the device involves large interactional space. In order to investigate on the interface signifier, several sections have been structured as follows. Section 1 presents the concept of signifier. This is followed by Sect. 2 that describes the relationship between interaction and interface, particularly those involving multitouch tabletop surface. Section 3 presents the existing related work on object interface signifier used for navigation. Section 4 describes the methods used in the study while Sect. 5 presents the findings and discusses the work in relation to interfaces for museum environments. Section 6 concludes the paper.

2 Literature Review

2.1 Interaction and Interface

In the virtual world, interaction design is an element that linked to the interface when it comes to interaction design. Interaction design is regarding how the product affect the way people work [1]. It is important to have a good interactive design as it could affect the process of learning, the efficiency of the interface and experience gain by users. As a designer, it is essential to follow basic principles of interaction design in producing a satisfying interaction between the user and the surface. Among the activities of the interaction design that need to be looked at are establishing requirement design, designing alternatives that meet the requirements, prototyping the alternative design and evaluating the developed prototype [2].

In establishing the requirements, a designer should know the target users and type of support an interactive product could equip. These are the fundamental step to a user-centered approach which forms the foundation of the product's necessity and supports the development. Besides target users and type of support that should be recognized, the form factor of the product, the basic posture of a product and the input method of the system should be considered as well [3]. Defining a form factor of a product is to know the hardware and software involved. For example, will the web application be displayed on a high-resolution screen? Or a phone need to be small and visible in dark and bright environment? A basic posture is the user's attention devote while interacting with the product and the product respond towards the devoted attention given. The input method is how the users will interact with the product, is it using a keyboard? Or is it by touching?

Designing the alternatives can be divided into two parts which are conceptual design and concrete design. The conceptual design part usually involves the conceptual model created for the product as the conceptual model is able to plan the user's activities by understanding how to interact with the product. The concrete design consists of details at every aspect of the product including the colors, sounds, images to use, menu design and icon design [2]. When it comes to the development of an interface, there are basic questions a designer should ask themselves before developing an interface, such as what do I want to accomplish? What are the alternative action sequences? What action can I do now? How do I do it? What happened? What does it mean? Is this okay? Have I accomplished my goal? According to [4], to ensure the questions are answered, a designer should concern to these seven aspects; discoverability, feedback, conceptual models, signifiers in the real world and virtual world, mapping and constraints.

A discoverability of the function should be perceivable and obvious for the users to determine the possible action applied for the interface. Feedback is the respond and information obtained after an action is executed that is used to improve the performance of the previous interface for the better. A conceptual model design all the information needed to improve the interface design, signifiers should be included as they are necessary elements that assure discoverability and feedback well interact. They are signs which reveals possible action that can be done on the interface. Mapping is related to the connection among controls and their impacts while constraints are equipped with guides action in using the interface [4]. Lastly, evaluating activity that identifies the usability and acceptability of the signifiers to be used in the future which is measured based on various criteria.

2.2   Multi Touch Tabletop Surface

Touch devices have been widely used and became part of our life due to its user-friendly aspect, attractive design and other beneficial reasons. The ordinary touch screen is only a visual display with a screen that sensitive to single pressure or touch. As technology advanced, a multitouch idea has been introduced that brought great excitement to the field and because of that people keep getting a new sight of making such multi-touch surface through Frustrated Total Internal Reflection (FTIR) technology [5]. The user is able to communicate with a system with more than one finger at a time over multi-touch sensing, as in chording and bi-manual operations. Such sensing devices are inherently capable to accommodate multiple users simultaneously, which is especially advantageous for larger shared-display systems such as interactive walls and tabletops [5].

Multi touch tabletop has been widely used in the various fields due to its ability to bring great advantages to the users. Multi touch tabletop is an interactive horizontal display that allows multiple users to interact while content is displayed on the table [6]. This technology is somewhat new in human computer interaction which is one of the post-WIMP (Window, Icon, Menu, and Pointer) technologies which acknowledge being natural and perceptive that equips flexible collaboration. Its large display affords with a shared surface that support communication among co-located users. [7]. The elements that multi touch tabletop have due to its large size of display and its inter-action is suitable for exhibition and learning purposes.

Concerning the size of the display, the large surface provides huge communication space that supports fluid activities of collaborative interaction [8]. Fluid activities are related to facilitating the transition process among the activities on the interface. For example, there are two to more activities at one time such as painting, writing and browsing, hence universal input device for all tabletop activities would make transitioning between activities smoother [9]. As the large display is able to smoothen the switching between the activities, it is also effective in supporting the information organization activities in the aspect of context-alertness, privacy and content relevance, and spontaneous and casual communication approach [10].

3   Related Work

As signifiers are a fundamentally an important element in a design, having them for navigation helps the user to disclose the sign and obtain the feedback that is well related and comprehensible [4]. Table 1 presented the effort done by researchers in the domain of museum application in relation to signifiers used for navigation. The focus of work ranging from broad issues such as issues that need to be considered when it comes to digitizing information for the virtual museum to a specific topic that involves browsing museum images on the tabletop.

Table 1. Focus of museum application in relation to signifier used for navigation

Focus of work	List of signifiers or characteristics of signifiers	Limitation	Authors
Virtual museums, a survey and some issues for consideration	→Text →Photo	• No obvious signifier to signify the important information	• Styliani et al. [11]
Multi-touch tables for exploring heritage content in public space	→Menu button →Size, rotation, and position of the image	• Difficult to discover the rotate, flick and resize gesture • No reset button to clear the messy or scattered image.	• Creed et al. [6]
Embodied interpretation: Gesture, social interaction, and meaning making in a national art museum	→Text →Images	• An unclear signifier that causes the users unable to perform required actions	• Steier et al. [12]
The development of an e-museum for contemporary arts	→Floor map	• Limited signifier used in navigating the interface	• Patias et al. [13]
Browsing museum image collections on a multi-touch table	→Small text →Icon button	• An unclear signifier that causes the users unable to perform a specific task	• Ciocca et al. [14]

All work included in Table 1 involves navigation in terms of moving around in the environment of the virtual museum. This includes navigation to find information, to browse specific image, and how two or more people interact with one another on the large display when finding the information and browsing the image.

The work presented has claimed that visible object interface signifiers did improve the performance of the user's interaction with the multi touch display. Signifiers help users to navigate the interface where menu button used to ease the users in facilitating the surface [6]. All the recorded works use a variety of signifiers in navigating the interface. Among the signifiers used are menu buttons [6, 14], images [6, 11, 14], floor maps [13] and text [12–14].

However, the signifiers used have their limitation that causes users to face difficulties while performing a certain task. Limitations include absence of obvious signifier to signify the necessary information [11], hard to discover the rotation, flick and resize gesture [6], unclear signifier to perform required actions [12], limited signifier used in navigating the interface [13] and less obvious signifiers [14]. These limitation of listed signifiers lead users to unable to perform required actions or notify the users of important information. Thus the existing work is still lacking in terms of certain features to signify the signifier on a large display.

4   Methodology

The objective of the study is to investigate the features related to signifiers that could be extracted from an existing museum application on a large display.

(i) Participants

Ten students (7 male, and 3 female) participated in this study. The participants were between 18 to 34 years old. All the participants were from Computer and Information

Sciences Department, Universiti Teknologi PETRONAS who use a computer on daily basis and have experience using touch-operated devices. However, some of the participants (40%) had no prior experience with the interactive tabletop.

(ii) Questionnaire survey

Before conducting the study, the participants were asked some questions about their experience in visiting the museum and on using the multi touch tabletop surface. The survey took about five minutes; participants filled the survey form. There are a total of nine questions that were divided into two parts. Six questions for Part 1 and three questions for Part 2 were designed to observe experienced participants and inexperienced participants in giving out opinion at the end of the study.

(iii)   An example of the interface use

Figure 2 is an example of the museum interface used for the preliminary study where there are four sections on it that are; time tunnel, dagger gallery, J.W.W Birch murder, and buildings surrounding the museum. These four sections are the information available at the Pasir Salak Museum.

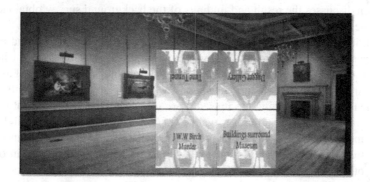

Fig. 2. Top view of museum's interface design for preliminary study

(iv) Research procedure

The study was conducted in a virtual reality laboratory of one postgraduate room for about two weeks. All ten students were divided into five small groups (i.e. with two students in each group) at the beginning of the study and each group did the study one at a time. All of them were briefly explained about Microsoft SUR40 tabletop surface used in the study, and the purpose of conducting the study. There are four sections regarding Pasir Salak museum which the participants need to perform interaction with the system and complete specific task alternately for each section. After two minutes of studying one section, the participants were invited to answer two to three simple quiz together related to the section they just explored. After completing the task, they have to continue and complete the next section. This activity was repeated until the participants completed all four sections. Before doing the study, the participants have been given a short practice with the multitouch table top (around 5 min) so that participants could get acquainted and experienced with the device. Participants were able to begin the collaborative task after we got their confirmation about their familiarities with the system and able to perform the collaborative task. Each group was given 40 min to complete the task. After performing the study, the participant will present their sense and response toward the multi touch digital tabletop through the questions asked. All collected data were then analysed.

(v) Interviews

All participants were interviewed to observe their opinion and preference towards the features of signifiers used during the study. Participants were asked open-ended questions about their experience navigating the surface and opinion about the features of signifiers on the task performed.

5 Result and Discussion

5.1 Questionnaire Survey

This section discusses the result and findings of the background survey obtained before allowing the participants to interact with the multitouch tabletop. Based on the survey conducted, it can be concluded that all ten respondents have experience and exposure towards the museum environment. However, none of the respondents have visited Pasir Salak's museum and thus shows the participants were not familiar with Pasir Salak museum. Art museum and history museum are popular among participants to visit. Among the reasons for visiting the museum are to gain information of what happened in the past, interested in sculpture, to gain experience, for a school visit and for fun. Usually, a museum has its own official website as a platform to disseminate information and eight from ten participants found that website did give them useful information while the other disagree with it. The reason they disagreed was that sometimes the information displayed on the website is not up to date and too general for them to understand. Somehow, if given a choice, the majority of them prefer to visit and experience themselves a visit to the museum.

On the other hand, all of the participants have experience in using touch screen devices. Among the devices are a smartphone, tablet, multitouch tabletop, computer and ATM machine. Lastly, related to user's involvement in using multitouch tabletop, only 40% of them have experienced it while 60% of them have no idea about multitouch tabletop.

5.2 A Set of Suitable Object Interface Signifier

Table 2 presents the findings of determining suitable visible object interface signifier. These are the signifiers that have been mentioned by the respondents to be included in the interface in order for them to navigate the interface. As listed above, the signifiers are arrow, text or number, menu button, and floor maps. A signifier can be words, a graphical illustration or any sign that unambiguous [4]. To navigate an interface, it is important to have more signifiers that provide signs to the user of possible actions that can be applied when interacting with the interface. Lack of signifier is a real drawback towards the interface as it causes lack of discoverability by the users for possible action. In navigating the interface during the study, solving the assigned task will be hard if there is no proper label; text or a number (R1 & R2), arrow and any possible sign to navigate (R1). The respondent also suggested to include a floor map into the interface for better direction to the museum. If floor map is included in the interface, the users can get a clearer picture of the real museum without the need to go there (R3 & R5). Navigating an interface must have text or iconic labels to make sense and users can rely on their instinct or intuition to solve the task [15]. Creating more menu buttons and give a meaningful interpretation on them is really necessary to give users direction while interacting with the surface (R1 & R7).

Having a menu button on an interface is necessary as good signifiers are able to keep users focused on learning rather than learning to operate the interface [16].

Table 2. Analysis of suitable object interface signifier

Signifiers	Respondents
• Arrow	➤ R1
• Text or number	➤ R1, R2
• Menu button	➤ R1, R7
• Floor map	➤ R3, R5

5.3   Features of Object Interface Signifier

Table 3 displays the findings in determining the characteristic of visible object signifier. The three characteristics listed above are the criteria mentioned by the respondents that should have been in the signifiers to make the signal more visible. The respondents said that to pay attention on the size of the arrows, menu buttons or any signifier later (R1) and labeling to improve the user's performance (R1 & R2). Colors also help the users to explain what a signifier might do (R9 & R10). This is because the color will change when the users want to click or clicked a button. These characteristics are believed to support the navigation on the interface since the signifiers become visible and perceivable when these characteristics are included. A signifier should be perceivable, else they will fail to serve its function. It also should be loud and bright enough to be realized as it could attract attention and also deliver information about the nature of the event that is signified. Lack of these criteria will lead to lack of discoverability, thus it might become a drawback of the design [4].

Table 3. Analysis of visible object interface signifier

Characteristics of signifiers	Respondents
• Size	➤ R1
• Labelling	➤ R1, R2
• Color	➤ R9, R10

6 Conclusion

A poorly design interface might frustrate users when navigating an environment. This could be addressed by integrating appropriate visible object interface signifiers into the design. This study has investigated the characteristics of visible object interface signifier used in designing virtual museum interface of a large display. Previous studies have included the concept of signifiers when designing the interface but the researchers probably were not aware of it. This situation happened due to the confusion of the term affordance and its application into design practice. Thus, in the earlier part of this paper, an introduction of the transition from affordance to signifier was presented. However, without an in depth studies on signifiers, the learning process could be delayed and causes difficulties in navigating the environment. This had led to the need of conducting this research. The study was conducted with ten participants to investigate their performance of collaborative learning using multi touch tabletop in order to help identifying suitable visible object interface signifier in supporting the interaction. The participants in the study have highlighted the visible signifiers that should be implemented in the virtual museum interface. Arrow is one of the visible signifiers mentioned. Other signifiers include text or numbers, menu buttons, and floor maps.

Future work will include finding a list of characteristics for visible object interface signifier for multitouch tabletop as they significantly help the signifiers become visible. This list will then be integrated into a museum interface.

Acknowledgements. We would like to thank our study participants for their participations in the study. This research was supported by funding from Universiti Teknologi PETRONAS.

References

1. Dix, A.: Human-computer interaction. In: Liu, L., Özsu, M.T. (eds.) Encyclopedia of Database Systems, pp. 1327–1331. Springer, Heidelberg (2009). doi:10.1007/978-0-387-39940-9_192
2. Preece, J., Sharp, H., Rogers, Y.: Interaction Design: Beyond Human-Computer Interaction. Wiley, Hoboken (2015)
3. Cooper, A., Reimann, R., Cronin, D.: About Face 3: The Essentials of Interaction Design. Wiley, Hoboken (2012)
4. Norman, D.: The Design of Everyday Things: Revised and, Expanded edn. Basic Books, New York (2013)
5. Han, J.Y.: Low-cost multi-touch sensing through frustrated total internal reflection. In: Proceedings of the 18th Annual ACM Symposium on User Interface Software and Technology, pp. 115–118 (2005)
6. Creed, C., Sivell, J., Sear, J.: Multi-touch tables for exploring heritage content in public spaces. In: Ch'ng, E., Gaffney, V., Chapman, H. (eds.) Visual Heritage in the Digital Age. SSCC, pp. 67–90. Springer, London (2013). doi:10.1007/978-1-4471-5535-5_5
7. Chen, W.: Multitouch tabletop technology for people with autism spectrum disorder: a review of the literature. Procedia Comput. Sci. **14**, 198–207 (2012)
8. Johanson, B., Fox, A., Winograd, T.: The interactive workspaces project: experiences with ubiquitous computing rooms. IEEE Pervasive Comput. **1**, 67–74 (2002)

9. Scott, S.D., Grant, K.D., Mandryk, R.L.: System guidelines for co-located, collaborative work on a tabletop display. In: Kuuti, K., Karsten, E.H., Fitzpatrick, G., Dourish, P., Schmidt, K. (eds.) ECSCW 2003, pp. 159–178. Springer, Heidelber (2003). doi:10.1007/978-94-010-0068-0_9

10. Mynatt, E.D., Huang, E.M., Voida, S., MacIntyre, B.: Large displays for knowledge work. In: O'Hara, K., Perry, M., Churchill, E., Russell, D. (eds.) Public and Situated Displays. The Kluwer International series on Computer Supported Cooperative Work, vol. 2, pp. 80–102. Springer, Heidelber (2003)

11. Styliani, S., Fotis, L., Kostas, K., Petros, P.: Virtual museums, a survey and some issues for consideration. J. Cult. Herit. **10**, 520–528 (2009)

12. Steier, R., Pierroux, P., Krange, I.: Embodied interpretation: gesture, social interaction, and meaning making in a national art museum. Learn. Culture Soc. Interact. **7**, 28–42 (2015)

13. Patias, P., Chrysanthou, Y., Sylaiou, S., Georgiades, C., Michael, D., Stylianidis, S., et al.: The development of an e-museum for contemporary arts. In: Proceedings of the 14th International Conference on Virtual Systems and Multimedia (2008)

14. Ciocca, G., Olivo, P., Schettini, R.: Browsing museum image collections on a multi-touch table. Inf. Syst. **37**, 169–182 (2012)

15. Neto, J.N., Neto, M.J.: Immersive cultural experience through innovative multimedia applications: the history of Monserrate Palace in Sintra (Portugal) presented by virtual agents. Int. J. Herit. Digit. Era **1**, 101–106 (2012)

16. Peters, D.: Interface Design for Learning: Design strategies for Learning Experiences. Pearson Education, London (2013)

Mathematics Education and Accessible Technologies for Visually Impaired Students in Bangladesh

Lutfun Nahar$^{(\boxtimes)}$, Azizah Jaafar, and Riza Sulaiman

Institute of Visual Informatics, Universiti Kebangsaan Malaysia (UKM),
43600 Bangi, Selangor, Malaysia
nahar.lutfun3@gmail.com, {azizahj,riza}@ukm.edu.my

Abstract. The learning process for the visually impaired students (VIS) is complicated because they are unable to get visual information. A lot of challenges and problems these VIS are facing to get education, especially in studying Mathematics. As a developing country, Bangladesh cannot afford for the costly Mathematics learning tools for VIS. The objective of this study is to analyze the current scenarios of learning Mathematics in different types of blind schools in Bangladesh. A survey is conducted in all three types of schools in order to achieve the objective. The survey was based on questionnaire comprising questions related to Mathematics learning, examination methods and learning difficulties. Survey results shows that they follow Braille system for reading and writing; however, they cannot write in Braille in the final examination. Taylor frame and abacus are the only options for counting numbers. This paper also tries to propose some key points to improve the current Mathematics learning process for the blind students.

1 Introduction

Disable community are considered the world's largest minority group. Approximately 650 million (10% of the world's population) people live with at least one disability [1]. Among them, a large portion (nearly 285 million) is visually impaired [2]. Approximately, 39 million of them are blind and rests are suffering from low vision. The developing world contains the largest portion of this visually impaired population, which is 90% [2]. Bangladesh is a low-income country with nearly 19.6% physically challenged people having at least one disability [3]. Approximately 750,000 people are visually impaired in Bangladesh [4]. The country has approximately 341,819 VI children in the 6–11 age group, which is about 19.7% of all disabled children in this age group [5].

According to UNESCO, almost 90% disable children in developing countries do not get the opportunity to attend school [1]. Additionally, lack of suitable technological tools and insufficient number of Special school are the two major challenges VI children of developing countries are facing. Bangladesh also struggles with rampant illiteracy along with a lot of people with different types of physical disabilities. The

H. Badioze Zaman et al. (Eds.): IVIC 2017, LNCS 10645, pp. 592–600, 2017.
https://doi.org/10.1007/978-3-319-70010-6_55

literacy rate is quite low (57.7%) in this country, which demands for ensuring education for all regardless of their disabilities [6, 7].

Visually impaired students (VIS) only depend on their touch and haring in their formal education. Braille is the universal method followed in visually impaired people's academia. Many Braille based technologies and methods have been introduced for studying mathematics throughout the world until now. However, VIS still facing many difficulties in studying mathematics specially while calculating the numbers manually. They cannot use calculators like the sighted children. Talking calculator and advanced technological devices are available nowadays in many countries of the world to assist VIS in learning mathematics and science. Bangladesh could not provide mathematics and science related education in tertiary level due to the lack of such assistive technologies for learning mathematics and science. However, VIS have to study mathematics in primary and secondary education and they face many difficulties while studying the subject. In order to know and understand the current scenario in mathematics education in primary and secondary schools for blinds, a survey is conducted. This paper presents the survey results as well as proposes some recommendations to elevate the current condition. The article also discuss about the accessible technologies for mathematics learning that can be implemented in the educational sector for them in Bangladesh.

2   Education for VIS in Bangladesh

Three types of education systems for the children with special needs are available in Bangladesh; namely special, integrated and inclusive education systems [8].

2.1   Special School

Special schools provide education only to students with learning difficulties and physical disabilities. These schools are situated in the 5 major divisional cities of the country. These special schools provide students an education in the Braille system. The MOSW is presently working to develop these schools and upgrade those to high school level [8].

2.2   Integrated School

Integrated Schools has been started in 1974 to provide education for VI children along with sighted children [8]. The program was established by the Department of Social Services (DSS). 47 units were established at the beginning; however, currently 64 are running in selected secondary schools in 64 districts. VI students are taught using Braille system in these schools.

2.3   Inclusive School

Inclusive schools were established to accommodate students with any type of disability. In inclusion schools, every student is treated equally regardless of their ethnic and cultural backgrounds, abilities, gender, age, religion, beliefs and behavior [9, 10]. The government has started to implement inclusive education in primary level of education from 2003. However, the progress of this program is not satisfactory due to the lack of necessary content related to disabilities; lack of skilled and trained teachers, etc [11].

3   Current Scenarios of Mathematics Education in Bangladesh

To analyze the present scenario, four blind schools in Bangladesh were visited to identify the challenges that blind students face, their needs and expectations. The survey was done through questionnaires with eight teachers (5 blind and 3 sighted) who are teaching the blind students in the schools. During this survey the questions were read one by one to the respondents and answers were recorded as some of them were blind. Summary of the questionnaires are given below in Fig. 1.

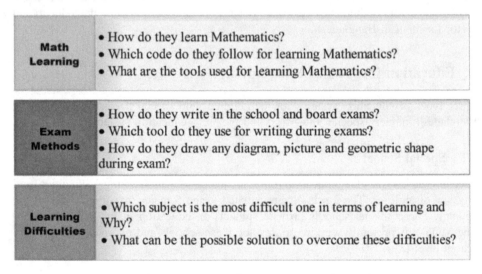

Fig. 1. Summary of survey questionnaire.

All the questions of the questionnaire are arranged in such a way that it can be able to find out all basic information of the three criteria including learning method, math learning, exam methods and learning difficulties. Teachers responded that the traditional slate and stylus remain the only option for students to learn Braille. Additionally, beginners learn numbers and counting by using Taylor Mathematical Slate and still secondary schools use Abacus for counting (Table 1). Due to the unavailable resource they are deprived of science education in Bangladesh. In college and university level they only study those subjects that they can memorize. However, the teachers added that blind students are very curious to know about science subjects. Summary of the response by the participants are given below in Table 1.

Table 1. Summary of responses from questionnaire survey.

Schools	Math learning	Exam methods	Learning difficulties
Special	• Using Taylor frame • UEB • Taylor frame & Abacus	• School exam- Slate & stylus; Board exam- writer • School exam- Slate & stylus • They cannot draw; just don't answer the questions	• Mathematics, because no calculator or any other technological tools • Talking Calculator or any other tools
Integrated	• Using Abacus • UEB • Taylor frame & Abacus	• School exam- Slate & stylus; Board exam- writer • School exam- Slate & stylus • Cannot answer the question as cannot draw	• Mathematics, because no technological tools and lack of efficient and trained teachers • Special Calculators or any technological tools
Inclusive	• Using Taylor frame • UEB • Taylor frame & Abacus	• School exam- Slate & stylus; Board exam- writer • School exam- Slate & stylus • They cannot draw and don't answer the questions	• Science especially Math, because no calculator or other technological tools for science learning • Talking Calculator or any other three dimensional models

4 Available Mathematics Learning Technologies for VIS

4.1 Mathematics Learning Tools Used in Bangladesh

Taylor Mathematical Slate
In mid 19th century Rev. William Taylor developed this device to teach mathematics to the VIS. The Taylor Mathematical Slate consisted of an aluminum frame and a set of metal pegs or type with the patterns. The frame has rows of opening each set out as an eight pointed star. The pegs could therefore be placed in the frame in one of eight orientations which could be used to represent numbers, letters or signs. Math can be composed in linear, vertical or in algebraic notation. Figure 2 shows a Taylor mathematical slate and corresponding algebraic notation.

Abacus
It is a device used by visually impaired children for doing basic mathematical calculations. Abacus is rectangular in shape. Abacuses with varied columns are used in different countries. This instructional material is written specifically for the abacus with 15 columns. The common operations for this abacus are same with those of the

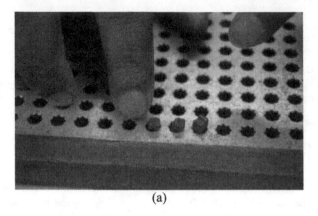

(a)

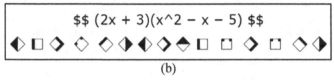

(b)

Fig. 2. (a) Taylor mathematical slate; (b) Algebraic notation.

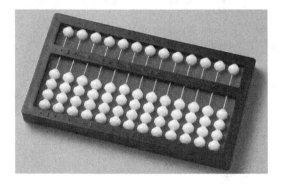

Fig. 3. Abacus for mathematical calculations.

abacuses with fewer columns, but the number of columns matters especially when fraction problems are solved. Figure 3 shows a typical abacus.

4.2   Mathematics Learning Tools Available Throughout the World

Math based Braille technological tools are very limited. However, a range of Technological initiatives and interventions have been introduced all over world to solve the problems and the issues associated with visual impairment and the people affected by it.

REMathEx

Gaura (2002) developed a system REMathEx to assist blind students to study complex mathematical expressions [12]. The system uses the combination of the Braille display and the speech synthesis outputs to provide all the required information about mathematical expressions to the visually impaired students.

Automatic Conversions of Mathematical Braille

Moço and Archambault [13] presented a general discussion on the automatic mathematical Braille translations [13]. There are several Braille notations and each Braille notations has specific rules which make them different than other notations. There are some rules that increase the difficulty of the translation on the side Braille to mainstream notation for blind reading. Using simple mathematical formulas, authors showed few particular rules but not all the specific rules.

ASTER

ASTER is an interactive computing system for writing rules for speaking various parts of text and mathematics. This system works for audio formatting electronic documents written in LATEX to produce audio documents. The effective speaking of mathematics is a key goal of ASTER. It can speak both literary texts and highly technical documents that contain complex mathematics. In an interactive way, using ASTER, an user can request any segments of text or mathematics to be spoken using several different rendering styles [14].

MathPlayer

MathPlayer converts the math into customizable speech or Braille for visually impaired. It is an add-in to Microsoft Internet Explorer that renders MathML visually containing a number of features that make mathematical expressions accessible to people with print-disabilities. MathPlayer integrates with many screen readers including JAWS and Window-Eyes and also works with a number of Text HELP!'s learning disabilities products [15].

Lambda

Lambda is a multimodal approach and it is based on 8-dot Braille cells. This means that nearly all of the Lambda symbols can be represented by a single cell and that there is a one-to-one correspondence between the Braille cells and the visual symbols. The study of mathematics is all but precluded to most blind students because of the reliance on visual notations. The Lambda System is an attempt to overcome this barrier to access through the development of a linear mathematical notation which can be manipulated by a multimodal mathematical editor. This provides access through Braille, synthetic speech and a visual display [16].

Talking Calculator

Figure 4 shows a talking calculator available in the market. It is a calculator used by visually impaired children for doing basic mathematical calculations. It gives voice feedback while giving input using any button. It also provides solution through voice feedback.

Fig. 4. Talking calculator [Picture taken at the Malaysian Association for Blind].

5   Recommendations

Proper use of the existing resources and the implementation of cheap recourses can contribute for the betterment of the present situation. Interview result represent that mathematics is the most difficult subject as there is a lack of technological tools to learn mathematics in this country. Through redesigning the educational infrastructure and implementing different accessible and affordable technologies, Govt. of Bangladesh can satisfy both teachers and students of the schools for blind. Figure 5 shows a strategy implementation model to elevate the current situation in mathematics learning.

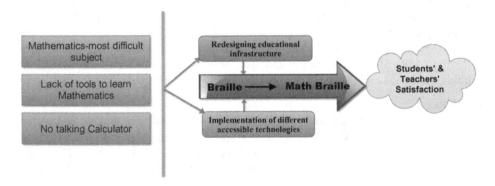

Fig. 5. Strategy implementation model.

5.1   Redesigning Educational Infrastructure

A significant finding in the needs assessment survey was that the blind students cannot write their board examination paper in Braille. The examiners for both the sighted and blind students are same. Therefore, they have to take assistance from another sighted person, who writes on behalf of them. Govt. of Bangladesh should make a separate educational board for the blind students as their writing method is different. If it is not possible to have different education board, then under each education board, Govt.

could make special unit for blind students. In this special unit all the examiner will be selected from blind schools or any schools where blind students study. Their question papers and the answer scripts both will be written in Braille. In this case, VIS will have the opportunity to proof their capabilities.

5.2 Implementation of Different Accessible Technologies

Along with the change in the educational infrastructure, Govt. can adapt some cheap and developed technologies that VIS are using in other countries. For example, Govt. can provide cheap Talking Calculator, as shown in above section, that Malaysian blind schools are using.

Bangladesh Govt. is currently producing DAISY book for the VIS. Along with the DAISY books, Govt. can recommend MathPlayer as it can easily convert mathematics book into both customizable speech and Braille format.

Govt. can introduce tactile graphics for the VIS to learn basic geometrical shapes. TactileView software can be one of the great solutions to produce tactile graphics for this purpose.

6 Conclusions

Students, who are visually impaired, face many challenges in mathematics education as they are deprived of most of the available teaching resources. Therefore, no visually impaired students in Bangladesh are participating in the Science education. Survey results also indicated that seating in the examinations is a big challenge for them as accessible assistive technologies are absent. This scenario can be changed by changing the educational infrastructure together with the implementation of few necessary accessible assistive technologies.

Acknowledgments. The authors acknowledge the funding provided by Universiti Kebangsaan Malaysia through the Zamalah Research University scholarship. The authors also acknowledge the blind schools for providing the information required for this study.

References

1. United Nations. Factsheet on Persons with Disabilities. http://www.un.org/disabilities/default.asp?id=18. Accessed 25 May 2013
2. WHO Media Centre. Visual impairment and blindness. http://www.who.int/mediacentre/factsheets/fs282/en/. Accessed 15 March 2014
3. Mitra, S., Posarac, A., Vick, B.: Disability and poverty in developing countries: a snapshsot from the World Health Survey. In: World Bank Sp Discussion Paper (1109) (2011)
4. Rahman, K.F.: Blindness, 'Vision 2020' and Bangladesh. Financ. Express **20**(436), 10 (2012)
5. Das, A.: Inclusion of student with disabilities in mainstream primary education of Bangladesh. J. Int. Dev. Coop. **17**(2), 1–10 (2011)

6. EFA Global Monitoring Report 2010. Reaching the Marginalized. United Nations Educational, Scientific and Cultural Organization. Oxford University Press (2010)
7. World Facts and Statistics on Disabilities and Disability Issues. http://www.disabled-world.com/disability/statistics/. Accessed 25 March 2013
8. Hossain, M.J.: Special education in Bangladesh: present trend and future needs. In: 28th Asia-Pacific International Seminar on Education for Individuals with Special Needs, Yokohama, Japan (2008)
9. Alam, K.J.: Country report Bangladesh. In: The 25th Asia-Pacific International Seminar on Special Education, Yokohama, Japan, pp. 37–41 (2005)
10. Malak, M.S.: Inclusive education reform in Bangladesh: pre-service teachers' responses to include students with special educational needs in regular classrooms. Int. J. Instruct. 6(1), 195–214 (2013)
11. Das, A., Ochiai, T.: Effectiveness of C-in-Ed course for inclusive education: viewpoint of in-service primary teachers in southern Bangladesh. Electron. J. Inclusive Educ. 2(10), 1–12 (2012)
12. Gaura, P.: REMathEx: reader and editor of the mathematical expressions for blind students. In: Miesenberger, K., Klaus, J., Zagler, W. (eds.) ICCHP 2002. LNCS, vol. 2398, pp. 486–493. Springer, Heidelberg (2002). doi:10.1007/3-540-45491-8_92
13. Moço, V., Archambault, D.: Automatic conversions of mathematical Braille: a survey of main difficulties in different languages. In: Miesenberger, K., Klaus, J., Zagler, W.L., Burger, D. (eds.) ICCHP 2004. LNCS, vol. 3118, pp. 638–643. Springer, Heidelberg (2004). doi:10.1007/978-3-540-27817-7_95
14. Raman, T.V., Gries, D.: Audio formatting—making spoken text and math comprehensible. Int. J. Speech Technol. 1, 21–31 (1995)
15. Soiffer, N.: MathPlayer: web-based math accessibility. In: Proceedings of the 7th International ACM SIGACCESS Conference on Computer and Accessibility, USA (2005)
16. Schweikhardt, W., Bernareggi, C., Jessel, N., Encelle, B., Gut, M.: LAMBDA: a European system to access mathematics with Braille and audio synthesis. In: Miesenberger, K., Klaus, J., Zagler, W.L., Karshmer, A.I. (eds.) ICCHP 2006. LNCS, vol. 4061, pp. 1223–1230. Springer, Heidelberg (2006). doi:10.1007/11788713_176

Designing an Interactive Learning to Enrich Children's Experience in Museum Visit

Zamratul Asyikin Amran[1(✉)] and Novia Admodisastro[2]

[1] Institut Visual Informatik, Universiti Kebangsaan Malaysia, Bangi, Malaysia
zamratul@gmail.com
[2] Faculty of Computer Science and Information Technology,
Universiti Putra Malaysia, Seri Kembangan, Malaysia
novia@upm.edu.my

Abstract. It has long been known that museum education has the ability to motivate and excite visitors whilst providing them with new insights and experiences. Nevertheless, activities that learning goal, for example, visiting a museum is found to disinterest, not appealing and give insignificant impact to children as compared to visiting the amusement park, playground, or even zoo. Thus, museums are increasingly being equipped with digital and mobile technologies. The main goal of using technologies is to improve the museum-going experience for visitors. In this research, we present a study of a museum interactive quest based on the proposed interaction design model. The study involves children in the age of 9 to 11 to visit a museum located in Malaysia. The findings from the study have highlighted the potential of the proposed interaction model that has affected the children enjoyment and engagement during the museum visit.

Keywords: Interaction design model · Museum · Children · Collaboration · User experience

1 Introduction

Nowadays, children have increasing access to television, Internet, video games which reduce the amount of time they spend on physical and perceptual activities that foster the children's cognitive development [1]. In addition, activities that have learning goal, for example, visiting museum or library is found to disinterest, not appealing and give insignificant impact to children as compared to visiting the amusement park, playground, or even zoo. Nevertheless, children are often brought by their parents or teachers to visit the museum to learn about history and artifacts [2]. The museum is an institution that conserves a collection of artifacts and other objects of scientific, artistic, cultural, or historical importance and makes them available for public viewing through exhibits that may be permanent or temporary. Usually, museums do not allow physical contact with the associated artifacts which makes the children feel boring and hinder participation from them.

So far, there are many research attempts to explore the adoption of digital and mobile technologies in many places including the museum. Nowadays museums were

© Springer International Publishing AG 2017
H. Badioze Zaman et al. (Eds.): IVIC 2017, LNCS 10645, pp. 601–611, 2017.
https://doi.org/10.1007/978-3-319-70010-6_56

increasingly equipped with interactive technology to improve the museum visit experience and learning by providing an active engagement process for children who come to visit. The Museon in Hague, Netherlands is one example that promotes interactive and encourages more hands-on approach [3]. The Museon aims to educate people, in particular children, in such a way that they also enjoy themselves. This is one way for museums to deal with these challenges to improve the museum-going experience for children by making children's visits more dynamic, engaging and enjoyable.

In this work, we describe and demonstrate an interaction design model to enrich children's experiences museum visit to promote fun and educational learning. The model emphases the notion of collaboration, engagement and active participation between the children throughout the museum tour. The study is conducted in one of the museums in Malaysia. The remainder of this paper is delivered in six sections. The Sect. 2 provides a brief literature review of previous works on enriching museum visit. The Sect. 3 describes the interaction design model and its prototype. The Sect. 4 discusses the experiment procedures and results. The Sect. 5 provides the discussion and limitations of the research. The Sect. 6 provides concluding remarks.

2 Related Works

The role of museums has shifted from mainly conserve, collect, research, and exhibit artefacts to institutions that are competitive and popular well compare to the library or science exhibition [4]. Nowadays, museums strive to make the place more relevant similar with other activities and cultural centres that focus on both education and entertainment [5]. Yet, in this increasing technology age, less emphasis has been given to the roles that museums have as credible sources of information like the history of war or world heritage [6]. One way for museums to deal with these challenges is to improve the museum-going experience for children by making the children's visits more dynamic, engaging and enjoyable [3]. In addition, social interaction has proven as an important part of learning [7] and therefore, there are growing interests in museums to use of technologies to support collaborative interaction between children [2]. Recently, the use of interactive multi-touch tables in museums receives considerable interest because of it able to facilitates collaborative interactions, open for new technologies by providing physical space and give access to multiple collocated visitors [8].

For example, Museon has developed PuppyIR a collaborative application using a multi-touch table that consists of two parts that were used before and after a museum tour throughout the exhibition space [9]. Touch table interface was found to be suitable for multi-user simultaneous interaction [10] that promote group interaction and discussion [11] and facilitate collaboration [12]. The tabletop interface was also found to be engaging [11] and allowing enjoyable user experience [13] while keeping the technology in the background. Enjoyment and fun have been found to support and deepen learning and to facilitate engagement and motivation [14]. The PuppyIR also developed tools that enable the children to access information about their museum tour via the internet after their visit at the museum. Another recent work, MuseumScouts [15] aims to provides learning experiences in different kinds of ways that focused on knowledge acquisition, transformation, and communication. The work using learner centred approach in the museum environment such as interactive multimedia presentation using a range of devices.

3   The Interaction Design Model

The proposed interaction design model relies on an electronic quest that encourages the children to collaborate, engage and participate actively throughout the museum tours throughout the museum tour (refers Fig. 1). A prototype application is developed based on the interaction design model. The prototype was developed on the Android platform to be deployed on mobile devices e.g. tablet, smart phones.

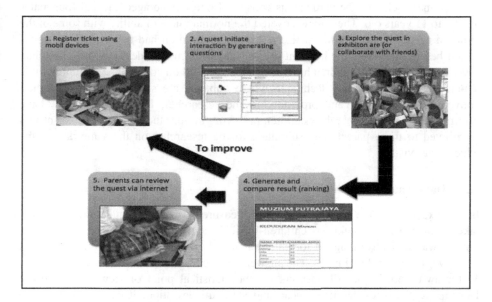

Fig. 1. Interaction design model of museum visit

The prototype is called Museum Quest (MQ). It has three main modules as follows:

a. *New Registration*. Children need to register before use the system. All the information will be kept in the database.
b. *Interactive Quest*. This module will generate five questions from the database.
c. *Check Result*. This module shows the result from the quest.

4   The Experiment

The experiment involves pre test and post-test for one group. A single selected group is under observation with a careful measurement being done before applying the experimental treatment and then measuring after. The experiment is described in details as follows:

4.1 Location

The Muzium Haiwan dan Mamalia in Putrajaya has been chosen to run the experiment as it met the criteria of the research where a museum is an educational place that aims to educate people, in particular children. The museum is a two-storey building with modern facilities. The ground floor consists of permanent exhibits on mammals of Malaysia. The first floor has exhibits of insects such as butterflies, stick insects, beetles, and bats.

4.2 Participants

There were five participants in total, aged between 9 to 11 years old that were in the same primary school. The participants consist of one female aged 11, and four males aged 9 to 11 years old. The sample covered the normal range of ability with some of the children needed help with instructions. All of the children had never used the application before but they are a frequent user of tablets or mobile devices with more than 1-year experience. The children have been chosen based on convenience sampling. It is a non-probability sampling technique where subjects are selected because of their convenient accessibility and proximity to the researcher. Prior the visit, we have informed the parents about their children partaking in this study. Letter of consent was distributed to these parents and submitted to the researcher on the same day of the educational visit.

4.3 Data Analysis Method

In the experiment, the user experience is measured using the Smileyometer which, taken from the Fun Toolkit for children by Read and MacFarlane [16]. The Smileyometer was specially designed for children. It is based on a 5-point Likert scale and uses five smileys (refers Fig. 2). The answers on the Smileyometer were re-coded from 1 (for awful) to 5 (for brilliant). As for the statistical point of view, we are using Descriptive Statistics describes mean and standard deviation. It can provide simple summaries about the sample and the measures. The interpretation of mean score is based on Nunnally and Bernstein [17] as shown in Table 1. For learning effects gained from the interactive application, we compared the result between before and after implementation of the application. The results of both quizzes of a paper-based and mobile device were compared.

Fig. 2. Smileyometer

Table 1. Mean interpretation scale by Nunnaly and Bernstein [17]

Mean score	Interpretation
1.00–2.00	Strongly disagree
2.01–3.00	Disagree
3.01–4.00	Agree
4.01–5.00	Strongly agree

4.4 Experiment Procedures

The Pre-test

(i)   The pre-test started by buying the entrance ticket and the participants explored the museum by themselves, monitored by the researcher as shown in Fig. 3(a).

(ii) After the museum tour finished, the participants were given a paper-based pop quiz as shown in Fig. 3(b), where they need to answer five questions related to the exhibitions. They were not allowed to discuss the answer among the participants.

(iii) Finally, pre-questionnaire forms were distributed to the participants. The form consists of six questions that intend to measures the participants' enjoyment and engagement of the museum visit.

(a)   **(b)**

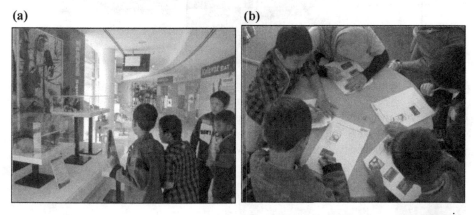

pop quiz

Fig. 3. (a) Children exploring the museum (b) Children answering paper-based pop quiz

The Post-test

(i) The post-test started by distributing the entrance ticket with QRCode that contains a password to access the MQ application. The participants were required to write their names on the ticket as shown in Fig. 4.

(ii) Next, a mobile device with Internet connection was given to the participants to access the MQ. They scanned the QRCode from the entrance ticket using the mobile device and a password was promoted as shown in Fig. 5. Then, they logged in to the system using the password.

Fig. 4. Children write their name on the ticket

Fig. 5. Children scanning the QRcode using mobile device and a password prompted

(iii) They were allowed to explore the exhibition area freely and looked for the answer for every question generated by MQ. They could answer the questions either by themselves or collaborate with their friends as shown in Fig. 6. They have three tries for each question.

Fig. 6. Children collaborating to play the museum quest

(iv) After the participants finished answering all the five questions in MQ, the post-questionnaire forms were distributed to the participants to measures their enjoyment and engagement when using the application.

4.5 Experiment Results

User Experience. The pre-test results in Table 2 presents the analysis of the children museum experience while touring the museum and answering the paper-based pop quiz. The findings showed that majority of the children is strongly agreed (M = 4.200, SD = 0.830) that it is easy to find all the answer given in the pop quiz. They also agreed (M = 3.800, SD = 1.090) that the animal hunt is fun. They also agreed that they prefer to do other activities besides animal hunt (M = 3.200, SD = 0.440), learn new things (M = 3.800, SD = 0.830), and the activities capture their attention (M = 3.400, SD = 0.540). In fact, they also agreed that they will come again to the museum (M = 3.400, SD = 0.890). From the findings, we can conclude that they did enjoy exploring the museum in traditional ways. However, during the pop quiz, they did not score well as shown in Fig. 7. This result showed that conventional tour did not give high impact to the children on the educational values.

Table 2. Mean analysis for pre-test

No.	Questions	Mean	Std deviation	Mean interpretation
1.	Do you think it is easy to find all the answers?	4.200	0.830	Strongly agree
2.	Do you think the animal hunt is fun?	3.800	1.090	Agree
3.	Do you prefer to do other activities besides animal hunt? E.g. coloring or puzzle?	3.200	0.440	Agree
4.	Do you learn new things during the animal hunt?	3.800	0.830	Agree
5.	Is the animal hunt capture your attention?	3.400	0.540	Agree
6.	Will you come again to the museum and play the animal hunt again	3.400	0.890	Agree

The post-test results in Table 3 present the analysis of participants' user experience using the MQ. The findings showed that majority of the children is strongly agreed (M = 4.800, SD = 0.440) that it is easy to find all the answer using the application. They also agreed (M = 3.400, SD = 0.540) that the animal hunt using the application is fun. They disagreed that they prefer to do other activities besides the animal hunt while using the application (M = 3.000, SD = 1.580). This result was contrary during the pre-test, where they preferred to do other activities than animal hunt. It is shown that MQ can improve engagement and enjoyment during the museum tour. They also strongly agreed (M = 4.800, SD = 0.440) that they learn new things during the animal

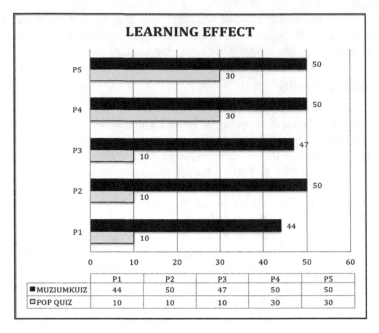

Fig. 7. Test scores for pre-test and post-test

Table 3. Mean analysis for post-test

No.	Questions	Mean	Std deviation	Mean interpretation
1.	Do you think it is easy to find all the answers using the application?	4.800	0.440	Strongly agree
2.	Do you think the animal hunt using the application is fun?	3.400	0.540	Agree
3.	Do you prefer to do other activities besides animal hunt while using the application? E.g. coloring or puzzle?	3.00	1.580	Disagree
4.	Do you learn new things during the animal hunt?	4.80	0.440	Strongly agree
5.	Is the animal hunt using the application capture your attention?	4.000	1.000	Agree
6.	Will you come again to the museum and play the animal hunt again	3.000	2.000	Disagree

hunt and agreed (M = 4.000, SD = 1.000) using the application capture their attention. However, they disagreed that they will come again to the museum. (M = 3.000, SD = 2.000). This happened because we conducted the pre- and post- tests at the same day that caused the smaller children (aged 8 and 9) to get detached. But significant changes for older children (aged 10 to 11) as they had been repeating the MQ several times to improve their marks. From the finding, we can conclude that the engagement and enjoyment during the museum tour have increased significantly.

Learning Effect. The learning effect was calculated based on the difference between the pre-test and post-test scores (refers Fig. 7). The results have shown that the educational values using the MQ have significantly increase compared to the traditional tour.

5 Discussion and Limitations

From the experiment conducted, we have identified several limitations of the developed prototype. We discovered that the children aged below 10 are easily distracted and impatience when using the MQ. From our observation, these happened due to the following reasons:

Too many words to read from the museum exhibition. Children are attracted to interactive stuff, but museum contains permanent exhibits that required them to read the information on the exhibits. They were easily distracted by something else like playing with their friends around the exhibition areas. Thus, the important of the museum visit has not been fulfilling.

The museum quiz is in question and answer format (A, B, C and D). The interactive quest is designed in objectives format where the children need to read the question and choose one of the four possible answers. Therefore, children need to read all the information related to the question around the exhibition areas where comes to the problem (a).

They don't feel the importance of answering all the questions. There was no motivation for them to complete the task. If there was a reward, the motivation will be escalated. Furthermore, there is no involvement of parents and schools in the museum visit, children do not feel it is essential to answer the questions. They took the museum quest slightly, therefore adult supervision throughout the museum visit are necessary.

Therefore, for future enhancement we would recommend as the following:

a. **The Interactive Quest**
   i. Improve the application by incorporating with various modality such as sight, hearing, touch, smell and taste.
   ii. Collaborate the prototype with other several museums in Malaysia. When the entrance ticket is scanned, it will download the questions from the cloud database for the respective museums.
   iii. Develop a set of questions based on age groups. Children aged below 9 years old can have a puzzle like questions like jigsaw puzzles.
b. **Parent, Teacher and Museum Involvement**
   i. Incorporate parents and schools in the museum activities. They can review the results and give comments.
   ii. Collaborate with museum institute to provide a monthly incentive such as a free ticket or a small token for those who achieve remarkable marks for motivation.

6 Conclusion

In this paper, we present a study of an interactive museum quest that involves children aged between 9 to 11. The museum quest carried out by the children using a prototype application called MQ that was being developed based on the proposed interaction design model. The aims of this work are to promote better interactivity, collaboration and engagement among children with the information exhibits in museums. Findings from the study indicate the proposed solution has effected the children enjoyment and engagement during the museum visit. We compared the experiments results between pre-test and post-test, and found the interaction model is comparable and gives promising results. Nevertheless, we highlighted some limitations and suggestions for work the enhancement.

References

1. Antle, A.N.: Research opportunities: embodied child–computer interaction. Int. J. Child-Comput. Interact. (2012)
2. Zancanaro, M., et al.: Children in the museum: an environment for collaborative storytelling. In: Stock, O., Zancanaro, M. (eds.) PEACH-intelligent Interfaces for Museum Visits. Cognitive Technologies, pp. 165–184. Springer, Heidelberg (2007). doi:10.1007/3-540-68755-6_8
3. Lingnau, A., et al.: Measuring enjoyment of an interactive museum experience. In: Proceedings of the ACM International Conference on Multimodal Interaction, pp. 249–256 (2012)
4. Kotler, N.: Can museums be all things to all people: missions, goals, and marketing's role. Museum Manag. Curatorship **18**(3), 271–287 (2000)
5. Hall, T., Bannon, L.: Designing ubiquitous computing to enhance children's interaction in museums. In: Proceedings of the Conference on Interaction Design and Children, New York, NY, pp. 62–69 (2005)
6. Haworth-Booth, M., MacCauley, A.: The Museum and The Photograph: Collecting Photography at the Victoria and Albert Museum, 1853–1900. Sterling and Francine Clark Art Museum, Williamstown (1998)
7. Gage, et al.: Educational Psychology, 6th edn. Wadsworth Publishing (1998)
8. Hornecker, E.: "I don't understand it either, but it is cool" - visitor interactions with a multi-touch table in a museum. In: Proceedings of the IEEE International Workshop on Horizontal Human-Computer Systems, pp. 113–120. IEEE (2008)
9. Lingnau, A., et al.: Enriching children's experiences during and after a museum visit. In: Proceedings of the Advanced Learning Technologies, pp. 288–292. IEEE (2012)
10. Hinrichs, U., et al.: Examination of text-entry methods for tabletop displays. In: Proceedings of the IEEE International Workshop on Horizontal Interactive Human-Computer Systems. IEEE (2007)
11. Zuckerman, O., et al.: Extending tangible interfaces for education: digital montessori-inspired manipulatives. In: Proceedings of the SIGCHI Conference on Human Factors in Computing Systems, pp. 859–868. ACM (2005)
12. Buisine, S., et al.: How do interactive tabletop systems influence collaboration? J. Comput. Hum. Behav. **28**(1), 49–59 (2012). Elsevier

13. Al Mahmud, A., et al.: Affective tabletop game: a new gaming experience for children. In: The Proceedings of the IEEE International Workshop on Horizontal Interactive Human-Computer Systems, pp. 44–51 (2007)
14. Klopfer, E., et al.: Mystery at the museum: a collaborative game for museum education. In: Proceedings of the 2005 Conference on Computer-Supported Collaborative Learning, pp. 316–320 (2005)
15. Wishart, J., Triggs, P.: MuseumScouts: exploring how schools, museums and interactive technologies can work together to support learning. J. Comput. Educ. **54**(3), 669–678 (2010)
16. Read, J.C., MacFarlane, S.: Endurability, engagement and expectations: measuring children's fun. In: Proceedings of the Conference on Interaction Design and Children. ACM (2002)
17. Nunnally, J., Bernstein, I.: Psychometric Theory, 3rd edn. McGraw-Hill, New York (1994)

Natural User Interface for Children: From Requirement to Design

Mohd Salihan Ab Rahman[1(✉)], Nazlena Mohamad Ali[1], and Masnizah Mohd[2]

[1] Institute of Visual Informatics, Bangi, Malaysia
salihan@yahoo.com, nazlena.ali@ukm.edu.my
[2] Faculty of Information Science & Technology,
Universiti Kebangsaan Malaysia, 43600 Bangi, Malaysia
masnizah.mohd@ukm.edu.my

Abstract. The emergence of natural user interface (NUI) provides children with more natural interaction. However, NUI developed are commonly inappropriate for their age, due to the lacking in understanding of their needs and the problems they face. This paper presents a research on natural user interface (NUI) for children where the understanding of the issues of usage and their requirement was gathered from literature review and analysis of a usability study. The identification of usability issues were gathered from an observation research of two types of NUI: free-form represented by Kinect; and touch-form represented by tablet iPad. Our observation from video recording analysis and interviews discovered that touch-form NUI is harder to recall, but its simple and straightforward gestures are easier to be performed as long as it does not involve finger-gestures. On the other hand, free-form NUI is more natural and easier to recall but unfortunately troubled by many unwanted gesture interpretations. By using analytical model, these findings were inter-related to input-system-output point of view that help us to propose recommendations to improve NUI interaction and proposes a NUI prototype design to aid children in learning.

Keywords: Natural user interface · HCI · Interaction design · User experience

1 Introduction

Computer interaction has entered an era in which we are no longer merely using a mouse and keyboard, but a more natural interaction like using tabs, gestures and voice. However, it should be noted that natural interaction doesn't mean only using natural input devices, but it should allow users to use it with their natural behaviour. For example, users can use the stylus to write using a pen as he wrote it on paper.

Natural user interface (NUI) is a system of human-computer interaction in which users act intuitively associated with common human behaviour or natural act [1]. NUI goal is to create a seamless interaction and quality of human and computer without any significant gap between each other, making the interface invisible between them [2].

Since NUI allows users to interact with the natural or common act, then we must first understand the users in terms of their behaviour, abilities and inclinations.

H. Badioze Zaman et al. (Eds.): IVIC 2017, LNCS 10645, pp. 612–624, 2017.
https://doi.org/10.1007/978-3-319-70010-6_57

However, existing studies conducted do not investigate the interaction itself, and did not focus on the user. For example, Zhang et al. [3] enhanced the ability of model appearance to get a more depth understanding of a field [3], a study of using reverse engineering Wiimote (Wii remote) [4], or studies in enhancing detection of inactivation patterns [5].

Nevertheless, there are studies conducted in human action recognition like [6] using Naive-Bayes classifier (NB) to recognise the movements of punch, clapping, throwing and collecting the ball. Review by Patsadu et al., comparing the classifier, the classifier among the back-propagation neural network (BPN), decision tree (DT) and NB for the motion standing, sitting and lying down [7]. Meanwhile, a survey conducted by Reyes et al. presented the real-time detection based on dynamic time wrapping of jump movement, bending and shaking [8]. However, these studies did not detail the characteristics of users, both in terms of the ability or lack of behaviour or conduct, bias or feeling or excitement as a result of the use of the NUI. Though research in computer vision and gesture interaction claims it provides more natural interactions, it still lacks to determine or explain the characteristics of the interaction, or how it affects the perception and feeling of the user [9, 10]. For instance, a research conducted by Farhadi-Niaki et al. studied the usability of gestures detection system between the arm and the fingers in a desktop environment. His research sampling utilised 10 participants aged between 26 to 36 years. They found that the gesture using fingers were more natural or more common and less tiring than the entire hand. He also found that there was no significant effect on the usability factors such as time duration, fatigue and overall satisfaction [11]. A question arises, whether the results of their study will be the same if children are taken into account?

With the proliferation of mobile applications and gestures that are designed for children, it should be an area of increasing focus in HCI research. However, in reality, many researchers pay more attention to adults, disabled and elderly [12]. Where else, children are rarely considered even though it is generally known that children requirements and needs are different from an adult. Thus, many design principles or guidelines used for adults may not be applicable for children technology [13, 14]. Since the research on children in NUI is scarce, there is uncertainty whether the problems identified among adult will be similar with children.

Among the most prominent problems occur in NUI interaction is how the computer processing can distinguish between individual gestures and gesture input. This was stated by Karam in his literature review covering 40 years of literature. According to him, this problem is very prominent in nearly every study of gestures, which involves determining the right time for the detection of gestures to start, when it should stop and when it should be interpreted as a gesture sequence of individual gestures [10]. In other words, there is a lot of misinterpretation of gestures detected in studies of NUI. Since the discovery of the problem that really stood out was recorded 10 years ago, we wanted to know whether the issue of the past still haunts the NUI today. Has the presence of NUI and advanced wireless technologies overcome this problem? To find this answer, inevitably, a user study of NUI and its quality of interaction should be carried out. The findings of the user study may provide a guide or baseline in designing a NUI system. A prototype can be built to get a realistic experience of how to represent the finding into a NUI product for children. This is because a prototype is not only a representation of a model or the release of a product built to test a concept or process, but it also allows or acts as a tool to enhance learning [15]. Therefore, this research action can benefit HCI and child-computer interaction (CCI). The prototype is designed to test and try out the new design to improve the ability of the system from the standpoint of system analysts and users. The prototype serves to provide specifications for a real working system, rather than merely relying on theory. In fact, the prototype can be designed and built to evaluate a theory or an idea [16].

2 Methodology

Research studies using a methodology known as mixed methods [17]. The methodology used in this research is a composition of quantitative and qualitative data collection and analysis [18]. The flow of research methodology is shown in Fig. 1. It starts with the collection of data from the literature review, where the lack of materials and data related to the study and the problems are identified (descriptive). Among them is the lack of detail regarding the interaction between NUI and children as users, the cause of the problem and its direct impact on the feelings and problems of user acceptance. Thus, a study of quantitative and qualitative observations on the use of two types of NUI is conducted. The two types of NUI are touch-based NUI and free-form NUI. This study aims to explore the scope of the research problems more thoroughly to obtain certainty on the issue of gestures. The study also aims to understand the needs of users and find the possible solution or opportunity (ideas) to solve the problem (description and analysis).

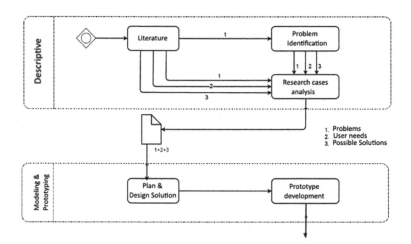

Fig. 1. Research method model.

Consequently, a separate study in the modelling and prototyping phase, the result of the observation of the user study and the literature of the previous studies are used to inter-relate them from input-system-output point of view by using an analytic model.

This approach enables us to observe each problem's element as a whole and its relationship with other elements.

The analysis from the analytic model is used to produce a prototype of free-form NUI. An assisted learning tool – teaching children how to pray; has been chosen as a prototype domain. A mechanism has been designed to cater the need of reducing unintentional gestures. The prototype has been designed to enable or disable the plug-in of the designed mechanism for evaluation purposes.

2.1   The User Study

The user study implemented a "within subject design" approach. Sixteen preschool children aged between five and six years old were divided into two groups. Participants in Group 1 used free-form Kinect first, followed by the touch-form tablet. Group 2 used the touch-form tablet first and then the free-form Kinect. This grouping was made because there were interview questions that required participants to remember and demonstrate the selected gestures in the user study, namely 'brush or wash', 'jump' and 'throw'. This study approach should be able to reduce error variance and previous experiences related to individual differences.

This study observed the Kinectimals game software usage from the start to the end of events of interaction. This study focused on the basic concept of NUI interaction as shown in Fig. 2. Three tasks have been assigned for various gesture manipulations which are brushing, jumping and throwing. These tasks are gestured by the children with body movements in front of Kinect camera for free-form; and fingers' sliding or swapping on a tablet for touch-form NUI.

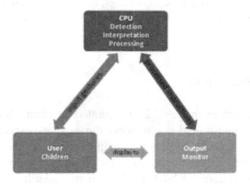

Fig. 2.   Basic concept of NUI interaction

2.2   Data Gathering

Data was gathered by analysing videos using video analysis software named Camtasia Studio 8, and interview session using certain methods and tools summarised in Table 1.

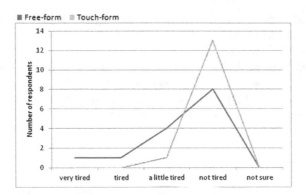

Fig. 3. Fatigue on usage

Table 1. Data collection.

Data	Observation	Interview session
Fatigue	Fatigue behaviour [11]	Borg scale [19]
Naturalness	–	Time to recall and demonstrate gestures [20]
Accuracy	Analysis of video recordings - the logged off right (*r*) & wrong (*w*) gestures recognition $Acc = r/r + w$ [20]	–
Duration	Time measure between start and end of each gesture movements [20]	–
Fun and satisfaction	User behaviour such as facial, feelings, body movements and expression of feelings [21]	Fun toolkit: smileyometer [22]

3 Result and Discussion

The results are summarised in Table 2 and plotted in charts below. Based on our observations, children find it hard to remember the gestures, especially on touch-form NUI. As a result, they decide to use dialogue help to remember the gesture needed. Our observations were strengthened by the quantitative findings on naturalness. The time required to recall the gesture for NUI touch-form was significantly longer than NUI free-form as shown in 2-way ANOVA and Fig. 4.

The children were observed to have limited motor skills as they cannot follow some manipulative gestures. The percentage of accuracy decreased when the touch gestures required more than one finger movements in touch-form NUI. Figure 5 shows the gesture 'roll' recorded a lower percentage accuracy compared to other gestures. The rolling gesture required users to move their fingers in a specific pattern as shown in the dialogue help or the instruction set system. This type of finger movement was not recognised by the children as they were still developing their motor skills. Free-form interaction also showed signs of the children's restricted motor skills, especially when

Table 2. Summary of results

Data	Touch-form	Free-form	Statistic test	Data plot
Fatigue	1 felt a little tired. The rest did not felt tired	4 felt little tired, 1 felt tired, 1 felt very tired, the rest did not felt tired		Fig. 3
Naturalness	brush (M = 4.752, SD = 7.30) jump (M = 9.368, SD = 10,593) throw (M = 8.330, SD = 10,296) respectively (n = 16)	brush (M = 2.180, SD = 0.926) jump (M = 2.651, SD = 1,971) throw (M = 1,411, SD = 0.402) respectively (n = 16)	2-way ANOVA F (1,90) = 17,835 p = 0.0005 where p < α (0.01). Post-hoc pairwise p < 0.001, 95% CI	Fig. 4
Accuracy	(M = 0.8419, SD = 0.126)	(M = 0.68, SD = 0.153)	Paired t-test t (15) = 2.999 p = 0.009 where p < α (0.05)	Fig. 5
Duration	The graph shows a similar pattern, in which clearly visible gesture that takes the longest time is 'brush'; NUI touch: 5.97 s; free-form: 14.24 s. While the average duration of the rest of the gestures takes less than 5 s			Fig. 6
Fun	OK: 6.25% Happy: 62.5% Very Happy: 31.25%	OK: 37.5% Happy: 12.5% Very Happy: 50%		Fig. 7
Satisfaction	78.57%	64.29%		Fig. 8

they explored the menu. The 'select' and 'swipe' gestures had low precision in NUI free-form as shown in Fig. 5. We discovered that these types of gestures required the children to raise their hands to select and keep their hands on the selection area. It was found to be a burden to them as many of the children displayed uncomfortable, sad, angry, or panicked expressions. Most of them dropped their hands, resulting in the selection being cancelled. In fact, there were a few incidents in which the detector recognised pairs of hands relaxing as a swipe to the left or the right. For example, if the user was in a 'care' or 'game' session, the system identified the relaxing hand movement as 'brush' or 'throw'. This is where the misinterpretation of movement

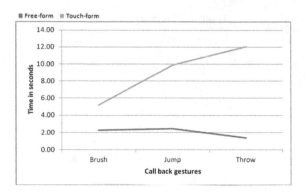

Fig. 4. Time to recall by gestures

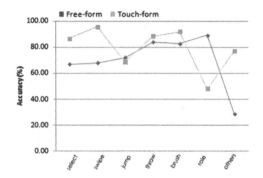

Fig. 5. Accuracy percentage by gestures

occurred. As a result, the children backed off or hid their hands because they felt worried or confused. Then they continued, but with more caution or with a slower movement. At the start, the children expressed their emotions by jumping up and down in excitement or raising their hands after successfully accomplishing a task objective. After the misinterpretation incident, they could not do so anymore as they were anxious that the detector would distinguish the movement as a throw or leap, affecting the game score. This is shown when they were halfway through a cheer, but pulled back anxiously. Some said "Oops!" or "Oh no!" when the system detected the gesture that was not meant to be done.

Although free-form NUI observed the gesture misinterpretation problem, it was still able to create a happy atmosphere. Based on Fig. 7, none of the participants felt sad or very sad, although the accuracy of the average for each user only reached 68% compared to the touch-form's 84% (Fig. 5). However, free-form NUI was able to record the highest amount of participants who felt 'very happy' at 50%, while touch-form NUI recorded 31%. The users were more satisfied with touch-form NUI (79%) than free-form NUI (64%). From these findings, we believe that the level of gesture qualities, experience and excitement can be boosted if the accuracy is improved and the misinterpretations corrected.

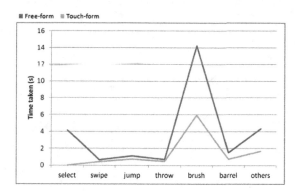

Fig. 6. Gesture duration by gestures

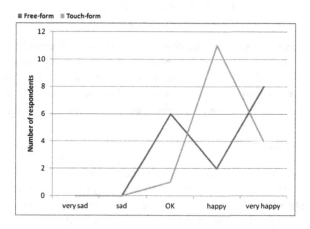

Fig. 7. Fun percentage

Gestures like 'select' and 'swipe' in touch-form NUI is easier and more reliable. By a single touch, the system detects the beginning plot of the interaction and ends when no longer in contact. The easy touch-form interaction style was excellent and should be adopted in the free-form gestures detection. However, the real challenge is how to achieve this kind of interaction system into free-form NUI.

4   Modeling to Design

"Modeling" is describing something you know. A good model makes correct assertions."

Alistair Cockburn [23]

In trying to understand and redesign software processes, it is often necessary to have an understanding of the "whys" that underlie the "whats" – the motivations, intents, and rationales behind the activities and input-system-output flows. Therefore,

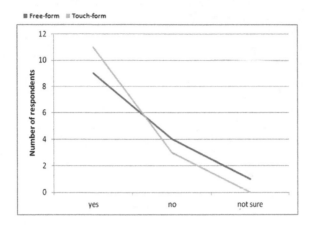

Fig. 8. Satisfaction percentage

we extend this paper to modelling to describe the process of converting the problem into a form that can be understood by showing the relationship between the various activities involved and the chosen approach for a solution. In line with the findings from the user study, we are certain about the children's requirement – providing the "whys" the problems or the issues occurred, certain behaviour in children, etc.

4.1   Analytic Model

We have produced a model of analysis (analytical model) hinges on the basic concept of NUI interaction (Fig. 2). This model is intended to provide an overview of the real issues, opportunities and challenges that have been found in the user study, the relationship between the input - system processing - output and design approach of these issues. Using this model, the findings of the first phase of the study can be seen more clearly from the three angles are shown in Fig. 9. As a result, the abstraction of the problem domain and the next steps can be planned systematically. Here are the results through systems thinking analytic model producing a design principle as follows:

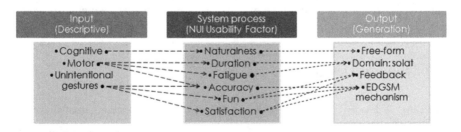

Fig. 9. NUI analytic model

1. Children have a limited cognitive ability. Cognitive ability is the ability to remember the purpose of the procedure, particularly the movements' pattern of the fingers on the touch NUI. Contrary to the free-form NUI, they have easily recalled the required gestures. This also proved that free-form NUI is more natural than touch-form. Thus, the proposed development of a prototype of a free-form interaction is desirable.
2. Children have limited motor ability. Motor limitation involved in fine motor skills, where children have difficulty moving their fingers according to the rules of the system. Movements' involving bigger motor ability larger than fingers is less problematic although the interaction did run for quite some time such as washing or brushing gestures in free-form interaction (Fig. 6). It is seen as an opportunity to build a prototype that uses a lot of big motor movements. Thus, the idea of the prototype development in the solat domain (prayers) involving large motor movements is coinciding with this opportunity.
3. Feedback system. Without the input device, the challenge of NUI is how to demonstrate applications for the NUI system responding to the motion-gesture shown by the user. If not, the user is unaware of the tracking being done against him that could affect the emotions of users.
4. Genesis misinterpretation of gestures is a problem that is very significant to evoke fear and discomfort to the child. This is a challenge that must be overcome with a design of a mechanism that can increase the accuracy of the system or reduce the incidence of misinterpretation of gestures in free-form NUI system, or both.
5. Free-form NUI potentially creates a more cheerful atmosphere. Based on the results of fun, behaviour and satisfaction from the user study, researchers believe the opportunity for free-form NUI to create a natural, interactive and cheerful atmosphere if the incident of misinterpretation of gestures can be overcome or reduced.

This model is like a bridge connecting the analysis stage to design stage, as illustrated in Fig. 10. The abstraction of the problem domain has successfully generated a list of potential solutions that can be used in the abstraction of the prototype design.

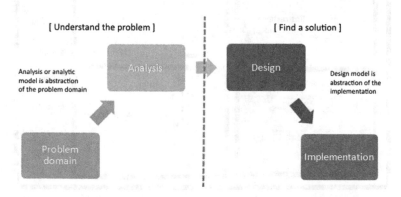

Fig. 10. Modeling to connect analysis to design stage

4.2   Prototype Design

The generation of the potential solutions from modelling are mapped to its design's part as follows:

- Result 1 and 2 determine the prototype will be in free-form NUI. The prototype domain is about learning solat (prayer) that uses full body interaction. We chose Kinect as the development platform since the Kinect camera has the ability to detect full body gestures.
- Result 3 and children's requirement motivate the GUI design to be like as Fig. 11.
  - Area 1 shows the teaching video so that the children can follow or imitate the step-by-step gestures' movement.
  - Area 2 is the enlightenment, assisting the video in showing the body part that needs to be a focus on by zooming into the body's part. It also shows the recitation that needs to be read at certain times.
  - Area 3 is the mirror image of the user, so that the user knows about his or her real-time condition. It is for the user to see whether it is similar to the instructional video or not.
  - Area 4 is the skeleton image of the user. This is part of the respond for the feedback to the user. With this skeleton, the user may know the system is detecting his/her gesture movement so that he/she knows that he/she is still in the game.
  - Area 5 is the task list that the user completed. This is also a part of feedback to the user.
  - Areas 6 is the right or wrong pop-up, recognition and start or finish alert as feedback to the user.

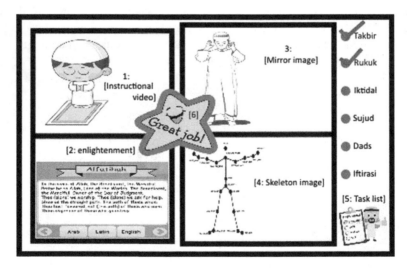

Fig. 11. GUI prototype design

- Result 4 and 5 require a design mechanism that can reduce the misinterpretation of unintentional gestures. The mechanism that been chosen to be embedded into the prototype originated from the idea of Davidson [24]. This concept is seen as very appropriate for the prayer learning concept. This is because, in prayer, there are many body gestures that need to be done with certain rules and in order, by following a strictly right sequence of movement. At the same time, the concept has the potential to prevent unintentional gesture movement.

5 Conclusion and Future Work

This paper represents the basis on NUI understanding for children. Our observation from video recording analysis and interviews suggested that free-form NUI should be invested since it more natural, easier to recall and has the potential to provide a better learning environment. The only obvious drawback was the problem with many unwanted gesture interpretations. By using analytical model, research findings were inter-related among input-system-output point of view that helped us to propose recommendations to improve NUI interaction and proposes a NUI prototype design to aid children in full body NUI learning.

For the future work, the prototype design will be expanded into a physical prototype with the detail working mechanism of reducing unwanted gestures to be embedded into it. Then the working prototype can be evaluated to see the level of children learning and their experiences. The measurement of the evaluation also can include the capability of the system to reduce the unintentional gestures and gesture detection accuracy.

References

1. Rouse, M.: Natural User Interface (NUI), April 2011. http://whatis.techtarget.com/definition/natural-user-interface-NUI. Accessed 2 Jan 2016
2. Christensson, P.: NUI Definition. TechTerms (2012). http://techterms.com/definition/nui. Accessed July 2016
3. Zhang, K., Zhai, Y., Leong, H.W., Wang, S.: An interaction educational computer game framework using hand gesture recognition. In: Proceedings of the 4th International Conference on Internet Multimedia Computing and Service, pp. 219–222. ACM (2012)
4. Lee, J.C.: Hacking the Nintendo Wii Remote. IEEE Pervasive Comput. 7, 39–45 (2008)
5. Lee, D.-H., Hong, K.-S.: Game interface using hand gesture recognition. In: 5th International Conference on Computer Sciences and Convergence Information Technology (ICCIT), pp. 1092–1097. IEEE (2010)
6. Yang, X., Tian, Y.: Eigenjoints-based action recognition using naive-bayes-nearest-neighbor. In: IEEE Computer Society Conference on Computer Vision and Pattern Recognition Workshops (CVPRW), pp. 14–19. IEEE (2012)
7. Patsadu, O., Nukoolkit, C., Watanapa, B.: Human gesture recognition using Kinect camera. In: International Joint Conference on Computer Science and Software Engineering (JCSSE), pp. 28–32. IEEE (2012)

8. Reyes, M., Dominguez, G., Escalera, S.: Featureweighting in dynamic timewarping for gesture recognition in depth data. In: IEEE International Conference on Computer Vision Workshops (ICCV Workshops), pp. 1182–1188. IEEE (2011)

9. Xie, L., Antle, A.N., Motamedi, N.: Are tangibles more fun?: comparing children's enjoyment and engagement using physical, graphical and tangible user interfaces, pp. 191–198. ACM (2008)

10. Karam, M.: A taxonomy of Gestures in Human Computer Interaction. ACM Trans. Comput. Hum. Interact. 1–45 (2005)

11. Farhadi-Niaki, F., Etemad, S.A., Arya, A.: Design and usability analysis of gesture-based control for common desktop tasks. In: Kurosu, M. (ed.) HCI 2013. LNCS, vol. 8007, pp. 215–224. Springer, Heidelberg (2013). doi:10.1007/978-3-642-39330-3_23

12. Bhuiyan, M., Picking, R.: Gesture-controlled user interfaces, what have we done and what's next? In: Proceedings of the Fifth Collaborative Research Symposium on Security, E-Learning, Internet and Networking (SEIN 2009), Darmstadt, Germany, pp. 26–27 (2009)

13. De Troyer, O., Janssens, E.: Supporting the requirement analysis phase for the development of serious games for children. Int. J. Child-Comput. Interact. 2, 76–84 (2014)

14. Chiasson, S., Gutwin, C.: Testing the media equation with children. In: Proceedings of the SIGCHI Conference on Human Factors in Computing Systems, pp. 829–838. ACM (2005)

15. Blackwell, A.H.: UXL Encyclopedia of Science. U.X.L, Farmington Hills (2015)

16. Rebelo, F., Soares, M.M.: Advances in Usability Evaluation. CRC Press, Boca Raton (2012)

17. Tashakkori, A., Teddlie, C.: SAGE Handbook of Mixed Methods in Social & Behavioral Research. Sage, Thousand Oaks (2010)

18. Creswell, J.W., Clark, V.L.P.: Designing and Conducting Mixed Methods Research. Sage, Thousand Oaks (2007). pp. 53–106

19. Borg, G.: Borg's Perceived Exertion and Pain Scales. Human Kinetics Publishers, Champaign (1998)

20. Barclay, K., Wei, D., Lutteroth, C., Sheehan, R.: A quantitative quality model for gesture based user interfaces. In: Proceedings of the 23rd Australian Computer-Human Interaction Conference, pp. 31–39. ACM (2011)

21. Deswal, S.: The science of how positive emotions affect content sharing. In: Adpushup Blog Test Optimize Grow, vol. 2016 (2014)

22. Read, J.C., MacFarlane, S.: Using the fun toolkit and other survey methods to gather opinions in child computer interaction. In: Proceedings of the 2006 Conference on Interaction Design and Children, pp. 81–88. ACM, Tampere, Finland (2006)

23. Cockburn, A.: Designing vs Modeling. GitHub, 28 September 2010. Accessed 28 Oct 2016

24. Davison, A.: Kinect Open Source Programming Secrets: Hacking the Kinect with OpenNI, NITE, and Java. McGraw Hill Professional, New York City (2012)

Improving Usability with TRIZ: A Review

Vanisri Batemanazan[✉], Azizah Jaafar, Rabiah Abdul Kadir,
and Norshita Mat Nayan

Institute of Visual Informatics,
National University of Malaysia (UKM), Bangi, Selangor, Malaysia
vanisri0127@gmail.com,
{azizahj,rabiahivi,norshita}@ukm.edu.my

Abstract. New innovations is unavoidable to persist in current world. Industries operate today, in a very challenging and complex environment with rapidly changing demanding and conditions. Thus, to play a significant role in the global market, it is essential to increase the impactful innovations, productivity and competitiveness in the development of new products. Therefore, collaboration between user and designer play important role in this situation. This perception brings innovative dimension for usability evaluations to accomplish the user's needs. To meet current requirements, usability needs to be improved to strengthen its impact. To achieve this, usability needs to be improved with a very effective model. Deep analysis is carried out to identify suitable model. TRIZ model identified as most appropriate collaborator for impactful effects. This paper presents a suggestion that describes how Usability can improve their outcomes with TRIZ.

Keywords: Usability · TRIZ · Parameter · Criteria · Metrics

1   Introduction

Usability is a most important concept in area of Human Computer Interaction HCI [1], which attempts to fulfil the gaps between human needs, demands and technologies evolution. Thus human issues been introduced into the design of interactive systems by inventing practical methods to observe human behaviour and their performance [2].

The demand of products increases along with increased human population as well as the power of the consumer also plays an important role in this factor. There are many factors in the user's rejection of unsatisfactory products. This rejection power occurs even though the product development process uses a high budget while undergoing a careful planning process by highly skilled experts. Usability is defined as the 'easy operation of a product by the user in addition to meet the needs of users'. Usability, does not have a complete and significant definition, either by researchers or by standardized organizations. Furthermore, there is no precise guidelines to define Usability. A latest usability survey accomplishes that 'authors have different views on how to measure usability'. Therefore this lack of harmony has led to a complicated of comparable definitions [3].

© Springer International Publishing AG 2017
H. Badioze Zaman et al. (Eds.): IVIC 2017, LNCS 10645, pp. 625–635, 2017.
https://doi.org/10.1007/978-3-319-70010-6_58

2   Challenges of Usability and Motivation

There has been lack of coordination on usability definition as claimed by Shackel [4]. Table below, exhibits comparable definitions of the term needed. But the challenging part is, there is no complete guideline for the designer used as to be a proper guidelines for them to follow. As a result, more complicated understanding with different models of different authors having the same criteria in different names. Furthermore, during the application of the models, designers usually unclear and confuse in selecting the criteria that suits the needs of the users. Even though it's has dissimilar names, some criteria may have the similar meaning and functions. Taxonomy of Usability Models listed as [5] in Table 1.

Table 1. Taxonomy of usability models

Constantine & Lockwood (1999)	ISO 9241-11 (1998)	Schneiderman (1992)	Nielsen (1993)	Preece et al. (1994)	Shackel (1991)
Efficiency in use	Efficiency	Speed of performance	Efficiency of use	Throughput	Effectiveness (Speed)
Learnability		Time to learn	Learnability (Ease of learning)	Learnability (Ease of learning)	Learnability (Time to learn)
Rememberability		Retention over time	Memorability		Learnability (Retention)
Reliability in use		Rate of errors by users	Errors/safety	Throughput	Effectiveness (Errors)
User satisfaction	Satisfaction (Comfort and acceptability of use)	Subjective satisfaction	Satisfaction	Attitude	Attitude

The variation of names can effect misunderstanding or propose a various perception for the same principle. Compilation criteria of Usability listed as in [6] Fig. 1. The variation or dissimilarity of criteria justified by the authors creates a difficult process in determining a collective name to particular parameter of all that criteria. Furthermore, by creating one more name, even to set up common criteria also can produce the same meaning over a dissimilar name for the criterion. Although each author has their own detailed method to usability, it indicated that there is great similarity between the definitions and terms, making them capable of grouping it into the same category [10]. Usability's criteria has not been fixed in a constant way [11]. Most of these various classifications or models do not contain all major aspects of Usability [12].

One significance of these weaknesses is that conceivably most developers do not apply appropriately any particular model in the evaluation of usability. As an alternative, actual practice tends to be informal such that developers may use usability models with which they are at ease with or thru their own experience [13]. These

Common criteria	Names given by authors
Consistency	• Uniformity and Consistency of Bastien and Scapin, 1993; • Consistency and standards Nielsen, 1994; • Predictability, Capacity of Synthesis and Capacity of Generalization of Dix et al, 1998; • Consistency of Shneiderman, 1998, • Efficient use of Preece et al, 2005; • Conformity to user expectations of ISO 9241-110, 2006.
User control	• Explicit control of Bastien and Scapin, 1993; • Freedom and User control of Nielsen, 1994; • Initiative Dialog of Dix et al, 1998; • Reversal of shares and User control of Shneiderman, 1998; • Efficient use of Preece et al, 2005; • User Control and Ease of individualization of ISO 9241-110, 2006.
Ease of learning	• Compatibility of Bastien and Scapin, 1993; • System compatibility with the real world, Rather than recognition memory of Nielsen, 1994; • Familiarity and Observability of Dix et al, 1998; • Easy to learn, easy to remember how to use and Efficiency in the use of Preece et al, 2005.
Flexibility	• Adaptability of Bastien and Scapin, 1993; • Flexibility and Efficiency in the use of Nielsen, 1994; • Capacity of Migration, Replacement and Configuration, and the Compliance task of Dix et al, 1998; • Shortcut to experienced users of Shneiderman, 1998; • Good value and Efficient use of Preece et al, 2005; • Adaptation and Adjustment to the task for learning of ISO 9241-110, 2006.
Errors management	• Erros management of Bastien and Scapin, 1993; • User help in the recognition, Prevention, Diagnosis and Correction of errors and Support and Documentation of Nielsen, 1994; • Recoverability of Dix et al, 1998; • Reversal of actions of Shneiderman, 1998; • Efficiency in the use and safety in the use of Preece et al, 2005; • Error tolerance of ISO 9241-110, 2006.
Reduction of excess	• Workload Bastien and Scapin, 1993; • Minimalist design and Recognition rather than memorization of Nielsen, 1994; • Ability to synthesis, Generalization and Replacement of Dix et al, 1998; • Low load of memorization of Shneiderman, 1998; • Efficiency in the use of Preece et al, 2005.
Visibility system status	• User guidance of Bastien and Scapin, 1993; • Visibility of system status of Nielsen, 1994; • Responsiveness of Dix et al, 1998; • Feedback informative and dialogues that indicate the end of action of Shneiderman, 1998; • Efficiency in the use of Preece et al, 2005; • Self-description of ISO 9241-110, 2006.

Fig. 1. Compilation of common criteria for usability

selections may not be appropriate in many circumstances and can lead to failure of the product even with lots of money spend in development process. Specifically, the effort to measure usability may be wasted without a reliable and consolidated framework for doing so.

3 Purpose for Improving

Functionality of Usability before 1980s was limited. Along with the rapid development of the changing and widening functionality technology, the ability to apply Usability on new products is still a debate. For examples, there is a noticeable difference between regular desktop computer, laptops and tabs. The user's functionality and functioning of a product has always changed over time.

Purpose for a combined model. There are four core reasons for a combined model of usability measurement. To identify the needs of users, a complete analysis needs to be done in earlier to avoid the failure of the product. Various criteria and standards need to be set to measure the level of efficiency [14].

Usability emphasizes context consists of four main elements as below:

- users,
- tools,
- task,
- environments.

These four contexts play a major role in the assessment of the Usability [15]. Lack of reliable information explains about evaluation to justify the degree of impact of Models influence, such as the role of Neilson's as opposed to Eight Golden Rules by Shneiderman in general context [16]. This lack of consistent operational definitions can make it difficult to practice usability in current situations. There is also difficulty to select a set of usability factors or metrics in considering aspects such as organization goals, business goals, and competition, economics, or resource constraints on development [17]. Problems could theoretically be addressed through an enhanced tool for use by individuals who are given the responsibility to evaluate usability. A consolidated model can also address this problem by integrating different perspectives on usability and its measurement in a consistent, constant way.

Secondly, the usability models defined, including the ISO/IEC 9126 standard, are static [18]. Also, none of these models typically give any direction concerning the use of usability measures and attributes in the identification and classification of risk [19].

Thirdly, it can be fairly challenging to relate usability standards in practice, that is, to adopt exactly how to measure the usability of a particular application. Specifically, it is not always clear how usability factors, criteria and metrics defined in numerous standards or models are related or whether one set of metrics may be more constructive than others [20]. A consolidated model should support the study of the relations among sets of factors, criteria, and metrics again in a reliable and clear way. This characteristic should also help to improve the problem that on effective application of usability standards in practice often seems to be influenced by on characteristic factors, such as the skills of individual practitioners.

Finally, a reliable usability model should also provide a complete guidelines for analysis of the data collected under it. A proper guidelines to allows person who are not usability engineers such as developers or quality assurance managers or anyone without usability knowledge to make correct selections on usability evaluation of particular applications in a specific situation successfully.

To overcome this problem, a problem solving model has been identified. The model is called TRIZ. TRIZ is proposed to be integrated with Usability to achieve the impactful enhancement.

4   Theory of Inventive Problem Solving (TRIZ)

TRIZ stands for the first letter of *Teoriya resheniya Izobreatatelskikh Zadatch* meaning "Theory of Inventive Problem Solving". TRIZ was proposed by Altshuller in 1946 from Russia. Now TRIZ is the backbone of the design of some of the world's leading brands such as Samsung, Motorola, Xerox and others.

TRIZ has its unique and distinct advantages over other methods used to solve such as brainstorming, mind maps, lateral thinking, morphological analysis, and other problems [21]. TRIZ offers a systematic framework of innovation and is fast resolving the problems efficiently. TRIZ systematic approach guides to designers during the troubleshooting process to avoid random solutions [22]. Souchkov (1997) explains that TRIZ covers the following three aspects [23]:

- Logical analysis,
- Knowledge-based philosophy,
- Systematic thinking.

As a means of solving non-specific problems, TRIZ does not support the concept of trial and error but based on the principles set out in the TRIZ guidelines. In addition, TRIZ also emphasizes that technological evolution is an unplanned process but adheres to several principles and has its own criteria. TRIZ has a special tool for resolving conflicts. Most importantly, the contradictory matrix which recommends which principles should be considered and capable of resolving about 1250 types of problems. TRIZ's Contradiction Analysis is an excellent solution tool in problem solving with the new dimension [24]. TRIZ be able to adapt easily in various fields and solve complex problems in a simple and systematic way. TRIZ is a skill capable of changing the perceptions and traditions practiced by the developers. It's contain 39 parameters, able to adjust accordingly to the problem. Thirty nine (39) Engineering parameters as listed in Table 2.

Table 2. Thirty nine (39) Engineering parameters

1. Weight of mobile object	21. Power supplied or consumed by object
2. Weight of stationary object	22. Energy loss by object
3. Length of mobile object	23. Substance loss by object
4. Length of stationary object	24. Information loss
5. Area of mobile object	25. Time loss
6. Area of stationary object	26. Quantity of matter
7. Volume of mobile object	27. Reliability of object
8. Volume of stationary object	28. Accuracy of measurement
9. Rate of change, speed	29. Precision of production
10. Force exerted by object	30. Harmful influence of object's environment
11. Stress, pressure exerted upon object	31. Harmful effects caused by object
12. Shape of object	32. Ease of production
13. Stability of object's composition	33. Convenience of use
14. Strength of object	34. Ease of repair and maintenance
15. Durability of mobile object	35. Adaptability, versatility of object
16. Durability of stationary object	36. Complexity of object
17. Temperature of object	37. Difficulties in measuring, inspection
18. Illumination of object	38. Level of automation
19. Energy consumption by mobile object	39. Production rate
20. Energy consumption by stationary object	

On the other hand, principles are used to guide the TRIZ practitioners in developing beneficial concepts of solution for inventive situations. Each solution is a recommendation on how to make a specific change to a system for eradicating a technical contradiction [25]. These principles originate from the Altshuller's analysis of patents. They have been derived from the study of the principles used in the top few percent's of the global patent literature, where an innovation invention had actually occurred. 40 Inventive principles are listed as in Table 3:

Table 3. Forty (40) Inventive principles

1. Segmentation	21. Skipping
2. Taking out	22. "Blessing in disguise"
3. Local Quality	23. Feedback
4. Asymmetry	24. 'Intermediary'
5. Merging	25. Self-service
6. Universality	26. Copying
7. "Nested doll"	27. Cheap short-living
8. Anti-weight	28. Mechanics substitution
9. Preliminary anti-action	29. Pneumatics and hydraulics
10. Preliminary action	30. Flexible shells and thin films
11. Beforehand cushioning	31. Porous materials
12. Equipotentiality	32. Color changes
13. The other way around	33. Homogeneity
14. Spheroidality	34. Discarding and recovering
15. Dynamics	35. Parameter changes
16. Partial or excessive actions	36. Phase transitions
17. Another dimension	37. Thermal expansion
18. Mechanical vibration	38. Strong oxidants
19. Periodic action	39. Inert atmosphere
20. Continuity of useful action	40. Composite material films

In TRIZ, problems can be defined in terms of contradictions [26]. An inventive problem contains at least one contradiction an inventive solution overcomes completely or partially this contradiction. A contradiction is a conflict in the system and it arises when two requirements or needs for a system are equally exclusive but both are required by the general function or in other words to reach the system objective [27].

Opposing to traditional methods for creativity stimulation, as brainstorming, trial and errors, TRIZ declines trade-offs and tries to reject the contradiction. TRIZ theory has specific tools to solve contradictions. The most significant one, the contradiction matrix, recommends which principles should be considered in solving approximately 1250 different types of contradictions [28]. Below are the part of contradiction matrix Fig. 2:

Worsening Feature ▸	1 Weight of a mobile object	7 Volume of mobile object	33 Convenience of use	36 Complexity of a device	38 Level of automation	39 Capacity/ Productivity
1 Weight of a mobile object		29, 2 40, 28	35, 3 2, 24	26, 30, 36, 34	26, 35 18, 19	35, 3 24, 37
7 Volume of mobile object	2, 26 29, 40		15, 13 30, 12	26, 1	35, 34 16, 24	10, 6 2, 34
33 Convenience of use	25, 2 13, 15	1, 16 35, 15		32, 26 12, 17	1, 34 12, 3	15, 1 28
36 Complexity of a device	26, 30 34, 36	34, 26 6	27, 9 26, 24		15, 1 24	12, 17 28
38 Level of automation	28, 26 18, 35	35, 13 16	1, 12 34, 3	15, 24 10		5, 12 35, 26
39 Capacity/ productivity	35, 26 24, 37	2, 6 34, 10	1, 28 7, 19	12, 17 28, 24	5, 12 35, 26	

Fig. 2. Part of contradiction matrix

5 Why TRIZ

In TRIZ is an extremely organized approach for innovation and problem solving, whereas Usability follows a less organized approach and in particular, it provides very small framework for identify the solutions. In contrast, TRIZ's structured approach and tracks in it other successes results in a more concrete exploration of the solution capacity. TRIZ's development from a historical analysis of design solutions also provides it with strong technology adaptation. While, Usability provides no formal meaning of technology forecasting, an in-depth understanding of consumer needs and experience to evaluate which types of products are more likely to succeed in the marketplace in current situation.

Usability refers to the methods and ease with users interact with a product [29]. It is more than just how easy a product is to use but also the function that are engaged, the contexts in which engagement occurs, and the satisfactions the product provides. A product is more than the sum of the functions it performs. In addition to consume the functionality of a product, users are purchasing a service either purposely entrenched in the product [30].

Although problem extractions is strength to TRIZ, Usability takes the specific user and context as its main principles. The usability needs, arising from subtleties and contradictions in human behavior, as the main point for development. The TRIZ practitioner places physical and technical contradictions and potential at the lead.

Both methodologies adhere to parallel development frameworks, in which research and analysis phases are followed by resolution generation then evaluation phases. Mann (2002) [31], set the structured innovation into four steps, which repeat iteratively:

1. Define,
2. Select Tool,
3. Generate Solutions,
4. Evaluate.

Within problem definition, Usability highlights problem finding. While a collection of TRIZ tools support the problem definition phase, in our knowledge, TRIZ practitioners often define the problem space based on inadequate information drawn from management imperatives, marketing perspectives or their own experience instead of user analysis [32]. TRIZ is a highly organized approach to innovation, while Usability follows a less structured approach and in specific, delivers very small structure for generating solutions.

6 Differences Between Usability and TRIZ

Whereas problem abstraction is essential to TRIZ method, Usability takes the specific user and context as its main objective. The Usability experts view's needs, arising from subtleties and contradictions in human behaviour, as the main point for development [33]. The TRIZ experts places theoretical and technical contradictions and potential at the forefront. Both methodologies apply similar development frameworks, in which research and analysis phases in initial stage are followed by resolution generation then evaluation phases and the final of process.

TRIZ's development from a huge data analysis of design solutions also provides it with robust technology forecasting records [34]. While Usability provides no formal means of technology forecasting data, an in-depth understanding of user needs allows one to evaluate the types of products are more intense to fulfil the needs and satisfied the end user. The key differences are:

A summary of several key differences between TRIZ and Usability [35] are shown in Table 4.

Table 4. Key differences between TRIZ and usability

TRIZ	Usability
Focus on functionally and technical side	Focus on human needs
Leverages prior technical successes	Leverages anthropological techniques
Emphasis abstraction	Emphasizes context
Highly structured approach	Free structured approach
Prescribes what and how	Describe why

- Usability are usable to all problems, whereas most TRIZ techniques are oriented toward technical problems, although they may be practical to solve nontechnical problems, as well.
- No precise Usability techniques are recommended for any given problem, whereas TRIZ seeks to characterize problems in order to determine the best techniques to apply.
- Usability does not offer specific solution ideas, whereas TRIZ typically offers selected principles, Standard Solutions, or effects.
- TRIZ is a form of huge data analysis of design solutions. While Usability provides no formal guidelines.

- TRIZ explain in detail on what and how the process occur meanwhile Usability are static with explanation on why.

7 Integrating TRIZ and Usability

The highlights of their connections and differences allowed the definition of the proposed method. It demonstrates that this integration of TRIZ and Usability is promising and it is quite clear that the functional approach problem solving method may be used for defining problems in a more structured way. In fact, the Usability theories consider the users' needs and expectations and TRIZ provides a list of systematic implements.

Moreover, the TRIZ approach to technical problem solving can give an major contribute to the creative phases of the Usability process, mostly if interaction matters concern physical aspect as in ergonomics, where example, the laws of evolution process represent real tools for pointing designers and developers towards enhanced and effective solutions. In general, the collaboration with TRIZ can improves usability lacks about technical issues or in other terms able to help in generating the 'what' and 'how' answers to the Usability 'why' questions.

Further motivations to form a combination model for usability measurement are to:

- Decrease the costs of usability testing by providing a base for understanding and comparing numerous usability metrics.
- Complement more subjective, expert-based evaluation of usability.
- Offer a base for clearer communication about usability measurement between developers and usability experts.
- Endorse usability measurement practices that are more reachable to developers who may not have strong backgrounds in usability engineering field.

8 Discussion and Conclusion

The beneficiaries of improvised usability are not just focused on end users but also organizations that develop Internet applications and software enhanced significantly indirectly at the same time. Some of the major benefits of usability are following:

- It can increase development productivity through more efficient design and fewer development repetition.
- It can help to discard over design by emphasizing the functionality required to meet the needs of actual users. Design problems can be perceived earlier in the development process, saving both time and money.
- It can deliver further cost savings through reduced support costs, reduced training requirements and greater user productivity.
- A usable product means more satisfied customers and a better status for the product and for the organization that developed it.

References

1. Nielsen, J.: Usability Engineering. Academic Press, London (1993)
2. Perlman, G.: Book review: human-computer interaction, by Jenny Preece, Yvonne Rogers, Helen Sharp, David Benyon, Simon Holland, and Tom Carey (Addison-Wesley, 1994). ACM SIGCHI Bull. **26**, 82–85 (1994)
3. Bevan, N., Macleod, M.: Usability measurement in context. Behav. Inf. Technol. **13**, 132–145 (1994)
4. Shackel, B.: Ergonomics in design for usability. In: Harrison, M.D., Monk, A.F. (ed.) Proceedings of the Second Conference of the British Computer Society Human Computer Interaction Specialist Group: people and Computers – Design for Usability Cambridge. British Computer Society Human Computer Interaction Specialist Group, pp. 44–64. Cambridge University Press, New York (1986)
5. Seffah, A., Donyaee, M., Kline, R., Padda, H.: Usability measurement and metrics: a consolidated model. Softw. Qual. J. **14**, 159–178 (2006)
6. Nassar, V.: Common criteria for usability review. Work **41**, 1053–1057 (2012). doi:10.3233/WOR-2012-0282-1053. IOS Press
7. Bligård, L.O., Strömberg, H., Karlsson, M.A.: Developers as users: exploring the experiences of using a new theoretical method for usability assessment. Adv. Hum.-Comput. Interact. **2017**, 13 (2017)
8. Nielsen, J.: Usability 101: Introduction to Usability, Alertbox, (2003). http://www.useit.com/alertbox/20030825.html. Accessed 5 Dec 2011
9. Shneiderman, B.: Designing the User Interface. Addison-Wesley Publishing Company, USA (1998)
10. Mayhew, D.: Usability Engineering Lifecycle. Morgan Kaufmann, San Francisco (1999)
11. Andre, T.S., Belz, S.M., McCreary, F.A., Hartson, H.R.: Testing a framework for reliable classification of usability problems. In: Proceedings of Human Factors and Ergonomics Society Annual Meeting. Human Factors and Ergonomics Society, Santa Monica, CA (2000, to Appear)
12. Rivera, B., Becker, P., Olsina, L.: Quality views and strategy patterns for evaluating and improving quality: usability and user experience case studies. J. Web Eng. **15**, 433–464 (2016)
13. Harrison, R., Flood, D., Duce, D.: Usability of mobile application: literature review and rationale for a new usability model. J. Interact. Sci. **1**, 1 (2013)
14. Kahn, M.J., Prail, A.: Formal usability inspections. In: Nielsen, J., Mack, R.L. (eds.) Usability Inspection Methods, pp. 141–171. Wiley, New York (1994)
15. Rubin, J.: Handbook of Usability Testing. Wiley, New York (1994)
16. Soares, M., et al.: Virtual reality in consumer product design: methods and applications. In: Human Factors and Ergonomics in Consumer Product Design: Methods and Techniques. CRC Press, Boca Raton (2011)
17. Seffah, A., Donayaee, M., Kline, R.B., Padda, H.K.: Usability measurement and metrics: a consolidated model. Softw. Qual. Control **14**(2), 159–178 (2006)
18. Jane, J.J.: Social context in usability evaluations: concepts, processes and products, Ph.D. thesis (2009). http://vbn.aau.dk/files/44026023/Jul_Jensen_PhD_thesis.pdf
19. Botman, H.: Do-it-yourself Usability Evaluation: Guiding Software Developers to Usability, pp. 59–66. Taylor & Francis, London (1996)
20. ISO 9241-11: Guidelines for Specifying and Measuring usability (1998)

21. Dey, A.K., Abowd, G.D.: Towards a better understanding of context and context-awareness. In: CHI2000 Workshop on What, Who, Where, When and How of Context-Awareness. ACM Press, New York (2000)
22. Tullis, T., Albert, B.: Tips and tricks for measuring the user experience usability and user experience. In: UPA-Boston's Seventh Annual Mini UPA Conference (2008)
23. Apte, P.R.: Introduction to TRIZ innovative problem solving. http://www.ee.iitb.ac.in/~apte/CV_PRA_TRIZ_INTRO.htm
24. Orloff, M.A.: Inventive Thinking Through TRIZ: A Practical Introduction. Springer, Heidelberg (2006). doi:10.1007/978-3-540-33223-7
25. Pala, S.: TRIZ: A New Framework For Innovation - Concepts and Cases Overview. ICFAI University Press, Hyderabad (2005). http://www.icfaipress.org/books/TRIZ-C&C_ov.asp
26. Mazur, G.: Theory of Inventive Problem Solving (TRIZ) (1995) http://www.mazur.net/triz/
27. Yang, K., Zhang, H.: A comparison of TRIZ and axiomatic design. TRIZ J. (2000)
28. Rantanen, K., Domb, E.: Simplified TRIZ: New Problem Solving Applications for Engineers and Manufacturing Professionals. St Lucie Press, Boca Raton (2002)
29. Altshuller, G.: Creativity As an Exact Science. Gordon & Breach, Philadelphia (1984)
30. Hipple, J.: The use of TRIZ principles in consumer product design. In: TRIZCON 2006, June 2006
31. Joshi, A., Sarda, N., Tripathi, S.: Measuring effectiveness of HCI integration in software development processes. J. Softw. Syst. (2010, in press) (Corrected Proof). https://doi.org/10.1016/j.jss.2010.03.078
32. Zhang, D., Adipat, B.: Challenges, methodologies, and issues in the usability testing of mobile applications. Int. J. Hum. Comput. Interact. 18(3), 293–308 (2005)
33. Mann, D.: Systematic (Software) Innovation, IFR Press, ISBN 978-1-906769-01-7 (2008)
34. Patnaik, D., Becker, R.: Needfinding: the why and how of uncovering people's needs. Des. Manag. J. 10(2), 37–43 (1999)
35. Virzi, R.A.: Refining the test phase of usability evaluation: how many subjects is enough? Hum. Factors 34(4), 457–468 (1992)
36. Runhua, T.: Voice of customers pushed by directed evolution. TRIZ J. (2002)
37. Batemanazan, V., Jaafar, A., Nayan, N.M., Kadir, R.A.: Synergy between TRIZ and usability: a review. In: Badioze Zaman, H., et al. (eds.) Advances in Visual Informatics. LNCS, vol. 9429, pp. 514–523. Springer, Cham (2015). doi:10.1007/978-3-319-25939-0_45

An Evaluation of Player Enjoyment in Game-Based Learning Arithmetic Drills via Racing Game

Nurul Hidayah Mat Zain[1]([⊠]), Razuan Harmy Johar[1],
Azlan Abdul Aziz[1], Aslina Baharum[2], Azizah Jaafar[3],
and Anita Mohd Yasin[1]

[1] Faculty of Computer and Mathematical Sciences,
Universiti Teknologi MARA (UiTM), Cawangan Melaka, Kampus Jasin,
77300 Merlimau, Melaka, Malaysia
nurulmz@tmsk.uitm.edu.my
[2] Faculty of Computing and Informatics, Universiti Malaysia Sabah (UMS),
Kota Kinabalu, Malaysia
[3] Institute of Visual Informatics, Universiti Kebangsaan Malaysia (UKM),
Bangi, Malaysia

Abstract. Arithmetic is the oldest branch of Mathematics which consists the study of numbers, specifically the properties of the basic traditional operations. According to a previous study, most of the users agree that Mathematics is considered as a difficult subject and there is a lack of enjoyment in practicing arithmetic drills. Therefore, this research has developed a racing game named *Need for Speed Arithmetic* for an enjoyable arithmetic drills experience. The racing game has implemented the Rapid Application Development (RAD) approach as it provided a stable and fast development process which is appropriate in developing the game. In this present study, the focus is on the evaluation of player enjoyment in game-based learning arithmetic drills. The evaluation scale adapted is based on EGameFlow Model which consists of seven dimensions: Immersion, challenge, goal clarity, feedback, concentration, control, and knowledge improvement. The social interaction dimension is excluded because the game is implemented on a standalone platform. The study findings indicate that the combination of gaming element with arithmetic drills in the Mathematics subject provide a sense of enjoyment to students in learning Mathematics through drill activities.

Keywords: Enjoyment · Game-based learning · Arithmetic drills · Racing game

1 Introduction

Arithmetic is a basic part of number theory. The number theory is one of the top-level divisions of modern mathematics, along with algebra, geometry and analysis. The terms arithmetic and higher arithmetic were used until the beginning of the 20th century as synonyms for number theory and are sometimes still used to refer to a wider part of

© Springer International Publishing AG 2017
H. Badioze Zaman et al. (Eds.): IVIC 2017, LNCS 10645, pp. 636–646, 2017.
https://doi.org/10.1007/978-3-319-70010-6_59

number theory. Arithmetic is taught to the students at a very young age to get them to know the numbers and developing the love towards it. The use of arithmetic is evident in a person's life in their everyday life routines such as counting the prices of an item, paying the bills and planning the expenditure of money on needs. The scope of this study covers the arithmetic syllabus for standard four school level which coincides with 10 years old student. The topic covers the basic arithmetic operations involving addition, subtraction, multiplication and division.

There is a common belief that majority of the students dislike mathematics [1]. An arithmetic is part of mathematics that deals with basic computation numbers such as addition, subtraction, multiplication and division. When the student dislike mathematics, they certainly have a bad perception about arithmetic. Some of the students also stated that learning mathematic such as arithmetic is not enjoyable [2, 3]. Besides, there is limited research evaluating the educational computer games itself [4]. Hence, the objective of this study is to evaluate player enjoyment in game-based learning arithmetic drills via racing games.

2 Related Study

2.1 Game-Based Learning

Trends in educational research indicate a growing curiosity in how games may impact learning [4–7]. Game-based learning (GBL) is a method used to present a subject matter through games [8]. GBL has been discovered to stimulate a positive attitude towards learning, develop memory skills and help student build self-constructed learning [9]. Since students are having the lack of enjoyment while doing mathematical questions or exercises, game-based learning incorporates both element of learning and enjoyment into one single design.

To date, several studies have been conducted regarding the benefits of GBL such as able to sustain the learners growing abilities [10], offered engagement experience in learning [4, 11], encourage motivation and prompt learners to actively process the learning content [6] and developing entrepreneurship sense to the users [7].

2.2 Enjoyment Experience

Enjoyment is important element in learning process when learning new tools since the user is more relax, motivated and willing to learn [12, 13]. The experience of enjoyment is very important not only for ordinary user but for extraordinary user [14, 15]. Prensky [12] also stated that the role that enjoyment plays regarding intrinsic motivation in education is twofold which is firstly, intrinsic motivation encourages the desire for return of the experience, secondly, fun can stimulate learners to engage themselves in activities with which they have little or no previous experience. Besides, Baek and Touati [16] also examined kids' enjoyment in the mobile game and focus the complexity of game enjoyment in mobile learning games.

2.3   Evaluation of Player Enjoyment

EGameFlow model is a game design model that is used to evaluate the user's learning cognition of enjoyment while playing a game [17]. This model is adapted for the purpose of evaluating *Need for Speed Arithmetic* game in this study. EGameFlow is a valid and reliable instrument to ensure the level of enjoyment brought to the learner by e-learning games [17]. An adapted EGameFlow Model that is implemented in this study consists of seven dimensions: immersion, challenge, goal clarity, feedback, concentration, control, and knowledge improvement. The following Table 1 gives a details description of all elements.

Table 1. The description of adapted EGameFlow model based on this study

Element	Criteria
Concentration	Player able to concentrate on the task
Goal Clarity	Games should provide the player with clear goals at appropriate times
Feedback	The task provides immediate feedback
Challenge	Perceived skills should match challenges and both must exceed a certain threshold
Autonomy	Allowed to exercise a sense of control over actions
Immersion	Deep but effortless involvement, reduced concern for self and sense of time
Knowledge Improvement	The improvement of knowledge after playing the game

3   Methodology

3.1   Participants

The 32 participants (11 female and 21 male) in Year Four primary students were recruited to participate in this study. All participants had experience playing computer games with 18 students categorized themselves as experience gamer, seven less experience gamers, and seven moderate experience gamers.

3.2   Instrument

The instrument for this study was adapted from EGameFlow Model. The adapted EGameFlow Model is self-administered questionnaire containing seven elements and 36 criteria to evaluate player enjoyment after playing a game. Since this game did not involve social interaction, the social interaction element was excluded. Table 2 shown all the enjoyment criteria. The instrument was written in bilingual which is English and Bahasa Melayu to make participants clearly understand each of the evaluation item. Most of the children were conversant in Bahasa Malaysia compared to English. The participant can ask guidance from their teachers, parents or the researcher on the entire evaluation process. Besides, the Likert Scale in the instrument was added with smiley emoji reaction feelings such as from very happy to very sad to make the questionnaires more fun and interactive for the participant to answer.

Table 2. The adapted EGameFlow model

Element	Code	Criteria
Concentration	C1	Most of the gaming activities are related to the learning task
	C2	No distraction from the task is highlighted
	C3	I can remain concentrated in the game
	C4	I am not distracted from tasks that the player should concentrate on
	C5	I am not burdened with tasks that seem unrelated
	C6	Workload in the game is adequate
Goal Clarity	G1	Game goals were presented in the beginning of the game
	G2	Game goals were presented clearly
	G3	Intermediate goals were presented in the beginning of each scene
	G4	Intermediate were presented clearly
Feedback	F1	I received feedback on my progress in the game
	F2	I received immediate feedback on my action
	F3	I am notified of new task immediately
	F4	I am notified of new event immediately
	F5	I received information on my success (or failure) of immediate goals immediately
Challenge	H1	The game provides "hints" in the text that help me overcome the challenges
	H2	The game provides "online support" that help me overcome the challenges
	H3	The game provides video or audio auxiliaries that help me overcome the challenges
	H4	The difficulty of challenges increases as my skills improved
	H5	The game provides new challenges with an appropriate pacing
	H6	The game provides different level of challenges that tailor to different player
Autonomy	A1	I feel a sense of control over the game
	A2	I know next step in the game
	A3	I feel a sense of control over the game
Immersion	I1	I forget about time passing while playing the game
	I2	I become unaware of my surrounding while playing the game
	I3	I temporarily forget worries everyday life while playing the game
	I4	I experienced an altered sense of time
	I5	I can be involved in the game
	I6	I feel emotionally involved in the game
	I7	I feel viscerally involved in the game

(continued)

Table 2. (*continued*)

Element	Code	Criteria
Knowledge Improvement	K1	The game increases my knowledge
	K2	I catch the basic ideas of the knowledge taught
	K3	I try to apply the knowledge in the game
	K4	The game motivates the player to integrate the knowledge taught
	K5	I want to know more about the knowledge taught

3.3   Evaluation Procedure

On the day of the evaluation process, consent forms and detailed procedures were given to the participants. All the participants were briefed and a demo was presented before they start playing the *Need for Speed Arithmetic* game. The desktop computer was prepared and ready for the participants to play the game. There is no duration time required for participants to complete their game. However, each participant took approximately five to seven minutes to finish the game. Once the participants finished the game, the participants were required to answer a post-questionnaire which is adapted from EGameFlow Model. They should answer it based on their experience while playing the game. The evaluation was conducted face to face individually between participant and the researcher. The presence of the researcher was to clarify any queries should there be any (Fig. 1).

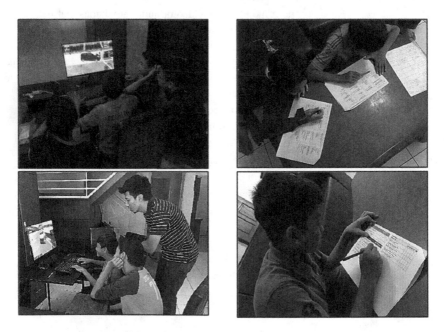

Fig. 1. Evaluation procedure in progress

4 Result and Discussion

The participants must answer 36 criteria to evaluate their enjoyment while playing the game. The data from the post-questionnaire were analyzed using the SPSS software tool. A standard descriptive statistical method was used to estimate the frequency (%) data. All the responses were tabulated and analyze according to all elements in EGameFlow Model. The total average from the evaluation were identified to determine the game enjoyment level. The detailed demographic data are shown in Table 3.

Table 3. The demographic data of participants

Questions	Range	Frequency (n)	Percentage (%)
Gender	Male	21	65.6
	Female	11	34.4
Time spend play computer games in a week	0 h per week	3	9.4
	1–3 h per week	20	62.5
	4–6 h per week	6	18.8
	7–9 h per week	3	9.4
	More than 10 h per week	0	0
Purpose of play games	To learn something	15	46.9
	For challenge	9	28.1
	For fun	17	53.1
	To fulfill my leisure time	7	21.9
Interest on games genre	Exploration	2	6.3
	Shooting game	14	43.8
	Sport (Racing Motorsport)	18	56.3
	Trivia (Board Game)	6	18.8
	Simulation	6	18.8
	Other	0	0
Level experience gamers	Experience gamers	18	56.3
	Less experience gamers	7	21.9
	Moderate experience gamers	7	21.9
	Novice gamers	0	0

The demographic data in Table 3 shown most participants are male (21, 65.6%) which is rather normal in today's gaming society. The demographic data showed most participants at this age play 1–3 h per week (20, 62.5%). Moreover, the demographic data also shows the highest purpose of playing games is for fun (17, 53.1%), followed by second highest which is to learn something with (15, 46.9%). The presented data brings positive result towards the determining one of *Need for Speed Arithmetic* game objectives, which is to bring enjoyment in drilling Arithmetic via racing game.

Additionally, positive result from the demographic exposed the highest genre score is Sport (Racing Motorsport) as much as (18, 56.3%) which is similar with developed game. The demographic data also presented the result with highest number of participants are experience gamers with (18, 56.3%) from the total of participants.

Table 4 showed the participants moderately agree that the gaming activities are related to the learning task with 46.9%. The results produced maybe because of the game is not fully contributing to learning but focus on arithmetic drills. The result also shown that the game indeed need a high level of concentration to finish with 37.5% of agreeability that the users able to remain concentrated in the game without any distraction. Table 4 also showed almost half participants (46.9%) agree that the game did not distract them from tasks that they should concentrate on. The results were predictable because the game nature itself makes the user fully focus and concentrate on the game. In racing sport nature or racing game, concentration is the main priority aspect to win the race. The game mission to get first place in the race also affected users' concentration while playing the game.

Table 4. Mean score and frequency (%) of responses for concentration element

Factor	Code	SD	D	MA	A	SA	Mean score	Std. deviation
Concentration	C1	6.3	0	46.9	21.9	25.0	3.59	1.073
	C2	12.5	12.5	46.9	15.6	12.5	3.03	1.150
	C3	0	6.3	28.1	37.5	28.1	3.88	.907
	C4	18.8	12.5	6.3	46.9	15.6	3.28	1.397
	C5	6.3	25.0	3.1	34.4	31.3	3.59	1.341
	C6	6.3	15.6	12.5	34.4	31.3	3.69	1.256
Total mean							**3.51**	

*SD-Strongly Disagree, D-Disagree, MA-Moderately Agree, A-Agree, SA-Strongly Agree

Based on the Table 5, the participant is most likely agree that the game goal is presented clearly in the game. The game goal and objective are presented at the early of the game in the *About* section to make the user know about the goals of the game clearly. The result produced a positive feedback which most of the participant agree on goals were presented in the beginning of each scene and were presented clearly. This demonstrate that the participant understands the goals of the game so that they able to play the game smoothly until the game ends.

Table 5. Mean score and frequency (%) of responses for goal clarity element

Factor	Code	SD	D	MA	A	SA	Mean score	Std. deviation
Goal clarity	G1	0	3.1	37.5	31.3	28.1	3.84	.884
	G2	25.0	18.8	21.9	34.4	25.0	3.66	1.208
	G3	6.3	6.3	25.0	37.5	25.0	3.69	1.120
	G4	0	12.5	21.9	31.3	34.4	3.88	1.040
Total mean							**3.71**	

*SD-Strongly Disagree, D-Disagree, MA-Moderately Agree, A-Agree, SA-Strongly Agree

Based on Table 6, in term of Feedback element, most criteria received a positive response with participants answered moderately agree, agree and strongly agree scale. The result showed that the game was provide a feedback to keep user on track and identify about player latest progress regarding the game. The score for these criteria are for strongly agree was 40.6% followed by agree with 34.4% and the lowest was 9.4%. The participants also strongly agree with 34.4% regarding the receiving information on users' success (or failure) of immediate goals immediately.

Table 6. Mean score and frequency (%) of responses for Feedback element

Factor	Code	SD	D	MA	A	SA	Mean score	Std. deviation
Feedback	F1	9.4	3.1	12.5	34.4	40.6	3.94	1.243
	F2	6.3	12.5	18.8	43.8	18.8	3.56	1.134
	F3	6.3	0	18.8	40.6	34.4	3.97	1.062
	F4	3.1	28.1	21.9	40.6	6.3	3.19	1.030
	F5	6.3	18.8	25.0	34.4	15.6	3.34	1.153
Total mean							**3.62**	

*SD-Strongly Disagree, D-Disagree, MA-Moderately Agree, A-Agree, SA-Strongly Agree

One of the criteria in Challenge element (Table 7) had received the highest positive score among other criteria with 43.8%. This support that the game indeed provided some hints to overcome the task challenges for the user. However, the Challenge element had received the highest negative score too among other criteria with 84.4%. This is about the disagreeability regarding the online support that help to overcome the challenges. This is because the game was built fully as an offline based game. The online features were put in the future work game.

Table 7. Mean score and frequency (%) of responses for Challenge element

Factor	Code	SD	D	MA	A	SA	Mean score	Std. deviation
Challenge	H1	3.1	6.3	31.3	15.6	43.8	3.91	1.146
	H2	84.4	3.1	6.3	3.1	3.1	1.38	.976
	H3	12.5	0	34.4	21.9	31.3	3.59	1.292
	H4	0	6.3	21.9	46.9	25.0	3.91	.856
	H5	3.1	15.6	21.9	28.1	31.3	3.69	1.176
	H6	3.1	12.5	18.8	28.1	37.5	3.84	1.167
Total mean							**3.39**	

*SD-Strongly Disagree, D-Disagree, MA-Moderately Agree, A-Agree, SA-Strongly Agree

The fifth element in EGameFlow model is Autonomy. Most of the result regarding the Autonomy element were received positive feedback. As shown in the Table 8, most of the response are mostly towards agree regarding all the criteria. Moreover, Table 8

Table 8. Mean score and frequency (%) of responses for Autonomy element

Factor	Code	SD	D	MA	A	SA	Mean score	Std. deviation
Autonomy	A1	3.1	3.1	28.1	28.1	37.5	3.94	1.045
	A2	12.5	3.1	43.8	40.6	12.5	4.13	.976
	A3	9.4	12.5	12.5	40.6	25.0	3.59	1.266
Total Mean							**3.76**	

*SD-Strongly Disagree, D-Disagree, MA-Moderately Agree, A-Agree, SA-Strongly Agree

showed 37.5% agreeability on the feel a sense of control over the game. These responses demonstrate that the game able to make the participant feel control of the game. The result also shown the positive result with 43.8% agreeability regarding the user know about the next step of the game. This shows that the user understands the flow of the game.

Table 9 shown the result of 40.6% agreeability regarding user forgets about time passing while playing the game. Besides, from the result, 34.4% participants strongly agree become unaware of surroundings while playing the game. This confirm that the participants enjoyed playing the game because they immerse with the game. The criteria on user temporarily forget the worries of everyday life while playing the game get the highest percentage with 43.8% in term of Immersion element. This is demonstrated that the game is really make the users very attracted and concentrate fully on the game.

Table 9. Mean score and frequency (%) of responses for Immersion element

Factor	Code	SD	D	MA	A	SA	Mean score	Std. deviation
Immersion	I1	9.4	3.1	18.8	40.6	28.1	3.75	1.191
	I2	6.3	12.5	21.9	25.0	34.4	3.69	1.256
	I3	3.1	15.6	9.4	43.8	28.1	3.78	1.128
	I4	21.9	18.8	25.0	18.8	15.6	2.88	1.385
	I5	6.3	0	25.0	31.3	37.5	3.94	1.105
	I6	12.5	21.9	12.5	21.9	31.3	3.38	1.454
	I7	6.3	12.5	25.0	31.3	25.0	3.56	1.190
Total Mean							**4.16**	

Table 10 presented the 40.6% agreeability of the participants about the game increases the users' knowledge. This showed that even the game was focus on drilling arithmetic skills, the game able to increase the user knowledge when playing the game. One of another benefit was the participants exposed with racing automotive environment. Table 10 also showed the result of agreeability about the user tries to apply the knowledge in the game which gives the most significant values which is as much as of 56.3%. This demonstrate that the user able to apply the basic knowledge of arithmetic to complete the challenges in the game.

Table 10. Mean score and frequency (%) of responses for Knowledge Improvement element

Factor	Code	SD	D	MA	A	SA	Mean score	Std. deviation
Knowledge Improvement	K1	3.1	6.3	12.5	40.6	37.5	4.03	1.031
	K2	9.4	9.4	28.1	31.3	21.9	3.47	1.218
	K3	0	0	12.5	56.3	31.3	4.19	.644
	K4	0	9.4	12.5	15.6	62.5	4.31	1.030
	K5	6.3	0	15.6	37.5	40.6	4.06	1.076
Total mean							3.34	
Overall							**3.64 (73%)**	

*SD-Strongly Disagree, D-Disagree, MA-Moderately Agree, A-Agree, SA-Strongly Agree

5   Conclusion

According to the findings, the total mean of all element was 3.64 which is in above average scale. The highest mean score among the seven elements are Immersion with a score of 4.16. The findings presented that the game was verified encourages player immersion. The increment of the degree of immersion is one of the important element that the learning tool provides student with a form of enjoyment [17]. The other element is also above agreeable level which proves that the game complies with the rules of every element in EGameFlow model. The overall average from total mean of seven element was computed to identify the agreeability of the enjoyment of this game. The result produces a value of 3.64 for the overall average which shows on agreeability level. This shows that 73% among the respondents agree that this game is enjoyable in terms of game-based learning.

References

1. Gafoor, K.A., Kurukkan, A.: Why high school students feel mathematics difficult? An exploration of affective beliefs. In: UGC Sponsored National Seminar on Pedagogy of Teacher Education-Trends and Challenges, pp. 1–6 (2015)
2. Vitasari, P., Herawan, T., Wahab, M.N.A., Othman, A., Sinnadurai, S.K.: Exploring mathematics anxiety among engineering students. Procedia – Soc. Behav. Sci. **8**, 482–489 (2010)
3. Markovits, Z., Forgasz, H.: "Mathematics is like a lion": elementary students' beliefs about mathematics. Educ. Stud. Math. **96**, 49–64 (2017)
4. Sampayo-Vargas, S., Cope, C.J., He, Z., Byrne, G.J.: The effectiveness of adaptive difficulty adjustments on students' motivation and learning in an educational computer game. Comput. Educ. **69**, 452–462 (2013). doi:10.1016/j.compedu.2013.07.004
5. Bourgonjon, J., De Grove, F., De Smet, C., Van Looy, J., Soetaert, R., Valcke, M.: Acceptance of game-based learning by secondary school teachers. Comput. Educ. **67**, 21–35 (2013). doi:10.1016/j.compedu.2013.02.010

6. Erhel, S., Jamet, E.: Digital game-based learning: impact of instructions and feedback on motivation and learning effectiveness. Comput. Educ. **67**, 156–167 (2013). doi:10.1016/j. compedu.2013.02.019
7. Romero, M.: Game based learning MOOC. Promoting entrepreneurship education. Elearning Pap. **33**, 1–5 (2013)
8. Qian, M., Clark, K.R.: Game-based learning and 21st century skills: a review of recent research. Comput. Hum. Behav. **63**, 50–58 (2016). doi:10.1016/j.chb.2016.05.023
9. Cojocariu, V.-M., Boghian, I.: Teaching the relevance of game-based learning to preschool and primary teachers. Procedia - Soc. Behav. Sci. **142**, 640–646 (2014). doi:10.1016/j. sbspro.2014.07.679
10. Hamari, J., Shernoff, D.J., Rowe, E., Coller, B., Asbell-Clarke, J., Edwards, T.: Challenging games help students learn: an empirical study on engagement, flow and immersion in game-based learning. Comput. Hum. Behav. **54**, 170–179 (2016). doi:10.1016/j.chb.2015. 07.045
11. Abdul Jabbar, A.I., Felicia, P.: Gameplay engagement and learning in game-based learning: a systematic review. Rev. Educ. Res. **85**, 1–40 (2015). doi:10.3102/0034654315577210
12. Prensky, M.: Types of learning and possible game styles. Digit. GameBased Learn. (2001)
13. Mat Zain, N.H., Jaafar, A., Abdul Razak, F.H.: Enjoyable game design: validation of motor-impaired user GameFlow model. Int. J. Comput. Theory Eng. **8**, 116–121 (2016). doi:10.7763/IJCTE.2016.V8.1029
14. Zain, N.H.M., Jaafar, A., Razak, F.H.A.: A user-centered design: methodological tools to design and develop computer games for motor-impaired users. In: Proceedings of 5th International Conference Computing Informatics, pp. 223–228 (2015)
15. Zain, N.H.M., Jaafar, A., Razak, F.H.A.: SGameFlow framework: how to experience enjoyment in serious game (SG) for motor impaired users (MIU). In: 2012 International Conference on Computer and Information Science, ICCIS 2012 - A Conference of World Engineering, Science and Technology Congress, ESTCON 2012 - Conference Proceedings, pp. 1020–1024 (2012)
16. Baek, Y., Touati, A.: Exploring how individual traits influence enjoyment in a mobile learning game. Comput. Hum. Behav. **69**, 347–357 (2017). doi:10.1016/j.chb.2016.12.053
17. Fu, F.L., Su, R.C., Yu, S.C.: EGameFlow: a scale to measure learners' enjoyment of e-learning games. Comput. Educ. **52**, 101–112 (2009). doi:10.1016/j.compedu.2008.07.004

Technological Intervention for Moral Education Among Teenagers: A Review

Sitti Hutari Mulyani[1,4(✉)], Billy Hendrik[2,4],
Muhammad Reza Putra[3,4], Gushelmi[3,4], Emil Naf'an[2,4],
Nazlena Mohamad Ali[2], and Khaidzir Ismail[1]

[1] Faculty Social Sciences and Humanities, Universiti Kebangsaan Malaysia,
Bangi, Malaysia
sittihutarimulyani@upiyptk.ac.id, izay@ukm.edu.my
[2] Institute Visual Informatic, Universiti Kebangsaan Malaysia, Bangi, Malaysia
m.haikalbilvy@yahoo.com, Emilnafan1974@gmail.com,
Nazlena.ali@ukm.edu.my
[3] Faculty of Information Science and Technology,
Universiti Kebangsaan Malaysia, Bangi, Malaysia
Mhd.rezaputra@gmail.com, Gushelmi@gmail.com
[4] Universitas Putra Indonesia "YPTK", Padang, Indonesia

Abstract. A good child is a dream for every family. Good moral education will encourage children to think and understand about what is allowed or forbidden things. A child who has a good education will be able to manage the management of emotions and the formation of his character. The main purpose of this study is to provide an alternative moral education in children, especially adolescents. Today's teenage morale is much damaged by juvenile delinquency as it happens and viral in social media, smoking behavior, dating, pre marital sex, piercing, taking drugs and things that violate the prevailing norms. Not all children get a good moral education from home or school. It requires effective moral education with technological intervention in improving and shaping the stage of moral development. Technology can not be separated from adolescents and greatly influence in adolescent moral formation. The positive actions they choose will help improve their attitude. Teens who have a good moral education in their social life will become more independent, and parents can give them the authority to choose more and act according to their choice. Moral education is the most important part in the stage of moral development of adolescents who are planted early on. The stage of moral development is divided into 3 levels: Conventional Level, Conventional Level and Post-Conventional Level. This research is more directed to developmental psychology and technological psychology. Interpersonal communication is the most important part in determining the outcome. The study concludes by suggesting a number of practical and theoretical recommendations for all related elements.

Keywords: Moral education · Technological intervention · Teenagers

© Springer International Publishing AG 2017
H. Badioze Zaman et al. (Eds.): IVIC 2017, LNCS 10645, pp. 647–657, 2017.
https://doi.org/10.1007/978-3-319-70010-6_60

1 Introduction

The child is a gift of God Almighty, which He left a family. Every family longs for children who have good moral, in order to be able to adapt to the social environment of society in accordance with prevailing norms. In general, teenagers will continue to vote and make decisions on each of their behaviors, but sometimes not all of their behavior is considered in accordance with the norms that apply to the community. Not infrequently their behavior is contrary to the custom and culture (read: Adab) that exist in an area where they live. In general, adolescents are also called transitional periods, the search period of identity, often they do coping strategies on the model he considers "present" or "true".

Gender, environmental, peer group differences are a factor that allows to influence moral development. Young women tend to be more embarrassed in expressing feelings, and boys tend to be more indifferent to the surroundings. The presence of technology is also able to influence behavior/behavior patterns among adolescents. With the presence of Technology, teenagers are more "able" to express feelings of sadness, happiness, anger through social media such as Instagram, twitter, Facebook etc. This is also the authors prove with the teen easily expressed feelings of sadness through the snippets or pieces of song lyrics uploaded on his personal Instagram. Surely this will trigger a quarrel among teenagers, so that moral development is not good. Another example of the moral damage factor of teenagers is smoking behavior and relationship goals are wrong, so adolescents are immediately coping on the wrong model. Most teenagers will imitate what has been viral in social media such as the case of blue whale, skip challenge, down another challenge that does not have an important purpose and leaves only the moral damage for teenagers [1]. According to Dion Hinchcliffe (2011) in an online article, the current trends in information communications technology and telecommunications sectors illustrate that social media or social networking services (SNS) is one of the five major achievements of the next half decade [9, 13, 29, 30]. When individuals abuse technology it will affect their own personal growth and development [12, 28, 30, 38]. The issue of adolescent morale and technology in the era of globalization is very exciting for us to discuss, from the problems faced with friends, family and society. Moral education among teenagers becomes very important, because to be able to make a state of character and good moral of course comes from good moral generation as well.

According to Berkowitz and Bier [41] In recent years, character and issues of morality among youth have received nationwide attention from the general public, policy makers, educators, and parents [2]. The original educational term comes from the Greek word "pedagogie" which means guidance given to the child. Education is the process of changing the attitude and conduct of a person or group of people in an effort to mature humans through teaching and training efforts; Processes, ways, actions educate. Human only through education can't be human. Education itself from specific (creator) whatever If she just is. Human but by people so they trained people are trained is remarkable (Kant 2015) [37]. Here a very important role for educators is. Educators in the context of universal morality that humanity needs an idealistic perspective, they be grasped. These trainers are not based on the natural tendency of individuals to

humanity, and to contribute to the future on behalf of generation must educate and instill in them the awareness that education should [37].

According to Ali and Asrori (2015) The moral word comes from the Latin, the mos. The word "mos" is a single word form, while its plural is morse. This means custom, moral. Customs are human actions that conform to general ideas about good or bad in society. Therefore morals are behaviors that conform to the measures of specific social or environmental actions accepted by society [4].

The word 'moral' is derived from the Latin *mos* (plural: *mores)* means the habit, custom. *mos* word *(mores)* in Latin is synonymous with the Greek word *ethos*. Dictionary of Education defines morality as a term used to delimit those characters, traits, intentions, or acts roommates Judgments can appropriately be designated as right, wrong, good, bad [14, 16].

Moral words in Arabic are often synonymous with the term "Akhlaq". Akhlaq is a plural word, but sometimes it is used in its singular form (khuluq) to mean character, innate disposition, or 'a state of the soul which causes it to perform its actions without thought or deliberation' (Miskawih, 1968, p. 30; cf. Omar, 1994, p. 103). [21] according to Djazwidi, *akhlāq* means 'good morals' *(al-akhlāq al-mahmūdah)* or 'bad character' *(al-akhlāq al-madzmūmah)* [16] Another term for morality is Adab, Adab al-islaˉm means 'the good manners adopted by Islam derived from its teachings and instructions' (al-Kaysi, 2003, p. 13) [21].

The moral according to Dewey (in Zuriah [40]) says that moral in moral education here is almost the same as rational, where moral reasoning is prepared as a principle of critical thinking to arrive at the choice and moral judgment that is regarded as the best mind and attitude. Moral always refers to the good of human as human being [20]. The field of morals is the field of human life in terms of human kindness. Moral norms are benchmarks for determining right-wrong human attitudes and actions viewed in terms of good and bad as a human and not as a role-specific and limited actors. So he thinks that the problem of the moral field is whether human is good or bad.

Morality is viewed as the system of rules that regulate the social interactions and social relationships of individuals within societies and is based on concepts of welfare (harm), trust, justice (comparative treatment and distribution) and rights. The concept of morality has been variously defined by philosophers and psychologist but in common terms it can be interpreted to mean a person's or society's view of what is perceived to be the highest good. Such a view is based on a set of principles, ideas and norms that are used to distinguish between right' and wrong'. Though the notion what is good' and what constitutes happiness has a definite cultural bias, morality generally refers to attitudes and predispositions that foster respect, responsibility, integrity and honesty [17, 24].

The Moral goodness, but it is possible to be virtuous. mentioned above, the existence virtue of the absence of natural tendency or can it be possible by reducing the possible. So who is really the freedom to obey the laws of morality, we're in it tend to adopt. In this case, the human being will require a disciplined. This disciplined state, based on the moral understanding of people's homework will help to capture the target [37].

According to Dreeben (in Zuriah [40]) if the goal of moral education would lead one to be moral, it is important that one be adapted to the purpose of community life. Therefore, in the early stages it is necessary to do moral conditioning and moral practice for habituation (in Zurian 2011). If we say about moral education that Islamic literature in the area of personality contains theories that direct man in certain ways as stated in two sources of Islam, which are the Qur'anic text and the Sunna [3].

Moral Education as part of grades education in schools, which helps learners to recognize, realize the importance, moral values that should be made A guide to his attitude and behavior as human beings, both individually and collectively in a society.

It can be concluded that moral education is a planned way and structured by an educator to form positive habits in learners, so as to form a good moral in accordance with the norms and character of the nation.

2 Teenagers

The word adolescent, also called adolescence and youth. The term adolescence comes from the Latin word adolescere which means to grow or grow into adulthood (in Hurlock [44]). Adolescence according to Mappiare (in Ali and Asrori 2015), between 12 years old up to 21 years for women and 13 years up to 22 years for men [4]. Based on the time span, adolescents are divided into 3 stages [8, 11, 32, 37]:

2.1 Early Adolescence (10–12 Years) [39]

a. Appear and do feel closer to peers.
b. Look and feel free.
c. Looks and does pay more attention to the state of his body and start thinking the imaginary (abstract).

2.2 Mid-Adolescence (13−15 Years) [30, 39]

a. Looks and wants to search for identity.
b. There is a desire for dating or interest in the opposite sex. There is a deep feeling of love.

2.3 The Final Adolescence (16−19 Years) [27, 30, 39]

a. Expressing self-deprecation.
b. In looking for more selective peers.
c. Has an image (picture, circumstances, role) against him.
d. Being able to manifest feelings of love.
e. Have the ability to think imaginary or abstract

Based on chronological age and various interests, there is a definition of adolescence that is:

a. In pediatric books, generally define teenagers is when a child has reached the age of 10–18 years and the age of 12−20 year boys.

b. According to the law no. 4 years 1979 on the welfare of children, adolescents are those who have not reached 21 years and not married.
c. Under the labor law, a child is considered a teenager if he has reached the age of 16–18 years or is married and has a place to live.
d. According to the marriage law No. 1 of 1979, children are considered to be teenagers if mature enough, i.e. age 16 years for women and 19 years for boys.
e. According to the office of the child's health, it is considered to be a teenager if the child is 18 years old, which is appropriate for the high school graduation.
f. According to the WHO (2011), adolescents when the child has reached the age of 10–18 years [35].

According to WHO, adolescence is a time in which:

a. The individual who develops from the moment he first signs his secondary sexual signs until he reaches sexual maturity.
b. Individuals experiencing psychological development and pattern identification from childhood to adulthood.
c. The transition from socio-economic dependence is full of relatively more independent conditions.

Adolescence is closely related to the development of "sense of identity versus role confusion," i.e. feeling or awareness of identity. Basically teenagers do not have a clear place, meaning he is among the group of children and adults. It is therefore often known as the "search for identity" phase. However, in this adolescent phase, adolescents are at a very potential stage of development, both in terms of cognitive, affective and physical. This is reinforced by Hurluck (in Ali and Asrori 2015) that the term adolescence actually has a broad meaning, including mental, emotional, social, and physical maturity [4].

3 Moral Development of Youth Period

According to Starbuck (in Jalaludin [42]), moral development in adolescents is based on guilt and efforts to seek protection. Moral types also seen in teenagers also include:

1. Self-directive, obedient to religion or morals based on personal considerations.
2. Adaptive, follow the environmental situation without making any criticism.
3. Submissive, sensing doubts about moral and religious teachings.
4. Unadjusted, not yet convinced of the truth of religious and moral teachings.
5. Deviant, rejects the basic and religious laws and moral order of society.

The stages of moral development according to Kohlberg (in Ali and Asrori 2015) are as follows [4]:

i. Pre-conventional Level: rules and moral expressions are still interpreted by the individual/child based on the physical consequences to be received, whether in the form of something painful or pleasurable. This level has two stages, namely punishment orientation and compliance as well as relativist-instrumental orientation.

ii. The initial conventional or conventional level: moral rules and expressions are adhered to on the basis of family, group or community expectations. This level has two stages, namely the orientation of agreement between the person or called "sweet child orientation" and the orientation of law and order.

iii. Post-conventional level: moral rules and expressions are formulated clearly based on legal values and principles that have validity and can be applied, regardless of the authority of the group or the person holding on to the principle and independent of self-identification with the group the. This level has two stages, namely the orientation of the social contract of legality and the orientation of universal ethical principles.

Factors Affecting the Achievement of Youth Identity

According to Waterman identity means having a clear self-image of the range of goods to be achieved, values, and beliefs chosen by the individual.

According to Prime unravels some of the factors that portray themselves teenagers include:

a. Family

Family circumstances can affect adolescents in self-esteem. There are some families who can portray themselves teenagers, among others:

(1) Socio-economic identity
(2) Family unity
(3) Attitudes & habits
(4) Child status

b. Social environment

Teenagers will try to expression to seek a social environment as a place for teenagers to express their identity. The teens feel with socializing teenagers can achieve their identity. In addition, within the social environment there are norms, values, ordinances also customs. In myself, adolescents will launder the values that apply in their social environment.

The way society around teenagers at the time of socializing can also portray adolescent identity.

c. Education

The way of thinking and behavior of a teenager can be known by the education of adolescents, adolescents who have a good education can consider the values and good in the environment. In adolescence the individual is at the stage of formal thinking. That is at this stage requires the ability of teenagers to think normally. With a good education will also be done teenagers who think formally operational feel challenged to achieve a unique identity. According to Asmau, Education, through which these moral values could be channelled from one generation to another is very important, being the first priority of Muslim parents, teachers and Islāmic institutions [6]. The process of identity-seeking processes in which a youth develops a unique personal identity or sense of self, separate and separate by others-is called individualization. These processes are [22, 33] (Table 1):

Table 1. The 5 C's of positive youth development

Asset	Definition	How to foster it
Competence	Perception that one has abilities and skills	Provide training and practice in specific skills, either academic or hands-on
Confidence	Internal sense of self efficacy and positive self-worth	Provide opportunities for young people to experience success when trying something new
Connection	Positive bonds with people and institutions	Build relationships between youth and peers, teachers and parents
Character	A sense of right and wrong (morality), integrity, and respect for standards of correct behaviour	Provide opportunities to practice increasing self-control and development of spirituality
Caring	A sense of sympathy and empathy for others	Care for young people

Source: Teen, 2009

4 Internet dan Morality

Internet provides human beings access to a large amount of data. Since the internet is not controlled by anyone, the type of data cannot be controlled. Therefore, all types of positive and negative information and objects are available on the web. Academic sources can be considered as positive aspect of the internet, whereas pornography, gambling and misappropriation are its negative aspects [1, 26]. Users need to make a choice to utilise the internet responsibly, wisely and intelligently [8, 19].

According to Longe et al. (2009): "Internet technology development in Sub-Saharan Africa has brought tremendous positive change in socio-economic growth and development in the region. Paradoxically, the internet has also evolved into a sophisticated tool in the hands of criminals for in various forms of cyber crime" [29].

According to research results Meena et al. and research results Hing Keung Ma: the internet is able to facilitate people to make a stronger face relationship without geographical, racial or social obstacles. This not only helps people to bond friendships but also emerges as a source to bridge different types of people from a little to a greater extent. But the results of this study indicate that children have negative effects, they are more likely to learn the language rough from their friends online, other than that children also often visit porn sites [1, 27].

The best filtering tool is having faith (Iman) and virtue (Taqwa) [19]. Good morals are faith [6]. Internet gives people the permission to act freely in almost everything. However, they are responsible for how they manage their freedom. Freedom and choice are related to responsibility, and everyone is responsible for his freedom and choice [5, 19]. We must understand that the internet can be a very enlightening platform, fun to surf, and can damage characters if not properly used [29]. So parents and teachers have more responsibility to help students learn how to use the internet safely and responsibly. For example, filtering is important for school and home computers. Teachers and parents should work together and discuss what types of restrictions are more efficient for students. Some people think we should protect our children from dangerous, offensive and inappropriate information [7].

Morality is one of the fundamental principles of Islām. Islām prescribes a number of rules and regulations to be observed by believers in all activities. To uphold these rules, Allah (SWT) in the Glorious Qur'ān provides the believers with a series of moral teachings regarding personal ethics, family, social, business and political ethics to name a few [8].

5   The Advantage of Technological Intervention for Moral Education

Teens are very easy to imitate parents, society, and the environment to make it as a lifestyle and even a habit. In moral education, with technological intervention, stakeholders will be able to play a role in realizing good moral education. On the web provided a variety of features that are able to maintain the moral of children. Teachers and educational leaders can also provide motivation for children to continue to enter into positive activities, in order to maintain adolescent morale. In the identification of Hamid et al. [43] states that "Based on recent crime trends and media portrayals, it seems that a problem underlying social ills in Malaysia is moral decay among the Malaysian youth". This confirms the importance of technological intervention in shaping and maintaining the moral of the child [18, 36].

Examples of current technological interventions are one of the faculties at the International Islamic University Malaysia that ICT has created an environment where the source of Islam can be converted to digital form so that it can be easily distributed globally in the form [19, 25]:

a. Muslim virtual class
   Getting education about Islam is made easier because it can be done from home through this virtual Muslim class [10, 32, 34].
b. Games and Video Islam for children [31].
c. Software - Interactive software to motivate Muslim children learn about Islam.
   Islamic software is available in the form of audio and text formats for mobile phones, IPods and laptops. Where islam software can also be accessed through the web for free and installation on the phone only takes time in just seconds [18, 31].
d. Online discussion on Islamic topics [15].

With the knowledge of Islam is expected parents and schools should take a role in preparing teenagers for success in the emerging information age with successful online ethical behavior outside of academia [23].

In addition teenagers need support from family and school, community, to building good relationship for moral education. The need for awareness of education programs that have been implemented by the Government through compulsory subjects of Citizenship Education, Education of Pancasila, etc. This awareness will also influence the government's decision in the rapid development of education. The more a good moral teenager the better a country will be in the future.

6   Conclusion

One of the goals of moral education with a technological theme is to help make the child moral good - honest, disciplined, responsible, and caring etc., according to the character of the nation. The tendency of teenagers is to imitate a model that he believes to be a real truth. Those who think that model is the most correct and contemporary in accordance with today's lifestyle. This ready-made model does not necessarily correspond to a good moral attitude.

This paper aims to discuss the importance of moral education for adolescents with technological intervention. This is because moral education with technological intervention (web-based) for adolescents can bring positive effects for adolescents in adolescent moral development. The goal is that teenagers are more rational, able to judge the good or bad, apply honesty, responsibility, compassion in social life. We know that teenagers are at a very potential stage of development, both cognitively, affectively and physically. But this can not develop properly, because it is associated with poverty and low levels of education.

References

1. Ma, H.: Internet addiction and antisocial internet behavior of adolescents. Sci. World J. **11**, 2187–2196 (2011). doi:10.1100/2011/308631
2. Park, N., Peterson, C.: Moral competence and character strengths among adolescents: the development and validation of the values in action inventory of strengths for youth. J. Adolesc. **29**(6), 891–909 (2006). doi:10.1016/j.adolescence.2006.04.011
3. Al-Ammar, F., Ahmed, I., Nordin, M.: Moral character of muslim personality: scale validation. J. Educ. Pract. **3**(16), 118–128 (2012). http://iiste.org/Journals/index.php/JEP/article/view/3704. Accessed 2 July 2017
4. Ali, M., Asrori, M.: Psikologi Remaja Perkembangan Peserta Didik. Jakarta: Bumi Aksara (2015)
5. Anderson, G., Phil, J.M.: Religion and morality in ghana : a reflection. Global J. Arts Humanit. Soc. Sci. **1**(3), 162–170 (2013). http://www.eajournals.org/wp-content/uploads/Religion-and-Morality-in-Ghana.pdf. Accessed 3 July 2017
6. Kabir, A.I.A.: The Qur'ānic approach to the inculcation of moral values: patterns for teacher education. QURANICA-Int. J. Quranic Res. **5**(2), 15–32 (2013)
7. Behiye, A.: Hubungan antara teknologi dan etika; dari masyarakat untuk sekolah, Turki. Online J. Distance Educ. -TOJDE **9**(4), 9 (2008). ISSN 1302-6488
8. Blackwell, L., Gardiner, E., Schoenebeck, S.: Managing expectations: technology tensions among parents and teens. In: Proceedings of the 19th ACM Conference on Computer-Supported Cooperative Work & Social Computing - CSCW 2016, pp. 1388–1399 (2016). doi:10.1145/2818048.2819928
9. Brandtzg, P.B.: Social networking sites: their users and social implications - a longitudinal study. J. Comput.-Mediat. Commun. **17**(4), 467–488 (2012). doi:10.1111/j.1083-6101.2012.01580.x
10. Cheung, C.-K., Chan, W.-T., Lee, T.-Y., Liu, S.-C., Leung, K.-K.: Structure of moral consciousness and moral intentions among youth in Hong Kong. Int. J. Adolesc. Youth **9** (2/3), 83–116 (2001). doi:10.1080/02673843.2001.9747870

11. Curtis, A.C.: Defining adolescence. J. Adolesc. Fam. Health 7(2), 1–39 (2015). http://scholar.utc.edu/jafh/vol7/iss2/2

12. Donovan, A.M.: Komunikasi Sosial dalam Masyarakat Teknologi Driven: A Philosophical Eksplorasi Faktor Dampak dan Konsekuensi. Amerika Komunikasi Journal 12 (2010)

13. Ellison, N.B.: Social network sites: definition, history, and scholarship 13, 210–230 (2008). doi:10.1111/j.1083-6101.2007.00393.x

14. George, I.N., Uyanga, U.D.: Youth and moral values in a changing society. IOSR J. Humanit. Soc. Sci. 19(6), 40–44 (2014)

15. Gulati, G., Cornish, R., Al-Taiar, H.: Web-based violence risk monitoring tool in psychoses: pilot study in community forensic patients. J. Forensic Psychol. Pract. 16(1), 49–59 (2016). doi:10.1080/15228932.2016.1128301. Taylor & Francis

16. Al Hamdani, D.: The character education in islamic education viewpoint. Jurnal Pendidikan Islam 1(1), 98–109 (2016). doi:10.15575/JPI.V1I1.614.G590

17. Hart, D., Carlo, G.: Moral development in adolescence. J. Res. Adolesc. 15(3), 223–233 (2005). doi:10.1111/j.1532-7795.2005.00094.x

18. Ho, J., Corden, M.E., Caccamo, L., Tomasino, K.N., Duffecy, J., Begale, M., Mohr, D.C.: Design and evaluation of a peer network to support adherence to a web based intervention for adolescents. Internet Interv. 6, 50–56 (2016). doi:10.1016/j.invent.2016.09.005

19. Hosseini, S.E., Ramchahi, A.A., Raja Yusuf, R.J.: The impact of information technology on islamic behaviour. J. Multidiscip. Eng. Sci. Technol. (JMEST) 1(5), 135–141 (2014). doi:10.13140/RG.2.1.4799.9603

20. Jamaluddin, D.: Character education in islamic perspective. Int. J. Sci. Technol. Res. 2(2), 187–189 (2013)

21. Halstead, J.M.: Islamic values: a distinctive framework for moral education. J. Moral Educ. 36(3), 283–296 (2007). doi:10.1080/03057240701643056

22. Jones, M., Dunn, J.G.H., Holt, N.L., Sullivan, P.J., Bloom, G.A.: Exploring the "5Cs" of positive youth development in sport. J. Sport Behav. 34(3), 250–267 (2011)

23. Judi, H.M., Asharari, N.S., Zin, N.A.M., Yusof, Z.M.: Framework of ICT impact on adolescent. Procedia Technol. 11, 1034–1040 (2013). doi:10.1016/j.protcy.2013.12.291. Elsevier B.V.

24. Kaur, S.: Moral values in education. IOSR J. Humanit. Soc. Sci. Ver. III 20(3), 21–26 (2015). doi:10.9790/0837-20332126

25. Komuda, R., Ptaszynski, M., Momouchi, Y., Rzepka, R., Araki, K.: Machine moral development : moral reasoning agent based on wisdom of web-crowd and emotions 1(3), 155–163 (2010). https://eprints.lib.hokudai.ac.jp/dspace/handle/2115/63641. Accessed 20 May

26. Salman, A., Abdullah, M.Y.H., Hasim, M.S., Pawanteh, L.: Sustainability of internet usage: a study among Malay Youth in Kota Bharu, Kelantan. Malays. J. Commun. 26, 62–72 (2001). http://journalarticle.ukm.my/300/. Accessed 20 May 2017

27. Meena, K.R, Chandio, M.S.: Penggunaan internet dan Dampaknya pada Masyarakat

28. Khurana, N.: The impact of social networking sites on the youth. J. Mass Commun. Journal. 5(12), 5–8 (2015). doi:10.4172/2165-7912.1000285

29. Opeoluwa, T.E., Nsima, S.U., Olugbenga, D.O.: Dampak Internet pada pendidikan dan kebudayaan Afrika. Int. J. Bus. Humaniora dan Teknologi 4(3) (2014)

30. Parvathy, J., Suchithra, R.: Impact of social networking sites on youth. Int. J. Comput. Appl. 129(3), 55–62 (2015). doi:10.15192/PSCP.ASR.2015.11.1.610

31. Pratt, M.W.: Handbook of Moral Development. Canadian Psychology (2006). doi:10.1080/03057240.2015.1053738

32. Portillo, J.A.R., Mufson, L., Greenhill, L.L., Gould, M.S., Fisher, P.W., Tarlow, N., Rynn, M.A.: Web-based interventions for youth internalizing problems: a systematic review. J. Am. Acad. Child Adolesc. Psychiatry **53**(12), 1254–1270.e5 (2014). doi:10.1016/j.jaac. 2014.09.005. Elsevier Inc

33. Robinson, A.M., Mckee, R.: An exploratory study of the five Cs model of positive youth development among Indiana 4-H youth. https://jyd.pitt.edu/ojs/jyd/article/viewFile/154/140. Accessed 20 May

34. Universitas Terbuka, Surabaya Regional Office: Academic dishonesty in distance higher education: challenges and models for moral education in the digital era, 176–195 (2013)

35. UNICEF: The state of the world's children 2011 adolescence an age of opportunity (2011)

36. Velea, S., Speran, Ġ:. Teacher's responsibility in moral and affective education of children **76**, 863–867 (2013). doi:10.1016/j.sbspro.2013.04.221

37. Whitmire, K.A.: Adolescence as a developmental phase: a tutorial. Top. Lang. Dis. **20**(2), 1–14 (2000). doi:10.1097/00011363-200020020-00003

38. Yönden, H.: Kant's conception of moral education assessment. Procedia – Soc. Behav. Sci. **174**, 2626–2628 (2015). doi:10.1016/j.sbspro.2015.01.943. Elsevier B.V.

39. Zeitel-Bank, N., Tat, U.: Social media and its effects on individuals and social systems. In: Management Knowledge and Learning International Conference, pp. 1183–1190 (2014). http://www.toknowpress.net/ISBN/978-961-6914-09-3/papers/ML14-714.pdf

40. Zuriah, N.: Pendidikan Moral & Budi Pekerti Dalam Perspektif Perubahan. Sinar Grafika Offset, Jakarta (2007)

41. Berkowitz, M.W., Bier, M.C.: Research-based character education. Ann. Am. Acad. Polit. Soc. Sci. **591**, 72–85 (2004)

42. Jalaludin, H.: Psikologi Agama, p. 72. PT Grafindo Persada, Jakarta, cet. (2009)

43. Hamid, R. et al.: Assessment of Psychomotor Domain in Materials Technology Laboratory Work. Published by Elsevier Ltd. Selection and/or peer-review under responsibility of Centre of Engineering Education, Universiti Teknologi Malaysia Open access under CC BY-NC-ND license (2012). doi:10.1016/j.sbspro.2012.09.708

44. Hurlock, E.B.: Psikologi Perkembangan Suatu Pendekatan Sepanjang Rentang Kehidupan, Edisi 5. Erlangga, Jakarta (1980)

Data Driven Cyber Security

IPv6 OS Fingerprinting Methods: Review

Omar E. Elejla[1(✉)], Bahari Belaton[1], Mohammed Anbar[2],
and Basem O. Alijla[3]

[1] School of Computer Science, Universiti Sains Malaysia,
Gelugor, Penang, Malaysia
oeoel4_com063@student.usm.my, bahari@usm.my
[2] National Advanced IPv6 Centre (NAv6),
Universiti Sains Malaysia, Gelugor, Penang, Malaysia
anbar@nav6.usm.my
[3] Faculty of Information Technology,
Islamic University of Gaza, Gaza City, Gaza Strip, Palestine, Israel
balijla@iugaza.edu.ps

Abstract. IPv6 is the new communication protocol which will eventually replace IPv4 is suffering from different security issues. As an initial step to understand IPv6 networks and their vulnerabilities it is of critical importance to identify the characteristics of the connected devices. Detecting the OS fingerprints of these devices is one of these characteristics that are essential to identifying the vulnerabilities of each of them. Currently, few OS detection methods have supported IPv6 protocol, as it did not fully replace IPv4 yet. This paper attempts to describe the existing methods of OS fingerprinting with IPv6, as well as their challenges and limitations. Moreover, this paper studies the available datasets that might be used for IPv6 OS fingerprinting. By understanding the existing methods and datasets, the reader can figure out the current needs for proposing new OS fingerprinting methods for IPv6 protocol.

Keywords: OS fingerprinting · IPv6 protocol · Network security

1 Introduction

IPv6 has been designed to replace IPv4 after IPv4 was criticized in terms of the addresses pool exhaustion and security issues. IPv6 has a four times longer header than IPv4, which can provide an address to every single device in the world. The world's devices count is expected to be 40.9 billion in 2020 [1]. The number of the IPv6 users is continuously increasing on a daily basis. An example of this is presented in Fig. 1 that illustrates the number of Google users who are currently using the IPv6 protocol. IPv6 has built-in security mechanisms such as IPSec protocol which serves to overcome some of IPv4 security issues. In addition, IPv6 introduced address auto configuration and mobility features for the nodes. Another main change in IPv6 compared to IPv4 is its major dependency on the ICMPv6 protocol, where it was optional in IPv4. These changes made the applicability of using IPv4 systems on IPv6 impossible [2].

Despite the security improvements of IPv6 over IPv4, it is still suffering from a set of attacks that exposes its reliability. Recently, several studies showed that IPv6 is

H. Badioze Zaman et al. (Eds.): IVIC 2017, LNCS 10645, pp. 661–668, 2017.
https://doi.org/10.1007/978-3-319-70010-6_61

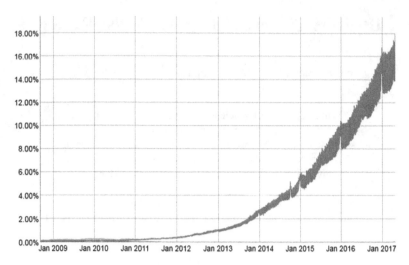

Fig. 1. Google IPv6 users

vulnerable to several types of attacks, which prevented it from being worthy to implement in real networks. IPv6 attacks are categized into two classes, which are either inherited from IPv4 protocol (performed in the same way of IPv4 attacks), or new attacks that depend on the new features of IPv6 [3]. Moreover, some of the IPv6 new features such as the multicast address contribute to making IPv6 attacks easy to perform. An example of this is Denial of Service (DoS) attacks.

Identifying the OS fingerprint is a technique that collects information from a network to determine the number of different hosts connected and the used OSes in the network. Determining the used OSes in the network helps the administrator to realize the security level of the network and find out potential vulnerabilities that the nodes are exposed to. Moreover, the OS fingerprinting detection provides the administrator with information about the unpatched or unauthorized and rogue devices that are attached to the network [4]. As IPv6 networks are vulnerable to many attacks, discovering the used OSes in the networks is a helpful step to improve its security and privacy.

This paper presents a review of the existing methods that are able to identify the fingerprints of the OSes based on IPv6 traffic, as well as studying the available IPv6 datasets for such use. To the best of the author's knowledge, this is the first paper that studied these methods in the light of IPv6 protocol. This paper aims to help in securing IPv6 by presenting this summarized review to the interesting readers for a faster understanding of the OS fingerprinting area. Moreover, having such review opens several questions about the existing methods and their worthiness to be applied to a real network.

OS fingerprinting methods are categorized based on the used technique of collecting the information into two main categories, which are active technique and passive technique. Active techniques depend on sending craft packets to the OSes and identify them based on their responses. Passive techniques prefer to be silent and depend on the normally generated traffics from the OSes. Passive techniques have the advantage over the active techniques that they do not affect the network performance as they do not generate any traffic (overhead) on the network. In addition, active techniques are never able to determine OSes that are located behind a firewall that crafted packets are unable to reach [5].

This paper is organized as follows: Sect. 2 details some of the existing OS fingerprinting methods and highlights some interesting point of their strength and weakness. Section 3 describes the availability of IPv6 datasets for OS fingerprinting purposes. Section 4 concludes the paper findings with opportunity for future promising technique.

2 IPv6 OS Fingerprinting Methods

IPv4 has been sufficiently studied in the light of OS fingerprinting, and several tools have been proposed for that purpose such as ETTERCAP [6] and Xprobe [7]. IPv4 addresses exhaustion problem is not the only addressed problem by IPv6. Many other features have been either improved, changed or added in the new protocol. Therefore, IPv4 OS fingerprinting methods are unsuitable to be directly applied to IPv6 networks, due to the major changes between the two protocols. However, some researchers have tried to adapt these methods to support IPv6 protocol by considering its new features and fields.

Security researchers realized that IPv6 needs more improvements to reach the goal of securing its networks. Therefore, several OS fingerprinting methods have supported IPv6 protocol as a step towards that goal. These methods are either IPv4 tools that were adapted to support IPv6 protocol by making use of its characteristics, or newly proposed IPv6 OS fingerprinting methods. All these methods are classified based on their information source into active or passive techniques. Figure 2 shows the taxonomy of the existing IPv6 OS fingerprinting methods.

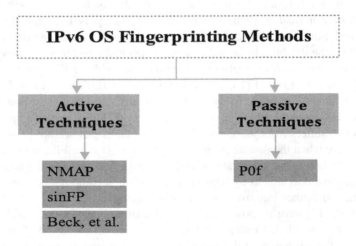

Fig. 2. Taxonomy of IPv6 OS fingerprinting existing methods

2.1   Active Techniques

Active fingerprinting is an aggressive method that probes the targeted devices by sending crafted packets to response with certain messages. The advantages of using such techniques is that they allow their systems to be located at any point of the network, as well as that system can learn more about the network compared to passive techniques. However, active techniques add overhead to the network because of the sent probe packets to the nodes. Moreover, IDSs might identify these packets as malicious behavior that leads to blocking or dropping them.

Several active OS fingerprinting methods have been adapted from IPv4 existing methods or exclusively proposed to identify OSes based on IPv6 traffic.

NMAP [8] is one of the most common free and open source tools that help in exploring and securing networks. It was released in 1998 to provide different services, including port scanning and active OS fingerprinting detection. NMAP uses raw IP packets in novel ways to determine the OSes. NMAP improved its OS detection accuracy compared to other tools by increasing the number of tests (probe packets) that are sent toward the targeted device (currently, 18 packets (TCP, UDP, ICMP) are sent). The devices' responses to the probe packets are compared to the NMAP database of OSes signatures and the closest match is chosen. IPv6 is started to be supported by NMAP since 2011.

The multiple tests that are used in NMAP have improved its detection ability to determine diverse types of OSes. However, these tests exposed the NMAP to be detected as an intrusion by IDS systems due to their suspicious behavior [9]. Moreover, the sent packet might lead to slowing down the performance and affecting the availability of the network. Despite, NMAP understands IPv6 traffic, and its IPv6 database is still considered small, and is unable to automatically determine the OSes based on IPv6 traffic [4, 10]. Although, NMAP has three scanning techniques for IPv6 protocol, practically, TCP scanning is the only working scan [10].

sinFP [11] was released by Patrice Auffret in 2006 mainly to overcome the problems of NMAP tool. sinFP has the ability to use both active and passive finger-printing techniques using a real SQLite database. In addition to IPv6 support, sinFP has the features of using a few probe packets (3 packets), apply the heuristic matching algorithm, and works in online and offline modes. Another advantage of sinFP is the ability to share the database to be utilized and integrated into other systems.

SinFP supported IPv6 by replacing its equivalent fields to IPv4 such as Identification (ID), Time to Live (TTL), and Don't Fragment (DF) with Flow Label, Hop Limit, and Traffic Class respectively. sinFP is one of the OSes detection tools that support IPv6 OS fingerprinting with its first versions. As SinFP depends on a database of signatures, it suffers from inaccurate detection of OSes that are not pre-recorded in the databases, or when the databases are not up-to-date. Also, sinFP has been criticized for the OS detection being inaccurate, as well as for the potential that the probe packets could be categorized as attacks by IDSs [12]. Therefore, it could not be considered as a reliable tool, and further improvements are still required.

Beck et al. [12] have proposed active OS detection methods exclusively for IPv6 traffics after they concluded that passive techniques are infeasible on IPv6. A simple tool namely osfinger6 has been developed using Python language and Scapy6 packet manipulation tool [13] to generate the required tests (probe packets). The authors conducted an experiment of sending 156 forged NS messages on a small testbed (6 OSes) using the osfinger6 tool. Based on the observations of the OSes responses, decision tree of the available OSes has been built.

The authors have figured out some surprising results about the OSes' responses to the sent NDP probe packets. However, applying such methods in real networks is irrational due to the same problem of NAMP tool of using a vast number of probe packets. These packets contribute in consuming the networks bandwidth and the possibility of classifying the tool as an intrusion by IDSs. Moreover, the proposed technique has not included the recent changes to the IPv6 extension headers that are defined in RFC 7045 and RFC 6564 [14]. To include the routers to the detected fingerprints, the authors promised to use NS and RS messages.

2.2 Passive Techniques

Passive fingerprinting techniques depend on analyzing the target devices traffics without calling them by sending probe packets. Passive techniques are preferred as the targeted devices are never bothered, thus, the network performance will not be affected. Also, the OS detection tool will be allowed to work normally by the IDSs. The disadvantages of passive techniques are that they could take a long waiting time to get the needed packets from the network to identify the OSes [15]. Moreover, passive techniques cannot work remotely as the tool must be located inside the targeted network to be able to capture the traffic [16].

Despite the advantages of passive OS fingerprinting, it has been applied for IPv6 traffic in one method which is p0f.

P0f (Passive OS Fingerprinting) [17] is the first effective passive OS detection tool. It is one of the most popular passive OS fingerprinting tools and was proposed by Zalewski in 2000. It depends on analyzing the TCP header to extract 9 features (mentioned in [18]) and compare them to a database of signatures to determine the OSes. It also has the ability to detect the OS version, firewall, Network Address Translation (NAT), and the distance to the remote system [12]. P0f does not have user graphical interface, it only can be used through command line prompt.

P0f has the advantage, compared to the active techniques, that it can detect the OSes that are located behind the firewall or NAT. However, the accuracy of identifying the OSes has been criticized as being inaccurate compared to active techniques [10]. In addition, P0f does not work for encrypted traffics where the TCP fields cannot be read. For IPv6 packets, p0f applies the same fingerprints of IPv4 with replacing its fields with their IPv4 equivalents [19]. Despite p0f understanding IPv6 traffic, it does not accurately detect OSes based on it traffics [12].

On summary, few OS fingerprinting methods have been proposed or adapted for IPv6 traffic.

As concluded from Table 1, insufficient research has been conducted on IPv6 OS fingerprinting. This could be due to the lake of implementation of IPv6 protocol on today's networks where most of the OSes still working with IPv4. The existing OS fingerprinting methods were either originally proposed for IPv6, or produced for IPv4 and then adapted to support IPv6. Both have several disadvantages that exposed their accuracy or affected network performance. Therefore, more work needs to be done to improve the existing methods and overcome their limitations and disadvantages.

Table 1. Summarizes the proposed IPv6 OS detection methods.

Method	Description	Disadvantages
NMAP	• Active OS fingerprinting • 18 probe packets • Understand IPv6 since 2011	• Might be detected as attacker • Might affect the network availability • Small database for IPv6 traffic • Unable to detect IPv6 OSes automatically
sinFP	• Active and passive OS fingerprinting • 3 probe packets • Support IPv6 • Sharable signatures database	• Might be detected as attacker • Might affect the network availability • Inaccurate OS detection
Beck et al. (osfinger6)	• Active OS fingerprinting • 156 probe packets (forged NS) • Support only IPv6 • OSes decision tree was built	• Might be detected as attacker • The probe packets might affect the network availability • Does not include the recent changes to IPv6 extension headers
P0f	• Passive OS fingerprinting • Understand IPv6 • Depends on analyzing 9 TCP features • Detect behind firewall and NAT OSes	• Inaccurate OS detection • Does not work for encrypted traffics • Unable to detect IPv6 OSes automatically

The traditional categorization of OS fingerprinting methods has been used in IPv6 fingerprinting methods. The used techniques have been classified into active and passive techniques. Active techniques have two main problems. One is being exposed to being blocked as an attacker, and the other one is their negative effects on the network. Passive techniques work silently to avoid these problems, and therefore they might be promising to be more applicable in IPv6 OS detection. Despite, the strengths of passive techniques they have been used in one IPv6 fingerprinting tool (p0f) only.

3 Datasets

Several OS fingerprinting methods depend on datasets of traffic to be used for design and evaluation of any new methods. Different IPv4 datasets have been used for this purpose such IRL dataset [20]. On the OS fingerprinting area, these datasets have different purpose which are;

- Understanding the traffic to propose better OS detection methods.
- Choosing the most related features (fingerprints).
- Training different classifiers to discover the most optimal one.
- Evaluating the efficiency of any new proposed method.
- Comparing two different methods by applying them to the same dataset.

In order to propose more IPv6 OS fingerprinting methods, there is an initial need to have a reference dataset with comprehensive OSes. However, to the best of our knowledge, there is a lack of availability of IPv6 datasets for such usage. This could be due to the privacy issues of the IPv6 information (such as IPv6 address and prefix) that might be included in the traffic which might expose the network to outside attacks. However, encryption or mapping techniques can solve such problem. Matoušek et al. [14] is the only research that has noticed this problem and promised to create an IPv6 dataset for OS fingerprinting purpose.

4 Conclusion

Sine IPv6 OS fingerprinting is not widely supported by the security community, this paper opens the door to motivate others to study it. By exploring the existing finger-printing methods that have the ability to understand and identify OSes based on IPv6 traffic, different points of interest have been highlighted. First, a small number of these methods support IPv6 which either were proposed for IPv6 or adapted from IPv4. Second, these methods are limited by several issues that need to be addressed before their employment on real networks. Third, the lake of the IPv6 datasets is another reason for this shortage of the IPv6 OS fingerprinting methods. Lastly, passive tech-niques seem more promising to be used in IPv6 OS detection compared to the active techniques due to their silent style, which saves their tools, as well as network resources.

References

1. ABI Research: The Internet of Things will Drive Wireless Connected Devices to 40.9 Billion in 2020. ABI Research (2014). https://www.abiresearch.com/press/the-internet-of-things-will-drive-wireless-connect/
2. Elejla, O.E., Anbar, M., Belaton, B.: ICMPv6-based DoS and DDoS attacks and defense mechanisms. IETE Tech. Rev. 1–18 (2016). doi:10.1080/02564602.2016.1192964
3. Elejla, O.E., Belaton, B., Anbar, M., Alnajjar, A.: Intrusion detection systems of ICMPv6-based DDoS attacks. Neural Comput. Appl. **28**, 1–12 (2016)
4. Schwartzenberg, J.: Using machine learning techniques for advanced passive operating system fingerprinting. Master thesis, University of Twente (2010)
5. Srisuresh, P., Egevang, K.: Traditional IP network address translator (Traditional NAT) (2000)
6. Ornaghi, A., Valleri, M.: Ettercap (2005). http://ettercap.github.io/ettercap/ (2017)
7. Yarochkin, F., Kydyraliev, M., Arkin, O.: Xprobe project (2014). http://x-probe.org/ (2017)

8. Lyon, G.: Nmap–free security scanner for network exploration & security audits (2009). https://nmap.org/ (2017)
9. Greenwald, L.G., Thomas, T.J.: Toward undetected operating system fingerprinting. WOOT **7**, 1–10 (2007)
10. Stopforth, R.: Techniques and countermeasures of TCP/IP OS fingerprinting on Linux Systems. Thesis, University of KwaZulu-Natal, Durban (2007)
11. Auffret, P.: SinFP, January 2007. http://www.gomor.org/sinfp (2017)
12. Beck, F., Festor, O., Chrisment, I.: IPv6 neighbor discovery protocol based OS fingerprinting, Inria (2007)
13. Biondi, P.: Scapy (2011). http://www.secdev.org/projects/scapy/ (2015)
14. Matoušek, P., Ryšavý, O., Grégr, M., Vymlátil, M.: Towards identification of operating systems from the internet traffic: IPFIX monitoring with fingerprinting and clustering. In: 2014 5th International Conference on Data Communication Networking (DCNET), pp. 1–7. IEEE (2014)
15. Prigent, G., Vichot, F., Harrouet, F.: IpMorph: fingerprinting spoofing unification. J. Comput. Virol. **6**(4), 329–342 (2010)
16. Nerakis, E.: IPv6 host fingerprint. Master DTIC Document, Naval Postgraduate School (2006)
17. Zalewski, M.: P0f: Passive OS Fingerprinting Tool (2006). http://lcamtuf.coredump.cx/p0f3/ (2017)
18. Jajodia, S., Subrahmanian, V.S., Swarup, V., Wang, C.: Cyber Deception: Building the Scientific Foundation. Springer International Publishing, Switzerland (2016). doi:10.1007/978-3-319-32699-3
19. Fifield, D., Geana, A., MartinGarcia, L., Morbitzer, M., Tygar, J.D.: Remote operating system classification over IPv6. In: Proceedings of the 8th ACM Workshop on Artificial Intelligence and Security, pp. 57–67. ACM (2015)
20. IRL Fingerprinting Dataset (2014). http://irl.cs.tamu.edu/projects/sampling/ (2017)

Body Matching Algorithm Using Normalize Dynamic Time Warping (NDTW) Skeleton Tracking for Traditional Dance Movement

A.S.A. Mohamed[1][✉], P.S. Chingeng[1], N.A. Mat Isa[1], and S.S. Surip[2]

[1] School of Computer Sciences, Universiti Sains Malaysia, Gelugor, Malaysia
sufril@usm.my
[2] School of the Arts, Universiti Sains Malaysia, Gelugor, Malaysia

Abstract. Traditional dance in Malaysia is generating considerable amount of interest due to its unique elements of heritage which have contributed to its diverse music and dance forms. For example, Zapin, Kuda Kepang, Mak Yong, Joget, Ngajat and much more. Recent developments in technology and ever-growing online community, traditional dance are undergoing a revolution where these dance form can be studied and observed easily especially when there are dance software that can help guide users to learn by performing the dance steps in real-time. However, the use of gesture sensor for accurately mapping the dance movements of traditional dance is not yet explored, since only modern dances are normally available to the masses in the form of computer games. This paper outlines a new approach to implement Normalize Dynamic Time Warping (NDTW) algorithm using skeleton tracking techniques to imitate the intricate movements of traditional dance and to assess the robustness of the algorithm. For this study, the traditional dance of Zapin was chosen because it consists of simple body movements and data were acquired using Microsoft Kinect. The results showed that the proposed algorithm gave the overall matching rate of 99.21% with maximum mean success rate of dancers gave 99.68% and non-dancers gave the percentage of 98.76%. This technique may be considered as a relatively unexplored application area, and the proposed system is an attempt to address the problem with reasonable accuracy and scopes for further research.

Keywords: Body matching · Motion capture · Traditional dance · Skeleton tracking · Kinect

1 Introduction

Dance is a performance art form consisting of selected sequences of human body movements. It can be performed individually, in a pair or a group of people. Every country has their specific traditional dance emerged from an ethnic. These dance movements represent an aesthetic and symbolic value within a culture. Malaysia has a unique culture and way of life, but globalization that hit's today's generation caused them to lose their identity, especially in learning traditional dances. With the advancement of technology, the development of accurate system is highly desirable to

© Springer International Publishing AG 2017
H. Badioze Zaman et al. (Eds.): IVIC 2017, LNCS 10645, pp. 669–680, 2017.
https://doi.org/10.1007/978-3-319-70010-6_62

address these issues based on two techniques which are dance recognition and the visual feedback to effectively assess dancer training and performance.

The comparison and analysis of captured motion data taken in real time from the real dancer against avatar data are the main issues in the virtual reality dance system. This paper focuses on how to match body joints coordinates captured from Kinect depth images based on real dancer from Kinect motion capture system that we consider here as the ground truth. The paper takes a new look at the accuracy of the proposed method using Normalize Dynamic Time Warping (NDTW) algorithm to compare the skeleton generated from the Kinect Sensor with the real dancer. The focus will be on how to retrieve body joint coordinates using an RGB skeleton sequence as a query and this methodology has only been applied to Zapin traditional dance.

In traditional dance teaching, the demonstration-performance method are employed to teach dancers, physical and mental skills [32]. Several demonstrations are performed by the professional dancer only then the non-dancer will have to perform under close supervision of the professional dancer and stored in a video form in the database. The evaluation of the accuracy of the dance steps and response will be directed based the degree of similarity between pre-stored coordinate sequences of dancer and non-dancer. As such, the application of computerized systems for assessment and training of dance remains a subject that attracts considerable research interest [17]. What is known as virtual dance is largely based on the visualization phase and therefore finding better virtual representations of dances is essential that leads to the importance of matching the dance steps between dancer and non-dancer that essentially requiring the user to follow the virtual dancer. Grounded along the idea, dance learning abilities are justified along the practical representation of characters driven by the non-dancer's motion capture information and the ability of the dancer to come after a virtual dancer. The integration of technology into dance is seen to break ground in terms of artistic creation this can be seen some of the approaches to integrate sensors into gaming based simulation to help in transferring knowledge effectively [20, 39, 40].

2   Literature Review

Few studies have been published on human body matching and many those reviews investigated different visual features to represent dance skeleton tracking such as angular representation of the skeleton design including hand and food trajectories [26], body characteristics calibration [1], real-time human movement retrieval [4], mixed of audio-visual and skeleton joint features [7]. Unfortunately, regardless of many approach have been proposed for dance performance evaluation none of those methods was based on the aspect of traditional dance.

Several researchers have expressed doubts regarding some approaches and applications to perceive human body motion and skeleton tracking. Their analysis has received general acceptance that skeleton tracking techniques utilizing a normal camera are not straightforward because it is time-consuming to set up. Capturing human motion data turn out to be common and a lot of method and algorithms have been used to accomplish a better outcome in term of robustness of the framework. To make the technology more supportive of human, researchers have spent much time to enhance the collaboration between innovative technology such as Microsoft Kinect, Asus Xtion, Intel RealSense camera R200 and much more while applying some technique and algorithm.

2.1 Time-Series Representation Body Matching

Time-Series Representation is generally a time series as a sequence of time dependent values [27] and understood to mean a gesture element is typically represented by a long multiple time-series. Therefore, to speed-up computation, simplified time series is often preferable. There has been growing interest to represent human body-part motion by utilizing the depth sensor camera, the stream of the skeleton feature to estimate data on stream produces by the camera sensor. This is due to the availability of the depth sensor camera such as the Microsoft Kinect. OpenNI was proposed to capture dataset recording where it can provide a high-level skeleton module which can be employed for detecting user and tracking his/her body joints [1, 6].

The convolution of the discrete-time position signals with a 1st Order Derivative of Gaussian (DOG) is utilized to calculate the instantaneous 3D velocities of the joints with the alignment of the dances are achieved by findings the time-lag that maximizes the Quaternionic Cross-Covariance (QCC) of each joint position signal vectors [1, 6, 27]. However, these methods suffer from several pitfalls because of skeleton calibration was not captured for each dancer. Therefore, custom skeletal tracking for the dancer is not possible as the captured dancer must stay still in a specific calibration pose.

A study was conducted using a real-time tracking based approach to human motion recognition, which receives an input contains a sequence of depth map captures from a single camera sensor which detects the position of 15 joints of the human body [23]. The technique employed the use of Hidden Markov Models (HMMs) which is quite efficient to perform action recognition. However, HMM-based recognition has a shorter duration compared with Kinect sensor capturing time and all proposed method is completed for the currently examined depth map before the next one is captured by the Kinect sensor.

Recently, experiments on the human action representation system were introduced using Bag of Words (BoWs) model representation of the action sequence along with the variance of the skeletal joints [30]. The feature vectors are independents of the duration of the action in the given action sequence. It has been suggested that motion capture data from the Multimodal Human Action database using Projection Based Learning Meta-Cognitive Radial Basis Function Network (PBL-McRBFN) classifier seems to be performing better than the state of the art approaches. Some preliminary work was carried out in 2011 [29] using interactive games based on 3D motion capture technology, which allows the virtual avatar to perform dance movement collaboratively by recognizing what a human player is dancing in real time using Finite State Machine (FSM) and applied to Progressive Block matching approach. Frame Matching Cost is introduced which forms part of the formulation of Block Matching cost.

More recent study [20] proposed the method of capturing the sides and frontal movement of the traditional dance and transfer the data stream position obtained from the central database using Microsoft Kinect. The accuracy of the movement of the dancer is based on scoring using the Normalize Cross Correlation (NCC) algorithm.

The method is based on the position of the body joints of the user matched with the movements of the avatar at every frame and estimated the difference between the two positions in terms of its Euclidean distance between the position of the user and the position of the avatar. The conclusion made from the study mentioned that the professional dancers can score the mean of 10.13% vs. the ground truth scoring while the non-dancers score 18.38% with the total difference (Dancers vs. Non-Dancers) <9%.

The Dynamic Time Warping (DTW) algorithm was also studied to overcome time and speed differences in the sequences and the underlying bone movements and can be used effectively for motion classification to generate and match the temporal description tracks of each bone in motion, without the need to have equal length, as DTW corrects for differences in speed [25].

2.2 Direct Body Matching Classification

There are three different types of sensing technologies, specifically optical motion capture, inertial motion capture and markerless motion capture [16]. The degree of precision of the capture motion and constraint posed are affected by these technologies. The motion skeleton are split into five different body joints and generate an automation of a posture vocabulary (code book) for each part to address the occlusion of problems using multiple Microsoft Kinect sensors and applied Hidden State Conditional Random Fields for the dance recognition [16]. The overall accuracy that has been obtained is 93.9% with 11 hidden states.

This has lead to investigation on human pose estimation for the first and second version of Kinect sensor along with standard motion capture technology with a Mixture of Gaussian and Uniform Distribution Models to evaluate the robustness of the pose tracking [31]. Experiments on body joint matching for 10 subjects with mean age 27-year-old while each subject was instructed to carry out some exercise via a video. The approach calculates the maximum likelihood of the parameters of the input data samples.

Another study look at the possibility of using markerless system to overcome the problem of a marker-based system by using model-based approaches (Myomotion) to track the 3D Degrees of Freedom (DoF) motion in a virtual reality environment [22]. By using Myomotion, 16 sensors track the motion of 15 joints and to calculate 22 anatomical angles. However, there are some accuracy issues for 3D kinematic of body segments with only limited number of body segments contributes to the major flaw.

A study of using the meta-heuristic approach to composing a dance by optimally selecting inter-gestures movement patterns from multiple dance gestures using fitness estimation and compare the performance of the proposed Differential Evolution (DE) was experimented to ensure a smooth transition of frames in the dance video [14]. The study also look at the measurement of the abruptness (TA) of inter-gesture transitions in a dance sequence which is by measuring the total difference between the two 3-dimensional body skeletal structures. The absolute transition abruptness of the gesture permutation is calculated by summing TA of each two-consecutive dance gesture. The approach indicated that smaller the TA value obtained, the smoother the inter-gesture transitions. The use of probabilistic deformable surface registration approach based on a patched of the reference human body model together with the body binding energy using (SVM) Support Vector Machine based classification scheme that partition target point cloud into the rigid body part and helps better correspondence search [31]. The reliability of the proposed method is confirmed by the experiments on Human Eva-II dataset and do not rely on the bone-length constraints to obtain decent results.

Dynamic Time Warping (DTW) is also used to determine block similarity of motion data [25] by mapping from an input sequence to a given sequence that minimizes the distance between the input sequence by using the Euclidean distance metric for sequence element distances. This method achieved 20–30% of error rates while working with data from real dance recordings which indicate that some movements were harder to distinguish than others. Some argument suggested that Hidden Markov Models (HMMs) might be more robust than Dynamic Time Warping (DTW) algorithm for gesture recognition [3]. Therefore, to analyse the accuracy of the assumptions, comparisons between HMMs and DTW using different criteria through the experiment with 50 samples was conducted and result showed that DTW gives higher performance compared to HMMs where the time taken to train HMMs with 50 samples was 3.6 ms but DTW only took 0.2 ms to compare two different gestures feature vectors.

3 Proposed Methodology

The proposed method look at enabling the comparison between two movement patterns of Zapin dance and allowing data to be extracted for body matching analyse the matching accuracy. By having Kinect sensor as the equipment, the acquired data and the corresponding sample motion of the Zapin dance can be used to extracts feature and perform matching between the acquired data and the corresponding sample motion of the Zapin dancer and non-dancer. These methods were chosen because it is one of the most rapid ways to test for the accuracy of body matching.

The accuracy of body matching between the motion data of avatars and real dancer is tested using the proposed Normalize Dynamic Time Warping (NDTW) algorithm. that does not fulfil the condition of DTW where it does not bound the beginning and end of the two sequences of time toward each other. The algorithm calculates the distance between each possible pair of points or features and constructing a cumulative matrix to find the alignment between two signals with a minimum overall cost and measurement of Optimal warping path (distance) can be found by tracking back the step where the algorithm starts from the end of the matching sequences. Therefore, this proposed method normalizes the scales of the skeleton through dividing the coordinates of each joint by the total number of connected bones. Figure 1 shows the process of the proposed algorithm.

The performance of the dance is based on the degree of similarity between pre-stored position sequence of the dancer and non-dancer's movement sequence. The experiments proceed following the steps and the feature vector consists of 3D coordinates of these 14 features as given below:

$$f_n = [X_1, Y_1, Z_1, X_2, Y_2, Z_2, \rightleftharpoons, X_{14}, Y_{14}, Z_{14}] \tag{1}$$

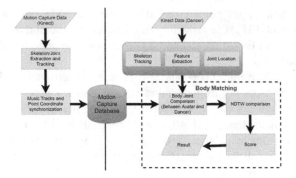

Fig. 1. The flow of the proposed algorithm

where n is the index of the skeleton frame at time t_n. A gesture sequence is the concatenation of N such feature vectors. After N feature vectors are concatenated to create the gesture sequence, they are pre-processed before the NDTW cost computation. The NDTW algorithm are used to determine the corresponding frames between the camera sensor and avatar skeletons. Figure 2 illustrates the allocation of the skeleton joints.

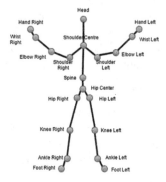

Fig. 2. Illustration of each joint of skeleton tracking

All feature vectors are normalized with the distance between the left and right shoulders to account for variations. The upper body and leg play essential roles of the dance movements. Therefore, shoulder, elbow, hand, knee and foot joint position of the Zapin dancer is considered. The relative 3D position of the shoulder (SL, S), elbow (EL, E), hand (HAL, HAR), knee (KL, KR), ankle (AL, AR) and foot (FL, FR) joints for both left and right are used to measure the distance in each frame (shoulder, elbow, hand, knee, ankle and foot for both left and right):

$$D_S = |S_L - S_R| \tag{2}$$

$$D_E = |E_L - E_R| \tag{3}$$

$$D_{HA} = |HA_L - HA_R| \tag{4}$$

$$D_K = |K_L - K_R| \tag{5}$$

$$D_A = |A_L - A_R| \tag{6}$$

$$D_F = |F_L - F_R| \tag{7}$$

To ensure invariance to dancer's height a specific normalization process is applied. Seven features set of body joints for both left and right which are input to NDTW separated to obtain distinct distance measures. Thus, the normalized-distance from shoulder $D3$, elbow $D4$, hand $D56$, knee $D7$, ankle $D6$ and foot $D8$ is dividing coordinates of each joints by the total of connected joints. The details of formula for normalizing coordinate distance is illustrated as below:

$$\hat{D}_S = \frac{D_S}{|S_L - N| + |N - S_R|} \tag{8}$$

$$\hat{D}_E = \frac{D_E}{|E_L - S_L| + |S_L - N| + |N - S_R| + |S_R - E_R|} \tag{9}$$

$$\hat{D}_{HA} = \frac{D_S}{|HA_L - E_L| + |E_L - S_L| + |S_L - N| + |N - S_R| + |S_R - E_R| + |E_R - HA_R|} \tag{10}$$

$$\hat{D}_K = \frac{D_K}{|K_L - H_L| + |H_L - W| + |W - H_R| + |H_R - K_R|} \tag{11}$$

$$\hat{D}_A = \frac{D_A}{|A_L - K_L| + |K_L - H_L| + |H_L - W| + |W - H_R| + |H_R - K_R| + |K_R - A_R|} \tag{12}$$

$$\hat{D}_F = \frac{D_F}{|F_L - A_L| + |A_L - K_L| + |K_L - H_L| + |H_L - W| + |W - H_R| + |H_R - K_R| + |K_R - A_R| + |A_R - F_R|} \tag{13}$$

Respectively, HL and HR are the left and right hip position and W is the waist position.

4 Results and Discussions

10 experienced Zapin dancers and 10 non-dancers were asked to perform both Ragam Acah and Ragam Melingkar dance movements. Thus, approximate of 40 video data and the corresponding motion data of 14 body joints consisting of mean distances were obtained. The system implemented in this work able to recognize four basic steps of Ragam Acah and six basic steps of Ragam Melingkar of the Zapin Dance as shown in Fig. 3. The recorded data consists of two parts which include repetition of six basic steps of Ragam Acah and four basic steps of Ragam Melingkar. The training and test set pattern is resulted for 32 frames.

(a)

(b)

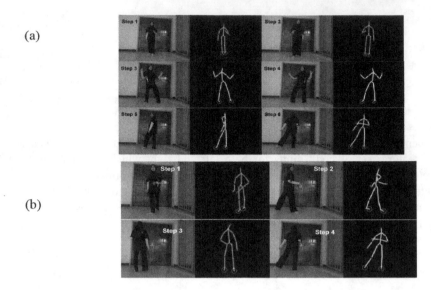

Fig. 3. Example of Zapin dance with (a) Ragam Acah and (b) Ragam Melingkar movements with its skeleton joint tracking representation.

The results indicated that mean joint values range between 90–99% for both Ragam Acah and Ragam Melingkar dance steps. Among all the body joints of Ragam Acah, the largest value in dancer are at the lower body part which are Left Knee, Left Ankle and Left Foot. Similar observation also can be made in Ragam Melingkar where the largest values in dancer are again consistently observed in lower body part, which includes Left Knee, Left Ankle and Left Foot. The non-dancer on the other hand has smaller values for those three body joints. In non-dancer, the largest values are observed in the following body joints: Left Hand and Left Knee. Figure 4(a) demonstrate the means of the body joints accuracy for dancer and non-dancer in Ragam Acah and (b) showing the Ragam Melingkar.

The mean value of non-dancer in both steps are close enough as compared to the mean value of the dancer. For overall result, dancer in Ragam Acah gives a higher mean accuracy which is 99.68% compare to Ragam melingkar with the mean accuracy of 99.64% for 14 body joints. Experimental results shown that using proposed algorithm, dancer and non-dancer are able to achieve accuracy with total mean of 99.21% for both dance steps. Although our results differ slightly from other literatures [3, 16, 31], it can be argued that the proposed algorithm for body matching has performed better. Figure 5 compares the accuracy of proposed body matching algorithm with another algorithm. The value of proposed algorithm gives the highest accuracy value compared to the other four algorithms which is 99.21%.

a)

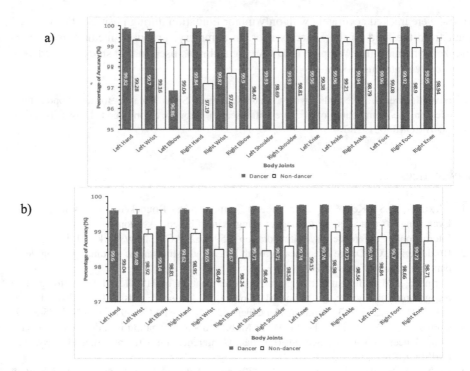

b)

Fig. 4. Percentage of accuracy between dancer and non-dancer in (a) Ragam Acah and (b) Ragam Melingkar

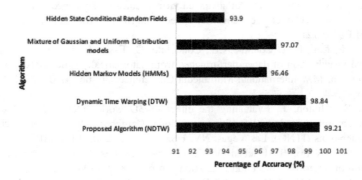

Fig. 5. Accuracy comparisons between the proposed algorithm with other algorithms.

5   Conclusion

This work has led to conclusion that joints are met accurately tracked during Zapin performance process. The results showed that body joints such as knee, ankle and foot joints were affected by inaccuracies, especially when there is high velocity during a dance performance. In addition to the findings, more static joints such as hand and elbow were tracked accurately with only minor limitation during positions that covered joint from the field of the Kinect sensor. In summary, proposed method using Normalize Dynamic Time Warping (NDTW) algorithm as used in this study showed very good body matching potential.

Acknowledgements. The author wish to thank Universiti Sains Malaysia for the support it has extended in the completion of the present research through Short Term University Grant No. 304/PKOMP/6313280.

References

1. Alexiadis, D.S., Kelly, P., Daras, P., O'Connor, N.E., Boubekeur, T., Moussa, M.B.: Evaluating a dancer's performance using kinect-based skeleton tracking. In: ACM International Conference on Multimedia, pp. 659–662. ACM, New York (2011)
2. Brodd-Reijer, C.: Dance quantification with kinect: adjusting music volume by using depth data from a kinect sensor (2012)
3. Carmona, J.M., Climent, J.: A performance evaluation of HMM and DTW for gesture recognition. In: Alvarez, L., Mejail, M., Gomez, L., Jacobo, J. (eds.) CIARP 2012. LNCS, vol. 7441, pp. 236–243. Springer, Heidelberg (2012). doi:10.1007/978-3-642-33275-3_29
4. Correa, D.S., Sciotti, D.F., Prado, M.G.: Mobile robots navigation in indoor environments using kinect sensor. In: Second Brazilian Conference on Critical Embedded Systems (CBSEC), Brazil, pp. 36–41 (2012)
5. Csaba, G., Somlyai, L., Vámossy, Z.: Differences between kinect and structured lighting sensor in robot navigation. In: 2012 IEEE 10th International Symposium Applied Machine Intelligence and Informatics (SAMI), Herl'any, Slovakia, pp. 85–90. IEEE (2012)
6. Essid, S., Alexiadis, D., Tournemenne, R., Gowing, M., Kelly, P., Monaghan, D., Daras, P., Drémeau, A., O'Connor, N.E.: An advanced virtual dance performance evaluator. In: 2012 IEEE International Conference Acoustics, Speech and Signal Processing (ICASSP), Kyoto, Japan. IEEE (2012)
7. Gowing, M., Kell, P., O'Connor, N.E., Concolato, C., Essid, S., Lefeuvre, J., Zhang, Q.: Enhanced visualisation of dance performance from automatically synchronised multimodal recordings. In: MM International Multimedia Conference, pp. 667–670. ACM, New York (2011)
8. Hani, B.-S., Clinton, J.: Evaluating the effect of 3D world integration within a social software environment. In: 2015 12th International Conference Information Technology - New Generations (ITNG), Las Vegas, NV, USA, pp. 255–260. IEEE (2015)
9. Higinio, G., Riveiro, B., Esteban, V.-F., Martinez-Sanchez, J., Pedro, A.: Metrological evaluation of microsoft kinect and asus xtion sensors, 1800–1806 (2013)
10. Hu, M.-C., Chen, C.-W., Cheng, W.-H., Chang, C.-H., Lai, J.-H., Wu, J.-L.: Real-time human movement retrieval and assessment with kinect sensor. IEEE Trans. Cybern. 742–753 (2014)
11. Huang, C.-H., Boyer, E., Ilic, S.: Robust human body shape and pose tracking. In: International Conference on 3D Vision, Washington, DC, USA, pp. 287–294. IEEE (2013)
12. Jia, W., Won-Jae, Y., Jafar, S., Erdal, O.: 3D image reconstruction and human body tracking using stereo vision and kinect technology. In: 2012 IEEE International Conference Electro/Information Technology (EIT), Indianapolis, IN, USA. IEEE (2012)
13. Jo, H., Yu, H., Kim, K., Sung, J.H.: Motion tracking system for multi-user with multiple kinects. Int. J. u-and e-Serv. Sci. Technol. 99–108 (2015)

14. Kar, R., Konar, A., Chakraborty, A.: Dance composition using microsoft kinect. In: Gavrilova, M.L., Tan, C.J.K., Saeed, K., Chaki, N., Shaikh, S.H. (eds.) Transactions on Computational Science XXV. LNCS, vol. 9030, pp. 20–34. Springer, Heidelberg (2015). doi:10.1007/978-3-662-47074-9_2

15. Adistambha, K., Ritz, C.H., Burnett, I.S.: Motion classification using dynamic time warping. In: 2008 IEEE 10th Workshop on Multimedia Signal Processing, Australia. IEEE (2008)

16. Kitsikidis, A., Dimitropoulos, K., Douka, S., Grammalidis, N.: Dance analysis using multiple Kinect sensors. In: Computer Vision Theory and Applications (VISAPP), pp. 789–795. IEEE (2014)

17. Kyan, M., Sun, G., Li, H., Zhong, L., Muneesawang, P., Dong, N., Guan, L.: An approach to ballet dance training through MS kinect and visualization in a cave virtual reality environment. ACM Trans. Intell. Syst. Technol. (TIST) 6, 23 (2015). Special Section on Visual Understanding with RGB-D Sensors. ACM, New York, NY, USA

18. Marija, M., Mile, J., Darko, M.: Analysis of the problem of Macedonian folk dance recognition. In: Conference for Informatics and Information Technology (2013)

19. Martin, C.C., Burkert, D.C., Choi, K.R.: A real-time ergonomic monitoring system using the microsoft kinect. In: Systems and Information Symposium (SIEDS), pp. 50–55. IEEE (2012)

20. Mohamed, A., Surip, S.: Real-time interactive cultural dance with gesture gaming elements via kinect-based skeleton tracking. In: 6th International Conference on Local Knowledge (ICLK), pp. 385–391 (2016)

21. Moran, A., Kamhi, G., Popov, A., Groscot, R.: Introducing Intel® RealSense™. Robotics Innovation Program (2015). http://roscon.ros.org/2015

22. Nazeeh, A., Khan, A., Alnowaimi, M., Morfeq, A.H., Ehab, A.H.: Accuracy of joint angles tracking using markerless motion system (2014)

23. Papadopoulos, G.T., Axenopoulos, A., Daras, P.: Real-time skeleton-tracking-based human action recognition using kinect data. In: Gurrin, C., Hopfgartner, F., Hurst, W., Johansen, H., Lee, H., O'Connor, N. (eds.) MMM 2014. LNCS, vol. 8325, pp. 473–483. Springer, Cham (2014). doi:10.1007/978-3-319-04114-8_40

24. Park, H., Lee, J., Bae, J.: Development of a dance rehabilitation system using kinect and a vibration feedback glove. In: 2015 15th International Conference Control, Automation and Systems (ICCAS), Busan, South Korea. IEEE (2015)

25. Pohl, H., Hadjakos, A.: Dance pattern recognition using dynamic time warping. In: Sound and Music Computing (2010)

26. Raptis, M., Kirovski, D., Hoppe, H.: Real-time classification of dance gestures from skeleton animation. In: Symposium on Computer Animation, pp. 147–156. ACM, New York (2011)

27. Schulz, S., Woerner, A.: Automatic motion segmentation for human motion synthesis. In: Perales, F.J., Fisher, R.B. (eds.) AMDO 2010. LNCS, vol. 6169, pp. 182–191. Springer, Heidelberg (2010). doi:10.1007/978-3-642-14061-7_18

28. Sungphill, M., Youngbin, P., Wook, K.D., Hong, S.I.: Multiple kinect sensor fusion for human. Int. J. Adv. Robot. Syst. (2015)

29. Tang, J.K., Chan, J.C., Leung, H.: Interactive dancing game with real-time recognition of continuous dance moves from 3D human motion capture. In: International Conference on Ubiquitous Information Management and Communication, p. 50. ACM, New York (2011)

30. Vantigodi, S., Radhakrishnan, V.B.: Action recognition from motion capture data using meta-cognitive RBF network classifier. In: 2014 IEEE Ninth International Conference Intelligent Sensors, Sensor Networks and Information Processing (ISSNIP), Singapore, pp. 1–6. IEEE (2014)

31. Wang, Q., Kurillo, G., Ofli, F., Bajcsy, R.: Evaluation of pose tracking accuracy in the first and second generations of microsoft kinect. In: Healthcare Informatics, pp. 380–389. IEEE (2015)

32. Yang, Y., Leung, H., Deng, L.: Automatic dance lesson generation. IEEE Trans. Learn. Technol. 191–198 (2011). IEEE

33. How often and why do people's eyes blink? - The Boston Globe. Archive.boston.com (2016). http://archive.boston.com/news/science/articles/2007/05/14/how_often_and_why_do_peoples_eyes_blink/. Accessed 07 Nov 2016

34. NEC Corporation of Malaysia introduces Neoface® facial recognition solutions for the first time in Malaysia. Sg.nec.com (2016). http://sg.nec.com/en_AP/press/201408/ap_20140812_01.html. Accessed 8 Oct 2016

35. Review: KeyLemon, Biometric-solutions.com (2016). http://www.biometric-solutions.com/software/reviews.php?story=keylemon. Accessed 8 Oct 2016

36. Makwana, H., Singh, T.: Comparison of different algorithm for face recognition. Global J. Comput. Sci. Technol. Graph. Vis. **13**(9) (2013)

37. Ahonen, T., Hadid, A., Pietikäinen, M.: Face recognition with local binary patterns. In: Pajdla, T., Matas, J. (eds.) ECCV 2004. LNCS, vol. 3021, pp. 469–481. Springer, Heidelberg (2004). doi:10.1007/978-3-540-24670-1_36

38. Singh, A.: Comparison of face recognition algorithms on dummy faces. Int. J. Multimed. Appl. **4**(4), 121–135 (2012)

39. Muhammad, M.A.N., Ruhaiyem, N.I.R., Mohamed, A.S.A.: Keeping curiosity in local historical knowledge alive by sensor based simulation game using flash actionscript 3. In: Proceedings of the International Conference Local Knowledge (2016)

40. Ravi, P.L., Ruhaiyem, N.I.R.: Intelligent gameplay for improved retro games. J. Telecommun. Electron. Comput. Eng. (JTEC) **8**(6), 23–26 (2016)

Data Driven Decision Analysis in Bank Financial Management with Goal Programming Model

Lam Weng Siew[1,2(✉)], Chen Jia Wai[1], and Lam Weng Hoe[1,2]

[1] Department of Physical and Mathematical Science, Faculty of Science,
Universiti Tunku Abdul Rahman, Kampar Campus, Jalan Universiti,
Bandar Barat, 31900 Kampar, Perak, Malaysia
lamws@utar.edu.my
[2] Centre for Mathematical Sciences, Centre for Business and Management,
Universiti Tunku Abdul Rahman, Kampar Campus, Jalan Universiti,
Bandar Barat, 31900 Kampar, Perak, Malaysia

Abstract. Financial management is important to the companies such as banks and financial institutions in managing the assets and liabilities. In optimizing the financial management, different goals have to be achieved simultaneously such as asset accumulation, liability reduction, equity, earning, profitability and total goal achievement. Therefore, goal programming model is introduced to solve the multiple objectives decision making problem in financial management. The objective of this study is to develop a goal programming model to optimize and compare the financial management of the banks in Malaysia based on the benchmark target value for each goal. In this study, six goals such as total assets, total liability, equity, profitability, earnings and total goal achievements are investigated for the period from year 2012 until 2016. The results of this study show that all banks are able to achieve the goal for total asset and equity. Moreover, the target value of equity can be increased further for all banks in future. This study is significant because it helps to determine the potential improvement on total liability, profit, earnings and total goal achievement for each bank in order to achieve the benchmark target value for future development.

Keywords: Goal programming · Financial management · LINGO software · Potential improvement

1 Introduction

Financial management is important to banks and financial institutions in managing the assets and liabilities. In optimizing the financial management, different goals have to be achieved simultaneously such as asset accumulation, liability reduction, equity, earning, profitability and total goal achievement [1]. Bank needs to monitor its financial management in order to control its liquidity and to achieve the desired profit. Therefore, financial planning is developed based on the past data driven decision analysis in order to hedge against the uncertainties [2]. The ability on fast and efficient interpretation on

© Springer International Publishing AG 2017
H. Badioze Zaman et al. (Eds.): IVIC 2017, LNCS 10645, pp. 681–689, 2017.
https://doi.org/10.1007/978-3-319-70010-6_63

the environment changes is one of the competitive advantages [3]. Bank and financial institution have to do data analysis on the latest trend and adjust their finance allocation for the best performance. Linear programming model was introduced to optimize the financial management of banks [4]. Since linear programming model is not able to handle multiple objectives, thus goal programming model has been introduced to solve multiple objectives decision problems in financial management. According to Naderi et al. [5], financial management enables the company to premeditate future risk based on data driven decision analysis with goal programming model. Kosmidou and Zopounidis [2] emphasized that different criteria should be considered in the bank financial management. Asset accumulation, liability reduction, equity, earning, profitability and total goal achievement are important goals in bank financial management [5]. Therefore, goal programming model [5, 6] is introduced to solve multiple objectives decision making problem in financial management.

Zaloom et al. [7] developed a goal programming model to optimize the fund management in bank. Besides that, goal programming model has been applied in other financial management such as portfolio management [8–10] and liquidity management [11]. For asset and liability management, the earliest study was carried out by Giokas and Vassiloglou [12] in Greece. Halim et al. [13] showed that goal programming model is able to identify the potential improvements on the goal achievement. Other than banking sector, goal programming model has been utilized in other optimization problems such as renewable energy production [14], assembly line [15], construction [16], manpower scheduling [17], inventory control [18] and so forth.

According to the past studies on bank financial management, goal programming model is only developed for the individual bank itself without comparing with other banks. The comparison among the peers or competitors is important because it helps to identify the potential improvement based on the benchmark [19–25]. In addition, goal programming model is able to determine the trade-off among the goals in bank financial management. Therefore, this study aims to fill the research gap by determining the benchmark target value for each goal in financial management. The objective of this study is to develop a goal programming model to optimize and compare the financial management of the banks in Malaysia based on the benchmark target value for each goal. Three highest financial status banks in Malaysia, namely CIMB Group Holding Berhad (CIMB), Malayan Banking Berhad (MAYBANK) and Public Bank Berhad (PBBANK) are investigated in this study for the period from year 2012 until 2016. The structure of the paper is organized as follows. The next section describes the data and methodology used in this study. Section 3 discusses about the empirical results of this study. Section 4 concludes the paper.

2   Data and Methodology

2.1   Goal Programming Model

Goal programming is a mathematical model which aims to solve multiple objectives decision making problems [6]. In this study, preemptive goal programming model is used by considering the priority of each goal [1, 5]. Preemptive goal programming model satisfies one goal at a time. Therefore, first priority goal will be satisfied followed by the second priority goal, third priority goal and so forth. The formulation of the preemptive goal programming model is shown as follows.

$$\text{Minimize } G_i = \rho_i \text{ where } i = 1, 2, 3, \ldots, n. \tag{1}$$

Subject to

$$\sum_{j=1}^{m} \left(a_{ij}x_j + d_i^- - d_i^+ \right) = g_i \tag{2}$$

$$x_j, d_i^-, d_i^+ \geq 0 \tag{3}$$

where

G_i	is i^{th} goal for $i = 1, 2, 3, \ldots, n$;
ρ_i	is deviation variable for $i = 1, 2, 3, \ldots, n$;
d_i^-	is negative deviation variable for $i = 1, 2, 3, \ldots, n$;
d_i^+	is positive deviation variable for $i = 1, 2, 3, \ldots, n$;
x_j	is decision variable for $j = 1, 2, 3, \ldots, m$;
a_{ij}	is parameter for decision variable; and
g_i	is target value for goal $i = 1, 2, 3, \ldots, n$.

2.2   Data

The data of this study consists of CIMB Group Holding Berhad (CIMB), Malayan Banking Berhad (MAYBANK) and Public Bank Berhad (PBBANK) which are listed banks in Malaysia stock market. The data is obtained from the financial statement of each bank for the period from year 2012 until 2016. Asset accumulation, liability reduction, equity, earning, profitability and total goal achievement are important goals in bank financial management [1]. The priority of the goals is listed as follows [13].

P1:   Maximize total assets (d_1^-),
P2:   Minimize total liabilities (d_2^+),
P3:   Maximize equity (d_3^-),
P4:   Maximize profitability (d_4^-),
P5:   Maximize earnings (d_5^-),
P6:   Maximize total goal achievements (d_6^-).

Based on the optimal solution of goal programming model, the goal is achieved if the respective deviation variable is zero. Tables 1, 2 and 3 present the financial data for CIMB, MAYBANK and PBBANK respectively in coded values.

Table 4 displays the comparison of financial data among the banks based on total values of each goal.

The benchmark target value for each goal is proposed based on the optimal value of comparison among the banks. As shown in Table 4, the benchmark target value for

Table 1. Financial data for CIMB

Goal	Group (RM'trillion)					Total
	2012	2013	2014	2015	2016	
Asset	0.3371	0.3709	0.4142	0.4616	0.4858	2.0695
Liability	0.3077	0.3397	0.3758	0.4193	0.4387	1.8812
Equity	0.0294	0.0312	0.0384	0.0422	0.0471	0.1883
Profit	0.0044	0.0046	0.0032	0.0029	0.0036	0.0187
Earnings	0.0135	0.0147	0.0141	0.0154	0.0161	0.0738
Total goal achievement	0.6920	0.7611	0.8456	0.9414	0.9912	4.2314

Table 2. Financial data for MAYBANK

Goal	Group (RM'trillion)					Total
	2012	2013	2014	2015	2016	
Asset	0.4949	0.5604	0.6403	0.7083	0.7360	3.1399
Liability	0.4509	0.5127	0.5856	0.6448	0.6655	2.8595
Equity	0.0440	0.0477	0.0547	0.0635	0.0705	0.2804
Profit	0.0059	0.0068	0.0069	0.0070	0.0070	0.0335
Earnings	0.0166	0.0185	0.0185	0.0212	0.0223	0.0972
Total goal achievement	1.0123	1.1462	1.3060	1.4449	1.5011	6.4105

Table 3. Financial data for PBBANK

Goal	Group (RM' trillion)					Total
	2012	2013	2014	2015	2016	
Asset	0.2746	0.3057	0.3457	0.3638	0.3801	1.6699
Liability	0.2560	0.2845	0.3168	0.3315	0.3447	1.5335
Equity	0.0186	0.0212	0.0289	0.0323	0.0354	0.1364
Profit	0.0039	0.0041	0.0046	0.0051	0.0053	0.0230
Earnings	0.0077	0.0082	0.0087	0.0095	0.0100	0.0441
Total goal achievement	0.5609	0.6237	0.7047	0.7422	0.7753	3.4068

Table 4. Comparison of financial data among the banks

Goal	Total values (RM' trillion)			Max	
	CIMB	MAYBANK	PBBANK		Min
Asset	2.0695	3.1399	1.6699	3.1399	
Liability	1.8812	2.8595	1.5335		1.5335
Equity	0.1883	0.2804	0.1364	0.2804	
Profit	0.0187	0.0335	0.0230	0.0335	
Earnings	0.0738	0.0972	0.0441	0.0972	
Total goal achievement	4.2314	6.4105	3.4068	6.4105	

each goal can be determined based on the maximum value for asset, equity, profit, earnings and total goal achievement as well as minimum value for liability.

Based on the financial data from Tables 1 2, 3 and 4 which serve as data driven decision analysis, goal programming model is developed for each bank and formulated as follows.

CIMB:

Minimize : $P1(d_1^-) + P2(d_2^+) + P3(d_3^-) + P4(d_4^-) + P5(d_5^-) + P6(d_6^-)$

Subject to

$0.3371x_1 + 0.3709x_2 + 0.4142x_3 + 0.4616x_4 + 0.4858x_5 + d_1^- - d_1^+ = 3.1399$
$0.3077x_1 + 0.3397x_2 + 0.3758x_3 + 0.4193x_4 + 0.4387x_5 + d_2^- - d_2^+ = 1.5335$
$0.0294x_1 + 0.0312x_2 + 0.0384x_3 + 0.0422x_4 + 0.0471x_5 + d_3^- - d_3^+ = 0.2804$
$0.0044x_1 + 0.0046x_2 + 0.0032x_3 + 0.0029x_4 + 0.0036x_5 + d_4^- - d_4^+ = 0.0335$
$0.0135x_1 + 0.0147x_2 + 0.0141x_3 + 0.0154x_4 + 0.0161x_5 + d_5^- - d_5^+ = 0.0972$
$0.6920x_1 + 0.7611x_2 + 0.8456x_3 + 0.9414x_4 + 0.9912x_5 + d_6^- - d_6^+ = 6.4105$

MAYBANK:

Minimize : $P1(d_1^-) + P2(d_2^+) + P3(d_3^-) + P4(d_4^-) + P5(d_5^-) + P6(d_6^-)$

Subject to

$0.4949x_1 + 0.5604x_2 + 0.6403x_3 + 0.7083x_4 + 0.7360x_5 + d_1^- - d_1^+ = 3.1399$
$0.4509x_1 + 0.5127x_2 + 0.5856x_3 + 0.6448x_4 + 0.6655x_5 + d_2^- - d_2^+ = 1.5335$
$0.0440x_1 + 0.0477x_2 + 0.0547x_3 + 0.0635x_4 + 0.0705x_5 + d_3^- - d_3^+ = 0.2804$
$0.0059x_1 + 0.0068x_2 + 0.0069x_3 + 0.0070x_4 + 0.0070x_5 + d_4^- - d_4^+ = 0.0335$
$0.0166x_1 + 0.0185x_2 + 0.0185x_3 + 0.0212x_4 + 0.0223x_5 + d_5^- - d_5^+ = 0.0972$
$1.0123x_1 + 1.1462x_2 + 1.3060x_3 + 1.4449x_4 + 1.5011x_5 + d_6^- - d_6^+ = 6.4105$

PBBANK:

Minimize : $P1(d_1^-) + P2(d_2^+) + P3(d_3^-) + P4(d_4^-) + P5(d_5^-) + P6(d_6^-)$

Subject to

$0.2746x_1 + 0.3057x_2 + 0.3457x_3 + 0.3638x_4 + 0.3801x_5 + d_1^- - d_1^+ = 3.1399$
$0.2560x_1 + 0.2845x_2 + 0.3168x_3 + 0.3315x_4 + 0.3447x_5 + d_2^- - d_2^+ = 1.5335$
$0.0186x_1 + 0.0212x_2 + 0.0289x_3 + 0.0323x_4 + 0.0354x_5 + d_3^- - d_3^+ = 0.2804$
$0.0039x_1 + 0.0041x_2 + 0.0046x_3 + 0.0051x_4 + 0.0053x_5 + d_4^- - d_4^+ = 0.0335$
$0.0077x_1 + 0.0082x_2 + 0.0087x_3 + 0.0095x_4 + 0.0100x_5 + d_5^- - d_5^+ = 0.0972$
$0.5609x_1 + 0.6237x_2 + 0.7047x_3 + 0.7422x_4 + 0.7753x_5 + d_6^- - d_6^+ = 6.4105$

In this study, LINGO software is used to solve the goal programming model. LINGO is an optimization software for solving linear programming model, non-linear programming model, goal programming model and integer programming model [26–31].

3 Result and Discussion

Tables 5, 6 and 7 present the goal achievement as well as the values of deviation variables for CIMB, MAYBANK and PBBANK respectively.

Table 5. CIMB goal achievements and deviation variables

Goals priority	d_i^-	d_i^+	Goal achievement
$P1$	0	0	Achieved
$P2$	0	1.3021	Not achieved
$P3$	0	2.3884×10^2	Achieved
$P4$	1.0067×10^2	0	Not achieved
$P5$	0	6.6684×10^3	Achieved
$P6$	3.3995×10^3	0	Not achieved

Table 6. MAYBANK goal achievements and deviation variables

Goals priority	d_i^-	d_i^+	Goal achievement
$P1$	0	0	Achieved
$P2$	0	1.3057	Not achieved
$P3$	0	2.0251×10^2	Achieved
$P4$	3.8385×10^3	0	Not achieved
$P5$	2.1892×10^3	0	Not achieved
$P6$	6.0244×10^3	0	Not achieved

Table 7. PBBANK goal achievements and deviation variables

Goals priority	d_i^-	d_i^+	Goal achievement
$P1$	0	0	Achieved
$P2$	0	1.3142	Not achieved
$P3$	0	1.1743×10^2	Achieved
$P4$	0	9.9647×10^3	Achieved
$P5$	1.4919×10^2	0	Not achieved
$P6$	4.9468×10^3	0	Not achieved

As shown in Tables 5, 6 and 7, three banks manage to achieve the first priority goal in maximizing total assets because d_1^- values are zero for all banks. In addition, zero value of d_1^+ shows that all banks' assets remain at RM3140 billion. For minimizing total liability goal, all banks are not able to achieve the goal since d_2^+ values are non-zero. However, all banks are able to achieve the third goal in maximizing equity. Based on the optimal solution, the target value of equity can be increased further for all banks in future. CIMB gives the highest increment (RM0.02388 trillion) followed by MAYBANK (RM0.02025 trillion) and PBBANK (RM0.01174 trillion). For the fourth goal in maximizing profitability, PBBANK is the only bank that achieves the goal. Besides that, the positive value of d_4^+ implies that the target value of profitability for PBBANK can be increased by RM0.00996 trillion. For the fifth goal in maximizing earnings, only CIMB is able to achieve the goal with increment of RM0.00667 trillion. However, all banks are not able to achieve the last goal which is maximizing total goal achievement.

Table 8 presents the potential improvement on total asset, total liability, equity, profit, earnings and total goal achievement for each bank based on the deviation from benchmark target value.

Table 8. Potential improvement based on the deviation from benchmark target value

Goals priority	CIMB (RM' trillion)	MAYBANK (RM' trillion)	PBBANK (RM' trillion)	Benchmark target value (RM' trillion)
Asset	0	0	0	3.1399
Liability	1.3021	1.3057	1.3142	1.5335
Equity	0	0	0	0.2804
Profit	1.0067×10^2	3.8385×10^3	0	0.0335
Earnings	0	2.1892×10^3	1.4919×10^2	0.0972
Total goal achievement	3.3995×10^3	6.0244×10^3	4.9468×10^3	6.4105

Based on the optimal solution of goal programming model, the potential improvement on each goal can be identified. As shown in Table 8, the potential improvement on each goal is given by the positive value of deviation. CIMB, MAYBANK and PBBANK are recommended to minimize RM1.3021 trillion, RM1.3057 trillion and RM1.3142 trillion respectively for total liability in order to achieve the benchmark target value of RM1.5335 trillion. Zero deviation for total asset and equity implies that no improvements are needed for all banks since both goals have been achieved. For total goal achievement, CIMB, MAYBANK and PBBANK are recommended to minimize RM3.3995×10^3 trillion, RM6.0244×10^3 trillion and RM4.9468×10^3 trillion respectively in order to achieve the benchmark target value of RM6.4105 trillion.

4   Conclusion

In this study, the goal programming model is developed to optimize and compare the financial management of CIMB, MAYBANK and PBBANK in Malaysia. The benchmark target value for each goal is proposed based on the optimal value of comparison among the banks. The results of this study show that all banks are able to achieve the goal for total asset and equity. Besides that, the target value of equity can be increased further for all banks in future. This study is significant because it helps to determine the potential improvement on total liability, profit, earnings and total goal achievement for each bank in order to achieve the benchmark target value. Therefore, the findings of this research help the banks to achieve the goals and enhance their competitive power in future.

References

1. Arewa, A., Owoputi, J.A., Torbira, L.L.: Financial statement management, liability reduction and asset accumulation: an application of goal programming model to a nigerian bank. Int. J. Finan. Res. **4**(4), 83–90 (2013)
2. Kosmidou, K., Zopounidis, C.: A multi objective methodology for bank asset liability management. In: Pardalos, P.M., Tsitsiringos, V.K. (eds.) Financial Engineering, E-commerce and Supply Chain. APOP, vol. 70, pp. 139–151. Kluwer Academic Publishers, Dordrecht (2002). doi:10.1007/978-1-4757-5226-7_9
3. Moradi, M., Janatifar, H.: Ranking of financial strategies based on linear goal programming and VIKOR. Int. J. Bus. Manag. Econ. **1**(1), 16–23 (2014)
4. Chambers, D., Charnes, A.: Inter temporal analysis and optimization of bank portfolios. Manag. Sci. **7**(11), 393–409 (1961)
5. Naderi, S., Minouei, M., Gashti, H.P.: Asset and liability optimal management mathematical modeling for bank. J. Basic Appl. Sci. Res. **3**(1), 484–493 (2013)
6. Charnes, A., Cooper, W.W., Ferguson, R.O.: Optimal estimation of executive compensation by linear programming. Manag. Sci. **1**(2), 138–151 (1955)
7. Zaloom, V., Tolga, A., Chu, H.: Bank funds management by goal programming. Comput. Ind. Eng. **11**(1–4), 132–135 (1986)
8. Lam, W.S., Lam, W.H.: Strategic decision making in portfolio management with goal programming model. Am. J. Oper. Manag. Inf. Syst. **1**(1), 34–38 (2016)
9. Lam, W.S., Jaaman, S.H., Ismail, H.: Portfolio optimization in enhanced index tracking with goal programming approach. In: The 2014 UKM FST Postgraduate Colloquium, vol. 1614, pp. 968–972. AIP Publishing, New York (2014)
10. Agarana, M.C., Bishop, S.A., Odetunmibi, O.A.: Optimization of banks loan portfolio management using goal programming technique. Int. J. Res. Appl. Natl. Soc. Sci. **2**(8), 43–52 (2014)
11. Mohammadi, R., Sherafati, M.: Optimization of bank liquidity management using goal programming and fuzzy AHP. Res. J. Recent Sci. **4**(6), 53–61 (2015)
12. Giokas, D., Vassiloglou, M.: A goal programming model for bank assets and liabilities. Eur. J. Oper. Res. **50**, 48–60 (1991)
13. Halim, B.A., Karim, H.A., Fahami, N.A., Mahad, N.F., Nordin, S.K.S., Hassan, N.: Bank financial statement management using a goal programming model. Procedia – Soc. Behav. Sci. **211**, 498–504 (2015)
14. Zografidou, E., Petridis, K., Petridis, N., Arabatzis, G.: A financial approach to renewable energy production in Greece using goal programming. Renew. Energy **108**, 37–51 (2017)
15. Polat, O., Mutlu, Ö., Özgörmüş, E.: A goal programming model for assembly line balancing problem type 2 under workload constraint. In: The 2015 Northeast Decision Sciences Conference, Cambridge, MA (2015)
16. Yahia-Berrouiguet, A., Tissourassi, K.: Application of goal programming model for allocating time and cost in project management: a case study from the company of construction seror. Yugoslav J. Oper. Res. **25**(2), 283–289 (2015)
17. Todovic, D., Makajic, N.D., Kostic, S.M., Martic, M.: Police officer scheduling using goal programming. Int. J. Police Strat. Manag. **38**, 295–313 (2015)
18. Choudhary, D., Shankar, R.: A goal programming model for joint decision making of inventory lot-size, supplier selection and carrier selection. Comput. Ind. Eng. **71**, 1–9 (2014)
19. Lam, W.S., Liew, K.F., Lam, W.H.: An empirical comparison on the efficiency of healthcare companies in Malaysia with data envelopment analysis model. Int. J. Serv. Sci. Manag. Eng. **4**(1), 1–5 (2017)

20. Memon, M.A., Tahir, I.M.: Relative efficiency of manufacturing companies in Pakistan using data envelopment analysis. Int. J. Bus. Commer. **1**(3), 10–27 (2011)
21. Lam, W.S., Liew, K.F., Lam, W.H.: Evaluation on the efficiency of healthcare companies in Malaysia with data envelopment analysis model. SCIREA J. Math. **1**(1), 95–106 (2016)
22. Mukta, M.: Efficiency of commercial banks in India: a DEA approach. Pertanika J. Soc. Sci. Humanit. **24**(1), 151–170 (2016)
23. Lam, W.S., Liew, K.F., Lam, W.H.: An empirical investigation on the efficiency of healthcare companies with data envelopment analysis model. Biomed. Stat. Inf. **1**(1), 19–23 (2016)
24. Liew, K.F., Lam, W.S., Lam, W.H.: Financial analysis on the company performance in Malaysia with multi-criteria decision making model. Syst. Sci. Appl. Math. **1**(1), 1–7 (2016)
25. Lam, W.S., Liew, K.F., Lam, W.H.: Evaluation on the financial performance of the Malaysian banks with TOPSIS model. Am. J. Serv. Sci. Manag. **4**(2), 11–16 (2017)
26. Lam, W.S., Lam, W.H.: Portfolio optimization for index tracking problem with mixed-integer programming model. J. Sci. Res. Dev. **2**(10), 5–8 (2015)
27. Lam, W.S., Lam, W.H.: Mathematical modeling of enhanced index tracking with optimization model. J. Numer. Anal. Appl. Math. **1**(1), 1–5 (2016)
28. Lam, W.H., Lam, W.S.: Mathematical modeling of risk in portfolio optimization with mean-extended Gini approach. SCIREA J. Math. **1**(2), 190–196 (2016)
29. Lam, W.S., Jaaman, S.H., Ismail, H.: Enhanced index tracking in portfolio optimization. In: International Conference on Mathematical Sciences and Statistics 2013, vol. 1557, pp. 469–472. AIP Publishing, New York (2013)
30. Lam, W.S., Jaaman, S.H., Ismail, H.: Index tracking modeling in portfolio optimization mixed integer linear programming. J. Appl. Sci. Agric. **9**(18), 47–50 (2014)
31. Lam, W.S., Jaaman, S.H., Lam, W.H.: A new enhanced index tracking model in portfolio optimization with sum weighted approach. In: The 4th International Conference on Mathematical Sciences 2016, vol. 1830, pp. 1–7. AIP Publishing, New York (2017)

Investigating Blind User Preference on Tactile Symbols for Landmarks on Audio-Tactile Map

Nazatul Naquiah Ahba Abd Hamid$^{(\boxtimes)}$, Fariza Hanis Abdul Razak,
and Wan Adilah Wan Adnan

Faculty of Computer and Mathematical Sciences,
Universiti Teknologi MARA (UiTM), 40450 Shah Alam, Selangor, Malaysia
nazatul84@gmail.com, {fariza,adilah}@tmsk.uitm.edu.my

Abstract. Tactile symbols are important in facilitating blind people to understand maps. With audio-tactile maps, the use of tactile symbols needs to be designed appropriately since the symbols are associated with speech. Although there are tactile symbols proposed in the literature, the design of these symbols are mainly for conventional tactile maps. As the literature suggests that the design of these symbols is based on user preferences which are largely influenced by culture and environment. Since there is no guideline for designing tactile symbols for our culture, we therefore conducted a user study with blind participants at Malaysian Association for the Blind (MAB) to investigate their preference on tactile symbols that can be used with audio-tactile maps. From the study, we found that in order for our blind participants to easily recognize a landmark, the landmark symbols should be filled with texture. Landmark symbol with texture inside can help convey information instantly through touch. Although audio can be used to convey information about the landmark, the audio on the tactile map is only a tool for confirming their tactile information. Since audio helps enhance their user experience with the tactile map, the placement of an audio label on the tactile map becomes crucial. This paper concludes by discussing some recommendations on how to improve the available landmark symbols according to their preferences.

Keywords: Tactile symbols · Audio-tactile maps · Blind users · Texture · Landmark symbols · Audio label

1 Introduction

Maps present geographical information of a place that can be used by a person for planning journeys. However, assessing information from maps can be difficult for people with no vision. Alternatively, special maps which are known as tactile maps have been proposed for the blind people. These tactile maps were designed with raised symbols to enable blind people to assess information through touch. Landmarks of a place can be presented as tactile symbols and braille labelling is used to provide the identification for the landmarks. There are many design guidelines that have been proposed in the literature on tactile symbols [1–3]. However, there is a lack of international standard on tactile symbols that can be used as guidelines for the designers or

© Springer International Publishing AG 2017
H. Badioze Zaman et al. (Eds.): IVIC 2017, LNCS 10645, pp. 690–701, 2017.
https://doi.org/10.1007/978-3-319-70010-6_64

researchers. Furthermore, these design guidelines are only meant for conventional tactile maps in which audio is not incorporated. Up to present, there is a limited study that focuses on designing tactile symbols for audio-tactile maps [4]. However, in [4], the study was presented as a work-in-progress and there was no update on the development of the study. Therefore, we replicated the study done by [4] to find out our own blind user preference on tactile symbols for audio-tactile maps.

2 Related Work

Tactile symbols are graphical representations developed for blind people who are unable to interpret pictures or written words [1]. The learning of tactile symbols is through touch. The symbols come in various shapes and textures to represent different meaning categories for instance, street, building and transport. The tactile symbols proposed in the literature were developed to be used on conventional tactile maps, however, the problems of clutter limit the information that can be presented on tactile maps [5].

Audio-tactile maps have been introduced to enhance the use of conventional tactile maps. Normally, in order for a user to read tactile maps, a blind person needs to be braille literate. With audio-tactile maps, a blind user is able to perceive information not only through touch but also hearing. The information represented by tactile symbols is translated into speech when a user presses on a particular area on the symbol.

Since tactile symbols for conventional tactile maps have been proposed, there is a lack of international standard on tactile symbols [2]. Different tactile symbols with different meanings have been proposed in literature. This could be due to the differences in user preferences where culture and environment influence the design of the symbols. Most tactile symbols proposed in the literature were mainly from Western countries and there is a lack of source on tactile symbols created for Asian countries. Therefore, this work was carried out to find out the preferences of blind people in Malaysia on tactile symbols.

The aim of this study is to investigate user preference on the tactile symbols for landmarks which can be used with audio-tactile maps. The study also focuses on the design of the tactile symbols in which speech label would be incorporated on the audio-tactile maps.

3 Methodology

To achieve our objectives, we carried out a qualitative user study with a group of blind people at Malaysian Association for the Blind (MAB) complex.

3.1 Blind Participants

Ten (10) totally blind people (3 females and 7 males) from Malaysian Association for the Blind (MAB) volunteered to take part in the study. All participants were new to both tactile and audio-tactile maps. The mean age of the participants was 21.4 years.

3.2   Audio-Tactile Maps

There were two (2) maps representing the same layout of a fictitious town but using tactile symbols with different textures. The first map (Map A) (Fig. 1) used tactile symbols with the same textures and the second map (Map B) (Fig. 2) used tactile symbols with different textures.

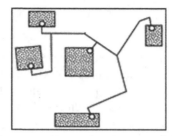

Fig. 1. Map A consists of tactile symbols with same textures.

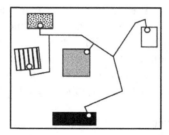

Fig. 2. Map B consists of tactile symbols with different textures.

There were thirteen (13) landmarks identified from our initial study on user requirements on landmarks [6]. There were seven (7) landmarks (road crossing, street, sidewalk, junction, telephone booth, fence and bridge) represented by five (5) different tactile symbols for each landmark. For landmarks of field, park, parking lot and building; they were represented by five (5) different textures. The symbols of these four (4) landmarks were based on the original shapes but had been simplified [1]. Landmark of water was represented by two (2) different textures (wavy and '+' patterns) as proposed in Edman's [1], and the entrance was represented by five (5) different symbols. The symbols were designed based on the guidelines by [1] for conventional tactile maps and [4] for audio-tactile maps. Some of the symbols suggested by Edman's were replicated in the current study due to the similarity of the symbols for certain landmarks. Apart from the landmark symbols and textures, the symbol of audio label was also tested where it was represented by an unfilled circle with 11 different sizes. All symbols used in this study were designed using Inkscape and printed using a laser printer before the symbols were embossed through a thermal fuser.

3.3   User Study

Each blind participant was first briefed about the study before they gave their consent. Upon their agreement, they then verbally completed a pre-test questionnaire. The questionnaire was constructed in different sections to obtain information on their demographics and their experiences in mobility and using both tactile and audio-tactile maps. After that, they were explained on the procedure of the study. Participants were introduced to a sample map (overlay) and a Talking Tactile Tablet (T3)[1]. The overlay presented a simple map of a town and the identification for each landmark was conveyed through speech. The blind participants needed to press on the unfilled circle on each landmark to acquire the information. They then were given some time to explore and familiarize with the use of the overlay with T3. Once they were confident, we started to begin the actual user study.

To begin with, we gave them two (2) different maps (Figs. 1 and 2) to explore using T3. Their task was to state their preference and reason for choosing the selected map. There were two (2) possible conditions that could be encountered. In the first condition, if a participant chose the map with same textures, they would be asked to select the most preferred textures available to represent the symbols. In the second condition, if a participant chose the map with different textures, they would be asked to do the same but for different landmarks.

The blind participants were required to explore every tactile symbol to identify which tactile symbol from the list was the best to represent for each landmark. They would also need to provide reason based on their selection. Upon the completion of the study, participants were interviewed to give their feedback on the design of the symbols. To appreciate their effort and support, we compensated them at the end of the study.

4   Results

(i)   Task 1: User Preference – Exploration with map with the same textures (Map A) and map with different textures (Map B)

All ten (10) participants chose Map B (Fig. 2) over Map A (Fig. 1). Based on the feedback from participants, they preferred a map with symbols that have different textures to avoid confusion. Moreover, map with different textures helped them to recognize, thus, differentiate landmarks on a map. The following are the comments from P1, P5 and P7.

P1:   "Map A is difficult, Map B is easy… When different textures are used for landmarks, it helps me to imagine the landmarks on the map. The tablet can be used for confirmation. If we used the same textures for landmarks, it can be troublesome especially when the landmarks are close to each other.. but if we used different textures, I feel more confident"

---

[1] http://www.touchgraphics.com.

P5:   "I chose Map B because it is easier for me to feel certain landmarks when different textures are used, so I would not be confused"

P7:   "To me, I prefer Map B to Map A because it is easier to recognize a landmark.... thus, making searching faster"

(ii)   Task 2: The placement of the audio label

There were different comments given by the participants regarding the placement of the audio label on the symbols that represented the landmarks. Three (3) participants preferred the audio label to be placed at the centre of the symbols meanwhile seven (7) participants preferred it to be at the edge of the symbols (Fig. 3).

Fig. 3. Audio label is placed at the edge of a tactile symbol and connected with a line that represents a path.

P1 and P4 thought that if the audio label was placed at the centre, it might 'block' their touch as they could not really feel the texture of a landmark. They preferred the audio label to be placed as Fig. 3. P5, P6, P7, P9 and P10 also agreed and added that it would be easier and faster if an audio label was placed at the edge of a symbol.

(iii)   Task 3: Symbol for Entrance

A triangle symbol was selected by five (5) participants to represent an entrance of a building (Fig. 4). P1 mentioned that it was selected due to the arrow points that the triangle has so it was easier to touch and feel and thus, easier to distinguish. P2 pointed out that the triangle was the best option due to the fact that buildings are usually represented by rectangle or square shape, so it is better to have an entrance with different shape that is pointy and simple. P4, P5 and P6 suggested that the triangle acted like an outward arrow that showed to the way in on a building symbol.

Fig. 4. Entrance of a building preferred by most participants.

(iv)   Task 4: Textures for landmarks

The textures were presented for five (5) landmarks; field, park, parking lot, building and water (e.g. river). The following are the preferred textures selected by the participants to represent these landmarks.

- Field

P3 pointed out the texture was rough, P4 mentioned the texture felt less flat and P5 felt that the texture made him imagined as grass and suitable to represent the inside of a field symbol (Fig. 5).

Fig. 5. Texture preferred by participants to represent the inside of a field symbol.

- Park

There were four (4) participants preferred the following texture to represent inside the park symbol. P3 mentioned that the surface of the texture was rough and it was suitable to represent inside of a park symbol. P4 and P8 agreed and added that the surface of the texture was flat whereas P10 stated that the surface was smooth. Rough but flat and smooth were the reasons they chose the texture to represent the inside of a park symbol (Fig. 6).

Fig. 6. Texture preferred by participants to represent the inside of a park symbol.

- Parking lot

Most participants (P1, P2, P5, P6 and P10) selected an empty texture to represent inside a parking lot symbol. P1 suggested that an empty space made him imagine it as a parking lot. P2, P6 and P10 also had the same opinion as P1. P5 mentioned that the empty space is spacious and that made him feel that it was suitable to represent the texture of a parking lot symbol (Fig. 7).

Fig. 7. Texture preferred by participants to represent the inside of a parking lot symbol.

- Building

Four (4) participants chose the following texture for building symbol. P1, P3, P5 and P9 mentioned that when touching the texture, it made them imagine like touching a wall of a building. Therefore, they selected the following texture as to represent inside a building landmark.

Fig. 8. Texture preferred by participants to represent the inside of a building symbol.

- Water

All ten (10) participants chose this texture as shown in Fig. 9 to represent inside water symbol. They said that the wavy texture made them think of water.

Fig. 9. Texture preferred by participants to represent the inside of a water symbol.

(v) Task 5: Symbol for landmarks

- Road crossing

Most participants chose the following symbol to represent road crossing. P1 mentioned that the symbol had vertical lines on the left and right of the audio label which helped him to distinguish between road and road crossing. Therefore, he felt the design was suitable for road crossing and included on a map. Other participants; P4, P5 and P8 also highlighted on the same aspect (Fig. 10).

Fig. 10. Tactile symbol preferred by participants to represent road crossing.

- Street

There were four (4) participants preferred the following symbol to represent street. P1 suggested that a symbol for street should be wide like Fig. 11. P3, P7 and P9 mentioned that they chose the symbol because it had a rough surface that reminded them of street.

Fig. 11. Tactile symbol preferred by participants to represent street.

- Sidewalk

Four (4) participants chose the symbol below for sidewalk. P1 said that it was easier to feel due to the design of the symbol. P3 stressed that it was the design of the symbol made him choose the symbol for sidewalk. Having filled squares on the line helped him feel the symbol. P6 mentioned that he chose the symbol because the design was suitable and P9 suggested it was ideal because it reminded him of tactile paving (Fig. 12).

Fig. 12. Tactile symbol preferred by participants to represent street.

- Junction

Four participants (P1, P4, P5 and P8) selected the following symbol for junction. P1 mentioned that the design was simple and it was easy for him to feel and identify it as junction. P4 felt that the symbol was easy to recognize as junction and understand where the lines were heading to. P5 said that the design was suitable since it was clear and can be felt through touch. P8 also gave the same opinion as P5. He said that it was easier for him to feel the shape of the line and understand that he was on a junction (Fig. 13).

Fig. 13. Tactile symbol preferred by participants to represent junction.

- Telephone booth

There were 5 participants preferred the symbol that is illustrated in Fig. 14 to represent telephone booth. P3 said that the symbol can be felt and the design was similar to the shape of a public phone. Other participants (P4, P5, P7 and P8) also mentioned the same reason because they could imagine it as public phone due to its shape.

Fig. 14. Tactile symbol preferred by participants to represent telephone booth.

- Fence

The symbol in Fig. 15 was preferred by four participants (P2, P6, P8 and P9). P2 expressed that the design of the symbol had both vertical and horizontal lines thus helped him to recognize it as fence compared to other symbols. P6 mentioned that the combination of the vertical and horizontal lines made him imagined as fence. P8 and P9 also provide the same comments on the design of the symbol that they selected.

Fig. 15. Tactile symbol preferred by participants to represent fence.

- Bridge

Five (50 participants (P1, P5, P6, P7 and P8) preferred the symbol illustrated in Fig. 16. P1 commented that the shape was easy to feel and imagine as bridge. P5 explained that because of having vertical lines and closer to each other enabled him to distinguish it from road. Therefore, it was perfect to represent bridge. P6, P7 and P8 mentioned that they could imagine a bridge when exploring the symbol.

Fig. 16. Tactile symbol preferred by participants to represent bridge.

(vi) Post-test questionnaire

1. Do you think that using tactile symbols will make it easier for you to remember the layout of a place?

All participants agreed with the above question. P2, P4, P5, P6 and P7 said that it would be easier for them to explore a map when tactile symbols were used. P4 mentioned that if symbols that were easy to remember were used, there would be no problem for him to remember the places on a map. P5 added that if tactile symbols were used to represent landmarks, it would help him understand the position of landmarks on a map.

2. Do you think that the tactile symbols can assist you in exploring a novel area?

All participants answered 'Yes' to this question.

3. Do you think the design of tactile symbols in representing landmarks used in this study was helpful to you?

All participants agreed. P3 added that he preferred if the symbols used can be designed based on real shape thus this will help the user to relate the symbol to its meaning.

4. Do you think the design of tactile symbols used in this study can be easily recognize? Why?

Most participants mentioned that they found the design of tactile symbols in this study can be easily recognized. However, P3 added that it would be good if the symbols were designed based on the real shape of landmarks. P6 said that the symbols used helped him imagine a landmark. The rest of participants mentioned that having different symbols for landmarks were good for differentiating among the landmarks.

5. What are the characteristics you prefer to be on tactile symbols?

There were many answers provided by the participants. P1 said that ideally, a symbol should be clear and simple. P2 mentioned that the size of symbols should be moderate. P4 suggested that the symbols should have textures and cannot be empty. The symbols also needed to be simple. P5 expressed his satisfaction with the symbols used in the study and the characteristics of the symbols used were already good enough. P7 highlighted that texture needs to be 2–3 types only because it is easier to memorize the shape of landmarks than its texture. P8 mentioned that he preferred if the symbol can represent nearly like the real landmark.

5   Discussion

We proposed a design model for landmark symbols on audio-tactile map:

(i)   Differentiate to recognize - Different texture for different landmark

Participants were presented with 2 maps of a fictitious town where the landmarks on each map were represented by tactile symbols, in which one map had symbols filled with same textures and the other one with different textures. Surprisingly, based on the results, all participants preferred the map with landmarks that represented by different textures. There were various comments provided by the participants however their main reason was to avoid confusion during exploring a map. When different textures were used to represent different landmarks, the textures provided them with recognition of certain landmarks and at the same time it helps them to differentiate between one landmark with another landmark. Although the participants were reminded that the landmarks were associated with speech to provide identification, they emphasized that using different textures provided them instant information during map exploration. This is because when a user has a map in front of him, the first thing he would do is scanning the map either using one hand or both hands. According to the participants, when landmarks have different textures, they would know that there are different landmarks available on the map during the scanning process. One of the participants mentioned that the tablet can be used to confirm the landmarks that are available through their identification. Even though audio can be used to distinguish the landmarks, the participants found it difficult to recognize the landmarks if it is solely based on audio.

Thus, at the initial scanning stage, landmarks with different textures provided them instant information on the landmarks that were presented on the map.

Most participants in this study preferred that the symbol for parking space, however, should not be filled by any texture. This was contrast with the findings by previous study where an empty space can lead to confusion [8]. There was only one participant (P4) commented that 'empty' gave a feeling that made them imagine that it is a parking lot due to its spaciousness.

(ii)   Familiarize to remember – familiar texture and shape for recognition

There were 5 different textures proposed for 5 landmarks (field, park, parking lot, building and water). Basically, the participants selected the textures for each landmark according to (1) whether the textures were able to provide them some imagination when they touched and felt the textures (e.g. roughness, smooth, embossed) and (2) the design of the textures (e.g. lines, polka-dots, wavy). For example, most participants chose the texture in Fig. 8 for building because of its roughness and the details of the texture reminded them of touching a wall. It is interesting to learn that one of the participants said that the texture needs to be 2 or 3 types only because memorizing many textures can be difficult. He further added that the regardless of the textures, it is fine as long as they can be differentiated with one another.

(iii)   Confirm - Audio for confirmation and at the edge of landmark symbol

Task 5 provided participants with different symbols for landmarks (road crossing, street, sidewalk, junction, telephone booth, fence and bridge). An audio label was put at the centre of each of the symbols. Since there were too many audio labels placed on a street or sidewalk symbol, they annoyed the blind participants during their map exploration. Some bridge symbols in this study were presented with audio labels, however, we found that the presence of the audio labels for bridge symbols was not suitable because they could confuse the blind participants. The blind participants felt that it was difficult for them to differentiate between the audio label and the bridge symbol. Therefore, most participants preferred the audio label to be placed at the edge of the symbol similar to what has been presented on Map A or Map B.

6   Conclusion

This study was conducted to obtain user preferences on tactile symbols to represent landmarks on an audio-tactile map. Tactile symbols were usually designed with textures. The feedback provided by the participants in this study were very useful to highlight that there were many factors that need to be considered when designing the tactile symbols to be used on audio-tactile maps. There were differences in the way the tactile symbols were designed when audio labels need to be included. User preferences were important in making the decision at the early phase and the suggestions provided were important to be considered to improve the design of the tactile symbols. The input gathered from the participants facilitate the design process of tactile maps to be used with an audio-tactile map for future work.

Acknowledgement. We would like to express our gratitude to Universiti Teknologi MARA (UiTM) for their support and funding of this paper: GIP grant code: 600.IRMI/MyRA 5/3/GIP (017/2017).

References

1. Edman, P.K.: Tactile Graphics. American Foundation for the Blind, New York (1992)
2. Perkins, C.: Cartography: progress in tactile mapping. Prog. Hum. Geogr. **26**, 521–530 (2002)
3. Lobben, A., Lawrence, M.: The use of environmental features on tactile maps by navigators who are blind. Prof. Geogr. **64**, 95–108 (2012)
4. Paladugu, D.A., Wang, Z., Li, B.: On presenting audio-tactile maps to visually impaired users for getting directions. In: CHI 2010 Extended Abstracts, pp. 3955–3960. ACM (2010)
5. Tatham, A.F.: The design of tactile maps: theoretical and practical considerations. In: Rybaczak, K., Blakemore, M. (eds.) Proceedings of International Cartographic Association: Mapping the Nations, pp. 157–166, ICA, London (1991)
6. Hamid, N.N.A., Adnan, W.A.W., Razak, F.H.A.: Case study: understanding the current learning techniques of wayfinding at Malaysian Association for the Blind (MAB). In: Proceeding of the International Conference on User Science and Engineering (2016) (to appear)
7. Wang, W., Li, B., Hedgpeth, T., Haven, T.: Instant tactile-audio map: enabling access to digital maps for people with visual impairment. In: ACM SIG ASSETS (2009)
8. Minatani, K., Watanabe, T., Yamaguchi, T., Watanabe, K., Akiyama, J., Miyagi, M., Oouchi, S.: Tactile map automated creation system to enhance the mobility of blind persons—its design concept and evaluation through experiment. In: Miesenberger, K., Klaus, J., Zagler, W., Karshmer, A. (eds.) ICCHP 2010. LNCS, vol. 6180, pp. 534–540. Springer, Heidelberg (2010). doi:10.1007/978-3-642-14100-3_80

An Improved Robust Image Watermarking Scheme Based on the Singular Value Decomposition and Genetic Algorithm

Atheer Bassel[1,2(✉)], Md Jan Nordin[1],
and Mohammed B. Abdulkareem[3]

[1] Faculty of Information Science and Technology,
Center for Artifical Intelligence Technology, Universiti Kebangsaan Malaysia,
43600 Bangi, Selangor Darul Ehsan, Malaysia
atheerbassel@siswa.ukm.edu.my, jan@ukm.edu.my
[2] Computer College, University of Anbar, Al Anbar, Iraq
[3] Department of Computer Engineering and Technology,
Almaaref University College, Al Anbar, Iraq
f_com22@yahoo.com

Abstract. This paper propose a robust image watermarking scheme based on the singular value decomposition (SVD) and genetic algorithm (GA). SVD based watermarking techniques suffer with an issue of false positive problem. This leads to even authentication the wrong owner. Prevention of false positive errors is a major challenge for ownership identification and proof of ownership application using digital watermarking. We employed GA algorithm to optimize the watermarked image quality (robustness) of the extracted watermarks. The former can be overcome by embedding the owner's components of the watermark into the host image, the latter is dependent on how much the quantity for the scaling factor of the principle components is embedded. To improve the quality of watermarking (robustness), GA is used for optimize the suitable scaling factor. Experimental result of the proposed technique proves the watermark image ownership and can be reliably identified even after severe attacks. The comparison of the proposed technique with the state of the art show the superiority of our proposed technique where it is outperforming the methods in comparison.

Keywords: Digital watermarking · Singular value decomposition (SVD) · Genetic algorithm (GA) · False positive problem

1 Introduction

The definitions of digital watermarking emerge while trying to overcome the limitations of encryption and steganography in the enforcement and protection of intellectual property rights [1, 2]. Compared to the idea of encryption, the watermark information is inserted into its original form and does not hinder users in listening to, viewing, watching, or manipulating the content. Unlike steganography, digital watermarking technologies are to establish the identity of information to avoid the unauthorized

© Springer International Publishing AG 2017
H. Badioze Zaman et al. (Eds.): IVIC 2017, LNCS 10645, pp. 702–713, 2017.
https://doi.org/10.1007/978-3-319-70010-6_65

embezzlement. Generally, additional information is embedded directly into the original multimedia or host signal which is useful and valuable, and the message itself is necessary to be secret.

With digital watermarking, image-related data are covertly embeddable via the manipulation of pixel values. However, this process is bound by a trade-off between the robustness against operations of image processing (attacks) and image quality. Considering that it is covert and comprises pixel values' manipulation, a watermark offers a way for enforcing certain image's integrity and authenticity. Generally, a robust watermark which can resist attacks is used for enforcing authenticity. Meanwhile, a fragile watermark that is easily destroyable by attacks is used for the detection of tampering; this enforces integrity. Within the watermarking community, there is a challenging issue associated to watermarking, that is, the issue of security. For the majority of watermarking systems available today, the processes of embedding and extraction are conducted on the plain media. Hence, it is compulsory that the watermark embedded is the owner of the original media or a trustworthy third party. This prevents the risk of the plain media being exposed. The processing conducted in the encrypted domain should not cause worry to the media owner. In relation to this, [3] mentioned that signal processing in the encrypted domain also termed as secure signal processing, offers a potential solution to this problem.

There are a lot of researchers who implemented SVD of watermark, especially during the embedding phase, and the watermark is in the host image [4, 5, 12, 14, 17, 18]. However, embedding via SVD can easily fail. Further, any reference watermark that is being explored for in an arbitrary image is easily discoverable by attackers. This strategy has led to the problem of false positive, when certain watermark was embedded. Here, the attacker can easily attest the ownership of the arbitrary watermarked image with no awareness of the initial watermark embedded in the host image. Therefore, the false positive rate for this application should be approximately zero and that proof of ownership cannot otherwise be reliable.

Another problem in ownership identification occurs in a situation where only scalar value of the scaling factor is employed in this trustworthy SVD-based image watermarking [5, 14, 17]. Employing the small value for scaling factor, the watermark's invisibility attained high peak signal to noise ratio (PSNR) of the watermarked image. However, the watermarked image is not as robust when there are some common attacks. The factor of scaling highly contributes to the control of the watermark images in terms of transparency and robustness [19]. It is worth mentioning that high scaling factor causes the quality of watermarked image to be unacceptable, and yet the watermark is robust [5, 12–15, 17, 18].

In addition, this work will provide more information for the false positive, false negative and scaling factor. The drawback for defining the false positive and false negative should be taken into account; the false position means false watermark detection while false negative denotes failure in detecting the already available watermark. In this work, a simple model is employed to enable an analysis for the estimation of the distribution of probability of false positive as well as false negative for the technique proposed. In short, correlation coefficient (NC) is to be employed in order to ascertain the degree of the similarity between the original and extracted watermark image. The problem of false positive emerges in nearly all the SVD-based algorithms caused by the fact that there is only the process of embedding watermark into the original image [22].

The scaling factor is very important applying with optimization because a decrease in the scale factor value during the optimization process can generate high quality final outcome [14, 17, 18]. The scaling factor in the proposed watermarking scheme employs control on the tradeoff between the imperceptibility and robustness.

Thus, based on the above, this work aims to:

1. Propose a GA for the embedding part of our process to make the system more robust.
2. Propose how the GA can define the chromosome (the population) and define the fitness function (objective) based on watermarking evaluation under the number of maximum iteration.
3. Evaluation and comparison with state of the art methods.

The rest of this paper is organized as follows. Section 2 introduces the review of singular value decomposition for image watermarking in the transform domain involved in this paper. Section 3 review and describe the GA. Section 4 describes the proposed method. Section 5 presents the experimental results and discussion. Finally, Sect. 6 gives the conclusion.

2   Singular Value Decomposition (SVD)

Singular value decomposition comprises a linear algebra technique for symmetric matrix diagonalization. A digital image is also a matrix of integer numbers. As such, SVD is performable on digital images right away. The attractive properties and unique features of SVD includes its stability with little disturbance. This is why SVD has been employed in numerous applications of signal processing. SVD is also a type of orthogonal transform and a numerical technique to diagonalizable matrix, and thus, it can be used as a technique for linear algebraic within the transformed domain which contain foundation states, which, in some sense, are optimal. SVD decomposes a specified matrix into three portions such as left singular matrix U, right singular matrix V and singular matrix S, on an image size A with size ($M \times N$). The expression is as the following.

$$A = USV^T \tag{1}$$

The matrix S comprises just the diagonal element and it is termed as singular values. The matrix S contains the singular values in downward order. Meanwhile, the matrix U and V comprise the image's decomposed and detailed information. Provide that A represents the rectangular matrix of the order ($n \times n$). Thus, matrix S is allowed to contain maximum n diagonal elements. In generally, these elements (S) symbolize the involvement of each layer of decomposed image in the final formation of image [6, 22]. The parent matrix (A) is reproducible with the smaller elements of matrix s but this reproduction of matrix $A*$ will reduce the quality.

$$A = USV^T = \begin{pmatrix} u_{1,1} & \cdots & u_{1,M} \\ \vdots & \ddots & \vdots \\ u_{M,1} & \cdots & u_{M,M} \end{pmatrix} \times \begin{pmatrix} s_{1,1} & \cdots & 0 \\ \vdots & \ddots & \vdots \\ 0 & \cdots & s_{M,N} \end{pmatrix} \times \begin{pmatrix} v_{1,1} & \cdots & v_{1,N} \\ \vdots & \ddots & \vdots \\ v_{N,1} & \cdots & v_{N,N} \end{pmatrix}^T$$

$$= \sum_{i=1}^{m} \sum_{j=1}^{n} \sum_{k=1}^{n} u_{i,k} \times s_{k,k} \times v_{k,j}$$

$$(2)$$

Where: U denotes a $(M \times M)$ matrix, V denotes a $(N \times N)$ matrix and S denotes a $(M \times N)$ diagonal matrix with positive elements from the first to ending row in downward order. The diagonal elements of S are termed SVs of A, which are non-negative and they are presumed to be downwardly organized. This fulfils the relation Eq. (2) where r denotes the matrix rank.

$$S_{1,1} \geq S_{2,2} \geq \ldots \ldots \geq S_{r,r} \geq S_{r+1,r+1} = S_{r+2,r+2} \cdots \ldots = S_{M,N} = 0 \qquad (3)$$

In watermarking that is grounded on SVD, a signal is treatable as a matrix and decomposed into three matrices. The SVD computation involves the discovery of the eigenvalues and eigenvectors of AA^T and $A^T A$. The eigenvectors of $A^T A$ consist of the columns of matrix V and the eigenvectors of AA^T consist of the columns of matrix U.

3 Genetic Algorithm (GA)

Genetic Algorithm (GA) is a population based meta-heuristic which impersonates the process of natural evolution. GA handles a population of individuals and each individual represents a potential solution. GA is a multipath algorithm that performs parallel searches in order to reduce the trapping in the local minima. GA works with a coding of parameters (chromosomes) that help in evolving the present state into the succeeding state with the smallest amount of calculations.

One chromosome (individual) represents one candidate solution. A gene represents a subsection of one chromosome that encodes the values of the shift patterns for one nurse. In order to guide the search, GA uses the fitness of each string. The search for an optimal solution typically begins with a set of individuals that are randomly produced, termed as initial population. Then, GA develops the population by applying three operators: (i) selection, (ii) crossover, and (iii) mutation to generate new individuals called offspring. At the end of each iteration, a new generation is created. This process keeps repeating until it reaches the termination criteria.

[9] Proposed an innovative watermarking scheme based on GA. It is robust against watermarking attacks and the watermarked image quality is also considered. The robustness of the proposed algorithm improved the watermarked image quality with GA. The simulation results for both the watermarked image quality and the correlation values of the extracted watermark after certain attacks was poor.

[21] Proposed the optimal watermarking embedding positions using GA to examine the correlation between the robustness and the quality of the digital image. It is a new approach to find the near optimal positions for embedding an authentication by GA.

[7] Introduced algorithms on optimized DWT-based image watermarking that can simulaneously offer perceptual transparency and robustness owing to the fact that these two watermarking requirements are contradictory, the DWT-based image watermarking problem as an optimization problem and its solution is via GA. In addition, an imperceptible and robust digital image watermarking system is described according to a combination of DWT.

[8] Introduced a technique of image watermarking according to SVD and Tiny-GA. The cover image SVD are modified to allow the embedding of the watermark. The Tiny-GA makes available the systematic consideration on the improvements of the factor of scaling so that the embedded watermark can be controlled in terms of strength. This proposed system allows the successful survival of embedded watermark following the attacks by image-processing operations.

[20] Proposed a new optimization method for digital images in the DWT domain based on GA algorithm. The watermark amplification factor is optimized and the quality of the watermarked images for a set of images is found to be good PSNR and correlation factor after different types of attacks.

4   The Proposed Method

This section illustrates the steps of the proposed scheme. The SVD with GA has been used in different application and performance of the SVD scheme and GA demonstrated better performance as opposed to the methods used in the past in each specific application. In the proposed the GA with watermarking, firstly, we deal with the scenario as set of solution in one population as optimization problem. Secondly, we calculate the fitness for each solution in my fitness including the image, watermark, attack image, extracted watermark and input parameter for SVD and GA. Finally, we compute the correlation between the original and extract watermark and the Peak signal to noise rate (PSNR), between the original image and after embedding image.

The procedure of the proposed technique as following, first, our technique finds the best solution in the population based on the objective function. Second, the algorithm will start the optimization process based on the GA procedure and update the population by adding the best solution obtained and delete the worst solution in the population. Finally, process will have terminated when stopping criteria meet.

Where, the Best X, refers to the index of the solution in population, L best represent the length of the solution and Best represent the best fitness for each solution.

The size for image was 512×512, the size of watermark image was 20×50, and this study searching for the best size of watermarking image (32 bit).

The proposed scheme is as elucidated below:

4.1   Watermarking Embedding

Presents the block diagram of the watermarking embedding of the SVD with GA scheme. SVD divide the image into three matrixes as U, S, and V, The $w - (w11, \ldots, w_{IJ}, \ldots, wnl \times nk)$ denotes a watermark and each bit $w_{ij} \in \{-1, 1\}$, in this case, the length of solution was $\{-1, 0, 1\}$ in the population of GA. Subsequently, a watermark bit w_{ij} is embedded in LL_{ij}.

For the embedding watermarking by using the GA generate the initial population by random. Here, each solution is a row vector of size $m \times m$ which equals to the watermark size. After this, for each solution i of the GA population, the execution of the watermark embedding algorithm is expressed as:

$$S' = S + \delta * Sw \qquad (4)$$

where δ is the scaling factor.

4.2   Watermarking Extraction

Watermark extraction is denoted by inverse watermark w'. In this paper, for the application of GA optimization, this discussion clearly demonstrates that any objective function that is utilized for optimizing watermark embedding should consider both PSNR and the correlation (watermark). This objective function is subsequently used to optimize the PSNR. The result of the proposed technique for PSNR optimization and correlation is better than the approaches used without optimization techniques. In addition, our result of our approach is better than the state of the art approaches which they used optimization.

The procedure of extracting watermark by GA is as following:

1. Apply type's image processing attacks on the signed image I' one by one attacks. This generates T different types of attacked watermarked images for the signed image I'.
2. Extract the watermarks from the attacked watermarked image.
3. Compare the PSNR between the original image I and signed image I' and the correlation values for attacked image.
4. Calculate the objective value of GA by using objective function is given in

$$\text{Objective function} = PSNR + 100 * \text{correlation} \qquad (5)$$

where: the correlation comprises the normalized cross-correlation between the original watermark and extracted watermark from each attacked signed image.

5. Choose the individuals with the best fitness values.
6. Create new population through the crossover and mutation on the select individuals.
7. Repeat the operations until the stopping criteria, the maximum amount of iteration (MAX-it) is achieved.

5 Experimental Results and Discussion

This section is dedicated to the performance evaluation of the recommended water-marking scheme and comparison with state of the art algorithms. In this experiment, the host images with size 512 × 512, (gray scale image) and 50 × 20 grey scale image alongside the 'copyright' watermark for owner's signature are to be used. All the schemes take into account the same size of the host image and watermark images for the experimental analysis. The schemes are all coded in MATLAB and executed on a personal computer (intel Pentium (R) Core i5 CPU at 3.40 GHz with 4 gigabyte RAM), running on windows 10 operating system (64-bit) (Fig. 1).

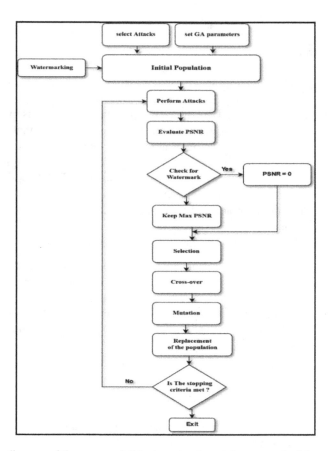

Fig. 1. Block diagram of the proposed GA steps, to attempt the removal of the watermark. The algorithm appears to be powerful against different types of attacks and proves the ownership image after attacks. In this paper, we improve the imperceptibility and robustness of watermark under the types of attacks by using SVD-GA, and by building the powerful system. For the imperceptibility, it is important that the visible watermarking and the embedded watermark are imperceptible. Generally, the watermark technique is said to be imperceptible, when the original and the water-marked image are mutually. As shown the literature, the imperceptible by way of objective process is performed by taking into account the quantitative index, peak signal to noise ratio (PSNR).

$$PSNR = 10 \cdot log_{10}\left(\frac{MAX^2}{MSE}\right) \tag{6}$$

where the Mean Square Error (MSE) represents the aggregate squared error amid the altered and the actual image. Meanwhile, PSNR represents the peak error measure while MAX denotes the highest pixel's value.

For the robustness watermark under types of attacks, normalized correlation (P), is employed in the similarity assessment between the original watermark (w) and the extracted watermark (w') as expressed below:

$$P(W, W') = \frac{\sum\limits_{i=1}^{N} W_i W_i'}{\sqrt{\sum\limits_{i=1}^{N} W_i^2 \sum\limits_{i=1}^{N} W_i'^2}} \tag{7}$$

where: ρ represents the introduced watermark w and abstracted watermark $\hat{w}$ in terms of correlation while N denotes the watermark image's measure. In addition, the probability of the detection of false watermark is expressed as:

$$P_{fp} = p\{NC(W, W') \geq T_p | no\, watermark\} \tag{8}$$

where: $p\{A \mid B\}$ denotes the probability of event A given that event B, Tp entails a threshold. Since $w(i)$ and $w'(i)$ are either 0 or 1, respectively, $w^2(i)$ and $w'^2(i)$ are either 0 or 1 (Table. 1).

Table 1. State of the art algorithms in comparison

#	Algorithm symbol	References	Description
1	DCT-GA	(Shieh et al. 2004) [9]	Discrete cosine transform with genetic algorithm to improve watermarked image quality
2	SVD-Tiny GA	(Chin Lai 2011) [11]	Singular value decomposition with tiny genetic algorithm to improve the visual quality of the watermarked image and the robustness of the watermark
3	LSB-GA	(Kanan and Nazeri 2014) [10]	Least significant bit with genetic algorithm to prpose a tunable visual image quality and data lossless method

We presented the discussion and comperisons between our algorithm and other previously published, we point out the superiority of our algorithm. The simulation result indicate that our watermarking is more robust and invisibility in the preoposed method.

In Fig. 2 show the embedding watermark imge inside the orginal image (Lena image) by using the SVD and GA. Our propose method was better then when compear with another technique from the litratuer review. In our proposed the ratio for the PSNR was **52.21** dB, and the correlation was **0.96** (Figs. 3, 4 and 5).

Original image	Watermark	Original image + watermark
![Original Lena image]	Copyright	![Lena image with watermark]
The (PSNR)=**52.218**		correlation = **0.968**

Fig. 2. Embedding watermark with original image using SVD-GA. In order to make a direct comparison of the proposed method against the above algorithm, (Kanan and Nazeri 2014) the author calculate the PSNR, the ratio for the PSNR (Lena image) was 45.12 dB. In 2011 by Chin Lai, the rate for the PSNR was 47.49 dB, and the correlation was 0.99. The (Shieh et al. 2004) proposed a GA based on discrete cosine transform (DCT), the PSNR was 34.79 dB, and the correlation was 0.74.

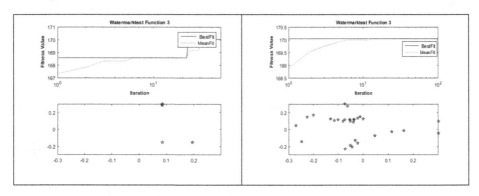

Fig. 3. Explain the evaluated performance of the optimization algorithm using Lena image 512 × 512 original image, testing and calculate the ratio of the best fitness. GA-based training procedure described, number of iteration was 100 and the population was 30 and the crossover was 0.7 and 0.1 for the mutation, where the ratio of another the population 30 and number of iteration 100, then the figure b was the population 10 and the number of iteration 50. In the end we choose the ratio of population 30 and the maximum iteration 100 when implementation the experiment under types of attack.

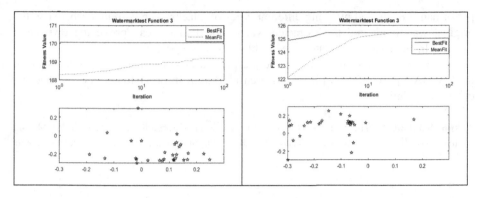

Fig. 4. After 0.2 for Gaussian noise attack, shown the value of best fitness after applying the Gaussian noise attack was 170. A Gaussian noise was added to the watermarked image. The result of the GA optimization indicates that the fitness function was maximum (170). This result was obtained at the 100th iteration and 30 population size of the GA optimization process. Also after 0.5 for Gaussian noise attack. A Gaussian noise was added to the watermarked image. The result of the GA optimization indicates that the fitness function was maximum (126). This result was obtained at the 100th iteration and 30 population size of the GA optimization process.

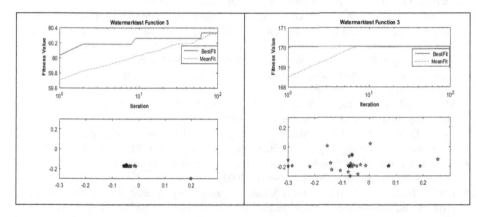

Fig. 5. Show the result of GA optimization process indicates that the fitness function was the maximum (60.4), after 60° of image rotation attack. The watermarked image was rotated with different angles. This result was obtained at the 100 iteration of GA optimization process and 30 of population size. The other side show the result of GA optimization process indicates that the fitness function was the maximum (170), after 90° of image rotation attack. The watermarked image was rotated with different angles. This result was obtained at the 100 iteration of GA optimization process and 30 of population size.

6 Conclusion

In this paper, we proposed GA for digital image watermarking scheme. The proposed GA used to optimize the performance of scaling factor in matrix form. The result obtained shows that the proposed GA got high robust watermarking image. The performance evaluated by using different types of attacks. The correlation between the original watermark and the extracted watermarked image can prove the ownership images. In addition, we treated the problem of false positive in SVD by using the proposed GA. For the future work, we are present to investigate the performance of modify GA by hybridize with local search algorithm in order to further improve the quality of solution.

Acknowledgement. The researchers wish to thank Universiti Kebangsaan Malaysia (UKM) and Ministry of Higher Education, Malaysia for their support on this work via research grants DIP-2016-018.

References

1. Cox, I.J., Kilian, J., Leighton, T., Shamoon, T.: A secure, robust watermark for multimedia. In: Anderson, R. (ed.) IH 1996. LNCS, vol. 1174, pp. 185–206. Springer, Heidelberg (1996). doi:10.1007/3-540-61996-8_41
2. Cox, I.J., Kilian, J., Leighton, F.T., Shamoon, T.: Secure spread spectrum watermarking for multimedia. IEEE Trans. Image Process. **6**(12), 1673–1687 (1997)
3. Guo, J., Zheng, P., Huang, J.: Secure watermarking scheme against watermark attacks in the encrypted domain. J. Vis. Commun. Image Represent. **30**, 125–135 (1997)
4. Emami, M.S., Omar, K.: A low-cost method for reliable ownership identification of medical images using SVM and Lagrange duality. Expert Syst. Appl. **40**(18), 7579–7587 (2013)
5. Run, R.-S., Horng, S.-J., Lai, J.-L., Kao, T.-W., Chen, R.-J.: An improved SVD-based watermarking technique for copyright protection. Expert Syst. Appl. **39**(1), 673–689 (2012)
6. Tian, J.: Reversible data embedding using a difference expansion. IEEE Trans. Circ. Syst. Video Technol. **13**(8), 890–896 (2003)
7. Mohammad, A.A., Alhaj, A., Shaltaf, S.: An improved SVD-based watermarking scheme for protecting rightful ownership. Sig. Process. **88**(9), 2158–2180 (2003)
8. Li, L., Qian, J., Pan, J.-S.: Characteristic region based watermark embedding with RST invariance and high capacity. AEU Int. J. Electron. Commun. **65**(5), 435–442 (2003)
9. Shih, F.Y., Wu, S.Y.: Combinational image watermarking in the spatial and frequency domains. Pattern Recogn. **36**(4), 969–975 (2003)
10. Kanan, H.R., Nazeri, B.: A novel image steganography scheme with high embedding capacity and tunable visual image quality based on a genetic algorithm. Expert Syst. Appl. **41**(14), 6123–6130 (2003)
11. Lai, C.C.: A digital watermarking scheme based on singular value decomposition and tiny genetic algorithm. Digit. Sig. Process. **21**(4), 522–527 (2011)
12. Atheer, B., Nordin, M.: Digital image watermark authentication using DWT-DCT. J. Eng. Appl. Sci. **11**, 3227–3232 (2016)
13. Hussein, E., Belal, M.A.: Digital watermarking techniques, applications and attacks applied to digital media: a survey. Int. J. Eng. Res. Technol. **1**, 1–8 (2012)
14. Mishra, A., Agarwal, C., Sharma, A., Bedi, P.: Optimized gray-scale image watermarking using DWT–SVD and Firefly algorithm. Expert Syst. Appl. **41**(17), 7858–7867 (2012)
15. Thabit, R., Khoo, B.E.: Robust reversible watermarking scheme using Slantlet transform matrix. J. Syst. Softw. **88**, 74–86 (2014)
16. Waleed, J., Jun, H.D., Abbas, T., Hameed, S., Hatem, H.: A survey of digital image watermarking optimization based on nature inspired algorithms NIAs. Int. J. Secur. Appl. **8**(6), 315–334 (2014)

17. Ali, M., Ahn, C.W., Pant, M., Siarry, P.: An image watermarking scheme in wavelet domain with optimized compensation of singular value decomposition via artificial bee colony. Inf. Sci. **301**, 44–60 (2015)
18. Ansari, I.A., Pant, M., Ahn, C.W.: Artificial bee colony optimized robust-reversible image watermarking. Multimed. Tools Appl. **76**(17), 18001–18025 (2017)
19. Jain, C., Arora, S., Panigrahi, P.K.: A reliable SVD based watermarking schem (2008). arXiv preprint arXiv:0808.0309
20. Surekha, P., Sumathi, S.: Application of GA and PSO to the analysis of digital image watermarking process. Int. J. Comput. Sci. Emerg. Technol. **1**, 350–362 (2010). (E-ISSN: 2044–6004)
21. Ni, Z., Shi, Y.Q., Ansari, N., Su, W.: Reversible data hiding. IEEE Trans. Circ. Syst. Video Technol. **16**(3), 354–362 (2006)
22. Moghaddasi, Z., Jalab, H.A., Noor, R.M.: A comparison study on SVD-based features in different transforms for image splicing detection. In: 2015 IEEE International Conference on Consumer Electronics-Taiwan (ICCE-TW), pp. 13–14. IEEE (June, 2015)

Methods of Evaluating the Usability of Human-Computer Interaction (HCI) Design in Mobile Devices for SAR Operation

Nur Syafikin Shaheera Mat Zaini,
Syed Nasir Alsagoff Syed Zakaria[✉], and Norshahriah Wahab[✉]

Department of Computer Science, Universiti Pertahanan Nasional Malaysia,
UPNM, 57000 Kuala Lumpur, Malaysia
n.syafikin.shaheera@gmail.com,
{syednasir,shahriah}@upnm.edu.my

Abstract. The evaluation process happens when the products need to be evaluated and tested to figure out whether the design meets the needs of user and usability goals established. In this paper, usability testing (real user tests) is conducted to implement the concept of human-computer interaction (HCI) using mobile devices by performing several tasks using an application developed which is HCI Test. HCI Test is a prototype of client-server system using Android mobile device as clients and Windows Tablet or laptop as a server to test the efficiency and effectiveness of command and control (C2) based on the accuracy of response and response time of the clients towards the server. The experiments were carried out using twenty-five (25) test participants supervised by the evaluator that controlled the server. The results obtained also been discussed in this paper.

Keywords: Human-computer interaction · Mobile devices · Usability testing

1 Introduction

In this day and age, people are exposed to human-computer interaction concept in line with the growth of mobile computing technology where people started to demand on their needs for applications used. In fact, mobile devices have shown a rapid development in computing technology world regarding processing power, memory capacity and battery life simultaneously with the new technology supplied such as improvement of the connectivity, external peripherals, GPS and location-based services and much more.

Igler et al. [1] have stated that the success or failure of application depends on how it will help to improve the user's task performance, ease of use and how it meets the user's requirements and satisfaction. A high level of usability is beneficial in terms of reducing development costs, increasing the level of user's satisfaction retention and reducing maintenance costs especially on user training [2].

In this paper, the experiment was carried out to determine the appropriate HCI parameter in an HCI interface consists of the background colour, font colour, font type and font style with similar font size for usage in the mobile application, based on the

© Springer International Publishing AG 2017
H. Badioze Zaman et al. (Eds.): IVIC 2017, LNCS 10645, pp. 714–726, 2017.
https://doi.org/10.1007/978-3-319-70010-6_66

speed and accuracy of response. This HCI interface is considered to provide an effective and efficient command and control (C2) process especially for SAR operation. Usability testing is selected to conduct the experiments in an open area, assigning the test participants as clients and the evaluator to control the server. The minimum brightness of mobile devices is set, and this experiment is conducted during the daylight, in particular, under direct sunlight.

2 Usability Evaluation Method

2.1 User-Centered Design (UCD) for the Mobile Approach

According to the [3], a user-centered design (UCD) explains the phases in the design and development lifecycle as well as focusing on obtaining an explicit understanding of users, tasks and environments. UCD involves several methods and tasks depending on the needs of developers which can help them to determine the tasks to perform and the arrangement in the way they perform it. Figure 1 shows the user-centered design (UCD) process for mobile application development.

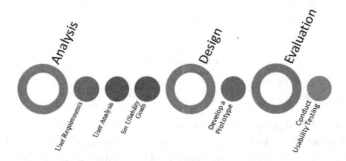

Fig. 1. User-centered design (UCD) process for the mobile approach (Adapted from Henry and Thorp (2006); U.S. Dept. of Health and Human Services (2006))

2.2 Analysis Phase

A field study is conducted during a field testing of an existing system called SAR-TAMS (Search and Rescue Tactical Management System) by directly observed the user participants' behaviours and their views are accounted for the further research. This system performing the concept of C4 which are command, control, coordination and communication involving a commander and few team members to perform a search and rescue operation that required a clear command and control process in the way they interact using mobile devices and their understanding towards the information displayed and further acted upon it. By collecting the user requirements, user demographics is provided as well as the usability goals for this experiment.

2.3   Design Phase

HCI Test is a client-server system using Android mobile device as clients and Windows Tablet or laptop as a server. The server provides the HCI parameters which are: (i) background colour, (ii) font colour, (iii) font type, (iv) font style and (v) font size. The server will send a bank of multiple-choice questions (MCQs) on the Android mobile device that needs to be answered by the test participants. Figure 2 shows the HCI Test layouts features. Figure 3 shows the two (2) different background colour, black and white. Each background colour consists of 144 questions in which all 288 questions need to be answered by the test participants.

HCI PARAMETERS (server controlled)	➤ Screen brightness ➤ Background colour ➤ Font colour ➤ Font type ➤ Font size ➤ Font style

MEASUREMENT TOOLS	➤ Timer at client (eliminates variable network delays)
	➤ Multiple choice (eliminates variable typing speed)
	➤ 3 types of similar logic question (eliminates variable question comprehension)
	➤ Practice questions (eliminates outliers)
	➤ Excel results with
	   ➤ Individual speed and accuracy
	   ➤ HCI set speed and accuracy
	   ➤ Overall speed and accuracy (eliminates outliers)

STRESS SIMULATION	➤ 10 seconds countdown timer with beeping sound
FEATURES	➤ HCI parameter change alert ➤ New question alert ➤ Battery monitor

Fig. 2. HCI test

2.4   Evaluation Phase

This experiment focusing on the user testing which involved one to one sessions with real users to perform the tasks. Usability testing is conducted based on the usability process design to implement the concept of HCI design using mobile devices by performing the tasks using HCI Test. This testing method used to test the speed and accuracy of responses by the test participants to show their understandings and reactions towards the commands given on their mobile HCI interface.

2.5   Usability Process Design

In this section, usability evaluation is a process that proposed by [4–6], to evaluate the activities based on the method used. This also can be referred as the test plan in conducting the user testing. It is important for the evaluator to be well-prepared by providing a test planning checklist in order to help them to track all the details. There are six main activities selected to conduct the usability testing in this research and can be referred to Fig. 4.

2.6   Select and Iterate Tasks

According to [5, 7, 8], there are three (3) criteria need to be emphasised during selecting tasks, which are:

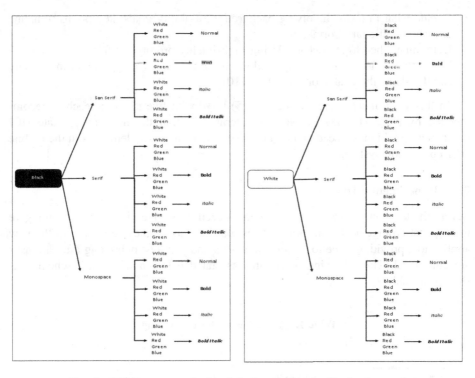

Fig. 3. HCI Parameters for black background and white background

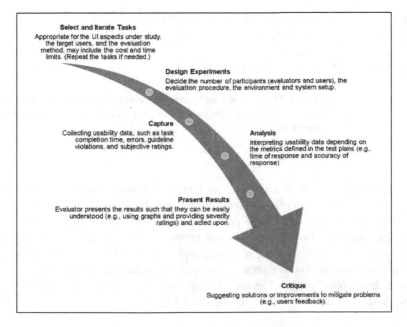

Fig. 4. Usability evaluation process [6]

- Decide what to test – Involving background, usability goals, key points, timeline and any additional information.
- Determine when to test what – Using high-fidelity prototype [9].
- Decide how many to test – May used not more than five (5) users and run as many small tests as the evaluator can afford [10].

In this experiment, there will be five (5) tasks with five (5) users each as recommended by [11]. The tasks need to be iterated to find the most appropriate HCI parameter with highest speed and accuracy so that it can be implemented in the mobile HCI application system.

2.7   Experimental Design

Before the test commences, a few procedures need to be taken in order to set up, give the pre-test arrangements and brief the test participants so they can adapt to the new application, providing time to perform the tasks and post-test debriefing after all tasks are completed. The following procedures as stated below and the task schedule as shown in Table 1.

Table 1. Task schedule for user testing

Application name	HCI Test
Hardware	1 × Surface Pro 3/Laptop 5 × Sony Xperia Z3 Compact
Time	11 pm–1 pm
Venue	Wide open area in the campus (UPNM)
Test participant	25 randomly selected male and female
Test session	6 sessions
Requirements	No cap for the male Dark coloured scarves for female Wipe the device screen each time before use to clear from the fingerprints Users may tilt the device but cannot cover the device screen using hands during testing Cannot wear glasses

The user is selected from university students which help to save costs and time to find and recruit the participants. In addition, test participants are the students of computer science course who have prior knowledge of mobile application development. As the students also is a cadet who underwent military training, they are exposed to knowledge about the process of command and control and even the establishment of discipline and commitment as a military cadet in which they tend to receive commands efficiently and professionally. The user demographics are shown in Table 2.

The process of the user testing as shown in Fig. 5.

Table 2. Characteristics and Number of Participants Required

Characteristic	Desired number of participants
Participant type	
Degree Student	25
Total number of participants	25
Age	
21–23	25
Gender	
Female	4
Male	21
Degree Course	
Computer Science	25
Year	
1	-
2	25
3	-

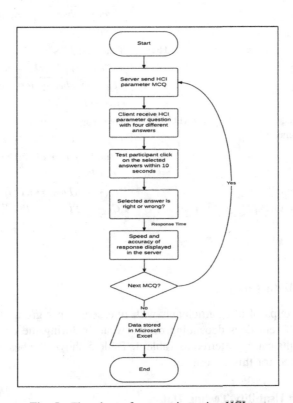

Fig. 5. Flowchart of user testing using HCI test

2.8   Capture Usability Data

Each HCI parameters consist of three (3) questions, and each of the questions needs to be answered by five (5) test participants. Once all the questions have been answered, the result will be calculated based on the three (3) questions of each of HCI parameter by five (5) test participants to find the mean. Mean is calculated for both of time to response (RT) and accuracy of response (PC) for each test participants. PC stands for the proportion of the correct responses [12]. The calculations are as follows in Table 3.

Table 3. Step of calculation to measure the accuracy and time to response

Step	Description	Calculation
1	Mean of time to response (RT) for HCI parameter/test participant	Total variables = 3 $$\frac{(RT_1 + RT_2 + RT_3)}{Total\ number\ of\ questions} = mean\ RT(s)$$
2	Mean of accuracy of response (PC) for HCI parameter/test participant	Total variables = 3 $$\frac{(PC_1 + PC_2 + PC_3)}{Total\ number\ of\ questions} = mean\ PC\ (\%)$$
3	Mean of time to response (RT) for HCI parameter	Total variables = 5 $$\frac{(RT_1 + RT_2 + RT_3 + RT_4 + RT_5)}{Total\ number\ of\ test\ participants} = mean\ RT(s)$$
4	Mean of accuracy of response (PC) for HCI parameter	Total variables = 5 $$\frac{(PC_1 + PC_2 + PC_3 + PC_4 + PC_5)}{Total\ number\ of\ test\ participants} = mean\ PC(\%)$$
5	Difference of RT	$RT_{HCl_1} - RT_{HCl_2} = RT(s)$
6	Difference of PC	$PC_{HCl_1} - PC_{HCl_2} = PC(\%)$

3   Results

3.1   Usability Data Analysis

There are five groups of test participants with five people per group. Each group has performed on different days depending on the weather during the daylight. The task sessions and results can be referred to Table 4. Table 5 shows the best ten (10) of HCI parameters selected for this experiment.

3.2   Presenting Usability Testing Data

(a) Task 1 vs. Task 2: Accuracy of Response vs. Time to Response vs. HCI Parameter.

Table 4. Task session of HCI test per group of five test participants

Group	Task session	HCI TEST	Accuracy of response (PC) (%)	Time to response (RT) (s)
1	1	HCI Parameters MCQs for black background colour	81.24	5.08
1	2	HCI Parameters MCQs for white background colour	86.40	5.26
2	3	Best ten (10) HCI parameters	100.00	3.34
3	4	Best ten (10) HCI parameters	86.68	6.66
4	5	Best ten (10) HCI parameters	93.34	3.28
S	6	Best ten (10) HCI parameters	100.00	4.86

Table 5. Best ten (10) of HCI parameters

Set	HCI parameter				
	Background colour	*Font colour*	*Font type*	*Font style*	*Font size*
1	Black	White	San Serif	Bold	14
2	Black	Green	San Serif	Bold	14
3	Black	White	San Serif	Italic	14
4	Black	Green	Serif	Normal	14
5	Black	White	Monospace	Bold	14
6	White	Black	Sans Serif	Italic	14
7	White	Black	Serif	Italic	14
8	White	Black	Serif	Bold Italic	14
9	White	Black	Monospace	Bold	14
10	White	Blue	Monospace	Bold	14

Based on the graph in Fig. 6, white background colour is 5.18% high accuracy of response than black background colour. However, white background colour is 1.8% slower than black background colour. According to [13, 14, 15], dark characters in a light background helps to reduce the focusing effort and improve the quality of a retinal image, which causes to less visual fatigue and better legibility.

(b) Task 3: Accuracy of Response vs. Time to Response vs. HCI Parameter.

Based on the graph in Fig. 7, set 1 until 10 used to represent the HCI parameter. Comparing for both background colour (can be referred in Table 5), set 9 is 13.32% more accurate than the Set 1. Set 9 is 3.32 s equal to 33.2% faster than set 1. Set 9 (**Background Colour: White; Font Colour: Black; Font Type: Monospace; Font Style: Bold; Font Size: 14**) is more accurate and faster which then selected as the best HCI parameter among all 10.

(c) Task 4: Accuracy of Response vs. Time to Response vs. HCI Parameter.

Based on the graph in Fig. 8, set 1 until 10 used to represent the HCI parameter. Comparing for both background colour (can be referred in Table 5),

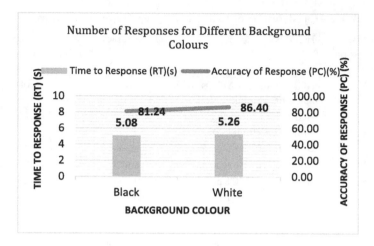

Fig. 6. Mean of responses for different background colours

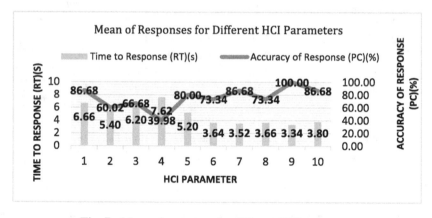

Fig. 7. Mean of responses for different HCI parameters

set 3 is 6.66% more accurate than set 8. Set 3 is 1.58 s equal to 15.8% faster than set 8. Set 3 (**Background Colour: Black; Font Colour: White; Font Type: Sans Serif; Font Style: Italic; Font Size: 14**) showed the most accurate response, but not the highest response speed among all 10.

(d) Task 5: Accuracy of Response vs. Time to Response vs. HCI Parameter.

Based on the graph Fig. 9, set 1 until 10 used to represent the HCI parameter. Comparing for both background colour (can be referred in Table 5), set 9 is 6.66% more accurate than set 1. Set 9 is 0.88 s equal to 8.80% faster than set 9. Set 9 (**Background Colour: White; Font Colour: Black; Font Type: Monospace; Font Style: Bold; Font Size: 14**) showed the most accurate with the highest speed of response which then selected as the best HCI parameter among all 10.

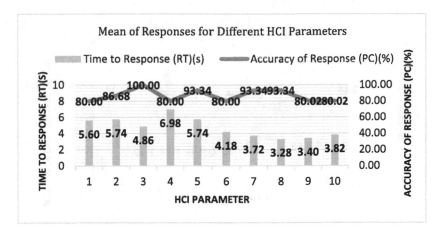

Fig. 8. Mean of responses for different HCI parameters

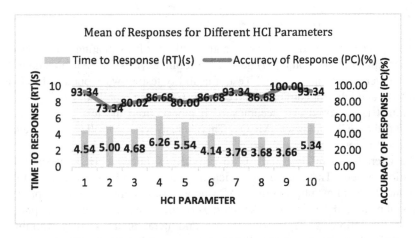

Fig. 9. Mean of responses for different HCI parameters

(e) Task 6: Accuracy of Response vs. Time to Response vs. HCI Parameter.

Based on the graph in Fig. 10, set 1 until 10 used to represent the HCI parameter. Comparing for both background colour (can be referred in Table 5), set 9 is 6.66% more accurate than set 1. Set 9 is 1.94 s equal to 19.4% faster than set 1. Set 9 **(Background Colour: White; Font Colour: Black; Font Type: Monospace; Font Style: Bold; Font Size: 14)** showed the most accurate with the highest speed of response which then selected as the best HCI parameter among all 10.

Based on all the results obtained, set 9 **(Background Colour: White; Font Colour: Black; Font Type: Monospace; Font Style: Bold; Font Size: 14)** is chosen as the best HCI parameter among all 10.

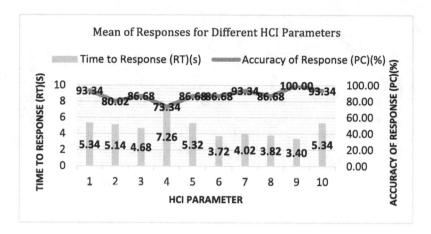

Fig. 10. Mean of responses for different HCI parameters

4 Discussion

The paper has proposed a system and method of evaluating the concept of human-computer interaction (HCI) design in mobile devices for SAR operation. Using a client-server system namely HCI Test, a usability testing was conducted to evaluate an effective and efficient command and control (C2) using mobile devices by analysing the parameters as speed and accuracy of response from the test participants while answering the HCI parameters MCQs. This system was controlled by the evaluator through a Windows server application.

The overall aim of this study is to provide an effective HCI interface for the application system. This ensures an efficient command and control among the team leader and the team members during SAR operations. Usability evaluation process is a successful method in helping to make findings of this research using the test plan which involved the following steps: (i) selecting and iterating tasks by performing user testing; (ii) design an experiment by choosing the suitable environment for system setup, (iii) recruiting participants and providing the testing procedures with time needed; (iv) capturing the usability data; (v) analyzing; (vi) presenting the results; and (vii) reviewing the user's behaviors and feedbacks.

Although **Background Colour: White; Font Colour: Black; Font Type: Monospace; Font Style: Bold; Font Size: 14** is the best HCI parameter obtained from the results, **Background Colour: Black; Font Colour: White; Font Type: Sans Serif; Font Style: Bold; Font Size: 14** is considering applied as an effective HCI interface display in mobile applications. The white background colour has a better legibility compared to the black background colour, black background colour also has its own advantages. Black background colour can provide a better night vision especially to be used while conducting SAR operation. Moreover, according to [15], black interface resulting in a less power consumption that helps to improve battery life.

HCI Test application has helped to evaluate the efficiency of command and control based on the results of speed and accuracy of response of the test participants which have showed the degree of understanding of the test participants while using the application and their rapid actions towards the commands given when answering the HCI Parameters questions controlled by the evaluator through a server.

5   Conclusion

In this paper, HCI Test is a client-server system developed for implementing HCI in mobile devices based on the current advancement of mobile technology. The process of command and control (C2) between team leaders and team members in SAR operation also emphasized based on the usability testing conducted.

Based on the results and findings obtained, this experiment is believed to provide the successful implementation of human-computer interaction (HCI) in mobile devices, especially for carrying out SAR operation. A further enhancement could take place for this useful mobile application so that it could be fully operational in future to provide more efficient and effective command, and control process for SAR operation as well can be used by other agencies that require the command and control processes in their mission.

References

1. Igler, B., Braumann, T., Böhm, S.: Evaluating the usability of mobile applications without affecting the user and the usage context. Int. J. Bus. Manag. Stud. **8047**, 92–102 (2013)
2. Bias, R.G., Mayhew, D.J.: Cost-justifying usability: an update for an Internet age. http://doi.org/ISBN-10:0120958112 (2005)
3. U.S. Dept. of Health and Human Services (ed.): The Research-Based Web Design & Usability Guidelines (Enlarged/E). U.S. Government Printing Office, Washington, DC (2006)
4. Nielsen, J.: Usability 101: introduction to usability why usability is important how to improve usability (2003)
5. Dix, A., Finlay, J., Abwod, G.D., Beale, R.: Human Computer Interaction (Third). Pearson Education Limited, London (2004). http://doi.org/10.1039/c1cc14592d
6. Shneiderman, B., Plaisant, C., Cohen, M., Jacobs, S.: Designing the User Interface: Strategies for Effective Human-Computer Interaction, 5th edn. Addison Wesley Longman, Boston (2010)
7. Shneiderman, B., Plaisant, C.: Designing the user interface: strategies for effective human-computer interaction. Br. Dent. J. **215** (2005). http://doi.org/10.1038/sj.bdj.2013.932
8. Craven, D.: Usability Testing Basics : An Overview (2016). http://webservices.itcs.umich.edu/drupal/wwwsig/sites/webservices.itcs.umich.edu.drupal.wwwsig/files/Usability-Testing-Basics.pdf
9. Ibragimova, E. High-fidelity prototyping: what, when, why and how? https://blog.prototypr.io/high-fidelity-prototyping-what-when-why-and-how-f5bbde6a7fd4. Accessed 30 Dec 2016
10. Nielsen, J.: How many test users in a usability study?. Nielsen Norman Group (2012). https://www.nngroup.com/articles/how-many-test-users/

11. Nielsen, J.: What Is usability? In: User Experience Re-Mastered, pp. 3–22. Elsevier (2010). http://doi.org/10.1016/B978-0-12-375114-0.00004-9
12. Bruyer, R., Brysbaert, M.: Combining speed and accuracy in cognitive psychology: is the inverse efficiency score (IES) a better dependent variable than the mean reaction time (RT) and the percentage of errors (PE). Psychol. Belg. **51**(1), 5–13 (2011). doi:10.5334/pb-51-1-5
13. Zuffi, S., Brambilla, C., Beretta, G., Scala, P.: Human computer interaction: legibility and contrast. In: Proceedings - 14th International Conference on Image Analysis and Processing, ICIAP 2007, pp. 241–246 (2007). http://doi.org/10.1109/ICIAP.2007.4362786
14. Buchner, A., Mayr, S., Brandt, M.: The advantage of positive text-background polarity is due to high display luminance. Ergonomics **52**(7), 882–886 (2009). doi:10.1080/00140130802641635
15. Piepenbrock, C., Mayr, S., Mund, I., Buchner, A.: Positive display polarity is advantageous for both younger and older adults. Ergonomics **56**(7), 1116–1124 (2003). doi:10.1080/00140139.2013.790485

Knowledge Driven Interface to Determine Degree of Exposure of Young Adult to Pedophile Online

Mat Razali Noor Afiza[✉], Nurjannatul Jannah Aqilah Md Saad,
Nor Asiakin Hasbullah, Norulzahrah Mohd Zainudin,
Suzaimah Ramli, Norshahriah Wahab, Mohd Nazri Ismail,
and Mohd Fahmi Mohamad Amran

National Defence University of Malaysia, Kuala Lumpur, Malaysia
noorafiza@upnm.edu.my

Abstract. In the era of Internet of Thing (IoT) which a lot of devices are connected to the internet, children are spending more hours online interacting in cyber space that increase exposure to cyber security including pedophile activity. Increase of time spend online could increase the potential of online sexual grooming behaviours of child molesters. Since that the behaviour are not easily identified prior to the abuse, this study gathers and collect information about child sexual abuse by pedophile and propose a comprehensive decision support system to educate children base on knowledge-driven method about online grooming by molesters. An interactive system is built to provide knowledge to children regarding child sexual abuse and pedophile in terms of definition and each characteristics of it. The main purpose of the system is compiling database about child sexual abuse and pedophiles in order to determine the level of child's exposure to pedophile in term of five attributes which is selection of victims, gaining access, grooming, trust and approach.

Keywords: Decision support system · Child sexual abuse · Pedophile · Online grooming

1 Introduction

World now are uproar with the rapid increase of child sexual abuse happened around the society. Not only that, pedophile issue also had been the main topic discussed not only in Malaysia in fact throughout the whole world. UNICEF classified child sexual abuse as any form of activity that involve child carried out without any consent on the victims by perpetrator. Child Act 2001 (Act 611) describe child sexual abuse act if child being obliged into any sexual activity (Syahirah et al. 2017).

Child abuse categorized into several types which is physical abuse, emotional abuse, sexual abuse and neglect (Hall and Martin 1981). From the statistic of child abuse cases by Ministry of Women, Family and Community Development of Malaysia, there are 3428 cases in 2011, 3831 in 2012 and 3841 cases that had been reported. This show a rapid increment in child abuse happened in Malaysia in three consecutive years

© Springer International Publishing AG 2017
H. Badioze Zaman et al. (Eds.): IVIC 2017, LNCS 10645, pp. 727–736, 2017.
https://doi.org/10.1007/978-3-319-70010-6_67

(Retrieved from Ministry of Women, Family and Community Development of Malaysia official site, 2014).

In Malaysia, the pedophile issue had been highlighted since the arrestment of Richard Huckle, a pedophile in Malaysia that had been sentenced 22 years of prison by one of the London's court for 71 charges on child sexual abuse that involve six months to twelve years of child (Retrieved from BBC News, 2016).

Pedophile are classified as an individual that have keen sexual interest into underage child. The general definition witnesses that the pedophiles word are commonly known as 'child molestation' or 'child sexual abuse'. The word pedophile are came from the Greek word which is 'pais' meaning child and 'philen' is meaning love. Hence, the real meaning of the word is 'love towards child' (Cooray and Apsara 2014). Pedophiles are divided into two category which is secondary pedophiles and primary pedophiles. Secondary pedophiles is based on the mental health and an individual behavior. While for primary pedophiles, there are two more categories which is invariant and pseudo neurotic. For invariant, usually a person who is and always involved with children or adolescent without feeling guilt or shame about his pedophiles activity. The pseudo neurotic pedophiles is an individual who is inclined towards heterosexual activities (Glasser 1990).

Pedophiles are often related to the process of online grooming as a method to engage with victims online (Abdul Rahim 2012). Usually, the predators will find victims through chat rooms on the Internet by masquerade as child who want to be friend with the victims. The predators may tried to attract attention from the victims to involve into a conversation and uses the online grooming method for sexual exploitations of the victims (Cooray and Apsara 2014). The online grooming is one of the phases that implemented by the predators in gaining sexual exploitation towards child.

Online grooming is a process where predators pretend to be a child on the Internet, attempt to engage with the victims through conversation made and to groom the victims for sexual exploitation purposes (Durber 2006). The grooming process is which predators gain attention, affection, interest and trust of child through kind of deeds and word (Conte et al. 1989). In this process, predators might present pornographic materials to the victims for desensitize purpose on sexualize content and normalized sexual contact (Durber 2006).

Therefore, there are a lot of preventive measurement withdrawn regarding to child sexual abuse. Education and exposure should be given to children earlier. Education is a kind form of communication between educator and children. Education can be handed out to children by educating them on how to surf the Internet safely, inform techniques and strategies that need to be done if they feel they have been involved in any sexual activity by perpetrators, telling them that even family members could be the abuser besides their friends (Wurtele and Kenny 2010). Parents also need to know about the online predator that could engaged with their children so that they can arms themselves with facts and strategy to help their child out. They could only talk with their child to tell what happened to them without making them feel scared or guilty (Elgersma 2017). This could be a problem as for a child that had been engaged in any sexual abuse, they might feel unsafe, low self-esteem, depressed, difficulty in talking about the abuse and eventually will result in reluctant of sexual abuse disclosure (Lovette 2004). But, the real things is that parents didn't know on what level does their child had been contacted or engaged by any online predators.

Thus, this study proposes a system that gather and collect information about the exposure of a child to a pedophiles through an interactive online questionnaire, which could help victims to disclose about the sexual engagement with online predator without need to talk to an adult. The main purpose of this system is to determine the level of exposure of child towards pedophiles and indirectly indicated that they are actually abused by the online predator according to the result printed. This proposed system is developed by using the concept of Decision Support System through the Knowledge Driven method. Target group of the user is child that age range from nine to fifteen years old that have any problem about sexual abuse.

2   Child Sexual Abuse

According to the common law of the Black's Law Dictionary, child is an individual who is below fourteen. In Osborn's Concise Law Dictionary, Roger Bird refer child to Children and Young Person Act 1993, section 107 as a person which is below the age of fourteen, while according to Children's Act 1975, section 107(1) young adult defined as an individual which is below the age of eighteen (Abas 2013).

Child sexual abuse is predefined as exposure of sexual stimulation towards children which is inappropriate to the child's age (Luther and James 1980). There are two types of child sexual abuse. The first type of child sexual abuse is familial where the abuser is from the victim's family member which is considered as incest and the other one is abuser are non-familial which could be the child's babysitter and parent's friends (Jones 2015).

Child sexual abuse are classified into three categories which is forced sexual attack, second, any sexual contact that concern around chest and sexual area, sodomy, exposing any sexual picture or videos that constituent to pornography or fondling genitals. The third category is sexual contact that logically prohibited due to the age of the child or because of the family relationship of the abuser to the child (Jones 1982).

The significant of pedophiles and child sexual abuse is both involving sexual exploitation (Nuetze et al. 2011). Child sexual abuse also happening in the online world where sexual exploitation were done through the usage of social media by the predators (Subrahmanyam et al. 2006). Online grooming is a process where predators pretend to be a child on the Internet, attempt to engage with the victims through conversation made and to groom the victims for sexual exploitation purposes (Durber 2006). The grooming process is which predators gain attention, affection, interest and trust of child through kind of deeds and word (Conte et al. 1989). In this process, predators might present pornographic materials to the victims for desensitize purpose on sexualize content and normalized sexual contact (Dombrowski et al. 2004).

Based on the research that was conducted by the EU Kids Online in 25 different EU state showed that the usage of Internet of child between 9–15 is very dominate in their life. The average of time that child spend on going online is about 88 min per day, 34% of the child added stranger into their friend list and about 54% of child had shared their personal information to people they have never met. Plus, about 14% of child had sent stranger picture or videos of themselves (Peersman et al. 2012). According to the CyberSAFE survey, about 90% of schooled child in Malaysia use Internet and 83% are susceptible to the danger of Internet such as the sexual exploitation (Thye 2016).

Mostly victims of sexual abuse become afraid and reluctant to disclosure about the abuse to elderly (Herman 1981). This is because, the child might feel untrusted if he or she report the truth situation in fact the victims might be accused for being the reason for the problem to occur in the first place. Other than that, the victims might feel terrified if the disclosure made will be the catalyst to the breakup of the it's own family institution (deFrancis 1969). Despite there are increasing number of sexual abuse case happened but just a few that had been reported (Kamaruddin 1996). This is due to the society sensitivity towards the case plus to protect the family's name if the abuser are the family members in which become the main inducer why such cases are not reported and need to be concealed (Shah 2005). Hence, to keep quiet is the best step for victims rather than to disclosure and the abuser will take advantage on the situation to sexual exploitation on the victims for a longer time (Lovette 2004).

Based on research through the The Norvold Abuse Questionnaire (NorAQ), level of sexual abuse of victims are divided into three which is mild, moderate and severe. For mild level, the sexual abuse happened through the sexual contact not included genitals area are performed by perpetrator toward victims by force. Perpetrator also may showed any pornographic materials towards the victims. For moderate, the sexual abuse take place as perpetrator performed sexual contact around body area including the genitals area towards the victim also by forced. Severe sexual abuse is declare if the any sexual contact that involve any kind of penetration into part of the victims body. Apart from that, the NorAQ questionnaire also state the relationship between emotional disturbance of the victim with the sexual abuse experienced by the victim. Below are the guideline of the NorAQ questionnaire (Swahnberg and Wajima 2003) (Fig. 1).

Sexual abuse	
Mild abuse, no genital contact	Has anybody *against your will* touched parts of your body other than the genitals in a 'sexual way' or forced you to touch other parts of his or her body in a 'sexual way'?
Mild abuse, emotional/ sexual humiliation	Have you in any other way been sexually humiliated; e.g. by being forced to watch a porno movie or similar *against your will*, forced to participate in a porno movie or similar, forced to show your body naked or forced to watch when somebody else showed his/her body naked?
Moderate abuse, genital contact	Has anybody *against your will* touched your genitals, used your body to satisfy him/herself sexually or forced you to touch anybody else's genitals?
Severe abuse, penetration	Has anybody *against your will* put his penis into your vagina, mouth or rectum or tried any of this; put in or tried to put an object or other part of the body into your vagina, mouth or rectum?

Fig. 1 Guideline of NorAQ questionnaire

3 Pedophile

The World Health Organization stated that pedophile are classified as an individual that have keen sexual interest towards child. The pedophilic term that have been used was describe on any sexual behavior which involved young adult that may or may not involve any sexual contact (Moen 2015).

Pedophiles are often related to the process of online grooming as a method to engage with victims online (Sandy et al. 2010). Usually, the predators will find victims through chat rooms on the Internet by masquerade as child who want to be friend with the victims. The predators may tried to attract attention from the victims to involve into a conversation and uses the online grooming method for sexual exploitations of the victims (Durber 2006). The online grooming is one of the phases that implemented by the predators in gaining sexual exploitation towards child.

The general definition witnesses that the pedophiles word are commonly known as 'child molestation' or 'child sexual abuse'. The word pedophile are came from the Greek word which is 'pais' meaning child and 'philen' is meaning love. Hence, the real meaning of the word is 'love towards child' (Cooray and Apsara 2014). Pedophiles are divided into two category which is secondary pedophiles and primary pedophiles. Secondary pedophiles is based on the mental health and an individual behavior. While for primary pedophiles, there are two more categories which is invariant and pseudo neurotic. For invariant, usually a person who is and always involved with children or adolescent without feeling guilt or shame about his pedophiles activity. The pseudo neurotic pedophiles is an individual who is inclined towards heterosexual activities (Glasser 1990).

Pedophiles used certain child sexual picture to lure other child to involve in the exploitation activity based on the instruction given by the predators. These pictures also used for a lifelong silence of the victims about the exploitations made (Ryan 2007). Collectors of child pornography are divided into two. Secure collectors and non-secure collectors. Secure collectors use security barriers such as encryption and password to access any child pornography. There are also required any person to submit required amount of child pornography in order to join the collectors community. As for non-secure collectors, they are contradicting with the secure collectors. They just access and download any child pornography item available on the Internet without any security barrier requirement (Krone 2004).

Basis on the Olson and Leatherman Models, there are five phases in online sexual predation which is gaining access, deceptive trust development, grooming, approach and isolation (McGhee et al. 2011). For the first phase of gaining access, the predators and the victims may exchange personal traits about each other. This process usually happened on the social media such as Facebook and Twitter. For instance, predators may pretend as child while communicating with victims (Winters and Jeglic 2016).

Deceptive trust development of predators towards victims by befriend with the victims, learning personal traits, show interests, giving gifts and sharing secret. This process is to give impression to the victims that they are having and exclusive relationship. The perpetrator portray himself as non-threaten person towards victims (Winters and Jeglic 2016). As for grooming process, it is a manipulation skill of victims and community so that sexual exploitation can be made without being detected. At this phase, the predators may use foul sexual language to the victims. Such as the predator could spelled "welcome" as "welcum" (McGhee et al. 2011). The approach phase is when the predators suggests that he and the victims should meet on the outside together. This meet is for sexual purpose of the predators (Winters and Jeglic 2016). Isolation take place as the predators isolate the victims by making the victims chats without any supervision (van Dam 2001).

Through this model, researcher had list out certain keywords that match with the characteristic of the phases stated. As for gaining access, topic as personal traits, which include age, address and relationships detail. For grooming, foul sexual language such as cum, penis, bra and sex are fall under this phases. Keywords for approach phases are included near, asking out, meet, and other that reflect the act of luring victims to meet the predators. For isolation, we might use the keyword alone, no parents, and other isolation adjectives.

4 Knowledge Driven

Knowledge Driven (KD) is one of the component is Decision Support System (Power 2000). KD is a computer based reasoning system which provide with information, understanding and suggestion to user (Power 1996).

KD contain an IF-ELSE rule which could help user to make a systematic choices based on the situation given. The example of the IF-ELSE rule are as below.

```
IF (Rule 1) {
Rule 1 is true;
} ELSEIF (Rule 2) {
Rule 2 is true;
} ELSE {
Rule 1 and Rule 2 are not true;
}
```

5 Method of Research

As said in the literature review, the Olson and Leatherman Models stated that there are five stage of online predation (McGhee et al. 2011). Online predation focused on using Internet to lure child for any sexual abuse and assault (Wolak et al. 2008). Based on the *Learning to Identify Internet Sexual Predation Journal* (McGhee et al. 2011), they used a software system, which is the ChatCoder in order to evaluate and categorize all five stages used by online sexual predators to expose any sexual assault or abuse through the Internet. ChatCoder is design by them to detect any word or lines online that contain any luring or exposing sexual of predators towards victims and categorized according to the Olson and Leatherman Models.

Thus form this idea, word that related to the five phases stated in literatures such as online grooming were used as questions in quizzes as a tool to determine level of exposure of child to pedophiles. The quizzes contain 25 questions for respondent to answer. In this study, system was developed by applying the KD rule method. This is to determine required result based on the specific rule assigned. The quiz score calculation is based on the NorAQ questionnaire on levelling the sexual abuse stage. The level of exposure towards pedophiles are determined through the overall percentage score of the total value of each categories which is selection of victims, gaining access, grooming, trust and approach that had been set on each selected question. The quizzes are consist of 25 question which is 5 question for each categories. Selection of answer of the quiz are based on the Likert method where each answer had 1–5 points assigned specifically (Cummins and Gullone 2000). The method to get the overall percentage score of the level of exposure to pedophiles is to calculate the individual value of each categories first. Below is the example of calculating individual value of categories, Selection of Victims (Fig. 2).

Question on Selection of Victims

    1.   Have you experienced any domestic violence in your family?

    2.   Is the perpetrator are someone from your family member?

    3.   Has anyone touch your chest purposely other than your parents?

    4.   Have you ever been neglected emotionally and physically in your family?

    5.   Do you have families with drugs, alcohol and gambling?

Selection of answer for all question:
1 = Never Experienced
2 = Mild Experienced
3 = Moderate Experienced
4 = Experienced
5 = Severe Experienced

Fig. 2 Example of question on Selection of Victims category

From the selection of answer chosen in Table 1, each answer points will be calculated using formula to determine the percentage of each categories. Below are the formula:

$$\%\textit{Selection of Victims} = \left[\frac{\sum_{i=1}^{5} X_a}{25}\right] \times 100$$

X_a = the points of answer that choose by user

$$\%\textit{Selection of Victims} = \left[\frac{a+b+c+d+e}{25}\right] \times 100$$

Table 1. Example of answered quiz

Questions	Answer
Have you experienced any domestic violence in your family	Severe Experienced = 5 point
Is the perpetrator are someone from your family member?	Mild Experienced = 2 point
Has anyone touch your chest purposely other than your parents?	Moderate Experienced = 3 point
Have you ever been neglected emotionally and physically in your family?	Severe Experienced = 5 point
Do you have families with drugs, alcohol and gambling?	Experienced = 4 point

Basically, the answer points are sum up as $5 + 2 + 3 + 5 + 4$ which hold the value of 19. After that, 19 will be divided by 25, which is the total value of all 5 answer's points. It will give the value of 0.76. After the value point of the answer were calculated, then to determine the percentage of possibility of being selected as a victim is determine which is by having the previous value multiply with 100 to get the percentage score of Selection of Victims category. Hence, here it shows that the child is having 76% of possibility to be selected as a target by the pedophiles.

For other categories which is gaining access, trust, grooming and approach, the same calculation will be made. After that, all the result of each categories will be represented into a graph for a better understanding. Next, all the categories result will be used to find the level of exposure to pedophiles. Below are the coding of the calculation to determine the level of exposure to pedophiles:

```
$ LevelOfAbuse = ($totalSelectionOfVictims + $TotalGainingAccess
                 + $TotalGrooming + $TotalTrust + $TotalApproach /
                 500) * 100

If ($LevelOfAbuse < 50) {print "Possibly Abused"}
If ($LevelOfAbuse > 50 && $LevelOfAbuse < 70) {print "Moderate
    Abused"}
If ($LevelOfAbuse > 70) {print "Severe Abused"}
```

The coding basically is to sum up all the individual value of each categories and to divide by 500 which is the total value of answer's point and then to be multiplied by 100 in order to get the percentage value. After that, the overall percentage score will determine the level of exposure to pedophiles. Question of each categories are retrieved based on the *Learning to Identify Internet Sexual Predation Journal* (McGhee et al. 2011) and *Stages of Sexual Grooming: Recognizing Potentially Predatory Behaviors of Child Molestors* (Winters and Jeglic 2016).

6   Conclusion

Lack of knowledge in sexual exploitation among youngster ignite the increasing number of child sex assault. Hence, this paper proposed knowledge driven based method in determining the level of exposure of young adult towards pedophile in virtual world. By using the quizzes by implementing the Likert method, the level of exposure is clustered into five categories which is selection of victims, gaining access, trust, grooming and approach. The result will be displayed in graph representing each categories individual value which could help people to understand it better at how much does a child were exposed to pedophiles.

References

Abas, A.: Child abuse in malaysia: legal measure for the prevention of the crime and protection of the victim. Int. J. Soc. Sci. Humanit. Stud. **4**, 1–10 (2013)

Abdul Rahim, A.: Jenayah Kanak-kanak dan Undang-undang Malaysia (2012)

Lovette, B.B.: Child sexual abuse disclosure: maternal response and other variables impacting the victim. Child Adolesc. Soc. Work J. **21**(4), 355–369 (2004)

van Dam, C.: Haworth Maltreatment and Trauma Press, Binghamton, New York (2001)

Elgersma, C.: What every parents need to know about online predators. New Straits Times, 3 September (2017). Accessed 3 Sept 2017

Peersman, C., Vaassen, F., Van Asch, V., Daelemans, W.: Conversation level constraints on pedophile detection in chat rooms. In: Notebook for PAN at CLEF 2012 (2012)

Cummins, R.A., Gullone, E.: Why we should not use 5-point Likert scales: the case for subjective quality of life measurement. In: Proceedings, Second International Conference on Quality of Life in Cities, pp. 74–93 (2000)

Power, D.: Decision support system (2000). http://www.mbaofficial.com/mba-courses/information-technology/what-are-group-decision-support-systems-what-are-its-components-and-features/

Power, D.J.: Web based model-driven decision support systems: concepts and issues. In: AMCIS 2000 Proceedings, vol. 387 (2000). http://aisle.aisnet.org/amcis2000/387

Durber, D.: Have You Checked the Children? Cyber Predator Laws and Very Strange Dangers (2006)

Bernard, F.: An enquiry among a group of pedophiles. J. Sex Res. **11**(3), 242–255 (1975)

Winters, G.M., Jeglic, E.L.: Stages of sexual grooming: recognizing potentially predatory behaviors of child molesters. Deviant Behav. J. **38**(6), 724–733 (2016)

Glasser, M.: Paedophilia. In: Principles and Practice of Forensic Psychiatry. Churchill Livingstone, Edinburgh (1990)

Boone, H.N., Boone, D.A.: Analyzing likert data. J. Ext. **50**(2), 1–5 (2012)

Swahnberg, I.M., Wijma, N.: The norvold abuse questionnaire (NorAQ). Eur. J. Publ. Health **13**(4), 361–366 (2003)

McGhee, I., Beyzick, J., Kontostathis, A., et al.: Learning to identify internet sexual predation. Int. J. Electron. Commer. **3**(3), 103–122 (2011)

Neutze, J., Seto, M.C., Schaeter, G.A., Mundt, I.A., Beier, K.M.: Predictors of child pornography offenses and child sexual abuse in a community sample of pedophiles and hebephiles. Sex. Abuse-J. Res. Treat. **23**(2), 212–242 (2011)

Wolak, J., Finkelhor, D., Mitchell, K.J.: Online "Predators" and their victims. Am. Psychol. **63** (2), 111–128 (2008)

Jones, J.G.: Sexual abuse of children: current concepts. Am. J. Dis. Child. **136**, 142–146 (1982)

Conte, J.R., Wolf, S., Smith, T.: What sexual offenders tells us about prevention strategies. Child Sex. Abuse Neglect **13**, 293–301 (1989)

Subrahmanyam, K., Smahel, D., Greenfield, P.: Connecting development constructions to the internet: identity presentation and sexual exploration in online teen chat rooms. Dev. Psychol. **42**(3), 395–406 (2006)

Freund, K., Watson, R., Dicky, R.: Does sexual abuse in childhood cause pedophilia: an exploratory study. Arch. Sex. Behav. **19**(6), 557–567 (1990)

Stermac, L.E., Segal, Z.V.: Adult sexual contact with children: an examination of cognitive factors. Behav. Ther. **20**, 573–584 (1989)

Thye, L.L.: Malaysia Must Enact Anti-grooming Law. New Straits Time, 17 June (2016). Accessed 20 Apr 2017

Cooray, E., Apsara, M.: Child pornography on the internet and the elusive world of pedophiles. Malay. Law J. Artic. **4**, 1–8 (2014)

Wurtele, S.K., Kenny, M.C.: Preventing online sexual victimization of youth. J. Behav. Anal. Offender Vict. Treat. Prev. **2**(1), 63–73 (2010)

Dombrowski, S.D., LeMasney, J.W., Ahia, C.E., Dickson, S.A.: Protecting children from online sexual predators: technologies, psychoeducational and legal considerations. Prof. Psychol.: Res. Pract. **35**(1), 65–73 (2004)

Krone, T.: A typology of online child pornography offendings. Trends Issues Crime Crim. Justice (279), 261–280 (2004)

Smart-Learning Networked Controllers for Centralized Air-Conditioning Systems Using Model-View-Controller Model

Tran Trong Tin[✉] ⓘ, Chen Zhi Yuan, and K.R. Selvaraj

University of Nottingham Malaysia Campus,
43500 Semenyih, Selangor, Malaysia
{Khcy5ttt,Zhiyuan.Chen,Kr.selvaraj}@nottingham.edu.my

Abstract. This paper presents a smart system iBeam which is a smart learning and networked air conditioning system designing by using a Model – View – Controller (MVC) model. This is a learning and networked Internet of Thing (IoT) system that can predict the thermal comfort of the occupants and regulate the air-conditioning temperature using Machine Learning algorithm in order to give an ideal thermal comfort and indoor air quality with the most minimal vitality cost. This system consists of an Android app to collect user's input, a server to run Machine Learning algorithm and to associate with a database that stores values from sensors such as temperature or humidity level. The app and the server communicate to each other through a Representational State Transfer web-service.

Keywords: Machine learning · M5P algorithm · Internet-of-things system · Heating Venting and Air-Conditioning (HVAC) · Smart-Learning system and model-view-controller

1 Introduction

The use and cost of energy affects each of us every day in our lives. Many issues arise from the use of energy such as in gas emissions, climate change, and dependency on deleting supplies of fossil fuels, which is the main resource to generate electricity and it is limited. Buildings in Malaysia consume more than industry and transport combined, in which cooling system accounts for 65%, triples as much as lighting. With the threat of global warming and increasing energy cost, keeping the room cool with less energy will become increasingly important in the future.

The purpose of this work is to develop a smart learning Internet of Things (IoT) system combined with machine learning algorithms to provide a solution that results in high energy efficiency, increased thermal comfort, and better indoor air quality. On the whole, the system is designed with a model-view-controller (MVC) software architectural pattern which contains 3 layers: an iBeam Network (iBN) – Model component, an iBeam Controller (iBK) – Controller component, and a mobile application – View component. iBN is an intelligent hub, unwired (or wired) systems which connects to iBK by means of a commander architecture and also acts as a database that accumulates data of five features: indoor and outdoor temperature, indoor and outdoor humidity, and preferable temperature from human. The View layer is represented by an Android mobile application called SpaceBeam. Through Graphic User Interfaces (GUI), users can suggest their desired temperature for the room, or examine data such as results of machine learning algorithms or current temperature. In terms of the controller, it is an implemented embedded server that would execute the learning algorithms to predict dew point temperature. The dataset for such execution is extracted from the database of the iBN.

This work has been explained in 6 sections. The introduction is covered in Sect. 1. Section 2 presents a brief review of literature as regards to related works, and machine learning overall. Section 3 illustrates the details of system design towards the achievement of this project aim and goals. The results of the implementation will be showed in Sect. 4. Section 5 draws the conclusion of this work.

2 Literature Review

Heating, ventilation, and air conditioning (HVAC) system is a well-known system that is being installed in a vast variety of buildings to provide high thermal comfort within the building. Compared with conventional air-conditioner concept (Variable-Air-Volume system), this HVAC system uses chilled beams which are chilled water pipes in modular units mounted to ceilings [1]. Basically, there are 2 types of chilled beam available and most commonly used by industry; typical examples are Dadanco Active Chilled Beam [2] from Australia and Semco Passive Chilled Beam [3] from Columbia. Chilled beam system uses water with a high specific heat capacity to absorb a large amount of heat. Water is considered to be the best transfer medium, which can remove the heat energy from the occupied space as the water is circulated to absorb it. This results in that humidity of the indoor air is controllable. No maintenance requirements and quietness are emblematic advantages of chilled beam. Furthermore, with the minimization of fan usage, consumed energy is remarkably reduced up to 30% [4]. In iBeam system, it makes a breakthrough by combining with data mining algorithm that learns and improves ability to provide appropriate thermal control and increase thermal comfort. Also, it totally removes the issue of condensation from active and passive chilled beam systems.

There are a number of researches have been done on HVAC systems. K.F. Fong [5] suggests that there have been several methods or different kind of optimization that have been developed in today's world. Based on their study, they were using the simulation-optimization approach to planning the perfect reset scheme for their system where the results of the first simulation will be used for evaluation and prediction for the next simulation. They implement predictive methods of the evolutionary algorithm using evolutionary programming that will find the accurate points of chilled water supply and supply air temperature to be reset for improved efficiency of the system. The result of their study, they found that with optimization of both chilled water supply and supply air temperature had a positive impact on energy saving, even better if the minimization is on a monthly basis where it could reach almost 7% of energy saving.

However, this works best only for HVAC that has constant speed chilled pumps, differential pressure bypass, and fixed speed supply air fans.

As electronic technologies are converging, the field of home automation is expanding. In terms of an Android application to control appliances, various smart systems have been proposed where the control is via Bluetooth [6–8], internet [9, 10], short message service (SMS) based [14], etc. Bluetooth capabilities are good and most of current laptop/notebook, tablets and cell phones have built-in adaptor that will indirectly reduce the cost of the system. However it limits the control to within the Bluetooth range of the environment while most other systems are not too feasible to be implemented as an intelligent system that can learn and train itself is needed. There are some other works also use Wi-Fi based controlled systems such as [15–17] which consists of a dedicated web server, a database and a web page for interconnecting and managing devices. They have remote control of air-conditioning system but lack of a smart algorithm to provide the best thermal comfort.

Therefore, in this research work a smart-learning system has been proposed with a view to provide a better system with a number of benefits. With the use of chilled beam, less energy is consumed and the temperature as well as humidity is controllable conveniently. The agreement of temperature in the room is made with the help of a smart-learning algorithm based on current indoor and outdoor temperature and humidity. Thereby, thermal comfort of human is significantly increased. An Android app is the mean for interaction between human and this system with friendly design and high security.

3 System Design

3.1 User Requirement

A requirement is a statement about an intended product that specifies what it should do or how to do it. For requirements to be effectively implemented and measured, they must be specific, unambiguous and clear. A good set of user requirements are needed for any project results in a reduction in time to process the software, which lead to a reduction in costs, or being able to better use the unique knowledge base belonging to a business. There are 3 different types of requirements which are listed by increasing detail level:

- Business requirements reflect sponsor points of view, scope of the project, or business objectives.
- User requirements show the user points of view, inputs and outputs, or goals.
- System requirements indicate functional (what the system does) and non-functional (how well the system does it) requirements.

In the proposed design, there are 7 features for the SpaceBeam application required by the client which could be treated as user requirements. They describe the business needs for what users require from the system. Those include authentication with login and logout function, tracking data such as outdoor temperature, statistics of learning algorithm, or history of adjusted temperature for a specific period of time. The user can also put forward a temperature at which they feel comfy the most to the system, or automatically sign in the system within a session.

3.2 System Architecture

Within the scope of this project, the system includes both client side (mobile application) and server side using Jetty and Jersey with regression supervised learning algorithm – M5P. Both sides communicate to each other through a Hyper Text Transfer Protocol (HTTP) method, named Application Programming Interface of Representational State Transfer (RESTful API).

An overview of the proposed system architecture is shown in Fig. 1. The system consists of an Android mobile app and a PC based for server side. The server is the controller performs essential actions such as retrieving data from the iBN, operating machine learning algorithms, getting and returning data to the Android app. The controller communicates with the app via the internet through specific MAC address of the server. Any internet connection through Wi-Fi or 3G/4G network can be used on the user device.

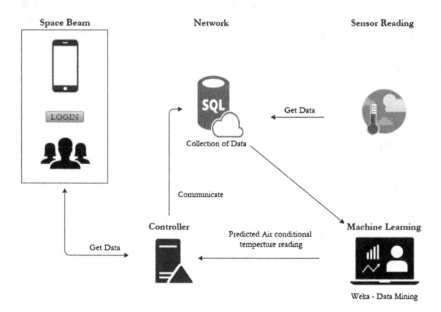

Fig. 1. Workflow of the proposed iBeam system

3.3 Software Development of the Android App

Android platform is chosen for the mobile app among Windows Phone, Symbian, or iOS as it is the most popular operating system for mobile nowadays. The app is built with the support of several tools:

- Software Development Kits (SDKs) which includes Application Programming Interface 21.0 (API 21.0 – the newest version of Android).
- Android Virtual Device manager (AVD) is used to manage and configure emulator instances.
- Android Debug Bridge (ADB) for connecting other tools with the emulator and devices.
- Android Emulator, which is an important tool to test on the appropriate target devices. This can also be used in conjunction with AVDs to simulate target devices.

An Integrated Development Environment (IDE) is indispensable for programming. Android Studio with IntelliJ built has been used. Together with Java programming language, it is more productive than other IDEs and offers outstanding framework-specific coding assistance and productivity-boosting features for Java EE, spring, GWT and other frameworks, along with deployment tools for most application servers. The screenshot of SpaceBeam app is shown in Fig. 2.

The designed app for the smart home system provides the following functionalities to the user:

- Remote connection to Jetty server via the Internet.
- User authentication.
- View the current outdoor temperature.
- View information of user account.
- Suggest the preferable temperature to system.
- View Machine Learning results.
- Check the history of adjusted temperature of the previous hour.

In order to use main features of the app, the user has to enter correct specific username and password. (Figure 2.a). If the Jetty server grants access to the app, a response packet containing HTTP status response code 200 will be received. Response 200 indicates the password is correct, and the app will send request for suitable iBK according to the information of user account. Automatic login will be enabled and the system will recognize the MAC address of the phone for future reference. If the user enters wrong password, the response code will be 404. After getting the information of iBK followed by room number (Fig. 2.b), the user confirm by pressing "Continue" button to switch to main control page.

There are 5 sections in the main control page. Each of them is presented by a tab. The meter in Fig. 2.c is showing the current temperature reading of the air – conditioner. For example, 21 °C is the current temperature of the air-conditioner. The refresh button can be used to manually update the current temperature. The user can slide the slider left or right to adjust their preferred temperature and then submit it to the server. Such value is sent through HTTP Post method to the server where regression process is executed right afterwards. The interface in Outdoor tab demonstrates the current outdoor temperature based on the user's specific location. The weather information is pulled down from OpenWeather API and is refreshed every time the user launches this application. Data is fetched via the link http://api.openweathermap.org/data/2.5/weather?q=%s&units=metric with specific requested x-api-key. 200 response code will be received from StringBuffer if there is no problem encountered, otherwise it

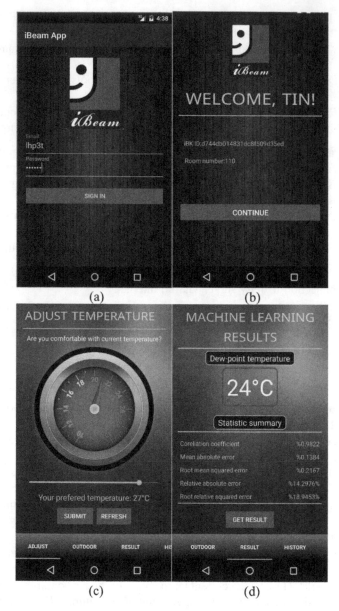

Fig. 2. Screenshots of the SpaceBeam app

would be 404. The humidity and pressure are also displayed with the icon of weather of the day. There is one page for retrieving data from the server of the learning progress with a "Get Result" button. The suggested temperature is displayed along with some brief statistics of regression process of Machine Learning. For tracking adjustment, the user can review history of previous hour of adjusted temperature reading and the time of other users by clicking on the "Reload" button in the page named "History". Finally, user can check their profile information in the last section shown in another interface.

Additionally for authentication system, SharedPreference feature on Android is taken into account to fulfill automatic login requirement. SharedPreference allows us to store private primitive application data in the form of key-value pair. Thereby, it is unnecessary to retype username and password each time within a session period. Other than that, the number of transaction made between the app and the server side needs minimized for speed optimization. There is a 30-min session for each user so that inactive users will be taken out of the system. Lastly, the password is one-way encrypted using md5-encryption for data security.

3.4 Software Development of the Jetty Server

The main controller hosting a server acts as the heart of iBeam system. This server runs on a PC which consists of server application software, regression algorithm of Machine Learning process, and extracted database from the iBN. The output response packet for communication between the app and the server is in JavaScript Object Notation (JSON) format. Commonly, there are 2 Utilizing Web Service to provide access to remote services or for enabling applications to communicate amongst each other: Simple Object Access Protocol (SOAP) and REpresentational State Transfer (REST). REST API takes more advantages by virtue of less coupling connection, protocol independence, and standardization.

Jetty and Jersey is a perfect couple for a REST web service. Similar to Apache Tomcat or Glassfish, Jetty is an open source HTTP server. However Jetty is just a stand-alone Java servlet container providing compact HTTP client side and powerful server methods. It focuses on performance, using annotation for HTTP verbs (such as @POST, @GET) and multi-connection HTTP rather than development of a full-blown Java Enterprise Edition (Java EE) container like Apache Tomcat. Such properties make it light, fast, and smaller memory footprint. Other prominent features of Jetty are the optimization of annotation classes, or automatic JSON file parsing and generating. Figure 3 below demonstrates how the communication works.

While Jetty is used for implementing server side, Jersey, on the other hand, associates with the client side on SpaceBeam app. Jersey is an open-source RESTful framework that provides its own API and extends Java API for RESTful Service (JAX-RS) toolkit with additional features and utilities to further simplify RESTful service and client development. For example, when the app sends request for user authentication, a web-target object is made based on a specific Uniform Resource Identifier (URI). The URI contains authority part (real IP of the hosting server), path part, and query part (if any). An invocation builder will parse it into a JSON file and send it to the server. Since then the connection is opened as a handshake is made from both side (Fig. 3). The server will execute Structure Query Language (SQL) statements from database then response to that request. The response message can be under any entity such as a String, an Integer, or even a particular Java object class, which needs to be coherent from both sides.

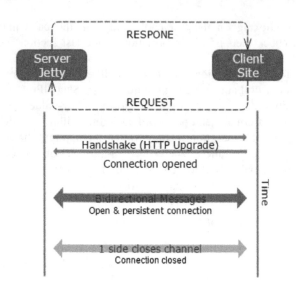

Fig. 3. Message exchange between client and server side

The controller starts off by initializing the Ethernet to establish connection between them. Data from humidity and temperature sensors is retrieved each 5 min and stored to the iBN. Simultaneously, it determines availability of the user. If the user is unavailable then the login session is brought about. The 404 response code will be sent if wrong username or password is entered. Otherwise the reponse code will be 200 and user status will be made available. Figure 4 shows the general flowchart fot eh Jetty server controller.

The controller starts off by initializing the Ethernet to establish connection between them. Data from humidity and temperature sensors is retrieved each 5 min and stored to the iBN. Simultaneously, it determines availability of the user. If the user is unavailable then the login session is brought about. The 404 response code will be sent if wrong username or password is entered. Otherwise the reponse code will be 200 and user status will be made available. Figure 4 shows the general flowchart of the Jetty server controller.

3.5   Software Development of the Machine Learning Algorithm

Approach

Machine learning is a study field that evolves from pattern recognition and computational learning theory in artificial intelligence. By and large, machine learning tasks are typically classified into three broad categories [10]. One of those is called "supervised learning" which analyzes the training data and produces an inferred function. Unsupervised learning is another one that infers a function to describe hidden structure from unlabeled data. The last one is "reinforcement learning" that interacts with a dynamic environment to perform a certain goal. With the objective of this project, regression analysis – a supervised learning task – is chosen to solve the problems by fitting the

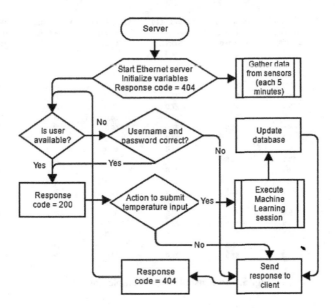

Fig. 4. Flowchart for the operation of the controller

training set to a continuous function describing a curve, so that the curve passes as much as possible to all of the data points. For example, to foresee the thermal comfort of the participants, the algorithm uses data from the past such as an occupant preferred a temperature of 25 °C on a rainy day to predict the dew-point temperature which satisfies everyone in the room (or building). The dew point temperature is the temperature at which the air can no longer "hold" all of the water vapor which is mixed with it, and some of the water vapor must condense into liquid water. The dew point is always lower than (or equal to) the air temperature. The humidity depends on the dew point temperature and current air temperature.

Dataset Description

The used sample dataset consists of 5 attributes and 7039 instances, sampled from 01/02/2016 to 25/02/2016. Each instance contains 5 attributes including Timestamp, Outdoor Temperature, Zone (indoor), Outdoor Humidity and User's Input Temperature of each floor such as a ground floor, first floor, and second floor. Vector input involves in user's input temperature, outdoor temperature, indoor and outdoor humidity. Desired output, also known as a supervisory signal, is the indoor temperature. There was no case of missing data in the dataset and it contains continuous variables for 5-min unit in terms of timestamp. The figure below shows a sample dataset (Fig. 5):

Algorithm Selected

In supervised learning, the final goal is to develop a finely tuned predictor hypothesis function h(x). The objective is to optimize the hypothesis so that, given input variable x about a certain domain (e.g. humidity), it will output the estimated value (the suitable temperature).

Timestamp	VAV-GF-107 Zone Temp (500:189)	VAV-GF-107 Zone Humidity (500:190)	VAV-GF-110 Zone Temp (500:55)	VAV-GF-110 Zone Humidity (500:56)	VAV-GF-112 Zone Temp (500:19)	VAV-GF-112 Zone Humidity (500:20)
2/1/2016 0:02	-68.5	81.5	27.0	67.0	26.3	81.0
2/1/2016 0:07	-72.2	81.5	27.0	66.0	26.3	81.0
2/1/2016 0:12	-69.8	81.5	27.0	66.0	26.3	81.0
2/1/2016 0:17	-123.7	81.5	27.0	66.0	26.3	81.0
2/1/2016 0:22	-136.3	81.5	27.0	67.0	26.3	81.0
2/1/2016 0:27	-79.2	81.5	27.0	66.0	26.3	81.0
2/1/2016 0:32	-82.5	81.5	27.0	66.0	26.3	81.0
2/1/2016 0:37	-68.6	81.5	27.0	66.0	26.3	81.0
2/1/2016 0:42	-69.3	81.5	27.0	66.0	26.3	81.0
2/1/2016 0:47	-70.6	81.5	27.0	66.0	26.3	81.0
2/1/2016 0:52	-68.5	81.5	27.0	66.0	26.3	81.0
2/1/2016 0:57	-105.8	81.5	27.0	67.0	26.3	81.0
2/1/2016 1:02	-76.2	81.5	27.0	67.0	26.3	81.0
2/1/2016 1:07	-83.1	81.5	27.0	67.0	26.3	81.0
2/1/2016 1:12	-80.1	81.5	27.0	67.0	26.3	81.0
2/1/2016 1:17	-99.9	81.5	27.0	66.0	26.3	81.0
2/1/2016 1:22	-90.6	81.5	27.0	67.0	26.3	81.0
2/1/2016 1:27	-88.2	81.5	27.0	67.0	26.3	81.0
2/1/2016 1:32	-72.5	81.5	27.0	67.0	26.3	81.0
2/1/2016 1:37	-124.2	81.5	27.0	67.0	26.3	81.0

Fig. 5. Screenshot of the sample dataset

This system takes M5P as the main algorithm for supervised training. M5P is an algorithm that is originated from Quinlan's M5 algorithm [11] and improved later to M5P [12]. It creates a model binary tree that will give the linear regression model at each leaf instead of a numerically predicted value. Prediction is calculated by trading the path on the tree to a leaf, and by using the linear model on that leaf. The M5P tree is built upon three stages which are illustrated in Fig. 6:

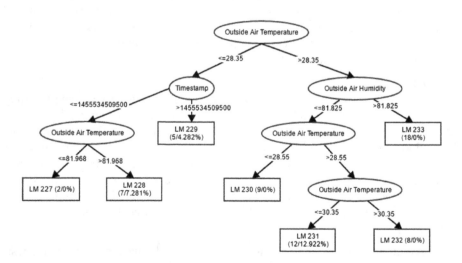

Fig. 6. Illustration of M5P algorithm processes

- Firstly, the algorithm is used to split the nodes recursively, following a criterion to minimize the intra-subset variation in the class values.
- Secondly, the tree is pruned to become simpler.
- Thirdly, a smoothing procedure is applied: linear models are measured for non-leaf nodes along the path back to the root, each predicted value will be combined with the leaf model prediction.

The outstanding benefit of M5P algorithm is that decision tree methods can handle both numeric and categorical data rather than only one type of variable for other methods [13]. By virtue of the steady rise of the dataset (1 new attribute each 5 min), M5P is superior to others by having a low training cost. Moreover, some pre-processing steps can be ignored such as normalization, converting from categorized to numerical variables, or deleting blank values.

Training and Evaluation

Cross Validation (CV) method was chosen in this case. In k-folds CV, the original dataset is randomly partitioned into k subsets (which is chosen to be 10) with the same size. This process then repeats for k times, in which each of the subset will be treated as the test set once for an iteration. Its high computational complexity is paid off by the well accurate assessment.

4 Result and Discussion

The iBeam system was fully developed and tested to demonstrate its feasibility and effectiveness. Screenshots of the mobile app has been presented in Fig. 2. As mentioned, authentication is required to access the smart home system. A notification will be displayed for wrong entered password. This message is based on the response received from the Jetty server. If correct authentication is provided, the app will proceed to look up for the appropriate iBK corresponding to the account.

The system is fully functional for sending to as well as fetching data from the server. It was also tested for the automatic logout feature after a specific period of time that has been set. The outdoor weather works properly as long as the using device is connecting to the Internet.

In terms of the server, Jetty has encountered with no problem when hosting the server in real time, or receiving authentication request from SpaceBeam app and sending response.

Last but not least is the result of the M5P learning algorithm. Output of the process would be a dew-point temperature that satisfies every people and it will be set to the centralized air-conditioner by the iBK. The total number of instance of this dataset is 7039. For each execution it takes about 2 s to run, which will be increased over time as the number of instance will rise rapidly through time. Thus such process is only called once per 30 min. Other than that, the retaining of relative absolute error around 15% for a 24-day dataset reflects that a good algorithm was applied since its predictions are usually closed to the human's comfort zone.

Table 1 illustrates the output result of different algorithms that are applied on the same dataset. The correlation index indicates how much the true value of interest and the estimated value are related. A value that is close to 1 or −1 means there is a perfect relationship between variables. M5P performs the best with highest correlation when compared to Decision Table, Linear Regression, or Lazy. The error indexes show accuracy amongst true and predicted value. Thus M5P algorithm gains more advantage with noticeably smaller error than the others.

Table 1. Comparison of some machine learning algorithms

	M5P – 30 min	M5P – 1 h	Decision table	Linear regression	Lazy (Ibk)
CC	0.9386	0.9632	0.9374	0.3716	0.5546
MAE	0.1458	0.1377	0.2228	0.8854	0.6058
RMSE	0.4008	0.3078	0.3985	1.0621	1.081
RAE	15.0609%	14.2187%	23.0073%	91.4353%	62.5624%
RRSE	35.0355%	26.9049%	34.8287%	92.8335%	94.4867%

5 Conclusion

In conclusion, an internet based smart-learning controller for air-conditioning was proposed and implemented. The system is proposed with a view to predicting the thermal comfort of the occupants and modulates the air-conditioning system to provide optimum thermal comfort and indoor air quality while operating at the lowest energy cost. This research is focused on developing such system with a mobile application, a network hub (iBN) that links with several sensors, a controller (iBK) with embedded Machine Learning algorithms, and a chilled beam system. The main contribution of this paper is building both client side (Android application) and server side using Jetty and Jersey with regression supervised learning algorithm – M5P. Both sides communicate to each other through a RESTful API web service. Users can use the app to suggest their comfort zone to the system for it to learn and automatically change the dew point temperature based on human contentment. Prospective future works include detecting occupancy via CO_2 sensors or motion sensors, associating with other systems such as fire detection, or lighting control. Other than that, GUI of the app and speed of the algorithm learning should also be improved.

Acknowledgements. Special thanks to our client, Blue Snow Energy Sendirian Berhad (Shn Bhd) who shares the project idea and provides experiments testing point and hardware support. I also would like to thank my friend – Thanh C. Ngo, Rutgers University – who supported me on designing the app. This paper is presented based on a G52GRP group project with Tran Phuong Dung, Ahmad Kamal Kamariza, Wong Wei Thong, and Lim Jyy Bing from the University of Nottingham, Malaysia Campus.

References

1. Roth, K., Dieckmann, J., Zogg, R., Brodrick, J.: Chilled beam cooling. ASHRAE J. **49**(9), 84 (2007)

2. Guan, Z., Wen, C.:Numerical investigation of geometry parameters for designing efficient terminal units in active chilled beam. In: 2014 9th IEEE Conference on Industrial Electronics and Applications, pp. 1114–1118 (2014)

3. Fischer, J.C., Mescher, K.T., Mitchell, R.K., Glen, S.P., Carroll, S.S.: Chilled beam pump module, system, and method (2013)

4. Murphy, J., Harshaw, J.: Applications Engineering. @BULLET providing insights for today's HVAC system designer. In: Trane Engineers Newsletter, vol. 42, no. 2 (2013)

5. Fong, K.F., Hanby, V.I., Chow, T.T.: HVAC system optimization for energy management by evolutionary programming. Energy Build. **38**(3), 220–231 (2006)

6. Anwaarullah, S., Altaf, S.V.: RTOS based home automation system using android. Int. J. Adv. Trends Comput. Sci. Eng. **2**(1), 480–484 (2013)

7. Ramlee, R.A., Othman, M.A., Leong, M.H., Ismail, M.M., Ranjit, S.S.S.: Smart home system using android application. In: 2013 International Conference of Information and Communication Technology, IColCT 2013, pp. 277–280 (2013)

8. Potts, J., Sukittanon, S.: Exploiting bluetooth on android mobile devices for home security application. In: 2012 Proceedings of IEEE Southeastcon, pp. 1–4 (2012)

9. Tan, K.K., Lee, T.H., Soh, C.Y.: Internet-based monitoring of distributed control systems-an undergraduate experiment. IEEE Trans. Educ. **45**(2), 128–134 (2002)

10. Swamy, N., Kuljaca, O., Lewis, F.L.: Internet-based educational control systems lab using NetMeeting. IEEE Trans. Educ. **45**(2), 145–151 (2002)

11. Tucker, A.B.: Computer science handbook. Chapman & Hall/CRC, Boca Raton (2004)

12. Quinlan, J.R.: Learning with continuous classes. In: Proceedings AI, pp. 343–348 (1992)

13. Wang, Y., Witten, I.H.: Induction of model trees for predicting continuous classes. In: Proceedings of the 9th European Conference on Machine Learning Poster Papers, pp. 128–137 (1997)

14. Khiyal, M.S.H., Khan, A., Shehzadi, E.: SMS based wireless home appliance control system (HACS) for automating appliances and security. Issues Inf. Sci. Inf. Technol. **6**, 887–894 (2009)

15. AAlkar, A.Z., Buhur, U.: An internet based wireless home automation system for multifunctional devices. IEEE Trans. Consum. Electron. **51**, 1169–1174 (2005)

16. Rajabzadeh, A., Manashty, A.R., Jahromi, Z.F.: A mobile application for smart house remote control system. In: World Academy of Science, Engineering and Technology, vol. 62 (2010)

17. Sharma, U., Reddy, S.R.N.: Design of home/office automation using wireless sensor network. Int. J. Comput. Appl. **43**, 53–60 (2012)

Analyzing and Detecting Network Intrusion Behavior Using Packet Capture

Zahidan Zabri$^{(\boxtimes)}$ and Puteri N.E. Nohuddin

Institute of Visual Informatics, National University of Malaysia, Bangi, Malaysia
zahidanzabri93@gmail.com, puteri.ivi@ukm.edu.my

Abstract. Network Intrusion is one of serious computer network security issues faced by almost all organizations or industries around the world. The big problem is that companies still have poor security to keep their network in good condition. Unfortunately, the management takes the simplest way by putting heavy responsibilities to network administrator rather than spending a high cost of computer security setup. In this paper describes a preliminary study for proposing a technique of analyzing network intrusion by using Packet Capture integrated with Network Intrusion Behavior Analysis Engine. This technique analyzes whether the flow of the network is healthy or malicious. The study consists of several components for implementing an effective and efficient network analyzing mechanism. Artificial Neural Network is selected as the main method for its behavior analysis engine. Then, it will illustrate the analysis result using an enhanced visualization method which gives more knowledge and understanding to the network administrators for effectively monitor network traffics.

Keywords: Network security · Threat · Behavior analysis · Intrusion detection · Artificial Neural Network

1 Introduction

Cyber world becomes increasingly challenging and unsecure due to the recent cutting edge and sophisticated network technology. Therefore, people use networked devices with connecting with others around the world. Unfortunately, there are still in low-security and they did not care about it that is the most important issue to keep the credential and other information always in good condition [1]. Network security is the most important thing in communication regardless of whether the user to user or within an organization because this will be more severe and getting worst in term of exploitation or leak of information.

Today, as we know that there are many organizations still have low network security and high network vulnerabilities which allow attackers to exploit. This may be caused by some reasons or lack of company funds to hardening their server from network traffic issues. However, the organizations which deployed the firewall or IDS to detect most known attacks, some of them are not desirable tools for security administrators, because they generate too many alerts with blow-level semantics, and most of them are false positives which is difficult to get a root or cause of security

© Springer International Publishing AG 2017
H. Badioze Zaman et al. (Eds.): IVIC 2017, LNCS 10645, pp. 750–761, 2017.
https://doi.org/10.1007/978-3-319-70010-6_69

threats [2]. In recent years, automatic IDS alerts analysis technique has become one of the hot topics in network security [3].

The main objective of this research is to develop network analysis inspector for capturing packet data. The proposed technique is used to determine whether packet data are healthy or not based on the detection of its anomaly activity. This console application will be integrated in real-time that triggered from packet capture or packet analyzer. Hence, this mechanism can help to reduce the redundant and irrelevant data that triggered from packet analyzer.

The data are collected based on artificial neural network concept or correlation rules in the engine and it will be visualized using an active view to determine whether it is a normal or malicious activity. Furthermore, when the console application integrated with the active view in real time, then the prototype of this mechanism will be released for the testing in the actual environment. The expected results or outcome of this research is a technique on network analysis behavior of packet data with enhanced visualization that integrated in real-time with packet analyzer.

The remainder of this paper is organized as follows. Section 2 discusses some related work and topics on network intrusion and data mining. Then, Sect. 3 discusses on the research objectives and methodology. Section 4 provides a description of the proposed research framework and its components. Section 5 discusses the expected result from this study. Finally, in Sect. 6, the paper will be concluded with a brief summary and future research work.

2 Background and Related Work

2.1 Network Intrusion Detection

Network intrusion can be described as cyber threats initiated by the attacker to gather information and deploy the attack to their victim to get the value or benefits. Furthermore, it can be any use of network to compromise the machines to intrude its stability or security information stored from it [4]. Hence, this paper describes that the flow of network and detection on intrusion by using packet capture and visualize whether it is suspicious or not is feasible. As we know that there are many thresholds of packet data to capture, but this research will solve the problem where it can capture the specific file or behavior based on what signature tagged in engine and the technique used.

Analyzing network intrusion is essential in order to have a more effective troubleshooting and resolving methods when the issue of network intrusion occurs. Furthermore, there is no need to bring down network services for extended periods of time [5]. Hence, the proposed research will be developed by analyzing network in real-time by using packet capture and retrieve the pcap file converted to json file in a network behavior analysis engine. So, the file will be retrieved based on signature tagged in engine and visualized with an analytics diagram on what the actual activity done by intruders to the compromised host.

In this proposed research, packet capture is essential because it will capture all of the packet data roughly through the network without filtering any specific activity for the network flow. Then, the packet data will be sent to the engine and matched with signature created to filter the irrelevant data. It will be visualized to the visualization graph platform Kibana as malicious activity instead of false alarm. According to Oluwabukola [6], packet capture is clarified as an assistant of network management with the features of monitoring and analyzing which can help to troubleshoot network, control traffics and detect intrusion. Besides, the packet capture is useful because it allows several mechanisms to analyze the network traffics thoroughly [7].

2.2   Network Intrusion Detection Using Data Mining

Basically, data mining is one of the tasks in data process that can be divided into two methods. The first is a predictive method, used to predict values based on known data to get the pattern of findings. For example, the classification models and regression models are used to get the pattern from predictive task. The second is a descriptive method which is to summarize data to get the relevant information. There are many categories that can be classified in this method such as probabilistic models, association rules, clustering and anomaly detection [8]. Hence, the proposed research is focused on the descriptive method because network intrusion analysis is more to summarize data and detects anomalous behaviors. Data mining is also a pattern finding as its core and very suitable with network intrusion to filter irrelevant data and redundant data. It is also can control and find regularities and irregularities in large data sets. There are several ways that how data mining related with network intrusion detection. For example, remove normal activities from alarm data to allow users to focus on real attacks, find anomaly traffics that uncovers a real attack and the others [9].

A network intrusion detection is a platform to monitor the network or system activities for malicious activities and unauthorized access to devices [10]. The goal of designing this mechanism is to protect the data's confidentiality and integrity. This proposed research focuses on these issues supported by data mining approaches.

Feature selection data analysis: Sindhu et al. [11] proposed a genetic based feature selection algorithm for minimizing the computational complexity of the classifier. Feature selection method can be divided into three categories named filter, wrapper and hybrid (embedded) method [12]. It can be used to evaluate features or feature subsets. Many feature subsets are determined based on classification performance. Based on this technique, it will be very complicated to resolve on this proposed mechanism because the method that has been used is not similar with the process flow concept. This approach is enough to enhance correlation rules in order to summarize data and classify packets in lowest amount of data network flow. In general, features selection data analysis is used in large amount of data network because it prevents the loss of importance of single features [13].

Clustering analysis: Clustering method is the one of the technique that identifying and extracting patterns in specific data, grouping those patterns and then identifying the "most interesting" pattern [14]. It also can be applied when the anomaly intrusion and misuse detection were detected which are also called as abnormal network behavior. The most common method that have been used in clustering method for the network intrusion detection is K-means algorithm [15]. It is used to discover new attacks which were not detected in previous instances [16]. Hence, it can produce the unknown source or intrusion model instead of known intrusion [17]. In this method, the new network normal behavior will be added to filter the common behavior sent to the network behavior analyzer, so only the abnormal data packets are taken and triggered to the visualization graph. Related to this proposed research, this method must be added with other data mining methods to get a better performance in network intrusion detection. However, it also can be used for future planning in which the mechanism needs to be enhanced on existing in-depth study.

Classification analysis: This method can be described with two main detections which are anomaly detection and signature based detection. The anomaly detection explores issues in threshold of network against to the normal traffics. The second employs signature detection to compare between anomaly or attack patterns (signatures) and it is more to be categorized as pattern based [18]. Hence, the proposed method will classify packet data for any previously unseen objects as accurately as possible. In classification analysis, there are many types of decision can be used to evaluate the pattern and flow of the data network intrusion. According to Srinivasulu *et al.* [19], the network intrusion can be performed and evaluated by many different data mining classification techniques such as CART, Naive Bayesian, and Artificial Neural Network Model classifier using a confusion matrix to test data for which the true values are known. In this proposed research, it analyzes network intrusion behavior using packet capture in the various data set are generated, specifically on attribute relation with the Source IP and Target IP parallel with an artificial neural network concept. However, the rules will be enhanced in-depth to detect new attack adversaries due to current global threats in cyber attacks.

2.3   Network Behavior Analysis Using Artificial Neural Network Concept

Artificial Neural Network (ANN) is a process to transform a set of input to come out with desired output supported by interconnection elements or pattern algorithm. The output is determined based on the characteristics and combination of algorithms. Hence, the neural network will be potential to resolve the problem and filter data parallel with intrusion analysis approaches [20]. The proposed research is motivated to develop the network intrusion detection based on artificial neural network concept. The recommended model will show as per below:

Figure 1 shows to define the artificial neurons as it receives a number of original data (data packets) via a connection which is correspond in a biological neuron [16]. Each neuron has a single threshold which is incoming packets triggered one by one from the packet capture. The sum of the inputs is formed and the threshold subtracted, to compose the activation of the neuron and the output of the neuron will be produced which is to show whether the incoming traffic is legitimate or not. Hence, if the activation function is used, the output will be 0 (legitimate) if the activation is equal to 1, and the output is 1 (suspicious) if the activation is more than 1. However, the activation function is depending on the behavior of packet (IP, Protocol, Port and Info) and the signature created. The activation function also known as the main configuration for the data structure and algorithm to make decisions in this proposed research.

Based on the reviews, we can deduce that it is feasible to establish an analyzing network intrusion behavior using packet capture based on artificial neural network concept.

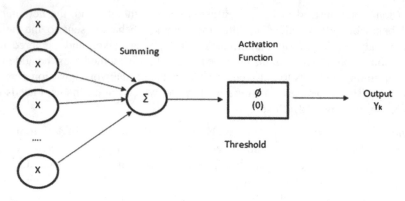

Fig. 1. Artificial neural network model

3 Research Objectives and Methodology

The network intrusion is becoming a challenging task due to increasing connectivity of systems that gives greater access to outsiders and makes it easier for intruders to steal information and illegal activity that gives benefit to them [21].

Network behavior analysis of packets can be used for network traffic monitoring, traffic analysis, troubleshooting and other useful purpose [22]. Even though, it is largely an internal threat in most organizations but sometimes a malicious third party may be able to eavesdrop as well as manipulate sensitive data during communication between machines in a LAN. Packet analyzer tool can handle the process of pattern capturing or traffics of connection. However, there are too many thresholds in minute (packet per second) that can lead many issues on network monitoring performance. Hence, the network behavior analysis is developed to get the pattern of traffics where there can visualize the result what actually happened that might be harmful to the internal network environment. To overcome this problem, this research proposes to use the concept of data mining techniques to collect data information and take out the result integrated with visualization graph in real-time. Thus, the objectives of this research are as follows:

(1) To investigate the network behaviors based on the result of intrusion when anomalous activity occurs.
(2) To adapt an appropriate mechanism and process in network behavior analysis.
(3) To propose the network intrusion behavior analysis framework in combination of packet analyzer with Elasticsearch and Kibana visualization.
4) To integrate packet analyzer into appropriate console application and active view (Kibana) to get the result of network intrusion whether in an internal and external environment.

In this study, several work stages have been identified for the methodology for the research. Initially, an investigation on the criteria of the proposed analyzing network intrusion behavior structure will be done.

Stage 1

Preliminary Study: This initial study will start by reviewing the sample of packet data, network behavior analysis framework and techniques involved in the network intrusion environment.

Stage 2

Software Design: In this stage, designs of framework, console application or engine and result of component development and active view system specification are done that are appropriate for network behavior analysis environment.

Stage 3

System Development: This stage involves with coding analysis on console and active view which are possible to be integrated into packet analyzer in real-time.

Stage 4

Prototype: At this stage, a prototype of console application or engine with enhanced active view analysis on stand-alone mode will be produced. The goal is to discover whether the system specification meets the requirement of the proposed research.

Stage 5

Visualization of active view results. The project will be managed show presentations on visualization of active view results integrated into network behavior analysis console in this stage.

4   The Network Intrusion Behavior Analysis Framework

The initial study focuses on understanding the mechanisms and characteristics of a network intrusion behavior analysis. A handful of papers related to the research and development of the network intrusion analysis will be studied [23, 24].

Figure 2 shows the proposed framework of Analyzing Network Intrusion Behavior using Packet Capture based on Artificial Neural Network Concept. The framework shows the work flow from the initial to the final experiment and it proves that the packet capture can be integrated with Elasticsearch to get the result [26]. The framework consists of five (5) main components which are:

(1) *Packet Capture/Analyzer.*

In this module, the packet data are captured by using a packet analyzer which is integrated in real-time. The gathered data includes Source IP, Target IP, Time, protocol, packet length and packet information. All packet data are captured and uploaded in excel file without any filtering or summarize and integrated to ElasticSearch server. Below is the example of packet data uploaded in excel file as shown in Fig. 3:

(2) *ElasticSearch Server.*

Elasticsearch is a search engine platform for integration or combination of any data with server depends on how is the process that the user want to configure

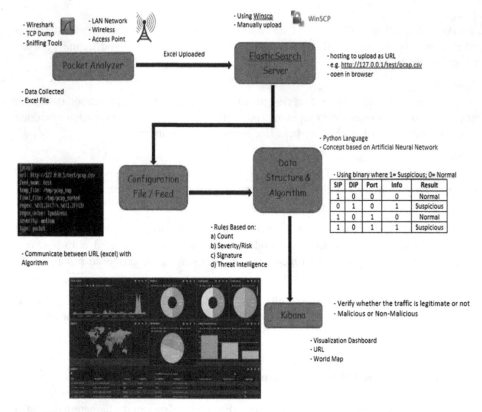

Fig. 2. The proposed framework of analyzing network intrusion behavior using packet capture based on artificial neural network concept

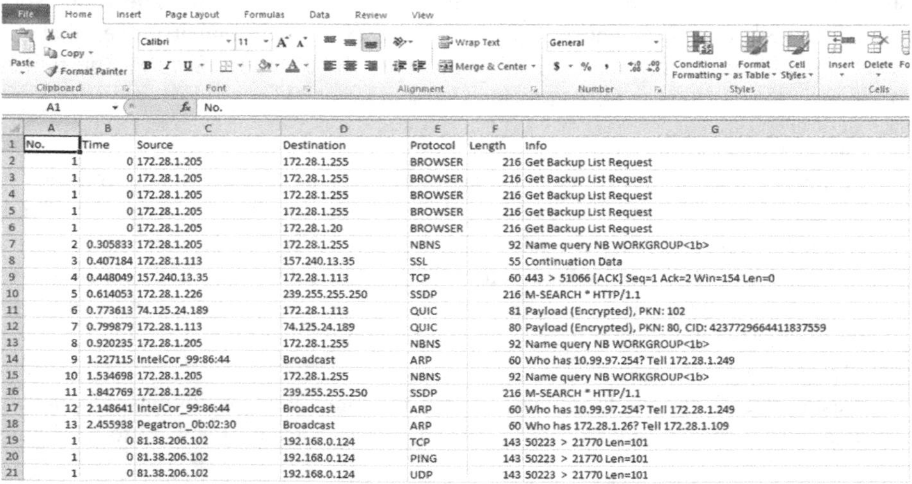

Fig. 3. Packet data in excel file

[27]. In this component, it will provide a method on how to gather packet data behavior for the analysis process. Packet data will be integrated in excel file and upload into this server. The server will be operated in Centos Linux platform by using Virtual Machine. The easiest way to upload in server is manually by using WinSCP as a platform to get into server because it can drag and drop file from physical machine to the server. Then, the excel file will be hosted to upload as URL for example http://127.0.0.1/test/pcap.csv. Figure 4 is an example of WinSCP screenshot in which the process of packet data is gathered.

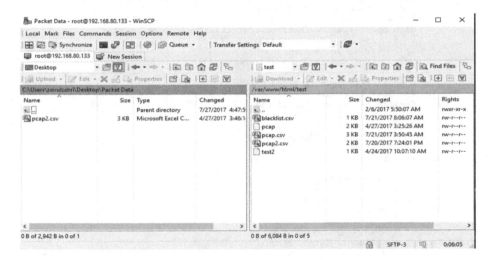

Fig. 4. WinSCP (division between physical machine with server)

(3) *Configuration File/ Feed.*
In this component, the relation between URL with algorithm will be configured. The URL should be defined. The configured should be also defined by name of configuration, temporary file, regular expression (regex) value as parser and type of configuration. All of this created as a simple way to make one by one process flow in mechanism. An example of configuration is as shown in Fig. 2.
(4) *Data Structure and Algorithm.*
This module is the most important element in the mechanism because this is the '*man in the middle*' which is an interconnection between data with visualization. Hence, the concept of Artificial Neural Network will be proved on this component. The Python language will be executed in this algorithm. The rules are based on count of traffics, severity/risk, signatures and threat intelligence and will be created in this stage to prove that which is the malicious traffics. Figure 5 shows the Pseudocode which is the simplified hardcoded for the initial experiment of this mechanism. It shows that the example of signature created, the comparison

```
                          ⎧ url: http://127.0.0.1/test/pcap.csv
                          ⎪ feed_name: test
  Configuration  ⎨ temp_file: /tmp/pcap_tmp
  File/Feed          ⎪ regex: "\d+.\d+.\d+.\d+","\d+.\d+.\d+.\d+","\w+","\d+",".*?"
                          ⎪ regex_value: ipaddress
                          ⎩ type: packet
```

```
data_type = Config.get(config_name,'regex_value')

if (data_type == "ipaddress"):
try:
        # Compare with threat intelligence excel file:
        import csv
        with open('/var/www/html/test/pcap.csv') as infile:
                    reader = csv.DictReader(infile)
        for a in reader:
        with open('/var/www/html/test/blacklist.csv') as csvfile:
                    reader = csv.DictReader(csvfile)
                    for b in reader:
                      (a['Source']) == (b['source']):

        # Split attribute in excel file:
        for line in infile:
        for log in extract_ips(line):
                    ip1 = log.split(',')
                    sip = ip1[0].replace('"','')
                    dip = ip1[1].replace('"','')
                    protocol = ip1[2].replace('"','')
                    info = ip1[4].replace('"','')

        # Index a document:
        es.index(
        index="threatelligence",
        doc_type=result_type,
        body={
                "Source_IP": sip,
                  "Source_info": ccode,
                "Destination": dip,
                  "Protocol": protocol,
                "country": ccountry,
                  "Info": info,
                "feed_src": parser_name,
                  "country_code": ccode,
                  "geolocate": longat,
                  "date": currdate
                  }
        )|
```

Fig. 5. Pseudocode

between Source IP in original packet data with Source IP that were blacklisted in global threat intelligence.

5) *Active View (Kibana)*

In the final component, the result will be visualized in a graph by using a software tool and combined with a search server to gather the packet data behavior. At this stage, we can conclude that the result whether the network is healthy or malicious through the investigation of network intrusion behavior analysis. For this situation, ElasticSearch will be combined with Kibana to visualize the result of network intrusion [25] (Fig. 6).

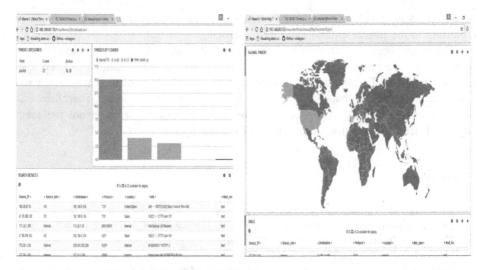

Fig. 6. Kibana dashboard and global threat map

5 Summary and Discussion

The expected outcome of the research is that the proposed technique will able to establish a network behavior analysis of packet capture which will be integrated into packet analyzer in real-time. At the same time, the active view also will be incorporated during the analysis to show the visualization graph. This proposed research helps to investigate the intrusion of network behavior by capturing the packet data which can be triggered based on signature and method used instead of false positive packet data.

Consequently, the proposed console application would be an effective reference for the network behavior analysis to operate does not matter whether the traffics in the internal or external environment.

6 Conclusion and Future Works

In this review paper, analyzing network intrusion using packet capture has been discussed along with the brief preliminary study of the process flow on network intrusion analysis and also with the enhanced visualization. This can be classified as a simplest process to achieve the objective of this proposed mechanism. Thus, it can ease task of network security analysts to analyze and to get essential information on network traffics.

In general, this mechanism can be one of the network monitoring to control the traffics from intrusion whether it from the internal or external environment. The proposed research would be one of the ways to solve this issue regarding the cost and network services provided. Network traffic also has many mechanisms in monitoring based on signature and behavior involved in the tools used. Hence, this mechanism will be deployed or developed with the correlation created following by phase-to-phase regarding to the implementation and enhancement.

The future work of the research can be extended in deploying this technique for the university to control and monitor the network by using this mechanism to keep it in healthy condition. The authors plan to enhance the technique in dealing with any issue due to denial of service that can be caused by a slow connection and etc. Therefore, this research will be developed in stages where it needs some time to ensure the main engine of network intrusion detection is fully tested.

References

1. Alfayyadh, B., Ponting, J., Alzomai, M., Jøsang, A.: Vulnerabilities in personal firewalls caused by poor security usability. In: 2010 IEEE International Conference on Information Theory and Information Security (ICITIS) (2010)
2. Stavroulakis, P., Stamp, M.: Handbook of Information and Communication Security (2010)
3. Peng, X., Zhao, H.: A framework of attacker centric cyber attack behavior analysis. In: 2007 IEEE International Conference on Communications (2007)
4. Portnoy, L., Eskin, E., Stolfo, S.: Intrusion detection with unlabeled data using clustering. Department of Computer Science, Columbia University (2001)
5. Cecil, A.: A summary of network traffic monitoring and analysis techniques. Whitepaper (2006)
6. Oluwabukola, O., Oludele, A., Ogbonna, A.C., Chigozirim, A., Amarachi, A.: A Packet Sniffer (PSniffer) Application for network security in Java. In: Cohen, E., Boyd, E. (eds.) Proceedings of Informing Science and Information Technology Education Conference 2013, pp. 389–400 (2013)
7. Turk, Y., Demir, O., Gören, S.: Real time wireless packet monitoring with raspberry Pi sniffer. Inf. Sci. Syst. **2014**, 185–192 (2014)
8. Sondwale, P.P.: Overview of predictive and descriptive data mining techniques. Int. J. Advanced Research in Computer Science and Software Engineering, IJARCSSE, vol. 5 no. 4 (2015)
9. Bloedorn, E., Christiansen, A.D., Hill, W., Skorupka, C., Talbot, L.M., Tivel, J.: Data mining for network intrusion detection: how to get started (2001)
10. Gupta, D., Singhai, S., Malik, S., Singh, A.: Network intrusion detection system using various data mining techniques. In: IEEE International Conference on Research Advances in Integrated Navigation Systems (RAINS) (2016)
11. Sindhu, S., Geetha, S., Kannan, A.: Decision tree based light weight intrusion detection using a wrapper approach. Expert Syst. Appl. **39**, 129–141 (2012)
12. Aggarwal, M., Amrita: Performance analysis of different feature selection methods in intrusion detection. Int. J. Sci. Technol. Res. **2**(6), 225–231 (2013)
13. Janecek, A.G.K., Gansterer, W.N., Demel, M.A., Ecker, G.F.: On the relationship between feature selection and classification accuracy. J. Mach. Learn. Res. **4**, 90–105 (2008)
14. Nohuddin, P.N.E., Christley, R., Coenen, F., Patel, Y., Setzkorn, C., Williams, S.: Frequent pattern trend analysis in social networks. In: Cao, L., Feng, Y., Zhong, J. (eds.) ADMA 2010. LNCS, vol. 6440, pp. 358–369. Springer, Heidelberg (2010). doi:10.1007/978-3-642-17316-5_35
15. Münz, G., Carle, G.: Traffic anomaly detection using kmeans clustering. In: GI/ITG Workshop MMBnet (2016)

16. Phutane, T., Pathan, A.: A survey of intrusion detection system using different data mining techniques. Int. J. Innov. Res. Comput. Commun. Eng. **2**, 11 (2014)
17. Bo, L., Dong-Dong, J.: The research of intrusion detection model based on clustering analysis. In: 2009 International Conference on Computer and Communications Security (2009)
18. Kaur, H., Sing, G., Minhas, J.: A review of machine learning based anomaly detection techniques. Int. J. Comput. Appl. Technol. Res. **2**(2), 185–187 (2013)
19. Srinivasulu, P., Nagaraju, D., Kumar, P.R., Rao, K.N.: Classifying the network intrusion attacks using data mining classification methods and their performance comparison. IJCSNS Int. J. Comput. Sci. Netw. Secur. **9**, 6 (2009)
20. Pervez, S., Ahmad, I., Akram, A., Swati, S.U.: Comparative analysis of artificial neural network technologies in intrusion detection systems. In: Proceedings of 6th WSEAS International Conference on Multimedia, Internet & Video Technologies (2006)
21. Moore, A.W., Zuev, D.: Internet traffic classification using bayesian analysis techniques. In: Proceedings of 2005 ACM SIGMETRICS International Conference on Measurement and Modeling of Computer Systems - SIGMETRICS 2005 (2005)
22. Gupta, A., Kumar, M., Rangra, A., Tiwari, V.K., Saxena, P.: Network intrusion detection types and analysis of their tools. Int. J. Eng. Res. Dev. **2**, 1 (2013)
23. Youssef, A., Emam, A.: Network intrusion detection using data mining and network behaviour analysis. Int. J. Comput. Sci. Inf. Technol. **3**(6), 87–98 (2011)
24. Northcutt, S., Novak, J.: Network Intrusion Detection, 3rd edn. Sams, Indianapolis (2002)
25. Reelsen, A.: Using Elasticsearch, Logstash and Kibana to Create Realtime Dashboards. Elasticsearch (2014)
26. Hargrave, V.: Packet Capture with Pyshark and Elasticsearch (2015)
27. Gormley, C., Tong, Z.: Elasticsearch: The Definitive Guide. O'Reilly Media, Inc., Sebastopol (2017)

Author Index

Printed in the United States
By Bookmasters